U0674269

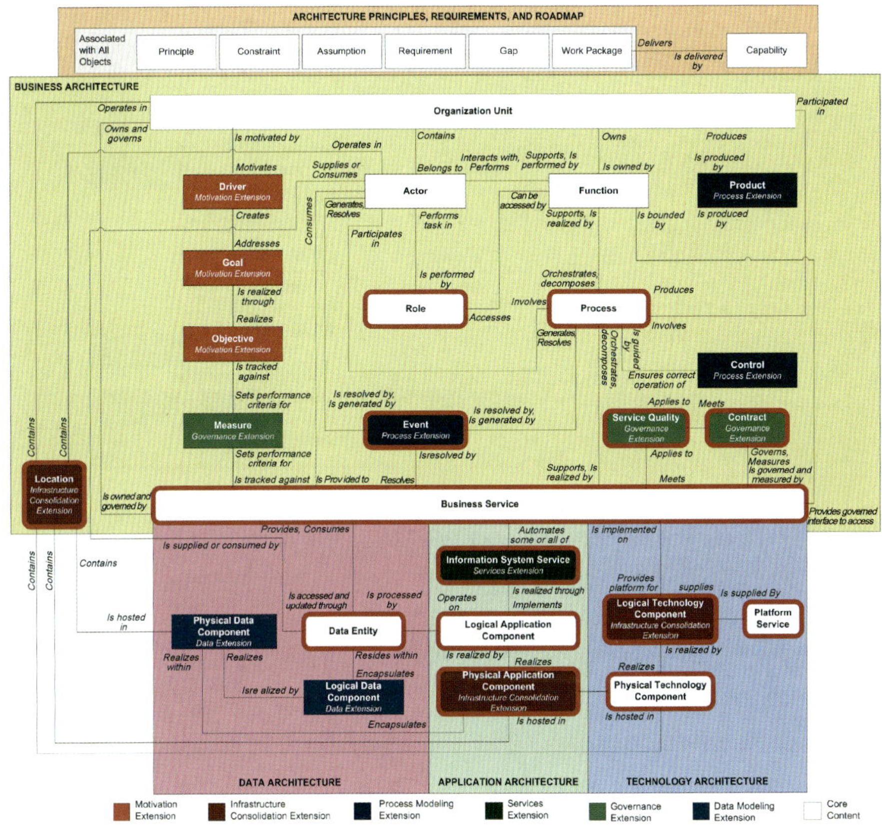

Figure 22-3 SOA Entities in the Content Metamodel

see page 430

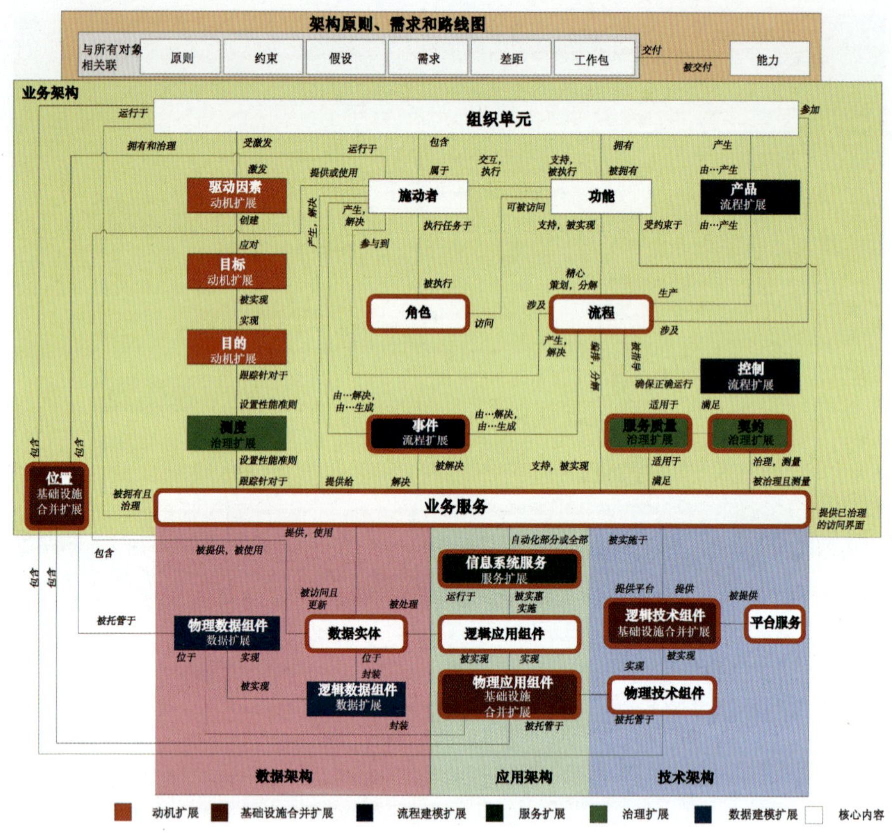

架构原则、需求和路线图
与所有对象相关联
原则
约束
假设
需求
差距
工作包
交付
被交付
能力
业务架构
运行于
组织单元
参加
拥有和治理
受激发
运行于
包含
交互，执行
支持，被执行
拥有
产生
激发
提供或使用
属于
被拥有
由…产生
驱动因素
动机扩展
施动者
功能
产品
流程扩展
创建
产生，解决
产生，解决
可被访问
执行任务于
支持，被实现
受约束于
由…产生
应对
参与到
目标
动机扩展
被执行
精心策划，分解
生产
被实现
角色
涉及
流程
实现
访问
涉及
目的
动机扩展
产生，解决
编排，分解
被指导
控制
流程扩展
确保正确运行
跟踪针对于
由…解决，由…生成
由…解决，由…生成
适用于
满足
设置性能准则
测度
治理扩展
事件
流程扩展
服务质量
治理扩展
契约
治理扩展
包含
包含
设置性能准则
被解决
支持，被实现
适用于
治理，测量
位置
基础设施合并扩展
跟踪针对于
提供给
解决
满足
被治理且测量
被拥有且治理
业务服务
提供已治理的访问界面
提供，使用
自动化部分或全部
被实施于
包含
被提供，被使用
信息系统服务
服务扩展
包含
包含
被访问且更新
被处理
运行于
被实惠实施
提供平台
提供
被提供
被托管于
物理数据组件
数据扩展
数据实体
逻辑应用组件
逻辑技术组件
基础设施合并扩展
平台服务
位于
实现
位于
被实现
实现
被实现
封装
实现
被实现
逻辑数据组件
数据扩展
物理应用组件
基础设施合并扩展
物理技术组件
封装
被托管于
被托管于
数据架构
应用架构
技术架构
动机扩展
基础设施合并扩展
流程建模扩展
服务扩展
治理扩展
数据建模扩展
核心内容

图 22-3　内容元模型中的 SOA 实体

见 431 页

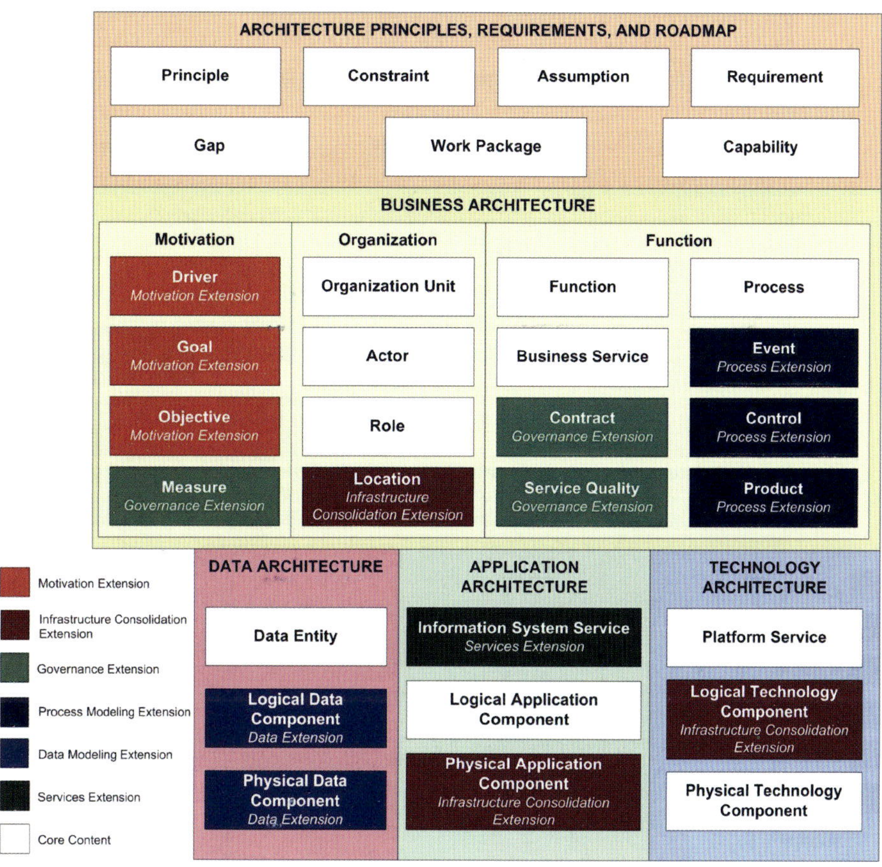

Figure 34-7 Content Metamodel with Extensions

see page 652

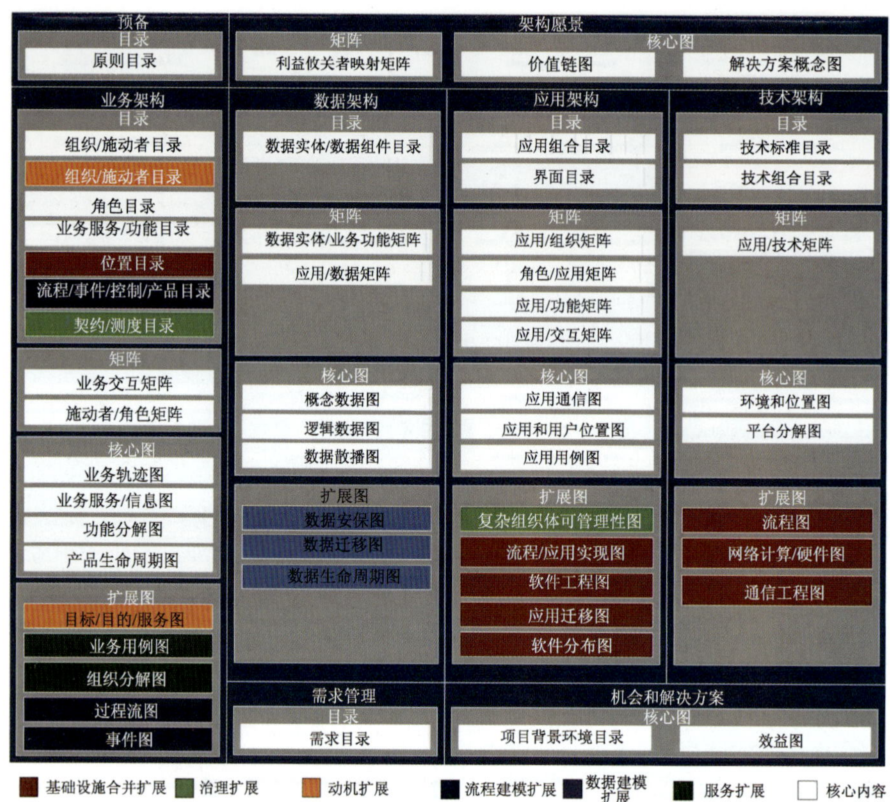
预备
目录
原则目录
架构愿景
矩阵
利益攸关者映射矩阵
核心图
价值链图
解决方案概念图
业务架构
目录
组织/施动者目录
组织/施动者目录
角色目录
业务服务/功能目录
位置目录
流程/事件/控制/产品目录
契约/测度目录
矩阵
业务交互矩阵
施动者/角色矩阵
核心图
业务轨迹图
业务服务/信息图
功能分解图
产品生命周期图
扩展图
目标/目的/服务图
业务用例图
组织分解图
过程流图
事件图
数据架构
目录
数据实体/数据组件目录
矩阵
数据实体/业务功能矩阵
应用/数据矩阵
核心图
概念数据图
逻辑数据图
数据散播图
扩展图
数据安保图
数据迁移图
数据生命周期图
应用架构
目录
应用组合目录
界面目录
矩阵
应用/组织矩阵
角色/应用矩阵
应用/功能矩阵
应用/交互矩阵
核心图
应用通信图
应用和用户位置图
应用用例图
扩展图
复杂组织体可管理性图
流程/应用实现图
软件工程图
应用迁移图
软件分布图
技术架构
目录
技术标准目录
技术组合目录
矩阵
应用/技术矩阵
核心图
环境和位置图
平台分解图
扩展图
流程图
网络计算/硬件图
通信工程图
需求管理
目录
需求目录
机会和解决方案
核心图
项目背景环境目录
效益图
基础设施合并扩展
治理扩展
动机扩展
流程建模扩展
数据建模扩展
服务扩展
核心内容

图 35-3 与核心内容元模型和扩展相关联的制品

见 731 页

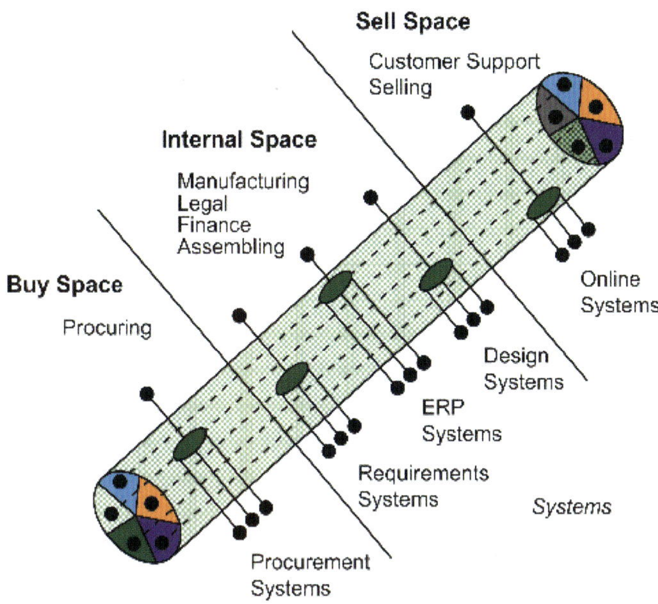

Figure 44-1 An approach to Boundaryless Information Flow (Enterprise Portals)

see page 1006

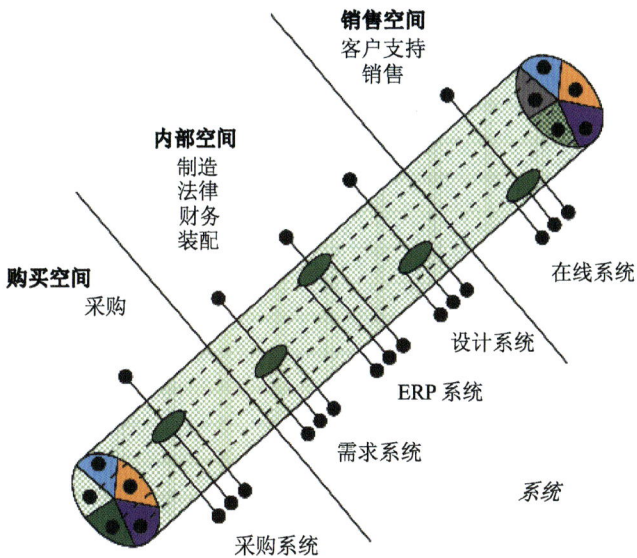

销售空间
客户支持
销售
内部空间
制造
法律
财务
装配
购买空间
采购
在线系统
设计系统
ERP 系统
需求系统
系统
采购系统

图 44-1 无边界信息流的实施途径（ENTERPRISE 门户）

见 1007 页

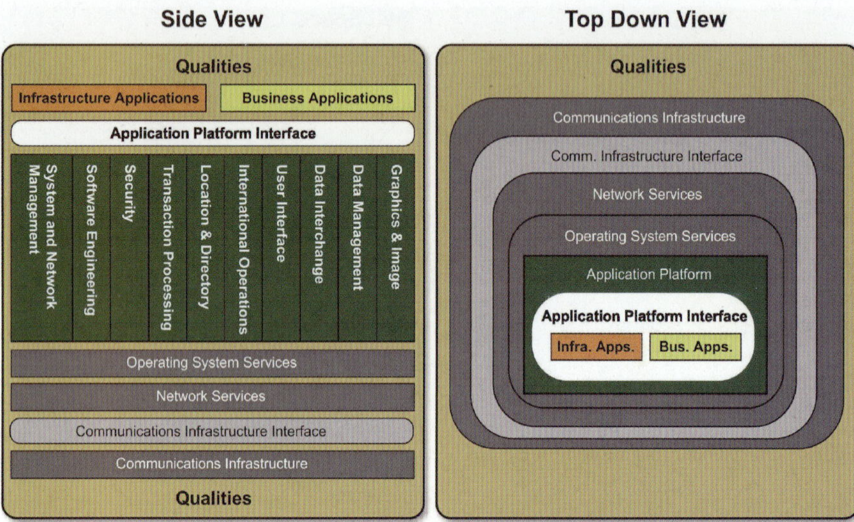
Side View
Top Down View
Qualities
Infrastructure Applications
Business Applications
Application Platform Interface
System and Network Management
Software Engineering
Security
Transaction Processing
Location & Directory
International Operations
User Interface
Data Interchange
Data Management
Graphics & Image
Operating System Services
Network Services
Communications Infrastructure Interface
Communications Infrastructure
Qualities
Qualities
Communications Infrastructure
Comm. Infrastructure Interface
Network Services
Operating System Services
Application Platform
Application Platform Interface
Infra. Apps.
Bus. Apps.

Figure 44-3 Focus of the III-RM

see page 1010

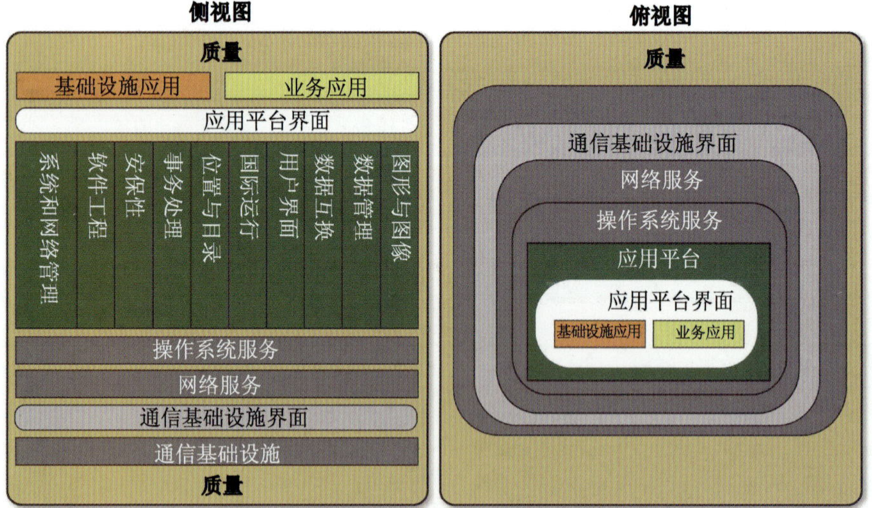
侧视图
俯视图
质量
基础设施应用
业务应用
应用平台界面
系统和网络管理
软件工程
安保性
事务处理
位置与目录
国际运行
用户界面
数据互换
数据管理
图形与图像
操作系统服务
网络服务
通信基础设施界面
通信基础设施
质量
质量
通信基础设施界面
网络服务
操作系统服务
应用平台
应用平台界面
基础设施应用
业务应用

图 44-3 III-RM 的聚焦点

见 1011 页

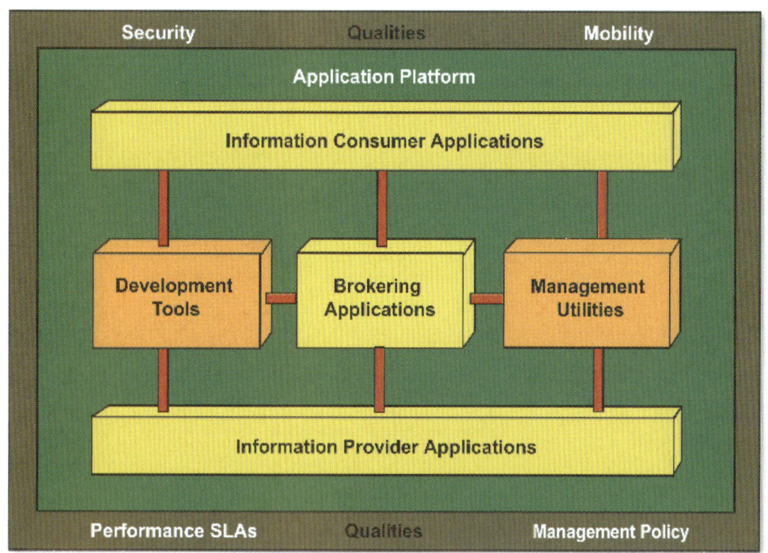

Figure 44-4 III-RM — High-Level

see page 1012

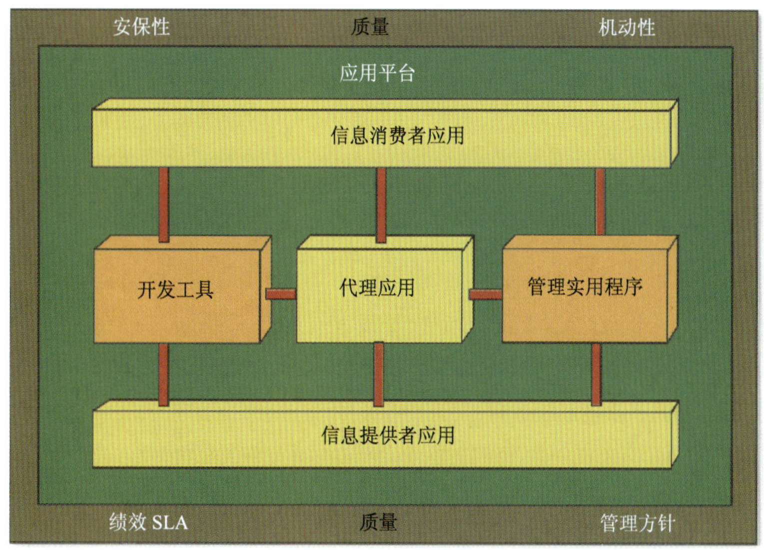

图 44-4 III-RM—高层级

见 1013 页

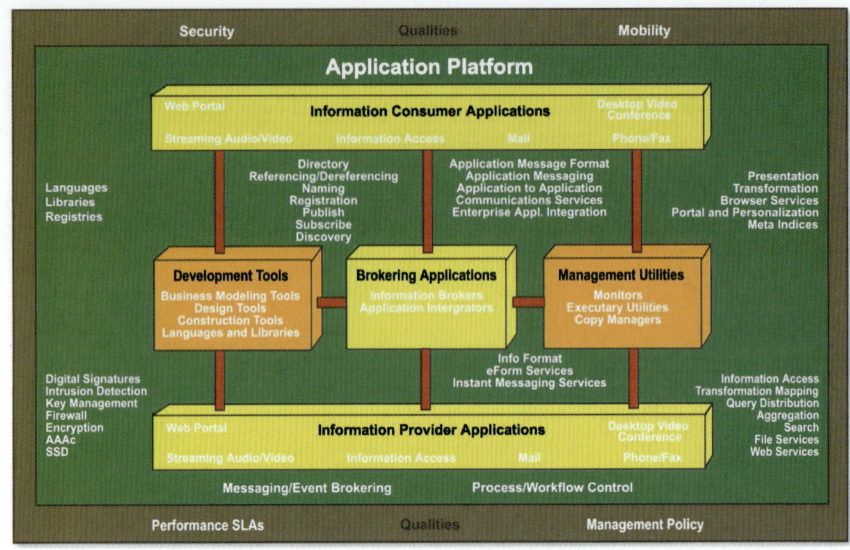

Figure 44-5　III-RM — Detailed

see page 1016

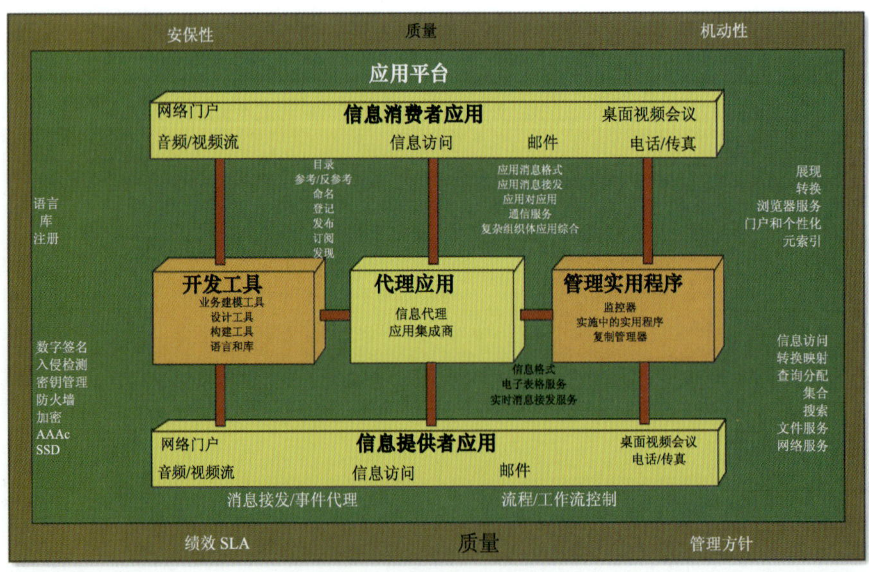

图 44-5　III-RM—细节说明

见 1017 页

TOGAF® 标准9.1版

TOGAF® VERSION 9.1

（中英对照版）

The Open Group 著

张新国 等译

TOGAF®标准 9.1 版（ENTERPRISE 版）是一个针对 ENTERPRISE 架构的、开放的业界共识框架，包含引言、架构开发方法、ADM 指南和技巧、架构内容框架、ENTERPRISE 的连续统一体和工具、TOGAF 参考模型和架构能力框架七个部分。旨在供 ENTERPRISE 架构师、业务架构师、IT 架构师、数据架构师、系统架构师、解决方案架构师以及负责组织内架构功能的任何人使用。

Open Group Standard
TOGAF® Version 9.1
ISBN: 978-90-8753-679-4
Document Number: G116
Published in the U.S. by The Open Group, 2011.

Any comments relating to the material contained in this document may be submitted by email to: OGspecs@opengroup.org

图书在版编目（CIP）数据

TOGAF 标准 9.1 版：汉英对照/开通集团（The Open Group）著；张新国等译. —北京：机械工业出版社，2016.9（2023.12 重印）
书名原文：TOGAF Version 9.1
ISBN 978-7-111-54793-8

Ⅰ.①T… Ⅱ.①开… ②张… Ⅲ.①企业管理—研究—汉、英 Ⅳ.①F272

中国版本图书馆 CIP 数据核字（2016）第 279213 号

机械工业出版社（北京市百万庄大街 22 号 邮政编码 100037）
策划编辑：廖 岩 责任编辑：廖 岩
责任印制：邓 博 责任校对：舒 莹
天津翔远印刷有限公司印刷
2023 年 12 月第 1 版第 12 次印刷
170mm×242mm • 83.25 印张 • 9 插页 • 1815 千字
标准书号：ISBN 978-7-111-54793-8
定价：580.00 元

凡购本书，如有缺页、倒页、脱页，由本社发行部调换

电话服务	网络服务
服务咨询热线：（010）88361066	机工官网：www.cmpbook.com
读者购书热线：（010）68326294	机工官博：weibo.com/cmp1952
（010）88379203	金书网：www.golden-book.com
封面无防伪标均为盗版	教育服务网：www.cmpedu.com

译者序

EA（Enterprise Architecture）在国际上已经发展了 30 多年，这个领域的知识和方法引入中国也已经有十余年，然而国内外在这一领域的技术认知与应用水平的差异，仍使我们在开始翻译这本国际知名架构体系 TOGAF®9.1 时感到责任重大、慎之又慎、希望尽量还原 EA 本身的涵义。同时，也感谢 The Open Group 及其中国区会员在翻译出版过程中给予的大力支持，使得在 TOGAF®9.1 中文版本面世之时，对一些专有名词的习惯用法进行了重新的认知和校准；其初衷是让更多的中文读者能够准确认知 EA，促进国内对 EA 应用能力的提升。

在大家开始阅读本书之前，我们希望和广大读者共同探讨几个方面的问题：

■ 关于外来词语的中文翻译

人类对任何事情的认知都是从概念开始的，概念是对我们世界万事万物的抽象和简化。根植于民族本身的事物，其概念我们往往最为清楚，但对于外来语，就必须保持一种审慎的态度进行语言的转换，以确保在语言转换后仍能保持准确的概念，这也是翻译中有音译和意译两种方式的缘由。一般做法是在汉语里能找到对应准确内涵的词时通常意译，因为我们深刻掌握了它的内涵；但对于无法准确对应到汉语词汇中的外来词，谨慎的做法是保持音译，例如，吉普、尼龙、博客、粉丝等词都是音译的结果。相比音译，意译需要承担的知识传播责任更为重大，译者必须殚精竭虑地避免由于理解的局限造成概念在转译中出现变化。例如英文的 quality 译作“质量”，质量一词从字面来看应译为 quality & quantity，其内涵与表现已出现偏差，quality 如果翻译成“品质”似乎更为准确。最近 Cyber 一词被广泛使用，该词是 20 世纪 40 年代由维纳在控制论研究中提出的，源于希腊语。Cyber 是由通信、控制、计算构成的。在 Cyber 空间，物理空间和系统对象之间公共传递的是信息，但国内普遍把 Çyber 等同于信息一词，显然是有所偏失的，不若音译为“赛博”更能有助于我们学习概念、厘清关系、促进进步。因此，在本书翻译中，我们都坚持忠于原文、力求精准、小心谨慎的原则，以反映原标准本来的内涵。而对于由多个国家的贡献者共同形成的 TOGAF®9.1 而言，语言严谨也是其本身的风格；以至于 TOGAF®9.1 标准中明确说明，当对任何词语含义产生模糊和争议时，建议参考韦氏词典进行判断。

■ 关于对“Enterprise Architecture”一词的理解

在此版译著中，最引人关注的莫过于未将 ENTERPRISE 一词译作常见的“企业”一词，而保留了英文原文，这是 The Open Group 组织在对其内涵与中文译法多次研讨后做出的不得已的决定，作为全文出现频率最高的词汇，我们在此与读者共同探讨其内涵及其可能的译法。

ENTERPRISE 一词在英文辞典及 TOGAF®9.1 里都明确是指：“一个组织或者一个组织群，其由所有权联系在一起，并有共同的底线。”如果简单从字面上就理解为企业，那现在国内外广泛应用架构方法的其他组织，如政府、军队、非营利性联合组织等就无法包括。对应地，在《现代汉语大词典》中对企业一词的定义为："能独立经营、自负盈亏的经济组织。拥有一定数量的固定资产和流动资产，具有法人资格，能独立承担民事责任等。"这一解释代表了国内普遍意义上对企业一词的理解。从概念上看，英文中 ENTERPRISE 一词代表具有一定复杂度的任何组织系统，指正式或非正式的各类社会组织，并不专指企业。ENTERPRISE 包含人、流程、组织、技术和资金等相互依赖的资源，并通过要素之间的相互作用来协调系统整体的功能、共享信息、创建工作流、分配资金和进行决策，以实现系统之目标。由此可见，不管是营利还是非营利，不管是政府还是非政府组织，不管是民间组织还是军队组织都属于 ENTERPRISE 的范畴。为表达在标准中对 ENTERPRISE 这一对象及其边界的强调，同时与 Complex organization 区别，我们推荐将其译为复杂组织体，TOGAF 介绍了进行复杂组织体架构设计的通用性方法及最佳实践，各企业单位应用该方法可以构建自身的企业架构，而政府采用该方法可以构建政府架构，军队也可依此构建军队架构。然而由于概念的转换涉及大量相关方共识的达成，在此版译文中，为表明原有"企业架构"一词已不再适用于 EA 的完整内涵，而此专有名词的翻译还需要进一步在更大范围上进行讨论、验证，故保留了 ENTERPRISE 一词的英文原文，未对其进行翻译。关于组织复杂性的内涵与特征，以及其与架构之间的必然联系，在本序的后面会深入谈到。

Architecture 一词的中文译法也易引起混淆。读者很容易把它理解为结构，但架构里包含结构，结构不能涵盖架构。架构是包含功能和行为的，从这个意义上讲一旦译为"体系结构"等，出现结构一词就已经将原意狭义化。架构是一个系统的基本组织，具体体现为组成部分部件和环境之间的关系，以及支配和设计、演进的原则。更重要的是架构不仅支配设计，还支配生命周期的演进，它是复杂系统进化的治理过程。在本次翻译过程中，Architecture 单独出现时采用了架构译法，但 Enterprise Architecture 作为一个专有名词保留了英文。我们希望以上遗留下来的缺憾能够成为 EA 方法深入研究和应用的一个契机，使对其的定义不只是一个词汇翻译问题，而是一个学术研究和概念定义问题。我们希望更多的人采用 EA 方法，与自身组织的实际情况相结合，形成相应的企业架构、政府架构、军队架构、大型复杂工程项目架构等。

TOGAF®9.1 为读者呈现了比较全面的架构设计和治理的方法与流程，理解 EA 理论与方法，首先要理解架构与系统论的关系以及架构的本体论特征。

■ 关于应对复杂性的挑战

我们今天面对的产品和组织都越来越复杂，复杂性是造成各种问题的原因。如果没有复杂性，可能架构并不是必须的，就如同要盖一间茅草屋是不需要蓝图的，如果盖几十层的现代化大楼，没有蓝图则无法实施。复杂性可以表达为组成系统的元素或者实体的数目，元素和元素之间的关系、内部和外部环境之间关系的数目总和。过去的机械产品，其复杂度量级最多是 10 的 4 次方，后来发展到机械、电子、软件综合系统，这样的系统复杂度量级在许多典型行业已达 10 的 8 次方，如果再加上网络就可能达到 10 的 9 次方以上。面对不断增加的客体复杂度，更要反思组织主体驾驭复杂度的能力，这是当前人类组织发展面临的很大挑战，如果我们的组织忽视这个本质问题，在实践中就会困难重重，这也是 EA 要在日益复杂的信息技术时代解决的问题。对复杂组织体进行深一层讨论，可以认为复杂组织体至少需具备两个层面的能力：第一层是要有满足外部需要的业务，第二层是业务要不仅能适应外部竞争与环境约束，还能最高效地运行。这两层的内容就是能力建设。我们之前因为落后，很多领域从无到有，所以能力建设往往在第一层，即所谓填补空白、达到国内一流。但当前国内各类复杂组织体都遇到第二层的挑战，就是达到在开放的国际环境下进行竞争的层次。综合以上论述，一方面组织管理的主客体复杂度不断提高，另一方面能力建设需求不断提高，这时就要考虑组织体的整体设计与管理，回答战略、能力建设、业务模型的对准问题，也就是目前广泛进行的变革设计，回答这些问题实际上就是在进行架构设计。

■ 关于架构的本体论基础

系统表现为实体及它们之间的关系。根据实体包含模块的组件关系不同可分为静态系统和动态系统两类，静态系统指构成系统的组件是相互连接的，动态系统指构成系统的组件是相互作用的。在一个开放的系统环境下，复杂的动态系统运行过程中会产生涌现性和自组织、自适应性。生物体参与的系统几乎都是复杂系统，ENTERPRISE 就是典型的高层级复杂系统。只有认识到其复杂系统的本质，才会促使我们将它显性化地当做一个系统来思考。这一部分和另外一部分是什么关系？本部分属于哪个更大的部分？在由更大的部分构成的环境下又包含哪些实体？它们之间又是什么关系？当所有的事情都能以联系的方式展开分析与设计，其实就是系统思维，今天的互联网思维本质上就是系统思维。

架构之所以能够在对复杂系统的理解、表达上发挥重要作用，原因是架构的本体论基础。本体论就是概念的规范化，规范就是要正规和正式地陈述表达，任何正式的知识都基于概念规范化。在表现上，本体论实际上也是确定一个领域的术语集合，例如谈到 Architecture 这个领域，一定要用这个领域的术语来表达，否则就难以达成共识。本体论是由主观知识到客观知识的桥梁，它传递一个领域共同的理解，而不是个体理解，它捕获共识问题，而不是个别问题。正由于这样，基于本体论的方法就为知识共享和复用提供了最为根本的基础。在信息化解决了信息复用与共享的手段背后，实际是关于各类数据、模型等的本体论解决了共享合作的基础。同时恰恰本体论在数字化环境里是最好实现的，因为它是知识的结构化抽象，不仅可实现知识的共享和复用，还可进一步解决异构对象的综合。如果没有本体论方法，未来赛博—物理系统难以建立。事实上，网络搜索引擎背后也是基于本体论方法。这种基于本体论的结构化定义，在网络里应用为搜索，在知识管理里应用为知识检索，在组织管理里就是战略与业务的对准，在系统工程里即从需求、设计到制造正向推进的数字线索，并可以实现全生命周期的可追溯，这也是架构发挥作用的重要原因。如果架构在正向设计之后没有可追溯性，就难于重复和提高成熟度，这是计算机软件工程，系统工程，还有人、组织在内的工程都需要架构方法的原因。

总结来说，EA 就是战略、业务与技术的综合，回答战略是什么、靠怎样的业务模型实现战略以及依靠什么技术支撑业务实现，从而保证战略和业务的对准。在解决复杂问题时，架构的本质作用是结构化，而不是结构。就像模块化一样，而不是模块本身。这是一种方法论，这种方法论贯彻到从形式到功能的设计，可以发挥三个方面的作用。一是促进组织管理从混乱到有序的转变。过去组织的业务结构和组织结构更多看到的是形式，架构更强调结构支撑下的功能变化与联系，明确功能与目标之间的联系。事实上，信息本身不能改变能量和物质，但是信息结构化程度的增加会改变物理的有序度，而任何事情只要有序，效率和效果都会更好，因此，架构设计与治理工作可以促进组织的高效有序发展。第二个作用是促进复杂组织体治理原则与业务模型共识的形成。架构工作将不同部分的想法、不同层级的想法、不同专业的想法转换成共享的工作模型和概念，通过显性化、结构化，促进组织体范围内架构设计结果的共享、执行或复用发展。第三方面的作用是促进政策连续性的组织治理。架构治理是面向战略、综合业务与技术应用的整体治理方式，所产生的结构化的创造性一定会比非结构化的创造性来得更有效，更能驾驭组织体不断增加的复杂性。

国际上架构方法的实践已经非常广泛，无论是大型企业、政府或是军队都有优秀的架构实践。其中 The Open Group 发布的 TOGAF（The Open Group Architecture Framework）是集成众多实践经验的具有通用性和实操性的架构标准。TOGAF 提出的架构开发方法及内容框架更是成为各类复杂组织体进行架构实践的主要参考。实践证明，架构及相关的模型理论在今天对广大的复杂型组织是通用的。为了促进国内架构方法的全面、深入理解与广泛传播，The Open Group 授权中航工业翻译并出版 TOGAF®9.1。我也非常荣幸能够继翻译引入 INCOSE 的《系统工程手册》后，再次组织翻译 TOGAF®9.1 这本庞大的架构标准，为架构方法在国内的推广和应用贡献一份力量。

在此次翻译过程中，我带领中航工业信息技术中心架构实践团队形成了一个翻译小组，坚持力求反映原著本意，力求中英文可对照互译，斟词琢句、慎之又慎地完成翻译工作。感谢中航工业信息技术中心团队在此过程中付出的辛劳。对我们翻译团队而言，这既是一个语言学习、转化的过程，更是一个架构方法全面认知和学习的历程。同时，在翻译与实践中的反复映射，加深了我们对架构方法的理解，促进了很多架构相关名词术语中文译法的修正。

ENTERPRISE 作为最高层次的复杂系统，正面临着严重的发展挑战，为获取竞争优势要保持一致的协同。这些协同包含组织战略变化和管理方式的协同，以及组织内部资源配置、组织文化建设到关系网络配置的协同。从总体能力建设角度出发，构建合适的系统输入与输出关系，并及时根据反馈调整、不断为顾客提供价值、实现股东利益，都需要组织采用全局分析、设计与治理的方法，形成从顶向下正向设计与变革的能力。架构的指导和战略的引领一定会帮助各类复杂组织更清楚地认知情况，分析需要，促进更为有序和有效的发展。

张新国
2016 年 10 月

序

TOGAF® 9.1 被中国译者翻译成简体中文，标志着 The Open Group 的重大里程碑。

首先，我想表达我对张新国博士（中航工业首席信息官）的感谢，因为他的引领和驱动使 TOGAF 翻译为中文成为可能，同时我也感谢 The Open Group 其他中国会员组织参与这项国际标准的推进工作。

EA 的实践和应用随着时间演进与完善，发挥出实用和示范价值。TOGAF 是在全球范围使用的 EA 标准和最佳实践，它并不代表单一组织的立场，而代表跨组织、行业与政府机构的共识。

该标准既是组织业务变革可以遵循的科学方法，也是指导企业推进业务与 IT 融合，进而推进两化深度融合的重要方法。本次将 TOGAF® 9.1 翻译成中文，是 The Open Group 在中国市场推广 TOGAF 的重大举措。

语言和文化并不总是容易沟通的。TOGAF 中的基本词汇“ENTERPRISE”，其理解和使用范围在英语原文中包含公共、私营、学术和慈善组织在内的多种涵义；而“Enterprise Architecture”多年前的中文翻译“企业架构”在当时起到了作用，但由于它侧重于“营利型”企业，此翻译方式潜在地排除了其他相关用法。

时至今日，“ENTERPRISE”和“Enterprise Architecture”的中文翻译并没有在审议过程中获得中国区会员的一致认可。因此，虽然此标准已经被翻译成中文，但是这两个最基本的术语将保持英文，兼顾英文包含的多个潜在译法。

基于原则的立场非常重要，具有多种观点和视角也很重要，但不应固执己见并以其作为停滞不前的理由。我们的世界变化太快，停滞不前的组织将无法生存或在竞争中胜出。

虽然在第一次本标准全文中文翻译中保留“ENTERPRISE”和“Enterprise Architecture”不做翻译不是理想的状况，但此次全文翻译工作很有必要，因为可以使大众知悉目前在中国被广泛理解和使用的现有翻译，并供其他中国组织使用和展望未来。本译著的潜在价值重大，而不仅限于“营利型”企业。

我们希望这本译著加速 TOGAF 这项管理修炼在中国更加深入和广泛地被接受，并使众多在中国政府、国家企事业单位和私营企业领域推进变革的领导者和其他个人受益。

Chris Forde
Enterprise Architecture 全球副总裁
亚太区总经理
The Open Group

鸣谢

本文件由 The Open Group 撰写，此次翻译管理人员包括：

Chris Forde，The Open Group 全球架构副总裁兼亚太区总经理

Andrew Josey, The Open Group 标准&认证副总裁

Sonia Gonzalez，The Open Group 论坛总监

高美华，The Open Group 亚太区商务总监

The Open Group 衷心感谢此 Open Group 标准的中文翻译团队：

张新国

高星海	程　燕
袁　蕾	沈欢欢
李　萍	孙向奎
张　哲	师荣华
张　迪	樊欣媛
姚轶峰	

The Open Group 衷心感谢在此中文翻译版正式审校过程中做出贡献的组织成员（以下排名不分先后，最终解释权归 The Open Group）：

金航数码科技有限责任公司
华为技术有限公司
Cognizant
Pan Asia Training

Contents

目 录

List of Figures

图 目 录

List of Tables

表 目 录

Preface

TOGAF Version 9.1, Enterprise Edition, is an open, industry consensus framework for enterprise architecture.

This Document

There are seven parts to the TOGAF document:

PART I (Introduction) This part provides a high-level introduction to the key concepts of enterprise architecture and in particular the TOGAF approach. It contains the definitions of terms used throughout TOGAF and release notes detailing the changes between this version and the previous version of TOGAF.

PART II (Architecture Development Method) This is the core of TOGAF. It descrybes the TOGAF Architecture Development Method (ADM) — a step-by-step approach to developing an enterprise architecture.

PART III (ADM Guidelines & Techniques) This part contains a collection of guidelines and techniques available for use in applying TOGAF and the TOGAF ADM.

PART IV (Architecture Content Framework)This part describes the TOGAF content framework, including a structured metamodel for architectural artifacts, the use of reusable architecture building blocks, and an overview of typical archi-tecture deliverables.

PART V (Enterprise Continuum & Tools) This part discusses appropriate taxonomies and tools to categorize and store the outputs of architecture activity within an enterprise.

PART VI (TOGAF Reference Models) This part provides a selection of architectural reference models, which includes the TOGAF Foundation Architecture, and the Integrated Information Infrastructure Reference Model (III-RM).

PART VII (Architecture Capability Framework) This part discusses the organization, processes, skills, roles, and responsibilities required to establish and operate an architecture function within an enterprise.

Intended Audience

TOGAF is intended for enterprise architects, business architects, IT architects, data architects, systems architects, solutions architects,and anyone responsible for the architecture function within an organization.

Keywords

architecture, architecture framework, architecture development method, architect, architecting, enterprise architecture, enterprise architecture framework, enterprise architecture method, method, methods, open, group, technical reference model, standards, standards information base.

前　言

TOGAF 9.1 版本（ENTERPRISE 版）是一个针对 Enterprise Architecture 的、开放的业界共识框架。

本文件

TOGAF 文件包含七个部分：

第一部分　（引言）本部分对 Enterprise Architecture 的关键概念，特别是 TOGAF 实施途径提供了概括性介绍。本部分包括在整个 TOGAF 中所使用术语的定义及对本 TOGAF 版本与之前 TOGAF 版本之间的变化进行详述的发布说明。

第二部分　（架构开发方法）本部分是 TOGAF 的核心，描述 TOGAF 架构开发方法（ADM）——一种开发 Enterprise Architecture 的循序渐进的实施途径。

第三部分　（ADM 指南和技巧）本部分包含在应用 TOGAF 和 TOGAF ADM 时可供使用的指南和技巧的集合。

第四部分　（架构内容框架）本部分描述 TOGAF 内容框架，包括一个用于架构制品的结构化元模型、可复用架构构建块的用法及典型架构交付物的概述。

第五部分　（ENTERPRISE 的连续统一体和工具）本部分论述对 ENTERPRISE 内架构活动的各种输出进行分类和存储的适用分类法和工具。

第六部分　（TOGAF 参考模型）本部分提供对架构参考模型的选择，包括 TOGAF 基础架构以及综合信息基础设施参考模型（III-RM）。

第七部分　（架构能力框架）本部分论述在 ENTERPRISE 内建立和运行架构功能所需的组织、流程、技能、角色和职责。

目标读者

TOGAF 旨在供 ENTERPRISE 架构师、业务架构师、IT 架构师、数据架构师、系统架构师、解决方案架构师以及负责组织内架构功能的任何人使用。

关键词

架构、架构框架、架构开发方法、架构师、架构开发、Enterprise Architecture、Enterprise Architecture 框架、Enterprise Architecture 方法、方法、方法集、开放、群组、技术参考模型、标准、标准信息库。

About The Open Group

The Open Group

The Open Group is a vendor-neutral and technology-neutral consortium, whose vision of Boundaryless Information Flow™ will enable access to integrated information within and between enterprises based on open standards and global interoperability. The Open Group works with customers, suppliers, consortia, and other standards bodies. Its role is to capture, understand, and address current and emerging requirements, establish policies, and share best practices; to facilitate interoperability, develop consensus, and evolve and integrate specifications and Open Source technologies; to offer a comprehensive set of services to enhance the operational efficiency of consortia; and to operate the industry's premier certification service, including UNIX® certification.

Further information on The Open Group is available at www.opengroup.org.

The Open Group has over 15 years' experience in developing and operating certification programs and has extensive experience developing and facilitating industry adoption of test suites used to validate conformance to an open standard or specification.

More information is available at www.opengroup.org/certification.

The Open Group publishes a wide range of technical documentation, the main part of which is focused on development of Technical and Product Standards and Guides, but which also includes white papers, technical studies, branding and testing documentation, and business titles. Full details and a catalog are available at www.opengroup.org/bookstore.

As with all live documents, Technical Standards and Specifications require revision to align with new developments and associated international standards. To distinguish between revised specifications which are fully backwards-compatible and those which are not:

- A new *Version* indicates there is no change to the definitive information contained in the previous publication of that title, but additions/extensions are included. As such, it *replaces* the previous publication.
- A new *Issue* indicates there is substantive change to the definitive information contained in the previous publication of that title, and there may also be additions/extensions. As such, both previous and new documents are maintained as current publications.

Readers should note that Corrigenda may apply to any publication.Corrigenda information is published at www.opengroup.org/corrigenda.

关于 The Open Group

The Open Group

The Open Group 是一个厂商中立和技术中立的联合体，其愿景“无边界信息流™”基于开放标准和全球互用性，促进对 ENTERPRISE 内或 ENTERPRISE 间综合信息的访问。The Open Group 与客户、供应商、联合体及其他标准机构共同工作，其角色是捕获、理解和应对当前及新兴的需求，建立方针，并分享最佳实践；促进互用性，发展共识，演进并综合各类规范和开源技术；提供一整套增强联合体运作效率的综合性服务，以及业界首屈一指的认证服务，包括 UNIX®认证。

更多关于 The Open Group 的信息可访问 www.opengroup.org。

The Open Group 在开发和运行认证程序方面拥有超过 15 年的经验，并且在开发和推动业界采用测试套件来确认与开放标准或规范的一致性方面，拥有丰富的经验。

更多信息可访问 www.opengroup.org/certification。

The Open Group 发布了各类技术文档，这些文档的主要部分聚焦于技术和产品标准及指南的开发，但也包括一些白皮书、技术研究、商标和测试文档，以及业务名称。更多详细内容和目录集可访问 www.opengroup.org/bookstore。

与所有现存的文件一样，技术标准和规范需要进行修订，以符合新进展和相关国际标准。在修订的规范中要区分哪些是完全向后兼容的，哪些不是完全向后兼容的：

- 新版本表示未对之前发行的出版物中所含的明确信息进行更改，但是包含了补充/扩展内容。因此，新版本取代了之前的出版物。
- 新版本发行表示对之前发行的出版物中所含的明确信息做出重要更改，并且也可能存在补充/扩展内容。因此，之前文件和新文件均被保留为当前出版物。

读者应注意勘误表可应用于任何出版物。勘误表信息发布在 www.opengroup.org/corrigenda 上。

Participants

This document was prepared by The Open Group Architecture Forum and incorporates TOGAF 9 and TOGAF 9 Technical Corrigendum No. 1. When The Open Group approved TOGAF 9 Technical Corrigendum No. 1 on July 21st, 2011, the membership of the Architecture Forum was as follows:

Dave Hornford, Conexiam, Chair

Tara Paider, Nationwide, Vice-Chair

Chris Forde, The Open Group, Forum Director

Andrew Josey, The Open Group, Director of Standards

Garry Doherty, The Open Group, TOGAF Product Manager

Cathy Fox, The Open Group, Technical Editor

Architecture Forum Technical Reviewers

Technical reviewers are those individuals who have submitted comments during the company review, or participated in a face-to-face issue resolution meeting during the development of TOGAF 9 Technical Corrigendum No. 1.

Andrew Josey	Dave van Gelder	Larry Bergen	Tara Paider
Arnold van Overeem	Garry Doherty	Maggie Huang	Tejpal S. Virdi
Bill Adams	Jack Fujieda	Mike Lambert	Thomas Obitz
Bill Estrem	Jane Varnus	Mike Turner	Timo Karvinen
Bob Weisman	Jason Broome	Paul van der Merwe	Tim O'Neill
Chris Armstrong	Judith Jones	Peter Kaufmann	Stephen Bennett
Chris Forde	Jörgen Dahlberg	Richard Hewardo	Harry Hendrickx
Chris Greenslade	Ken Street	Roger Griessen	Steve Else
Paul Homan	Kevin Sevigny	Roland Fabri	Ed Harrington
Dave Hornford	Kirk Hansen	Sarina Viljoen	Heather Kreger

Architecture Forum Members

The following organizations were members of the Architecture Forum at the time of approval.

参与方

本文件由 The Open Group 架构论坛编制并纳入 TOGAF 9 和 TOGAF 9 第 1 号技术勘误表。在 The Open Group 于 2011 年 7 月 21 日批准 TOGAF 9 第 1 号技术勘误表时，架构论坛包括如下成员：

Dave Hornford， Conexiam，主席

Tara Paider， Nationwide，副主席

Chris Forde， The Open Group，论坛负责人

Andrew Josey， The Open Group，标准负责人

Garry Doherty， The Open Group，TOGAF 产品经理

Cathy Fox， The Open Group，技术编辑

架构论坛技术审视人员

技术审视人员是在公司审视期间已提交意见或在编制 TOGAF 9 第 1 号技术勘误表期间参与到面对面议题解决方案会议的个人。

Andrew Josey	Dave van Gelder	Larry Bergen	Tara Paider
Arnold van Overeem	Garry Doherty	Maggie Huang	Tejpal S. Virdi
Bill Adams	Jack Fujieda	Mike Lambert	Thomas Obitz
Bill Estrem	Jane Varnus	Mike Turner	Timo Karvinen
Bob Weisman	Jason Broome	Paul van der Merwe	Tim O'Neill
Chris Armstrong	Judith Jones	Peter Kaufmann	Stephen Bennett
Chris Forde	Jörgen Dahlberg	Richard Hewardo	Harry Hendrickx
Chris Greenslade	Ken Street	Roger Griessen	Steve Else
Paul Homan	Kevin Sevigny	Roland Fabri	Ed Harrington
Dave Hornford	Kirk Hansen	Sarina Viljoen	Heather Kreger

架构论坛成员

下列组织在本文件被批准时是架构论坛的成员。

1Plug, USA
act! consulting GmbH, Germany
alfabet AG, Germany
ARISMORE, France
AT&T ITAS, USA
Aalto University, School of Science & Technology, Finland
Abu Dhabi Retirement Pensions & Benefits Fund, UAE
Acando AS, Norway
Accelare, USA Accenture, USA
Ahead Technology Inc., Canada
Allianz Global Corporate & Specialty, Germany
Altertech, Saudi Arabia American
Express, USA Anywhere, Czech
Republic Aoyama Gakuin University, Japan
Apollo Group, USA
Applied Technology Solutions Inc., USA
ArchiXL, Netherlands
Architecting the Enterprise, UK
Armscor, South Africa
Armstrong Process Group Inc., USA
Aspire Technology, China
Astra Zeneca, UK
Athr IT Consulting, Saudi Arabia
Austin Energy, USA
Auto Trader.com, USA
Avolution, Australia
BIZZ design Holding, Netherlands
BNP PARIBAS, France
BP Oil International Ltd., UK
BSI SA, Switzerland
Bank of America, USA
Bank of Montreal, Canada
Biner Consulting, Sweden
Bizcon, Denmark
Boston University, USA
British Telecom Plc, UK
Build The Vision Inc., Canada
Business Connexion, South Africa
CA Inc., Canada
CC and C Solutions, Australia
CEISAR, France
CGI Group Inc., Canada
CLARS Ltd., UK
CPP Investment Board, Canada
CS Interactive Training, South Africa
CSC, USA
Capgemini, Netherlands
Capita IT Services, UK
Casewise Systems Ltd., USA
CeRTAE ULaval, Canada
Celestial Consulting Ltd., UK
Centre for Open Systems, Australia
Chem China, China
Chengdu GKHB Computer Systems, China
Cisco Systems Inc., USA
Cognizant CTS, India
Colorado Technical University, USA
Conexiam, Canada
DMTF, USA
DNV CIBIT, Netherlands
DUX DILIGENS, Mexico

Participants
DWP Programme & Systems Delivery Group, UK
Deccan Global Solutions LLC, USA
Deloitte Consulting LLP, USA
Department of Information Management, Ming Chuan University, Taiwan
Detecon International GmbH, Germany
Detica, UK
Devoteam Consulting, Denmark
EA Global Ltd., UK
EA Principals Inc., USA
EA Dynamics UK Ltd., UK
EASD-CIOB (Treasury Board of Canada Secretariat), Canada
ETNIC, Belgium
Edutech Enterprises, Singapore
Eli Lilly & Company Ltd., USA
Elparazim, USA
Energistics, USA
Energy Consulting/Corporate IT Solutions, Russian Federation
Enterprise Architects Pty Ltd., Australia
Enterprise Architects, UK
Enterprise Architecture Consulting, UK
Enterprise Architecture Solutions Ltd., UK
Eskom, South Africa
Estrat TI SA DE CV, Mexico
FEAC Institute, USA
Faculty Training Institute, South Africa
Firstrand Bank Ltd., South Africa
Forefront Consulting Group AB, Sweden
France Telecom, France
Fraunhofer SIT, Germany
Fujitsu Services, UK
Getronics, Netherlands
Gijima, South Africa
Global Info Tech Co. Ltd., China
Gnosis IT Knowledge Solutions, Brazil
Grant MacEwan College, Canada
Hebei Wangxun Digital Technology Ltd., China
Hewlett-Packard, USA
Hotel Technology Next Generation, USA
IBM, USA
iCMG Private Ltd., India
Infosys Ltd., India
Infovide SA, Poland
ING Group, Netherlands
INVITALIA, Italy
IRM AB, Sweden
IRM UK, UK
ISES, Netherlands
ISNordic A/S, Denmark
Itera-IT Institute Iberoamerica, Mexico
ITM Beratungsgesellschaft mbH, Germany
IT preneurs, Netherlands
JISC ,UK

Jodayn Consulting, Saudi Arabia
JourneyOne, Australia
Kamehameha Schools, USA
Kirk Hansen Consulting, Canada
Knotion Consulting, South Africa
KU-INOVA, Thailand
Kyoto University, Japan
Lawrence Technological University, USA
LoQutus, Belgium
Mainline Information Systems Inc, USA
Maptech, UAE
Marathon Oil Corporation, USA
Marriott International, USA
Mega International, France
Meraka Institutue, South Africa
Metaplexity Associates, USA
MetLife, USA
MIC Business Solutions Inc, USA
Microsoft Corporation, USA
Mizuho Information & Research Institute Inc, Japan
Molimax Consulting Ltd., UK
NAF, Netherlands Architecture Forum, Netherlands
NASA SEWP, USA
National IT and Telecom Agency, IT-Architecture Division, Denmark
National Policing Improvement Agency, UK
National University of Singapore, Institute of Systems Science, Singapore
Nationwide, USA
Nedbank, South Africa
NEHTA, Australia
NEOXIA, Morocco
NGN Technologies, India
NII Holdings Inc., USA
Nedbank, South Africa
Nippon Telegraph & Telephone Corporation, Japan
Nomura Research Institute Ltd., Japan
Norwegian University of Science & Technology, Norway
OFFIS, Germany
OMG, USA
Online Business Systems, Canada
Open GIS Consortium Inc., USA
Open Text Inc., Canada
Oracle Corporation, USA
Orbus Software, UK
Ovations, South Africa
Oxford Brookes University, UK
PATH ITTS, Brazil
Penn State (College of IST), USA
plenum Management Consulting, Germany
Price water house Coopers LLP, South Africa
Procter & Gamble Company, USA Promis,
Switzerland
Proya Profesyonel Yazilim Cozumleri ve Danismanlik Ltd., Turkey

Participants
QA Ltd., UK
QR Systems Inc., Canada
Qernel nv, Belgium
QualiWare ApS, Denmark
Raytheon, USA
ReGIS Inc., Japan
Real IRM Solutions (Pty) Ltd., South Africa
Redd Consulting, UK
Reply Ltd., UK
Resultex Ltd., New Zealand
Rio Tinto, UK
Rococo Co Ltd., Japan
Roehampton University, UK
Rolls-Royce plc, USA
Royal Philips Electronics, Netherlands
SAP, Germany
SARS, South Africa
SIF Association, USA
SIM University, Singapore
SIOS Technology Inc., Japan
SKLSE (Wuhan University), China
SMME, Belgium
SNA Technologies Inc., USA
SYRACOM Consulting AG, Germany
Senacor Technologies AG, Germany
Shenzhen Kingdee Middleware, China
Shift Technologies LLC, UAE
Sidra Medical & Research Center, Qatar
Sinapse, Canada
Sirius Computer Solutions, USA
Skills Funding, UK
Smart421 Ltd., UK
Software AG, Germany
Sogeti SAS, Netherlands
Soluta.Net srl, Italy
Solvera Solutions, Canada
South African Reserve Bank, South Africa
Sparx Systems, Australia
State Information Technology Agency (Pty) Ltd., South Africa
Steria Ltd., UK
Swiss Federal Administration, Switzerland
Systems Flow Inc., USA
T-Systems, South Africa
TONEX, USA
TRM Technologies Inc., Canada
TSYS, USA
Tata Consultancy Services, India
Teamcall Ltd., Belgium
Technology & HR Consultancy Ltd., UK
TeleManagement Forum, UK
Telkom SA Ltd., South Africa
The Boeing Company, USA

The Capital Group Companies Inc., USA
The MITRE Corporation, USA
The Marlo Group, Australia
The Salamander Organization Ltd., UK
The Unit bv, Netherlands
Tieto EA Consulting, Finland
Tieturi OY, Finland
triVector (Pty) Ltd., South Africa
Troux Technologies, USA
Turkcell, Turkey
UDEF-IT, USA
US DoD-CIO (Office of the CIO), USA
Unilever Group plc, UK
University of Colorado at Boulder, USA
University of Denver, USA
University of Johannesburg, South Africa
University of Nordland Norway
University of Pretoria, South Africa
University of South Africa, South Africa
University of Washington, USA
Vale Brazil, Brazil
Van Haren Publishing, Netherlands
Web Age Solutions Inc., Canada
Wells Fargo Bank, USA
Wipro Technologies, India
World Vision International, USA
Xantus Consulting, UK

Trademarks

Boundaryless Information Flow™ is a trademark and ArchiMate®, Jericho Forum®, Making Standards Work®, Motif®, OSF/1®, The Open Group®, TOGAF®, UNIX®, and the "X" device are registered trademarks of The Open Group in the United Sta-tes and other countries.

COBIT® is a registered trademark of the Information Systems Audit and Control Ass-ociation and the IT Governance Institute.

CORBA®, MDA®, Model Driven Architecture®, Object Management®, OMG®, and UML® are registered trademarks and BPMN™, Business Process Modeling Notation™, and Unified Modeling Language™ are trademarks of the Object Management Group.

Energistics™ is a trademark of Energistics.

FICO® is a registered trademark of Fair Isaac Corporation.

IBM® and WebSphere® are registered trademarks of International Business Machines Corporation.

IEEE® is a registered trademark of the Institute of Electrical and Electronics Engine-ers, Inc.

ITIL® is a registered trademark of the Office of Government Commerce in the United Kingdom and other countries.

Java® is a registered trademark of Sun Microsystems, Inc.

Merriam-Webster's Collegiate Dictionary® is a trademark of Merriam-Webster, Incor-porated.

Microsoft® is a registered trademark of Microsoft Corporation.

OAGIS® is a registered trademark of the Open Applications Group, Inc.

OpenGL® is a registered trademark of SGI.

PRINCE® is a registered trademark and PRINCE2™ is a trademark of the Office of Government Commerce in the United Kingdom and other countries.

SAP® is a registered trademark of SAP AG in Germany and in several other coun-tries.

The following are registered trademarks of the Software Engineering Institute (SEI):

- CMMI® (Capability Maturity Model Integration)
- IPD-CMM® (Integrated Product Development Capability Maturity Model)
- P-CMM® (People Capability Maturity Model)
- SA-CMM® (Software Acquisition Capability Maturity Model)
- SCAMPI® (Standard CMMI Appraisal Method for Process Improvement)
- SE-CMM® (Systems Engineering Capability Maturity Model)
- SW-CMM® (Capability Maturity Model for Software)

The Open Group acknowledges that there may be other company names and pro-ducts that might be covered by trademark protection and advises the reader to verify them independently.

商标

无边界信息流™是一个商标，ArchiMate®、Jericho Forum®、Making Standards Work®、Motif®、OSF/1®、The Open Group®、TOGAF®、UNIX®以及“X”图案是 The Open Group 在美国和其他国家的注册商标。

COBIT®是信息系统审计和控制协会与 IT 治理协会的注册商标。

CORBA®、MDA®、Model Driven Architecture®、Object Management®、OMG®以及 UML®是注册商标，BPMN™、Business Process Modeling Notation™和 Unified Modeling Language™是对象管理组织（OMG）的商标。

Energistics™是 Energistics 公司的商标。

FICO®是 Fair Isaac 公司的注册商标。

IBM®和 WebSphere®是国际商业机器公司（IBM）的注册商标。

IEEE®是电气与电子工程师协会的注册商标。

ITIL®是英国政府商务部在英国和其他国家的注册商标。

Java®是 Sun Microsystems 公司的注册商标。

Merriam-Webster's Collegiate Dictionary®是 Merriam-Webster 公司的商标。

Microsoft®是微软公司的商标。

OAGIS®是 Open Applications Group 公司的注册商标。

OpenGL®是 SGI 的注册商标。

PRINCE®是一个注册商标，PRINCE2™是英国政府商务部在英国和其他国家的商标。

SAP®是 SAP 股份公司在德国和其他几个国家使用的注册商标。

以下商标是软件工程协会（SEI）的注册商标：

- CMMI®（能力成熟度模型综合）
- IPD-CMM®（集成产品开发能力成熟度模型）
- P-CMM®（人力资源能力成熟度模型）
- SA-CMM®（软件采办能力成熟度模型）
- SCAMPI®（标准 CMMI 流程改进评估方法）
- SE-CMM®（系统工程能力成熟度模型）
- SW-CMM®（软件能力成熟度模型）

The Open Group 承认可能存在商标保护所涵盖的其他公司名称和产品，并建议读者对这些公司名称和产品进行独立验证。

Acknowledgements

The Open Group gratefully acknowledges The Open Group Architecture Forum for developing TOGAF.

The Open Group gratefully acknowledges the contribution of the US Air Force for its Headquarters AirForce Principles.

The Open Group gratefully acknowledges those past and present members of the Architecture Forum who have served as its officers (Chairs and Vice-Chairs) since its inception. In alphabetical order:

Mick Adams
Christer Askerfjord
Terence Blevins
Bill Estrem
Hugh Fisher
Chris Forde
Chris Greenslade
Ed Harrington
Dave Hornford
David Jackson
Stuart Macgregor
Ian McCall
Tara Paider
Barry Smith
Walter Stahlecker
Paul van der Merwe
Dave van Gelder
Jane Varnus
Vish Viswanathan
Hal Wilson

The Open Group gratefully acknowledges the following individuals who have made contributions in the development of this and earlier versions of TOGAF 9:

Mick Adams
Christopher Blake
Stuart Crawford
Bill Estrem
Kirk Hansen
Dave Hornford
Judith Jones
Mike Lambert
Andrew Macaulay
Mike Turner
Paul van der Merwe
Robert Weisman

The Open Group gratefully acknowledges the following organizations that have made contributions in the development of this and earlier versions of TOGAF 9:

American Express
Architecting-the-Enterprise
Bank of Montreal
Capgemini
CGI Group
Conexiam
Metaplexity Associates
Nationwide
Real IRM Solutions
SAP

致谢

The Open Group 向开发 TOGAF 的 The Open Group 架构论坛表示衷心感谢。

The Open Group 衷心地感谢对美国空军总部原则做出贡献的美国空军。

The Open Group 诚挚地感谢那些自架构论坛成立以来，曾经和现在担任其工作人员（主席和副主席）的成员。按字母顺序：

- Mick Adams
- Christer Askerfjord
- Terence Blevins
- Bill Estrem
- Hugh Fisher
- Chris Forde
- Chris Greenslade
- Ed Harrington
- Dave Hornford
- David Jackson
- Stuart Macgregor
- Ian McCall
- Tara Paider
- Barry Smith
- Walter Stahlecker
- Paul van der Merwe
- Dave van Gelder
- Jane Varnus
- Vish Viswanathan
- Hal Wilson

The Open Group 向以下曾在开发本 TOGAF 9 版本和更早版本的过程中做出贡献的个人表示诚挚的感谢：

- Mick Adams
- Christopher Blake
- Stuart Crawford
- Bill Estrem
- Kirk Hansen
- Dave Hornford
- Judith Jones
- Mike Lambert
- Andrew Macaulay
- Mike Turner
- Paul van der Merwe
- Robert Weisman

The Open Group 向以下曾在开发本 TOGAF 9 版本和更早版本的过程中做出贡献的组织表示诚挚的感谢：

- American Express
- Architecting-the-Enterprise
- Bank of Montreal
- Capgemini
- CGI Group
- Conexiam
- Metaplexity Associates
- Nationwide
- Real IRM Solutions
- SAP

Referenced Documents

The following documents are referenced in the TOGAF specification:

- Analysis Patterns — Reusable Object Models, M. Fowler, ISBN: 0-201-89542-0, Addison-Wesley.
- A Pattern Language: Towns, Buildings, Construction, Christopher Alexander, ISBN: 0-19-501919-9, Oxford University Press, 1979.
- Books of Knowledge — Project Management and System Engineering, Project Management Institute (refer to www.pmi.org) and the International Council of Systems Engineers (refer to http://g2sebok.incose.org).
- Business Transformation Enablement Program (BTEP), Canadian Government; refer to www.tbs-sct.gc.ca/btep-pto/index_e.asp.
- Business Process Modeling Notation (BPMN) Specification, Object Management Group (OMG);refer to www.bpmn.org.
- Common Object Request Broker Architecture (CORBA), Object Management Group (OMG); refer to www.corba.org.
- Control Objectives for Information and related Technology (COBIT), Version 4.0, IT GovernanceInstitute, 2005.
- Corporate Governance, Ranami Naidoo, ISBN: 1-919-903-0086, Double Storey, 2002.
- Design Patterns: Elements of Reusable Object-Oriented Software, Erich Gamma, Richard Helm, Ralph Johnson, & John Vlissides, ISBN: 0-201-63361-2, Addison-Wesley, October 1994.
- Enterprise Architecture as Strategy, Jeanne Ross, Peter Weill, & David C. Robertson, ISBN: 1-59139-839-8, Harvard Business School Press, 2006.
- Enterprise Architecture Capability Maturity Model (ACMM), Version 1.2, United States Department of Commerce, December 2007.
- Enterprise Architecture Maturity Model, Version 1.3, National Association of State CIOs (NASCIO), December 2003.
- Enterprise Architecture Planning (EAP): Developing a Blueprint for Data, Applications, and Technology, Steven H. Spewak & Steven C. Hill, ISBN: 0-47-159985-9, John Wiley & Sons, 1993.
- Federal Enterprise Architecture Framework (FEAF), Version 1.1, US Federal Chief Information Officer (CIO) Council, September 1999; refer to www.cio.gov/documents/fedarch1.pdf.
- Headquarters Air Force Principles for Information Management, US Air Force, June 29, 1998.
- IEEE Std 1003.0-1995, Guide to the POSIX Open System Environment (OSE), identical to ISO/IEC TR 14252 (administratively withdrawn by IEEE).
- IEEE Std 1003.23-1998, Guide for Developing User Organization Open System Environment (OSE) Profiles (administratively withdrawn by IEEE)

引用文件

本 TOGAF 规范引用了下述文件：

- Analysis Patterns — Reusable Object Models, M. Fowler, ISBN: 0-201-89542-0, Addison-Wesley.
- A Pattern Language: Towns, Buildings, Construction, Christopher Alexander, ISBN: 0-19-501919-9, Oxford University Press, 1979.
- Books of Knowledge — Project Management and System Engineering, Project Management Institute (refer to www.pmi.org) and the International Council of Systems Engineers (refer to http://g2sebok.incose.org).
- Business Transformation Enablement Program (BTEP), Canadian Government; refer to www.tbs-sct.gc.ca/btep-pto/index_e.asp.
- Business Process Modeling Notation (BPMN) Specification, Object Management Group (OMG);refer to www.bpmn.org.
- Common Object Request Broker Architecture (CORBA), Object Management Group (OMG); refer to www.corba.org.
- Control Objectives for Information and related Technology (COBIT), Version 4.0, IT Governance Institute, 2005.
- Corporate Governance, Ranami Naidoo, ISBN: 1-919-903-0086, Double Storey, 2002.
- Design Patterns: Elements of Reusable Object-Oriented Software, Erich Gamma, Richard Helm, Ralph Johnson, & John Vlissides, ISBN: 0-201-63361-2, Addison-Wesley, October 1994.
- Enterprise Architecture as Strategy, Jeanne Ross, Peter Weill, & David C. Robertson, ISBN: 1-59139-839-8, Harvard Business School Press, 2006.
- Enterprise Architecture Capability Maturity Model (ACMM), Version 1.2, United States Department of Commerce, December 2007.
- Enterprise Architecture Maturity Model, Version 1.3, National Association of State CIOs (NASCIO), December 2003.
- Enterprise Architecture Planning (EAP): Developing a Blueprint for Data, Applications, and Technology, Steven H. Spewak & Steven C. Hill, ISBN: 0-47-159985-9, John Wiley & Sons, 1993.
- Federal Enterprise Architecture Framework (FEAF), Version 1.1, US Federal Chief Information Officer (CIO) Council, September 1999; refer to www.cio.gov/documents/fedarch1.pdf.
- Headquarters Air Force Principles for Information Management, US Air Force, June 29, 1998.
- IEEE Std 1003.0-1995, Guide to the POSIX Open System Environment (OSE), identical to ISO/IEC TR 14252 (administratively withdrawn by IEEE).
- IEEE Std 1003.23-1998, Guide for Developing User Organization Open System Environment (OSE) Profiles (administratively withdrawn by IEEE).

- Implementing Enterprise Architecture — Putting Quality Information in the Hands of Oil and Gas Knowledge Workers (SPE 68794), G.A. Cox, R.M. Johnston, SPE, & R. M. Palermo, Aera Energy LLC, Copyright 2001, Society of Petroleum Engineers, Inc.
- Interoperable Enterprise Business Scenario Business Scenario, October 2002 (K022), published by The Open Group; refer to www.opengroup.org/bookstore/catalog/k022.htm.
- ISO 10303, Industrial Automation Systems and Integration — Product Data Representation and Exchange.
- ISO/IEC 10746-1: 1998, Information Technology — Open Distributed Processing — Reference Model: Overview.
- ISO/IEC 10746-4: 1998, Information Technology — Open Distributed Processing — Reference Model: Architectural Semantics.
- ISO/IEC TR 14252: 1996, Information Technology — Guide to the POSIX Open System Environment (OSE) (identical to IEEE Std 1003.0).
- ISO/IEC 17799: 2005, Information Technology — Security Techniques — Code of Practice for Information Security Management.
- ISO/IEC 20000: 2005, Information Technology — Service Management.
- ISO/IEC 42010: 2007, Systems and Software Engineering — Recommended Practice for Architectural Description of Software-Intensive Systems, Edition 1 (technically identical to ANSI/IEEE Std 1471-2000).
- IT Portfolio Management Facility (ITPMF) Specification, Object Management Group (OMG); refer to www.omg.org/spec/ITPMF.
- Mapping of TOGAF 8.1 with COBIT 4.0 by the IT Governance Institute (ITGI) White Paper, July 2007 (W072), published by The Open Group; refer to www.opengroup.org/bookstore/catalog/w072.htm.
- Webster's Collegiate Dictionary, Merriam-Webster, English Language, 11th Edition, April 2008, ISBN-10: 0877798095, ISBN-13: 978-0877798095; refer to www.merriam-webster.com.
- Model Driven Architecture (MDA) Specification, Object Management (OMG); refer to www.omg.org/mda.
- OECD Principles of Corporate Governance, Organization for Economic Cooperation and Development, December 2001; refer to www.oecd.org.
- Pattern-Oriented Software Architecture: A System of Patterns, F. Buschmann, R. Meunier, H.Rohnert, P. Sommerlad, & M. Stal, ISBN: 0-471-95869-7, John Wiley & Sons, 1996.
- Patterns and Software: Essential Concepts and Terminology, Brad Appleton; refer to www.cmcrossroads.com/bradapp/docs/patterns-intro.html.
- Practical Guide to Federal Enterprise Architecture, Version 1.0, US Federal Chief Information Officer (CIO) Council, February 2001; a cooperative venture with the General Accounting Office (GAO) and the Office of Management and Budget (OMB).
- REA: A Semantic Model for Internet Supply Chain Collaboration, Robert Haugen and William E.McCarthy, January 2000; refer to www.jeffsutherland.org/oopsla2000/mccarthy/mccarthy.htm.
- Resource-Event-Agent (REA) Business Model, William E. McCarthy; refer to www.msu.edu/user/mccarth4.

- Implementing Enterprise Architecture — Putting Quality Information in the Hands of Oil and Gas Knowledge Workers (SPE 68794), G.A. Cox, R.M. Johnston, SPE, & R. M. Palermo, Aera Energy LLC, Copyright 2001, Society of Petroleum Engineers, Inc.
- Interoperable Enterprise Business Scenario Business Scenario, October 2002 (K022), published by The Open Group; refer to www.opengroup.org/bookstore/catalog/k022.htm.
- ISO 10303, Industrial Automation Systems and Integration — Product Data Representation and Exchange.
- ISO/IEC 10746-1: 1998, Information Technology — Open Distributed Processing — Reference Model: Overview.
- ISO/IEC 10746-4: 1998, Information Technology — Open Distributed Processing — Reference Model: Architectural Semantics.
- ISO/IEC TR 14252: 1996, Information Technology — Guide to the POSIX Open System Environment (OSE) (identical to IEEE Std 1003.0).
- ISO/IEC 17799: 2005, Information Technology — Security Techniques — Code of Practice for Information Security Management.
- ISO/IEC 20000: 2005, Information Technology — Service Management.
- ISO/IEC 42010: 2007, Systems and Software Engineering — Recommended Practice for Architectural Description of Software-Intensive Systems, Edition 1 (technically identical to ANSI/IEEE Std 1471-2000).
- IT Portfolio Management Facility (ITPMF) Specification, Object Management Group (OMG); refer to www.omg.org/spec/ITPMF.
- Mapping of TOGAF 8.1 with COBIT 4.0 by the IT Governance Institute (ITGI) White Paper, July2007 (W072), published by The Open Group; refer to www.opengroup.org/bookstore/catalog/w072.htm.
- Webster's Collegiate Dictionary, Merriam-Webster, English Language, 11th Edition, April 2008, ISBN-10: 0877798095, ISBN-13: 978-0877798095; refer to www.merriam-webster.com.
- Model Driven Architecture (MDA) Specification, Object Management (OMG); refer to www.omg.org/mda.
- OECD Principles of Corporate Governance, Organization for Economic Cooperation and Development, December 2001; refer to www.oecd.org.
- Pattern-Oriented Software Architecture: A System of Patterns, F. Buschmann, R. Meunier, H.Rohnert, P. Sommerlad, & M. Stal, ISBN: 0-471-95869-7, John Wiley & Sons, 1996.
- Patterns and Software: Essential Concepts and Terminology, Brad Appleton; refer to www.cmcrossroads.com/bradapp/docs/patterns-intro.html.
- Practical Guide to Federal Enterprise Architecture, Version 1.0, US Federal Chief Information Officer (CIO) Council, February 2001; a cooperative venture with the General Accounting Office (GAO) and the Office of Management and Budget (OMB).
- REA: A Semantic Model for Internet Supply Chain Collaboration, Robert Haugen and William E.McCarthy, January 2000; refer to www.jeffsutherland.org/oopsla2000/mccarthy/mccarthy.htm.
- Resource-Event-Agent (REA) Business Model, William E. McCarthy; refer to www.msu.edu/user/mccarth4.

- Re-usable Asset Specification (RAS), Version 2.2, Object Management Group (OMG), November2005; refer to www.omg.org/spec/RAS.
- Service Component Architecture (SCA) Specification, Version 1.0, published by OSOA, March2007.
- Service Data Objects (SDO) for C Specification, Version 2.1, published by OSOA, September 2007.
- Service Data Objects (SDO) for C++ Specification, Version 2.1, published by OSOA, December 2006.
- Service Data Objects (SDO) for COBOL Specification, Version 2.1, published by OSOA, September 2007.
- Service Data Objects (SDO) for Java Specification, Version 2.1, published by OSOA, November 2006.
- Software Processing Engineering Metamodel (SPEM) Specification, Version 2.0, Object Management Group (OMG), April 2008; refer to www.omg.org/spec/SPEM/2.0.
- Standard for the Exchange of Product model data (STEP); also ISO 10303, Industrial Automation Systems and Integration — Product Data Representation and Exchange.
- The Art of Systems Architecting, Eberhardt Rechtin & Mark W. Maier.
- The Command and Control System Target Architecture (C2STA), Electronic Systems Center (ESC), US Air Force, 2000.
- The Open Group SOA Source Book, Version 2, Guide, April 2010 (G102), published by The Open Group; refer to www.opengroup.org/bookstore/catalog/g102.htm.
- The Open Group Service Integration Maturity Model (OSIMM), Technical Standard, August 2009 (C092), published by The Open Group; refer to www.opengroup.org/bookstore/catalog/c092.htm.
- The Open Group SOA Governance Framework, Technical Standard, August 2009 (C093), published by The Open Group; refer to www.opengroup.org/bookstore/catalog/c093.htm.
- The Open Group SOA Ontology, Technical Standard, October 2010 (C104), published by The Open Group; refer to www.opengroup.org/bookstore/catalog/c104.htm.
- The Oregon Experiment, Christopher Alexander, ISBN: 0-19-501824-9, Oxford University Press,1975.
- The Timeless Way of Building, Christopher Alexander, ISBN: 0-19-502402-8, Oxford University Press, 1979.
- UML Profile and Metamodel for Services (UPMS) RFP (OMG soa/2006-09-09), Object Management Group (OMG), June 2007.
- Unified Modeling Language (UML) Specification, Object Management Group (OMG); refer to www.uml.org.
- US Treasury Architecture Development Guidance (TADG), formerly known as the Treasury Information System Architecture Framework (TISAF).

The following web sites provide useful reference material:

- IBM Patterns for e-business: www.ibm.com/framework/patterns
- IBM Patterns for e-business Resources (also known as the “RedBooks”): www. ibm.com/developerworks/patterns/library

- Re-usable Asset Specification (RAS), Version 2.2, Object Management Group (OMG), November2005; refer to www.omg.org/spec/RAS.
- Service Component Architecture (SCA) Specification, Version 1.0, publicshed by OSOA, March 2007.
- Service Data Objects (SDO) for C Specification, Version 2.1, published by OSOA, September 2007.
- Service Data Objects (SDO) for C++ Specification, Version 2.1, published by OSOA, December 2006.
- Service Data Objects (SDO) for COBOL Specification, Version 2.1, publicshed by OSOA, September 2007.
- Service Data Objects (SDO) for Java Specification, Version 2.1, published by OSOA, November 2006.
- Software Processing Engineering Metamodel (SPEM) Specification, Version 2.0, Object Management Group (OMG), April 2008; refer to www.omg.org/spec/SPEM/2.0.
- Standard for the Exchange of Product model data (STEP); also ISO 10303, Industrial Automation Systems and Integration — Product Data Representation and Exchange.
- The Art of Systems Architecting, Eberhardt Rechtin & Mark W. Maier.
- The Command and Control System Target Architecture (C2STA), Electronic Systems Center (ESC), US Air Force, 2000.
- The Open Group SOA Source Book, Version 2, Guide, April 2010 (G102), published by The Open Group; refer to www.opengroup.org/bookstore/catalog/g102.htm.
- The Open Group Service Integration Maturity Model (OSIMM), Technical Standard, August 2009 (C092), published by The Open Group; refer to www.opengroup.org/bookstore/catalog/c092.htm.
- The Open Group SOA Governance Framework, Technical Standard, August 2009 (C093), published by The Open Group; refer to www.opengroup.org/bookstore/catalog/c093.htm.
- The Open Group SOA Ontology, Technical Standard, October 2010 (C104), published by The Open Group; refer to www.opengroup.org/bookstore/catalog/c104.htm.
- The Oregon Experiment, Christopher Alexander, ISBN: 0-19-501824-9, Oxford University Press,1975.
- The Timeless Way of Building, Christopher Alexander, ISBN: 0-19-502402-8, Oxford UniversityPress, 1979.
- UML Profile and Metamodel for Services (UPMS) RFP (OMG soa/2006-09-09), Object Management Group (OMG), June 2007.
- Unified Modeling Language (UML) Specification, Object Management Group (OMG); refer to www.uml.org.
- US Treasury Architecture Development Guidance (TADG), formerly known as the Treasury Information System Architecture Framework (TISAF).

下列网址提供有用的参考材料：

- IBM 的电子商务特征模式：www.ibm.com/framework/patterns.
- IBM 的电子商务资源特征模式（也被称为“红皮书”）：www. ibm.com/developerworks/patterns/library.

- The Information Technology Governance Institute: www.itgi.org

This web site has many resources that can help with corporate assessment of both IT and governance in general.

- The Patterns Home Page: hillside.net/patterns.

This web site is hosted by The Hillside Group and provides information about patterns, links to online patterns, papers, and books dealing with patterns, and patterns-related mailing lists.

- The Patterns-Discussion FAQ: g.oswego.edu/dl/pd-FAQ/pd-FAQ.html

This web site is maintained by Doug Lea and provides a thorough and highly readable FAQ about patterns.

- The Volere web site has a useful list of leading requirements tools: www.volere.co.uk/tools.htm.

- 信息技术治理协会: www.itgi.org

此网站拥有多种资源，一般有助于 IT 与治理的公司级评价。

- 特征模式主页: hillside.net/patterns

此网址由 hillside 组托管，并为特征模式、在线特征模式的链接、论文、处理特征模式的书籍以及与特征模式相关的邮件清单提供信息。

- 特征模式讨论的常见问答: g.oswego.edu/dl/pd-FAQ/pd-FAQ.html

此网址由 Doug Lea 维护，提供全面且可读性高的关于相关模式的常见问答。

- Volere 网站拥有一系列有用且先进的需求工具: www.volere.co.uk/tools.htm.

TOGAF Version 9.1

Part I Introduction

The Open Group

TOGAF 9.1 版本

第一部分　引言

The Open Group

Chapter 1
Introduction

TOGAF is a framework — a detailed method and a set of supporting tools — for developing an enterprise architecture. It may be used freely by any organization wishing to develop an enterprise architecture for use within that organization (see Section 4.5.1).

TOGAF is developed and maintained by members of The Open Group, working within the Architecture Forum (refer to www.opengroup.org/architecture).The original development of TOGAF Version 1 in 1995 was based on the Technical Architecture Framework for Information Management (TAFIM), developed by the US Department of Defense (DoD).The DoD gave The Open Group explicit permission and encouragement to create TOGAF by building on the TAFIM, which itself was the result of many years of development effort and many millions of dollars of US Government investment.

Starting from this sound foundation,the members of The Open Group Architecture Forum have developed successive versions of TOGAF and published each one on The Open Group public web site.

If you are new to the field of enterprise architecture and/or TOGAF, you are recommended to read the Executive Overview (refer to Section 1.2), where you will find answers to questions such as:

- What is an enterprise?
- Why do I need an enterprise architecture?
- Why do I need TOGAF as a framework for enterprise architecture?

1.1 Structure of the TOGAF Document

The structure of the TOGAF documentation reflects the structure and content of an Architecture Capability within an enterprise, as shown in Figure 1-1.

第 1 章 简 介

TOGAF 是一个框架——一种详细方法和一套支持工具——用于开发 Enterprise Architecture。该框架可以被任何希望开发用于组织内部的 Enterprise Architecture 的组织免费使用（见 4.5.1 节）。

TOGAF 由在架构论坛（见 www.opengroup.org/architecture）工作的 The Open Group 成员开发和维护。1995 年，TOGAF 第 1 版的初始开发，基于美国国防部（DoD）开发的信息管理技术架构框架（TAFIM）。DoD 给予 The Open Group 明确的许可和鼓励以在 TAFIM 上创建 TOGAF，TAFIM 本身是在美国政府投资数百万美元支持下经多年开发工作而形成的成果。

从这个良好的基础开始，The Open Group 架构论坛的成员已经开发了多个 TOGAF 连续版本，并将每个版本发布在 The Open Group 公共网站上。

如果是初次接触 Enterprise Architecture 和/或 TOGAF 领域，建议你阅读执行概述（见 1.2 节），在该节中你会找到如下问题的答案：

- 什么是 ENTERPRISE？
- 为什么需要 Enterprise Architecture？
- 为什么需要 TOGAF 作为 Enterprise Architecture 的框架？

1.1 TOGAF 文件的结构

TOGAF 文件的结构是反映一个 ENTERPRISE 内架构能力的结构和内容，如图 1-1 所示。

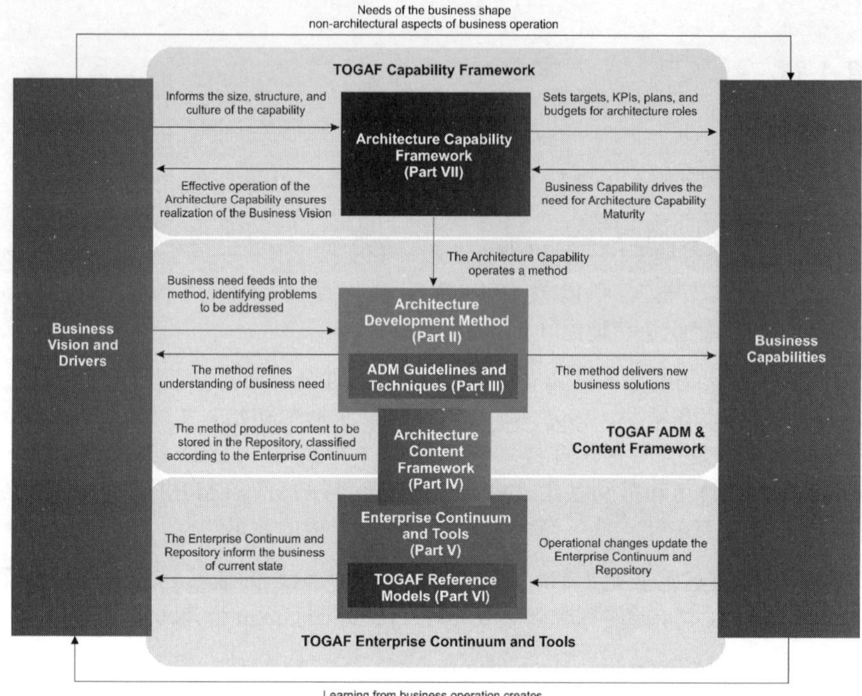

Figure 1-1 Structure of the TOGAF Document

There are seven parts to the TOGAF document:

PART I (Introduction) This part provides a high-level introduction to the key concepts of enterprise architecture and in particular the TOGAF approach. It contains the definitions of terms used throughout TOGAF and release notes detailing the changes between this version and the previous version of TOGAF.

PART II (Architecture Development Method) This part is the core of TOGAF. It describes the TOGAF Architecture Development Method (ADM) — a step-by-step approach to developing an enterprise architecture.

PART III (ADM Guidelines and Techniques) This part contains a collection of guidelines and techniques available for use in applying TOGAF and the TOGAF ADM.

PART IV (Architecture Content Framework) This part describes the TOGAF content framework, including a structured metamodel for architectural artifacts, the use of re-usable architecture building blocks, and an overview of typical architecture deliverables.

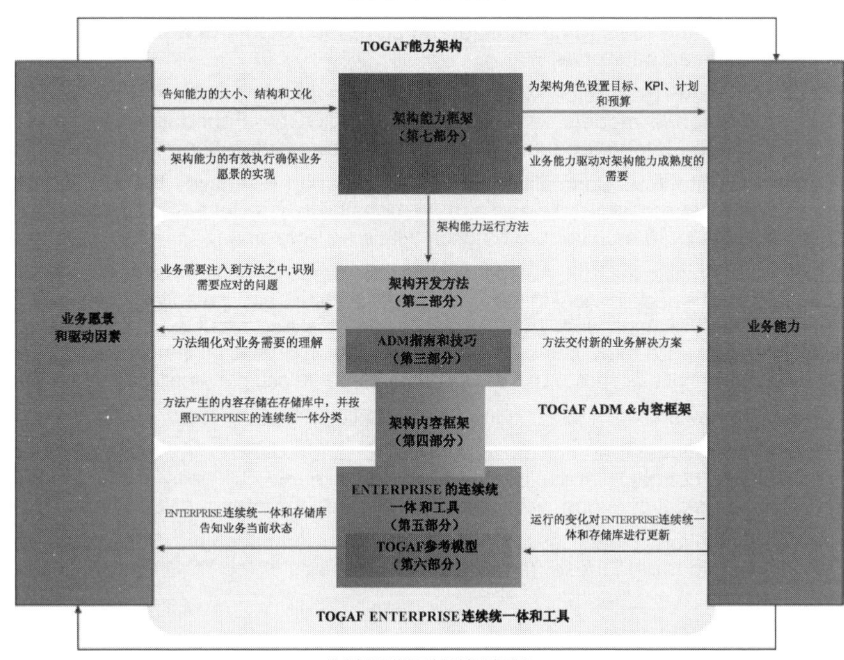

图 1-1　TOGAF 文件的结构

TOGAF 文件包含七个部分：

第一部分　（引言）本部分对 Enterprise Architecture 的关键概念，特别是 TOGAF 实施途径提供概括性介绍。本部分包括在整个 TOGAF 中所使用术语的定义，以及对本 TOGAF 版本与之前 TOGAF 版本之间的变化进行详述的发布说明。

第二部分　（架构开发方法）本部分是 TOGAF 的核心，描述 TOGAF 架构开发方法（ADM）——一种开发 Enterprise Architecture 的循序渐进的实施途径。

第三部分　（ADM 指南和技巧）本部分包含在应用 TOGAF 和 TOGAF ADM 时可供使用的指南和技巧的集合。

第四部分　（架构内容框架）本部分描述 TOGAF 内容框架，包括一个用于架构制品的结构化元模型、可复用架构构建块的用法及典型架构交付物的概述。

PART V (Enterprise Continuum & Tools) This part discusses appropriate taxonomies and tools to categorize and store the outputs of architecture activity within an enterprise.

PART VI (TOGAF Reference Models)This part provides a selection of architectural refe-rence models, which includes the TOGAF Foundation Architecture, and the Integrated Information Infrastructure Reference Model (III-RM).

PART VII (Architecture Capability Framework)This part discusses the organization, processes, skills, roles, and responsibilities required to establish and operate an architecture function within an enterprise.

The intention of dividing the TOGAF specification into these independent parts is to allow for different areas of specialization to be considered in detail and potentially addressed in isolation. Although all parts work together as a whole, it is also feasible to select particular parts for adoption while excluding others. For example, an organization may wish to adopt the ADM process, but elect not to use any of the materials relating to Architecture Capability.

As an open framework, such use is encouraged, particularly in the following situa-tions:

- Organizations that are new to TOGAF and wish to incrementally adopt TOGAF concepts are expected to focus on particular parts of the specifica-tion for initial adoption, with other areas tabled for later consideration.
- Organizations that have already deployed architecture frameworks may choose to merge these frameworks with aspects of the TOGAF specification.

1.2 Executive Overview

This section provides an executive overview of enterprise architecture, the basic concepts of what it is (not just another name for IT Architecture), and why it is needed. It provides a summary of the benefits of establishing an enterprise architecture and adopting TOGAF to achieve that.

What is an enterprise?

TOGAF defines "enterprise" as any collection of organizations that has a common set of goals. For example, an enterprise could be a government agency, a whole corporation, a division of a corporation, a single department, or a chain of geographically distant organizations linked together by common ownership.

The term "enterprise" in the context of "enterprise architecture" can be used to denote both an entire enterprise — encompassing all of its information and technology services, processes, and infrastructure — and a specific domain within the enterprise. In both cases, the architecture crosses multiple systems, and multiple functional groups within the enterprise.

Confusion often arises from the evolving nature of the term "enterprise". An extended enterprise nowadays frequently includes partners, suppliers, and custom-mers. If the goal is to integrate an extended enterprise, then the enterprise comprises the partners, suppliers, and customers, as well as internal business units.

The business operating model concept is useful to determine the nature and scope of the enterprise architecture within an organization. Large corporations and govern-ment agencies may comprise multiple enterprises, and may develop and maintain a number of independent enterprise architectures to address each one. However, there is often much in common about the information systems in each enterprise, and there is usually great potential for gain in the use of a common architecture framework. For example, a common framework can provide a basis for the development of an Architecture Repository for the integration and re-use of models, designs, and baseline data.

第五部分 （ENTERPRISE 的连续统一体和工具）本部分论述对 ENTERPRISE 内架构活动的各种输出进行分类和存储的适用分类法和工具。

第六部分 （TOGAF 参考模型）本部分提供对架构参考模型的选择，包括 TOGAF 基础架构以及综合信息基础设施参考模型（III-RM）。

第七部分 （架构能力框架）本部分论述在 ENTERPRISE 内建立和运行架构功能所需的组织、流程、技能、角色和职责。

将 TOGAF 规范划分成这些独立的部分的意图，就是允许对专门化的不同领域进行详细考量并有可能分别处理。尽管所有部分作为一个整体进行工作，但是选择采用某些特殊部分而排除其余部分，仍是可行的。例如，一个组织可能希望采用 ADM 流程，但是选择不使用与架构能力相关的任何资料。

对一个开放框架，鼓励上述使用方法，特别是在下述情况下：

- 那些不熟悉 TOGAF，并希望逐步采用 TOGAF 概念的组织，期望在初期采用时关注本规范的某些特殊部分，并在之后将其他领域列入考虑范围。
- 那些已部署架构框架的组织，可能选择将这些框架与 TOGAF 规范的一些方面合并。

1.2 执行概述

本节提供 Enterprise Architecture 的执行概述、Enterprise Architecture 的基本概念（不只是 IT 架构的另一个名称）和为什么需要 Enterprise Architecture，对建立 Enterprise Architecture 和采用 TOGAF 的益处进行归纳。

什么是 ENTERPRISE？

TOGAF 将“ENTERPRISE”定义为具有一系列共同目标的任何组织的集合。例如，一个 ENTERPRISE 可能是政府机构、整个公司、公司的一个分部、单一部门，或由共同所有权联系在一起的一系列地理上相距较远的组织。

术语“ENTERPRISE”在“Enterprise Architecture”背景环境下，既可被用于意指一个完整的 ENTERPRISE——包括 ENTERPRISE 的所有信息和技术服务、流程及基础设施——也可以意指 ENTERPRISE 内一个特定领域。在以上两种情况下，架构跨越 ENTERPRISE 内多重系统和多重功能组。

“ENTERPRISE”的演进本质经常引起混淆。现今，扩展型 ENTERPRISE 往往包括合作伙伴、供应商和客户。如果目标是整合扩展型 ENTERPRISE，那么 ENTERPRISE 就包含合作伙伴、供应商和客户以及内部业务单元。

业务运行模型概念对于确定组织内 Enterprise Architecture 的本质和范围是非常有用的。大型公司和政府机构可包含多重 ENTERPRISE，并可开发和维护应对每一个 ENTERPRISE 的若干独立的 Enterprise Architecture。然而，每个 ENTERPRISE 的信息系统常常具有许多共同之处，并且在使用共同架构框架过程中通常会获得巨大潜力。例如，一个共同框架可为开发针对模型、设计和基线数据的整合和复用的架构库提供基础。

Why do I need an enterprise architecture?

The purpose of enterprise architecture is to optimize across the enterprise the often fragmented legacy of processes (both manual and automated) into an integrated environment that is responsive to change and supportive of the delivery of the business strategy.

Today's CEOs know that the effective management and exploitation of information through IT is a key factor to business success, and an indispensable means to achieving competitive advantage. An enterprise architecture addresses this need, by providing a strategic context for the evolution of the IT system in response to the constantly changing needs of the business environment.

Furthermore, a good enterprise architecture enables you to achieve the right balance between IT efficiency and business innovation. It allows individual business units to innovate safely in their pursuit of competitive advantage. At the same time, it ensures the needs of the organization for an integrated IT strategy are met, permitting the closest possible synergy across the extended enterprise.

The advantages that result from a good enterprise architecture bring important business benefits, which are clearly visible in the net profit or loss of a company or organiza-tion:

- A more efficient business operation:
  - Lower business operation costs.
  - More agile organization.
  - Business capabilities shared across the organization.
  - Lower change management costs.
  - More flexible workforce.
  - Improved business productivity.
- A more efficient IT operation:
  - Lower software development, support, and maintenance costs.
  - Increased portability of applications.
  - Improved interoperability and easier system and network management.
  - Improved ability to address critical enterprise-wide issues like security.
  - Easier upgrade and exchange of system components.
- Better return on existing investment, reduced risk for future investment:
  - Reduced complexity in the business and IT.
  - Maximum return on investment in existing business and IT infrastructure.
  - The flexibility to make, buy, or out-source business and IT solutions.
  - Reduced risk overall in new investments and their cost of ownership.

为什么需要 Enterprise Architecture？

Enterprise Architecture 的目的是，在贯穿整个 ENTERPRISE 范围内，将通常碎片化的已有流程（手动和自动）优化为一个对变化做出响应并支持业务战略达成的综合环境。

今天的 CEO 都明白，通过 IT 对信息的有效管理和利用是取得业务成功的关键因素，并且是获取竞争优势的一个必不可少的手段。Enterprise Architecture 业务环境不断变化的需要，通过提供 IT 系统演进的战略背景环境来应对。

与此同时，一个良好的 Enterprise Architecture，使你能够在 IT 效率和业务创新之间达成适当的平衡。它使得单个业务单元在追求竞争优势时能够有把握地创新。同时，架构确保组织对综合 IT 战略的需要得以满足，使得在贯穿整个扩展型 ENTERPRISE 内获得最大可能的协同。

良好的 Enterprise Architecture 产生的优势会带来重要的业务效益，其在公司或组织的净损益中清晰可见：

- 更高效的业务运行：
  - 更低的业务运行成本。
  - 更敏捷的组织。
  - 穿越组织而共享的业务能力。
  - 更低的变更管理成本。
  - 更加灵活的员工队伍。
  - 提高业务生产率。
- 更高效的 IT 运行：
  - 更低的软件开发、支持和维护成本。
  - 已提高的应用可移植性。
  - 改进的互用性和更容易的系统与网络管理。
  - 提高应对整个 ENTERPRISE 范围的关键问题的能力诸如安保性。
  - 更易于升级和交换系统组件。
- 更好的现有投资回报，降低了未来投资风险：
  - 降低业务和 IT 的复杂性。
  - 最大化现有业务和 IT 基础设施的投资回报。
  - 自制、购买或外包业务和 IT 解决方案的灵活性。
  - 降低了新投资及其拥有成本的总体风险。

- Faster, simpler, and cheaper procurement:
  - Buying decisions are simpler, because the information governing procurement is readily available in a coherent plan.
  - The procurement process is faster — maximizing procurement speed and flexibility without sacrificing architectural coherence.
  - The ability to procure heterogeneous, multi-vendor open systems.
  - The ability to secure more economic capabilities.

What specifically would prompt me to develop an enterprise architecture?

Typically, preparation for business transformation needs or for radical infrastructure changes initiates an enterprise architecture review or development. Often key people identify areas of change required in order for new business goals to be met. Such people are commonly referred to as the "stakeholders" in the change. The role of the architect is to address their concerns by:

- Identifying and refining the requirements that the stakeholders have.
- Developing views of the architecture that show how the concerns and requirements are going to be addressed.
- Showing the trade-offs that are going to be made in reconciling the potentially conflicting concerns of different stakeholders.

Without the enterprise architecture, it is highly unlikely that all the concerns and requirements will be considered and met.

What is an architecture framework?

An architecture framework is a foundational structure, or set of structures, which can be used for developing a broad range of different architectures. It should describe a method for designing a target state of the enterprise in terms of a set of building blocks, and for showing how the building blocks fit together. It should contain a set of tools and provide a common vocabulary. It should also include a list of recommended standards and compliant products that can be used to implement the building blocks.

Why do I need TOGAF as a framework for enterprise architecture?

TOGAF has been developed through the collaborative efforts of over 300 Architecture Forum member companies from some of the world's leading companies and organizations. Using TOGAF results in enterprise architecture that is consistent, reflects the needs of stakeholders, employs best practice, and gives due consideration both to current requirements and the perceived future needs of the business.

Developing and sustaining an enterprise architecture is a technically complex process which involves many stakeholders and decision processes in the organization. TOGAF plays an important role in standardizing and de-risks the architecture development process. TOGAF provides a best practice framework for adding value, and enables the organization to build workable and economic solutions which address their business issues and needs.

- 更快、更简单和更便宜的采购：
  - — 采购决策更简单，因为采购管控的信息在协调一致的计划中易于获取。
  - — 采购流程更快速——使采购速度和灵活性最大化，而无需牺牲架构整体一致性。
  - — 采购多样化、多厂商开放系统的能力。
  - — 确保更经济性的能力。

什么会特别地促使我们开发 Enterprise Architecture？

典型情况下，对业务转型需要或彻底的基础设施变革的准备，可以启动 Enterprise Architecture 的审视或开发。通常情况下，关键人员识别出为满足新业务目标所需要变革的领域。在变革过程中，这些人员通常被称为“利益攸关者”，架构师的作用是通过以下方式应对其关注点：

- 识别和细化利益攸关者的需求。
- 开发多个表明要如何应对关注点和需求的架构视图。
- 展示在协调不同利益攸关者关注点的潜在冲突中要做出的权衡。

如果没有 Enterprise Architecture，要考虑并满足所有关注点和需求几乎是不可能的。

什么是架构框架？

架构框架是一个基础结构或结构集合，可被用于开发更大范围的不同架构。架构框架应描述一种方法，用于基于一系列构建块来设计 ENTERPRISE 的目标状态，并表明构建块如何适配地结合在一起。它应包含一系列工具，并提供一个常用词汇表，也应包括能够用于实现构建块的推荐标准和合规产品的列表。

为什么需要 TOGAF 作为 Enterprise Architecture 的框架？

TOGAF 是由超过 300 家来自于一些世界领先公司和组织的架构论坛的成员公司共同努力开发的。使用 TOGAF 产生的 Enterprise Architecture 是连续一致的，反映利益攸关者的需要，应用最佳实践并适当考虑该业务的当前需求和所预知的未来需要。

开发和维持 Enterprise Architecture，在技术上是一个复杂过程，它涉及组织中的许多利益攸关者和决策过程。TOGAF 在标准化方面发挥着重要作用，并降低架构开发流程风险。TOGAF 提供的最佳实践框架，是一个以增加价值为目的，并使组织能够构建应对其业务问题和需要的可行且经济的解决方案。

Who would benefit from using TOGAF?

Any organization undertaking, or planning to undertake, the development and implementation of an enterprise architecture for the support of business transformation will benefit from use of TOGAF.

Organizations seeking Boundaryless Information Flow can use TOGAF to define and implement the structures and processes to enable access to integrated information within and between enterprises.

Organizations that design and implement enterprise architectures using TOGAF are assured ofa design and a procurement specification that can facilitate an open systems implementation, thus enabling the benefits of open systems with reduced risk.

谁会从使用 TOGAF 中受益？

任何正在从事或计划从事支持业务转型的 Enterprise Architecture 的开发和实施的组织，均会从 TOGAF 的使用中受益。

寻求无边界信息流的组织，可以使用 TOGAF 来定义和实施体系与流程，以便能够访问 ENTERPRISE 内部及其之间的综合信息。

设计和实施 Enterprise Architecture 的组织，使用 TOGAF 保证设计和采购规范，有助于一个开放系统的实施，从而能够在具有降低了风险的开放系统中受益。

Chapter 2
Core Concepts

For the purposes of TOGAF 9, the core concepts provided in this chapter apply.

2.1 What Is TOGAF?

TOGAF is an architecture framework. TOGAF provides the methods and tools for assisting in the acceptance, production, use, and maintenance of an enterprise architecture. It is based on an iterative process model supported by best practices and a reusable set of existing architecture assets.

2.2 What Is Architecture in the Context of TOGAF?

ISO/IEC 42010: 2007 defines "architecture" as:

> "The fundamental organization of a system, embodied in its components, their relation-ships to each other and the environment, and the principles governing its design and evolution."

TOGAF embraces but does not strictly adhere to ISO/IEC 42010: 2007 terminology. In TOGAF," architecture" has two meanings depending upon the context:

1. A formal description of a system, or a detailed plan of the system at component level to guide its implementation.
2. The structure of components, their inter-relationships, and the principles and guidelines governing their design and evolution over time.

TOGAF considers the enterprise as a system and endeavors to strike a balance between promoting the concepts and terminology of ISO/IEC 42010: 2007 — ensuring that usage of terms defined by ISO/IEC 42010: 2007 is consistent with the standard — and retaining other commonly accepted terminology that is familiar to the majority of the TOGAF readership. For more on terminology, refer to Chapter 3 and Part IV, Chapter 35.

第 2 章
核心概念

本章中提供的核心概念适用于 TOGAF 9。

2.1 什么是 TOGAF？

TOGAF 是一种架构框架。TOGAF 提供方法和工具，有助于 Enterprise Architecture 的认可、构建、使用和维护。它基于多个最佳实践所支持的迭代的流程模型，以及一套可复用的现有架构资产。

2.2 在 TOGAF 背景环境下，什么是架构？

ISO/IEC 42010: 2007 将“架构”定义为：

> “一个系统的基础组织，体现在系统组件、组件之间及组件与环境之间的相互关系，以及对系统设计和演进进行治理的原则中。”

TOGAF 采纳但不严格遵循 ISO/IEC 42010: 2007 中的术语。在 TOGAF 中，根据背景环境，“架构”具有两种含义：

1. 一个系统的正式描述，或指导系统实施的组件层级详细计划。
2. 组件结构、组件之间相互关系，以及对这些组件的设计和随时间演进的治理原则和指南。

TOGAF 将 ENTERPRISE 视为一个系统，并尽力在使用 ISO/IEC 42010:2007 的概念和术语（确保 ISO/IEC 42010: 2007 所定义术语的使用与标准中一致）与保留已被大多数 TOGAF 读者普遍接受且所熟悉的术语之间达成平衡。关于术语更多的信息，见第 3 章以及第四部分第 35 章。

2.3 What Kind of Architecture Does TOGAF Deal with?

There are four architecture domains that are commonly accepted as subsets of an overall enterprise architecture, all of which TOGAF is designed to support:

- The **Business Architecture** defines the business strategy, governance, organization, and key business processes.
- The **Data Architecture** describes the structure of an organization's logical and physical data assets and data management resources.
- The **Application Architecture** provides a blueprint for the individual applications to be deployed, their interactions, and their relationships to the core business processes of the organization.
- The **Technology Architecture** describes the logical software and hardware capabilities that are required to support the deployment of business, data, and application services. This includes IT infrastructure, middleware, networks, communications, processing, standards, etc.

2.4 Architecture Development Method

The TOGAF Architecture Development Method (ADM) provides a tested and repeatable process for developing architectures. The ADM includes establishing an architecture framework, developing architecture content, transitioning, and governing the realization of architectures.

All of these activities are carried out within an iterative cycle of continuous architecture definition and realization that allows organizations to transform their enterprises in a controlled manner in response to business goals and opportunities.

Phases within the ADM are as follows:

- The **Preliminary Phase** describes the preparation and initiation activities required to create an Architecture Capability including customization of TOGAF and definition of Architecture Principles.
- **Phase A: Architecture Vision** describes the initial phase of an architecture development cycle. It includes information about defining the scope of the architecture development initiative, identifying the stakeholders, creating the Architecture Vision, and obtaining approval to proceed with the architecture development.
- **Phase B: Business Architecture** describes the development of a Business Architecture to support the agreed Architecture Vision.
- **Phase C: Information Systems Architectures** describes the development of Information Systems Architectures to support the agreed Architecture Vision.
- **PhaseD:Technology Architecture** describes the development of the Technology Architecture to support the agreed Architecture Vision.
- **Phase E: Opportunities & Solutions** conducts initial implementation planning and the identification of delivery vehicles for the architecture defined in the previous phases.
- **Phase F: Migration Planning** addresses how to move from the Baseline to the Target Architectures by finalizing a detailed Implementation and Migration Plan.

2.3 TOGAF 涉及哪些种类的架构？

有四种通常被认为是一个总体 Enterprise Architecture 子集的架构域，TOGAF 支持这四种架构域：

- **业务架构**，定义业务战略、治理、组织和关键业务流程。
- **数据架构**，描述组织的逻辑与物理数据资产及数据管理资源的结构。
- **应用架构**，提供包含待部署的独立应用及其之间交互作用和与组织的核心业务流程间的关系的蓝图。
- **技术架构**，描述支持业务、数据和应用服务部署所需的逻辑的软件与硬件能力，包括 IT 基础设施、中间件、网络、通信、处理和标准等。

2.4 架构开发方法

TOGAF 架构开发方法（ADM）提供用于开发架构的一个经测试的并可重复的流程。ADM 包括建立架构框架、开发架构内容、架构过渡及对架构实现进行管控。

所有这些活动均在一个连续的架构定义与实现的迭代周期内实施，使得组织能以一种受控的方式实施 ENTERPRISE 转型，以响应业务目标和机遇。

ADM 各阶段如下所述：

- **预备阶段**描述创建架构能力所需的准备和启动活动，包括 TOGAF 的定制化和架构原则的定义。
- **阶段 A：架构愿景**描述架构开发周期的初始阶段。该阶段包括定义架构开发举措的范围、识别利益攸关者、创建架构愿景，并获得继续推进架构开发的批准。
- **阶段 B：业务架构**描述支持被认同的架构愿景的业务架构的开发。
- **阶段 C：信息系统架构**描述支持被认同的架构愿景的信息系统架构的开发。
- **阶段 D：技术架构**描述支持被认同的架构愿景的技术架构的开发。
- **阶段 E：机会和解决方案**引导初始的实施规划，并为在之前阶段中定义的架构进行交付载体的识别。
- **阶段 F：迁移规划**涉及如何通过最终确定的详细实施和迁移计划来实现从基线架构向目标架构的转移。

- **Phase G: Implementation Governance** provides an architectural oversight of the implementation.
- **Phase H:Architecture Change Management** establishes procedures form an aging change to the new architecture.
- **Requirements Management** examines the process of managing architecture requirements throughout the ADM.

2.5 Deliverables, Artifacts, and Building Blocks

Architects executing the ADM will produce a number of outputs as a result of their efforts, such as process flows, architectural requirements, project plans, project compliance assessments, etc. The TOGAF Architecture Content Framework (see Part IV, Chapter 33) provides a structural model for architectural content that allows major work products to be consistently defined, structured, and presented.

The Architecture Content Framework uses the following three categories to describe the type of architectural work product within the context of use:

- A **deliverable** is a work product that is contractually specified and in turn formally reviewed, agreed, and signed off by the stakeholders. Deliverables represent the output of projects and those deliverables that are in documentation form will typically be archived at completion of a project, or transitioned into an Architecture Repository as a reference model, standard, or snapshot of the Architecture Landscape at a point in time.
- An **artifact** is an architectural work product that describes an aspect of the architecture.

  Artifacts are generally classified as catalogs (lists of things), matrices (showing relationships between things), and diagrams (pictures of things). Examples include a requirementscatalog, business interaction matrix, and a use-case diagram. An architectural deliverable may contain many artifacts and artifacts will form the content of the Architecture Repository.
- A **building block** represents a (potentially reusable) component of business, IT, or architectural capability that can be combined with other building blocks to deliver architectures and solutions.

  Building blocks can be defined at various levels of detail, depending on what stage of architecture development has been reached. For instance, at an early stage, a building block can simply consist of a name or an outline description. Later on, a building block may be decomposed into multiple supporting building blocks and may be accompanied by a full specification. Building blocks can relate to “architectures” or “solutions” .

  — **Architecture Building Blocks (ABBs)** typically describe required capability and shape the specification of Solution Building Blocks (SBBs). For example, a customer services capability may be required within an enterprise, supported by many SBBs, such as processes, data, and application software.

  — **Solution Building Blocks (SBBs)** represent components that will be used to implement the required capability. For example, a network is a building block that can be described through complementary artifacts and then put to use to realize solutions for the enterprise.

The relationships between deliverables, artifacts, and building blocks are shown in Figure 2-1.

- **阶段 G：实施治理**为实施提供架构的监管。
- **阶段 H：架构变更管理**为管理达到新架构的变更建立程序。
- **需求管理**对管理架构需求的流程的审查贯穿于整个 ADM。

2.5　交付物、制品和构建块

执行 ADM 的架构师会产生很多输出作为其工作的结果，例如，过程流、架构需求、项目计划、项目合规性评估等。TOGAF 架构内容框架（见第四部分第 33 章）为架构内容提供一种结构化模型，从而使主要的工作产物可被一致地定义、结构化和表达。

架构内容框架，使用下列三个分类描述在所使用的背景环境之中的架构工作产物类型：

- **交付物**是以契约方式规定的工作产物，并由利益攸关者依次正式审视、同意并签发。交付物代表项目的输出，文件形式的交付物通常在项目完成时存档，或过渡到架构库中当作参考模型、标准或作为架构全景在某个时点的“快照”。
- **制品**是描述架构的某一方面的架构工作产物。

  制品通常可分为目录集（事物的列表）、矩阵（表明事物之间的关系）和图表（事物的图像）。例如，需求目录集、业务交互矩阵和用例图。一个架构交付物可包含多个制品，制品构成架构库的内容。
- **构建块**代表业务、IT 或架构能力的一种（潜在可复用的）组件，它可以与其他构建块进行结合，以交付架构和解决方案。

  构建块可以在不同细节层级上被定义，这取决于架构开发所达到的阶段。例如，在初期阶段，构建块可以只包括名称或概述。其后，一个构建块可分解成多重支持的构建块，并可随附一份完整的规范。构建块可以与“架构”或“解决方案”相关。

  — **架构构建块（ABB）**，通常描述所需的能力，并对解决方案构建块（SBBs）的规范进行塑形。例如，ENTERPRISE 可能需要客户服务能力，它由多个 SBB 支持，如流程、数据和应用软件。

  — **解决方案构建块（SBB）**，代表用于实现所需能力的组件。例如，网络是一个能够通过互补的制品来描述的构建块，并用于实现 ENTERPRISE 的解决方案。

交付物、制品和构建块之间的关系如图 2-1 所示。

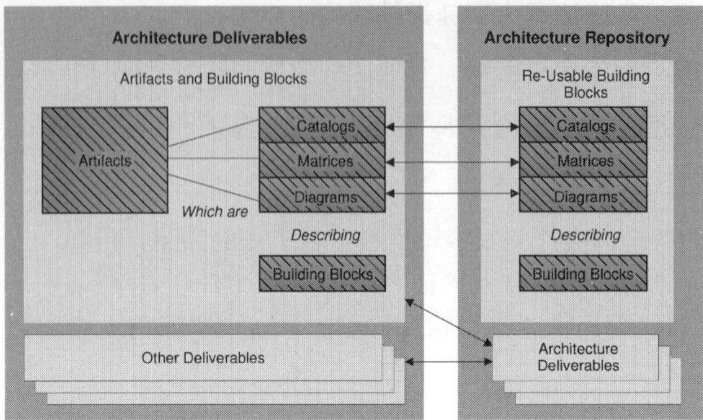

Figure 2-1 Relationships between Deliverables, Artifacts, and Building Blocks

For example, an Architecture Definition Document is a deliverable that documents an architecture description. This document will contain a number of complementary artifacts that are views of the building blocks relevant to the architecture. For example, a process flow diagram (an artifact) may be created to describe the target call handling process (a building block). This artifact may also describe other building blocks, such as the actors involved in the process (e.g.,a Customer Services Representative). An example of the relationships between deliverables, artifacts, and building blocks is illustrated in Figure 2-2.

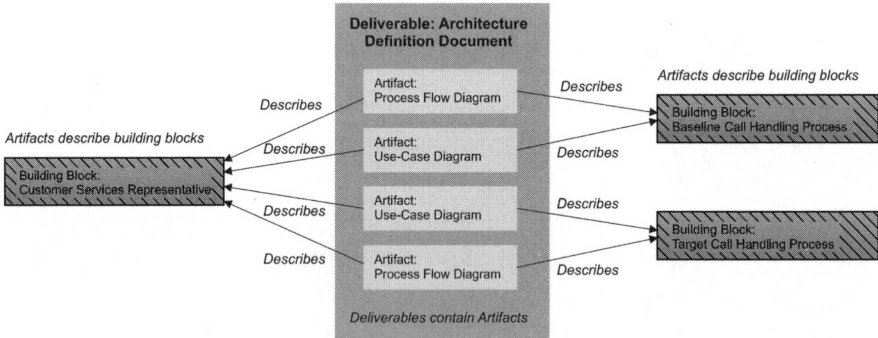

Figure 2-2 Example — Architecture Definition Document

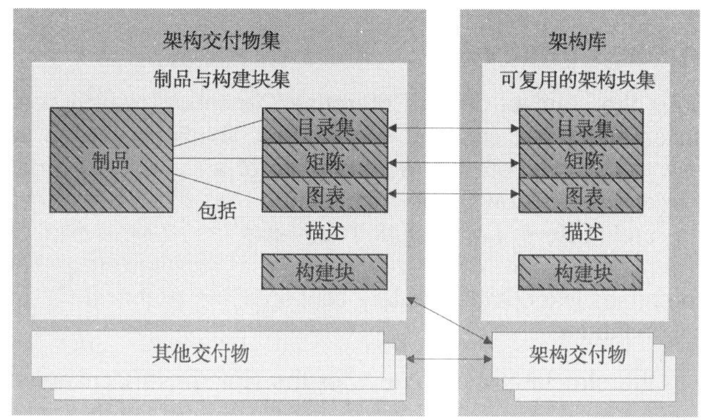

图 2-1　交付物、制品和构建块之间的关系

例如，架构定义文件是一种将架构描述文件化的交付物。该文件会包含多个互补的制品，它们是与架构相关的构建块的视图。例如，可创建一个流程图（制品）用以描述目标呼叫处理过程流（构建块）。该制品还可描述其他构建块，如参与该流程的施动者（如客户服务代表）。图 2-2 阐明了交付物、制品和构建块之间的关系示例。

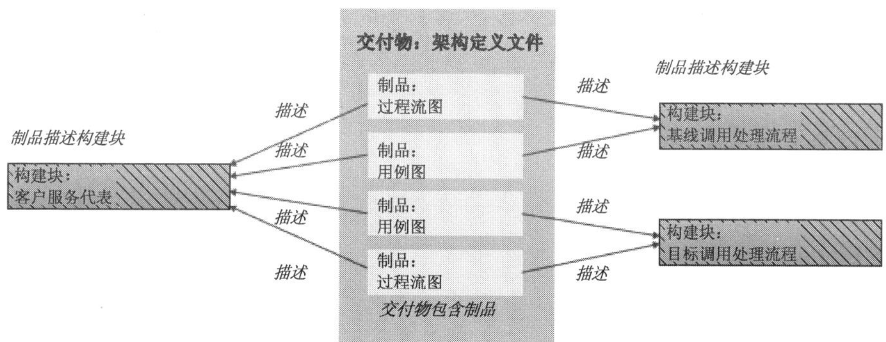

图 2-2　示例——架构定义文件

2.6 Enterprise Continuum

TOGAF includes the concept of the Enterprise Continuum, which sets the broader context for an architect and explains how generic solutions can be leveraged and specialized in order to support the requirements of an individual organization. The Enterprise Continuum is a view of the Architecture Repository that provides methods for classifying architecture and solution artifacts as they evolve from generic Foundation Architectures to Organization-Specific Architectures. The Enterprise Continuum comprises two complementary concepts: the Architecture Continuum and the Solutions Continuum.

An overview of the structure and context for the Enterprise Continuum is shown in Figure 2-3.

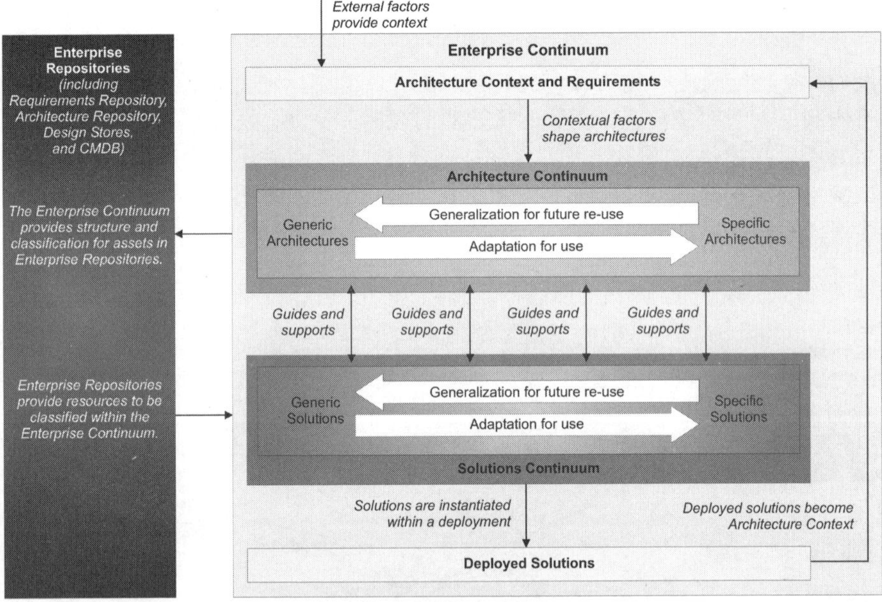

Figure 2-3 Enterprise Continuum

2.6 ENTERPRISE 的连续统一体

TOGAF 包括 ENTERPRISE 的连续统一体的概念，这为架构师提供了更广泛的背景环境，并说明如何更好地利用一般性的解决方案并使其特定化，以支持单个组织的需求。ENTERPRISE 的连续统一体是架构库的一种视图，它提供架构和解决方案的制品从一般基础性架构演变为组织特定架构时的分类方法。ENTERPRISE 的连续统一体包含两个补充概念：架构连续统一体和解决方案连续统一体。

ENTERPRISE 的连续统一体的结构和背景环境概述如图 2-3 所示。

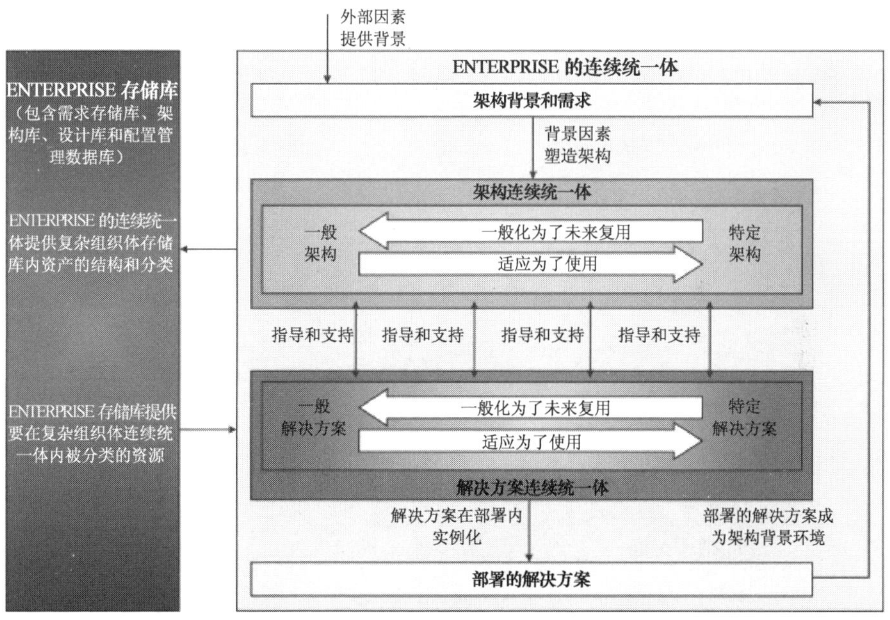

图 2-3 ENTERPRISE 的连续统一体

2.7 Architecture Repository

Supporting the Enterprise Continuum is the concept of an Architecture Repository which can be used to store different classes of architectural output at different levels of abstraction, created by the ADM. In this way, TOGAF facilitates understanding and cooperation between stakeholders and practitioners at different levels.

By means of the Enterprise Continuum and Architecture Repository, architects are encouraged to leverage all other relevant architectural resources and assets in developing an Organization-Specific Architecture.

In this context, the TOGAF ADM can be regarded as describing a process lifecycle that operates at multiple levels within the organization, operating within a holistic governance framework and producing aligned outputs that reside in an Architecture Repository. The Enterprise Continuum provides a valuable context for understanding architectural models: it shows building blocks and their relationships to each other, and the constraints and requirements on a cycle of architecture development.

The structure of the TOGAF Architecture Repository is shown in Figure 2-4.

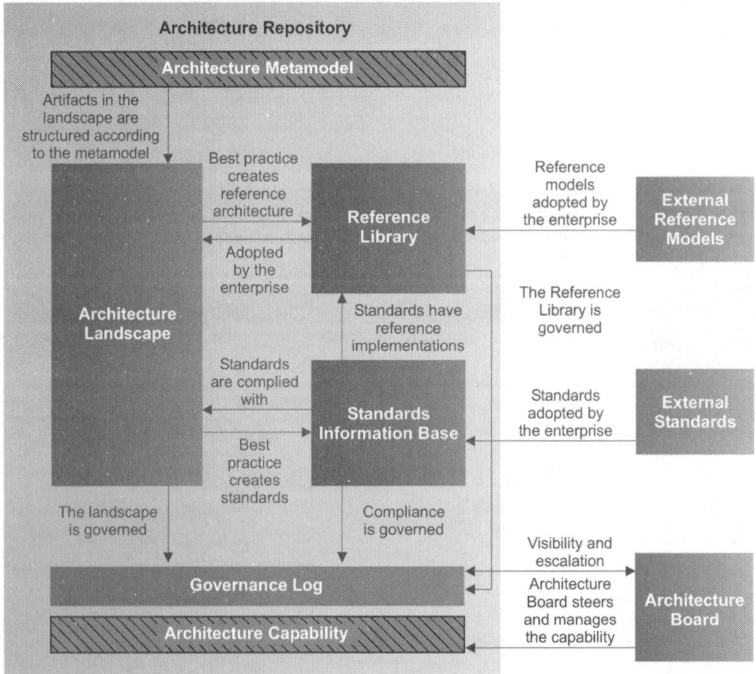

Figure 2-4 TOGAF Architecture Repository Structure

2.7 架构库

支持 ENTERPRISE 的连续统一体是架构库的设计理念，架构库可被用于将 ADM 创建的不同类别的架构输出存储在不同的抽象层级上。TOGAF 以这种方式促进不同层级的利益攸关者与实践者之间的理解和合作。

借助于 ENTERPRISE 的连续统一体和架构库，鼓励架构师在开发组织特定架构的过程中更好地利用所有其他相关的架构资源和资产。

在这一背景环境中，TOGAF ADM 可以被当作是描述在组织内的多层级上运行的流程生命周期，在整体治理框架内运行，并产生协调一致的输出，存放于架构库中。ENTERPRISE 的连续统一体提供了一个对理解架构模型有价值的背景环境：它展示了构建块及构建块间相互关系，以及在架构开发周期中的约束和需求。

TOGAF 架构库的结构如图 2-4 所示。

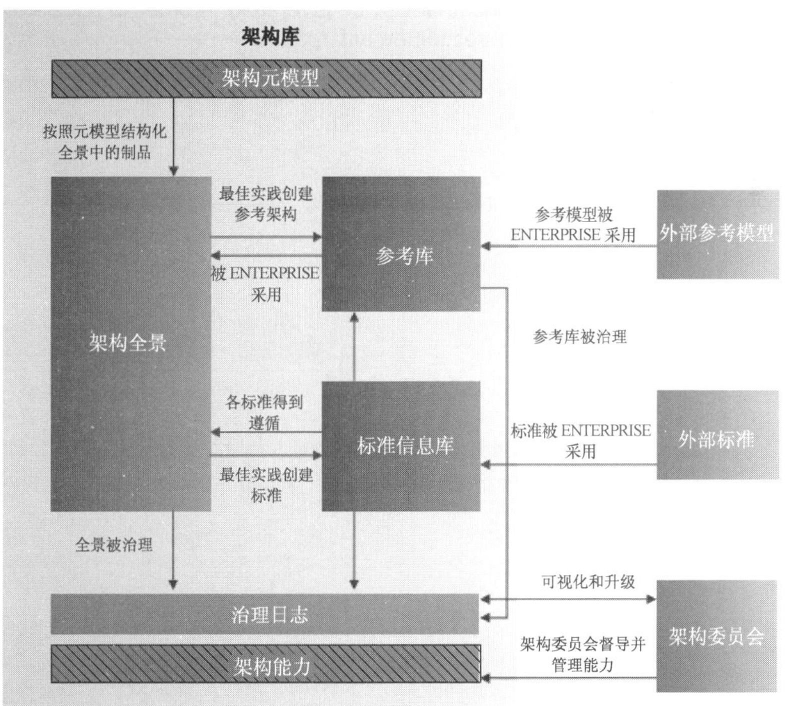

图 2-4 TOGAF 架构库结构

The major components within an Architecture Repository are as follows:

- The **Architecture Metamodel** describes the organizationally tailored application of an architecture framework, including a metamodel for architecture content.
- The **Architecture Capability** defines the parameters, structures, and processes that support governance of the Architecture Repository.
- The **Architecture Landscape** is the architectural representation of assets deployed within the operating enterprise at a particular point in time. The landscape is likely to exist at multiple levels of abstraction to suit different architecture objectives.
- The **Standards Information Base** (SIB) captures the standards with which new architectures must comply, which may include industry standards, selected products and services from suppliers, or shared services already deployed within the organization.
- The **Reference Library** provides guidelines, templates, patterns, and other forms of reference material that can be leveraged in order to accelerate the creation of new architectures for the enterprise.
- The **Governance Log** provides a record of governance activity across the enterprise.

架构库内的主要组件如下所述：

- **架构元模型**，描述架构框架在组织上的剪裁应用，包括架构内容元模型。
- **架构能力**，定义支持架构库治理的参数、结构和流程。
- **架构全景**，在一个特定时点部署于运行着的 ENTERPRISE 内的资产的架构表达。架构全景可能存在于多重抽象层级以适应不同的架构目的。
- **标准信息库（SIB）**，获取新架构必须遵守的标准，包括行业标准、选定的供应商产品和服务或已部署在该组织内的共享服务。
- **参考库**，提供指南、模板、特征模式和可更好利用的其他参考资料形式，以便加速 ENTERPRISE 新架构的创建。
- **治理日志**，提供贯穿整个 ENTERPRISE 的治理活动记录。

2.8 Establishing and Maintaining an Enterprise Architecture Capability

In order to carry out architectural activity effectively within an enterprise, it is necessary to put in place an appropriate business capability for architecture, through organization structures, roles, responsibilities, skills, and processes. An overview of the TOGAF Architecture Capability is shown in Figure 2-5.

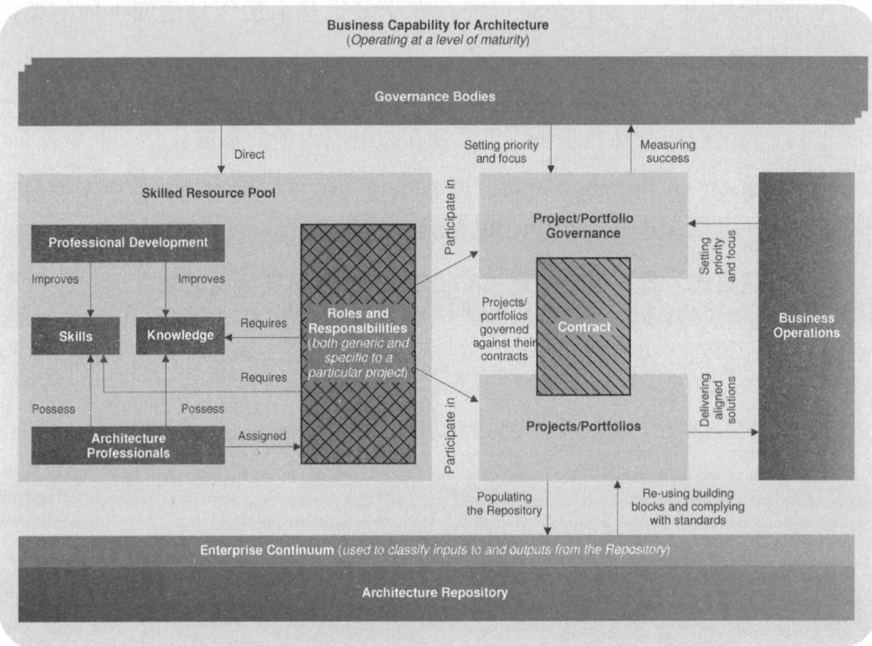

Figure 2-5 TOGAF Architecture Capability Overview

2.8 建立和维护 Enterprise Architecture 能力

为在 ENTERPRISE 内有效实施架构活动，有必要通过组织结构、角色、职责、技能和流程，将合适的架构的业务能力落实到位。TOGAF 架构能力概述如图 2-5 所示。

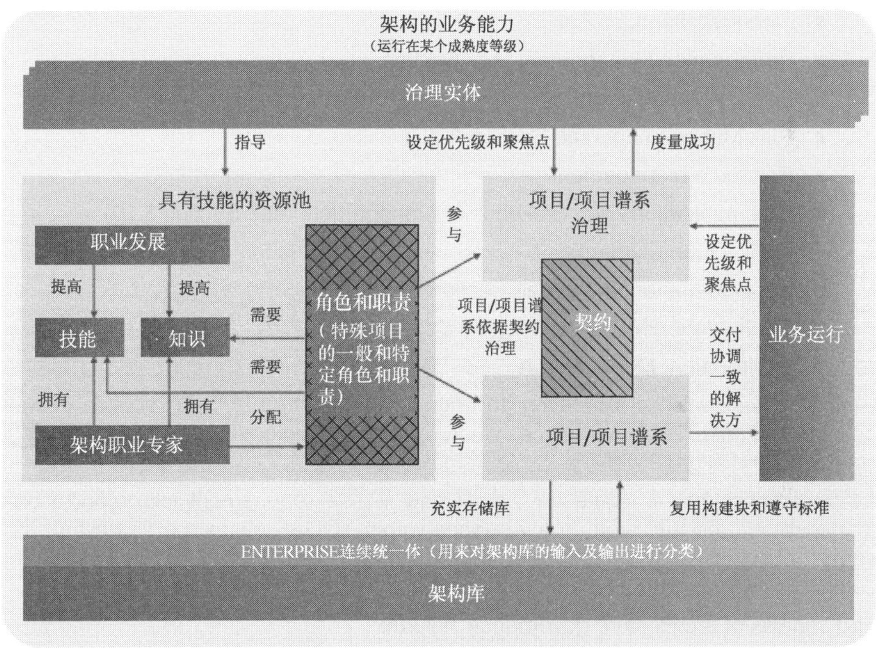

图 2-5 TOGAF 架构能力概述

2.9 Establishing the Architecture Capability as an Operational Entity

Barring architecture capabilities set up to purely support change delivery programs, it is increasingly recognized that a successful enterprise architecture practice must sit on a firm operational footing. In effect, an enterprise architecture practice must be run like any other operational unit within a business; i.e., it should be treated like a business. To this end, and over and above the core processes defined within the ADM, an enterprise architecture practice should establish capabilities in the following areas:

- Financial Management
- Performance Management (see Section 3.52)
- Service Management
- Risk Management (see Section A.75)
- Resource Management
- Communications and Stakeholder Management (see Section 3.29)
- Quality Management
- Supplier Management (see Section A.82)
- Configuration Management (see Section A.15)
- Environment Management

Central to the notion of operating an ongoing architecture is the execution of well-defined and effective governance, whereby all architecturally significant activity is controlled and aligned within a single framework.

As governance has become an increasingly visible requirement for organizational management, the inclusion of governance within TOGAF aligns the framework with current business best practice and also ensures a level of visibility, guidance, and control that will support all architecture stakeholder requirements and obligations.

The benefits of architecture governance include:

- Increased transparency of accountability, and informed delegation of authority.
- Controlled risk management.
- Protection of the existing asset base through maximizing reuse of existing architectural components.
- Proactive control, monitoring, and management mechanisms.
- Process, concept, and component reuse across all organizational business units.
- Value creation through monitoring, measuring, evaluation, and feedback.
- Increased visibility supporting internal processes and external parties' requirements; in particular, increased visibility of decision-making at lower levels ensures oversight at an appropriate level within the enterprise of decisions that may have far-reaching strategic consequences for the organization.
- Greater shareholder value; in particular, enterprise architecture increasingly represents the core intellectual property of the enterprise — studies have demonstrated a correlation between increased shareholder value and well-governed enterprises.

2.9 将架构能力建立为运行实体

除非将架构能力的建立仅用于支持变更交付项目，否则，应逐渐认识到一个成功的 Enterprise Architecture 实践必须建立在坚实的运行基础之上。实际上，Enterprise Architecture 实践必须如同业务内任何其他运行单元一样运行，即 Enterprise Architecture 实践应被视为一种业务。为此，除了 ADM 内定义的核心流程外，Enterprise Architecture 实践还应在下述领域建立能力：

- 财务管理
- 绩效管理（见 3.52 节）
- 服务管理
- 风险管理（见 A.75 节）
- 资源管理
- 沟通和利益攸关者管理（见 3.29 节）
- 质量管理
- 供应商管理（见 A.82 节）
- 构型管理（见 A.15 节）
- 环境管理

对一个运行中的架构进行运作的核心要点是，执行已明确定义且有效的治理体系，从而使所有架构重要活动受控，并在单一框架内保持协调一致。

由于治理已经成为一个日益明显的组织管理需求，TOGAF 内包含的治理使框架与当前业务最佳实践相一致，并且还确保可见性、引导和控制水平，以支持所有架构利益攸关者的需求和义务。

架构治理的好处包括：

- 增加责任的透明度并告知授权。
- 受控的风险管理。
- 通过现有架构组件的最大化复用来保护现有资产基础。
- 前瞻性的控制、监控和管理机制。
- 跨越所有组织业务单元复用流程、概念与组件。
- 通过监控、衡量、评价和反馈来创造价值。
- 增加对内部流程和外部各方需求支撑的可见性；特别是，较低层级上增加的决策可见性确保那些可能对该组织具有深远战略影响的决策在 ENTERPRISE 内的适当层级得到监督。
- 更显著的股东价值；特别是，Enterprise Architecture 越来越多地代表 ENTERPRISE 的核心知识产权——研究已经表明，增加的股东价值与治理良好的 ENTERPRISE 之间的相关性。

- Integrates with existing processes and methodologies and complements functionality by adding control capabilities.

Further detail on establishing an enterprise Architecture Capability is given in Part VII, Chapter45.

2.10 Using TOGAF with Other Frameworks

Two of the key elements of any enterprise architecture framework are:

- A definition of the deliverables that the architecting activity should produce.
- A description of the method by which this should be done.

With some exceptions, the majority of enterprise architecture frameworks focus on the first of these — the specific set of deliverables — and are relatively silent about the methods to be used to generate them (intentionally so, in some cases).

Because TOGAF is a generic framework and intended to be used in a wide variety of environments, it provides a flexible and extensible content framework that underpins a set of generic architecture deliverables.

As a result, TOGAF may be used either in its own right, with the generic deliverables that it describes; or else these deliverables may be replaced or extended by a more specific set, defined in any other framework that the architect considers relevant.

In all cases, it is expected that the architect will adapt and build on the TOGAF framework in order to define a tailored method that is integrated into the processes and organization structures of the enterprise. This architecture tailoring may include adopting elements from other architecture frameworks, or integrating TOGAF methods with other standard frameworks, such as ITIL, CMMI, COBIT, PRINCE2, PMBOK, and MSP. Guidelines for adapting the TOGAF ADM in such a way are given in Part II, Section 5.3.

As a generic framework and method for enterprise architecture, TOGAF provides the capability and the collaborative environment to integrate with other frameworks. Organizations are able to fully utilize vertical business domains, horizontal technology areas (such as security or manageability), or application areas (such as e-Commerce) to produce a competitive enterprise architecture framework which maximizes their business opportunities.

- 整合现有流程和方法论，并通过增加控制能力来完善其功能性。

在第七部分第45章中有更多的关于建立ENTERPRISE的架构能力的详细内容。

2.10 使用TOGAF与其他框架

任何Enterprise Architecture框架的两个关键要素都是：

- 架构活动应产生的交付物的定义。
- 完成架构活动应采用的方法描述。

除一些例外情况，大多数Enterprise Architecture框架关注于第一种要素——特定的交付物集合——并且相对很少提及用于生成这些交付物的方法（在一些情况下是有意的）。

因为TOGAF是一个一般框架，且旨在用于多种多样的环境，所以TOGAF提供一个灵活且可扩展的内容框架，用以支撑一系列一般架构交付物。

因此，TOGAF可在其自身范围内与其所描述的一般交付物一起使用，或者可由一个更特定的集合替代或扩展这些交付物，这里所说的更特定的集合，可以是架构师认为相关的、在任何其他框架中定义的交付物。

在所有情况下，架构师应当基于TOGAF框架进行调整和构建，以定义一种被整合到ENTERPRISE的流程和组织结构中的剪裁方法。这一架构剪裁过程，可包括采用其他架构框架的元素或将TOGAF方法与其他标准框架进行综合，例如ITIL、CMMI、COBIT、PRINCE2、PMBOK和MSP。第二部分的第5.3节给出了以上述方式调整TOGAF ADM的指南。

作为Enterprise Architecture的一般框架和方法，TOGAF提供与其他框架进行综合的能力和协同环境。各类组织能够全面地利用垂直业务域、水平技术领域（如安保性和可管理性）或应用领域（如电子商务），以产生一个使ENTERPRISE业务机会最大化的具有竞争力的Enterprise Architecture框架。

Chapter 3 Definitions

For the purposes of TOGAF 9,the following terms and definitions apply. Appendix A should be referenced for supplementary definitions not defined in this chapter. Merriam-Webster's Collegiate Dictionary should be referenced for terms not defined in this section or Appendix A.

3.1 Abstraction

The technique of providing summarized or generalized descriptions of detailed and complex content.

Abstraction, as in " level of abstraction " , can also mean providing a focus for analysis that is concerned with a consistent and common level of detail or abstraction. Abstraction in this sense is typically used in architecture to allow a consistent level of definition and understanding to be achieved in each area of the architecture in order to support effective communication and decision-making. It is especially useful when dealing with large and complex architectures as it allows relevant issues to be identified before further detail is attempted.

3.2 Actor

A person, organization, or system that has a role that initiates or interacts with activities; for example, a sales representative who travels to visit customers. Actors may be internal or external to an organization.In the automotive industry, an original equipment manufacturer would be considered an actor by an automotive dealership that interacts with its supply chain activities.

3.3 Application

A deployed and operational IT system that supports business functions and services; for example, a payroll. Applications use data and are supported by multiple technology components but are distinct from the technology components that support the application.

第3章 定 义

下述术语和定义适用于 TOGAF 9。对于未在本章中规定的补充定义，应参考附录 A。对于未在本节或附录 A 中定义的术语，应参考韦氏大学词典。

3.1 抽象

对详细而又复杂的内容进行总结性或概括性描述的技术。

“抽象层次”中的抽象，还可表示为进行一致且共同的详细或抽象层级上的分析而提供聚焦点。这种意义上的抽象在架构中的典型使用，使得架构每个领域中定义和理解的一致，以支持有效沟通和决策。当处理大型且复杂的架构时，抽象是特别有用的，因为它使得对相关议题的识别在试图进一步地展开细节前就能进行。

3.2 施动者

以某种角色发起活动或与活动进行交互的个人、组织或系统，例如旅行访问客户的销售代表。施动者可以处于组织内部或外部。在汽车行业，汽车经销商就将原始设备制造商视为与其供应链活动进行交互的一个施动者。

3.3 应用

一个已部署和运行的 IT 系统，用以支持各种业务功能和服务，例如薪资系统。应用使用数据并被多重技术组件支持，但与支持其的技术组件截然不同。

3.4 Application Architecture

A description of the structure and interaction of the applications as groups of capabilities that provide key business functions and manage the data assets.

Note: Application Architecture is described in Part II, Chapter 11.

3.5 Application Platform

The collection of technology components of hardware and software that provide the services used to support applications.

3.6 Application Platform Interface (API)

The interface, or set of functions, between application software and/or the application platform.

3.7 Architectural Style

The combination of distinctive features in which architecture is performed or expressed.

3.8 Architecture

1. A formal description of a system, or a detailed plan of the system at component level, to guide its implementation (source: ISO/IEC 42010: 2007).
2. The structure of components, their inter-relationships, and the principles and guidelines governing their design and evolution over time.

3.9 Architecture Building Block (ABB)

A constituent of the architecture model that describes a single aspect of the overall model. See also Section 3.21.

3.4 应用架构

对应用结构和应用间交互的描述，这些应用作为能力群组提供关键业务功能并管理数据资产。

注：在第二部分第 11 章中描述应用架构。

3.5 应用平台

提供支持各类应用的多种服务的硬件和软件的技术组件集合。

3.6 应用平台界面（API）

应用软件和/或应用平台之间的界面或功能集。

3.7 架构风格

在架构的执行或表达中的独特特征组合。

3.8 架构

1. 一个系统的正式描述，或指导系统实施的组件层级的详细计划（来源：ISO/IEC 42010:2007）。
2. 组件结构、组件之间相互关系，以及对这些组件的设计和随时间演进进行治理的原则和指南。

3.9 架构构建块（ABB）

描述总体模型单一方面的架构模型的一种构成要素。还可参见 3.21 节。

3.10 Architecture Continuum

A part of the Enterprise Continuum. A repository of architectural elements with increasing detail and specialization. This Continuum begins with foundational definitions like reference models, core strategies, and basic building blocks. From there it spans to Industry Architectures and all the way to an organization's specific architecture.

See also Section 3.35.

3.11 Architecture Development Method (ADM)

The core of TOGAF. A step-by-step approach to develop and use an enterprise architecture.

Note: The ADM is described in Part II: Architecture Development Method (ADM).

3.12 Architecture Domain

The architectural area being considered. There are four architecture domains within TOGAF:

business, data, application, and technology.

3.13 Architecture Framework

A conceptual structure used to develop, implement, and sustain an architecture.

3.14 Architecture Governance

The practice and orientation by which enterprise architectures and other architectures are managed and controlled at an enterprise-wide level. It is concerned with change processes (design governance) and operation of product systems (operational governance).

See also Section 3.39.

3.15 Architecture Landscape

The architectural representation of assets in use, or planned, by the enterprise at particular points in time.

3.10 架构连续统一体

ENTERPRISE 的连续统一体的一部分。它是具有不断增加的细节和特定性的架构元素的存储库。架构连续统一体以诸如参考模型、核心策略和基本构建块等基础定义开始，在此基础上扩展到行业架构，并最终扩展成为组织特定架构。

还可参见 3.35 节。

3.11 架构开发方法（ADM）

TOGAF 的核心。开发和使用 Enterprise Architecture 的一种循序渐进的实施途径。

注：在第二部分：架构开发方法（ADM）中描述 ADM。

3.12 架构域

架构开发中需要考虑的架构领域。TOGAF 中包括四个架构域：业务、数据、应用和技术。

3.13 架构框架

用于开发、实施并维持架构的概念性结构。

3.14 架构治理

在整个 ENTERPRISE 范围层级管理和控制 Enterprise Architecture 和其他架构的实践和定位。架构治理关注变革流程（设计治理）和产品系统运行（运行治理）。

还可参见 3.39 节。

3.15 架构全景

在特定时点下对 ENTERPRISE 使用或计划的资产的架构表达。

3.16 Architecture Principles

A qualitative statement of intent that should be met by the architecture. Has at least a supporting rationale and a measure of importance.

Note: A sample set of Architecture Principles is defined in Part III, Chapter 23.

3.17 Architecture Vision

A succinct description of the Target Architecture that describes its business value and the changes to the enterprise that will result from its successful deployment. It serves as an aspirational vision and a boundary for detailed architecture development.

Note: Phase A (Architecture Vision) is described in Part II, Chapter 7.

3.18 Artifact

An architectural work product that describes an aspect of the architecture. See also Section 3.21.

3.19 Baseline

A specification that has been formally reviewed and agreed upon, that there after serves as the basis for further development or change and that can be changed only through formal change control procedures or a type of procedure such as configuration management.

3.20 Boundaryless Information Flow

1. A trademark of The Open Group.
2. A shorthand representation of "access to integrated information to support business process improvements" representing a desired state of an enterprise's infrastructure specific to the business needs of the organization.

An infrastructure that provides Boundaryless Information Flow has open standard components that provide services in a customer's extended enterprise that:

- Combine multiple sources of information.
- Securely deliver the information whenever and wherever it is needed, in the right context for the people or systems using that information.

Note: The need for Boundaryless Information Flow is described in Part VI, Chapter 44.

3.16 架构原则

对架构应满足的意图的定性申明，至少具备一个支持的理由和一个重要性的测度。

注：在第三部分第 23 章中定义架构原则的样本集。

3.17 架构愿景

对目标架构的简要描述，架构愿景描述目标架构的业务价值，以及 ENTERPRISE 因目标架构的成功部署而出现的变化。架构愿景是详细架构开发的强烈渴望的愿景和边界。

注：在第二部分第 7 章中描述阶段 A（架构愿景）。

3.18 制品

描述架构某一方面的一种架构工作产物。还可参见 3.21 节。

3.19 基线

已经过正式审视并且取得一致认可的规范，基线确立后，将作为进一步开发或变更的基础，而且它仅可通过正式的变更控制程序或如构型管理等程序进行变更。

3.20 无边界信息流

1. The Open Group 的商标。
2. “访问综合信息以支持业务流程改进”的一种简短表达，它表达满足特定的组织业务需要的一种 ENTERPRISE 的基础设施期望状态。

提供无边界信息流的基础设施，具有开放标准组件，这些标准组件为客户扩展型 ENTERPRISE 提供下述服务：

- 整合多重信息来源。
- 在使用该信息的人员或系统的正确背景环境下，无论何时何地需要，均安全地传递信息。

注：在第二部分第 44 章中描述对无边界信息流的需要。

3.21 Building Block

Represents a (potentially reusable) component of business, IT, or architectural capability that can be combined with other building blocks to deliver architectures and solutions.

Building blocks can be defined at various levels of detail,depending on what stage of architecture development has been reached. For instance, at an early stage, a building block can simply consist of a name or an outline description. Lateron, a building block maybe decomposed into multiple supporting building blocks and may be accompanied by a full specification. Building blocks can relate to "architectures" or "solutions" .

See also Section 3.18.

Note: Building blocks are described in Part IV, Chapter 37.

3.22 Business Architecture

A description of the structure and interaction between the business strategy, organization, functions, business processes, and information needs.

Note: Business Architecture is described in Part II, Chapter 8.

3.23 Business Function

Delivers business capabilities closely aligned to an organization, but not necessarily explicitly governed by the organization.

3.24 Business Governance

Concerned with ensuring that the business processes and policies (and their operation) deliver the business outcomes and adhere to relevant business regulation.

3.25 Business Service

Supports business capabilities through an explicitly defined interface and is explicitly governed by an organization.

3.26 Capability

An ability that an organization, person, or system possesses. Capabilities are typically expressed in general and high-level terms and typically require a combination of organization, people, processes, and technology to achieve. For example, marketing, customer contact, or outbound telemarketing.

3.21 构建块

代表业务、IT 或架构能力的一种（潜在可复用的）组件，它能够与其他构建块进行结合，以交付架构和解决方案。

构建块可以在不同细节层级上被定义，这取决于架构开发所达到的阶段。例如，在初期阶段，构建块可以只包括名称或概述。其后，一个构建块可分解成多重支持的构建块，并可随附一份完整的规范。构建块可以与“架构”或“解决方案”相关。

还可参见 3.18 节。

注：在第四部分第 37 章描述构建块。

3.22 业务架构

对业务战略、组织、功能、业务流程和信息需要之间的结构和交互的描述。

注：在第二部分第 8 章中描述业务架构。

3.23 业务功能

交付与组织密切协调一致的业务能力，但这些能力并非必须由该组织明确治理。

3.24 业务治理

致力于确保业务流程和策略（及其运行）交付业务产出并遵循相关的业务规定。

3.25 业务服务

通过明确定义的界面支持业务能力，并由组织明确管控。

3.26 能力

组织、个人或系统拥有的能力。能力常常以一般且高度概括的术语表达，并且，能力通常需要将组织、人员、流程和技术结合起来才能达成。例如，市场营销、客户联络或推式电话营销等。

3.27 Capability Architecture

A highly detailed description of the architectural approach to realize a particular solution or solution aspect.

3.28 Capability Increment

A discrete portion of a capability architecture that delivers specific value. When all increments have been completed, the capability has been realized.

3.29 Communications and Stakeholder Management

The management of needs of stakeholders of the enterprise architecture practice. It also manages the execution of communication between the practice and the stakeholders and the practice and the consumers of its services.

Note: Architecture stakeholder management is described in Chapter 24.

3.30 Concerns

The key interests that are crucially important to the stakeholders in a system, and determine the acceptability of the system. Concerns may pertain to any aspect of the system's functioning, development, or operation, including considerations such as performance, reliability, security, distribution, and evolvability.

See also Section 3.68.

3.31 Constraint

An external factor that prevents an organization from pursuing particular approaches to meet its goals. For example, customer data is not harmonized within the organization, regionally or nationally, constraining the organization's ability to offer effective customer service.

3.27 能力架构

对实现特定解决方案或解决方案某方面的架构途径的非常详细的描述。

3.28 能力增量

交付特定价值的能力架构的一个离散部分。当完成所有增量时，就已经实现了这种能力。

3.29 沟通和利益攸关者管理

对 Enterprise Architecture 实践中利益攸关者的需要进行的管理。同时，它对 Enterprise Architecture 实践与利益攸关者之间，以及 Enterprise Architecture 实践与其服务使用者之间的沟通执行进行管理。

注：在第 24 章中描述架构利益攸关者管理。

3.30 关注点

在系统中，对利益攸关者至关重要并决定该系统可接受性的关键兴趣点。关注点可与系统的功能、开发或运行的任何方面相关，包括对如性能、可靠性、安保性、分布和可演进性等方面的考虑。

还可参见 3.68 节。

3.31 约束

阻碍组织寻求满足其目标的特定途径的外部因素。例如，客户数据在地区性或全国性范围的组织内部不一致，限制组织提供有效客户服务的能力。

3.32 Data Architecture

A description of the structure and interaction of the enterprise's major types and sources of data, logical data assets, physical data assets, and data management resources.

Note: Data Architecture is described in Part II, Chapter 10.

3.33 Deliverable

An architectural work product that is contractually specified and in turn formally reviewed, agreed, and signed off by the stakeholders. Deliverables represent the output of projects and those deliverables that are in documentation form will typically be archived at completion of a project, or transitioned into an Architecture Repository as a reference model, standard, or snapshot of the Architecture Landscape at a point in time.

3.34 Enterprise

The highest level (typically) of description of an organization and typically covers all missions and functions. An enterprise will often span multiple organizations.

3.35 Enterprise Continuum

A categorization mechanism useful for classifying architecture and solution artifacts,both internal and external to the Architecture Repository, as they evolve from generic Foundation Architectures to Organization-Specific Architectures.

See also Section 3.10 and Section 3.67.

3.36 Foundation Architecture

Generic building blocks, their inter-relationships with other building blocks, combined with the principles and guidelines that provide a foundation on which more specific architectures can be built.

3.37 Framework

A structure for content or process that can be used as a tool to structure thinking, ensuring consistency and completeness.

3.32 数据架构

对 ENTERPRISE 的主要数据类型及来源、逻辑数据资产、物理数据资产，以及数据管理资源的结构及交互的描述。

注：在第二部分第 10 章中描述数据架构。

3.33 交付物

以契约方式规定，并依次由利益攸关者正式审视、同意并签发的架构工作产物。交付物代表项目的输出，文档形式的交付物通常在项目完成时存档，或过渡到架构库中当作参考模型、标准或作为架构全景在某个时点的“快照”。

3.34 ENTERPRISE

对组织的最高层级（通常是）描述，通常涵盖所有使命和职能。一个 ENTERPRISE 通常跨越多重组织。

3.35 ENTERPRISE 的连续统一体

在架构和解决方案制品从一般基础性架构演变为组织特定架构时，可用于对架构库内部或外部的架构和解决方案制品进行归类的分类机制。

还可参见 3.10 节和 3.67 节。

3.36 基础架构

由一般构建块、通用构建块与其他构建块的相互关系以及有关的原则和指南构成，并为在其之上构建更具体的架构提供了基础。

3.37 框架

一种可用作结构化思考工具的内容或流程的结构，从而确保一致性和完整性。

3.38 Gap

A statement of difference between two states. Used in the context of gap analysis, where the difference between the Baseline and Target Architecture is identified.

Note: Gap analysis is described in Part III, Chapter 27.

3.39 Governance

The discipline of monitoring, managing, and steering a business (or IS/IT landscape) to deliver the business outcome required.

See also Section 3.14, Section 3.24, and Section A.60 in Appendix A.

3.40 Information

Any communication or representation of facts, data, oropinions, in any medium or form, including textual, numerical, graphic, cartographic, narrative, or audio-visual forms.

3.41 Information Technology (IT)

1. The lifecycle management of information and related technology used by an organization.
2. An umbrella term that includes all or some of the subject areas relating to the computer industry, such as Business Continuity, Business IT Interface, Business Process Modeling and Management, Communication, Compliance and Legislation, Computers, Content Management, Hardware, Information Management, Internet, Offshoring, Networking, Programming and Software, Professional Issues, Project Management, Security, Standards, Storage, Voice and Data Communications. Various countries and industries employ other umbrella terms to describe this same collection.
3. A term commonly assigned to a department within an organization tasked with provisioning some or all of the domains described in (2) above.
4. Alternate names commonly adopted include Information Services, Information Management, et al.

3.38 差距

对两种状态之间差异的陈述。用于差距分析的背景环境，识别基线和目标架构之间的差异的情况。

注：在第三部分第27章中描述差距分析。

3.39 治理

监控、管理和指导业务（或IS/IT全景）以交付所需业务产出的规程。

还可参见3.14节、3.24节以及附录A中的A.60节。

3.40 信息

利用包括文字、数值、图形、制图、叙述或视听形式在内的任意介质或形式对各种事实、数据或观念的传达或表达。

3.41 信息技术（IT）

1. 对组织所使用的信息和相关技术的生命周期管理。
2. 一种涵盖性术语，包括与计算机行业有关的所有或部分主题领域，例如业务的持续性、业务IT界面、业务流程建模和管理、通信、合规性和立法、计算机、内容管理、硬件、信息管理、互联网、离岸外包、网络化、编程和软件、专业议题、项目管理、安保性、标准、存储、语音和数据通信。不同国家和行业使用其他的涵盖性术语描述这一相同的集合。
3. 通常指派到组织内的一个部门的术语，该组织负责规定上文（2）中所述的部分或全部域。
4. 通常采用的别称包括信息服务、信息管理等。

3.42 Interoperability

1. The ability to share information and services.
2. The ability of two or more systems or components to exchange and use information.
3. The ability of systems to provide and receive services from other systems and to use the services so interchanged to enable them to operate effectively together.

3.43 Logical

An implementation-independent definition of the architecture, often grouping related physical entities according to their purpose and structure. For example, the products from multiple infrastructure software vendors can all be logically grouped as Java application server platforms.

3.44 Metadata

Data about data, of any sort in any media, that describes the characteristics of an entity.

3.45 Metamodel

A model that describes how and with what the architecture will be described in a structured way.

3.46 Method

A defined, repeatable approach to address a particular type of problem.

See also Section 3.47.

3.47 Methodology

A defined, repeatable series of steps to address a particular type of problem, which typically centers on a defined process, but may also include definition of content.

See also Section 3.46.

3.42 互用性

1. 共享信息和服务的能力。
2. 两个或多个系统或组件交换和使用信息的能力。
3. 系统向其他系统提供服务、从其他系统接收服务以及使用如此互换的服务，促进彼此有效协同运行的能力。

3.43 逻辑的

架构的一种与实施无关的定义，通常按照相关物理实体的目的和结构对它们进行分组。例如，多重基础设施软件厂商所提供的产品都可以在逻辑上分组成 Java 应用服务器平台。

3.44 元数据

任何介质中存在的任何类型的“数据的数据”，描述实体的特征。

3.45 元模型

一种说明如何以及使用什么元素以结构化方式描述架构的模型。

3.46 方法

应对特定类型问题而被定义且可重复的一种实施途径。

还可参见 3.47 节。

3.47 方法论

为应对特定类型问题而被定义且可重复的一系列步骤。方法论通常以某个定义的流程为中心，但也可以包括对内容的定义。

还可参见 3.46 节

3.48 Model

A representation of a subject of interest. A model provides a smaller scale, simplified, and/or abstract representation of the subject matter. A model is constructed as a "means to an end" . In the context of enterprise architecture, the subject matter is a whole or part of the enterprise and the end is the ability to construct "views" that address the concerns of particular stakeholders; i.e., their "viewpoints" in relation to the subject matter.

See also Section 3.68, Section 3.75, and Section 3.76.

3.49 Modeling

A technique through construction of models which enables a subject to be represented in a form that enables reasoning, insight, and clarity concerning the essence of the subject matter.

3.50 Objective

A time-bounded milestone for an organization used to demonstrate progress towards a goal; for example, "Increase Capacity Utilization by 30% by the end of 2009 to support the planned increase in market share" .

3.51 Patterns

A technique for putting building blocks into context; for example, to describe a re-usable solution to a problem. Building blocks are what you use: patterns can tell you how you use them, when, why, and what trade-offs you have to make in doing so.

See also Section 3.21.

3.52 Performance Management

The monitoring, control, and reporting of the enterprise architecture practice performance. Also concerned with continuous improvement.

3.53 Physical

A description of a real-world entity. Physical elements in an enterprise architecture may still be considerably abstracted from Solution Architecture, design, or implementation views.

3.54 Platform

A combination of technology infrastructure products and components that provides that prerequisites to host application software.

3.48 模型

对所感兴趣的主题的一种表达。模型为主题提供了一种较小的尺度、简化的和/或抽象的表达。模型被构造为一种“达到目的的手段”。在 Enterprise Architecture 的背景环境中，主题是整个或部分 ENTERPRISE，而目的则是构造涉及特定利益攸关者关注点的“视图”的能力，即构造与主题相关联的“视角”的能力。

还可参见 3.68 节、3.75 节以及 3.76 节。

3.49 建模

一种模型构建技术，它使得能够通过对主题本质进行推理、洞察和明晰的形式表达主题。

3.50 目的

组织的一个有时限性的里程碑，用于展示朝着目标的进展，例如，“2009 年年底前产能利用率提高 30%，以支持市场份额按计划增长。”

3.51 特征模式

一种将构建块置入背景环境中的技术，例如为了描述某个问题的可复用的解决方案。构建块是回答“用什么”，特征模式则告诉你“如何、何时、为什么使用它们，以及在使用中你必须做出何种权衡”。

还可参见 3.21 节。

3.52 绩效管理

对 Enterprise Architecture 实践绩效的监控、控制和报告，同时也关注持续改进。

3.53 物理的

对真实实体的描述。Enterprise Architecture 中的物理元素在很大程度上仍然可从解决方案架构、设计或实施视图中抽象出来。

3.54 平台

一种技术基础设施产品与组件的组合，平台为部署应用软件提供先决条件。

3.55 Platform Service

A technical capability required to provide enabling infrastructure that supports the delivery of applications.

3.56 Principle

See Section 3.16.

3.57 Reference Model (RM)

A reference model is an abstract framework for understanding significant relationships among the entities of [an] environment, and for the development of consistent standardsor specifications supporting that environment. A reference model is based on a small number of unifying concepts and may be used as a basis for education and explaining standards to a non-specialist. A reference model is not directly tied to any standards, technologies, or other concrete implementation details, but it does seek to provide common semantics that can be used unambiguously across and between different implementations.

Note: The source of this definition is OASIS; refer to www.oasis-open.org/committees/tc_ home.php?wg_abbrev=soa-rm.

3.58 Repository

A system that manages all of the data of an enterprise, including data and process models and other enterprise information. Hence, the data in a repository is much more extensive than that in a data dictionary, which generally defines only the data making up a database.

3.59 Requirement

A statement of need that must be met by a particular architecture or work package.

3.60 Roadmap

An abstracted plan for business or technology change, typically operating across multiple disciplines over multiple years. Normally used in the phrases Technology Roadmap, Architecture Roadmap, etc.

3.55 平台服务

为了提供支持应用交付的使能性基础设施必需的一种技术能力。

3.56 原则

见 3.16 节。

3.57 参考模型（RM）

参考模型是一种抽象框架，旨在帮助理解环境中实体之间的重要关系和开发支持该环境的一致标准或规范。参考模型基于少量统一概念，并可以作为基础，用来对非专业人员进行教育和解释标准。参考模型并不直接绑定任何标准、技术或其他具体实施细节，但它试图提供可跨越不同实施以及在不同实施之间明确使用的常用语义。

注：本定义的来源是 OASIS，参见 www.oasis-open.org/committees/tc_home.php?wg_abbrev=soa-rm。

3.58 存储库

一个管理 ENTERPRISE 所有数据的系统，包括数据和流程模型，以及其他 ENTERPRISE 信息。因此，存储库中的数据比数据字典中的数据更加广泛，数据字典一般只定义构成数据库的数据。

3.59 需求

对必须通过特定架构或工作包来满足的需要的陈述。

3.60 路线图

业务变革或技术变革的抽象计划，通常历时数年跨越多个学科。一般用于技术路线图、架构路线图等短语。

3.61 Role

1. The usual or expected function of an actor, or the part somebody or something plays in a particular action or event. An Actor may have a number of roles.
2. The part an individual plays in an organization and the contribution they make through the application of their skills, knowledge, experience, and abilities.

See also Section 3.2.

3.62 Segment Architecture

A detailed, formal description of areas within an enterprise, used at the program or portfolio level to organize and align change activity.

See also Section 3.70.

3.63 Service Orientation

A way of thinking in terms of services and service-based development and the outcomes of services.

See also Section 3.64.

3.64 Service Oriented Architecture (SOA)

An architectural style that supports service orientation. It has the following distinctive features:

- It is based on the design of the services — which mirror real-world business activities —comprising the enterprise (or inter-enterprise) business processes.
- Service representation utilizes business descriptions to provide context (i.e., business process, goal, rule, policy, service interface, and service component) and implements services using service orchestration.
- It places unique requirements on the infrastructure — it is recommended that implementations use open standards to realize interoperability and location transparency.
- Implementations are environment-specific — they are constrained or enabled by context and must be described within that context.
- It requires strong governance of service representation and implementation.
- It requires a "Litmus Test" , which determines a "good service" .

See also Section 3.7 and Section 3.63.

3.61 角色

1. 施动者通常具有的或被期望的职能，或某个人或某件事在特定行动或事件中扮演的角色。一个施动者可具有多种角色。

2. 个人在组织中所起的作用以及他们通过应用自身技能、知识、经验和能力所做出的贡献。

还可参见 3.2 节。

3.62 分部架构

对 ENTERPRISE 内各区域正式而详细的描述。分段架构在项目群或项目谱系层级使用，旨在对变更活动进行组织和使其协调一致。

还可参见 3.70 节。

3.63 面向服务

一种根据服务、基于服务的开发和服务的产出来思考问题的方式。

还可参见 3.64 节。

3.64 面向服务架构（SOA）

一种支持面向服务的架构方式。它具有以下独特特征：

- 以服务设计为基础，这些服务反映真实世界的业务活动，包括 ENTERPRISE（或 ENTERPRISE 间）的业务流程。
- 服务表达利用业务描述提供背景环境（即业务流程、目标、规则、方针、服务界面和服务组件），并使用服务编排实现服务。
- 它对基础设施提出了独特需求——推荐在实施中利用开放标准实现互用性和位置透明性。
- 实施与特定环境相关——它们受背景环境约束，或由背景环境实现，并且必须在该背景环境中描述。
- 它需要对服务表达和实施进行强有力的管控。
- 它需要一个判定“良好服务”的“试金石”。

还可参见 3.7 节和 3.63 节。

3.65 Solution Architecture

A description of a discrete and focused business operation or activity and how IS/IT supports that operation. A Solution Architecture typically applies to a single project or project release, assisting in the translation of requirements into a solution vision, high-level business and/or IT system specifications, and a portfolio of implementation tasks.

3.66 Solution Building Block (SBB)

A candidate solution which conforms to the specification of an Architecture Building Block (ABB).

3.67 Solutions Continuum

A part of the Enterprise Continuum. A repository of re-usable solutions for future implementation efforts. It contains implementations of the corresponding definitions in the Architecture Continuum.

See also Section 3.35 and Section 3.10.

3.68 Stakeholder

An individual, team, or organization (or classes thereof) with interests in, or concerns relative to, the outcome of the architecture. Different stakeholders with different roles will have different concerns.

See also Section A.85 in Appendix A.

3.69 Standards Information Base (SIB)

A database of standards that can be used to define the particular services and other components of an Organization-Specific Architecture.

Note: The Standards Information Base is described in Part V, Section 41.4.

3.70 Strategic Architecture

A summary formal description of the enterprise, providing an organizing framework for operational and change activity, and an executive-level, long-term view for direction setting.

3.71 Target Architecture

The description of a future state of the architecture being developed for an organization. There may be several future states developed as a roadmap to show the evolution of the architecture to a target state.

3.65 解决方案架构

对目标明确且独立的业务运行或活动以及对 IS/IT 如何支持该业务运行的描述。解决方案架构通常应用于一个单一的项目或项目发布，协助将需求转变为一个解决方案愿景、高层级业务和/或 IT 系统规范和一个实施任务谱系。

3.66 解决方案构建块（SBB）

一种符合架构构建块（ABB）规范的候选解决方案。

3.67 解决方案连续统一体

ENTERPRISE 的连续统一体的一部分。一个用于未来实施工作并可复用的解决方案的存储库。它包含架构连续统一体中对应定义的实现。

还可参见 3.35 节和 3.10 节。

3.68 利益攸关者

与架构产出利益相关或关注架构产出的个人、团队或组织（或其中的某些群体）。角色各异的不同利益攸关者，其关注点也不相同。

还可参见附录 A 中的 A.85 节。

3.69 标准信息库（SIB）

各种标准的数据库，可用于定义组织特定架构的特定服务和其他组件。

注：在第五部分的 41.4 节中描述标准信息库。

3.70 战略架构

对 ENTERPRISE 的概括性正式描述，提供面向运行和变革活动的组织框架以及用于制定方向的执行层级长期视图。

3.71 目标架构

针对组织开发的架构的未来状态的描述。若干未来状态可形成路线图，以展示架构向目标状态的演进。

3.72 Taxonomy of Architecture Views

The organized collection of all views pertinent to an architecture.

3.73 Technology Architecture

A description of the structure and interaction of the platform services, and logical and physical technology components.

Note: Technology Architecture is described in Part II, Chapter 12.

3.74 Transition Architecture

A formal description of one state of the architecture at an architecturally significant point in time. One or more Transition Architectures may be used to describe the progression in time from the Baseline to the Target Architecture.

Note: Transition Architecture is described in Part IV, Section 36.2.3.

3.75 View

The representation of a related set of concerns. A view is what is seen from a viewpoint. An architecture view may be represented by a model to demonstrate to stakeholders their areas of interest in the architecture. A view does not have to be visual or graphical in nature.

See also Section 3.68 and Section 3.76.

3.76 Viewpoint

A definition of the perspective from which a view is taken. It is a specification of the conventions for constructing and using a view (often by means of an appropriate schema or template). A view is what you see; a viewpoint is where you are looking from — the vantage point or perspective that determines what you see.

See also Section A.56 in Appendix A.

3.77 Work Package

A set of actions identified to achieve one or more objectives for the business. A work package can be a part of a project, a complete project, or a program.

3.72　架构视图分类法

与架构相关的所有视图的有序集合。

3.73　技术架构

对平台服务、逻辑技术组件以及物理技术组件的结构和它们之间交互作用的描述。

注：在第二部分第 12 章中描述技术架构。

3.74　过渡架构

对架构在某个重要时点的某一种状态的正式描述。可以使用一个或多个过渡架构描述从基线架构向目标架构的时间演进。

注：在第四部分 36.2.3 节描述过渡架构。

3.75　视图

一组相关关注点的表达。视图是从某一视角看到的结果。架构视图可以用模型表达，以展示利益攸关者在架构中所关注的领域。视图本质上不一定必须是可视的或图形化的。

还可参见 3.68 节和 3.76 节。

3.76　视角

对获得视图的角度的定义。视角是对构造和使用视图的惯例的规范（经常采用适当的图表或模板）。视图是看到的结果，视角是观察点——决定所见结果的有利位置或角度。

还可参见附录 A 中的 A.56 节。

3.77　工作包

为达成一个或多个业务目的所识别的一组行动。工作包可以是某个项目的一部分，也可以是一个完整项目或一个项目群。

Chapter 4
Release Notes

For the purposes of TOGAF 9, the release notes provided in this chapter apply.

4.1 What's New in TOGAF 9?

This section provides an overview of the major new features within TOGAF 9.

Modular Structure

One focus of TOGAF 9 development has been to ensure that the specification content is structured in a modular way. The modular seven-part structure of TOGAF allows for the concepts in each part to be developed with limited impacts on other parts. Content that was contained within the TOGAF 8.1.1 Resource Base has been classified and moved into parts that have a defined purpose (as opposed to generic "resources").

The modular structure in TOGAF is intended to support greater usability, as each part has a defined purpose and can be read in isolation as a stand-alone set of guidelines. The modular structure is also expected to support incremental adoption of the TOGAF specification. Finally, the modular structure supports more sophisticated release management of the TOGAF specification. In future, individual parts may evolve at different speeds and the current specification structure is intended to allow changes in one area to take place with limited impacts across the specification.

Content Framework

A significant addition of new content to the TOGAF specification is the content framework. The TOGAF content framework provides a detailed model of architectural work products, including deliverables, artifacts within deliverables, and the architectural building blocks that artifacts represent. The intention of including a content framework within TOGAF is to drive greater consistency in the outputs that are created when following an Architecture Development Method (ADM).

The benefit of including a content framework applies at a number of levels. Firstly, within a single architecture development initiative the content framework provides a comprehensive checklist of architecture outputs that could be created and consequently reduce the risk of gaps within the final architecture deliverable set.

The second major benefit of inclusion of a content framework applies when attempting to integrate architectural work products across an enterprise. The content framework is intended to be adapted and then adopted by an enterprise in order to mandate standard architectural concepts, terms, and deliverables. If all architecture initiatives use the same models for content, their outputs can be combined much more easily than in situations where each architect uses a completely different approach.

第 4 章 发布说明

本章中提供的发布说明适用于 TOGAF 9。

4.1 TOGAF 9 的新特征是什么?

本节提供对 TOGAF 9 中的主要新特征的概述。

模块化结构

TOGAF 9 开发的一个聚焦点就是确保规范内容以模块形式结构化。TOGAF 的七部分模块化结构，使得每部分的概念是以对其他部分影响有限的方式提出的。包含在 TOGAF 8.1.1 资源库中的内容已经被分类，并被移动到具有明确目的的部分（而不再是一般“资源”）。

TOGAF 中的模块化结构旨在支持更好的可用性，因为每一部分均具有明确目的并能够作为独立指南集单独阅读。模块化结构也期望能够支持渐进的方式采用 TOGAF 规范。最后，模块化结构支持更复杂的 TOGAF 规范发布管理。未来，独立的每部分可能以不同的速度演进，并且当前规范结构旨在使得一个领域的变革以对整个规范影响有限的方式发生。

内容框架

TOGAF 规范中一个新增加的重要内容是内容框架。TOGAF 内容框架提供架构工作产物的一个详细模型，包括交付物、交付物中的制品以及制品所代表的架构构建块。在 TOGAF 内加入一个内容框架的意图是，在遵循架构开发方法（ADM）时驱使所创建的输出具有更好的一致性。

内容框架的加入可使多个层级受益。首先，在单一架构开发举措中，内容框架提供了一份全面的架构输出检查单，该份检查单可以在最终架构交付物集中创建，因此可以降低最终架构交付物集的差距风险。

加入内容框架的第二个好处是，在尝试综合贯穿整个 ENTERPRISE 的架构工作产物时应用它。内容框架旨在被 ENTERPRISE 适应后采用，以便强制执行标准架构概念、术语和交付物。相比每个架构师使用完全不同的实施途径的情况，如果所有架构举措均使用相同的内容模型，将更易于组合所有架构举措的输出。

Finally, a substantial benefit of the inclusion of a content framework within TOGAF is that it provides (for the first time) a detailed open standard for how architectures should be described. The existence of this standard allows tools vendors, product vendors, and service vendors to adopt consistent ways of working, which in turn will result in greater consistency between architecture tools, better tool interoperability, more consistent reference architectures, and better comparability between related reference architectures.

Extended Guidance on Adopting TOGAF within an Enterprise

Within larger organizations, the practice of enterprise architecture requires a number of individuals and teams that work together on many architectures. Although each architecture will address a specific problem, in an ideal situation architectures can be considered as a group in order to develop an overall integrated view of how the enterprise is changing.

This version of TOGAF features an extended set of concepts and guidelines to support the establishment of an integrated hierarchy of architectures being developed by teams that operate within an overarching architectural governance model. In particular, the following concepts are introduced:

- **Partitioning**: In order to develop architectures that have manageable levels of cost and complexity, it is necessary to partition the enterprise into specific architectures. TOGAF discusses the concept of partitioning and provides a variety of techniques and considerations on how to partition the various architectures within an enterprise.
- **Architecture Repository**: TOGAF provides a logical information model for an Architecture Repository, which can be used as an integrated store for all outputs created by executing the ADM.
- **Capability Framework**: This version of TOGAF provides a more structured definition of theorganization, skills, roles, and responsibilities required to operate an effective enterprise Architecture Capability. The new TOGAF materials also provide guidance on a process that can be followed to identify and establish an appropriate Architecture Capability.

Explicit Consideration of Architectural Styles, Including SOA and Security Architecture

The new Part III: ADM Guidelines & Techniques brings together a set of supporting materials that show in more detail how the ADM can be applied to specific situations. The new guidelines discuss:

- The varying uses of iteration that are possible within the ADM and when each technique should be applied.
- The linkages between the TOGAF ADM and Service Oriented Architecture (SOA).
- The specific considerations required to address security architecture within the ADM.
- The various types of architecture development required within an enterprise and how these relate to one another.

最后，TOGAF 中包括内容框架的一个重要好处是该内容框架提供（第一次）一个关于应如何描述架构的详细开放标准。该标准的存在使得工具厂商、产品厂商以及服务厂商能采用一致的工作方式，继而将产生架构工具之间更大的一致性、更好的工具互用性、更一致的参考架构，以及相关参考架构之间更好的可比性。

在 ENTERPRISE 内采用 TOGAF 的扩展引导

在更大的组织内，Enterprise Architecture 的实践需要许多个人和团队针对多个架构开展合作。虽然每个架构都会应对一个特定问题，但是在理想的情况下，可以将这些架构视为一个群组，以便开发关于 ENTERPRISE 如何变革的总体综合视图。

本版 TOGAF 重点介绍一组扩展的概念和指南，以支持由多个团队开发的在一个首要架构治理模型中运行的一套综合的、层次化架构的建立。特别是引入了下述概念：

- 划分：为了开发具有可管理的成本和复杂性层级的架构，有必要将 ENTERPRISE 划分成特定架构。TOGAF 论述划分的概念并提供关于如何划分一个 ENTERPRISE 内不同架构的各种技巧和考量因素。
- 架构库：TOGAF 提供一个架构库的逻辑信息模型，可被用作通过执行 ADM 所创建的所有输出的一个综合存储器。
- 能力框架：本版 TOGAF 提供关于运行一个有效的 ENTERPRISE 的架构能力所需的组织、技能、角色和职责的更结构化的定义。新的 TOGAF 资料还提供了关于可遵循的流程的引导，以识别和建立适当的架构能力。

明确考虑架构风格，包括 SOA 和安保架构

新的第三部分：ADM 指南和技巧汇集了一组支持资料，更详细地表明了如何将 ADM 应用于特定情况。新的指南论述了：

- ADM 中可以使用的不同迭代用法以及每个技巧应何时使用。
- TOGAF ADM 和面向服务架构（SOA）之间的联系。
- 在 ADM 内应对安保架构所需的特定考量因素。
- ENTERPRISE 内所需不同类型的架构开发以及彼此间如何关联。

Additional ADM Detail

This version of the TOGAF specification includes more detailed information supporting the execution of the ADM. Particular areas of enhancement are:

- The Preliminary Phase, which features extended guidance on establishing an enterprise architecture framework and planning for architecture development. The extended Preliminary Phase also provides pointers to the definition of a governance model for architecture benefit realization and also discusses the linkage between TOGAF and other management frameworks.
- The Opportunities & Solutions phase and Migration Planning phase, which feature a more detailed and robust method for defining and planning enterprise transformation, based on the principles of capability-based planning.

4.1.1 Changes Applied in this Edition

This edition of TOGAF 9 includes a set of maintenance updates based on feedback received on the 2009 publication. A separate detailed document of the changes is available as TOGAF 9 Technical Corrigendum No. 1 (Document U112). A summary list of the changes is included below:

- Definitions of terms where usage by TOGAF is not distinctive from the common dictionary definition have been removed.
- The usage of the terms "application" *versus* "system" have been reviewed and made consistent.
- The Phase E and F descriptions have been reworked to match the level of detail in other phases.
- The uses of terminology for Transition Architecture/Roadmap/Implementation Strategy have been clarified and made consistent.
- The concepts of levels/iterations/partitions have been clarified and made consistent. This includes a reorganization of material in Part III, Chapter 19 and Chapter 20, and Part V, Chapter 40.
- The "Objectives" sections of the phases have been reworked to focus on actual objectives rather than techniques or a list of steps.
- The possible artifacts (viewpoints) for each phase are now listed in the description of that phase, not just in Part IV, Chapter 35.
- The terms "artifact" *versus* "viewpoint" have been clarified and made consistent. This includes a restructuring of Part IV, Chapter 35.
- The SOA chapter (Part III, Chapter 22) has been updated to describe the latest SOA WorkGroup output.
- Additional introductory text on architectural styles has been added in Part III, Chapter 18.
- Minor changes have been made to the Security Architecture chapter (Part III, Chapter 21) for consistency with the ADM.
- Corrections have been made to metamodel diagrams.
- Corrections have been applied to aspects of the metamodel.

更多的 ADM 细节

本版 TOGAF 规范包括更多支持 ADM 执行的详细信息。增加的特定领域包括：

- 预备阶段，重点介绍的是对建立 Enterprise Architecture 框架和规划架构开发的扩展引导。扩展的预备阶段还提供了对用于架构益处实现的治理模型定义的指示，并论述了 TOGAF 和其他管理架构之间的联系。
- 机会和解决方案阶段和迁移规划阶段，重点介绍的是根据基于能力的规划原则定义和规划 ENTERPRISE 转型的更详细和稳健的方法。

4.1.1　本版中应用的变更

本版 TOGAF 9 包括一组基于接收到的针对 2009 年出版物的反馈的维护更新。这些变更的独立详细说明文件作为 TOGAF 9 第 1 号技术勘误表（文件 U112）使用。以下是所包括的变更的汇总列表：

- 已经删除了 TOGAF 所使用的、与常用词典定义截然不同的术语。
- 术语“应用”与“系统”的使用已经过审视并达成一致。
- 已经修正了阶段 E 和阶段 F 的描述，以便与其他阶段中的细节层级相匹配。
- 对术语过渡架构/路线图/实施策略的使用已做过分类并达成一致。
- 层级/迭代/划分的概念已经得到阐明并达成一致。这包括重新组织第三部分第 19 章和第 20 章以及第五部分第 40 章中的资料。
- 已经修正了各阶段的“目的”一节以关注于实际目的而不是技巧或一系列步骤。
- 将每个阶段的可能制品（视角）列入所在阶段的描述中，而不仅是第四部分的第 35 章。
- 术语“制品”与“视角”已经得到阐明并达成一致。这包括对第四部分第 35 章的重新调整。
- 已经更新了 SOA 一章（第三部分第 22 章）以描述最新的 SOA 工作组输出。
- 已经在第三部分第 18 章增加了关于架构风格的更多介绍性文本。
- 已经对安保架构一章（第三部分第 21 章）进行了小范围变更，以便与 ADM 保持一致。
- 已经对元模型图进行了修正。
- 已经将这些修正应用于元模型的多个方面。

- The Building Blocks example has been removed.
- The Document Categorization Model has been removed.
- Duplicate text in several places has been replaced with an appropriate reference:
  — Gap Analysis in Phases B, C, and D now references Part III, Chapter 27.
  — Requirements Management in several phases now references Part II, Section 17.2.2 in the Requirements Management phase.
- Some of the artifacts have been renamed to better reflect their usage:
  — System/Data matrix becomes Application/Data matrix.
  — Class diagram has been replaced with Conceptual Data diagram and Logical Data diagram.
  — System/Organization matrix becomes Application/Organization matrix.
  — Role/System matrix becomes Role/Application matrix.
  — System/Function matrix becomes Application/Function matrix.
  — Process/System Realization diagram becomes Process/Application Realization diagram.
  — System Use-Case diagram becomes Application Use-Case diagram.
  — System/Technology matrix becomes Application/Technology matrix.
- The descriptionof Architecture Principles now divides the min to two types only — Enterprise and Architecture — whereas before they called out IT Principles separately. IT Principles are now seen as just part of Enterprise Principles.
- The Stakeholder Map included in the Stakeholder Management chapter (Part III, Chapter24) is now explicitly referred to as an example, the table has been highlighted to refer to Stakeholder Concerns, and the list of artifacts for each stakeholder updated.
- The Business Scenarios chapter (Part III, Chapter 26) has been renamed to Business Scenarios and Business Goals to better reflect the contents of the chapter.
- The relationship of the Enterprise Repository to the Architecture Repository is clarified in Part V, Chapter 41.
- The Evaluation Criteria and Guidelines have been removed from Part V, Chapter 42.
- The chapter on Architecture Maturity Models (Part VII, Chapter 51) has been editorially revised for consistency and clarity.

- 已经删除了构建块示例。
- 已经删除了文件分类模型。
- 已经将若干位置的重复文本替换为一个适当的参考：
  - — 阶段 B、C 和 D 中的差距分析现参照第三部分第 27 章。
  - — 若干阶段的需求管理现参照第二部分需求管理阶段的 17.2.2 节。
- 一些制品已被重新命名，以更好地反映其用途：
  - — 系统/数据矩阵变为应用/数据矩阵。
  - — 类图已经被替换为概念数据图和逻辑数据图。
  - — 系统/组织矩阵变为应用/组织矩阵。
  - — 角色/系统矩阵变为角色/应用矩阵。
  - — 系统/功能矩阵变为应用/功能矩阵。
  - — 流程/系统实现图变为流程/应用实现图。
  - — 系统用例图变为应用用例图。
  - — 系统/技术矩阵变为应用/技术矩阵。
- 架构原则的描述现在只分成两种类型——ENTERPRISE 和架构——然而是在它们分别调出 IT 原则前。目前，IT 原则仅仅被视为 ENTERPRISE 原则的一部分。
- 在利益攸关者管理一章（第三部分第 24 章）中包括的利益攸关者映射被明确地称为一个示例，该表格已经突出强调了参照利益攸关者关注点以及更新的每个利益攸关者的制品列表。
- 业务场景一章（第三部分第 26 章）已被重新命名为业务场景和业务目标，以更好地反映本章的内容。
- 在第五部分第 41 章阐明 ENTERPRISE 存储库与架构库之间的关系。
- 已经从第五部分第 42 章中删除了评价标准和指南。
- 为了一致和清晰，已经明确修订了架构成熟度模型一章（第七部分第 51 章）。

4.2 The Benefits of TOGAF 9

TOGAF 9 provides a wide-ranging set of revisions to the TOGAF specification. When combined, these edits seek to achieve a set of objectives to improve the value of the TOGAF framework.

Greater Usability

A number of enhancements within TOGAF 9 support greater usability of the overall specification. Firstly, the modular structure of the specification makes it easier for an architect to consider a specific aspect of the Architecture Capability. In all areas, the specification seeks to add detail and clarity above and beyond previous TOGAF versions.

More Focus on Holistic Enterprise Change

TOGAF has a solid history in IT architecture, considering the ways in which IT can support enterprise change. However, as TOGAF has grown in depth and maturity it has become a framework for managing the entire spectrum of change required to transform an enterprise towards a target operating model. TOGAF 9 continues this evolution and incorporates a broader perspective of change that allows enterprise architecture to be used to specify transformation across the business, data, applica-tion, and technology domains.

More Consistency of Output

Previous versions of TOGAF focused on providing a consistent process for develop-ing architectures.TOGAF 9 includes a greatly enhanced consideration of architectural work products to ensure that a consistent process is used to produce consistent outputs. The Architecture Content Framework provides a detailed model of the outputs to be created by the ADM. Additionally, the Enterprise Continuum, Architecture Partitioning, and Architecture Repository sections provide detailed guidance on how architectural deliverables can be scoped, governed, and integrated.

4.3 Mapping of the TOGAF 8.1.1 Structure to TOGAF 9

Listed below are the Parts of the TOGAF 8 specification. For each Part, a description is given to explain where the TOGAF 8 content can be found within the current specification.

Part I: Introduction

The Introduction part of the TOGAF 8.1.1 specification has been used as the basis for creation of Part I: Introduction in TOGAF 9. The introduction to TOGAF 9 reflects the content of TOGAF 9 rather than the content of TOGAF 8.1.1, and also features a number of enhancements to improve accessibility.

Part II: Architecture Development Method

The essence of the TOGAF 8.1.1 ADM has been retained in TOGAF 9. Part II: Architecture Development Method (ADM) within TOGAF 9 is structured along similar lines to Part II of the TOGAF 8.1.1 document. TOGAF ADM phase inputs and outputs (Chapter 16 of TOGAF 8.1.1) have been moved from the ADM section of TOGAF 8.1.1 to Part IV: Architecture Content Framework of TOGAF 9.

TOGAF 9 ADM features additional content in the majority of ADM phases, which in the most part adds further detail and clarification to the same approach that was described in TOGAF 8.1.1.

4.2 TOGAF 9 的效益

TOGAF 9 提供一个范围广泛的 TOGAF 规范修订集。当被组合在一起时，这些修订力图达成一系列提升 TOGAF 框架价值的目的。

更大的使用性

TOGAF 9 内大量增加的内容支持总体规范具有更好的使用性。首先，本规范的模块化结构使得架构师更容易考虑架构能力的一个特定方面。在所有领域，本规范力图增加超出之前 TOGAF 版本的细节和清晰度。

更关注 ENTERPRISE 整体变革

考虑到 IT 能够支持 ENTERPRISE 变革所采用的方式，TOGAF 具有一个稳固的 IT 架构历史。然而，随着 TOGAF 在深度和成熟度方面的提高，它已经成为用于管理 ENTERPRISE 向目标运行模型转型所需的完整变革谱系的一个框架。TOGAF 9 继续这种演进并结合更广阔的变革角度，以使 Enterprise Architecture 能用于指定跨业务、数据、应用和技术域的转型。

更一致的输出

TOGAF 的之前版本关注于提供一致的架构开发流程。TOGAF 9 包括对架构工作产物的更多考虑，以确保一致的流程用于产生一致的输出。架构内容框架提供一个通过 ADM 创建的各类输出的详细模型。另外，ENTERPRISE 的连续统一体、架构划分以及架构库三节提供架构交付物如何被界定、管控和整合的详细指南。

4.3 TOGAF 8.1.1 结构到 TOGAF 9 的映射

以下列出的是 TOGAF 8 规范的各部分。对于每一个部分均给出了说明，以解释可在当前规范的哪个位置找到 TOGAF 8 的内容。

第一部分：引言

TOGAF 8.1.1 规范的引言部分被用作创建 TOGAF 9“第一部分：引言”的基础。TOGAF 9 的引言反映 TOGAF 9 的内容而不是 TOGAF 8.1.1 的内容，并且重点介绍了大量增加内容来提高易用性。

第二部分：架构开发方法

已经将 TOGAF 8.1.1 ADM 的要素保留在 TOGAF 9 中。按照与 TOGAF 8.1.1 文件的第二部分相似的方式对 TOGAF 9 中的“第二部分：架构开发方法（ADM）”进行了结构化。已经将 TOGAF ADM 阶段的输入和输出（TOGAF 8.1.1 的第 16 章）从 TOGAF 8.1.1 的 ADM 一节移动到了 TOGAF 9 的“第四部分：架构内容框架”。

TOGAF 9 ADM 重点介绍在大多数 ADM 阶段增加了更多关于 TOGAF 8.1.1 所描述的相同途径的细节及对该方法的阐述的内容。

Part III: Enterprise Continuum

The TOGAF 8.1.1 Enterprise Continuum has seen a substantial degree of change. The Enterprise Continuum concept is retained within Part V: Enterprise Continuum & Tools. The TOGAF Technical Reference Model and Integrated Information Infrastructure Reference Model are extracted and placed within Part VI: TOGAF Reference Models in TOGAF 9.

TOGAF 9 adds new materials that describe an approach to architecture partitioning and also provides a structured model of an Architecture Repository. These concepts support and elaborate on the original intent of the Enterprise Continuum.

TOGAF 9 removes the Standards Information Base from the TOGAF specification. However, an example SIB remains at The Open Group web site (www.opengroup.org). The concept of a Standards Information Base is important within TOGAF, but the breadth and speed of change of relevant architectural standards mean that it is impractical to maintain a current and relevant collection of standards within a specification such as TOGAF.

Part IV: Resource Base

The Resource Base is not included in this version of TOGAF. Some elements of the Resource Base have been deprecated from the TOGAF specification, but will still be available in White Paper form. Other elements of the Resource Base have been moved to other areas of the specification.

The following table illustrates where TOGAF 8.1.1 Resource Base content can now be located.

TOGAF 8.1.1 Resource	Current Location
Architecture Board	Moved to Part VII: Architecture Capability Framework
Architecture Compliance	Moved to Part VII: Architecture Capability Framework
Architecture Contracts	Moved to Part VII: Architecture Capability Framework
Architecture Governance	Moved to Part VII: Architecture Capability Framework
Architecture Maturity Models	Moved to Part VII: Architecture Capability Framework
Architecture Patterns	Moved to Part III: ADM Guidelines & Techniques
Architecture Principles	Moved to Part III: ADM Guidelines & Techniques
Architecture Skills Framework	Moved to Part VII: Architecture Capability Framework
Developing Architecture Views	Elements retained within Part IV: Architecture Content Framework
Building Blocks	Elements retained within Part IV: Architecture Content Framework
Business Process Domain Views	Elements retained within Part IV: Architecture Content Framework
Business Scenarios	Moved to Part III: ADM Guidelines & Techniques
Case Studies	Removed. Case Studies will be available on The Open Group web site
Glossary	Moved to Part I: Introduction
Other Architectures & Frameworks	Removed. This material will be available on The Open Group web site as a White Paper
Tools for Architecture Development	Moved to Part V: Enterprise Continuum & Tools
ADM and the Zachman Framework	Removed. This material will be available on The Open Group web site as a White Paper

第三部分：ENTERPRISE 的连续统一体

TOGAF 8.1.1ENTERPRISE 的连续统一体观察到了实质变化的程度。ENTERPRISE 的连续统一体概念保留在“第五部分：ENTERPRISE 的连续统一体和工具”中。TOGAF 技术参考模型和综合信息基础设施参考模型被提取并放置在 TOGAF 9 的“第六部分：TOGAF 参考模型”中。

TOGAF 9 增加描述架构划分途径的新资料并提供架构库的结构化模型。这些概念支持并详细阐述 ENTERPRISE 的连续统一体的原始意图。

TOGAF 9 从 TOGAF 规范中删除了标准信息库（SIB）。然而，示例 SIB 仍保留在 The Open Group 网站（www.opengroup.org）上。标准信息库的概念在 TOGAF 中非常重要，但是，相关架构标准变化的幅度和速度意味着在诸如 TOGAF 的规范内保持当前和相关标准集是不现实的。

第四部分：资源库

资源库未包括在本版 TOGAF 内。已从 TOGAF 规范中删除了资源库的一些元素，但仍可以白皮书形式获取到。资源库的其他元素已被移动到本规范的其他区域。

下表阐明了 TOGAF 8.1.1 资源库的内容目前所在的位置。

TOGAF 8.1.1 资源	当前位置
架构委员会	移动到第七部分：架构能力框架
架构合规性	移动到第七部分：架构能力框架
架构契约	移动到第七部分：架构能力框架
架构治理	移动到第七部分：架构能力框架
架构成熟度模型	移动到第七部分：架构能力框架
架构模式	移动到第三部分：ADM 指南和技巧
架构原则	移动到第三部分：ADM 指南和技巧
架构技能框架	移动到第七部分：架构能力框架
开发架构视图	元素保留在第四部分：架构内容框架
构建块	元素保留在第四部分：架构内容框架
业务流程域视图	元素保留在第四部分：架构内容框架
业务场景	移动到第三部分：ADM 指南和技巧
案例研究	已删除。可在 The Open Group 网站中获得案例研究
术语表	移动到第一部分：引言
其他架构和框架	已删除。本资料可从 The Open Group 网站以白皮书的形式获得
架构开发工具	移动到第五部分：ENTERPRISE 的连续统一体和工具
ADM 和 Zachman 框架	已删除。本资料可从 The Open Group 网站以白皮书的形式获得

4.4 Mapping of TOGAF 9 Structure to TOGAF 8.1.1

The following table illustrates where TOGAF 9 chapters map to those of TOGAF 8.1.1.

	TOGAF 9 Chapter	Derivation from TOGAF 8.1.1
	Part I: Introduction	
1	Introduction	Material revised; based on Chapter 1
2	Core Concepts	New chapter
3	Definitions	Material derived from Chapter 36, reworked into formal definitions and abbreviations sections
4	Release Notes	New chapter
	Part II: Architecture Development Method	
5	Introduction	Material revised; based on Chapter 3
6	Preliminary Phase	Material revised; based on Chapter 4
7	Phase A: Architecture Vision	Material revised; based on Chapter 5
8	Phase B: Business Architecture	Material revised; based on Chapter 6
9	Phase C: Information Systems Architectures	Material revised; based on Chapter 7
10	Phase C: Data Architecture	Material revised; based on Chapter 8
11	Phase C: Application Architecture	Material revised; based on Chapter 9
12	Phase D: Technology Architecture	Material revised; based on Chapter 10
13	Phase E: Opportunities & Solutions	Material revised; based on Chapter 11
14	Phase F: Migration Planning	Material revised; based on Chapter 12
15	Phase G: Implementation Governance	Material revised; based on Chapter 13
16	Phase H: Architecture Change Management	Material revised; based on Chapter 14
17	ADM Architecture Requirements Management	No material change; maps to Chapter 15
	Part III: ADM Guidelines & Techniques	
18	Introduction	New chapter
19	Applying the ADM across the Architecture Landscape	New chapter
20	Applying the ADM at Different Enterprise Levels	New chapter
21	Security Architecture and the ADM	New chapter; derived from Security White Paper (W055)
22	Using TOGAF to Define & Govern SOAs	New chapter
23	Architecture Principles	No material change; maps to Chapter 29
24	Stakeholder Management	New chapter
25	Architecture Patterns	No material change; maps to Chapter 28
26	Business Scenarios	No material change; maps to Chapter 34
27	Gap Analysis	New chapter; derived from Gap Analysis
28	Migration Planning Techniques	New chapter
29	Interoperability Requirements	New chapter
30	Business Transformation Readiness Assessment	New chapter
31	Risk Management	New chapter
32	Capability-Based Planning	New chapter
	Part IV: Architecture Content Framework	
33	Introduction	New chapter
34	Content Metamodel	New chapter
35	Architectural Artifacts	Derived from Chapter 31, plus new material
36	Architecture Deliverables	Revised; was Chapter 16
37	Building Blocks	Revised from Chapter 32

4.4 TOGAF 9 结构到 TOGAF 8.1.1 的映射

下表阐明了 TOGAF 9 各章到 TOGAF 8.1.1 各章的映射。

TOGAF9 中的章节		与 TOGAF 8.1.1 的偏差
	第一部分：引言	
1	简介	修订资料；根据第 1 章
2	核心概念	新章节
3	定义	资料来自第 36 章，修改为正式定义和缩写章节
4	发布说明	新章节
	第二部分：架构开发方法	
5	简介	修订资料；根据第 3 章
6	预备阶段	修订资料；根据第 4 章
7	阶段 A：架构愿景	修订资料；根据第 5 章
8	阶段 B：业务架构	修订资料；根据第 6 章
9	阶段 C：信息系统架构	修订资料；根据第 7 章
10	阶段 C：数据架构	修订资料；根据第 8 章
11	阶段 C：应用架构	修订资料；根据第 9 章
12	阶段 D：技术架构	修订资料；根据第 10 章
13	阶段 E：机会和解决方案	修订资料；根据第 11 章
14	阶段 F：迁移规划	修订资料；根据第 12 章
15	阶段 G：实施治理	修订资料；根据第 13 章
16	阶段 H：架构变更管理	修订资料；根据第 14 章
17	ADM 架构需求管理	无资料变更；映射到第 15 章
	第三部分：ADM 指南和技巧	
18	简介	新章节
19	贯穿架构全景应用 ADM	新章节
20	在不同 ENTERPRISE 层级应用 ADM	新章节
21	安保架构和 ADM	新章节；来自“安保白皮书”（W055）
22	使用 TOGAF 定义和治理 SOA	新章节
23	架构原则	无资料变更；映射到第 29 章
24	利益攸关者管理	新章节
25	架构模式	无资料变更；映射到第 28 章
26	业务场景	无资料变更；映射到第 34 章
27	差距分析	新章节；来自“差距分析”
28	迁移规划技巧	新章节
29	互用性需求	新章节
30	业务转型准备度评估	新章节
31	风险管理	新章节
32	基于能力的规划	新章节
	第四部分：架构内容框架	
33	简介	新章节
34	内容元模型	新章节
35	架构制品	来自第 31 章，以及新资料
36	架构交付物	修订；之前是第 16 章
37	构建块	根据第 32 章修订

	TOGAF 9 Chapter	Derivation from TOGAF 8.1.1
	Part V: Enterprise Continuum & Tools	
38	Introduction	New chapter
39	Enterprise Continuum	Derived from Chapters 17 and 18 with subs-tantial revisions
40	Architecture Partitioning	New chapter
41	Architecture Repository	New chapter
42	Tools for Architecture Development	Derived from Chapter 38, with the evaluation guidelines removed.
	Part VI: TOGAF Reference Models	
43	Foundation Architecture: Technical Reference Model	No material change; maps to Chapters 19 and 20
44	Integrated Information Infrastructure Reference Model	No material change; maps to Chapter 22
	Part VII: Architecture Capability Framework	
45	Introduction	New chapter
46	Establishing an Architecture Capability	New chapter
47	Architecture Board	Minimal change; maps to Chapter 23
48	Architecture Compliance	Minimal change; maps to Chapter 24
49	Architecture Contracts	Minimal change; maps to Chapter 25
50	Architecture Governance	Minimal change, maps to Chapter 26
51	Architecture Maturity Models	Minimal change; maps to Chapter 27
52	Architecture Skills Framework	Some cosmetic changes; maps to Chapter 30
A	Glossary of Supplementary Definitions	Derived from Chapter 36
B	Abbreviations	Derived from Chapter 36

4.5 Using TOGAF

4.5.1 Conditions of Use

The TOGAF documentation is freely available for viewing online without a license. Alternatively, the complete TOGAF documentation set may be downloaded and stored under license, as explained on the TOGAF information web site.

In either case, the TOGAF documentation may be used freely by any organization wishing to do so to develop an architecture for use within that organization. No part of it may be reproduced, stored in a retrieval system, or transmitted, in any form or by any means, electronic, mechanical, photocopying, recording, or otherwise, for any other purpose including, but not by way of limitation, any use for commercial gain, without the prior permission of the copyright owners.

4.5.2 How Much Does TOGAF Cost?

The Open Group operates as a not-for-profit consortium committed to delivering greater bu-siness efficiency by bringing together buyers and suppliers of information systems to lower the barriers of integrating new technology across the enterprise. Its goal is to realize the vision of Boundaryless Information Flow.

TOGAF is a key part of its strategy for achieving this goal, and The Open Group wants TOGAF to be taken up and used in practical architecture projects, and the experience from its use fed back to help improve it.

	TOGAF9 中的章节	与 TOGAF 8.1.1 的偏差
	第五部分：ENTERPRISE 的连续统一体和工具	
38	简介	新章节
39	ENTERPRISE 的连续统一体	来自第 17 章和第 18 章，且进行了大量修订
40	架构划分	新章节
41	架构库	新章节
42	架构开发工具	来自第 38 章，删除了评价指南
	第六部分：TOGAF 参考模型	
43	基础架构：技术参考模型	无资料变更；映射到第 19 章和第 20 章
44	综合信息基础设施参考模型	无资料变更；映射到第 22 章
	第七部分：架构能力框架	
45	简介	新章节
46	建立架构能力	新章节
47	架构委员会	最少变更；映射到第 23 章
48	架构合规性	最少变更；映射到第 24 章
49	架构契约	最少变更；映射到第 25 章
50	架构治理	最少变更；映射到第 26 章
51	架构成熟度模型	最少变更；映射到第 27 章
52	架构技能框架	一些修饰性变更；映射到第 30 章
A	补充定义的术语表	来自第 36 章
B	缩略语	来自第 36 章

4.5　使用 TOGAF

4.5.1　使用条件

TOGAF 文档可在无许可证情况下免费在线查看。或者，按照 TOGAF 信息网站中的说明，可在获得许可证的情况下下载和存储完整的 TOGAF 文档集。

在任意一种情况下，TOGAF 文档均可供任何希望这样做的组织免费使用，以开发在该组织内使用的架构。在未得到版权所有者预先许可的情况下，TOGAF 文档的任何部分不得以任何形式或任何手段，如电子、机械、影印、记录或其他方式，进行复制、存储在检索系统中或传输，用于任何其他目的，包括但不限于获得商业利益的目的。

4.5.2　TOGAF 花费多少成本？

The Open Group 以非营利性联合体的形式运营，致力于通过汇集信息系统的买方和供应商提供更高的业务效率，以减少在贯穿整个 ENTERPRISE 范围内整合新技术的障碍。其目标是实现无边界信息流的愿景。

TOGAF 是 The Open Group 用于实现该目标的策略的一个关键部分，The Open Group 希望在实际架构项目中采纳和使用 TOGAF，并且反馈从使用中获得的经验，以帮助改进 TOGAF。

The Open Group therefore publishes TOGAF on its public web server, and allows and encourages its reproduction and use free-of-charge by any organization wishing to use it internally to develop an enterprise architecture. (There are restrictions on its commercial exploitation, however; see Section 4.5.1.)

4.5.3 Downloads

Downloads of the TOGAF documentation, including a printable PDF file, are available under license from the TOGAF information web site (refer to www.opengroup.org/architecture/togaf). The license is free to any organization wishing to use TOGAF entirely for internal purposes (for example, to develop an enterprise architecture for use within that organization).

4.6 Why Join The Open Group?

Organizations wishing to reduce the time, cost, and risk of implementing multi-vendor solutions that integrate within and between enterprises need The Open Group as their key partner.

The Open Group brings together the buyers and suppliers of information systems worldwide, and enables them to work together, both to ensure that IT solutions meet the needs of customers, and to make it easier to integrate IT across the enterprise. TOGAF is a key enabler in this task.

Yes, TOGAF itself is freely available. But how much will you spend on developing or updating your enterprise architecture using TOGAF? And how much will you spend on procurements based on that architecture?The price of membership of The Open Group is insignificant in comparison with these amounts.

In addition to the general benefits of membership, as a member of The Open Group you will be eligible to participate in The Open Group Architecture Forum, which is the development program within which TOGAF is evolved, and in which TOGAF users come together to exchange information and feedback.

Members of the Architecture Forum gain:

- Immediate access to the fruits of the current TOGAF work program (not publicly available until publication of the next edition of the TOGAF document) — in effect, the latest information on TOGAF
- Exchange of experience with other customer and vend or organizations involved in enterprise architecture in general, and networking with architects using TOGAF in significant architecture development projects around the world.
- Peer review of specific architecture case study material.

因此，The Open Group 在其公共 web 服务器上发布了 TOGAF，并允许和鼓励任何希望在内部使用 TOGAF 开发 Enterprise Architecture 的组织免费复制和使用。（但是，对于商业开发有许多限制，见 4.5.1 节）

4.5.3 下载

在从 TOGAF 信息网站（见 www.opengroup.org/architecture/togaf）获得许可证的情况下，下载 TOGAF 文档，包括可打印的 PDF 文件。对于任何希望在内部完全使用 TOGAF（例如，开发一个在该组织内使用的 Enterprise Architecture）的组织，该许可证是免费的。

4.6 为什么加入 The Open Group?

希望在 ENTERPRISE 内部和 ENTERPRISE 之间整合的多厂商解决方案的实现中减少时间、成本和风险的组织，需要 The Open Group 作为其关键合作伙伴。

The Open Group 汇集全世界范围内信息系统的买方和供应商，并使他们能进行合作，以确保 IT 解决方案满足客户需要，并使得在贯穿整个 ENTERPRISE 的范围内整合 IT 更容易。TOGAF 是本任务中的关键使能项。

是的，TOGAF 本身是可以免费得到的。但是在使用 TOGAF 时开发或更新 Enterprise Architecture 会花费多少？以及基于该架构，会在采购上花费多少？The Open Group 成员的花费与这些数额相比是微不足道的。

除了一般成员权益，The Open Group 的成员有资格参加作为开发项目的 The Open Group 架构论坛，在这个项目中，TOGAF 会得到演进并且 TOGAF 用户会在这个项目中交换信息和反馈。

架构论坛的成员获得以下权益：

- 立即访问当前 TOGAF 工作项目（在下一个 TOGAF 文件版本出版前未公开）的成果——实际上是关于 TOGAF 的最新信息。
- 与 Enterprise Architecture 通常涉及的其他客户和厂商组织进行经验交流，并与全球范围内在重要架构开发项目中使用 TOGAF 的架构师进行交流。
- 特定架构实例研究资料的同行审视。

TOGAF Version 9.1

Part II Architecture Development Method(ADM)

The Open Group

TOGAF9.1 版本

第二部分　架构开发方法（ADM）

The Open Group

Chapter 5 Introduction

This chapter describes the Architecture Development Method (ADM) cycle, adapting the ADM, architecture scope, and architecture integration.

5.1 ADM Overview

The TOGAF ADM is the result of continuous contributions from a large number of architecture practitioners. It describes a method for developing and managing the lifecycle of an enterprise architecture, and forms the core of TOGAF. It integrates elements of TOGAF described in this document as well as other available architectural assets, to meet the business and IT needs of an organization.

5.1.1 The ADM, Enterprise Continuum, and Architecture Repository

The Enterprise Continuum provides a framework and context to support the leverage of relevant architecture assets in executing the ADM. These assets may include architecture descriptions, models, and patterns taken from a variety of sources, as explained in Part V: Enterprise Continuum & Tools.

The Enterprise Continuum categorizes architectural source material — both the contents of the organization's own enterprise repositories and the set of relevant, available reference models and standards in the industry.

The practical implementation of the Enterprise Continuum will typically take the form of an Architecture Repository (see Part V, Chapter 41) that includes reference architectures, models, and patterns that have been accepted for use within the enterprise, and actual architectural work done previously within the enterprise. The architect would seek to re-use as much as possible from the Architecture Repository that was relevant to the project at hand. (In addition to the collection of architecture source material, the repository would also contain architecture development work-in-progress.)

At relevant places throughout the ADM, there are reminders to consider which, if any, architecture assets from the Architecture Repository the architect should use. In some cases — for example, in the development of a Technology Architecture — this may be the TOGAF Foundation Architecture (see Part VI: TOGAF Reference Models). In other cases — for example, in the development of a Business Architecture — it may be a reference model for e-Commerce taken from the industry at large.

The criteria for including source materials in an organization's Architecture Repository will typically form part of the enterprise architecture governance process. These governance processes should consider available resources both within and outside the enterprise in order to determine when general resources can be adapted for specific enterprise needs and also to determine where specific solutions can be generalized to support wider re-use.

第 5 章
简介

本章描述架构开发方法（ADM）周期、ADM 的适应性调整、架构范围和架构综合。

5.1 ADM 概述

TOGAF ADM 是众多架构实践者持续努力贡献的成果，它描述一种开发和管理 Enterprise Architecture 生命周期的方法，并构成 TOGAF 的核心。它综合本文件中描述的 TOGAF 元素和其他可用的架构资产，以满足组织的业务和 IT 需要。

5.1.1 ADM、ENTERPRISE 的连续统一体和架构库

ENTERPRISE 的连续统一体提供在执行 ADM 的过程中支持更强有力地发挥相关架构资产作用的框架和背景环境。按照“第五部分：ENTERPRISE 的连续统一体和工具”中的解释，这些资产可包括架构描述、模型以及从各种来源中抽取的特征模式。

ENTERPRISE 的连续统一体对架构源资料进行分类——这些素材包括组织自身的 ENTERPRISE 存储库的内容以及行业内一系列相关可用的参考模型和标准。

ENTERPRISE 的连续统一体的实际实施通常会采用架构库（见第五部分，第 41 章）的形式，包括已在 ENTERPRISE 内部采用的参考架构、模型和特征模式，以及之前在 ENTERPRISE 内已做的实际架构工作。架构师将寻求尽可能地从架构库中复用与当前项目相关的内容。（除了收集架构源资料，存储库也将包含架构开发过程制品。）

在整个 ADM 中的相关位置，提示架构师考虑应使用架构存储库中的哪些架构资产（如果有）。在某些情况下，例如在技术架构的开发过程中，这可能是 TOGAF 基础架构（见第六部分：TOGAF 参考模型）。在其他情况下，例如在业务架构的开发过程中，它可能是取自整个行业内的电子商务参考模型。

在组织的架构库中，包含源资料的准则通常会构成 Enterprise Architecture 治理流程的一部分。这些治理流程应考虑 ENTERPRISE 内部和外部的可用资源，以确定通用资源何时可适应于特定 ENTERPRISE 的需要，并确定可在何处对特定解决方案进行一般化，以支持更大范围的复用。

While using the ADM, the architect is developing a snap shot of the enterprise's decisions and their implications at particular points in time. Each iteration of the ADM will populate an organization-specific landscape with all the architecture assets identified and leveraged through the process, including the final organization-specific architecture delivered.

Architecture development is a continuous, cyclical process, and in executing the ADM repeatedly over time, the architect gradually adds more and more content to the organization's Architecture Repository. Although the primary focus of the ADM is on the development of the enterprise-specific architecture, in this wider context the ADM can also be viewed as the process of populating the enterprise's own Architecture Repository with relevant re-usable building blocks taken from the "left", more generic side of the Enterprise Continuum.

In fact, the first execution of the ADM will often be the hardest, since the architecture assets available for re-use will be relatively scarce. Even at this stage of development, however, there will be architecture assets available from external sources such as TOGAF, as well as the IT industry at large, that could be leveraged in support of the effort.

Subsequent executions will be easier, as more and more architecture assets become identified, are used to populate the organization's Architecture Repository, and are thus available for future re-use.

5.1.2 The ADM and the Foundation Architecture

The ADM is also useful to populate the Foundation Architecture of an enterprise. Business requirements of an enterprise may be used to identify the necessary definitions and selections in the Foundation Architecture. This could be a set of re-usable common models, policy and governance definitions, or even as specific as overriding technology selections (e.g., if mandated by law). Population of the Foundation Architecture follows similar principles as for an enterprise architecture, with the difference that requirements for a whole enterprise are restricted to the overall concerns and thus less complete than for a specific enterprise.

It is important to recognize that existing models from these various sources, when integrated, may not necessarily result in a coherent enterprise architecture. "Integratability" of architecture descriptions is considered in Section 5.6.

5.1.3 ADM and Supporting Guidelines and Techniques

Part III: ADM Guidelines & Techniques is a set of resources — guidelines, templates, checklists, and other detailed materials — that support application of the TOGAF ADM.

The individual guidelines and techniques are described separately in Part III: ADM Guidelines & Techniques so that they can be referenced from the relevant points in the ADM as necessary, rather than having the detailed text clutter the description of the ADM itself.

在使用 ADM 的同时，架构师在特定时点“显像”ENTERPRISE 决策及其内涵的一幅“快照”。每轮 ADM 迭代都将使用通过流程识别和得以更好利用的所有架构资产充实组织特有的全景，包括最终交付组织特有的架构。

架构开发是一个连续的循环流程，并且在随着时间推移而反复执行 ADM 的过程中，架构师逐渐向组织架构库中添加越来越多的内容。虽然 ADM 的主要聚焦点是 ENTERPRISE 特有架构的开发，但是在这个更广泛的背景环境中，ADM 还可以被视为使用取自“左侧”（ENTERPRISE 的连续统一体更一般的一侧）的相关可复用构建块来填充 ENTERPRISE 自身的架构库的流程。

实际上，因为可复用的架构资产相对稀缺，第一次执行 ADM 往往将是最艰难的。但是，即便是在本开发阶段，也会有来自于外部来源诸如 TOGAF 以及整个 IT 行业内的架构资产，可以更好地被利用来支持这项工作。

随着越来越多的架构资产被识别，用来充实组织架构库并因此可用于未来的复用，后续执行将会更容易。

5.1.2 ADM 和基础架构

ADM 对于充实 ENTERPRISE 的基础架构也是有用的。ENTERPRISE 的业务需求可用于识别基础架构中必需的定义和选择。这可能是一系列可复用的公用模型、方针和治理定义，或者甚至具体到首要技术选择（例如，如果法律规定）。基础架构的充实遵循类似 Enterprise Architecture 原则，区别是，整个 ENTERPRISE 的需求被限定在总体关注点，因此不如特定 ENTERPRISE 的需求完整。

重要的是认识到，在综合时来自于不同来源的现有模型可能不一定会产生协调一致的 Enterprise Architecture。在 5.6 节中描述了架构“可综合性”。

5.1.3 ADM 和支持指南和技巧

“第三部分：ADM 指南和技巧”是支持 TOGAF ADM 应用的一系列资源——指南、模板、检查清单和其他详细资料。

在“第三部分：ADM 指南和技巧”中分别描述指南和技巧，以便可以根据需要从 ADM 中相关位置引用这些指南和技巧，而不会因详细的文本干扰对 ADM 本身的描述。

5.2 Architecture Development Cycle

5.2.1 Key Points

The following are the key points about the ADM:

- The ADM is iterative, over the whole process, between phases, and within phases (see Part III, Chapter 19). For each iteration of the ADM, a fresh decision must be taken as to:
  - The breadth of coverage of the enterprise to be defined
  - The level of detail to be defined.
  - The extent of the time period aimed at, including the number and extent of any intermediate time periods.
  - The architectural assets to be leveraged, including:
    - Assets created in previous iterations of the ADM cycle within the enterprise.
    - Assets available elsewhere in the industry (other frameworks, systems models, vertical industry models, etc.).
- These decisions should be based on a practical assessment of resource and competence availability, and the value that can realistically be expected to accrue to the enterprise from the chosen scope of the architecture work.
- As a generic method, the ADM is intended to be used by enterprises in a wide variety of different geographies and applied in different vertical sectors/ industry types. As such, it may be, but does not necessarily have to be, tailored to specific needs. For example, it may be used in conjunction with the set of deliverables of another framework, where these have been deemed to be more appropriate for a specific organization. (For example, many US federal agencies have developed individual frameworks that define the deliverables specific to their particular departmental needs.)

These issues are considered in detail in Section 5.3.

5.2.2 Basic Structure

The basic structure of the ADM is shown in Figure 5-1.

Throughout the ADM cycle, there needs to be frequent validation of results against the original expectations, both those for the whole ADM cycle, and those for the particular phase of the process.

5.2 架构开发周期

5.2.1 关键点

以下内容是关于 ADM 的关键点：

- ADM 在整个流程中、各个阶段之间以及各个阶段内（见第三部分，第 19 章）是迭代的。对于 ADM 的每轮迭代，必须按照以下因素采取新的决策：
  - — 待定义的 ENTERPRISE 覆盖范围的广度。
  - — 待定义的细节层级。
  - — 目标时间区间范围，包括任何中间时间区间的数量和范围。
  - — 更大程度利用架构资产，包括：
    - — ENTERPRISE 内以往的 ADM 周期迭代所创建的资产。
    - — 在行业其他地方可用的资产（其他的框架、系统模型、垂直行业模型等）。
- 这些决策均应基于对资源和能力可用性的实际评估以及实际期望从选定的架构工作范围内增加到该 ENTERPRISE 的价值。
- 作为一种一般化的方法，ADM 旨在由位于各种不同地理位置的 ENTERPRISE 来使用并应用于不同的垂直部门/行业类型。如此一来，它也许是按照特定需要进行剪裁，但不一定必须如此。例如，ADM 可以与另一个框架的交付物集结合使用，这些交付物已被视为更适合于某个特定组织。（例如，许多美国联邦机构已经开发出了多个独立架构，用于定义其特殊部门需要的特有交付物。）

这些问题在 5.3 节中详细论述。

5.2.2 基本结构

ADM 的基本结构如图 5-1 所示。

在 ADM 整个周期中，需要根据原始期望对结果进行经常的确认，既包括整体 ADM 周期，也包括该流程的特定阶段。

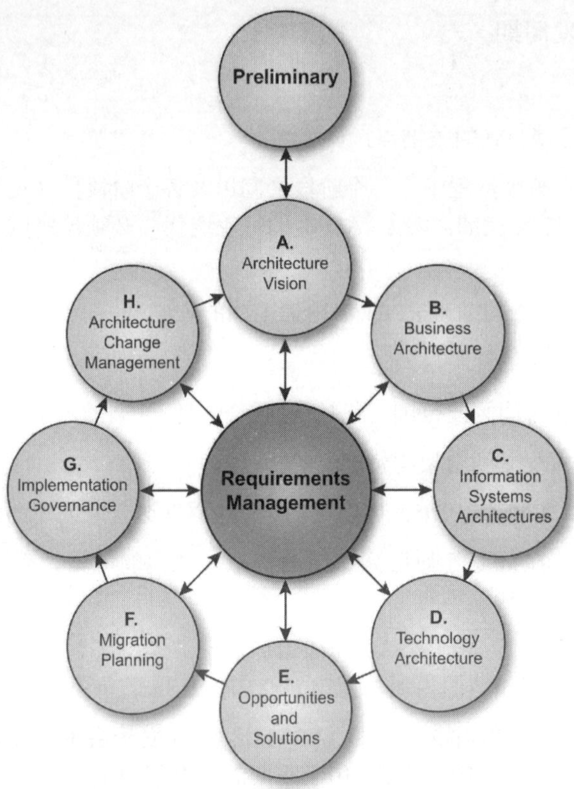

Figure 5-1 Architecture Development Cycle

The phases of the ADM cycle are further divided into steps; for example, the steps within the architecture development phases (B, C, D) are as follows:

- Select reference models, viewpoints, and tools
- Develop Baseline Architecture Description
- Develop Target Architecture Description
- Perform gap analysis
- Define candidate roadmap components
- Resolve impacts across the Architecture Landscape
- Conduct formal stakeholder review

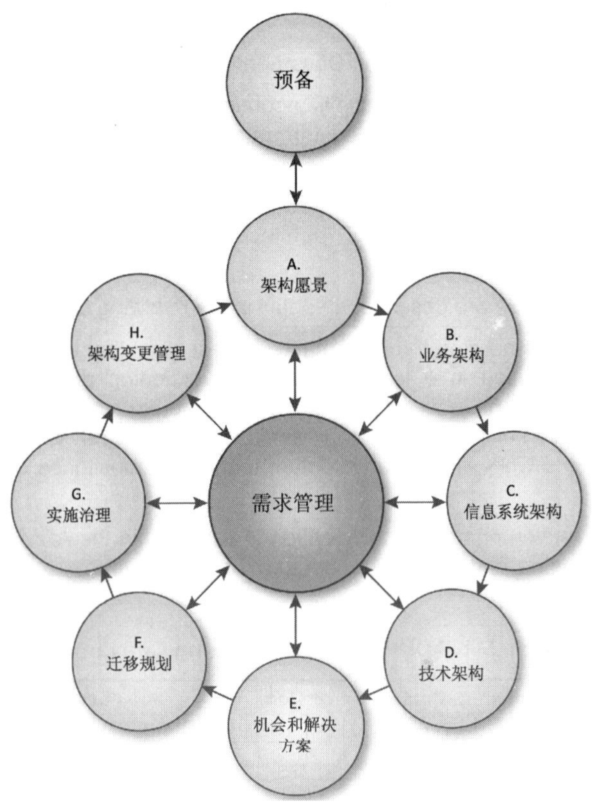

图 5-1 架构开发周期

ADM 周期的各个阶段被进一步划分为以下步骤；例如，架构开发阶段（B、C、D）内的步骤如下：

- 选择参考模型、视角和工具
- 开发基线架构描述
- 开发目标架构描述
- 进行差距分析
- 定义候选路线图组件
- 化解贯穿架构全景的影响
- 进行正式的利益攸关者审视

- Finalize the Architecture
- Create Architecture Definition Document

The Requirements Management phase is a continuous phase which ensures that any changes to requirements are handled through appropriate governance processes and reflected in all other phases.

An enterprise may choose to record all new requirements, including those which are in scope of the current Statement of Architecture Work through a single Requirements Repository.

The phases of the cycle are described in detail in the following chapters within Part II.

Note that output is generated throughout the process, and that the output in an early phase may be modified in a later phase. The versioning of output is managed through version numbers. In all cases, the ADM numbering scheme is provided as an example. It should be adapted by the architect to meet the requirements of the organization and to work with the architecture tools and repositories employed by the organization.

In particular, a version numbering convention is used within the ADM to illustrate the evolution of Baseline and Target Architecture Definitions. Table 5-1 describes how this convention is used.

Table 5-1 ADM Version Numbering Convention

<table>
<tr><th>Phase</th><th>Deliverable</th><th>Content</th><th>Version</th><th>Description</th></tr>
<tr><td rowspan="4">A: Architecture Vision</td><td rowspan="4">Architecture Vision</td><td>Business Architecture</td><td>0.1</td><td>Version 0.1 indicates that a high-level outline of the architecture is in place.</td></tr>
<tr><td>Data Architecture</td><td>0.1</td><td>Version 0.1 indicates that a high-level outline of the architecture is in place.</td></tr>
<tr><td>Application Architecture</td><td>0.1</td><td>Version 0.1 indicates that a high-level outline of the architecture is in place.</td></tr>
<tr><td>Technology Architecture</td><td>0.1</td><td>Version 0.1 indicates that a high-level outline of the architecture is in place.</td></tr>
<tr><td>B: Business Architecture</td><td>Architecture Definition Document</td><td>Business Architecture</td><td>1.0</td><td>Version 1.0 indicates a formally reviewed, detailed architecture.</td></tr>
<tr><td rowspan="2">C: Information Systems Architecture</td><td rowspan="2">Architecture Definition Document</td><td>Data Architecture</td><td>1.0</td><td>Version 1.0 indicates a formally reviewed, detailed architecture.</td></tr>
<tr><td>Application Architecture</td><td>1.0</td><td>Version 1.0 indicates a formally reviewed, detailed architecture.</td></tr>
<tr><td>D: Technology Architecture</td><td>Architecture Definition Document</td><td>Technology Architecture</td><td>1.0</td><td>Version 1.0 indicates a formally reviewed, detailed architecture.</td></tr>
</table>

- 最终确定架构
- 创建架构定义文件

需求管理阶段是一个连续阶段，它确保通过适当的治理流程来处理任何需求变更并反映在所有其他阶段中。

ENTERPRISE 可选择记录所有新的需求，包括通过单个需求存储库来记录当前架构工作说明书范围内的那些需求。

在第二部分的以下章节中详细描述 ADM 周期的这些阶段。

注意，在流程中各处均产生输出且早期阶段产生的输出可在以后的阶段中进行修改。通过版本号管理输出的版本。在所有情况下，ADM 编号方案作为一个示例提供。ADM 编号方案应由架构师进行调整以满足组织的需求，并与组织所采用的架构工具和存储库一同使用。

特别地，在 ADM 内，版本编号协定被用来阐明基线架构定义和目标架构定义的演进。表 5-1 描述如何使用本协定。

表 5-1　ADM 版本编号约定

阶段	交付物	内容	版本	描述
A：架构愿景	架构愿景	业务架构	0.1	版本 0.1 表明架构的高层级概要已形成
		数据架构	0.1	版本 0.1 表明架构的高层级概要已形成
		应用架构	0.1	版本 0.1 表明架构的高层级概要已形成
		技术架构	0.1	版本 0.1 表明架构的高层级概要已形成
B：业务架构	架构定义文件	业务架构	1.0	版本 1.0 表明经正式审视的详细架构
C：信息系统架构	架构定义文件	数据架构	1.0	版本 1.0 表明经正式审视的详细架构
		应用架构	1.0	版本 1.0 表明经正式审视的详细架构
D：技术架构	架构定义文件	技术架构	1.0	版本 1.0 表明经正式审视的详细架构

5.3 Adapting the ADM

The ADM is a generic method for architecture development, which is designed to deal with most system and organizational requirements. However, it will often be necessary to modify or extend the ADM to suit specific needs. One of the tasks before applying the ADM is to review its components for applicability, and then tailor them as appropriate to the circumstances of the individual enterprise. This activity may well produce an "enterprise-specific" ADM.

One reason for wanting to adapt the ADM, which it is important to stress, is that the order of the phases in the ADM is to some extent dependent on the maturity of the architecture discipline within the enterprise. For example, if the business case for doing architecture at all is not well recognized, then creating an Architecture Vision is almost always essential; and a detailed Business Architecture often needs to come next, in order to underpin the Architecture Vision, detail the business case for remaining architecture work, and secure the active participation of key stakeholders in that work. In other cases a slightly different order may be preferred; for example, a detailed inventory of the baseline environment may be done before undertaking the Business Architecture.

The order of phases may also be defined by the architecture principles and business principles of an enterprise. For example, the business principles may dictate that the enterprise be prepared to adjust its business processes to meet the needs of a packaged solution, so that it can be implemented quickly to enable fast response to market changes. In such a case, the Business Architecture (or at least the completion of it) may well follow completion of the Information Systems Architecture or the Technology Architecture.

Another reason for wanting to adapt the ADM is if TOGAF is to be integrated with another enterprise framework (as explained in Part I, Section 2.10). For example, an enterprise may wish to use TOGAF and its generic ADM in conjunction with the well-known Zachman Framework, or another enterprise architecture framework that has a defined set of deliverables specific to a particular vertical sector: Government, Defense, e-Business, Telecommunications, etc. The ADM has been specifically designed with this potential integration in mind.

Other possible reasons for wanting to adapt the ADM include:

- The ADM is one of the many corporate processes that make up the corporate governance model. It is complementary to, and supportive of, other standard program management processes, such as those for authorization, risk management, business planning and budgeting, development planning, systems development, and procurement.
- The ADM is being mandated for use by a prime or lead contractor in an outsourcing situation, and needs to be tailored to achieve a suitable com-promise between the contractor's existing practices and the contracting enterprise's requirements.
- The enterprise is a small-to-medium enterprise, and wishes to use a "cut-down" method more attuned to the reduced level of resources and system complexity typical of such an environment.
- The enterprise is very large and complex, comprising many separate but interlinked "enterprises" within an overall collaborative business framework, and the architecture method needs to be adapted to recognize this. Different approaches to planning and integration may be used in such cases, including the following (possibly in combination):
    - Top-down planning and development — designing the whole interconnected meta-enterprise as a single entity (an exercise that typically stretches the limits of practicality).

5.3 ADM 的适应性调整

ADM 是一种一般化的架构开发方法，被设计用于处理大多数系统和组织需求。然而，修改或扩展 ADM 以适应特定需要常常是必需的。应用 ADM 前，一个任务是审视各组成部分的适用性，然后按照 ENTERPRISE 各自的环境适当剪裁。本活动有可能产生一个“ENTERPRISE 特有的”ADM。

想要适应性调整 ADM 且重点强调的一个原因是，ADM 中各个阶段的顺序在某种程度上依赖于 ENTERPRISE 内架构规程的成熟度。例如，如果架构开发的业务案例尚未得到充分识别，那么创建一个架构愿景几乎总是必不可少的；并且详细的业务架构通常要随之而来，以便支撑架构愿景，详细说明其余架构工作的业务案例，并确保关键的利益攸关者主动参与到这项工作之中。在其他情况下，对顺序稍做调整可能更为可取；例如，详细的基线环境库目录可在进行业务架构开发之前完成。

阶段的顺序也可根据 ENTERPRISE 的架构原则和业务原则来定义。例如，业务原则可要求 ENTERPRISE 做好调整其业务流程的准备，以满足打包解决方案的需要，以便为快速应对市场变化来迅速实施该解决方案。在这种情况下，业务架构（或至少业务架构的完成）也许在信息系统架构或技术架构完成之后会很好形成。

需要适应性调整 ADM 的另一个原因是，TOGAF 是否将与另一个 ENTERPRISE 框架（在第一部分，2.10 节中解释）综合。例如，ENTERPRISE 可能希望使用 TOGAF 及其通用 ADM 结合著名的 Zachman 框架，或另一个具有特定于特殊垂直部门（政府、国防部、电子商务、电信等）的一系列确定交付物的 Enterprise Architecture。ADM 在进行专门设计时已经意识到有这种综合的可能性。

需要调整 ADM 的其他可能的原因包括：

- ADM 是组成公司治理模型的众多公司级流程之一。它与其他标准程序管理流程互补并提供支持，例如那些用于授权、风险管理、业务规划和预算、开发规划、系统开发和采购的流程。
- ADM 经委托由主要或总承包商在外包条件下使用，并且需要剪裁，以在承包商现有实践和承包的 ENTERPRISE 需求之间达成适当的折中。
- ENTERPRISE 属于中小型 ENTERPRISE，并希望使用更加适合中小型 ENTERPRISE 这类环境下特有的资源水平和系统复杂度均较低的“精简”方法。
- ENTERPRISE 规模庞大且复杂，包含一个整体协作的业务框架内的众多独立但相互联系的“ENTERPRISE”，并需要对架构方法进行调整以认识到这种情况。在这种情况下，可使用不同的规划和途径，包括以下方法（可结合使用）：
  - 自顶向下规划和开发——将整体互连的元 ENTERPRISE 设计为一个单一实体（一种训练实际情况限定的运用）。

- — Development of a "generic" or "reference" architecture, typical of the enterprises within the organization, but not representing any specific enterprise, which individual enterprises are then expected to adapt in order to produce an architecture "instance" suited to the particular enterprise concerned.
- — Replication — developing a specific architecture for one enterprise, implementing it as a proof-of-concept, and then taking that as a "reference architecture" to be cloned in other enterprises.

- In a vendor or production environment, a generic architecture for a family of related products is often referred to as a "Product Line Architecture", and the analogous process to that outlined above is termed "(Architecture-based) Product Line Engineering". The ADM is targeted primarily at archi-tects in IT user enterprises, but a vendor organization whose products are IT-based might well wish to adapt it as a generic method for a Product Line Architecture development.

5.4 Architecture Governance

The ADM, whether adapted by the organization or used as documented here, is a key process to be managed in the same manner as other architecture artifacts classified through the Enterprise Continuum and held in the Architecture Repository. The Architecture Board should be satisfied that the method is being applied correctly across all phases of an architecture development iteration. Compliance with the ADM is fundamental to the governance of the architecture, to ensure that all considerations are made and all required deliverables are produced.

The management of all architectural artifacts, governance, and related processes should be supported by a controlled environment. Typically this would be based on one or more repositories supporting versioned object and process control and status.

The major information areas managed by a governance repository should contain the following types of information:

- **Reference Data** (collateral from the organization's own repositories/Enterprise Continuum, including external data; e.g., COBIT, ITIL): Used for guidance and instruction during project implementation. This includes the details of information outlined above. The reference data includes a description of the governance procedures themselves.
- **Process Status**: All information regarding the state of any governance processes will be managed; examples of this include outstanding compliance requests, dispensation requests, and compliance assessments investigations.
- **Audit Information**: This will record all completed governance process actions and will be used to support:
  - — Key decisions and responsible personnel for any architecture project that has been sanctioned by the governance process.
  - — A reference for future architectural and supporting process developments, guidance, and precedence.

The governance artifacts and process are themselves part of the contents of the Architecture Repository.

— “一般”或“参考”架构的开发，组织内的 ENTERPRISE 具有代表性，但不代表任何特定 ENTERPRISE，然后期望各个 ENTERPRISE 进行适应性调整，以便产生一个适于所关注的特指 ENTERPRISE 的架构“实例”。

— 复制——为一个 ENTERPRISE 开发特定架构，将该架构作为方案验证来实施，然后在其他 ENTERPRISE 中当作“参考架构”进行克隆。

- 在供应商或生产环境中，用于相关产品族的一般架构通常被称为“产品线架构”，并且以上列出的相似流程被称为“（基于架构的）产品线工程”。ADM 主要面向 IT 用户 ENTERPRISE 中的架构师，但是其产品基于 IT 的供应商组织很有可能希望将 ADM 调整为产品线架构开发的一种一般方法。

5.4 架构治理

无论是由组织适应性调整还是按本文所记录的这样使用，ADM 都是一个按照与在 ENTERPRISE 的连续统一体中分类并在架构库中保存的其他架构制品相同的方式管理的关键流程。架构委员会应确信在架构开发迭代的所有阶段中均在正确应用方法。符合 ADM 是治理架构的基础，以确保进行了周全的考虑并产生所有需要的交付物。

对所有架构制品、治理和相关流程的管理均应由受控环境所支持。典型情况下，这将会基于支持受版本控制的对象和流程控制及状态的一个或多个存储库。

由治理存储库管理的主要信息领域应包含以下类型的信息：

- 参考数据（从组织拥有的存储库/ENTERPRISE 的连续统一体中收集，包括外部数据，如 COBIT、ITIL）：用于项目实施期间的引导和指令。参考数据包括以上列出的信息的详细说明，也包括对治理程序本身的描述。
- 流程状态：与治理流程的状态有关的所有信息均会被管理；流程状态的示例包括重要的合规性要求、特许请求以及合规性评估调查。
- 审核信息：审核信息会记录所有完整的治理流程活动并用于支持：

— 经由治理流程正式认可的任何架构项目的关键决策和负责人员。

— 作为未来架构的和支持流程的开发、引导和排序的参考。

治理制品和流程本身是架构库内容的一部分。

5.5 Scoping the Architecture

There are many reasons to constrain (or restrict) the scope of the architectural activity to be undertaken, most of which relate to limits in:

- The organizational authority of the team producing the architecture
- The objectives and stakeholder concerns to be addressed within the archite-cture
- The availability of people, finance, and other resources

The scope chosen for the architecture activity should ideally allow the work of all architects within the enterprise to be effectively governed and integrated. This requires a set of aligned "architecture partitions" that ensure architects are not working on duplicate or conflicting activities. It also requires the definition of re-use and compliance relationships between architecture partitions.

The division of the enterprise and its architecture-related activity is discussed in more detail inChapter 40.

Four dimensions are typically used in order to define and limit the scope of an architecture:

- **Breadth**: What is the full extent of the enterprise, and what part of that extent will this architecting effort deal with?
  - — Many enterprises are very large, effectively comprising a federation of organizational units that could validly be considered enterprises in their own right.
  - — The modern enterprise increasingly extends beyond its traditional boun-daries, to embrace a fuzzy combination of traditional business enterprise combined with suppliers, customers, and partners.
- **Depth**: To what level of detail should the architecting effort go? How much architecture is "enough"? What is the appropriate demarcation between the architecture effort and other, related activities (system design, system engineering, system development)?
- **Time Period**: What is the time period that needs to be articulated for the Architecture Vision, and does it make sense (in terms of practicality and resources) for the same period to be covered in the detailed architecture description? If not, how many Transition Architectures are to be defined, and what are their time periods?
- **Architecture Domains**: A complete enterprise architecture description should contain all four architecture domains (business, data, application, technology), but the realities of resource and time constraints often mean there is not enough time, funding, or resources to build a top-down, all-inclusive architecture description encompassing all four architecture domains, even if the enterprise scope is chosen to be less than the full extent of the overall enterprise.

Typically, the scope of an architecture is first expressed in terms of breadth, depth, and time. Once these dimensions are understood, a suitable combination of architec-ture domains can be selected that are appropriate to the problem being addressed. Techniques for using the ADM to develop a number of related architectures are discussed in Chapter 20.

The four dimensions of architecture scope are explored in detail below. In each case, particularly in largescale environments where architectures are necessarily develo-ped in a federated manner, there is a danger of architects optimizing within their own scope of activity, instead of at the level of the overall enterprise. It is often necessary to sub-optimize in a particular area, in order to optimize at the enterprise level. The aim should always be to seek the highest level of commonality and focus on scalable and re-usable modules in order to maximize re-use at the enterprise level.

5.5 界定架构的范围

有多个原因约束（或限制）待执行架构活动的范围，大部分原因与下面的限制有关：

- 架构创建团队的组织权限
- 在该架构内所涉及的目的和利益攸关者关注点
- 人员、财务和其他资源的可用性

在理想情况下，架构活动选用的范围应允许对所有架构师在该 ENTERPRISE 范围内的工作进行有效治理和综合。这就需要一系列协调一致的“架构划分”，确保架构师不会从事重复的或冲突的活动。这也需要定义各架构划分之间的复用和合规性关系。

ENTERPRISE 及其架构相关活动的划分将在第 40 章进行更详细的论述。

典型情况下，使用四个维度来定义并界定架构范围：

- 广度：ENTERPRISE 的完整扩展广度是什么，本架构工作会涉及该扩展广度的哪一部分？
  - 许多 ENTERPRISE 非常庞大，实际上包括一个由若干组织单元构成的联盟，这些组织单元在其自身范围内就可以被视为 ENTERPRISE。
  - 现代 ENTERPRISE 日益延伸到传统边界以外，包括一种由传统业务 ENTERPRISE 与供应商、客户和合作伙伴结合在一起的模糊组合。
- 深度：架构工作应该进行到什么样的细节层级？多少个架构是“足够”的？架构工作和其他相关活动（系统设计、系统工程、系统开发）之间的适当界限是什么？
- 时间区间：什么是描绘架构愿景所需的时间区间？在详细架构描述中涵盖同一时区间是否有意义（就现实性和资源而言）？如果没有意义，将定义多少个过渡架构？它们各自的时间区间是什么？
- 架构域：一个完整的 Enterprise Architecture 描述应当包括全部四个架构域（业务、数据、应用、技术），但是资源和时间约束的现实情况往往意味着没有足够的时间、资金或资源来建立一个涵盖所有四个架构域的自顶向下的全面架构描述，即便是选定的 ENTERPRISE 范围比整个 ENTERPRISE 的总体范围要小得多。

通常，首先在广度、深度和时间方面表达架构的范围。一旦理解了这些维度，可选定适于正在应对的问题的适当架构域组合。在第 20 章中论述使用 ADM 开发多个相关架构的技巧。

下面详细探究架构范围的四个维度。在每种情况下，特别是在必须以一种联合的方式开发架构的大规模环境中，架构师在自身活动范围内而并非在总体 ENTERPRISE 层级上进行优化，会存在一定风险。通常有必要在特定领域内进行局部优化，以便在 ENTERPRISE 层级上优化。目标应始终是寻求最高层级的共用性，并聚焦于可扩展且可复用的模块以便使 ENTERPRISE 层级的复用最大化。

5.5.1 Breadth

One of the key decisions is the focus of the architecture effort, in terms of the breadth of overall enterprise activity to be covered (which specific business sectors, functions, organizations, geographical areas, etc.).

It is often necessary to have a number of different architectures existing across an enterprise, focused on particular timeframes, business functions, or business require-ments.

For large complex enterprises federated architectures — independently developed, maintained, and managed architectures that are subsequently integrated within an integration framework — are typical. Such a framework specifies the principles for interoperability, migration, and conformance. This allows specific business units to have architectures developed and governed as stand-alone architecture projects. More details and guidance on specifying the interoperability requirements for different solutions can be found in Part III, Chapter 29.

The feasibility of a single enterprise-wide architecture for every business function or purpose may be rejected as too complex and unwieldy. In these circumstances it is suggested that a number of different enterprise architectures exist across an enterprise. These enterprise architectures focus on particular timeframes, business segments or functions, and specific organizational requirements. In such a case we need to create the overarching enterprise architecture as a "federation" of these enterprise architectures. An effective way of managing and exploiting these enterprise architectures is to adopt a publish-and-subscribe model that allows architecture to be brought under a governance framework. In such a model, architecture developers and architecture consumers in projects (the supply and demand sides of architecture work) sign up to a mutually beneficial framework of governance that ensures that:

- Architectural material is of good quality, up-to-date, fit-for-purpose, and published (reviewed and agreed to be made public).
- Usage of architecture material can be monitored, and compliance with standards, models, and principles can be exhibited, via:
  - A Compliance Assessment process that describes what the user is subscribing to, and assesses their level of compliance.
  - A dispensation process that may grant dispensations from adherence to architecture standards and guidelines in specific cases (usually with a strong business imperative).

Publish and subscribe techniques are being developed as part of general IT governance and specifically for the Defense sphere.

5.5.2 Depth

Care should be taken to judge the appropriate level of detail to be captured, based on the intended use of the enterprise architecture and the decisions to be made based on it. It is important that a consistent and equal level of depth be completed in each architecture domain (business, data, application, technology) included in the architecture effort. If pertinent detail is omitted, the architecture may not be useful. If unnecessary detail is included, the architecture effort may exceed the time and resources available, and/or the resultant architecture may be confusing or cluttered. Developing architectures at different levels of detail within an enterprise is discussed in more detail in Chapter 20.

It is also important to predict the future uses of the architecture so that, within resource limitations, the architecture can be structured to accommodate future tailoring, extension, or re-use. The depth and detail of the enterprise architecture needs to be sufficient for its purpose, and no more.

5.5.1 广度

依据所涵盖的总体 ENTERPRISE 活动的广度（特定的业务部门、功能、组织、地理区域等），其中一个关键决策是架构工作的聚焦点。

通常有必要使存在于整个 ENTERPRISE 中的多个不同的架构聚焦于特定时间区间、业务功能或业务需求。

对于复杂的大型 ENTERPRISE，联邦架构是典型架构——在一个集成框架内依次综合的独立开发、维护和管理的多个架构。这样的框架规定互用性、迁移和一致性的原则。这允许特定的业务单元将这些架构作为独立的架构项目进行开发和治理。更多关于规定不同解决方案互用性需求的详细说明和指南可在第三部分的第 29 章中找到。

针对每个业务功能或目的的单一的整个 ENTERPRISE 范围的架构的可行性，因过于复杂和不实用可能被拒绝。在这些情形下，建议整个 ENTERPRISE 中存在多个不同的 Enterprise Architecture。这些 Enterprise Architecture 聚焦于特定时间区间、业务区域或功能，以及特定的组织需求。在这种情况下，我们需要将首要的 Enterprise Architecture 创建为这些 Enterprise Architecture 的一个“联邦”。管理和开拓这些 Enterprise Architecture 的有效途径是采用一个允许架构被纳入治理框架的发布—订阅模型。在这样一个模型中，项目中的架构开发者和架构使用者（架构工作的供方和需方）签订一个互惠互利的治理框架，以确保：

- 架构资料是优质的、最新的、适用的和发布的（经审视并同意公开的）。
- 通过以下流程，可监控架构资料的使用，并可体现与标准、模型和原则的一致性：
  - 合规性评估流程，描述用户正在“订阅”什么，并评估其合规性等级。
  - 特许流程，可根据是否遵守特定情况（通常带有强烈的业务需要）的架构标准和指南来授予特许。

发布和订阅技巧正在作为一般 IT 治理的一部分进行开发，特别是用于国防领域。

5.5.2 深度

应关切根据 Enterprise Architecture 的预期用途和由此做出的决策来判定将要捕获的适当的细节层级。重要的是，应在包含在架构工作中的每个架构域（业务、数据、应用、技术）中完成一致且对等的深度层级。如果省略相关的细节，那么架构可能会不再有用。如果包括不必要的细节，那么架构工作可能超出可用的时间和资源，和/或得到的架构可能是令人迷惑或凌乱的。第 20 章更详细地论述在 ENTERPRISE 范围内的不同细节层级上开发架构。

预测架构的未来用途同样重要，以便在资源限制范围内，架构可被结构化以适应未来剪裁、扩展或复用。Enterprise Architecture 的深度和细节只需要足以满足其目的。

Iterations of the ADM will build on the artifacts and the capabilities created during previous iteration.

There is a need to document all the models in an enterprise, to the level of detail appropriate to the need of the current ADM cycle. The key is to understand the status of the enterprise's architecture work, and what can realistically be achieved with the resources and competencies available, and then focus on identifying and delivering the value that is achievable. Stakeholder value is a key focus: too broad a scope may deter some stakeholders (no return on investment).

5.5.3 Time Period

The ADM is described in terms of a single cycle of Architecture Vision, and a set of Target Architectures (Business, Data, Application, Technology) that enable the implementation of the vision.

In such cases, a wider view may be taken, whereby an enterprise is represented by several different architecture instances (for example, strategic, segment, capability), each representing the enterprise at a particular point in time. One architecture instance will represent the current enterprise state (the "as-is", or baseline). Another architecture instance, perhaps defined only partially, will represent the ultimate target end-state (the "vision"). In-between, intermediate or "Transition Architecture" instances may be defined, each comprising its own set of Target-Architecture Descriptions. An example of how this might be achieved is given in Part III, Chapter 20.

By this approach, the Target Architecture work is split into two or more discrete stages:

1. First, develop Target Architecture Descriptions for the overall (largescale) system, demonstrating a response to stakeholder objectives and concerns for a relatively distant timeframe (for example, a six-year period).
2. Then develop one or more "Transition Architecture" descriptions, as increments or plateaus, each in line with and converging on the Target Architecture Descriptions, and describing the specifics of the increment concerned.

In such an approach, the Target Architectures are evolutionary in nature, and require periodic review and update according to evolving business requirements and developments in technology, whereas the Transition Architectures are (by design) incremental in nature, and in principle should not evolve during the implementation phase of the increment, in order to avoid the "moving target" syndrome. This, of course, is only possible if the implementation schedule is under tight control and relatively short (typically less than two years).

The Target Architectures remain relatively generic, and because of that are less vulnerable to obsolescence than the Transition Architectures. They embody only the key strategic architectural decisions, which should be blessed by the stakeholders from the outset, whereas the detailed architectural decisions in the Transition Architectures are deliberately postponed as far as possible (i.e., just before imple-mentation) in order to improve responsiveness *vis a vis* new technologies and products.

The enterprise evolves by migrating to each of these Transition Architectures in turn. As each Transition Architecture is implemented, the enterprise achieves a consistent, operational state on the way to the ultimate vision. However, this vision itself is periodically updated to reflect changes in the business and technology environment, and in effect may never actually be achieved, as originally described. The whole process continues for as long as the enterprise exists and continues to change.

Such a breakdown of the architecture description into a family of related architecture products of course requires effective management of the set and their relationships.

ADM 的迭代将会建立在前一轮迭代中所创建的制品和能力之上。

需要对 ENTERPRISE 中的所有模型进行文件化，细节层级适合当前 ADM 周期的需要。关键是理解 ENTERPRISE 的架构工作的状态，以及通过可用的资源和能力可以在实际上达成什么，然后聚焦于识别和交付可实现的价值。利益攸关者价值是一个关键聚焦点：过度宽泛的范围可能会使某些利益攸关者感到沮丧（无投资回报）。

5.5.3 时间区间

根据单一架构愿景周期以及使该愿景能够实现的一系列目标架构（业务、数据、应用、技术）来描述 ADM。

在这种情况下，可采用更宽广的视野，由此，ENTERPRISE 可通过若干不同的架构实例（例如，战略、分部、能力）表达，每个实例代表特定时点的 ENTERPRISE。一个架构实例将表示当前的 ENTERPRISE 状态（“现状”或基线）。另一个架构实例，也许仅部分定义，将表示最终目标的最终状态（“愿景”）。在两者之间可定义中间的或“过渡架构”实例，每个实例包括其拥有的目标架构描述集。在第三部分第 20 章中给出如何达成这一点的示例。

通过这种途径，目标架构工作分成两个或更多个离散的阶段：

1. 首先，开发总体（大规模）系统的目标架构描述，表明对相对久远的时间区段（例如，六年）内的利益攸关者的目的和关注点的响应。
2. 然后，开发一个或更多个“过渡架构”描述，作为增量或稳定状态，每个“过渡架构”描述都与目标架构保持一致且汇聚焦于目标架构描述，并描述所关注的增量的特性。

在这种实施途径中，目标架构在本质上是演进的，并要求根据演进的业务需求和技术发展定期审视和更新，虽然过渡架构在本质上（按照设计）是递增的，并且在原则上不应在递增的实施阶段演进，以避免存在“移动的目标”的综合症状。当然，这只在实施进度被严格控制并相对较短（通常是小于两年）的情况下是可能的。

目标架构保持相对的通用性，正因如此，相比过渡架构，其不易被淘汰。目标架构仅体现利益攸关者从一开始所拥有的关键战略架构决策，而过渡架构中的详细架构决策则被有意识地尽可能延后（即刚好在实施之前），以便面对新技术和产品时提高响应性。

ENTERPRISE 通过依次迁移至每个过渡架构进行演进。当实施每个过渡架构时，ENTERPRISE 在通往最终愿景的过程中达成一致的运行状态。然而，愿景本身是定期更新的，以反映业务和技术环境的变化，并在实际上从未按照初始的描述真正实现过。只要 ENTERPRISE 存在并继续变革，整个流程就持续进行。

当然，这样一种使架构描述成为一系列相关架构产物的分解，要求对该集合及其相互关系进行有效管理。

5.5.4 Architecture Domains

A complete enterprise architecture should address all four architecture domains (business, data, application, technology), but the realities of resource and time constraints often mean there is not enough time, funding, or resources to build a topdown, all-inclusive architecture description encompassing all four architecture domains.

Architecture descriptions will normally be built with a specific purpose in mind — a specific set of business drivers that drive the architecture development — and clarifying the specific issue(s) that the architecture description is intended to help explore, and the questions it is expected to help answer, is an important part of the initial phase of the ADM.

For example, if the purpose of a particular architecture effort is to define and examine technology options for achieving a particular capability, and the fundamental business processes are not open to modification, then a full Business Architecture may well not be warranted. However, because the Data, Application, and Technology Architectures build on the Business Architecture, the Business Architecture still needs to be thought through and understood.

While circumstances may sometimes dictate building an architecture description not containing all four architecture domains, it should be understood that such an architecture cannot, by definition, be a complete enterprise architecture. One of the risks is lack of consistency and therefore ability to integrate. Integration either needs to come later — with its own costs and risks — or the risks and trade-offs involved in not developing a complete and integrated architecture need to be articulated by the architect, and communicated to and understood by the enterprise management.

5.6 Architecture Integration

Architectures that are created to address a subset of issues within an enterprise require a consistent frame of reference so that they can be considered as a group as well as point deliverables. The dimensions that are used to define the scope boundary of a single architecture (e.g., level of detail, architecture domain, etc.) are typically the same dimensions that must be addressed when considering the integration of many architectures. Figure 5-2 illustrates how different types of architecture need to co-exist.

At the present time, the state of the art is such that architecture integration can be accomplished only at the lower end of the integratability spectrum. Key factors to consider are the granularity and level of detail in each artifact, and the maturity of standards for the interchange of architectural descriptions.

5.5.4 架构域

一个完整的 Enterprise Architecture 应该应对四个架构域（业务、数据、应用、技术），但是资源和时间约束的现实情况，往往意味着没有足够的时间、资金或资源来建立一个涵盖所有四个架构域的自顶向下的详尽架构描述。

通常架构描述的建立都考虑到特定目的——驱动架构开发的一系列特定业务驱动因素——并明晰架构描述，旨在帮助探索的特定议题以及期望帮助解答的问题，这是 ADM 初始阶段的一个重要部分。

例如，如果特定架构工作的目的是定义和审查用于实现特定能力的技术选项，并且基础业务流程并不对修改开放，那么完整业务架构很可能得不到保障。然而，由于数据、应用和技术架构建立在业务架构上，业务架构仍然需要全面地考虑和理解业务架构。

虽然有时一些情况可能指定构建一个不包含全部四个架构域的架构描述，但应该明白的是，根据定义，这样的架构不可能是一个完整的 Enterprise Architecture。其中一个风险是缺乏一致性并因此缺乏综合的能力。综合或需要在之后进行——具有自身的成本和风险——或需要由架构师清楚表达出与未开发出一个完整和综合的架构有关的风险和权衡对象，传达至 ENTERPRISE 管理部门并被管理部门理解。

5.6 架构综合

为处理 ENTERPRISE 内的问题子集而创建的架构需要一致的参照框架，以便这些架构和指定交付物被视为一个群组。通常，用于界定单一架构（例如细节层级、架构域等）范围边界的维度与在考虑综合多个架构时必须涉及的维度相同。图 5-2 阐明不同类型的架构需要如何共存。

目前，现有技术水平使得架构综合只能够在综合能力谱系的较低端完成。要考虑的关键因素是每个制品的粒度和细节层级，以及用于架构描述互换标准的成熟度。

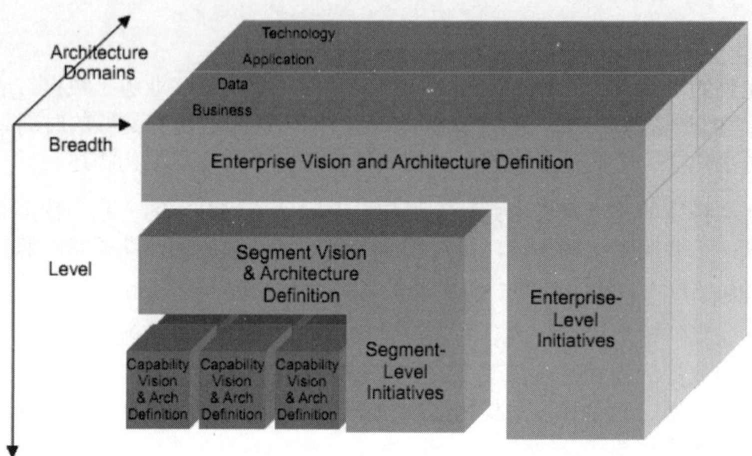

Figure 5-2 Integration of Architecture Artifacts

As organizations address common themes (such as Service Oriented Architecture (SOA), and integrated information infrastructure), and universal data models and standard data structures emerge, integration toward the high end of the spectrum will be facilitated. However, there will always be the need for effective standards governance to reduce the need for manual co-ordination and conflict resolution.

5.7 Summary

The TOGAF ADM defines a recommended sequence for the various phases and steps involved in developing an architecture, but it cannot recommend a scope — this has to be determined by the organization itself, bearing in mind that the recommended sequence of development in the ADM process is an iterative one, with the depth and breadth of scope and deliverables increasing with each iteration. Each iteration will add resources to the organization's Architecture Repository.

While a complete framework is useful (indeed, essential) to have in mind as the ultimate long-term goal, in practice there is a key decision to be made as to the scope of a specific enterprise architecture effort. This being the case, it is vital to understand the basis on which scoping decisions are being made, and to set expectations right for what is the goal of the effort.

The main guideline is to focus on what creates value to the enterprise, and to select horizontal and vertical scope, and time periods, accordingly. Whether or not this is the first time around, understand that this exercise will be repeated, and that future iterations will build on what is being created in the current effort, adding greater width and depth.

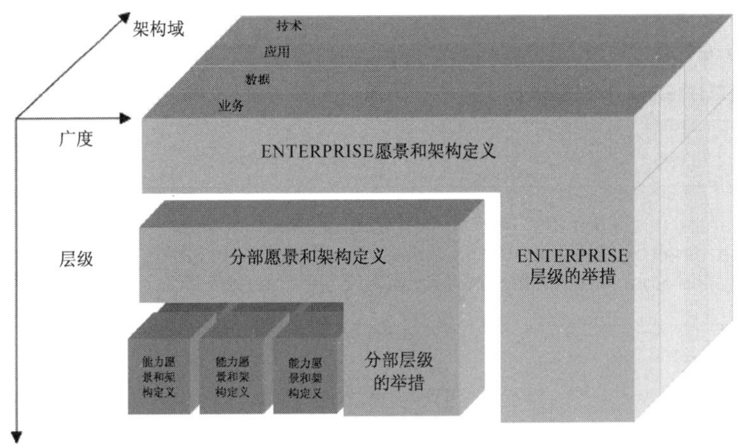

图 5-2 架构制品的综合

当组织应对共用主题[例如面向服务架构（SOA）和集成信息基础设施]并且通用数据模型和标准数据结构出现时，将会促进对谱系高端的综合。然而，总是需要有效的标准治理来减少对人工协调与冲突解决的需要。

5.7 概要总结

TOGAF ADM 为开发架构中涉及的不同阶段和步骤定义了一个推荐的顺序，但不能推荐一个范围——这必须由组织自己来确定，需要牢记的是推荐的 ADM 流程开发顺序是迭代的，且范围的深度、广度和交付物随着每轮迭代而增加。每轮迭代将会向组织架构存储库增添资源。

尽管一个完整的框架对于将其考虑作为最终长期目标是有用的（确实很重要），但实际上，需要依据特定 Enterprise Architecture 工作的范围做出关键决策。因此，至关重要的是，必须理解界定范围的决策所依据的基础以及设定适于该工作的目标的期望。

主要指南将聚焦于“什么为 ENTERPRISE 创造了价值”，并据此选择水平和垂直范围及时间区间。无论这是否是第一轮，要知道这样的训练将会重复进行，并且未来迭代将会建立于当前的工作所创造的内容之上，增加宽度和深度。

Chapter 6
Preliminary Phase

This chapter describes the preparation and initiation activities required to meet the business directive for a new enterprise architecture, including the definition of an Organization-Specific Architecture framework and the definition of principles.

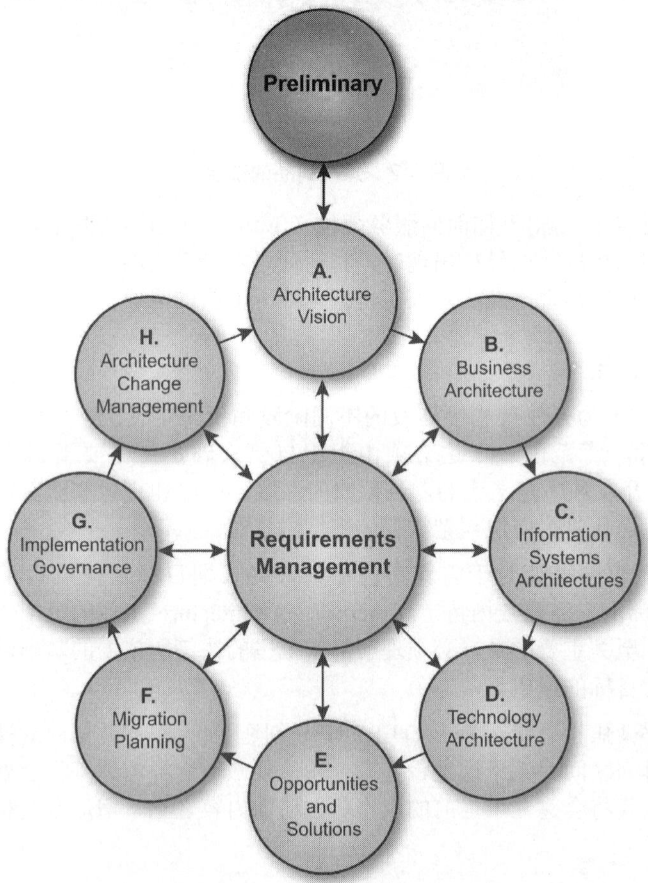

Figure 6-1 Preliminary Phase

第6章
预备阶段

本章描述为满足一个新的 Enterprise Architecture 业务方针所需的准备和发起活动，包括组织特定架构框架定义和原则定义。

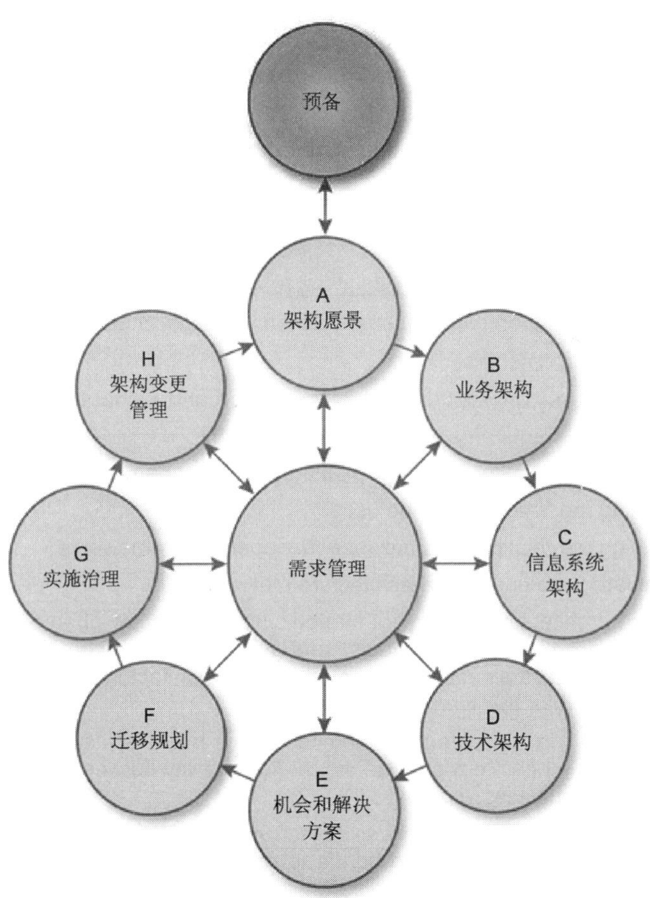

图6-1　预备阶段

6.1 Objectives

The objectives of the Preliminary Phase are:

1. Determine the Architecture Capability desired by the organization:

- Review the organizational context for conducting enterprise architecture
- Identify and scope the elements of the enterprise organizations affected by the Architecture Capability
- Identify the established frameworks, methods, and processes that intersect with the Architecture Capability
- Establish Capability Maturity target

2. Establish the Architecture Capability:

- Define and establish the Organizational Model for Enterprise Architecture
- Define and establish the detailed process and resources for architecture governance
- Select and implement tools that support the Architecture Capability
- Define the Architecture Principles

6.2 Approach

This Preliminary Phase is about defining "where, what, why, who, and how we do architecture" in the enterprise concerned. The main aspects are as follows:

- Defining the enterprise
- Identifying key drivers and elements in the organizational context
- Defining the requirements for architecture work
- Defining the Architecture Principles that will inform any architecture work
- Defining the framework to be used
- Defining the relationships between management frameworks
- Evaluating the enterprise architecture maturity

The enterprise architecture provides a strategic, top-down view of an organization to enable executives, planners, architects, and engineers to coherently co-ordinate, integrate, and conduct their activities. The enterprise architecture framework provides the strategic context for this team to operate within.

Therefore, developing the enterprise architecture is not a solitary activity and the enterprise architects need to recognize the interoperability between their frameworks and the rest of the business.

Strategic, interim, and tactical business objectives and aspirations need to be met. Similarly, the enterprise architecture needs to reflect this requirement and allow for operation of architecture discipline at different levels within the organization.

Depending on the scale of the enterprise and the level of budgetary commitment to enterprise architecture discipline, a number of approaches may be adopted to sub-divide or partition architecture teams, processes, and deliverables. Approaches for architecture partitioning are discussed in Part V, Chapter 40. The Preliminary Phase should be used to determine the desired approach to partitioning and to establish the groundwork for the selected approach to be put into practice.

6.1 目的

预备阶段的目的是：

1. 确定组织所期望的架构能力：

- 审视开展 Enterprise Architecture 的组织背景环境
- 识别并确定受架构能力影响的 ENTERPRISE 组织元素及范围
- 识别与架构能力相交叉的已有框架、方法及流程
- 建立能力成熟度目标

2. 建立架构能力：

- 定义并建立 Enterprise Architecture 的组织模型
- 定义并建立用于架构治理的详细流程和资源
- 选择并应用支持架构能力的工具
- 定义架构原则

6.2 实施途径

预备阶段是在所关注的 ENTERPRISE 中定义“何处、何事、为何、何人以及如何进行架构”。主要内容如下：

- 定义 ENTERPRISE
- 识别组织背景环境中的关键驱动因素和元素
- 定义架构工作的需求
- 定义架构原则以作为任何架构工作的依据
- 定义要使用的框架
- 定义管理框架间的关系
- 评估 Enterprise Architecture 成熟度

Enterprise Architecture 为一个组织提供了自顶向下的战略视图，使高层管理者、计划者、架构师和工程师能够连贯地协调、综合和进行他们的活动。Enterprise Architecture 框架为团队提供在其中运行的战略背景环境。

因此，开发 Enterprise Architecture 不是一个孤立的活动，ENTERPRISE 架构师需要认识到他们的框架和其他业务之间的互用性。

战略的、过渡的和战术的业务目的及渴望需要被满足。同样地，Enterprise Architecture 需要反映上述需求并允许架构规程在组织内不同层级的运行。

依据 ENTERPRISE 的规模和投入 Enterprise Architecture 规程的预算水平，可采用多种途径方法细分或划分架构团队、流程和交付物。第五部分的第 40 章论述架构划分的方法。预备阶段应该用于确定所期望的划分方法并为即将投入实践的备选方法建立基础。

The Preliminary Phase may be revisited, from the Architecture Vision phase (see Part III, Chapter 19), in order to ensure that the organization's Architecture Capability is suitable to address a specific architecture problem.

6.2.1 Enterprise

One of the main challenges of enterprise architecture is that of enterprise scope.

The scope of the enterprise, and whether it is federated, will determine those stakeholders who will derive most benefit from the enterprise Architecture Capability. It is imperative that a sponsor is appointed at this stage to ensure that the resultant activity has resources to proceed and the clear support of the business management. The enterprise may encompass many organizations and the duties of the sponsor are to ensure that all stakeholders are included in defining, establishing, and using the Architecture Capability.

6.2.2 Organizational Context

In order to make effective and informed decisions about the framework for architecture to be used within a particular enterprise, it is necessary to understand the context surrounding the architecture framework. Specific areas to consider would include:

- The commercial models for enterprise architecture and budgetary plans for enterprise architecture activity. Where no such plans exist, the Preliminary Phase should be used to develop a budget plan.
- The stakeholders for architecture in the enterprise; their key issues and concerns.
- The intentions and culture of the organization, as captured within board business directives, business imperatives, business strategies, business principles, business goals, and business drivers.
- Current processes that support execution of change and operation of the enterprise, including the structure of the process and also the level of rigor and formality applied within the organization. Areas for focus should include:
  - Current methods for architecture description
  - Current project management frameworks and methods
  - Current systems management frameworks and methods
  - Current project portfolio management processes and methods
  - Current application portfolio management processes and methods
  - Current technology portfolio management processes and methods
  - Current information portfolio management processes and methods
  - Current systems design and development frameworks and methods
- The Baseline Architecture landscape, including the state of the enterprise and also how the landscape is currently represented in documentation form.

应从架构愿景阶段（见第三部分，第 19 章）回顾预备阶段，以确保组织架构能力可以应对特定架构问题。

6.2.1 ENTERPRISE

Enterprise Architecture 的主要挑战之一就是 ENTERPRISE 的范围。

ENTERPRISE 的范围，无论是否是联邦的，均将确定那些将从 ENTERPRISE 的架构能力中得到最大利益的利益攸关者。当务之急是在本阶段指定发起人，以确保有资源推进后续的活动并明晰业务管理的支持。ENTERPRISE 可包括众多组织，并且发起人的职责是确保所有利益攸关者被包括在定义、建立和使用架构能力的过程中。

6.2.2 组织的背景环境

为了对特定 ENTERPRISE 范围内使用的架构框架做出有效的和有依据的决策，有必要理解架构框架周边的背景环境。考虑的特定领域包括：

- Enterprise Architecture 的商业模型和 Enterprise Architecture 活动的预算计划。在不存在这样计划的情况下，预备阶段应开发一个预算计划。
- ENTERPRISE 中的架构利益攸关者；他们的关键议题和关注点。
- 在委员会业务方针、业务关键、业务战略、业务原则、业务目标和业务驱动因素范畴内捕获的组织意图和文化。
- 支持执行 ENTERPRISE 变革和运行的当前流程，包括流程的结构以及在该组织内应用的严谨程度和正式程度。聚焦的领域应包括：
  - 用于架构描述的当前方法
  - 当前项目管理框架和方法
  - 当前系统管理框架和方法
  - 当前项目谱系管理流程和方法
  - 当前应用谱系管理流程和方法
  - 当前技术谱系管理流程和方法
  - 当前信息谱系管理流程和方法
  - 当前系统设计和开发框架和方法
- 基线架构全景，包括 ENTERPRISE 状态及当前如何以文档形式表达该全景。

- The skills and capabilities of the enterprise and specific organizations that will be adopting the framework.

Review of the organizational context should provide valuable requirements on how to tailor the architecture framework in terms of:

- Level of formality and rigor to be applied.
- Level of sophistication and expenditure required.
- Touch-points with other organizations, processes, roles, and responsibilities.
- Focus of content coverage.

6.2.3 Requirements for Architecture Work

The business imperatives behind the enterprise architecture work drive the require-ments and performance metrics for the architecture work. They should be sufficiently clear so that this phase may scope the business outcomes and resource require-ments, and define the outline enterprise business information requirements and associated strategies of the enterprise architecture work to be done. For example, these may include:

- Business requirements
- Cultural aspirations
- Organization intents
- Strategic intent
- Forecast financial requirements

Significant elements of these need to be articulated so that the sponsor can identify all the key decision-makers and stakeholders involved in defining and establishing an Architecture Capability.

6.2.4 Principles

The Preliminary Phase defines the Architecture Principles that will form part of the constraints on any architecture work undertaken in the enterprise. The issues involved in this are explained in Part III, Chapter 23.

The definition of Architecture Principles is fundamental to the development of an enterprise architecture. Architecture work is informed by business principles as well as Architecture Principles. The Architecture Principles themselves are also normally based in part on business principles. Defining business principles normally lies outside the scope of the architecture function. However, depending on how such principles are defined and promulgated within the enterprise, it may be possible for the set of Architecture Principles to also restate, or cross-refer to a set of business principles, business goals, and strategic business drivers defined elsewhere within the enterprise. Within an architecture project, the architect will normally need to ensure that the definitions of these business principles, goals, and strategic drivers are current, and to clarify any areas of ambiguity.

The issue of architecture governance is closely linked to that of Architecture Principles. The body responsible for governance will also normally be responsible for approving the Architecture Principles, and for resolving architecture issues. The issues involved in governance are explained in Part VII, Chapter 50.

- 正在采用基线框架的 ENTERPRISE 与特定组织的技能和能力。

组织背景环境的审视应如何依据以下方面剪裁架构框架而提供有价值的需求：

- 应用的正式程度和严谨程度。
- 所需的精致和开销程度。
- 与其他组织、流程、角色和职责的结合点。
- 内容覆盖的聚焦点。

6.2.3 架构工作的需求

Enterprise Architecture 工作背后的业务关键驱动着架构工作的需求和性能指标。这些业务关键应足够清晰，以便确定本阶段的业务成果和资源需求的范围，并定义要完成的 Enterprise Architecture 工作的概要 ENTERPRISE 业务信息需求和相关策略。例如，这些业务关键包括：

- 业务需求
- 文化渴望
- 组织意图
- 战略意图
- 预测的财务需求

需要清楚表达这些业务需要的重要元素，以便于发起人可以识别出涉及定义和建立架构能力的全部关键决策人和利益攸关者。

6.2.4 原则

预备阶段定义架构原则，其会构成 ENTERPRISE 进行各种架构工作的部分约束。第三部分第 23 章解释这一方面所涉及的议题。

架构原则的定义是 Enterprise Architecture 开发的基础。业务原则以及架构原则为架构工作之依据。架构原则自身也通常部分地基于业务原则，定义业务规则一般在架构功能的范围之外。然而，根据在 ENTERPRISE 内定义和发布这种原则方式，架构原则集也可能重新申明，或与 ENTERPRISE 内其他定义的一系列业务原则、业务目标和战略业务驱动因素交叉引用。在架构项目范围内，架构师将通常需要确保这些业务原则、目标和战略驱动因素的定义是现行有效的，并且需要明晰任何含糊不清之处。

架构治理议题与架构原则议题是紧密关联的。负责治理的主体通常也会负责批准架构原则和解决架构议题。第七部分第 50 章解释治理中涉及的议题。

6.2.5 Management Frameworks

The TOGAF Architecture Development Method (ADM) is a generic method, intended to be used by enterprises in a wide variety of industry types and geographies. It is also designed for use with a wide variety of other enterprise architecture frameworks, if required (although it can be used perfectly well in its own right, without adaptation).

TOGAF has to co-exist with and enhance the operational capabilities of other management frameworks that are present within any organization either formally or informally. In addition to these frameworks, most organizations have a method for the development of solutions, most of which have an IT component. The significance of systems is that it brings together the various domains (also known as People, Processes, and Material/Technology) to deliver a business capability.

The main frameworks suggested to be co-ordinated with TOGAF are:

- **Business Capability Management** (Business Direction and Planning) that determines what business capabilities are required to deliver business value including the definition of return on investment and the requisite control/ performance measures.
- **Portfolio/Project Management Methods** that determine how a company manages its change initiatives.
- **Operations Management Methods** that describe how a company runs its day-to-day operations, including IT.
- **Solution Development Methods** that formalize the way that business systems are delivered in accordance with the structures developed in the IT architecture.

As illustrated in Figure 6-2, these frameworks are not discrete and there are significant overlaps between them and the Business Capability Management. The latter includes the delivery of performance measured business value.

The overall significance is that the enterprise architect applying TOGAF cannot narrowly focus on the IT implementation, but must be aware of the impact that the architecture has on the entire enterprise.

6.2.5 管理框架

TOGAF 架构开发方法（ADM）是一种一般方法，旨在由处于多种行业类型和多个地理位置的 ENTERPRISE 使用。如果需要（虽然该方法本身就可完美使用，无须调整），该方法也被设计用于与多种其他 Enterprise Architecture 框架一同使用。

TOGAF 必须与任何正式或非正式组织内存在的其他管理框架的运行能力共存并提高运行能力。除了这些框架，大部分组织还具有一种用于开发解决方案的方法，大部分解决方案都具有 IT 组件。系统的重要性是集合各种不同领域（亦即人员、流程和资料/技术）来交付业务能力。

建议与 TOGAF 相协调的主要框架是：

- **业务能力管理**（业务方向和规划），确定交付业务价值需要什么业务能力，包括投资收益率的定义以及必要的控制/绩效指标。
- **项目谱系/项目管理方法**，确定一个公司如何管理其变革举措。
- **运行管理方法**，描述一个公司如何进行其日常运作，包括 IT。
- **解决方案开发方法**，形成根据 IT 架构中开发的结构化交付业务系统的方式。

如图 6-2 所示，这些框架不是彼此分离的，并且这些框架与业务能力管理之间存在明显重叠。后者包括用绩效衡量的业务价值的交付。

至关重要的是，架构师在应用 TOGAF ENTERPRISE 中不能仅关注 IT 实施，还必须意识到该架构对总体 ENTERPRISE 的影响。

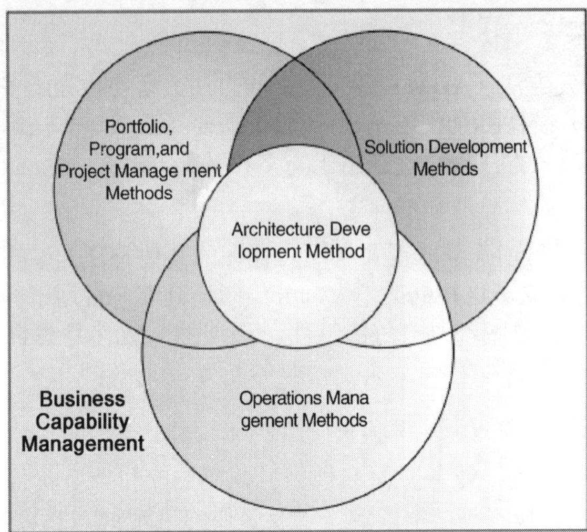

Figure 6-2 Management Frameworks to Co-ordinate with TOGAF

The Preliminary Phase therefore involves doing any necessary work to adapt the ADM to define an organization-specific framework, using either the TOGAF deliverables or the deliverables of another framework. The issues involved in this are discussed in Section 5.3.

6.2.6 Relating the Management Frameworks

Figure 6-3 illustrates a more detailed set of dependencies between the various frameworks and business planning activity that incorporates the enterprise's strategic plan and direction. The enterprise architecture can be used to provide a structure for all of the corporate initiatives, the Portfolio Management Framework can be used to deliver the components of the architecture, and the Operations Management Framework supports incorporation of these new components within the corporate infrastructure.

The business planners are present throughout the process and are in a position to support and enforce the architecture by retaining approval for resources at the various stages of planning and development.

The solution development methodology is used within the Portfolio Management Framework to plan, create, and deliver the architectural components specified in the portfolio and project charters. These deliverables include, but are not exclusively, IT; for example, a new building, a new set of skills, production equipment, hiring, marketing, and so on. Enterprise architecture potentially provides the context for all enterprise activities.

The management frameworks are required to complement each other and work in close harmony for the good of the enterprise.

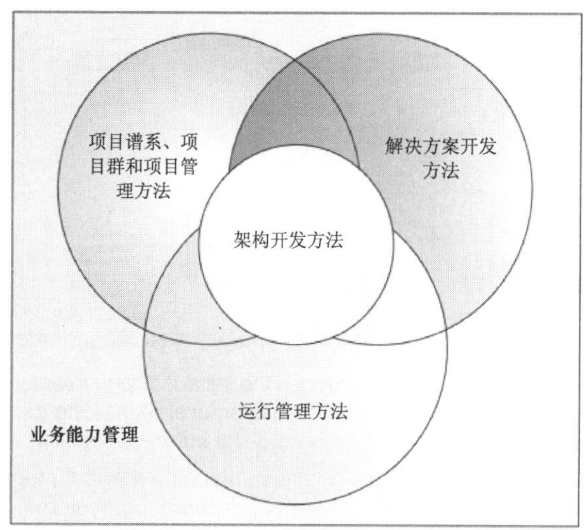

图 6-2　与 TOGAF 相协调的管理框架

因此，预备阶段涉及为使 ADM 适于定义一个组织特有的框架而执行的所有必要的工作，并使用 TOGAF 交付物或另一个框架的交付物。5.3 节已论述涉及这一方面的议题。

6.2.6　使管理框架相关联

图 6-3 阐明各种不同框架和纳入 ENTERPRISE 战略计划和方向的业务规划活动之间的更详细的依赖关系集合。Enterprise Architecture 用于提供一个针对公司级所有举措的结构，项目谱系管理框架可用于交付该架构的组件，并且运行管理框架支持在公司级基础设施中纳入新的组件。

业务计划者在整个流程中随处可见，通过保留对各种不同的规划和开发阶段资源的批准，支持和执行该架构。

在项目谱系管理框架内使用解决方案开发方法论，以计划、创建和交付项目谱系和项目章程特定的架构组件。这些交付物包含但不限于 IT，如一个新的建筑、一系列新技能、生产设备、招聘和营销等。Enterprise Architecture 可为所有的 ENTERPRISE 活动提供背景环境。

为了 ENTERPRISE 的利益，需要管理框架之间相互补充和紧密和谐地工作。

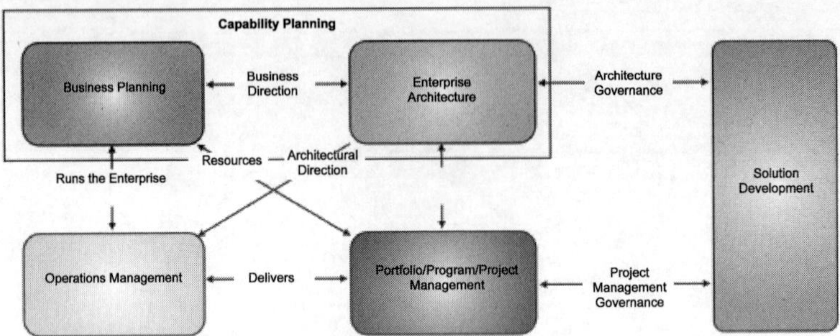

Figure 6-3 Interoperability and Relationships between Management Frameworks

Business planning at the strategy level provides the initial direction to enterprise architecture. Updates at the annual planning level provide a finer level of ongoing guidance. Capability-based Planning is one of many popular techniques for business planning.

Enterprise architecture structures the business planning into an integrated framework that regards the enterprise as a system or system of systems. This integrated approach will validate the business plan and can provide valuable feedback to the corporate planners. In some organizations, the enterprise architects have been moved to or work very closely with the strategic direction groups. TOGAF delivers a framework for enterprise architecture.

Portfolio/project management is the delivery framework that receives the structured, detailed direction that enables them to plan and build what is required, knowing that each assigned deliverable will be in context (i.e., the piece of the puzzle that they deliver will fit into the corporate puzzle that is the enterprise architecture). Often this framework is based upon the Project Management Institute or UK Office of Government Commerce (PRINCE2) project management methodologies. Project architectures and detailed out-of-context design are often based upon systems design methodologies.

Operations management receives the deliverables and then integrates and sustains them within the corporate infrastructure. Often the IT service management services are based upon ISO20000 or BS15000 (ITIL).

6.2.7 Planning for Enterprise Architecture/Business Change Maturity Evaluation

Capability Maturity Models (detailed in Part VII, Chapter 51) are useful ways of assessing the ability of an enterprise to exercise different capabilities.

Capability Maturity Models typically identify selected factors that are required to exercise a capability. An organization's ability to execute specific factors provides a measure of maturity and can be used to recommend a series of sequential steps to improve a capability. It is an assessment that gives executives an insight into pragmatically improving a capability.

A good enterprise architecture maturity model covers the characteristics necessary to develop and consume enterprise architecture. Organizations can determine their own factors and derive the appropriate maturity models, but it is recommended to take an existing model and customize it as required.

Several good models exist, including NASCIO, and the US Department of Commerce Architecture Capability Maturity Model.

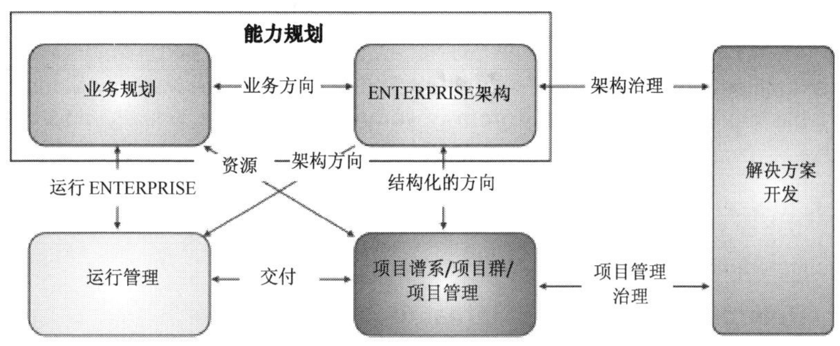

图 6-3 管理框架之间的互用性和关系

战略层级的业务规划为 Enterprise Architecture 提供初始方向。年度规划层级的更新提供一个更细层级的持续的引导。基于能力的规划是众多流行的业务规划方法之一。

Enterprise Architecture 将业务规划结构化为一个视 ENTERPRISE 为系统或系统之系统的综合框架。此综合途径会确认业务计划并向公司级计划者提供有价值的反馈。在一些组织中，ENTERPRISE 架构师已经被调动到战略指导组，或与战略指导群组开展紧密合作。TOGAF 交付 Enterprise Architecture 框架。

项目谱系/项目管理是获得结构化和具有细节指导的一种交付框架，使得架构师能够计划和构建所需要的内容，了解每个指派的交付物所处的背景环境（即，架构师交付的这部分框架将会与作为 Enterprise Architecture 的公司级框架适配）。通常这种框架基于美国项目管理协会或英国政府商务办公室（PRINCE2）的项目管理方法论。项目架构和合详细的脱离背景环境的设计通常基于系统设计方法论。

运行管理获得交付物后，将这些交付物在公司级基础设施内集成和维护。IT 服务管理服务通常基于 ISO20000 或 BS15000（ITIL）。

6.2.7 Enterprise Architecture/业务变革成熟度评估规划

能力成熟度模型（在第七部分第 51 章中详细说明）是评估 ENTERPRISE 训练不同能力的有效方式。

能力成熟度模型通常识别需要训练一种能力的选定因素。组织执行特定要素的能力提供对成熟度的测量并能够用来建议一系列改进能力的顺序步骤。这个评估使高层管理者深度透视实用改进一种能力。

一个良好的 Enterprise Architecture 成熟度模型涵盖开发和使用 Enterprise Architecture 所必要的特征。组织能够确定其特有的因素并得到适当的成熟度模型，但是建议采取现有模型并按用户要求进行定制化。

有许多好的模型，包括 NASCIO 以及美国商务部架构能力成熟度模型。

The use of Capability Maturity Models is detailed in Part VII, Chapter 51.

Other examples include the US Federal Enterprise Architecture Maturity Model. Even though the models are originally from government, they are equally applicable to industry.

6.3 Inputs

This section defines the inputs to the Preliminary Phase.

6.3.1 Reference Materials External to the Enterprise

- TOGAF
- Other architecture framework(s), if required

6.3.2 Non-Architectural Inputs

- Board strategies and board business plans, business strategy, IT strategy, business principles, business goals, and business drivers, when pre-existing
- Major frameworks operating in the business; e.g., portfolio/project management
- Governance and legal frameworks, including architecture governance strategy, when pre-existing
- Architecture capability
- Partnership and contract agreements

6.3.3 Architectural Inputs

Pre-existing models for operating an enterprise Architecture Capability can be used as a baseline for the Preliminary Phase. Inputs would include:

- Organizational Model for Enterprise Architecture (see Part IV, Section 36.2.16), including:
  - Scope of organizations impacted
  - Maturity assessment, gaps, and resolution approach
  - Roles and responsibilities for architecture team(s)
  - Budget requirements
  - Governance and support strategy
- Existing Architecture Framework, if any, including:
  - Architecture method
  - Architecture content
  - Configured and deployed tools

在第七章第 51 节中，详细说明能力成熟度模型的使用。

其他示例包括美国联邦政府 Enterprise Architecture 成熟度模型。尽管这些模型最初来源于政府，但是它们同样适用于工业界。

6.3 输入

本节定义对预备阶段的输入。

6.3.1 ENTERPRISE 的外部参考资料

- TOGAF
- 其他架构框架（若需要）

6.3.2 非架构输入

- 委员会战略和委员会业务计划、业务战略、IT 战略、业务原则、业务目标和业务驱动因素（当预先存在时）
- 业务中运行的主要框架；例如，项目谱系/项目管理
- 治理和法律框架，包括架构治理战略（当预先存在时）
- 架构能力
- 合作和承包协议

6.3.3 架构输入

预先存在的用于运行 ENTERPRISE 的架构能力的模型，其可被用作预备阶段的基线。输入将包括：

- Enterprise Architecture 的组织模型（见第四部分 36.2.16 节），包括：
  - 受影响的组织的范围
  - 成熟度评估、差距和解决途径
  - 架构团队的角色和职责
  - 预算需求
  - 治理和支持战略
- 现有的架构框架（如果有），包括：
  - 架构方法
  - 架构内容
  - 经配置和部署的工具

— Architecture Principles
— Architecture Repository

6.4 Steps

The TOGAF ADM is a generic method, intended to be used by a wide variety of different enterprises, and in conjunction with a wide variety of other architecture frameworks, if required. The Preliminary Phase therefore involves doing any necessary work to initiate and adapt the ADM to define an organization-specific framework. The issues involved with adapting the ADM to a specific organizational context are discussed in detail in Section 5.3.

The level of detail addressed in the Preliminary Phase will depend on the scope and goals of the overall architecture effort.

The order of the steps in the Preliminary Phase (see below) as well as the time at which they are formally started and completed should be adapted to the situation at hand in accordance with the established architecture governance.

The steps within the Preliminary Phase are as follows:

- Scope the enterprise organizations impacted (see Section 6.4.1)
- Confirm governance and support frameworks (see Section 6.4.2)
- Define and establish enterprise architecture team and organization (see Section 6.4.3)
- Identify and establish architecture principles (see Section 6.4.4)
- Tailor TOGAF and, if any, other selected Architecture Frameworks (see Section 6.4.5)
- Implement architecture tools (see Section 6.4.6)

6.4.1 Scope the Enterprise Organizations Impacted

- Identify core enterprise (units) — those who are most affected and achieve most value from the work
- Identify soft enterprise (units) — those who will see change to their capability and work with core units but are otherwise not directly affected
- Identify extended enterprise (units) — those units outside the scoped enterprise who will be affected in their own enterprise architecture
- Identify communities involved (enterprises) — those stakeholders who will be affected and who are in groups of communities
- Identify governance involved, including legal frameworks and geographies (enterprises)

— 架构原则

— 架构存储库

6.4 步骤

TOGAF ADM 是一个通用方法，旨在用于各种不同的 ENTERPRISE，并与各种其他架构框架结合（如果需要）。因此，预备阶段包括为启动并使 ADM 的适应性调整于定义一个组织特有的框架而执行的所有必要的工作。该议题涉及按特定的组织背景环境调整 ADM，将在 5.3 节中详细论述。

预备阶段所划分的细节层级将取决于总体架构工作的范围和目标。

预备阶段中的步骤顺序（见下文）和这些步骤正式开始与完成的时间应按已建立的架构治理来适应当前情况。

预备阶段中的步骤如下：

- 界定受影响的 ENTERPRISE 组织的范围（见 6.4.1 节）
- 确认治理和支持框架（见 6.4.2 节）
- 定义并建立 Enterprise Architecture 团队和组织（见 6.4.3 节）
- 识别和建立架构原则（见 6.4.4 节）
- 剪裁 TOGAF 以及其他选定的架构框架（如果有）（见 6.4.5 节）
- 实施架构工具（见 6.4.6 节）

6.4.1 界定受影响的 ENTERPRISE 组织的范围

- 识别核心 ENTERPRISE（单元）——那些受该工作影响最大并从该工作得到最大价值的
- 识别“软”ENTERPRISE（单元）——那些将会看到对其能力的改变并与核心单元合作但不直接受到影响的
- 识别扩展 ENTERPRISE（单元）——那些在界定的 ENTERPRISE 范围外、受其自身 Enterprise Architecture 影响的
- 识别涉及的团体（ENTERPRISE）——那些会受到影响并属于团体群组成员的利益攸关者
- 识别涉及的治理，包括法律框架和地理范围（ENTERPRISE）

6.4.2 Confirm Governance and Support Frameworks

The architecture framework will form the keystone to the flavor (centralized or federated, light or heavy, etc.) of architecture governance organization and guidelines that need to be developed. Part of the major output of this phase is a framework for architecture governance. We need to understand how architectural material (standards, guidelines, models, compliance reports, etc.) is brought under governance; i.e., what type of governance repository characteristics are going to be required, what relationships and status recording are necessary to ascertain which governance process (dispensation, compliance, take-on, retirement, etc.) has ownership of an architectural artifact.

It is likely that the existing governance and support models of an organization will need to change to support the newly adopted architecture framework.

To manage the organizational change required to adopt the new architectural framework, the current enterprise governance and support models will need to be assessed to understand their overall shape and content. Additionally, the sponsors and stakeholders for architecture will need to be consulted on potential impacts that could occur.

Upon completion of this step, the architecture touch-points and likely impacts should be understood and agreed by relevant stakeholders.

6.4.3 Define and Establish Enterprise Architecture Team and Organization

- Determine existing enterprise and business capability
- Conduct an enterprise architecture/business change maturity assessment, if required
- Identify gaps in existing work areas
- Allocate key roles and responsibilities for enterprise Architecture Capability management and governance
- Define requests for change to existing business programs and projects:
  - Inform existing enterprise architecture and IT architecture work of stakeholder requirements
  - Request assessment of impact on their plans and work
  - Identify common areas of interest
  - Identify any critical differences and conflicts of interest
  - Produce requests for change to stakeholder activities
- Determine constraints on enterprise architecture work
- Review and agree with sponsors and board
- Assess budget requirements

6.4.2 确认治理和支持框架

架构框架会构成需要开发的架构治理组织和指南的特色（集中的或联邦的，轻的或重的等）的“拱心石”。本阶段主要输出的部分是架构治理的框架。我们需要理解架构资料（标准、指南、模型、合规报告等）如何得到治理，即，将需要什么类型的治理存储库特征，什么关系和状态记录对于确定哪种治理流程（分配、合规、采用、退役等）具有架构制品所有权是十分必要的。

组织的现有治理和支持模型，为支持新采用的架构框架很可能将会需要改变。

为采纳新的架构框架而管理所需的组织变革，就需要对当前 ENTERPRISE 的治理和支持模型进行评估以理解这些模型的总体形态和内容。另外，对于有可能出现的潜在影响需要与架构发起人和利益攸关者商议。

一旦完成本步骤，相关的利益攸关者应理解和接受架构结合点和可能的影响。

6.4.3 定义并建立 Enterprise Architecture 团队和组织

- 确定现有 ENTERPRISE 和业务能力
- 如果需要，进行 Enterprise Architecture/业务变革成熟度评价
- 识别现有工作领域中的差距
- 为 ENTERPRISE 的架构能力管理和治理分配关键角色和责任
- 定义现有业务项目群和项目的变更要求：
  - 向现有 Enterprise Architecture 和 IT 架构工作通告利益攸关者的需求
  - 要求对其计划和工作的影响进行评估
  - 识别所关注的共用领域
  - 识别所关注的所有关键差异和冲突
  - 生成利益攸关者活动的变更要求
- 确定 Enterprise Architecture 工作的约束
- 审视并与发起人和委员会达成一致
- 评估预算需求

6.4.4 Identify and Establish Architecture Principles

Architecture Principles (see Part III, Chapter 23) are based on business principles and are critical in setting the foundation for architecture governance. Once the organizational context is understood, define a set of Architecture Principles that is appropriate to the enterprise.

6.4.5 Tailor TOGAF and, if Any, Other Selected Architecture Framework(s)

In this step, determine what tailoring of TOGAF is required. Consider the need for:

- **Terminology Tailoring**: Architecture practitioners should use terminology that is generally understood across the enterprise. Tailoring should produce an agreed terminology set for description of architectural content.
- **Process Tailoring**: The TOGAF ADM provides a generic process for carrying out architecture. Process tailoring provides the opportunity to remove tasks that are already carried out elsewhere in the organization, add organization-specific tasks (such as specific checkpoints) and to align the ADM processes to external process frameworks and touch-points. Key touch-points to be addressed would include:
    - Links to (project and service) portfolio management processes
    - Links to project lifecycle
    - Links to operations handover processes
    - Links to operational management processes (including configuration management, change management, and service management)
    - Links to procurement processes
- **Content Tailoring**: Using the TOGAF Architecture Content Framework and Enterprise Continuum as a basis, tailoring of content structure and classification approach allows adoption of third-party content frameworks and also allows for customization of the framework to support organization-specific requirements.

6.4.6 Implement Architecture Tools

The level of formality used to define and manage architecture content will be highly dependent on the scale, sophistication, and culture of the architecture function within the organization. With an understanding of the desired approach to architecture, it is possible to select appropriate architecture tools to underpin the architecture function.

The approach to tools may be based on relatively informal usage of standard office productivity applications, or may be based on a customized deployment of specialist architecture tools. Depending on the level of sophistication, the implementation of tools may range from a trivial task to a more involved system implementation activity.

Issues in tools standardization are discussed in Part V, Chapter 42.

6.4.4 识别和建立架构原则

架构原则（见第三部分，第 23 章）基于业务原则，且对建立架构治理基础极其关键。一旦理解了组织的背景环境，就可以定义一系列适合 ENTERPRISE 的架构原则。

6.4.5 剪裁 TOGAF 以及其他选定的架构框架（如果有）

在这一步骤中，确定需要什么样的 TOGAF。考虑需要何种剪裁：

- 术语剪裁：架构实践者应使用在整个 ENTERPRISE 内被普遍理解的术语。剪裁应产生一套共同约定的术语集合，用于描述架构内容。
- 流程剪裁：TOGAF ADM 提供用于实施架构的通用流程。在对删除已经在组织其他地方执行过的任务、增加组织特定任务（如特定检查点）以及使 ADM 流程与外部流程框架和结合点相一致等方法，流程剪裁均为此提供机会。需要应对的关键结合点将包括：
  - 与（项目和服务）项目谱系管理流程的联系
  - 与项目生命周期的联系
  - 与运行工作交接流程的联系
  - 与运行管理流程（包括配置管理、变更管理和服务管理）的联系
  - 与采购流程的联系
- 内容剪裁：以 TOGAF 架构内容框架和 ENTERPRISE 的连续统一体作为基础，内容结构和分类方法的剪裁允许采纳第三方的内容框架，并允许对该框架进行定制化以支持组织特定的需求。

6.4.6 实施架构的工具

用于定义和管理架构内容的正规程度将高度依赖于组织内部架构功能的规模、复杂性和文化。理解期望的架构实施途径，就可能选择适当的架构工具来支撑架构功能。

工具的使用途径可能以标准办公效率应用的相对非正式使用作为基础，或以专家架构工具的定制化部署作为基础。依靠复杂程度，工具实施范围可从一个细小的任务到一个更复杂的系统实施活动。

在第五部分第 42 章中论述了工具标准化议题。

6.5 Outputs

The outputs of the Preliminary Phase may include, but are not restricted to:

- Organizational Model for Enterprise Architecture (see Part IV, Section 36.2.16), including:
  - Scope of organizations impacted
  - Maturity assessment, gaps, and resolution approach
  - Roles and responsibilities for architecture team(s)
  - Constraints on architecture work
  - Budget requirements
  - Governance and support strategy
- Tailored Architecture Framework (see Part IV, Section 36.2.21), including:
  - Tailored architecture method
  - Tailored architecture content (deliverables and artifacts)
  - Architecture Principles (see Part IV, Section 36.2.4)
  - Configured and deployed tools
- Initial Architecture Repository (see Part IV, Section 36.2.5), populated with framework content
- Restatement of, or reference to, business principles, business goals, and business drivers(see Part IV, Section 36.2.9)
- Request for Architecture Work (optional) (see Part IV, Section 36.2.17)
- Architecture Governance Framework (see (Part VII, Section 50.2) The outputs may include some or all of the following:
- Catalogs:
  - Principles catalog

6.5 输出

预备阶段的输出可包括但不限于：

- Enterprise Architecture 的组织模型（见第四部分 36.2.16 节），包括：
  - 受影响的组织的范围
  - 成熟度评估、差距和解决途径
  - 架构团队的角色和职责
  - 对架构工作的约束
  - 预算需求
  - 治理和支持战略
- 经剪裁的架构框架（见第四部分 36.2.21 节），包括：
  - 经剪裁的架构方法
  - 经剪裁的架构内容（交付物和制品）
  - 架构原则（见第四部分 36.2.4 节）
  - 经配置和部署的工具
- 用框架内容充实的初始架构存储库（见第四部分 36.2.5 节）
- 对业务原则、业务目标和业务驱动因素（见第四部分 36.2.9 节）的重新申明或重新引用
- 架构工作要求书（可选）（见第四部分 36.2.17 节）
- 架构治理框架（见第七部分 50.2 节）

输出可包括下列内容中的部分或全部内容：

- 目录：
  - 原则目录

Chapter 7
Phase A: Architecture Vision

This chapter describes the initial phase of the Architecture Development Method (ADM). It includes information about defining the scope, identifying the stakeholders, creating the Architecture Vision, and obtaining approvals.

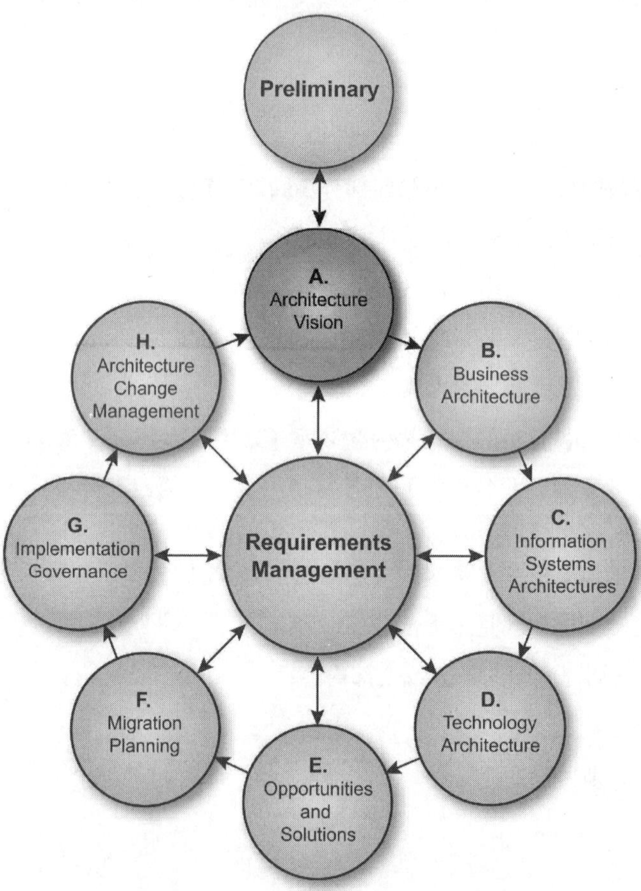

Figure 7-1 Phase A: Architecture Vision

第 7 章
阶段 A：架构愿景

本章描述架构开发方法（ADM）的初始阶段。它包括关于定义范围、识别利益攸关者、创建架构愿景和获得批准的信息。

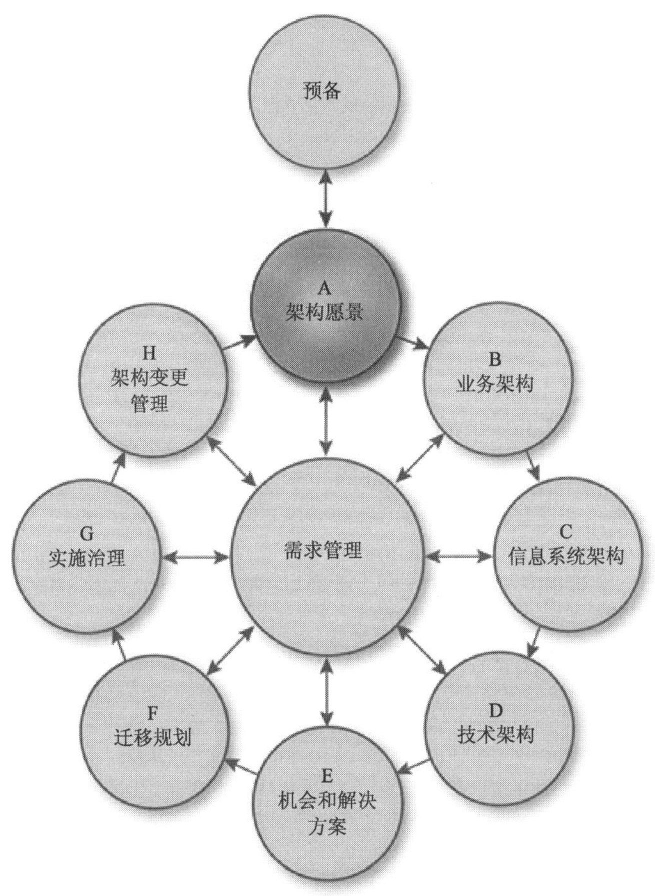

图 7-1　阶段 A：架构愿景

7.1 Objectives

The objectives of Phase A are to:

- Develop a high-level aspirational vision of the capabilities and business value to be delivered as a result of the proposed enterprise architecture.
- Obtain approval for a Statement of Architecture Work that defines a program of works to develop and deploy the architecture outlined in the Architecture Vision.

7.2 Approach

7.2.1 General

Phase A starts with receipt of a Request for Architecture Work from the sponsoring organization to the architecture organization.

The issues involved in ensuring proper recognition and endorsement from corporate management, and the support and commitment of line management, are discussed in Part VII, Section 50.1.4.

Phase A also defines what is in and what is outside the scope of the architecture effort and the constraints that must be dealt with. Scoping decisions need to be made on the basis of a practical assessment of resource and competence availability, and the value that can realistically be expected to accrue to the enterprise from the chosen scope of architecture work. The issues involved in this are discussed in Section 5.5. Scoping issues addressed in the Architecture Vision phase will be restricted to the specific objectives for this ADM cycle and will be constrained within the overall scope definition for architecture activity as established within the Preliminary Phase and embodied within the architecture framework.

In situations where the architecture framework in place is not appropriate to achieve the desired Architecture Vision, revisit the Preliminary Phase and extend the overall architecture framework for the enterprise.

The constraints will normally be informed by the business principles and Architecture Principles, developed as part of the Preliminary Phase (see Chapter 6).

Normally, the business principles, business goals, and strategic drivers of the organization are already defined elsewhere in the enterprise. If so, the activity in Phase A is involved with ensuring that existing definitions are current, and clarifying any areas of ambiguity. Otherwise, it involves defining these essential items for the first time.

Similarly, the Architecture Principles that form part of the constraints on architecture work will normally have been defined in the Preliminary Phase (see Chapter 6). The activity in Phase A is concerned with ensuring that the existing principles definitions are current, and clarifying any areas of ambiguity. Otherwise, it entails defining the Architecture Principles for the first time, as explained in Part III, Chapter 23.

7.1 目的

阶段 A 的目的是：

- 开发待交付的能力和业务价值的高层级强烈渴望的愿景，作为所建议的 Enterprise Architecture 的结果。
- 获得对定义工作计划的架构工作说明书的批准，以开发和部署在架构愿景中概述的架构。

7.2 实施途径

7.2.1 概述

阶段 A 开始于架构组织从发起组织接收到架构工作要求书。

在第七部分 50.1.4 节中，论述了涉及确保公司级管理层的适当认可和担保，以及各级管理层的支持和承诺的议题。

阶段 A 还规定了什么是在架构工作的范围内，什么是在架构工作的范围外以及必须应对的约束。需要基于对资源和能力可用性的实际评估以及根据选定的架构工作范围实际期望累积形成 ENTERPRISE 的价值来做出界定范围的决策。5.5 节论述了涉及这一方面的议题。在架构愿景阶段所应对的界定范围议题将被限于本轮 ADM 周期的特定目的之内，并且限制在建立初始阶段内和体现在架构框架内的架构活动定义的总体范围之内。

在架构框架不适于达成所期望的架构愿景的情况下，重新回顾预备阶段并扩展该 ENTERPRISE 的总体架构框架。

约束通常将以预备阶段（见第 6 章）部分开发的业务原则和架构原则为其依据。

通常，已在 ENTERPRISE 中其他地方定义了组织业务原则、业务目标以及战略驱动因素。如此一来，阶段 A 中的活动涉及确保现有定义现行有效并明晰任何含糊不清的地方。否则，就涉及首次定义这些重要的内容项。

同样地，通常在预备阶段对构成架构工作约束部分的架构原则已经进行了定义（见第 6 章）。阶段 A 中的活动关注于确保现有原则定义现行有效并明晰任何含糊不清的地方。否则，按照第三部分第 23 章的解释，就需要首次定义架构原则。

7.2.2 Creating the Architecture Vision

The Architecture Vision provides the sponsor with a key tool to sell the benefits of the proposed capability to stakeholders and decision-makers within the enterprise. Architecture Vision describes how the new capability will meet the business goals and strategic objectives and address the stakeholder concerns when implemented.

Clarifying and agreeing the purpose of the architecture effort is one of the key parts of this activity, and the purpose needs to be clearly reflected in the vision that is created. Architecture projects are often undertaken with a specific purpose in mind — a specific set of business drivers that represent the return on investment for the stakeholders in the architecture development. Clarifying that purpose, and demonstrating how it will be achieved by the proposed architecture development, is the whole point of the Architecture Vision.

Normally, key elements of the Architecture Vision — such as the enterprise mission, vision, strategy, and goals — have been documented as part of some wider business strategy or enterprise planning activity that has its own lifecycle within the enterprise. In such cases, the activity in Phase A is concerned with verifying and understanding the documented business strategy and goals, and possibly bridging between the enterprise strategy and goals on the one hand, and the strategy and goals implicit within the current architecture reality.

In other cases, little or no Business Architecture work may have been done to date. In such cases, there will be a need for the architecture team to research, verify, and gain buy-in to the key business objectives and processes that the architecture is to support. This may be done as a free-standing exercise, either preceding architecture development, or as part of the ADM initiation phase (Preliminary Phase).

The Architecture Vision provides a first-cut, high-level description of the Baseline and Target Architectures, covering the business, data, application, and technology domains. These outline descriptions are developed in subsequent phases.

Business scenarios are an appropriate and useful technique to discover and document business requirements, and to articulate an Architecture Vision that responds to those requirements. Business scenarios are described in Part III, Chapter 26.

Once an Architecture Vision is defined and documented in the Statement of Architecture Work, it is critical to use it to build a consensus, as described in Part VII, Section 50.1.4. Without this consensus it is very unlikely that the final architecture will be accepted by the organization as a whole. The consensus is represented by the sponsoring organization signing the Statement of Architecture Work.

7.2.3 Business Scenarios

The ADM has its own method (a "method-within-a-method") for identifying and articulating the business requirements implied in new business capability to address key business drivers, and the implied architecture requirements. This process is known as "business scenarios", and is described in Part III, Chapter 26. The technique may be used iteratively, at different levels of detail in the hierarchical decomposition of the Business Architecture.

7.2.2 创建架构愿景

架构愿景为发起人提供一个关键工具，以向 ENTERPRISE 内的利益攸关者和决策者举荐所提供能力的益处。架构愿景描述新能力将如何满足业务目标和战略目的，以及在实施时如何应对利益攸关者关注点。

明晰和商议架构工作的目的是本活动的关键部分之一，并且需要在创建的愿景中清晰地反映该目的。通常按照考虑的特定目的承担架构项目——一系列表示利益攸关者在架构开发过程中的投资回报的特定业务驱动因素。明晰该目的，并表明如何通过所推荐的架构开发达成这个目的，是架构愿景的重点。

通常，架构愿景的关键元素——诸如 ENTERPRISE 的使命、愿景、战略和目标——已被记录为 ENTERPRISE 内具有自身生命周期的一些更广泛的业务战略或 ENTERPRISE 规划活动的部分。在这种情况下，阶段 A 中的活动关注验证和理解已文件化的业务战略和目标，并且在另一方面，可能还关注在 ENTERPRISE 战略和目标与当前架构现实中隐含的战略和目标之间搭建桥梁。

在其他情况下，到目前为止，可能几乎没有开展业务架构工作。在这种情况下，架构团队需要对架构要支持的关键业务目的和流程进行研究、验证和使其获得认同。这可能被作为一次独立的训练来执行，或者在架构开发之前或者作为 ADM 起始阶段（预备阶段）的一部分。

架构愿景提供基线架构和目标架构的初步的高层级描述，涵盖业务域、数据域、应用域和技术域。这些概要描述在后续阶段开发。

业务场景是一种用以发现和记录业务需求并清楚地表述响应那些需求的架构愿景的合适且有用的技巧。业务场景在第三部分第 26 章中描述。

一旦在架构工作说明书中定义和文件化架构愿景，那么关键的是使用该架构愿景构建共识，如第七部分 50.1.4 节所述。如果未达成共识，那么总体而言，组织不太可能接受最终架构。由发起组织签订架构工作说明书来表达共识。

7.2.3 业务场景

ADM 具有其自身的、用于识别和清楚表述隐含在涉及关键业务驱动因素的新业务能力中和隐含着架构需求的业务需求的方法（一个“方法中的方法”）驱动因素。这种流程被称为“业务场景”，在第三部分第 26 章中描述。该技巧可在业务架构层级结构分解中的不同细节层级上迭代使用。

7.3 Inputs

This section defines the inputs to Phase A.

7.3.1 Reference Materials External to the Enterprise

- Architecture reference materials (see Part IV, Section 36.2.5)

7.3.2 Non-Architectural Inputs

- Request for Architecture Work (see Part IV, Section 36.2.17)
- Business principles, business goals, and business drivers (see Part IV, Section 36.2.9)

7.3.3 Architectural Inputs

- Organizational Model for Enterprise Architecture (see Part IV, Section 36.2.16), including:
  - Scope of organizations impacted
  - Maturity assessment, gaps, and resolution approach
  - Roles and responsibilities for architecture team(s)
  - Constraints on architecture work
  - Re-use requirements
  - Budget requirements
  - Requests for change
  - Governance and support strategy
- Tailored Architecture Framework (see Part IV, Section 36.2.21), including:
  - Tailored architecture method
  - Tailored architecture content (deliverables and artifacts)
  - Architecture principles (see Part IV, Section 36.2.4), including business principles, when pre-existing
  - Configured and deployed tools
- Populated Architecture Repository (see Part IV, Section 36.2.5) — existing architectural documentation (framework description, architectural descriptions, baseline descriptions, ABBs, etc.)

7.3 输入

本节定义了对阶段A的输入。

7.3.1 ENTERPRISE 外部的参考资料

- 架构参考资料（见第四部分36.2.5节）

7.3.2 非架构输入

- 架构工作要求书（见第四部分36.2.17节）
- 业务原则、业务目标和业务驱动因素（见第四部分36.2.9节）

7.3.3 架构输入

- Enterprise Architecture 的组织模型（见第四章36.2.16节），包括：
  - 受影响的组织的范围
  - 成熟度评估、差距和解决途径
  - 架构团队的角色和职责
  - 对架构工作的约束
  - 复用需求
  - 预算需求
  - 变更要求
  - 治理和支持战略
- 经剪裁的架构框架（见第四部分36.2.21节），包括：
  - 经剪裁的架构方法
  - 经剪裁的架构内容（交付物和制品）
  - 架构原则（见第四部分36.2.4节），包括业务原则（当之前存在时）
  - 经配置和部署的工具
- 经充实的架构存储库（见第四部分 36.2.5 节）——现有架构文档（框架描述、架构说明、基线描述、ABB等）

7.4 Steps

The level of detail addressed in Phase A will depend on the scope and goals of the Request for Architecture Work, or the subset of scope and goals associated with this iteration of architecture development.

The order of the steps in Phase A (see below) as well as the time at which they are formally started and completed should be adapted to the situation at hand in accordance with the established architecture governance.

The steps in Phase A are as follows:

- Establish the architecture project (see Section 7.4.1)
- Identify stakeholders, concerns, and business requirements (see Section 7.4.2)
- Confirm and elaborate business goals, business drivers, and constraints (see Section7.4.3)
- Evaluate business capabilities (see Section 7.4.4)
- Assess readiness for business transformation (see Section 7.4.5)
- Define scope (see Section 7.4.6)
- Confirm and elaborate Architecture Principles, including business principles (see Section7.4.7)
- Develop Architecture Vision (see Section 7.4.8)
- Define the Target Architecture value propositions and KPIs (see Section 7.4.9)
- Identify the business transformation risks and mitigation activities (see Section 7.4.10)
- Develop Statement of Architecture Work; secure approval (see Section 7.4.11)

7.4.1 Establish the Architecture Project

Execution of ADM cycles should be conducted within the project management framework of the enterprise. In some cases, architecture projects will be stand-alone. In other cases, architectural activities will be a subset of the activities within a larger project. In either case, architecture activity should be planned and managed using accepted practices for the enterprise.

Conduct the necessary procedures to secure recognition of the project, the endorsement of corporate management, and the support and commitment of the necessary line management. Include references to other management frameworks in use within the enterprise, explaining how this project relates to those frameworks.

7.4.2 Identify Stakeholders, Concerns, and Business Requirements

Identify the key stakeholders and their concerns/objectives, and define the key business requirements to be addressed in the architecture engagement. Stakeholder engagement at this stage is intended to accomplish three objectives:

- To identify candidate vision components and requirements to be tested as the ArchitectureVision is developed
- To identify candidate scope boundaries for the engagement to limit the extent of architectural investigation required

7.4 步骤

阶段 A 中所划分的细节层级取决于架构工作要求书的范围和目标，或者与架构开发本轮迭代相关的范围和目标的子集。

阶段 A 中的步骤顺序（见下文）和这些步骤正式开始和完成的时间应按已建立的架构治理来适应当前情况。

阶段 A 中的步骤如下：

- 建立架构项目（见 7.4.1 节）
- 识别利益攸关者、关注点和业务需求（见 7.4.2 节）
- 确认和详细阐述业务目标、业务驱动因素和约束（见 7.4.3 节）
- 评价业务能力（见 7.4.4 节）
- 评估业务转型准备度情况（见 7.4.5 节）
- 定义范围（见 7.4.6 节）
- 确认和详细阐述架构原则，包括业务原则（见 7.4.7 节）
- 开发架构愿景（见 7.4.8 节）
- 定义目标架构价值主张和 KPI（见 7.4.9 节）
- 识别业务转型风险和缓解活动（见 7.4.10 节）
- 开发架构工作说明书；确保批准（见 7.4.11 节）

7.4.1 建立架构项目

ADM 周期的执行应在 ENTERPRISE 的项目管理框架内进行。在某些情况下，架构项目会是独立的存在。在其他情况下，架构活动会是大型项目中活动的子集。不论哪种情况，均应使用已接受的 ENTERPRISE 实践对架构活动进行计划和管理。

执行必要的程序以确保对项目的认可、公司级管理层赞同和必要的一线管理层的支持和承诺。将使用中的其他管理框架的参考文献包括在 ENTERPRISE 范围内，解释本项目是如何与那些框架相关联的。

7.4.2 识别利益攸关者、关注点和业务需求

识别关键利益攸关者及其关注点/目的，并定义将在架构工作中所涉及的关键业务需求。本阶段的利益攸关者介入旨在实现三个目的：

- 识别在开发架构愿景时要测试的候选愿景组件和需求
- 识别该工作的候选范围边界以限制所需架构研究的广度

- To identify stakeholder concerns, issues, and cultural factors that will shape how the architecture is presented and communicated

The major product resulting from this step is a stakeholder map for the engagement, showing which stakeholders are involved with the engagement, their level of involvement, and their key concerns (see Part III, Section 24.3 and Section 24.4). The stakeholder map is used to support various outputs of the Architecture Vision phase, and to identify:

- The concerns and viewpoints that are relevant to this project; this is captured in the Architecture Vision (see Part IV, Section 36.2.8)
- The stakeholders that are involved with the project and as a result form the starting point for a Communications Plan (see Part IV, Section 36.2.12)
- The key roles and responsibilities within the project, which should be included within the Statement of Architecture Work (see Part VII, Section 36.2.20)

Another key task will be to consider which architecture views and viewpoints need to be developed to satisfy the various stakeholder requirements. As described in Part III, Chapter 24, understanding at this stage which stakeholders and which views need to be developed is important in setting the scope of the engagement.

During the Architecture Vision phase, new requirements generated for future architecture work within the scope of the selected requirements need to be documented within the Architecture Requirements Specification, and new requirements which are beyond the scope of the selected requirements must be input to the Requirements Repository for management through the Requirements Management process.

7.4.3 Confirm and Elaborate Business Goals, Business Drivers, and Constraints

Identify the business goals and strategic drivers of the organization.

If these have already been defined elsewhere within the enterprise, ensure that the existing definitions are current, and clarify any areas of ambiguity. Otherwise, go back to the originators of the Statement of Architecture Work and work with them to define these essential items and secure their endorsement by corporate management.

Define the constraints that must be dealt with, including enterprise-wide constraints and project-specific constraints (time, schedule, resources, etc.). The enterprise-wide constraints may be informed by the business and Architecture Principles developed in the Preliminary Phase or clarified as part of Phase A.

7.4.4 Evaluate Business Capabilities

It is valuable to understand a collection of capabilities within the enterprise. One part refers to the capability of the enterprise to develop and consume the architecture. The second part refers to the baseline and target capability level of the enterprise.

Gaps identified in the Architecture Capability require iteration between Architecture Vision and Preliminary Phase to ensure that the Architecture Capability is suitable to address the scope of the architecture project (see Part III, Chapter 19).

Gaps, or limitations, identified in the enterprise's capability to execute on change will inform the architect on the description of the Target Architecture and on the Imple-mentation and Migration Plan (see Part IV, Section 36.2.14) created in Phase E and Phase F.

- 识别将会塑形架构被表达和沟通方式的利益攸关者的关注点、议题和文化因素

由本步骤产生的主要产物是利益攸关者介入的映射，表明哪些利益攸关者参与介入、其参与程度以及其关键关注点（见第三部分 24.3 节和 24.4 节）。利益攸关者映射被用于支持架构愿景阶段的各种不同输出，并识别：

- 与该项目相关的关注点和视角；在架构愿景阶段被捕获（见第四部分 36.2.8 节）
- 与该项目有关并由此形成沟通计划起点的利益攸关者（见第四章 36.2.12 节）
- 项目内的关键角色和责任，应包括在架构工作说明书内（见第七部分 36.2.20 节）

另一个关键任务将是考虑需要开发哪些架构视图和视角，用以满足各种利益攸关者需求。如第三部分第 24 章所述，在本阶段理解需要开发哪些利益攸关者和哪些视图对于设定工作范围是重要的。

在架构愿景阶段期间，需在架构需求规范中记录选定需求范围内的未来架构工作产生的新需求，并且，必须在整个需求管理流程中将不在选定需求范围内的新需求输入到用于管理的需求存储库中。

7.4.3 确认和详细阐述业务目标、业务驱动因素和约束

识别组织的业务目标和战略驱动因素。

如果已经在 ENTERPRISE 的其他地方定义了这些业务目的和战略驱动因素，那么确保现有定义是有效的，明晰任何模糊不清的方面。否则，就要追溯到架构工作说明书的发起人并与其合作来定义这些重要项，并确保公司级管理层对这些重要项的赞同。

定义必须处理的约束，包括整个 ENTERPRISE 范围的约束以及项目特定的约束（时间、进度、资源等）。业务和架构原则在预备阶段开发或在阶段 A 某一环节中被予以阐明，为整个 ENTERPRISE 范围的约束提供依据。

7.4.4 评价业务能力

理解 ENTERPRISE 内的能力集合是很有价值的。能力集合的一部分是指 ENTERPRISE 开发架构和使用架构的能力，另一部分是指 ENTERPRISE 的基线能力和目标能力水平。

在架构能力中，确定的差距需要在架构愿景和预备阶段之间迭代，以确保架构能力适于要涉及的架构项目的范围（见第三部分第 19 章）。

在 ENTERPRISE 执行变革的能力中识别出的差距或限制，会作为架构师目标架构描述以及在阶段 E 和阶段 F 中创建的实施和迁移计划的依据（见第四部分 36.2.14 节）。

This step seeks to understand the capabilities and desires of the enterprise at an appropriate level of abstraction (see Chapter 20). Consideration of the gap between the baseline and target capability of the enterprise is critical. Showing the baseline and target capabilities within the context of the overall enterprise can be supported by creating Value Chain diagrams that show the linkage of related capabilities.

The results of the assessment are documented in a Capability Assessment (see Part IV, Section36.2.10).

7.4.5 Assess Readiness for Business Transformation

A Business Transformation Readiness Assessment can be used to evaluate and quantify the organization's readiness to undergo a change. This assessment is based upon the determination and analysis/rating of a series of readiness factors, as described in Chapter 30.

The results of the readiness assessment should be added to the Capability Assessment (see Part IV, Section 36.2.10). These results are then used to shape the scope of the architecture, to identify activities required within the architecture project, and to identify risk areas to be addressed.

7.4.6 Define Scope

Define what is inside and what is outside the scope of the Baseline Architecture and Target Architecture efforts, understanding that the baseline and target need not be described at the same level of detail. In many cases, the Baseline is described at a higher level of abstraction, so more time is available to specify the Target in sufficient detail. The issues involved in this are discussed in Section 5.5. In particular, define:

- The breadth of coverage of the enterprise
- The level of detail required
- The partitioning characteristics of the architecture (see Part V, Chapter 40 for more details)
- The specific architecture domains to be covered (business, data, application, technology)
- The extent of the time period aimed at, plus the number and extent of any intermediate time period
- The architectural assets to be leveraged, or considered for use, from the organization's Enterprise Continuum:
  - Assets created in previous iterations of the ADM cycle within the enter-prise
  - Assets available elsewhere in the industry (other frameworks, systems models, vertical industry models, etc.)

7.4.7 Confirm and Elaborate Architecture Principles, including Business Principles

Review the principles under which the architecture is to be developed. Architecture principles are normally based on the principles developed as part of the Preliminary Phase. They are explained, and an example set given, in Part III, Chapter 23. Ensure that the existing definitions are current, and clarify any areas of ambiguity. Otherwise, go back to the body responsible for architecture governance and work with them to define these essential items for the first time and secure their endorsement by corporate management.

本步骤试图在适当的抽象层级上理解 ENTERPRISE 的能力和愿望（见第 20 章）。考量因素 ENTERPRISE 基线能力与目标能力之间的差距是至关重要的。通过创建表明相关能力联系的价值链图，能够支持呈现总体 ENTERPRISE 的背景环境中的基线和目标能力。

评估的结果记录在能力评估中（见第四部分 36.2.10 节）。

7.4.5　评估业务转型准备度

业务转型准备度评估可用于评价并量化组织对接受变革的准备度。如第 30 章所述，本评估基于一系列准备度因素的确定和分析/评级。

准备度评估的结果应增加到能力评估中（见第四部分 36.2.10 节）。然后，这些结果被用来形成架构的范围，以识别架构项目内所需的活动以及要应对的风险领域。

7.4.6　定义范围

定义什么在基线架构和目标架构范围之内以及什么在范围之外，理解基线和目标不必以相同的细节层级来描述。在许多情况中，在较高的抽象层级上描述基线，因此，更多的时间可以用来足够详细地设定目标。5.5 节论述了涉及这一方面的议题。尤其是定义：

- ENTERPRISE 覆盖范围的广度
- 所需的细节层级
- 架构的划分特征（对于更多详细说明，见第五部分第 40 章）
- 待涵盖的特定架构域（业务、数据、应用、技术）
- 目标对准的时间区间范围，以及任何中间时间区间的数量和范围
- 根据组织的 ENTERPRISE 的连续统一体充分利用或考虑使用的架构资产：
  — ENTERPRISE 内以前的 ADM 周期迭代所创建的资产
  — 行业中其他可用的资产（其他框架、系统模型、垂直行业模型等）

7.4.7　确认和详细阐述架构原则，包括业务原则

审视开发的架构所依据的原则。架构原则通常基于作为预备阶段的部分所开发的原则。第三部分第 23 章解释这些原则并给出示例集。确保现有定义现行有效，并明晰任何模糊不清的方面。否则，就要追溯到负责架构治理的机构并与其合作以首次定义这些重要内容项并获得公司级管理层的赞同。

7.4.8 Develop Architecture Vision

Based on the stakeholder concerns, business capability requirements, scope, constraints, and principles, create a high-level view of the Baseline and Target Architec-tures. The Architecture Vision typically covers the breadth of scope identified for the project, at a high level. Informal techniques are often employed. A common practice is to draw a simple solution concept diagram that illustrates concisely the major components of the solution and how the solution will result in benefit for the enter-prise.

Business scenarios are an appropriate and useful technique to discover and document business requirements, and to articulate an Architecture Vision that responds to those requirements. Business scenarios may also be used at more detailed levels of the architecture work (e.g., in Phase B) and are described in Part III, Chapter 26.

This step generates the first, very high-level definitions of the baseline and target environments, from a business, information systems, and technology perspective, as described in Section 7.5.

These initial versions of the architecture should be stored in the Architecture Repository, organized according to the standards and guidelines established in the architecture framework.

7.4.9 Define the Target Architecture Value Propositions and KPIs

- Develop the business case for the architectures and changes required
- Produce the value proposition for each of the stakeholder groupings
- Assess and define the procurement requirements
- Review and agree the value propositions with the sponsors and stakeholders concerned
- Define the performance metrics and measures to be built into the enterprise architecture to meet the business needs
- Assess the business risk (see Part III, Chapter 31)

The outputs from this activity should be incorporated within the Statement of Architecture Work to allow performance to be tracked accordingly.

7.4.10 Identify the Business Transformation Risks and Mitigation Activities

Identify the risks associated with the Architecture Vision and assess the initial level of risk (e.g., catastrophic, critical, marginal, or negligible) and the potential frequency associated with it. Assign a mitigation strategy for each risk. A risk management framework is described in Part III, Chapter 31.

There are two levels of risk that should be considered, namely:

- **Initial Level of Risk**: Risk categorization prior to determining and implementing mitigating actions
- **Residual Level of Risk**: Risk categorization after implementation of mitigating actions (if any)

Risk mitigation activities should be considered for inclusion within the Statement of Architecture Work.

7.4.8 开发架构愿景

基于利益攸关者的关注、业务能力需求、范围、约束和原则创建一个高层级的基线架构和目标架构的视图。架构愿景通常涵盖已识别的高层级项目的范围的广度，常常采用非正式的技巧。普遍的做法是绘制简单的解决方案概念图，以简要阐明解决方案的主要组件以及该解决方案如何使 ENTERPRISE 受益。

业务场景是一种用以发现和记录业务需求并清楚地表达响应那些需求的架构愿景的恰当且有用的技巧。业务场景也可在更多架构工作（如在阶段 B）的细节层级上使用，并在第三部分第 26 章中描述。

本步骤从业务、信息系统和技术的层面产生第一个非常高层级的基线和目标环境的定义，如 7.5 节所述。

这些架构的初始版本应保存在架构存储库中，根据架构框架中建立的标准和指南进行组织。

7.4.9 定义目标架构价值主张和 KPI

- 开发用于所需架构和变革的业务案例
- 产生每个利益攸关者群组的价值主张
- 评估和定义采购需求
- 审视并与有关发起人和利益攸关者商议价值主张
- 定义为满足业务需要而被构建到 Enterprise Architecture 中的性能衡量标准和测度
- 评估业务风险（参见第三部分第 31 章）

本活动的输出应被纳入到架构工作说明书内，以允许据此跟踪绩效。

7.4.10 识别业务转型风险和缓解活动

识别与架构愿景有关的风险并评估风险的初始等级（如，灾难性的、关键性的、不重要的或可忽略的）以及与之相关联的潜在频率。为每个风险指派一个缓解策略。在第三部分第 31 章描述风险管理框架。

应考虑两个风险等级，即：

- **风险的初始等级**：确定和实施缓解行动前的风险等级
- **风险的残余等级**：实施缓解行动后的风险等级（如果有）

应考虑在架构工作说明书中包含风险缓解活动。

7.4.11 Develop Statement of Architecture Work; Secure Approval

Assess the work products that are required to be produced (and by when) against the set of business performance requirements. This will involve ensuring that:

- Performance metrics are built into the work products.
- Specific performance-related work products are available. Then, activities will include:
  - — Identify new work products that will need to be changed
  - — Provide direction on which existing work products, including building blocks, will need to be changed and ensure that all activities and dependencies on these are co-ordinated
  - — Identify the impact of change on other work products and dependence on their activities
  - — Based on the purpose, focus, scope, and constraints, determine which architecture domains should be developed, to what level of detail, and which architecture views should be built
  - — Assess the resource requirements and availability to perform the work in the timescale required; this will include adhering to the organization's planning methods and work products to produce the plans for performing a cycle of the ADM
  - — Estimate the resources needed, develop a roadmap and schedule for the proposed development, and document all these in the Statement of Architec-ture Work
  - — Define the performance metrics to be met during this cycle of the ADM by the enterprise architecture team
  - — Develop the specific enterprise architecture Communications Plan and show where, how, and when the enterprise architects will communicate with the stakeholders, including affinity groupings and communities, about the progress of the enterprise architecture developments
  - — Review and agree the plans with the sponsors, and secure formal approval of the Statement of Architecture Work under the appropriate governance procedures
  - — Gain sponsor's sign-off to proceed

7.5 Outputs

The outputs of Phase A may include, but are not restricted to:

- Approved Statement of Architecture Work (see Part IV, Section 36.2.20), including in particular:
  - — Architecture project description and scope
  - — Overview of Architecture Vision
  - — Architecture project plan and schedule
- Refined statements of business principles, business goals, and business drivers (seePart IV, Section 36.2.9).
- Architecture principles (see Part IV, Chapter 23).

7.4.11 开发架构工作说明书；确保批准

评估根据业务绩效需求集产生（以及至何时）的所需的工作产物。这将涉及确保：

- 绩效衡量标准被构建到工作产物中。
- 与绩效相关的特定工作产物是可用的。那么，活动会包括：
  — 识别需要变更的新的工作产物
  — 提供包括构建块在内的现有工作产物将会变化的方向，并确保所有活动及其依赖性是协调的
  — 识别变更对其他工作产物及其活动的依赖度的影响
  — 基于目的、聚焦点、范围和约束，确定应开发哪些架构域，开发到什么细节层级并且应构建何种架构视图
  — 评估在所需时间区间内执行工作的资源需求和可用性，包括遵守组织规划方法和工作产物以产生执行 ADM 周期的计划
  — 预估所需的资源，为所建议的开发制定路线图和进度安排，并在架构工作说明书中记录全部的内容
  — 定义在 ADM 周期内将由 Enterprise Architecture 团队达成的绩效衡量标准
  — 开发特定 Enterprise Architecture 沟通计划并表明 ENTERPRISE 架构师在何处、用何种方式以及何时与利益攸关者（包括关联组和群体）就 Enterprise Architecture 开发的进展进行沟通
  — 审视并与发起人商议计划，并按照适当的治理程序确保对架构工作说明书的正式批准
  — 获得发起人的签字以便继续进行

7.5 输出

阶段 A 的输出可包括但不限于：

- 批准的架构工作说明书（见第四部分 36.2.20 节），尤其包括：
  — 架构项目描述和范围
  — 架构愿景的概述
  — 架构项目计划和进度安排
- 业务原则、业务目标和业务驱动因素的细化说明（见第四部分，36.2.9 节）。
- 架构原则（见第四部分第 23 章）。

- Capability Assessment (see Part IV, Section 36.2.10).
- Tailored Architecture Framework (see Part IV, Section 36.2.21) (for the engagement), including:
  - Tailored architecture method
  - Tailored architecture content (deliverables and artifacts)
  - Configured and deployed tools
- Architecture Vision (see Part IV, Section 36.2.8), including:
  - Problem description
  - Objective of the Statement of Architecture Work
  - Summary views
  - Business Scenario (optional)
  - Refined key high-level stakeholder requirements
- Draft Architecture Definition Document, including (when in scope):
  - Baseline Business Architecture, Version 0.1
  - Baseline Technology Architecture, Version 0.1
  - Baseline Data Architecture, Version 0.1
  - Baseline Application Architecture, Version 0.1
  - Target Business Architecture, Version 0.1
  - Target Technology Architecture, Version 0.1
  - Target Data Architecture, Version 0.1
  - Target Application Architecture, Version 0.1
- Communications Plan (see Part IV, Section 36.2.12).
- Additional content populating the Architecture Repository (see Part IV, Section 36.2.5).

Note: Multiple business scenarios may be used to generate a single Architecture Vision.

The outputs may include some or all of the following:

- Matrices:
  - Stakeholder Map matrix
- Diagrams:
  - Value Chain diagram
  - Solution Concept diagram

- 能力评估（见第四部分 36.2.10 节）。
- 经剪裁的架构框架（见第四部分 36.2.21 节）（用于该工作），包括：
  - 经剪裁的架构方法
  - 经剪裁的架构内容（交付物和制品）
  - 经配置和部署的工具
- 架构愿景（见第四部分 36.2.8 节），包括：
  - 问题描述
  - 架构工作说明书的目的
  - 概要视图
  - 业务场景（可选）
  - 细化的关键高层级利益攸关者需求
- 草拟的架构定义文件，包括（当在范围中时）：
  - 基线业务架构，版本 0.1
  - 基线技术架构，版本 0.1
  - 基线数据架构，版本 0.1
  - 基线应用架构，版本 0.1
  - 目标业务架构，版本 0.1
  - 目标技术架构，版本 0.1
  - 目标数据架构，版本 0.1
  - 目标应用架构，版本 0.1
- 沟通计划（见第四部分 36.2.12 节）。
- 充实架构存储库的增加内容（见第四部分 36.2.5 节）。

注：多重业务场景可被用于产生一个单一架构愿景。

输出可包括下列的一些或全部内容：

- 矩阵：
  - 利益攸关者映射矩阵
- 图：
  - 价值链图
  - 解决方案概念图

Chapter 8
Phase B: Business Architecture

This chapter describes the development of a Business Architecture to support an agreed Architecture Vision.

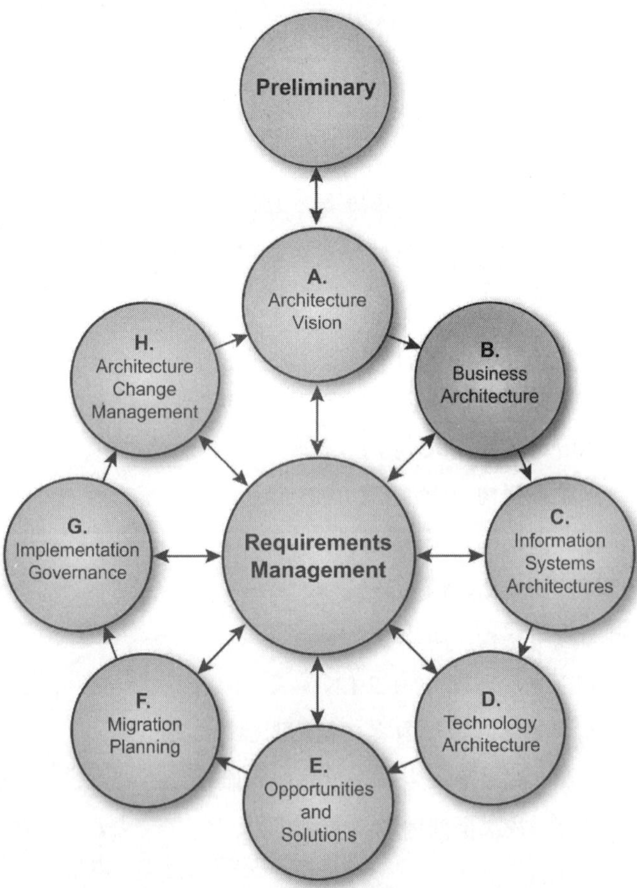

Figure 8-1 Phase B: Business Architecture

第 8 章 阶段 B：业务架构

本章描述用以支持商定的架构愿景的业务架构的开发。

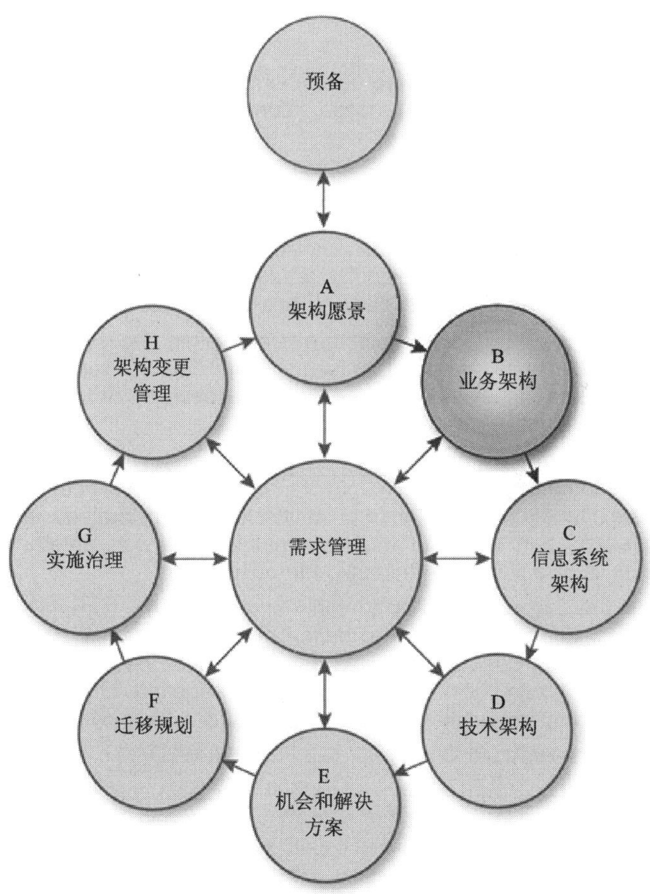

图 8-1 阶段 B：业务架构

8.1 Objectives

The objectives of Phase B are to:

- Develop the Target Business Architecture that describes how the enterprise needs to operate to achieve the business goals, and respond to the strategic drivers set out in the Architecture Vision, in a way that addresses the Request for Architecture Work and stakeholder concerns.
- Identify candidate Architecture Roadmap components based upon gaps between the Baseline and Target Business Architectures.

8.2 Approach

In summary, the Business Architecture describes the product and/or service strategy, and the organizational, functional, process, information, and geographic aspects of the business environment.

8.2.1 General

A knowledge of the Business Architecture is a prerequisite for architecture work in any other domain (Data, Application, Technology), and is therefore the first architec-ture activity that needs to be undertaken, if not catered for already in other organ-izational processes (enterprise planning, strategic business planning, business process re-engineering, etc.).

In practical terms, the Business Architecture is also often necessary as a means of demonstrating the business value of subsequent architecture work to key stakeholders, and the return on investment to those stakeholders from supporting and participating in the subsequent work.

The scope of the work in Phase B will depend to a large extent on the enterprise environment. In some cases, key elements of the Business Architecture may be done in other activities; for example, the enterprise mission, vision, strategy, and goals may be documented as part of some wider business strategy or enterprise planning activity that has its own lifecycle within the enterprise.

In such cases, there may be a need to verify and update the currently documented business strategy and plans, and/or to bridge between high-level business drivers, business strategy, and goals on the one hand, and the specific business requirements that are relevant to this architecture development effort. The business strategy typically defines what to achieve — the goals and drivers, and the metrics for success — but not how to get there. That is role of the Business Architecture.

In other cases, little or no Business Architecture work may have been done to date. In such cases, there will be a need for the architecture team to research, verify, and gain buy-in to the key business objectives and processes that the architecture is to support. This may be done as a free-standing exercise, either preceding architecture development, or as part of Phase A.

In both of these cases, the business scenario technique (see Part III, Chapter 26) of the TOGAF ADM, or any other method that illuminates the key business require-ments and indicates the implied technical requirements for IT architecture, may be used.

A key objective is to re-use existing material as much as possible. In architecturally more mature environments, there will be existing Architecture Definitions, which (hopefully) will have been maintained since the last architecture development cycle. Where architecture descriptions exist, these can be used as a starting point, and verified and updated if necessary; see Part V, Section 39.4.1.

8.1 目的

阶段B的目的是：

- 开发目标业务架构，该架构描述ENTERPRISE需要如何运行，从而以表达架构工作要求书和利益攸关者关注点的方式达成业务目标，并响应架构愿景中设定的战略驱动因素。
- 基于基线业务架构与目标业务架构之间的差距来识别候选架构路线图组件。

8.2 实施途径

概括来说，业务架构描述产品和/或服务战略，以及业务环境的组织、功能、流程、信息和地理方面。

8.2.1 概述

对业务架构的了解是在任何其他领域（数据、应用、技术）进行架构工作的前提，因此，如果在其他组织流程（ENTERPRISE规划、战略业务规划、业务流程再造等）中不满足需要，业务架构则是需要进行的第一个架构活动。

实际上，作为向关键利益攸关者表明后续架构工作的业务价值，以及向支持和参与后续工作的利益攸关者表明投资收益的一种手段，业务架构通常也很有必要。

阶段B中的工作范围将在很大程度上依赖于ENTERPRISE环境。在一些情况下，业务架构的关键元素可能在其他活动中开展，如ENTERPRISE使命、愿景、战略和目标可能已被文件化，作为在ENTERPRISE内具有其自身生命周期的一些更广泛的业务战略或ENTERPRISE规划活动的部分。

在这种情况下，可能需要验证和更新目前已被文件化的业务战略和计划，和/或在另一方面，需要在高层级业务驱动因素、业务战略和目标与本架构开发工作相关的特定业务需求之间建立桥梁。业务战略通常定义达成什么——目标和驱动因素，以及成功的衡量标准——而不是如何达到，那是业务架构的工作。

在其他情况下，到现阶段为止，可能几乎没有开展任何架构工作。在这种情况下，架构团队需要对架构支持的关键业务目的和流程进行研究、验证和获得认同。这可能被作为一次独立活动来训练，或者在架构开发之前或者作为阶段A的部分来完成。

在这两种情况下，可使用TOGAF ADM的业务场景技巧（见第三部分第26章）或任何阐明关键业务需求并指出隐含的IT架构技术需求的其他方法。

一个关键目的是尽可能复用现有的资料。在架构方面更成熟的环境中，将存在（但愿如此）自最后一个架构开发周期起保留至今的现有架构定义。在存在架构描述的情况下，这些描述可作为起点使用，必要时可进行验证和更新；见第五部分，39.4.1节。

Gather and analyze only that information that allows informed decisions to be made relevant to the scope of this architecture effort. If this effort is focused on the defini-tion of (possibly new) business processes, then Phase B will necessarily involve a lot of detailed work. If the focus is more on the Target Architectures in other domains (data/information, application systems, infrastructure) to support an essentially exist-ing Business Architecture, then it is important to build a complete picture in Phase B without going into unnecessary detail.

8.2.2 Developing the Baseline Description

If an enterprise has existing architecture descriptions, they should be used as the basis for the Baseline Description. This input may have been used already in Phase A in developing an Architecture Vision, and may even be sufficient in itself for the Baseline Description.

Where no such descriptions exist, information will have to be gathered in whatever format comes to hand.

The normal approach to Target Architecture development is top-down. In the Baseline Description, however, the analysis of the current state often has to be done bottom-up, particularly where little or no architecture assets exist. In such a case, the architect simply has to document the working assumptions about high-level architectures, and the process is one of gathering evidence to turn the working assumptions into fact, until the law of diminishing returns sets in.

Business processes that are not to be carried forward have no intrinsic value. However, when developing Baseline Descriptions in other architecture domains, architectural components (principles, models, standards, and current inventory) that are not to be carried forward may still have an intrinsic value, and an inventory may be needed in order to understand the residual value (if any) of those components.

Whatever the approach, the goal should be to re-use existing material as much as possible, and to gather and analyze only that information that allows informed decisions to be made regarding the Target Business Architecture. It is important to build a complete picture without going into unnecessary detail.

8.2.3 Business Modeling

Business models should be logical extensions of the business scenarios from the Architecture Vision, so that the architecture can be mapped from the high-level business requirements down to the more detailed ones.

A variety of modeling tools and techniques may be employed, if deemed appropriate (bearing in mind the above caution not to go into unnecessary detail). For example:

- **Activity Models** (also called **Business Process Models**) describe the functions associated with the enterprise's business activities, the data and/or information exchanged between activities (internal exchanges), and the data and/or information exchanged with other activities that are outside the scope of the model (external exchanges). Activity models are hierarchical in nature. They capture the activities performed in a business process, and the ICOMs (inputs, controls, outputs, and mechanisms/resources used) of those activities. Activity models can be annotated with explicit statements of business rules, which represent relationships among the ICOMs. For example, a business rule can specify who can do what under specified conditions, the combina-tion of inputs and controls needed, and the resulting outputs. One technique for creating activity models is the IDEF (Integrated Computer Aided Manufac-turing (ICAM) DEFinition) modeling technique.

只采集和分析那些能够做出与本架构工作范围相关的有依据的决策信息。如果本工作聚焦于（可能是新的）业务流程的定义，那么阶段 B 将必然涉及许多细节工作。如果聚焦点更多的是关于其他领域（数据/信息、应用系统、基础设施）中的目标架构以支持一个基本的现有业务架构，那么重要的是在阶段 B 中构建一个完整图像，而不陷入不必要的细节。

8.2.2 开发基线描述

如果一个 ENTERPRISE 具有架构描述，那么这些描述应被用作基线描述的基础。这个输入可能已经用于阶段 A 中开发架构愿景，甚至可能足以将其本身用于基线描述。

如果不存在这样的描述，则应不论格式的采集信息。

开发目标架构的正常途径是自顶向下。然而，在基线描述中，对当前状态的分析通常必须自底向上完成，特别是在几乎不存在架构资产的情况下。在这种情况下，架构师只是必须将关于高层级架构的工作假设文件化，直到边际效用递减规律出现前，该过程是将工作假设转变为事实而收集的证据之一。

未继续执行的业务流程不具有内在价值。然而，在其他架构域中开发基线描述时，未继续执行的架构组件（原则、模型、标准和当前存储清单）可能仍然具有内在价值，并且可能需要存储清单以了解这些组件的剩余价值（如果有）。

无论是什么途径，目标应是尽可能复用现有资料，只采集和分析有助于做出与目标业务架构相关的有依据的决策信息。重点在于构建一个完整图像，而不陷入不必要的细节。

8.2.3 业务建模

业务模型应是根据架构愿景对业务场景进行的逻辑扩展，以便该架构能够从高层级业务需求向下映射至更详细的需求。

如果认为适当，记住上述关于不要陷入不必要细节的警告，可采用各种建模工具和技巧。例如：

- **活动模型**（也称为**业务流程模型**）描述与 ENTERPRISE 业务活动相关联的功能、活动之间交换的数据和/或信息（内部交换）以及与模型范围之外的其他活动交换的数据和/或信息（外部交换）。活动模型在本质上是层级化的，它们捕获在业务流程中所进行的活动，以及那些活动的 ICOMs（输入、控制、输出和机制/所使用的资源）。活动模型可注释有显性的业务规则说明，以表示 ICOMs 间的关系。例如，业务规则可规定在指定条件下由谁做什么、所需输入与控制项的组合以及产生输出。一种用于创建活动模型的技巧是 IDEF［集成计算机辅助制造（ICAM）定义］的建模技术。

The Object Management Group (OMG) has developed the Business Process Model-ing Notation (BPMN), a standard for business process modeling that includes a lang-uage with which to specify business processes, their tasks/steps, and the documents produced.

- **Use-Case Models** can describe either business processes or systems func-tions, depending on the focus of the modeling effort. A use-case model describes the business processes of an enterprise in terms of use-cases and actors corresponding to business processes and organizational participants (people, organizations, etc.). The use-case model is described in use-case diagrams and use-case specifications.
- **Class Models** are similar to logical data models. A class model describes static information and relationships between information. A class model also describes informational behaviors. Like many of the other models, it can also be used to model various levels of granularity. Depending on the intent of the model, a class model can represent business domain entities or systems implementation classes. A business domain model represents key business information (domain classes), their characteristics (attributes), their behaviors (methods or operations), and relationships (often referred to as multiplicity, describing how many classes typically participate in the relationship), and cardinality (describes required or optional participation in the relationship). Specifications further elaborate and detail information that cannot be repres-ented in the class diagram.

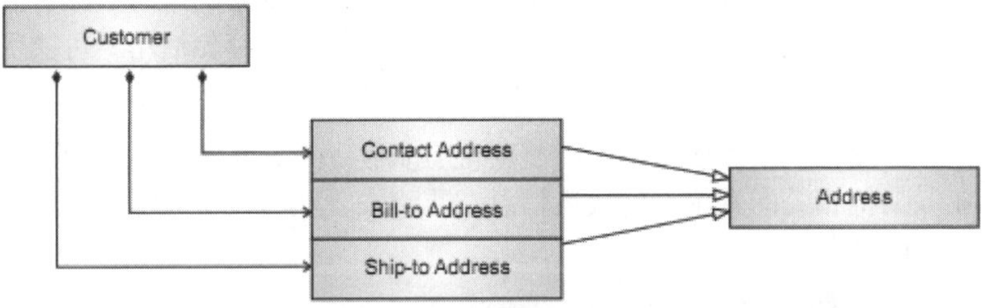

Figure 8-2 UML Business Class Diagram

All three types of model above can be represented in the Unified Modeling Language (UML), and a variety of tools exist for generating such models.

Certain industry sectors have modeling techniques specific to the sector concerned. For example, the Defense sector uses the following models. These models have to be used carefully, especially if the location and conduct of business processes will be altered in the visionary Business Architecture.

- The **Node Connectivity Diagram** describes the business locations (nodes), the "needlines" between them, and the characteristics of the information exchanged. Node connectivity can be described at three levels: conceptual, logical, and physical. Each needline indicates the need for some kind of information transfer between the two connected nodes. A node can represent a role (e.g., a CIO), an organizational unit, a business location or facility, and so on. An arrow indicating the direction of information flow is annotated to describe the characteristics of the data or information — for example, its content, media, security or classification level, timeliness, and requirements for information system interoperability.

对象管理组（OMG）已开发了业务流程建模符号（BPMN），是一种用于业务流程建模的标准，包括一种规定业务流程及其任务/步骤以及生成文件的语言。

- **用例模型**可依据建模的聚焦点描述业务流程或系统功能。用例模型依据于业务流程和组织参与者（人员、组织等）的用例和施动者描述ENTERPRISE的业务流程。以用例图和用例规范描述用例模型。
- **类模型**与逻辑数据模型相似。类模型描述静态信息以及信息间的关系，类模型还描述信息的行为。类似于许多其他模型，类模型还可用于各种粒度级的建模。依据模型的意图，类模型可表示业务域实体或系统实施类别。业务域模型表示关键业务信息（域类别）、业务特征（属性）及其行为（方法或运行）和关系（通常被称为多重性，描述典型情况下有多少类参与到该关系之中）以及基数（描述关系中所需或可选的参与项）。规范进一步详细阐述和详细说明在该类图中不能表示的信息。

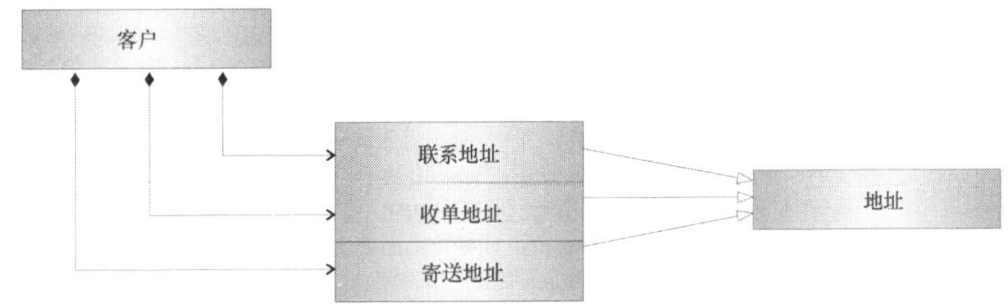

图 8-2　UML 业务类图

上述这三种类型的模型均可使用统一建模语言（UML）表达，并且存在各种用于生成这种模型的工具。

某些行业对所关注的领域有特定的建模技巧。例如，防务领域使用下述模型。这些模型必须谨慎地使用，特别是如果业务流程的位置和执行将会在未来的业务架构中发生改变的情况。

- **节点连接图**描述业务位置（节点）、位置间的“需求线”以及所交换信息的特征。节点连接性可在三个层级上描述：概念、逻辑和物理层级。每个需求线均表示两个连接节点间信息传输的某类需求。一个节点可表达一个角色（如 CIO）、一个组织单元、一个业务位置或设施等。标注出表示信息流方向的箭头，以描述数据或信息的特征——例如，其内容、介质、安保性或分类等级、时间线和对信息系统互用性的需求。

- The **Information Exchange Matrix** documents the information exchange requirements for an enterprise architecture. Information exchange require-ments express the relationships across three basic entities (activities, business nodes and their elements, and information flow), and focus on characteristics of the information exchange, such as performance and security. They identify who exchanges what information with whom, why the information is necessary, and in what manner.

Although originally developed for use in the Defense sector, these models are finding increasing use in other sectors of government, and may also be considered for use in non-government environments.

8.2.4 Architecture Repository

As part of Phase B, the architecture team will need to consider what relevant Business Architecture resources are available from the Architecture Repository (see Part V, Chapter 41), in particular:

- Generic business models relevant to the organization's industry sector. These are "Industry Architectures", in terms of the Enterprise Continuum. They are held in the Reference Library of the Architecture Repository (see Part V, Section 41.3). For example:
  - The Object Management Group (OMG) — www.omg.org — has a number of vertical Domain Task Forces developing business models relevant to specific vertical domains such as Healthcare, Transportation, Finance, etc.
  - The TeleManagement Forum (TMF) — www.tmforum.org — has developed detailed business models relevant to the Telecommunications industry.
  - Government departments and agencies in different countries have reference models and frameworks mandated for use, intended to promote cross-departmental integration and interoperability. An example is the Federal Enterprise Architecture Business Reference Model, which is a function-driven framework for describing the business operations of the Federal Government independent of the agencies that perform them.
- Business models relevant to common high-level business domains. For exa-mple:
  - The Resource-Event-Agent (REA) business model was originally created by William E. McCarthy (refer to www.msu.edu/user/mccarth4) of Michigan State University, mainly for modeling of accounting systems. It has proved so useful for better understanding of business processes that it has become one of the major modeling frameworks for both traditional enterprises and e-Commerce systems.
  - The STEP Framework (STandard for the Exchange of Product model data) is concerned with product design and supply chain interworking. STEP is an ISO standard (ISO 10303). Implementation of the STEP standard has been led by some large aerospace manufacturers, and has also been taken up in other industries that have a need for complex graphic and process data, such as the construction industry.
  - RosettaNet — www.rosettanet.org — is a consortium created by leading companies in the computer, electronic component, and semiconductor manufacturing supply chains. Its mission is to develop a complete set of standard e-Business processes for these supply chains, and to promote and support their adoption and use.
- Enterprise-specific building blocks (process components, business rules, job descriptions, etc.).

- **信息交换矩阵**记录使 Enterprise Architecture 的信息交换需求文件化。信息交换需求表达了三个基本实体（活动、业务节点及其元素和信息流）间的关系，并聚焦于信息交换的特征（诸如性能和安保性）识别谁与谁交换了什么信息、为什么该信息是必要的，以及采用的方式。

虽然这些模型最初开发用于防务领域，但是，越来越多地被政府的其他部门使用，并且也可能被考虑用于非政府环境。

8.2.4 架构存储库

作为阶段 B 的部分，架构团队需要考虑从架构存储库（参见第五部分第 41 章）中可获得哪些相关的业务架构资源，尤其是：

- 一般业务模型与组织所属行业领域有关。依照 ENTERPRISE 的连续统一体，这些属于“行业架构”。通用业务模型被保存在架构存储库的参考库中（见第五部分 41.3 节）。例如：
  - 对象管理组（OMG）——www.omg.org——拥有很多垂直域任务组来开发与特定垂直域（诸如医疗保健、交通、金融等）有关的业务模型。
  - 电信管理论坛（TMF）——www.tmforum.org——已开发了与电信行业有关的详细业务模型。
  - 不同国家的政府部门和机构强制使用的参考模型和框架，旨在促进跨部门的综合和协同工作能力。例如，联邦 Enterprise Architecture 业务参考模型，这是一个功能驱动的框架，用于描述独立于业务运行机构的联邦政府所进行的业务运行。
- 与常用高层级业务域有关的业务模型。例如：
  - 资源—事件—代理人（REA）业务模型最初由密歇根州立大学的 WilliamE.McCarthy 创建（参照 www.msu.edu/user/mccarth4），主要用于会计系统的建模。该模型已被证明对于更好地理解业务流程是十分有用的，从而成为传统 ENTERPRISE 和电子商务系统的主要建模框架之一。
  - STEP 框架（产品模型数据交换标准）关注于产品设计和供应链交互工作。STEP 是一个 ISO 标准（ISO10303）。STEP 标准的实施已经由一些大型航空航天制造商所引领，并且也被诸如建筑业等其他需要复杂图形和流程数据的行业所接纳。
  - RosettaNet——www.rosettanet.org——是由在计算机、电子组件以及半导体制造供应链方面的领先企业所创建的企业联盟。RosettaNet 的任务是开发用于这些供应链的一系列完整的标准电子商务流程，并促进和支持这些流程的采纳和使用。
- ENTERPRISE 特定构建块（流程组件、业务规则、工作描述等）。

- Applicable standards.

8.3 Inputs

This section defines the inputs to Phase B.

8.3.1 Reference Materials External to the Enterprise

- Architecture reference materials (see Part IV, Section 36.2.5)

8.3.2 Non-Architectural Inputs

- Request for Architecture Work (see Part IV, Section 36.2.17)
- Business principles, business goals, and business drivers (see Part IV, Section 36.2.9)
- Capability Assessment (see Part IV, Section 36.2.10)
- Communications Plan (see Part IV, Section 36.2.12)

8.3.3 Architectural Inputs

- Organizational Model for Enterprise Architecture (see Part IV, Section 36.2.16), including:
  - Scope of organizations impacted
  - Maturity assessment, gaps, and resolution approach
  - Roles and responsibilities for architecture team(s)
  - Constraints on architecture work
  - Budget requirements
  - Governance and support strategy
- Tailored Architecture Framework (see Part IV, Section 36.2.21), including:
  - Tailored architecture method
  - Tailored architecture content (deliverables and artifacts)
  - Configured and deployed tools
- Approved Statement of Architecture Work (see Part IV, Section 36.2.20)
- Architecture principles (see Part IV, Section 36.2.4), including business principles, when pre-existing
- Enterprise Continuum (see Part V, Chapter 39)
- Architecture Repository (see Part IV, Section 36.2.5), including:
  - Re-usable building blocks
  - Publicly available reference models

- 可用的标准。

8.3 输入

本节定义了对阶段 B 的输入。

8.3.1 ENTERPRISE 外部参考资料

- 架构参考资料（见第四部分 36.2.5 节）

8.3.2 非架构输入

- 架构工作要求书（见第四部分 36.2.17 节）
- 业务原则、业务目标和业务驱动因素（见第四部分 36.2.9 节）
- 能力评估（见第四部分 36.2.10 节）
- 沟通计划（见第四部分 36.2.12 节）

8.3.3 架构输入

- Enterprise Architecture 的组织模型（见第四部分 36.2.16 节），包括：
  - — 组织受影响的范围
  - — 成熟度评估、差距和解决途径
  - — 架构团队的角色和职责
  - — 对架构工作的约束
  - — 预算需求
  - — 治理和支持战略
- 经剪裁的架构框架（见第四部分 36.2.21 节），包括：
  - — 经剪裁的架构方法
  - — 经剪裁的架构内容（交付物和制品）
  - — 经配置和部署的工具
- 经批准的架构工作说明书（见第四部分 36.2.20 节）
- 架构原则（见第四部分 36.2.4 节），包括业务原则（当预先存在时）
- ENTERPRISE 的连续统一体（见第五部分第 39 章）
- 架构存储库（见第四部分 36.2.5 节），包括：
  - — 可复用的构建块
  - — 公开可用的参考模型

  - Organization-specific reference models
  - Organization standards
- Architecture Vision (see Part IV, Section 36.2.8), including:
  - Problem description
  - Objective of the Statement of Architecture Work
  - Summary views
  - Business Scenario (optional)
  - Refined key high-level stakeholder requirements
- Draft Architecture Definition Document, including (when in scope):
  - Baseline Business Architecture, Version 0.1
  - Baseline Technology Architecture, Version 0.1
  - Baseline Data Architecture, Version 0.1
  - Baseline Application Architecture, Version 0.1
  - Target Business Architecture, Version 0.1
  - Target Technology Architecture, Version 0.1
  - Target Data Architecture, Version 0.1
  - Target Application Architecture, Version 0.1

8.4 Steps

The level of detail addressed in Phase B will depend on the scope and goals of the overall architecture effort.

New business processes being introduced as part of this effort will need to be defined in detail during Phase B. Existing business processes to be carried over and supported in the target environment may already have been adequately defined in previous architectural work; but, if not, they too will need to be defined in Phase B.

The order of the steps in Phase B (see below) as well as the time at which they are formally started and completed should be adapted to the situation at hand, in accordance with the established architecture governance. In particular, determine whether in this situation it is appropriate to conduct Baseline or Target Architecture development first, as described in Part III, Chapter 19.

All activities that have been initiated in these steps must be closed during the Finalize the Business Architecture step (see Section 8.4.8). The documentation generated from these steps must be formally published in the Create Architecture Definition Document step (see Section8.4.9).

The steps in Phase B are as follows:

- Select reference models, viewpoints, and tools (see Section 8.4.1)
- Develop Baseline Business Architecture Description (see Section 8.4.2)

  - 组织特定参考模型
  - 组织标准
- 架构愿景（见第四部分 36.2.8 节），包括：
  - 问题描述
  - 架构工作说明书的目的
  - 概要视图
  - 业务场景（可选）
  - 细化的关键高层级利益攸关者需求
- 草拟的架构定义文件，包括（当在范围中时）：
  - 基线业务架构，0.1 版本
  - 基线技术架构，0.1 版本
  - 基线数据架构，0.1 版本
  - 基线应用架构，0.1 版本
  - 目标业务架构，0.1 版本
  - 目标技术架构，0.1 版本
  - 目标数据架构，0.1 版本
  - 目标应用架构，0.1 版本

8.4 步骤

阶段 B 中所涉及的细节层级取决于总体架构工作的范围和目标。

作为这项工作的部分而被引入的新的业务流程需要在阶段 B 期间被详细定义。在目标环境中延用并被支持的现有业务流程，可能已经在之前的架构工作中被充分定义；但是如果没有，它们也需要在阶段 B 中被定义。

阶段 B 中的步骤顺序（见下文）及其正式开始和完成的时间应适应于当前情况，秉承已经建立的架构治理。尤其是，在这种情况下确定首先实施基线架构开发还是实施目标架构开发更合适，如第三部分第 19 章所述。

在这些步骤中已经启动的所有活动必须在最终确定业务架构步骤（见 8.4.8 节）时结束。这些步骤生成的文档必须在创建架构定义文件步骤（见 8.4.9 节）中正式发布。

阶段 B 中的步骤如下：

- 选择参考模型、视角和工具（见 8.4.1 节）
- 开发基线业务架构描述（见 8.4.2 节）

- Develop Target Business Architecture Description (see Section 8.4.3)
- Perform gap analysis (see Section 8.4.4)
- Define candidate roadmap components (see Section 8.4.5)
- Resolve impacts across the Architecture Landscape (see Section 8.4.6)
- Conduct formal stakeholder review (see Section 8.4.7)
- Finalize the Business Architecture (see Section 8.4.8)
- Create Architecture Definition Document (see Section 8.4.9)

8.4.1 Select Reference Models, Viewpoints, and Tools

Select relevant Business Architecture resources (reference models, patterns, etc.) from the Architecture Repository, on the basis of the business drivers, and the stakeholders and concerns.

Select relevant Business Architecture viewpoints (e.g., operations, management, financial); i.e., those that will enable the architect to demonstrate how the stakeholder concerns are being addressed in the Business Architecture.

Identify appropriate tools and techniques to be used for capture, modeling, and analysis, in association with the selected viewpoints. Depending on the degree of sophistication warranted, these may comprise simple documents or spreadsheets, or more sophisticated modeling tools and techniques, such as activity models, business process models, use-case models, etc.

8.4.1.1 Determine Overall Modeling Process

For each viewpoint, select the models needed to support the specific view required, using the selected tool or method.

Ensure that all stakeholder concerns are covered. If they are not, create new models to address concerns not covered, or augment existing models (see Section 8.2.3). Business scenarios are a useful technique to discover and document business requirements, and may be used iteratively, at different levels of detail in the hierarchical decomposition of the Business Architecture. Business scenarios are described in Part III, Chapter 26.

Activity models, use-case models, and class models are mentioned earlier as techniques to enable the definition of an organization's business architecture. In many cases, all three approaches can be utilized in sequence to progressively decompose a business.

- **Structured Analysis**: Identifies the key business functions within the scope of the architecture, and maps those functions onto the organizational units within the business.
- **Use-case Analysis**: The breakdown of business-level functions across actors and organizations allows the actors in a function to be identified and permits a breakdown into services supporting/delivering that functional capability.
- **Process Modeling**: The breakdown of a function or business service through process modeling allows the elements of the process to be identified, and permits the identification of lower-level business services or functions.

The level and rigor of decomposition needed varies from enterprise to enterprise, as well as within an enterprise, and the architect should consider the enterprise's goals, objectives, scope, and purpose of the enterprise architecture effort to determine the level of decomposition.

- 开发目标业务架构描述（见 8.4.3 节）
- 进行差距分析（见 8.4.4 节）
- 定义候选路线图组件（见 8.4.5 节）
- 化解贯穿整个架构全景中的影响（见 8.4.6 节）
- 进行正式的利益攸关者审视（见 8.4.7 节）
- 最终确定业务架构（见 8.4.8 节）
- 创建架构定义文件（见 8.4.9 节）

8.4.1 选择参考模型、视角和工具

基于业务驱动因素、利益攸关者和关注点从架构存储库中选择相关的业务架构资源（参考模型、特征模式等）。

选择相关的业务架构视角（如运行、管理、财务）；即，使架构师能够展示利益攸关者的关注点在业务架构中如何得到处理的那些视角。

结合选定的视角，识别用于捕获、建模和分析的适当工具和技巧。根据认可的复杂程度，这些工具和技巧可包括简单的文件或电子表格，或更复杂的建模工具和技巧，如活动模型、业务流程模型、用例模型等。

8.4.1.1 确定总体建模流程

针对每个视角，使用选定的工具或方法来选择所需模型以支持所要求的特定视角。

确保所有利益攸关者的关注点都被涵盖。若没有，就要创建新模型以应对未涵盖的关注点或扩展现有模型（见 8.2.3 节）。业务场景是一种发现和记录业务需求的有用技巧，并且可在业务架构层级分解中的不同细节层级上迭代使用。业务场景在第三部分第 26 章中描述。

活动模型、用例模型和类模型之前作为使能组织业务架构定义的技巧被提及。在许多情况下，这三种途径均可按顺序加以利用，以逐步分解一个业务。

- **结构化分析**：识别架构范围内的关键业务功能，并将这些功能映射到业务内的组织单元。
- **用例分析**：贯穿一个功能中多个施动者和组织的业务层级功能的分解，允许将其分解成支持/交付多个功能能力的服务。
- **流程建模**：通过流程建模中一个功能或业务服务的分解能够识别该流程的元素，并允许识别低层级的业务服务或功能。

在不同 ENTERPRISE 之间以及在 ENTERPRISE 内，所需分解的层级和严格程度是不同的。架构师应考虑 Enterprise Architecture 的目标、目的、范围以及 ENTERPRISE 努力确定分解层级的目的。

8.4.1.2 Identify Required Service Granularity Level, Boundaries, and Contracts

The TOGAF content framework differentiates between the functions of a business and the services of a business. Business services are specific functions that have explicit, defined boundaries that are explicitly governed. In order to allow the architect flexibility to define business services at a level of granularity that is appropriate for and manageable by the business, the functions are split as follows: micro-level functions will have explicit, defined boundaries, but may not be explicitly governed. Likewise, macro business functions may be explicitly governed, but may not have explicit, defined boundaries.

The Business Architecture phase therefore needs to identify which components of the architecture are functions and which are services. Services are distinguished from functions through the explicit definition of a service contract. When Baseline Architectures are being developed, it may be the case that explicit contracts do not exist and it would therefore be at the discretion of the architect to determine whether there is merit in developing such contracts before examining any Target Architectures.

A service contract covers the business/functional interface and also the technology/ data interface. Business Architecture will define the service contract at the business/ functional level, which will be expanded on in the Application and Technology Architecture phases.

The granularity of business services should be determined according to the business drivers, goals, objectives, and measures for this area of the business. Finer-grained services permit closer management and measurement (and can be combined to create coarser-grained services), but require greater effort to govern. Guidelines for identification of services and definition of their contracts can be found in Part III, Chapter 22.

8.4.1.3 Identify Required Catalogs of Business Building Blocks

Catalogs capture inventories of the core assets of the business. Catalogs are hierarchical in nature and capture the decomposition of a building block and also decompositions across related building blocks (e.g., organization/actor).

Catalogs form the raw material for development of matrices and views and also act as a key resource for portfolio managing business and IT capability.

The following catalogs should be considered for development within a Business Architecture:

- Organization/Actor catalog
- Driver/Goal/Objective catalog
- Role catalog
- Business Service/Function catalog
- Location catalog
- Process/Event/Control/Product catalog
- Contract/Measure catalog

The structure of catalogs is based on the attributes of metamodel entities, as defined in Part IV, Chapter 34.

8.4.1.2 识别所需的服务粒度层级、边界和契约

TOGAF 内容框架在业务功能和业务服务之间是有区别的。业务服务是特定功能，这些功能具有被明确治理的清晰且限定的边界。为有助于架构师在适于业务并可由该业务管理的粒度层级上灵活定义业务服务，这些功能按如下划分：微观层级的功能将具有明确且限定的边界，但是可能无法被明确治理。与此类似，宏观业务功能可被明确治理，但是可能不具有明确且限定的边界。

因此，业务架构阶段需要识别哪些架构组件是功能，哪些是服务。通过明确定义服务契约，将服务与功能区别开来。开发基线架构时可能不存在明确的契约，因此，在审查目标架构前，应依据架构师的意见来确定开发这样的契约是否值得。

服务契约涵盖业务/功能界面以及技术/数据界面。业务架构在业务/功能层级上定义服务契约，并在应用和技术架构阶段展开。

业务服务的粒度应根据本业务领域的业务驱动因素、目标、目的和测度确定。更细粒度的服务有助于使管理和衡量更紧密（并且可被组合产生粗粒度服务），但是就要求在治理方面付诸更多的努力。识别服务并定义其契约的指南可在第三部分第 22 章中找到。

8.4.1.3 识别所需的业务构建块目录集

目录集捕获业务的核心资产清单。目录集本质上是分层级的，并贯穿单个构建块的分解以及相关构建块（如组织/施动者）之间的分解。

目录集构成用于矩阵和视图开发的原始资料，并充当项目谱系管理业务和 IT 能力的关键资源。

应考虑在业务架构内开发下列目录集：

- 组织/施动者目录集
- 驱动因素/目标/目的目录集
- 角色目录集
- 业务服务/功能目录集
- 位置目录集
- 流程/事件/控制/产品目录集
- 契约/测度目录集

目录集结构基于元模型实体的属性，如第四部分第 34 章所定义。

8.4.1.4 Identify Required Matrices

Matrices show the core relationships between related model entities.

Matrices form the raw material for development of views and also act as a key resource for impact assessment, carried out as a part of gap analysis.

The following matrices should be considered for development within a Business Architecture:

- Business interaction matrix (showing dependency and communication between organizations and actors).
- Actor/role matrix (showing the roles undertaken by each actor).

The structure of matrices is based on the attributes of metamodel entities, as defined in Part IV, Chapter 34.

8.4.1.5 Identify Required Diagrams

Diagrams present the Business Architecture information from a set of different perspectives (viewpoints) according to the requirements of the stakeholders.

The following Diagrams should be considered for development within a Business Architecture:

- Business Footprint diagram.
- Business Service/Information diagram.
- Functional Decomposition diagram.
- Goal/Objective/Service diagram.
- Use-case diagram.
- Organization Decomposition diagram.
- Process Flow diagram.
- Events diagram.

The structure of diagrams is based on the attributes of metamodel entities, as defined in Part IV, Chapter 34.

8.4.1.6 Identify Types of Requirement to be Collected

Once the Business Architecture catalogs, matrices, and diagrams have been developed, architecture modeling is completed by formalizing the business-focused requirements for implementing the Target Architecture.

These requirements may:

- Relate to the business domain.
- Provide requirements input into the Data, Application, and Technology Architectures.
- Provide detailed guidance to be reflected during design and implementation to ensure that the solution addresses the original architecture requirements.

Within this step, the architect should identify requirements that should be met by the architecture(see Section 17.2.2).

In many cases, the Architecture Definition will not be intended to give detailed or comprehensive requirements for a solution (as these can be better addressed through general requirements management discipline). The expected scope of requirements content should be established during the Architecture Vision phase and documented in the approved Statement of Architecture Work.

8.4.1.4 识别所需的矩阵

矩阵表明相关模型实体之间的核心关系。

矩阵形成视图开发的原始资料，并充当作为差距分析的一部分而被实施的影响评估的关键资源。

应考虑为在业务架构内开发下列矩阵：

- 业务交互矩阵（表明组织与施动者之间的依赖性和沟通）。
- 施动者/角色矩阵（表明每个施动者承担的角色）。

矩阵结构基于元模型实体的属性，如第四部分第 34 章所定义。

8.4.1.5 识别所需的图

根据利益攸关者的需求，图代表从一系列不同的关注层面（视角）展示的业务架构信息。

为在业务架构内开发，应考虑下列图：

- 业务印迹图。
- 业务服务/信息图。
- 功能分解图。
- 目标/目的/服务图。
- 用例图。
- 组织分解图。
- 过程流图。
- 事件图。

图结构基于元模型实体的属性，如第四部分第 34 章所定义。

8.4.1.6 识别待收集的需求类型

一旦开发了业务架构目录集、矩阵和图，通过将为了实施目标架构而聚焦于业务的需求进行正规化来完成架构建模。

这些需求可以：

- 与业务域相关。
- 提供对数据架构、应用架构和技术架构的需求输入。
- 提供将在设计和实施期间要被反映的详细引导，以确保解决方案应对最初的架构需求。

在本步骤中，架构师应识别该架构应满足的需求（见 17.2.2 节）。

在许多情况下，架构定义并非旨在给出对解决方案的详细或全面需求（因为这些需求可通过一般需求管理规程更好地应对）。期望的需求内容范围应在架构愿景阶段建立，并记录在已批准的架构工作说明书中。

Any requirement or change in requirement that is outside of the scope defined in the Statement of Architecture Work must be submitted to the Requirements Repository for management through the governed Requirements Management process.

8.4.2 Develop Baseline Business Architecture Description

Develop a Baseline Description of the existing Business Architecture, to the extent necessary to support the Target Business Architecture. The scope and level of detail to be defined will depend on the extent to which existing business elements are likely to be carried over into the Target Business Architecture, and on whether architecture descriptions exist, as described in Section 8.2. To the extent possible, identify the relevant Business Architecture building blocks, drawing on the Architecture Repository (see Part V, Chapter 41).

Where new architecture models need to be developed to satisfy stakeholder concerns, use the models identified within Step 1 as a guideline for creating new architecture content to describe the Baseline Architecture.

8.4.3 Develop Target Business Architecture Description

Develop a Target Description for the Business Architecture, to the extent necessary to support the Architecture Vision. The scope and level of detail to be defined will depend on the relevance of the business elements to attaining the Target Architecture Vision, and on whether architectural descriptions exist. To the extent possible, identify the relevant Business Architecture building blocks, drawing on the Architecture Repository (see Part V, Chapter 41).

Where new architecture models need to be developed to satisfy stakeholder concerns, use the models identified within Step 1 as a guideline for creating new architecture content to describe the Target Architecture.

8.4.4 Perform Gap Analysis

Verify the architecture models for internal consistency and accuracy:

- Perform trade-off analysis to resolve conflicts (if any) among the different views.
- Validate that the models support the principles, objectives, and constraints.
- Note changes to the viewpoint represented in the selected models from the Architecture Repository, and document.
- Test architecture models for completeness against requirements.

Identify gaps between the baseline and target, using the Gap Analysis technique as described in Part III, Chapter 27.

在架构工作说明书所定义的范围之外的任何需求或需求变更必须提交至需求存储库，以通过受治理的需求管理流程进行管理。

8.4.2 开发基线业务架构描述

开发现有业务架构的一种基线描述，达到支持目标业务架构所必需的程度。待定义的范围和细节层级，将取决于现有的业务元素有可能延用到目标业务架构中的程度，并取决于架构描述是否存在，如 8.2 节所述。尽可能地利用架构存储库（参见第五部分第 41 章）识别相关的业务架构构建块。

当需要开发新架构模型以满足利益攸关者的关注点时，使用步骤 1 中识别的模型作为创建用于描述基线架构的新架构内容的指南。

8.4.3 开发目标业务架构描述

为业务架构开发一种目标描述，达到支持架构愿景所必需的程度。待定义的范围和细节层级，将取决于业务元素与实现目标架构愿景之间的相关性，并取决于架构描述是否存在。尽可能地利用架构存储库（见第五部分第 41 章）识别相关的业务架构构建块。

当需要开发新的架构模型以满足利益攸关者的关注点时，使用步骤 1 中识别的模型作为创建用于描述目标架构的新架构内容的指南。

8.4.4 进行差距分析

验证架构模型的内部一致性和准确度：

- 进行权衡分析，以解决不同视图间的冲突（如果有）。
- 确认模型支持的原则、目的和约束。
- 对以架构存储库中选定模型中所表达的视角变更进行注释，并文件化。
- 按需求测试架构模型的完整性。

使用第三部分第 27 章中描述的差距分析技巧识别基线与目标之间的差距。

8.4.5 Define Candidate Roadmap Components

Following creation of a Baseline Architecture, Target Architecture, and gap analysis results, a business roadmap is required to prioritize activities over the coming phases.

This initial Business Architecture roadmap will be used as raw material to support more detailed definition of a consolidated, cross-discipline roadmap within the Opportunities & Solutions phase.

8.4.6 Resolve Impacts Across the Architecture Landscape

Once the Business Architecture is finalized, it is necessary to understand any wider impacts or implications.

At this stage, other architecture artifacts in the Architecture Landscape should be examined to identify:

- Does this Business Architecture create an impact on any pre-existing architectures?
- Have recent changes been made that impact on the Business Architecture?
- Are there any opportunities to leverage work from this Business Architecture in other areas of the organization?
- Does this Business Architecture impact other projects (including those planned as well as those currently in progress)?
- Will this Business Architecture be impacted by other projects (including those planned as well as those currently in progress)?

8.4.7 Conduct Formal Stakeholder Review

Check the original motivation for the architecture project and the Statement of Architecture Work against the proposed Business Architecture, asking if it is fit for the purpose of supporting subsequent work in the other architecture domains. Refine the proposed Business Architecture only if necessary.

8.4.8 Finalize the Business Architecture

- Select standards for each of the building blocks, re-using as much as possible from the reference models selected from the Architecture Repository.
- Fully document each building block.
- Conduct final cross-check of overall architecture against business goals; document rationale for building block decisions in the architecture document.
- Document final requirements traceability report.
- Document final mapping of the architecture within the Architecture Repository; from the selected building blocks, identify those that might be re-used (working practices, roles, business relationships, job descriptions, etc.), and publish via the Architecture Repository.
- Finalize all the work products, such as gap analysis results.

8.4.5 定义候选路线图组件

创建基线架构、目标架构和差距分析结果之后，需要一个业务路线图，以确定后续阶段中活动的优先顺序。

这个初始业务架构路线图，将用作支持机会和解决方案阶段中合并的、跨学科路线图的更详细定义的原始资料。

8.4.6 化解贯穿整个架构全景中的影响

一旦最终确定了业务架构终结，理解更广泛的影响或含义是很有必要的。

在这个阶段，应审查架构全景中的其他架构制品以期识别：

- 这个业务架构是否对之前存在的架构产生影响？
- 是否已经做出影响业务架构的最新变革？
- 是否有机会更有力地发挥本业务架构中的工作在该组织其他领域中的作用？
- 本业务架构是否影响其他项目（包括已计划的和目前正在进行的项目）？
- 本业务架构是否受到其他项目（包括已计划的和目前正在进行的项目）的影响？

8.4.7 进行正式的利益攸关者审视

根据建议的业务架构检查架构项目和架构工作说明书的原始动机，询问其是否适于支持其他架构域中后续工作的目的。仅在必要时对建议的业务架构进行细化。

8.4.8 最终确定业务架构

- 为每个构建块选择标准，尽可能复用从架构存储库中选择的参考模型。
- 完整每个构建块的文件记录。
- 根据业务目标对总体架构进行最终交叉检查；在架构文件中记录构建块决策的理由依据。
- 文件化最终的需求可追溯性报告。
- 文件化架构存储库中架构的最终映射，在选定的构建块中识别可能复用的部分（工作实践、角色、业务关系、职位描述等），并通过架构存储库发布。
- 最终确定所有的工作产物，如差距分析结果。

8.4.9 Create Architecture Definition Document

- Document rationale for building block decisions in the Architecture Definition Document.
- Prepare the business sections of the Architecture Definition Document, comprising some or all of:
  - A business footprint (a high-level description of the people and locations involved with key business functions)
  - A detailed description of business functions and their information needs
  - A management footprint (showing span of control and accountability)
  - Standards, rules, and guidelines showing working practices, legislation, financial measures, etc.
  - A skills matrix and set of job descriptions

If appropriate, use reports and/or graphics generated by modeling tools to demonstrate key views of the architecture. Route the document for review by relevant stakeholders, and incorporate feedback.

8.5 Outputs

The outputs of Phase B may include, but are not restricted to:

- Refined and updated versions of the Architecture Vision phase deliverables, where applicable, including:
  - Statement of Architecture Work (see Part IV, Section 36.2.20), updated if necessary
  - Validated business principles, business goals, and business drivers (see Part IV, Section 36.2.9), updated if necessary
  - Architecture principles (see Part IV, Section 36.2.4)
- Draft Architecture Definition Document (see Part IV, Section 36.2.3), including:
  - Baseline Business Architecture, Version 1.0 (detailed), if appropriate
  - Target Business Architecture, Version 1.0 (detailed), including:
  - Organization structure — identifying business locations and relating them to organizational units
  - Business goals and objectives — for the enterprise and each organizational unit
  - Business functions — a detailed, recursive step involving successive decomposition of major functional areas into sub-functions
  - Business services — the services that the enterprise and each enterprise unit provides to its customers, both internally and externally
  - Business processes, including measures and deliverables
  - Business roles, including development and modification of skills require-ments
  - Business data model

8.4.9 创建架构定义文件

- 在架构定义文件中记录构建块决策的理由依据
- 准备架构定义文件的业务章节，包括部分或全部下列内容：
  - — 业务印迹（对涉及关键业务功能的人员和位置的高层级描述）
  - — 业务功能及其信息需求的详细描述
  - — 管理印迹（表明控制的幅度和可追究的责任）
  - — 表明工作实践、法规和财务测度等的标准、规则和指南
  - — 技能矩阵和一系列职位描述

如适用，使用由建模工具生成的用来展现架构的关键视图的报告和/或图。分发文件以供相关利益攸关者审视，并纳入反馈。

8.5 输出

阶段 B 的输出可包括但不限于：

- 架构愿景阶段交付物的经过细化和更新的版本，在适用情况下，包括：
  - — 架构工作说明书（见第四部分，36.2.20 节），必要时进行更新
  - — 确认的业务原则、业务目标和业务驱动因素（见第四部分 36.2.9 节），必要时进行更新
  - — 架构原则（见第四部分 36.2.4 节）
- 草拟的架构定义文件（见第四部分 36.2.3 节），包括：
  - — 基线业务架构，版本 1.0（详细），如适用
  - — 目标业务架构，版本 1.0（详细），包括：
  - — 组织结构——识别业务位置并使其与组织单元相关联
  - — 业务目标和目的——用于 ENTERPRISE 和每个组织单元
  - — 业务功能——一个详细的递归步骤，包括将主要功能领域逐步分解为子功能
  - — 业务服务——ENTERPRISE 和每个 ENTERPRISE 单元向其内部和外部客户提供的服务
  - — 业务流程，包括测度和交付物
  - — 业务角色，包括技能需求的开发和修改
  - — 业务数据模型

- — Correlation of organization and functions — relate business functions to organizational units in the form of a matrix report
- — Views corresponding to the selected viewpoints addressing key stakeholder concerns

- Draft Architecture Requirements Specification (see Part IV, Section 36.2.6), including such Business Architecture requirements as:
  - — Gap analysis results
  - — Technical requirements — identifying, categorizing, and prioritizing the implications for work in the remaining architecture domains; for example, by a dependency/priority matrix (for example, guiding trade-off between speed of transaction processing and security); list the specific models that are expected to be produced (for example, expressed as primitives of the Zachman Framework)
  - — Updated business requirements
- Business Architecture components of an Architecture Roadmap (see Part IV, Section 36.2.7).

The outputs may include some or all of the following:

- Catalogs:
  - — Organization/Actor catalog
  - — Driver/Goal/Objective catalog
  - — Role catalog
  - — Business Service/Function catalog
  - — Location catalog
  - — Process/Event/Control/Product catalog
  - — Contract/Measure catalog
- Matrices:
  - — Business Interaction matrix
  - — Actor/Role matrix
- Diagrams:
  - — Business Footprint diagram
  - — Business Service/Information diagram
  - — Functional Decomposition diagram
  - — Product Lifecycle diagram
  - — Goal/Objective/Service diagram
  - — Use-case diagram
  - — Organization Decomposition diagram
  - — Process Flow diagram
  - — Event diagram

  — 与所选择的视角相对应的涉及关键利益攸关者关注点的视图

- 草拟的架构需求规范（见第四部分 36.2.6 节），包括如下这类业务架构需求：
  — 差距分析结果
  — 技术需求——识别、分类和优先排序剩余架构域工作的含义，例如，通过依赖性/优先级矩阵（例如，指导对事务处理速度和安保性之间进行的权衡）；列出期望产生的特定模型（例如，表示为 Zachman 框架的原始形式）
  — 经过更新的业务需求
- 架构路线图的业务架构组件（见第四部分 36.2.7 节）。

输出可包括部分或全部下列内容：

- 目录集：
  — 组织/施动者目录集
  — 驱动因素/目标/目的目录集
  — 角色目录集
  — 业务服务/功能目录集
  — 位置目录集
  — 流程/事件/控制/产品目录集
  — 契约/测度目录集
- 矩阵：
  — 业务交互矩阵
  — 施动者/角色矩阵
- 图：
  — 业务印迹图
  — 业务服务/信息图
  — 功能分解图
  — 产品生命周期图
  — 目标/目的/服务图
  — 用例图
  — 组织分解图
  — 过程流图
  — 事件图

Chapter 9
Phase C: Information Systems Architectures

This chapter describes the Information Systems Architectures for an architecture project, including the development of Data and Application Architectures.

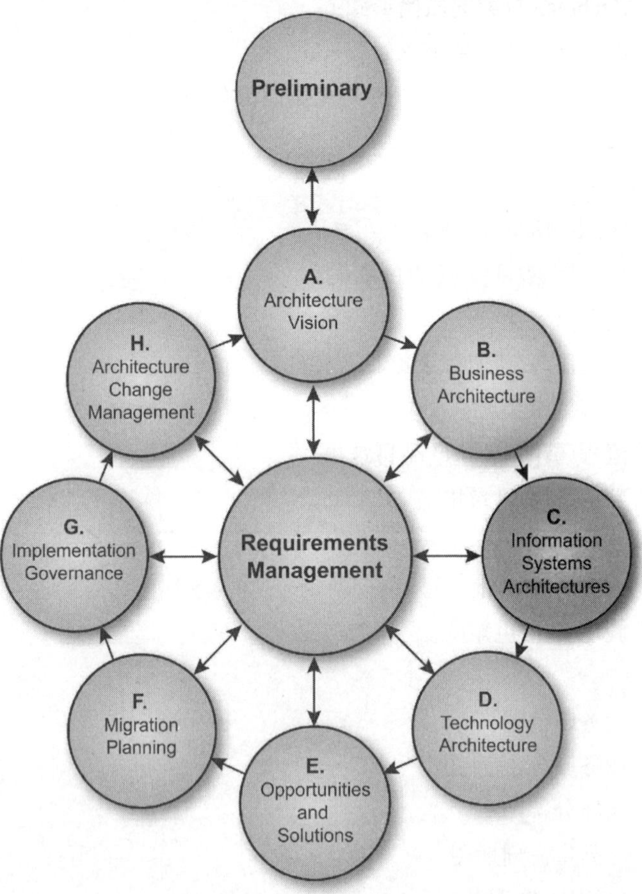

Figure 9-1 Phase C: Information Systems Architectures

第 9 章
阶段 C：信息系统架构

本章描述架构项目的信息系统架构，包括数据架构和应用架构的开发。

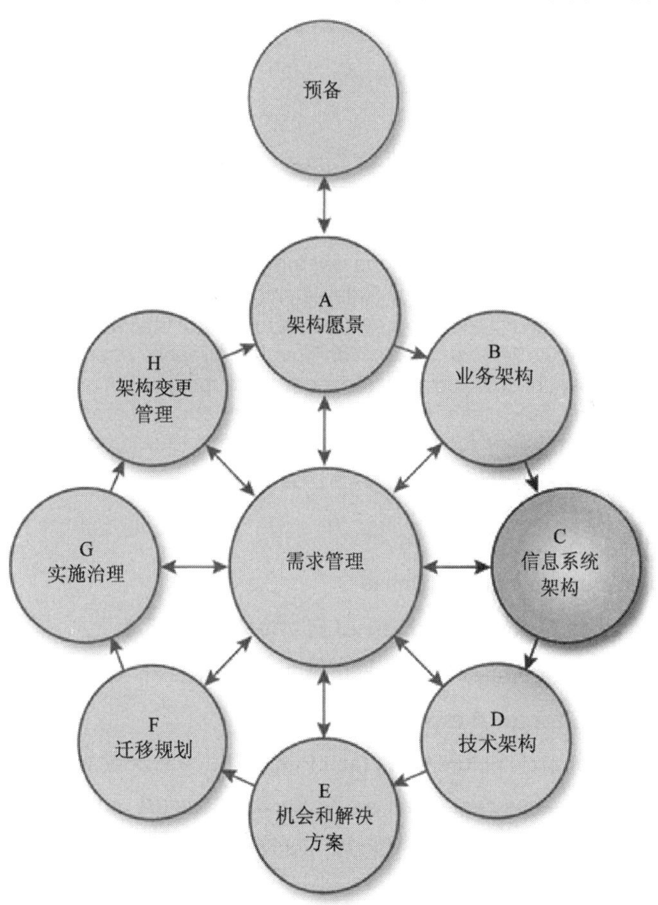

图 9-1　阶段 C：信息系统架构

9.1 Objectives

The objectives of Phase C are to:

- Develop the Target Information Systems (Data and Application) Architecture, describing how the enterprise's Information Systems Architecture will enable the Business Architecture and the Architecture Vision, in a way that addresses the Request for Architecture Work and stakeholder concerns.
- Identify candidate Architecture Roadmap components based upon gaps between the Baseline and Target Information Systems (Data and Application) Architectures.

9.2 Approach

Phase C involves some combination of Data and Application Architecture, in either order. Advocates exist for both sequences. For example, Steven Spewak's Enterprise Architecture Planning (EAP) recommends a data-driven approach.

On the other hand, major applications systems — such as those for Enterprise Resource Planning (ERP), Customer Relationship Management (CRM), etc. — often provide a combination of technology infrastructure and business application logic, and some organizations take an application-driven approach, whereby they recognize certain key applications as forming the core underpinning of the mission-critical business processes, and take the implementation and integration of those core applications as the primary focus of architecture effort (the integration issues often constituting a major challenge).

9.3 Inputs

This section defines the inputs to Phase C.

9.3.1 Reference Materials External to the Enterprise

- Architecture reference materials (see Part IV, Section 36.2.5)

9.3.2 Non-Architectural Inputs

- Request for Architecture Work (see Part IV, Section 36.2.17)
- Capability Assessment (see Part IV, Section 36.2.10)
- Communications Plan (see Part IV, Section 36.2.12)

9.1 目的

阶段 C 的目的是：

- 开发目标信息系统（数据和应用）架构，描述 ENTERPRISE 的信息系统架构如何实现业务架构和架构愿景（以应对架构工作要求书和利益攸关者关注点的方式进行描述）。
- 基于基线信息系统架构和目标信息系统（数据和应用）架构之间的差距，识别候选架构路线图组件。

9.2 实施途径

阶段 C 包括数据架构和应用架构以任一顺序的若干组合，每个顺序都有拥护者。例如，Steven Spewak 的 Enterprise Architecture 规划（EAP）推荐一种数据驱动的途径。

另一方面，主要的应用系统——诸如企业资源规划（ERP）、客户关系管理（CRM）等——通常提供技术基础设施和业务应用逻辑的组合，在形成任务—关键业务流程的核心支撑时，一些组织采用应用驱动的途径识别已确定的关键应用，且将这些核心应用的实施和集成视为架构工作的主要聚焦点（集成工作通常构成主要挑战）。

9.3 输入

本节定义了对阶段 C 的输入。

9.3.1 ENTERPRISE 外的参考资料

- 架构参考资料（见第四部分 36.2.5 节）

9.3.2 非架构输入

- 架构工作要求书（见第四部分 36.2.17 节）
- 能力评估（见第四部分 36.2.10 节）
- 沟通计划（见第四部分 36.2.12 节）

9.3.3 Architectural Inputs

- Organizational Model for Enterprise Architecture (see Part IV, Section 36.2.16), including:
  - Scope of organizations impacted
  - Maturity assessment, gaps, and resolution approach
  - Roles and responsibilities for architecture team(s)
  - Constraints on architecture work
  - Budget requirements
  - Governance and support strategy
- Tailored Architecture Framework (see Part IV, Section 36.2.21), including:
  - Tailored architecture method
  - Tailored architecture content (deliverables and artifacts)
  - Configured and deployed tools
- Application principles (see Part III, Section 23.6.3), if existing
- Data principles (see Part III, Section 23.6.2), if existing
- Statement of Architecture Work (see Part IV, Section 36.2.20)
- Architecture Vision (see Part IV, Section 36.2.8)
- Architecture Repository (see Part IV, Section 36.2.5), including:
  - Re-usable building blocks
  - Organization-specific reference models
  - Organization standards
- Draft Architecture Definition Document (see Part IV, Section 36.2.3), including:
  - Baseline Business Architecture, Version 1.0 (detailed), if appropriate
  - Target Business Architecture, Version 1.0 (detailed)
  - Baseline Data Architecture, Version 0.1
  - Target Data Architecture, Version 0.1
  - Baseline Application Architecture, Version 0.1
  - Target Application Architecture, Version 0.1
- Draft Architecture Requirements Specification (see Part IV, Section 36.2.6), including:
  - Gap analysis results (from Business Architecture)
  - Relevant technical requirements that will apply to Phase C
- Business Architecture components of an Architecture Roadmap (see Part IV, Section 36.2.7)

9.3.3 架构输入

- Enterprise Architecture 的组织模型（见第四部分，36.2.16 节），包括：
  - 组织受影响的范围
  - 成熟度评估、差距和解决途径
  - 架构团队的角色和职责
  - 对架构工作的约束
  - 预算需求
  - 治理和支持战略
- 经剪裁的架构框架（见第四部分 36.2.21 节），包括：
  - 经剪裁的架构方法
  - 经剪裁的架构内容（交付物和制品）
  - 经配置和部署的工具
- 应用原则（见第三部分 23.6.3 节），如存在
- 数据原则（见第三部分 23.6.2 节），如存在
- 架构工作说明书（见第四部分 36.2.20 节）
- 架构愿景（见第四部分 36.2.8 节）
- 架构存储库（见第四部分 36.2.5 节），包括：
  - 可复用的构建块
  - 组织特定的参考模型
  - 组织标准
- 草拟的架构定义文件（见第四部分 36.2.3 节），包括：
  - 基线业务架构，版本 1.0（详细），如适用
  - 目标业务架构，版本 1.0（详细）
  - 基线数据架构，版本 0.1
  - 目标数据架构，版本 0.1
  - 基线应用架构，版本 0.1
  - 目标应用架构，版本 0.1
- 草拟的架构需求规范（见第四部分 36.2.6 节），包括：
  - 差距分析结果（来自于业务架构）
  - 适用于阶段 C 的相关技术需求
- 架构路线图的业务架构组件（见第四部分 36.2.7 节）

9.4 Steps

Detailed steps for Phase C are given separately for each architecture domain:

- Data Architecture (see Chapter 10)
- Application Architecture (see Chapter 11)

9.5 Outputs

The main outputs of Phase C are:

- Refined and updated versions of the Architecture Vision phase deliverables, where applicable, including:
  - Statement of Architecture Work (see Part IV, Section 36.2.20), updated if necessary
- Draft Architecture Definition Document (see Part IV, Section 36.2.3), including:
  - Baseline Data Architecture, Version 1.0
  - Target Data Architecture, Version 1.0
  - Baseline Application Architecture, Version 1.0
  - Target Application Architecture, Version 1.0
  - Data Architecture views corresponding to the selected viewpoints addressing key stakeholder concerns
  - Application Architecture views corresponding to the selected viewpoints addressing key stakeholder concerns
- Draft Architecture Requirements Specification (see Part IV, Section 36.2.6), including such Information Systems Architecture requirements as:
  - Gap analysis results
  - Relevant technical requirements that will apply to this evolution of the architecture development cycle
  - Constraints on the Technology Architecture about to be designed
  - Updated business requirements, if appropriate
- Information systems components of an Architecture Roadmap (see Part IV, Section 36.2.7)

9.4 步骤

分别为每个架构域给出阶段 C 的详细步骤：

- 数据架构（见第 10 章）
- 应用架构（见第 11 章）

9.5 输出

阶段 C 的主要输出有：

- 架构愿景阶段交付物经过细化和更新的版本，在适用情况下，包括：
  - 架构工作说明书（见第四部分 36.2.20 节），必要时进行更新
- 草拟的架构定义文件（见第四部分 36.2.3 节），包括：
  - 基线数据架构，版本 1.0
  - 目标数据架构，版本 1.0
  - 基线应用架构，版本 1.0
  - 目标应用架构，版本 1.0
  - 与选定视角相对应的应对关键利益攸关者关注点的数据架构视图
  - 与选定视角相对应的应对关键利益攸关者关注点的应用架构视图
- 草拟的架构需求规范（见第四部分 36.2.6 节），包括如下这类信息系统架构需求：
  - 差距分析结果
  - 适用于本轮架构开发周期演进的相关技术需求
  - 对将要设计的技术架构的约束
  - 经过更新的业务需求，如适用
- 架构路线图的信息系统组件（见第四部分 36.2.7 节）

Chapter 10 Phase C: Information Systems Architectures — Data Architecture

This chapter describes the Data Architecture part of Phase C.

10.1 Objectives

The objectives of the Data Architecture part of Phase C are to:

- Develop the Target Data Architecture that enables the Business Architecture and the Architecture Vision, while addressing the Request for Architecture Work and stakeholder concerns
- Identify candidate Architecture Roadmap components based upon gaps between the Baseline and Target Data Architectures

10.2 Approach

10.2.1 Key Considerations for Data Architecture

10.2.1.1 Data Management

When an enterprise has chosen to undertake largescale architectural transformation, it is important to understand and address data management issues. A structured and comprehensive approach to data management enables the effective use of data to capitalize on its competitive advantages.

Considerations include:

- A clear definition of which application components in the landscape will serve as the system of record or reference for enterprise master data.
- Will there be an enterprise-wide standard that all application components, including software packages, need to adopt (in the main packages can be prescriptive about the data models and may not be flexible)?
- Clearly understand how data entities are utilized by business functions, processes, and services.
- Clearly understand how and where enterprise data entities are created, stored, transported, and reported.

第 10 章
阶段 C：信息系统架构——数据架构

本章描述阶段 C 的数据架构部分。

10.1 目的

阶段 C 的数据架构部分的目的是：

- 开发实现业务架构和架构愿景的目标数据架构，同时应对架构工作要求书和利益攸关者关注点。
- 基于基线数据架构和目标数据架构之间的差距识别候选架构路线图组件。

10.2 实施途径

10.2.1 数据架构的考量因素

10.2.1.1 数据管理

当 ENTERPRISE 选择进行大规模架构转型时，理解并应对数据管理议题是很重要的。数据管理的一种结构化和综合的实施途径能有效利用数据，积累竞争优势。

考量因素包括：

- 明确定义全景中哪些应用组件将充当 ENTERPRISE 主数据的记录或参考的系统。
- 是否存在所有应用组件（包括软件包）需要采用的整个 ENTERPRISE 范围的标准（该标准在主要的程序包中可规定数据模型但可能不灵活）？
- 清晰地理解业务功能、流程和服务如何利用数据实体。
- 清晰地理解如何以及在哪里创建、存储、传递和报告 ENTERPRISE 的数据实体。

- What is the level and complexity of data transformations required to support the information exchange needs between applications?
- What will be the requirement for software in supporting data integration with the enterprise's customers and suppliers (e.g., use of ETL tools during the data migration, data profiling tools to evaluate data quality, etc.)?

10.2.1.2 Data Migration

When an existing application is replaced, there will be a critical need to migrate data (master, transactional, and reference) to the new application. The Data Architecture should identify data migration requirements and also provide indicators as to the level of transformation, weeding, and cleansing that will be required to present data in a format that meets the requirements and constraints of the target application. The objective being that the target application has quality data when it is populated. Another key consideration is to ensure that an enterprise-wide common data definition is established to support the transformation.

10.2.1.3 Data Governance

Data governance considerations ensure that the enterprise has the necessary dimensions in place to enable the transformation, as follows:

- **Structure**: This dimension pertains to whether the enterprise has the necessary organizational structure and the standards bodies to manage data entity aspects of the transformation.
- **Management System**: Here enterprises should have the necessary management system and data-related programs to manage the governance aspects of data entities throughout its lifecycle.
- **People**: This dimension addresses what data-related skills and roles the enterprise requires for the transformation. If the enterprise lacks such resources and skills, the enterprise should consider either acquiring those critical skills or training existing internal resources to meet the requirements through a well-defined learning program.

10.2.2 Architecture Repository

As part of this phase, the architecture team will need to consider what relevant Data Architecture resources are available in the organization's Architecture Repository (see Part V, Chapter 41), in particular, generic data models relevant to the organization's industry "vertical" sector. For example:

- ARTS has defined a data model for the Retail industry.
- Energistics has defined a data model for the Petrotechnical industry.

- 支持多种应用之间信息交换所需的数据转换的层级和复杂度如何？
- 在支持与 ENTERPRISE 的客户和供应商的数据集成方面，对软件的需求是什么（例如，数据迁移期间使用 ETL 工具，以及使用数据分析工具评估数据质量等）？

10.2.1.2 数据迁移

当现有应用被取代时，关键的需要是将数据（主数据、交互数据和引用数据）迁移到新的应用。数据架构应识别数据迁移需求并提供关于转换、清除和净化等级的指标，这在以符合目标应用需求和约束的格式来提供数据时很有必要。其目的是在充实目标应用时保证数据质量。另一个考量因素是确保建立整个 ENTERPRISE 范围的共用数据定义，以支持转换。

10.2.1.3 数据治理

数据治理的考量确保 ENTERPRISE 具有必要的维度，以使能转型，如下所示：

- **结构**：本维度涉及 ENTERPRISE 是否具有必要的组织结构和标准体系来管理转换的数据实体方方面面。
- **管理系统**：此处的 ENTERPRISE 应具有必要的管理系统和与数据相关的程序，从而在数据全生命周期内管理数据实体的治理方方面面。
- **人员**：本维度表明 ENTERPRISE 的数据转换所需的与数据相关的技能和角色。如果 ENTERPRISE 缺乏这些资源和技能，就应考虑获取这些关键技能，或通过制定明确的学习计划来培训现有的内部资源以满足需求。

10.2.2 架构存储库

作为本阶段的部分，架构团队需要考虑在组织的架构存储库（见第五部分第 41 章）中可获得哪些相关的数据架构资源，尤其是与组织所处行业“垂直”区域有关的一般数据模型。例如：

- ARTS 已经定义了一个零售业的数据模型。
- 能源流组织已经定义了一个油田技术行业的数据模型。

10.3 Inputs

This section defines the inputs to Phase C (Data Architecture).

10.3.1 Reference Materials External to the Enterprise

- Architecture reference materials (see Part IV, Section 36.2.5)

10.3.2 Non-Architectural Inputs

- Request for Architecture Work (see Part IV, Section 36.2.17)
- Capability Assessment (see Part IV, Section 36.2.10)
- Communications Plan (see Part IV, Section 36.2.12)

10.3.3 Architectural Inputs

- Organizational Model for Enterprise Architecture (see Part IV, Section 36.2.16), including:
  - Scope of organizations impacted
  - Maturity assessment, gaps, and resolution approach
  - Roles and responsibilities for architecture team(s)
  - Constraints on architecture work
  - Budget requirements
  - Governance and support strategy
- Tailored Architecture Framework (see Part IV, Section 36.2.21, on page 449), including:
  - Tailored architecture method
  - Tailored architecture content (deliverables and artifacts)
  - Configured and deployed tools
- Data principles (see Part III, Section 23.6.2), if existing
- Statement of Architecture Work (see Part IV, Section 36.2.20)
- Architecture Vision (see Part IV, Section 36.2.8)
- Architecture Repository (see Part IV, Section 36.2.5), including:
  - Re-usable building blocks (in particular, definitions of current data)
  - Publicly available reference models
  - Organization-specific reference models
  - Organization standards
- Draft Architecture Definition Document (see Part IV, Section 36.2.3), including:
  - Baseline Business Architecture, Version 1.0 (detailed), if appropriate

10.3 输入

本节定义了对阶段 C（数据架构）的输入。

10.3.1 ENTERPRISE 外的参考资料

- 架构参考资料（见第四部分，36.2.5 节）

10.3.2 非架构输入

- 架构工作要求书（见第四部分，36.2.17 节）
- 能力评估（见第四部分，36.2.10 节）
- 沟通计划（见第四部分，36.2.12 节）

10.3.3 架构输入

- Enterprise Architecture 的组织模型（见第四部分，36.2.16 节），包括：
  - — 组织受影响的范围
  - — 成熟度评估、差距和解决途径
  - — 架构团队的角色和职责
  - — 对架构工作的约束
  - — 预算需求
  - — 治理和支持战略
- 经剪裁的架构框架（见第 449 页中的第四部分，36.2.21 节），包括：
  - — 经剪裁的架构方法
  - — 经剪裁的架构内容（交付物和制品）
  - — 经配置和部署的工具
- 数据原则（见第三部分，23.6.2 节），如存在
- 架构工作说明书（见第四部分，36.2.20 节）
- 架构愿景（见第四部分，36.2.8 节）
- 架构存储库（见第四部分，36.2.5 节），包括：
  - — 可复用的构建块（尤其是当前数据的定义）
  - — 公开可用的参考模型
  - — 组织特定参考模型
  - — 组织标准
- 草拟的架构定义文件（见第四部分，36.2.3 节），包括：
  - — 基线业务架构，1.0 版本（详细），如适用

  - Target Business Architecture, Version 1.0 (detailed)
  - Baseline Data Architecture, Version 0.1, if available
  - Target Data Architecture, Version 0.1, if available
  - Baseline Application Architecture, Version 1.0 (detailed) or Version 0.1 (Vision)
  - Target Application Architecture, Version 1.0 (detailed) or Version 0.1 (Vision)
  - Baseline Technology Architecture, Version 0.1 (Vision)
  - Target Technology Architecture, Version 0.1 (Vision)
- Draft Architecture Requirements Specification (see Part IV, Section 36.2.6), including:
  - Gap analysis results (from Business Architecture)
  - Relevant technical requirements that will apply to this phase
- Business Architecture components of an Architecture Roadmap (see Part IV, Section36.2.7)

10.4 Steps

The level of detail addressed in Phase C will depend on the scope and goals of the overall architecture effort.

New data building blocks being introduced as part of this effort will need to be defined in detail during Phase C. Existing data building blocks to be carried over and supported in the target environment may already have been adequately defined in previous architectural work; but, if not, they too will need to be defined in Phase C.

The order of the steps in this phase (see below) as well as the time at which they are formally started and completed should be adapted to the situation at hand in accordance with the established architecture governance. In particular, determine whether in this situation it is appropriate to conduct Baseline Description or Target Architecture development first, as described in Part III, Chapter 19.

All activities that have been initiated in these steps must be closed during the Finalize the Data Architecture step (see Section 10.4.8). The documentation generated from these steps must be formally published in the Create Architecture Definition Document step (see Section 10.4.9).

The steps in Phase C (Data Architecture) are as follows:

- Select reference models, viewpoints, and tools (see Section 10.4.1)
- Develop Baseline Data Architecture Description (see Section 10.4.2)
- Develop Target Data Architecture Description (see Section 10.4.3)
- Perform gap analysis (see Section 10.4.4)
- Define candidate roadmap components (see Section 10.4.5)
- Resolve impacts across the Architecture Landscape (see Section 10.4.6)
- Conduct formal stakeholder review (see Section 10.4.7)
- Finalize the Data Architecture (see Section 10.4.8)

— 目标业务架构，1.0 版本（详细）
— 基线数据架构，0.1 版本，如可用
— 目标数据架构，0.1 版本，如可用
— 基线应用架构，1.0 版本（详细）或 0.1 版本（愿景）
— 目标应用架构，1.0 版本（详细）或 0.1 版本（愿景）
— 基线技术架构，0.1 版本（愿景）
— 目标技术架构，0.1 版本（愿景）

- 草拟的架构需求规范（见第四部分，36.2.6 节），包括：
  - 差距分析结果（来自于业务架构）
  - 适用于本阶段的相关技术需求
- 架构路线图的业务架构组件（见第四部分，36.2.7 节）

10.4 步骤

阶段 C 中所划分的细节层级取决于总体架构工作的范围和目标。

作为本项工作的部分所列入的新数据构建块需要在阶段 C 中详细定义。延用到目标环境且被其支持的现有数据构建块，可能在之前的架构工作中已被充分定义，如果没有，就需要在阶段 C 中定义。

本阶段中的步骤顺序（见下文）和这些步骤正式开始和完成的时间，应按已确定的架构治理，以适应当前情况。尤其是，确定在这种情况下首先实施基线描述或目标架构开发是否合适，如第三部分第 19 章所述。

在这些步骤中，已经开始的所有活动必须在最终确定数据架构步骤（见 10.4.8 节）中结束。这些步骤中生成的文档必须在创建架构定义文件步骤（见 10.4.9 节）中正式发布。

阶段 C（数据架构）中的步骤如下：

- 选择参考模型、视角和工具（见 10.4.1 节）
- 开发基线数据架构描述（见 10.4.2 节）
- 开发目标数据架构描述（见 10.4.3 节）
- 进行差距分析（见 10.4.4 节）
- 定义候选路线图组件（见 10.4.5 节）
- 化解贯穿整个架构全景中的影响（见 10.4.6 节）
- 进行正式的利益攸关者审视（见 10.4.7 节）
- 最终确定数据架构（见 10.4.8 节）

- Create Architecture Definition Document (see Section 10.4.9)

10.4.1 Select Reference Models, Viewpoints, and Tools

Review and validate (or generate, if necessary) the set of data principles. These will normally form part of an overarching set of architecture principles. Guidelines for developing and applying principles, and a sample set of data principles, are given in Part III, Chapter 23.

Select relevant Data Architecture resources (reference models, patterns, etc.) on the basis of the business drivers, stakeholders, concerns, and Business Architecture.

Select relevant Data Architecture viewpoints (for example, stakeholders of the data — regulatory bodies, users, generators, subjects, auditors, etc.; various time dimensions — real-time, reporting period, event-driven, etc.; locations; business processes); i.e., those that will enable the architect to demonstrate how the stakeholder concerns are being addressed in the Data Architecture.

Identify appropriate tools and techniques (including forms) to be used for data capture, modeling, and analysis, in association with the selected viewpoints. Depending on the degree of sophistication warranted, these may comprise simple documents or spreadsheets, or more sophisticated modeling tools and techniques such as data management models, data models, etc. Examples of data modeling techniques are:

- Entity-relationship diagram.
- Class diagrams.

10.4.1.1 Determine Overall Modeling Process

For each viewpoint, select the models needed to support the specific view required, using the selected tool or method.

Ensure that all stakeholder concerns are covered. If they are not, create new models to address concerns not covered, or augment existing models (see above).

The recommended process for developing a Data Architecture is as follows:

- Collectdata-related models from existing Business Architecture and Application Architecture materials.
- Rationalize data requirements and align with any existing enterprise data catalogs and models; this allows the development of a data inventory and entity relationship.
- Update and develop matrices across the architecture by relating data to business service, business function, access rights, and application.
- Elaborate Data Architecture views by examining how data is created, distributed, migrated, secured, and archived.

10.4.1.2 Identify Required Catalogs of Data Building Blocks

The organization's data inventory is captured as a catalog within the Architecture Repository. Catalogs are hierarchical in nature and capture a decomposition of a metamodel entity and also decompositions across related model entities (e.g., logical data component → physical data component → data entity).

Catalogs form the raw material for development of matrices and diagrams and also act as a key resource for portfolio managing business and IT capability.

- 创建架构定义文件（见 10.4.9 节）

10.4.1 选择参考模型、视角和工具

审视并确认（或生成，如有必要）一组数据原则。这些原则通常构成首要架构原则组的一部分。第三部分第 23 章给出了开发和应用原则的指南以及一组数据原则示例。

基于业务驱动因素、利益攸关者、关注点和业务架构选择相关的数据架构资源（参考模型、特征模式等）。

选择相关的数据架构视角（例如，数据的利益攸关者——监管机构、使用者、生成者、隶属者、审核者等；不同的时间维度——实时、报告周期、事件驱动等；位置；业务流程）；即架构师能说明在数据架构中，如何应对利益攸关者的关注点的视角。

结合所选视角，识别用于数据捕获、建模和分析的适当工具和技巧（包括形式）。根据认可的复杂程度，这些工具和技巧可包括简单的文件或电子表格，或较为复杂的建模工具和技巧（如数据管理模型、数据模型等）。数据建模技巧的示例为：

- 实体关系图。
- 类图。

10.4.1.1 确定总体建模流程

针对每个视角，使用选定的工具或方法来选择支持所要求的特定视图所需的模型。

确保所有利益攸关者的关注点被涵盖。若没有，就要创建新模型以应对未涵盖的关注点或扩展现有模型（见上文）。

开发数据架构的建议流程如下：

- 从现有的业务架构和应用架构资料中收集与数据相关的模型。
- 将数据需求合理化并与现有 ENTERPRISE 的数据目录集和模型保持一致，这有助于数据存储清单和实体关系的开发。
- 通过将数据与业务服务、业务功能、访问权和应用关联起来从而使更新和开发矩阵贯穿整个架构。
- 通过审查数据被如何创建、分布、迁移、保护并存档从而详细阐述数据架构视图。

10.4.1.2 识别所需的数据构建块目录集

捕获组织的数据存储清单作为架构存储库内的一个目录集。目录集本质上是分层次的，并捕获元模型实体的分解以及相关模型实体之间的分解（例如，逻辑数据组件→物理数据组件→数据实体）。

目录集形成用于开发矩阵和图的原始资料，并充当项目谱系管理的业务能力和 IT 能力的关键资源。

During the Business Architecture phase, a Business Service/Information diagram was created showing the key data entities required by the main business services. This is a prerequisite to successful Data Architecture activities.

Using the traceability from application to business function to data entity inherent in the content framework, it is possible to create an inventory of the data needed to be in place to support the Architecture Vision.

Once the data requirements are consolidated in a single location, it is possible to refine the data inventory to achieve semantic consistency and to remove gaps and overlaps.

The following catalogs should be considered for development within a Data Architec-ture:

- Data Entity/Data Component catalog.

The structure of catalogs is based on the attributes of metamodelentities, as defined in Part IV, Chapter 34.

10.4.1.3 Identify Required Matrices

Matrices show the core relationships between related model entities.

Matrices form the raw material for development of diagrams and also act as a key resource for impact assessment.

At this stage, an entity to applications matrix could be produced to validate this mapping. How data is created, maintained, transformed, and passed to other applications, or used by other applications, will now start to be understood. Obvious gaps such as entities that never seem to be created by an application or data created but never used, need to be noted for later gap analysis.

The rationalized data inventory can be used to update and refine the architectural diagrams of how data relates to other aspects of the architecture.

Once these updates have been made, it may be appropriate to drop into a short iteration of Application Architecture to resolve the changes identified.

The following matrices should be considered for development within a Data Architec-ture:

- Data Entity/Business Function (showing which data supports which functions and which business function owns which data).
- Business Service/Information (developed during the Business Architecture phase).
- Application/Data (developed across the Application Architecture and Data Architecture phases).

The structure of matrices is based on the attributes of metamodel entities, as defined in Part IV, Chapter 34.

10.4.1.4 Identify Required Diagrams

Diagrams present the Data Architecture information from a set of different perspectives (viewpoints) according to the requirements of the stakeholders.

Once the data entities have been refined, a diagram of the relationships between entities and their attributes can be produced.

It is important to note at this stage that information may be a mixture of enterprise-level data(from system service providers and package vendor information) and local-level data held in personal databases and spreadsheets.

在业务架构阶段创建一个表明主要业务服务所需的关键数据实体的业务服务/信息图。这是数据架构活动成功的前提。

使用内容框架内固有的应用—业务功能—数据实体的可追溯性，就可能创建支持架构愿景所需要的数据存储清单。

一旦在单一位置合并了数据需求，就可能细化数据存储清单，以实现语义一致性并消除差距和重叠。

应考虑在数据架构内开发下列目录集：

- 数据实体/数据组件目录集。

目录集结构基于元模型实体的属性，如第四部分第 34 章所定义。

10.4.1.3 识别所需的矩阵

矩阵表明相关模型实体之间的核心关系。

矩阵形成用于开发图的原始资料，并充当影响评估的关键资源。

本阶段生成应用矩阵实体以确认本映射。从现在开始理解数据被如何创建、维护、转换并传递至其他应用，或由其他应用使用。需要注意用于后续差距分析的明显差距，比如看起来永远不会由应用创建的实体或已经创建但从未使用的数据。

合理化的数据存储清单可用于更新并细化关于数据如何与架构其他方面相关联的架构图。

一旦经过更新，则适合进入应用架构的短期迭代以解决已识别的变更。

应考虑在数据架构中开发下列矩阵：

- 数据实体/业务功能（表明哪些数据支持哪些功能，以及哪些业务功能拥有哪些数据）。
- 业务服务/信息（在业务架构阶段开发）。
- 应用/数据（在应用贯穿架构和数据架构阶段开发）。

矩阵结构基于元模型实体的属性，如第四部分第 34 章所定义。

10.4.1.4 识别所需的图

根据利益攸关者的需求，图代表从一组不同关注层面（视角）展现出的数据架构信息。

一旦数据实体被细化，则可生成实体及其属性之间的关系图。

重要的是，注意本阶段的信息可能是 ENTERPRISE 层级数据（来自系统服务提供者和程序包供应商信息）与在个人数据库和电子表格中保存的本地层级数据的混合体。

The level of detail modeled needs to be carefully assessed. Some physical system data models will exist down to a very detailed level; others will only have core entities modeled. Not all data models will have been kept up-to-date as applications were modified and extended over time. It is important to achieve a balance in the level of detail provided (e.g., reproducing existing detailed system physical data schemas or presenting high-level process maps and data requirements, highlight the two extreme views).

The following diagrams should be considered for development within a Data Architec-ture:

- Conceptual Data diagram.
- Logical Data diagram.
- Data Dissemination diagram.
- Data Lifecycle diagram.
- Data Security diagram.
- Data Migration diagram.

10.4.1.5 Identify Types of Requirement to be Collected

Once the Data Architecture catalogs, matrices, and diagrams have been developed, architecture modeling is completed by formalizing the data-focused requirements for implementing the Target Architecture.

These requirements may:

- Relate to the data domain.
- Provide requirements input into the Application, and Technology Architectures.
- Provide detailed guidance to be reflected during design and implementation to ensure that the solution addresses the original architecture requirements.

Within this step, the architect should identify requirements that should be met by the architecture(see Section 17.2.2).

10.4.2 Develop Baseline Data Architecture Description

Develop a Baseline Description of the existing Data Architecture, to the extent necessary to support the Target Data Architecture. The scope and level of detail to be defined will depend on the extent to which existing data elements are likely to be carried over into the Target Data Architecture, and on whether architectural descriptions exist, as described in Section 10.2. To the extent possible, identify the relevant Data Architecture building blocks, drawing on the Architecture Repository (see Part V, Chapter 41).

Where new architecture models need to be developed to satisfy stakeholder concerns, use the models identified within Step 1 as a guideline for creating new architecture content to describe the Baseline Architecture.

需要仔细评估建模的细节层级。某些物理系统数据模型将细化到非常详细的层级，其他的仅对核心实体进行建模。由于应用将随时间修改和扩展，因此，并不是所有的数据模型都会保持最新状态。重要的是在提供的细节层级中达到平衡（例如，复制现有的详细系统物理数据模式或展现高层级流程映射和数据需求，强调这两个极端的视图）。

应考虑在数据架构内开发下列图：

- 概念数据图。
- 逻辑数据图。
- 数据传播图。
- 数据生命周期图。
- 数据安保图。
- 数据迁移图。

10.4.1.5 识别待收集的需求类型

一旦开发了数据架构目录集、矩阵和图，就可通过对用于目标架构实施且以数据为聚焦点的需求进行标准化来完成架构建模。

这些需求可能：

- 与数据域相关。
- 提供对应用架构和技术架构的需求输入。
- 提供在设计和实施期间反映出的详细引导，以确保解决方案应对最初的架构需求。

在本步骤中，架构师应识别该架构应满足的需求（见 17.2.2 节）。

10.4.2 开发基线数据架构描述

开发现有数据架构的基线描述，以达到支持目标数据架构所必需的程度。待定义的范围和细节层级取决于现有的数据元素在多大程度上有可能延用到目标数据架构中，以及架构描述是否存在，如 10.2 节所述。尽可能地利用架构存储库（见第五部分第 41 章）识别相关的数据架构构建块。

当需要开发新架构模型以满足利益攸关者的关注点时，使用步骤 1 中识别的模型作为创建用于描述基线架构的新架构内容的指南。

10.4.3 Develop Target Data Architecture Description

Develop a Target Description for the Data Architecture, to the extent necessary to support the Architecture Vision and Target Business Architecture. The scope and level of detail to be defined will depend on the relevance of the data elements to attaining the Target Architecture, and on whether architectural descriptions exist. To the extent possible, identify the relevant Data Architecture building blocks, drawing on the Architecture Repository (see Part V, Chapter 41).

Where new architecture models need to be developed to satisfy stakeholder concerns, use the models identified within Step 1 as a guideline for creating new architecture content to describe the Target Architecture.

10.4.4 Perform Gap Analysis

Verify the architecture models for internal consistency and accuracy:

- Perform trade-off analysis to resolve conflicts (if any) among the different views.
- Validate that the models support the principles, objectives, and constraints.
- Note changes to the view point represented in the selected models from the Architecture Repository, and document.
- Test architecture models for completeness against requirements.

Identify gaps between the baseline and target, using the Gap Analysis technique as described inPart III, Chapter 27.

10.4.5 Define Candidate Roadmap Components

Following creation of a Baseline Architecture, Target Architecture, and gap analysis, a data roadmap is required to prioritize activities over the coming phases.

This initial Data Architecture roadmap will be used as raw material to support more detailed definition of a consolidated, cross-discipline roadmap within the Opportunities & Solutions phase.

10.4.6 Resolve Impacts Across the Architecture Landscape

Once the Data Architecture is finalized, it is necessary to understand any wider impacts or implications.

At this stage, other architecture artifacts in the Architecture Landscape should be examined to identify:

- Does this Data Architecture create an impact on any pre-existing architectures?
- Have recent changes been made that impact the Data Architecture?
- Are there any opportunities to leverage work from this Data Architecture in other areas of the organization?
- Does this Data Architecture impact other projects (including those planned as well as those currently in progress)?

10.4.3 开发目标数据架构描述

开发数据架构的目标描述，以达到支持架构愿景和目标业务架构所必需的程度。待定义的范围和细节层级将取决于数据元素与实现目标架构之间的关联性，以及架构描述是否存在。尽可能地利用架构存储库（参见第五部分第 41 章）识别相关的数据架构构建块。

当需要开发新的架构模型以满足利益攸关者关注点时，使用步骤 1 中识别的模型作为创建用于描述目标架构的新架构内容的指南。

10.4.4 进行差距分析

验证架构模型的内部一致性和准确度：

- 进行权衡分析，以解决不同视图间的冲突（如果有）。
- 确认模型支持的原则、目的和约束。
- 对架构存储库中选定模型里表达出的视角变更进行注释，并文档化。
- 根据需求测试架构模型的完整性。

使用第三部分第 27 章中描述的差距分析技巧，识别基线与目标之间的差距。

10.4.5 定义候选路线图组件

创建基线架构、目标架构和差距分析之后，需要一个数据路线图来确定后续阶段中活动的优先顺序。

本初始数据架构路线图将作为原始资料，支持在机会和解决方案阶段中合并的，跨学科的路线图的更详细定义。

10.4.6 解析贯穿整个架构全景中的影响

一旦最终确定了数据架构，有必要理解任何更广泛的影响或后果。

在本阶段，应审查架构全景中的其他架构制品以识别：

- 本数据架构是否对先前存在的架构产生影响？
- 是否已经做出影响数据架构的最新变更？
- 是否有机会在该组织的其他领域中更有力地发挥来自数据架构的工作的作用？
- 本数据架构是否影响其他项目（包括已计划的和当前正在进行的项目）？

- Will this Data Architecture be impacted by other projects (including those planned as well as those currently in progress)?

10.4.7 Conduct Formal Stakeholder Review

Check the original motivation for the architecture project and the Statement of Architecture Work against the proposed Data Architecture. Conduct an impact analysis to identify any areas where the Business and Application Architectures (e.g., business practices) may need to change to cater for changes in the Data Architecture (for example, changes to forms or procedures, applications, or database systems).

If the impact is significant, this may warrant the Business and Application Architectures being revisited.

Identify any areas where the Application Architecture (if generated at this point) may need to change to cater for changes in the Data Architecture (or to identify constraints on the Application Architecture about to be designed).

If the impact is significant, it may be appropriate to drop into a short iteration of the Application Architecture at this point.

Identify any constraints on the Technology Architecture about to be designed, refining the proposed Data Architecture only if necessary.

10.4.8 Finalize the Data Architecture

- Select standards for each of the building blocks, re-using as much as possible from the reference models selected from the Architecture Repository.
- Fully document each building block.
- Conduct final cross-check of overall architecture against business requirements; document rationale for building block decisions in the architecture document.
- Document final requirements traceability report.
- Document final mapping of the architecture within the Architecture Repository; from the selected building blocks, identify those that might be re-used, and publish via the Architecture Repository.
- Finalize all the work products, such as gap analysis.

10.4.9 Create Architecture Definition Document

Document rationale for building block decisions in the Architecture Definition Document.

Prepare Data Architecture sections of the Architecture Definition Document, comprising some or all of:

- Business data model.
- Logical data model.
- Data management process model.
- Data Entity/Business Function matrix.

- 本数据架构是否会受到其他项目（包括已计划的和当前正在进行的项目）的影响？

10.4.7 进行正式的利益攸关者审视

根据建议的数据架构来检查架构项目和架构工作说明书的原始动机。进行影响分析，以识别可能需要改变业务架构和应用架构（例如，业务实践）的区域来迎合数据架构内的变更要求（例如，对形式和步骤、应用或数据库系统的变更）。

如果影响很显著，也许要保证业务架构和应用架构被重新回顾。

识别出为应对数据架构内变更而可能需要改变应用架构（若此时生成）的领域（或识别对将要设计的应用架构的约束）。

如果影响很显著，那么此时可能适合进入应用架构的短迭代。

识别对将要设计的技术架构的约束，仅在必要时对建议的数据架构进行细化。

10.4.8 最终确定数据架构

- 选择每个构建块的标准，尽可能复用从架构存储库中选择的参考模型。
- 完整地文件化每个构建块。
- 根据业务需求对总体架构进行最终交叉检查，在架构文件中记录构建块决策的理由依据。
- 记录最终的需求可追溯性报告。
- 记录架构存储库中架构的最终映射，从选定的构建块中识别可复用的构建块，并通过架构存储库发布。
- 最终确定所有的工作产物，如差距分析。

10.4.9 创建架构定义文件

在架构定义文件中记录构建块决策的理由依据。

准备架构定义文件的数据架构章节，包括以下部分或全部内容：

- 业务数据模型。
- 逻辑数据模型。
- 数据管理流程模型。
- 数据实体/业务功能矩阵。

- Data interoperability requirements (e.g., XML schema, security policies).
- If appropriate, use reports and/or graphics generated by modeling tools to demonstrate key views of the architecture; route the document for review by relevant stakeholders, and incorporate feedback.

10.5 Outputs

The outputs of Phase C (Data Architecture) may include, but are not restricted to:

- Refined and updated versions of the Architecture Vision phase deliverables, where applicable:
  - Statement of Architecture Work (see Part IV, Section 36.2.20), updated if necessary
  - Validated data principles (see Part III, Section 23.6.2), or new data principles (if generated here)
- Draft Architecture Definition Document (see Part IV, Section 36.2.3), including:
  - Baseline Data Architecture, Version 1.0, if appropriate
  - Target Data Architecture, Version 1.0
  - Business data model
  - Logical data model
  - Data management process models
  - Data Entity/Business Function matrix
  - Views corresponding to the selected viewpoints addressing key stakeholder concerns
- Draft Architecture Requirements Specification (see Part IV, Section 36.2.6), including such Data Architecture requirements as:
  - Gap analysis results
  - Data interoperability requirements
  - Relevant technical requirements that will apply to this evolution of the architecture development cycle
  - Constraints on the Technology Architecture about to be designed
  - Updated business requirements, if appropriate
  - Updated application requirements, if appropriate
- Data Architecture components of an Architecture Roadmap (see Part IV, Section 36.2.7)

The outputs may include some or all of the following:

- Catalogs:
  - Data Entity/Data Component catalog
- Matrices:
  - Data Entity/Business Function matrix

- 数据互用性需求（例如，XML 模式、安保策略）。
- 如适用，使用建模工具生成的报告和/或图说明架构的关键视图，分发文件，以供相关利益攸关者审视，并纳入反馈。

10.5 输出

阶段 C（数据架构）的输出可包括但不限于：

- 架构愿景阶段交付物的经过细化和更新的版本，如适用：
  - — 架构工作说明书（见第四部分，36.2.20 节），必要时进行更新
  - — 经过确认的数据原则（见第三部分，23.6.2 节）或新的数据原则（若在此阶段生成）
- 草拟的架构定义文件（见第四部分，36.2.3 节），包括：
  - — 基线数据架构，版本 1.0，如适用
  - — 目标数据架构，版本 1.0
  - — 业务数据模型
  - — 逻辑数据模型
  - — 数据管理流程模型
  - — 数据实体/业务功能矩阵
  - — 与应对关键的利益攸关者关注点所选定的视角相对应的视图
- 草拟的架构需求规范（见第四部分，36.2.6 节），包括以下各类数据架构需求：
  - — 差距分析结果
  - — 数据互用性需求
  - — 适用于本架构开发周期演进的相关技术需求
  - — 对将要设计的技术架构的约束
  - — 经过更新的业务需求，如适用
  - — 经过更新的应用需求，如适用
- 架构路线图的数据架构组件（见第四部分 36.2.7 节）

输出可包括以下部分或全部内容：

- 目录集：
  - — 数据实体/数据组件目录
- 矩阵：
  - — 数据实体/业务功能矩阵

- Application/Data matrix

- Diagrams:
  - Conceptual Data diagram
  - Logical Data diagram
  - Data Dissemination diagram
  - Data Security diagram
  - Data Migration diagram
  - Data Lifecycle diagram

  — 应用/数据矩阵

- 图：
  — 概念数据图
  — 逻辑数据图
  — 数据传播图
  — 数据安保图
  — 数据迁移图
  — 数据生命周期图

Chapter 11
Phase C: Information Systems Architectures — Application Architecture

This chapter describes the Application Architecture part of Phase C.

11.1 Objectives

The objectives of the Application Architecture part of Phase C are to:

- Develop the Target Application Architecture that enables the Business Architecture and the Architecture Vision, while addressing the Request for Architecture Work and stakeholder concerns
- Identify candidate Architecture Roadmap components based upon gaps between theBaseline and Target Application Architectures

11.2 Approach

11.2.1 Architecture Repository

As part of this phase, the architecture team will need to consider what relevant Application Architecture resources are available in the Architecture Repository (see Part V, Chapter 41). In particular:

- Generic business models relevant to the organization's industry "vertical" sector; for example:
  - The TeleManagement Forum (TMF) — www.tmforum.org — has developed detailed applications models relevant to the Telecommunications industry.
  - The Object Management Group (OMG) — www.omg.org — has a number of vertical Domain Task Forces developing software models relevant to specific vertical domains such as Healthcare, Transportation, Finance, etc.
- Application models relevant to common high-level business functions, such as electronic commerce, supply chain management, etc.

The Open Group has a Reference Model for Integrated Information Infrastructure (III-RM) — see Part VI, Chapter 44 — that focuses on the application-level components and services necessary to provide an integrated information infrastructure.

第 11 章
阶段 C：信息系统架构——应用架构

本章描述阶段 C 的应用架构部分。

11.1 目的

阶段 C 的应用架构部分的目的是：

- 在应对架构工作要求书和利益攸关者关注点的同时，开发使能业务架构和架构愿景的目标应用架构。
- 基于基线应用架构和目标应用架构之间的差距识别候选架构路线图组件。

11.2 实施途径

11.2.1 架构存储库

作为本阶段的一部分，架构团队需要考虑在架构存储库（见第五部分第 41 章）中哪些相关的应用架构资源是可用的。尤其是：

- 与组织所属行业“垂直”的区域有关的通用业务模型；例如：
  - 电信管理论坛（TMF）——www.tmforum.org——已开发了与电信行业有关的详细应用模型。
  - 对象管理组（OMG）——www.omg.org——拥有多个垂直域任务组，例如医疗保健、交通、金融等，开发与特定垂直域有关的软件模型。
- 与诸如电子商务、供应链管理等共用高层级业务功能有关的应用模型。

The Open Group 具有综合信息基础设施的参考模型（III-RM）——参见第四部分第 44 章——该模型聚焦于提供综合信息基础设施必需的应用层级的组件和服务。

11.3 Inputs

This section defines the inputs to Phase C (Application Architecture).

11.3.1 Reference Materials External to the Enterprise

- Architecture reference materials (see Part IV, Section 36.2.5)

11.3.2 Non-Architectural Inputs

- Request for Architecture Work (see Part IV, Section 36.2.17)
- Capability Assessment (see Part IV, Section 36.2.10)
- Communications Plan (see Part IV, Section 36.2.12)

11.3.3 Architectural Inputs

- Organizational Model for Enterprise Architecture (see Part IV, Section 36.2.16), including:
  - Scope of organizations impacted
  - Maturity assessment, gaps, and resolution approach
  - Roles and responsibilities for architecture team(s)
  - Constraints on architecture work
  - Budget requirements
  - Governance and support strategy
- Tailored Architecture Framework (see Part IV, Section 36.2.21), including:
  - Tailored architecture method
  - Tailored architecture content (deliverables and artifacts)
  - Configured and deployed tools
- Application principles (see Part III, Section 23.6.3), if existing
- Statement of Architecture Work (see Part IV, Section 36.2.20)
- Architecture Vision (see Part IV, Section 36.2.8)
- Architecture Repository (see Part IV, Section 36.2.5), including:
  - Re-usable building blocks
  - Publicly available reference models
  - Organization-specific reference models
  - Organization standards
- Draft Architecture Definition Document (see Part IV, Section 36.2.3), including:
  - Baseline Business Architecture, Version 1.0 (detailed), if appropriate

11.3 输入

本节定义了对阶段 C（应用架构）的输入。

11.3.1 ENTERPRISE 外部参考资料

- 架构参考资料（见第四部分 36.2.5 节）

11.3.2 非架构输入

- 架构工作要求书（见第四部分 36.2.17 节）
- 能力评估（见第四部分 36.2.10 节）
- 沟通计划（见第四部分 36.2.12 节）

11.3.3 架构输入

- Enterprise Architecture 的组织模型（见第四部分 36.2.16 节），包括：
  - — 组织受影响的范围
  - — 成熟度评估、差距和解决途径
  - — 架构团队的角色和职责
  - — 对架构工作的约束
  - — 预算需求
  - — 治理和支持战略
- 经剪裁的架构框架（见第四部分 36.2.21 节），包括：
  - — 经剪裁的架构方法
  - — 经剪裁的架构内容（交付物和制品）
  - — 经配置和部署的工具
- 应用原则（见第三部分 23.6.3 节），如存在
- 架构工作说明书（见第四部分 36.2.20 节）
- 架构愿景（见第四部分 36.2.8 节）
- 架构存储库（见第四部分 36.2.5 节），包括：
  - — 可复用的构建块
  - — 公开可用的参考模型
  - — 组织特定的参考模型
  - — 组织标准
- 起草架构定义文件（见第四部分 36.2.3 节），包括：
  - — 基线业务架构，版本 1.0（详细），如适用

  - Target Business Architecture, Version 1.0 (detailed)
  - Baseline Data Architecture, Version 1.0 (detailed), or Version 0.1 (Vision)
  - Target Data Architecture, Version 1.0 (detailed), or Version 0.1 (Vision)
  - Baseline Application Architecture, Version 0.1, if appropriate and if available
  - Target Application Architecture, Version 0.1, if available
  - Baseline Technology Architecture, Version 0.1 (Vision)
  - Target Technology Architecture, Version 0.1 (Vision)
- Draft Architecture Requirements Specification (see Part IV, Section 36.2.6), including:
  - Gap analysis results (from Business Architecture and Data Architecture, if available)
  - Relevant technical requirements that will apply to this phase
- Business and Data Architecture components of an Architecture Roadmap, if available (seePart IV, Section 36.2.7)

11.4 Steps

The level of detail addressed in Phase C will depend on the scope and goals of the overall architecture effort.

New application building blocks being introduced as part of this effort will need to be defined in detail during Phase C. Existing application building blocks to be carried over and supported in the target environment may already have been adequately defined in previous architectural work; but, if not, they too will need to be defined in Phase C.

The order of the steps in this phase (see below as well as the time at which they are formally started and completed should be adapted to the situation at hand in accordance with the established architecture governance. In particular, determine whether in this situation it is appropriate to conduct Baseline Description or Target Architecture development first, as described in Part III, Chapter 19.

All activities that have been initiated in these steps must be closed during the Finalize the Application Architecture step (see Section 11.4.8). The documentation generated from these steps must be formally published in the Create Architecture Definition Document step (see Section 11.4.9).

The steps in Phase C (Application Architecture) are as follows:

- Select reference models, viewpoints, and tools (see Section 11.4.1)
- Develop Baseline Application Architecture Description (see Section 11.4.2)
- Develop Target Application Architecture Description (see Section 11.4.3)
- Perform gap analysis (see Section 11.4.4)
- Define candidate roadmap components (see Section 11.4.5)
- Resolve impacts across the Architecture Landscape (see Section 11.4.6)
- Conduct formal stakeholder review (see Section 11.4.7)

  — 目标业务架构，版本 1.0（详细）
  — 基线数据架构，版本 1.0（详细）或版本 0.1（愿景）
  — 目标数据架构，版本 1.0（详细）或版本 0.1（愿景）
  — 基线应用架构，版本 0.1，如适用且可用
  — 目标应用架构，版本 0.1，如可用
  — 基线技术架构，版本 0.1（愿景）
  — 目标技术架构，版本 0.1（愿景）
- 起草架构需求规范（见第四部分 36.2.6 节），包括：
  — 差距分析结果（来自于业务架构和数据架构，如可用）
  — 适用于本阶段的相关技术需求
- 架构路线图的业务和数据架构组件（见第四部分 36.2.7 节），如可用

11.4 步骤

阶段 C 中所划分的细节层级将取决于总体架构工作的范围和目标。

作为本项工作的部分引入的新应用构建块需要在阶段 C 中详细定义。将在目标环境中延用并被支持的现有应用构建块可能已经在之前的架构工作中充分定义，但如果没有，则需要在阶段 C 中定义。

本阶段中的步骤顺序（见下文）及其正式开始和完成的时间，应按已确定的架构治理根据当前情况进行适应性调整。尤其是，确定在这种情况下首先实施基线描述或目标架构开发是否合适，如第三部分第 19 章所述。

在这些步骤中，已经开始的所有活动必须在最终确定应用架构步骤（见 11.4.8 节）结束。这些步骤中生成的文档必须在创建架构定义文件步骤（见 11.4.9 节）正式发布。

阶段 C（应用架构）中的步骤如下：

- 选择参考模型、视角和工具（见 11.4.1 节）
- 开发基线应用架构描述（见 11.4.2 节）
- 开发目标应用架构描述（见 11.4.3 节）
- 进行差距分析（见 11.4.4 节）
- 定义候选路线图组件（见 11.4.5 节）
- 化解整个贯穿架构全景中的影响（见 11.4.6 节）
- 进行正式的利益攸关者审视（见 11.4.7 节）

- Finalize the Application Architecture (see Section 11.4.8)
- Create Architecture Definition Document (see Section 11.4.9)

11.4.1 Select Reference Models, Viewpoints, and Tools

Review and validate (or generate, if necessary) the set of application principles. These will normally form part of an overarching set of architecture principles. Guidelines for developing and applying principles, and a sample set of application principles, are given in Part III, Chapter 23.

Select relevant Application Architecture resources (reference models, patterns, etc.) from the Architecture Repository, on the basis of the business drivers, the stakeholders, and their concerns.

Select relevant Application Architecture viewpoints (for example, stakeholders of the applications— viewpoints relevant to functional and individual users of applications, etc.); i.e., those that will enable the architect to demonstrate how the stakeholder concerns are being addressed in the Application Architecture.

Identify appropriate tools and techniques to be used for capture, modeling, and analysis, in association with the selected viewpoints. Depending on the degree of sophistication warranted, these may comprise simple documents or spreadsheets, or more sophisticated modeling tools and techniques.

Consider using platform-independent descriptions of business logic. For example, the OMG's Model Driven Architecture (MDA) offers an approach to modeling Application Architectures that preserves the business logic from changes to the underlying platform and implementation technology.

11.4.1.1 Determine Overall Modeling Process

For each viewpoint, select the models needed to support the specific view required, using the selected tool or method.

Ensure that all stakeholder concerns are covered. If they are not, create new models to address concerns not covered, or augment existing models (see above).

The recommended process for developing an Application Architecture is as follows:

- Understand the list of applications or application components that are required, based on the baseline Application Portfolio, what the requirements are, and the business architecture scope.
- Simplify complicated applications by decomposing them into two or more applications.
- Ensure that the set of application definitions is internally consistent, by removing duplicate functionality as far as possible, and combining similar applications into one.
- Identify logical applications and the most appropriate physical applications.
- Develop matrices across the architecture by relating applications to business service, business function, data, process, etc.
- Elaborate a set of Application Architecture views by examining how the application will function, capturing integration, migration, development, and operational concerns.

The level and rigor of decomposition needed varies from enterprise to enterprise, as well as within an enterprise, and the architect should consider the enterprise's goals, objectives, scope, and purpose of the enterprise architecture effort to determine the level of decomposition.

- 最终确定应用架构（见 11.4.8 节）
- 创建架构定义文件（见 11.4.9 节）

11.4.1 选择参考模型、视角和工具

审视并确认（或生成——如有必要）一组应用原则。这些原则通常形成一组首要架构原则的部分。第三部分第 23 章给出开发和应用原则的指南以及一组应用原则示例。

基于业务驱动因素、利益攸关者及其关注点，从架构存储库中选择相关的应用架构资源（参考模型、特征模式等）。

选择相关的应用架构视角（例如，应用的利益攸关者——与应用的功能和个人使用者有关的视角等）；即架构师能够说明在应用架构中如何应对利益攸关者的关注点的视角。

结合选定的视角，识别适合用于捕获、建模和分析的适当工具和技巧。根据认可的复杂程度，这些工具和技术可包括简单的文件或电子表格，或较为复杂的建模工具和技巧。

考虑使用与平台无关的业务逻辑描述。例如，OMG 的模型驱动架构（MDA）提供了一种对应用架构进行建模的途径，可保护业务逻辑免受基础平台和实施技术变更的影响。

11.4.1.1 确定总体建模流程

针对每个视角，使用选定的工具或方法来选择需要的模型，支持所要求的特定视图。

确保所有利益攸关者的关注点被涵盖。如没有，就要创建新模型以应对未涵盖的关注点或扩展现有模型（见上文）。

由于开发应用架构的建议流程如下：

- 基于基线应用谱系、需求以及业务架构范围，理解所需的应用或应用组件列表。
- 通过将复杂的应用分解为两个或更多的应用对其进行简化。
- 通过尽可能删除重复的功能并合并相似的应用，确保应用定义组在内部是协调一致的。
- 识别逻辑应用和最恰当的物理应用。
- 通过贯穿应用与业务服务、业务功能、数据和流程等，从而在架构内开发矩阵。
- 通过审查应用将如何行使功能，捕获综合、迁移、开发以及运行关注点，从而详细阐述一组应用架构视图。

在 ENTERPRISE 之间以及在 ENTERPRISE 内部，所需分解的层级和严格程度是不同的，架构师应考虑 ENTERPRISE 的目标、目的、范围和 Enterprise Architecture 工作的用途，以确定分解层级。

The level of granularity should be sufficient to enable identification of gaps and the scope of candidate work packages.

11.4.1.2 Identify Required Catalogs of Application Building Blocks

The organization's Application Portfolio is captured as a catalog within the Architec-ture Repository. Catalogs are hierarchical in nature and capture a decomposition of a metamodel entity and also decompositions across related model entities (e.g., logical application component → physical application component → information system service).

Catalogs form the raw material for development of matrices and diagrams and also act as a key resource for portfolio managing business and IT capability.

The structure of catalogs is based on the attributes of metamodel entities, as defined in Part IV, Chapter 34.

The following catalogs should be considered for development within an Application Architecture:

- Application Portfolio catalog
- Interface catalog

11.4.1.3 Identify Required Matrices

Matrices show the core relationships between related model entities.

Matrices form the raw material for development of diagrams and also act as a key resource for impact assessment.

Once the baseline Application Portfolio has been assembled, it is necessary to map the applications to their purpose in supporting the business. The initial mapping should focus on business services within the Business Architecture, as this is the level of granularity where architecturally significant decisions are most likely to be needed.

Once applications are mapped to business services, it will also be possible to make associations from applications to data, through the business-information diagrams developed during Business Architecture.

If readily available, baseline application data models may be used to validate the BusinessArchitecture and also to identify which data is held locally and which is accessed remotely.

The Data Architecture phase will focus on these issues, so at this point it may be appropriate to drop into a short iteration of Data Architecture if it is deemed to be valuable to scope of the architecture engagement.

Using existing information in the baseline application catalog, the Application Archi-tecture should identify user and organizational dependencies on applications. This activity will support future state planning by determining impacted user communities and also facilitating the grouping of application by user type or user location.

A key user community to be specifically considered is the operational support organ-ization. This activity should examine application dependencies on shared operations capabilities and produce a diagram on how each application is effectively operated and managed.

Specifically considering the needs of the operational community may identify requirements for new or extended governance capabilities and applications.

粒度层级应足以识别差距和候选工作包的范围。

11.4.1.2 识别所需的应用构建块目录集

捕获组织的应用谱系作为架构存储库内的目录集。目录集本质上是分层级的，并捕获元模型实体的分解以及相关模型实体之间的分解（例如，逻辑应用组件→物理应用组件→信息系统服务）。

目录集构成开发矩阵和图的原始资料，并作为项目谱系管理业务和 IT 能力的关键资源。

目录集结构基于元模型实体的属性，如第四部分第 34 章所定义。

应考虑在应用架构内开发下列目录集：

- 应用谱系目录集
- 界面目录集

11.4.1.3 识别所需的矩阵

矩阵表明相关模型实体之间的核心关系。

矩阵形成用作开发图的原始资料，并充当影响评估的关键资源。

一旦组建了基线应用谱系，就有必要将应用映射到其支持的业务方面的用途中去。初始映射应聚焦于业务架构内的业务服务，因为这是在架构上做重要决策时最有可能需要的粒度层级。

一旦将应用映射到业务服务中，还有可能通过业务架构期间开发的业务信息图来关联应用与数据。

若容易可用，就可使用基线应用数据模型确认业务架构，并用于识别哪些数据被本地保存以及哪些数据被远程访问。

数据架构阶段将聚焦于这些议题，故此时若认为对界定架构工作的范围有价值，则适合进入数据架构的短迭代。

应用架构应使用基线应用目录中的现有信息来识别用户和组织对应用的依赖性。本活动将通过确定受影响的用户群体并按用户类型或用户位置促进应用分组来支持未来状态规划。

需要特别考虑的关键用户团体是运行的支持组织。本活动应审查应用对共享运行能力的依赖性，并生成如何有效运行和管理每个应用的图。

特别考虑运行团体的需要可识别出对新的或扩展的治理能力和应用的需求。

The following matrices should be considered for development within an Application Architecture:

- Application/Organization matrix
- Role/Application matrix
- Application Interaction matrix
- Application/Function matrix

The structure of matrices is based on the attributes of metamodel entities, as defined in Part IV, Chapter 34.

11.4.1.4 Identify Required Diagrams

Diagrams present the Application Architecture information from a set of different perspectives(viewpoints) according to the requirements of the stakeholders.

Once the desired functionality of an application is known, it is necessary to perform an internal assessment of how the application should be best structured to meet its requirements.

In the case of packaged applications, it is likely to be the case that the application supports a number of configuration options, add-on modules, or application services that may be applied to the solution. For custom developed applications, it is necessary to identify the high-level structure of the application in terms of modules or sub-systems as a foundation to organize design activity.

The following diagrams should be considered for development within an Application Architecture:

- Application Communication diagram
- Application and User Location diagram
- Enterprise Manageability diagram
- Process/Application Realization diagram
- Application Migration diagram
- Software Distribution diagram
- Software Engineering diagram
- Application Use-Case diagram

The structure of diagrams is based on the attributes of metamodel entities, as defined in Part IV, Chapter 34.

11.4.1.5 Identify Types of Requirement to be Collected

Once the Application Architecture catalogs, matrices, and diagrams have been developed, architecture modeling is completed by formalizing the application-focused requirements for implementing the Target Architecture.

These requirements may:

- Relate to the application domain.
- Provide requirements input into the Data and Technology Architectures.
- Provide detailed guidance to be reflected during design and implementation to ensure that the solution addresses the original architecture requirements.

Within this step, the architect should identify requirements that should be met by the architecture(see Section 17.2.2).

应考虑在应用架构内开发下列矩阵：

- 应用/组织矩阵
- 角色/应用矩阵
- 应用交互矩阵
- 应用/功能矩阵

矩阵结构基于元模型实体的属性，如第四部分第34章所定义。

11.4.1.4　识别所需的图

根据利益攸关者的需求，图从一组不同的关注层面（视角）表达应用架构信息。

一旦了解一个期望的应用功能性，有必要就如何最佳地构建应用架构以满足其需求进行内部评估。

在打包应用的情况下，应用可能支持多个可用于解决方案的配置选项、附加模块或应用服务。对于定制开发的应用，有必要根据模块或子系统将应用的高层级结构识别为组织设计活动的基础。

应考虑在应用架构内开发下列图：

- 应用通信图
- 应用和用户位置图
- ENTERPRISE 可管理性图
- 流程/应用实现图
- 应用迁移图
- 软件分布图
- 软件工程图
- 应用用例图

图的结构基于元模型实体的属性，如第四部分第34章所定义。

11.4.1.5　识别待收集的需求类型

一旦开发了应用架构目录集、矩阵和图，通过对所实施目标架构聚焦于应用的需求进行正规化表达，完成架构建模。

这些需求可以：

- 与应用域关联。
- 为数据架构和技术架构提供需求输入。
- 提供将在设计和实施期间反映出的详细引导，以确保解决方案在本步骤中应对最初的架构需求。

在此步骤内，架构师应识别架构应满足的需求（见17.2.2节）。

11.4.2 Develop Baseline Application Architecture Description

Develop a Baseline Description of the existing Application Architecture, to the extent necessary to support the Target Application Architecture. The scope and level of detail to be defined will depend on the extent to which existing applications are likely to be carried over into the Target Application Architecture, and on whether architecture descriptions exist, as described in Section 11.2.To the extent possible, identify the relevant Application Architecture building blocks, drawing on the Architecture Repository (see Part V, Chapter 41). If not already existing within the Architecture Repository, define each application in line with the Application Portfolio catalog (see Part IV, Chapter 34).

Where new architecture models need to be developed to satisfy stakeholder concerns, use the models identified within Step 1 as a guideline for creating new architecture content to describe the Baseline Architecture.

11.4.3 Develop Target Application Architecture Description

Develop a Target Description for the Application Architecture, to the extent necessary to support the Architecture Vision, Target Business Architecture, and Target Data Architecture. The scope and level of detail to be defined will depend on the relevance of the applications elements to attaining the Target Architecture Vision, and on whether architectural descriptions exist. To the extent possible, identify the relevant Application Architecture building blocks, drawing on the Architecture Repository (see Part V, Chapter 41).

Where new architecture models need to be developed to satisfy stakeholder concerns, use the models identified within Step 1 as a guideline for creating new architecture content to describe the Target Architecture.

11.4.4 Perform Gap Analysis

Verify the architecture models for internal consistency and accuracy:

- Perform trade-off analysis to resolve conflicts (if any) among the different views.
- Validate that the models support the principles, objectives, and constraints.
- Note changes to the viewpoint represented in the selected models from the Architecture Repository, and document.
- Test architecture models for completeness against requirements.

Identify gaps between the baseline and target, using the Gap Analysis technique as described in Part III, Chapter 27.

11.4.2 开发基线应用架构描述

开发现有应用架构的基线描述，达到支持目标应用架构所必需的程度。待定义的范围和细节层级将取决于现有应用有可能延用到目标应用架构中的程度，以及是否存在架构描述，如 11.2 节所述。尽可能地利用架构存储库（见第五部分第 41 章）识别相关的应用架构构建块。若架构存储库中尚不存在架构描述，则根据应用谱系目录集（参见第四部分第 34 章）定义每个应用。

如需开发新架构模型以满足利益攸关者的关注点，使用步骤 1 中识别的模型作为创建用以描述基线架构的新架构内容的指南。

11.4.3 开发目标应用架构描述

开发应用架构的目标描述，达到支持架构愿景、目标业务架构和目标数据架构所必需的程度。待定义的范围和细节层级将取决于应用元素与实现目标架构愿景之间的关联性，以及架构描述是否存在。尽可能地利用架构存储库（见第五部分第 41 章）识别相关的应用架构构建块。

如需开发新的架构模型，以满足利益攸关者的关注点，使用步骤 1 中识别的模型作为创建用于描述目标架构的新架构内容的指南。

11.4.4 进行差距分析

验证架构模型的内部一致性和准确性：

- 进行权衡分析，以解决不同视图间的冲突（如有）。
- 确认模型支持原则、目的和约束。
- 对架构存储库中选定模型里表达出的视角变更进行注释，并文件化。
- 根据需求测试架构模型的完整性。

使用第三部分第 27 章中描述的差距分析技巧来识别基线与目标之间的差距。

11.4.5 Define Candidate Roadmap Components

Following creation of a Baseline Architecture, Target Architecture, and gap analysis, an application roadmap is required to prioritize activities over the coming phases.

This initial Application Architecture roadmap will be used as raw material to support more detailed definition of a consolidated, cross-discipline roadmap within the Opportunities & Solutions phase.

11.4.6 Resolve Impacts Across the Architecture Landscape

Once the Application Architecture is finalized, it is necessary to understand any wider impacts or implications.

At this stage, other architecture artifacts in the Architecture Landscape should be examined to identify:

- Does this Application Architecture create an impact on any pre-existing architectures?
- Have recent changes been made that impact the Application Architecture?
- Are there any opportunities to leverage work from this Application Architecture in other areas of the organization?
- Does this Application Architecture impact other projects (including those planned as well as those currently in progress)?
- Will this Application Architecture be impacted by other projects (including those planned as well as those currently in progress)?

11.4.7 Conduct Formal Stakeholder Review

Check the original motivation for the architecture project and the Statement of Architecture Work against the proposed Application Architecture. Conduct an impact analysis, to identify any areas where the Business and Data Architectures (e.g., business practices) may need to change to cater for changes in the Application Architecture (for example, changes to forms or procedures, applications, or database systems). If the impact is significant, this may warrant the Business and Data Architectures being revisited.

Identify any constraints on the Technology Architecture (especially the infrastructure) about to be designed.

11.4.8 Finalize the Application Architecture

- Select standards for each of the building blocks, re-using as much as possible from the reference models selected from the Architecture Repository.
- Fully document each building block.
- Conduct final cross-check of overall architecture against business require-ments; document rationale for building block decisions in the architecture document.
- Document final requirements traceability report.
- Document final mapping of the architecture within the Architecture Repository; from the selected building blocks, identify those that might be re-used, and publish via the Architecture Repository.

11.4.5 定义候选路线图组件

创建基线架构、目标架构和差距分析后，则需要一个应用路线图来对后续阶段的活动进行优先级排序。

该初始应用架构路线图会作为原始资料，用以支持在机会和解决方案阶段中合并的跨学科的路线图的更详细定义。

11.4.6 化解贯穿整个架构全景中的影响

一旦最终确定了应用架构，就有必要理解更广泛的影响或含义。

在本阶段，应审查架构全景中的其他架构制品以识别：

- 本应用架构对所有先前存在的架构是否产生影响？
- 最近作出的变更是否影响应用架构？
- 在组织的其他领域是否有机会利用本应用架构中的工作？
- 该应用架构是否影响其他项目（包括已计划的和当前正在进行的项目）？
- 本应用架构是否会受到其他项目（包括已计划的和当前正在进行的项目）的影响？

11.4.7 进行正式的利益攸关者审视

根据建议的应用架构，检查架构项目和架构工作说明书的原始动机。进行影响分析，以识别业务和数据架构（例如业务实践）可能需要改变的任何领域来应对应用架构内的变更（例如，形式或程序、应用或数据库系统的变更）。如果影响很显著，则会确保对业务和应用架构进行回顾。

识别对将要设计的技术架构（尤其是基础设施）的所有约束。

11.4.8 最终确定应用架构

- 为每个构建块选择标准，尽可能复用从架构存储库中选择的参考模型。
- 完整地文件化每个构建块。
- 根据业务需求，对总体架构进行最终的交叉检查；在架构文件中记录构建块决策的理由依据。
- 文件化最终的需求可追溯性报告。
- 文件化架构存储库中架构的最终映射；从选定的构建块中识别可复用的构建块，并通过架构存储库发布。

- Finalize all the work products, such as gap analysis.

11.4.9 Create Architecture Definition Document

- Document rationale for building block decisions in the Architecture Definition Document.
- Prepare Application Architecture sections of the Architecture Definition Document; if appropriate, use reports and/or graphics generated by modeling tools to demonstrate key views of the architecture; route the document for review by relevant stakeholders, and incorporate feedback.

11.5 Outputs

The outputs of Phase C (Application Architecture) may include, but are not restricted to:

- Refined and updated versions of the Architecture Vision phase deliverables, where applicable:
  - Statement of Architecture Work (see Part IV, Section 36.2.20), updated if necessary
  - Validated application principles, or new application principles (if generated here)
- Draft Architecture Definition Document (see Part IV, Section 36.2.3), including:
  - Baseline Application Architecture, Version 1.0, if appropriate
  - Target Application Architecture, Version 1.0
  - Process systems model
  - Place systems model
  - Time systems model
  - People systems model
  - Views corresponding to the selected viewpoints, addressing key stakeholder concerns
- Draft Architecture Requirements Specification (see Part IV, Section 36.2.6), including such Application Architecture requirements as:
  - Gap analysis results
  - Applications interoperability requirements
  - Relevant technical requirements that will apply to this evolution of the architecture development cycle
  - Constraints on the Technology Architecture about to be designed
  - Updated business requirements, if appropriate
  - Updated data requirements, if appropriate
- Application Architecture components of an Architecture Roadmap (see Part IV, Section 36.2.7)

- 最终确定所有的工作产物，例如差距分析。

11.4.9 创建架构定义文件

- 在架构定义文件中记录构建块决策的理由依据。
- 准备架构定义文件的应用架构章节；如适用，使用建模工具生成的报告和/或图说明架构的关键视图；分发文件以供相关利益攸关者审视，并纳入反馈。

11.5 输出

阶段 C（应用架构）的输出可包括但不限于：

- 如适用，架构愿景阶段交付物的经过细化和更新的版本：
  - 架构工作说明书（见第四部分 36.2.20 节），必要时更新
  - 经过确认的应用原则，或新的应用原则（若在此阶段生成）
- 起草架构定义文件（见第四部分 36.2.3 节），包括：
  - 基线应用架构，版本 1.0，如适用
  - 目标应用架构，版本 1.0
  - 流程系统模型
  - 位置系统模型
  - 时间系统模型
  - 人员系统模型
  - 与选定的视角对应并应对关键的利益攸关者关注点的视图
- 起草架构需求规范（见第四部分 36.2.6 节），包括以下各类应用架构需求：
  - 差距分析结果
  - 应用互用性需求
  - 适用于本架构开发周期演进的相关技术需求
  - 对即将设计的技术架构的约束
  - 经过更新的业务需求，如适用
  - 经过更新的数据需求，如适用
- 架构路线图（见第四部分 36.2.7 节）的应用架构组件

The outputs may include some or all of the following:

- Catalogs:
  - Application Portfolio catalog
  - Interface catalog
- Matrices:
  - Application/Organization matrix
  - Role/Application matrix
  - Application/Function matrix
  - Application Interaction matrix
- Diagrams:
  - Application Communication diagram
  - Application and User Location diagram
  - Application Use-Case diagram
  - Enterprise Manageability diagram
  - Process/Application Realization diagram
  - Software Engineering diagram
  - Application Migration diagram
  - Software Distribution diagram

输出可包括下列部分或全部内容：

- 目录集：
  - 应用谱系目录集
  - 界面目录集
- 矩阵：
  - 应用/组织矩阵
  - 角色/应用矩阵
  - 应用/功能矩阵
  - 应用交互矩阵
- 图：
  - 应用通信图
  - 应用和用户位置图
  - 应用用例图
  - ENTERPRISE 可管理性图
  - 流程/应用实现图
  - 软件工程图
  - 应用迁移图
  - 软件分布图

Chapter 12
Phase D: Technology Architecture

This chapter describes the development of a Technology Architecture for an architecture project.

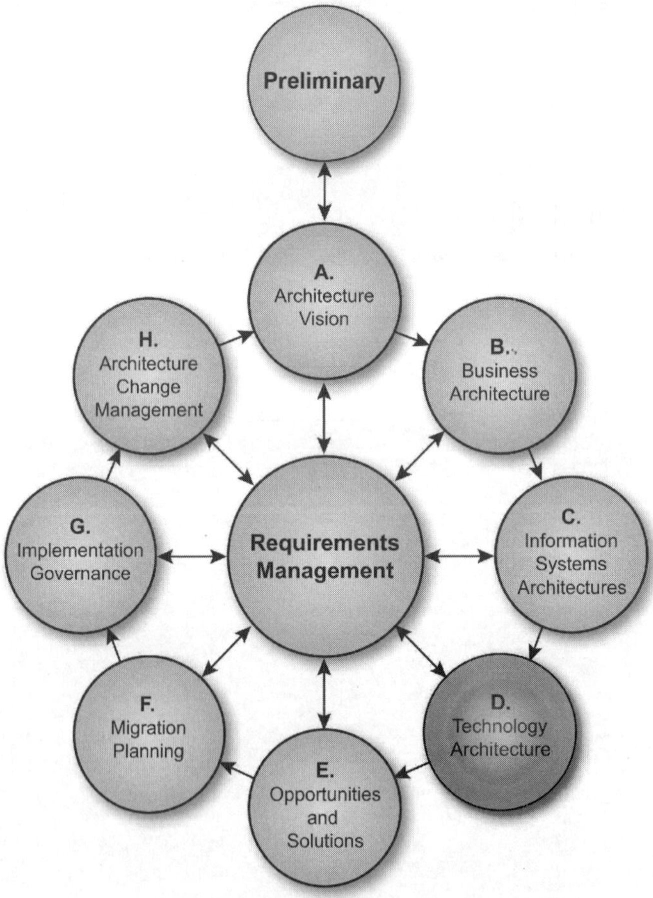

Figure 12-1 Phase D: Technology Architecture

第 12 章
阶段 D：技术架构

本章描述架构项目中技术架构的开发。

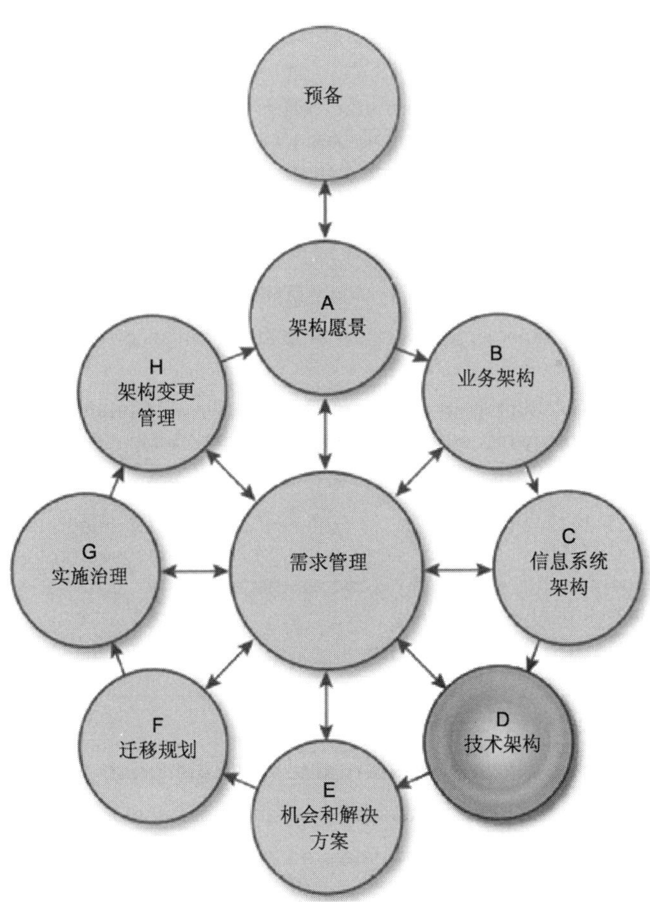

图 12-1　阶段 D：技术架构

12.1 Objectives

The objectives of Phase D are to:

- Develop the Target Technology Architecture that enables the logical and physical application and data components and the Architecture Vision, addressing the Request for Architecture Work and stakeholder concerns.
- Identify candidate Architecture Roadmap components based upon gaps between theBaseline and Target Technology Architectures.

12.2 Approach

12.2.1 Architecture Repository

As part of Phase D, the architecture team will need to consider what relevant Technology Architecture resources are available in the Architecture Repository (see Part V, Chapter 41).

In particular:

- Existing IT services as documented in the IT repository or IT service catalog.
- TOGAF Technical Reference Model (TRM).
- Generic technology models relevant to the organization's industry "vertical" sector.

For example, the TeleManagement Forum (TMF) — www.tmforum.org — has developed detailed technology models relevant to the Telecommunications industry.

- Technology models relevant to Common Systems Architectures.

For example, The Open Group has a Reference Model for Integrated Information Infrastructure (III-RM) — see Part VI, Chapter 44 — that focuses on the application-level components and underlying services necessary to provide an integrated information infrastructure.

12.3 Inputs

This section defines the inputs to Phase D.

12.3.1 Reference Materials External to the Enterprise

- Architecture reference materials (see Part IV, Section 36.2.5)
- Product information on candidate products

12.1 目的

阶段D的目的是：

- 开发能实现逻辑和物理应用、数据组件和架构愿景的目标技术架构，涉及架构工作要求和利益攸关者关注点。
- 基于基线技术架构和目标技术架构之间的差距识别候选架构路线图组件。

12.2 实施途径

12.2.1 架构存储库

作为阶段 D 的一部分，架构团队需要考虑可从架构存储库（见第五部分第 41 章）中获得哪些相关的技术架构资源。

尤其是：

- 在 IT 存储库或 IT 服务目录集中记录的现有 IT 服务。
- TOGAF 技术参考模型（TRM）。
- 与组织所属行业“垂直”区域有关的通用技术模型。

例如，电信管理论坛（TMF）——www.tmforum.org——已开发了与电信行业有关的详细技术模型。

- 与共用系统架构有关的技术模型。

例如，The Open Group 具有综合信息基础设施的参考模型（III-RM）——见第六部分，第 44 章——该模型聚焦于对提供综合信息基础设施必要的应用层级的组件和基础服务。

12.3 输入

本节定义了对阶段 D 的输入。

12.3.1 ENTERPRISE 外部参考资料

- 架构参考资料（见第四部分，36.2.5 节）
- 候选产品的产品信息

12.3.2 Non-Architectural Inputs

- Request for Architecture Work (see Part IV, Section 36.2.17)
- Capability Assessment (see Part IV, Section 36.2.10)
- Communications Plan (see Part IV, Section 36.2.12)

12.3.3 Architectural Inputs

- Organizational Model for Enterprise Architecture (see Part IV, Section 36.2.16), including:
  - Scope of organizations impacted
  - Maturity assessment, gaps, and resolution approach
  - Roles and responsibilities for architecture team(s)
  - Constraints on architecture work
  - Budget requirements
  - Governance and support strategy
- Tailored Architecture Framework (see Part IV, Section 36.2.21), including:
  - Tailored architecture method
  - Tailored architecture content (deliverables and artifacts)
  - Configured and deployed tools
- Technology principles (see Part III, Section 23.6.4), if existing
- Statement of Architecture Work (see Part IV, Section 36.2.20)
- Architecture Vision (see Part IV, Section 36.2.8)
- Architecture Repository (see Part IV, Section 36.2.5), including:
  - Re-usable building blocks
  - Publicly available reference models
  - Organization-specific reference models
  - Organization standards
- Draft Architecture Definition Document (see Part IV, Section 36.2.3), including:
  - Baseline Business Architecture, Version 1.0 (detailed)
  - Target Business Architecture Version 1.0 (detailed)
  - Baseline Data Architecture, Version 1.0 (detailed)
  - Target Data Architecture, Version 1.0 (detailed)
  - Baseline Application Architecture, Version 1.0 (detailed)
  - Target Application Architecture, Version 1.0 (detailed)
  - Baseline Technology Architecture, Version 0.1 (vision)
  - Target Technology Architecture, Version 0.1 (vision)

12.3.2 非架构输入

- 架构工作要求书（见第四部分，36.2.17 节）
- 能力评估（见第四部分，36.2.10 节）
- 沟通计划（见第四部分，36.2.12 节）

12.3.3 架构输入

- Enterprise Architecture 的组织模型（见第四部分，36.2.16 节），包括：
  — 受影响的组织的范围
  — 成熟度评估、差距和解决途径
  — 架构团队的角色和职责
  — 对架构工作的约束
  — 预算需求
  — 治理和支持战略
- 经剪裁的架构框架（见第四部分，36.2.21 节），包括：
  — 经剪裁的架构方法
  — 经剪裁的架构内容（交付物和制品）
  — 经配置和部署的工具
- 技术原则（见第三部分，23.6.4 节），如存在
- 架构工作说明书（见第四部分，36.2.20 节）
- 架构愿景（见第四部分，36.2.8 节）
- 架构存储库（见第四部分，36.2.5 节），包括：
  — 可复用的构建块
  — 公开可用的参考模型
  — 组织特定参考模型
  — 组织标准
- 起草架构定义文件（见第四部分，36.2.3 节），包括：
  — 基线业务架构，版本 1.0（详细）
  — 目标业务架构，版本 1.0（详细）
  — 基线数据架构，版本 1.0（详细）
  — 目标数据架构，版本 1.0（详细）
  — 基线应用架构，版本 1.0（详细）
  — 目标应用架构，版本 1.0（详细）
  — 基线技术架构，版本 0.1（愿景）
  — 目标技术架构，版本 0.1（愿景）

- Draft Architecture Requirements Specification (see Part IV, Section 36.2.6), including:
  - — Gap analysis results (from Business, Data, and Application Architectures)
  - — Relevant technical requirements from previous phases
- Business, Data, and Application Architecture components of an Architecture Roadmap(see Part IV, Section 36.2.7)

12.4 Steps

The level of detail addressed in Phase D will depend on the scope and goals of the overall architecture effort.

New technology building blocks being introduced as part of this effort will need to be defined in detail during Phase D. Existing technology building blocks to be supported in the target environment may need to be redefined in Phase D to ensure interoperability and fit-for-purpose within this specific Technology Architecture.

The order of the steps in Phase D (see below) as well as the time at which they are formally started and completed should be adapted to the situation at hand in accordance with the established architecture governance. In particular, determine whether in this situation it is appropriate to conduct Baseline Description or Target Architecture development first, as described in Part III, Chapter 19.

All activities that have been initiated in these steps must be closed during the Finalize the Technology Architecture step (see Section 12.4.8). The documentation generated from these steps must be formally published in the Create Architecture Definition Document step (see Section 12.4.9).

The steps in Phase D are as follows:

- Select reference models, viewpoints, and tools (see Section 12.4.1)
- Develop Baseline Technology Architecture Description (see Section 12.4.2)
- Develop Target Technology Architecture Description (see Section 12.4.3)
- Perform gap analysis (see Section 12.4.4)
- Define candidate roadmap components (see Section 12.4.5)
- Resolve impacts across the Architecture Landscape (see Section 12.4.6)
- Conduct formal stakeholder review (see Section 12.4.7)
- Finalize the Technology Architecture (see Section 12.4.8)
- Create Architecture Definition Document (see Section 12.4.9)

- 起草架构需求规范（见第四部分，36.2.6 节），包括：
  - 差距分析结果（来自业务架构、数据架构和应用架构）
  - 来自之前阶段的相关技术需求
- 架构路线图（见第四部分，36.2.7 节）的业务、数据和应用架构组件

12.4 步骤

阶段 D 中所划分的细节层级会取决于总体架构工作的范围和目标。

作为本项工作一部分引入的新技术构建块需要在阶段 D 中详细定义。将在目标环境中被支持的现有技术构建块可能需要在阶段 D 中重新定义，以确保本特定技术架构内的互用性和适用性。

阶段 D 中的步骤顺序（见下文）及其正式开始和完成的时间，应按已确定的架构治理根据当前情况进行调整。尤其是，确定在这种情况下首先实施基线描述或目标架构开发是否合适，如第三部分第 19 章所述。

在这些步骤中，已经开始的所有活动必须在最终确定技术架构步骤（见 12.4.8 节）结束。这些步骤中生成的文档必须在创建架构定义文件步骤（见 12.4.9 节）正式发布。

阶段 D 中的步骤如下：

- 选择参考模型、视角和工具（见 12.4.1 节）
- 开发基线技术架构描述（见 12.4.2 节）
- 开发目标技术架构描述（见 12.4.3 节）
- 进行差距分析（见 12.4.4 节）
- 定义候选路线图组件（见 12.4.5 节）
- 化解贯穿整个架构全景中的影响（见 12.4.6 节）
- 进行正式的利益攸关者审视（见 12.4.7 节）
- 最终确定技术架构（见 12.4.8 节）
- 创建架构定义文件（见 12.4.9 节）

12.4.1 Select Reference Models, Viewpoints, and Tools

Review and validate the set of technology principles. These will normally form part of an overarching set of architecture principles. Guidelines for developing and applying principles, and a sample set of technology principles, are given in Part III, Chapter 23.

Select relevant Technology Architecture resources (reference models, patterns, etc.) from the Architecture Repository (see Part V, Chapter 41), on the basis of the business drivers, stakeholders, and their concerns.

Select relevant Technology Architecture viewpoints that will enable the architect to demonstrate how the stakeholder concerns are being addressed in the Technology Architecture.

Identify appropriate tools and techniques to be used for capture, modeling, and analysis, in association with the selected viewpoints. Depending on the degree of sophistication required, these may comprise simple documents and spreadsheets, or more sophisticated modeling tools and techniques.

12.4.1.1 Determine Overall Modeling Process

For each viewpoint, select the models needed to support the specific view required, using the selected tool or method. Ensure that all stakeholder concerns are covered. If they are not, create new models to address them, or augment existing models (see above).

The process to develop a Technology Architecture incorporates the following steps:

- Define a taxonomy of platform services and logical technology components (including standards).
- Identify relevant locations where technology is deployed.
- Carry out a physical inventory of deployed technology and abstract up to fit into the taxonomy.
- Look at application and business requirements for technology.
- Is the technology in place fit-for-purpose to meet new requirements (i.e., does it meet functional and non-functional requirements)?
  - Refine the taxonomy
  - Product selection (including dependent products)
- Determine configuration of the selected technology.
- Determine impact:
  - Sizing and costing
  - Capacity planning
  - Installation/governance/migration impacts

In the earlier phases of the ADM, certain decisions made around service granularity and service boundaries will have implications on the technology component and the platform service. The areas where the Technology Architecture may be impacted will include the following:

- **Performance**: The granularity of the service will impact on platform service requirements.Coarse-grained services contain several units of functionality with potentially varying non-functional requirements, so platform performance should be considered. In addition, coarse-grained services can sometimes contain more information than actually required by the requesting system.

12.4.1 选择参考模型、视角和工具

审视并确认一组技术原则。这些原则通常构成首要架构原则集的一部分。第三部分第 23 章给出开发并应用原则的指南以及一组技术原则示例。

基于业务驱动因素、利益攸关者及其关注点从架构存储库（见第五部分，第 41 章）中选择相关的技术架构资源（参考模型、特征模式等）。

选择将使架构师能够说明在技术架构中如何应对利益攸关者的关注点的相关技术架构视角。

结合选定的视角，识别用于捕获、建模和分析的适当工具和技巧。根据所需的复杂程度，这些工具和技巧可包括简单的文件或电子表格，或较为复杂的建模工具和技巧。

12.4.1.1 确定总体建模流程

针对每个视角，使用选定的工具或方法来选择支持所要求的特定视图所需的模型。确保涵盖所有利益攸关者的关注点。若没有，创建新模型以应对它们或扩展现有模型（见上文）。

开发技术架构的流程包含下列步骤：

- 定义平台服务和逻辑技术组件的分类法（包括标准）。
- 识别部署技术的相关位置。
- 执行已部署技术的实际清单并提取至符合该分类/层法。
- 考虑应用和业务的技术需求。
- 适当的技术是否适用于满足新需求（即其是否满足功能性和非功能性需求）？
  - 细化分类/层法
  - 产物选择（包括从属产物）
- 确定选定技术的配置。
- 确定影响：
  - 规模和成本
  - 能力规划
  - 安装/治理/迁移影响

在 ADM 的早期阶段，围绕服务粒度和服务边界作出的某些决策将对技术组件和平台服务产生影响。技术架构可能受影响的领域将包括如下方面：

- **性能**：服务粒度将影响平台服务需求。粗粒度服务包含若干具有可能变化的非功能性需求的功能单元，因此，应该考虑平台性能。此外，粗粒度服务有时可包含比要求系统实际所需更多的信息。

- **Maintainability**: If service granularity is too coarse, then introducing changes to that service becomes difficult and impacts the maintenance of the service and the platform on which it is delivered.
- **Location and Latency**: Services might interact with each other over remote links and inter-service communication will have in-built latency. Drawing service boundaries and setting the service granularity should consider platform/location impact of these inter-service communications.
- **Availability**: Service invocation is subject to network and/or service failure. So high communication availability is an important consideration during service decomposition and defining service granularity

Product selection processes may occur within the Technology Architecture phase where existing products are re-used, incremental capacity is being added, or product selection decisions are a constraint during project initiation.

Where product selection deviates from existing standards, involves significant effort, or has wide-ranging impact, this activity should be flagged as an opportunity and addressed through the Opportunities & Solutions phase.

12.4.1.2 Identify Required Catalogs of Technology Building Blocks

Catalogs are inventories of the core assets of the business. Catalogs are hierarchical in nature and capture a decomposition of a metamodel entity and also decompositions across related model entities (e.g., platform service → logical technology component → physical technology component).

Catalogs form the raw material for development of matrices and diagrams and also act as a key resource for portfolio managing business and IT capability.

The Technology Architecture should create technology catalogs as follows:

- Based on existing technology catalogs and analysis of applications carried out in theApplication Architecture phase, collect a list of products in use.
- If the requirements identified in the Application Architecture are not met by existing products, extend the product list by examining products available on the market that provide the functionality and meet the required standards.
- Classify products against the TOGAF TRM if appropriate, extending the model as necessary to fit the classification of technology products in use.
- If technology standards are currently in place, apply these to the technology component catalog to gain a baseline view of compliance with technology standards.

The following catalogs should be considered for development within a Technology Architecture:

- Technology standards
- Technology portfolio

The structure of catalogs is based on the attributes of metamodel entities, as defined in Part IV, Chapter 34.

- **可维护性**：如果服务粒度过粗，则向该服务引入变更将变得非常困难，且影响服务以及交付服务的平台的维护。
- **位置和时延**：服务可能通过远程链接进行彼此交互，且服务内通信将具有内置时延。如绘制服务边界和设定服务粒度，应考虑这些服务内通信的平台/位置影响。
- **可用性**：服务调用受到网络和/或服务失败的影响。因此，高通信可用性是服务分解并定义服务粒度期间的一个重要考量因素。

产品选择流程可能出现在技术架构阶段中，在该阶段，现有产品被复用，增量能力正在增加，或产品选择决策是项目启动期间的一个约束条件。

当产品选择偏离现有标准、涉及大量的工作投入或具有广泛影响时，本活动应被标记为机会并在机会和解决方案阶段来应对。

12.4.1.2 识别所需的技术构建块目录

目录集是业务的核心资产清单。目录集本质上是分层级的，并捕获元模型实体的分解以及相关模型实体之间的分解（例如，平台服务→逻辑技术组件→物理技术组件）。

目录集构成用于开发矩阵和图的原始资料，并充当项目谱系管理业务和 IT 能力的关键资源。

技术架构应创建如下技术目录集：

- 基于现有的技术目录集和在应用架构阶段中进行的应用分析，收集使用中的产品列表。
- 如果现有产品不满足应用架构中识别的需求，则通过审查市场上可用的、提供功能性并满足所需标准的产品来扩展产品列表。
- 如适用，按照 TOGAF TRM 对产品进行分类，必要时扩展模型以适合使用中的技术产品分类。
- 如果技术标准目前合适，则将其用于技术组件目录以获得符合技术标准的基线视图。

应考虑在技术架构内开发下列目录：

- 技术标准
- 技术谱系

目录结构基于元模型实体属性，如第四部分第 34 章所定义。

12.4.1.3 Identify Required Matrices

Matrices show the core relationships between related model entities.

Matrices form the raw material for development of diagrams and also act as a key resource for impact assessment.

The following matrix should be considered for development within a Technology Architecture:

- Application/Technology matrix

12.4.1.4 Identify Required Diagrams

Diagrams present the Technology Architecture information from a set of different perspectives(viewpoints) according to the requirements of the stakeholders.

This activity provides a link between platform requirements and hosting requirements, as a single application may need to be physically located in several environments to support local access, development lifecycles, and hosting requirements.

For major baseline applications or application platforms (where multiple applications are hosted on the same infrastructure stack), produce a stack diagram showing how hardware, operating system, software infrastructure, and packaged applications combine.

If appropriate, extend the Application Architecture diagrams of software distribution to show how applications map onto the technology platform.

For each environment, produce a logical diagram of hardware and software infras-tructure showing the contents of the environment and logical communications between components. Where available, collect capacity information on the deployed infrastru-cture.

For each environment, produce a physical diagram of communications infrastructure, such as routers, switches, firewalls, and network links. Where available, collect capacity information on the communications infrastructure.

The following diagrams should be considered for development within a Technology Architecture:

- Environments and Locations diagram
- Platform Decomposition diagram
- Processing diagram
- Networked Computing/Hardware diagram
- Communications Engineering diagram

The structure of diagrams is based on the attributes of metamodel entities, as defined in Part IV, Chapter 34.

12.4.1.5 Identify Types of Requirement to be Collected

Once the Technology Architecture catalogs, matrices, and diagrams have been developed, architecture modeling is completed by formalizing the technology-focused requirements for implementing the Target Architecture.

These requirements may:

- Relate to the technology domain.

12.4.1.3 识别所需的矩阵

矩阵表明相关模型实体之间的核心关系。

矩阵构成用于开发图的原始资料，并充当影响评估的关键资源。

应考虑在技术架构内开发下列矩阵：

- 应用/技术矩阵

12.4.1.4 识别所需的图

根据利益攸关者的需求，图从一组不同关注层级（视角）表达技术架构信息。

由于单个应用可能需要在物理上位于支持本地访问、开发生命周期和托管需求的若干环境中，因此本活动提供了平台需求和托管需求之间的联系。

对于主要的基线应用或应用平台（在相同的基础设施栈上托管多重应用被），生成栈图来表明硬件、操作系统、软件基础设施和打包应用如何结合。

如适用，扩展软件分布的应用架构图来表明应用如何映射到技术平台上。

针对每个环境，生成软硬件基础设施的逻辑图来表明组件间环境与逻辑通信的内容。如果可用，收集已部署的基础设施的能力信息。

针对每个环境，生成诸如路由器、交换机、防火墙和网络链路的通信基础设施的物理图。如果可用，收集通信基础设施的能力信息。

应考虑在技术架构内开发下列图：

- 环境和位置图
- 平台分解图
- 流程图
- 网络计算/硬件图
- 通信工程图

图的结构基于元模型实体属性，如第四部分第 34 章所定义。

12.4.1.5 识别待收集的需求类型

一旦开发了技术架构目录集、矩阵和图，则通过对实施目标架构的以技术为聚焦点的需求进行正规化表达来完成架构建模。

这些需求可以：

- 与技术域相关。

- Provide detailed guidance to be reflected during design and implementation to ensure that the solution addresses the original architecture requirements.

Within this step, the architect should identify requirements that should be met by the architecture(see Section 17.2.2).

12.4.1.6 Select Services

The services portfolios are combinations of basic services from the service categories in the TOGAF TRM that do not conflict. The combination of services are again tested to ensure support for the applications. This is a prerequisite to the later step of defining the architecture fully.

The previously identified requirements can provide more detailed information about:

- Requirements for organization-specific elements or pre-existing decisions (as applicable)
- Pre-existing and unchanging organizational elements (as applicable)
- Inherited external environment constraints

Where requirements demand definition of specialized services that are not identified in TOGAF, consideration should be given to how these might be replaced if standardized services become available in the future.

For each building block, build up a service description portfolio as a set of non-conflicting services. The set of services must be tested to ensure that the functionality provided meets application requirements.

12.4.2 Develop Baseline Technology Architecture Description

Develop a Baseline Description of the existing Technology Architecture, to support the Target Technology Architecture. The scope and level of detail to be defined will depend on the extent to which existing technology components are likely to be carried over into the Target Technology Architecture, and on whether architectural descriptions exist, as described in Section 12.2.

Identify the relevant Technology Architecture building blocks, drawing on any artifacts held in the Architecture Repository. If nothing exists within the Architecture Repository, define each application in line with the Technology Portfolio catalog (see Part IV, Chapter 34).

Begin by converting the description of the existing environment into the terms of the organization's Foundation Architecture (e.g., the TOGAF Foundation Architecture's TRM). This will allow the team developing the architecture to gain experience with the model and to understand its component parts. The team may be able to take advantage of a previous architectural definition, but it is assumed that some adaptation may be required to match the architectural definition techniques described as part of this process. Another important task is to set down a list of key questions which can be used later in the development process to measure the effectiveness of the new architecture.

Where new architecture models need to be developed to satisfy stakeholder concerns, use the models identified within Step 1 as a guideline for creating new architecture content to describe the Baseline Architecture.

- 提供将在设计和实施期间反映出的详细引导，以确保解决方案应对最初的架构需求。

在本步骤中，架构师应识别架构应满足的需求（见 17.2.2 节）。

12.4.1.6 选择服务

服务谱系是 TOGAF TRM 的服务类别中互不冲突的基本服务的组合。对服务组合进行再次测试以确保支持应用。这是全面定义架构的后续步骤的前提。

之前识别的需求可提供以下更详细的信息：

- 组织特定的元素或先前存在决策的需求（如适用）
- 先前存在和不变更的组织元素（如适用）
- 既有的外部环境约束

如在 TOGAF 中未识别需求需要的专业化服务的定义，则应考虑如果标准化服务在未来可用，该如何取代专业化服务。

针对每个构建块，将服务描述谱系构建为一组非冲突服务。必须对这组服务进行测试来确保所提供的功能性满足应用需求。

12.4.2 开发基线技术架构描述

开发现有技术架构的基线描述，以支持目标技术架构。待定义的范围和细节层级，将取决于现有的技术组件可能延用到目标技术架构中的程度，以及架构描述是否存在，如 12.2 节所述。

利用架构存储库中保存的制品，识别相关的技术架构构建块。若架构存储库中不存在制品，则根据技术谱系目录集（见第四部分，第 34 章）定义每个应用。

首先，将现有环境的描述转换成组织基础架构的术语（例如，TOGAF 基础架构的 TRM）。这将使得开发架构的团队获得模型方面的经验并理解其组成部分。团队也许能够利用之前的架构定义，但假定需要适应性调整，以匹配作为本流程部分所描述的架构定义技巧。另一个重要任务是制定关键问题列表，稍后可在开发流程中使用以衡量新架构的有效性。

如需开发新架构模型以满足利益攸关者的关注时，使用步骤 1 中识别的模型作为创建新架构内容用以描述基线架构的指南。

12.4.3 Develop Target Technology Architecture Description

Develop a Target Description for the Technology Architecture, to the extent necessary to support the Architecture Vision, Target Business Architecture, and Target Informa-tion Systems Architecture. The scope and level of detail to be defined will depend on the relevance of the technology elements to attaining the Target Architecture, and on whether architectural descriptions exist. To the extent possible, identify the relevant Technology Architecture building blocks, drawing on the Architecture Repository (see Part V, Chapter 41).

A key process in the creation of a broad architectural model of the target system is the conceptualization of building blocks. Architecture Building Blocks (ABBs) describe the functionality and how they may be implemented without the detail introduced by configuration or detailed design. The method of defining building blocks, along with some general guidelines for their use in creating an architectural model, is described in Part IV, Section 37.3.

Where new architecture models need to be developed to satisfy stakeholder concerns, use the models identified within Step 1 as a guideline for creating new architecture content to describe the Target Architecture.

12.4.4 Perform Gap Analysis

Verify the architecture models for internal consistency and accuracy:

- Perform trade-off analysis to resolve conflicts (if any) among the different views.
- Validate that the models support the principles, objectives, and constraints.
- Note changes to the viewpoint represented in the selected models from the Architecture Repository, and document.
- Test architecture models for completeness against requirements.

Identify gaps between the baseline and target, using the Gap Analysis technique as described inPart III, Chapter 27.

12.4.5 Define Candidate Roadmap Components

Following creation of a Baseline Architecture, Target Architecture, and gap analysis, a Technology Roadmap is required to prioritize activities over the coming phases.

This initial Technology Architecture roadmap will be used as raw material to support more detailed definition of a consolidated, cross-discipline roadmap within the Opportunities & Solutions phase.

12.4.6 Resolve Impacts Across the Architecture Landscape

Once the Technology Architecture is finalized, it is necessary to understand any wider impacts or implications.

At this stage, other architecture artifacts in the Architecture Landscape should be examined to identify:

- Does this Technology Architecture create an impact on any pre-existing architectures?

12.4.3 开发目标技术架构描述

开发技术架构的目标描述，达到支持架构愿景、目标业务架构和目标信息系统架构所必需的程度。待定义的范围和细节层级，将取决于技术元素与实现目标架构之间的关联性，以及是否存在架构描述。尽可能地利用架构存储库（见第五部分，第 41 章）识别相关的技术架构构建块。

在目标系统的一个宽广架构模型的创建中，一个关键流程是构建块的概念化。架构构建块（ABB）描述功能性以及在没有配置或详细设计的细节介绍的情况下，如何实施这些构建块。定义构建块的方法和其在创建架构模型时使用的一般指南在第四部分第 37.3 节中描述。

当需要开发新的架构模型以满足利益攸关者的关注点时，使用步骤 1 中识别的模型作为创建新架构内容用以描述目标架构的指南。

12.4.4 进行差距分析

验证架构模型的内部一致性和准确性：

- 进行权衡分析，以解决不同视图间的冲突（如有）。
- 确认模型支持原则、目的和约束。
- 对架构存储库中选定模型里表达出的视角变更进行注释，并文件化。
- 根据需求测试架构模型的完整性。

使用第三部分第 27 章中描述的差距分析技巧识别基线与目标之间的差距。

12.4.5 定义候选路线图组件

创建基线架构、目标架构和差距分析后，需要一个技术路线图对后续阶段的活动进行优先级排序。

本初始技术架构路线图会用作原始资料，支持机会和解决方案阶段中合并且跨学科的路线图的更详细定义。

12.4.6 化解贯穿整个架构全景中的影响

一旦最终确定了技术架构，就有必要理解更广泛的影响或含义。

在本阶段，应审查架构全景中的其他架构制品以识别：

- 本技术架构是否对先前存在的架构产生影响？

- Have recent changes been made that impact the Technology Architecture?
- Are there any opportunities to leverage work from this Technology Architecture in other areas of the organization?
- Does this Technology Architecture impact other projects (including those planned as well as those currently in progress)?
- Will this Technology Architecture be impacted by other projects (including those planned as well as those currently in progress)?

12.4.7 Conduct Formal Stakeholder Review

Check the original motivation for the architecture project and the Statement of Architecture Work against the proposed Technology Architecture, asking if it is fit for the purpose of supporting subsequent work in the other architecture domains. Refine the proposed Technology Architecture only if necessary.

12.4.8 Finalize the Technology Architecture

- Select standards for each of the building blocks, re-using as much as possible from the reference models selected from the Architecture Repository.
- Fully document each building block.
- Conduct final cross-check of overall architecture against business goals; document rationale for building block decisions in the architecture document.
- Document final requirements traceability report.
- Document final mapping of the architecture within the Architecture Repository; from the selected building blocks, identify those that might be re-used (working practices, roles, business relationships, job descriptions, etc.), and publish via the Architecture Repository.
- Finalize all the work products, such as gap analysis.

12.4.9 Create Architecture Definition Document

Document the rationale for building block decisions in the Architecture Definition Document.

Prepare the technology sections of the Architecture Definition Document, comprising some or allof:

- Fundamental functionality and attributes — semantic, unambiguous including security capability and manageability.
- Dependent building blocks with required functionality and named interfaces.
- Interfaces — chosen set, supplied (APIs, data formats, protocols, hardware interfaces, standards).
- Map to business/organizational entities and policies.

If appropriate, use reports and/or graphics generated by modeling tools to demonstrate key views of the architecture. Route the document for review by relevant stakeholders, and incorporate feedback.

- 是否已经作出影响技术架构的最新变更？
- 是否有机会在该组织的其他领域中，更好地利用本技术架构中的工作？
- 本技术架构是否影响其他项目（包括已计划的和当前正在进行的项目）？
- 本技术架构是否会受到其他项目（包括已计划的和当前正在进行的项目）的影响？

12.4.7 进行正式的利益攸关者审视

根据建议的技术架构检查架构项目和架构工作说明书的原始动机，询问其是否适于支持其他架构域中后续工作的目的。仅在必要时对建议的技术架构进行细化。

12.4.8 最终确定技术架构

- 为每个构建块选择的标准，尽可能复用从架构存储库中选择的参考模型。
- 完整地文件化每个构建块。
- 根据业务目标对总体架构进行最终交叉检查；在架构文件中记录构建块决策的理由依据。
- 记录最终的需求可追溯性报告。
- 记录架构存储库中架构的最终映射；从选定的构建块中识别可能复用的构建块（工作实践、角色、业务关系、工作描述等），并通过架构存储库发布。
- 最终确定所有的工作产物，如差距分析。

12.4.9 创建架构定义文件

在架构定义文件中记录构建块决策的理由依据。

准备架构定义文件的技术章节，包括以下部分或全部内容：

- 基础功能性和属性——语义，清晰准确且包括安保能力和可管理性。
- 具有所需功能性和已命名界面的依赖性构建块。
- 界面——已供应的选定系列（API、数据格式、协议、硬件界面、标准）。
- 业务/组织实体和策略的映射。

如适用，使用建模工具生成的报表和/或图形说明架构的关键视图。分发文件以供相关利益攸关者审视，并纳入反馈。

12.5 Outputs

The outputs of Phase D may include, but are not restricted to:

- Refined and updated versions of the Architecture Vision phase deliverables, where applicable:
  - Statement of Architecture Work (see Part IV, Section 36.2.20), updated if necessary
  - Validated technology principles, or new technology principles (if generated here)
- Draft Architecture Definition Document (see Part IV, Section 36.2.3), including:
  - Target Technology Architecture, Version 1.0 (detailed), including:
  - Technology Components and their relationships to information systems
  - Technology platforms and their decomposition, showing the combinations of technology required to realize a particular technology "stack"
  - Environments and locations — a grouping of the required technology into computing environments (e.g., development, production)
  - Expected processing load and distribution of load across technology components
  - Physical (network) communications
  - Hardware and network specifications
  - Baseline Technology Architecture, Version 1.0 (detailed), if appropriate
  - Views corresponding to the selected viewpoints addressing key stakeholder concerns
- Draft Architecture Requirements Specification (see Part IV, Section 36.2.6), including such Technology Architecture requirements as:
  - Gap analysis results
  - Requirements output from Phases B and C
  - Updated technology requirements
- Technology Architecture components of an Architecture Roadmap (see Part IV, Section 36.2.7)

The outputs may include some or all of the following:

- Catalogs:
  - Technology Standards catalog
  - Technology Portfolio catalog
- Matrices:
  - Application/Technology matrix
- Diagrams:
  - Environments and Locations diagram
  - Platform Decomposition diagram
  - Processing diagram

12.5 输出

阶段 D 的输出可包括但不限于：

- 架构愿景阶段交付物的细化和更新版本，如适用：
  - 架构工作说明书（见第四部分，36.2.20 节），必要时更新
  - 经确认的技术原则，或新的技术原则（若在此阶段生成）
- 起草架构定义文件（见第四部分，36.2.3 节），包括：
  - 目标技术架构，版本 1.0（详细），包括：
  - 技术组件及其与信息系统的关系
  - 技术平台及其分解，以表明实现特定技术“栈”所需的技术组合
  - 环境和位置——所需技术到计算环境的分组（如开发、生产）
  - 期望的处理负载和负载在技术组件中的分布
  - 物理（网络）通信
  - 硬件和网络规范
  - 基线技术架构，版本 1.0（详细），如适用
  - 与选定视角对应且应对关键的利益攸关者关注点的视图
- 起草架构需求规范（见第四部分 36.2.6 节），包括以下各类技术架构需求：
  - 差距分析结果
  - 阶段 B 和 C 的需求输出
  - 经过更新的技术需求
- 架构路线图的技术架构组件（见第四部分 36.2.7 节）

输出可包括以下部分或全部内容：

- 目录：
  - 技术标准目录
  - 技术谱系目录
- 矩阵：
  - 应用/技术矩阵
- 图：
  - 环境和位置图
  - 平台分解图
  - 流程图

- — Networked Computing/Hardware diagram
- — Communications Engineering diagram

12.6 Postscript

Choosing the scope of an architecture development cycle carefully will accelerate the pay-back. In contrast, an excessively large scope is unlikely to lead to successful implementation.

— 网络计算/硬件图

— 通信工程图

12.6 附言

仔细选择架构开发周期的范围将加快获得回报的速度。相反，过大的范围不可能实施成功。

Chapter 13
Phase E: Opportunities & Solutions

This chapter describes the process of identifying delivery vehicles (projects, programs, or portfolios) that effectively deliver the Target Architecture identified in previous phases.

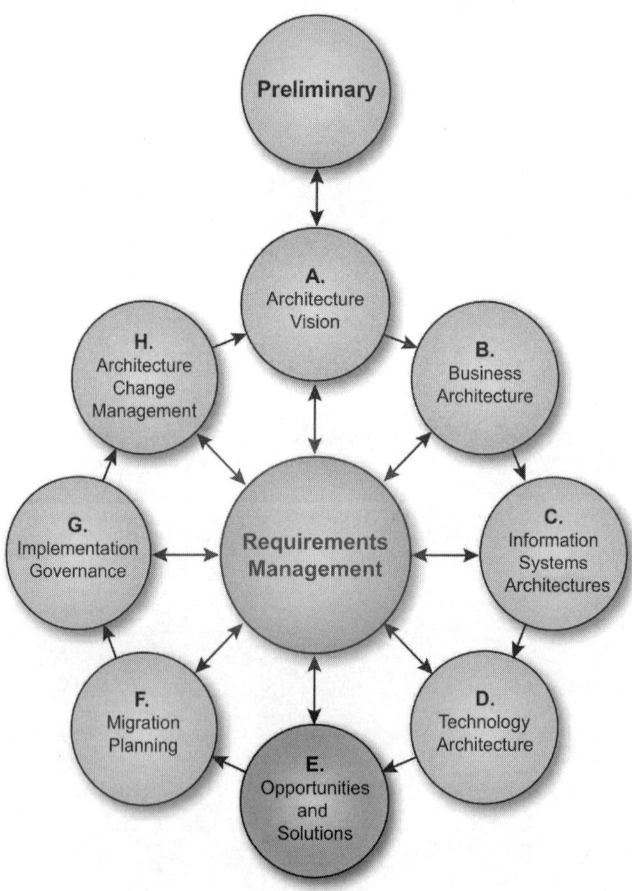

Figure 13-1 Phase E: Opportunities & Solutions

第 13 章
阶段 E：机会和解决方案

本章描述识别各种交付载体（项目、项目群或项目谱系）的流程，以有效地交付此前各阶段识别的目标架构。

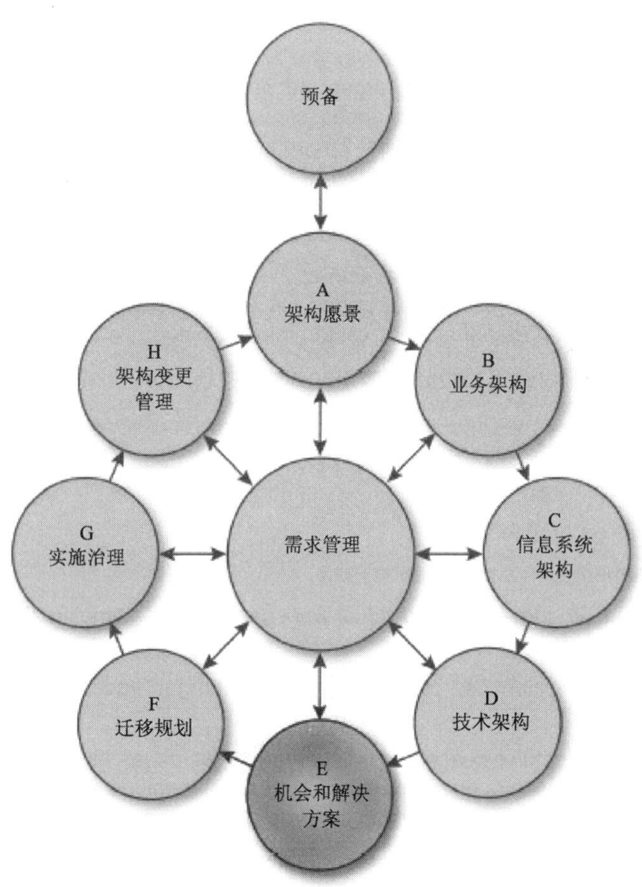

图 13-1　阶段 E：机会和解决方案

13.1 Objectives

The objectives of Phase E are to:

- Generate the initial complete version of the Architecture Roadmap, based upon the gap analysis and candidate Architecture Roadmap components from Phases B, C, and D.
- Determine whether an incremental approach is required, and if so identify Transition Architectures that will deliver continuous business value.

13.2 Approach

Phase E concentrates on how to deliver the architecture. It takes into account the complete set of gaps between the Target and Baseline Architectures in all architecture domains, and logically groups changes into work packages within the enterprise's portfolios. This is an effort to build a best-fit roadmap that is based upon the stakeholder requirements, the enterprise's business transformation readiness, identified opportunities and solutions, and identified implementation constraints. The key is to focus on the final target while realizing incremental business value.

Phase E is the initial step on the creation of the Implementation and Migration Plan which is completed in Phase F. It provides the basis of a well considered Implementation and Migration Plan that is integrated into the enterprise's portfolio in Phase F.

The following four concepts are key to transitioning from developing to delivering a Target Architecture:

- Architecture Roadmap
- Work Packages
- Transition Architectures
- Implementation and Migration Plan

The Architecture Roadmap lists individual work packages in a timeline that will realize the Target Architecture.

Each work package identifies a logical group of changes necessary to realize the Target Architecture.

A Transition Architecture describes the enterprise at an architecturally significant state between the Baseline and Target Architectures. Transition Architectures provide interim Target Architectures upon which the organization can converge.

The Implementation and Migration Plan provides a schedule of the projects that will realize the Target Architecture.

13.1 目的

阶段E的目的在于：

- 基于阶段 B、C 和 D 的差距分析和候选架构路线图组件，生成架构路线图初始的完整版本。
- 确定是否需要增量方法，如需要，则识别要交付连续业务价值的过渡架构。

13.2 实施途径

阶段 E 集中于如何交付架构，将考虑所有架构域内的目标架构与基线架构之间差距的完整集合，并且在 ENTERPRISE 项目谱系内从逻辑上将变更组合成工作包。这是一项基于利益攸关者需求、ENTERPRISE 业务转型准备度、识别的机会和解决方案以及识别的实施约束来构建最佳适配路线图的工作。关键是聚焦于最终目标，同时实现业务价值增值。

阶段 E 是关于在阶段 F 中完成创建实施与迁移计划的初始步骤。其提供在阶段F中整合到ENTERPRISE项目谱系中充分考虑的实施与迁移计划的基础。

以下四种概念是从开发目标架构向交付目标架构过渡的关键。

- 架构路线图
- 工作包
- 过渡架构
- 实施和迁移计划

架构路线图按实现目标架构的时间线列出各个工作包。

每个工作包识别实现目标架构所需变更的逻辑群组。

过渡架构在基线架构和目标架构之间，以架构方面的重要状态来描述ENTERPRISE。过渡架构提供组织可收敛的临时目标架构。

实施和迁移计划提供一个实现目标架构的项目进度表。

13.3 Inputs

This section defines the inputs to Phase E.

13.3.1 Reference Materials External to the Enterprise

- Architecture reference materials (see Part IV, Section 36.2.5)
- Product information

13.3.2 Non-Architectural Inputs

- Request for Architecture Work (see Part IV, Section 36.2.17)
- Capability Assessment (see Part IV, Section 36.2.10)
- Communications Plan (see Part IV, Section 36.2.12)
- Planning methodologies

13.3.3 Architectural Inputs

- Organizational Model for Enterprise Architecture (see Part IV, Section 36.2.16), including:
  - Scope of organizations impacted
  - Maturity assessment, gaps, and resolution approach
  - Roles and responsibilities for architecture team(s)
  - Constraints on architecture work
  - Budget requirements
  - Governance and support strategy
- Governance models and frameworks for:
  - Corporate Business Planning
  - Enterprise Architecture
  - Portfolio, Program, Project Management
  - System Development/Engineering
  - Operations (Service)
- Tailored Architecture Framework (see Part IV, Section 36.2.21), including:
  - Tailored architecture method
  - Tailored architecture content (deliverables and artifacts)
  - Configured and deployed tools
- Statement of Architecture Work (see Part IV, Section 36.2.20)
- Architecture Vision (see Part IV, Section 36.2.8)

13.3 输入

本节定义阶段 E 的输入。

13.3.1 ENTERPRISE 外部参考资料

- 架构参考资料（见第四部分 36.2.5 节）
- 产品信息

13.3.2 非架构输入

- 架构工作要求书（见第四部分 36.2.17 节）
- 能力评估（见第四部分 36.2.10 节）
- 沟通计划（见第四部分 36.2.12 节）
- 规划方法论

13.3.3 架构输入

- Enterprise Architecture 的组织模型（见第四部分 36.2.16 节），包括：
  - 组织受影响的范围
  - 成熟度评估、差距和解决途径
  - 架构团队的角色和职责
  - 对架构工作的约束
  - 预算需求
  - 治理和支持战略
- 治理模型和框架用于：
  - 公司级业务规划
  - Enterprise Architecture
  - 项目谱系、项目群和项目的管理
  - 系统开发/工程
  - 运行（服务）
- 经剪裁的架构框架（见第四部分 36.2.21 节），包括：
  - 经剪裁的架构方法
  - 经剪裁的架构内容（交付物和制品）
  - 经配置和部署的工具
- 架构工作说明书（见第四部分 36.2.20 节）
- 架构愿景（见第四部分 36.2.8 节）

- Architecture Repository (see Part IV, Section 36.2.5), including:
  - Re-usable building blocks
  - Publicly available reference models
  - Organization-specific reference models
  - Organization standards
- Draft Architecture Definition Document (see Part IV, Section 36.2.3), including:
  - Baseline Business Architecture, Version 1.0 (detailed)
  - Target Business Architecture, Version 1.0 (detailed)
  - Baseline Data Architecture, Version 1.0 (detailed)
  - Target Data Architecture, Version 1.0 (detailed)
  - Baseline Application Architecture, Version 1.0 (detailed)
  - Target Application Architecture, Version 1.0 (detailed)
  - Baseline Technology Architecture, Version 1.0 (detailed)
  - Target Technology Architecture, Version 1.0 (detailed)
- Draft Architecture Requirements Specification (see Part IV, Section 36.2.6), including:
  - Architectural requirements
  - Gap analysis results (from Business, Data, Application, and Technology Architecture)
  - IT Service Management requirements
- Change Requests for existing business programs and projects (see Part IV, Section 36.2.11)
- Candidate Architecture Roadmap components from Phases B, C, and D

13.4 Steps

The level of detail addressed in Phase E will depend on the scope and goals of the overall architecture effort.

The order of the steps in Phase E (see below) as well as the time at which they are formally started and completed should be adapted to the situation at hand in accordance with the established architecture governance.

All activities that have been initiated in these steps must be closed during the Create theArchitecture Roadmap & Implementation and Migration Plan step (see Section 13.4.11).

The steps in Phase E are as follows:

- Determine/confirm key corporate change attributes (see Section 13.4.1)
- Determine business constraints for implementation (see Section 13.4.2)
- Review and consolidate gap analysis results from Phases B to D (see Section 13.4.3)
- Review consolidated requirements across related business functions (see Section 13.4.4)

- 架构存储库（见第四部分 36.2.5 节），包括：
  - 可复用的构建块
  - 公开可用的参考模型
  - 组织特定参考模型
  - 组织标准
- 起草架构定义文件（见第四部分 36.2.3 节），包括：
  - 基线业务架构，版本 1.0（详细）
  - 目标业务架构，版本 1.0（详细）
  - 基线数据架构，版本 1.0（详细）
  - 目标数据架构，版本 1.0（详细）
  - 基线应用架构，版本 1.0（详细）
  - 目标应用架构，版本 1.0（详细）
  - 基线技术架构，版本 1.0（详细）
  - 目标技术架构，版本 1.0（详细）
- 起草架构需求规范（参见第四部分 36.2.6 节），包括：
  - 架构需求
  - 差距分析结果（来自业务、数据、应用和技术架构）
  - IT 服务管理需求
- 现有业务项目群和项目的变更要求（见第四部分 36.2.11 节）
- 来自阶段 B、C 和 D 的候选架构路线图组件

13.4 步骤

阶段 E 中所划分的细节层级将取决于总体架构工作的范围和目标。

阶段 E 中的步骤的顺序（见下文）及其正式开始和结束的时间应按照已确定的架构治理且适应于当前情况。

所有在这些步骤中已经开始的活动均必须在创建架构路线图与实施和迁移计划步骤（参见 13.4.11 节）结束。

阶段 E 中的步骤如下：

- 确定/确认关键的公司级变革属性（见 13.4.1 节）
- 确定用于实施的业务约束（见 13.4.2 节）
- 审视且合并来自阶段 B～D 的差距分析结果（见 13.4.3 节）
- 审视相关业务功能的合并需求（见 13.4.4 节）

- Consolidate and reconcile interoperability requirements (see Section 13.4.5)
- Refine and validate dependencies (see Section 13.4.6)
- Confirm readiness and risk for business transformation (see Section 13.4.7)
- Formulate Implementation and Migration Strategy (see Section 13.4.8)
- Identify and group major work packages (see Section 13.4.9)
- Identify Transition Architectures (see Section 13.4.10)
- Create the Architecture Roadmap & Implementation and Migration Plan (see Section 13.4.11)

13.4.1 Determine/Confirm Key Corporate Change Attributes

This step determines how the enterprise architecture can be best implemented to take advantage of the organization's business culture. This should include the creation of an Implementation Factor Assessment and Deduction matrix (see Part III, Section 28.1) to serve as

a repository for architecture implementation and migration decisions. The step also includes assessments of the transition capabilities of the organization units involved (including culture and abilities), and assessments of the enterprise (including culture and skill sets).

The resulting factors from the assessments should be documented in the Implementation Factor Assessment and Deduction matrix. For organizations where enterprise architecture is well established, this step can be simple, but the matrix has to be established so that it can be used as an archive and record of decisions taken.

13.4.2 Determine Business Constraints for Implementation

Identify any business drivers that would constrain the sequence of implementation. This should include a review of the business and strategic plans, at both a corporate and line-of-business level, and a review of the Enterprise Architecture Maturity Ass-essment.

13.4.3 Review and Consolidate Gap Analysis Results from Phases B to D

Consolidate and integrate the gap analysis results from the Business, Information Systems, and Technology Architectures (created in Phases B to D) and assess their implications with respect to potential solutions and inter-dependencies. This should be done by creating a Consolidated Gaps, Solutions, and Dependencies matrix, as shown in Part III, Section 28.2, which will enable the identification of Solution Building Blocks (SBBs) that could potentially address one or more gaps and their associated Architecture Building Blocks (ABBs).

Review the Phase B, C, and D gap analysis results and consolidate them in a single list. The gaps should be consolidated along with potential solutions to the gaps and dependencies. A recommended technique for determining the dependencies is to use sets of views such as the Business Interaction matrix, the Data Entity/Business Function matrix, and the Application/Function matrix to completely relate elements from different architectural domains.

Rationalize the Consolidated Gaps, Solutions, and Dependencies matrix. Once all of the gaps have been documented, re-organize the gap list and place similar items together. When grouping the gaps, refer to the Implementation Factor Assessment and Deduction matrix and review the implementation factors. Any additional factors should be added to the Implementation Factor Assessment and Deduction matrix.

- 合并和调和互用性需求（见 13.4.5 节）
- 细化和确认依赖性（见 13.4.6 节）
- 确认业务转型的准备度和风险（见 13.4.7 节）
- 制定实施和迁移策略（见 13.4.8 节）
- 识别主要工作包并将其分组（见 13.4.9 节）
- 识别过渡架构（见 13.4.10 节）
- 创建架构路线图及实施和迁移计划（见 13.4.11 节）

13.4.1 确定/确认关键的公司级变革属性

该步骤决定如何能够最好地实施 Enterprise Architecture 以利用组织的业务文化。这应包括创建实施因素评估和推绎矩阵（见第三部分 28.1 节），以充当架构实施和迁移决策的存储库。该步骤还包括对所涉及的组织单元的过渡能力（包括文化和能力）的评估和对 ENTERPRISE（包括文化和技能组合）的评估。

应在实施因素评估和推绎矩阵中记录从评估中得出的因素。对于 Enterprise Architecture 构建良好的组织，本步骤可能是简单的，但是必须建立该矩阵以便能够用作已做决策的档案和记录。

13.4.2 确定关于实施的业务约束

识别所有约束实施顺序的业务驱动因素，应包括公司级和业务线层面上的业务和战略计划的审视，以及 Enterprise Architecture 成熟度评估的审查。

13.4.3 审视和合并阶段 B～D 的差距分析结果

对业务、信息系统以及技术架构（在阶段 B～D 中创建）的差距分析结果进行合并与综合，并且针对潜在解决方案和相互依赖性评估其影响。这应通过创建合并的差距、解决方案和依赖性矩阵（如第三部分 28.2 节所示）来完成，这些合并的差距、解决方案和依赖性矩阵，能够识别潜在地应对一个或多个差距的解决方案构建块（SBB）及其相关架构构建块（ABB）。

审视阶段 B、C 和 D 差距分析结果并将这些结果合并在一个单一列表中。应将这些差距以及这些差距和依赖性的潜在解决方案合并。一种确定依赖性的推荐技巧是使用多组视图（诸如业务交互矩阵、数据实体/业务功能矩阵及应用/功能矩阵）使不同架构域中的元素完全相关联。

对合并的差距、解决方案和依赖性矩阵进行合理化。一旦记录了所有的差距，就要重新编制差距列表并将相似项排列在一起。当对差距分组时，参考实施因素评估和推绎矩阵并审视实施因素。应将所有附加因素添加至实施因素评估和推绎矩阵。

13.4.4 Review Consolidated Requirements Across Related Business Functions

Assess the requirements, gaps, solutions, and factors to identify a minimal set of requirements whose integration into work packages would leadto a more efficient and effective implementation of the Target Architecture across the business functions that are participating in the architecture. This functional perspective leads to the satisfaction of multiple requirements through the provision of shared solutions and services. The implications of this consolidation of requirements with respect to architectural components can be significant with respect to the provision of resources. For example, several requirements raised by several lines of business can be resolved through the provision of a shared set of Business Services and Information System Services within a work package or project.

13.4.5 Consolidate and Reconcile Interoperability Requirements

Consolidate the interoperability requirements identified in previous phases. The Architecture Vision and Target Architectures, as well as the Implementation Factor Assessment and Deduction matrix and Consolidated Gaps, Solutions, and Dependencies matrix, should be consolidated and reviewed to identify any constraints on interoperability required by the potential set of solutions.

A key outcome is to minimize interoperability conflicts, or to ensure such conflicts are addressed in the architecture. Re-used Solution Building Blocks (SBBs), Commercial Off-The-Shelf (COTS) products, and third-party service providers typically impose interoperability requirements that conflict. Any such conflicts must be addressed in the architecture, and conflicts must be considered across all architecture domains (Business, Applications, Data, and Technology).

There are two basic approaches to interoperability conflicts; either create a building block that transforms or translates between conflicting building blocks, or make a change to the specification of the conflicting building blocks.

13.4.6 Refine and Validate Dependencies

Refine the initial dependencies, ensuring that any constraints on the Implementation and Migration Plans are identified. There are several key dependencies that should be taken into account, such as dependencies on existing implementations of Business Services and Information System Services or changes to them. Dependencies should be used for determining the sequence of implementation and identifying the coordination required. A study of the dependencies should group activities together, creating a basis for projects to be established. Examine the relevant projects and see whether logical increments of deliverables can be identified. The dependencies will also help to identify when the identified increments can be delivered. Once finished, an assessment of these dependencies should be documented as part of the Architecture Roadmap and any necessary Transition Architectures.

Addressing dependencies serves as the basis for most migration planning.

13.4.4 审视所有相关业务功能的合并需求

评估需求、差距、解决方案及因素来识别一组最低需求，把这些需求整合进工作包，将使参与该架构所有业务功能的目标架构的实施工作效率更高、效果更好。这种功能的关注层级，通过提供共享的解决方案和服务来满足多重需求。相对于提供资源，这种需求的合并对于架构组件的影响可能是显著的。例如，可通过在一个工作包或项目中提供一套共享的业务服务和信息系统服务，解决由若干业务线提出的若干需求。

13.4.5 合并和调和互用性需求

合并此前各阶段识别的互用性需求。应合并和审视架构愿景和目标架构、实施因素评估和推绎矩阵以及合并的差距、解决方案和依赖性矩阵，以识别对一组潜在解决方案所需的互用性的所有约束。

关键的成果是最小化互用性冲突或确保在架构中应对这些冲突。可复用解决方案构建块（SBB）、商用货架（COTS）产品及第三方服务供应商通常会产生冲突的互用性需求。必须在该架构中应对所有这类冲突，并且必须在所有架构域（业务、应用、数据及技术）中考虑冲突。

存在两种解决互用性冲突的基本途径——在冲突的构建块之间创建转换或转化的构建块，或对冲突构建块的规范进行更改。

13.4.6 细化和确认依赖性

细化初始依赖性，以确保识别出所有对实施和迁移计划的约束。存在若干应考虑的关键依赖性，诸如对现有业务服务和信息系统服务的实施或变更的依赖性。应将依赖性用于确定实施的顺序及识别所需要的协调。对依赖性的研究应将活动组合到一起，为待建立的项目创建基础。审查相关项目，查看是否能够识别交付物的逻辑增量。这些依赖性还将有助于识别何时可交付识别的增量。一旦完成此工作，应将这些依赖性的评估文件化，作为架构路线图和所有必要的过渡架构的部分。

应对依赖性充当着大多数迁移规划的基础。

13.4.7 Confirm Readiness and Risk for Business Transformation

Review the findings of the Business Transformation Readiness Assessment previously conducted in Phase A and determine their impact on the Architecture Roadmap and the Implementation and Migration Strategy. It is important to identify, classify, and mitigate risks associated with the transformation effort. Risks should be documented in the Consolidated Gaps, Solutions, and Dependencies matrix.

13.4.8 Formulate Implementation and Migration Strategy

Create an overall Implementation and Migration Strategy that will guide the implementation of the Target Architecture, and structure any Transition Architectures. The first activity is to determine an overall strategic approach to implementing the solutions and/or exploiting opportunities. There are three basic approaches as follows:

- Greenfield: A completely new implementation.
- Revolutionary: A radical change (i.e., switch on, switch off).
- Evolutionary: A strategy of convergence, such as parallel running or a phased approach to introduce new capabilities.

Next, determine an approach for the overall strategic direction that will address and mitigate the risks identified in the Consolidated Gaps, Solutions, and Dependencies matrix. The most common implementation methodologies are:

- Quick win (snapshots).
- Achievable targets.
- Value chain method.

These approaches and the identified dependencies should become the basis for the creation of the work packages. This activity terminates with agreement on the Implementation and Migration Strategy for the enterprise.

13.4.9 Identify and Group Major Work Packages

Key stakeholders, planners, and the enterprise architects should assess the missing business capabilities identified in the Architecture Vision and Target Architecture.

Using the Consolidated Gaps, Solutions, and Dependencies matrix together with the Implementation Factor Assessment and Deduction matrix, logically group the various activities into work packages.

Fill in the "Solution" column in the Consolidated Gaps, Solutions, and Dependencies matrix to recommend the proposed solution mechanisms. Indicate for every gap/activity whether the solution should be oriented towards a new development, or be based on an existing product, and/or use a solution that can be purchased. An existing system may resolve the requirement with minor enhancements. For new development this is a good time to determine whether the work should be conducted in-house or through a contract.

Classify every current system that is under consideration as:

- Mainstream: Part of the future information system.

13.4.7 确认业务转型的准备度和风险

审视之前在阶段 A 中进行的业务转型准备度评估的研究结果，并确定其对架构路线图及实施和迁移策略的影响。对与转型工作有关的风险进行识别、分类和缓解是很重要的。应在合并的差距、解决方案和依赖性矩阵中记录风险。

13.4.8 制定实施和迁移战略

创建一种将引导目标架构实施的总体实施和迁移策略，并构建过渡架构。第一个活动是确定一种实施解决方案和/或利用机会的总体战略途径。三种基本途径如下：

- 新建的：一种全新的实施。
- 革命性的：一种彻底的改变（即，开启、关闭）。
- 演进的：一种收敛的战略，例如并行运行或一种引进新能力的分阶段的途径。

其次，为总体战略方向确定一种途径，以应对和缓解在合并的差距、解决方案和依赖性矩阵中识别的风险。最常用的实施方法论是：

- 快速复制法（快照）。
- 可实现的目标。
- 价值链方法。

这些途径和已识别的依赖性应成为创建工作包的基础。该活动与 ENTERPRISE 的实施和迁移策略达成一致后则终止。

13.4.9 识别主要工作包并将其分组

关键的利益攸关者、计划者及 ENTERPRISE 架构师应评估在架构愿景和目标架构中识别到的缺失的业务能力。

使用已合并的差距、解决方案和依赖性矩阵，连同实施因素评估和推绎矩阵，在逻辑上将不同活动组合成工作包。

填写合并的差距、解决方案和依赖性矩阵中的“解决方案”栏，以推荐建议的解决方案机制。针对每个差距/活动，表明该解决方案是否应面向新的开发，或基于现有产品，和/或使用可购买的解决方案。一个现有系统可通过较小的改进来解决需求。对于新的开发，这是一个决定是否应在内部开发或外包工作的好时机。

将每个正在考虑中的当前系统分类为：

- 主流：未来信息系统的一部分。

- Contain: Expected to be replaced or modified in the planning horizon (next three years).
- Replace: To be replaced in the planning horizon.

Supporting top-level work packages should then in turn be decomposed into incre-ments to deliver the capability increments. Analyze and refine these work packages, or increments with respect to their business transformation issues and the strategic implementation approach. Finally, group the work packages into portfolios and projects within a portfolio, taking into consideration the dependencies and the strategic imple-mentation approach.

13.4.10 Identify Transition Architectures

Where the scope of change to implement the Target Architecture requires an incre-mental approach, then one or more Transition Architectures may be necessary. These provide an ability to identify clear targets along the roadmap to realizing the Target Architecture. The Transition Architectures should provide measurable business value. The time-span between successive Transition Architectures does not have to be of uniform duration.

Development of Transition Architectures must be based upon the preferred implementation approach, the Consolidated Gaps, Solutions, and Dependencies matrix, the listing of projects and portfolios, as well as the enterprise's capacity for creating and absorbing change.

Determine where the difficult activities are, and unless there are compelling reasons, implement them after other activities that most easily deliver missing capability.

13.4.11 Create the Architecture Roadmap & Implementation and Migration Plan

Consolidate the work packages and Transition Architectures into the Architecture Roadmap, Version 0.1, which describes a timeline of the progression from the Baseline Architecture to the Target Architecture. The timeline informs the Implementation and Migration Plan. The Architecture Roadmap frames the migration planning in Phase F. Identified Transition Architectures and work packages should have a clear set of outcomes. The Architecture Roadmap must demonstrate how the selection and timeline of Transition Architectures and work packages realizes the Target Architecture.

The detail of the Architecture Roadmap, Version 0.1 should be expressed at a similar level of detail to the Architecture Definition Document developed in Phases B, C, and D. Where significant additional detail is required before implementation the architecture is likely transitioning to a different level. See Part III, Chapter 19 and Chapter 20 for techniques to manage iteration and different levels of detail.

The Implementation and Migration Plan must demonstrate the activity necessary to realize the Architecture Roadmap. The Implementation and Migration Plan forms the basis of the migration planning in Phase F. The detail of the Implementation and Migration Plan, Version 0.1 must be aligned to the detail of the Architecture Roadmap and be sufficient to identify the necessary projects and resource requirements to realize the roadmap.

When creating the Implementation and Migration Plan there are many approaches to consider, such as a data-driven sequence, where application systems that create data are implemented first, then applications that process the data. A clear understanding of the dependencies and lifecycle of in-place SBBs is required for an effective Implementation and Migration Plan.

Finally, update the Architecture Vision, Architecture Definition Document, and Architecture Requirements Specification with any additional relevant outcomes from this phase.

- 包含：期望在规划远景（未来三年）内替换或改进。
- 替换：将在规划远景中替换。

然后，支持性的顶层工作包应被依次分解成增量来交付能力增量。应分析并细化这些工作包，或关于其业务转型议题和战略实施途径的增量。最后，考虑到依赖性和战略实施途径，将工作包组合成多个项目谱系和各项目谱系中的多个项目。

13.4.10 识别过渡架构

如果实施目标架构的变更范围需要一种增量递增方法，则可能需要一个或多个过渡架构，这提供一种沿着实现目标架构的路线图识别明确目标的能力。这些过渡架构应提供可衡量的业务价值。相继的过渡架构之间的时间跨度不必具有统一的期限。

开发过渡架构必须基于首选的实施途径，合并的差距、解决方案和依赖性矩阵，以及项目和项目谱系列表以及 ENTERPRISE 创建和吸收变革的能力。

确定困难活动所在，除非具有说服力的理由，应在其他最容易交付缺失能力的活动后实施这些活动。

13.4.11 创建架构路线图及实施和迁移计划

将工作包和过渡架构合并到架构路线图 0.1 版本中，该架构路线图描述了从基线架构向目标架构演进的时间线。该时间线是实施和迁移计划的依据。该架构路线图框定了阶段 F 中的迁移规划。已识别的过渡架构和工作包应具有一系列明确的成果。该架构路线图必须说明过渡架构和工作包的选择和时间线是如何实现目标架构的。

应按与阶段 B、C 和 D 中开发的架构定义文件相似的细节层级来表达架构路线图 0.1 版本的细节。如果在实施前需要大量的增加细节，该架构可能过渡到一个不同的层级。对迭代和不同细节层级进行管理的技巧，见第三部分第 19 章和第 20 章。

实施和迁移计划必须说明实现该架构路线图所必需的活动。该实施和迁移计划形成了阶段 F 中的迁移规划的基础。实施和迁移计划的细节（版本 0.1）必须与架构路线图的细节相一致，并且足以识别必要的项目和资源需求以实现该路线图。

当创建实施和迁移计划时，需要考虑多种途径——如数据驱动序列，首先实施创建数据的应用系统，然后是处理数据的应用。对于有效的实施和迁移计划，需要清楚理解原 SBB 的依赖性和生命周期。

最后，使用本阶段所有附加的相关成果更新架构愿景、架构定义文件及架构需求规范。

13.5 Outputs

The outputs of Phase E may include, but are not restricted to:

- Refined and updated version of the Architecture Vision phase deliverables, where applicable, including:
  - Architecture Vision, including definition of types and degrees of interope-rability
  - Statement of Architecture Work (see Part IV, Section 36.2.20), updated if necessary
- Draft Architecture Definition Document (see Part IV, Section 36.2.3), including:
  - Baseline Business Architecture, Version 1.0 updated if necessary
  - Target Business Architecture, Version 1.0 updated if necessary
  - Baseline Data Architecture, Version 1.0 updated if necessary
  - Target Data Architecture, Version 1.0 updated if necessary
  - Baseline Application Architecture, Version 1.0 updated if necessary
  - Target Application Architecture, Version 1.0 updated if necessary
  - Baseline Technology Architecture, Version 1.0 updated if necessary
  - Target Technology Architecture, Version 1.0 updated if necessary
  - Transition Architecture, number and scope as necessary
  - Views corresponding to the selected viewpoints addressing key stakeh-older concerns
- Draft Architecture Requirements Specification (see Part IV, Section 36.2.6), including:
  - Consolidated Gaps, Solutions, and Dependencies Assessment
- Capability Assessments, including:
  - Business Capability Assessment
  - IT Capability Assessment
- Architecture Roadmap (see Part IV, Section 36.2.7), including:
  - Work package portfolio:
    - Work package description (name, description, objectives)
    - Functional requirements
    - Dependencies
    - Relationship to opportunity
    - Relationship to Architecture Definition Document and Architecture Requirements Specification
    - Relationship to any capability increments
    - Business value
    - Implementation Factor Assessment and Deduction Matrix
    - Impact
  - Identification of Transition Architectures, if any, including:

13.5 输出

阶段 E 的输出可包括但不限于：

- 架构愿景阶段交付物的细化和更新版本，如适用，包括：
  - 架构愿景，包括互用性的类型和程度的定义
  - 架构工作说明书（见第四部分 36.2.20 节），必要时进行更新
- 起草架构定义文件（见第四部分 36.2.3 节），包括：
  - 基线业务架构，版本 1.0，必要时进行更新
  - 目标业务架构，版本 1.0，必要时进行更新
  - 基线数据架构，版本 1.0，必要时进行更新
  - 目标数据架构，版本 1.0，必要时进行更新
  - 基线应用架构，版本 1.0，必要时进行更新
  - 目标应用架构，版本 1.0，必要时进行更新
  - 基线技术架构，版本 1.0，必要时进行更新
  - 目标技术架构，版本 1.0，必要时进行更新
  - 过渡架构，必要的数量和范围
  - 对应选定视角并应对关键的利益攸关者关注点的视图
- 起草架构需求规范（见第四部分 36.2.6 节），包括：
  - 合并的差距、解决方案和依赖性评估
- 能力评估，包括：
  - 业务能力评估
  - IT 能力评估
- 架构路线图（见第四部分 36.2.7 节），包括：
  - 工作包谱系：
    - 工作包描述（名称、描述、目的）
    - 功能需求
    - 依赖性
    - 与机会的关系
    - 与架构定义文件和架构需求规范的关系
    - 与所有能力增量的关系
    - 业务价值
    - 实施因素评估和推绎矩阵
    - 影响
  - 过渡架构的识别（如果有），包括：

    - Relationship to Architecture Definition Document
  - Implementation recommendations:
    - Criteria measures of effectiveness
    - Risks and issues
    - Solution Building Blocks (SBBs)
- Implementation and Migration Plan, Version 0.1, including:
  - Implementation and Migration Strategy

The outputs may include some or all of the following:

- Diagrams:
  - Project Context diagram
  - Benefits diagram

    - 与架构定义文件的关系
  - 实施建议：
    - 有效性标准测量指标
    - 风险和议题
    - 解决方案构建块（SBB）
- 实施和迁移计划，版本 0.1，包括：
  - 实施和迁移策略

输出可包括以下部分或全部内容：

- 图：
  - 项目背景环境图
  - 效益图

Chapter 14
Phase F: Migration Planning

This chapter addresses migration planning; that is, how to move from the Baseline to the Target Architectures by finalizing a detailed Implementation and Migration Plan.

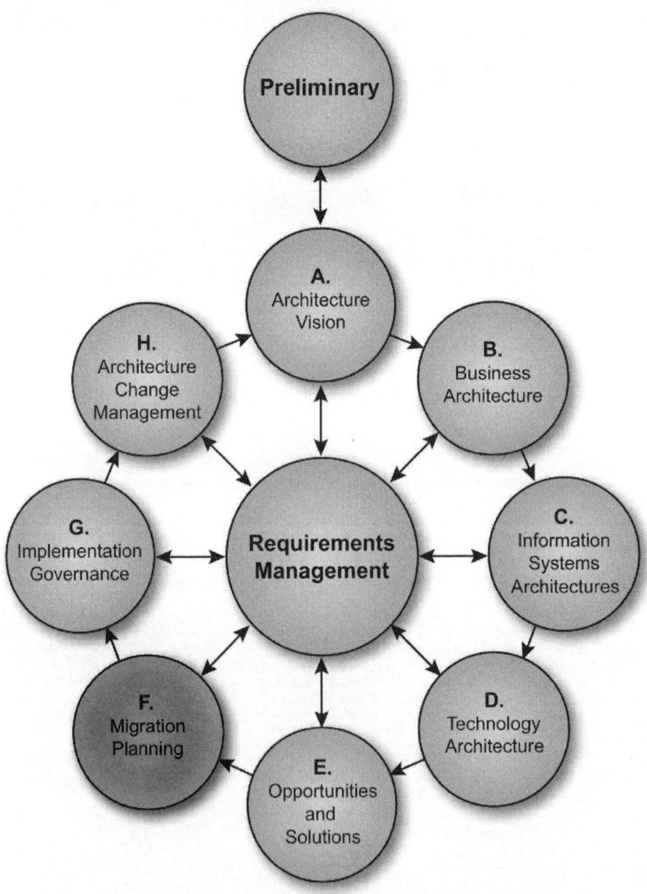

Figure 14-1 Phase F: Migration Planning

第 14 章
阶段 F：迁移规划

本章论述迁移规划，即如何通过最终确定一个详细的实施和迁移计划将基线架构迁移至目标架构。

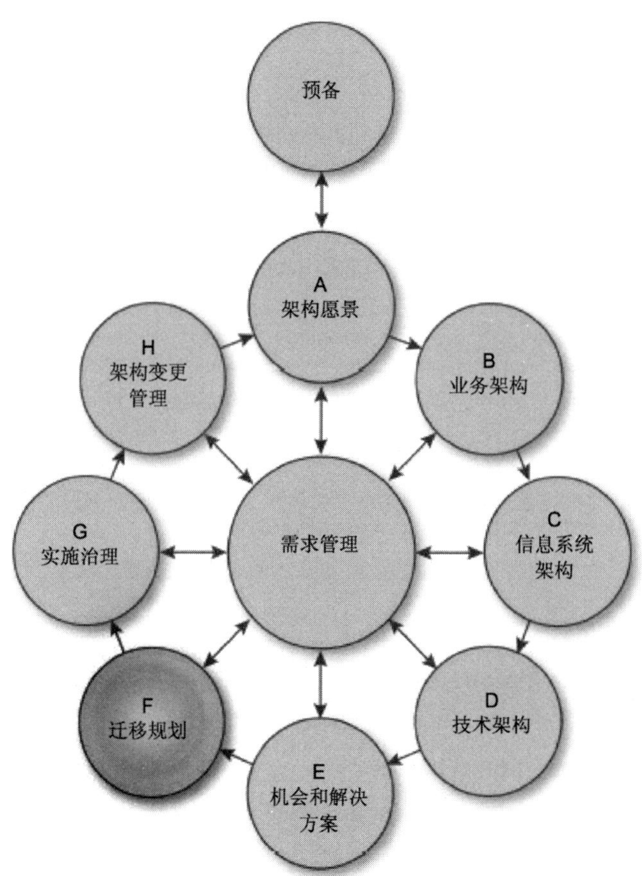

图 14-1 阶段 F：迁移规划

14.1 Objectives

The objectives of Phase F are to:

- Finalize the Architecture Roadmap and the supporting Implementation and Migration Plan.
- Ensure that the Implementation and Migration Plan is coordinated with the enterprise's approach to managing and implementing change in the enterprise's overall change portfolio.
- Ensure that the business value and cost of work packages and Transition Architectures is understood by key stakeholders.

14.2 Approach

The focus of Phase F is the creation of an Implementation and Migration Plan in co-operation with the portfolio and project managers.

Phase E provides an incomplete Architecture Roadmap and Implementation and Migration Plan that address the Request for Architecture Work. In Phase F this Roadmap and the Implementation and Migration Plan are integrated with the enterprise's other change activity.

Activities include assessing the dependencies, costs, and benefits of the various migration projects within the context of the enterprise's other activity. The Architecture Roadmap, Version0.1 and Implementation and Migration Plan, Version 0.1 from Phase E will form the basis of the final Implementation and Migration Plan that will include portfolio and project-level detail.

The architecture development cycle should then be completed and lessons learned documented to enable continuous process improvement.

14.3 Inputs

This section defines the inputs to Phase F.

14.3.1 Reference Materials External to the Enterprise

- Architecture reference materials (see Part IV, Section 36.2.5)

14.3.2 Non-Architectural Inputs

- Request for Architecture Work (see Part IV, Section 36.2.17)
- Capability Assessment (see Part IV, Section 36.2.10)
- Communications Plan (see Part IV, Section 36.2.12)

14.1 目的

阶段 F 的目的是：

- 最终确定架构路线图和支持的实施和迁移计划。
- 确保实施和迁移计划与 ENTERPRISE 在 ENTERPRISE 总体变革谱系中管理和实施变更途径相协调。
- 确保关键利益攸关者理解工作包和过渡架构的业务价值和成本。

14.2 实施途径

阶段 F 的聚焦点是配合项目谱系经理和项目经理创建实施和迁移计划。

阶段 E 提供不完整的架构路线图以及实施和迁移计划来应对架构工作要求书。在阶段 F 中，本路线图以及实施和迁移计划将与 ENTERPRISE 其他变革活动集成。

活动包括在 ENTERPRISE 其他活动的背景环境之中评估不同迁移项目的依赖性、成本和效益。阶段 E 中的架构路线图 0.1 版本及实施和迁移计划 0.1 版本将形成最终实施和迁移计划的基础，最终实施和迁移计划包括项目谱系和项目层级细节。

然后，应完成架构开发周期并记录经验教训，以实现流程持续改进。

14.3 输入

本节定义了对阶段 F 的输入。

14.3.1 ENTERPRISE 外部参考资料

- 架构参考资料（见第四部分 36.2.5 节）

14.3.2 非架构输入

- 架构工作要求书（见第四部分 36.2.17 节）
- 能力评估（见第四部分 36.2.10 节）
- 沟通计划（见第四部分 36.2.12 节）

14.3.3 Architectural Inputs

- Organizational Model for Enterprise Architecture (see Part IV, Section 36.2.16), including:
  - Scope of organizations impacted
  - Maturity assessment, gaps, and resolution approach
  - Roles and responsibilities for architecture team(s)
  - Constraints on architecture work
  - Budget requirements
  - Governance and support strategy
- Governance models and frameworks for:
  - Corporate Business Planning
  - Enterprise Architecture
  - Portfolio, Program, Project Management
  - System Development/Engineering
  - Operations (Service)
- Tailored Architecture Framework (see Part IV, Section 36.2.21), including:
  - Tailored architecture method
  - Tailored architecture content (deliverables and artifacts)
  - Configured and deployed tools
- Statement of Architecture Work (see Part IV, Section 36.2.20)
- Architecture Vision (see Part IV, Section 36.2.8)
- Architecture Repository (see Part IV, Section 36.2.5), including:
  - Re-usable building blocks
  - Publicly available reference models
  - Organization-specific reference models
  - Organization standards
- Draft Architecture Definition Document (see Part IV, Section 36.2.3), including:
  - Baseline Business Architecture, Version 1.0 (detailed)
  - Target Business Architecture, Version 1.0 (detailed)
  - Baseline Data Architecture, Version 1.0 (detailed)
  - Target Data Architecture, Version 1.0 (detailed)
  - Baseline Application Architecture, Version 1.0 (detailed)
  - Target Application Architecture, Version 1.0 (detailed)
  - Baseline Technology Architecture, Version 1.0 (detailed)
  - Target Technology Architecture, Version 1.0 (detailed)

14.3.3 架构输入

- Enterprise Architecture 的组织模型（见第四部分 36.2.16 节），包括：
  - — 受影响的组织的范围
  - — 成熟度评估、差距和解决途径
  - — 架构团队的角色和职责
  - — 对架构工作的约束
  - — 预算需求
  - — 治理和支持战略
- 治理模型和框架用于：
  - — 公司级业务规划
  - — Enterprise Architecture
  - — 项目谱系、项目群、项目管理
  - — 系统开发/工程
  - — 操作（服务）
- 经剪裁的架构框架（见第四部分 36.2.21 节），包括：
  - — 经剪裁的架构方法
  - — 经剪裁的架构内容（交付物和制品）
  - — 经配置和部署的工具
- 架构工作说明书（见第四部分 36.2.20 节）
- 架构愿景（见第四部分 36.2.8 节）
- 架构存储库（见第四部分 36.2.5 节），包括：
  - — 可复用的构建块
  - — 公开可用的参考模型
  - — 组织特定参考模型
  - — 组织标准
- 起草架构定义文件（见第四部分 36.2.3 节），包括：
  - — 基线业务架构，版本 1.0（详细）
  - — 目标业务架构，版本 1.0（详细）
  - — 基线数据架构，版本 1.0（详细）
  - — 目标数据架构，版本 1.0（详细）
  - — 基线应用架构，版本 1.0（详细）
  - — 目标应用架构，版本 1.0（详细）
  - — 基线技术架构，版本 1.0（详细）
  - — 目标技术架构，版本 1.0（详细）

  - Transition Architectures, if any
- Draft Architecture Requirements Specification (see Part IV, Section 36.2.6), including:
  - Architectural requirements
  - Gap analysis results (from Business, Data, Application, and Technology Architecture)
  - IT Service Management requirements
- Change Requests for existing business programs and projects (see Part IV, Section 36.2.11)
- Architecture Roadmap, Version 0.1 (see Part IV, Section 36.2.7), including:
  - Identification of work packages
  - Identification of Transition Architectures
  - Implementation Factor Assessment and Deduction Matrix
- Capability Assessment (see Part IV, Section 36.2.10), including:
  - Business Capability Assessment
  - IT Capability Assessment
- Implementation and Migration Plan, Version 0.1 (see Part IV, Section 36.2.14) including the high-level Implementation and Migration Strategy.

14.4 Steps

The level of detail addressed in Phase F will depend on the scope and goals of the overall architecture effort.

The order of the steps in Phase F (see below) as well as the time at which they are formally started and completed should be adapted to the situation at hand in accordance with the established architecture governance.

All activities that have been initiated in these steps must be closed during the Complete the architecture development cycle and document lessons learned step (see Section 14.4.7).

The steps in Phase F are as follows:

- Confirm management framework interactions for Implementation and Migration Plan (see Section 14.4.1).
- Assign a business value to each work package (see Section 14.4.2)
- Estimate resource requirements, project timings, and availability/delivery vehicle (see Section 14.4.3).
- Prioritize the migration projects through the conduct of a cost/benefit assessment and risk validation (see Section 14.4.4).
- Confirm Architecture Roadmap and update Architecture Definition Document (see Section 14.4.5).
- Complete the Implementation and Migration Plan (see Section 14.4.6).
- Complete the architecture development cycle and document lessons learned (see Section 14.4.7).

— 过渡架构（如果有）

- 起草架构需求规范（见第四部分 36.2.6 节），包括：
  - — 架构需求
  - — 差距分析结果（来自业务、数据、应用和技术架构）
  - — IT 服务管理需求
- 现有业务项目群和项目的变更要求（见第四部分 36.2.11 节）
- 架构路线图，版本 0.1（见第四部分 36.2.7 节），包括：
  - — 工作包的识别
  - — 过渡架构的识别
  - — 实施因素评估和推绎矩阵
- 能力评估（见第四部分 36.2.10 节），包括：
  - — 业务能力评估
  - — IT 能力评估
- 实施和迁移计划，版本 0.1（见第四部分 36.2.14 节），包括高层级实施和迁移策略。

14.4 步骤

阶段 F 中所划分的细节层次，取决于总体架构工作的范围和目标。

阶段 F 中的步骤顺序（见下文）及其正式开始和结束的时间应按照已确定的架构治理来适应当前情况。

所有在这些步骤中已开始的活动均必须在完成架构开发周期中结束并记录经验教训步骤（见 14.4.7 节）。

阶段 F 中的步骤如下：

- 为实施和迁移计划确认管理框架的交互作用（见 14.4.1 节）。
- 为每个工作包指派业务价值（见 14.4.2 节）。
- 评估资源需求、项目时间安排和可用性/交付载体（见 14.4.3 节）。
- 通过进行成本/效益评估和风险验证对迁移项目进行优先级排序（见 14.4.4 节）。
- 确认架构路线图并更新架构定义文件（见 14.4.5 节）。
- 完成实施和迁移计划（见 14.4.6 节）。
- 完成架构开发周期并记录经验教训（见 14.4.7 节）。

14.4.1 Confirm Management Framework Interactions for the Implementation and Migration Plan

This step is about coordinating the Implementation and Migration Plan with the mana-gement frameworks within the organization. There are typically four management frameworks that have to work closely together for the Implementation and Migration Plan to succeed:

- **Business Planning** that conceives, directs, and provides the resources for all of the activities required to achieve concrete business objectives/outco-mes.
- **Enterprise Architecture** that structures and gives context to all enterprise activities delivering concrete business outcomes primarily but not exclusively in the IT domain.
- **Portfolio/Project Management** that co-ordinates, designs, and builds the business systems that deliver the concrete business outcomes.
- **Operations Management** that integrates, operates, and maintains the deliverables that deliver the concrete business outcomes.

The Implementation and Migration Plan will impact the outputs of each of these frameworks and consequently has to be reflected in them. In the course of this step, understand the frameworks within the organization and ensure that these plans are coordinated and inserted (in a summary format) within the plans of each one of these frameworks.

The outcome of this step may well be that the Implementation and Migration Plan could be part of a different plan produced by another one of the frameworks with enterprise architecture participation.

14.4.2 Assign a Business Value to Each Work Package

Establish and assign business values to all of the work packages. The intent is to first establish what constitutes business value within the organization, how value can be measured, and then apply this to each one of the projects and project increments.

If Capability-Based Planning has been used, then the business values associated with the capabilities and associated capability increments should be used to assign the business values for deliverables.

There are several issues to address in this activity:

- **Performance Evaluation Criteria** are used by portfolio and capability managers to approve and monitor the progress of the architecture transfor-mation.
- **Return-on-Investment Criteria** have to be detailed and signed off by the various executive stakeholders.
- **Business Value** has to be defined as well as techniques, such as the value chain, which are to be used to illustrate the role in achieving tangible business outcomes. Business value will be used by portfolio and capability managers to allocate resources and, in cases where there are cut backs, business value in conjunction with return on investment can be used to determine whether an endeavor proceeds, is delayed, or is canceled.
- **Critical Success Factors (CSFs)** should be established to define success for a project and/or project increment. These will provide managers and impl-ementers with a gauge as to what constitutes a successful implementation.
- **Measures of Effectiveness (MOE)** are often performance criteria and many corporations include them in the CSFs. Where they are treated discretely, it should be clear as to how these criteria are to be grouped.

14.4.1 为实施和迁移计划确认管理框架交互

该步骤是关于协调实施和迁移计划与组织内的管理框架的。

典型情况下，存在如下四种为实施和迁移计划取得成功而必须密切合作的管理框架：

- 对为达成具体业务目的/成果所需的所有活动进行构思、指引和提供资源的业务规划。
- 对主要而并非仅仅在 IT 域交付具体业务成果的所有 ENTERPRISE 活动进行结构化并提供背景环境的 Enterprise Architecture。
- 协调、设计和构建交付具体业务成果的业务系统的项目谱系/项目管理。
- 集成、运行和维护交付具体业务成果的交付物的操作管理。

实施和迁移计划会影响这些框架中每个框架的输出，因此，必须反映在这些输出中。在本步骤中，理解组织内的框架，确保在这些框架中每个框架的计划内（以概要格式）协调并插入这些计划。

本步骤的成果很可能是，实施和迁移计划可能是不同计划的一部分，该计划由 Enterprise Architecture 参与的框架的另一个计划产生。

14.4.2 为每个工作包指派业务价值

为所有工作包建立和指派业务价值。意图在于，首先确定组织内的业务价值由什么构成、如何测量，然后将该业务价值应用到每一个项目和项目增量。

如果已使用基于能力的规划，则应利用与这些能力和相关能力增量有关的业务价值为交付物指派业务价值。

在该活动中存在需要应对的若干议题：

- 由项目谱系管理人员和能力管理人员使用**绩效评价准则**来批准并监控架构转型的进展。
- **投资回报准则**必须由不同执行利益攸关者详细说明并签字。
- 必须定义**业务价值**和技巧，此外，诸如价值链等技术将被用于说明在获得切实的业务成果中的作用。将由项目谱系管理人员和能力管理人员使用业务价值来分配资源，在削减的情况下，可使用业务价值连同投资回报来确定是否继续、延迟或取消所进行的努力。
- 应建立**关键成功因素（CSF）**，以定义项目和/或项目增量的成功。这些关键成功因素会为管理者和实施者提供衡量构成成功实施的标准。
- **有效性测量指标（MOE）**通常是性能标准，许多公司将其包括在 CSF 中。在离散处理这些标准的情况下，应明确如何把这些标准分组。

- **Strategic Fit** based upon the overall enterprise architecture (all tiers) will be the critical factor for allowing the approval of any new project or initiative and for determining the value of any deliverable.

Use the work packages as a basis of identifying projects that will be in the Implementation and Migration Plan. The identified projects will be fully developed in other steps in Phase F. The projects, and project increments, may require adjustment of the Architecture Roadmap and Architecture Definition Document.

Risks should then be assigned to the projects and project increments by aggregating risks identified in the Consolidated Gaps, Solutions, and Dependencies Matrix (from Phase E).

Estimate the business value for each project using the Business Value Assessment Technique(see Part III, Section 28.5).

14.4.3 Estimate Resource Requirements, Project Timings, and Availability/Delivery Vehicle

This step determines the required resources and times for each project and their increments and provides the initial cost estimates. The costs should be broken down into capital (to create the capability) and operations and maintenance (to run and sustain the capability). Opportunities should be identified where the costs associated with delivering new and/or better capability can be offset by decommissioning existing systems. Assign required resources to each activity and aggregate them at the project increment and project level.

14.4.4 Prioritize the Migration Projects through the Conduct of a Cost/Benefit Assessment and Risk Validation

Prioritize the projects by ascertaining their business value against the cost of delivering them. The approach is to first determine, as clearly as possible, the net benefit of all of the SBBs delivered by the projects, and then verify that the risks have been effectively mitigated and factored in. Afterwards, the intent is to gain the requisite consensus to create a prioritized list of projects that will provide the basis for resource allocation.

It is important to discover all costs, and to ensure that decision-makers understand the net benefit over time.

Review the risks to ensure that the risks for the project deliverables have been mitigated as much as possible. The project list is then updated with risk-related comments.

Have the stakeholders agree upon a prioritization of the projects. Prioritization criteria will use elements identified in creation of the draft Architecture Roadmap in Phase E as well as those relating to individual stakeholders' agendas. Notice that it is possible for a project to earn a high priority if it provides a critical deliverable on the path to some large benefit, even if the immediate benefit of the project itself is small.

Formally review the risk assessment and revise it as necessary ensuring that there is a full understanding of the residual risk associated with the prioritization and the projected funding line.

- 基于总体 Enterprise Architecture（所有层）的战略协调性，将是允许任何新项目或举措的批准以及确定任何交付物价值的关键因素。

将工作包用作识别要纳入实施和迁移计划中的项目的基础。在阶段 F 中的其他步骤中被充分地开发已识别的项目。这些项目和项目增量可能需要调整架构路线图和架构定义文件。

然后，应通过合计（在阶段 E 中）已合并的差距、解决方案和依赖性矩阵中识别的风险，将风险指派至项目群和项目增量。

利用业务价值评估技术为每个项目评估业务价值（见第三部分 28.5 节）。

14.4.3 评估资源需求、项目时间安排和可用性/交付载体

该步骤为每个项目及其增量确定所需资源和时间，并提供最初成本估算。应将成本分为资本（创建能力）和运行及维护（运行并维持能力）。在那些与交付新的和/或更好能力相关的成本能够通过使现有系统退役来抵消的机会，应该被识别。将所需资源指派给每个活动，并在项目增量和项目层级上合计所需资源。

14.4.4 通过成本/效益评估和风险验证对迁移项目进行优先级排序

通过根据交付项目的成本确定其业务价值，对项目进行优先级排序。这种途径首先尽可能清楚地确定项目所交付的所有 SBB 的净效益，然后，证实已有效地缓解风险并将其考虑在内。其后，意图是获得创建优先项目列表的必要共识，来为资源分配提供基础。

重要的是发现所有成本，并确保决策人随着时间的推移而理解净效益。

审视风险以确保已尽可能地缓解项目交付物的风险。然后，利用风险相关的意见更新项目列表。

应使利益攸关者对项目的优先级排序达成一致意见。优先准则将使用于阶段 E 创建架构路线图草稿中识别的元素以及有关个体利益攸关者议题的元素。注意，如果一个项目在获得某种较大效益的过程中提供关键交付物，那么，即使这个项目本身的直接效益很小，也可能获得高优先级。

正式审视风险评估并根据需要进行修订，以确保充分理解与优先排序和预计资金线有关的残留风险。

14.4.5 Confirm Architecture Roadmap and Update Architecture Definition Document

Update the Architecture Roadmap including any Transition Architectures. Review the work to date to assess what the time-spans between Transition Architecture should be, taking into consideration the increments in business value and capability and other factors, such as risk. Once the capability increments have been finalized, consolidate the deliverables by project. This will result in a revised Architecture Roadmap.

This is needed in order to co-ordinate the development of several concurrent instances of the various architectures. A Transition Architecture State Evolution Table (see Part III, Section 28.4) can be used to show the proposed state of the domain architectures at various levels of detail.

If the implementation approach has shifted as a result of confirming the implementation increments, update the Architecture Definition Document. This may include assigning project objectives and aligning projects and their deliverables with the Transition Architectures to create an Architecture Definition Increments Table (see Part III, Section 28.3).

14.4.6 Generate the Implementation and Migration Plan

Generate the completed Implementation and Migration Plan. Much of the detail for the plan has already been gathered and this step brings it all together using accepted planning and management techniques.

This should include integrating all of the projects and activities as well as dependencies and impact of change into a project plan. Any Transition Architectures will act as portfolio milestones.

All external dependencies should be captured and included, and the overall availability of resources assessed. Project plans may be included within the Implementation and Migration Plan.

14.4.7 Complete the Architecture Development Cycle and Document Lessons Learned

This step transitions governance from the development of the architecture to the realization of the architecture. If the maturity of the Architecture Capability warrants, an Implementation Governance Model may be produced (see Part IV, Section 36.2.15).

Lessons learned during the development of the architecture should be documented and captured by the appropriate governance process in Phase H as inputs to managing the Architecture Capability.

The detail of the Architecture Roadmap and the Implementation and Migration Plan should be expressed at a similar level of detail to the Architecture Definition Document developed in Phases B, C, and D. Where significant additional detail is required by the next phase the architecture is likely transitioning to a different level. Depending upon the level of the Target Architecture and Implementation and Migration Plan it may be necessary to iterate another ADM cycle at a lower level of detail. See Part III, Chapter 19 and Chapter 20 for techniques to manage iteration and different levels of detail.

14.4.5 确认架构路线图并更新架构定义文件

更新包括过渡架构的架构路线图。审视到目前为止的工作，以评估过渡架构之间的时间跨度应为多少，应把业务价值和能力增量及诸如风险的其他因素考虑在内。一旦最终确定能力增量，则应根据项目合并交付物。以上工作产生修订的架构路线图。

这对协调多个并发的不同架构实例的开发工作是必要的。一种过渡架构状态演进表（见第三部分 28.4 节）可用来说明不同细节层级的域架构的建议状态。

如果实施途径由于确认实施增量而转变，应更新架构定义文件。这可能包括指派项目目的和使项目及其交付物与过渡架构一致，以创建架构定义增量表（见第三部分 28.3 节）。

14.4.6 生成实施和迁移计划

生成完整的实施和迁移计划。已收集本计划的大量细节，本步骤利用公认的规划和管理技术将所有细节整合到一起。

这应包括将所有项目和活动以及变更的依赖性和影响综合到一个项目计划中。任何过渡架构都会充当项目谱系里程碑。

所有外部依赖性均应被捕获和包括在内，并应评估资源的总体可用性。在实施和迁移计划中可包含多个项目计划。

14.4.7 完成架构开发周期并记录经验教训

本步骤将架构开发的治理过渡到架构实现的治理。如果保证架构能力的成熟度，可生成实施治理模型（见第四部分 36.2.15 节）。

应通过阶段 H 中适当的治理流程，记录和捕获在架构开发期间得到的经验教训，作为对管理架构能力的输入。

对该架构路线图及该实施和迁移计划的细节的表达，应与阶段 B、C 和 D 中开发的架构定义文件具有相似的细节层级。如果下一个阶段需要重要的附加细节，该架构可能过渡到不同的层级。根据该目标架构及实施和迁移计划的层级，可能有必要在一个较详细的细节层级上迭代另一轮 ADM 周期。关于管理迭代和不同细节层级的技术，参见第三部分第 19 章和第 20 章。

14.5 Outputs

The outputs of Phase F may include, but are not restricted to:

- Implementation and Migration Plan, Version 1.0 (see Part IV, Section 36.2.14), including:
  - Implementation and Migration Strategy
    - Project and portfolio breakdown of the implementation:
    - Allocation of work packages to project and portfolio
    - Capabilities delivered by projects
    - Relationship to Target Architecture and any Transition Architectures
    - Milestones and timing
    - Work breakdown structure
  - Project charters (optional):
    - Related work packages
    - Business value
    - Risk, issues, assumptions, dependencies
    - Resource requirements and costs
    - Benefits of migration
    - Estimated costs of migration options
- Finalized Architecture Definition Document (see Part IV, Section 36.2.3), including:
  - Finalized Transition Architectures, if any
- Finalized Architecture Requirements Specification (see Part IV, Section 36.2.6)
- Finalized Architecture Roadmap (see Part IV, Section 36.2.7)
- Re-Usable Architecture Building Blocks (see Part IV, Section 36.2.1)
- Requests for Architecture Work (see Part IV, Section 36.2.17) for a new iteration of the ADM cycle (if any)
- Implementation Governance Model (if any) (see Part IV, Section 36.2.15)
- Change Requests for the Architecture Capability arising from lessons learned

14.5 输出

阶段 F 的输出可能包括但不限于：

- 实施和迁移计划，版本 1.0（见第四部分 36.2.14 节），包括：
  - — 实施和迁移策略
  - — 实施的项目和项目谱系分解：
    - — 为项目和项目谱系分配工作包
    - — 按项目交付的能力
    - — 与目标架构和过渡架构的关系
    - — 里程碑和时间安排
    - — 工作分解结构
  - — 项目章程（可选）：
    - — 相关工作包
    - — 业务价值
    - — 风险、议题、假设、依赖性
    - — 资源需求和成本
    - — 迁移的效益
    - — 迁移选项的估计成本
- 最终确定的架构定义文件（见第四部分 36.2.3 节），包括：
  - — 最终确定的过渡架构，如果有
- 最终确定的架构需求规范（见第四部分 36.2.6 节）
- 最终确定的架构路线图（见第四部分 36.2.7 节）
- 可复用的架构构建块（见第四部分 36.2.1 节）
- ADM 周期新一轮迭代的架构工作要求书（如果有）（见第四部分 36.2.17 节）
- 实施治理模型（如果有）（见第四部分 36.2.15 节）
- 由经验教训产生的架构能力变更要求

Chapter 15
Phase G: Implementation Governance

This chapter provides an architectural oversight of the implementation.

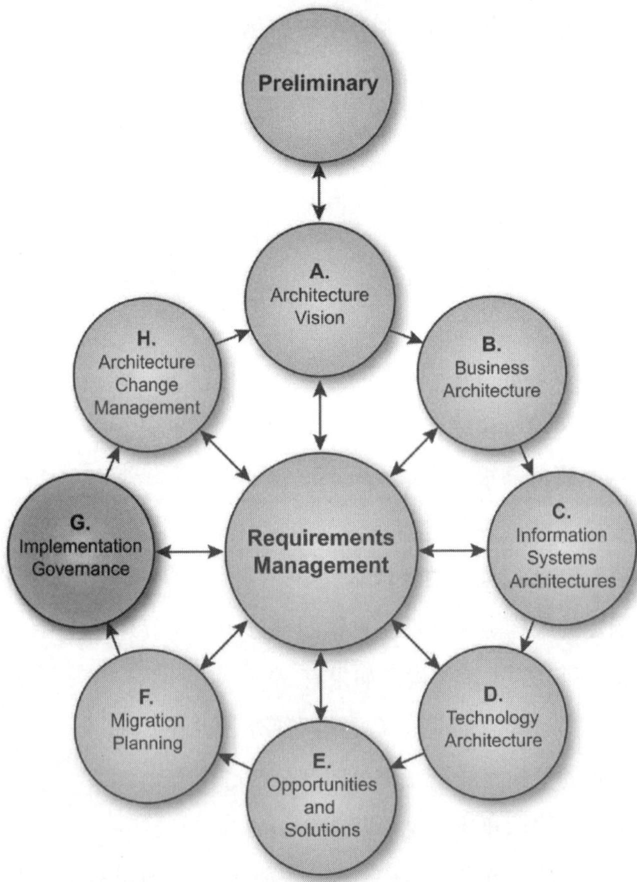

Figure 15-1 Phase G: Implementation Governance

第 15 章
阶段 G：实施治理

本章提供对实施的架构化监督。

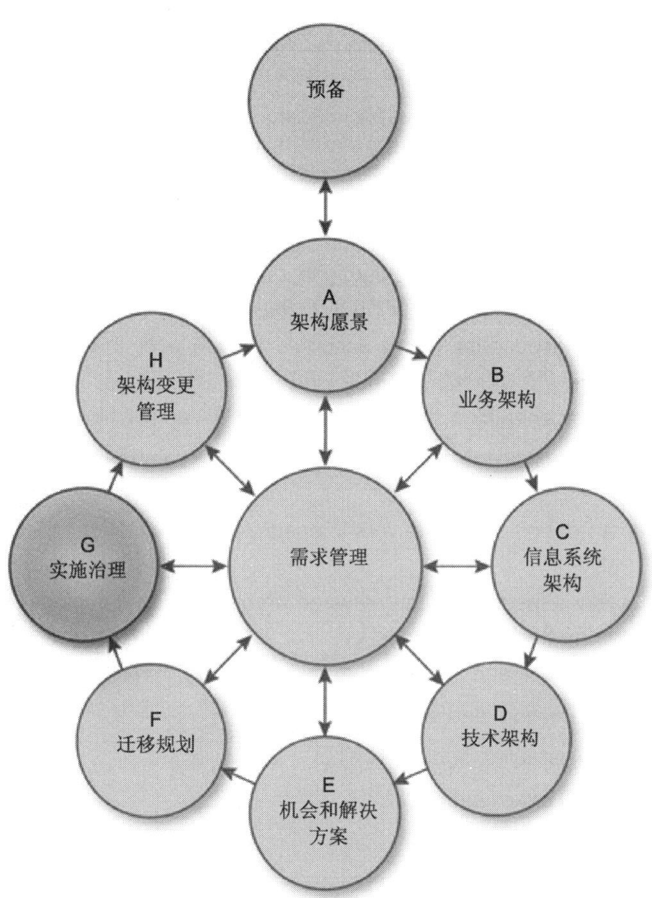

图 15-1　阶段 G：实施治理

15.1 Objectives

The objectives of Phase G are to:

- Ensure conformance with the Target Architecture by implementation projects.
- Perform appropriate Architecture Governance functions for the solution and any implementation-driven architecture Change Requests.

15.2 Approach

It is here that all the information for successful management of the various imple-mentation projects is brought together. Note that, in parallel with Phase G, there is the execution of an organizational-specific development process, where the actual devel-opment happens.

To enable early realization of business value and benefits, and to minimize the risk in the transformation and migration program, the favored approach is to deploy the Target Architecture as a series of transitions. Each transition represents an incremental step towards the target, and each delivers business benefit in its own right. Therefore, the overall approach in Phase G is to:

- Establish an implementation program that will enable the delivery of the Transition Architectures agreed for implementation during the Migration Plan-ning phase.
- Adopt a phased deployment schedule that reflects the business priorities embodied in the Architecture Roadmap.
- Follow the organization's standard for corporate, IT, and architecture govern-ance.
- Use the organization's established portfolio/program management approach, where this exists.
- Define an operations framework to ensure the effective long life of the deployed solution.

Phase G establishes the connection between architecture and implementation organization, through the Architecture Contract.

Project details are developed, including:

- Name, description, and objectives.
- Scope, deliverables, and constraints.
- Measures of effectiveness.
- Acceptance criteria.
- Risks and issues.

Implementation governance is closely allied to overall architecture governance, which is discussed in Part VII, Chapter 50.

A key aspect of Phase G is ensuring compliance with the defined architecture(s), not only by the implementation projects, but also by other ongoing projects within the enterprise. The considerations involved with this are explained in detail in Part VII, Chapter 48.

15.1 目的

阶段 G 的目的是：

- 通过实施项目确保与目标架构的一致性。
- 为解决方案和实施驱动的架构变更要求，执行适当的架构治理功能。

15.2 实施途径

在本阶段中，所有关于不同实施项目的成功管理的信息将被整合在一起。注意：与阶段 G 并行的，是发生实际开发的组织特定开发流程的执行。

为了能够尽早实现业务价值和效益，以及为了使转型和迁移项目群中的风险最小化，所推崇的途径是将目标架构部署为一系列过渡。每次过渡表示向目标递增的一步，且在其自身范围内提供业务效益。因此，阶段 G 中的总体途径是：

- 建立一个能使过渡架构的交付与迁移规划阶段的实施相匹配的实施项目群。
- 采用一种反映架构路线图中所体现的业务优先级的分阶段部署进度表。
- 遵循公司级、IT 和架构治理的组织标准。
- 使用组织已建立的项目谱系/项目群管理途径（如果方法存在）。
- 定义一种运行框架，以确保已部署的解决方案长期有效。

阶段 G 通过架构契约在架构与实施组织之间建立联系。

制定项目细节，包括：

- 名称、描述和目的。
- 范围、交付物和约束。
- 有效性测量指标。
- 验收标准。
- 风险和问题。

实施治理与总体架构治理紧密相联，第七部分第 50 章对此进行了论述。

阶段 G 的关键是：不仅通过实施项目，而且还通过该 ENTERPRISE 内其他正在进行的项目确保与已定义的架构的一致性。在第七部分第 48 章中，详细解释了涉及这一方面的考量因素。

15.3 Inputs

This section defines the inputs to Phase G.

15.3.1 Reference Materials External to the Enterprise

- Architecture reference materials (see Part IV, Section 36.2.5)

15.3.2 Non-Architectural Inputs

- Request for Architecture Work (see Part IV, Section 36.2.17)
- Capability Assessment (see Part IV, Section 36.2.10)

15.3.3 Architectural Inputs

- Organizational Model for Enterprise Architecture (see Part IV, Section 36.2.16), including:
  — Scope of organizations impacted
  — Maturity assessment, gaps, and resolution approach
  — Roles and responsibilities for architecture team(s)
  — Constraints on architecture work
  — Budget requirements
  — Governance and support strategy
- Tailored Architecture Framework (see Part IV, Section 36.2.21), including:
  — Tailored architecture method
  — Tailored architecture content (deliverables and artifacts)
  — Configured and deployed tools
- Statement of Architecture Work (see Part IV, Section 36.2.20)
- Architecture Vision (see Part IV, Section 36.2.8)
- Architecture Repository (see Part IV, Section 36.2.5), including:
  — Re-usable building blocks
  — Publicly available reference models
  — Organization-specific reference models
  — Organization standards
- Architecture Definition Document (see Part IV, Section 36.2.3)
- Architecture Requirements Specification (see Part IV, Section 36.2.6), including:
  — Architectural requirements
  — Gap analysis results(from Business, Data, Application, and Technology Architectures)

15.3 输入

本节定义了对阶段 G 的输入。

15.3.1 ENTERPRISE 外的参考资料

- 架构参考资料（见第四部分 36.2.5 节）

15.3.2 非架构输入

- 架构工作要求书（见第四部分 36.2.17 节）
- 能力评估（见第四部分 36.2.10 节）

15.3.3 架构输入

- Enterprise Architecture 的组织模型（见第四部分 36.2.16 节），包括：
  — 受影响的组织的范围
  — 成熟度评估、差距和解决途径
  — 架构团队的角色和职责
  — 对架构工作的约束
  — 预算需求
  — 治理和支持战略
- 经剪裁的架构框架（见第四部分 36.2.21 节），包括：
  — 经剪裁的架构方法
  — 经剪裁的架构内容（交付物和制品）
  — 经配置和部署的工具
- 架构工作说明书（见第四部分 36.2.20 节）
- 架构愿景（见第四部分 36.2.8 节）
- 架构存储库（见第四部分 36.2.5 节），包括：
  — 可复用的构建块
  — 公开可用的参考模型
  — 组织特定参考模型
  — 组织标准
- 架构定义文件（见第四部分 36.2.3 节）
- 架构需求规范（见第四部分 36.2.6 节），包括：
  — 架构需求
  — 差距分析结果（来自业务、数据、应用和技术架构）

- Architecture Roadmap (see Part IV, Section 36.2.7)
- Implementation Governance Model (see Part IV, Section 36.2.15)
- Architecture Contract (standard) (see Part VII, Chapter 49)
- Request for Architecture Work (see Part IV, Section 36.2.17) identified during Phases Eand F
- Implementation and Migration Plan (see Part IV, Section 36.2.14)

15.4 Steps

The level of detail addressed in Phase G will depend on the scope and goals of the overall architecture effort.

The order of the steps in Phase G (see below) as well as the time at which they are formally started and completed should be adapted to the situation at hand in accordance with the established architecture governance.

The steps in Phase G are as follows:

- Confirm scope and priorities for deployment with development management (see Section15.4.1)
- Identify deployment resources and skills (see Section 15.4.2)
- Guide development of solutions deployment (see Section 15.4.3)
- Perform enterprise architecture compliance reviews (see Section 15.4.4)
- Implement business and IT operations (see Section 15.4.5)
- Perform post-implementation review and close the implementation (see Section 15.4.6)

15.4.1 Confirm Scope and Priorities for Deployment with Development Management

- Review migration planning outputs and produce recommendations on deployment
- Identify enterprise architecture priorities for development teams
- Identify deployment issues and make recommendations
- Identify building blocks for replacement, update, etc.
- Perform gap analysis on enterprise architecture and solutions framework

The gaps in the existing enterprise solutions framework need to be identified and the specific Solution Building Blocks (SBBs) required to fill these gaps will be the identified by the solutions architects. These SBBs may have a one-to-one or many-to-one relationship with the projects. The solutions architects need to define exactly how this will be done. There may be other projects working on these same capabilities and the solutions architects need to ensure that they can leverage best value from these investments.

- Produce a gap analysis report

- 架构路线图（见第四部分 36.2.7 节）
- 实施治理模型（见第四部分 36.2.15 节）
- 架构契约（标准）（见第七部分第 49 章）
- 阶段 E 和 F 中识别的架构工作要求书（见第四部分 36.2.17 节）
- 实施和迁移计划（见第四部分 36.2.14 节）

15.4 步骤

阶段 G 中划分的细节层级取决于总体架构工作的范围和目标。

阶段 G 中步骤的顺序（见下文）及其正式开始和结束的时间，应按照已确定的架构治理来适应当前情况。

阶段 G 中的步骤如下：

- 利用开发管理来确认部署的范围和优先级（见 15.4.1 节）
- 识别部署资源和技能（见 15.4.2 节）
- 指导解决方案部署的开发（见 15.4.3 节）
- 执行 Enterprise Architecture 合规审视（见 15.4.4 节）
- 实施业务和 IT 运行（见 15.4.5 节）
- 执行实施后审视并结束实施（见 15.4.6 节）

15.4.1 利用开发管理来确认部署的范围和优先级

- 审视迁移规划输出并提出部署建议
- 为开发团队识别 Enterprise Architecture 优先级
- 识别部署议题并提出建议
- 识别用于替换、更新等的构建块
- 对 Enterprise Architecture 和解决方案框架进行差距分析

需要识别现有 ENTERPRISE 解决方案框架中的差距，并由解决方案架构师来识别用于填补这些差距所需的特定解决方案构建块（SBB）。这些 SBB 与项目可能是一对一或多对一的关系。解决方案架构师需要准确定义如何完成。其他项目也可能实现相同的能力，解决方案架构师需要确保这些投资产生最优价值。

- 生成差距分析报告

15.4.2 Identify Deployment Resources and Skills

The project resources will include the development resources which will need to be educated in the overall enterprise architecture deliverables and expectations from the specific development and implementation projects.

The following considerations should be addressed in this step:

- Identify system development methods required for solutions development

Note: There are a range of systems development methods and tools available to the project teams. The method should ideally be able to interoperate with the architecture outputs; for example, generate code from architecture artifacts delivered to date. This could be achieved through the use of modeling languages used for the enterprise architecture development that may be captured as inputs to the systems development tools and thereby reduce the cost of solutions development.

- Ensure that the systems development method enables feedback to the architecture team on designs

15.4.3 Guide Development of Solutions Deployment

- Formulate project recommendation

For each separate implementation and deployment project, do the following:

  - Document scope of individual project in impact analysis
  - Document strategic requirements (from the architectural perspective) in impact analysis
  - Document change requests (such as support for a standard interface) in impact analysis
  - Document rules for conformance in impact analysis
  - Document timeline requirements from roadmap in impact analysis

- Document Architecture Contract
  - Obtain signature from all developing organizations and sponsoring organization
- Update Enterprise Continuum directory and repository for solutions
- Guide development of business & IT operating models for services
- Provide service requirements derived from enterprise architecture
- Guide definition of business & IT operational requirements
- Carry out gap analysis between the Solution Architecture and operations
- Produce Implementation Plan

15.4.2 识别部署资源和技能

项目资源包括开发资源，这些开发资源需要在总体 Enterprise Architecture 交付物和来自特定开发和实施项的期望中进行培养。

应在该步骤中考量以下因素：

- 识别解决方案开发所需的系统开发方法

注： 项目团队具有一系列可用的系统开发方法和工具。在理想的情况下，这些方法应能与架构输出互操作；例如，从截至目前交付的架构制品中生成代码。这一点可通过使用建模语言达成，这种语言可用于 ENTERPRISE 的架构开发并被捕获作为对系统开发工具的输入，从而降低解决方案开发成本。

- 确保该系统开发方法能向架构团队进行设计反馈

15.4.3 指导解决方案部署的开发

- 制定项目建议

对每个单独实施和部署的项目进行以下工作：

  — 在影响分析中记录单个项目的范围

  — 在影响分析中（从架构的关注层级）记录战略需求

  — 在影响分析中记录变更要求（如对标准界面的支持）

  — 在影响分析中记录一致性规则

  — 在影响分析中记录路线图的时间线要求

- 记录架构契约

  — 从所有开发组织和发起组织获得签名

- 为多个解决方案更新 ENTERPRISE 的连续统一体目录集和存储库
- 为服务指导业务和 IT 运营模型的开发
- 提供源自 Enterprise Architecture 的服务需求
- 指导业务和 IT 运行要求的定义
- 在解决方案架构和实际运行之间进行差距分析
- 生成实施计划

15.4.4 Perform Enterprise Architecture Compliance Reviews

- Review ongoing implementation governance and architecture compliance for each building block.
- Conduct post-development reviews.
- Close development part of deployment projects.

15.4.5 Implement Business and IT Operations

- Carry out the deployment projects including: IT services delivery implementation; business services delivery implementation; skills development & training implementation; communications documentation publication.
- Publish new Baseline Architectures to the Architecture Repository and update other impacted repositories, such as operational configuration management stores.

15.4.6 Perform Post-Implementation Review and Close the Implementation

- Conduct post-implementation reviews.
- Publish reviews and close projects.

Closure on Phase G will be when the solutions are fully deployed once.

15.5 Outputs

The outputs of Phase G may include, but are not restricted to:

- Architecture Contract (signed) (see Part VII, Chapter 49), as recommended in the architecture-compliant implemented architectures.
- Compliance Assessments (see Part IV, Section 36.2.13).
- Change Requests (see Part IV, Section 36.2.11).
- Architecture-compliant solutions deployed including:
  — The architecture-compliant implemented system

Note: The implemented system is actually an output of the development process. However, given the importance of this output, it is stated here as an output of the ADM. The direct involvement of architecture staff in implementation will vary according to organizational policy, as described in Part VII, Chapter 50.

  — Populated Architecture Repository

  — Architecture compliance recommendations and dispensations

  — Recommendations on service delivery requirements

  — Recommendations on performance metrics

  — Service Level Agreements (SLAs)

  — Architecture Vision, updated post-implementation

15.4.4 执行 Enterprise Architecture 合规审视

- 为每个构建块审视正在进行的实施治理和架构的合规性。
- 进行开发后审视。
- 结束部署项目的开发部分。

15.4.5 实施业务和 IT 运行

- 实施部署项目，包括 IT 服务交付实施、业务服务交付实施、技能发展和培训实施和通信文档发布。
- 向架构存储库发布新的基线架构并更新其他受影响的存储库，例如运行构型管理存储器。

15.4.6 执行实施后审视并结束实施

- 执行实施后审视。
- 发布审视并结束项目。

当这些解决方案被全面部署一次之后，阶段 G 也随之结束。

15.5 输出

阶段 G 的输出可包括但不限于：

- 架构契约（已签署）（见第七部分第 49 章），如在已实施架构合规性的架构中所推荐的。
- 合规评估（见第四部分 36.2.13 节）。
- 变更要求（见第四部分 36.2.11 节）。
- 所部署的符合架构的解决方案包括：
  — 符合架构的已实施系统。

注：该实施系统，实际上是该开发流程的一个输出。然而，考虑到该输出的重要性，该输出在此被指定为 ADM 的一个输出。如第七部分第 50 章所描述，架构人员对实施的直接参与将根据组织策略而变化。

  — 已充实的架构存储库
  — 架构合规建议和特许
  — 服务交付需求的建议
  — 绩效衡量标准的建议
  — 服务水平协议（SLA）
  — 根据实施后情况更新的架构愿景

- Architecture Definition Document, updated post-implementation
- Business and IT operating models for the implemented solution

— 根据实施后情况更新的架构定义文件
— 已实施的解决方案的业务和 IT 运行模型

Chapter 16
Phase H: Architecture Change Management

This chapter looks at establishing procedures for managing change to the new architecture.

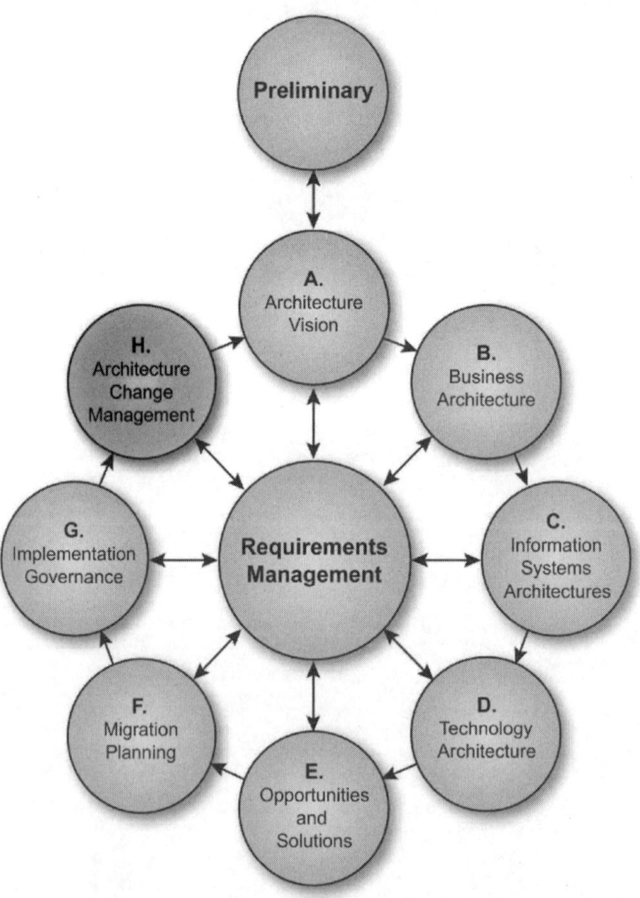

Figure 16-1 Phase H: Architecture Change Management

第 16 章
阶段 H：架构变更管理

本章着眼于为管理变更以达到新架构而建立程序。

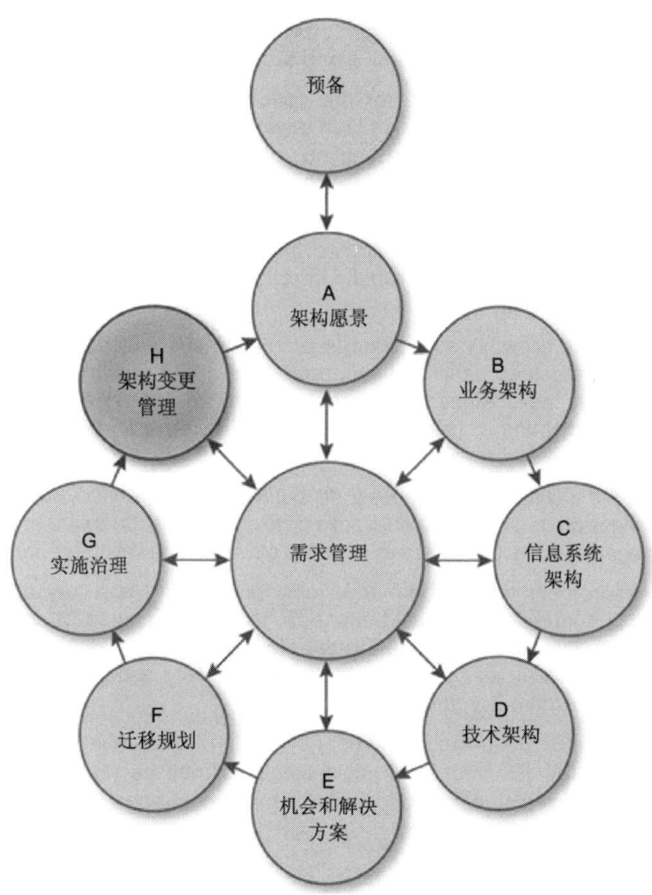

图 16-1　阶段 H：架构变更管理

16.1 Objectives

The objectives of Phase H are to:

- Ensure that the architecture lifecycle is maintained.
- Ensure that the Architecture Governance Framework is executed.
- Ensure that the enterprise Architecture Capability meets current requirements.

16.2 Approach

The goal of an architecture change management process is to ensure that the architecture achieves its original target business value. This includes managing changes to the architecture in a cohesive and architected way.

This process will typically provide for the continual monitoring of such things as governance requests, new developments in technology, and changes in the business environment. When changes are identified, change management will determine whether to formally initiate a new architecture evolution cycle.

Additionally, the architecture change management process aims to establish and support the implemented enterprise architecture as a dynamic architecture; that is, one having the flexibility to evolve rapidly in response to changes in the technology and business environment.

Monitoring business growth and decline is a critical aspect of this phase. Usage of the enterprise architecture is the most important part of the architecture development cycle. All too often the business has been left with an enterprise architecture that works for the organization of yesterday but may not give back sufficient capability to meet the needs of the enterprise of today and tomorrow.

In many cases the architecture continues to fit, but the solutions underlying them may not, and some changes are required. The enterprise architect needs to be aware of these change requirements and considers this an essential part of constant renewal of the architecture.

Capacity measurement and recommendations for planning is a key aspect of this phase. While the architecture has been built to deliver a steady state Business Architecture with agreed capacity during the lifecycle of this enterprise architecture, the growth or decline in usage needs to be continually assessed to ensure that maximum business value is achieved.

For example, some Solution Architectures may not lend themselves to be scalable by a large factor — say 10 — or alternative solutions may be more economic when scaled up. While the architecture specifications may not change, the solutions or their operational context may change.

If the performance management and reporting has been built into the work products through previous phases, then this phase is about ensuring the effectiveness of these. If there needs to be additional monitoring or reporting, then this phase will handle the changes.

The value and change management process, once established, will determine:

- The circumstances under which the enterprise architecture, or parts of it, will be permitted to change after deployment, and the process by which that will happen.
- The circumstances under which the architecture development cycle will be initiated again to develop a new architecture.

16.1 目的

阶段 H 的目的是：

- 确保架构生命周期得以维持。
- 确保架构治理框架得以执行。
- 确保 ENTERPRISE 的架构能力满足当前需求。

16.2 实施途径

架构变更管理流程的目标是确保架构达成其原始目标业务价值，包括以紧密并且架构化的方式管理对架构的变更。

该流程通常对诸如治理要求、新的技术开发和业务环境变化等提供持续监控。当变更被识别时，变更管理会决定是否正式启动一个新的架构演进周期。

此外，该架构变更管理流程旨在建立并支持已实施的 Enterprise Architecture 成为动态的架构，即其具有能迅速演进以响应技术和业务环境变化的柔性。

监控业务的增长和下降是本阶段的一个关键方面。使用 Enterprise Architecture 是架构开发周期的最重要部分。业务时常交由一个 Enterprise Architecture 来处理，其服务于过去的组织，但是可能不会恢复足够的能力来满足现在与将来的 ENTERPRISE 需求。

该架构在多种情况下继续适用，但是构成其基础的解决方案可能不适合，并需要进行一些变更。ENTERPRISE 架构师需要意识到这些变更需求，并且将其视为架构不断更新的一个根本性的部分。

对规划进行能力测量和建议是本阶段的一个关键方面。虽然架构已被构建以在 Enterprise Architecture 的生命周期中交付具有商定能力的稳态业务架构，但仍需要持续评估使用率的增长或下降，以确保实现最大业务价值。

例如，某些解决方案架构可能不适合进行较大倍数的扩展——例如 10 倍——或在规模扩展时多个替代解决方案可能更为经济。虽然架构规范可能没有改变，但是这些解决方案或其运行背景环境可能改变。

如果绩效管理和报告在此前各阶段已成为工作产物的一部分，则本阶段是确保这些工作产物的有效性。如果需要额外的监控或报告，则本阶段会处理这些变化。

价值和变更管理流程一旦建立便会决定：

- 允许在部署后变更或部分变更 Enterprise Architecture 及其将要发生的流程的情境。
- 将要再次启动架构开发周期以开发一个新的架构的情境。

The architecture change management process is very closely related to the architecture governance processes of the enterprise, and to the management of the Architecture Contract (see Part VII, Chapter 49) between the architecture function and the business users of the enterprise.

In Phase H it is critical that the governance body establish criteria to judge whether a Change Request warrants just an architecture update or whether it warrants starting a new cycle of the Architecture Development Method (ADM). It is especially important to avoid "creeping elegance", and the governance body must continue to look for changes that relate directly to business value.

An Architecture Compliance report should state whether the change is compliant to the current architecture. If it is non-compliant, an exemption may be granted with valid rationale. If the change has high impact on the architecture, then a strategy to manage its impact should be defined.

Guidelines for establishing these criteria are difficult to prescribe, as many companies accept risk differently, but as the ADM is exercised, the maturity level of the governance body will improve, and criteria will become clear for specific needs.

16.2.1 Drivers for Change

The main purpose for the development of the enterprise architecture so far has been strategic direction and top-down architecture and project generation to achieve corporate capabilities. However, enterprise architecture does not operate in a vacuum. There is usually an existing infrastructure and business which is already providing value.

There are also probably drivers for change which are often bottom-up, based upon modifying the existing infrastructure to enhance functionality. Enterprise architecture changes this paradigm by a strategic top-down approach to a degree, although the delivery of increments makes the equation more complex.

There are three ways to change the existing infrastructure that have to be integrated:

- Strategic, top-down directed change to enhance or create new capability (capital).
- Bottom-up changes to correct or enhance capability (operations and maintenance) for infrastructure under operations management.
- Experiences with the previously delivered project increments in the care of operations management, but still being delivered by ongoing projects.

Governance will have to handle the co-ordination of these Requests for Change, plus there needs to be a lessons learned process to allow for problems with the recently delivered increments to be resolved and changes made to the Target Architectures being designed and planned.

A lessons learned process ensures that mistakes are made once and not repeated. They can come from anywhere and anyone and cover any aspect of the enterprise architecture at any level (strategic, enterprise architecture definition, transition, or project). Often an enterprise architecture-related lesson may be an indirect outcome of a lesson learned elsewhere in the organization.

The Architecture Board (see Part VII, Chapter 47) assesses and approves Requests for Change (RFC). An RFC is typically in response to known problems but can also include improvements. A challenge for the Architecture Board when handling an RFC is to determine whether it should be approved or whether a project in a Transition Architecture will resolve the issue.

架构变更管理流程与 ENTERPRISE 的架构治理流程密切相关，且与 ENTERPRISE 的架构功能和业务使用者之间的架构契约（见第七部分第 49 章）的管理密切相关。

在阶段 H 中，至关重要的是治理主体建立准则，以判断变更要求书是否只是有必要更新架构，还是有必要启动架构开发方法（ADM）的一个新周期。避免“完美蠕行”是尤其重要的，并且，该治理主体必须继续寻找与业务价值直接相关的变更。

一份架构合规报告应说明该变更是否与当前架构合规。如果其不合规，可利用有效的理由依据予以豁免。如果该变更对该架构产生重大影响，则应定义管理其影响的策略。

许多公司接受风险的程度不同，因此建立这些准则的指南是难以规定的，但是由于实施了 ADM，治理主体的成熟度会提高，并且准则对于特定需要会变得明确。

16.2.1 变更的驱动因素

到目前为止，开发 Enterprise Architecture 的主要目的是通过战略方向和自顶向下的架构及产生项目来达成公司级能力。然而，Enterprise Architecture 并非在真空中运行。通常存在一种已经持续提供价值的现有基础设施和业务。

基于修改现有基础设施以增强功能，还可能存在多个变更的驱动因素，它们通常是自底向上的。虽然多个增量的交付使得综合考虑更为复杂，但是 Enterprise Architecture 通过战略性自顶向下的途径在一定程度上改变了这种范式。

三种改变必须集成的现有基础设施的方式如下：

- 增强或创建新能力（资本）的战略性自顶向下的定向变更。
- 在运行管理下，为基础设施校正或增强能力（运行和维护）的自底向上的变更。
- 受运行管理控制且已于先前交付的、但仍由正在进行的项目交付的项目增量方面的经验。

治理必须处理这些变更请求的协调，另外需要经验教训学习流程，使得最近交付增量的问题能解决并对正在设计和计划的目标架构进行变更。

经验教训学习流程确保已出现过一次的错误不会重复出现。这些错误可能由任何地方和任何人产生，涵盖任何层级的 Enterprise Architecture 的任何方面（战略、Enterprise Architecture 定义、过渡或项目）。通常，一个 ENTERPRISE 的与架构相关的经验教训可能是在组织内其他地方所得到的经验教训的间接结果。

架构委员会（见第七部分，第 47 章）评估并批准变更请求（RFC）。一个 RFC 在通常情况下是对已知问题进行响应，但也可包括多个改进措施。架构委员会在处理 RFC 时的挑战是，决定其是否被批准或某个过渡架构中的项目是否会解决该问题。

When assessing project or solution fit into the architecture, there may also be the case when an innovative solution or RFC drives a change in the architecture.

In addition, there are many technology-related drivers for architecture Change Requests. For example:

- New technology reports
- Asset management cost reductions
- Technology withdrawal
- Standards initiatives

This type of Change Request is normally manageable primarily through an enterprise's change management and architecture governance processes.

In addition, there are business drivers for architecture change, including:

- Business-as-usual developments
- Business exceptions
- Business innovations
- Business technology innovations
- Strategic change

This type of Change Request often results in a complete re-development of the architecture, or at least in an iteration of a part of the architecture development cycle, as explained below.

16.2.2 Enterprise Architecture Change Management Process

The enterprise architecture change management process needs to determine how changes are to be managed, what techniques are to be applied, and what metho-dologies used. The process also needs a filtering function that determines which phases of the architecture development process are impacted by requirements. For example, changes that affect only migration may be of no interest in the architecture development phases.

There are many valid approaches to change management, and various management techniques and methodologies that can be used to manage change; for example, project management methods such as PRINCE2, service management methods such as ITIL, management consultancy methods such as Catalyst, and many others. An enterprise that already has a change management process in place in a field other than architecture (for example, in systems development or project management) may well be able to adapt it for use in relation to architecture.

The following describes an approach to change management, aimed particularly at the support of a dynamic enterprise architecture, which may be considered for use if no similar process currently exists.

The approach is based on classifying required architectural changes into one of three categories:

- **Simplification change**: A simplification change can normally be handled via change management techniques.
- **Incremental change**: An incremental change may be capable of being handled via change management techniques, or it may require partial re-architecting, depending on the nature of the change (see Section 16.2.3 for guidelines).

当评估适合架构的项目或解决方案时，还可能存在创新解决方案或 RFC 驱动架构发生变更的情况。

此外，架构变更请求具有多个与技术相关的驱动因素。例如：

- 新技术报告
- 资产管理成本缩减
- 技术退出
- 标准举措

这种变更要求通常主要通过 ENTERPRISE 的变更管理和架构治理流程进行管理。

此外，存在多个架构变更的业务驱动因素，包括：

- 常规业务开发
- 业务异常
- 业务创新
- 业务技术创新
- 战略变革

这种变更请求常常导致架构的完全重新开发或至少导致一部分架构开发周期的迭代，下面会作出解释。

16.2.2 Enterprise Architecture 变更管理流程

Enterprise Architecture 变更管理流程需要决定如何管理变更、将应用何种技术、使用何种方法。该流程还需要一种过滤功能来确定架构开发流程的哪些阶段受需求影响。例如，仅影响迁移的变更在架构开发阶段可能不需关注。

存在许多变更管理的有效途径和可用于管理变更的不同管理技巧和方法论；例如，诸如 PRINCE2 的项目管理方法、诸如 ITIL 的服务管理方法、诸如 Catalyst 的管理咨询方法以及许多其他方法。在不同于架构的其他领域（例如，在系统开发或项目管理领域）已有适当的变更管理流程的 ENTERPRISE 较能使其与架构相关的使用相适应。

下面描述一种变更管理的途径，旨在特别地支持一种动态 Enterprise Architecture，如果目前不存在类似流程，可考虑使用该方法。

该途径基于所需的架构变更分为以下三个类别之一：

- **简化变更：**简化变更通常可通过变更管理技术进行处理。
- **增量变更：**增量变更可能能够通过变更管理技术进行处理，或其可能需要部分重新进行架构开发，这取决于变更的性质（关于指南，见 16.2.3 节）。

- **Re-architecting change**: A re-architecting change requires putting the whole architecture through the architecture development cycle again.

Another way of looking at these three choices is to say that a simplification change to an architecture is often driven by a requirement to reduce investment; an incremental change is driven by a requirement to derive additional value from existing investment; and a re-architecting change is driven by a requirement to increase investment in order to create new value for exploitation.

To determine whether a change is simplification, incremental, or re-architecting, the following activities are undertaken:

1. Registration of all events that may impact the architecture.
2. Resource allocation and management for architecture tasks.
3. The process or role responsible for architecture resources has to make assessment of what should be done.
4. Evaluation of impacts.

16.2.3 Guidelines for Maintenance versus Architecture Redesign

A good rule-of-thumb is:

- If the change impacts two stakeholders or more, then it is likely to require an architecture redesign and re-entry to the ADM.
- If the change impacts only one stakeholder, then it is more likely to be a candidate for change management.
- If the change can be allowed under a dispensation, then it is more likely to be a candidate for change management.

For example:

- If the impact is significant for the business strategy, then there may be a need to redo the whole enterprise architecture — thus a re-architecting approach.
- If a new technology or standards emerge, then there may be a need to refresh the Technology Architecture, but not the whole enterprise architecture — thus an incremental change.
- If the change is at an infrastructure level — for example, ten systems reduced or changed to one system — this may not change the architecture above the physical layer, but it will change the Baseline Description of the Technology Architecture. This would be a simplification change handled via change management techniques.

In particular, a refreshment cycle (partial or complete re-architecting) may be required if:

- The Foundation Architecture needs to be re-aligned with the business strategy.
- Substantial change is required to components and guidelines for use in deployment of the architecture.
- Significant standards used in the product architecture are changed which have significant end-user impact; e.g., regulatory changes.

If there is a need for a refreshment cycle, then a new Request for Architecture Work must be issued (to move to another cycle).

- **重新开发架构的变更：**重新开发架构的变更需要再次将整体架构经过架构开发周期进行开发。

考虑这三种选择的另一种方式是，架构的简化变更往往通过减少投资的需求来驱动；增量变更通过从现有投资获取附加价值的需求来驱动；重新开发架构变更通过增加投资（为使开发创造新价值）的需求来驱动。

为确定变更是否简化、增量或重新开发架构，进行以下活动：

1. 对可能影响架构的所有事件的注册。
2. 架构任务的资源分配和管理。
3. 负责多种架构资源的流程或角色必须评估应该完成什么。
4. 影响的评价。

16.2.3 维护vs.架构再设计的指南

合理的经验法则如下：

- 如果变更影响两方或多方利益攸关者，则可能需要进行架构重新设计和重返ADM。
- 如果变更仅影响一方利益攸关者，则较可能成为变更管理的候选。
- 如果变更可在特许中被允许，则较可能成为变更管理的候选。

例如：

- 如果该影响对业务战略很重要，则可能需要重新开发整个Enterprise Architecture——因此是一种重新开发架构的途径。
- 如果出现一种新技术或多个新标准，则可能需要更新技术架构，但并非整个Enterprise Architecture——因此是一种增量变更。
- 如果变更处于基础设施水平——例如，十个系统减少或变更为一个系统——这可能不会变更物理层之上的架构，但会变更技术架构的基线描述。这将是一个通过变更管理技术处理的简化变更。

尤其是，可能需要一个更新周期（部分或全部重新开发架构），如果：

- 基础架构需要与业务战略重新保持对准。
- 在架构部署中使用的组件和指南要求实质性变更。
- 产品架构所用的重要标准发生变更，对最终用户产生重大影响；例如，监管变更。

如果需要更新周期，则必须发布一个新的架构工作要求书（以转移到另一个周期）。

16.3 Inputs

This section defines the inputs to Phase H.

16.3.1 Reference Materials External to the Enterprise

- Architecture reference materials (see Part IV, Section 36.2.5)

16.3.2 Non-Architectural Inputs

- Request for Architecture Work (see Part IV, Section 36.2.17)

16.3.3 Architectural Inputs

- Organizational Model for Enterprise Architecture (see Part IV, Section 36.2.16), including:
    - Scope of organizations impacted
    - Maturity assessment, gaps, and resolution approach
    - Roles and responsibilities for architecture team(s)
    - Constraints on architecture work
    - Budget requirements
    - Governance and support strategy
- Tailored Architecture Framework (see Part IV, Section 36.2.21), including:
    - Tailored architecture method
    - Tailored architecture content (deliverables and artifacts)
    - Configured and deployed tools
- Statement of Architecture Work (see Part IV, Section 36.2.20)
- Architecture Vision (see Part IV, Section 36.2.8)
- Architecture Repository (see Part IV, Section 36.2.5), including:
    - Re-usable building blocks
    - Publicly available reference models
    - Organization-specific reference models
    - Organization standards
- Architecture Definition Document (see Part IV, Section 36.2.3)
- Architecture Requirements Specification (see Part IV, Section 36.2.6), including:
    - Gap analysis results(from Business, Data, Application, and Technology Architectures)
    - Architectural requirements
- Architecture Roadmap (see Part IV, Section 36.2.7)

16.3 输入

本节定义了对阶段 H 的输入。

16.3.1 ENTERPRISE 外部参考资料

- 架构参考资料（见第四部分 36.2.5 节）

16.3.2 非架构输入

- 架构工作要求书（见第四部分 36.2.17 节）

16.3.3 架构输入

- Enterprise Architecture 的组织模型（见第四部分 36.2.16 节），包括：
  - 受影响的组织的范围
  - 成熟度评估、差距和解决途径
  - 架构团队的角色和职责
  - 对架构工作的约束
  - 预算需求
  - 治理和支持战略
- 经剪裁的架构框架（见第四部分 36.2.21 节），包括：
  - 经剪裁的架构方法
  - 经剪裁的架构内容（交付物和制品）
  - 经配置和部署的工具
- 架构工作说明书（见第四部分 36.2.20 节）
- 架构愿景（见第四部分 36.2.8 节）
- 架构存储库（见第四部分 36.2.5 节），包括：
  - 可复用的构建块
  - 公开可用的参考模型
  - 组织特定的参考模型
  - 组织标准
- 架构定义文件（见第四部分 36.2.3 节）
- 架构需求规范（见第四部分 36.2.6 节），包括：
  - 差距分析结果（来自业务、数据、应用和技术架构）
  - 架构需求
- 架构路线图（见第四部分 36.2.7 节）

- Change Request (see Part IV, Section 36.2.11), — technology changes:
  - New technology reports
  - Asset management cost reduction initiatives
  - Technology withdrawal reports
  - Standards initiatives
- Change Request (see Part IV, Section 36.2.11), — business changes:
  - Business developments
  - Business exceptions
  - Business innovations
  - Business technology innovations
  - Strategic change developments
- Change Request (see Part IV, Section 36.2.11), — from lessons learned
- Implementation Governance Model (see Part IV, Section 36.2.15)
- Architecture Contract (signed) (see Part VII, Chapter 49)
- Compliance Assessments (see Part IV, Section 36.2.13)
- Implementation and Migration Plan (see Part IV, Section 36.2.14)

16.4 Steps

The level of detail addressed in Phase H will depend on the scope and goals of the overall architecture effort.

The order of the steps in Phase H (see below) as well as the time at which they are formally started and completed should be adapted to the situation at hand in accordance with the established architecture governance.

The steps in Phase H are as follows:

- Establish value realization process (see Section 16.4.1)
- Deploy monitoring tools (see Section 16.4.2)
- Manage risks (see Section 16.4.3)
- Provide analysis for architecture change management (see Section 16.4.4)
- Develop change requirements to meet performance targets (see Section 16.4.5)
- Manage governance process (see Section 16.4.6)
- Activate the process to implement change (see Section 16.4.7)

- 变更要求（见第四部分 36.2.11 节）——技术变更：
  - — 新技术报告
  - — 资产管理成本降低举措
  - — 技术撤回报告
  - — 标准举措
- 变更要求（见第四部分 36.2.11 节）——业务变更：
  - — 业务发展
  - — 业务异常
  - — 业务创新
  - — 业务技术创新
  - — 战略变革发展
- 变更要求（见第四部分 36.2.11 节）——来自经验教训
- 实施治理模型（见第四部分 36.2.15 节）
- 架构契约（已签署）（见第七部分第 49 章）
- 合规评估（见第四部分 36.2.13 节）
- 实施和迁移计划（见第四部分 36.2.14 节）

16.4 步骤

阶段 H 中所划分的细节层级将取决于总体架构工作的范围和目标。

阶段 H 中的步骤顺序（见下文）及其正式开始和结束的时间，应按照已确定的架构治理来适应当前情况。

阶段 H 中的步骤如下：

- 建立价值实现流程（见 16.4.1 节）
- 部署监控工具（见 16.4.2 节）
- 管理风险（见 16.4.3 节）
- 为架构变更管理提供分析（见 16.4.4 节）
- 开发满足绩效目标的变更需求（见 16.4.5 节）
- 管理治理流程（见 16.4.6 节）
- 为实施变更而启动流程（见 16.4.7 节）

16.4.1 Establish Value Realization Process

Influence business projects to exploit the enterprise architecture for value realization (outcomes).

16.4.2 Deploy Monitoring Tools

Ensure monitoring tools are deployed and applied to enable the following:

- Monitor technology changes which could impact the Baseline Architecture.
- Monitor business changes which could impact the Baseline Architecture.
- Business value tracking; e.g., investment appraisal method to determine value metrics for the business objectives.
- Monitor enterprise Architecture Capability maturity.
- Track and assess asset management programs.
- Track the QoS performances and usage.
- Determine and track business continuity requirements.

16.4.3 Manage Risks

Manage enterprise architecture risks and provide recommendations for IT strategy.

16.4.4 Provide Analysis for Architecture Change Management

Provide analysis for architecture change management:

- Analyze performance.
- Conduct enterprise architecture performance reviews with service management.
- Assess Change Requests and reporting to ensure that the expected value realization and Service Level Agreement (SLA) expectations of the customers are met.
- Undertake a gap analysis of the performance of the enterprise architecture.
- Ensure change management requests adhere to the enterprise architecture governance and framework.

16.4.5 Develop Change Requirements to Meet Performance Targets

Make recommendations on change requirements to meet performance targets and development of position to act.

16.4.1 建立价值实现流程

影响业务项目，以利用 Enterprise Architecture 实现价值（成果）。

16.4.2 部署监控工具

确保部署并应用监控工具以实现以下内容：

- 监控可影响基线架构的技术变更。
- 监控可影响基线架构的业务变更。
- 业务价值跟踪，如用以确定业务目的的价值衡量标准的投资评估方法。
- 监控 ENTERPRISE 的架构能力成熟度。
- 跟踪和评估资产管理计划。
- 跟踪 QoS 绩效和使用率。
- 确定和跟踪业务连续性需求。

16.4.3 管理风险

管理 Enterprise Architecture 风险并为 IT 战略提供建议。

16.4.4 为架构变更管理提供分析

为架构变更管理提供分析：

- 分析性能。
- 进行关于服务管理的 Enterprise Architecture 绩效审视。
- 评估变更要求和报告，以确保实现用户预期价值和满足服务水平协议（SLA）期望。
- 对 Enterprise Architecture 的绩效进行差距分析。
- 确保变更管理要求符合 Enterprise Architecture 治理和框架。

16.4.5 开发满足绩效目标的变更需求

对满足绩效目标的变更需求和实施变更位置的开发提出建议。

16.4.6 Manage Governance Process

Manage governance process and framework for architecture:

- Arrange meeting of Architecture Board (or other Governing Council).
- Hold meeting of the Architecture Board with the aim of the meeting to decide on handling changes (technology and business and dispensations).

16.4.7 Activate the Process to Implement Change

Activate the architecture process to implement change:

- Produce a new Request for Architecture Work and request for investment.
- Ensure any changes implemented in this phase are captured and documented in the Architecture Repository.

16.5 Outputs

The outputs of Phase H may include, but are not restricted to:

- Architecture updates (for maintenance changes).
- Changes to architecture framework and principles (for maintenance changes).
- New Request for Architecture Work (see Part IV, Section 36.2.17), to move to another cycle (for major changes).
- Statement of Architecture Work (see Part IV, Section 36.2.20), updated if necessary.
- Architecture Contract (see Part IV, Chapter 49), updated if necessary.
- Compliance Assessments (see Part IV, Section 36.2.13), updated if necessary.

16.4.6 管理治理流程

管理架构的治理流程和框架：

- 安排架构委员会（或其他治理委员会）的会议。
- 召开架构委员会会议，会议的目的在于决定处理变更（技术、业务和特许）。

16.4.7 为实施变更启动流程

为实施变更启动架构流程：

- 生成一份新的架构工作要求书和投资要求书。
- 确保在该架构存储库中捕获并记录在此阶段实施的任何变更。

16.5 输出

阶段 H 的输出可包括但不限于：

- 架构更新（针对维护变更）。
- 对架构框架和原则的变更（针对维护变更）。
- 新的架构工作要求书（见第四部分 36.2.17 节），以转移到另一个周期（针对重大变更）。
- 架构工作说明书（见第四部分 36.2.20 节），必要时进行更新。
- 架构契约（见第四部分第 49 章），必要时进行更新。
- 合规评估（见第四部分 36.2.13 节），必要时进行更新。

Chapter 17
ADM Architecture Requirements Management

This chapter looks at the process of managing architecture requirements throughout the ADM.

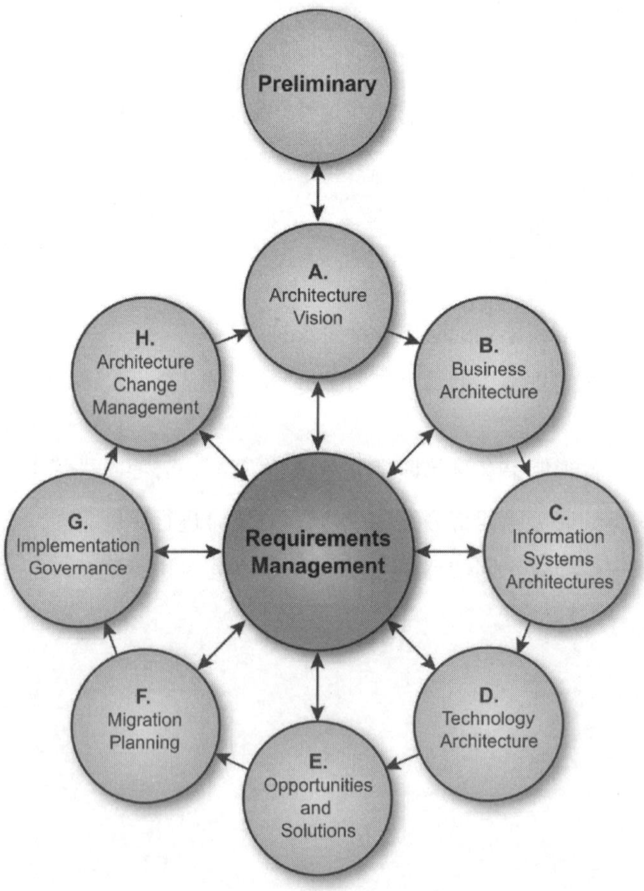

Figure 17-1 ADM Architecture Requirements Management

第 17 章
ADM 架构需求管理

本章关注于贯穿 ADM 始终的架构需求管理流程。

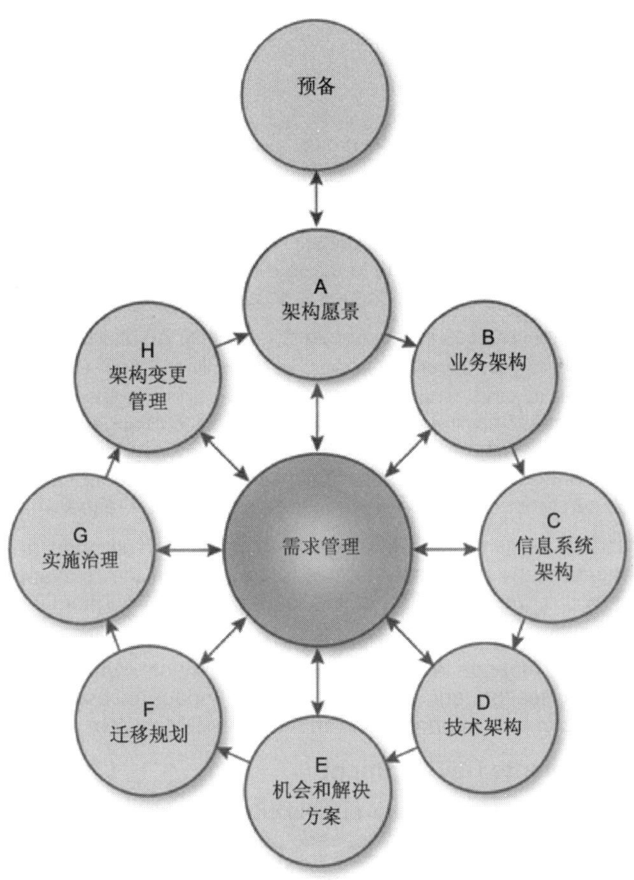

图 17-1　ADM 架构需求管理

17.1 Objectives

The objectives of the Requirements Management phase are to:

- Ensure that the Requirements Management process is sustained and operates for all relevant ADM phases.
- Manage architecture requirements identified during any execution of the ADM cycle or a phase.
- Ensure that relevant architecture requirements are available for use by each phase as the phase is executed.

17.2 Approach

17.2.1 General

As indicated by the "Requirements Management" circle at the center of the ADM graphic, the ADM is continuously driven by the requirements management process.

It is important to note that the Requirements Management circle denotes not a static set of requirements, but a dynamic process whereby requirements for enterprise architecture and subsequent changes to those requirements are identified, stored, and fed into and out of the relevant ADM phases, and also between cycles of the ADM.

The ability to deal with changes in requirements is crucial. Architecture is an activity that by its very nature deals with uncertainty and change — the "grey area" between what stakeholders aspire to and what can be specified and engineered as a solution. Architecture requirements are therefore invariably subject to change in practice. Moreover, architecture often deals with drivers and constraints, many of which by their very nature are beyond the control of the enterprise (changing market conditions, new legislation, etc.), and which can produce changes in requirements in an unforeseen manner.

Note also that the Requirements Management process itself does not dispose of, address, or prioritize any requirements; this is done within the relevant phase of the ADM. It is merely the process for managing requirements throughout the overall ADM.

It is recommended that a Requirements Repository (see Part IV, Section 41.6.1) is used to record and manage all architecture requirements. Unlike the Architecture Requirements Specification, and the Requirements Impact Assessment, the Requirements Repository can hold information from multiple ADM cycles.

17.2.2 Requirements Development

The first high-level requirements are articulated as part of the Architecture Vision, generated by means of the business scenario or analogous technique.

Each phase of the ADM, from Preliminary to Phase H, must select the approved requirements for that phase as held in the Requirements Repository and Architecture Requirements Specification. At the completion of the phase the status of all such requirements needs to be updated. During the phase execution new requirements generated for future architecture work within the scope of the current Statement of Architecture Work need to be documented within the Architecture Requirements Specification, and new requirements which are outside of the scope of the current Statement of Architecture Work must be input to the Requirements Repository for management through the Requirements Management process.

17.1 目的

需求管理阶段的目的是：

- 确保需求管理流程在所有相关 ADM 阶段得以维持并运行。
- 管理在执行 ADM 周期或其中一个阶段期间识别的架构需求。
- 确保在执行该阶段时相关架构需求可供每个阶段使用。

17.2 实施途径

17.2.1 概述

如 ADM 图形中心的“需求管理”圆圈所示，ADM 由需求管理流程持续驱动。

重要的是，注意需求管理圆圈表示的并非一组静态需求，而是一个动态流程，通过该流程可识别、存储 Enterprise Architecture 的需求及其后续变更，并在相关的 ADM 阶段和 ADM 周期之间进行输入和输出。

处理需求变更的能力是至关重要的。架构在本质上是处理不确定性和变革的一项活动——是介于利益攸关者所渴望的因素与可规定和设计为解决方案的因素之间的“灰色区域”。因此，架构需求总是受到实际变更的影响。此外，架构通常涉及驱动因素和约束，就其本质而言，其中许多因素不受 ENTERPRISE 的控制（变化的市场情况、新的立法等），这就会不可预见地产生需求变更。

还要注意的是，需求管理流程本身并不处理、应对任何需求或对需求进行优先级排序，这是在 ADM 的相关阶段中完成的。需求管理流程仅仅是贯穿于 ADM 始终的管理需求的流程。

建议使用需求存储库（见第四部分 41.6.1 节）来记录和管理所有架构需求。与架构需求规范和需求影响评估不同，需求存储库可保存来自多重 ADM 周期的信息。

17.2.2 需求开发

最高层级的需求被表述为架构愿景的一部分，由业务场景或模拟技术生成。

ADM 从预备阶段到阶段 H 的每个阶段，都必须为该阶段选择已批准的需求（保存在需求存储库和架构需求规范中）。在完成该阶段时，需要更新所有这些需求的状态。在阶段执行期间，针对当前架构工作说明书范围之内的未来架构工作产生的新需求，需要记录在架构需求规范中；针对当前架构工作说明书范围之外的新需求，必须输入需求存储库中，以通过需求管理流程进行管理。

In each relevant phase of the ADM the architect should identify types of requirement that must be met by the architecture, including applicable:

- Functional requirements
- Non-functional requirements

When defining requirements the architect should take into account:

- Assumptions for requirements
- Constraints for requirements
- Domain-specific principles that drive requirements
- Policies affecting requirements
- Standards that requirements must meet
- Organization guidelines for requirements
- Specifications for requirements

Deliverables in later ADM phases also contain mappings to the design requirements, and may also generate new types of requirements (for example, conformance requirements, time windows for implementation).

17.2.3 Resources

The world of requirements engineering is rich with emerging recommendations and processes for requirements management. TOGAF does not mandate or recommend any specific process or tool; it simply states what an effective requirements management process should achieve (i.e., the "requirements for requirements", if you like).

17.2.3.1 Business Scenarios

One effective technique that is described in TOGAF itself is business scenarios, which are an appropriate and useful technique to discover and document business requirements, and to articulate an Architecture Vision that responds to those requirements. Business scenarios are described in detail in Part III, Chapter 26.

17.2.3.2 Requirements Tools

There is a large, and increasing, number of Commercial Off-The-Shelf (COTS) tools available for the support of requirements management, albeit not necessarily designed for architecture requirements. The Volere web site has a very useful list of leading requirements tools (see www.volere.co.uk/tools.htm).

在 ADM 的各相关阶段中，架构师应识别必须由该架构满足的各种需求，包括适用的：

- 功能需求
- 非功能需求

当定义需求时，架构师应考虑：

- 需求的假设
- 需求的约束
- 驱动需求的域特定原则
- 影响需求的策略
- 需求必须满足的标准
- 需求的组织指南
- 需求规范

ADM 后期阶段内的交付物还包含与设计需求的映射，还可能产生各种新的需求（例如，一致性需求、实施的时间窗）。

17.2.3 资源

需求工程的领域富有新兴的需求管理建议和流程。TOGAF 不要求或建议任何特定的流程或工具，而仅说明有效的需求管理流程应达成的方面（即“需求之需求”）。

17.2.3.1 业务场景

TOGAF 本身所描述的一种有效的技术是业务场景。业务场景是一种适当且有用的技术，用以发现并记录业务需求，并清楚地表述了响应那些需求的架构愿景。在第三部分第 26 章中详细描述了业务场景。

17.2.3.2 需求工具

大量的、越来越多的商用货架（COTS）工具可用于支持需求管理，虽然这些工具未必为架构需求所设计。Volere 网站上具有一个非常实用的领先需求工具列表（见 www.volere.co.uk/tools.htm）。

17.3 Inputs

Inputs to the Requirements Management phase are:

- A populated Architecture Repository (see Part IV, Section 36.2.5).
- Organizational Model for Enterprise Architecture (see Part IV, Section 36.2.16), including:
  - Scope of organizations impacted
  - Maturity assessment, gaps, and resolution approach
  - Roles and responsibilities for architecture team(s)
  - Constraints on architecture work
  - Budget requirements
  - Governance and support strategy
- Tailored Architecture Framework (see Part IV, Section 36.2.21), including:
  - Tailored architecture method
  - Tailored architecture content (deliverables and artifacts)
  - Configured and deployed tools
- Statement of Architecture Work (see Part IV, Section 36.2.20).
- Architecture Vision (see Part IV, Section 36.2.8).
- Architecture requirements, populating an Architecture Requirements Specification (see Part IV, Section 36.2.6).
- Requirements Impact Assessment (see Part IV, Section 36.2.18).

17.4 Steps

The steps in the Requirements Management phase are described in the table below:

	Requirements Management Steps	ADM Phase Steps
Step 1		Identify/document requirements — use business scenarios, or an analogous technique
Step 2	Baseline requirements: a. Determine priorities arising from current phase of ADM b. Confirm stakeholder buy-in to resultant priorities c. Record requirements priorities and place in Requirements Repository	
Step 3	Monitor baseline requirements	

17.3 输入

对需求管理阶段的输入是：

- 一个已充实的架构库（见第四部分 36.2.5 节）。
- Enterprise Architecture 的组织模型（见第四部分 36.2.16 节），包括：
  - 受影响的组织的范围
  - 成熟度评估、差距和解决途径
  - 架构团队的角色和职责
  - 对架构工作的约束
  - 预算需求
  - 治理和支持战略
- 经剪裁的架构框架（见第四部分 36.2.21 节），包括：
  - 经剪裁的架构方法
  - 经剪裁的架构内容（交付物和制品）
  - 经配置和部署的工具
- 架构工作说明书（见第四部分 36.2.20 节）。
- 架构愿景（见第四部分 36.2.8 节）。
- 填充一个架构需求规范的架构需求（见第四部分 36.2.6 节）。
- 需求影响评估（见第四部分 36.2.18 节）。

17.4 步骤

在下列表格中描述了需求管理阶段的步骤：

	需求管理步骤	ADM 阶段步骤
步骤 1		识别/记录需求——使用多个业务场景或类似的技术
步骤 2	基线需求： a. 确定由 ADM 的当前阶段产生的优先级 b. 确认利益攸关者对得到的优先级的认同 c. 记录需求优先级并将其置入需求存储库	
步骤 3	监控基线需求	

	Requirements Management Steps	ADM Phase Steps
Step 4		Identify changed requirements: a. Remove or re-assess priorities b. Add requirements and re-assess priorities c. Modify existing requirements
Step 5	Identify changed requirements andrecord priorities: a. Identify changed requirements and ensure the requirements are prioritized by the architect(s) responsible for the current phase, and by the relevant stakeholders b. Record new priorities c. Ensure that any conflicts are identified and managed through the phases to a successful conclusion and prioritization d. Generate Requirements Impact Statement (see Section 36.2.18) for steering the architecture team **Notes** ■ Changed requirements can come in through any route. To ensure that the requirements are properly assessed and prioritized, this process needs to direct the ADM phases and record the decisions related to the requirements ■ The Requirements Management phase needs to determine stakeholder satisfaction with the decisions. Where there is dissatisfaction, the phase remains accountable to ensure the resolution of the issues and determine next steps	

	需求管理步骤	ADM 阶段步骤
步骤 4		识别变更的需求： a. 删除或重新评估优先级 b. 添加需求并重新评估优先级 c. 修改现有的需求
步骤 5	识别变更的需求并记录优先级： a. 识别变更的需求并确保这些需求由负责当前阶段的架构师和相关利益攸关者进行优先级排序 b. 记录新的优先级 c. 确保在这些阶段中识别并管理所有冲突，直至成功做出结论并进行优先级排序 d. 生成需求影响说明书（见 36.2.18 节），以指导架构团队 **注** ■ 变更的需求可通过任何途径得以实现。为了确保对这些需求进行适当地评估和优先级排序，该流程需要指导 ADM 阶段并记录与需求有关的决策 ■ 需求管理阶段需要确定利益攸关者对这些决策的满意度。如果不满意，该阶段仍有责任确保这些问题得到解决，然后确定接下来的步骤	

	Requirements Management Steps	ADM Phase Steps
Step 6		a. Assess impact of changed requirements on current (active) phase b. Assess impact of changed requirements on previous phases c. Determine whether to implement change, or defer to later ADM cycle; if decision is to implement, assess timescale for change management implementation d. Issue Requirements Impact Statement, Version *n*+1
Step 7		Implement requirements arising from Phase H The architecture can be changed through its lifecycle by the Architecture Change Management phase (Phase H). The requirements management process ensures that new or changing requirements that are derived from Phase H are managed accordingly
Step 8	Update the Requirements Repository with information relating to the changes requested, including stakeholder views affected	
Step 9		Implement change in the current phase

	需求管理步骤	ADM 阶段步骤
步骤 6		a. 评估变更的需求对当前（现行）阶段的影响 b. 评估变更的需求对前几个阶段的影响 c. 确定是否实施变更，或推迟到 ADM 后期；如果决定实施，评估变更管理实施的时间表 d. 发布需求影响说明书，*n*+1 版
步骤 7		实施由阶段 H 产生的需求 架构可通过架构变更管理阶段（阶段 H）在其整个架构生命周期内进行变更。需求管理流程确保源自阶段 H 的新需求或变更的需求被相应地管理
步骤 8	利用与所要求的变更有关的信息，包括受影响的利益攸关者视图来更新需求存储库	
步骤 9		在当前阶段中实施变更

	Requirements Management Steps	ADM Phase Steps
Step 10		Assess and revise gap analysis forpast phases The gap analysis in the ADM Phases B through D identifies the gaps between Baseline and Target Architectures. Certain types of gap can give rise to gap requirements. The ADM describes two kinds of gap: ■ Something that is present in the baseline, but not in the target (i.e., eliminated — by accident or design) ■ Something not in the baseline, but present in the target (i.e., new) A "gap requirement" is anything that has been eliminated by accident, and therefore requires a change to the Target Architecture. If the gap analysis generates gap requirements, then this step will ensure that they are addressed, documented, and recorded in the Requirements Repository, and that the Target Architecture is revised accordingly

17.5 Outputs

The outputs of the Requirements Management process may include, but are not restricted to:

- Requirements Impact Assessment (see Part IV, Section 36.2.18).
- Updated Architecture Requirements Specification(see Part IV,Section 36.2.6),if necessary.

The Requirements Repository will be updated as part of the Requirements Management phase and should contain all requirements information.

When new requirements arise, or existing ones are changed, a Requirements Impact Statement is generated, which identifies the phases of the ADM that need to be revisited to address the changes. The statement goes through various iterations until the final version, which includes the full implications of the requirements (e.g., costs, timescales, and business metrics) on the architecture development. Once requirements for the current ADM cycle have been finalized then the Architecture Requirements Specification should be updated.

	需求管理步骤	ADM 阶段步骤
步骤 10		评估并修订已结束阶段的差距分析 ADM 阶段 B～D 中的差距分析识别了基线架构和目标架构之间的差距。某些类型的差距可产生差距需求。 ADM 描述了两种差距： ■ 基线架构中存在但目标架构中不存在（即被偶然或刻意淘汰的）的某个事物 ■ 基线架构中不存在而目标架构中存在（即新的）的某个事物 “差距需求”是被偶然淘汰的任何事物，因此需要对该目标架构进行变更。 如果差距分析产生了差距需求，则本步骤会确保这些差距需求在需求存储库中得到应对、文件化和记录，并确保相应地修订该目标架构

17.5 输出

需求管理流程的输出可包括但不限于：

- 需求影响评估（见第四部分 36.2.18 节）。
- 如必要，更新的架构需求规范（见第四部分 36.2.6 节）。

需求存储库会作为需求管理阶段的一部分被更新，并且应包含所有需求信息。

当提出新需求或变更现有需求时，应生成一份需求影响说明书来识别为应对变更而需要回顾的 ADM 各阶段。该需求说明书经过多轮迭代直到最终版本，包括这些需求对架构开发的全面影响（例如，成本、时间表和业务衡量标准）。一旦最终确定当前 ADM 周期的需求，则应更新架构需求规范。

TOGAF Version 9.1

Part III ADM Guidelines and Techniques

The Open Group

TOGAF 9.1 版本

第三部分　ADM 指南和技巧

The Open Group

Chapter 18
Introduction

This chapter provides an overview of the contents of Part III.

18.1 Guidelines for Adapting the ADM Process

The Architecture Development Method (ADM) process can be adapted to deal with a number of different usage scenarios, including different process styles (e.g., the use of iteration) and also specific specialist architectures (such as security). Guidelines included within this part of TOGAF are as follows:

- Applying Iteration to the ADM (see Chapter 19) discusses the concept of iteration and shows potential strategies for applying iterative concepts to the ADM.
- Applying the ADM across the Architecture Landscape (see Chapter 20) discusses the different types of architecture engagement that may occur at different levels of the enterprise. This section then also discusses how the ADM process can be focused to support different types of engagement.
- Security Architecture and the ADM (see Chapter 21) provides an overview of specific security considerations that should be considered during different phases of the ADM.
- Using TOGAF to Define & Govern SOAs (see Chapter 22) shows how SOA concepts can be supported by the TOGAF framework and the specific SOA considerations for different phases of the ADM.

18.2 Techniques for Architecture Development

The following techniques are described within Part III: ADM Guidelines & Techniques to support specific tasks within the ADM:

- Architecture Principles (see Chapter 23) — principles for the use and deployment of IT resources across the enterprise — describes how to develop the set of general rules and guidelines for the architecture being developed.
- Stakeholder Management (see Chapter 24) describes Stakeholder Management, an important discipline that successful architecture practitioners can use to win support for their projects.
- Architecture Patterns (see Chapter 25) provides guidance on using architectural patterns.
- Business Scenarios (see Chapter 26) describes the Business Scenarios technique, a method for deriving business requirements for architecture and the implied technical requirements.

第 18 章 简 介

本章提供第三部分内容的概述。

18.1 ADM 的适应性调整指南

可以调整架构开发方法（ADM）流程，以处理诸多不同的使用场景，包括不同的流程风格（如迭代的使用）以及特定的专业架构（如安保架构）。TOGAF 本部分内包含的指南如下：

- “对 ADM 应用迭代”（见第 19 章）论述迭代的概念并表明将迭代概念应用于 ADM 的潜在策略。
- “贯穿架构全景应用 ADM”（见第 20 章）论述可能在 ENTERPRISE 的不同层级上发生的不同类型的架构介入。本节还论述如何能聚焦 ADM 流程以支持不同类型的介入。
- “安保架构和 ADM”（见第 21 章）针对应在 ADM 的不同阶段考虑的特定安保考量因素提供一个概述。
- “使用 TOGAF 定义和治理 SOA”（见第 22 章）表明 SOA 概念如何能够在 ADM 的不同阶段得到 TOGAF 框架和特定 SOA 考量因素的支持。

18.2 架构开发技巧

在“第三部分：ADM 指南和技巧”中描述下列技巧以支持 ADM 中的特定任务：

- “架构原则”（见第 23 章）——使用和部署贯穿整个 ENTERPRISE 的 IT 资源的原则——描述如何为正在开发的架构制定一套一般规则和指南。
- “利益攸关者管理”（见第 24 章）描述利益攸关者管理，即成功的架构实践者可用于赢得对其项目支持的一种重要修炼。
- “架构特征模式”（见第 25 章）提供关于使用架构特征模式的引导。
- “业务场景”（见第 26 章）描述业务场景技巧，即一种获取架构业务需求和隐含技术需求的方法。

- Gap Analysis (see Chapter 27) describes the technique known as gap analysis. It is widely used in the TOGAF ADM to validate an architecture that is being developed.
- Migration Planning Techniques (see Chapter 28) describes a number of techniques to support migration planning in Phases E and F.
- Interoperability Requirements (see Chapter 29) describes a technique for determining interoperability requirements.
- Business Transformation Readiness Assessment (see Chapter 30) describes a technique for identifying business transformation issues.
- Risk Management (see Chapter 31) describes a technique for managing risk during an architecture/business transformation project.
- Capability-Based Planning (see Chapter 32) describes the technique of capability-based planning.

18.3 Using TOGAF with Different Architectural Styles

TOGAF is designed to be flexible and it can be used with various architectural styles. This part of TOGAF includes two chapters that are intended as useful examples.

- Security Architecture and the ADM (see Chapter 21)
- Using TOGAF to Define & Govern SOAs (see Chapter 22)

Architectural styles differ in terms of focus, form, techniques, materials, subject, and time period. Some styles can be considered as fashionable, others focused on particular aspects of enterprise architecture. TOGAF is a generic framework and intended to be used in a wide variety of environments. It is a flexible and extensible framework that can be readily adapted to a number of architectural styles.

An organization's Architecture Landscape can be expected to contain architecture work that is developed in many architectural styles. TOGAF ensures that the needs of each stakeholder are appropriately addressed in the context of other stakeholders and the Baseline Architecture.

When using TOGAF to support a specific architectural style the practitioner must take into account the combination of distinctive features in which architecture is performed or expressed. As a first step, the distinctive features of a style must be identified.

For example, The Open Group definition for SOA identifies the following distinctive features:

- It is based on the design of the services — which mirror real-world business activities — comprising the enterprise (or inter-enterprise) business processes.
- Service representation utilizes business descriptions to provide context (i.e., business process, goal, rule, policy, service interface, and service component) and implements services using service orchestration.
- It places unique requirements on the infrastructure — it is recommended that implementations use open standards to realize interoperability and location transparency.
- Implementations are environment-specific — they are constrained or enabled by context and must be described within that context.

The second step is determining how these distinctive features will be addressed. Addressing a distinctive style should not call for significant changes to TOGAF; instead it should adjust the models, viewpoints, and tools used by the practitioner.

- “差距分析”（见第 27 章）描述被称为差距分析的技巧，它在 TOGAF ADM 中被广泛用于确认一个正在开发中的架构。
- “迁移规划技巧”（见第 28 章）描述在阶段 E 和阶段 F 中多种用于支持迁移规划的技巧。
- “互用性需求”（见第 29 章）描述一种确定互用性需求的技巧。
- “业务转型准备度评估”（见第 30 章）描述一种识别业务转型问题的技巧。
- “风险管理”（见第 31 章）描述在架构/业务转型项目中管理风险的一种技巧。
- “基于能力的规划”（见第 32 章）描述基于能力进行规划的技巧。

18.3 配合不同架构风格使用 TOGAF

TOGAF 设计灵活并且可配合不同架构风格使用。本部分 TOGAF 包括两个章节，旨在给出有用的示例。

- “安保架构和 ADM”（见第 21 章）
- “使用 TOGAF 定义和治理 SOA”（见第 22 章）

架构风格在聚焦点、形式、技巧、资料、主题和时间区间方面存在差异。某些风格被认为是流行的，而其他风格则聚焦于 Enterprise Architecture 的特定方面。TOGAF 是一种一般框架并且旨在用于多种环境中。TOGAF 是一种可易于被调整成多种架构风格的灵活且可扩展的框架。

预期组织架构全景会包含以多种架构风格开发的架构工作。TOGAF 确保在其他利益攸关者和基线架构的背景环境下适当地应对每个利益攸关者的需要。

当使用 TOGAF 支持一种特定的架构风格时，实践者必须考虑到执行或表达架构所依据的独特性特征的组合。作为第一步，必须识别出一种风格的独特性特征。

例如，The Open Group 的 SOA 定义识别出下列独特性特征：

- 它是基于服务（其是真实世界业务活动的“镜像”）的设计，并包括 ENTERPRISE（或 ENTERPRISE 间）的业务流程。
- 服务的表达是利用业务描述来提供背景环境（即业务流程、目标、规则、方针、服务界面和服务组件），并使用服务编排来实施服务。
- 它对基础设施提出特殊需求——建议实施使用开放标准来实现互用性和位置透明性。
- 实施是特定于环境的，它们受到背景环境的约束，或由背景环境使能，并且必须在所处的背景环境中描述。

第二步是确定如何应对独特性特征。应对一种独特的风格不应要求对 TOGAF 进行重大变更，而应调整实践者所使用的模型、视角和工具。

In Phase B, Phase C, and Phase D the practitioner is expected to select the relevant architecture resources, including models, viewpoints, and tools, to properly describe the architecture domain and demonstrate that stakeholder concerns are addressed (see Part II, Section 8.4.1, Section 10.4.1, Section 11.4.1, and Section 12.4.1). Depending upon the distinctive features, different architectural styles will add new elements that must be described, highlight existing elements, adjust the notation used to describe the architecture, and focus the architect on some stakeholders or stakeholder concerns.

Addressing the distinctive features will usually include extensions to the Architecture Content Metamodel and the use of specific notation or modeling techniques and the identification of viewpoints. Whether the style is dominant will determine whether it is necessary to revisit the Preliminary Phase and make changes to the Architecture Capability or whether support for the distinctive feature is possible within the scope of selection expected within a single ADM cycle.

Style-specific reference models and maturity models are commonly used tools that support a practitioner.

Over time new architectural styles are expected to arise to address the key problems facing practitioners. Some styles will be transitory, some will endure in a niche, and some will merge into the mainstream. The Open Group Forums and Work Groups exist to address the challenges facing the industry. These bodies produce a wide range of material that is useful to a practitioner interested in adapting TOGAF, or a particular ADM cycle, to a particular architectural style for current materials, including White Papers and Standards that are applicable (see www.opengroup.org/togaf_docs).

在阶段 B、阶段 C 和阶段 D 中，期望实践者选择相关架构资源（包括模型、视角和工具），以恰当地描述架构域并证明利益攸关者关注点得以涉及（见第二部分，8.4.1 节、10.4.1 节、11.4.1 节和 12.4.1 节）。根据这些区别性特征，不同的架构风格将添加必须描述的新元素，强调现有元素，调整用来描述该架构的符号，并使架构师聚焦于某些利益攸关者或利益攸关者关注点。

应对这些区别性特征通常将包括架构内容元模型的扩展、特定符号或建模技巧的使用以及视角的识别。风格是否起决定作用会决定是否有必要回顾预备阶段并对架构能力进行改变，或决定在单一 ADM 周期内期望的选择范围中是否可能支持区别性特征。

特定风格的参考模型和成熟度模型是支持实践者的常用工具。

经过一段时间后，期望产生多种新的架构风格，应对实践者所面临的关键问题。有些风格将是暂时的，有些风格将在某种环境下持续使用，而有些风格将融入主流。The Open Group 论坛和工作组的存在是为了应对各行业所面临的挑战。这些机构制作对实践者有用的各式各样的资料，实践者感兴趣的是，将 TOGAF 或特定的 ADM 周期适应性调整为当前资料（包括适用的白皮书和标准，参见 www.opengroup.org/togaf_docs）的一种特定架构风格。

Chapter 19
Applying Iteration to the ADM

19.1 Overview

The graphical representation of the TOGAF ADM, as shown in Figure 5-1, and the description of the ADM phases discretely in order in Part II, can be read to imply a deterministic waterfall methodology. This method of presentation is provided for the purpose of quickly communicating the basics of architecture development and the architecture lifecycle. In practice, two key concepts are used to manage the complexity of developing an enterprise architecture and managing its lifecycle — iteration and levels (see Chapter 20). The two concepts are tightly linked.

The ADM supports a number of concepts that are characterized as iteration. First, iteration describes the process of both describing a comprehensive Architecture Landscape through multiple ADM cycles based upon individual initiatives bound to the scope of the Request for Architecture Work. Second, iteration describes the integrated process of developing an architecture where the activities described in different ADM phases interact to produce an integrated architecture. In order to concisely describe the activity and outputs, this latter iteration is described in sequential terms. Third, iteration describes the process of managing change to the organization's Architecture Capability.

Iteration to develop a comprehensive Architecture Landscape:

- Projects will exercise through the entire ADM cycle, commencing with Phase A. Each cycle of the ADM will be bound by a Request for Architecture Work. The architecture output will populate the Architecture Landscape, either extending the landscape described, or changing the landscape where required.
- Separate projects may operate their own ADM cycles concurrently, with relationships between the different projects.
- One project may trigger the initiation of another project. Typically, this is used when higher-level architecture initiatives identify opportunities or solutions that require more detailed architecture, or when a project identifies landscape impacts outside the scope of its Request for Architecture Work.

Iteration within an ADM cycle (Architecture Development iteration):

- Projects may operate multiple ADM phases concurrently. Typically, this is used to manage the inter-relationship between Business Architecture, Information Systems Architecture, and Technology Architecture.
- Projects may cycle between ADM phases, in planned cycles covering multiple phases. Typically, this is used to converge on a detailed Target Architecture when higher-level architecture does not exist to provide context and constraint.

第 19 章
对 ADM 应用迭代

19.1 概述

第二部分中，TOGAF ADM 的图形表达（如图 5-1 所示）和对按序离散排列的 ADM 阶段的描述，可以解读为暗示一种确定性的瀑布方法。提供这种表达方法是为了快速传达架构开发的基本要素和架构生命周期。在实践中，用两个关键概念来管理 Enterprise Architecture 开发及其生命周期管理的复杂性——迭代和层级（参见第 20 章）。这两个概念紧密相联。

ADM 支持多个被特征化为迭代的概念。第一，对于受架构工作要求书范围所限的各举措，迭代描述了通过多个 ADM 周期描述一个完整架构全景的流程。第二，迭代描述开发架构的综合流程，在该流程中，不同 ADM 阶段内描述的活动相互作用而产生一个综合架构。为了简明扼要地描述活动和输出，第二种迭代按顺序描述。第三，迭代描述管理变化组织的架构能力的流程。

开发完整架构全景的迭代：

- 项目会从阶段 A 着手并在整个 ADM 周期中进行训练。ADM 的每轮周期都受一个架构工作要求书的约束。架构输出将充实架构全景，或扩展所描述的全景，或在需要时变更该全景。
- 独立的项目可同时运行各自的 ADM 周期，不同项目之间具有联系。
- 一个项目可触发另一个项目的启动。典型情况下，当较高层级的架构举措识别出需要更详细的架构的机会或解决方案时，或当一个项目识别出其架构工作要求书范围之外的全景影响时，使用这种迭代。

一个 ADM 周期内的迭代（架构开发迭代）：

- 项目可能同时运行多个 ADM 阶段。典型情况下，这种迭代被用来管理业务架构、信息系统架构和技术架构之间的相互关系。
- 在涵盖多个阶段的计划周期内项目可在 ADM 阶段之间循环。典型情况下，当没有较高层级的架构提供背景环境和约束时，这种迭代被用来在详细的目标架构上收敛。

- Projects may return to previous phases in order to circle back and update work products with new information. Typically, this is used to converge on an executable Architecture Roadmap or Implementation and Migration Plan, when the implementation details and scope of change trigger a change or re-prioritization of stakeholder requirements.

Iteration to manage the Architecture Capability (Architecture Capability iteration):

- Projects may require a new iteration of the Preliminary Phase to (re-) establish aspects of the Architecture Capability identified in Phase A to address a Request for Architecture Work.
- Projects may require a new iteration of the Preliminary Phase to adjust the organization's Architecture Capability as a result of identifying new or changed requirements for Architecture Capability as a result of a Change Request in Phase H.

19.2 Iteration Cycles

The suggested iteration cycles for the TOGAF ADM are shown in Figure 19-1, and can be used to effectively group related architectural activities to achieve a specific purpose. These iteration cycles are referenced in Section 19.3 and Section 19.5.

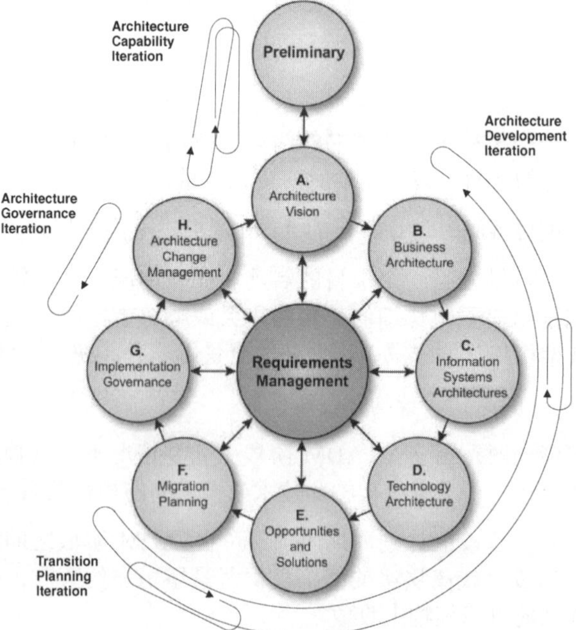

Figure 19-1 Iteration Cycles

- 项目可返回到之前的阶段，以便循回并用新的信息更新工作产物。典型情况下，当实施细节和变更范围触发利益攸关者需求的变更或重新排列优先顺序时，这种迭代被用来在可执行的架构路线图或实施与迁移计划上收敛。

架构能力管理的迭代（架构能力迭代）：

- 项目可能需要预备阶段的一个新的迭代来（重新）建立在阶段 A 中识别的架构能力的多个方面，为架构工作要求书做准备。
- 由于新的或变更的架构能力需求是在阶段 H 中的变更要求中识别的，因此，项目可能需要预备阶段的一个新的迭代来调整组织的架构能力。

19.2 迭代周期

TOGAF ADM 的建议迭代周期如图 19-1 所示，并且可被用来有效地对相关架构活动进行分组，以达成一个特定的目的。在 19.3 节和 19.5 节中引用这些迭代周期。

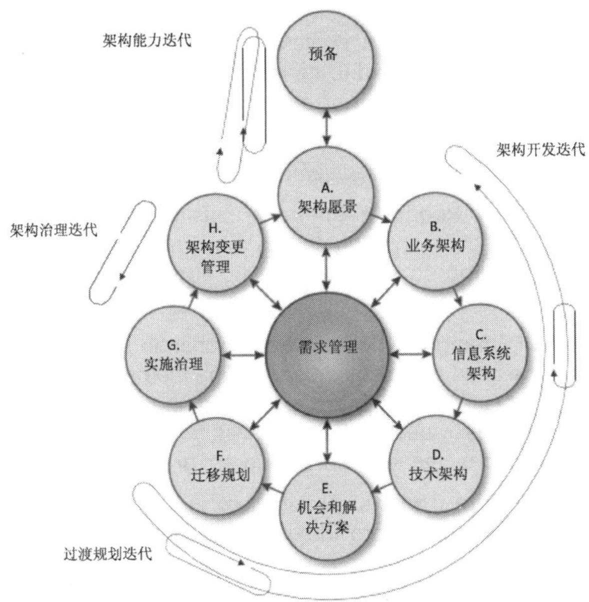

图 19-1 迭代周期

- **Architecture Capability** iterations support the creation[1] and evolution of the required Architecture Capability. This includes the initial mobilization of the architecture activity for a given purpose or architecture engagement type by establishing or adjusting the architecture approach, principles, scope, vision, and governance.
- **Architecture Development** iterations allow the creation of architecture content by cycling through, or integrating, Business, Information Systems, and Technology Architecture phases. These iterations ensure that the architecture is considered as a whole. In this type of iteration stakeholder reviews are typically broader. As the iterations converge on a target, extensions into the Opportunities and Solutions and Migration Planning phases ensure that the architecture's implementability is considered as the architecture is finalized.
- **Transition Planning** iterations support the creation of formal change roadmaps for a defined architecture.
- **Architecture Governance** iterations support governance of change activity progressing towards a defined Target Architecture.

19.3 Classes of Architecture Engagement

An architecture function or services organization may be called on to assist an enterprise in a number of different contexts, as the architectures developed can range from summary to detail, broad to narrow coverage, and current state to future state. In these contexts the concept of iteration should be used in developing the architecture.

Typically, there are three areas of engagement for architects:

- **Identification of Required Change:** Outside the context of any change initia-tive, architecture can be used as a technique to provide visibility of the IT capability in order to support strategic decision-making and alignment of execution.
- **Definition of Change:** Where a need to change has been identified, architecture can be used as a technique to define the nature and extent of change in a structured fashion. Within largescale change initiatives, architectures can be developed to provide detailed Architecture Definition for change initiatives that are bounded by the scope of a program or portfolio.
- **Implementation of Change:** Architecture at all levels of the enterprise can be used as a technique to provide design governance to change initiatives by providing big-picture visibility, supplying structural constraints, and defining criteria on which to evaluate technical decisions.

Figure 19-2 and the following table show the classes of enterprise architecture engagement.

---

1. Guidance on how to use a full ADM cycle for initially establishing an organization's Architecture Capability is found in Part VII, Chapter 46.

- **架构能力**迭代支持所需架构能力的创建[1]和演进。这包括通过建立或调整架构途径、原则、范围、愿景和治理，针对给定的目的或架构介入类型对架构活动进行的最初启动。
- **架构开发**迭代使得通过在业务、信息系统和技术架构阶段中循环或对这些阶段进行综合能创建架构内容。这些迭代确保架构被作为一个整体来考虑。在这类迭代中，利益攸关者审查通常较为广泛。随着这些迭代在目标上收敛，向机会及解决方案阶段和迁移规划阶段中的扩展确保在最终确定架构时考虑架构的可实施性。
- **过渡规划**迭代支持为已定义的架构创建正式的变更路线图。
- **架构治理**迭代支持向已定义的目标架构的变更活动进展进行管控。

19.3 架构介入的类别

由于所开发的架构的范围从概要到详细，覆盖面从宽到窄、状态从当前到未来，因此，可请求一个架构功能或服务组织在多个不同背景环境下协助一个 ENTERPRISE。在这些背景环境下，迭代的概念应用于开发该架构。

典型情况下，有三个领域需要架构师介入：

- **所需变革的识别**：在变革举措的背景环境之外，架构可被用作一种技巧来提供 IT 能力的可见性，以便支持战略决策和执行的对准。
- **变革的定义**：当一个变革的需要被识别时，架构可被用作一种以结构化的方式定义变革的本质和程度的技巧。在大规模变革举措的范围内，可开发多个架构，为受项目群或项目谱系的范围约束的变革举措提供详细的架构定义。
- **变革的实施**：通过提供"大图像"可见性、结构约束及定义评论技术决策所依据的准则，ENTERPRISE 所有层级上的架构可作为一种提供对变革举措进行设计治理的技巧。

图 19-2 和下列表格表明 Enterprise Architecture 介入的类别。

1. 关于如何将 ADM 全周期用于初步建立一个组织的架构能力的指南，可在第三部分第 46 章中查找到。

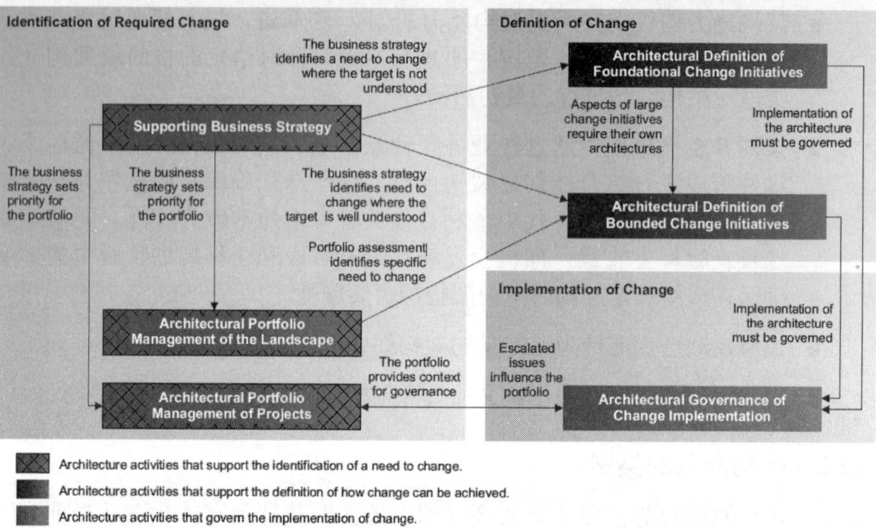

Figure 19-2 Classes of Enterprise Architecture Engagement

Each of these architecture engagement types is described in the table below.

Area of Engagement	Architecture Engagement	Description
Identification of Required Change	Supporting Business Strategy	As the business strategies, objectives, goals, and drivers change, it is necessary for the enterprise to change in order to maintain alignment. The creation of new business strategies can be supported by enterprise architecture by: ▪ Providing visibility of change opportunities ▪ Providing elaboration on the practical impacts of a particular strategic choice ▪ Providing tests on the feasibility or viability of a particular strategic direction

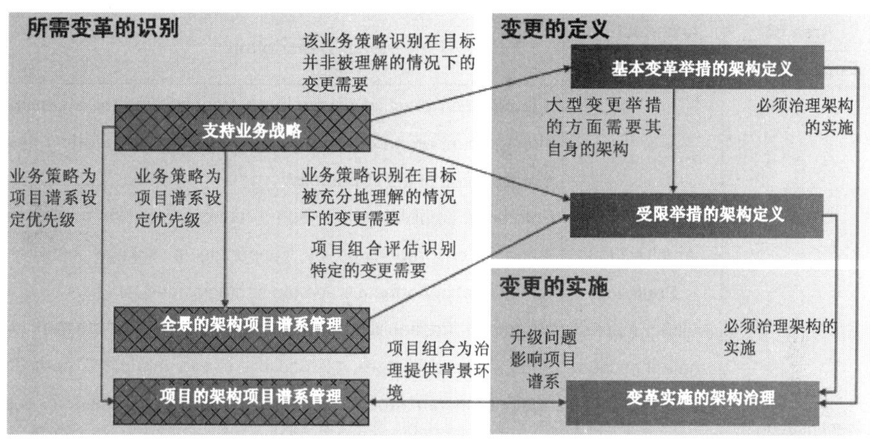

图 19-2　Enterprise Architecture 介入的类别

每个架构介入的类型如下表所描述。

介入领域	架构介入	描述
所需变革的识别	支持业务战略	随着业务战略、目的、目标和驱动因素的变化，ENTERPRISE 有必要为了保持对准而做出变化。 新的业务战略的创建可通过下列方式得到 Enterprise Architecture 的支持： ▪ 提供变革机会的可见性 ▪ 提供对特殊战略选择的实际影响的详细阐述 ▪ 提供对特殊战略方向的可行性或生命力的试验

Area of Engagement	Architecture Engagement	Description
Identification of Required Change	Architectural Portfolio Management of the Landscape	It is common practice across large organizations for a service management organization to provide operational reporting and management of the IT portfolio. Enterprise architecture can add a further dimension to service management reporting, by supporting a linkage between operational performance and the strategic need for IT. Using the traceability between IT and business inherent in enterprise architecture, it is possible to evaluate the IT portfolio against operational performance data and business needs (e.g., cost, functionality, availability, responsiveness) to determine areas where misalignment is occurring and change needs to take place.
	Architectural Portfolio Management of Projects	It is common practice across large organizations for a program management organization to provide operational reporting and management of the change portfolio. Enterprise architecture can add a further dimension to project portfolio management reporting, by supporting a linkage between project scope, architectural impact and business value. Architectural factors can be added to other quantitative project factors to support strategic decision-making on project priority and funding levels.
Definition of Change	Architectural Definition of Foundational Change Initiatives	Foundational change initiatives are change efforts that have a known objective, but are not strictly scoped or bounded by a shared vision or requirements. In foundational change initiatives, the initial priority is to understand the nature of the problem and to bring structure to the definition of the problem. Once the problem is more effectively understood, it is possible to define appropriate solutions and to align stakeholders around a common vision and purpose.

介入领域	架构介入	描述
所需变革的识别	全景的架构谱系管理	在贯穿多个大型组织中，服务管理组织的共用的实践是提供 IT 项目谱系的运行报告和管理。 通过支撑运营绩效和 IT 战略需要之间的联系，Enterprise Architecture 可向服务管理报告添加一个额外维度。 利用 Enterprise Architecture 内固有的 IT 和业务之间的可追溯性，有可能根据运营绩效数据和业务需求（例如，成本、功能性、可用性、响应性）评价 IT 项目谱系，以确定发生不一致和需要进行变更的领域
	项目的架构谱系管理	在跨多个大型组织中，项目群管理组织的共用的实践是提供变更项目谱系的运行报告和管理。 通过支撑项目范围、架构影响和业务价值之间的联系，Enterprise Architecture 可向项目谱系管理报告添加一个额外维度。 架构因素可添加到其他量化项目因素上，以支持对项目优先级和资金水平的战略决策
变革的定义	基础变革举措的架构定义	基础变革举措是具有已知目的的变革，但并不受共享的愿景或需求的严格限制或约束。 在基础变革举措中，最初的优先事项是理解问题的本质并将使问题的定义结构化。 一旦更为有效地理解问题，有可能定义适当的解决方案并使多个利益攸关者对准公用的愿景和目标努力

Area of Engagement	Architecture Engagement	Description
Definition of Change	Architectural Definition of Bounded Change Initiatives	Bounded change initiatives are change efforts that typically arise as the outcome of a prior architectural strategy, evaluation, or vision. In bounded change initiatives, the desired outcome is already understood and agreed upon. The focus of architectural effort in this class of engagement is to effectively elaborate a baseline solution that addresses the identified requirements, issues, drivers, and constraints
Implementation of Change	Architectural Governance of Change Implementation	Once an architectural solution model has been defined, it provides a basis for design and implementation. In order to ensure that the objectives and value of the defined architecture are appropriately realized, it is necessary for continuing architecture governance of the implementation process to support design review, architecture refinement, and issue escalation

Different classes of architecture engagement at different levels of the enterprise will require focus in specific areas, as shown below.

Engagement Type	Focus Iteration Cycles	Scope Focus
Supporting Business Strategy	Architecture Capability Architecture Development (Baseline First)	Broad, shallow consideration given to the Architecture Landscape in order to address a specific strategic question and define terms for more detailed architecture efforts to address strategy realization
Architectural Portfolio Management of the Landscape	Architecture Capability Architecture Development (Baseline First)	Focus on physical assessment of baseline applications and technology infrastructure to identify improvement opportunities, typically within the constraints of maintaining business as usual
Architectural Portfolio Management of Projects	Transition Planning Architecture Governance	Focus on projects, project dependencies, and landscape impacts to align project sequencing in a way that is architecturally optimized

介入领域	架构介入	描述
变革的定义	受限变革举措的架构定义	典型情况下，受限变革举措是起源于先前架构策略、评价或愿景的结果的变革工作。 在受限变革举措中，已经理解期望结果并进行了商定。该类介入中的架构工作聚焦于有效地详细阐述了涉及识别的需求、问题、驱动因素和约束的基线解决方案
变革的实施	变革实施的架构治理	一旦定义架构解决方案模型，其便为设计和实施提供基础。 为了确保适当地实现已定义架构的目的和价值，有必要实施流程的持续架构治理以支持设计审查、架构细化和议题升级

ENTERPRISE 不同层级的不同类别架构介入需要聚焦于特定领域，如下表所示。

介入类型	聚焦点迭代周期	聚焦点范围
支持业务战略	架构能力 架构开发 （基线先行）	为了应对特定战略问题并为更详细的架构工作来定义术语以应对战略实现，所给予架构全景的广泛的、浅显的考量因素
全景的架构谱系管理	架构能力 架构开发 （基线先行）	典型情况下，在保持正常业务的约束范围内，聚焦于应用和技术基础设施基线的物理评估来识别改进机会
项目的架构谱系管理	过渡规划 架构治理	聚焦于项目、项目依赖性和全景影响来以架构优化的方式对准项目顺序

Engagement Type	Focus Iteration Cycles	Scope Focus
Architectural Definition of Foundational Change Initiatives	Architecture Capability Architecture Development (Baseline First) Transition Planning	Focus on elaborating a vision through definition of baseline and identifying what needs to change to transition the baseline to the target
Architectural Definition of Bounded Change Initiatives	Architecture Development (Target First) Transition Planning	Focus on elaborating the target to meet a previously defined and agreed vision, scope, or set of constraints. Use the target as a basis for analysis to avoid perpetuation of baseline, suboptimal architectures
Architectural Governance of Change Implementation	Architecture Governance	Use the Architecture Vision, constraints, principles, requirements, Target Architecture definition, and transition roadmap to ensure that projects realize their intended benefit, are aligned with each other, and are aligned with wider business need

19.4 Approaches to Architecture Development

Two approaches can be adopted within the ADM for the development of architectures:

- **Baseline First:** In this style, an assessment of the baseline landscape is used to identify problem areas and improvement opportunities. This process is most suitable when the baseline is complex, not clearly understood, or agreed upon. This approach is common where organizational units have had a high degree of autonomy.
- **Targ et First:** In this style, the target solution is elaborated in detail and then mapped back to the baseline, in order to identify change activity. This process is suitable when a target state is agreed at a high level and where the enterprise wishes to effectively transition to the target model.

Typically, if the baseline is broadly understood a higher value will be obtained focusing on the target first then baseline to the extent necessary to identify changes.

In practical terms, an architecture team will always give informal consideration to the baseline when analyzing the target (and *vice versa*). In situations where baseline and target are expected to be considered in parallel by stakeholders, it is recommended that the architecture team focuses priority on one state in order to maintain focus and consistency of execution.

介入类型	聚焦点迭代周期	聚焦点范围
基础变革举措的架构定义	架构能力 架构开发 （基线先行） 过渡规划	聚焦于通过基线定义详细阐述愿景并识别哪些需要变革以使基线过渡到目标
受限变革举措的架构定义	架构开发 （目标先行） 过渡规划	聚焦于详细阐述目标来满足先前定义且达成一致的愿景、范围或约束集。将目标用作分析的基础，以避免基线、次优架构的固化
变革实施的架构治理	架构治理	使用架构愿景、约束、原则、需求、目标架构定义和过渡路线图来确保项目实现其预期效益、相互一致并且与更广泛的业务需要一致

19.4 架构开发的途径

可在 ADM 内针对架构开发采用两种途径：

- **基线先行**：在这种方式中，利用基线全景的评估来识别问题领域和改进机会。当基线比较复杂、未被充分理解或达成一致时，该流程最为合适。在组织单元已经高度自治的情况下，这种途径是很常用的。
- **目标先行**：在这种方式中，详细地阐述目标解决方案，然后将其映射回基线，以便识别变革活动。当目标状态在高层级达成一致并且 ENTERPRISE 希望有效地向目标模型过渡的情况下，这种流程是合适的。

典型情况是，如果基线被广泛理解，通过首先聚焦于目标、然后聚焦于基线并达到识别变革所需程度，而获得更高价值。

实际上，当分析目标时，架构团队将始终对基线进行非正式的考量因素（反之亦然）。在基线和目标预期由利益攸关者并行考虑的情况下，建议架构团队将优先级集中于一种状态，以便保持执行的聚焦点和连贯性。

19.5 Iteration Considerations

Some iteration cycles can be executed once, whereas others have a natural minimum number of cycles. For some iteration cycles, each iteration follows the same process; where there is more than one iteration within a cycle, the process differs slightly for each of the iterations.

When considering the usage of iteration cycles, it is also necessary to consider where to place appropriate checkpoints within the process. If the expected level of stakeholder involvement is high, it may be sensible to carry out very frequent but informal checkpoints to ensure that the process is moving in the intended direction. If stakeholders are less closely involved, then checkpoints may be less frequent but more formal. Checkpoints at the completion of each iteration cycle, or at the end of several iteration cycles, are common.

19.5.1 Iteration between ADM Cycles

Each iteration completes an ADM cycle at a single level of architecture description. This approach to the ADM uses Phase F (Migration Planning) to initiate new more detailed architecture development projects. This approach is illustrated in Figure 19-3. This type of iteration highlights the need for higher-level architecture to guide and constrain more detailed architecture. It also highlights that the complete Architecture Landscape is developed by multiple ADM iterations.

19.5 迭代考量因素

某些迭代周期可被执行一次，然而，其他迭代周期具有自然的最小周期数。对于某些迭代周期，每次迭代都遵循相同的流程；在一个周期具有一轮以上的迭代时，每次迭代的流程略有不同。

当考虑使用迭代周期时，还有必要考虑在流程内何处设置适当的检查点。如果预期的利益攸关者参与度的预期水平很高，则执行非常频繁而非正式的检查点可能是明智的，以确保该流程按预期方向推进。如果利益攸关者并非紧密参与，则检查点可能并非频繁但较为正式。每个迭代周期结束时的检查点或若干迭代周期结束时的检查点是很常见的。

19.5.1 ADM 周期之间的迭代

每次迭代在架构描述的一个单一层级上完成一个 ADM 周期。这种 ADM 的实施途径是使用阶段 F（迁移规划）来启动更为详细的新架构开发项目。这种实施途径如图 19-3 所示。这种类型的迭代强调较高层级架构指导和约束更为详细的架构的必要性。还强调完整的架构全景通过多轮 ADM 迭代来开发。

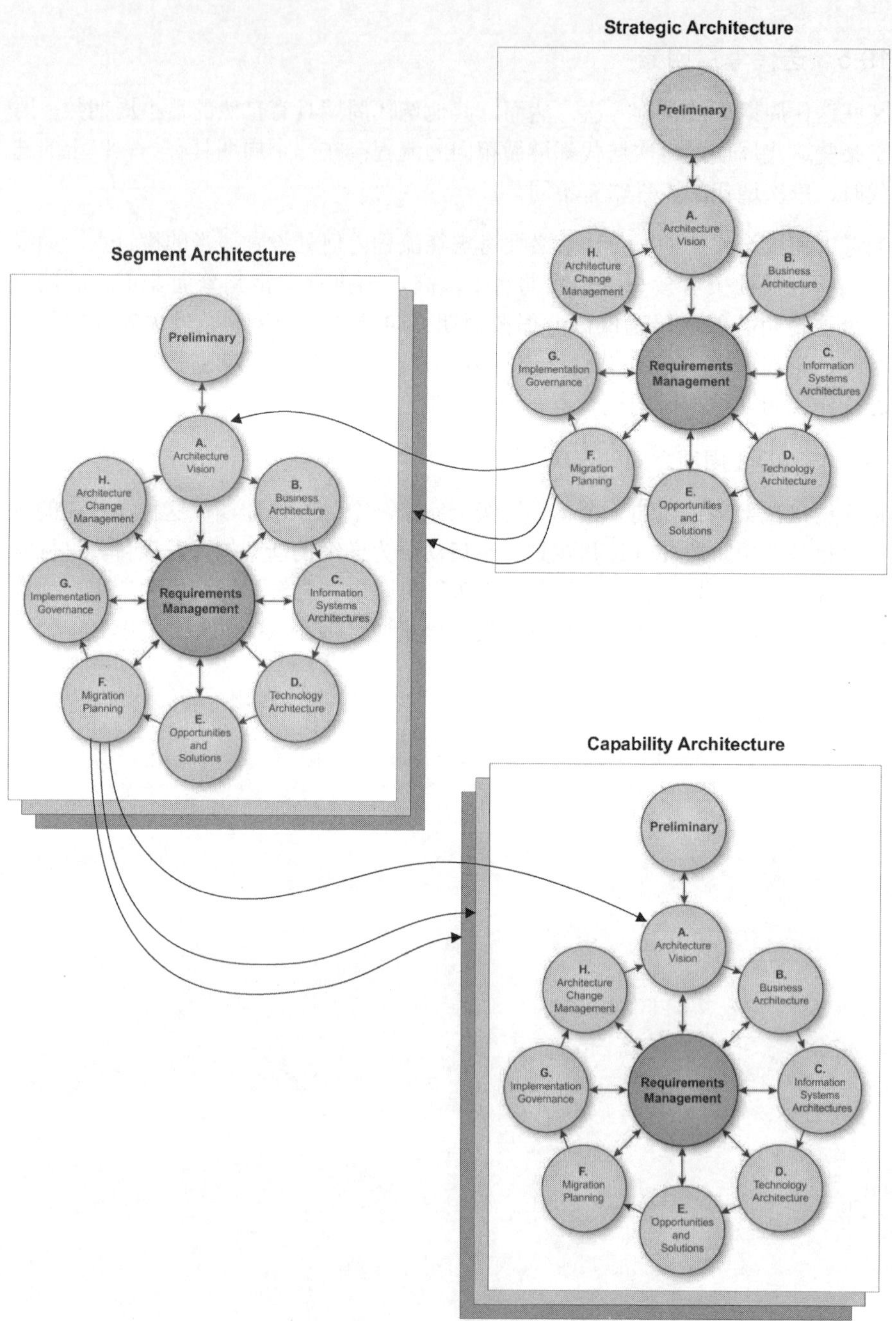

Figure 19-3 A Hierarchy of ADM Processes Example

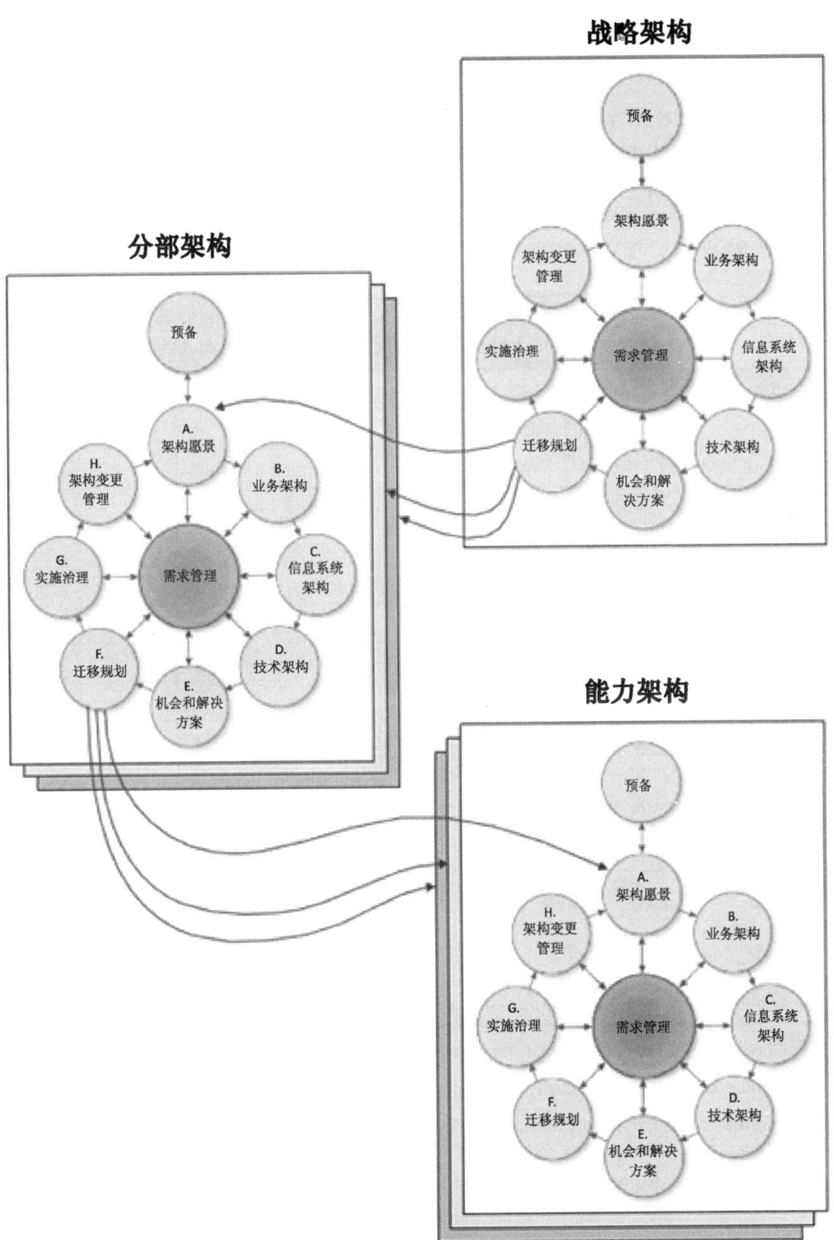

图 19-3　ADM 流程层级结构的示例

19.5.2 Iteration within an ADM Cycle

Each iteration cycle crosses multiple TOGAF ADM phases. The following tables show at a high level which phases should be completed for which iteration cycle, showing activity that is core (i.e., the primary focus of the iteration), activity that is light (i.e., the secondary focus of the iteration), and activity that may be informally conducted (i.e., some activity may be carried out, but it is not explicitly mentioned in the ADM).

		Architecture Development			Transition Planning		Architecture Governance	
TOGAF Phase		Iteration 1	Iteration 2	Iteration *n*	Iteration 1	Iteration *n*	Iteration 1	Iteration *n*
Preliminary		Informal	Informal	Informal				Light
Architecture Vision		Informal	Informal	Informal	Informal	Informal		Light
Business Architecture	Baseline	Core	Light	Core	Informal	Informal		Light
	Target	Informal	Core	Core	Informal	Informal		Light
Application Architecture	Baseline	Core	Light	Core	Informal	Informal		Light
	Target	Informal	Core	Core	Informal	Informal		Light
Data Architecture	Baseline	Core	Light	Core	Informal	Informal		Light
	Target	Informal	Core	Core	Informal	Informal		Light
Technology Architecture	Baseline	Core	Light	Core	Informal	Informal		Light
	Target	Informal	Core	Core	Informal	Informal		Light
Opportunities and Solutions		Light	Light	Light	Core	Core	Informal	Informal
Migration Planning		Light	Light	Light	Core	Core	Informal	Informal
Implementation Governance					Informal	Informal	Core	Core
Change Management		Informal	Informal	Informal	Informal	Informal	Core	Core

Core: primary focus activity for the iteration

Light: secondary focus activity for the iteration

Informal: potential activity for the iteration, not formally mentioned in the method

Figure 19-4 Activity by Iteration for Baseline First Architecture Definition

19.5.2 在一个 ADM 周期内的迭代

每个迭代周期跨越多个 TOGAF ADM 阶段。下列表格在高层级上表明应针对哪个迭代周期完成哪些阶段，表明了核心的活动（即迭代的主要聚焦点）、轻度的活动（即迭代的次要聚焦点）和可能非正式执行的活动（即某个活动可能被执行，但其并未在该 ADM 中明确提及）。

		架构开发			过渡规划		架构治理	
TOGAF 阶段		迭代 1	迭代 2	迭代 *n*	迭代 1	迭代 *n*	迭代 1	迭代 *n*
预备		非正式	非正式	非正式				轻量
架构愿景		非正式	非正式	非正式	非正式	非正式		轻量
业务架构	基线	核心	轻量	核心	非正式	非正式		轻量
	目标	非正式	核心	核心	非正式	非正式		轻量
应用架构	基线	核心	轻量	核心	非正式	非正式		轻量
	目标	非正式	核心	核心	非正式	非正式		轻量
数据架构	基线	核心	轻量	核心	非正式	非正式		轻量
	目标	非正式	核心	核心	非正式	非正式		轻量
技术架构	基线	核心	轻量	核心	非正式	非正式		轻量
	目标	非正式	核心	核心	非正式	非正式		轻量
机会和解决方案		轻量	轻量	轻量	核心	核心	非正式	非正式
迁移规划		轻量	轻量	轻量	核心	核心	非正式	非正式
实施治理					非正式	非正式	核心	核心
变更管理		非正式	非正式	非正式	非正式	非正式	核心	核心

核心：该迭代的主要聚焦点活动

轻量：该迭代的次要聚焦点活动

非正式：该迭代的潜在活动，并未在该方法中正式提到

图 19-4 用于基线先行架构定义的迭代活动

		Architecture Development			Transition Planning		Architecture Governance	
TOGAF Phase		Iteration 1	Iteration 2	Iteration *n*	Iteration 1	Iteration *n*	Iteration 1	Iteration *n*
Preliminary		Informal	Informal	Informal				Light
Architecture Vision		Informal	Informal	Informal	Informal	Informal		Light
Business Architecture	Baseline	Informal	Core	Core	Informal	Informal		Light
	Target	Core	Light	Core	Informal	Informal		Light
Application Architecture	Baseline	Informal	Core	Core	Informal	Informal		Light
	Target	Core	Light	Core	Informal	Informal		Light
Data Architecture	Baseline	Informal	Core	Core	Informal	Informal		Light
	Target	Core	Light	Core	Informal	Informal		Light
Technology Architecture	Baseline	Informal	Core	Core	Informal	Informal		Light
	Target	Core	Light	Core	Informal	Informal		Light
Opportunities and Solutions		Light	Light	Light	Core	Core	Informal	Informal
Migration Planning		Light	Light	Light	Core	Core	Informal	Informal
Implementation Governance					Informal	Informal	Core	Core
Change Management		Informal	Informal	Informal	Informal	Informal	Core	Core

Core: primary focus activity for the iteration

Light: secondary focus activity for the iteration

Informal: potential activity for the iteration, not formally mentioned in the method

Figure 19-5 Activity by Iteration for Target First Architecture Definition

The suggested iteration cycles mapped to the TOGAF phases are described in the following table:

Iteration Cycle	Iteration	Purpose	Description
Architecture Development (Baseline First)	Iteration 1	Define the Baseline Architecture	This iteration comprises a pass through the Business Architecture, Information Systems Architecture, and Technology Architecture phases of the ADM, focusing on definition of the baseline. Opportunities, solutions, and migration plans are also considered to drive out the focus for change and test feasibility

TOGAF 阶段		架构开发 迭代 1	架构开发 迭代 2	架构开发 迭代 *n*	过渡规划 迭代 1	过渡规划 迭代 *n*	架构治理 迭代 1	架构治理 迭代 *n*
预备		非正式	非正式	非正式				轻量
架构愿景		非正式	非正式	非正式	非正式	非正式		轻量
业务架构	基线	非正式	核心	核心	非正式	非正式		轻量
	目标	核心	轻量	核心	非正式	非正式		轻量
应用架构	基线	非正式	核心	核心	非正式	非正式		轻量
	目标	核心	轻量	核心	非正式	非正式		轻量
数据架构	基线	非正式	核心	核心	非正式	非正式		轻量
	目标	核心	轻量	核心	非正式	非正式		轻量
技术架构	基线	非正式	核心	核心	非正式	非正式		轻量
	目标	核心	轻量	核心	非正式	非正式		轻量
机会和解决方案		轻量	轻量	轻量	核心	核心	非正式	非正式
迁移规划		轻量	轻量	轻量	核心	核心	非正式	非正式
实施治理					非正式	非正式	核心	核心
变更管理		非正式	非正式	非正式	非正式	非正式	核心	核心

核心：该迭代的主要聚焦点活动

轻量：该迭代的次要聚焦点活动

非正式：该迭代的潜在活动，并未在该方法中正式提到

图 19-5 用于目标先行架构定义的迭代活动

映射到 TOGAF 各阶段的建议迭代周期如下表所述：

迭代周期	迭代	目的	描述
架构开发（基线先行）	迭代 1	定义基线架构	此迭代贯穿 ADM 的业务架构阶段、信息系统架构阶段和技术架构阶段，聚焦于基线的定义。 机会、解决方案和迁移计划还被认为超出变革和试验可行性的聚焦点之外

Iteration Cycle	Iteration	Purpose	Description
Architecture Development（Baseline First）	Iteration 2	Define the Target Architecture and gaps	This iteration comprises a pass through the Business Architecture, Information Systems Architecture, and Technology Architecture phases of the ADM, focusing on definition of the target and analyzing gaps against the baseline. Opportunities, solutions, and migration plans are also considered to test viability
	Iteration *n*	Refine baseline, target, and gaps	Subsequent Architecture Development iterations attempt to correct and refine the target to achieve an outcome that is beneficial, feasible, and viable
Architecture Development (Target First)	Iteration 1	Define the Target Architecture	This iteration comprises a pass through the Business Architecture, Information Systems Architecture, and Technology Architecture phases of the ADM, focusing on definition of the target. Opportunities, solutions, and migration plans are also considered to drive out the focus for change and test feasibility
	Iteration 2	Define the Baseline Architecture and gaps	This iteration comprises a pass through the Business Architecture, Information Systems Architecture, and Technology Architecture phases of the ADM, focusing on definition of the baseline and analyzing gaps against the target. Opportunities, solutions, and migration plans are also considered to test viability
	Iteration *n*	Refine baseline, target, and gaps	Subsequent Architecture Development iterations attempt to correct and refine the target to achieve an outcome that is beneficial, feasible, and viable
Transition Planning	Iteration 1	Define and agree a set of improvement opportunities, aligned against a provisional Transition Architecture	The initial iteration of Transition Planning seeks to gain buy-in to a portfolio of solution opportunities in the Opportunities & Solutions phase of ADM. This iteration also delivers a provisional Migration Plan

迭代周期	迭代	目的	描述
架构开发（基线先行）	迭代 2	定义目标架构和差距	此迭代包括贯穿 ADM 的业务架构阶段、信息系统架构阶段和技术架构阶段，聚焦于目标的定义并根据基线来分析差距。 机会、解决方案和迁移计划也被考虑用于测试（目标架构）生命力
	迭代 n	细化基线、目标和差距	后续架构开发迭代试图修正和细化目标，以达成一个有利的、可行的和有生命力的结果
架构开发（目标先行）	迭代 1	定义目标架构	此迭代包括贯穿 ADM 的业务架构阶段、信息系统架构阶段和技术架构阶段，聚焦于目标的定义。 机会、解决方案和迁移计划也被认为超出变更和试验可行性的焦点之外
	迭代 2	定义基线架构和差距	此迭代包括贯穿 ADM 的业务架构阶段、信息系统架构阶段和技术架构阶段，聚焦于基线的定义并根据目标分析差距。 机会、解决方案和迁移计划还被认为用于检验（目标架构）生命力
	迭代 n	细化基线、目标和差距	后续架构开发迭代试图修正和细化目标，以达成一个有利的、可行的和有生命力的结果
过渡规划	迭代 1	定义并议定一系列改进机会，根据临时过渡架构使其对准	过渡规划的初始迭代寻求获得对 ADM 的机会和解决方案阶段中的解决方案机会项目谱系的认同。 此迭代也交付一份临时迁移计划

Iteration Cycle	Iteration	Purpose	Description
Transition Planning	Iteration *n*	Agree the Transition Architecture, refining the identified improvement opportunities to fit	Subsequent iterations of Transition Planning seek to refine the migration plan, feeding back issues into the Opportunities & Solutions phase for refinement
Architecture Governance	Iteration 1	Mobilize architecture governance and change management processes	The initial Architecture Governance iteration establishes a process for governance of change and also puts in place the appropriate people, processes, and technology to support managed access to and change of the defined architecture
	Iteration *n*	Carry out architecture governance and change control	Subsequent iterations of the Architecture Governance cycle focus on periodic reviews of change initiatives to resolve issues and ensure compliance. Results of a change request may trigger another phase to be revisited; for example, feeding back a new requirement to the Preliminary Phase to improve the Architecture Capability, or a new requirement for the architecture into the Architecture Development phases

19.6 Conclusions

All of these techniques are valid applications of the ADM. Combined together, they represent how the ADM can be used in practice. The ADM should always be used in an iterative process. How this process is exercised is dependent upon organizational factors. Particular factors for consideration include:

- **The formality and nature of established process checkpoints within the organization.** Does the organization mandate that certain groups of activities are carried out between checkpoints? Does the organization mandate that certain activities must be finalized before other activities can be carried out?
- **The level of stakeholder involvement expected within the process.** Are stakeholders expecting to be closely involved within the development of a solution, or are they expecting to see a complete set of deliverables for review and approval?
- **The number of teams involved and the relationships between different teams.** Is the entire architecture being developed by a specific team, or is there a hierarchy of teams with governance relationships between them?
- **The maturity of the solution area and the expected amount of rework and refinement required to arrive at an acceptable solution.** Can the solution be achieved in a single pass, or does it require extensive proof-of-concept and prototyping work to evolve a suitable outcome?

迭代周期	迭代	目的	描述
过渡规划	迭代 *n*	议定过渡架构，细化识别的改进机会以达到适配	过渡规划的后续迭代寻求细化迁移计划，将议题反馈到机会和解决方案阶段来细化。
架构治理	迭代 1	动员架构治理以及变更管理流程	初始架构治理迭代建立一个变更管控流程并将适当的人员、流程和技术落实到位，以支持对已定义架构的管理访问和变更
	迭代 *n*	执行架构治理及变更控制	架构治理周期的后续迭代聚焦于变革举措的定期审查，以解决问题并确保合规性。变更要求的结果可能触发回顾另一个阶段；例如，将新的需求反馈到预备阶段以改进架构能力，或将架构的新需求反馈到架构开发阶段

19.6 结论

所有这些技巧是 ADM 的有效应用。这些技巧组合在一起表达如何在实践中应用 ADM。ADM 应始终在迭代流程中使用。如何演练此流程，取决于多个组织因素。特定考量因素包括：

- **组织内建立的流程检查点的形式和本质**。组织是否要求在检查点之间进行某些活动群组？组织是否要求在进行其他活动之前必须最终确定某些活动？
- **利益攸关者在流程内的预期参与度**。利益攸关者是否期望紧密参与解决方案的开发，或其是否期望看到一整套用于审视和批准的交付物？
- **参与的团队数量及不同团队之间的关系**。整个架构是否正由特定团队开发，或是否存在互相具有治理关系的团队的层级结构？
- **解决方案领域的成熟度及获得可接受的解决方案所需的返工和细化的预期工作量**。解决方案是否能够获得一次性通过，或其是否需要大量的方案论证和原型构建工作以演进到合适的结果？

- **Attitude to risk.** Does the organizational culture react negatively to partially complete work products being circulated? Does the organizational culture require solutions to be proved in a trial environment before they can be implemented for mainstream application?
- **The class of engagement.** What is the context for development of the enterprise architecture?

- **对风险的态度**。组织文化对正在循环的部分完成的工作产物是否反应消极？组织文化是否需要在主流应用实施之前将解决方案在试用环境中得到证明？
- **介入类别**。Enterprise Architecture 开发的背景环境是什么？

Chapter 20 Applying the ADM across the Architecture Landscape

20.1 Overview

In a typical enterprise, many architectures will be described in the Architecture Landscape at any point in time. Some architectures will address very specific needs; others will be more general. Some will address detail; some will provide a big picture. To address this complexity TOGAF uses the concepts of levels and the Enterprise Continuum to provide a conceptual framework for organizing the Architecture Landscape. These concepts are tightly linked with organizing actual content in the Architecture Repository and any architecture partitions discussed in Part V

20.2 Architecture Landscape

Levels provide a framework for dividing granular the Architecture Landscape into three levels of granularity:

1. **Strategic Architecture** provides an organizing framework for operational and change activity and allows for direction setting at an executive level.
2. **Segment Architecture** provides an organizing framework for operational and change activity and allows for direction setting and the development of effective architecture roadmaps at a program or portfolio level.
3. **Capability Architecture** provides an organizing framework for change activity and the development of effective architecture roadmaps realizing capability increments.

Figure 20-1 shows a summary of the classification model for Architecture Landscapes.

第 20 章 贯穿架构全景应用 ADM

20.1 概述

在一个典型的 ENTERPRISE 中，在任何时点都有许多架构在架构全景中被描述。一些架构将应对非常特定的需要；其他架构则更具有普遍性。一些架构涉及细节，另一些则提供“大图像”。为应对复杂性，TOGAF 使用层级的概念和 ENTERPRISE 的连续统一体为搭建架构全景提供一个概念框架。这些概念与第五部分所论述的在架构库和架构划分中所组织的实际内容紧密联系。

20.2 架构全景

层级提供了一个框架，将架构全景分成三个粒度层级：

1. **战略架构**为运行和变革活动提供一个组织框架并且允许在一个执行层级上进行方向设置。
2. **分部架构**为运行和变革活动提供一个组织框架并且允许在项目群或项目谱系层级上进行方向设置和开发有效的架构路线图。
3. **能力架构**为变革活动和实现能力增量的有效架构路线图的开发提供一个组织框架。

图 20-1 展示了架构全景的分类模型概要。

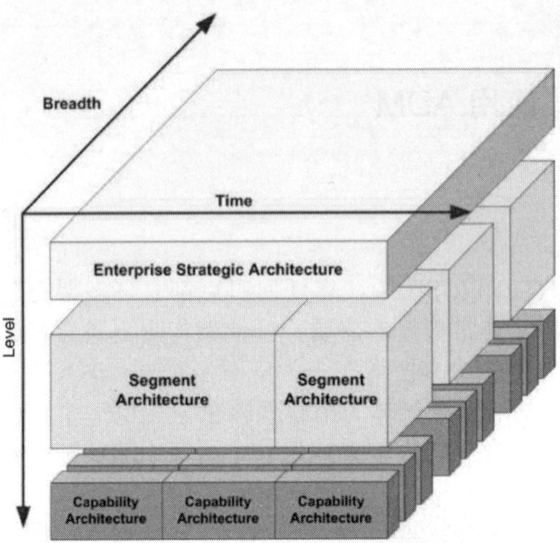

Figure 20-1 Summary Classification Model for Architecture Landscapes

The Architecture Continuum provides a method of dividing each level of the Architecture Landscape (see Section 39.4.1) by abstraction. It offers a consistent way to define and understand the generic rules, representations, and relationships in an architecture, including traceability and derivation relationships. The Architecture Continuum shows the relationships from foundation elements to organization-specific architecture, as shown in Figure 20-2.

The Architecture Continuum is a useful tool to discover commonality and eliminate unnecessary redundancy.

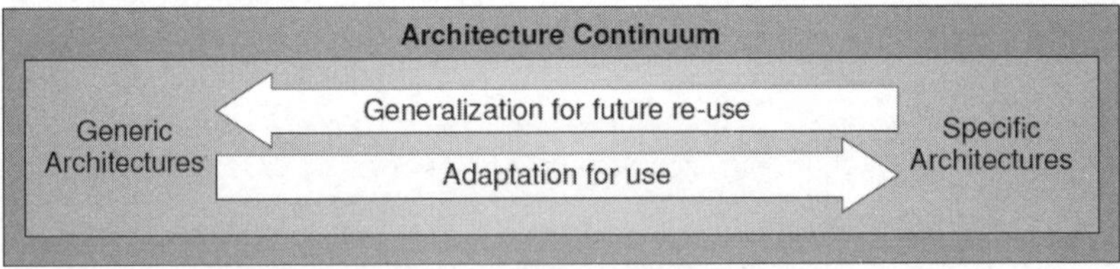

Figure 20-2 Summary of Architecture Continuum

Levels and the Architecture Continuum provide a comprehensive mechanism to describe and classify the Architecture Landscape. These concepts can be used to organize the Architecture Landscape into a set of related architectures with:

- Manageable complexity for each individual architecture or solution.
- Defined groupings.

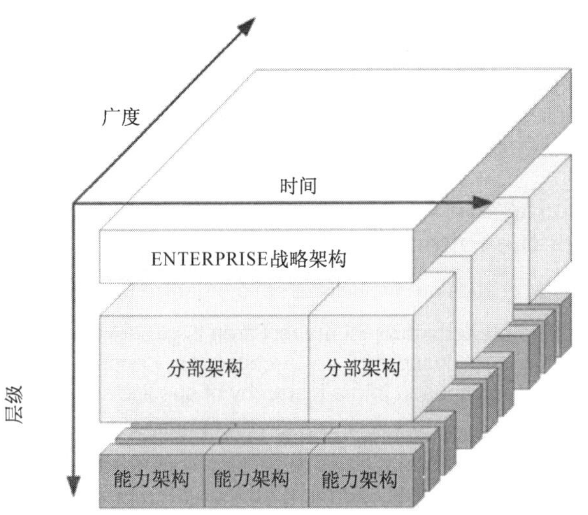

图 20-1 架构全景的概要分类模型

架构连续统一体提供一种方法，通过抽象方式来划分架构全景（见 39.4.1 节）各层级。它提供一种一致的方式来定义并理解架构中的一般规则、表示法和关系，包括可追溯性关系和衍生关系。架构连续统一体表示出了从基础元素到特定于组织的架构的关系，如图 20-2 所示。

架构连续统一体是一种可发现公共性并消除不必要冗余的有用工具。

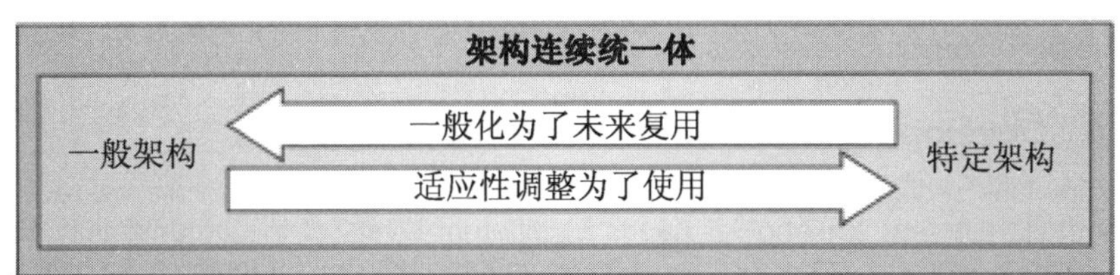

图 20-2 架构连续统一体的概要

层级和架构连续统一体提供一种可描述架构全景并将其分类的综合机制。这些概念可用来搭建架构全景，形成一系列具有下列内容的相关架构：

- 每个单独架构或解决方案可管理的复杂性。
- 已定义的分组。

- Defined hierarchies and navigation structures.
- Appropriate processes, roles, and responsibilities attached to each grouping.

There is no definitive organizing model for architecture, as each enterprise should adopt a model that reflects its own operating model.

20.3 Organizing the Architecture Landscape to Understand the State of the Enterprise

The following characteristics are typically used to organize the Architecture Landscape:

- Breadth: The breadth (subject matter) area is generally the primary organiz-ing characteristic for describing an Architecture Landscape. Architectures are functionally decomposed into a hierarchy of specific subject areas or segments.
- Depth: With broader subject areas, less detail is needed to ensure that the architecture has a manageable size and complexity. More specific subject matter areas will generally permit (and require) more detailed architectures.
- Time: For a specific breadth and depth an enterprise can create a Baseline Architecture and a set of Target Architectures that stretch into the future. Broader and less detailed architectures will generally be valid for longer periods of time and can provide a vision for the enterprise that stretches further into the future.
- Recency: Finally, each architecture view will progress through a development cycle where it increases in accuracy until finally approved. After approval, an architecture will begin to decrease in accuracy if not actively maintained. In some cases recency may be used as an organizing factor for historic architectures.

Using the criteria above, architectures can be grouped into Strategic, Segment, and Capability Architecture levels, as described in Figure 20-1.

20.4 Developing Architectures at Different Levels

The previous sections have identified that different types of architecture are required to address different stakeholder needs at different levels of the organization. Each architecture typically does not exist in isolation and must therefore sit within a governance hierarchy. Broad, summary architectures set the direction for narrow and detailed architectures.

A number of techniques can be employed to use the ADM as a process that supports such hierarchies of architectures. Essentially there are two strategies that can be applied:

1. Architectures at different levels can be developed through iterations within a single cycle of the ADM process.
2. Architectures at different levels can be developed through a hierarchy of ADM processes, executed concurrently.

At the extreme ends of the scale, either of these two options can be fully adopted. In practice, an architect is likely to need to blend elements of each to fit the exact requirements of their Request for Architecture Work. Each of these approaches is described in Chapter 19.

- 已定义的层级结构和导航结构。
- 每个分组所附带的适当的流程、角色和责任。

没有确定的架构的组织模型，因为每个 ENTERPRISE 应采用一种能够反映其自身运行模型的模型。

20.3 绘编架构全景以理解 ENTERPRISE 的状态

下列特征通常被用于搭建架构全景：

- 广度：广度（主题内容）区域通常是用于描述架构全景的主要组织特征。架构在功能上分解成特定主题区域或分部的层级结构。
- 深度：对于更广泛的主题领域，需要较少细节来确保架构具有可管理的尺寸和复杂性。更具体的主题内容领域通常允许（并且需要）更为详细的架构。
- 时间：为了特定的广度和深度，ENTERPRISE 可创建一个基线架构和一系列延伸到未来的目标架构。较为广泛且不甚详细的架构通常有效期更长，并且能够为进一步向未来延伸的 ENTERPRISE 提供愿景。
- 新近性：最后，每个架构视图将经历一个开发周期以提高其准确度直至最终批准。经批准后，如果未积极地维护，架构准确度将开始降低。某些情况下，新近性可被用作历史架构的组成因素。

使用以上准则，架构可被分成战略架构层级、分部架构层级和能力架构层级，如图 20-1 所述。

20.4 开发不同层级的架构

前几节已识别了需要不同类型架构在组织不同层级上应对不同利益攸关者的需要。典型情况下，每个架构并非孤立存在，因此，必须位于一个治理层级结构内。广泛且概括性的架构为有限且详细的架构设定了方向。

可利用多种技巧，将 ADM 用作一个支持这种架构层级结构的流程。本质上，可采用两种策略：

1. 可在 ADM 流程的单一周期内，通过迭代的方式开发不同层级的架构。
2. 可通过 ADM 流程的层级结构以并行的方式开发不同层级的架构。

在极端情况下，可完全采用这两个选项中的任意一个。实际上，一个架构师可能需要混合使用这两种方法的元素，以匹配其架构工作要求书的确切需求。第 19 章中分别描述了这些方法。

Chapter 21
Security Architecture and the ADM

21.1 Overview

The goal of this chapter is to explain the security considerations that need to be addressed during application of the TOGAF Architecture Development Method (ADM).

21.2 Introduction

Architecture development methods are tools in the hands of the security practitioner to be used to create best practice and organization-specific security capability.

The guidance included here is intended to help both enterprise architects and security practitioners to avoid missing critical security concerns.

This chapter informs the enterprise architect of what the security architect will need to carry out during the security architecture work.

Often the security architecture is treated as a separate architecture domain within the enterprise architecture while needing to be fully integrated in it. The focus of the security architect is enforcement of security policies of the enterprise without inhibiting value.

Security architectures generally have the following characteristics:

- Security architecture has its own discrete security methodology.
- Security architecture composes its own discrete views and viewpoints.
- Security architecture addresses non-normative flows through systems and among applications.
- Security architecture introduces its own normative flows through systems and among applications.
- Security architecture introduces unique, single-purpose components in the design.
- Security architecture calls for its own unique set of skills and competencies of the enterprise and IT architects.

第 21 章 安保架构和 ADM

21.1 概述

本章的目标是解释需要在应用 TOGAF 架构开发方法（ADM）过程中解决的安保考量因素。

21.2 简介

架构开发方法是安保实践者所掌握的用于创建最佳实践和组织特定安保能力的工具。

此处包含的引导，旨在帮助 ENTERPRISE 架构师和安保实践者避免遗漏关键的安保关注点。

本章向 ENTERPRISE 架构师告知安保架构师在安保架构工作中需要实施的内容。

通常，安保架构被视为 Enterprise Architecture 内的一个独立架构领域，同时需要完全整合在 Enterprise Architecture 内。安保架构师的聚焦点是，在不抑制价值的情况下执行 ENTERPRISE 的安保策略。

安保架构通常具有下列特性：

- 安保架构具有自己的独立安全方法论。
- 安保架构构成其自己的独立视图和视角。
- 安保架构应对跨系统及在应用之间的非规范流。
- 安保架构引入其自己的跨系统及在应用之间的规范流。
- 安保架构在设计中引入独特的、专用的组件。
- 安保架构需要具有其自身的独特技能和才干 ENTERPRISE 和 IT 架构师。

21.3 Guidance on Security for the Architecture Domains

Security concerns are pervasive throughout the architecture domains and in all phases of the architecture development. Security is called out separately because it is infrastructure that is rarely visible to the business function. Its fundamental purpose is to protect the value of the systems and information assets of the enterprise. Often the nature of security in the enterprise is that it is deemed successful if either nothing happens that is visible to the user or other observer, and/or no damage or losses occur to the enterprise. For example, the data in a customer records database is not leaked or damaged — or an intangible issue such as the company name appears in an article in the news saying that its data systems had been compromised.

The security architecture does have its own single-purpose components and is experienced as a quality of systems in the architecture. The Enterprise Security view of the architecture has its own unique building blocks, collaborations, and interfaces. These security-unique elements must interface with the business systems in a balanced and cost-effective way, so as to maintain the security policies of the enterprise, yet not interfere with system operations and functions. It is least costly and most effective to plan for and implement security-specific functions in the Target Architecture as early as possible in the development cycle to avoid costly retrofit or rework because required building blocks for security were not added or used during systems development and deployment. The approach of the security architect considers not only the normal flow of the application, but also the abnormal flows, failure modes, and ways the systems and applications can be interrupted and fail.

All groups of stakeholders in the enterprise will have security concerns and it is desirable to bring a security architect into the project as early as possible. Throughout the phases of the ADM, guidance will be offered on security-specific information which should be gathered, steps which should be taken, and artifacts which should be created. Architecture decisions related to security should be traceable to business and policy decisions and their risk management.

The generally accepted areas of concern for the security architect are:

- Authentication: The substantiation of the identity of a person or entity related to the enterprise or system in some way.
- Authorization: The definition and enforcement of permitted capabilities for a person or entity whose identity has been established.
- Audit: The ability to provide forensic data attesting that the systems have been used in accordance with stated security policies.
- Assurance: The ability to test and prove that the enterprise architecture has the security attributes required to uphold the stated security policies.
- Availability: The ability of the enterprise to function without service interrupttion or depletion despite abnormal or malicious events.
- Asset Protection: The protection of information assets from loss or unintended disclosure, and resources from unauthorized and unintended use.
- Administration: The ability to add and change security policies, add or change how policies are implemented in the enterprise, and add or change the persons or entities related to the systems.
- Risk Management: The organization's attitude and tolerance for risk. (This risk management is different from the special definition found in financial markets and insurance institutions that have formal risk management departments.)

21.3 关于架构领域安保性的引导

安保问题在整个架构领域和在所有架构开发阶段中是普遍存在的。由于安保性是基础设施且对于业务功能几乎不可见，因此，被单独提出。其根本目的是保护 ENTERPRISE 的系统和信息资产的价值。ENTERPRISE 的安保本质通常在于，如果没有发生用户或其他观察者可见的问题，和/或 ENTERPRISE 没有发生损坏或损失，则是成功的。例如，客户记录数据库中的数据未被泄露或损坏——或诸如公司名称出现在一篇称其数据系统已被损害的新闻文章中等无形问题。

安保架构确实具有其自己的专用组件并且被视为架构内系统的一种质量。架构的 ENTERPRISE 安保性视图具有其自己的独特构建块、协作关系和界面。这些独特的安保性元素必须以平衡且具有成本效益的方式与业务系统交互，以便维护 ENTERPRISE 的安保策略，且不干扰系统运行和功能。由于在系统开发和部署过程中，未添加或使用安保性所需的构建块，因此为避免昂贵的改造或返工而尽早在开发周期中计划并实施目标架构中特定的安保性的功能，是成本最低且最为有效的。安保架构师的实施途径不仅考虑到应用的常规流，而且考虑到异常流、失效模式以及系统和应用可被中断和失效的方式。

ENTERPRISE 中各组利益攸关者都具有安保关注点，使安保架构师尽快投入到项目中是非常值得的。在 ADM 的阶段，为应收集的特定的安保性的信息、应采取的措施和应创建的制品提供引导。与安保性有关的架构决策应可追溯到业务决策和方针决策及其风险管理。

安保架构师普遍接受的关注领域是：

- 认证：以某种方式对与 ENTERPRISE 或系统相关的某个人或实体的身份的证实。
- 授权：对已经确认身份的某个人或实体的所准许能力的定义和执行。
- 审计：提供证明系统的使用符合规定安保策略的法定数据的能力。
- 保证：试验并证明 Enterprise Architecture 具有支撑规定的安保策略所需安全属性的能力。
- 可用性：尽管发生异常或恶意事件，ENTERPRISE 在运行中也不会出现服务中断或丧失的能力。
- 资产保护：使信息资产免于遭受损失或非预期的泄漏以及使资源免于未授权和非预期的使用的保护。
- 管理：增加和变更安保策略、增加或变更策略在 ENTERPRISE 中的实施方式、以及增加或变更与系统相关的个人或实体的能力。
- 风险管理：组织对风险的态度和承受能力。（此风险管理不同于具有正式风险管理部门的金融市场和保险机构中所给出的特殊定义。）

Typical security architecture artifacts would include:

- Business rules regarding handling of data/information assets.
- Written and published security policy.
- Codified data/information asset ownership and custody.
- Risk analysis documentation.
- Data classification policy documentation.

21.4 ADM Architecture Requirements Management

The security policy and security standards become part of the enterprise requirements management process. Security policy is established at an executive level of the business, is long-lived, and resistant to whimsical change. Security policy is not tied to any specific technology. Once the security policies are established, they can be referred to as requirements for all architecture projects.

Security standards change more frequently and state technology preferences used to support security policies. New technologies that support the implementation of security policies in a better way can be adopted as needed. The improvements can be in reduced costs or increased benefits. Security standards will manifest themselves as security-related building blocks in the Enterprise Continuum. Security patterns for deploying these security-related building blocks are referred to in the Security Guidance to Phase E.

New security requirements arise from many sources:

1. A new statutory or regulatory mandate.
2. A new threat realized or experienced.
3. A new IT architecture initiative discovers new stakeholders and/or new requirements.

In the case where 1. and 2. above occur, these new requirements would be drivers for input to the change management system discussed in Phase H. A new architecture initiative might be launched to examine the existing infrastructure and applications to determine the extent of changes required to meet the new demands. In the case of 3. above, a new security requirement will enter the requirements management system.

Is our security good?

This question inevitably comes from management to the security architect. No security measures are ever perfect, and the potential exists for the amount of money and effort expended to become very large for little additional return. Security assurance testing should be in place so that the security systems can be measured to ensure that they keep the security policies for which they were designed. Security policy audits should be held and might be mandatory by statute or regulation. These security audits and possible security policy changes are the exact reason why separation of policy enforcement from application code is so strongly emphasized.

典型的安保架构制品包括：

- 关于处理数据/信息资产的业务规则。
- 书面的和发布的安保方针。
- 编码数据/信息资产所有权和保管。
- 风险分析文件。
- 数据分类策略文件。

21.4 ADM 架构需求管理

安保策略和安保标准成了 ENTERPRISE 需求管理流程的一部分。安保策略在业务的执行层级上制定，其长期有效且不受反复无常变化的影响。安保策略并非与特定技术绑定。一旦安保策略被制定，便可被称为所有架构项目的需求。

安保标准变化日益频繁并且规定了用于支持安保策略的技术偏好。可根据需要，采用以更好的方式支持安保策略实施的新技术。这种改进可降低成本或增加效益。安保标准将在 ENTERPRISE 的连续统一体中作为安保相关构建块来表示。部署这些安保相关构建块的安保特征模式在阶段 E 的安保引导中提及。

新的安保需求由多个源头产生：

1. 新的法令或法规要求。
2. 所意识到的或经历的新威胁。
3. 新的 IT 架构举措发现新的利益攸关者和/或新需求。

在上述第 1 项和第 2 项发生时，这些新需求将成为阶段 H 中所论述的变更管理系统的输入的驱动因素。为了审查现有的基础设施和应用来确定满足新要求所需变更的程度，可以发起一项新的架构举措。在上述第 3 项的情况下，一个新的安保需求将输入到需求管理系统中。

我们的安保性是否良好？

这个问题不可避免地来自对安保架构师的管理。没有任何安保措施是始终完美的，并且存在投入大量金钱和工作却只得到很少的附加回报的可能性。应采用安保保证试验以便衡量安保系统，确保其保持为其设计的安保方针。应根据法令或法规进行安保方针审计，并且可能是强制性的。这些安保审计和可能的安保方针变更是如此着重强调应将策略执行与应用系统代码分离的确切原因。

Nothing useful can be said about a security measure outside the context of an application, or a system and its environment

The efficacy of a security measure is considered in relation to the risk it mitigates. An enterprise cannot determine how much it will be willing to spend on securing an asset until it understands the asset value. For example, the use of that asset in an application and the concomitant risk the asset is exposed to as a result, will determine the true requirements for security. Additionally, the organization's tolerance for risk is a factor. In other words, the question asked should not be: "Is it secure?" but rather: "Is it secure enough?" The latter is ultimately a question to be answered by risk analysis.

21.5 Preliminary Phase

Scope the enterprise organizations impacted by the security architecture

- Identify core enterprise (units) — those who are most affected and achieve most value from the security work.
- Identify soft enterprise (units) — those who will see change to their capability and work with core units but are otherwise not directly affected.
- Identify extended enterprise (units) — those units outside the scoped enter-prise who will need to enhance their security architecture for interoperability purposes.
- Identify communities involved (enterprises) — those stakeholders who will be affected by security capabilities and who are in groups of communities.
- Identify the security governance involved, including legal frameworks and geographies(enterprises).

If the business model of the organization does encompass federation with other organizations, the extent of the security federation should be established at this point in the process. Contractual federation agreements should be examined for their security implications and agreements. It may be necessary to establish joint architec-ture meetings with other members ofa federation to establish interfaces and protocols for exchange of security information related to federated identity, authentication, and authorization.

Define and document applicable regulatory and security policy requirements

The framework and principles rarely change, and so the security implications called out in the objectives of this phase should be fairly straightforward. A written security policy for the organization must be in place, and there should be regular notification and education established for employees. ISO/IEC 17799: 2005 is a good place to start the formation of a security policy, and can be used to assess the security readiness of an organization. Without a written and published security policy, enforcement is difficult. Security policies refer to many aspects of security for the organization — such as physical premises security — that are remotely related to security of systems and applications. The security policy should be examined to find relevant sections, and updated if necessary. Architecture constraints established in the security policy must be communicated to the other members of the architecture team.

In a similar fashion, there may be regulatory requirements that specify obligations the system must fulfil or actions that must be taken. Whether the system will be subject to regulation will depend upon the functionality of the system and the data collected or maintained. In addition, the jurisdiction where the system or service is deployed, where the users reside, or under which the deploying entity is chartered or incorporated will inform this decision. It may be wise to obtain legal counsel regarding these obligations at the outset of activities.

脱离应用背景环境或系统及其环境的背景，无法对安保措施进行任何有用的说明

安保措施的效能被认为与其减轻的风险有关。一个 ENTERPRISE 需理解资产价值后，才能够确定愿意花费多少资金来保护资产。例如，资产在应用中的使用和该资产因此所面临的伴随风险将决定安保性的真正需求。此外，组织对风险的承受能力是一个因素。换言之，所提出的问题不应是“是否安全” 而是“是否足够安全？”，后者是风险分析最终所要回答的问题。

21.5 预备阶段

界定受安保架构影响的 ENTERPRISE 组织的范围

- 识别核心 ENTERPRISE（单元）——那些最受影响且从安保工作中达成最大价值的 ENTERPRISE。
- 识别“软”ENTERPRISE（单元）——那些可以看到其能力变化并与核心单元合作但不直接受到影响的 ENTERPRISE。
- 识别扩展 ENTERPRISE（单元）——那些为实现互用性而需增强其安保架构的界定的有限范围的 ENTERPRISE 之外的单元。
- 识别所涉及的群体（ENTERPRISE）——那些受到安保能力影响且处于各组群体之中的利益攸关者。
- 识别所涉及的安保治理，包括法律框架和地理位置（ENTERPRISE）。

如果组织的业务模型的确包括与其他组织的联盟，应在流程中就这一点确定安保联盟的程度。应针对安保内涵和协议审查契约联盟协议。可能有必要与联盟其他成员建立联合架构会议，以便为与联邦身份识别、认证和授权有关的安保信息的交换建立界面和协议。

定义适用的法规要求和安保策略需求并将其文件化

框架和原则很少变化，因此，在该阶段目的中相呼应的安保内涵应是相当直接的。组织的书面安保方针必须到位，并且应为雇员进行定期通知和培训。ISO/IEC 17799:2005 是形成安保方针的良好起点，并且可用来评估组织的安保准备度。如果没有书面发布的安保策略，则难以执行。安保方针涉及组织安保性的多个方面——例如，物理场所安保性——这些与系统和应用的安保性几乎不相关。审查安保方针以便找出相关部分，并在必要时进行更新。安保方针中建立的架构约束必须传达给架构团队的其他成员。

以此类推，可能具有法规要求，使得规定系统必须履行的职责或必须采取的行动。系统是否将受到法规的制约，取决于系统的功能性和所收集或维护的数据。此外，系统或服务在哪里部署，用户在哪里驻留或者哪个部署实体被许可或合并的管辖权将为决策提供依据。在活动开始时获得关于这些义务的法律指导可能是明智的。

Define the required security capability as part of Architecture Capability

Agreement on the role of the security architect in the enterprise architecture process and in the architecture and IT governance should also be established. Security considerations can conflict with functional considerations and a security advocate is required to ensure that all issues are addressed and conflicts of interest do not prevent explicit consideration of difficult issues. Executive policy decisions should be established at this point about what security policies can be negotiable and which policies must be enforced for regulatory or statutory reasons.

Implement security architecture tools

The level of formality used to define and manage security architecture content will be highly dependent on the scale, sophistication, and culture of the security architecture function.

The approach to security tools may be based on relatively informal usage of standard office productivity applications, or may be based on a customized deployment of specialist security architecture tools and techniques.

21.5.1 Security Inputs

- Written security policy
- Relevant statutes
- List of applicable jurisdictions

21.5.2 Security Outputs

- List of applicable regulations
- List of applicable security policies
- Security team roster
- List of security assumptions and boundary conditions

21.6 Phase A: Architecture Vision

Security considerations have an impact on Phases A to H of the TOGAF ADM. The following security specifics appropriate to the security architecture must be addressed within each phase in addition to the generic phase activities.

The steps of the Architecture Vision phase are applicable to ensuring that security requirements are addressed in subsequent phases of the ADM. Security considerations will have an effect on the enterprise such that all enterprise architecture development needs to be informed and utilize the security policy, constraints, governance, artifacts, and building blocks.

After establishing any enterprise architecture project, the following specific security-related activities need to be undertaken.

Definition of relevant stakeholders and discovery of their concerns and objectives will require development of a high-level scenario. Key business requirements will also be established through this early scenario work. The TOGAF ADM business scenario process may be useful here and at later stages.

将所需安保能力定义为架构能力的一部分

还应就安保架构师在 Enterprise Architecture 流程和在架构及 IT 治理中的角色达成一致意见。安保考量因素可能与功能考量因素冲突，并且安保倡议者需要确保所有问题得到解决且利益冲突不会妨碍对困难问题的明确考量因素。应在这一点上就何种安保方针可协商和哪些方针必须由于法规或法令原因得以执行而确定执行方针决策。

实施安保架构工具

用来定义和管理安保架构内容的正式程度将高度依赖于安保架构功能的规模、复杂性和文化。

安保工具的实施途径可能以标准办公效率应用的相对非正式使用为基础，或可能以专家安保架构工具和技巧的自定义部署为基础。

21.5.1 安保输入

- 书面安保方针
- 相关法令
- 适用管辖权的列表

21.5.2 安保输出

- 适用法规的列表
- 适用安保方针的列表
- 安保团队名册
- 安保假设和边界条件的列表

21.6 阶段 A：架构愿景

安保考量因素对 TOGAF ADM 的阶段 A～阶段 H 产生影响。除了一般阶段活动之外，还必须在各阶段涉及下列适于安保架构的安保细节。

架构愿景阶段的步骤适用于确保安保需求在 ADM 的后续阶段得到应对。安保考量因素将对 ENTERPRISE 产生影响，因此，所有 Enterprise Architecture 开发均需被告知，并且需要利用安保方针、约束、治理、制品和构建块。

在建立 Enterprise Architecture 项目后，需要着手下列与安保相关的特定活动。

需要开发高层级场景来定义相关利益攸关者并发现其关注点和目的。关键业务需求还将通过早期场景工作来确定。TOGAF ADM 业务场景流程可能在此处和后期有用。

Obtain management support for security measures

In similar fashion to obtaining management recognition and endorsement for the overall architecture project, so too endorsement of the security-related aspects of the architecture development effort should be obtained. Recognition that the project might have development and infrastructure impact that are not readily visible by looking solely at the systems in question should be made clear. Thorough consideration and mitigation of issues related to risk and security may be perceived as a waste of resources and time; the level of management support must be understood and communicated throughout the team.

Define necessary security-related management sign-off milestones of this architecture development cycle

The traceability of security-related architecture decisions should be documented and the appropriate executives and line management who need to be informed of security-related aspects of the project need to be identified and the frequency of reporting should be established. It should be recognized that the tension between delivery of new business function and enforcement of security policies does exist, and that a process for resolving such disputes that arise should be established early in the project. Such tensions often have the result of putting the security architect seemingly "in the way of completing the project". It needs to be understood by management and the other architects involved that the role of the security architect is to safeguard the assets of the enterprise.

Determine and document applicable disaster recovery or business continuity plans/requirements

Any existing disaster recovery and business continuity plans must be understood and their relationship with the planned system defined and documented.

Identify and document the anticipated physical/business/regulatory environment(s) in which the system(s) will be deployed

All architecture decisions must be made within the context of the environments within which the system will be placed and operate. Physical environments that should be documented may include battlefield environments, commercial environments, outdoor environments, mobile environments, and the like. In a similar fashion, the business environment must be defined. Potential business environments may include different assumptions regarding users and interfaces, and those users or interfaces may carry the onus of regulatory environments in which the system must operate (users under the age of thirteen in the US, for example).

Determine and document the criticality of the system: safety-critical/mission-critical/non-critical

Safety-critical systems place lives in danger in case of failure or malfunction.

Mission-critical systems place money, market share, or capital at risk in case of failure.

Non-critical systems have little or no consequence in case of failure.

获取对安保测度的管理层支持

采用与获取管理层对总体架构项目的认可和批准相似的方式，获得对架构开发工作的安保性相关方面的批准。应清楚认识到，项目可能具有开发和基础设施的影响，这在单独观察有疑问的系统时是无法充分可见的。对与风险和安保性有关的问题进行全面考虑和缓解可能被视为浪费资源和时间；必须在整个小组中理解并传达管理层支持的程度。

在架构开发周期中定义必需的安保性相关的管理层签署同意的里程碑

安保性相关架构决策的可追溯性应被文件化，需要被告知，项目安保性相关方面的相应执行层和各级管理层都需要被识别出来并且应确定报告的频率。应认识到，在交付新的业务功能和执行安保方针之间确实存在紧张关系，并且应认识到，解决出现的这些争端的流程应在项目初期建立。这种紧张关系通常导致安保架构师似乎“妨碍了项目的完成”。管理层和其他参与的架构师需要理解安保架构师的角色是保护 ENTERPRISE 的资产。

确定适用的灾难恢复或业务连续性计划/需求并将其文件化

必须理解现有灾难恢复和业务连续性计划，并且定义和文件化其与计划系统的关系。

识别将要部署的系统的预期物理/业务/法规环境，并将其文件化

所有架构决策都必须在将要布置且运行系统的环境背景下做出。应被文件化的物理环境可能包括战场环境、商业环境、户外环境、移动环境等等。与此相似，必须定义业务环境。潜在业务环境可能包括关于用户和界面的不同假设，以及那些可能对系统运行必须所处的法规环境承担责任的用户或界面（例如美国 13 岁以下的用户）。

确定系统的关键性：安全关键性/任务关键性/非关键性，并将其文件化

安全关键性系统如果失效或故障会危及生命。

任务关键性系统如果失效会危及资金、市场份额或资本。

非关键性系统如果失效引发很少或不会产生任何后果。

21.6.1 Security Inputs

- List of applicable security policies
- List of applicable jurisdictions
- Complete disaster recovery and business continuity plans

21.6.2 Security Outputs

- Physical security environment statement
- Business security environment statement
- Regulatory environment statement
- Security policy cover letter signed by CEO or delegate
- List of architecture development checkpoints for security sign-off
- List of applicable disaster recovery and business continuity plans
- Systems criticality statement

21.7 Phase B: Business Architecture

Determine who are the legitimate actors who will interact with the product/ service/process

Development of the business scenarios and subsequent high-level use-cases of the project concerned will bring to attention the people actors and system actors involved. Many subsequent decisions regarding authorization will rely upon a strong understanding of the intended users, administrators, and operators of the system, in addition to their expected capabilities and characteristics. It must be borne in mind that users may not be humans; software applications may be legitimate users. Those tending to administrative needs, such as backup operators, must also be identified, as must users outside boundaries of trust, such as Internet-based customers.

Assess and baseline current security-specific business processes (enhancement of existing objective)

The business process regarding how actors are vetted as proper users of the system should be documented. Consideration should also be made for actors from outside the organization who are proper users of the system. The outside entities will be determined from the high-level scenarios developed as part of Phase A.

Determine whom/how much it is acceptable to inconvenience in utilizing security measures

Security measures, while important, can impose burden on users and administrative personnel. Some will respond to that burden by finding ways to circumvent the measures. Examples include administrators finding ways to create “back doors” or customers choosing a competitor to avoid the perceived burden of the infrastructure. The trade-offs can require balancing security advantages against business advantages and demand informed judicious choice.

21.6.1 安保输入

- 适用安保方针的列表
- 适用管辖区的列表
- 完整的灾难恢复和业务连续性计划

21.6.2 安保输出

- 物理安保环境说明书
- 业务安保环境说明书
- 法规环境说明书
- CEO 或委托代表所签署的安保方针附函
- 针对安保性签署同意的架构开发检查点的列表
- 适用的灾难恢复和业务连续性计划的列表
- 系统关键性说明书

21.7 阶段 B：业务架构

确定将与产品/服务/流程交互的合法施动者

开发有关项目的业务场景和后续高层级用例将引起参与的人为施动者和系统施动者的注意。关于授权的多个后续决策将依靠对系统的指定用户、管理者和操作者及其预期的能力和特征的充分理解。必须记住用户可能并非人类，软件应用程序可能是合法用户。如同信任边界之外的用户（诸如基于互联网的客户）必须被识别一样，诸如备份操作人员的那些倾向于管理性需求的用户同样必须被识别。

评估当前安保特定的业务流程（现有目的的增强）并建立基线

关于施动者如何作为系统的适当用户进行审查的业务流程应被文件化。还应考虑来自组织外的作为系统适当用户的施动者。将根据作为阶段 A 的一部分进行开发的高层级场景确定外部实体。

确定在使用安保措施中带来的不便对谁/在多大程度上是可接受的

尽管安保措施很重要，却会为用户和管理人员增加负担。一些人员通过设法回避这些措施来应对负担。例如，管理人员设法创建“后门”或客户选择竞争者，避免已察觉的基础设施负担。做权衡可要求使安保优势与业务优势保持平衡并需要明智合理的选择。

Identify and document interconnecting systems beyond project control

Every cybernetic or business system must rely upon existing systems beyond the control of the project. These systems possess advantages and disadvantages, risks and benefits. Examples include the Domain Name System (DNS) that resolves computer and service names to Internet addresses, or paper currency issued by the local treasury. The address returned by the host or service DNS may not always be trustworthy; paper currency may not always be genuine, and recourse will vary in efficacy between jurisdictions. These interfaces must be understood and documented.

Determine the assets at risk if something goes wrong — "What are we trying to protect?"

Assets are not always tangible and are not always easy to quantify. Examples include: loss of life, loss of customer good will, loss of a AAA bond rating, loss of market share.

Determine the cost (both qualitative and quantitative) of asset loss/impact in failure cases

It must be remembered that those assets most challenging to quantify can be the most valuable and must not be neglected. Even qualitative estimates will prove valuable in assessing comparative risks.

Identify and document the ownership of assets

Assets may be owned by outside entities, or by inside entities. Inside entities may be owned by individuals or by organizations. Determine:

- Where trust is assumed
- How it is established
- How it is communicated

Always trace it to the real world; i.e.:

- Assessment (credit searches, personal vouching)
- Liability (monetary damages, jail terms, sanctions)

All security decisions rely upon trust that has been established in some fashion. No trust assumptions have any value if they cannot be rooted in real-world assessment and liability. In most business environments, trust is established through contracts that define liability where the trust is breached. The onus for assessing trust is the responsibility of those choosing to enter into the contracts and their legal counsel. It is important to note that technology (e.g., digital certificates, SAML, etc.) cannot create trust, but can only convey in the electronic world the trust that already exists in the real world through business relationships, legal agreements, and security policy consistencies.

Determine and document appropriate security forensic processes

To be able to enforce security policies, breaches of security need to be properly captured so that problem determination and possible policy or legal action can be taken against the entity causing the breach. Forensic practices suitable to provide evidence where necessary need to be established and documented. Security personnel should be trained to follow the forensic procedures and training material regarding the need to collect evidence should be considered for the standard security education given to employees.

识别项目控制范围之外的互连系统并将其文件化

每个控制系统或业务系统必须依赖项目控制范围之外的现有系统。这些系统有利有弊，有风险也有收益。例如，将计算机和服务名称解析成互联网地址的域名系统（DNS），或地方国库发行的纸币。通过主机或服务 DNS 返回的地址可能并不总是可信赖的；纸币可能并不总是真实的，并且追索权的效能在管辖区之间将有所不同。必须理解这些界面并将其文件化。

如果出现错误，确定有风险的资产——“我们在努力保护什么？”

资产并非始终有形且并不总是易于量化。例如，寿命损失、客户商誉的损失、AAA 债券评级的损失、市场份额的损失。

确定失效情况下的资产损失/影响的成本（定性和定量）

必须记住，那些最难以量化的资产可能是最有价值且不得忽视的。甚至定性评价在评估相对风险时是具有价值的。

识别资产所有权并将其文件化

资产可由外部实体或由内部实体所有。内部实体可由个人或由组织所有。确定以下内容：

- 在何处假设信任
- 如何建立信任
- 如何传达信任

始终将其追溯到真实世界；即：

- 评估（信用搜索、个人担保）
- 责任（货币损失、刑期、处罚）

所有安保决策依靠以某种方式建立的信任。如果信任假设不能植根于真实世界的评估和责任，则没有任何价值。在大多数业务环境中，通过定义在违背信任时所应承担责任的契约来建立信任。评估信任的责任是那些选择签订契约的人员及其法律顾问的职责。重要的是，注意技术（例如，数字证书、SAML 等）不能创建信任，而仅可通过业务关系、法律协议和安保方针一致性在电子世界中传达已经存在于真实世界中的信任。

确定适当的安保取证流程并将其文件化

为了能够执行安保策略，需要适当捕获安保违规行为，以便可对导致违规的实体进行问题确认并采取可能的方针或法律行为。需要建立适合于在必要时提供证据的法庭实践并将其文件化。为了遵守鉴定流程，安保人员应经过培训，并且应考虑将有关收集证据所需的培训资料提供给雇员进行标准安保教育。

Identify the criticality of the availability and correct operation of the overall service

The risks associated with loss of availability may have already been adequately considered in the foregoing mission-critical/safety-critical assessment.

Determine and document how much security (cost) is justified by the threats and the value of the assets at risk

A risk analysis (an understanding of the value of assets at risk and the likelihood of potential threats) provides an important guideline for investments in mitigation strategies for the identified threats.

Reassess and confirm Architecture Vision decisions

Business analysis involves a number of rigorous thought exercises and may call into question the initial assumptions identified in the Architecture Vision.

Assess alignment or conflict of identified security policies with business goals

The security policies identified in the Preliminary Phase may have provisions that are difficult or impossible to reconcile with the business goals in light of the identified risks. Possible responses include alteration of aspects of the business environment, modification of the intended user population, or technical mitigation of risks (addressed in Phase C).

Determine "what can go wrong?"

Perform a threat analysis that identifies the high-level threats bearing upon the system and their likelihood.

21.7.1 Security Inputs

- Initial business and regulatory security environment statements
- List of applicable disaster recovery and business continuity plans
- List of applicable security policies and regulations

21.7.2 Security Outputs

- List of forensic processes
- List of new disaster recovery and business continuity requirements
- Validated business and regulatory environment statements
- List of validated security policies and regulations
- List of target security processes
- List of baseline security processes
- List of security actors
- List of interconnecting systems
- Statement of security tolerance for each class of security actor

识别可用性的关键度临界点及修正整体服务的运行

在上述任务关键性/安全关键性的评估中，可能已充分考虑与损失可用性相关的风险。

由威胁和处于风险中的资产价值确定合理的安保性（成本）是多少，并将其文件化

风险分析（对处于危险中的资产价值和潜在威胁的可能性的一种理解）为在所识别威胁的缓解策略上的投资提供重要指南。

重新评估并确认架构愿景决策

业务分析涉及大量严格的思维训练并可质疑架构愿景中所识别的最初假设。

评估所识别的安保方针与业务目标的一致性或冲突

根据已识别的风险，在预备阶段中所识别的安保方针可能具有难以或不可能与业务目标相调和的规定。对比可能的响应包括业务环境多方面的变更、指定用户群的更改或风险的技术性缓解（在阶段 C 中应对）。

确定“什么可能出错？”

执行威胁分析，识别对系统及其可能性产生影响的高层级威胁。

21.7.1 安保输入

- 初始业务及法规安保环境说明书
- 适用灾难恢复和业务连续性计划的列表
- 适用的安保方针与规定的列表

21.7.2 安保输出

- 取证流程列表
- 新灾难恢复与业务连续性需求的列表
- 确认的业务与监管环境说明书
- 确认的安保方针和规定的列表
- 目标安保流程的列表
- 基线安保流程的列表
- 安保施动者的列表
- 互连系统的列表
- 各类安保施动者的安保容忍度说明书

- Asset list with values and owners
- List of trust paths
- Availability impact statement(s)
- Threat analysis matrix

21.8 Phase C: Information Systems Architectures

Assess and baseline current security-specific architecture elements (enhancement of existing objective)

A full inventory of architecture elements that implement security services must be compiled in preparation for a gap analysis.

Identify safe default actions and failure states

Every state change in any system is precipitated by some trigger. Commonly, an enumerated set of expected values of that trigger initiates a change in state. However, there are likely other potential trigger inputs that must be accommodated in non-normative cases. Additionally, system failure may take place at any point in time. Safe default actions and failure modes must be defined for the system informed by the current state, business environment, applicable policies, and regulatory obligations. Safe default modes for an automobile at zero velocity may no longer be applicable at speed. Safe failure states for medical devices will differ markedly from safe failure states for consumer electronics.

Identify and evaluate applicable recognized guidelines and standards

Standards are justly credited for reducing cost, enhancing interoperability, and leveraging innovation. From a security standpoint, standard protocols, standard object libraries, and standard implementations that have been scrutinized by experts in their fields help to ensure that errors do not find their way into implementations. From a security standpoint, errors are security vulnerabilities.

Revisit assumptions regarding interconnecting systems beyond project control

In light of the risk assessments performed, assumptions regarding interconnecting systems may require modification.

Determine and document the sensitivity or classification level of information stored/created/used

Information stored, created, or manipulated by the system may or may not be subject to an official classification that defines its sensitivity and the obligations to which the system and its owners are subject. The absence of any official classification does not necessarily absolve the onus on maintaining the confidentiality of data. Consideration must be made for different legislative burden that may hold jurisdiction over the system and the data stored.

- 列出价值和拥有者的资产列表
- 信任路径列表
- 可用性影响说明书
- 威胁分析矩阵

21.8 阶段 C：信息系统架构

评估当前安保特定架构元素（现有目的的增强）并建立基线

在准备差距分析时，必须编制实施安保服务的架构元素完整存储清单。

识别安全默认行为和失效状态

任何系统中的每次状态变更均由某次触发而促成。通常，对触发期望值的列举启动了状态的改变。然而，以可能存在必须适应非规范情况的其他潜在触发输入。此外，系统故障可能在任何时点发生。必须由当前状态、业务环境、适用方针和法规义务为依据的系统来定义安全默认行为和失效模式。零速度下的汽车安全默认模式在高速情况下可能不再适用。医疗器械的安全失效状态与消费性电子产品的安全失效状态将明显不同。

识别和评价适用的得到认可的指南和标准

标准理应被用于降低成本、提高互用性和更好地促进创新。从安保的立场考虑，已经由相应领域的专家仔细审查的标准协议、标准对象库和标准贯彻有助于确保实施中不会发生错误。从安保的立场考虑，错误属于安保漏洞。

回顾项目控制范围之外的关于互连系统的假设

根据所实施的风险评估，关于互连系统的假设可能需要修改。

确定所储存/创建/使用的信息的灵敏度或分类等级并将其文件化

由系统储存、创建或操作的信息可能受正式分类的约束，也可能不受约束，这种分类定义其灵敏度和系统及其所有人所承担的义务。缺少正式分类，不一定免除维持数据机密性的责任。必须考虑不同立法责任，其可能对系统和所储存数据拥有管辖权。

Identify and document custody of assets

All assets of value are kept and maintained on behalf of the owner. The specific persons or organizations charged with this responsibility must be identified.

Identify the criticality of the availability and correct operation of each function

Presumably, in the event of system failure or loss of functionality, some value is lost to stakeholders. The cost of this opportunity loss should be quantified, if possible, and documented.

Determine the relationship of the system under design with existing business disaster/continuity plans

Existing business disaster/continuity plans may accommodate the system under consideration. If not, some analysis is called for to determine the gap and the cost if that gap goes unfilled.

Identify what aspects of the system must be configurable to reflect changes in policy/business environment/access control

No environment is static and systems must evolve to accommodate change. Systems architected for ready reconfiguration will better reflect that change and result in lower cost over the life of the system. Security is enhanced when security-related changes can be implemented inexpensively and are, hence, not sidelined. Security is also enhanced when changes require no changes to code; changes to code introduce bugs and bugs introduce security vulnerabilities.

Identify lifespan of information used as defined by business needs and regulatory requirements

Information maintained beyond its useful lifespan represents wasted resources and, potentially, business decisions based upon suboptimal data. Regulation, however, sometimes mandates the timetable for maintenance of information as archival data.

Determine approaches to address identified risks:

- Mitigate
- Accept
- Transfer
- Avoid

There are several standard ways to address identified and quantified risk. The list above is not intended to be exhaustive for all approaches.

Identify actions/events that warrant logging for later review or triggering forensic processes

Anomalous actions and states will outnumber planned actions and states. These transitions will warrant logging to reconstruct chains of events, facilitate root cause analysis, and, potentially, establish evidence for civil or criminal action. It must be borne in mind that logs must be regularly reviewed to be introduced as evidence into a court of law in some jurisdictions.

识别并文件化资产的保管

为了拥有者的利益，保持并维护所有有价资产。必须识别承担该责任的特定人员或组织。

识别每个功能的可用性的关键度临界点和正确运行的关键性

据推测，如果发生系统故障或功能损失，利益攸关者便损失一些价值。应量化机会损失的成本，如可能，将其文件化。

确定正在设计中的系统与现有业务灾难/连续性计划的关系

现有业务灾难/连续性计划可能适应正在考量因素之中的系统。若非如此，需要在差距未填补的情况下进行一些分析来确定差距和成本。

识别系统的哪些方面必须是可配置的，以反映方针/业务环境/访问控制的变化

没有任何环境是静止的，而且系统必须逐步演进以适应变化。针对准备就绪的重新配置所构建的系统，会更好地反映变化并使得整个系统寿命的成本更低。当安保性相关变更可被经济地实施而且不会因此被迫退出时，安保性得到增强。当变化无须代码变更时，安保性也会得到增强；代码变更产生缺陷，而缺陷产生安保漏洞。

识别按照业务需要和法定要求的规定所使用信息的寿命

在其有用寿命之外所保存的信息代表浪费的资源，且潜在地代表基于次优数据的业务决策。然而，法规有时强制执行作为档案数据的信息维护时间表。

确定方法以应对已识别的风险：

- 缓解
- 接受
- 转移
- 避免

有若干种标准方法来应对已识别和量化的风险。上述列表并非旨在穷举所有途径。

识别证明后期审视日志或触发取证流程合理的行为/事件

异常行为和状态在数量上将超过计划的行为和状态。这些过渡态将确保具有日志重构事件链、促进根本原因分析，并潜在地为民事或刑事行为提供的证据的记录是合理的。必须牢记的是，必须定期审查日志，以在某些管辖区作为证据提供给法院。

Identify and document requirements for rigor in proving accuracy of logged events (non-repudiation)

Since malicious tampering of systems is commonly accompanied by tampering of logged data to thwart investigation and apprehension, the ability to protect and establish the veracity of logs through cryptographic methods will remove uncertainty from investigations and bolster cases in legal proceedings.

Identify potential/likely avenues of attack

Thinking like an adversary will prepare the architect for creation of a robust system that resists malicious tampering and, providentially, malfunction arising from random error.

Determine "what can go wrong?"

21.8.1 Security Inputs

- Threat analysis matrix
- Risk analysis
- Documented forensic processes
- Validated business policies and regulations
- List of interconnecting systems
- New disaster recovery and business continuity requirements

21.8.2 Security Outputs

- Event log-level matrix and requirements
- Risk management strategy
- Data lifecycle definitions
- List of configurable system elements
- Baseline list of security-related elements of the system
- New or augmented security-related elements of the system
- Security use-case models:
  - Normative models
  - Non-normative models
- List of applicable security standards:
  - Protocols
  - Object libraries
  - Others ...
- Validated interconnected system list
- Information classification report

识别严格证明所记录事件（不可否认）准确度的需求并将其文件化

由于系统的恶意篡改通常伴随着已记录数据的篡改，以致妨碍调查研究和理解，因此通过加密方法来保护和建立日志真实性的能力将消除调查研究中的不确定性并支持法律程序中的案件。

识别潜在的/可能的攻击途径

从对手的角度思考会使架构师做好准备来创建具有鲁棒性的系统，以阻止恶意篡改并及时阻止由于随机错误而引起的故障。

确定“什么会出现错误？”

21.8.1 安保输入

- 威胁分析矩阵
- 风险分析
- 文件化的取证流程
- 确认的业务方针及规定
- 互连系统列表
- 新的灾难恢复与业务连续性需求

21.8.2 安保输出

- 事件的日志级别矩阵和需求
- 风险管理战略
- 数据生命周期定义
- 可配置系统元素的列表
- 系统安保性相关元素的基线列表
- 新的或增强的系统安保性相关元素
- 安保用例模型：
  - 规范性模型
  - 非规范模型
- 适用安保标准的列表：
  - 协议
  - 对象库
  - 其他
- 确认的互连系统列表
- 信息分类报告

- List of asset custodians
- Function criticality statement
- Revised disaster recovery and business continuity plans
- Refined threat analysis matrix

21.9 Phase D: Technology Architecture

Assess and baseline current security-specific technologies (enhancement of existing objective)

Revisit assumptions regarding interconnecting systems beyond project control

Identify and evaluate applicable recognized guidelines and standards

Identify methods to regulate consumption of resources

Every system will rely upon resources that may be depleted in cases that may or may not be anticipated at the point of system design. Examples include network bandwidth, battery power, disk space, available memory, and so on. As resources are utilized approaching depletion, functionality may be impaired or may fail altogether. Design steps that identify non-renewable resources, methods that can recognize resource depletion, and measures that can respond through limiting the causative factors, or through limiting the effects of resource depletion to non-critical functionality, can enhance the overall reliability and availability of the system.

Engineer a method by which the efficacy of security measures will be measured and communicated on an ongoing basis

As systems are deployed and operated in dynamic environments, security measures will perform to varying degrees of efficacy as unexpected threats arise and as expected threats change in the environment. A method that facilitates ongoing evaluation of the value of security measures will inform ongoing changes to the system in response to changing user needs, threat patterns, and problems found.

Identify the trust (clearance) level of:

- All users of the system
- All administrators of the system
- All interconnecting systems beyond project control

Regulatory requirements, information classification levels, and business needs of the asset owners will all influence the required level of trust that all interactive entities will be required to fulfil to qualify for access to data or services.

- 资产保管人名单
- 功能关键性说明书
- 修订的灾难恢复与业务连续性计划
- 细化的威胁分析矩阵

21.9 阶段 D：技术架构

评估当前安保特定的技术（现有目的的增强）并建立基线

回顾项目控制范围之外的关于互连系统的假设

识别并评价适用的已认可的指南和标准

识别用于调整资源消耗的方法

每个系统将依靠在系统设计时可能或不可能预先考虑的情况下可能消耗的资源。例如，网络带宽、电池电量、磁盘空间、可用内存等。当资源使用接近耗尽时，功能可能受损或完全失效。用以识别不可再生资源的设计步骤、用以确认资源耗尽的方法，以及用以通过限制诱发因素或通过限制资源耗尽对非关键功能的影响来进行响应的措施，均能够增强系统的整体可靠性和可用性。

工程化建立一种基于可持续基础之上的测度的效能可被测量和沟通的方法

在动态环境中部署和运行系统时，随着意外威胁的发生及预期威胁在环境中的变化，安保措施将按不同程度的有效性实行。一种有助于持续评估安保措施价值的方法将为系统进行持续变化提供依据，以响应对用户需求、威胁特征模式和所发现问题的变化。

识别下列内容的信任（许可）等级：

- 系统的所有用户
- 系统的所有管理人员
- 项目控制范围之外的所有互连系统

资产拥有人的法定要求、信息分类等级和业务需要均将影响所需信任等级，该信任等级是所有交互实体为了有资格访问数据或服务需要达到的。

Identify minimal privileges required for any entity to achieve a technical or business objective

Granting sweeping capabilities to any user, application, or other entity can simplify successful transaction completion at the cost of complicating or precluding effective control and audit. Many regulatory obligations are more challenging to demonstrate compliance where privileges are sweeping and controls are loose.

Identify mitigating security measures, where justified by risk assessment

This objective is where the classic security services of identification, authentication, authorization, data confidentiality, data integrity, non-repudiation, assurance, and audit are brought into play, after their applicability is determined and the cost/value of protection has been identified.

Determine "what can go wrong?"

21.9.1 Security Inputs

- List of security-related elements of the system
- List of interconnected systems
- List of applicable security standards
- List of security actors
- Risk management strategy
- Validated security policies
- Validated regulatory requirements
- Validated business policies related to trust requirements

21.9.2 Security Outputs

- Baseline list of security technologies
- Validated interconnected systems list
- Selected security standards list
- Resource conservation plan
- Security metrics and monitoring plan
- User authorization policies
- Risk management plan
- User trust (clearance) requirements

识别实体为达成技术或业务目的所需的最小特权

向用户、应用或其他实体提供全面能力，可以使事物的成功完成变得简单，付出的代价是，使有效控制和审计变得复杂或受到阻碍。在特权影响广泛且控制松懈的情况下，法规义务更难以验证其合规性。

在通过风险评估证明合理的情况下，识别缓解安保措施

该目的是在确定适用性和识别保护的成本/价值后，发挥识别、认证、授权、数据保密、数据完整性、不可否认性、保证和审计等典型安保服务的作用。

确定"什么会出现错误？"

21.9.1 安保输入

- 系统安保性相关元素的列表
- 互连系统列表
- 适用安保标准的列表
- 安保施动者列表
- 风险管理策略
- 经确认的安保策略
- 经确认的监管要求
- 经确认的有关信任需求的业务方针

21.9.2 安保输出

- 安保技术的基线列表
- 确认的互连系统列表
- 所选安保标准的列表
- 资源保护计划
- 安保衡量标准和监控计划
- 用户授权策略
- 风险管理计划
- 用户信任（许可）需求

21.10 Phase E: Opportunities & Solutions

Identify existing security services available for re-use

From the Baseline Security Architecture and the Enterprise Continuum, there will be existing security infrastructure and security building blocks that can be applied to the requirements derived from this architecture development engagement. For example, if the requirement exists for application access control external to an application being developed, and such a system already exists, it can be used again. Statutory or regulatory requirements may call for physical separation of domains which may eliminate the ability to re-use existing infrastructure. Known products, tools, building blocks, and patterns can be used, though newly implemented.

Engineer mitigation measures addressing identified risks

Having determined the risks amenable to mitigation and evaluated the appropriate investment in that mitigation as it relates to the assets at risk, those mitigation measures must be designed, implemented, deployed, and/or operated.

Evaluate tested and re-usable security software and security system resources

Since design, code, and configuration errors are the roots of many security vulnerabilities, taking advantage of any problem solutions already engineered, reviewed, tested, and field-proven will reduce security exposure and enhance reliability.

Identify new code/resources/assets that are appropriate for re-use

Populate the Architecture Repository with new security building blocks.

Determine "what can go wrong?"

21.11 Phase F: Migration Planning

Assess the impact of new security measures upon other new components or existing leveraged systems

In a phased implementation the new security components are usually part of the infrastructure in which the new system is implemented. The security infrastructure needs to be in a first or early phase to properly support the project.

Implement assurance methods by which the efficacy of security measures will be measured and communicated on an ongoing basis

During the operational phases, mechanisms are utilized to monitor the performance of many aspects of the system. Its security and availability are no exception.

Identify correct secure installation parameters, initial conditions, and configurations

Security of any system depends not on design and implementation alone, but also upon installation and operational state. These conditions must be defined and monitored not just at deployment, but also throughout operation.

21.10 阶段 E：机会和解决方案

识别可复用的现有安保服务

从基线安保架构和 ENTERPRISE 的连续统一体来看，将存在的现有安保基础设施和安保构建块，可应用于源自架构开发介入而来的需求。例如，如果对正在开发的应用之外存在应用访问控制需求并且这种系统已经存在，则安保服务可被再次使用。法令或法规需求可能要求域物理隔离，其可能消除复用现有基础设施的能力。虽然已知的产出物、工具、构建块和特征模式是新近实现的，但仍可以被使用。

设计缓解措施以应对已识别的风险

一旦确定易于缓解的风险以及评价处于风险中资产有关的缓解措施的合理投资，则必须设计、实施、部署和/或操作那些缓解措施。

评价经测试且可复用的安保软件和安保系统资源

由于设计、编码和配置错误是许多安保漏洞的根源，利用任何已设计、审查、测试和现场验证的问题解决方案将减少安保漏洞并提高可靠性。

识别适合复用的新代码/资源/资产

利用新的安保构建块充实架构库。

确定“什么会出现错误？”

21.11 阶段 F：迁移规划

评估新的安保措施对其他新组件或已得到更好利用的现有系统的影响

在分阶段实施中，新的安保组件通常是实现新系统的基础设施的一部分。该安保基础设施需要在第一阶段或早期阶段正确地支持该系统项目。

实施保证方法，使得在一持续的基础上安保测度效能能被测量和传达

在运行阶段，使用多个机制来监控系统多个方面的绩效，其安保性和可用性也不例外。

识别正确的安保安装参数、初始化条件和配置

任何系统的安保性并不仅仅依赖设计和实施，还依赖安装和运行状态。不仅在部署时而且在整个运行过程中，这些条件都必须被定义并被监控。

Implement disaster recovery and business continuity plans or modifications

Determine "what can go wrong?"

21.12 Phase G: Implementation Governance

Establish architecture artifact, design, and code reviews and define acceptance criteria for the successful implementation of the findings

Many security vulnerabilities originate as design or code errors and the simplest and least expensive method to locate and find such errors is generally an early review by experienced peers in the craft. Locating such errors, of course, is the first step and implementing corrections at an appropriate point in the development lifecycle is necessary to benefit from the investment. Follow-on inspections or formalized acceptance reviews may be warranted in high-assurance or safety-critical environments.

Implement methods and procedures to review evidence produced by the system that reflects operational stability and adherence to security policies

While planning and specification is necessary for all aspects of a successful enterprise, they are insufficient in the absence of testing and audit to ensure adherence to that planning and specification in both deployment and operation. Among the methods to be exercised are:

- Review system configurations with security impact which can be modified to ensure configuration changes have not compromised security design
- Audit the design, deployment, and operations against security policies
- Audit the design, deployment, and operations against business objectives
- Run test cases against systems to ensure the security systems have been implemented as designed
- Run disaster recovery tests
- Run business continuity tests

Implement necessary training to ensure correct deployment, configuration, and operations of security-relevant subsystems and components; ensure awareness training of all users and non-privileged operators of the system and/or its components

Training is not necessary simply to preclude vulnerabilities introduced through operations and configuration error, though this is critical to correct ongoing secure performance. In many jurisdictions, proper training must be performed and documented to demonstrate due diligence and substantiate corrective actions or sanctions in cases where exploits or error compromise business objectives or to absolve contributory responsibility for events that bring about harm or injury.

实施或修改灾难恢复和业务连续性计划

确定“什么会出现错误？”

21.12 阶段 G：实施治理

建立架构制品、设计和代码审查并为所做成果的成功实施定义验收准则

很多安保漏洞源于设计或代码错误，而用以定位并找到这些错误的最简单且成本最低的方法通常是行业内富有经验的同行所进行的早期审查。当然，定位这些错误是第一步，还需要在开发生命周期的适当时刻来执行修正，以便从投资中受益。后续检验或正式验收审查可在高可信度或安全关键环境中得到保证。

实施方法和程序，以审视由系统所产生的反映运行稳定性和安保方针遵循度的证据

虽然规划和规范对于一个成功的 ENTERPRISE 的各方面而言是必要的，然而，在缺少测试和审计的情况下，不足以确保在部署和运行中遵守该规划和规范。所要训练的方法包括：

- 审视具有安保影响的系统配置，并可修改以确保配置变更不会危及安保设计
- 针对安保方针来审计设计、部署和运行
- 针对业务目的审计设计、部署和运行
- 针对系统运行试验用例，以确保已按设计实施安保系统
- 运行灾难恢复试验
- 运行业务连续性试验

实施必要的培训以确保正确部署、配置和运行与安保性相关的子系统和组件；确保对系统和/或其组件的所有用户和非特权操作者进行认知培训

虽然培训对修正持续的安保绩效至关重要，但是这对于仅避免运行中产生的漏洞和配置错误并非必要。在多个管辖区中，必须进行适当的培训并将其文件化，以表明尽到责任并证明在非法手段或错误危及业务目的的情况下采取了纠正措施或处罚，或者免除了带来损害或损伤的事件的分担责任。

Determine "what has gone wrong?"

The very purpose of governance is the establishment of a feedback loop that determines the efficacy of plan execution and implements corrections, where required. It must be borne in mind that the imperfections in plans executed are rooted both in human processes and cybernetic processes.

21.13 Phase H: Architecture Change Management

As stated in Part II, Chapter 17 (Requirements Management), change is driven by new requirements. Changes in security requirements are often more disruptive than a simplification or incremental change. Changes in security policy can be driven by statute, regulation, or something that has gone wrong.

Changes in security standards are usually less disruptive since the trade-off for their adoption is based on the value of the change. However, standards changes can also be mandated. Similar approaches to these changes as mentioned above are good rules of thumb for security as well. However, security changes are often infrastructure changes, and can have a greater impact. A seemingly small security requirement change can easily trigger a new architecture development cycle.

Determine "what has gone wrong?"

Good security forensics practices in conjunction with a written published security policy make determination of what has gone wrong possible. Further, they make enforcement possible. As the guidance above suggests, minor changes can be made in the context of change management and major changes will require a new architecture effort.

Incorporate security-relevant changes to the environment into the requirements for future enhancement (enhancement of existing objective)

Changes that arise as a result of a security problem or new security technology will feed into the Requirements Management process.

21.14 References

- NIST 80018: Guide for Developing Security Plans for Information Technology Systems
- NIST 80027: Engineering Principles for Information Technology Security (A Baseline forAchieving Security)
- NIST 80030: Guide for Risk Management for Information Technology Systems

确定“什么出了错？”

治理的真正目的是，在需要时建立确定计划执行有效性并实施修正的反馈回路。必须记住，所执行计划中的不足来源于人工流程和控制流程。

21.13 阶段 H：架构变更管理

如第二部分第 17 章（需求管理）所述，变更由新的需求所驱动。安保需求的变更通常比简化或增量变更更具有破坏性。安保方针的变更可由法令、法规或出现问题的某些方面所驱动。

安保标准的变更通常破坏性较小，这是因为，权衡标准的采纳是基于变更的价值的。然而，也可强制执行标准变更。上述这些变更的类似途径还是良好的安保经验法则。然而，安保变更通常是基础设施变更，并且可产生较大影响。一个看似微小的安保需求变更很容易触发一个新的架构开发周期。

确定“什么出了错？”

良好的安保取证实践与发布的书面安保方针相结合，使得确定什么出现了问题成为可能，也使得执行成为可能。如上述引导所建议的，可能在变更管理的背景环境下进行微小变更，而重大变更将需要新的架构工作。

将对环境的安保性相关变更合并入对未来增强（现有目的的增强）的需求

安保问题或新的安保技术所引起的变更将纳入需求管理流程。

21.14 参考文献

- NIST 80018：信息技术系统安保计划开发指南
- NIST 80027：信息技术安保工程原则（实现安保性的基线）
- NIST 80030：信息技术系统风险管理指南

Chapter 22
Using TOGAF to Define & Govern SOAs

22.1 Overview

This chapter discusses:

- Service-Oriented Architecture (SOA) as an architectural style.
- Factors relating to the adoption and deployment of SOA within the enterprise.
- Using the TOGAF Architecture Development Method (ADM) to develop your SOA.

This chapter, where appropriate, includes references to Technical Standards and Guides developed by The Open Group SOA Work Group.

22.2 Introduction

As the business environment becomes more sophisticated, the challenges facing organizations are shifting away from questions of efficiency and automation towards questions of complexity management and business agility.

Complex webs of existing applications and interfaces create highly complex landscapes where change becomes more and more difficult and the impacts of change become harder to predict and understand.

The concept of SOA provides an architectural style that is specifically intended to simplify the business and the interoperation of different parts of that business. By structuring capability as meaningful, granular services as opposed to opaque, silo'ed business units, it becomes possible to quickly identify functional capabilities of an organization, avoid duplicating similar capabilities across the organization and quickly assemble new capabilities.

By standardizing the behavior and interoperation of services, it is possible to limit the impacts of change and also to understand in advance the likely chain of impacts.

From a software development perspective, SOA focuses on structuring applications in a way that facilitates system flexibility and agility — a necessity in today's complex and fast-moving business environment. SOA aims to break down traditional application silos into portfolios of more granular services that operate in open and interoperable ways, while extracting commodity capability into a virtualized infrastructure platform of shared re-usable utility services.

第 22 章 使用 TOGAF 定义和治理 SOA

22.1 概述

本章论述：

- 作为一种架构风格的面向服务架构（SOA）。
- 与在 ENTERPRISE 内部采用和部署 SOA 相关的因素。
- 使用 TOGAF 架构开发方法（ADM）开发您的 SOA。

本章在适当位置包含 The Open Group SOA 工作组所制定的技术标准和指南的参考文献。

22.2 简介

随着业务环境日渐复杂，组织所面临的挑战从效率和自动化问题正在向复杂性管理和业务敏捷性问题转移。

现有应用和界面的复杂网络创建高度复杂的全景，而其中的变更变得越来越复杂，且变更的影响变得更加难以预测和理解。

SOA 的概念提供了一种架构风格，专门用于简化业务及其不同部分之间的互操作。通过将能力结构化为有意义、精细的服务而非晦涩的竖井式业务单元，能够快速识别组织的功能性能力，避免贯穿整个组织复制相似的能力，以及快速聚合新的能力。

通过将服务的行为和互操作进行标准化，就可能限制变更的影响并且事先理解可能的系列影响。

从软件开发的关注层级而言，SOA 聚焦于以促进系统灵活性和敏捷性的方式来结构化应用程序，这是当今复杂且快速变化的业务环境的迫切需要。SOA 旨在将传统的应用竖井分解为多个以开放和可互操作的方式运行的更加精细服务的项目谱系，同时将提取商品化能力到共有共享的可复用的实用服务的虚拟化基础设施平台之中。

22.3 SOA Definition

Note: This section is provided for reader convenience. Part I, Chapter 3 should be referred to for the formal definitions.

Service-Oriented Architecture (SOA) is an architectural style that supports service-orientation. Service-orientation is a way of thinking in terms of services and service-based development andthe outcomes of services.

A service is a logical representation of a repeatable business activity that has a specified outcome (e.g., check customer credit, provide weather data, consolidate drilling reports, etc.) and:

- Is self-contained
- May be composed of other services
- Is a “black box” to consumers of the service

An architectural style is the combination of distinctive features in which architecture is performed or expressed.

22.4 SOA Features

SOA is based on the design of the services — which mirror real-world business activities — comprising the enterprise (or inter-enterprise) business processes. Service representation utilizes business descriptions to provide context (i.e., business process, goal, rule, policy, service interface, service component, etc.).

SOA places unique requirements on the infrastructure. Because of this, it is recommended that implementations use open standards to realize interoperability and location transparency. For instance, the availability of services must somehow be documented in a place easily accessible by those requiring the use of those services. An SOA-specific Directory Service and an Enterprise Service Bus (ESB) are two examples of technology implementations that require adherence to relevant open standards to achieve the interoperability that SOA promises.

Implementations are enterprise environment-specific — they are constrained or enabled by context and must be described within that context. Given that, SOA requires strong governance of service representation and implementation.

22.3 SOA 定义

注：本节是为读者提供方便。正式定义应参考第一部分第 3 章。

面向服务架构（SOA）是一种支持面向服务的架构风格。面向服务是一种以服务、基于服务开发以及服务结果为因素的思考方式。

服务是一种具有特定结果的可重复业务活动的逻辑表达（例如，检查客户信用、提供天气数据、合并钻取报告等），且：

- 是独立完整的
- 可由其他服务组成
- 对其用户来说是一个“黑盒”

架构风格是架构执行或表达的独特性特征的组合。

22.4 SOA 特征

SOA 以反映真实世界的业务活动的服务的设计为基础，包括 ENTERPRISE（或 ENTERPRISE 间）的业务流程。服务的表达利用业务描述来提供背景环境（即业务流程、目标、规则、方针、服务界面、服务组件等）。

SOA 对基础设施提出特殊需求。由于这一点，建议使用开放标准来实施，以实现互用性和位置的透明性。例如，服务的可用性必须以某种方式由需要使用服务者记录在易于访问处。SOA 特定目录服务和企业服务总线（ESB）是两个技术实施的示例，需遵守相关开放标准以达成 SOA 所承诺的互用性。

实施是特定于 ENTERPRISE 环境的——它们受背景环境的约束或由其实现，且必须在相应背景环境中被描述。考虑到这点，SOA 需要对服务的表达和实施进行强有力的管控。

22.5 Enterprise Architecture and SOA

Enterprise architecture provides frameworks, tools, and techniques to assist organizations with the development and maintenance of their SOAs. Some of the key benefits that enterprise architecture provides include:

- Consistent abstractions of high-level strategies and deliverables to support planning and analysis.
- Linkage of different perspectives to a single business problem (e.g., business, information systems, technology, breadth, depth, level of detail, etc.) providing a consistent model to address various domains and tests for completeness.
- Identification of clear roadmaps to achieve future state.
- Traceability that links IT and other assets to the business they support.
- Support for impact assessment, risk/value analysis, and portfolio management.
- Identified and documented principles, constraints, frameworks, patterns, and standards.
- Governance frameworks and processes that ensure appropriate authority for decision-making.

Enterprise architecture becomes a foundation for service-orienting an organization, because it links stakeholders together, ensuring that the needs of each stakeholder community are met and that each stakeholder community is aware of appropriate context. This linkage is the foundation for interoperability and re-use.

Through its linking of the business context to IT, enterprise architecture readily identifies and provides justification for the cost of change programs in relation to the business value to be derived from the effort. Enterprise architecture may provide the context and analysis capabilities to:

- Show how SOA solutions can be effectively architected to support business capabilities.
- Show which services should be built and which should be re-used.
- Show how services should be designed.

Without enterprise architecture, the negative effects may include one or more of the following:

- Limited agility.
- Difficulty identifying and orchestrating SOA services.
- Service sprawl.
- Exponentially growing governance challenges.
- Limited SOA service interoperability.
- Limited SOA service re-use.
- Multiple silo'ed SOAs.
- Difficulty evolving and changing SOA implementations.

22.5 Enterprise Architecture 和 SOA

Enterprise Architecture 提供框架、工具和技巧，用以辅助组织开发和维护其 SOA。Enterprise Architecture 所提供的一些关键益处包括：

- 高层级战略和交付物的一致性抽象，以支持规划和分析。
- 从不同关注层级对单一业务问题进行联系（例如，业务、信息系统、技术、广度、深度、细节层级等），以提供一种一致性模型来应对各种域和试验的完整性。
- 识别出清晰的路线图以达成未来状态。
- 对 IT 和其他资产与其所支持的业务之间联系的可追溯性。
- 对影响评估、风险/价值分析和项目谱系管理的支持。
- 已识别并文件化的原则、约束、框架、特征模式和标准。
- 确保恰当决策权限的治理框架和流程。

Enterprise Architecture 成为使组织面向服务的基础，因为其将多个利益攸关者联系在一起，确保满足每个利益攸关者团体的需求且确保每个利益攸关者团体意识到适当的背景环境。这种联系是互用性和复用的基础。

通过将业务背景环境与 IT 联系起来，Enterprise Architecture 更容易识别并提供正当理由，说明与源自该工作的业务价值有关的变更计划的成本。Enterprise Architecture 可提供背景环境和分析能力以便：

- 表明如何有效地对 SOA 解决方案构建架构以支持业务能力。
- 表明哪些服务应被构建以及哪些服务应被复用。
- 表明应如何设计服务。

若没有 Enterprise Architecture，负面影响可能包括下列内容中的一个或多个：

- 有限的敏捷性。
- 难以识别和编排 SOA 服务。
- 服务的无序扩张。
- 指数级增长的治理挑战。
- 有限的 SOA 服务互用性。
- 有限的 SOA 服务复用。
- 多个竖井式 SOA。
- 难以演进和变更 SOA 的实施。

22.6 SOA and Levels

The size and complexity of an enterprise affects the way the Enterprise Architect develops its architecture. Where there are many different organizational and business models, it is not practical to integrate them within a single architecture. There are very few infrastructure items, with the exception of the Internet and the World-Wide Web, that can be applied across the whole of a large organization. Even these provide only a basic level of support for business processes. Generally, it may not be appropriate to develop a single, integrated SOA for a large and complex enterprise.

For such an enterprise, assuming an architecture landscape as shown in Figure 20-1, the architect should look first at developing a strategic architecture that gives a summary formal description of the enterprise, providing an organizing framework for operational and change activity, and an executive-level, long-term view for direction setting. This might, for example, identify particular segments where SOA should be used, and call for use of services for interaction between segments, but it is highly unlikely to specify particular services or groups of services, or to prescribe a detailed infrastructure for SOA.

The architect could then develop segment architectures, each of which gives a detailed, formal description of areas within an enterprise, used at the program or portfolio level to organize and align change activity. Each of these segment architectures could be a single, integrated SOA.

For a smaller and less complex enterprise whose business operations can share a common infrastructure, you can use TOGAF to create an integrated SOA with groups of services that support the business activities.

From here on it is assumed that the scope is an enterprise of this kind. It could be self-standing or a segment of a larger enterprise.

22.6.1 Level of Detail of Implementation Specification

How completely should the architecture define what to implement? At one extreme, it could specify the future of the enterprise, and define all the changes to reach the target, including the projects that will produce the changes, and a detailed time plan. At the other extreme, it could just indicate areas where work is needed, and suggest priorities for addressing them.

Architecture development could fall anywhere between these two extremes. For the kind of enterprise SOA that we are considering here, it is likely that you would specify the infrastructure and define the projects to implement it, with a detailed time plan. You might do the same for some or all of the solutions. Alternatively, particularly where agility is important, you might identify solutions, and perhaps specify initial versions of them, but allow for additional solutions to be identified later, and for implementation projects to develop further versions of the solutions without having to ask for changes to the architecture.

22.6.2 SOA Activities at Different Levels

At the level of Strategic Architecture the basic SOA issue is identifying whether you need SOA and in which Segments. In the Strategic Architecture we identify:

- The high-level relationships and boundaries within the organization.
- Cross-segment SOA capability requirements (what information and functionality is needed across segments).

22.6 SOA 和层级

ENTERPRISE 的规模和复杂度影响 ENTERPRISE 架构师开发其架构的方式。在具有多个不同的组织模型和业务模型的情况下，在单一架构内综合这些模型是不切实际的。除了互联网和万维网，几乎没有贯穿整个大型组织应用的基础设施项目。甚至这些基础设施项目仅为业务流程提供基础层级的支持。通常，为一个复杂的大型 ENTERPRISE 开发一个单一、综合的 SOA 可能是不合适的。

对这种 ENTERPRISE，假设架构全景如图 20-1 所示，架构师应首先考虑开发一个战略架构来对 ENTERPRISE 提供概要的正式描述，为运行和变更活动提供一个组织框架并为方向设定提供一个执行层级的长期视图。例如，这样可以识别应使用 SOA 的特定分段并且要求各分段之间使用服务进行交互，但是，几乎不可能指定特定服务或服务组，或者为 SOA 规定详细的基础设施。

架构师能够开发多个分部架构，每个分部架构为 ENTERPRISE 内的多个区域提供详细、正式的描述，在项目群或项目谱系层级上用来组织和协调变更活动。其中的每个分部架构都可能是一个单一、综合的 SOA。

对于规模较小、复杂度较低的且其业务运行可共享一个公用的基础设施的 ENTERPRISE，您可以使用 TOGAF 创建一个具有多个支持业务活动的服务组的综合 SOA。

从现在起，假设范围是这类 ENTERPRISE。其可能是独立的 ENTERPRISE 或是规模较大的 ENTERPRISE 的一个分部。

22.6.1 实施规范的细节层级

架构对实施内容的定义应达到怎样的完备程度？在一种极端情况下，其可说明该 ENTERPRISE 的未来，并且定义为了达到目标的所有变革，包括将产生变革的项目以及一个详细的时间计划。在另一种极端情况下，其仅指示需要开展工作的领域以及应对这些领域的优先级。

架构开发可介于这两种极端情况之间的任何程度。对于此处考虑的这一类 ENTERPRISE SOA，可能您会指定基础设施并且为实施该架构定义多个项目，同时具有详细时间计划。您也可对一些或所有解决方案采用相同的做法。或者，特别是在敏捷性很重要时，您可以识别解决方案，也可说明这些解决方案的最初版本，但是允许后续识别更多的解决方案，且允许实施项目在不必要求变更架构的情况下能开发这些解决方案的更新版本。

22.6.2 不同层级上的 SOA 活动

在战略架构的层级上，基本的 SOA 议题是识别您是否需要 SOA 以及在哪些分段中需要 SOA。在该战略架构中应识别：

- 组织内的高层级关系和边界。
- 跨分部的 SOA 能力需求（跨分部需要何种信息和功能）。

- Key capabilities best addressed by SOA.
- Key capabilities required for SOA.
- Segments best addressed by SOA.
- Principles and patterns of SOA service development and description, which may be defined at the Segment and Capability levels.
- The roles, responsibilities, processes, and tools of SOA governance.
- The organization-specific Reference Architecture.

At the Segment level the basic SOA issue is describing the structure of SOA. In the Segment Architectures we define:

- Which capabilities will use SOA as an architecture style.
- Cross-capability relationships (what information and functionality is needed across capabilities).
- More detailed cross-segment relationships (what information and functionality is needed across Segment).
- Cross-capability SOA service re-use possibilities.
- Principles and patterns of SOA service development and description, which may be defined at the Strategic and Capability levels; it is most common to define these as part of Segment Architecture.

For Capability Architecture the basic SOA issue is which services will be available. In theCapability Architectures we will describe:

- The functional and non-functional requirements of the capability.
- Cross-capability SOA service requirements.
- SOA services that enable cross-capability re-use.
- SOA services that enable the capability.
- Principles and patterns of SOA service development and description, which may be defined at the Strategic and Segment levels.

Regardless of the level of architecture being pursued it is possible to identify SOA solutions that will best service the requirements of the enterprise.

22.7 Using TOGAF for SOA

This section describes, for each phase of the TOGAF ADM, what should be considered when looking to apply the principle of service-orientation, and how this affects the phase. This is not intended as a self-standing description and should be read in conjunction with other sections of this document.

- 由 SOA 最有效地应对的关键能力。
- SOA 所需的关键能力。
- 由 SOA 最有效应对的分部。
- SOA 服务开发和描述的原则及特征模式，可在分部层级和能力层级上定义。
- SOA 治理的作用、责任、流程和工具。
- 组织特定的参考架构。

在分部层级上，基本的 SOA 议题是描述 SOA 的结构。在该分部架构中应定义：

- 哪些能力将 SOA 用作一种架构风格。
- 跨能力的关系（跨能力需要何种信息和功能）。
- 更详细的跨分部的关系（跨分部需要何种信息和功能）。
- 跨能力 SOA 服务的复用可能性。
- 可在战略层级和能力层级上定义的 SOA 服务开发和描述的原则及特征模式，最常见的是将这些定义为分部架构的一部分。

对于能力架构，基本的 SOA 议题是哪些服务将是可用的。在该能力架构中将描述：

- 能力的功能性及非功能性需求。
- 跨能力 SOA 服务需求。
- 实现跨能力复用的 SOA 服务。
- 实现能力的 SOA 服务。
- 可在战略层级和分段层级上定义的 SOA 服务开发和描述的原则及特征模式。

不管正在寻求什么架构层级，都有可能识别将最有效地服务于该 ENTERPRISE 需求的 SOA 解决方案。

22.7 将 TOGAF 用于 SOA

本节针对 TOGAF ADM 的每个阶段，描述在思考应用面向服务的原则时，应考虑什么内容及这些内容如何影响该阶段。本节并非旨在作为独立描述，应结合本文其他章节一起来阅读。

22.7.1 Preliminary Phase

The Preliminary Phase is where the Architecture Capability is adapted to support SOA. The key outputs of this phase are the principles, organizational structure, governance, and initial content of the Architecture Repository.

22.7.1.1 Principle of Service-Orientation

The starting point for SOA development with TOGAF is that the enterprise adopts service-orientation as an architecture principle (see Principle 6: Service Orientation, 23.6.1). An enterprise wishing to use TOGAF for SOA should include this principle, either as it stands or in modified form, in its set of architecture principles.

If the architect is introducing TOGAF to an enterprise that is already committed to SOA, or that is part of a larger enterprise that has made a strategic decision to use SOA, then adoption of the principle of service-orientation is straightforward. If, on the other hand, SOA is being introduced to an enterprise that is not already committed to it, then the decision to adopt this principle should not be taken lightly.

Successful SOA depends in part on the readiness of the enterprise to become service-oriented. The organization can conduct an SOA maturity assessment during the Preliminary Phase, using The Open Group Service Integration Maturity Model (OSIMM) as part of the review of the organizational context for conducting enterprise architecture. This will help to establish the rationale for the enterprise to adopt the principle of service-orientation.

Even though an enterprise may be committed to SOA, it is not always appropriate to use the SOA style to address every architectural problem. As the section on levels identified specific segments, or capabilities may be best served by SOA in an organization not otherwise committed; or specific segments or capabilities may not be well suited to SOA in an organization committed to SOA.

From here on it is assumed that the principle of service-orientation is adopted.

22.7.1.2 Governance and Support Strategy

A review should occur of the existing governance procedures, confirming that they are appropriate for SOA. If they are not, then recommendations should be made for change to make them appropriate.

The Open Group has a standardized governance framework that focuses on SOA and may be used to enhance existing governance frameworks (see The Open Group SOA Governance Framework Technical Standard). This provides a high-level reference model of how SOA governance extends and supports both enterprise architecture and IT governance. It also includes an SOA Governance Vitality Method (SGVM) that can be used to define a specific SOA governance regimen adapted to the organization's view of governance.

22.7.1 预备阶段

预备阶段是调整架构能力以支持 SOA 的阶段。该阶段的关键输出是原则、组织结构、治理和架构库的初始内容。

22.7.1.1 面向服务的原则

利用 TOGAF 进行 SOA 开发的起点是 ENTERPRISE 采用面向服务作为一种架构原则（见 23.6.1 节 “原则 6：面向服务”）。一个希望为 SOA 使用 TOGAF 的 ENTERPRISE 应按目前的情况或以修正的形式，将面向服务的原则包括在它的一套架构原则中。

对于已致力于 SOA 的 ENTERPRISE，或对于已就使用 SOA 作出战略决策的规模较大 ENTERPRISE 的一部分 ENTERPRISE，如果架构师正将 TOGAF 引入其中，采用面向服务的原则是顺理成章的。相反，如果 SOA 正被引入已不再致力于 SOA 的 ENTERPRISE，则不应轻率做出采用该原则的决策。

成功的 SOA 部分取决于将要转变成面向服务的 ENTERPRISE 的准备度。组织可在预备阶段进行 SOA 成熟度评估，将 The Open Group 服务集成成熟度模型（OSIMM）用作 ENTERPRISE 进行架构的组织背景环境审视的一部分。这将有助于 ENTERPRISE 对采用面向服务原则建立理由依据。

即使一个 ENTERPRISE 可致力于 SOA，也并非始终适合于使用 SOA 风格应对每个架构问题。正如关于识别层级的章节所述，特定分部或能力在一个不致力于其他方面的组织中可由 SOA 最大程度地服务；或特定分段或能力在一个致力于 SOA 的组织中可能并非极其适合于 SOA。

从此处开始，假设采用面向服务的原则。

22.7.1.2 治理和支持战略

应对现有治理程序进行审视，确认其适合于 SOA。如果不适合，则应提出变更的建议，以使现有的治理程序变得合适。

The Open Group 具有一个标准化治理框架，该框架聚焦于 SOA 并可用来加强现有的治理框架（见 The Open Group SOA 治理框架技术标准）。它提供一个关于 SOA 治理如何扩展和支持 Enterprise Architecture 和 IT 治理的高层级参考模型，还包括一种 SOA 治理活力法（SGVM），用来定义一种适于组织治理视图的特定 SOA 治理方案。

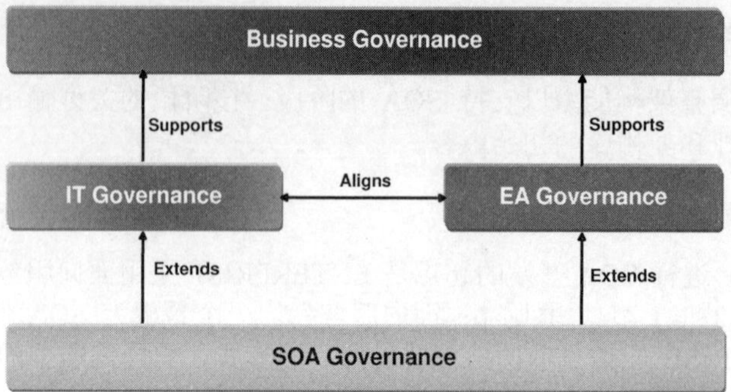

Figure 22-1 The Open Group SOA Governance Framework

22.7.1.3 Partitions and Centers of Excellence

Different teams will work on different elements of architecture at the same time. Partitions allow for specific groups of architects to own and develop specific elements of the architecture. It is suggested that the team start with a focused initiative before implementing on a wide scale. The team responsible for SOA should initially be structured as a Center of Excellence (CoE).

A successful CoE will have several key attributes:

- A clear definition of the CoE's mission: why it exists, its scope of responsibility, and what the organization and the architecture practice should expect from the CoE.
- Clear goals for the CoE including measurements and Key Performance Indicators (KPIs). It is important to ensure that the measures and KPIs of the CoE do not drive inappropriate selection of SOA as the architecture style.
- The CoE will provide the "litmus test" of a good service.
- The CoE will disseminate the skills, experience, and capabilities of the SOA center to the rest of the architecture practice.
- Identify how members of the CoE, and other architecture practitioners, will be rewarded for success.
- Recognition that, at the start, it is unlikely the organization will have the necessary skills to create a fully functional CoE. The necessary skills and experience must be carefully identified, and where they are not present, acquired. A fundamental skill for leading practitioners within the CoE is the ability to mentor other practitioners transferring knowledge, skills, and experience.
- Close-out plan for when the CoE has fulfilled its purpose.

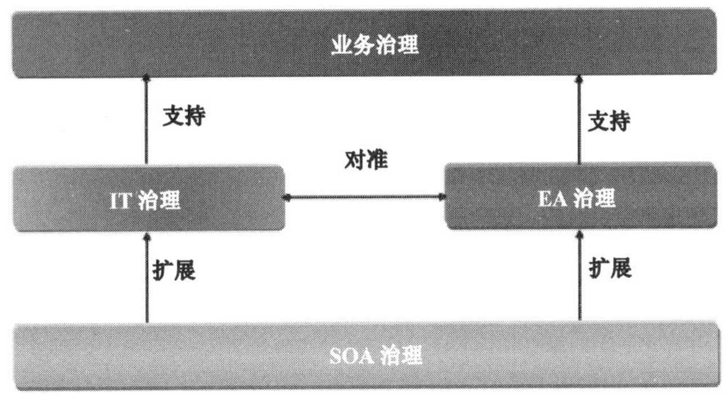

图 22-1 The Open Group SOA 治理框架

22.7.1.3 划分和卓越中心

不同团队将同时致力于不同的架构元素。划分使得特定分组的架构师能拥有并开发架构的特定元素。建议团队在大规模实施前从焦点举措开始推进。负责 SOA 的团队在成立之初应构建为卓越中心（CoE）。

一个成功的 CoE 将具有若干关键属性：

- CoE 任务的明确定义：其存在的原因、责任范围及组织和架构实践应期望从该 CoE 中得到的内容。
- CoE 的清晰目标包括测度和关键绩效指标（KPI）。重要的是，确保 CoE 的测度和 KPI 未导致不恰当选择 SOA 作为架构风格。
- CoE 会提供良好服务的"试金石"。
- CoE 会向其余架构实践传播 SOA 中心的技能、经验和能力。
- 识别 CoE 的成员和其他架构实践者如何因成功而得到奖励。
- 要认识到，组织不可能在一开始就具有创建功能全面 CoE 的必要技能。必须仔细识别必要的技能和经验，如果没有就需要获取。一种在 CoE 内引领实践者的基础性技能是指导其他实践者传递知识、技能和经验的能力。
- CoE 何时实现其目的的完工计划。

22.7.1.4 Architecture Repository

There are a number of SOA resources that should be considered when initially populating the Architecture Repository as described in The Open Group SOA Reference Architecture (see The Open Group SOA Source Book). These include:

- **The Building Blocks of SOA**, which describes a set of ABBs that represent the key elements of SOA.
- **A High-Level Perspective of the SOA Reference Architecture**, which gives an overview of the nine layers of the reference architecture, with examples and rationale describing the main responsibilities of the layers and their primary building blocks.
- **Detailed Building Blocks of the SOA Reference Architecture**, which presents detailed models that show how some of the features of SOA can be implemented using the reference architecture.
- **Infrastructure for SOA**, which describes Architecture Building Blocks (ABBs) that correspond to infrastructure products that are available today to support service-oriented applications.
- **Industry SOA Standards**, such as the TeleManagement Forum Integration Framework.

A high-level graphic that describes The Open Group SOA Reference Architecture follows:

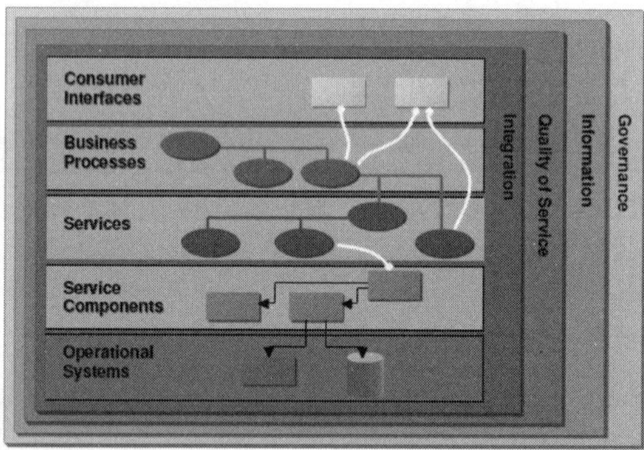

Figure 22-2 The Open Group SOA Reference Architecture

22.7.1.4 架构库

如 The Open Group SOA 参考架构（见 The Open Group SOA 源手册）中所述，许多 SOA 资源应在初次填充架构库时进行考虑。这些 SOA 资源包括：

- **SOA 的构建块**，描述一套表达 SOA 关键元素的 ABB。
- SOA **参考架构中的一个高层级的关注层级**，提供对参考架构九个分层的概述，用示例和理由依据描述各分层及其基本构建块的主要职责。
- **SOA 参考架构的详细构建块**，提供详细模型来表明如何利用该参考架构实现 SOA 的某些特征。
- **SOA 基础设施**，描述与当前可用于支持面向服务应用的基础设施产品对应的架构构建块（ABB）。
- **SOA 行业标准**，例如电信管理论坛集成框架。

一种描述 The Open Group SOA 参考架构的高层级图示如下所示。

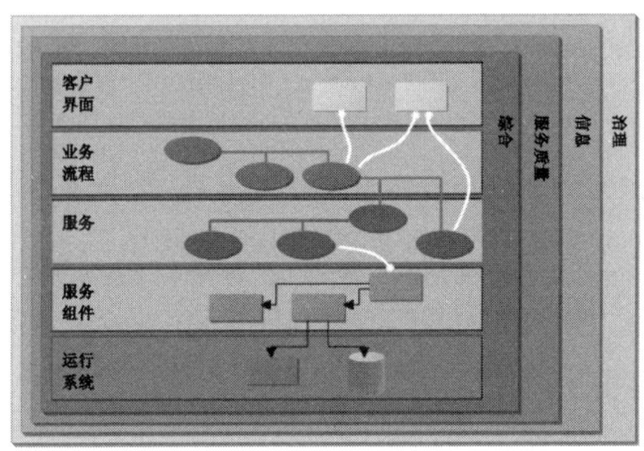

图 22-2　The Open Group SOA 参考架构

22.7.2 Phase A: Architecture Vision

The high-level description produced in Phase A will reflect the service-oriented nature of the architecture that is envisaged. One obvious difference between an SOA architecture description and a description of an architecture of another style is the language. The SOA description uses different language, with words such as "policy", "composition", and "task", and it has different models, such as matrices showing use of services by business processes and use of applications by services. The Open Group SOA Ontology provides a taxonomy and ontology for SOA.

In an SOA project it is important to ensure that stakeholders understand the implications of SOA and are prepared for the organizational impacts of composable SOA services. This impact is applicable whether SOA services are made available as wrapped legacy applications, using exposed services on purchased products, bespoke services, Cloud Computing Software as a Service (SaaS), etc.

22.7.2.1 Stakeholders, Concerns, and Business Requirements

The stakeholders to consult, the requirements to address, and the models, artifacts, and views to develop vary from one architecture engagement to another. There are some concerns that are specific to SOA, or are more likely to arise in SOA developments. The *Addressing Stakeholder Concerns in SOA* section of The Open Group SOA Source Book is a good resource for addressing this topic.

22.7.3 Architecture Development: Phases B, C, and D

In this section we consider the SOA impact on Phases B, C, and D, the architecture development domains. The following graphic of the TOGAF Content Metamodel identifies (outlined in red) entities that are key to SOA.

22.7.2 阶段 A：架构愿景

阶段 A 中生成的高层级描述将反映所设想架构的面向服务的本质。SOA 架构描述与另一种风格的架构描述之间的一个明显差异就是语言。SOA 描述使用不同语言，用到诸如“方针”“组成”和“任务”等词汇，且其具有不同模型，诸如表明通过业务流程使用服务以及通过服务使用应用的矩阵。The Open Group SOA 本体论为 SOA 提供分类法和本体论。

在一个 SOA 项目中，重要的是确保利益攸关者理解 SOA 的意义，并且对可组合 SOA 服务带来的组织影响做好准备。使得无论是使用购买产品的公开服务、预定服务、云计算软件即服务（SaaS）等，还是使打包遗留应用的 SOA 服务可用，这种影响都是适当的。

22.7.2.1 利益攸关者、关注点和业务需求

待咨询的利益攸关者、待应对的需求及待开发的模型、制品和视图在不同架构介入之间各不相同。有一些关注点是特定于 SOA 的，或更可能在 SOA 开发中出现。《The Open Group SOA 源手册》的“在 SOA 中应对利益攸关者的关注点”一节是应对此类主题的良好资源。

22.7.3 架构开发：阶段 B、C 和 D

本节考虑了 SOA 对阶段 B、C 和 D 架构开发域的影响。以下 TOGAF 内容元模型图识别了对于 SOA 而言关键的实体（用红色标出）。

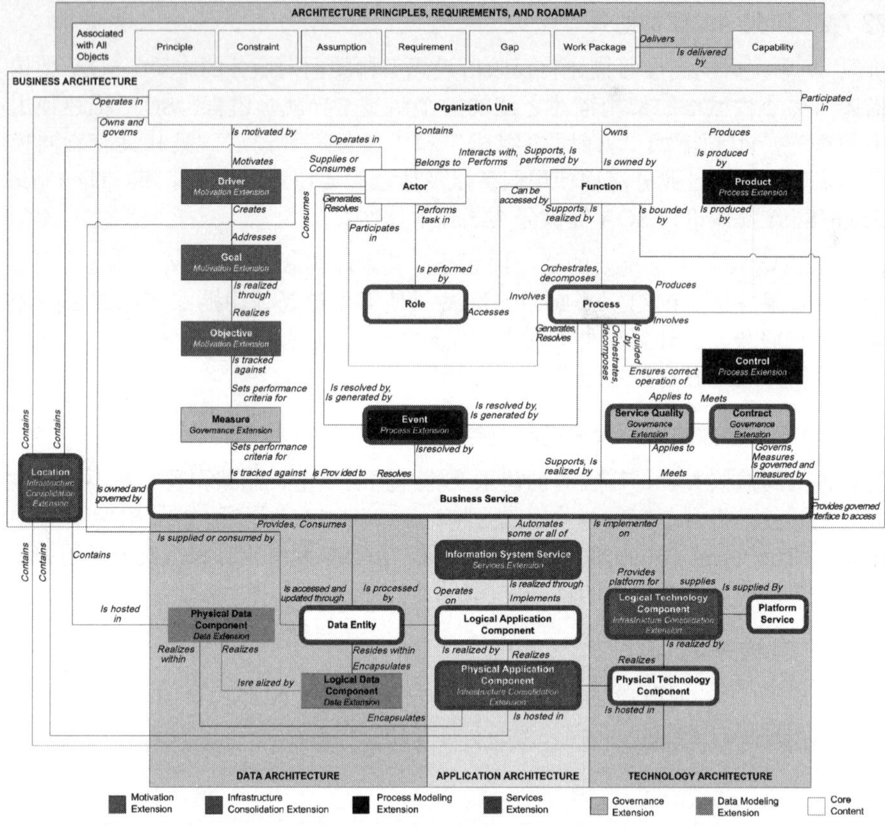

Figure 22-3 SOA Entities in the Content Metamodel

Key entities include:

- Event
- Process
- Business Service
- IS Service
- Platform service
- Logical Application and Technology Component
- Physical Application and Technology Component
- Data entity
- Role

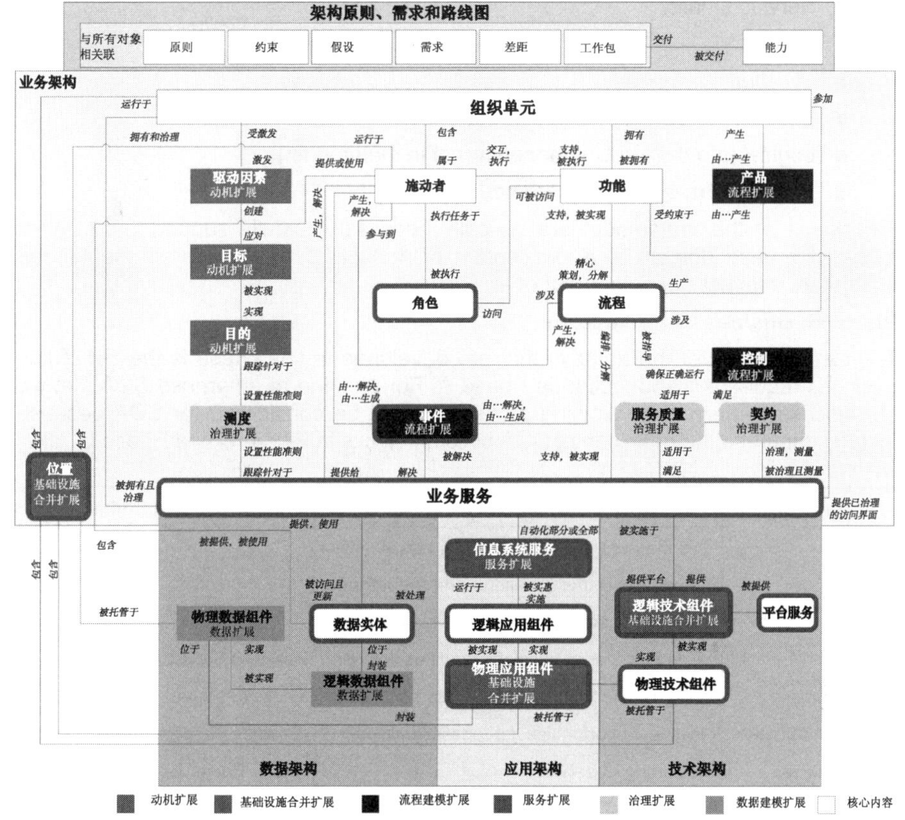

图 22-3　内容元模型中的 SOA 实体

见彩色插图 ii 页

关键实体包括：

- 事件
- 流程
- 业务服务
- IS 服务
- 平台服务
- 逻辑应用和技术组件
- 物理应用和技术组件
- 数据实体
- 角色

- Service Quality
- Contract
- Location
- Business Information (not in metamodel)
- Logical Information Components (not in metamodel)
- Business Rules (not in metamodel)

Extensions of the metamodel are typically necessary to fully support SOA. What follows for each domain is a description of artifacts that are appropriate for the enterprise architect's development of an SOA.

Phase B: Business Architecture

The starting point for the artifacts that are developed in this phase is the set of key business requirements identified in Phase A. For the kind of enterprise SOA that we are discussing here, the following artifacts should be considered for SOA because they contribute to the definition of SOA building blocks in Phase C and Phase D.

Artifact	Purpose	Metamodel Entities
Business ServiceInteraction Diagram	This diagram shows all thebusiness services in scope and their relations and the information flowing between thebusiness services. It will indicate what business services are commonly re-used by other business services indicating opportunities for possible re-use of supporting IS services. The diagram will also be used to define business processes and the relationships between those business processes since each process is composed by a subset of this model	Business Services, Contracts, Business Information (Business Information is mentioned in Phase B, but there is not a metamodel entity.)
Business Process Diagram	This is a set of diagrams thatshow the business processes and their decomposition, their interactions, and the information with which they are concerned	Subset of Business Service Model showing the Business Se-r vices and Contracts involved in the processes and the Business Inf-ormation passed between the Bu-siness Services

- 服务质量
- 契约
- 位置
- 业务信息（不在元模型之中）
- 逻辑信息组件（不在元模型之中）
- 业务规则（不在元模型之中）

通常，需要扩展元模型以完全支持 SOA。对每个域而言，接下来是描述适合 ENTERPRISE 架构师开发 SOA 的制品。

阶段 B：业务架构

该阶段开发制品的起始点是阶段 A 中所识别的一系列关键业务需求。对于本处讨论的此类 ENTERPRISESOA，应针对 SOA 考虑以下制品，因为它们有助于定义阶段 C 和阶段 D 中的 SOA 构建块。

制品	目的	元模型实体
业务服务交互图	该图显示范围内的所有业务服务及其关系以及业务服务之间流动的信息。表明哪些业务服务通常被其他业务服务复用，为有可能支持 IS 服务的复用指明机会。 由于每个流程由本模型的子集组成，因此该图还将被用来定义业务流程和那些业务流程之间的关系	业务服务、契约、业务信息 （在阶段 B 中提到业务信息，但不存在元模型实体。）
业务流程图	这是一套表明业务流程及其分解、交互和其所涉及信息的图	业务服务模型的子集，用以表明这些流程中所涉及的业务服务和契约及在业务服务之间传递的业务信息

Artifact	Purpose	Metamodel Entities
Business Vocabulary Catalog	This is a list of the key termsused in describing the business processes and information. It is important that the Business Architecture phase establishes the information context for the software services, as described in the *Information Architecture for SOA* section of The Open Group Source Book, and a catalog of business terms is an important part of this context. The business vocabulary can be derived while developing the business service model	This is a list of Business Information elements and descriptions of those elements (Business Information is mentioned in Phase B, but there is not a metamodel entity.)
Business Services Catalog	This is a list of the enterprise's business services and their non-functional requirements. It is used to analyze the non-functional requirements	List of Business Services and their Service Qualities
Business Service/ Location Catalog	To understand where the Business Services need to be executed	Business Service, Location
Event/ Process Catalog	To understand which process is run in relation to an event	Lists Event and their effected Business Process
Contract/ Service Quality Catalog	To understand the non-functional properties of a contract	Lists Contracts and their relevant Service Qualities
Business Service Interaction Matrix	To show relations between Business Services	Business Services on both axisand Contracts in the cross point
Business Service/ Information Matrix (CRUD)	To show how information elements are used by Business Services and to find faults in that model	Business Services and Business Information elements (Business Information is mentioned in Phase B, but there is not a current TOGAF metamodel entity.)
Information Component Model	To define the logical structure ofthe information in the organization. It can be used as an input to the exchange model defining the input and outputs from SOA services	Business Information elements, Logical Information Components, and their relations (None of these exist in the current metamodel.)

The appropriate views should be produced to enable demonstration to stakeholders of how their SOA-specific concerns relating to the Business Architecture are addressed. In doing this the architect addresses the requirements that can be satisfied by the Business Architecture. The remaining architecture requirements will be addressed in Phase C and Phase D.

制品	目的	元模型实体
业务词汇表目录	这是一个用于描述业务流程和信息的关键术语列表。重要的是，如《The Open Group 源手册》的 SOA 信息架构一节中所述，业务架构阶段为软件服务建立信息背景环境，并且业务术语目录是该背景环境的一个重要部分。业务词汇表可在开发业务服务模型时被导出	这是一个业务信息元素及那些元素描述的列表 （在阶段 B 中提到业务信息，但不存在元模型实体。）
业务服务目录	这是 ENTERPRISE 业务服务及其非功能性需求的列表。其被用于分析这些非功能性需求	业务服务及其服务质量的列表
业务服务/位置目录	理解需要执行业务服务的位置	业务服务，位置
事件/流程目录	理解哪个流程的运行与一个事件有关	列出事件及其受影响的业务流程
契约/服务质量目录	理解一个契约的非功能属性	列出契约及其相关服务质量
业务服务交互矩阵	表明业务服务之间的关系	位于轴线和契约交叉点上的业务服务
业务服务/信息矩阵（CRUD）	表明信息元素如何被业务服务使用并且找出模型中的错误	业务服务和业务信息元素 （在阶段 B 中提到业务信息，但不存在当前的 TOGAF 元模型实体。）
信息组件模型	定义组织中信息的逻辑结构。在定义 SOA 服务中输入和输出的交换模型中，本模型可被用作一个输入	业务信息元素，逻辑信息组件及其关系 （这些项均未存在于当前元模型之中。）

应生成适当的视图，向利益攸关者展示如何应对与业务架构有关的 SOA 特定关注点。在此阶段时，架构师应对可由业务架构满足的需求。其余的架构需求将在阶段 C 和阶段 D 中得以应对。

Phase C: Information Systems Architectures

The phase is split into two sub-phases, Data Architecture and Applications Architecture. SOA makes little difference to the Data Architecture sub-phase, but it has a major impact on the Applications Architecture. As well as affecting the artifacts that are developed, the views that are produced, the concerns that are discussed, and the requirements that are identified, SOA affects the way that the architect does the gap analysis between Baseline and Target Architectures in Phase C.

With SOA, the traditional software applications are replaced by sets of loosely-coupled services. Existing applications should still be described, as should any new applications of a traditional kind that are required, and these applications should be included in the applications portfolio. In addition, areas of application functionality that are covered by services should be identified. These will (probably as part of the implementation) be decomposed into services, which will be included in the services portfolio.

But SOA is not only about services, it is also the solutions created by using combinations of services. These solutions are usually structured using the Business Processes and Business Services defined in Phase B.

SOA-Specific Phase C Artifacts

Artifact	Purpose	Metamodel Entity Usage
IS Service-Interaction Diagram	This shows requirements forpotential SOA services (IS Services) and the interactions between them, and their use of information. It is used to show the full set of requirements for the solution and the relationships between the requirements	IS Services and the Contracts between them The Contracts indicate what Business Information is communicated. Preferably the Service Quality entity for both IS Services and Contracts are derived from the Business Services and their Contracts and related Service Qualities
Business Process/ IS Service Matrix	This matrix shows the relation between each Business Process and the IS Services supporting the process. It is used to show the full set of requirements for SOA services for a given Business Process	Business Process and itsrelation to IS Service(s)
IS Service Contract Catalog	The catalog lists all IS Services,their Contracts, and the related Service Qualities to enable analysis of the non-functional requirements (e.g., security, performance, loading, availability, policies, etc.) for potential SOA Services. This catalog is an important input to the Service Portfolio Management process in SOA governance	List of IS Services and their related Service Qualities Additionally, IS Service Contracts for each IS Service are included

阶段 C：信息系统架构

本阶段被分成两个子阶段，即数据架构和应用架构。SOA 对数据架构子阶段几乎不产生影响，但是对应用架构影响重大。SOA 影响了阶段 C 中架构师在基线架构和目标架构之间进行差距分析的方式，还影响所开发的制品、所生成的视图、所讨论的关注点和所识别的需求。

应用 SOA，传统软件应用被多套松耦合的服务所替代。现有应用仍应按所需任何传统类型的新应用一样被描述，并且这些应用应包括在应用组合中。此外，应识别服务所覆盖的应用功能区域。这些应用（可能作为实施的一部分）将被分解成多个服务，这些服务被包括在服务谱系之中。

但 SOA 不仅与服务相关，也是使用服务组合创建的解决方案。通常，使用阶段 B 中所定义的业务流程和业务服务对这些解决方案进行结构化。

阶段 C 的 SOA 特定制品

制品	目的	元模型实体使用
IS 服务交互图	表明对潜在 SOA 服务（IS 服务）的需求和这些需求之间的交互及其信息使用。用来表明解决方案的一整套需求和这些需求之间的关系	IS 服务和服务之间的契约 这些契约表明传达什么业务信息。最可取的是，IS 服务和契约的服务质量实体源于业务服务及其契约以及相关的服务质量
业务流程/IS 服务矩阵	该矩阵表明各业务流程与支持该流程的 IS 服务之间的关系。用来表明给定业务流程的 SOA 服务的一整套需求	业务流程及其与 IS 服务的关系
IS 服务契约目录集	本目录集列出所有 IS 服务及其契约和相关服务质量，以对潜在 SOA 服务的非功能性需求（例如，安保性、性能、加载、可用性、方针等）进行分析。该目录是对 SOA 治理中的服务项目谱系管理流程的一个重要输入	IS 服务及其相关服务质量的列表 此外，包括每个 IS 服务的多个 IS 服务契约

Artifact	Purpose	Metamodel Entity Usage
IS Service/ Application (existing) Catalog	This catalog connects IS Services (potential SOA Services), Contracts, and Service Qualities with existing applications (as-is Physical Application Components). It is used to specify wrapping scenarios on existing applications and to analyze non-functional requirements	IS Service(s), related Contracts,and Service Qualities connected with as-is Physical Application Components
IS Service/ Data Entity Matrix	This matrix shows what data is handled by potential SOA Services (IS Services). It is used to identify potential data handling SOA Services	IS Services and its related Data Entities
Logical SOA Component Matrix	This matrix shows the relationship between the logical SOA Components (Logical Application Components) and the potential SOA Services (IS Services). It is used to structure Logical Components from the requirements	IS Services, Logical Application Components, and Principles and Business Drivers (used to find criteria to do grouping) A Logical SOA Component (Logical Application Component) would be a candidate for an SOA Serviceon capability-level architectures
Logical SOA Solution Diagram	This diagram shows the relations between the logical SOA components (Logical Application Components) and other logical solutions (Logical Application Components). It is used to show and analyze the functional and non-functional requirements of the interfaces between solutions	Logical Application Components and Contracts and their Service Qualities Logical Technology Components and their mapping to Contracts are used for the interface mechanisms
Service Distribution Matrix	This matrix shows the services distributed on physical locations to fulfil legal or other requirement. The purpose is to show and analyze if there are any location requirements on services. This can be done on either IS Services or Logical Application Components	IS Service, Logical Application Component, Physical Application Component, and Location

Using the artifacts, the architect should develop views that demonstrate to stakeholders how their SOA-specific concerns relating to the Applications Architecture are addressed. Models that enable discussion of concerns relating to the Data Architecture should also be developed as part of Phase C. These are similar to the models that would be developed for a traditional architecture based on software applications.

In doing this, this addresses the requirements that can be satisfied by the Information Systems Architectures. The remaining architecture requirements will be addressed in Phase D: Technology Architecture.

制品	目的	元模型实体使用
IS 服务/数据实体矩阵	本矩阵表明哪些数据由潜在 SOA 服务（IS 服务）处理。用来识别处理 SOA 服务的潜在数据	IS 服务及其相关数据实体
逻辑 SOA 组件矩阵	本矩阵表明逻辑 SOA 组件（逻辑应用组件）和潜在 SOA 服务（IS 服务）之间的关系。用来对来自需求的逻辑组件进行结构化	IS 服务、逻辑应用组件、原则和业务驱动因素（用于发现进行分组的准则） 一个逻辑 SOA 组件（逻辑应用组件）将是多个能力层级架构上的一个 SOA 服务的候选组件
逻辑 SOA 解决方案图	本图表明逻辑 SOA 组件（逻辑应用组件）和其他逻辑解决方案（IS 服务）之间的关系。用来表明和分析解决方案之间界面的功能性和非功能性需求	逻辑应用组件和契约及其服务质量 逻辑技术组件及其与契约的对应关系被用于界面机制
服务分布矩阵	本矩阵表明为满足法律或其他需求而在物理位置上分布的服务。其目的是表明和分析是否具有对服务的任何位置需求。这可针对 IS 服务或逻辑应用组件中的任何一项进行	IS 服务、逻辑应用组件、物理应用组件和位置

架构师应使用这些制品来开发视图，向利益攸关者展示其与应用架构有关的 SOA 特定关注点如何得以应对。能用于讨论与数据架构相关的关注点的模型还应作为阶段 C 的一部分来开发。这些模型与将为基于软件应用的传统架构而开发的模型相似。

该执行过程应对可被信息系统架构所满足的需求。其余的架构需求将在阶段 D：技术架构中应对。

In each of Phases B, C, and D a gap analysis should be performed between the Baseline and Target Architectures to determine what needs to be done to move from the baseline to the target. For Phases B and D, and the Data Architecture sub-phase of Phase C, this is not much affected by SOA. For the Applications Architecture sub-phase of Phase C, however, SOA makes a difference to the way that the gap analysis is performed.

The ABBs defined in Phase C will include traditional applications and groups of services covering areas of application functionality. Both kinds of building block should be included in the gap analysis. However, it may be the intent that a group of services be implemented as a "wrapper" over existing applications. This situation, which is special for SOA, should be indicated in the gap analysis, as well as situations where old applications are to be removed or replaced, or new applications are to be added.

Phase D: Technology Architecture

For SOA, the Technology Architecture defines the software and hardware infrastructure needed to support the portfolio of services. A starting point for the Technology Architecture is The Open Group SOA Reference Architecture which contains most platform services possible for an SOA infrastructure. Each organization will need to customize the SOA Reference Architecture to their needs.

SOA-Specific Phase D Artifacts

Artifact	Purpose	Metamodel Entity Usage
Logical Technology Architecture Diagram	This diagram is used to show and analyze the instance of The Open Group SOA Reference Architecture. It will contain all ABBs and capabilities deemed necessary for the SOA solution	Platform Service (Capability),Logical Technology Component(ABB)
Logical Applicationand Technology Matrix	This matrix is used to show and analyze the relations between the Logical Application Components and the Logical Technology Components to ensure the architect understands what technology will be used for the Logical Application Components. It will also be used to derive and validate the non-functional requirements for the technology components	Logical Application Componentsand their relations to Logical Technology Components, including derivations of the Service Qualities

The Open Group has produced additional information concerning adapting an organization's infrastructure for service-orientation, including The Open Group Service-Oriented Infrastructure (SOI) Reference Model (consult The Open Group SOA Source Book for guidance).

Using the artifacts and SOI Reference Model, the architect should develop views that demonstrate to the stakeholders how their SOA-specific concerns relating to the Technology Architecture are addressed.

在阶段 B、C 和 D 中，应在基线架构和目标架构之间进行差距分析，以确定从基线架构到目标架构转移而需完成的内容。对于阶段 B 和 D 及阶段 C 的数据架构子阶段，将不会受到 SOA 的很大影响。然而，对于阶段 C 的应用架构子阶段，SOA 对差距分析的执行方式产生影响。

阶段 C 中所定义的 ABB 将包括传统应用及覆盖多个应用功能区域的多组服务。这两种构建块应包括在差距分析之中。然而，其意图可能是执行一组服务，在多个现有的应用上用作“封装器”。应在差距分析中指出这种对于 SOA 而言特殊的情况，并指出将删除或替代旧应用的情况或将添加新应用的情况。

阶段 D：技术架构

对于 SOA，技术架构定义支持服务谱系所需的软件和硬件基础设施。技术架构的起始点是 The Open Group SOA 参考架构，其包含对 SOA 基础设施可能实现的大多数平台服务。每个组织需要按其需求定制 SOA 参考架构。

阶段 D 特定于 SOA 的制品

制品	目的	元模型实体使用
逻辑技术架构图	本图被用来表明和分析 The Open Group SOA 参考架构的实例。其包含所有被认为 SOA 解决方案所必需的 ABB 和能力	平台服务（能力）、逻辑技术组件（ABB）
逻辑应用和技术矩阵	本矩阵被用来表明和分析逻辑应用组件和逻辑技术组件之间的关系，以确保架构师理解何种技术将用于逻辑应用组件。还用来推导并确认这些技术组件的非功能性需求	逻辑应用组件及其与逻辑技术组件的关系，包括服务质量的派生

The Open Group 已产生关于为面向服务调整组织基础设施的附加信息，包括 The Open Group 面向服务基础设施（SOI）参考模型（参考《The Open Group SOA 源手册》作为指导）。

架构师应使用这些制品和 SOI 参考模型来开发视图，向利益攸关者展示其与技术架构有关的 SOA 特定关注点如何得以应对。

In doing this, the architect adds further requirements to those identified in Phases A, B, and C, and addresses the requirements that can be satisfied by the Technology Architecture. All architecture requirements should have been addressed by the end of this phase. If there are still outstanding architecture requirements, then it is necessary to go back to Phase B or Phase C to address them. Implementation requirements will be addressed by the projects that are identified in Phase E.

Phase E: Opportunities and Solutions

The identification of SOA solutions is a key task for SOA. The questions of what SOA solutions the enterprise will have, and how they will be managed, should be considered in this phase.

Solution delivery options are normally considered as part of this phase. A delivery option that should be considered particularly for SOA is the use of services provided by external companies, as opposed to the development of services in-house or the acquisition of software products that perform the services.

SOA-Specific Phase E Artifacts

Artifact	Purpose	Metamodel Entity Usage
Physical SOASolution Matrix	This matrix shows the relationship between the physical SOA solutions (Physical Application Components) and the Logical SOA Components. It is used to define the physical structure of the SOA solution	IS Services, Logical Application Components, Physical Application Components and Principles & Business Drivers (used to find criteria to do structuring)
Physical SOASolution Diagram	This diagram shows the relations between the physical SOA solution (Physical Application Components) and other solutions (Physical Application Components). It is used to show and analyze the functional and non-functional requirements of the interfaces between solutions	Physical Application Components and Contracts and their Service Qualities Physical Technology Components and their mapping to Contracts are used for the interface mechanisms
Physical Service Solution Matrix	This matrix shows which existing services are re-used, which services could be provided by external services (SaaS), and which services need to be developed as wrappings of new/existing applications and which need to be developed. It is an input to the SOA Governance Service Portfolio Management process	IS Services, Physical Application Components (as-is SOA services for re-use), other Physical Application Components (new and existing applications to be wrapped), and new Physical Application Components (new services to be developed or purchased externally)

在执行过程中，架构师将更多的需求添加至阶段 A、B 和 C 已识别的需求中，并且应对可由该技术架构满足的需求。所有架构需求应在该阶段结束前已得到应对。如果仍存在未解决的架构需求，则有必要返回到阶段 B 或阶段 C 来应对这些需求。通过在阶段 E 中所识别的项目来应对实施需求。

阶段 E：机会和解决方案

识别 SOA 解决方案是 SOA 的一项关键任务。应在本阶段考虑关于 ENTERPRISE 应具有何种 SOA 解决方案及其如何管理的问题。

通常认为解决方案交付选项是该阶段的一部分。一个为 SOA 特别考虑的交付选项是使用外部公司所提供的服务，而非开发内部服务或采办执行这些服务的软件产品。

阶段 E 特定于 SOA 的制品

制品	目的	元模型实体使用
物理 SOA 解决方案矩阵	本矩阵表明物理 SOA 解决方案（物理应用组件）和逻辑 SOA 组件之间的关系。用来定义 SOA 解决方案的物理结构	IS 服务、逻辑应用组件、物理应用组件及原则和业务驱动因素（用于找到进行结构化的准则）
物理 SOA 解决方案图	本图表明物理 SOA 解决方案（物理应用组件）和其他解决方案（物理应用组件）之间的关系。用来表明和分析解决方案之间界面的功能性和非功能性需求	物理应用组件和契约及其服务质量 物理技术组件及其与契约的对应关系 用于界面机制
物理服务解决方案矩阵	本矩阵表明哪些现有服务可被复用，哪些服务可由外部服务（SaaS）提供，哪些服务需要包装新的/现有的应用来开发以及哪些服务需要被开发。 这是对 SOA 治理服务项目谱系管理流程的一个输入	IS 服务、物理应用组件（为了复用的当前 SOA 服务）、其他物理应用组件（待封装的新的和现有的应用）和新的物理应用组件（待外部开发或购买的新服务）

Artifact	Purpose	Metamodel Entity Usage
Application Guidelines	This document provides guidelines on how to develop SOA solutions and services. Suggestions of possible guidelines can be found in Appendix A of The Open Group SOA Governance Framework	
Physical Technology Architecture Diagram	This diagram is used to showand analyze the physical technical solution for the SOA infrastructure	Platform Service, Logical Technology Component, Physical Technology Component
Physical Applicationand Technology Matrix	This matrix is used to show and analyze the physical infrastructure used to run the physical application and to ensure that the non-functional requirements are derived properly and understood	Physical Application Components and their relations to Physical Technology Components, including derivations of the Service Qualities
Technology Portfolio Catalog	This is a list of products and kinds of product that will be used in the implementation, including SOA run-time infrastructure, SOA development environment, service component technology, and service interface (portal, channel, etc.) technology. It will also include non-functional requirements	Physical Application Components and their relation with Service Qualities
Technology Guidelines	This document provides guidelines on how to use SOA infrastructure. Suggestions of possible guidelines can be found in Appendix A of The Open Group SOA Governance Framework	

The implementation projects that are identified, and the implementation and migration strategy, will depend on the decisions taken on the level of detail of implementation specification when the architect team scoped the architecture development in Phase A.

Phase F: Migration Planning

The implementation governance model is reviewed in Phase F in order to ensure that it is in place before the next phase — Implementation Governance — commences. SOA requires particular governance rules and procedures. The governance and support strategy is reviewed in the Preliminary Phase. If it needs to be updated for SOA, then this should be done before implementation starts. This should use the same resources identified in Secton 22.7.1.2.

制品	目的	元模型实体使用
应用指南	本文件对如何开发 SOA 解决方案和服务提供指南。关于可能的指南的建议可在 The Open Group SOA 治理框架的附录 A 中找到	
物理技术架构图	本图用来表明和分析 SOA 基础设施的物理技术解决方案	平台服务、逻辑技术组件、物理技术组件
物理应用和技术矩阵	本矩阵用来表明和分析用于运行物理应用的物理基础设施，并且用来确保适当地导出和理解非功能性需求	物理应用组件及其与物理技术组件的关系，包括服务质量的派生
项目谱系目录集	这是一个实施所用产品和产品种类的列表，包括 SOA 运行时间基础设施、SOA 开发环境、服务组件技术和服务界面（门户、信道等）技术。还包括非功能性需求	物理应用组件及其与服务质量的关系
技术指南	本文件对如何使用 SOA 基础设施提供指南。关于可能的指南的建议可在 The Open Group SOA 治理框架的附录 A 中找到	

架构师团队在阶段 A 中界定架构开发时，对实施规范的细节层级所做的决策决定所识别的实施项目及实施和迁移战略。

阶段 F：迁移规划

在阶段 F 审查实施治理模型，以便确保其在下一个阶段——实施治理——开始前落实到位。SOA 需要多个特殊的治理规则和程序。在预备阶段中审查治理和支持策略，如果为了 SOA 需要将其更新，则在开始实施之前需要进行这一步。这应使用 22.7.1.2 节中所识别的相同资源。

Phase G: Implementation Governance

The activities performed in the Implementation Governance phase will depend in part on the decisions taken on the level of detail of implementation specification when the architect team scoped the architecture development in Phase A. During the Implementation Governance phase, the monitoring part of the SGVM should be put in operation to ensure that the SOA governance activities are performed at the correct level.

Phase H: Architecture Change Management

It is at this point that the architect should determine whether it is necessary to revisit the Preliminary Phase to adjust the Architecture Capability. Where SOA has not previously been used within an enterprise, Phase H of an architecture development is an opportunity to assess the contribution that SOA could make, and to consider adopting the principle of service-orientation.

22.8 Summary

There are a number of SOA methods, tools, and reference materials available to help the Enterprise Architect develop SOA. The Open Group standards and publications are suggested. Some are directly focused on SOA — such as the SOA Source Book, OSIMM, or the SGVM — others are not directly focused but regularly useful, such as outputs of The Open Group Security Forum.

Using TOGAF to create SOA requires adapting TOGAF to address the requirements of a particular style. Addressing a style will require:

- Identifying key metamodel entries
- Identifying extensions to the content metamodel
- Identifying key artifacts
- Identifying style-specific reference materials and maturity models

The adaption of an Architecture Capability to support SOA requires considerable activity in the Preliminary Phase of TOGAF. These activities and SOA-specific Open Group SOA Work Group tools include:

- Adapting the principle of service-orientation
- Determining organization readiness for SOA: OSIMM
- Governance: The Open Group SGVM
- Partitions: Utilize a specialist Center of Excellence to support SOA

In the rest of the TOGAF ADM phases, what changes is how an architecture is described, analyzed, and documented. During an iteration of the ADM the practitioner needs to consider the key metamodel entities identified, and the artifacts identified. At different levels of granularity the purpose of the ADM cycle will vary. In Strategic-level work the purpose is identifying whether SOA is needed, and in which Segments. In Segment-level work the purpose is describing the structure and capability requirements of SOA. Finally, in the Capability-level work to identify and describe the requirements of the SOA services that will be available.

When delivering SOA with TOGAF, the practitioner should never lose sight of the final objective: SOA solutions that address managing the enterprise's complexity and provide business agility.

阶段 G：实施治理

架构师团队在阶段 A 中界定架构开发时，对实施规范的细节层级所做的决策部分地决定在实施治理阶段执行的活动。在该实施治理阶段中，SGVM 的监控部分应投入运行，以确保在正确的层级上执行 SOA 治理活动。

阶段 H：架构变更管理

正是在这一阶段，架构师应确定是否有必要回顾“预备阶段”以调整架构能力。在 ENTERPRISE 先前未使用过 SOA 的情况下，架构开发的阶段 H 是评估 SOA 可做的贡献和考虑采用面向服务原则的一个机会。

22.8 概要总结

有许多 SOA 方法、工具和参考资料可用于帮助 ENTERPRISE 架构师开发 SOA。建议参考 The Open Group 标准和出版物，一些直接聚焦于 SOA——诸如 SOA 源手册、OSIMM 或 SGVM——其他的并非直接聚焦于 SOA 但频繁使用，诸如 The Open Group 安保讨论会的输出。

使用 TOGAF 创建 SOA，需要调整 TOGAF 来应对特定风格的需求。应对一种风格将需要：

- 识别关键元模型实体
- 识别对内容元模型的扩展
- 识别关键制品
- 识别风格特定的参考资料和成熟度模型

调整架构能力以支持 SOA 要求在 TOGAF 的预备阶段进行大量的活动。这些活动和 SOA 特定的 Open Group SOA 工作组工具包括：

- 调整面向服务的原则
- 为 SOA：OSIMM 确定组织准备情况
- 治理：The Open Group SGVM
- 划分：利用专业的卓越中心支持 SOA

在 TOGAF ADM 的其余阶段，发生变化的内容是如何描述、分析一个架构并将其文件化。在 ADM 迭代中，实践者需要考虑所识别的关键元模型实体和制品。ADM 循环的目的将在不同粒度层级上变化。在战略层级工作中，其目的在于识别是否需要 SOA 和在哪些分段中需要 SOA。在分段层级工作中，其目的在于描述 SOA 的结构和能力需求。最后，在能力层级工作中识别和描述可用的 SOA 服务的需求。

当利用 TOGAF 交付 SOA 时，实践者不应忽视最终目的：SOA 解决方案应对管理 ENTERPRISE 的复杂性并提供业务敏捷性。

Chapter 23
Architecture Principles

This chapter describes principles for use in the development of an enterprise architecture.

23.1 Introduction

Principles are general rules and guidelines, intended to be enduring and seldom amended, that inform and support the way in which an organization sets about fulfilling its mission.

In their turn, principles may be just one element in a structured set of ideas that collectively define and guide the organization, from values through to actions and results.

Depending on the organization, principles may be established within different domains and at different levels. Two key domains inform the development and utilization of architecture:

- **Enterprise** principles provide a basis for decision-making throughout an enterprise, and inform how the organization sets about fulfilling its mission. Such principles are commonly found as a means of harmonizing decision-making across an organization. In particular, they are a key element in a successful architecture governance strategy (see Chapter 50).

  Within the broad domain of enterprise principles, it is common to have subsidiary principles within a business or organizational unit. Examples include IT, HR, domestic operations, or overseas operations. These principles provide a basis for decision-making within the subsidiary domain and will inform architecture development within the domain. Care must be taken to ensure that the principles used to inform architecture development align to the organizational context of the Architecture Capability.

- **Architecture** principles are a set of principles that relate to architecture work. They reflect a level of consensus across the enterprise, and embody the spirit and thinking of existing enterprise principles. Architecture principles govern the architecture process, affecting the development, maintenance, and use of the enterprise architecture.

  It is common to have sets of principles form a hierarchy, in that segment principles will be informed by, and elaborate on, the principles at the enterprise level. Architecture principles will be informed and constrained by enterprise principles.

Architecture principles may restate other enterprise guidance in terms and form that effectively guide architecture development.

The remainder of this section deals exclusively with architecture principles.

第 23 章 架构原则

本章描述用于 Enterprise Architecture 开发的原则。

23.1 简介

原则是持久的、极少修改的一般规则和指南，其告知并支持组织着手履行任务的方式。

而这些原则可能只是一套结构化思想中的一个元素，这些结构化思想从价值观到行动和结果共同地定义和指导组织。

根据不同组织，在不同域内和不同层级上建立多个原则。两个关键域为架构的开发和利用提供依据：

- ENTERPRISE 原则为整个 ENTERPRISE 的决策提供基础，并且为组织如何着手履行任务提供依据。这些原则通常被认为是协调贯穿组织进行决策的一种手段。特别地，这些原则是一个成功架构治理战略（见第 50 章）中的关键元素。

  在广泛的 ENTERPRISE 原则的范围内，一个业务或组织单元内具有多个辅助性原则是很常见的。例如，IT、HR、国内运行或海外运行。这些原则为该子域内的决策提供依据并将贯彻到该域内的架构开发。必须要注意，确保这些用于为架构开发提供依据的原则与该架构能力的组织背景环境相对准。

- **架构**原则是与架构工作有关的一套原则。它们反映贯穿 ENTERPRISE 的共识程度，并且体现现有 ENTERPRISE 原则的精髓和思维方式。架构原则管控架构流程，影响 Enterprise Architecture 的开发、维护和使用。

  将多套原则构成一个层级结构是很普遍的，分部原则在这种层级结构上被 ENTERPRISE 层级的原则贯彻和详细阐述。架构原则将由 ENTERPRISE 原则贯彻并受其约束。

架构原则可使用有效指导架构开发的术语和形式来重申其他 ENTERPRISE 的引导。

本节的其余部分专门论述架构原则。

23.2 Characteristics of Architecture Principles

Architecture principles define the underlying general rules and guidelines for the use and deployment of all IT resources and assets across the enterprise. They reflect a level of consensus among the various elements of the enterprise, and form the basis for making future IT decisions.

Each architecture principle should be clearly related back to the business objectives and key architecture drivers.

23.3 Components of Architecture Principles

It is useful to have a standard way of defining principles. In addition to a definition statement, each principle should have associated rationale and implications statements, both to promote understanding and acceptance of the principles themselves, and to support the use of the principles in explaining and justifying why specific decisions are made.

A recommended template is given in Table 23-1.

Table 23-1 Recommended Format for Defining Principles

Name	Should both represent the essence of the rule as well as be easy to remember. Specific technology platforms should not be mentioned in the name or statement of a principle. Avoid ambiguous words in the Name and in the Statement such as: "support", "open", "consider", and for lack of good measure the word "avoid", itself, be careful with "manage(ment)", and look for unnecessary adjectives and adverbs (fluff)
Statement	Should succinctly and unambiguously communicate the fundamental rule. For the most part, the principles statements for managing information are similar from one organization to the next. It is vital that the principles statement be unambiguous
Rationale	Should high light the business benefits of adhering to the principle, using business terminology. Point to the similarity of information and technology principles to the principles governing business operations. Also describe the relationship to other principles, and the intentions regarding a balanced interpretation. Describe situations where one principle would be given precedence or carry more weight than another for making a decision
Implications	Should high light the requirements, both for the business and IT, for carrying out the principle — in terms of resources, costs, and activities/tasks. It will often be apparent that current systems, standards, or practices would be in congruent with the principle upon adoption. The impact to the business and consequences of adopting a principle should be clearly stated. The reader should readily discern the answer to: "How does this affect me?" It is important not to over simplify, trivialize, or judge the merit of the impact. Some of the implications will be identified as potential impacts only, and may be speculative rather than fully analyzed

An example set of architecture principles following this template is given in Section 23.6.

23.2 架构原则的特征

架构原则对贯穿 ENTERPRISE 所有 IT 资源和资产的使用和部署定义出深层的通用规则和指南。这些架构原则，反映 ENTERPRISE 各个元素之间的共识程度，并构成未来 IT 决策的基础。

每个架构原则应反过来与业务目的和关键的架构驱动因素具有明确的关联。

23.3 架构原则的组成部分

有一个定义原则的标准方式是很有用的。除一个定义说明之外，每个原则还应具有多个相关的理由依据和含义说明，以加强对原则本身的理解和认可，并支持使用这些原则，解释做出特定决策的原因并证明其合理性。

表 23-1 中给出了建议的模板。

表 23-1 定义原则的建议格式

名称	应表达该规则的实质并使其便于记忆。特定技术平台不应在原则的名称或说明中提到。避免在名称和说明中使用歧义词，例如“支持”“公开”“考虑”，并且由于缺乏良好的测度，避免使用“避免”这个词本身，谨慎使用“管理”并寻找不必要的形容词和副词（无用的词语）
说明	应简洁且准确地传达基础性的规则。在多数情况下，这些用于管理信息的原则说明在不同组织之间是相似的。至关重要的是，该原则说明应是准确的
理由依据	应使用业务术语来强调遵循该原则的业务好处。应表明信息和技术原则与管控业务运行原则的相似性。还应描述与其他原则的关系和关于平衡解释的意图。描述在决策时一个原则获得优先或比另一个原则更有影响力的情况
含义	应强调对业务和 IT 的需求，以便从资源、成本和活动/任务的角度贯彻该原则。若当前的系统、标准或实践在采用时不符合该原则，通常是很明显的。采用一个原则对业务和后果的影响应明确说明。读者应易于辨别“这如何对我产生影响？”的答案。重要的是，不要过分简单化、轻视或断定该影响的优点。其中的一些意义将仅被识别为潜在影响，并且，可能是推测性的而并非是经过充分分析的

遵循该模板的一个架构原则示例集在第 23.6 节中给出。

23.4 Developing Architecture Principles

Architecture principles are typically developed by the enterprise architects, in conjunction with the key stakeholders, and are approved by the Architecture Board.

Architecture principles will be informed by principles at the enterprise level, if they exist. Architecture principles must be clearly traceable and clearly articulated to guide decision-making. They are chosen so as to ensure alignment of the architecture and implementation ofthe Target Architecture with business strategies and visions.

Specifically, the development of architecture principles is typically influenced by the following:

- **Enterprise mission and plans**: the mission, plans, and organizational infrastructure of the enterprise.
- **Enterprise strategic initiatives**: the characteristics of the enterprise — its strengths, weaknesses, opportunities, and threats — and its current enterprisewide initiatives (such as process improvement and quality management).
- **External constraints**: market factors (time-to-market imperatives, customer expectations, etc.); existing and potential legislation.
- **Current systems and technology**: the set of information resources deployed within the enterprise, including systems documentation, equipment inventories, network configuration diagrams, policies, and procedures.
- **Emerging industry trends**: predictions about economic, political, technical, and market factors that influence the enterprise environment.

23.4.1 Qualities of Principles

Merely having a written statement that is called a principle does not mean that the principle is good, even if everyone agrees with it.

A good set of principles will be founded in the beliefs and values of the organization and expressed in language that the business understands and uses. Principles should be few in number, future-oriented, and endorsed and championed by senior management. They provide a firm foundation for making architecture and planning decisions, framing policies, procedures, and standards, and supporting resolution of contradictory situations. A poor set of principles will quickly become disused, and the resultant architectures, policies, and standards will appear arbitrary or self-serving, and thus lack credibility. Essentially, principles drive behavior.

There are five criteria that distinguish a good set of principles:

- **Understandable**: the underlying tenets can be quickly grasped and understood by individuals throughout the organization. The intention of the principle is clear and unambiguous, so that violations, whether intentional or not, are minimized.
- **Robust**: enable good quality decisions about architectures and plans to be made, and enforceable policies and standards to be created. Each principle should be sufficiently definitive and precise to support consistent decision-making in complex, potentially controversial situations.
- **Complete**: every potentially important principle governing the management of information and technology for the organization is defined. The principles cover every situation perceived.

23.4 开发架构原则

架构原则通常由 ENTERPRISE 架构师与关键的利益攸关者联合开发，并且经架构委员会批准。

架构原则将由 ENTERPRISE 层级上的原则（如果其存在）进行贯彻。架构原则必须是可明确追溯的且被明确地表达以指导决策。选择这些原则，以便确保目标架构的构建和实施与业务策略和愿景对准。

具体地说，架构原则的开发通常受以下内容所影响：

- **ENTERPRISE 任务和计划**：ENTERPRISE 的任务、计划和组织基础设施。
- **ENTERPRISE 战略举措**：ENTERPRISE 的特征——其优势、劣势、机会和威胁——及其当前整个 ENTERPRISE 范围的举措（诸如流程改进和质量管理）。
- **外部约束**：市场因素（上市时间迫切需要、客户期望等）；现有和潜在的法律。
- **当前系统和技术**：部署在 ENTERPRISE 内的一组信息资源，包括系统文件、设备清单、网络配置图、策略和程序。
- **新兴行业趋势**：影响 ENTERPRISE 环境的关于经济、政治、技术和市场因素的预测。

23.4.1 原则的质量

仅具有一个称为原则的书面说明并不意味着该原则是好的，即使每个人都认同它。

一套良好的原则将建立在组织的信仰与价值观上，并且用业务所理解和使用的语言表达。原则应当为数不多、面向未来并得到高级管理层的认可和支持。这些原则为做出架构和规划决策，选定方针、程序和标准，以及支持解决矛盾情况提供一个坚实的基础。一套不良的原则将被迅速地废弃，而由此产生的架构、策略和标准将显得独断的或利己的，也因此缺乏可信度。本质上，原则驱动行为。

辨别一套良好原则的五个准则如下：

- **可理解**：基本宗旨可被整个组织所有人迅速掌握并理解。该原则应目的清晰，以便使有意或无意的违背最小化。
- **健壮**：能够对将进行的架构和计划、创建的可执行方针和标准做出高质量决策。每个原则应足够明确且精确，以支持在复杂、有潜在争议的情况下的一致决策。
- **完整**：为组织治理其信息和技术管理每个潜在重要的原则都被定义。这些原则涵盖感知到的每种情况。

- **Consistent**: strict adherence to one principle may require a loose interpretation of another principle. The set of principles must be expressed in a way that allows a balance of interpretations. Principles should not be contradictory to the point where adhering to one principle would violate the spirit of another. Every word in a principle statement should be carefully chosen to allow consistent yet flexible interpretation.
- **Stable**: principles should be enduring, yet able to accommodate changes. An amendment process should be established for adding, removing, or altering principles after they are ratified initially.

23.5 Applying Architecture Principles

Architecture principles are used to capture the fundamental truths about how the enterprise will use and deploy IT resources and assets. The principles are used in a number of different ways:

1. To provide a framework within which the enterprise can start to make conscious decisions about enterprise architecture and projects that implement the target enterprise architecture.
2. As a guide to establishing relevant evaluation criteria, thus exerting strong influence on the selection of products, solutions, or solution architectures in the later stages of managing compliance to the enterprise architecture.
3. As drivers for defining the functional requirements of the architecture.
4. As an input to assessing both existing implementations and the strategic portfolio, for compliance with the defined architectures; these assessments will provide valuable insights into the transition activities needed to implement an architecture, in support of business goals and priorities.
5. The Rationale statements within an Architecture Principle highlight the business value of implementations consistent with the principle and provide guidance for difficult decisions with conflicting drivers or objectives.
6. The Implications statements within an Architecture Principle provide an outline of the key tasks, resources, and potential costs to the enterprise of following the principle; they also provide valuable inputs to future transition initiative and planning activities.
7. Support the architecture governance activities in terms of:
   — Providing a “back-stop” for the standard Architecture Compliance assessments where some interpretation is allowed or required.
   — Supporting the decision to initiate a dispensation request where the implications of a particular architecture amendment cannot be resolved within local operating procedure.

Principles are inter-related, and need to be applied as a set.

Principles will sometimes compete; for example, the principles of “accessibility” and “security” tend towards conflicting decisions. Each principle must be considered in the context of “all other things being equal”.

At times a decision will be required as to which principle will take precedence on a particular issue. The rationale for such decisions should always be documented.

A common reaction on first reading of a principle is “this is obvious and does not need to be documented”. The fact that a principle seems self-evident does not mean that the guidance in a principle is followed. Having principles that appear obvious helps ensure that decisions actually follow the desired outcome.

- **一致**：严格遵守一个原则可能需要对另一个原则进行不严谨的解释。该系列原则必须以允许解释平衡的方式进行表达。原则不应相矛盾，不能由于遵守一个原则就将违背另一个原则的精髓。原则说明中的每个字都应仔细选择，以使得解释能一致而灵活。
- **稳定**：原则应是持久的，但是能够适应变化。在最初被批准后，应针对添加、删除或更改原则建立一个修正流程。

23.5 架构原则的应用

架构原则被用来捕获关于 ENTERPRISE 将如何使用和部署 IT 资源和资产的基本事实。这些原则以多种不同方式被应用：

1. 提供一个框架，在此框架内，ENTERPRISE 可以就 Enterprise Architecture 实施和目标 Enterprise Architecture 的项目做出有意识的决策。
2. 作为一个建立相关评价准则的指南，在管理 Enterprise Architecture 合规性的后期阶段，对产品、解决方案或解决方案架构的选择产生巨大影响。
3. 作为定义架构功能性需求的驱动因素。
4. 作为评估现有实施和战略性项目谱系的输入，以使与所定义的架构相吻合；这些评估对实现架构所需过渡活动提供有价值的理解，以支持多个业务目标及优先级。
5. 一个架构原则中的理由依据申明强调了与该原则一致的实施的业务价值，并在驱动因素或目的相冲突而很难做决策时提供引导。
6. 架构原则中的含义说明，为遵守该原则的 ENTERPRISE 提供对关键任务、资源和潜在成本的概览，还对未来过渡举措和规划活动提供多个有价值的输入。
7. 从以下维度支持架构治理活动：
   - 在允许或需要某种解释的情况下，为标准架构合规性评估提供“支援”。
   - 在特定架构修正的含义无法在本地运行程序内被解析的情况下，支持发起一个豁免要求的决策。

原则是相互关联的，并且需要作为一个集合来应用。

原则有时相互冲突，例如，“易用性”和“安保性”的原则往往会引起决策冲突。必须在“其他所有事物皆平等”的背景环境下考虑每个原则。

有时，需要对哪个原则在一个特定问题上取得优先权做出决策。这些决策的理由依据应始终被文件化。

对初次阅读一个原则的普遍反应是“这是很明显的且无需文件化”。一个原则似乎不言自明的事实并不意味着遵循了原则中的引导。具有看似易理解的原则有助于确保决策确实符合期望的结果。

Although specific penalties are not prescribed in a declaration of principles, violations of principles generally cause operational problems and inhibit the ability of the organization to fulfil its mission.

23.6 Example Set of Architecture Principles

Too many principles can reduce the flexibility of the architecture. Many organizations prefer to define only high-level principles, and to limit the number to between 10 and 20.

The following example illustrates both the typical content of a set of architecture principles, and the recommended format for defining them, as explained above.

23.6.1 Business Principles

Principle 1: Primary of Principles

Statement: These principles of information management apply to all organizations within the enterprise.

Rationale: The only way we can provide a consistent and measurable level of quality information to decision-makers is if all organizations abide by the principles.

Implications:

- Without this principle, exclusions, favoritism, and inconsistency would rapidly undermine the management of information.
- Information management initiatives will not begin until they are examined for compliance with the principles.
- A conflict with a principle will be resolved by changing the framework of the initiative.

Principle 2: Maximize Benefit to the Enterprise

Statement: Information management decisions are made to provide maximum benefit to the enterprise as a whole.

Rationale: This principle embodies " service above self" . Decisions made from an enterprise-wide perspective have greater long-term value than decisions made from any particular organizational perspective. Maximum return on investment requires information management decisions to adhere to enterprise-wide drivers and priorities. No minority group will detract from the benefit of the whole. However, this principle will not preclude any minority group from getting its job done.

Implications:

- Achieving maximum enterprise-wide benefit will require changes in the way we plan and manage information. Technology alone will not bring about this change.
- Some organizations may have to concede their own preferences for the greater benefit of the entire enterprise.

虽然在原则声明中未规定特定的处罚，但是违背原则通常会引起运行问题并抑制组织履行其任务的能力。

23.6 架构原则示例集

过多原则可降低架构的灵活性。许多组织更愿意仅定义高层级的原则，且将数量限制在 10～20 个之间。

以下示例阐明一套架构原则的典型内容，以及如上所述的用于定义这些架构原则的建议格式。

23.6.1 业务原则

原则 1：以原则为主

说明：	这些信息管理的原则应用于 ENTERPRISE 内所有组织。
理由依据：	可向决策人提供一致且可测量层级的质量信息的唯一方式是所有组织是否遵守该原则。
含义：	■ 如果没有本原则，排斥、偏好或不一致将会迅速减损对信息的管理。 ■ 在审查是否符合原则前，将不会开始这些信息管理举措。 ■ 与原则的冲突将通过改变该举措的框架来解决。

原则 2：最大化 ENTERPRISE 的利益

说明：	做出信息管理决策，以向整个 ENTERPRISE 提供最大利益。
理由依据：	本原则体现了“超我服务”。从全 ENTERPRISE 的关注层级做出的决策比根据任何特定组织的关注层级所做出的决策具有更高的长期价值。最大投资回报要求信息管理决策遵守整个 ENTERPRISE 范围的驱动因素和优先级。少数群组不会减损整体的利益。然而，本原则将不妨碍任何少数群组完成其工作。
含义：	■ 实现整个 ENTERPRISE 范围的利益最大化，需要以计划和管理信息的方式进行的变革。单凭技术不会带来这种变革。 ■ 一些组织可能必须为整个 ENTERPRISE 的更大利益而在其自身偏好方面做出让步。

- Application development priorities must be established by the entire enterprise for the entire enterprise.
- Applications components should be shared across organizational boundaries.
- Information management initiatives should be conducted in accordance with the enterprise plan. Individual organizations should pursue information management initiatives which conform to the blueprints and priorities established by the enterprise. We will change the plan as we need to.
- As needs arise, priorities must be adjusted. A forum with comprehensive enterprise representation should make these decisions.

Principle 3: Information Management is Everybody's Business

Statement: All organizations in the enterprise participate in information management decisions needed to accomplish business objectives.

Rationale: Information users are the key stakeholders, or customers, in the application of technology to address a business need. In order to ensure information management is aligned with the business, all organizations in the enterprise must be involved in all aspects of the information environment. The business experts from across the enterprise and the technical staff responsible for developing and sustaining the information environment need to come together as a team to jointly define the goals and objectives of IT.

Implications:

- To operate as a team, every stakeholder, or customer, will need to accept responsibility for developing the information environment.
- Commitment of resources will be required to implement this principle.

Principle 4: Business Continuity

Statement: Enterprise operations are maintained in spite of system interrupttions.

Rationale: As system operations become more pervasive, we become more dependenton them; therefore, we must consider the reliability of such systems throughout their design and use. Business premises throughout the enterprise must be provided with the capability to continue their business functions regardless of external events. Hardware failure, natural disasters, and data corruption should not be allowed to disrupt or stop enterprise activities. The enterprise business functions must be capable of operating on alternative information delivery mechanisms.

Implications:

- Dependency on shared system applications mandates that the risks of business interruption must be established in advance and managed. Management includes but is not limited to periodic reviews, testing for vulnerability and exposure, or designing mission-critical services to ensure business function continuity through redundant or alternative capabilities.
- Recoverability, redundancy, and maintainability should be addersed at the time of design.
- Applications must be assessed for criticality and impact on the enterprise mission, in order to determine what level of continuity is required and what corresponding recovery plan is necessary.

- 整个 ENTERPRISE 的应用开发优先级必须由整个 ENTERPRISE 确定。
- 应用组件应穿越组织边界进行共享。
- 信息管理举措应按照 ENTERPRISE 计划执行。单个组织应执行符合由 ENTERPRISE 建立的蓝图和优先级的信息管理举措。将在需要时改变计划。
- 当需求出现时，必须调整优先级。广泛代表 ENTERPRISE 的讨论会应作出这些决策。

原则 3：信息管理关系到每个人

说明： ENTERPRISE 中的所有组织均参与实现业务目的所需的信息管理决策。

理由依据： 在应用技术以应对业务需要的过程中，信息用户是关键利益攸关者或客户。为了确保信息管理与业务对准，ENTERPRISE 中的所有组织必须参与信息环境的所有方面。跨 ENTERPRISE 中的业务专家以及负责开发和维持信息环境的技术人员需要组成一个团队，共同定义 IT 目标和目的。

含义：

- 为了以团队的方式工作，每个利益攸关者或客户将需接受开发信息环境的责任。
- 实施本原则将需要资源投入。

原则 4：业务连续性

说明： 不管系统是否中断，ENTERPRISE 均保持运行。

理由依据： 随着系统运行变得无处不在，我们变得愈发依赖于这些系统运行；因此，我们必须考虑这样的系统在其设计和使用中的可靠性。贯穿于 ENTERPRISE 的业务前提，必须具备继续其业务功能的能力，无论是否有外部事件发生。不应允许硬件故障、自然灾害以及数据损坏，以免中断或终止 ENTERPRISE 活动。ENTERPRISE 业务功能必须能够在可替代的信息交付机制上运行。

含义：

- 对共享系统应用的依赖性，要求业务中断风险必须预先确定和管理。管理包括但不限于定期审查、易损性和暴露测试或设计关键任务服务，以通过冗余或可替代的能力确保业务功能的连续性。
- 应在设计时应对可恢复性、冗余和可维护性。
- 必须评估应用的关键性以及对 ENTERPRISE 任务的影响，以便确定何种层级的连续性是所需的、以及何种相应恢复计划是必要的。

Principle 5: Common Use Applications

Statement: Development of applications used across the enterprise is preferred over the development of similar or duplicative applications which are only provided to a particular organization.

Rationale: Duplicative capability is expensive and proliferates conflicting data.

Implications:

- Organizations which depend on a capability which does not serve theentire enterprise must change over to the replacement enterprise-widecapability. This will require establishment of and adherence to a policy requiring this.
- Organizations will not be allowed to develop capabilities for their own use which are similar/duplicative of enterprise-wide capabilities. In this way, expenditures of scarce resources to develop essentially the same capability in marginally different ways will be reduced.
- Data and information used to support enterprise decision-making will be standardized to a much greater extent than previously. This is because the smaller, organizational capabilities which produced different data (which was not shared among other organizations) will be replaced by enterprise-wide capabilities. The impetus for adding to the set of enterprise-wide capabilities may well come from an organization making a convincing case for the value of the data/information previously produced by its organizational capability, but the resulting capability will become part of the enterprise-wide system, and the data it produces will be shared across the enterprise.

Principle 6: Service Orientation

Statement: The architecture is based on a design of services which mirror real-world business activities comprising the enterprise (or inter-enterprise) business processes.

Rationale: Service orientation delivers enterprise agility and Boundaryless Information Flow.

Implications:

- Service representation utilizes business descriptions to provide context (i.e., business process, goal, rule, policy, service interface, and service component) and implements services using service orchestration.
- Service orientation places unique requirements on the infrastructure, and implementations should use open standards to realize interoperability and location transparency.
- Implementations are environment-specific; they are constrained or enabled by context and must be described within that context.
- Strong governance of service representation and implementation is required.
- A “Litmus Test”, which determines a “good service”, is required.

原则 5：共用使用应用

说明： 对在贯穿 ENTERPRISE 中使用的应用开发，其优先于仅提供给特定组织的类似或重复应用的开发。

理由依据： 重复能力昂贵并增加冲突数据。

含义：

- 那些所依赖的能力并非服务于整个 ENTERPRISE 的组织必须转换替代为 ENTERPRISE 范围内的能力，这要求建立并遵守于一个要求如此的方针。
- 不允许组织开发其自身使用且与整个 ENTERPRISE 范围的能力相似/重复的能力。这样，以略微不同的方式开发基本相同能力所用的稀缺资源支出将会减少。
- 用于支持 ENTERPRISE 决策的数据和信息将被标准化到一个比之前更大的范围。这是因为，产生不同数据（不在其他组织间共享）的较小组织能力将由整个 ENTERPRISE 范围的能力取代。增加整个 ENTERPRISE 范围的能力集合的推动力可能正是来自于一个对组织自身能力在之前所产生数据/信息的价值上做出有说服力案例的组织，但是得到的能力将成为整个 ENTERPRISE 范围系统的一部分，并且该能力产生的数据将贯穿 ENTERPRISE 内共享。

原则 6：面向服务

说明： 该架构基于服务的设计，这些服务“镜像”由 ENTERPRISE（或 ENTERPRISE 间）业务流程组成的真实世界业务活动。

理由依据： 面向服务实现 ENTERPRISE 敏捷性和无边界信息流。

含义：

- 服务的表达利用业务描述来提供背景环境（即业务流程、目标、规则、策略、服务界面和服务组件），并使用服务编排来实施服务。
- 面向服务对基础设施设置特殊需求，并且实施应使用开放标准来实现互用性和位置的透明性。
- 实施是环境特有的，它们受到背景环境的约束或由背景环境实现，并且必须在那个背景环境中描述。
- 需要对服务的表达和实施进行有力的管控。
- 需要一个能够判定“良好服务”的“试金石”。

Principle 7: Compliance with Law

Statement: Enterprise information management processes comply with all relevant laws, policies, and regulations.

Rationale: Enterprise policy is to abide by laws, policies, and regulations. This will not preclude business process improvements that lead to changes in policies and regulations.

Implications:

- The enterprise must be mindful to comply with laws, regulations, and external policies regarding the collection, retention, and management of data.
- Education and access to the rules. Efficiency, need, and common sense are not the only drivers. Changes in the law and changes in regulations may drive changes in our processes or applications.

Principle 8: IT Responsibility

Statement: The IT organization is responsible for owning and implementing IT processes and infrastructure that enable solutions to meet user-defined requirements for functionality, service levels, cost, and delivery timing.

Rationale: Effectively align expectations with capabilities and costs so that all projects are cost-effective. Efficient and effective solutions have reasonable costs and clear benefits.

Implications:

- A process must be created to prioritize projects.
- The IT function must define processes to manage business unit expectations.
- Data, application, and technology models must be created to enable integrated quality solutions and to maximize results.

Principle 9: Protection of Intellectual Property

Statement: The enterprise's Intellectual Property (IP) must be protected. This protection must be reflected in the IT architecture, implementation, and governance processes.

Rationale: A major part of an enterprise's IP is hosted in the IT domain.

Implications:

- While protection of IP assets is everybody's business, much of the actual protection is implemented in the IT domain. Even trust in non-IT processes can be managed by IT processes (email, mandatory notes, etc.).
- A security policy, governing human and IT actors, will be required that can substantially improve protection of IP. This must be capable of both avoiding compromises and reducing liabilities.
- Resources on such policies can be found at the SANS Institute (refer to www.sans.org/newlook/home.php).

原则 7：法律合规性

说明：　ENTERPRISE 信息管理流程遵守所有相关法律、方针和法规。

理由依据：　ENTERPRISE 方针将遵守法律、方针和法规。这不会妨碍那些导致政策和法规变化的业务流程改进。

含义：

- ENTERPRISE 必须注意遵守与数据收集、保存和管理相关的法律、法规和外部方针。
- 教育和获取规则。效率、需要和常识不是仅有的驱动因素，法律以及法规的变更可驱动流程或应用的变更。

原则 8：IT 责任

说明：　IT 组织有责任拥有和实施 IT 流程和基础设施，使得解决方案能够满足用户定义的功能性、服务水平、成本和交付时间需求。

理由依据：　将期望与能力和成本进行有效匹配，以便所有项目都具有成本效益。有效率且有成效的解决方案具有合理的成本和明确的效益。

含义：

- 必须创建流程，以对项目进行优先排序。
- IT 功能必须定义管理业务单元期望的流程。
- 必须创建数据、应用和技术模型，以实现综合质量解决方案并使结果最大化。

原则 9：知识产权保护

说明：　必须保护 ENTERPRISE 的知识产权（IP）。这种保护必须反映在 IT 架构、实施和治理流程中。

理由依据：　ENTERPRISEIP 的主要部分托管在 IT 领域中。

含义：

- 虽然保护 IP 资产是每个人的职责，但是大部分实际保护是在 IT 域中实施的。甚至非 IT 流程中的托管也可以由 IT 流程（电子邮件、强制性指令等）管理。
- 管治人员和 IT 施动者的安保方针，需要在实质上改进 IP 保护。这必须既能避免妥协，又能减少负担。
- 可在 SANS 协会（见 www.sans.org/newlook/home.php）中找到类似方针的资源。

23.6.2 Data Principles

Principle 10: Data is an Asset

Statement: Data is an asset that has value to the enterprise and is managed accordingly.

Rationale: Data is a valuable corporate resource; it has real, measurable value. In simpleterms, the purpose of data is to aid decision-making. Accurate, timely data is critical to accurate, timely decisions. Most corporate assets are carefully managed, and data is no exception. Data is the foundation of our decision-making, so we must also carefully manage data to ensure that we know where it is, can rely upon its accuracy, and can obtain it when and where we need it.

Implications:

- This is one of three closely-related principles regarding data: data is an asset; data is shared; and data is easily accessible. The implication is that there is an education task to ensure that all organizations within the enterprise understand the relationship between value of data, sharing of data, and accessibility to data.
- Stewards must have the authority and means to manage the data for which they are accountable.
- We must make the cultural transition from "data ownership" thinking to "data stewardship" thinking.
- The role of data steward is critical because obsolete, incorrect, or inconsistent data could be passed to enterprise personnel and adversely affect decisions across the enterprise.
- Part of the role of data steward, who manages the data, is to ensure data quality. Procedures must be developed and used to prevent and correct errors in the information and to improve those processes that produce flawed information. Data quality will need to be measured and steps taken to improve data quality — it is probable that policy and procedures will need to be developed for this as well.
- A forum with comprehensive enterprise-wide representation should decide on process changes suggested by the steward.
- Since data is an asset of value to the entire enterprise, data stewards accountable for properly managing the data must be assigned at the enterprise level.

Principle 11: Data is Shared

Statement: Users have access to the data necessary to perform their duties; therefore, data is shared across enterprise functions and organizations.

Rationale: Timely access to accurate data is essential to improving the quality and efficiency of enterprise decision-making. It is less costly to maintain timely, accurate data in a single application, and then share it, than it is to maintain duplicative data in multiple applications. The enterprise holds a wealth of data, but it is stored in hundreds of incompatible stovepipe databases. The speed of data collection, creation, transfer, and assimilation is driven by the ability of the organization to efficiently share these islands of data across the organization.

23.6.2 数据原则

原则 10：数据是一种资产

说明：数据是一种对 ENTERPRISE 有价值的资产，因此应进行管理。

理由依据：数据是一种有价值的公司资源，具有实际、可测量的价值。简言之，数据的用途是辅助决策。准确及时的数据对于准确及时的决策至关重要。大部分公司资产都被仔细地管理，而数据也不例外。数据是我们决策的基础，因此，我们还必须仔细管理数据，以确保我们知道数据位于何处、其准确度可依靠，且在我们需要数据时能够随时随地获得。

含义：

- 这是关于数据的三个密切相关的原则之一：数据是一种资产；数据是共享的；并且数据是易于访问的。这就暗示着，要有一个教育任务来确保 ENTERPRISE 内所有组织都理解数据价值、数据共享和数据可访问性之间的关系。
- 管理员必须具有权限和手段来管理其所负责的数据。
- 我们必须由“数据所有权”思维向“数据管理”思维进行文化过渡。
- 数据管理员的作用是关键的，因为作废的、不正确的或不一致的数据可能会被传递给 ENTERPRISE 全体人员，并对贯穿 ENTERPRISE 的决策产生不利影响。
- 管理数据的数据管理员的部分作用是确保数据质量。必须开发和使用程序，防止和纠正信息中的错误并改进那些产生有缺陷信息的流程。需要测量并采取步骤提高数据质量——同样有可能需要为此开发策略和程序。
- 全面代表整个 ENTERPRISE 范围的讨论会应针对管理员建议的流程变更做出决定。
- 由于数据是对整个 ENTERPRISE 有价值的一种资产，所以必须在 ENTERPRISE 层级上委派负责适当管理数据的数据管理员。

原则 11：数据是共享的

说明：用户有权使用对执行其职责非常必要的数据；因此，数据贯穿 ENTERPRISE 功能和组织之间共享。

理由依据：及时获取准确的数据，对于改进 ENTERPRISE 决策的质量和效率是必要的。相较于在多个应用中保留重复数据，在单一应用中保留及时且准确的数据并共享该数据所花费的成本更少。ENTERPRISE 拥有丰富的数据，但是，这些数据保存在数以百计不兼容的烟囱式数据库中。数据收集、创建、传输和吸收的速度由组织在整个组织内有效共享这些数据孤岛的能力所驱动。

Shared data will result in improved decisions since we will rely on fewer(ultimately one virtual) sources of more accurate and timely managed data for all of our decision-making. Electronically shared data will result in increased efficiency when existing data entities can be used, without re-keying, to create new entities.

Implications:

- This is one of three closely-related principles regarding data: data is an asset; data is shared; and data is easily accessible. The implication is that there is an education task to ensure that all organizations within the enterprise understand the relationship between value of data, sharing of data, and accessibility to data.
- To enable data sharing we must develop and abide by a common set of policies, procedures, and standards governing data management and access for both the short and the long term.
- For the short term, to preserve our significant investment in legacy systems, we must invest in software capable of migrating legacy system data into a shared data environment.
- We will also need to develop standard data models, data elements, and other metadata that defines this shared environment and develop a repository system for storing this metadata to make it accessible.
- For the long term, as legacy systems are replaced, we must adopt and enforce common data access policies and guidelines for new application developers to ensure that data in new applications remains available to the shared environment and that data in the shared environment can continue to be used by the new applications.
- For both the short term and the long term we must adopt common methods and tools for creating, maintaining, and accessing the data shared across the enterprise.
- Data sharing will require a significant cultural change.
- This principle of data sharing will continually "bump up against" the principle of data security. Under no circumstances will the data sharing principle cause confidential data to be compromised.
- Data made available for sharing will have to be relied upon by all users to execute their respective tasks. This will ensure that only the most accurate and timely data is relied upon for decision-making. Shared data will become the enterprise-wide "virtual single source" of data.

Principle 12: Data is Accessible

Statement: Data is accessible for users to perform their functions.

Rationale: Wide access to data leads to efficiency and effectiveness in decision-making, and affords timely response to information requests and service delivery. Using information must be considered from an enterprise perspective to allow access by a wide variety of users. Staff time is saved and consistency of data is improved.

Implications:

- This is one of three closely-related principles regarding data: data is an asset; data is shared; and data is easily accessible. The implication is that there is an education task to ensure that all organizations within the enterprise understand the relationship between value of data, sharing of data, and accessibility to data.

共享数据将产生改进的决策，因为，我们将依靠更少（最终是一个虚拟的）、更准确且及时管理的数据来源来做出所有决策。当现有数据实体可用于（无须密钥更新）产生新的实体时，电子共享数据将使得效率增加。

含义：

- 这是关于数据的三个密切相关的原则之一：数据是一种资产；数据是共享的；并且数据是易于访问的。这就暗示着，具有一个教育任务来确保 ENTERPRISE 内所有组织都理解数据价值、数据共享和数据可访问性之间的关系。
- 为了使数据能够共享，我们必须制定并遵守一系列短期和长期管控数据管理和访问的公共策略、程序和标准。
- 从短期看，为了保护在遗留系统中的重要投资，我们必须投资于能够将遗留系统数据迁移至共享数据环境中的软件。
- 我们还需要开发标准数据模型、数据元素和定义此共享环境的其他元数据，并需要开发存储库系统，用于存储此元数据以使其可供访问。
- 从长期看，在替换遗留系统时，我们必须采用并实施供新应用开发人员使用的公用的数据访问策略和指南，以确保新应用中的数据仍可用于共享环境，并且共享环境中的数据可继续被新应用使用。
- 无论从短期还是长期看，我们必须采用用于跨 ENTERPRISE 创建、维护和访问共享数据的公用的方法和工具。
- 数据共享需要一个显著的文化变迁。
- 这一数据共享的原则将持续“触碰”数据安保原则。在任何情况下，数据共享原则均不应导致机密数据泄漏。
- 在所有用户执行其各自任务时，可用于共享的数据必须是可依靠的。这确保决策时，依靠的只有最精确和及时的数据。共享数据将变成整个 ENTERPRISE 范围的数据“虚拟单一来源”。

原则 12：数据是可访问的

说明： 数据可供用户访问以执行其功能。

理由依据： 广泛访问数据会使决策效率更高效果更好和有效，并对信息要求和服务交付给予及时响应。使用信息必须从 ENTERPRISE 的关注层级来考虑，使得各种用户能访问。工作人员的时间被节省并且数据一致性也在提高。

含义：

- 这是关于数据的三个密切相关的原则之一：数据是一种资产；数据是共享的；并且数据是易于访问的。这就暗示着，教育任务是确保 ENTERPRISE 内所有组织都理解数据价值、数据共享和数据可访问性之间的关系。

- Accessibility involves the ease with which users obtain information.
- The way information is accessed and displayed must be sufficiently adaptable to meet a wide range of enterprise users and their corresponding methods of access.
- Access to data does not constitute understanding of the data. Personnel should take caution not to misinterpret information.
- Access to data does not necessarily grant the user access rights to modify or disclose the data. This will require an education process and a change in the organizational culture, which currently supports a belief in "ownership" of data by functional units.

Principle 13: Data Trustee

Statement: Each data element has a trustee accountable for data quality.

Rationale: One of the benefits of an architected environment is the ability to share data (e.g., text, video, sound, etc.) across the enterprise. As the degree of data sharing grows and business units rely upon common information, it becomes essential that only the data trustee makes decisions about the content of data. Since data can lose its integrity when it is entered multiple times, the data trustee will have sole responsibility for data entry which eliminates redundant human effort and data storage resources.

Note: A trustee is different than a steward — a trustee is responsible for accuracy and currency of the data, while responsibilities of a steward may be broader and include data standardization and definition tasks.

Implications:

- Real trusteeship dissolves the data "ownership" issues and allows the data to be available to meet all users' needs. This implies that a cultural change from data "ownership" to data "trusteeship" may be required.
- The data trustee will be responsible for meeting quality requirements levied upon the data for which the trustee is accountable.
- It is essential that the trustee has the ability to provide user confidence in the data based upon attributes such as "data source".
- It is essential to identify the true source of the data in order that the data authority can be assigned this trustee responsibility. This does not mean that classified sources will be revealed nor does it mean the source will be the trustee.
- Information should be captured electronically once and immediately validated as close to the source as possible. Quality control measures must be implemented to ensure the integrity of the data.
- As a result of sharing data across the enterprise, the trustee is accountable and responsible for the accuracy and currency of their designated data element(s) and, subsequently, must then recognize the importance of this trusteeship responsibility.

- 可访问性涉及用户获取信息的难易程度。
- 访问和显示信息的方式必须充分适应于满足大范围的 ENTERPRISE 用户及其对应的访问方法。
- 访问数据不构成对数据的理解。全体人员应注意，不要曲解信息。
- 访问数据不必授予用户修改或公开数据的访问权。这需要一个教育过程且需要改变组织文化，该组织文化目前支持功能单元对数据有“所有权”的观点。

原则 13：数据受托人

说明：　　每个数据元均具有一个负责数据质量的受托人。

理由依据：　　架构环境的好处之一是跨 ENTERPRISE 共享数据（如文本、视频、声音等）的能力。随着数据共享程度的增加以及业务单元对公用的信息的依赖，仅由数据受托人对数据内容做出决策变得至关重要。由于被多次输入时，数据可能失去其完整性，所以，数据受托人将只负责消除冗余人员工作和数据存储资源的数据输入。

注：受托人不同于管理员——受托人负责数据的准确度和流动性，而管理员的责任可能更为广泛并且包括数据标准化和定义的任务。

含义：

- 实际托管机制解决数据“所有权”问题并允许数据用于满足所有用户需要。这意味着，可能需要从数据“所有制”到数据“托管制”的文化变迁。
- 数据受托人将对其所负责数据达到所规定的质量要求承担责任。
- 受托人有能力基于诸如“数据源”的属性使用户信任数据是至关重要的。
- 至关重要的是，识别数据的真正来源，以便可以将数据权限指定此受托人负责。这不意味着将揭示分类的来源，也不意味着该来源将是受托人。
- 信息应以电子化的方式一次捕获，并立即尽可能以接近于来源的方式进行确认。必须实施质量控制措施以确保数据的完整性。
- 由于跨 ENTERPRISE 共享数据，所以受托人有责任并负责其指定数据元的准确度和流动性，因此，必须认识到此托管责任的重要性。

Principle 14: Common Vocabulary and Data Definitions

Statement: Data is defined consistently throughout the enterprise, and the definitions are understandable and available to all users.

Rationale: The data that will be used in the development of applications must have a common definition throughout the Headquarters to enable sharing of data. A common vocabulary will facilitate communications and enable dialog to be effective. In addition, it is required to interface systems and exchange data.

Implications:

- We are lulled into thinking that this issue is adequately addressed because there are people with "data administration" job titles and forums with charters implying responsibility. Significant additional energy and resources must be committed to this task. It is key to the success of efforts to improve the information environment. This is separate from but related to the issue of data element definition, which is addressed by a broad community — this is more like a common vocabulary and definition.
- The enterprise must establish the initial common vocabulary for the business. The definitions will be used uniformly through-out the enterprise.
- Whenever a new data definition is required, the definition effort will be co-ordinated and reconciled with the corporate "glossary" of data descriptions. The enterprise data administrator will provide this co-ordination.
- Ambiguities resulting from multiple parochial definitions of data must give way to accepted enterprise-wide definitions and understanding.
- Multiple data standardization initiatives need to be co-ordinated.
- Functional data administration responsibilities must be assigned.

Principle 15: Data Security

Statement: Data is protected from unauthorized use and disclosure. In addition to the traditional aspects of national security classification, this includes, but is not limited to, protection of pre-decisional, sensitive, source selection-sensitive, and proprietary information.

Rationale: Open sharing of information and the release of information via relevant legislation must be balanced against the need to restrict the availability of classified, proprietary, and sensitive information.

Existing laws and regulations require the safeguarding of national security and the privacy of data, while permitting free and open access. Pre-decisional (work-in-progress, not yet authorized for release) information must be protected to avoid unwarranted speculation, misinterpretation, and inappropriate use.

Implications:

- Aggregation of data, both classified and not, will create a large target requiring review and de-classification procedures to maintain appropriate control. Data owners and/or functional users must determine whether the aggregation results in an increased classification level. We will need appropriate policy and procedures to handle this review and de-classification. Access to information based on a need-to-know policy will force regular reviews of the body of information.

原则 14：公用的词汇表和数据定义

说明：数据在整个 ENTERPRISE 中一致地定义，并且这些定义可被所有用户理解和使用。

理由依据：将在应用开发中使用的数据，必须在整个总部机构中具有公用的定义以能够分享数据。公共词汇表将会促进沟通并使对话有效。此外，需要连接系统并交换数据。

含义：

- 我们浸入认为存在职务为“数据管理”的人员以及章程中隐含责任的讨论会的思维中，此议题得以充分涉及。必须将重要的额外精力和资源投入到该任务中，这对于改进信息环境工作的成功是非常关键的。这与由广泛团体应对的数据元定义问题相独立但又相关，更像是一个公用的词汇表和定义。
- ENTERPRISE 必须为业务创建初始的公用的词汇表。这些定义将在整个 ENTERPRISE 内被统一使用。
- 无论何时需要新的数据定义，均将会协调定义工作并使其与数据描述的整体“术语表”一致。ENTERPRISE 数据管理者将进行这种协调。
- 多个狭隘的数据定义所导致的模棱两可必须被已接受的整个 ENTERPRISE 范围的定义和理解所替代。
- 需要协调多重数据标准化举措。
- 必须指定功能数据管理责任。

原则 15：数据安保性

说明：防止数据被未授权使用和泄露。除了国家安保分类的传统方面外，这还包括但不限于之前决策的信息、敏感信息、对来源选择敏感的信息以及专有信息的保护。

理由依据：必须根据限制分类信息、专有信息和敏感信息可用性的需要，使开放信息共享和经由相关法规进行信息发布相平衡。

现有法律、法规需要保障国家安全和数据私密性，同时允许自由和开放的访问。必须保护预先决策（在制品，尚未授权发布）的信息，以避免毫无根据的猜测、曲解和不适当使用。

含义：

- 无论分类还是未分类的数据集合将产生一个巨大的目标，该目标需要审视和解密的程序，以保持适当控制。数据所有者和/或功能用户必须确定集合是否导致分类层级的增加。我们将需要适当的方针和程序来处理这类审查和解密。基于须知策略访问信息将强制对信息体进行定期审查。

- The current practice of having separate systems to contain different classifications needs to be rethought. Is there a software solution to separating classified and unclassified data? The current hardware solution is unwieldy, inefficient, and costly. It is more expensive to manage unclassified data on a classified system. Currently, the only way to combine the two is to place the unclassified data on the classified system, where it must remain.
- In order to adequately provide access to open information while maintaining secure information, security needs must be identified and developed at the data level, not the application level.
- Data security safeguards can be put in place to restrict access to "view only", or "never see". Sensitivity labeling for access to pre-decisional, decisional, classified, sensitive, or proprietary information must be determined.
- Security must be designed into data elements from the beginning; it cannot be added later. Systems, data, and technologies must be protected from unauthorized access and manipulation. Headquarters information must be safeguarded against inadvertent or unauthorized alteration, sabotage, disaster, or disclosure.
- Need new policies on managing duration of protection for pre-decisional information and other works-in-progress, in consideration of content freshness.

23.6.3 Application Principles

Principle 16: Technology Independence

Statement: Applications are independent of specific technology choices and therefore can operate on a variety of technology platforms.

Rationale: Independence of applications from the underlying technology allows applications to be developed, upgraded, and operated in the most cost-effective and timely way. Otherwise technology, which is subject to continual obsolescence and vendor dependence, becomes the driver rather than the user requirements themselves.

Realizing that every decision made with respect to IT makes us dependent on that technology, the intent of this principle is to ensure that Application Software is not dependent on specific hardware and operating systems software.

Implications:

- This principle will require standards which support portability.
- For Commercial Off-The-Shelf (COTS) and Government Off-The-Shelf (GOTS) applications, there may be limited current choices, as many of these applications are technology and platform-dependent.
- Subsystem interfaces will need to be developed to enable legacy applications to interoperate with applications and operating environments developed under the enterprise architecture.
- Middleware should be used to decouple applications from specific software solutions.

- 需要重新思考使独立系统包含不同分类的现行实践。是否存在分离已分类数据和未分类资料的软件解决方案？当前硬件解决方案是不实用的、无效率的和昂贵的。在一个分类系统上管理未分类资料更是昂贵。目前，合并两类解决方案的唯一方式是，将未分类数据放在必须保留该未分类数据的分类系统上。
- 为了在维护安保信息的同时充分提供访问开放信息的机会，必须在数据层级而非应用层级上识别和开发安保需要。
- 可实施数据安保防护措施，以便将访问限制为“仅查看”或“不允许查看”的数据。必须确定用于访问预先决策信息、决策信息、分类信息、敏感信息或专有信息的敏感标签。
- 安保性必须从一开始即设计成数据元；随后，不能进行添加。必须防止对操作系统、数据和技术进行未经授权的访问和篡改。必须保护总部机构信息不会受到无意或未授权的改动、破坏、灾难或泄露。
- 考虑到内容新鲜度，需要一些关于管理预先决策信息和其它在制品的保护期限的新策略。

23.6.3 应用原则

原则 16：技术独立性

说明：　应用独立于特定技术选择，并因此能够在各种技术平台上运行。

理由依据：　来自基础技术的应用独立性允许以最符合成本效益和最及时的方式开发、升级和运行应用程序。否则，持续淘汰且依赖厂商的技术——而不是用户需求本身——将变为驱动因素。

意识到每个根据 IT 做出的决策均使我们依赖于那个技术，本原则的意图是，确保应用软件不依赖特定的硬件和操作系统软件。

含义：

- 本原则需要支持可移植性的标准。
- 对于商用货架（COTS）和政府现货（GOTS）应用，存在有限的当前选择，因为许多这些应用取决于技术和平台。
- 需要开发子系统界面，使已有应用能够与按 Enterprise Architecture 开发的应用和操作环境进行互操作。
- 中间件应用于从特定的软件解决方案中分离应用。

- As an example, this principle could lead to use of Java, and future Java-like protocols, which give a high degree of priority to platform-independence.

Principle 17: Ease-of-Use

Statement: Applications are easy to use. The underlying technology is transparent to users, so they can concentrate on tasks at hand.

Rationale: The more a user has to understand the underlying technology, the less productive that user is. Ease-of-use is a positive incentive for use of applications. It encourages users to work within the integrated information environment instead of developing isolated systems to accomplish the task outside of the enterprise's integrated information environment. Most of the knowledge required to operate one system will be similar to others. Training is kept to a minimum, and the risk of using a system improperly is low.

Using an application should be as intuitive as driving a different car.

Implications:

- Applications will be required to have a common " look-and-feel" andsupport ergonomic requirements. Hence, the common look-and-feelstandard must be designed and usability test criteria must be developed.
- Guidelines for user interfaces should not be constrained by narrow assumptions about user location, language, systems training, or physical capability. Factors such as linguistics, customer physical infirmities (visual acuity, ability to use keyboard/mouse), and proficiency in the use of technology have broad ramifications in determining the ease-of-use of an application.

23.6.4 Technology Principles

Principle 18: Requirements-Based Change

Statement: Only in response to business needs are changes to applications and technology made.

Rationale: This principle will foster an atmosphere where the information environment changes in response to the needs of the business, rather than having the business change in response to IT changes. This is to ensure that the purpose of the information support — the transaction of business — is the basis for any proposed change. Unintended effects on business due to IT changes will be minimized. A change in technology may provide an opportunity to improve the business process and, hence, change business needs.

Implications:

- Changes in implementation will follow full examination of the proposed changes using the enterprise architecture.
- We don't fund a technical improvement or system development unless a documented business need exists.
- Change management processes conforming to this principle will be developed and implemented.
- This principle may bump up against the responsive change principle. We must ensure the requirements documentation process does not hinder responsive change to meet legitimate business needs. The purpose of this principle is to keep us focused on business, not technology needs — responsive change is also a business need.

- 作为一个示例，本原则可带来对 Java 的使用以及未来类似 Java 的协议，这为平台独立性提供高度优先级。

原则 17：易用性

说明： 应用是易于使用的。基础技术对用户是透明的，因此用户可专注于手头的任务。

理由依据： 用户必须理解的基础技术越多，用户的效率越低。易用性是使用应用的正向激励。它鼓励用户在集成信息环境中工作而非开发单独系统，以完成 ENTERPRISE 集成信息环境以外的任务。运行一个系统所需的大部分知识会与其他系统类似。将培训保持在最小限度，并且系统使用不当的风险很低。

使用一种应用程序应如同开一辆不同的汽车一样直观。

含义：

- 应用需要有一个常见的“界面外观”并支持人类工程学需求。因此，必须设计常见的界面外观标准并且必须形成可用性测试准则。
- 用户界面指南不应受有关用户位置、语言、系统培训或物理能力的有限假设的约束。诸如语言、客户身体疾病（视觉分辨力、使用键盘和鼠标的能力）以及使用技术的熟练程度等因素在确定应用是否易用方面具有广泛的影响。

23.6.4 技术原则

原则 18：基于需求的变更

说明： 应用和技术的变更仅为响应业务需要而发生。

依据： 本原则将推动一种氛围，即信息环境因响应业务需要而变化，而不是使业务变化以响应 IT 变化。这确保信息支持的目的——业务事项——是任何所提出变化的基础。IT 变化对业务造成的计划之外的影响将会被最小化。技术变化可提供一个改进业务流程的机会，并因此改变业务需要。

含义：

- 实施变更将使用 Enterprise Architecture 对所提出变化采用全面审查。
- 除非存在一个文件化的业务需要，否则，我们不对技术改进或系统开发提供资金。
- 开发和实施符合本原则的变更管理流程。
- 本原则可能碰到响应变更原则。我们必须确保需求文件化流程不妨碍满足正规业务需要的响应变更。本原则的目的是使我们保持对业务需要而非技术需要的关注——响应变更也是一种业务需要。

Principle 19: Responsive Change Management

Statement: Changes to the enterprise information environment are implemented in a timely manner.

Rationale: If people are to be expected to work within the enterprise information environment, that information environment must be responsive to their needs.

Implications:

- We have to develop processes for managing and implementing change that do not create delays.
- A user who feels a need for change will need to connect with a "business expert" to facilitate explanation and implementation of that need.
- If we are going to make changes, we must keep the architectures updated.
- Adopting this principle might require additional resources.
- This will conflict with other principles (e.g., maximum enterprise-wide benefit, enterprise-wide applications, etc.).

Principle 20: Control Technical Diversity

Statement: Technological diversity is controlled to minimize the non-trivial cost of maintaining expertise in and connectivity between multiple processing environments.

Rationale: There is a real, non-trivial cost of infrastructure required to support alternative technologies for processing environments. There are further infrastructure costs incurred to keep multiple processor constructs interconnected and maintained.

Limiting the number of supported components will simplify maintainability and reduce costs.

The business advantages of minimum technical diversity include: standard packaging of components; predictable implementation impact; predictable valuations and returns; redefined testing; utility status; and increased flexibility to accommodate technological advancements. Common technology across the enterprise brings the benefits of economies of scale to the enterprise. Technical administration and support costs are better controlled when limited resources can focus on this shared set of technology.

Implications:

- Policies, standards, and procedures that govern acquisition of technology must be tied directly to this principle.
- Technology choices will be constrained by the choices available within the technology blueprint. Procedures for augmenting the acceptable technology set to meet evolving requirements will have to be developed and put in place.
- We are not freezing our technology baseline. We welcome technology advances and will change the technology blueprint when compatibility with the current infrastructure, improvement in operational efficiency, or a required capability has been demonstrated.

原则 19：响应变更管理

说明：　以一种及时的方式实施 ENTERPRISE 信息环境的变更。

理由依据：　如果期望人员在 ENTERPRISE 信息环境内工作，那么该信息环境必须对人员需要做出响应。

含义：
- 我们必须开发用于管理和实施不会产生延迟的变更的流程。
- 感觉需要变更的用户需要与“业务专家”联络，以促进对该需要的解释和实施。
- 如果将要做出变更，那么我们必须保持架构被更新。
- 采用本原则可能需要更多的资源。
- 这将与其他原则（如整个 ENTERPRISE 范围的利益最大化、整个 ENTERPRISE 范围的应用等）发生冲突。

原则 20：控制技术的多样性

说明：　控制技术多样性，使维护多个处理环境中的专业知识以及这些环境间的连通性的关键成本最小化。

理由依据：　需要实际的关键基础设施成本来支持用于处理环境的替代技术，产生更多的基础设施成本，以保持多个处理器构成互连并得到维护。

限制支持组件的数量将简化可维护性并降低成本。

最低技术多样性业务优势包括：组件的标准封装；可预测的实施影响；可预测的价值和收益；重新定义的测试；效用状态；以及为适应技术进步增加的灵活性。贯穿 ENTERPRISE 的公用的技术为 ENTERPRISE 带来大规模的经济效益。当限制的资源集中于共享技术集合时，技术管理和支持成本将被更好地控制。

含义：
- 管控技术采办的方针、标准和程序必须与本原则直接绑定。
- 技术选择将受到技术蓝图内可用选择的约束。必须开发为满足演进需求而扩大可接受技术集合的程序并将其落实到位。
- 我们未冻结我们的技术基线。我们欢迎技术进步并将在与当前基础设施的兼容性、运营效率提高或所需能力得到证明时，改变技术蓝图。

Principle 21: Interoperability

Statement: Software and hardware should conform to defined standards that promote interoperability for data, applications, and technology.

Rationale: Standards help ensure consistency, thus improving the ability to manage systems and improve user satisfaction, and protect existing IT investments, thus maximizing return on investment and reducing costs. Standards for interoperability additionally help ensure support from multiple vendors for their products, and facilitate supply chain integration.

Implications:

- Interoperability standards and industry standards will be followed unless there is a compelling business reason to implement a non-standard solution.
- A process for setting standards, reviewing and revising them periodically, and granting exceptions must be established.
- The existing IT platforms must be identified and documented.

原则 21：互用性

说明：软件和硬件均应符合已规定的提高数据、应用和技术互用性的标准。

理由依据：标准有助于确保一致性，从而提高管理系统的能力，并且有助于提高用户满意度和保护现有的 IT 投资，从而最大化投资收益并降低成本。用于互用性的标准还有助于确保多家厂商对其产品的支持，并促进供应链整合。

含义：

- 应遵守互用性标准和行业标准，除非存在强制业务理由而实施非标准的解决方案。
- 必须确定一个用于设定标准、定期审查和修订标准并批准例外情况的流程。
- 必须识别现有的 IT 平台，并将其文件化。

Chapter 24
Stakeholder Management

24.1 Introduction

Stakeholder Management is an important discipline that successful architecture practitioners can use to win support from others. It helps them ensure that their projects succeed where others fail.

The benefits of successful Stakeholder Management are that:

- The most powerful stakeholders can be identified early and their input can then be used to shape the architecture; this ensures their support and improves the quality of the models produced.
- Support from the more powerful stakeholders will help the engagement win more resource, thus making the architecture engagement more likely to succeed.
- By communicating with stakeholders early and frequently, the architecture team can ensure that they fully understand the architecture process, and the benefits of enterprise architecture; this means they can support the architecture team more actively when necessary.
- The architecture team can more effectively anticipate likely reactions to the architecture models and reports, and can build into the plan the actions that will be needed to capitalize on positive reaction while avoiding or addressing any negative reactions.
- The architecture team can identify conflicting or competing objectives among stakeholders early and develop a strategy to resolve the issues arising from them.

It is essential in any initiative to identify the individuals and groups within the organization who will contribute to the development of the architecture, identify those that will gain and those that will lose from its introduction, and then develop a strategy for dealing with them.

第 24 章 利益攸关者管理

24.1 简介

利益攸关者管理是一门重要的修炼，成功的架构实践者可以用其赢得他人的支持。它有助于架构实践者确保他们的项目能取得成功，否则就会失败。

成功的利益攸关者管理的益处是：

- 可提早识别出最有权力的利益攸关者，并且随后他们的输入可被用来进行架构塑形，以此确保他们的支持并提高所产生模型的质量。
- 来自更有权力的利益攸关者的支持将帮助架构工作赢得更多资源，从而使架构工作更有可能取得成功。
- 通过提早与利益攸关者频繁地沟通，架构团队可以确保他们充分地理解架构流程以及 Enterprise Architecture 的好处；这意味着，利益攸关者可以在必要时更主动地支持架构团队。
- 架构团队可以更有效地预计利益攸关者对架构模型和报告的可能反应，将需要利用利益攸关者的积极反应且避免或应对任何消极反应的行动编入计划。
- 架构团队可以提早识别利益攸关者之间相互冲突或相互竞争的目的，并制定战略来解决他们产生的问题。

在任何举措中，根本性的是识别组织内有助于架构开发的个体和群组，识别因架构引入而受益或受损的个体和群组，然后制定一项处理它们的战略。

24.2 Approach to Stakeholder Management

Stakeholder analysis should be used during Phase A (Architecture Vision) to identify the key players in the engagement, and also be updated throughout each phase; different stakeholders may be uncovered as the engagement progresses through into Opportunities & Solutions, Migration Planning, and Architecture Change Management.

Complex architectures are extremely hard to manage, not only in terms of the architecture development process itself, but also in terms of obtaining agreement from the large numbers of stakeholders touched by it.

For example, just as a building architect will create wiring diagrams, floor plans, and elevations to describe different facets of a building to its different stakeholders (electricians, owners, planning officials), so an enterprise architect must create different views of the business, information system, and technology architecture for the stakeholders who have concerns related to these aspects.

TOGAF specifically identifies this issue throughout the ADM through the following concepts (as defined in Section 35.1):

- Stakeholders
- Concerns
- Views
- Viewpoints

24.3 Steps in the Stakeholder Management Process

The following sections detail recommended Stakeholder Management activity.

24.3.1 Identify Stakeholders

Identify the key stakeholders of the enterprise architecture.

The first task is to brainstorm who the main enterprise architecture stakeholders are. As part of this, think of all the people who are affected by it, who have influence or power over it, or have an interest in its successful or unsuccessful conclusion.

It might include senior executives, project organization roles, client organization roles, system developers, alliance partners, suppliers, IT operations, customers, etc.

When identifying stakeholders there is a danger of concentrating too heavily on the formal structure of an organization as the basis for identification. Informal stakeholder groups may be just as powerful and influential as the formal ones.

Most individuals will belong to more than one stakeholder group, and these groups tend to arise as a result of specific events.

Look at who is impacted by the enterprise architecture project:

- Who gains and who loses from this change?
- Who controls change management of processes?

24.2 利益攸关者管理的实施途径

在阶段 A（架构愿景）中，利益攸关者分析应被用来识别架构介入的关键参与者，并且还应在每个阶段得到更新；随着架构工作进展到机会和解决方案、迁移规划以及架构变更管理阶段，可能会有不同的利益攸关者被发现。

复杂的架构极难管理，不仅架构开发流程本身如此，而且获得受该流程影响的众多相关利益攸关者的同意也很困难。

例如，正如建筑架构师将创建布线图、楼层平面图和立面图来向其不同的利益攸关者（电工、业主、规划官员）描述一个建筑的不同方面一样，ENTERPRISE 架构师必须为关注点与这些方面相关的利益攸关者创建业务、信息系统和技术架构的不同视图。

通过以下概念（如第 35.1 节中所定义），TOGAF 在整个 ADM 中明确识别出该问题：

- 利益攸关者
- 关注点
- 视图
- 视角

24.3 利益攸关者管理流程的步骤

下面几节详述推荐的利益攸关者管理活动。

24.3.1 识别利益攸关者

识别出 Enterprise Architecture 的关键利益攸关者。

第一项任务是，头脑风暴出谁是主要的 Enterprise Architecture 利益攸关者。作为本任务的一部分，考虑受 Enterprise Architecture 影响、对 Enterprise Architecture 产生影响或控制或对其成功或失败结果感兴趣的全体人员。

可能包括高级管理人员、项目组织角色、客户组织角色、系统开发人员、合作伙伴、供应商、IT 运维人员、客户等。

识别利益攸关者时，存在过度关注组织的正式结构并以此作为识别工作基础的风险。非正式的利益攸关者群组可能恰好与正式的利益攸关者群组具有同等权力和影响力。

大多数个体将属于一个以上利益攸关者群组，这些群组往往由特定事件引起。

考虑谁受到 Enterprise Architecture 项目的影响：

- 谁会在此变革中受益或受损？
- 谁控制流程的变革管理？

- Who designs new systems?
- Who will make the decisions?
- Who procures IT systems and who decides what to buy?
- Who controls resources?
- Who has specialist skills the project needs?
- Who has influence?

In particular, influencers need to be identified. These will be well respected and moving up, participate in important meetings and committees (look at meeting minutes), know what's going on in the company, be valued by their peers and superiors, and not necessarily be in any formal position of power.

Although stakeholders may be both organizations and people, ultimately the enterprise architecture team will need to communicate with people. It is the correct individual stakeholders within a stakeholder organization that need to be formally identified.

24.3.1.1 Sample Stakeholder Analysis

A sample stakeholder analysis that distinguishes 22 types of stakeholder, in five broad categories, is shown in Figure 24-1. Any particular architecture project may have more, fewer, or different stakeholders; and they may be grouped into more, fewer, or different categories.

- 谁设计新系统？
- 谁将做决策？
- 谁采购 IT 系统，以及谁决定买什么 IT 系统？
- 谁控制资源？
- 谁具有项目所需的专业技能？
- 谁具有影响力？

尤其需要识别出有影响力的人。这些人将会被充分尊重并持续参与架构工作，参与重要会议和委员会（检查会议记录），了解公司进展，受到同事和上级的重视，并且未必就任任何正式的重要职位。

虽然利益攸关者既可以是组织也可以是个人，但最终 Enterprise Architecture 团队需要与个人进行沟通。在利益攸关者组织中，需要正式识别出正确的单个利益攸关者。

24.3.1.1 利益攸关者分析示例

将 22 种利益攸关者分成五大类的利益攸关者分析示例如图 24-1 所示。任何特殊的架构项目都可能有更多、更少或不同的利益攸关者；且这些利益攸关者可被分成更多、更少或不同的类别。

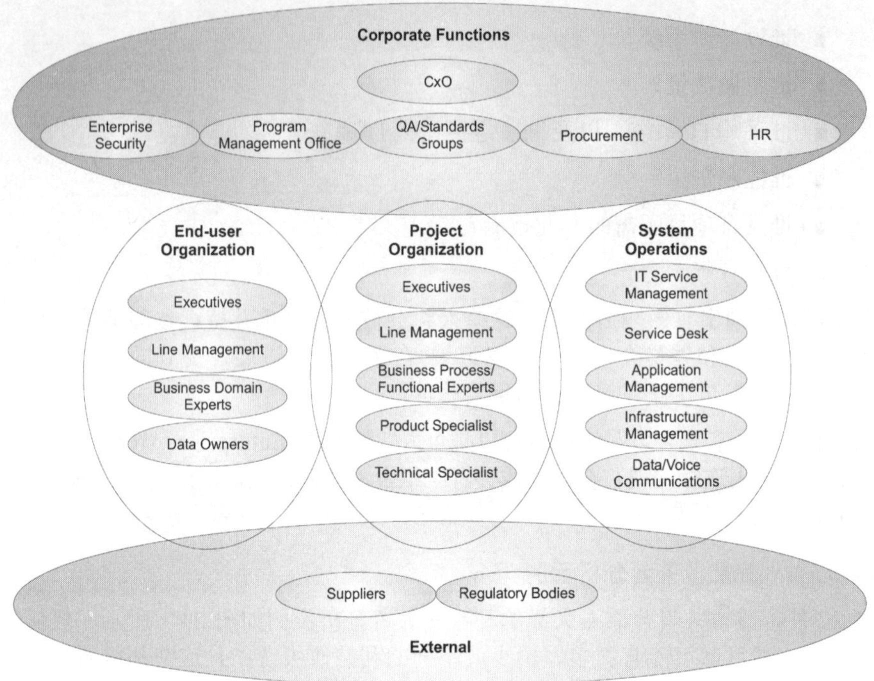

Figure 24-1 Sample Stakeholders and Categories

Consider both the Visible team — those obviously associated with the project/ change — and the Invisible team — those who must make a real contribution to the project/change for it to be successful but who are not obviously associated with it (e.g., providers of support services).

24.3.2 Classify Stakeholder Positions

Develop a good understanding of the most important stakeholders and record this analysis for reference and refresh during the project. An example stakeholder analysis is shown in Table24-1.

Table 24-1 Example Stakeholder Analysis

Stakeholder Group	Stakeholder	Ability to Disrupt Change	Current Unders-tanding	Required Unders-tanding	Current Commitment	Required Commitment	Required Support
CIO	John Smith	H	M	H	L	M	H
CFO	Jeff Brown	M	M	M	L	M	M

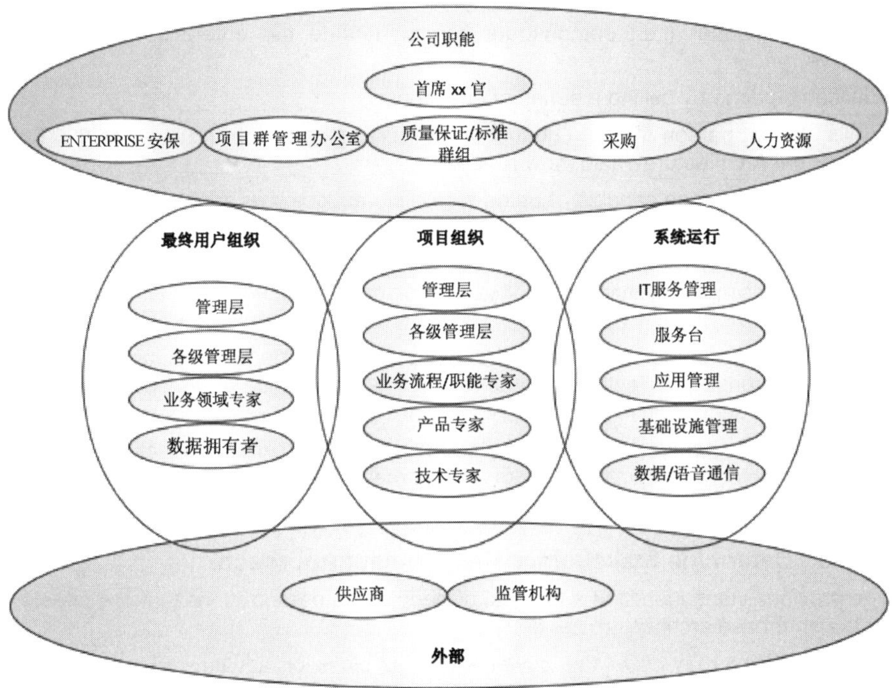

图 24-1 利益攸关者和类别的示例

考虑有形团队（与项目/变更明显相关的那些人）和无形团队（对项目/变更的成功必须作出实际贡献，但并不与其明显相关的那些人，例如，支持服务的提供者）。

24.3.2 对利益攸关者职位分类

形成对最重要的利益攸关者的深入认识并记录该分析，以供在项目中参考和更新。利益攸关者分析示例如表 24-1 所示。

表 24-1 利益攸关者分析示例

利益攸关者群组	利益攸关者	破坏变更的能力	目前的认识	所需认识	目前的投入	所需投入	所需支持
首席信息官	约翰·史密斯	高	中	高	低	中	高
首席财务官	杰夫·布朗	中	中	中	低	中	中

It is also important to assess the readiness of each stakeholder to behave in a supportive manner (i.e., demonstrate commitment to the enterprise architecture initiative).

This can be done by asking a series of questions:

- Is that person ready to change direction and begin moving towards the Target Architecture? If so, how ready?
- Is that person capable of being a credible advocate or agent of the proposed enterprise architecture initiative? If so, how capable?
- How involved is the individual in the enterprise architecture initiative? Are they simply an interested observer, or do they need to be involved in the details?
- Has that person made a contractual commitment to the development of the enterprise architecture, and its role in the governance of the development of the organization?

Then, for each person whose commitment is critical to ensure success, make a judgment as to their current level of commitment and the desired future level of commitment.

24.3.3 Determine Stakeholder Management Approach

The previous steps identified a long list of people and organizations that are affected by the enterprise architecture project.

Some of these may have the power either to block or advance. Some may be interested in what the enterprise architecture initiative is doing; others may not care. This step enables the team to easily see which stakeholders are expected to be blockers or critics, and which stakeholders are likely to be advocates and supporters of the initiative.

Work out stakeholder power, influence, and interest, so as to focus the enterprise architecture engagement on the key individuals. These can be mapped onto a power/interest matrix, which also indicates the strategy to adopt for engaging with them. Figure 24-2 shows an example power grid matrix.

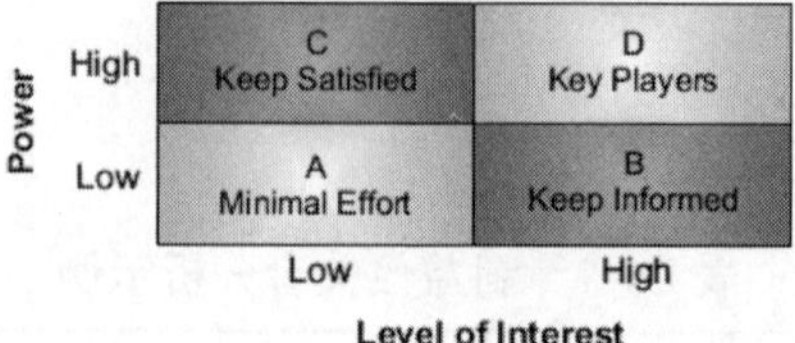

Figure 24-2 Stakeholder Power Grid

同样重要的是，评估每个利益攸关者以支持方式表现出的准备度（即，展示其对 Enterprise Architecture 举措的投入）。

这可以通过询问一系列问题完成：

- 该人员是否准备改变方向并开始接近目标架构？如果是，准备得如何？
- 该人员是否能成为提议的 Enterprise Architecture 举措的可信提倡者或代理人？如果是，能力如何？
- 个体在 Enterprise Architecture 举措中的参与程度？他们是否只是感兴趣的观察者亦或需要他们参与到细节中？
- 该人员是否对开发 Enterprise Architecture 以及其在组织开发治理中的角色作出契约性承诺？

然后，对于其投入对确保成功至关重要的每个人而言，针对其目前的投入层级和所需的未来投入层级作出判断。

24.3.3 确定利益攸关者管理途径

之前的步骤识别出一长串受 Enterprise Architecture 项目影响的个人和组织的名单。

其中，一些个人和组织可能拥有阻碍或促进的权力。有些个人或组织可能对 Enterprise Architecture 举措正在进行的工作感兴趣，其他个人和组织可能毫不关心。此步骤使团队能够轻易地看出哪些利益攸关者有望成为阻碍者或批评者，以及哪些利益攸关者有可能成为架构举措的提倡者和支持者。

确定利益攸关者的权力、影响力和利益，以便于将 Enterprise Architecture 介入聚焦于关键个体。这些可映射到权力/利益矩阵中，该矩阵也表明了与他们互相作用时应采取的策略。图 24-2 表明一个权力网格矩阵的示例。

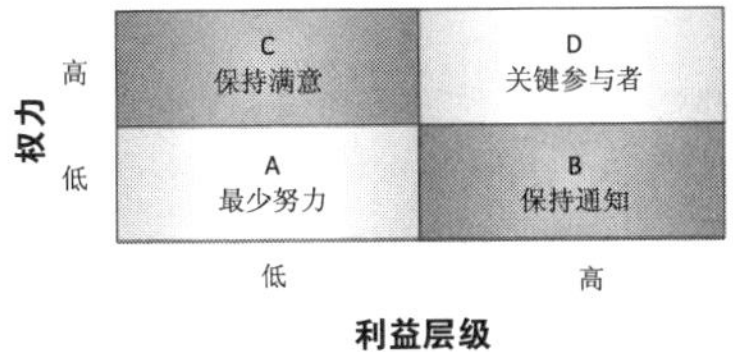

图 24-2 利益攸关者权力网格

24.3.4 Tailor Engagement Deliverables

Identify catalogs, matrices, and diagrams that the architecture engagement needs to produce and validate with each stakeholder group to deliver an effective architecture model.

It is important to pay particular attention to stakeholder interests by defining specific catalogs, matrices, and diagrams that are relevant for a particular enterprise architecture model. This enables the architecture to be communicated to, and understood by, all the stakeholders, and enables them to verify that the enterprise architecture initiative will address their concerns.

24.4 Template Stakeholder Map

The following table provides an example stakeholder map for a TOGAF architecture project which has stakeholders as identified in Figure 24-1.

Stakeholder	Key Concerns	Class	Catalogs, Matrices, and Diagrams
CxO (Corporate Functions); e.g., CEO, CFO, CIO, COO	The high-level drivers,goals, and objectives of the organization, and how these are translated into an effective process and IT architecture to advance the business	KEEP SATISFIED	Business Footprint diagram Goal/Objective/ Service diagram Organization Decomposition diagram
Program Management Office (Corporate Functions); e.g., Project Portfolio Managers	Prioritizing, funding, andaligning change activity. An understanding of project content and technical dependencies between projects supports portfolio management decision-making	KEEP SATISFIED	Requirements catalog Project Context diagram Benefits diagram Business Footprint diagram Application Communication diagram Functional Decomposition diagram

24.3.4 剪裁工作交付物

识别架构介入需要生成的目录集、矩阵和图，并与每一个利益攸关者群组进行确认，以交付一个有效的架构模型。

重要的是，通过定义与特殊 Enterprise Architecture 模型有关的特定目录、矩阵和图，对利益相关者的利益予以特别关注。这能够将架构传达至所有利益攸关者，并使其理解架构，且使他们能够验证：Enterprise Architecture 举措将应对其关注点。

24.4 利益攸关者映射模板

下表针对具有如图 24-1 所识别的利益有关者的 TOGAF 架构项目提供利益攸关者映射示例。

利益攸关者	关键关注点	分类	目录、矩阵和图
首席××官（公司职能）； 如：首席执行官（CEO）、首席财务官（CFO）、首席信息官（CIO）、首席运营官（COO）	组织的高层级驱动因素、目标和目的，以及如何将这些转化为一个有效流程和 IT 架构以推进业务发展	保持满意	业务足迹图 目标/目的/服务图 组织分解图
项目群管理办公室（公司职能）； 例如项目谱系管理者	对变革活动进行优先级排序、资金支持和调整。对项目内容和项目之间的技术依赖性的理解可支持项目谱系管理决策	保持满意	需求目录集 项目背景环境图 效益图 业务足迹图 应用通信图 功能分解图

Stakeholder	Key Concerns	Class	Catalogs, Matrices,and Diagrams
Procurement (Corporate Functions); e.g., Acquirers	Understanding what building blocks of the architecture can be bought, and what constraints (or rules) are relevant to the purchase. Acquirers will shop with multiple vendors looking for the best cost solution while adhering to the constraints (or rules) derived from the architecture, such as standards. The key concern is to make purchasing decisions that fit the architecture	KEY PLAYERS	Technology Portfolio catalog Technology Standards catalog
Human Resources(HR) (Corporate Functions); e.g., HR Managers, Training & Development Managers	The roles and actors arerequired to support the architecture and changes to it. The key concern is managing people transitions	KEEP INFORMED	Organization Decomposition diagram Organization/ Actor catalog Location catalog Application and User Location diagram
Enterprise Security (Corporate Functions); e.g., Corporate Risk Management, Security Officers, IT Security Managers	Ensuring that the information, data, and systems of the organization are available to only those that have permission, and protecting the information, data, and systems from unauthorized tampering	KEY PLAYERS	Product Lifecycle diagram Data Dissemination diagram Data Security diagram Actor/Role matrix Networked Computing Hardware diagram Communications Engineering diagram

利益攸关者	关键关注点	分类	目录、矩阵和图
采购（公司职能）；例如采办方	理解架构的哪些构建块可以购买，以及与采购有关的约束（或规则）有哪些。采办方将向多家厂商进行采购，寻求最佳成本解决方案，同时遵循源自架构的约束，例如各类标准。关键关注点是作出符合架构的购买决策	关键参与者	技术谱系目录集 技术标准目录集
人力资源（HR）（公司职能）；例如 HR 经理、培训与发展经理	需要这些角色和施动者支持架构及对架构作出的变更。其关键关注点是管理人事变动	保持通知	组织分解图 组织/施动者目录集 位置目录 应用和用户位置图
ENTERPRISE 安保（公司职能）；如公司风险管理、安保官员、IT 安保经理	确保组织的信息、数据和系统仅供有权限的人使用，并保护这些信息、数据和系统免受未授权的篡改	关键参与者	产品生命周期图 数据分发图 数据安保图 施动者/角色矩阵 网络计算硬件图 通信工程图

Stakeholder	Key Concerns	Class	Catalogs, Matrices, and Diagrams
QA/Standards Group (Corporate Functions); e.g., Data Owners, Process Owners, Technical Standards Bodies	Ensuring the consistent governance of the organization's business, data, application, and technology assets	KEY PLAYERS	Process/Event/Control/ Product catalog Contract/Measure catalog Application Portfolio catalog Interface catalog Technology Standards catalog Technology Portfolio catalog
Executive(End User Organization); e.g., Business Unit Directors, Business Unit CxOs,Business Unit Head of IT/Architecture	The high-level drivers,goals, and objectives of the organization, and how these are translated into an effective process and architecture to advance the business	KEEP SATISFIED	Business Footprint diagram Goal/Objective/ Service diagram Organization Decomposition diagram Process Flow diagram Application Communication diagram
Line Management (End User Organization); e.g., Senior Business Managers, Operations Regional Managers, IT Managers	Top-level functions and processes of the organization, and how the key applications support these processes	KEY PLAYERS	Business Footprint diagram Organization Decomposition diagram Functional Decomposition diagram Process Flow diagram Application Communication diagram Application and User Location diagram

利益攸关者	关键关注点	分类	目录、矩阵和图
质量保证/标准群组 （公司职能）； 例如数据拥有者、 流程拥有者、 技术标准机构	确保组织的业务、数据、应用和技术资产的统一管控	关键 参与者	流程/事件/控制/产品目录集 契约/测度目录集 应用谱系目录集 界面目录集 技术标准目录集 技术谱系目录集
管理层 （最终用户组织）； 例如 IT/架构的业务部主任、 业务部首席××官、 业务部负责人	组织的高层级驱动因素、目标和目的，以及如何将这些转化为一个有效流程和架构以推进业务发展	保持满意	业务足迹图 目标/目的/服务图 组织分解图 过程流图 应用通信图
各级管理层 （最终用户组织）； 例如高级业务经理、 区域运行经理、IT 经理	组织的顶层功能和流程，以及关键应用如何支持这些流程	关键 参与者	业务足迹图 组织分解图 功能分解图 过程流图 应用通信图 应用和用户位置图

Stakeholder	Key Concerns	Class	Catalogs, Matrices, and Diagrams
Business Domain Experts (End User Organization); e.g., Business Process Experts, Business/Process Analyst, ProcessArchitect, Process Designer, Functional Managers, Business Analyst	Functional aspects of processes and supporting systems. This can cover the human actors involved inthe system, the user processes involved in the system, the functions required to support the processes, and the information required to flow in support of the processes	KEY PLAYERS	Business Interaction matrix Actor/Role matrix Business Service/ Information diagram Functional Decomposition diagram Product Lifecycle diagram Business Use-case diagram Application Use-case diagram Application Communication diagram Data Entity/ Business Function matrix
IT Service Management (Systems Operations); e.g., Service Delivery Manager	Ensuring that IT services provided to the organization meet the service levels required by that organization to succeed in business	KEEP INFORMED	Technology Standards catalog Technology Portfolio catalog Contract/Measure catalog Process/Application Realization diagram Enterprise Manageability diagram

利益攸关者	关键关注点	分类	目录、矩阵和图
业务领域专家（最终用户组织）；例如业务流程专家、业务/流程分析师、流程架构师、流程设计师、功能经理、业务分析师	流程和支持系统的功能方面。这可涵盖系统涉及的人员施动者、系统涉及的用户流程、支持流程所需的功能以及支持这些流程所需流通的信息	关键参与者	业务交互矩阵 施动者/角色矩阵 业务服务/信息图 功能分解图 产品生命周期图 业务用例图 应用用例图 应用通信图 数据实体/业务功能矩阵
IT 服务管理（系统运行）；例如服务交付经理	确保提供给组织的 IT 服务满足组织为取得业务成功所需的服务水平	保持通知	技术标准目录集 技术谱系目录集 契约/测度目录集 流程/应用实现图 ENTERPRISE 可管理性图

Stakeholder	Key Concerns	Class	Catalogs, Matrices, and Diagrams
IT Operations — Applications (System Operations); e.g., Application Architecture,System & Software Engineers	Development approach, software modularity and re-use, portability migration, and interoperability	KEY PLAYERS	Process/Application Realization diagram Application/Data matrix Application Migration diagram Software Engineering diagram Platform decomposition Diagram Networked Computing/ Hardware diagram Software distribution Diagram
IT Operations — Infrastructure (System Operations); e.g., Infrastructure Architect, Wintel support, Mid-range support, Operational DBA, Service Desk	Location, modifiability, re-usability, and availability of all components of the system. Ensuring that the appropriate components are developed and deployed within the system in an optimal manner	KEY PLAYERS	Platform Decomposition diagram Technology Standards catalog Technology Portfolio catalog Enterprise Manageability diagram Networked Computing/ Hardware diagram Processing diagram Environments and Locations diagram
IT Operations — Data/Voice Communications (System Operations); e.g., Network Management	Location, modifiability, re-usability, and availability of communications and networking services. Ensuring that the appropriate communications and networking services are developed and deployed within the system in an optimal manner	KEY PLAYERS	Communications Engineering diagram

利益攸关者	关键关注点	分类	目录、矩阵和图
IT 运行——应用（系统运行）；例如应用架构、系统和软件工程师	开发途径、软件模块化和复用、可移植性迁移和互用性	关键参与者	流程/应用实现图 应用/数据矩阵 应用迁移图 软件工程图 平台分解图 网络计算/硬件图 软件分布图
IT 运行——基础设施（系统运行）；例如基础设施架构师、Wintel 支持、中端支持、工作 DBA、服务台	系统所有组件的位置、可修改性、可复用性和可用性。确保以最优方式在系统内开发并部署了适当组件	关键参与者	平台分解图 技术标准目录集 技术谱系目录集 ENTERPRISE 可管理性图 网络计算/硬件图 处理图 环境和位置图
IT 运行——数据/语音通信（系统运行）；例如网络管理	通信和网络服务的位置、可修改性、可复用性和可用性。确保以最优方式在系统内开发并部署了适当的通信和网络服务	关键参与者	通信工程图

Stakeholder	Key Concerns	Class	Catalogs, Matrices, and Diagrams
Executive (Project Organization); e.g., Sponsor, Program Manager	On-time, on-budget deliveryof a change initiative that will realize expected benefits for the organization	KEEP INFORMED	Requirements catalog Principles catalog Value Chain diagram Solution Concept diagram Functional Decomposition diagram Application and User Location diagram
Line Management (Project Organization); e.g., Project Manager	Operationally achieving on-time, on-budget delivery of a change initiative with an agreed scope	KEEP INFORMED	Application Communication diagram Functional Decomposition diagram Environments and Locations diagram
Business Process/ Functional Expert (Project Organization); e.g., Financials FICO Functional Consultant, HR Functional Consultant	Adding more detail to the functional requirements of a change initiative based on experience and interaction with business domain experts in the end-user organization	KEY PLAYERS	Process Flow diagram Business Use-case diagram Business Service/ Information diagram Functional Decomposition diagram Application Communication diagram

利益攸关者	关键关注点	分类	目录、矩阵和图
高级管理层 （项目组织）； 例如发起人、 项目群经理	将实现组织预期利益的一项变革举措的准时、预算内交付	保持通知	需求目录集 解决方案概念图 功能分解图 应用和用户位置图
各级管理层 （项目组织）； 例如项目经理	在商定范围内，在运行上实现变革举措的准时、预算内交付	保持通知	应用通信图 功能分解图 环境和位置图
业务流程/功能专家 （项目组织）； 例如金融 FICO 职能顾问、 HR 职能顾问	基于经验以及与终端用户组织内的业务领域专家进行的交流，向变革举措的功能性需求中添加更多的细节	关键参与者	过程流图 业务用例图 业务服务/信息图 功能分解图 应用通信图

Stakeholder	Key Concerns	Class	Catalogs, Matrices, and Diagrams
Product Specialist (Project Organization); e.g., Portal Product Specialist	Specifying technology product designs in order to meet project requirements and comply with the Architecture Vision of the solution. In a packages and packaged services environment, product expertise can be used to identify product capabilities that can be readily leveraged and can provide guidance on strategies for product customization	KEY PLAYERS	Software Engineering diagram Application/ Data matrix
Technical Specialist (Project Organization); e.g., Application Architect	Specifying technology product designs in order to meet project requirements and comply with the Architecture Vision of the solution	KEY PLAYERS	Software Engineering diagram Platform Decomposition diagram Process/ Application Realization diagram Application/ Data matrix Application Migration diagram
Regulatory Bodies (Outside Services); e.g., Financial Regulator, Industry Regulator	Receipt of the informationthey need in order to regulate the client organization, and ensuring that their information requirements are properly satisfied. Interested in reporting processes, and the data and applications used to provide regulatory return information	KEEP SATISFIED	Business Footprint diagram Application Communication diagram
Suppliers (Outside Services); e.g., Alliance Partners, Key Suppliers	Ensuring that their information exchange requirements are met in order that agreed service contracts with the client organizations can be fulfilled	KEEP SATISFIED	Business Footprint diagram Business Service/ Information diagram Application Communication diagram

利益攸关者	关键关注点	分类	目录、矩阵和图
产品专家 （项目组织）； 例如门户产品专家	规定技术产品设计，以满足项目需求并遵从解决方案的架构愿景。 在成套服务和打包服务环境中，产品专家意见可用于识别可迅速得到更好利用并可为产品定制战略提供指南的产品能力	关键参与者	软件工程图 应用/数据矩阵
技术专家 （项目组织）； 例如应用架构师	规定技术产品设计，以满足项目需求并遵从解决方案的架构愿景	关键参与者	软件工程图 平台分解图 流程/应用实现图 应用/数据矩阵 应用迁移图
监管机构 （外部服务）； 例如金融监管机构、行业监管机构	收到他们为调整客户组织所需的信息，并确保适当满足他们的信息需求。对报告流程以及用于提供返回调整信息的数据和应用感兴趣	保持满意	业务足迹图 应用通信图
供应商 （外部服务）； 例如联盟合作者、关键供应商	确保他们对信息交换的需求得到了满足，以便可以履行与客户组织商定的服务契约	保持满意	业务足迹图 业务服务/信息图 应用通信图

Chapter 25
Architecture Patterns

This chapter provides guidelines for using architecture patterns.

25.1 Introduction

Patterns for system architecting are very much in their infancy. They have been introduced into TOGAF essentially to draw them to the attention of the systems architecture community as an emerging important resource, and as a placeholder for hopefully more rigorous descriptions and references to more plentiful resources in future versions of TOGAF.

They have not (as yet) been integrated into TOGAF. However, in the following, we attempt to indicate the potential value to TOGAF, and to which parts of the TOGAF Architecture Development Method (ADM) they might be relevant.

25.1.1 Background

A "pattern" has been defined as: "an idea that has been useful in one practical context and will probably be useful in others" [*Analysis Patterns — Re-usable Object Models*].

In TOGAF, patterns are considered to be a way of putting building blocks into context; for example, to describe a re-usable solution to a problem. Building blocks are what you use: patterns can tell you how you use them, when, why, and what trade-offs you have to make in doing so.

Patterns offer the promise of helping the architect to identify combinations of Architecture and/or Solution Building Blocks (ABBs/SBBs) that have been proven to deliver effective solutions in the past, and may provide the basis for effective solutions in the future.

Pattern techniques are generally acknowledged to have been established as a valuable architectural design technique by Christopher Alexander, a buildings architect, who described this approach in his book *The Timeless Way of Building*, published in 1979. This book provides an introduction to the ideas behind the use of patterns, and Alexander followed it with two further books (*A Pattern Language* and *The Oregon Experiment*) in which he expanded on his description of the features and benefits of a patterns approach to architecture.

Software and buildings architects have many similar issues to address, and so it was natural for software architects to take an interest in patterns as an architectural tool. Many papers and books have been published on them since Alexander's 1979 book, perhaps the most renowned being *Design Patterns: Elements of Re-usable Object-Oriented Software*. This book describes simple and elegant solutions to specific problems in object-oriented software design.

第 25 章
架构特征模式

本章提供架构特征模式的使用指南。

25.1 简介

系统架构的特征模式在很大程度上处于萌芽阶段。这些模式已基本引入 TOGAF 中，作为一种重要的新兴资源，并作为 TOGAF 未来版本中对更丰富资源进行可能更严格的描述和引用的“占位符”，而引起系统架构团体的注意。

它们并未（迄今为止）整合到 TOGAF 中。然而，下面将尝试说明它们对 TOGAF 的潜在价值，以及它们可能与 TOGAF 架构开发方法（ADM）的哪些部分相关。

25.1.1 背景

“特征模式”已经被定义为：“在一种实际背景环境中有用的认知内涵/认知内容，并在其他背景环境中也可能有用”[分析特征模式——可复用的对象模型]。

在 TOGAF 中，特征模式被认为是一种将构建块置入背景环境的方式；例如，描述某个问题的可复用解决方案。构建块是“用什么”，特征模式可告诉你：“如何使用它们，在使用中何时、为何必须做出权衡以及必须做出何种权衡。”

特征模式提供以下承诺：帮助架构师识别过去已被证明能交付有效解决方案和在未来可能提供有效解决方案基础的架构和/或解决方案构建块（ABB/SBB）的组合。

普遍认为，特征模式技巧已由建筑架构师克里斯托佛•亚历山大建立为一种有价值的架构设计技巧，在其 1979 年出版的《建筑的永恒之道》书中描述了这种实施途径。本书介绍了使用特征模式背后的想法，并且亚历山大在另外两本书（《特征模式语言》和《俄勒冈实验》）中沿用了该介绍，在这两本书中，他对架构特征模式实施途径的特征和好处的描述进行了扩展。

软件和建筑架构师有很多相似的议题需要应对，因此软件架构师对作为架构工具的特征模式感兴趣是一件很自然的事。继亚历山大 1979 年出版的书以后，关于特征模式已经出版了许多论文和书籍，也许最著名的就是《设计特征模式：可复用面向对象软件的基础》。本书描述了面向对象的软件设计中的特定问题的简单且简洁的解决方案。

25.1.2 Content of a Pattern

Several different formats are used in the literature for describing patterns, and no single format has achieved widespread acceptance. However, there is broad agreement on the types of things that a pattern should contain. The headings which follow are taken from *Pattern-Oriented Software Architecture: A System of Patterns*. The elements described below will be found in most patterns, even if different headings are used to describe them.

Name
: A meaningful and memorable way to refer to the pattern, typically a single word or short phrase.

Problem
: A description of the problem indicating the intent in applying the pattern — the intended goals and objectives to be reached within the context and forces described below (perhaps with some indication of their priorities).

Context
: The preconditions under which the pattern is applicable — a description of the initial state before the pattern is applied.

Forces
: A description of the relevant forces and constraints, and how they interact/conflict with each other and with the intended goals and objectives. The description should clarify the intricacies of the problem and make explicit the kinds of trade-offs that must be considered. (The need for such trade-offs is typically what makes the problem difficult, and generates the need for the pattern in the first place.) The notion of "forces" equates in many ways to the "qualities" that architects seek to optimize, and the concerns they seek to address, in designing architectures. For example:

- — Security, robustness, reliability, fault-tolerance
- — Manageability
- — Efficiency, performance, through put, band width requirements, space utilization
- — Scalability (incremental growth on-demand)
- — Extensibility, evolvability, maintainability
- — Modularity, independence, re-usability, openness, composability (plug-and-play), portability
- — Completeness and correctness
- — Ease-of-construction
- — Ease-of-use
- — etc., . ..

Solution
: A description, using text and/or graphics, of how to achieve the intended goals and objectives. The description should identify both the solution's static structure and its dynamic behavior — the people and computing actors, and their collaborations. The description may include guidelines for implementing the solution. Variants or specializations of the solution may also be described.

Resulting Context
: The post-conditions after the pattern has been applied. Implementing the solution normally requires trade-offs among competing forces. This element describes which forces have been resolved and how, and which remain unresolved. It may also indicate other patterns that may be applicable in the new context. (A pattern may be one step in accomplishing some larger goal.) Any such other patterns will be described in detail under Related Patterns.

25.1.2 特征模式内容

为了描述特征模式，在文献中使用了若干不同的版式，但没有一种版式得到广泛接受。然而，对一种特征模式应包含的内容类型却有广泛共识。下列标题摘自《面向特征模式的软件架构：特征模式系统》。以下描述的元素将在大多数特征模式中找到，即使描述它们的标题是不同的。

名称 指代特征模式的一种有意义且好记的方式，通常是一个单词或一个短语。

问题 对表明应用特征模式意图的问题的描述——在下述背景环境和影响力中待实现的预期目标和目的（可能根据它们优先顺序的若干指示）。

背景环境 特征模式适用的前提——对应用特征模式前初始状态的描述。

影响力 对相关影响力和约束力、彼此之间以及与预期目标和目的之间如何相互影响/冲突的描述。该描述应阐明问题的错综复杂之处，并明确说明必须考虑的权衡种类。（对这种权衡的需要通常使问题很困难，并率先产生对特征模式的需要）。“影响力”的概念在许多方面等同于架构师在设计架构过程中力图优化的“品质”，以及他们力图应对的关注点。例如：

- 安保性、鲁棒性、可靠性、容错性
- 可管理性
- 效率、绩效、吞吐量、带宽需求、空间利用率
- 可伸缩性（按需递增扩展）
- 可扩展性、可演化性、可维护性
- 模块性、独立性、可复用性、公开性、可组合性（即插即用）、可移植性
- 完整性和正确性
- 施工简便性
- 易用性
- 等等

解决方案 采用文字和/或图形对如何达成预期目标和目的进行的描述。该描述应识别解决方案的静态结构及其动态行为——即人工施动者和计算施动者以及他们之间的协作。该描述可包括实施该解决方案的指南。也可描述解决方案的变体或专门化。

产生的背景环境

应用特征模式后的后续条件。实施解决方案通常需要在相互竞争的影响力之间作出权衡。本元素描述已经解决了哪些影响力、如何解决的以及哪些未解决。它同样表明在新的背景环境中，可能适用的其他特征模式。（特征模式可能是实现某个更远大目标中的一个步骤）。任何这类其他的特征模式都将在“相关特征模式”中详细描述。

Examples One or more sample applications of the pattern which illustrate each of the other elements: a specific problem, context, and set of forces; how the pattern is applied; and the resulting context.

Rationale An explanation/justification of the pattern as a whole, or of individual components within it, indicating how the pattern actually works, and why — how it resolves the forces to achieve the desired goals and objectives, and why this is "good". The Solution element of a pattern describes the external structure and behavior of the solution: the Rationale provides insight into its internal workings.

Related Patterns

The relationships between this pattern and others. These may be predecessor patterns, whose resulting contexts correspond to the initial context of this one; or successor patterns, whose initial contexts correspond to the resulting context of this one; or alternative patterns, which describe a different solution to the same problem, but under different forces; or co-dependent patterns, which may/must be applied along with this pattern.

Known Uses Known applications of the pattern within existing systems, verifying that the pattern does indeed describe a proven solution to a recurring problem. Known Uses can also serve as Examples.

Patterns may also begin with an Abstract providing an overview of the pattern and indicating the types of problems it addresses. The Abstract may also identify the target audience and what assumptions are made of the reader.

25.1.3 Terminology

Although design patterns have been the focus of widespread interest in the software industry for several years, particularly in the object-oriented and component-based software fields, it is only recently that there has been increasing interest in architecture patterns — extending the principles and concepts of design patterns to the architecture domain.

The technical literature relating to this field is complicated by the fact that many people in the software field use the term "architecture" to refer to software, and many patterns described as

"architecture patterns" are high-level software design patterns. This simply makes it all the more important to be precise in use of terminology.

25.1.3.1 Architecture Patterns and Design Patterns

The term "design pattern" is often used to refer to any pattern which addresses issues of software architecture, design, or programming implementation. In *Pattern-Oriented Software Architecture: A System of Patterns*, the authors define these three types of patterns as follows:

- An **Architecture Pattern** expresses a fundamental structural organization or schema for software systems. It provides a set of predefined subsystems, specifies their responsibilities, and includes rules and guidelines for organizing the relationships between them.
- A **Design Pattern** provides a scheme for refining the subsystems or components of a software system, or the relationships between them. It describes a commonly recurring structure of communicating components that solves a general design problem within a particular context.

示例　　阐明特定问题、背景环境和一系列影响力等其他每一个元素的特征模式的一种或多种示例应用，如何应用特征模式，以及产生的背景环境。

依据　　对整个特征模式或特征模式内单独组件的解释/判断，它说明模式实际上是如何运作的，以及为什么这么运作——它如何解决影响力以达成预期目标和目的，以及为什么这样是“好的”。特征模式的解决方案元素描述了解决方案的外部结构和行为：理由依据提供对其内部工作的深入了解。

相关特征模式

本模式与其他模式之间的关系。这些特征模式可能是原有模式，其产生的背景环境与本特征模式的初始背景环境相对应；或者是后继特征模式，其初始背景环境与本特征模式的产生背景环境相对应；或者是备选特征模式，其描述同一问题的不同解决方案，但是在不同的影响力下；或者是互相依赖特征模式，其可能/必须与本特征模式一起应用。

已知用途　　特征模式在现有系统中的已知应用，验证了特征模式确实描述对重复出现问题的已证实的解决方案。已知用途也可用作示例。

特征模式也可能开始于一个提供特征模式综述并说明其应对的问题类型的摘要。此摘要也可能识别目标受众以及读者作出的假设。

25.1.3　术语

虽然设计特征模式在多年来一直是软件行业广泛关注的重点，尤其是在面向对象和基于组件的软件领域，但直到最近，对架构特征模式的兴趣才逐渐增加——将设计特征模式的原则和概念扩展到架构领域。

由于软件领域很多人使用术语“架构”来指软件，并且很多被描述为“架构特征模式”的特征模式是高层级软件设计特征模式，因此，有关该领域的技术文献十分复杂。这只会使得准确使用术语变得愈加重要。

25.1.3.1　架构特征模式和设计特征模式

术语“设计特征模式”常常用于指应对软件架构、设计或编程实现等议题的任何特征模式。在《面向特征模式的软件架构：特征模式系统》中，作者定义了如下三种特征模式：

- 架构特征模式，表示软件系统的基础结构组织或范式。它提供一系列预定义子系统，规定它们的责任，并包括用于组织它们之间关系的规则和指南。
- 设计特征模式，为细化软件系统的子系统或组件或其之间的关系提供方案。它描述通信组件经常反复出现的结构，这种结构解决了特殊背景环境中的一般设计问题。

- An **Idiom** is a low-level pattern specific to a programming language. An idiom describes how to implement particular aspects of components or the relationships between them using the features of the given language.

These distinctions are useful, but it is important to note that architecture patterns in this context still refers solely to software architecture. Software architecture is certainly an important part of the focus of TOGAF, but it is not its only focus.

In this section we are concerned with patterns for enterprise system architecting. These are analogous to software architecture and design patterns, and borrow many of their concepts and terminology, but focus on providing re-usable models and methods specifically for the architecting of enterprise information systems — comprising software, hardware, networks, and people — as opposed to purely software systems.

25.1.3.2 Patterns and the Architecture Continuum

Although architecture patterns have not (as yet) been integrated into TOGAF, each of the first four main phases of the ADM (Phases A through D) gives an indication of the stage at which relevant re-usable architecture assets from the enterprise Architecture Continuum should be considered for use. Architecture patterns are one such asset.

An enterprise that adopts a formal approach to use and re-use of architecture patterns will normally integrate their use into the enterprise Architecture Continuum.

25.1.3.3 Patterns and Views

Architecture views are selected parts of one or more models representing a complete system architecture, focusing on those aspects that address the concerns of one or more stakeholders. Patterns can provide help in designing such models, and in composing views based on them.

25.1.3.4 Patterns and Business Scenarios

Relevant architecture patterns may well be identified in the work on business scenarios.

25.1.4 Architecture Patterns in Use

Two examples of architecture patterns in use are outlined in the following subsections, one from the domain of an IT customer enterprise's own architecture framework, and the other from a major system vendor who has done a lot of work in recent years in the field of architecture patterns.

- The US Treasury Architecture Development Guidance (TADG) document (see Section25.2) provides a number of explicit architecture patterns, in addition to explaining a rationale, structure, and taxonomy for architectural patterns as they relate to the US Treasury.
- The IBM Patterns for e-Business web site (see Section 25.3) gives a series of architecture patterns that go from the business problem to specific solutions, firstly at a generic level and then in terms of specific IBM product solutions. A supporting resource is IBM's set of *Red Books*.

The following material is intended to give the reader pointers to some of the places where architecture patterns are already being used and made available, in order to help readers make their own minds up as to the usefulness of this technique for their own environments.

- 惯用语，是一种特定于编程语言的低层级特征模式。惯用语描述如何利用规定语言的特征来实现组件的特定方面或其之间的关系。

这些区别十分有用，但重要的是应注意到，在这种背景环境中，架构特征模式仍然仅仅指软件架构。软件架构无疑是 TOGAF 聚焦点的一个重要部分，但并不是 TOGAF 唯一的聚焦点。

在本节中，我们关注的是 ENTERPRISE 系统架构开发的特征模式。这些模式类似于软件架构特征模式和设计特征模式，并借用了它们的许多概念和术语，但这些特征模式着重于专门为 ENTERPRISE 信息系统的架构开发——包括软件、硬件、网络和人员——提供与纯软件系统完全不同的可复用的模型和方法。

25.1.3.2 特征模式和架构连续统一体

虽然架构特征模式尚未（迄今为止）整合到 TOGAF 中，但 ADM 前四个主要阶段（阶段 A～阶段 D）中的每个阶段均指出，在哪个阶段应考虑使用来自 ENTERPRISE 的架构连续统一体的相关可复用架构资产。架构特征模式是这类资产中的一种。

采用一种正式途径使用或复用架构特征模式的 ENTERPRISE，通常将它们的使用整合到 ENTERPRISE 的架构连续统一体中。

25.1.3.3 特征模式和视图

架构视图是代表完整系统架构的一个或多个模型的选定部分，它聚焦于那些应对一个或多个利益攸关者关注点的方面。特征模式可以在设计这些模型和基于这些模型组成视图的方面提供帮助。

25.1.3.4 特征模式和业务场景

相关的架构特征模式很有可能在业务场景的工作中识别出来。

25.1.4 使用中的架构特征模式

下列小节概述了使用中的架构特征模式的两个示例，一个来自于 IT 客户 ENTERPRISE 自身的架构框架领域，另一个来自于近年在架构特征模式领域中做了大量工作的主要系统厂商。

- 美国财务部架构开发指导（TADG）文件（见 25.2 节），除了解释与美国财务部有关的架构特征模式的依据、结构和分类法外，还提供了多个明确的架构特征模式。
- IBM 电子商务网站特征模式（见 25.3 节）首先按一般级别，然后根据具体的 IBM 产品解决方案提供一系列从业务问题到特定解决方案的架构特征模式。支持资源可在 IBM 的一套《红皮书》中找到。

下列资料旨在提示读者已经使用并可得到的架构特征模式所在的若干位置，目的是帮助读者自行决定本技巧在其自身环境中的有用性。

25.2 US Treasury Architecture Development Guidance (TADG)

The *US Treasury Architecture Development Guidance* (TADG) document — formerly known as the *Treasury Information System Architecture Framework* (TISAF) — provides a number of explicit architecture patterns.

Section 7 of the TADG document describes a rationale, structure, and taxonomy for architecture patterns, while the patterns themselves are formally documented in Appendix D. The architecture patterns presented embrace a larger set of systems than just object-oriented systems. Some architecture patterns are focused on legacy systems, some on concurrent and distributed systems, and some on real-time systems.

25.2.1 TADG Pattern Content

The content of an architecture pattern as defined in the TADG document contains the following elements:

Name — Each architecture pattern has a unique, short descriptive name. The collection of architecture pattern names can be used as a vocabulary for describing, verifying, and validating Information Systems Architectures.

Problem — Each architecture pattern contains a description of the problem to be solved.

The problem statement may describe a class of problems or a specific problem.

Rationale — The rationale describes and explains a typical specific problem that is representative of the broad class of problems to be solved by the architecture pattern. For a specific problem, it can provide additional details of the nature of the problem and the requirements for its resolution.

Assumptions — The assumptions are conditions that must be satisfied in order for the architecture pattern to be usable in solving the problem. They include constraints on the solution and optional requirements that may make the solution more easy to use.

Structure — The architecture pattern is described in diagrams and words in as much detail as is required to convey to the reader the components of the pattern and their responsibilities.

Interactions — The important relationships and interactions among the components of the pattern are described and constraints on these relationships and interactions are identified.

Consequences — The advantages and disadvantages of using this pattern are described, particularly in terms of other patterns (either required or excluded) as well as resource limitations that may arise from using it.

Implementation — Additional implementation advice that can assist designers in customizing this architectural design pattern for the best results.

25.2 美国财政部架构开发指导（TADG）

《美国财政部架构开发指导》（TADG）文件——以前称为《美国财务部信息系统架构框架》（TISAF）——提供多个明确的架构特征模式。

TADG 文件的第 7 节描述了架构特征模式的依据、结构和分类法，而特征模式本身在附录 D 中被正式文件化。提出的架构特征模式包括更大范围的系统，而并非仅仅是面向对象的系统。一些架构特征模式专注于已有系统，一些专注于并行系统和分布式系统，还有一些则专注于实时系统。

25.2.1 TADG 特征模式内容

TADG 文件中定义的架构特征模式的内容包含以下元素：

名称　　每个架构特征模式具有一个唯一的、简洁的描述性名称。架构模式名称的集合可用作描述、验证和确认信息系统架构的词汇表。

问题　　每个架构特征模式都包含对待解决问题的描述。

问题说明可描述一类问题或一个特定问题。

理由依据　　理由依据描述并解释了由架构特征模式解决的广义类问题所代表的一个典型特定问题。对于一个特定问题，它可以提供问题本质及其解决办法需求的更多细节。

假设　　假设是为使架构特征模式在解决问题中可用而必须满足的条件。它们包括对解决方案的约束和可使解决方案更容易使用的可选需求。

结构　　按要求尽可能详细地用图和文字描述架构特征模式，以向读者传达特征模式的各个组件及其责任。

交互　　描述特征模式各个组件之间重要的关系和交互，并且识别对这些关系和交互的约束。

后果　　描述使用该模式的优缺点，尤其在其他特征模式（需要的或排除在外的）和使用本特征模式可能引起的资源限制方面进行描述。

实施　　可帮助设计师在定制本架构设计特征模式中取得最佳结果的附加实施建议。

25.2.2 TADG Architecture Patterns

The TADG document contains the following patterns.

Architectural Design Pattern Name	Synopsis
Client-Proxy Server	Acts as a concentrator for many low-speed links to access aserver.
Customer Support	Supports complex customer contact across multiple organizations.
Reactor	Decouples an event from its processing.
Replicated Servers	Replicates servers to reduce burden on central server.
Layered Architecture	A decomposition of services such that most interactions occur only between neighboring layers.
Pipe and Filter Architecture	Transforms information in a series of incremental steps or processes.
Subsystem Interface	Manages the dependencies between cohesive groups of functions (subsystems).

25.3 IBM Patterns for e-Business

The *IBM Patterns for e-Business* web site (refer to www.ibm.com/framework/patterns) provides a group of re-usable assets aimed at speeding the process of developing eBusiness applications. A supporting IBM web site is *Patterns for e-Business Resources* (refer to www.ibm.com/developerworks/patterns/library). This is also known as the "Red Books".

The rationale for IBM's provision of these patterns is to:

- Provide a simple and consistent way to translate business priorities and requirements into technical solutions.
- Assist and speed up the solution development and integration process by facilitating the assembly of a solution and minimizing custom one-of-a-kind implementations.
- Capture the knowledge and best practices of experts and make it available for use by less experienced personnel.
- Facilitate the re-use of intellectual capital such as reference architectures, frameworks, and other architecture assets.

IBM's patterns are focused specifically on solutions for e-Business; i.e., those which allow an organization to leverage web technologies in order to re-engineer business processes, enhance communications, and lower organizational boundaries with:

- Customers and shareholders (across the Internet)
- Employees and stakeholders (across a corporate Intranet)
- Vendors, suppliers, and partners (across an Extranet)

They are intended to address the following challenges encountered in this type of environment:

- High degree of integration with legacy systems within the enterprise and with systems outside the enterprise.

25.2.2 TADG 架构特征模式

TADG 文件包含下列特征模式。

架构设计特征模式名称	概要
客户端代理服务器	作为多个低速链路访问服务器的集中器
客户支持	支持跨多个组织的复杂客户联系
反应器	从事件处理中解耦事件
复制的服务器	复制服务器，以减少中央服务器的负担
分层架构	服务的分解，使得大多数交互仅发生在相邻层之间
管道和过滤器架构	以一系列递增步骤或流程转换信息
子系统界面	管理功能的凝聚群组（子系统）之间的依赖性

25.3 IBM 电子商务特征模式

IBM 电子商务特征模式网站（见 www.ibm.com/framework/patterns），提供一组旨在加速开发电子商务应用流程的可复用资产。支持 IBM 网站的是电子商务资源模式（见 www.ibm.com/developerworks/patterns/library）。这也被称为“红皮书”。

IBM 提供这些特征模式的理由依据是：

- 提供一种简单且一致的方法，将业务优先级和需求转化为技术解决方案。
- 通过促进解决方案组装并最小化定制的独一无二的实施，帮助并加速解决方案的开发和集成流程。
- 抓取专家知识和最佳实践并使其可供经验较少的人员使用。
- 促进诸如参考架构、框架以及其他架构资产等知识资本的复用。

IBM 特征模式特别关注电子商务的解决方案；即为了与以下人员重构业务流程，加强沟通并降低组织边界，使得组织能更强有力地发挥网络技术作用的解决方案：

- 客户和利益攸关者（通过互联网）
- 员工和利益攸关者（通过公司内网）
- 厂商、供应商和合作者（通过外网）

他们旨在应对这类环境中遇到的下列挑战：

- 与 ENTERPRISE 内已有系统以及与 ENTERPRISE 外系统的高度集成。

- The solutions need to reach users faster; this does not mean sacrificing quality, but it does mean coming up with better and faster ways to develop these solutions.
- Service Level Agreements (SLAs) are critical.
- Need to adapt to rapidly changing technologies and dramatically reduced product cycles.
- Address an acute shortage of the key skills needed to develop quality solutions.

IBM defines five types of pattern:

- **Business Patterns**, which identify the primary business actors, and describe the interactions between them in terms of different archetypal business interactions such as:
  - Service (a.k.a. user-to-business) — users accessing transactions on a 24x7 basis
  - Collaboration (a.k.a. user-to-user) — users working with one another to share data and information
  - Information Aggregation (a.k.a. user-to-data) — data from multiple sources aggregated and presented across multiple channels
  - Extended Enterprise (a.k.a. business-to-business) — integrating data and processes across enterprise boundaries
- **Integration Patterns**, which provide the " glue " to combine business patterns to form solutions. They characterize the business problem, business processes/rules, and existing environment to determine whether front-end or back-end integration is required.
  - Front-end integration (a.k.a. access integration) — focused on providing seamless and consistent access to business functions. Typical functions provided include single sign-on, personalization, transcoding, etc
  - Back-end integration (a.k.a. application integration) — focused on connecting, interfacing, or integrating databases and systems. Typical integration can be based on function, type of integration, mode of integration, and by topology
- **Composite Patterns**, which are previously identified combinations and selections of business and integration patterns, for previously identified situations such as: electronic commerce solutions, (public) enterprise portals, enterprise intranet portal, collaboration ASP, etc.
- **Application Patterns**: Each business and integration pattern can be implemented using one or more application patterns. An application pattern characterizes the coarse-grained structure of the application — the main application components, the allocation of processing functions and the interactions between them, the degree of integration between them, and the placement of the data relative to the applications.
- **Runtime Patterns**: Application patterns can be implemented by run-time patterns, which demonstrate non-functional, service-level characteristics, such as performance, capacity, scalability, and availability. They identify key resource constraints and best practices.

The IBM web site also provides specific (IBM) product mappings for the run-time patterns, indicating specific technology choices for implementation.

- 这些解决方案需要更快地交付给用户；这不意味着牺牲质量，而意味着找出更好且更快的方法来开发这些解决方案。
- 服务水平协议（SLA）至关重要。
- 需要适应技术快速变化和产品周期大幅缩短。
- 应对开发质量解决方案所需的关键技能急剧短缺问题。

IBM 定义五种类型的特征模式：

- 业务特征模式，该模式识别主要的业务施动者，并根据不同的原型业务交互描述施动者之间的交互，例如：
  - 服务（又称用户到企业）——用户可全天候（24×7）访问事务
  - 合作（又称用户到用户）——用户相互协作，以共享数据和信息
  - 信息聚合（又称用户到数据）——来自多源的数据跨多重信道聚合并表达
  - 扩展的 ENTERPRISE（又称企业到企业）——跨 ENTERPRISE 边界集成数据和流程
- 集成特征模式，该模式提供合并业务特征模式的“粘胶剂”，以形成解决方案。它们描述了业务问题、业务流程/规则，以及现有环境的特征，以确定是否需要前端集成或后端集成。
  - 前端集成（又称访问集成）——聚焦于提供对业务功能无缝且一致的访问。所提供的典型功能包括单点登录、个性化、转码等
  - 后端集成（又称应用集成）——聚焦于连接、联系或集成数据库和系统。典型的集成可基于功能、集成类型、集成模式或通过拓扑实现
- 复合特征模式，该模式是以前识别的业务和集成模式的组合及选择，适合于以往识别的诸如电子商务解决方案、（公共）ENTERPRISE 门户、ENTERPRISE 内网门户、ASP 合作等情况。
- 应用特征模式：可使用一个和多个应用特征模式实现每种业务和集成特征模式。应用特征模式描述了应用的粗粒度结构特征——主要的应用组件、处理功能的分配及其之间的交互、集成度以及数据相对于应用的位置。
- 运行时特征模式：应用特征模式可通过运行时模式实现，运行时模式证明了非功能性、服务水平特征，例如绩效、能力、可伸缩性和可用性。它们识别出关键的资源约束和最佳实践。

IBM 网站还为运行时特征模式提供特定的（IBM）产品映射，表明了用于实施的特定技术选择。

25.4 Some Pattern Resources

- The Patterns Home Page (refer to hillside.net/patterns) hosted by the Hillside Group provides information about patterns, links to online patterns, papers, and books dealing with patterns, and patterns-related mailing lists.
- The Patterns-Discussion FAQ (refer to g.oswego.edu/dl/pd-FAQ/pd-FAQ.html) maintained by Doug Lea provides a very thorough and highly readable FAQ about patterns.
- *Patterns and Software: Essential Concepts and Terminology* by Brad Appleton (refer to www.cmcrossroads.com/bradapp/docs/patterns-intro.html) provides another thorough and readable account of the patterns field.

25.4 若干特征模式资源

- 由 Hillside 集团托管的特征模式首页（见 hillside.net/patterns）提供关于特征模式的信息、在线特征模式的链接、涉及特征模式的论文和书籍以及与特征模式相关的邮件列表。
- 由 Doug Lea 维护的关于特征模式讨论的常见问题（见 g.oswego.edu/dl/pd-FAQ/pd-FAQ.html）提供关于特征模式的非常全面且可读性较强的常见问题。
- 特征模式和软件：Brad Appleton 所著的根本性的概念和术语（见 www.cmcrossroads.com/bradapp/docs/patterns-intro.html）提供特征模式领域的另一种全面且可读的解释。

Chapter 26 Business Scenarios and Business Goals

This chapter describes a method for deriving business requirements for architecture and the implied technical requirements. It also provides guidelines on defining goals and objectives for architecture development.

26.1 Introduction

A key factor in the success of an enterprise architecture is the extent to which it is linked to business requirements, and demonstrably supporting and enabling the enterprise to achieve its business objectives.

Business scenarios are an important technique that may be used at various stages of the enterprise architecture, principally the Architecture Vision and the Business Architecture, but in other architecture domains as well, if required, to derive the characteristics of the architecture directly from the high-level requirements of the business. They are used to help identify and understand business needs, and thereby to derive the business requirements that the architecture development has to address.

A business scenario describes:

- A business process, application, or set of applications that can be enabled by the architecture.
- The business and technology environment.
- The people and computing components (called “actors”) who execute the scenario.
- The desired outcome of proper execution.

A good business scenario is representative of a significant business need or problem, and enables vendors to understand the value to the customer organization of a developed solution.

A good business scenario is also “SMART”:

- **Specific**, by defining what needs to be done in the business.
- **Measurable**, through clear metrics for success.
- **Actionable, by:**
  - Clearly segmenting the problem
  - Providing the basis for determining elements and plans for the solution
- **Realistic**, in that the problem can be solved within the bounds of physical reality, time, and cost constraints.

第 26 章
业务场景和业务目标

本章描述获得架构的业务需求和暗含的技术需求的方法。本章还提供关于定义架构开发的目标和目的的指南。

26.1　简介

Enterprise Architecture 成功的关键因素在于其与业务需求相关联的程度，以及明确支持 ENTERPRISE 并使其能够达成业务目的的程度。

业务场景是一种重要的技巧，可用在 Enterprise Architecture 的不同阶段，主要是架构愿景和业务架构，但需要时也可用在其他架构领域，以从高层级业务需求中直接提取架构特征。使用业务场景有助于识别并理解业务需求，从而导出架构开发必须处理的业务需求。

业务场景描述：

- 架构能够启用的业务流程、应用或应用集。
- 业务和技术环境。
- 执行该场景的人员和计算组件（称为“施动者”）。
- 适当执行的期望结果。

良好的业务场景表达重大的业务需要或问题，并使厂商能够理解成熟解决方案对客户组织的价值。

良好的业务场景同样是“SMART”的：

- **具体的**，通过定义业务中需要完成什么。
- **可衡量的**，通过成功的明确衡量标准。
- **可付诸行动的**，通过：
  - —　明确地划分问题
  - —　为确定解决方案的元素和计划提供基础
- **切实可行的**，在于问题可在物理现实、时间和成本约束的范围内解决。

- **Time-bound**, in that there is a clear statement of when the solution opportunity expires.

Section 26.9 provides detailed examples on objectives that could be considered. Whatever objectives you use, the idea is to make those objectives SMART.

26.2 Benefits of Business Scenarios

A business scenario is essentially a complete description of a business problem, both in business and in architectural terms, which enables individual requirements to be viewed in relation to one another in the context of the overall problem. Without such a complete description to serve as context:

- There is a danger of the architecture being based on an incomplete set of requirements that do not add up to a whole problem description, and that can therefore misguide architecture work.
- The business value of solving the problem is unclear.
- The relevance of potential solutions is unclear.

Also, because the technique requires the involvement of business line management and other stakeholders at an early stage in the architecture project, it also plays an important role in gaining the buy-in of these key personnel to the overall project and its end-product — the enterprise architecture.

An additional advantage of business scenarios is in communication with vendors. Most architecture nowadays is implemented by making maximum use of Commercial Off-The-Shelf (COTS) software solutions, often from multiple vendors, procured in the open market. The use of business scenarios by an IT customer can be an important aid to IT vendors in delivering appropriate solutions. Vendors need to ensure that their solution components add value to an open solution and are marketable. Business scenarios provide a language with which the vendor community can link customer problems and technical solutions. Besides making obvious what is needed, and why, they allow vendors to solve problems optimally, using open standards and leveraging each other's skills.

26.3 Creating the Business Scenario

26.3.1 Overall Process

Creating a business scenario involves the following, as illustrated in Figure 26-1.

1. Identifying, documenting, and ranking the problem driving the scenario.
2. Identifying the business and technical environment of the scenario and documenting it in scenario models.
3. Identifying and documenting desired objectives (the results of handling the problems successfully); get "SMART".
4. Identifying the human actors (participants) and their place in the business model.
5. Identifying computer actors (computing elements) and their place in the technology model.

- 有时限的，对解决方案机会何时失效有明确的说明。

26.9 节对可考虑到的目的提供详细示例。无论你使用的目的是什么，理念都是使那些目的 SMART。

26.2 业务场景的益处

业务场景基本上是用业务术语和架构术语对业务问题的一个完整描述，能够在整个问题的背景环境中，将单个需求与其他需求关联起来进行观察。如果缺乏这样一个作为背景环境的完整描述，那么：

- 基于一系列未加入整个问题描述中的不完整需求所建立的架构存在危险，因此会误导架构工作。
- 解决问题带来的业务价值不明确。
- 潜在解决方案的相关性不明确。

同样，因为本技巧要求业务各级管理层和其他利益攸关者在早期阶段参与到架构项目，因此，它在获得这些关键人员对整个项目和项目最终产物——Enterprise Architecture 的支持方面发挥重要作用。

业务场景的另一个好处是与厂商保持沟通。现在大多数架构是通过最大限度地使用通常由多家厂商提供的、从公开市场上采购的商用货架（COTS）软件解决方案来实现。IT 客户使用业务场景，对 IT 厂商交付合适的解决方案而言是一个重要的帮助。厂商需要确保他们的解决方案组件增加了公开解决方案的价值并且是可销售的。业务场景提供了一种厂商群体可用来将客户问题与技术解决方案建立联系的语言。除了清楚说明所需内容以及原因外，业务场景使厂商能使用公开标准并更好地利用彼此的技能以最佳方式解决问题。

26.3 创建业务场景

26.3.1 整体流程

创建一个业务场景包括以下内容，如图 26-1 所示。

1. 对驱动该场景的问题进行识别、文件化和定级。
2. 识别该场景的业务和技术环境，并在场景模型中使其文件化。
3. 识别并文件化预期目的（成功解决问题的结果）；达到“SMART”。
4. 识别人员施动者（参与者）及其在业务模型中的位置。
5. 识别计算机施动者（计算元素）及其在技术模型中的位置。

6. Identifying and documenting roles, responsibilities, and measures of success per actor; documenting the required scripts per actor, and the results of handling the situation.
7. Checking for "fitness-for-purpose" and refining only if necessary.

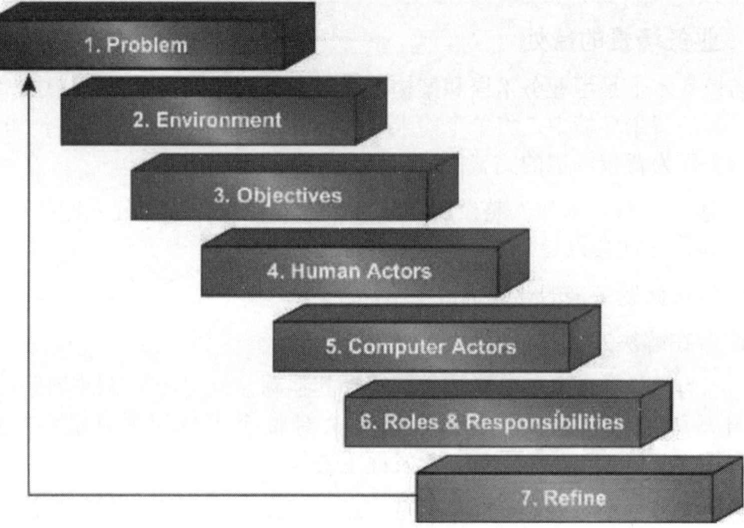

Figure 26-1 Creating a Business Scenario

A business scenario is developed over a number of iterative phases of Gathering, Analyzing, and Reviewing the information in the business scenario.

In each phase, each of the areas above is successively improved. The refinement step involves deciding whether to consider the scenario complete and go to the next phase, or whether further refinement is necessary. This is accomplished by asking whether the current state of the business scenario is fit for the purpose of carrying requirements downstream in the architecture process.

The three phases of developing a business scenario are described in detail below, and depicted in Figure 26-2.

6. 识别并文件化每个施动者的角色、职责和成功的衡量标准；使每个施动者所需的脚本文件化，以及处理该情况的结果。

7. 检查“适用性”，并且仅在必要时进行细化。

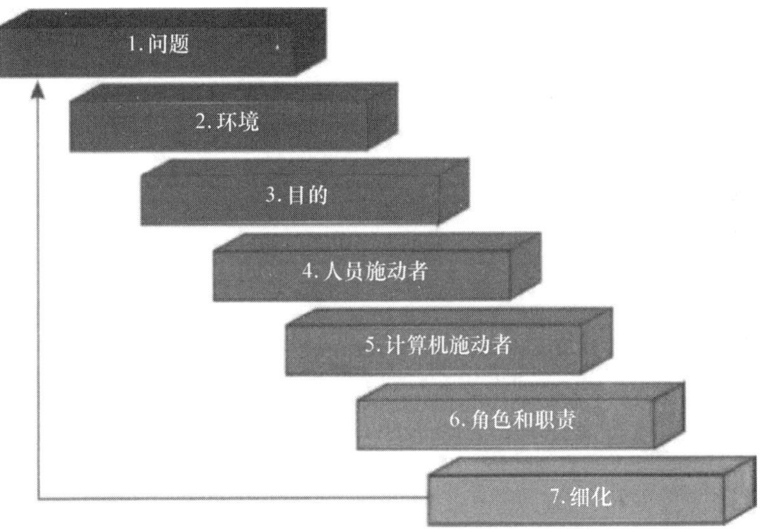

图 26-1　创建一个业务场景

业务场景经过多个迭代阶段的收集、分析并审查业务场景中的信息而被开发出来。

在每个阶段中，上述每个方面都相继得以改善。细化步骤包括决定是否认为该场景是完整的并进入下一阶段，或是否有必要进一步细化，这可以通过询问业务场景的当前状态是否符合将需求在架构流程中向下传递的目的来完成。

下面详细描述了开发业务场景的三个阶段，并在图 26-2 中予以描绘。

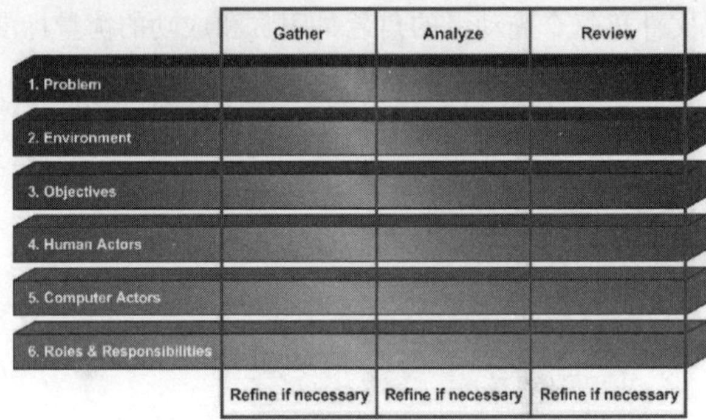

Figure 26-2 Phases of Developing Business Scenarios

26.3.2 Gathering

The Gathering phase is where information is collected on each of the areas in Figure 26-1. If information gathering procedures and practices are already in place in an organization — for example, to gather information for strategic planning — they should be used as appropriate, either during business scenario workshops or in place of business scenario workshops.

Multiple techniques may be used in this phase, such as information research, qualitative analysis, quantitative analysis, surveys, requests for information, etc. As much information as possible should be gathered and preprocessed "off-line" prior to any face-to-face workshops (described below). For example, a request for information may include a request for strategic and operational plans. Such doc-uments typically provide great insights, but the information that they contain usually requires significant preprocessing. The information may be used to generate an initial draft of the business scenario prior to the workshop, if possible. This will increase the understanding and confidence of the architect, and the value of the workshop to its participants.

A very useful way to gather information is to hold business scenario workshops, whereby a business scenario consultant leads a select and small group of business representatives througha number of questions to elicit the information surrounding the problem being addressed by the architecture effort. The workshop attendees must be carefully selected from high levels in the business and technical sides of the organization. It is important to get people that can and will provide information openly and honestly. Where a draft of the business scenario already exists— for example, as a result of preprocessing information gathered during this phase, as described above — the workshop may also be used to review the state of the business scenario draft.

Sometimes it is necessary to have multiple workshops: in some cases, to separate the gathering of information on the business side from the gathering of information on the technical side; and in other cases simply to get more information from more people.

When gathering information, the architect can greatly strengthen the business scenario byobtaining "real-world examples" ; i.e., case studies to which the reader can easily relate. When citing real-world examples, it is important to maintain a level of anonymity of the parties involved, to avoid blame.

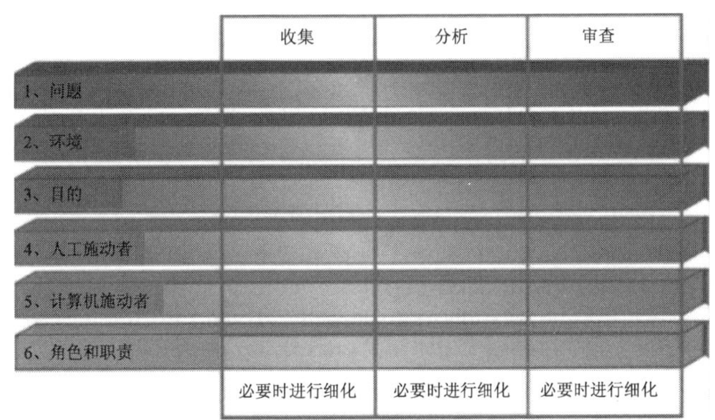

图 26-2　开发业务场景的阶段

26.3.2　收集

收集阶段是收集有关图 26-1 中各方面信息的阶段。如果组织内已经存在信息收集程序和实践——例如，收集用于战略规划的信息——它们应适当用在业务场景研讨会期间或代替业务场景研讨会。

在这一阶段，可以使用多种技巧，诸如信息研究、定性分析、定量分析、调查、信息要求等。在进行任何面对面研讨会（描述如下）之前，应“离线”收集并预处理尽可能多的信息。例如，信息要求可能包括对战略计划和运行计划的要求。这类文件通常提供深入见解，但是，这类文件包含的信息经常需要进行工作量相当大的预处理。如可能，这些信息可用于在研讨会之前生成业务场景的初步草图。这会提高架构师的理解力和自信心，以及研讨会对其参与者的价值。

收集信息的一个十分有用的方法是举行业务场景研讨会，借助研讨会，业务场景顾问通过多个问题引导挑选出的一小组业务代表，从而引出围绕架构工作正涉及的问题的信息。研讨会的参加者必须是从业务高层和组织技术人员中挑选出来的。重要的是，选出能够且愿意公开并诚实地提供信息的人。已经存在业务场景草图时——例如，由该阶段收集的预处理信息所产生，如上所述——研讨会也可用于审查该业务场景草图的状态。

有时必须举办多次研讨会：在某些情况下，将业务方的信息收集与技术方的信息收集分开进行；在其他情况下，仅仅是从更多人那里获得更多信息。

收集信息时，架构师可以通过获取“现实世界的示例”（即，读者可轻易涉及的案例研究）极大地强化业务场景。引用现实世界的示例时，重要的是保持有关当事人一定的匿名性，以避免被指责。

26.3.3 Analyzing

The Analyzing phase is where a great deal of real Business Architecture work is actually done. This is where the information that is gathered is processed and documented, and where the models are created to represent that information, typically visually.

The Analyzing phase takes advantage of the knowledge and experience of the business scenario consultant using past work and experience to develop the models necessary to depict the information captured. Note that the models and documentation produced are not necessarily reproduced *verbatim* from interviews, but rather filtered and translated according to the real underlying needs.

In the Analyzing phase it is important to maintain linkages between the key elements of the business scenario. One technique that assists in maintaining such linkages is the creation of matrices that are used to relate business processes to each of:

- Constituencies
- Human Actors
- Computer Actors
- Issues
- Objectives

In this way, the business process becomes the binding focal point, which makes a great deal of sense, since in most cases it is business process improvement that is being sought.

26.3.4 Reviewing

The Reviewing phase is where the results are fed back to the sponsors of the project to ensure that there is a shared understanding of the full scope of the problem, and the potential depth of the technical impact.

Multiple business scenario workshops or "readout" meetings with the sponsors and involved parties are recommended. The meetings should be set up to be open and interactive. It is recommended to have exercises built into meeting agendas, in order to test attendees' understanding and interest levels, as well as to test the architect's own assumptions and results.

This phase is extremely important, as the absence of shared expectations is in many cases the root cause of project failures.

26.3.3 分析

分析阶段是真正完成大量实际业务架构工作的阶段。这是收集的信息被处理和文件化的阶段，也是创建模型来表达该信息的阶段，这种表达通常是形象化的。

分析阶段利用业务场景顾问的知识和经验的优势，使用过去的工作和经验来开发描述所捕获信息所需的模型。应注意，产生的模型和文件无须从访谈中逐字复制，而是按照实际的基本需要进行筛选和转化。

在分析阶段，重要的是保持业务场景关键元素之间的联系。帮助保持这类联系的一种技巧是创建用于将业务流程与下列各项联系起来的矩阵：

- 拥护者
- 人员施动者
- 计算机施动者
- 议题
- 目的

用这种方法，业务流程就会成为非常有意义且有约束力的聚焦点，因为在大多数情况下，正在寻求的正是业务流程的改进。

26.3.4 审查

审查阶段是将结果反馈给项目发起人，以确保对问题的全部范围和技术影响的潜在深度具有共同理解的阶段。

建议召开由发起人和相关方参加的多个业务场景研讨会或“读出”会议。会议应被安排成公开且互动的。建议在会议议程中加入演练，以便测试参会者的理解和利益层级，同时测试架构师自己的假设和结果。

本阶段极其重要，因为缺少共同期望在很多情况下是项目失败的根本原因。

26.4 Contents of a Business Scenario

The documentation of a business scenario should contain all the important details about the scenario. It should capture, and sequence, the critical steps and interactions between actors that address the situation. It should also declare all the relevant information about all actors, specifically: the different responsibilities of the actors; the key pre-conditions that have to be met prior to proper system functionality; and the technical requirements for the service to be of acceptable quality.

There are two main types of content: graphics (models), and descriptive text. Both have a part to play.

- **Business Scenario Models** capture business and technology views in a graphical form, to aid comprehension. Specifically, they relate actors and interactions, and give a starting point to confirm specific requirements.
- **Business Scenario Descriptions** capture details in a textual form. A typical contents list for a business scenario is given below.

26.4 业务场景内容

业务场景的文档应包含有关场景的所有重要细节。它应该捕获那些处理该情况的施动者之间的关键步骤和交互并将其排序。它同样应该声明关于全部施动者的所有相关信息，尤其是：施动者的不同责任；满足适当的系统功能性之前必须满足的关键前提条件；以及使服务具有可接受质量的技术需求。

主要有两种类型的内容：图形（模型）和说明性文字。二者均具有一定作用。

- 业务场景模型以图形格式捕获业务和技术视图以辅助理解。特别地，它们涉及施动者和交互，并给出确认特定需求的起点。
- 业务场景描述以文本格式捕获细节。下面给出了业务场景的一个典型内容列表。

Table of Contents

- PREFACE
  - EXECUTIVE SUMMARY
  - DOCUMENT ROADMAP
- BUSINESS SCENARIO
  - BUSINESS SCENARIO OVERVIEW
    - BACKGROUND OF SCENARIO
    - PURPOSE OF SCENARIO
    - DEFINITIONS/DESCRIPTIONS OF TERMS USED
  - VIEWS OF ENVIRONMENTS AND PROCESSES
    - BUSINESS ENVIRONMENT
      - Constituencies
    - PROCESS DESCRIPTIONS
      - Process "a"
      - etc.
    - TECHNICAL ENVIRONMENT
      - Technical environment "a"
      - etc. . . .
    - ACTORS AND THEIR ROLES AND RESPONSIBILITIES
    - COMPUTER ACTORS AND ROLES
    - RELATIONSHIP OF COMPONENTS AND PROCESSES
    - HUMAN ACTORS AND ROLES
    - RELATIONSHIP OF HUMANS AND PROCESSES
    - INFORMATION FLOW ANALYSIS
    - PRINCIPLES AND CONSTRAINTS
      - IT Principles
      - Constraints
    - REQUIREMENTS
- BUSINESS SCENARIO ANALYSIS
  - PROBLEM SUMMARY
    - Issues
    - Objectives
- SUMMARY
- APPENDIXES
  - APPENDIX A: BUSINESS SCENARIOS — ADDITIONAL INFORMATION
  - APPENDIX B-n: BUSINESS SCENARIO WORKSHOP NOTES

26.5 Contributions to the Business Scenario

It is important to realize that the creation of a business scenario is not solely the province of the architect. As mentioned previously, business line management and other stakeholders in the enterprise are involved, to ensure that the business goals are accurately captured. In addition, depending on the relationship that an organization has with its IT vendors, the latter also may be involved, to ensure that the roles of technical solutions are also accurately captured, and to ensure communication with the vendors.

Typically, the involvement of the business management is greatest in the early stages, while the business problems are being explored and captured, while the involvement of the architect is greatest in the later stages, and when architectural solutions are being described. Similarly, if vendors are involved in the business scenario process, the involvement of the customer side (business management plus enterprise architects) is greatest in the early stages, while that of the vendors is greatest in the later stages, when the role of specific technical solutions is being explored and captured. This concept is illustrated in Figure 26-3.

内容列表

- 前言
  - 执行概要
  - 文件路线图
- 业务场景
  - 业务场景综述
    - 场景的背景
    - 场景的目的
    - 所使用术语的定义/描述
  - 环境和流程视图
    - 业务环境
      - 拥护者
    - 流程描述
      - 流程“a”
      - 等等。
    - 技术环境
      - 技术环境“a”
      - 等等。
    - 施动者及其角色和职责
    - 计算机施动者和角色
    - 组件和流程之间的关系
    - 人员施动者和角色
    - 人员和流程之间的关系
    - 信息流分析
    - 原则和约束
      - IT 原则
      - 约束
    - 需求
- 业务场景分析
  - 问题概要
    - 议题
    - 目的
- 概要
- 附录
  - 附录 A：业务场景——附加信息
  - 附录 B～n：业务场景研讨会注释

26.5 对业务场景的贡献

重要的是，认识到创建业务场景并不仅仅是架构师的职权。正如前面所提到的，ENTERPRISE 内的各级业务管理层和其他利益攸关者都参与其中，以确保捕获业务目标。此外，根据组织与其 IT 厂商之间所具有的关系，后者也可能参与其中，以确保同样准确地捕获技术解决方案的作用，并确保与厂商之间的沟通。

典型情况下，早期阶段中业务管理部门的参与是最多的，随着业务问题逐渐被探究和捕获以及架构解决方案逐渐被描述，后期阶段中架构师的参与是最多的。相似地，如果厂商参与到业务场景流程中，那么，早期阶段中客户方（业务管理部门和 ENTERPRISE 架构师）的参与是最重要的，但在探究和记录特定技术解决方案的作用的后期阶段，厂商的参与是最重要的。图 26-3 阐明了本概念。

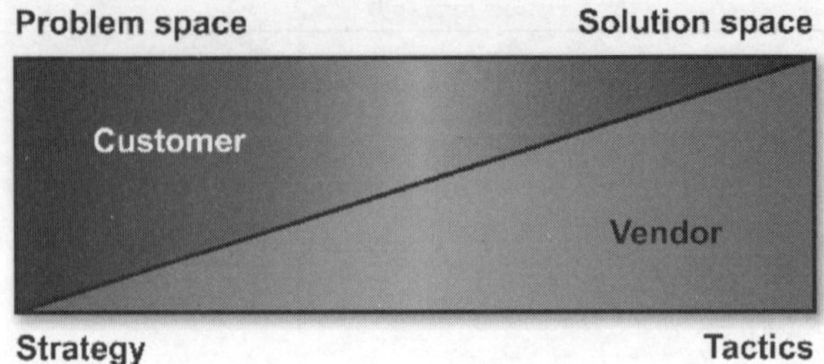

Figure 26-3 Relative Contributions to a Business Scenario

Vendor IT architects might be able to assist enterprise IT architects with integration of the vendors' products into the enterprise architecture. This assistance most probably falls in the middle of the timeline in Figure 26-3.

26.6 Business Scenarios and the TOGAF ADM

Business scenarios figure most prominently in the initial phase of the Architecture Development Method (ADM), Architecture Vision, when they are used to define relevant business requirements, and to build consensus with business management and other stakeholders.

However, the business requirements are referred to throughout all phases of the ADM cycle, as illustrated in Figure 26-4.

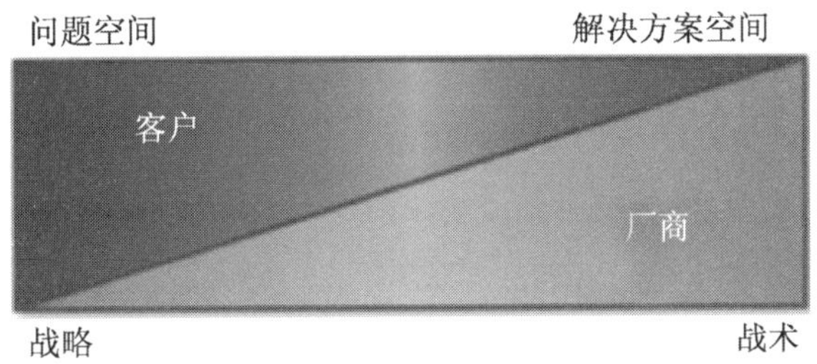

图 26-3 对业务场景的相对贡献

厂商 IT 架构师也许能够帮助 ENTERPRISE IT 架构师将厂商产品整合到 Enterprise Architecture 之中。这一帮助最有可能落在图 26-3 中时间线的中间。

26.6 业务场景和 TOGAF ADM

当业务场景用于定义相关业务需求并与业务管理部门和其他利益攸关者达成共识时，它们在架构开发方法（ADM）、架构愿景的初始阶段占有最重要的地位。

然而，在 ADM 周期的所有阶段中均提及了业务需求，如图 26-4 所示。

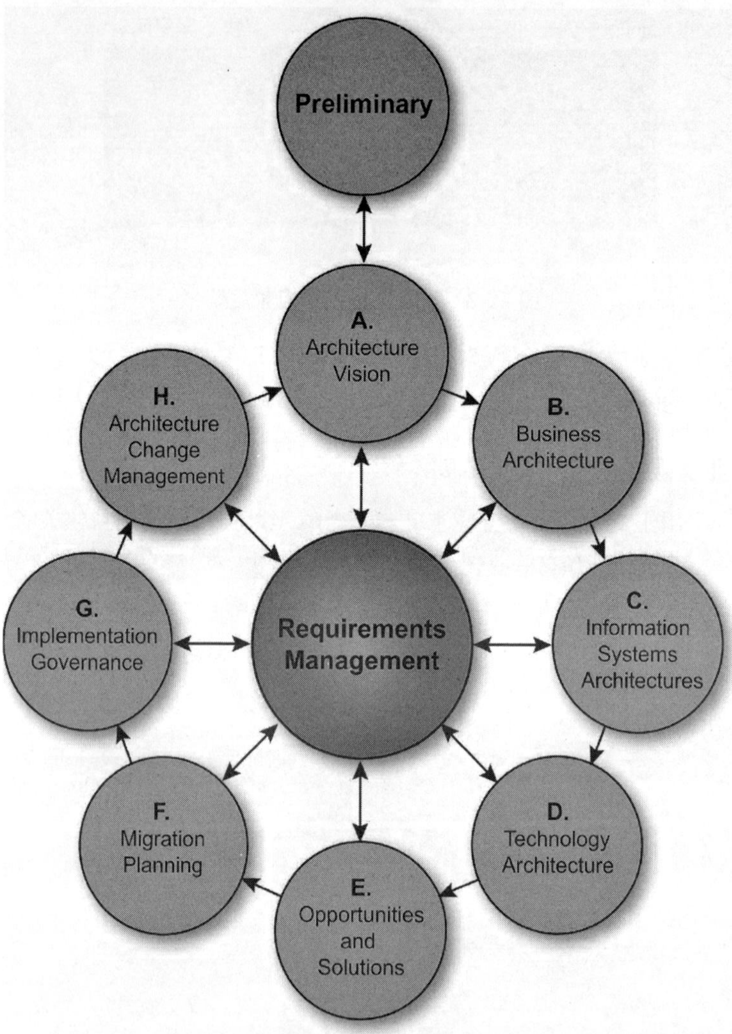

Figure 26-4 Relevance of Requirements Throughout the ADM

Because business requirements are important throughout all phases of the ADM cycle, the business scenario technique has an important role to play in the TOGAF ADM, by ensuring that the business requirements themselves are complete and correct.

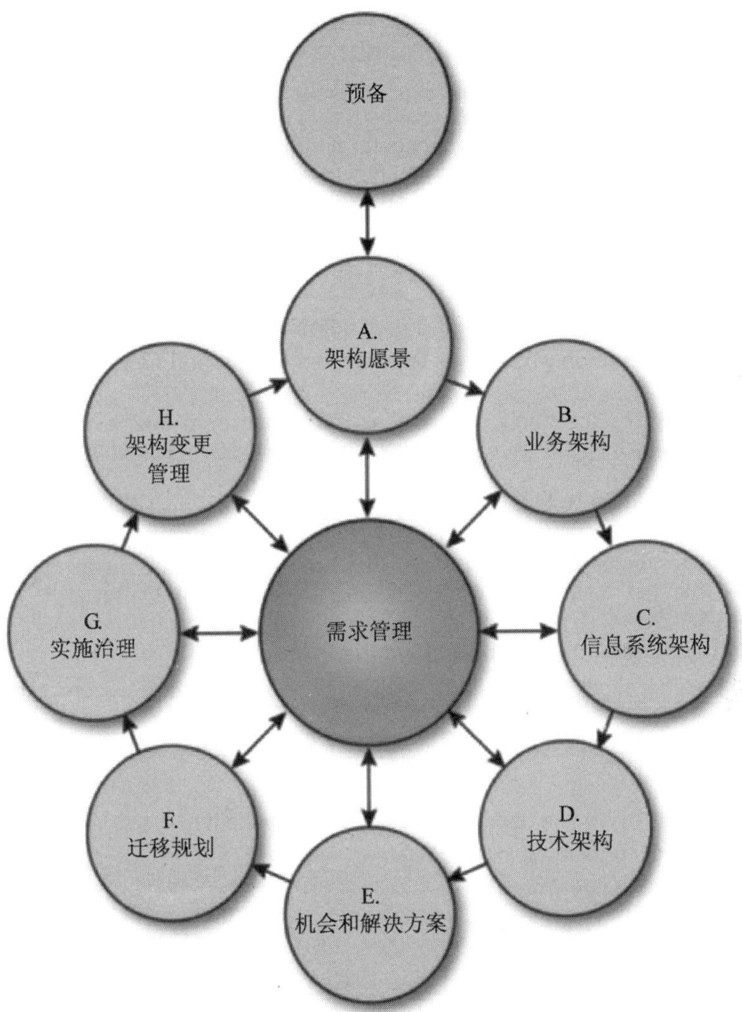

图 26-4 贯穿整个 ADM 的需求相关性

因为业务需求在 ADM 周期的所有阶段中都十分重要，使得业务场景技巧通过确保业务需求本身是完整和正确的，而在 TOGAF ADM 中发挥重要作用。

26.7 Developing Business Scenarios

26.7.1 General Guidelines

The stakeholders (e.g., business managers, end users) will tell you what they want, but as an architect you must still gain an understanding of the business, so you must know the most important actors in the system. If the stakeholders do not know what they want:

- Take time, observe, and record how they are working today
- Structure information in such a way that it can be used later
- Uncover critical business rules from domain experts
- Stay focused on what needs to be accomplished, and how it is to be accomplished

This effort provides the anchor for a chain of reason from business requirements through to technical solutions. It will pay off later to be diligent and critical at the start.

26.7.2 Questions to Ask for Each Area

The business scenario workshops mentioned above in the Gathering phase are really structured interviews. While there is no single set of appropriate questions to ask in all situations, the following provides some guidance to help business scenario consultants in asking questions.

Identifying, Documenting, and Ranking the Problem

Is the problem described as a statement of *what* needs to be accomplished, like steps in a process, and not *how* (with technology "push")?

If the problem is too specific or a "how":

- Raise a red flag
- Ask "Why do you need to do it that way?" questions

If the problem is too vague or not actionable:

- Raise a red flag
- Ask "What is it you need to do, or will be able to do if this problem is solved?" questions

Ask questions that help to identify where and when the problem exists:

- Where are you experiencing this particular problem? In what business process?
- When do you encounter these issues? During the beginning of the process, the middle, the end?

Ask questions that help to identify the costs of the problem:

- Do you account for the costs associated with this problem? If so, what are they?
- Are there hidden costs? If so, what are they?
- Is the cost of this problem covered in the cost of something else? If so, what and how much?
- Is the problem manifested in terms of poor quality or a perception of an ineffective organization?

26.7 开发业务场景

26.7.1 一般指南

利益攸关者（例如业务经理、最终用户）将告诉你他们想要什么，但是作为一名架构师，你同样也必须不断理解业务，因此你必须知道系统中最重要的施动者。如果利益攸关者不知道他们想要什么，那么：

- 花时间观察并记录他们今天是如何工作的
- 以可供日后使用的方式使信息结构化
- 从领域专家那里发现关键的业务规则
- 保持聚焦于需要完成什么，以及它是如何完成的

这项工作为从业务需求到技术解决方案的原因链条提供了“锚点”。在开始时持有勤奋且批判的态度将在日后得益。

26.7.2 每个领域需要提问的问题

上述收集阶段中提到的业务场景研讨会是真正的结构化访谈。虽然没有一组在所有情况下均适合询问的问题，但下面提供了一些指南，来帮助业务场景顾问询问问题。

对问题进行识别、文件化和定级

问题是否被描述成类似流程步骤一样的“需要完成什么”的说明，而不是“如何完成”（用“推送”技术）？

如果问题太具体，或是一个“如何完成”的问题，则：

- 升起红标
- 询问“为什么需要以那种方式完成它？”

如果问题太含糊或不可付诸行动，则：

- 升起红标
- 询问“你需要做的是什么，或如果解决了这个问题将能够做什么？”

询问有助于识别问题存在于何处以及何时存在的问题：

- 在哪里遇到的这个特殊问题？在哪个业务流程中？
- 什么时候遇到的这些问题？在流程开始、中间还是末尾？

询问有助于识别问题成本的问题：

- 是否说明了有关这个问题的成本？如果是，它们都是什么？
- 存在隐性成本吗？如果存在，它们都是什么？
- 这个问题的成本是否涵盖在其他事情的成本中？如果是，这个成本是什么以及是多少？
- 是否从劣质方面或无效组织的认知方面表明了问题？

Identifying the Business & Technical Environment, and Documenting in Models

Questions to ask about the business environment:

- What key process suffers from the issues? What are the major steps that need to be processed?
- Location/scale of internal business departments?
- Location/scale of external business partners?
- Any specific business rules and regulations related to the situation?

Ques-tions to ask about the current technology environment:

- What technology components are already presupposed to be related to this problem?
- Are there any technology constraints?
- Are there any technology principles that apply?

Identifying and Documenting Objectives

Is the "what" sufficiently backed up with the rationale for "why"? If not, ask for measurable rationale in the following areas:

- Return on investment
- Scalability
- Performance needs
- Compliance to standards
- Ease-of-use measures

Identifying Human Actors and their Place in the Business Model

An actor represents anything that interacts with or within the system. This can be a human, or a machine, or a computer program. Actors initiate activity with the system, for example:

- Computer user with the computer
- Phone user with the telephone
- Payroll clerk with the payroll system
- Internet subscriber with the web browser

An actor represents a role that a user plays; i.e., a user is someone playing a role while using the system (e.g., John (user) is a dispatcher (actor)). Each actor uses the system in different ways (otherwise they should be the same actor). Ask about the humans that will be involved, from different viewpoints, such as:

- Developer
- Maintainer
- Operator
- Administrator
- User

识别业务和技术环境，并文件化在模型中

关于业务环境需要问的问题：

- 哪些关键流程受到这些问题的影响？需要处理的主要步骤是什么？
- 内部业务部门的位置/规模？
- 外部业务合作者的位置/规模？
- 是否存在有关该情况的任何具体业务规则和章程？

关于当前技术环境需要问的问题：

- 已经预设了哪些与此问题有关的技术组件？
- 是否存在任何技术约束？
- 是否存在任何应用到的技术原则？

识别并记录目的

“为什么”的理由依据是否充分支持“是什么”？如果否，寻找在下列方面可衡量的依据：

- 投资收益
- 可伸缩性
- 绩效需要
- 与标准的合规性
- 易用性测度

识别人员施动者及其在业务模型中的位置

施动者代表与系统交互或在系统内交互的任何事物。施动者可以是一个人，或是一台机器，或是一个计算机程序。施动者发起与系统交互的活动，例如：

- 计算机用户与计算机
- 电话用户与电话
- 工资结算员与工资管理系统
- 互联网用户与网页浏览器

施动者代表用户扮演的角色；即用户是在使用系统的同时扮演一种角色的人[即，John（用户）是一名调度员（施动者）]。每个施动者以不同方式使用系统（否则，他们应该是同一类施动者）。从不同视角询问将涉及的人员，例如：

- 开发人员
- 维护人员
- 操作员
- 管理员
- 用户

Identifying Computer Actors and their Place in the Technology Model

Ask about the computer components likely to be involved, again from different points of view. What must they do?

Documenting Roles, Responsibilities, Measures of Success, Required Scripts

When defining roles, ask questions like:

- What are the main tasks of the actor?
- Will the actor have to read/write/change any information?
- Will the actor have to inform the system about outside changes?
- Does the actor wish to be informed about unexpected changes?

Checking for Fitness-for-Purpose, and refining if necessary

Is there enough information to identify who/what could fulfil the requirement? If not, probe more deeply.

Is there a description of when, and how often, the requirement needs to be addressed? If not, ask about timing.

26.8 Business Scenario Documentation

26.8.1 Textual Documentation

Effective business scenario documentation requires a balance between ensuring that the detail is accessible, and preventing it from overshadowing the results and overwhelming the reader. To this end, the business scenario document should have the main findings in the body of the document and the details in appendices.

In the appendices:

- Capture all the important details about a business scenario:
  - Situation description and rationale
  - All measurements
  - All actor roles and sub-measurements
  - All services required
- Capture the critical steps between actors that address the situation, and sequence the interactions
- Declare relevant information about all actors:
  - Partition the responsibility of the actors
  - List pre-conditions that have to be met prior to proper system functionality
  - Provide technical requirements for the service to be of acceptable quality

In the main body of the business scenario:

- Generalize all the relevant data from the detail in the appendices

识别计算机施动者及其在技术模型中的位置

再一次从不同视角询问可能涉及的计算机组件。它们必须做什么？

记录角色、职责、成功衡量标准、所需脚本

当定义角色时，询问类似如下问题：

- 施动者的主要任务是什么？
- 施动者是否必须读/写/变更任何信息？
- 施动者是否必须向系统告知外部变更？
- 施动者是否希望收到意外变更的通知？

检查适用性，仅在必要时进行细化

是否具有充足信息来识别谁/什么可以满足该需求？若没有，进行更深入的探查。

是否存在对何时以及多久需要处理一次需求的描述？若没有，询问时间安排。

26.8 业务场景文档

26.8.1 文本文档

有效的业务场景文档，需要在确保可获得细节和在防止细节掩盖结果并使读者不知所措之间取得平衡。为此，业务场景文件应在文件主体中包含主要的调查结果并在附录中包含细节。

在附录中：

- 捕获关于业务场景的所有重要细节：
  - 情况描述和依据
  - 全部测量结果
  - 施动者的全部角色和子测量结果
  - 所需的全部服务
- 捕获处理该情况的施动者之间的关键步骤，并将交互按序排列。
- 声明关于全部施动者的相关信息：
  - 划分施动者的职责
  - 列出满足适当的系统功能性之前必须满足的前提条件
  - 提供使服务具有可接受质量的技术需求

在业务场景的主体中：

- 从附录的细节中归纳所有相关数据

26.8.2 Business Scenario Models

- Remember the purpose of using models:
  - Help comprehension
  - Give a starting point to confirm requirements
  - Relate actors and interactions
- Keep drawings clear and neat:
  - Do not put too much into one diagram
  - Simpler diagrams are easier to understand
- Number diagrams for easy reference:
  - Maintain a catalog of the numbers to avoid duplicates

26.9 Guidelines on Goals and Objectives

26.9.1 Importance of Goals

One of the first steps in the development of an architecture is to define the overall goals and objectives for the development. The objectives should be derived from the business goals of the organization, and the way in which IT is seen to contribute to meeting those goals.

Every organization behaves differently in this respect, some seeing IT as the driving force for the enterprise and others seeing IT in a supporting role, simply automating the business processes which already exist. The essential thing is that the architectural objectives should be very closely aligned with the business goals and objectives of the organization.

26.9.2 Importance of SMART Objectives

Not only must goals be stated in general terms, but also specific measures need to be attached to them to make them SMART, as described above.

The amount of effort spent in doing this will lead to greater clarity for the sponsors of the architecture evolution cycle. It will pay back by driving proposed solutions much more closely toward the goals at each step of the cycle. It is extremely helpful for the different stakeholders inside the organization, as well as for suppliers and consultants, to have a clear yardstick for measuring fitness-for-purpose. If done well, the ADM can be used to trace specific decisions back to criteria, and thus yield their justification.

The goals below have been adapted from those given in previous versions of TOGAF. These are categories of goals, each with a list of possible objectives. Each of these objectives should be made SMART with specific measures and metrics for the task. However, since the actual work to be done will be specific to the architecture project concerned, it is not possible to provide a list of generic SMART objectives that will relate to any project.

Instead, we provide here some example SMART objectives.

26.8.2 业务场景模型

- 牢记使用模型的目的：
  - 帮助理解
  - 给出确认需求的起点
  - 使施动者和交互相关联
- 保持图纸清晰整洁：
  - 不要在一个图中加入过多内容
  - 简单的图更容易理解
- 对图进行编号，以便于参考：
  - 保留编号目录集，以免重复

26.9 目标和目的指南

26.9.1 目标的重要性

开发架构的首要步骤之一是定义开发的总体目标和目的。目的应源于组织的业务目标以及如何看待 IT 将有助于满足那些目标。

每个组织在这方面表现各不相同，一些组织将 IT 视为 ENTERPRISE 的驱动力，而另一些组织将 IT 视为一种支持作用，仅仅使已经存在的业务流程自动化。根本性的问题在于架构目的应与组织的业务目标和目的保持紧密对准。

26.9.2 SMART 目的的重要性

不仅必须用一般术语来表述目标，而且需要在其中加入特定的测度使其遵循 SMART 原则，如上所述。

这么做所花费的精力将使发起人更清楚架构演进周期。通过在周期各阶段驱动所提出的解决方案更接近目标方向而获得回报。这极其有助于组织内的不同利益攸关者以及供应商和顾问拥有衡量适用性的明确尺度。如果完成得当，ADM 可用于将特定决策追溯到准则，从而产生这些决策的正当理由。

下列目标改编自 TOGAF 之前版本所给出的那些目标。这些是目标类别，每个类别具有一系列可能的目的。应使这些目的中的每一个都遵循“SMART”原则，并具有任务的特定测度和指标。然而，由于需要完成的实际工作将特定于所关注的架构项目，因此，不太可能提供将与任何项目都有关的一系列通用 SMART 目标。

作为替代，我们在此提供一些 SMART 目标的示例。

Example of Making Objectives SMART

Under the general goal heading "Improve User Productivity" below, there is an objective to provide a "Consistent User Interface" and it is described as follows:

> "A consistent user interface will ensure that all user-accessible functions and services will appear and behave in a similar, predictable fashion regardless of application or site. This will lead to better efficiency and fewer user errors, which in turn may result in lower recovery costs."

To make this objective SMART, we ask whether the objective is specific, measurable, actionable, realistic, and time-bound, and then augment the objective appropriately.

The following captures an analysis of these criteria for the stated objective:

- **Specific**: The objective of providing "a consistent user interface that will ensure all user accessible functions and services will appear and behave in a similar, predictable fashion regardless of application or site". is pretty specific. However, the measures listed in the second sentence could be more specific . ..
- **Measurable**: As stated above, the objective is measurable, but could be more specific. The second sentence could be amended to read (for example): "This will lead to 10% greater user efficiency and 20% fewer order entry user errors, which in turn may result in 5% lower order entry costs".
- **Actionable**: The objective does appear to be actionable. It seems clear that consistency of the user interface must be provided, and that could be handled by whoever is responsible for providing the user interface to the user device.
- **Realistic**: The objective of providing "a consistent user interface that will ensure all user accessible functions and services will appear and behave in a similar, predictable fashion regardless of application or site" might not be realistic. Considering the use today of PDAs at the user end might lead us to augment this objective to ensure that the downstream developers don't unduly create designs that hinder the use of new technologies. The objective could be re-stated as "a consistent user interface, across user interface devices that provide similar functionality, that will ensure . . ." etc.
- **Time-bound**: The objective as stated is not time-bound. To be time-bound the objective could be re-stated as "By the end of Q3, provide a consistent . . .".

The above results in a SMART objective that looks more like this (again remember this is an example):

> "By the end of Q3, provide a consistent user interface across user interface devices that provide similar functionality to ensure all user accessible functions and services appear and behave in a similar way when using those devices in a predictable fashion regardless of application or site. This will lead to 10% greater user efficiency and 20% fewer order entry user errors, which in turn may result in 5% lower order entry costs."

使目的 SMART 的示例

在下面的"提高用户生产力"为标题的一般目标下，有一个提供"一致的用户界面"的目的，它的描述如下：

> "无论应用程序或网站如何，一致的用户界面将确保所有用户可访问的功能和服务将以相似、可预测的方式呈现并运行。这将产生更高的效率和更少的用户错误，转而会产生更低的回收成本。"

为使这一目的 SMART，我们询问目的是否是具体的、可衡量的、可付诸行动的、切实可行的以及有时限的，然后适当扩大目的。

下面捕获了所述目的的这些准则的分析：

- **特定的**：提供"无论应用程序和网站如何，一致的用户界面将确保所有用户可访问的功能和服务将以相似、可预测的方式出现并运行。"的目的是相当明确的。然而，第二句话列出的测度可能更加具体。
- **可衡量的**：如上所述，目的是可衡量的，但可以是更具体的。第二句话可被修正为（例如）："这将导致用户效率提高 10%以及订单输入用户错误减少 20%，转而会导致订单输入成本降低 5%"。
- **可付诸行动的**：目的看起来确实是可付诸行动的。显而易见的是，必须提供用户界面的一致性，且这可由负责向用户设备提供用户界面的任何人来处理。
- **切实可行的**：提供"无论应用程序或网站如何，一致的用户界面将确保所有的用户可访问的功能和服务将以相似、可预测的方式呈现并运行。"的目的可能不太切实可行。考虑当今在用户端使用的 PDA 可能使我们扩大这个目的，以确保后期开发人员不会不当地创作出阻碍新技术使用的设计。该目的可以被重新表述为"一致的用户界面，贯穿于提供相似功能性的用户界面设备，将确保……"等。
- **有时限的**：表述的目的没有时限。为使其有时限，该目的可被重新表述为"到 Q3 结束的时候，提供一个一致的……"。

在一个 SMART 的目的中，上述结果更倾向于这个表述（再次牢记这只是一个示例）：

> "到 Q3 结束的时候，在提供相似功能性的用户界面设备之间提供一个一致的用户界面，以确保当以可预测的方式使用这些设备时，无论应用或网站如何，所有用户可访问的功能和服务将以相似的方式呈现并运行。这将使得用户效率提高 10%以及订单输入用户错误减少 20%，转而会导致订单输入成本降低 5%。"

26.9.3 Categories of Goals and Objectives

Although every organization will have its own set of goals, some examples may help in the development of an organization-specific list. The goals given below are categories of goals, each with a list of possible objectives, which have been adapted from the goals given in previous versions of TOGAF.

Each of the objectives given below should be made SMART with specific measures and metrics for the task involved, as illustrated in the example above. However, the actual work to be done will be specific to the architecture project concerned, and it is not possible to provide a list of generic SMART objectives that will relate to any project.

Goal: Improve Business Process Performance

Business process improvements can be realized through the following objectives:

- Increased process throughput
- Consistent output quality
- Predictable process costs
- Increased re-use of existing processes
- Reduced time of sending business information from one process to another process

Goal: Decrease Costs

Cost improvements can be realized through the following objectives:

- Lower levels of redundancy and duplication in assets throughout the enterprise
- Decreased reliance on external IT service providers for integration and customization
- Lower costs of maintenance

Goal: Improve Business Operations

Business operations improvements can be realized through the following objectives:

- Increased budget available to new business features
- Decreased costs of running the business
- Decreased time-to-market for products or services
- Increased quality of services to customers
- Improved quality of business information

Goal: Improve Management Efficacy

Management efficacy improvements can be realized through the following objectives:

- Increased flexibility of business
- Shorter time to make decisions
- Higher quality decisions

26.9.3 目标和目的类别

虽然每个组织都有自己的一系列目标，但一些示例可在开发组织特有列表方面有所帮助。下面给出的目标是目标类别，每个类别都具有一系列改编自TOGAF之前版本中给出的目标的可能目的。

应使下面所给出的每一个目的都遵循 SMART 原则，且具有用于所涉及任务的特定测度和指标，如上述示例所阐述的那样。然而，由于需要完成的实际工作将特定于所关注的架构项目，因此，不太可能提供与任何项目都有关的一系列通用的 SMART 目的。

目标：提高业务流程绩效

业务流程的改进可以通过下列目的实现：

- 增加流程吞吐量
- 一致的输出质量
- 可预测的流程成本
- 增加现有流程的复用
- 缩短从一个流程向另一个流程发送业务信息的时间

目标：减少成本

成本改善可通过下列目的实现：

- 降低整个 ENTERPRISE 中资产的冗余和重复度
- 在综合和定制方面减少对外部 IT 服务提供者的依赖
- 降低维护成本

目标：改善业务运行

业务运行的改善可通过下列目的实现：

- 在新业务特征上增加可用的预算
- 降低运行业务的成本
- 缩短产品或服务的上市时间
- 提高对客户的服务质量
- 改善业务信息的质量

目标：提高管理效能

管理效能的提高可通过下列目的实现：

- 增加业务的灵活性
- 缩短决策时间
- 提高质量决策

Goal: Reduce Risk

Risk improvements can be realized through the following objectives:

- Ease of implementing new processes
- Decreased errors introduced into business processes through complex and faulty systems
- Decreased real-world safety hazards (including hazards that cause loss of life)

Goal: Improve Effectiveness of IT Organization

IT organization effectiveness can be realized through the following objectives:

- Increased rollout of new projects
- Decreased time to rollout new projects
- Lower cost in rolling out new projects
- Decreased loss of service continuity when rolling out new projects
- Common development: applications that are common to multiple business areas will be developed or acquired once and re-used rather than separately developed by each business area.
- Open systems environment: a standards-based common operating environment, which accommodates the injection of new standards, technologies, and applications on an organization-wide basis, will be established. This standards-based environment will provide the basis for development of common applications and facilitate software re-use.
- Use of products: as far as possible, hardware-independent, off-the-shelf items should be used to satisfy requirements in order to reduce dependence on custom developments and to reduce development and maintenance costs.
- Software re-use: for those applications that must be custom developed, development of portable applications will reduce the amount of software developed and add to the inventory of software suitable for re-use by other systems.
- Resource sharing: data processing resources (hardware, software, and data) will be shared by all users requiring the services of those resources. Resource sharing will be accomplished in the context of security and operational considerations.

Goal: Improve User Productivity

User productivity improvements can be realized through the following objectives:

- Consistent user interface: a consistent user interface will ensure that all user-accessible functions and services will appear and behave in a similar, predictable fashion regardless of application or site. This will lead to better efficiency and fewer user errors, which in turn may result in lower recovery costs.
- Integrated applications: applications available to the user will behave in a logically consistent manner across user environments, which will lead to the same benefits as a consistent user interface.
- Data sharing: databases will be shared across the organization in the context of security and operational considerations, leading to increased ease-of-access to required data.

目标：减少风险

风险改善可通过下列目的实现：

- 轻松地实施新流程
- 减少通过复杂和故障系统引入业务流程的错误
- 减少现实世界的安全隐患（包括导致生命损失的隐患）

目标：提高 IT 组织的有效性

IT 组织的有效性可通过下列目的实现：

- 增加新项目的推出
- 缩短推出新项目的时间
- 降低推出新项目的成本
- 减少推出新项目时服务连续性的损失
- 共同开发：多重业务领域共用的应用将被开发或采办一次并复用，而不是由每个业务领域单独开发。
- 开放系统环境：将建立一个基于标准的公共运行环境，该环境在整个组织的基础上容纳新标准、新技术和新应用的引入。这个基于标准的环境将为共用应用的开发提供基础并促进软件复用。
- 产品的使用：应尽可能使用独立于硬件的、现有的产品来满足需求，以便减少对定制开发的依赖性并降低开发和维护成本。
- 软件复用：对于必须定制开发的应用，开发可移植的应用将减少开发的软件数量并增加适合其他系统复用的软件存储清单。
- 资源共享：数据处理资源（硬件、软件和数据）将被需要这些资源的服务的所有用户共享。资源共享将在安保性和操作考量因素的背景环境中完成。

目标：提高用户生产力

用户生产力的提高可通过下列目的实现：

- 一致的用户界面：无论应用程序或网站如何，一致的用户界面将确保所有用户可访问的功能和服务以相似、可预测的方式呈现并运行。这将产生更高的效率和更少的用户错误，产生更低的回收成本。
- 集成的应用：可供用户使用的应用将在用户环境中以逻辑一致的方式运行，这将产生与一致的用户界面相同的效益。
- 数据共享：数据库将在安保性和操作考量因素的背景环境中在组织内被共享，使所需数据的易访问性提高。

Goal: Improve Portability and Scalability

The portability and scalability of applications will be through the following objectives:

- Portability: applications that adhere to open systems standards will be portable, leading to increased ease-of-movement across heterogeneous computing platforms. Portable applications can allow sites to upgrade their platforms as technological improvements occur, with minimal impact on operations.
- Scalability: applications that conform to the model will be configurable, allowing operation on the full spectrum of platforms required.

Goal: Improve Interoperability

Interoperability improvements across applications and business areas can be realized through the following objectives:

- Common infrastructure: the architecture should promote a communications and computing infrastructure based on open systems and systems transparency including, but not limited to, operating systems, database management, data interchange, network services, network management, and user interfaces.
- Standardization: by implementing standards-based platforms, applications will be provided with and will be able to use a common set of services that improve the opportunities for interoperability.

Goal: Increase Vendor Independence

Vendor independence will be increased through the following objectives:

- Interchangeable components: only hardware and software that have standards-based interfaces will be selected, so that upgrades or the insertion of new products will result in minimal disruption to the user's environment.
- Non-proprietary specifications: capabilities will be defined in terms of non-proprietary specifications that support full and open competition and are available to any vendor for use in developing commercial products.

Goal: Reduce Lifecycle Costs

Lifecycle costs can be reduced through most of the objectives discussed above. In addition, the following objectives directly address reduction of lifecycle costs:

- Reduced duplication: replacement of isolated systems and islands of automation with interconnected open systems will lead to reductions in overlapping functionality, data duplication, and unneeded redundancy because open systems can share data and other resources.
- Reduced software maintenance costs: reductions in the quantity and variety of software used in the organization will lead to reductions in the amount and cost of software maintenance. Use of standard off-the-shelf software will lead to further reductions in costs since vendors of such software distribute their product maintenance costs across a much larger user base.
- Incremental replacement: common interfaces to shared infrastructure components allow for phased replacement or upgrade with minimal operational disturbance.
- Reduced training costs: common systems and consistent Human Computer Interfaces(HCIs) will lead to reduced training costs.

目标：提高可移植性和可伸缩性

应用的可移植性和可伸缩性可通过下列目的提高：

- 可移植性：遵守开放系统标准的应用将是可移植的，使跨异构计算平台的易移动性提高。当出现技术改进时，可移植的应用使得网站在对运行产生最小影响的情况下更新其平台。
- 可伸缩性：符合模型的应用将是可配置的，使得能对所需的全部平台进行操作。

目标：提高互用性

跨应用和业务领域的互用性的改进可通过下列目的实现：

- 公共基础设施：架构应基于开放系统和系统透明度来改进通信和计算基础设施，包括但不限于操作系统、数据库管理、数据交换、网络服务、网络管理和用户界面。
- 标准化：通过实现基于标准的平台，应用将具有并能够使用一系列提高互用性机会的公共服务。

目标：提高厂商独立性

厂商独立性将通过下列目的提高：

- 可互换的组件：只有具有基于标准界面的硬件和软件才将被选择，因此，新产品的升级或输入将对用户环境造成最小程度的破坏。
- 非专有规范：将根据支持全面公开竞争且在开发商业产品过程中可供任何厂商使用的非专有规范来定义能力。

目标：降低生命周期成本

降低生命周期成本可通过上面讨论的大多数目的来实现。此外，下列目的可以直接降低生命周期成本。

- 减少复制：因为开放系统可以共享数据和其他资源，因此，用互连开放系统替代隔离系统和自动化孤岛，将使重叠功能、数据复制和不需要的冗余减少。
- 降低软件维护成本：减少组织内使用的软件的数量和种类，将使软件维护数量和成本减少。使用标准的现有软件将导致成本的进一步降低，这是因为这类软件的厂商在跨越更大用户基础范围内分配其产品维护成本。
- 增量式更换：共享的基础设施组件的公共界面，能在操作干扰最小的情况下进行阶段性的更换或升级。
- 降低培训成本：公共系统和一致的人机界面（HCIs）将使培训成本降低。

Goal: Improve Security

Security can be improved in the organization's information through the following objectives:

- Consistent security interfaces for applications: consistent security interfaces and procedures will lead to fewer errors when developing applications and increased application portability. Not all applications will need the same suite of security features, but any features used will be consistent across applications.
- Consistent security interfaces for users: a common user interface to security features will lead to reduced learning time when moving from system to system.
- Security independence: application deployment can use the security policy and mechanisms appropriate to the particular environment if there is good layering in the architecture.
- A 25% reduction in calls to the help desk relating to security issues.
- A 20% reduction in "false positives" detected in the network (a false positive is an event that appears to be an actionable security event, but in fact is a false alarm).

Goal: Improve Manageability

Management improvement can be realized through the following objectives:

- Consistent management interface: consistent management practices and procedures will facilitate management across all applications and their underlying support structures. A consistent interface can simplify the management burden, leading to increased user efficiency.
- Reduced operation, administration, and maintenance costs: operation, administration, and maintenance costs may be reduced through the availability of improved management products and increased standardization of the objects being managed.

26.10 Summary

Business scenarios help address one of the most common issues facing IT executives: aligning IT with the business.

The success of any major IT project is measured by the extent to which it is linked to business requirements, and demonstrably supports and enables the enterprise to achieve its business objectives. Business scenarios are an important technique that may be used at various stages of defining enterprise architecture, or any other major IT project, to derive the characteristics of the architecture directly from the high-level requirements of the business. Business scenarios are used to help identify and understand business needs, and thereby to derive the business requirements that the architecture development, and ultimately the IT, has to address.

However, it is important to remember that business scenarios are just a tool, not the objective. They are a part of, and enable, the larger process of architecture development. The architect should use them, but not get lost in them. The key is to stay focused — watch out for "feature creep", and address the most important issues that tend to return the greatest value.

目标：提高安保性

安保性可在组织的信息内通过下列目的提高：

- 应用的一致安保界面：开发应用并提高应用的可移植性时，一致的安保界面和程序将产生更少的错误。并不是所有的应用都需要同一套安保特征，但所用的任何特征将在所有应用中保持一致。
- 一致的安保用户界面：从一个系统移动到另一个系统时，安保特征的公共用户界面将缩短学习时间。
- 安保独立性：如果架构分层良好，则应用的部署可使用适用于特殊环境的安保策略和机制。
- 向服务台发出的关于安保问题的呼叫减少 25%。
- 网络中检测到的“误报”减少 20%（误报看似是一个可付诸行动的安保事件，但实际上是一个虚报）。

目标：提高可管理性

可管理性的提高可通过下列目的实现：

- 一致的管理界面：一致的管理实践和程序将在跨越所有应用及其基础支持结构之间促进管理。一致的界面可以简化管理负担，从而提高用户效率。
- 降低运行、管理和维护成本：运行、管理和维护成本可通过改进的管理产品的可用性和增强的被管理对象的标准化来降低。

26.10 概要总结

业务场景帮助处理 IT 管理层面临的大多数常见问题之一：使 IT 与业务精准对接。

主要 IT 项目的成功是通过其与业务需求联系并能明确的支持和确保 ENTERPRISE 达成其业务目的的程度来衡量的。业务场景一种重要的技巧，可用在定义 Enterprise Architecture 的不同阶段，或任何其他主要的 IT 项目中，以从高层级业务需求中直接获得架构特征。业务场景用于帮助识别并理解业务需要，从而获取架构开发以及最终 IT 必须处理的业务需求。

然而，重要的是要牢记业务场景仅仅是一种工具，而不是目的。它们是较大的架构开发流程的一部分并能启用该流程。架构师应使用业务场景，而不是迷失其中。关键在于保持聚焦——提防“特征销声匿迹”，并处理倾向于返回最大价值的最重要的问题。

Chapter 27
Gap Analysis

The technique known as gap analysis is widely used in the TOGAF Architecture Development Method (ADM) to validate an architecture that is being developed. The basic premise is to highlight a shortfall between the Baseline Architecture and the Target Architecture; that is, items that have been deliberately omitted, accidentally left out, or not yet defined.

27.1 Introduction

A key step in validating an architecture is to consider what may have been forgotten. The architecture must support all of the essential information processing needs of the organization. The most critical source of gaps that should be considered is stakeholder concerns that have not been addressed in prior architectural work.

Potential sources of gaps include:

- Business domain gaps:
  - People gaps (e.g., cross-training requirements)
  - Process gaps (e.g., process inefficiencies)
  - Tools gaps (e.g., duplicate or missing tool functionality)
  - Information gaps
  - Measurement gaps
  - Financial gaps
  - Facilities gaps (buildings, office space, etc.)
- Data domain gaps:
  - Data not of sufficient currency
  - Data not located where it is needed
  - Not the data that is needed
  - Data not available when needed
  - Data not created
  - Data not consumed
  - Data relationship gaps
- Applications impacted, eliminated, or created

第 27 章
差距分析

被称为差距分析的技巧在 TOGAF 架构开发方法（ADM）中被广泛应用，以确认正在开发的架构。基本前提是，强调基线架构和目标架构之间的差异；即被故意省略、意外遗漏或尚未定义的条目。

27.1 简介

确认架构的一个关键步骤是考虑可能忘记了什么。架构必须支持组织的全部基本信息处理需要。应考虑的差距的最重要来源是在之前的架构工作中未被涉及的利益攸关者关注点。

差距的潜在来源包括：

- 业务域差距：
  - 人员差距（例如，交叉培训需求）
  - 流程差距（例如，流程的低效率）
  - 工具差距（例如，重复的或缺失的工具功能）
  - 信息差距
  - 测量结果差距
  - 资金差距
  - 设施差距（楼宇、办公空间等）
- 数据域差距：
  - 数据没有得到充分传播
  - 数据没有位于其被需要的位置
  - 不是所需要的数据
  - 数据在需要时不可用
  - 数据未被创建
  - 数据未被使用
  - 数据关系差距
- 影响、消除或创建的应用

- Technologies impacted, eliminated, or created

27.2 Suggested Steps

The suggested steps are as follows:

- Draw up a matrix with all the Architecture Building Blocks (ABBs) of the Baseline Architecture on the vertical axis, and all the ABBs of the Target Architecture on the horizontal axis.
- Add to the Baseline Architecture axis a final row labeled "New", and to the Target Architecture axis a final column labeled "Eliminated".
- Where an ABB is available in both the Baseline and Target Architectures, record this with "Included" at the intersecting cell.
- Where an ABB from the Baseline Architecture is missing in the Target Architecture, each must be reviewed. If it was correctly eliminated, mark it as such in the appropriate "Eliminated" cell. If it was not, an accidental omission in the Target Architecture has been uncovered that must be addressed by reinstating the ABB in the next iteration of the architecture design — mark it as such in the appropriate "Eliminated" cell.
- Where an ABB from the Target Architecture cannot be found in the Baseline Architecture, mark it at the intersection with the "New" row as a gap that needs to filled, either by developing or procuring the building block.

When the exercise is complete, anything under "Eliminated" or "New" is a gap, which should either be explained as correctly eliminated, or marked as to be addressed by reinstating or developing/procuring the function.

27.3 Example

Figure 27-1 shows an example analysis for ABBs that are services from the Network Services category of the Technical Reference Model (TRM), and shows a number of services from the Baseline Architecture missing from the Target Architecture.

- 影响、消除或创建的技术

27.2 建议的步骤

建议的步骤如下：

- 绘制一个矩阵，将所有基线架构的架构构建块（ABB）放在垂直轴，将所有目标架构的架构构建块（ABB）放在水平轴。
- 在基线架构轴的最后增加一行，标示为“新增”，在目标架构轴的最后增加一列，标示为“消除”。
- 如果一个 ABB 同时存在于基线架构和目标架构中，在交叉单元格将其记录为“已包括”。
- 如果基线架构中的 ABB 在目标架构中缺失，必须检查每一个 ABB。如果确实应该将其消除，则在“消除”列的适当单元格中对其进行相应标记。如果不该将其消除，则发现了目标架构中的一个意外遗漏，必须通过在下一轮架构设计迭代中恢复 ABB 来处理——在“消除”列的适当单元格中对其进行相应标记。
- 当基线架构中找不到目标架构中的 ABB 时，在“新增”行的交叉单元格上将 ABB 作为差距进行标记，该差距需要通过开发或外购构建块的方式进行填充。

当完成上述演练后，所有出现在“消除”列或“新增”行中的都是差距，这些差距要么解释为应该被消除，要么被标记出来，以便通过复原或开发/采购其功能来处理。

27.3 示例

图 27-1 表明了 ABB 作为技术参考模型（TRM）中网络服务目录内服务的一个分析示例，并表明了在目标构架中出现缺失的基线构架中的多个服务。

Target → Architecture Baseline Architecture ↓	**Video Conferencing Services**	**Enhanced Telephony Services**	**Mailing List Services**	**Eliminated Services ↓**
Broadcast Services				Intentionally eliminated
Video Conferencing Services	Included			
Enhanced Telephony Services		Potential match		
Shared Screen Services				Unintentionally excluded —a gap in Target Architecture
New →		Gap: Enhanced services to be developed or produced	Gap: To be developed or produced	

Figure 27-1 Gap Analysis Example

目标架构→ 基线架构 ↓	视频会议服务	增强电话服务	邮件列表服务	消除的服务 ↓
广播服务				有意消除
视频会议服务	已包括			
增强电话服务		潜在匹配		
共享屏幕服务				无意被排除—— 目标架构中的一个差距
新增→		差距：待开发或 产生的增强服务	差距：待开发或产生	

图 27-1　差距分析示例

Chapter 28
Migration Planning Techniques

This chapter contains a number of techniques used to support migration planning in Phases E and F.

28.1 Implementation Factor Assessment & Deduction Matrix

The technique of creating an Implementation Factor Assessment and Deduction matrix can be used to document factors impacting the architecture Implementation and Migration Plan.

The matrix should include a list of the factors to be considered, their descriptions, and the deductions that indicate the actions or constraints that have to be taken into consideration when formulating the plans.

Factors typically include:

- Risks
- Issues
- Assumptions
- Dependencies
- Actions
- Impacts

An example matrix is shown in Figure 28-1.

Implementation Factor Assessment and Deduction Matrix		
External	**Description**	**Deduction**
<Name of Factor>	<Description of Factor>	<Impact on Migration Plan>
Change in Technology	Shut down the messagecenters, saving 700 personnel, and have them replaced by email.	• Need for personnel training, reassignment • Email has major personnel savings and should be given priority
Consolidation of Services		
Introduction of New Customer Service		

Figure 28-1 Implementation Factor Assessment and Deduction Matrix

第 28 章 迁移规划技巧

本章包括多个用于支持阶段 E 和 F 中迁移规划的技巧。

28.1 实施因素评估和推论矩阵

创建实施因素评估和推论矩阵的技巧，可用于记录影响架构实施和迁移计划的各种因素。

矩阵应包括需要考虑的因素列表、它们的描述以及表明制定计划时必须考虑的行动或约束的推论。

因素通常包括：

- 风险
- 议题
- 假设
- 依赖性
- 行动
- 影响

示例矩阵如图 28-1 所示。

实施因素评估和推论矩阵		
外部	**描述**	**推论**
<因素的名称>	<因素的描述>	<对迁移计划的影响>
技术变更	关闭信息中心，节约 700 名人员，并用电子邮件代替	• 需要对人员进行培训、重新分配 • 电子邮件可大量节省人工成本，应优先考虑
服务的合并		
新型客户服务的引入		

图 28-1　实施因素评估和推论矩阵

28.2 Consolidated Gaps, Solutions, & Dependencies Matrix

The technique of creating a Consolidated Gaps, Solutions, and Dependencies matrix allows the architect to group the gaps identified in the domain architecture gap analysis results and assess potential solutions and dependencies to one or more gaps.

This matrix can be used as a planning tool when creating work packages. The identified dependencies will drive the creation of projects and migration planning in Phases E and F.

An example matrix is shown in Figure 28-2.

Consolidated Gaps, Solutions, and Dependencies Matrix				
No.	**Architecture**	**Gap**	**Potential Solutions**	**Dependencies**
1	Business	New Order Processing Process	Use COTS software toolprocess Implement customsolution	Drives applications (2)
2	Application	New Order Processing Application	COTS software tool X Develop in-house	
3	Information	Consolidated CustomerIn-formation Base	Use COTS customerbase Develop customer datamart	

Figure 28-2 Consolidated Gaps, Solutions, and Dependencies Matrix

28.3 Architecture Definition Increments Table

The technique of creating an Architecture Definition Increments table allows the architect to plana series of Transition Architectures outlining the status of the enterprise architecture at specified times.

A table should be drawn up, as shown in Figure 28-3, listing the projects and then assigning their incremental deliverables across the Transition Architectures.

28.2 合并的差距、解决方案和依赖性矩阵

创建合并的差距、解决方案和依赖性矩阵的技巧，使得架构师能对主要架构差距分析结果中所识别的差距进行分组，并评估潜在解决方案以及对一个或多个差距的依赖性。

在创建工作包时，可将这种矩阵作为一种规划工具。识别出的依赖性将驱动阶段 E 和 F 中的项目创建和迁移规划。

示例矩阵如图 28-2 所示。

合并的差距、解决方案和依赖性矩阵				
序号	**架构**	**差距**	**潜在解决方案**	**依赖性**
1	业务	新订单处理流程	使用 COTS 软件工具流程 实施定制的解决方案	驱动应用（2）
2	应用	新订单处理应用	COTS 软件工具 X 内部开发	
3	信息	合并的客户信息库	使用 COTS 客户库 开发客户数据集市	

图 28-2　合并的差距、解决方案和依赖性矩阵

28.3 架构定义增量表

创建架构定义增量表的技巧，使得架构师能计划出一系列概述 ENTERPRISE 在特定时间点上状态的过渡架构。

应绘制如图 28-3 所示的表，列出各个项目，然后跨过渡架构分配其增量交付物。

Architecture Definition - Project Objectives by Increment (Example Only)				
	April 2007/2008	April 2008/2009	April 2009/2010	
Project	**Transition Architecture 1: Preparation**	**Transition Architecture 2: Initial Operational Capability**	**Transition Architecture 3: Benefits**	**Comments**
Enterprise e-Services Capability	Training and Business Process	e-Licensing Capability	e-Employment Benefits	
IT e-Forms	Design and Build			
IT e-Information Environment	Design and Build Information Environment	Client Common Data Web Content Design and Build	Enterprise Common Data Component Management Design and Build	
. . .	. . .	. . .	. . .	. . .

Figure 28-3　Architecture Definition Increments Table

28.4 Transition Architecture State Evolution Table

The technique of creating the Transition Architecture State Evolution table allows the architect to show the proposed state of the architectures at various levels using the Technical Reference Model (TRM).

A table should be drawn, listing the services from the TRM used in the enterprise, the TransitionArchitectures, and proposed transformations, as shown in Figure 28-4.

All Solution Building Blocks (SBBs) should be described with respect to their delivery and impact on these services. They should also be marked to show the progression of the enterprise architecture. In the example, where target capability has been reached, this is shown as "new" or "retain"; where capability is transitioned to a new solution, this is marked as "transition"; and where a capability is to be replaced, this is marked as "replace".

Architectural State using the Technical Reference Model				
Sub-Domain	**Service**	**Transition Architecture 1**	**Transition Architecture 2**	**Transition Architecture 3**
Infrastructure Applications	Information Exchange Services	Solution System A (replace)	Solution System B-1 (transition)	Solution System B-2 (new)
	Data Management Services	Solution System D (retain)	Solution System D (retain)	Solution System D (retain)
. . .	. . .	. . .	. . .	. . .

Figure 28-4　Transition Architecture State Evolution Table

Another technique (not shown here) is to use color coding in the matrix; for example:

架构定义——递增的项目目的（仅为示例）				
项目	2007 年 4 月—2008 年	2008 年 4 月—2009 年	2009 年 4 月—2010 年	注释
	过渡架构 1：准备	过渡架构 2：初始的运行能力	过渡架构 3：收益	
ENTERPRISE 电子服务能力	培训和业务流程	电子许可能力	电子化就业收益	
IT 电子表单	设计并构造			
IT 电子信息环境	设计并构建信息环境	客户公共 数据网页内容 设计并构建	ENTERPRISE 公共 数据组件管理 设计并构建	
……	……	……	……	……

图 28-3 架构定义增量表

28.4 过渡架构状态演进表

创建过渡架构状态演进表的技巧，有助于架构师使用技术参考模型（TRM）在不同层级表明建议的架构状态。

应绘制一个表，列出 ENTERPRISE 所用的 TRM 中的服务、各过渡架构和建议的转型，如图 28-4 所示。

应当描述所有解决方案构建块（SBB）的交付及其对这些服务的影响。同样，应对它们进行标记，以表明该 Enterprise Architecture 的进展。在下面的示例中，当已经达到目标能力时，将该 SBB 标记为“新增”或“保留”；当能力过渡到新的解决方案时，将 SBB 标记为“过渡”；且当能力将被替换时，将 SBB 标记为“替换”。

使用技术参考模型的架构状态				
子域	服务	过渡架构 1	过渡架构 2	过渡架构 3
基础设施应用	信息交换服务	解决方案系统 A （替换）	解决方案系统 B-1 （过渡）	解决方案系统 B-2 （新增）
	数据管理服务	解决方案系统 D （保留）	解决方案系统 D （保留）	解决方案系统 D （保留）
……	……	……	……	……

图 28-4 过渡架构状态演进表

另一种技巧（未在此示出）是在矩阵中采用颜色编码；例如：

- Green: Service SBB in place (either new or retained).
- Yellow: Service being transitioned into a new solution.
- Red: Service to be replaced.

28.5 Business Value Assessment Technique

A technique to assess business value is to draw up a matrix based on a value index dimension and a risk index dimension. An example is shown in Figure 28-5. The value index should include criteria such as compliance to principles, financial contribution, strategic alignment, and competitive position. The risk index should include criteria such as size and complexity, technology, organizational capacity, and impact of a failure. Each criterion should be assigned an individual weight.

The index and its criteria and weighting should be developed and approved by senior management. It is important to establish the decision-making criteria before the options are known.

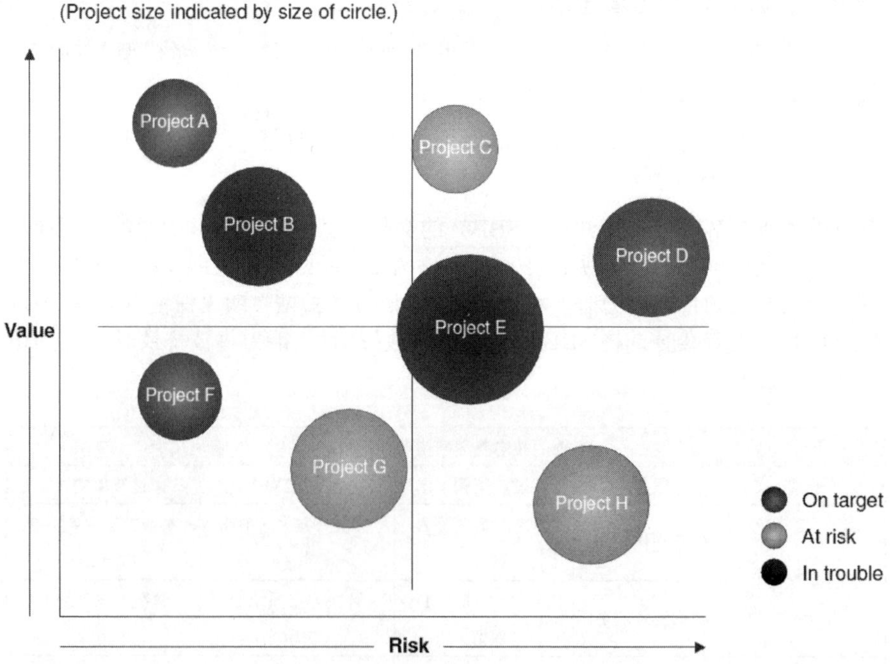

(Project size indicated by size of circle.)

Figure 28-5 Sample Project Assessment with Respect to Business Value and Risk

- 绿色：恰当的服务 SBB（新增或保留）。
- 黄色：正过渡到新的解决方案的服务。
- 红色：待替换的服务。

28.5 业务价值评估技巧

一种评估业务价值的技巧是，基于价值指标维度和风险指标维度来绘制一个矩阵，如图 28-5 所示。价值指标应包括诸如与原则的合规性、财务贡献、战略对准以及竞争地位等准则。风险指标应当包括诸如规模和复杂性、技术、组织能力和失败影响等准则。应对每个准则分配单独的权重。

指标及其准则和权重都应由高级管理层制定并批准。重要的是，在知晓选项前制定决策的准则。

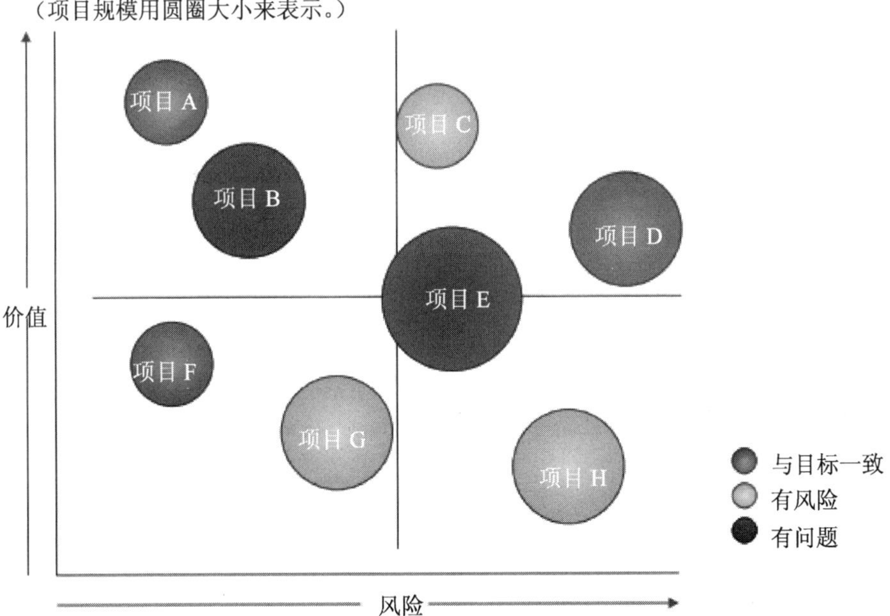

图 28-5 关于业务价值和风险的项目评估示例

Chapter 29
Interoperability Requirements

This chapter provides guidelines for defining and establishing interoperability requirements.

29.1 Overview

A definition of interoperability is "the ability to share information and services". Defining the degree to which the information and services are to be shared is a very useful architectural requirement, especially in a complex organization and/or extended enterprise.

The determination of interoperability is present throughout the Architecture Development Method(ADM) as follows:

- In the Architecture Vision (Phase A), the nature and security considerations of the information and service exchanges are first revealed within the business scenarios.
- In the Business Architecture (Phase B), the information and service exchanges are further defined in business terms.
- In the Data Architecture (Phase C), the content of the information exchanges are detailed using the corporate data and/or information exchange model.
- In the Application Architecture (Phase C), the way that the various applications are to share the information and services is specified.
- In the Technology Architecture (Phase D), the appropriate technical mechanisms to permit the information and service exchanges are specified.
- In Opportunities & Solutions (Phase E), the actual solutions (e.g., Commercial Off-The-Shelf (COTS) packages) are selected.
- In Migration Planning (Phase F), the interoperability is logically implemented.

第 29 章
互用性需求

本章提供定义并制定互用性需求的指南。

29.1 综述

互用性的定义是"共享信息和服务的能力"。定义共享信息和服务的程度是一个非常有用的架构需求，尤其是在复杂的组织和/或扩展的 ENTERPRISE 中。

对互用性的确定贯穿于整个架构开发方法（ADM），具体如下：

- 在架构愿景阶段（阶段 A）中，信息和服务交换的本质和安保考量因素在业务场景中首次出现。
- 在业务构架阶段（阶段 B）中，进一步用业务术语定义信息和服务交换。
- 在数据架构阶段（阶段 C）中，使用公司级数据和/或信息交换模型详细说明信息交换的内容。
- 在应用构架阶段（阶段 C）中，规定不同的应用共享信息和服务的方式。
- 在技术架构阶段（阶段 D）中，对允许信息和服务交换的适当技术机制做出规定。
- 在机会和解决方案阶段（阶段 E）中，选择实际的解决方案［例如，商用货架（COTS）包］。
- 在迁移规划阶段（阶段 F）中，逻辑上实现互用性。

29.2 Defining Interoperability

There are many ways to define interoperability and the aim is to define one that is consistently applied within the enterprise and extended enterprise. It is best that both the enterprise and the extended enterprise use the same definitions.

Many organizations find it useful to categorize interoperability as follows:

- **Operational or Business Interoperability** defines how business processes are to be shared.
- **Information Interoperability** defines how information is to be shared.
- **Technical Interoperability** defines how technical services are to be shared or at least connect to one another.

From an IT perspective, it is also useful to consider interoperability in a similar vein to Enterprise Application Integration (EAI); specifically:

- **Presentation Integration/Interoperability** is where a common look-and-feel approach through a common portal-like solution guides the user to the underlying functionality of the set of systems.
- **Information Integration/Interoperability** is where the corporate information is seamlessly shared between the various corporate applications to achieve, for example, a common set of client information. Normally this is based upon a commonly accepted corporate ontology and shared services for the structure, quality, access, and security/privacy for the information.
- **Application Integration/Interoperability** is where the corporate functionality is integrated and shareable so that the applications are not duplicated (e.g., one change of address service/component; not one for every application) and are seamlessly linked together through functionality such as workflow. This impacts the business and infrastructure applications and is very closely linked to corporate business process unification/interoperability.
- **Technical Integration/Interoperability** includes common methods and shared services for the communication, storage, processing, and access to data primarily in the application platform and communications infrastructure domains. This interoperability is premised upon the degree of rationalization of the corporate IT infrastructure, based upon standards and/or common IT platforms. For example, multiple applications sharing one infrastructure or 10,000 corporate web sites using one centralized content management/web server (rather than thousands of servers and web masters spread throughout the country/globe).

Many organizations create their own interoperability models, such as illustrated in the example below from the Canadian Government. They have a high-level definition of the three classes of interoperability and identify the nature of the information and services that they wish to share. Interoperability is coined in terms of e-enablers for e-Government. Their interoperability breakdown is as follows:

- Information Interoperability:
  - Knowledge management
  - Business intelligence
  - Information management
  - Trusted identity

29.2 定义互用性

定义互用性有很多方法，目的是在 ENTERPRISE 和扩展的 ENTERPRISE 内定义一种一贯应用的互用性。最好是 ENTERPRISE 和扩展的 ENTERPRISE 使用相同的定义。

许多组织发现将互用性分成以下几类很有用：

- 运行或业务互用性，定义如何共享业务流程。
- 信息互用性，定义如何共享信息。
- 技术互用性，定义技术服务如何共享或至少如何相互连接。

从 IT 关注层级看，以类似于 ENTERPRISE 应用综合（EAI）的方式考虑互用性同样很有用；特别是：

- **表达综合/互用性**，是普通观感途径通过类似门户的公共解决方案指导用户使用系统集的基础功能。
- **信息综合/互用性**，是公司级信息在不同公司级应用之间被无缝共享而达成的，例如公共客户信息集。通常，这基于一种被普遍认可的公司级本体论和信息的结构、质量、访问和安保性/隐秘性的共享服务。
- **应用综合/互用性**，是综合且共享公司级功能，使得应用不会重复（例如，地址服务/组件的一个变更；并非是每个应用的变更）且通过诸如工作流的功能被无缝地联系起来。这影响业务和基础设施应用，并与公司级的业务流程统一化/互用性密切相关。
- **技术综合/互用性**，包括对主要存在于应用平台和通信基础设施领域内的数据进行通信、存储、处理和访问的公共方法和共享服务。这种互用性的前提是公司级 IT 基础设施基于标准和/或公共 IT 平台的合理化程度。例如，多个应用共享一个基础设施，或 10 000 个公司级网站使用一个集中式内容管理/网络服务器（而不是遍布整个国家/世界的数以千计的服务器和网站管理员）。

许多组织创建它们自己的互用性模型，如下列来自加拿大政府的示例所阐述的那样。这些组织拥有三类互用性的高层级定义，并识别出它们想要共享的信息和服务的本质。互用性根据电子政务的电子赋能者创造。它们的互用性分解如下：

- 信息互用性：
  - 知识管理
  - 业务智能
  - 信息管理
  - 信任的身份

- Business Interoperability:
  - Delivery networks
  - e-Democracy
  - e-Business
  - Enterprise resource management
  - Relationship and case management
- Technical Interoperability:
  - IT infrastructure

In certain architectural approaches, such as system of systems or a federated model, interoperability is a strongly recommended best practice that will determine how the systems interact with each other. A key consideration will be the enterprise's business operating model.

29.3 Enterprise Operating Model

Key to establishing interoperability is the determination of the corporate operating model, where the operating model is "the necessary level of business process integration and standardization for delivering goods and services to customers. An operating model describes how a company wants to thrive and grow. By providing a more stable and actionable view of the company than strategy, the operating model drives the design of the foundation for execution." [2]

For example, if lines of business or business units only need to share documents, then the Architecture and Solution Building Blocks (ABBs and SBBs) may be simpler than if there is a need to share structured transaction data. Similarly, if the Architecture Vision includes a shared services environment, then it is useful to define the level the services are to be shared.

The corporate operating model will normally indicate what type of interoperability approach will be appropriate. This model should be determined in Phase A (Architecture Vision) if not in Phase B (Business Architecture), and definitely by Phase E (Opportunities & Solutions).

Complex enterprises and/or extended enterprises (e.g., supply chain) may have more than one type of operating model. For example, it is common for the internal operating model (and supporting interoperability model) to differ from the one used for the extended enterprise.

---

2. Enterprise Architecture as Strategy provides potential models.

- 业务互用性：
  - 交付网络
  - 电子民主
  - 电子商务
  - ENTERPRISE 资源管理
  - 关系和案例管理
- 技术互用性：
  - IT 基础设施

在诸如系统之系统或联邦模型的某些架构实施途径中，强烈建议将互用性作为确定各系统之间如何交互的最佳实践。关键考量因素将是 ENTERPRISE 的业务运行模型。

29.3 ENTERPRISE 运行模型

建立互用性的关键是确定公司级的运行模型，其中运行模型是“向客户交付商品或服务的业务流程综合和标准化的必要层级。运行模型描述一个公司想要如何兴盛和成长。相比战略而言，运行模型通过提供一个更加稳定且可付诸行动的公司视图，驱动对执行基础的设计。”[2]

例如，如果业务线或业务单位只需要共享文件，那么与假设需要共享结构性交易数据相比，架构和解决方案构建块（ABB 和 SBB）可能更加简单。同样，如果架构愿景包括共享的服务环境，那么定义这些服务的共享水平是有用的。

公司级的运行模型通常将表明何种类型的互用性途径会是合适的。该模型即便未在阶段 B（业务架构）中也应在阶段 A（架构愿景）中确定，并由阶段 E（机会和解决方案）明确地确定。

复杂的 ENTERPRISE 和/或扩展的 ENTERPRISE（如供应链）可能具有不止一种类型的运行模型。例如，常见的是，内部运行模型（和支持互用性模型）不同于扩展的 ENTERPRISE 使用的模型。

2.作为战略的 Enterprise Architecture 提供潜在模型。

29.4 Refining Interoperability

Implementing interoperability requires the creation, management, acceptance, and enforcement of realistic standards that are SMART (Specific, Measurable, Actionable, Realistic, and Time- bound). Clear measures of interoperability are key to success.

Architecture is the key for identifying standards and facilitated sessions (brainstorming) will examine potential pragmatic ways (that fit within the current or emerging business culture) to achieve the requisite degree of interoperability.

Interoperability should be refined so that it meets the needs of the enterprise and/or extended enterprise in an unambiguous way. The refined interoperability measures (degrees, types, and high-level targets) should be part of or referred to the enterprise architecture strategic direction.

These measures are instantiated within a transformation strategy that should be embedded within the Target Architecture definition and pragmatically implemented in the Transition Architectures. Upon completion, also update the consolidated gap analysis results and dependencies to ensure that all of the brainstorming nuggets are captured.

An example of specifying interoperability is the Degrees of Interoperability (used within the Canadian Department of National Defense and NATO). These organizations were focused on the sharing of information and came up with four degrees of interoperability as follows:

- **Degree 1: Unstructured Data Exchange** involves the exchange of human-interpretable unstructured data, such as the free text found in operational estimates, analysis, and papers.
- **Degree 2: Structured Data Exchange** involves the exchange of human-interpretable structured data intended for manual and/or automated handling, but requires manual compilation, receipt, and/or message dispatch.
- **Degree 3: Seamless Sharing of Data** involves the automated sharing of data amongst systems based on a common exchange model.
- **Degree 4: Seamless Sharing of Information** is an extension of Degree 3 to the universal interpretation of information through data processing based on co-operating applications.

These degrees should be further refined and made technically meaningful for each of the degrees. An example refinement of degree 3 with four subclassifications follows:

- 3A: Formal Message Exchange
- 3B: Common Data Exchange
- 3C: Complete Data Exchange
- 3D: Real-time Data Exchange

The intent is to specify the detailed degrees of interoperability to the requisite level of detail so that they are technically meaningful.

These degrees are very useful for specifying the way that information has to be exchanged between the various systems and provide critical direction to the projects implementing the systems.

Similar measures should be established to determine service/business and technical interoperability.

29.4 细化互用性

实施互用性需要创建、管理、认可并执行 SMART（具体的、可衡量的、可付诸行动的、切实可行的以及有时限的）的切实可行的标准。互用性的明确测度是成功的关键。

架构是识别标准的关键，并且引导会议（头脑风暴）将审查可能的实用方法（适应当前或新兴的业务文化），以达到所需的互用性程度。

应细化互用性，以便其以明确的方式满足 ENTERPRISE 和/或扩展 ENTERPRISE 的需要。细化的互用性测度（程度、类型和高层级目标）应是 Enterprise Architecture 战略方向的一部分或指 Enterprise Architecture 战略方向。

这些测度在应当嵌入目标架构定义，并在过渡架构中实际实施的转型战略中进行实例化。完成后，还要更新合并的差距分析结果和依赖性，以确保捕获所有头脑风暴中有价值的想法。

规定互用性的一个示例是“互用性的程度”（用在加拿大国防部和北约中）。这些组织聚焦于信息共享并提出四个互用性程度，如下所示：

- **程度 1：非结构化数据交换**，涉及人类可解释的非结构化数据的交换，例如在运行报价单、分析结果和论文中发现的自由文本。
- **程度 2：结构化数据交换**，涉及用于手动和/或自动处理的人类可解释的结构化数据的交换，但是要求手动编译、接收和/或信息调度。
- **程度 3：数据的无缝共享**，涉及基于公共交换模型的在系统之间的数据自动化共享。
- **程度 4：信息的无缝共享**，是基于协同操作应用通过数据处理将程度 3 扩展到信息的普遍解释。

这些程度应被进一步细化，并使每个程度在技术上具有意义。用四个子分类对程度 3 进行细化的一个示例如下：

- 3A：正式信息交换
- 3B：公共数据交换
- 3C：完整数据交换
- 3D：实时数据交换

意图是将互用性的详细程度明确到必要的细节层级，使其在技术上具有意义。

这些程度对于明确在不同系统之间交换信息的方式来说十分有用，并为实现系统的项目提供了关键方向。

应设定相似的测度以确定服务/业务以及技术互用性。

29.5 Determining Interoperability Requirements

Co-existence between emerging and existing systems, especially during transformation, will be a major challenge and brainstorming should attempt to figure out what has to be done to reduce the pain. It is imperative to involve the operations management staff and architects in this step as they will be responsible for operating the portfolio deliverables.

For example, there might be a need for a "wrapper" application (an application that acts as the interface [a.k.a. interpreter] between the legacy application and the emerging infrastructure). Indeed, pragmatically, in the "if it works do not fix it" world, the "wrapper" might become a permanent solution.

Regardless, using the gap analysis results and business scenarios as a foundation, brainstorm the IT issues and work them through to ensure that all of the gaps are clearly identified and addressed and verify that the organization-specific requirements will be met.

It is important to note that the ensuing development process must include recognition of dependencies and boundaries for functions and should take account of what products are available in the marketplace. An example of how this might be expressed can be seen in the building blocks example (see Part III, Chapter 37).

If a mechanism such as the Degrees of Interoperability is used, then a matrix showing the interoperability requirements is a useful tool, as illustrated in Figure 29-1 and Figure 29-2, noting that the degree of information sharing is not necessarily symmetrical or bidirectional between systems and/or stakeholders.

The matrix below can be used within the enterprise and/or within the extended enterprise as a way of detailing that information and/or services can be shared. The matrix should start in the Business Architecture (Phase B) to capture the nature of the sharing of information between stakeholders, and evolve to determine the what systems share what information in Phase C.

Phase B: Inter-stakeholder Information Interoperability Requirements(Using degrees of information interoperability)

Phase B: Inter-stakeholder Information Interoperability Requirements (Using degrees of information interoperability)							
Stakeholders	A	B	C	D	E	F	G
A		2	3	2	3	3	3
B	2		3	2	3	2	2
C	3	3		2	2	2	3
D	2	2	2		3	3	3
E	4	4	2	3		3	3
F	4	4	2	3	3		2
G	2	2	3	3	3	3	

Figure 29-1 Business Information Interoperability Matrix

Figure 29-1 shows that Stakeholder A requires structured data exchange (degree 2) with Stakeholders/Systems B and D, and seamless sharing of data (degree 3) with Stakeholders/Systems C, E, F, and G.

The business information interoperability matrix should be refined within the Information Systems Architecture using refined measures and specifying the actual systems used by the stakeholders. A sample is shown in Figure 29-2.

29.5 确定互用性需求

新兴系统和现有系统之间的共存性（尤其在转型期间）将是一个主要挑战，并且头脑风暴应试图明白必须做什么来减少损失。当务之急是使运行管理人员和架构师参与本步骤，因为他们将对运行项目谱系交付物负责。

例如，可能需要“封装”应用［一种充当遗留应用和新兴基础设施之间界面(又称解释器)的应用］。事实上，从实用角度而言，在“如果奏效，就不要去改变”的世界中，该“封装”可能成为一个永久的解决方案。

不管怎样，使用差距分析结果和业务场景作为基础，对 IT 问题进行头脑风暴并将其解决，以确保明确识别并处理了所有差距并证明将满足组织特有需求。

重要的是，要注意确保开发流程必须包括功能依赖性和边界的识别，并应考虑在市场上可购买到什么产品。如何表达这一点的示例可在构建块示例中看到（见第三部分第 37 章）。

如果使用诸如互用性程度的机制，那么表明互用性需求的矩阵就是一个有用工具，如图 29-1 和图 29-2 所示，注意，信息共享的程度在系统和/或利益攸关者之间并不一定是对称的或双向的。

在 ENTERPRISE 中和/或扩展的 ENTERPRISE 中，下面的矩阵可用作详细说明可共享的信息和/或服务的一种方式。此矩阵应从业务架构（阶段 B）中开始，以捕获在利益攸关者之间共享信息的本质，并演进以确定在阶段 C 中哪些系统共享哪些信息。

阶段 B：利益攸关者之间的信息互用性需求（使用信息互用性的程度）							
利益攸关者	A	B	C	D	E	F	G
A		2	3	2	3	3	3
B	2		3	2	3	2	2
C	3	3		2	2	2	3
D	2	2	2		3	3	3
E	4	4	2	3		3	3
F	4	4	2	3	3		2
G	2	2	3	3	3	3	

图 29-1 业务信息互用性矩阵

图 29-1 表明利益攸关者 A 需要与利益攸关者/系统 B 和 D 进行结构化数据交换（程度 2），并与利益攸关者/系统 C、E、F 和 G 进行数据的无缝共享（程度 3）。

应通过使用细化的测度并规定利益攸关者使用的实际系统，在信息系统内细化业务信息互用性矩阵。示例矩阵如图 29-2 所示。

Phase C: Inter-system Interoperability Requirements							
	System A	System B	System C	System D	System E	System F	System G
System A		2A	3D	2B	3A	3A	3B
System B	2E		3F	2C	3A	2B	2C
System C	3E	3F		2B	2A	2A	3B
System D	2B	2B	2B		3A	3A	3B
System E	4A	4B	2B	3A		3B	3B
System F	4A	4A	2B	3B	3A		2D
System G	2B	2B	3A	3A	3B	3B	

Figure 29-2 Information Systems Interoperability Matrix

In Figure 29-2, both the nature of the exchange is more detailed (e.g., Degree 3A *versus* only Degree 3) and the sharing is between specific systems rather than stakeholders. For example, System A shares information with the other systems in accordance with enterprise technical standards.

In many organizations the Business Architectures describe the nature of the information shared between stakeholders and/or organizations (e.g., in defense the term is "operational node"), and the Data Architecture specifies the information shared between systems.

Update the defined target data and Application Architecture (Version 1.0) with the interoperability issues that were raised.

29.6 Reconciling Interoperability Requirements with Potentia Solutions

The enterprise architect will have to ensure that there are no interoperability conflicts, especially if there is an intention to re-use existing SBBs and/or COTS.

The most significant issue to be addressed is in fact business interoperability. Most SBBs or COTS will have their own business processes embedded. Changing the embedded business processes will often require so much work, that the advantages of re-using solutions will be lost. There are numerous examples of this in the past.

Furthermore, there is the workflow aspect between the various systems that has to be taken into account. The enterprise architect will have to ensure that any change to the business interoperability requirements is signed off by the business architects and architecture sponsors in a revised Statement of Architecture Work.

阶段 C：系统间的互操作性需求							
	系统A	系统B	系统C	系统D	系统E	系统F	系统G
系统A		2A	3D	2B	3A	3A	3B
系统B	2E		3F	2C	3A	2B	2C
系统C	3E	3F		2B	2A	2A	3B
系统D	2B	2B	2B		3A	3A	3B
系统E	4A	4B	2B	3A		3B	3B
系统F	4A	4A	2B	3B	3A		2D
系统G	2B	2B	3A	3A	3B	3B	

图 29-2　信息系统互用性矩阵

在图 29-2 中，交换的本质被进一步细化（例如，程度 3A 仅与程度 3 相对），且这种共享是在特定的系统之间而不是在利益攸关者之间。例如，系统 A 根据 ENTERPRISE 技术标准与其他系统共享信息。

在许多组织中，业务架构描述在利益攸关者和/或组织之间共享的信息的本质（例如，在国防领域该术语为“作战节点”），而数据架构规定在系统之间共享的信息。

根据提出的互用性问题更新已定义的目标数据和应用架构（1.0 版本）。

29.6　使互用性需求与潜在的解决方案保持一致

ENTERPRISE 架构师将必须确保不存在任何互用性冲突，尤其是在打算复用现有 SBB 和/或 COTS 的情况下。

实际上，将处理的最重要的问题是业务互用性。大多数 SBB 或 COTS 将拥有自己的嵌入式业务流程。改变嵌入式业务流程通常会需要太多工作，以致将失去复用解决方案的优势。过去有大量这方面的示例。

此外，还必须考虑不同系统之间的工作流方面。ENTERPRISE 架构师必须确保对业务互用性需求作出的任何变更需经业务架构师和架构发起人在已修订的架构工作说明书上签字同意。

29.7 Summary

Defining interoperability in a clear unambiguous manner at several levels (business/service, information, and technical) is a useful architecture planning tool. The notions of interoperability will become ever more important in the Service Oriented Architecture (SOA) environment where services will be shared internally and externally in ever more inter-dependent extended enterprises.

29.7 概要总结

以清晰准确的方式在若干层级（业务/服务、信息和技术）上定义互用性是一个有用的架构规划工具。互用性概念将在面向服务架构（SOA）环境中变得越来越重要，在该环境下，服务将在越来越多的相互依赖的扩展的ENTERPRISE 内部和外部共享。

Chapter 30
Business Transformation Readiness Assessment

This chapter describes a technique known as Business Transformation Readiness Assessment, used for evaluating and quantifying an organization's readiness to undergo change.

This chapter builds on work by the Canadian Government and its Business Transformation Enablement Program (BTEP).[3]

30.1 Introduction

Enterprise architecture is a major endeavor within an organization and most often an innovative Architecture Vision (Phase A) and supporting Architecture Definition (Phases B to D) will entail considerable change. There are many dimensions to change, but by far the most important is the human element. For example, if the enterprise envisages a consolidation of information holdings and a move to a new paradigm such as service orientation for integrated service delivery, then the human resource implications are major. Potentially coupled with a change-averse culture and a narrowly skilled workforce, the most sound and innovative architecture could go nowhere.

Understanding the readiness of the organization to accept change, identifying the issues, and then dealing with them in the Implementation and Migration Plans is key to successful architecture transformation in Phases E and F. This will be a joint effort between corporate (especially human resources) staff, lines of business, and IT planners.

The recommended activities in an assessment of an organization's readiness to address business transformation are:

- Determine the readiness factors that will impact the organization.
- Present the readiness factors using maturity models.
- Assess the readiness factors, including determination of readiness factor ratings.
- Assess the risks for each readiness factor and identify improvement actions to mitigate the risk.
- Work these actions into Phase E and F Implementation and Migration Plan.

3. Refer to www.tbs-sct.gc.ca/btep-pto/index_e.asp.

第 30 章 业务转型准备度评估

本章描述被称为“业务转型准备度评估”的一种技巧，用来评估并量化一个组织经受变革的准备度。

本章以加拿大政府及其业务转型使能计划（BTEP）的研究为基础。[3]

30.1 简介

Enterprise Architecture 是组织内的一项重大努力，很多时候，一种新颖的架构愿景（阶段 A）和相支持的架构定义（阶段 B 和 D）会牵涉相当多的变革。有许多需要变革的维度，但到目前为止最重要的是人员元素。例如，如果 ENTERPRISE 想合并信息存量并转换为诸如用于集成服务交付的面向服务的新范例，那么人力资源影响是主要的。潜在地，伴随而来的是抵触变革的文化和技能有限的劳动力，最合理且最创新的架构可能不起什么作用。

在实施和迁移计划阶段中理解组织接受变革的准备度、识别问题并随后处理这些问题，是阶段 E 和 F 中架构转型成功的关键。这将是公司层级的（尤其是人力资源）员工、业务线和 IT 计划人员之间的共同努力成果。

在评估组织应对业务转型的准备工作中建议的活动包括：

- 确定将影响组织的准备度因素。
- 使用成熟度模型来表达这些准备度因素。
- 评估准备度因素，包括对准备度因素评定的确定。
- 评估每个准备度因素的风险，并识别缓解风险的改善行动。
- 在阶段 E 和 F——实施和迁移计划中实施这些行动。

3.见：www.tbs-sct.gc.ca/btep-pto/index_e.asp.

30.1.1 Business Transformation Enablement Program (BTEP)

The Canadian Government Business Transformation Enablement Program (BTEP) provides guidance on how to identify the business transformation-related issues.

The BTEP recommends that all projects conduct a transformation readiness assessment to at least uncover the business transformation issues. This assessment is based upon the determination and analysis/rating of a series of readiness factors. The outcome is a deeper understanding of the challenges and opportunities that could be presented in the course of the endeavor. Many of the challenges translate directly into risks that have to be addressed, monitored, and, if possible, mitigated.

The following sections describe Business Transformation Readiness Assessment using the BTEP method, including some lessons learned. Readers should keep in mind that most organizations will have their own unique set of factors and criteria, but most are similar.

30.2 Determine Readiness Factors

The first step is to determine what factors will impact on the business transformation associated with the migration from the Baseline to Target Architectures.

This can be best achieved through the conduct of a facilitated workshop with individuals from different parts of the organization. It is important that all perspectives are sought as the issues will be varied. In this workshop it is very useful to start off with a tentative list of factors that participants can re-use, reject, augment, or replace.

An example set of factors drawn from the BTEP follows:

- **Vision** is the ability to clearly define and communicate what is to be achieved. This is where management is able to clearly define the objectives, in both strategic and specific terms. Leadership in defining vision and needs comes from the business side with IT input. Predictable and proven processes exist for moving from vision to statement of requirements. The primary drivers for the initiative are clear. The scope and approach of the transformation initiative have been clearly defined throughout the organization.
- **Desire, Willingness, and Resolve** is the presence of a desire to achieve the results, willingness to accept the impact of doing the work, and the resolve to follow through and complete the endeavor. There is active discussion regarding the impact that executing the project may have on the organization, with clear indication of the intent to accept the impacts. Key resources (e.g., financial, human, etc.) are allocated for the endeavor and top executives project the clear message that the organization will follow through; a message that identifies the effort as well as the benefits. Organizationally there is a history of finishing what is started and of coming to closure on issues in the timeframes needed and there is agreement throughout the organization that the transformation initiative is the" right" thing to do.
- **Need**, in that there is a compelling need to execute the endeavor. There are clear statements regarding what the organization will not be able to do if the project does not proceed, and equally clear statements of what the project will enable the organization to do. There are visible and broadly understood consequences of endeavor failure and success criteria have been clearly identified and communicated.
- **Business Case** exists that creates a strong focus for the project, identifying benefits that must be achieved and thereby creating an imperative to succeed. The business case document identifies concrete benefits (revenues or savings) that the organization is committed to deliver and clearly and unquestionably points to goals that the organization is committed to achieving.

30.1.1 业务转型使能计划（BTEP）

加拿大政府业务转型使能计划（BTEP）就如何识别业务转型相关问题提供指南。

BTEP 建议所有的项目都进行转型准备度评估，从而至少发现业务转型问题。本评估基于对一系列准备度因素的确定和分析/评定。结果是，更深入地理解可能出现在努力过程中的挑战和机遇。许多挑战直接转换成必须得到应对、监控和缓解（若可能）的风险。

下面几节描述使用 BTEP 方法进行的业务转型准备度评估，包括一些经验教训。读者应记住，大部分组织将拥有他们自己独特的一套因素和准则，但是大部分是相似的。

30.2 确定准备度因素

第一步是确定哪些因素将影响到与从基线构架到目标构架的迁移有关的业务转型。

实现这一步骤的最佳途径是通过与来自组织中不同部门的个人召开引导式研讨会。重要的是，随着问题的变化，寻找到所有的观点。在这个研讨会上，以参与者能够复用、拒绝、补充或替换的临时因素列表作为开始是十分有用的。

从 BTEP 中抽取出的一组因素的示例如下：

- **愿景**是明确定义并传达将要达成什么的能力。在愿景中，管理层能够用战略术语和特定术语明确定义目的。对愿景和需要进行定义的领导层来自具有 IT 输入的业务方。存在可预测和已证明的流程，用以从愿景转移到需求说明。此举措的主要驱动因素是明确的。转型举措的范围和途径已经在整个组织内进行了明确定义。
- **愿望、意愿和决心**是表达对达成结果的愿望、接受开展工作带来影响的意愿和贯彻到底并完成努力的决心。对于执行此项目可能对组织造成的影响进行积极讨论，并明确表明接受这些影响的意图。应为这项尝试分配关键资源（例如，资金、人员等），且高管层设计了组织将贯彻到底的明确消息；识别付出和收益的消息。在组织上有一段发展史，在要求时间段内完成已开始的工作并结束议题，并且在整个组织内一致认为转型举措是需要做的“正确”事情。
- **需要**是执行努力的强制性需要。存在关于如果项目未继续的话组织不能做什么的明确说明，并且同样存在项目将促使组织能够完成什么的明确说明。存在已经明确识别并传达的尝试失败和成功准则的可见且被广泛理解的后果。
- **业务案例**的存在为项目创建了一个强有力的聚焦点，以识别必须达成的效益从而产生成功需要。业务案例文件识别组织承诺交付的具体效益（收入或存款），并明确且毫无疑问地指出组织承诺实现的目标。

- **Funding**, in the form of a clear source of fiscal resources, exists that meets the endeavor's potential expenditures.
- **Sponsorship and Leadership** exists and is broadly shared, but not so broad as to diffuse accountability. Leadership keeps everyone "on board" and keeps all focused on the strategic goals. The endeavor is sponsored by an executive who is appropriately aligned to provide the leadership the endeavor needs and able to articulate and defend the needs of the endeavor at the senior management level. These executive sponsors are and will remain engaged throughout.
- **Governance** is the ability to engage the involvement and support of all parties with an interest in or responsibility to the endeavor with the objective of ensuring that the corporate interests are served and the objectives achieved. There are clearly identified stakeholders and a clear sense of their interest in and responsibility to the project; a culture that encourages participation towards corporate rather than local objectives; a history of being able to successfully manage activities that cross interest areas; a culture that fosters meaningful, as opposed to symbolic, participation in management processes; and a commitment to ongoing project review and challenge and openness to outside advice.
- **Accountability** is the assignment of specific and appropriate responsibility, recognition of measurable expectations by all concerned parties, and alignment of decision-making with areas of responsibility and with where the impact of the decisions will be felt. Accountability is aligned with the area where the benefits of success or consequences of failure of the endeavor will be felt as well as with the responsibility areas.
- **Workable Approach and Execution Model** is an approach that makes sense relative to the task, with a supporting environment, modeled after a proven approach. There are clear notions of the client and the client's role relative to the builder or prime contractor and the organization is experienced with endeavors of this type so that the processes, disciplines, expertise, and governance are already in place, proven, and available to apply to the transformation endeavor. All the players know their roles because they have played them before with success. In particular, the roles of "client" and "systems builder" are mature and stable. There is a communication plan covering all levels of the organization and meeting the needs ranging from awareness to availability of technical detail. There is a reward and recognition plan in place to recognize teams and individuals who use good change management practices, planning and prevention of crisis behaviors, and who reinforce behaviors appropriate to the new way of doing business. It is clear to everyone how implementation will occur, how it will be monitored, and how realignment actions will be made and there are adequate resources dedicated for the life of the transformation.
- **IT Capacity to Execute** is the ability to perform all the IT tasks required by the project, including the skills, tools, processes, and management capability. There has been a recent successful execution of a similar endeavor of similar size and complexity and there exist appropriate processes, discipline, skills, and a rationale model for deciding what skills and activities to source externally.
- **Enterprise Capacity to Execute** is the ability of the enterprise to perform all the tasks required by the endeavor, in areas outside of IT, including the ability to make decisions within the tight time constraints typical to project environments based upon the recent successful execution of a similar endeavor of at least half the size and complexity. There exist non-IT-specific processes, discipline, and skills to deal with this type of endeavor. The enterprise has a demonstrated ability to deal with the type of ongoing portfolio/project management issues and requirements. There is a recognition of the need for knowledge and skill-building for the new way of working as well as the value of a formal gap analysis for skills and behavior.

- **资金**以财政资源的明确来源形式存在以满足尝试的潜在支出。
- **发起层与领导层**存在并被广泛共享，但并未达到分散责任的广泛程度。领导层保持每个人都“在岗”，并保持所有人都聚焦于战略目标。这种努力由一个执行者发起，该执行者被适当调整，以向领导层提供努力的需要并且能够在高级管理层级上明确表达并捍卫努力的需要。这些执行发起人参与并将持续参与整个流程。
- **治理**是从事将所有对尝试感兴趣或对其负有责任的当事人包含在内并支持的能力，治理的目的是确保服务于公司级利益并达成目的。存在明确识别出的利益攸关者及其对项目利益和职责的清楚认识；鼓励为公司级而不是局部目的而参与的文化；能够成功管理跨利益领域活动的历史；推动管理流程中有意义的（而不是象征性的）参与的文化；以及致力于持续项目审查和挑战以及外部建议的公开性。
- **责任**是特定和适当的职责分配，各方可衡量的期望的识别，以及决策与职责领域与将受到决策影响的领域所保持的一致性。责任与获得尝试的成功收益或失败后果的领域以及与职责领域保持一致。
- **可行途径和执行模型**是理解任务、具备支持环境、采用经验证的方法建模的一种实施途径。对于客户和有关建造者或主要承包商扮演的客户角色具有明确的概念，且组织对这类尝试很有经验，因此，流程、规程、专业知识和治理已经到位并经过证明，且可应用在转型尝试中。所有参与者都知道他们的角色，因为他们之前已经成功地扮演了这些角色。特别是，“客户”和“系统建造者”角色是成熟且稳定的。存在一项通信计划，该计划覆盖组织各个层级并满足从意识到技术细节可用性的所有需要。存在一项恰当的奖励和识别计划，以识别出团体和个人，其使用良好的变更管理实践、规划和预防危机行为，以及加强适合全新业务经营方式的行为。每个人都很清楚实施将如何出现、如何监控以及如何作出重新调整行动，并且存在专门用于转型生命期的充足资源。
- **IT 执行能力**是项目所需的执行所有 IT 任务的能力，包括技能、工具、流程和管理能力。已经有最近成功执行了具有相似规模和复杂性的相似尝试，且存在决定从外部获得哪些技能和活动的适当流程、规程、技能和理论依据模型。
- **ENTERPRISE 执行能力**是 ENTERPRISE 在 IT 领域外执行尝试所要求的所有任务的能力，包括在项目环境较为典型的紧迫时间约束内做出决策的能力，这种约束基于最近成功执行的相关尝试，且至少具有其一半规模和复杂性。存在处理这类尝试的非 IT 特有的流程、规程和技能。ENTERPRISE 拥有处理这类持续的项目谱系/项目管理问题和需求的已表明的能力。人们认识到需要全新工作方式所用的知识和技能建设，以及技能和行为的正式差距分析的价值。

- **Enterprise Ability to Implement and Operate** the transformation elements and their related business processes, absorb the changes arising from implementation, and ongoing ability to operate in the new environment. The enterprise has a recent proven ability to deal with the change management issues arising from new processes and systems and has in place a solid disciplined and process-driven service management program that provides operations, maintenance, and support for existing systems.

Once the factors have been identified and defined, it is useful to call a follow-on workshop where the factors shall be assessed in some detail in terms of their impact/risk. The next section will deal with preparing for an effective assessment of these factors.

30.3 Present Readiness Factors

Once the factors are determined, it is necessary to present them in such a way that the assessment is clear and the maximum value is derived from the participants.

One such presentation is through the use of maturity models. If each factor is converted into a maturity model (a re-usable governance asset as well) accompanied by a standard worksheet template containing all of the information and deductions that have to be gathered, it can be a very useful tool.

The maturity model should enable participants to:

- Assess their current (Baseline Architecture) maturity level.
- Determine the target maturity level that would have to be achieved to realize the Target Architecture.
- Determine an intermediate target that would be achievable in a lesser timeframe.

The care spent preparing the models (which is not insignificant) will be recouped by a focused workshop that will rapidly go through a significant number of factors.

It is important that each factor be well-defined and that the scope of the enterprise architecture endeavor (preliminary planning) be reflected in the models to keep the workshop participants focused and productive.

Circulating the models before the workshop for comments would be useful, if only to ensure that they are complete as well as allowing the participants to prepare for the workshop. Note that the model shown below also has a recommended target state put in by the enterprise architect; this again acts as governance.

An example of a maturity model is shown in Figure 30-1 for one of the BTEP factors:

- **ENTERPRISE 实施和运行**转型元素及其相关业务流程的能力、吸收实施所引起的变更的能力以及在新环境中持续运行的能力。ENTERPRISE 拥有最近已被证明的处理新流程和系统引起的变更管理问题的能力，并且确立了一个为现有系统提供操作、维护和支持的稳定有条理且由流程驱动的服务管理程序。

一旦识别和定义了因素，召开后续研讨会十分有用，在该研讨会上，将根据其影响/风险在细节上评估这些因素。下一节将处理有效评估这些因素的准备工作。

30.3 表达准备度因素

一旦因素被确定，有必要通过这样一种方式表达它们：评估是明确的且最大价值源自参与者。

通过使用成熟度模型来完成这样一种表达。如果将每个因素转化成成熟度模型（同时也是一种可复用的治理资产），附有包含必须收集的全部信息和推论的标准工作表模板，则其可能是一个十分有用的工具。

成熟度模型应使参与者能够：

- 评估他们当前（基线架构）的成熟度层级。
- 确定要实现目标架构所必须达成的目标成熟度层级。
- 确定在较短的时间段内可实现的中期目标。

在模型（并不是无关紧要的）的准备上所付心血将在快速查看大量因素的集中研讨会上得到补偿。

重要的是，每个因素应该是明确定义的，而且 Enterprise Architecture 尝试（预备规划）的范围应反映到模型中，从而使研讨会参与者全神贯注并富有成效。

如果只是为了确保模型是完整的并有助于参与者为研讨会做准备，那么在研讨会前传阅这些模型以获得评论将十分有用。应注意，下面展示的模型同样具有由 ENTERPRISE 架构师加入的建议目标状态；这再一次起到治理的作用。

BTEP 因素之一的成熟度模型的示例如图 30-1 所示。

<table>
<tr><th colspan="6">Business Transformation Readiness Assessment - Maturity Model</th></tr>
<tr><td colspan="3" rowspan="2">Factor 2: Need for Enterprise Information Architecture</td><td>Class</td><td colspan="2">Organizational Context</td></tr>
<tr><td>BTEP Readiness Factor</td><td colspan="2">YES</td></tr>
<tr><td>Definition</td><td colspan="5">There is recognition by the organization that information is a strategic corporate asset requiring stewardship.
There is also recognition that the data is not universally understandable, of requisite quality, and accessible.</td></tr>
<tr><th colspan="6">Maturity Model Levels</th></tr>
<tr><th>0
Not defined</th><th>1
Ad Hoc</th><th>2
Repeatable</th><th>3
Defined</th><th>4
Managed</th><th>5
Optimized</th></tr>
<tr><td>Information is not recognized as an asset.

There is no clear stewardship of data</td><td>Data Management (DM) concepts are intuitively understood and practiced on an ad hoc basis.

Stewardship of the data is informal.

Data is recognized by certain internal experts and senior management as being of strategic importance to the organization.

Focus is primarily on technically managing redundant data at the applications level</td><td>Many parts of the organization value information/data as a strategic asset.

Internal DM experts maintain clear lines of responsibility and stewardship of the data, organized along lines of business and at all senior levels.

Staff put into practice DM principles and standards in their daily activities</td><td>Data is recognized as a strategic asset in most parts of the organization, and throughout most levels from operations to senior management.

Resources are committed to ensuring strong stewardship of data at the lower management and information expert levels</td><td>Data is recognized as a strategic asset in all parts of the organization, and throughout most levels from operations to senior management.

Resources are committed to ensuring strong stewardship of data at the senior management and information expert levels</td><td>Data is treated in all levels throughout the organization as a strategic asset to be exploited and re-used.

Data products and services are strongly integrated with the management practice of the organization.

All staff are empowered and equipped to take stewardship of information, and are seen as "knowleg workers"</td></tr>
<tr><td></td><td></td><td></td><td></td><td>Recommended Target State</td><td></td></tr>
</table>

Figure 30-1 Business Transformation Readiness Assessment — Maturity Model

30.4 Assess Readiness Factors

Ideally, the factors should be assessed in a multi-disciplinary workshop. Using a mechanism such as maturity models, enterprise architects will normally have to cover a great deal of ground in little time.

The use of a series of templates for each factor would expedite the assessment, and ensure consistency across the wide range of factors.

The assessment should address three things, namely:

- Readiness Factor Vision
- Readiness Factor Rating
- Readiness Factor Risks & Actions

30.4.1 Readiness Factor Vision

The vision for a readiness factor is the determination of where the enterprise has to evolve to address the factor. First, the factor should be assessed with respect to its base state and then its target state.

For example, if the "IT capacity to execute" factor is rated as low, the factor should ideally be at "high" to realize the Target Architecture Vision. An intermediate target might be useful to direct the implementation. Maturity models are excellent vehicles to guide this determination.

<table>
<tr><th colspan="6">业务转型准备度评估——成熟度模型</th></tr>
<tr><td colspan="3" rowspan="2">因素 2：ENTERPRISE 信息架构的需要</td><td>分类</td><td colspan="2">组织的背景环境</td></tr>
<tr><td>BTEP
准备度因素</td><td colspan="2">是</td></tr>
<tr><td>定义</td><td colspan="5">组织认为信息是一种需要管理的战略性公司级资产。
组织同样认为数据未得到普遍理解，未达到必需质量且不可访问</td></tr>
<tr><td colspan="6">成熟度模型层级</td></tr>
<tr><td>0
未定义</td><td>1
随意的</td><td>2
可重复</td><td>3
已定义</td><td>4
已管理</td><td>5
已优化</td></tr>
<tr><td>信息未被视为一种资产。

没有明确的数据管理</td><td>数据管理（DM）概念被直观理解并在随意的基础上进行实践。

数据管理是非正式的。

某些内部专家和高级管理层认为数据对组织具有战略重要性。

聚焦点主要在于在应用层级上技术性地管理冗余数据</td><td>组织的许多部门将信息/数据估价为一种战略资产。

内部 DM 专家对沿业务线并在全部高层级中组织的数据保持明确职责和管理工作。

员工在其日常活动中践行 DM 原则和标准</td><td>在组织大多数部门内以及从运行到高级管理层的大多数层级中，均将数据视为一种资产。

将资源致力于确保在较低管理层和信息专家层级上对数据进行有力地管理</td><td>在组织的所有部门内以及从运行到高级管理层的大多数层级中，将数据视为一种战略资产。

将资源致力于确保在高级管理层和信息专家层级上对数据进行有力地管理</td><td>在整个组织的全部层级中，将数据作为一种待开发和复用的战略资产。

数据产品和服务与组织管理实践强有力地结合起来。

所有员工均被授权并有资格管理信息，且被视为“知识工作者”</td></tr>
<tr><td></td><td></td><td></td><td></td><td>建议的目标状态</td><td></td></tr>
</table>

图 30-1　业务转型准备度评估——成熟度模型

30.4　评估准备度因素

理想上，这些因素应在多学科研讨会中被评估。使用诸如成熟度模型的机制，ENTERPRISE 架构师通常必须在极短时间内将大量内容涵盖在内。

为每个因素使用一系列模板会加快评估，并确保在范围广泛的多个因素之间保证一致性。

评估应涉及三件事情，即：

- 准备度因素愿景
- 准备度因素评定
- 准备度风险和行动

30.4.1　准备度因素愿景

准备度因素愿景是，确定 ENTERPRISE 必须从哪里开始演进以应对该因素。首先，应对因素的基础状态进行评估，然后对其目标状态进行评估。

例如，如果“IT 执行能力”因素被评定为低，而其在理想上应为“高”以实现目标架构愿景。中期目标对指导实施可能十分有用。成熟度模型是指导此测定的极佳工具。

30.4.2 Readiness Factor Rating

Once the factor visions are established, then it is useful to determine how important each factor is to the achievement of the Target Architecture as well as how challenging it will be to migrate the factor into an acceptable visionary state.

The BTEP uses a Readiness Rating Scheme that can be used as a start point for any organization in any vertical. Each one of the readiness factors are rated with respect to:

- **Urgency**, whereby if a readiness factor is urgent, it means that action is needed before a transformation initiative can begin.
- **Readiness Status**, which is rated as either Low (needs substantial work before proceeding), Fair (needs some work before proceeding), Acceptable (some readiness issues exist; no showstoppers), Good (relatively minor issues exist), or High (no readiness issues).
- **Degree of Difficulty to Fix** rates the effort required to overcome any issues identified as either No Action Needed, Easy, Moderate, or Difficult.

Although a more extensive template can be used in the workshop, it is useful to create a summary table of the findings to consolidate the factors and provide a management overview. A like summary is shown in Figure 30-2.

Business Factor Assessment Summary				
Ser	**Readiness Factor**	**Urgency**	**Readiness Status**	**Degree of Difficulty to Fix**
1	Vision			
2	Desire/willingness/resolve			
3	Need			
4	Business case			
5	Funding			
6	Sponsorship and leadership			
7	Governance			
8	Accountability			
9	Workable approach and execution model			
10	IT capacity to execute			
11	Departmental capacity to execute			
12	Ability to implement and operate			

Figure 30-2 Summary Table of Business Transformation Readiness Assessment

30.4.2 准备度因素评定

一旦确定了因素愿景，则确定每个因素对达成目标架构有多重要以及将该因素迁移到可接受的愿景状态具有多大挑战性是有用的。

BTEP 采用准备度评定方案，该方案可用作任何领域中任何组织的起始点。应评定每个准备度因素的以下方面：

- **紧急性**，如果一个准备度因素十分紧急，则意味着在可以开始转型举措前需要采取行动。
- **准备度状态**，被评定为低（在继续进行前需要大量工作）、合理（继续进行前需要一些工作）、可接受（存在一些准备度问题，但可以继续进行）、良好（存在相对细微的问题），或高（无准备度问题）。
- **确定的困难程度**，将克服任何识别出的问题所需的工作评定为不需要行动、容易的、中等的，或困难的。

虽然在研讨会中可以使用更广泛的模板，但建立合并因素的结果概要表并提供管理综述是非常有用的。一个类似的概要如图 30-2 所示。

业务因素评估概要				
序号	**准备度因素**	**紧急性**	**准备度状态**	**确定的困难程度**
1	愿景			
2	愿望/意愿/决心			
3	需要			
4	业务案例			
5	资金			
6	发起层与领导层			
7	治理			
8	责任			
9	可行途径和执行模型			
10	IT 执行能力			
11	部门的执行能力			
12	实施和运行能力			

图 30-2　业务转型准备度评估概要表

30.4.3 Readiness Factor Risks & Actions

Once the factors have been rated and assessed, derive a series of actions that will enable the factors to change to a favorable state.

Each factor should be assessed with respect to risk using the process highlighted in Part III, Chapter 31, including an estimate of impact and frequency.

Each factor should be discretely assessed and a series of improvement actions outlined. Before starting anew, existing actions outlined in the architectures should be checked first before creating new ones.

These newly identified actions should then be formally incorporated into the emergingImplementation and Migration Plan.

From a risk perspective, these actions are designed to mitigate the risks and produce an acceptable residual risk. As risks, they should be part of the risk management process and closely monitored as the enterprise architecture is being implemented.

30.5 Readiness and Migration Planning

The assessment exercise will provide a realistic assessment of the organization and will be a key input into the strategic migration planning that will be initiated in Phase E and completed in Phase F. It is important to note whether the business transformation actions will be on the vision's critical path and, if so, determine how they will impact implementation. There is no point deploying new IT capability without employees trained to use it and support staff ready to sustain it.

The readiness factors, as part of an overall Implementation and Migration Plan, will have to be continuously monitored (Phase G) and rapid corrective actions taken through the IT governance framework to ensure that the defined architectures can be implemented.

The readiness factors assessment will be a living document and during the migration planning and execution of the Transition Architectures, the business transformation activities will play a key role.

30.6 Marketing the Implementation Plan

The Architecture Definition should not be widely circulated until the business transformation issues are identified and mitigated, and the associated actions part of an overall "marketing" plan for the vision and the Implementation and Migration Plan.

For example, the consolidation of information holdings could result in hundreds of lost jobs and this vision should not be announced before a supporting business transformation/human resources plan is formulated to retrain or support the workers' quest for new employment.

The business transformation workshops are a critical part of the Communications Plan whereby key individuals from within the organization gather to assess the implications of transforming the enterprise. To do this they will become aware of the Architecture Vision and architecture definition (if they were not already involved through the business scenarios and Business Architecture). This group will feel ownership of the enterprise architecture, recognizing the enterprise architect as a valuable steward.

30.4.3 准备度因素风险和行动

一旦因素已被评定和评估，则衍生出一系列使因素变为有利状态的行动。

应使用第三部分第 31 章强调的流程来评估每个因素的风险，包括对影响和频率的估计。

应分别评估每个因素并概述一系列改进行动。在重新开始之前，应在创建新行动之前首先检查架构中概述的现有行动。

然后，应将这些新确定的行动正式归并到新兴的实施和迁移计划阶段中。

从风险的观点看，设计这些行动以迁移风险并产生可接受的残留风险。作为风险，这些行动应成为风险管理流程的一部分，并在实施 Enterprise Architecture 时密切监控。

30.5 准备度和迁移规划

评估训练将提供对组织的一个实际评估，并将作为在阶段 E 发起并在阶段 F 完成的战略迁移规划的关键输入。重要的是，注意业务转型行动是否将处于愿景的关键路径上，如果是，则确定它们将如何影响实施。如果不对使用 IT 能力进行员工培训，并且支持人员没有准备好保持 IT 能力，那么部署新的 IT 能力毫无意义。

作为总体实施和迁移计划一部分的准备度因素必须被持续监控（阶段 G），并且必须通过 IT 治理框架采取快速纠正行动，以确保可以实施已定义的架构。

准备度因素评估将是一个长期存在的文件，且在迁移规划期间和过渡架构执行过程中，业务转型活动将起到关键作用。

30.6 推广实施计划

在业务转型议题被识别和减轻，以及在整个“推广”的联合行动部分为愿景与实施和迁移计划拟定计划前，架构定义不应被广泛传阅。

例如，合并信息存量会导致数以百计的人失业，并且在制定一项支持业务转型/人力资源计划以重新培训或支持工作者寻找新工作前，不应宣布此愿景。

业务转型研讨会是沟通计划的一个重要部分，通过该计划，组织内的关键人员聚集在一起，评估 ENTERPRISE 转型的影响。为了完成这个目的，他们将意识到架构愿景和架构定义（如果其还未被业务场景和业务架构涉及）。此群组将觉得对 Enterprise Architecture 拥有所有权，从而将 ENTERPRISE 架构师视为有价值的管理员。

Their determination of the factors will again create a culture of understanding across the enterprise and provide useful insights for the Implementation and Migration Plan.

The latter plan should include a Communications Plan, especially to keep the affected personnel informed. In many cases collaborating with the unions and shop stewards will further assist a humane (and peaceful) transition to the target state.

30.7 Conclusion

In short, enterprise architecture implementation will require a deep knowledge and awareness of all of the business transformation factors that impact transitioning to the visionary state. With the evolution of IT, the actual technology is not the real issue any more in enterprise architecture, but the critical factors are most often the cultural ones. Any Implementation and Migration Plan has to take both into consideration. Neglecting these and focusing on the technical aspects will invariably result in a lackluster implementation that falls short of realizing the real promise of a visionary enterprise architecture.

对因素的确定将再次创建理解整个 ENTERPRISE 的文化，并对实施和迁移计划提供有用的深入见解。

后一个计划应包括沟通计划，特别是要知会受影响的人员。在很多情况下，与工会和工会管理员合作将进一步辅助向目标状态的人性化（及和平的）过渡。

30.7 结论

简而言之，Enterprise Architecture 实施将需要对影响向愿景状态过渡的所有业务转型因素具有深入了解和认识。随着 IT 的演进，实际技术不再是 Enterprise Architecture 中的一个真正议题，而关键因素往往是文化因素。任何实施和迁移计划均要对二者进行考虑。将此忽略而聚焦于技术方面必然导致实施乏善可陈，不足以实现愿景中 Enterprise Architecture 的真正承诺。

Chapter 31
Risk Management

This chapter describes risk management, which is a technique used to mitigate risk when implementing an architecture project.

31.1 Introduction

There will always be risk with any architecture/business transformation effort. It is important to identify, classify, and mitigate these risks before starting so that they can be tracked throughout the transformation effort.

Mitigation is an ongoing effort and often the risk triggers may be outside the scope of the transformation planners (e.g., merger, acquisition) so planners must monitor the transformation context constantly.

It is also important to note that the enterprise architect may identify the risks and mitigate certain ones, but it is within the governance framework that risks have to be first accepted and then managed.

There are two levels of risk that should be considered, namely:

1. **Initial Level of Risk**: Risk categorization prior to determining and implementing mitigating actions.
2. **Residual Level of Risk**: Risk categorization after implementation of mitigateing actions (if any).

The process for risk management is described in the following sections and consists of the following activities:

- Risk classification
- Risk identification
- Initial risk assessment
- Risk mitigation and residual risk assessment
- Risk monitoring

第 31 章 风险管理

本章描述风险管理，它是在实施架构项目时用于缓解风险的一种技巧。

31.1 简介

在任何架构/业务转型工作中，总是存在风险。重要的是应在工作开始前识别、归类并缓解这些风险，以便可以在整个转型期间进行跟踪。

缓解风险是一项持续的工作，而且风险触发因素可能经常超出转型计划人员的范围（例如合并、采购），因此计划人员必须不断地监控转型背景环境。

同样重要的是注意到，ENTERPRISE 架构师可识别出风险并缓解某些风险，但风险必须在治理框架内首先接受并随后管理。

有两个风险等级应该被考虑，即：

1. **风险的初始等级**：在确定并实施缓解行动之前的风险类别。
2. **风险的残余等级**：在实施缓解行动（若有）之后的风险类别。

风险管理流程在下几节中描述并由下列活动组成：

- 风险分类
- 风险识别
- 初始风险评估
- 风险缓解及残留风险评估
- 风险监控

31.2 Risk Classification

Risk is pervasive in any enterprise architecture activity and is present in all phases within the Architecture Development Method (ADM). From a management perspective, it is useful to classify the risks so that the mitigation of the risks can be executed as expeditiously as possible.

One common way for risks to be classified is with respect to impact on the organization (as discussed in Section 31.4), whereby risks with certain impacts have to be addressed by certain levels of governance.

Risks are normally classified as time (schedule), cost (budget), and scope but they could also include client transformation relationship risks, contractual risks, technological risks, scope and complexity risks, environmental (corporate) risks, personnel risks, and client acceptance risks.

Another way of delegating risk management is to further classify risks by architecture domains. Classifying risks as business, information, applications, and technology is useful but there may be organizationally-specific ways of expressing risk that the corporate enterprise architecture directorate should adopt or extend rather than modify.

Ultimately, enterprise architecture risks are corporate risks and should be classified and as appropriate managed in the same or extended way.

31.3 Risk Identification

The maturity and transformation readiness assessments will generate a great many risks. Identify the risks and then determine the strategy to address them throughout the transformation.

The use of Capability Maturity Models (CMMs) is suitable for specific factors associated with architecture delivery to first identify baseline and target states and then identify the actions required to move to the target state. The implications of *not* achieving the target state can result in the discovery of risks. Refer to Chapter 30 for specific details.

Risk documentation is completed in the context of a Risk Management Plan, for which templates exist in standard project management methodologies (e.g., Project Management Book of Knowledge and PRINCE2) as well as with the various government methodologies.

Normally these methodologies involve procedures for contingency planning, tracking and evaluating levels of risk; reacting to changing risk level factors, as well as processes for documenting, reporting, and communicating risks to stakeholders.

31.2 风险分类

风险普遍存在于任何 Enterprise Architecture 活动中，并出现在架构开发方法（ADM）的全部阶段中。从管理视角看，对风险分类以便尽可能迅速地执行风险缓解是非常有用的。

对风险分类的一个常用方法是考虑其对组织的影响（如 31.4 节所讨论），通过该方法，具有某种影响的风险必须通过某个层级的治理来应对。

风险通常分为时间风险（进度表）、成本风险（预算）和范围风险，但它们也可包括客户转型关系风险、契约风险、技术风险、范围和复杂性风险、环境（公司级）风险、人员风险和客户验收风险。

委托风险管理的另一种方式是根据架构领域对风险进行进一步分类。把风险分为业务风险、信息风险、应用风险和技术风险非常有用，但可能存在组织特定的方式来表达风险，公司级的 Enterprise Architecture 董事会可采用或扩展该方法，但不能对其进行修改。

最终，Enterprise Architecture 风险是公司级风险，并应以相同或扩展的方式对其分类并进行适当管理。

31.3 风险识别

成熟度和转型准备度评估将产生很多风险。识别出这些风险，然后确定在整个转型期间用于应对它们的策略。

能力成熟度模型（CMM）的使用适用于与架构交付有关的特定因素，以首先识别基线和目标状态，然后确定转换到目标状态所需的行动。没有达到目标状态所产生的影响会导致发现风险。特定细节见第 30 章。

在风险管理计划的背景环境下完成了风险记录，其模板存在于标准的项目管理方法论（例如，知识和 PRINCE2 项目管理手册）中并具有各种不同的治理方法论。

这些方法论通常涉及对风险等级进行应急规划、跟踪及评价的程序；并包括对改变风险等级因素的反应，以及向利益攸关者记录、报告并沟通风险的流程。

31.4 Initial Risk Assessment

The next step is to classify risks with respect to effect and frequency in accordance with scales used within the organization. Combine effect and frequency to come up with a preliminary risk assessment.

There are no hard and fast rules with respect to measuring effect and frequency. The following guidelines are based upon existing risk management best practices. Effect could be assessed using the following example criteria:

- **Catastrophic** infers critical financial loss that could result in bankruptcy of the organization.
- **Critical** infers serious financial loss in more than one line of business leading to a loss in productivity and no return on investment on the IT investment.
- **Marginal** infers a minor financial loss in a line of business and a reduced return on investment on the IT investment.
- **Negligible** infers a minimal impact on a line of business' ability to deliver services and/or products.

Frequency could be indicated as follows:

- **Frequent**: Likely to occur very often and/or continuously.
- **Likely**: Occurs several times over the course of a transformation cycle.
- **Occasional**: Occurs sporadically.
- **Seldom**: Remotely possible and would probably occur not more than once in the course of a transformation cycle.
- **Unlikely**: Will probably not occur during the course of a transformation cycle.

Combining the two factors to infer impact would be conducted using a heuristically-based but consistent classification scheme for the risks. A potential scheme to assess corporate impact could be as follows:

- **Extremely High Risk (E)**: The transformation effort will most likely fail with severe consequences.
- **High Risk (H)**: Significant failure of parts of the transformation effort resulting in certain goals not being achieved.
- **Moderate Risk (M)**: Noticeable failure of parts of the transformation effort threatening the success of certain goals.
- **Low Risk (L)**: Certain goals will not be wholly successful.

These impacts can be derived using a classification scheme, as shown in Figure 31-1.

31.4 初始风险评估

下一步是根据组织内采用的衡量尺度，按影响和频率对风险进行分类。将影响和频率结合，从而提出初步的风险评估。

在衡量影响和频率方面，没有固定不变的规则。下列指南基于现有的风险管理最佳实践。可使用下列示例准则评估影响：

- **灾难性的**，指可导致组织破产的重大财务损失。
- **关键的**，指导致生产力损失以及 IT 投资无投资收益率的多个业务线的严重财务损失。
- **微小的**，指一个业务线中轻微的财务损失以及较低的 IT 投资收益率。
- **可忽略的**，指对业务线交付服务和/或产品的能力的影响最小。

频率应如下所示：

- **频繁的**：可能经常和/或连续发生。
- **可能的**：在转型周期过程中发生多次。
- **偶尔的**：零星地发生。
- **很少的**：在转型周期过程中发生的可能性极小并有可能发生不超过一次。
- **不太可能的**：在转型周期中可能不会发生。

将这两个因素结合，以推断出可使用基于启发式但一致的风险分类方案来实施影响。评估公司级影响的一个潜在方案如下：

- **极高的风险（E）**：转型工作最有可能失败，带来严重后果。
- **高风险（H）**：导致某些目标没有达成的部分转型工作的重大失败。
- **中等风险（M）**：威胁到某些目标成功的部分转型工作的明显失败。
- **低风险（L）**：某些目标不会完全成功。

可使用分类方案得出这些影响，如图 31-1 所示。

Corporate Risk Impact Assessment					
Effect	Frequency				
	Frequent	Likely	Occasional	Seldom	Unlikely
Catastrophic	E	E	H	H	M
Critical	E	H	H	M	L
Marginal	H	M	M	L	L
Negligible	M	L	L	L	L

Figure 31-1 Risk Classification Scheme

31.5 Risk Mitigation and Residual Risk Assessment

Risk mitigation refers to the identification, planning, and conduct of actions that will reduce the risk to an acceptable level.

The mitigation effort could be a simple monitoring and/or acceptance of the risk to a full-blown contingency plan calling for complete redundancy in a Business Continuity Plan (with all of the associated scope, cost, and time implications).

Due to the implications of this risk assessment, it has to be conducted in a pragmatic but systematic manner. With priority going to frequent high impact risks, each risk has to be mitigated in turn.

31.6 Conduct Residual Risk Assessment

Once the mitigation effort has been identified for each one of the risks, re-assess the effect and frequency and then recalculate the impacts and see whether the mitigation effort has really made an acceptable difference. The mitigation efforts will often be resource-intensive and a major outlay for little or no residual risk should be challenged.

Once the initial risk is mitigated, then the risk that remains is called the "residual risk". The key consideration is that the mitigating effort actually reduces the corporate impact and does not just move the risk to another similarly high quadrant. For example, changing the risk from frequent/catastrophic to frequent/critical still delivers an Extremely high risk. If this occurs, then the mitigation effort has to be reconsidered.

The final deliverable should be a transformation risk assessment that could be structured as a worksheet, as shown in Figure 31-2.

公司级风险影响评估					
影响	频率				
	频繁的	可能的	偶尔的	很少的	不太可能的
灾难性的	极高	极高	高	高	中等
关键的	极高	高	高	中等	低
微小的	高	中等	中等	低	低
可忽略的	中等	低	低	低	低

图 31-1　风险分类方案

31.5　风险缓解及残余风险评估

风险缓解指的是将风险降低到可接受等级的行动的识别、规划和实施。

缓解工作可能是简单地监控和/或接受在业务连续性计划中，要求完整冗余的成熟应急计划中的风险（具有全部相关的范围、成本和时间影响）。

由于此风险评估的影响，必须以实用但系统的方式实施风险评估。由于频繁的高影响风险具有优先级，因此必须依次缓解每个风险。

31.6　实施残留风险评估

一旦针对每一个风险识别了缓解工作，则重新评估影响和频率，然后重新估计影响并查看缓解工作是否确实带来了可接受的差别。缓解工作通常是资源密集型的，并且用于几乎不存在的残留风险的主要费用应受到质疑。

一旦缓解了初始风险，那么剩余的风险被称为“残留风险”。关键考量因素是缓解工作确实减少了公司级影响，而并非仅仅将风险转移到另一个同样高风险的象限中。例如，将风险从“频繁的/灾难性的”转变为“频繁的/关键的”，仍然可能交付一个极高的风险。如果发生这种情况，则必须重新考虑缓解工作。

最终的交付物应该是一个可结构化为工作表形式的转型风险评估，如图 31-2 所示。

Risk ID	Risk	Preliminary Risk			Mitigation	Residual Risk		
		Effect	Frequency	Impact		Effect	Frequency	Impact

Figure 31-2 Sample Risk Identification and Mitigation Assessment Worksheet

31.7 Risk Monitoring and Governance (Phase G)

The residual risks have to be approved by the IT governance framework and potentially in corporate governance where business acceptance of the residual risks is required.

Once the residual risks have been accepted, then the execution of the mitigating actions has to be carefully monitored to ensure that the enterprise is dealing with residual rather than initial risk.

The risk identification and mitigation assessment worksheets are maintained as governance artifacts and are kept up-to-date in Phase G (Implementation Governance) where risk monitoring is conducted.

Implementation governance can identify critical risks that are not being mitigated and might require another full or partial ADM cycle.

31.8 Summary

Risk Management is an integral part of enterprise architecture. Practitioners are encouraged to use their corporate risk management methodology or extend it using the guidance in this chapter. In the absence of a formal corporate methodology, architects can use the guidance in this chapter as a best practice.

风险 ID	风险	初始风险			缓解	残留风险		
		影响	频率	严重影响		影响	频率	严重影响

图 31-2 风险识别和缓解评估工作表示例

31.7 风险监控和治理（阶段 G）

残留风险必须由 IT 治理框架批准，并潜在地存在于需要对残留风险进行业务验收的公司级治理中。

一旦接受了残留风险，则必须仔细地监控缓解活动的执行，以确保 ENTERPRISE 正在处理的是残余风险而不是初始风险。

风险识别和缓解评估工作表作为治理制品被保留，且在实施风险监控的阶段 G（实施治理）中保持最新状态。

实施治理可以识别出未被缓解的、并可能需要另一个完整或部分 ADM 周期处理的关键风险。

31.8 概要总结

风险管理是 Entorprise Architecture 的一个组成部分。鼓励实践者使用其公司级的风险管理方法论或使用本章中的指南对该方法论进行扩展。在缺乏正式的公司级方法论的情况下，架构师可以使用本章中的指南作为最佳实践。

Chapter 32
Capability-Based Planning

This chapter provides an overview of capability-based planning, a business planning technique that focuses on business outcomes. It also copes well with the friction of co-ordinating projects across corporate functional domains that together enable the enterprise to achieve that capability (for example, electronic service delivery).

32.1 Overview

Capability-based planning focuses on the planning, engineering, and delivery of strategic business capabilities to the enterprise. It is business-driven and business-led and combines the requisite efforts of all lines of business to achieve the desired capability. Capability-based planning accommodates most, if not all, of the corporate business models and is especially useful in organizations where a latent capability to respond (e.g., an emergency preparedness unit) is required and the same resources are involved in multiple capabilities. Often the need for these capabilities are discovered and refined using business scenarios (see Part III, Chapter 26).

From an IT perspective, capability-based planning is particularly relevant. For example, setting up a data center is really about consolidating corporate data and providing the related services. Lead enterprise architects for this capability will find themselves involved in managing construction, personnel training, and other change management tasks as well as IT architecture tasks. In the past, many IT projects were less than successful even though the actual IT implementation was brilliant, but the associated other tasks (business process re-engineering, client training, support training, infrastructure, and so on) were not controlled by the enterprise architects and planners and often were not satisfactorily completed.

On the other hand, IT projects were often described in terms of technical deliverables not as business outcomes, making it difficult for business to appreciate what was being delivered and often the IT architects lost sight of the ultimate business goal. Capability-based planning frames all phases of the architecture development in the context of business outcomes, clearly linking the IT vision, architectures (ABBs and SBBs), and the Implementation and Migration Plans with the corporate strategic, business, and line of business plans.

In many governments, horizontal interoperability and shared services are emerging as cornerstones of their e-Government implementations and capability-based management is also prominent although under many guises. In the private sector, the concepts of supply chain management and Service Oriented Architecture (SOA) are increasingly forcing planners/managers to govern horizontally as well as vertically.

第 32 章
基于能力的规划

本章提供对基于能力的规划的综述，这是一种专注于业务成果的业务规划技巧。它同样能较好地应对公司级功能域间协作项目中的摩擦，这些功能域共同促使 ENTERPRISE 达成此能力（例如，电子服务交付）。

32.1 综述概述

基于能力的规划聚焦于 ENTERPRISE 战略性业务能力的规划、设计和交付。它是业务驱动和业务引领的，并结合所有业务线的必要工作来达成期望的能力。基于能力的规划适用于大多数（若不是全部）的公司级业务模型，尤其在需要具备潜在响应能力（例如，应急准备单元）并且相同的资源被投入到多种能力中的组织中特别有用。常常使用业务场景（见第三部分第 26 章）发现并细化对这些能力的需要。

从 IT 关注层级看，基于能力的规划尤其恰当。例如，设立数据中心实际上与合并公司级数据及提供相关服务有关。该能力的 ENTERPRISE 首席架构师将发现自己参与到管理建设、人员培训及其他变革管理任务和 IT 架构任务中。在过去，许多 IT 项目仍不甚成功，尽管实际的 IT 实施十分杰出，其他有关的任务（业务流程再设计、客户培训、支持培训、基础设施等）并非由 ENTERPRISE 架构师和计划人员控制，且通常并没有圆满完成。

另一方面，IT 项目通常根据技术交付物来描述，而不是作为业务成果，这使业务很难去鉴别正在交付什么，并且 IT 架构师通常看不到最终的业务目标。基于能力的规划在业务成果的背景环境下框定架构开发的所有阶段，明确地将 IT 愿景、架构（ABB 和 SBB）以及实施和迁移计划与公司级策略计划、业务和业务线计划联系起来。

在很多政府中，水平的互用性和共享服务正逐渐出现并作为其电子政务实施的基石，且基于能力的管理虽然以多种形式存在，但同样十分显著。在私营机构中，供应链管理和面向服务架构（SOA）的概念日益促使计划人员/管理人员进行水平以及垂直的管控。

32.2 Capability-Based Planning Paradigm

Capability-based planning has long been entrenched in the Defense realm in the US, UK, Australia, and Canada. The associated governance mechanisms, as well as rigorous capability derivation (capability engineering), are emerging primarily in the systems engineering domain. These concepts are readily transferable into other domains, such as IT.

32.3 Concept of Capability-Based Planning

From an enterprise architecture and IT perspective, capability-based planning is a powerful mechanism to ensure that the strategic business plan drives the enterprise from a top-down approach. It is also adaptable with capability engineering to leverage emerging bottom-up innovations.

No matter how the corporation structures itself, it will have to cope with the delivery of business capabilities whose delivery will require co-ordination and alignment across business verticals.

Capabilities are business-driven and ideally business-led. One of the main challenges is that the benefits are often reaped at the enterprise and not the line of business level. Consequently, projects within line of business-led portfolios tend to take a line of business rather than corporate perspective. Managing the delivery of a capability is challenging, but the entrenchment of a capability-based perspective within an organization is a powerful mechanism to deliver synergistically derived business value that will resonate in profitability and stock value.

Capabilities should be specified using the same discipline in the specification of objectives as in business scenarios; specifically, they should follow the SMART guidelines to avoid ambiguity.

As shown in Figure 32-1, many capabilities are "horizontal" and go against the grain of normal vertical corporate governance. Most often, management direction as well as the corporate management accountability framework are based upon line of business metrics, not enterprise metrics. Enterprise architecture is also a horizontal function that looks at enterprise-level (as well as line of business-level) optimization and service delivery. Not surprisingly, capability-based planning and enterprise architecture are mutually supportive. Both often operate against the corporate grain and both have to cope with challenging business environments. Business support of enterprise architecture is crucial for its success and it is logical that it aligns with the corporate capability planners as well as provide support for those within the vertical lines of business.

32.2 基于能力的规划范例

基于能力的规划早已在美国、英国、澳大利亚和加拿大的国防领域中确立。相关的治理机制以及严密的能力推论（能力工程）最初出现在系统工程领域。这些概念被迅速转移到其他领域中，例如 IT 领域。

32.3 基于能力的规划的概念

从 Enterprise Architecture 和 IT 的视角看，基于能力的规划是一种确保战略性业务计划根据自顶向下的途径驱动 ENTERPRISE 的强大机制。它同样适用于能力工程，以更强有力地发挥新兴的自底向上的创新的作用。

无论公司结构本身如何，公司必须处理业务能力的交付，这些能力的交付将需要跨垂直业务协调和对准。

能力是业务驱动的，且在理想上是业务导向的。主要挑战之一是，常常在 ENTERPRISE 层级而不是业务线层级获得效益。因此，业务线导向的项目谱系内的项目倾向于采用业务线的视角而不是公司级的视角。对能力交付的管理具有挑战性，但组织内确立基于能力的视角是一种交付将在盈利能力和股票价值方面取得反响的、以协同方式得出业务价值的强大机制。

应使用目的规范中与业务场景中相同的规程来规定能力；特别地，它们应遵循 SMART 指南，以避免歧义。

如图 32-1 所示，许多能力是“水平的”并与正常的垂直公司级治理背道而驰。管理方向和公司级管理责任框架往往基于业务指标线，而非 ENTERPRISE 指标。Enterprise Architecture 同样是一种着眼于 ENTERPRISE 层级（以及业务线层级）优化和服务交付的水平功能。毫不奇怪的是，基于能力的规划与 Enterprise Architecture 是互相支持的。二者的运行通常与公司级运行背道而驰，且二者均应对挑战性的业务环境。对 Enterprise Architecture 的业务支持对其成功至关重要，并且其与公司级能力计划人员保持一致，为垂直业务线内的那些能力提供支持是合乎逻辑的。

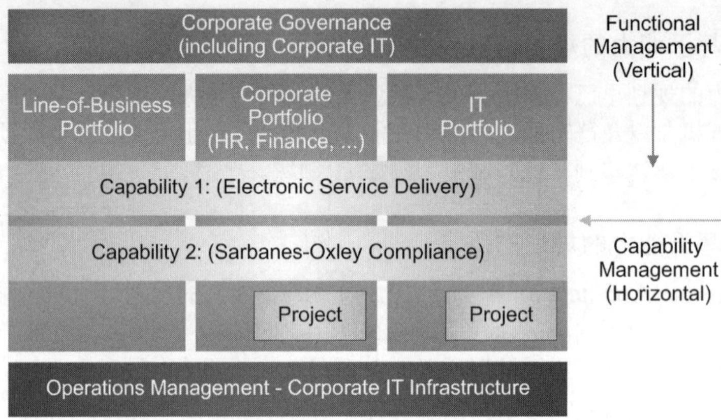

Figure 32-1 Capability-Based Planning Concept

Capabilities can also be vertical and handled in the context of the business organizational structure. In fact, capability requirements often drive organizational design, but within an organization in the process of business transformation, the organization may be trailing the capability needs.

Vertical capabilities are easier to handle and support by the enterprise architecture function, but still challenging when services are rationalized at the enterprise level and lines of business receive shared services that they do not directly control (they provide indirect control through IT governance in the Architecture Board as created in preliminary planning and used in Phase G (Implementation Governance).

For capability-based planning to succeed, it has to be managed with respect to dimensions and increments, as explained in the following two sections.

32.3.1 Capability Dimensions

Capabilities are engineered/generated taking into consideration various dimensions that straddle the corporate functional portfolios.

Every organization has a different but similar set of dimensions. An example set (based upon the Canadian Department of National Defense) could include personnel, research & development, infrastructure/facilities, concepts/processes, information management, and material. Whatever dimensions are selected, they should be well explained and understood.

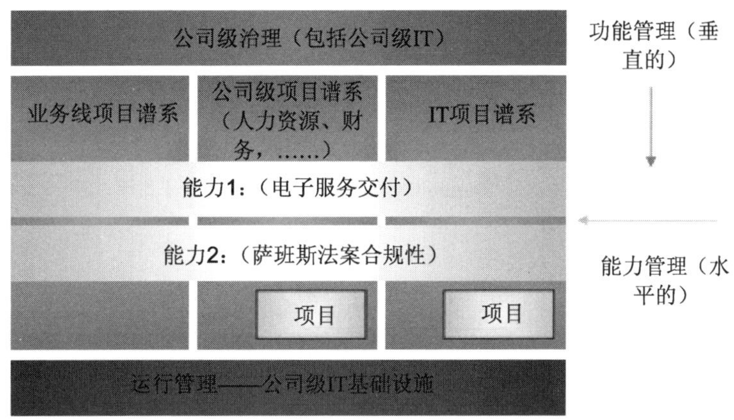

图 32-1　基于能力的规划的概念

能力同样可以是垂直的，并可在业务组织结构的背景环境下被处理。事实上，能力需求经常会驱动组织设计，但在业务转型过程的组织内，该组织可能追踪能力需要。

垂直能力更容易由 Enterprise Architecture 功能处理和支持，但当服务在 ENTERPRISE 层级被合理化并且业务线接收其不直接控制（业务线通过在初步规划中所创建并在阶段 G“实施治理”中所使用的架构委员会中的 IT 治理来提供间接控制）的共享服务时，这些垂直能力仍具有挑战性。

为了使基于能力的规划取得成功，必须在维度和增量方面如以下两节说明的那样对其进行管理。

32.3.1　能力维度

能力是通过考虑跨越公司级功能项目谱系的各种不同维度设计/产生的。

每个组织具有不同但相似的维度集。一个示例集（基于加拿大国防部）可包括人员、研究与开发、基础设施/设备、概念/流程、信息管理和资料。无论选择哪些维度，它们应被很好地说明与理解。

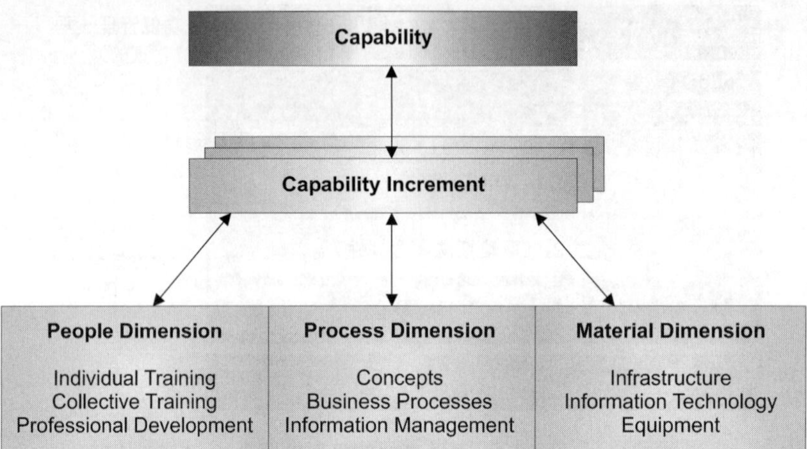

Figure 32-2 Capability Increments and Dimensions

32.3.2 Capability Increments

A capability will take an extended time to deliver (specifics will be a function of the organization and industry vertical) and will normally involve many projects delivering numerous increments. In addition, the capability needs to provide real business value to stakeholders as soon as possible and maintain momentum to achieve the Target Architecture as well as the associated executive support and corporate funding. Therefore, it is useful to break the capability into capability increments that deliver discrete, visible, and quantifiable outcomes as well as providing the focus for Transition Architectures and the deliverables from numerous inter-dependent projects. These outcomes are the Critical Success Factors (CSFs) for continued capability support.

Communicating the potentially complex incremental evolution of a capability to the stakeholder community is essential to establish buy-in at the start and to maintain their buy-in during the transition. The Capability Increment "Radar" diagram (see Figure 32-3) is a proven approach to describing how a capability will evolve over time. The architect selects the aspects of capability that are important to the stakeholder community as lines radiating from the center. Against each line, the architect draws points that represent significant "capability points" ("lower" capability points nearest the center; "higher" capability points farthest from the center). With these "markers" in place the architect can, by joining up the capability points into a closed loop, demonstrate in a simple form how each "capability increment" will extend on the previous increment. This, of course, requires that each capability point is formally defined and "labeled" ina way that is meaningful to the stakeholders. In the diagram below, we have depicted Capability Increment 0 as the starting capability.

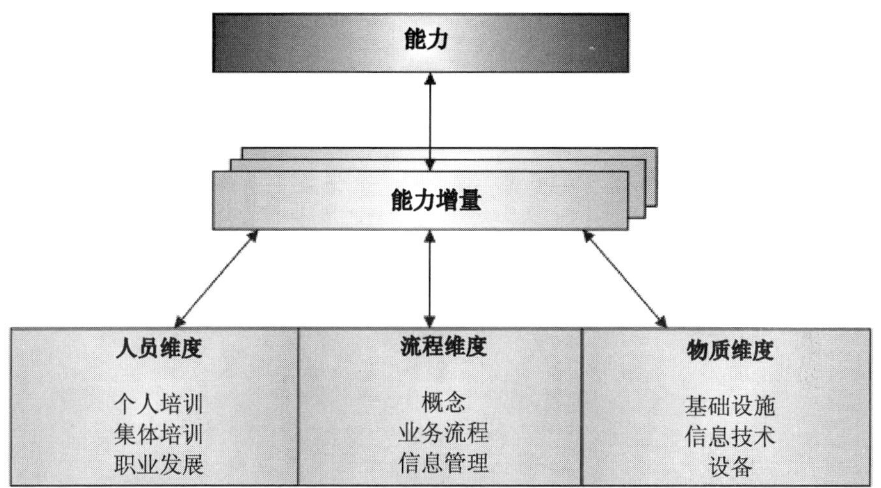

图 32-2　能力增量和维度

32.3.2　能力增量

能力会花费更长的时间来交付（细节会是垂直组织和行业的功能），并通常会涉及交付大量增量的许多项目。此外，能力需要尽快向利益攸关者提供实际的业务价值，保持达成目标架构以及相关联的执行支持和公司级资金的动力。因此，将能力分解成用于交付离散的、可见的、可量化成果的能力增量，并为大量相互依赖的项目中的过渡架构和交付物提供聚焦点十分有用。这些成果是持续能力支持的关键成功因素（CSF）。

向利益攸关者群体传达潜在的复杂能力增量演进，这对在一开始建立认同并在过渡期间维护其认同而言是至关重要的。能力增量“雷达”图（见图 32-3）是一种描述能力如何随时间演进的已被验证的途径。架构师选择出对利益攸关者群体而言非常重要的能力方面作为从中心辐射出来的直线。架构师根据每条直线画出代表重要的“能力点”的点（“低”能力点离中心最近；“高”能力点离中心最远）。架构师可根据这些适当“标记”，将能力点连成一个闭环，以简单形式证明每个“能力增量”是如何在以往增量基础上扩大的。当然，这要求以一种对利益攸关者有意义的方式正式定义及“标记”每个能力点。在下面的图中，我们将能力增量 0 描绘成起始能力。

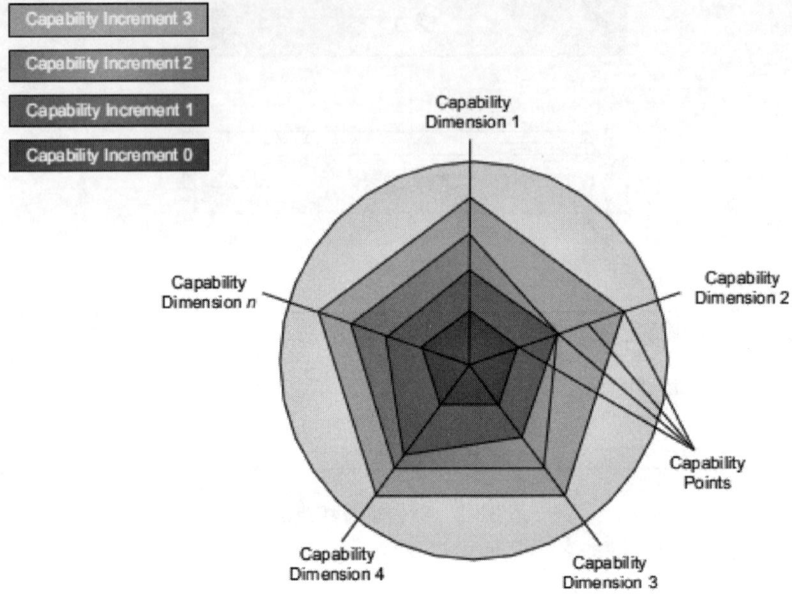

Figure 32-3 Capability Increment "Radar"

32.4 Capabilities in an Enterprise Architecture Context

The capabilities are directly derived from the corporate strategic plan by the corporate strategic planners that are and/or include the enterprise architects and satisfy the enterprise goals, objectives, and strategies. Most organizations will also have an annual business plan that describes how the organization intends to proceed over the next fiscal period in order to meet the enterprise strategic goals.

Figure 32-4 illustrates the crucial relationships between capability-based planning, enterprise architecture, and portfolio/project management. On the left hand side, capability management is aligned with enterprise architecture. The key is that all of the architectures will be expressed in terms of business outcomes and value rather than in IT terms (e.g., establishment of a server farm), thereby ensuring IT alignment with the business.

The intent is that the corporate strategic direction drives the Architecture Vision in Phase A, as well as the corporate organization which will be the basis for the creation of portfolios.

Specific capabilities targeted for completion will be the focus of the Architecture Definition (Phases B, C, and D) and, based upon the identified work packages, Phase E projects will be conceived.

The capability increments will be the drivers for the Transition Architectures (Phase E) that will structure the project increments. The actual delivery will be co-ordinated through the Implementation and Migration Plans (Phase F).

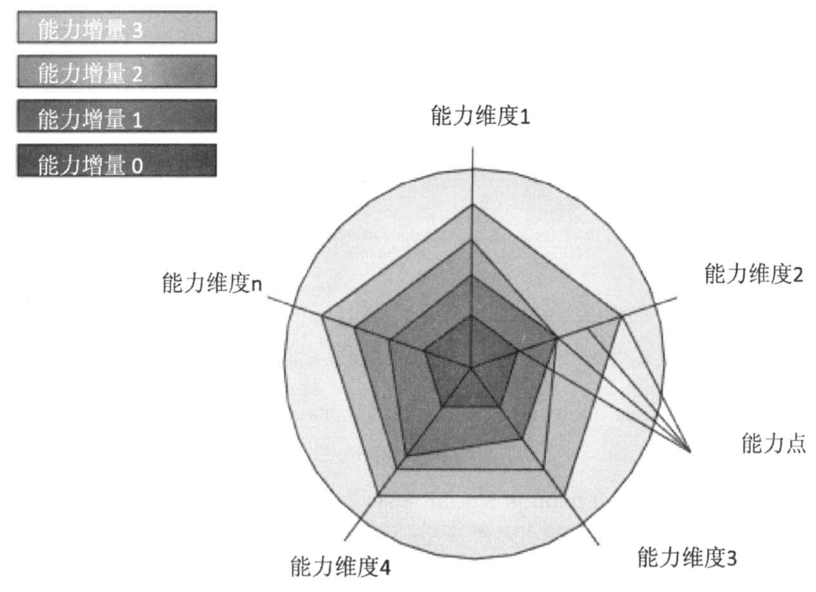

图 32-3　能力增量“雷达”图

32.4　Enterprise Architecture 背景环境下的能力

这种能力直接来源于公司级战略计划人员（或包括 ENTERPRISE 架构师）制定的公司级战略计划，并满足 ENTERPRISE 目标、目的和战略。大部分组织还拥有年度业务计划，该计划描述组织打算在下一个财务期间如何进展，以满足 ENTERPRISE 战略目标。

图 32-4 阐明基于能力的规划、Enterprise Architecture 与项目谱系/项目管理之间的决定性关系。在左侧，能力管理与 Enterprise Architecture 保持一致。关键在于所有的架构将用业务成果和价值来表示，而不是用 IT 术语（例如服务器集群的建立），从而确保 IT 与业务的对准。

意图在于，公司级战略方向驱动阶段 A 中的架构愿景，以及即将成为创建项目谱系基础的公司级组织。

目标在于完成的特定能力将成为架构定义（阶段 B、C 和 D）的聚焦点，且基于已识别的工作包构思阶段 E 中的项目。

能力增量将成为项目增量结构化的过渡架构（阶段 E）的驱动因素。实际交付将通过实施情况和迁移计划（阶段 F）来协调。

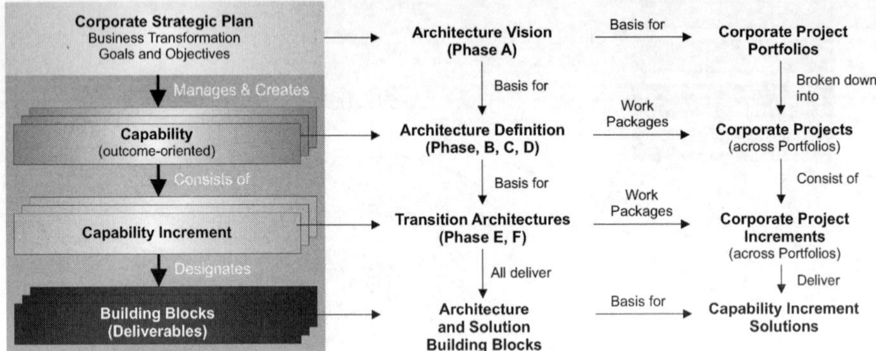

Figure 32-4 Relationship Between Capabilities, Enterprise Architecture, and Projects

Capability managers will perform similar tasks to that of the portfolio managers, but across the portfolios aligning the projects and project increments to deliver continuous business value. Whereas the portfolio managers will be concerned with the co-ordination of their projects to optimally design, build, and deliver the Solution Building Blocks (SBBs). Ideally, capability managers will also manage funding that can use the Transition Architectures as gates. Co-ordination between the portfolio and capability managers will have to be provided at the corporate level.

32.5 Summary

Capability-based planning is a versatile business planning paradigm that is very useful from an enterprise architecture perspective. It assists in aligning IT with the business and helps focus IT architects on the continuous creation of business value.

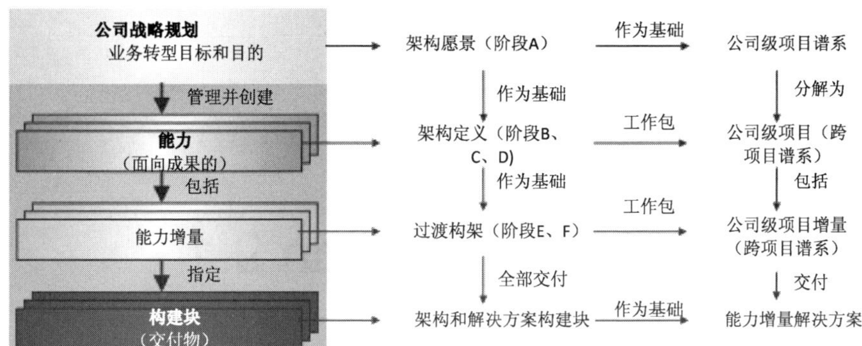

图 32-4　能力、Enterprise Architecture 和项目之间的关系

能力管理者会执行与项目谱系管理者相似的任务，但将跨越项目谱系使项目与项目增量对准，以交付连续的业务价值。而项目谱系管理者将关注其项目的协作，以最佳地设计、构建并交付解决方案构建块（SBB）。理想情况下，能力管理者也会管理可将过渡架构用作传送作用的资金。必须在公司层级上在项目谱系管理者和能力管理者之间提供协调。

32.5　概要总结

从 Enterprise Architecture 的关注层级来看，基于能力的规划是一个十分有用的多用途业务规划范例。它有助于使 IT 与业务对准，并帮助 IT 架构师聚焦于业务价值的连续创造。

TOGAF Version 9.1

Part IV Architecture Content Framework

The Open Group

TOGAF 9.1 版本

第四部分　架构内容框架

The Open Group

Chapter 33
Introduction

33.1 Overview

Architects executing the Architecture Development Method (ADM) will produce a number of outputs as a result of their efforts, such as process flows, architectural requirements, project plans, project compliance assessments, etc. The content framework provides a structural model for architectural content that allows the major work products that an architect creates to be consistently defined, structured, and presented.

The content framework provided here is intended to allow TOGAF to be used as a stand-alone framework for architecture within an enterprise. However, other content frameworks exist (such as the Zachman Framework) and it is anticipated that some enterprises may opt to use an external framework in conjunction with TOGAF. In these cases, the content framework provides a useful reference and starting point for TOGAF content to be mapped to other frameworks.

The Architecture Content Framework uses the following three categories to describe the type of architectural work product within the context of use:

- A **deliverable** is a work product that is contractually specified and in turn formally reviewed, agreed, and signed off by the stakeholders. Deliverables represent the output of projects and those deliverables that are in documentation form will typically be archived at completion of a project, or transitioned into an Architecture Repository as a reference model, standard, or snap shot of the Architecture Landscape at a point in time.
- An **artifact** is an architectural work product that describes an aspect of the architecture. Artifacts are generally classified as catalogs (lists of things), matrices (showing relationships between things), and diagrams (pictures of things). Examples include a requirements catalog, business interaction matrix, and a use-case diagram. An architectural deliverable may contain many artifacts and artifacts will form the content of the Architecture Repository.
- A **building block** represents a (potentially re-usable) component of business, IT, or architectural capability that can be combined with other building blocks to deliver architectures and solutions.

Building blocks can be defined at various levels of detail, depending on what stage of architecture development has been reached. For instance, at an early stage, a building block can simply consist of a name or an outline description. Later on, a building block may be decomposed into multiple supporting building blocks and may be accompanied by a full specification. Building blocks can relate to "architectures" or "solutions".

— Architecture Building Blocks (ABBs) typically describe required capability and shape the specification of Solution Building Blocks (SBBs). For example, a customer services capability may be required within an enterprise, supported by many SBBs, such as processes, data, and application software.

第 33 章
简　介

33.1　概述

执行架构开发方法（ADM）的架构师的工作结果会产生大量输出，例如过程流、架构需求、项目计划、项目合规性评估等。内容框架为架构内容提供一种结构化模型，从而使架构师创建的主要工作产物可被一致地定义、结构化和表达。

本文提供的内容框架，旨在 ENTERPRISE 内将 TOGAF 用作一个独立的架构框架。然而，存在其他的内容框架（如 Zachman 框架），预计有些 ENTERPRISE 可能会选择把其他的框架与 TOGAF 联合起来使用。在这些情况下，内容框架提供一个有用的参考和出发点，将 TOGAF 内容映射到其他框架。

架构内容框架使用下列三个类别描述在使用的背景环境之中架构工作产物的类型：

- **交付物**：是以契约方式规定并依次由利益攸关者正式审视、同意并签发的工作产物。交付物代表项目的输出，那些文档形式的交付物通常在项目完成时存档，或过渡到架构库中作为参考模型、标准或作为架构全景在某个时点的“快照”。
- **制品**：是描述架构某一方面的架构工作产物。制品通常可分为目录集（事物的列表）、矩阵（表明事物之间的关系）和图（事物的图片）。示例包括需求目录集、业务交互矩阵和用例图。一个架构交付物可包含多个制品，且制品将构成架构库的内容。
- **构建块**代表业务能力、IT 能力或架构能力的一个（潜在可复用的）组件，可与其他构建块结合以交付架构和解决方案。

构建块可以在不同细节层级上被定义，这取决于架构开发已达到的阶段。例如，在初期阶段，构建块可以只包括名称或概述。随后，构建块可分解成多个支持构建块，并可随附一份完整的规范。构建块可以与“架构”或“解决方案”相关联。

— 架构构建块（ABB）通常描述所需的能力并塑造解决方案构建块（SBB）规范。例如，ENTERPRISE 内可能需要客户服务能力，它由多个 SBB 支持，如流程、数据和应用软件。

— Solution Building Blocks (SBBs) represent components that will be used to implement the required capability. For example, a network is a building block that can be described through complementary artifacts and then put to use to realize solutions for the enterprise.

The relationships between deliverables, artifacts, and building blocks are shown in Figure 33-1.

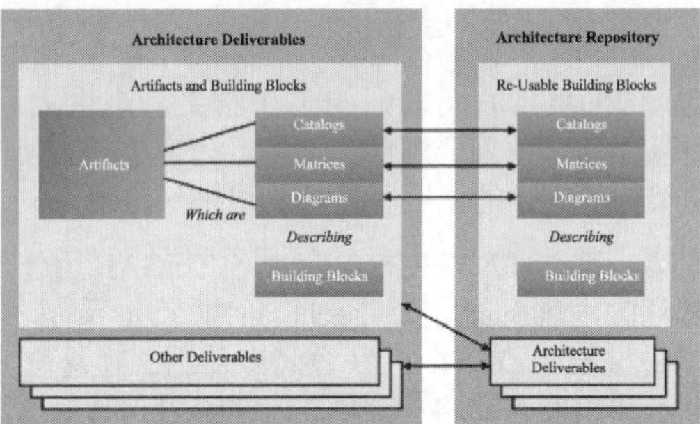

Figure 33-1 Relationships between Deliverables, Artifacts, and Building Blocks

For example, an Architecture Definition Document is a deliverable that documents an architecture description. This document will contain a number of complementary artifacts that are views of the building blocks relevant to the architecture. For example, a process flow diagram (an artifact) may be created to describe the target call handling process (a building block). This artifact may also describe other building blocks, such as the actors involved in the process (e.g.,a Customer Services Representative). An example of the relationships between deliverables, artifacts, and building blocks is illustrated in Figure 33-2.

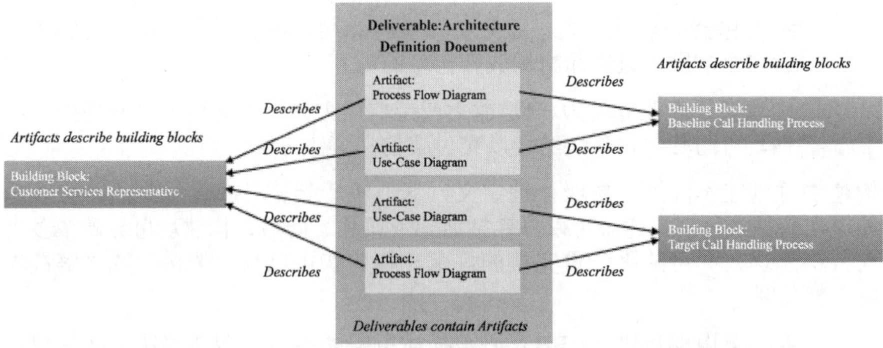

Figure 33-2 Example — Architecture Definition Document

— 解决方案构建块（SBB）代表用于实现所需能力的组件。例如，网络是一个能够通过互补的制品来描述的构建块，并可用于实现 ENTERPRISE 的解决方案。

交付物、制品和构建块之间的关系如图 33-1 所示。

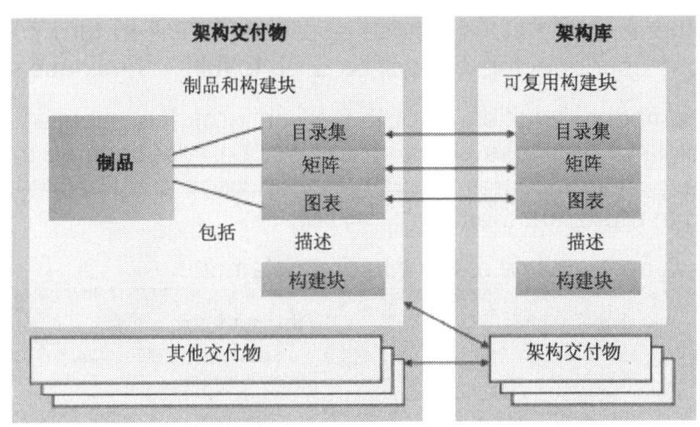

图 33-1　交付物、制品和构建块之间的关系

例如，架构定义文件是一种将架构描述文件化的交付物。该文件包含多个互补的制品，它们是与架构相关的构建块的视图。例如，可创建一个过程流图（制品）以描述目标调用处理流程（构建块）。该制品还可描述其他构建块，如参与该流程的施动者（例如，客户服务代表）。图 33-2 阐明交付物、制品和构建块之间的关系示例。

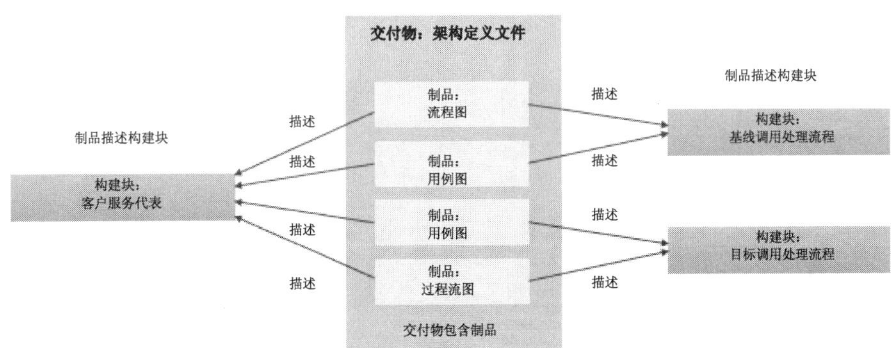

图 33-2　示例——架构定义文件

33.2 Content Metamodel

The content metamodel provides a definition of all the types of building blocks that may exist within an architecture, showing how these building blocks can be described and related to one another. For example, when creating an architecture, an architect will identify applications, "data entities" held within applications, and technologies that implement those applications. These applications will in turn support particular groups of business user or actor, and will be used to fulfil "business services".

The content metamodel identifies all of these concerns (i.e., application, data entity, technology, actor, and business service), shows the relationships that are possible between them (e.g., actors consume business services), and finally identifies artifacts that can be used to represent them.

Figure 33-3 shows an overview of the content metamodel.

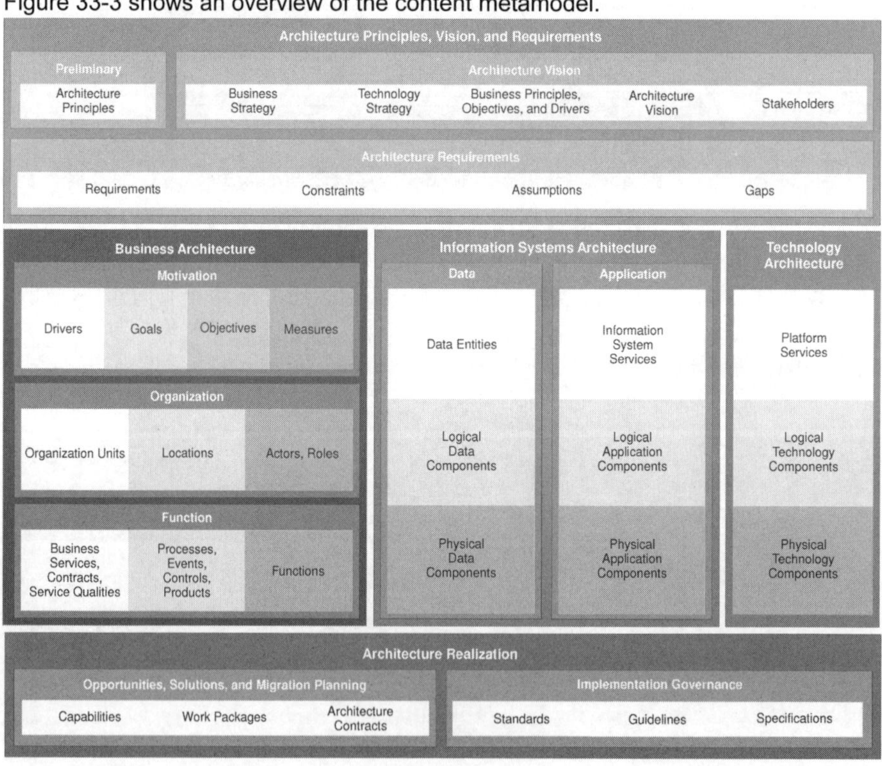

Figure 33-3 Content Metamodel Overview

33.2 内容元模型

内容元模型提供对架构中可能存在的所有构建块类型的定义，表明可以如何描述这些构建块以及彼此之间如何相关联。例如，在创建架构时，架构师将识别应用、应用内保留的“数据实体”和实现这些应用的技术。这些应用反过来支持特定群组的业务用户或施动者，并将用于履行“业务服务”。

内容元模型识别所有这些关注点（即应用、数据实体、技术、施动者和业务服务），表明它们之间可能的关系（如施动者使用业务服务），并最终识别可用来代表它们的制品。

图 33-3 表明内容元模型的概述。

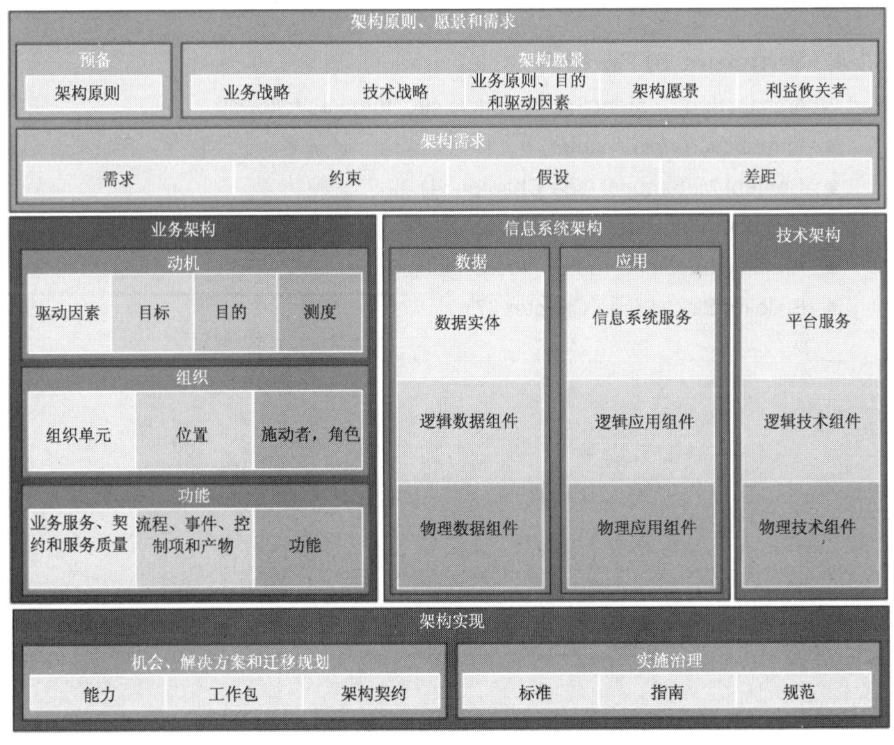

图 33-3 内容元模型概述

33.3 Content Framework and the TOGAF ADM

The TOGAF ADM describes the process of moving from a baseline state of the enterprise to a target state of the enterprise. The ADM will address a business need through a process of visioning, architecture definition, transformation planning, and architecture governance. At each stage in this process, the ADM requires information as inputs and will create outputs as a result of executing a number of steps. The content framework provides an underlying structure for the ADM that defines inputs and outputs in more detail and puts each deliverable into the context of the holistic architecture view of the enterprise.

The content framework should therefore be used as a companion to the ADM. The ADM describes what needs to be done to create an architecture and the content framework describes what the architecture should look like once it is done.

33.4 Structure of Part IV

Part IV: Architecture Content Framework is structured as follows:

- Introduction (this chapter)
- Content Metamodel (see Chapter 34)
- Architectural Artifacts (see Chapter 35)
- Architecture Deliverables (see Chapter 36)
- Building Blocks (see Chapter 37)

33.3 内容框架和 TOGAF ADM

TOGAF ADM 描述从 ENTERPRISE 基线状态到目标状态的迁移流程。ADM 通过建立愿景、架构定义、转型规划和架构治理来应对业务需要。在此流程的每个阶段，ADM 要求将信息作为输入，并经过执行多个步骤来创建输出。内容框架为 ADM 提供底层结构，更详细地定义输入和输出并将每个交付物放入 ENTERPRISE 的整体架构视图的背景环境中。

因此，内容框架应该被用作 ADM 的伴随物。ADM 描述创建架构需要做什么，内容框架描述架构一旦完成应该是什么样子。

33.4 第四部分的结构

第四部分：架构内容框架的结构如下：

- 简介（本章）
- 内容元模型（见第 34 章）
- 架构制品（见第 35 章）
- 架构交付物（见第 36 章）
- 构建块（见第 37 章）

Chapter 34
Content Metamodel

34.1 Overview

The TOGAF Architecture Development Method (ADM) provides a process lifecycle to create and manage architectures within an enterprise. At each phase within the ADM, a discussion of inputs, outputs, and steps describes a number of architectural work products or artifacts, such as process and application. The content metamodel provided here defines a formal structure for these terms to ensure consistency within the ADM and also to provide guidance for organizations that wish to implement their architecture within an architecture tool.

34.2 Content Metamodel Vision and Concepts

This section provides an overview of the objectives of the content metamodel, the concepts that support the metamodel, and an overview of the metamodel itself. Subsequent sections then go on to discuss each area of the metamodel in more detail. Contents of this section are as follows:

- Core content metamodel concepts (see Section 34.2.1) identifies the key concepts within the core content metamodel, including:
  - Core and extension content
  - Formal and informal modeling
  - Core metamodel entities
  - Catalog, matrix, and diagram concept
- Overview of the TOGAF content metamodel (see Section 34.2.2) provides a high-level overview of the content of the metamodel.

34.2.1 Core Content Metamodel Concepts

A TOGAF architecture is based on defining a number of architectural building blocks within architecture catalogs, specifying the relationships between those building blocks in architecture matrices, and then presenting communication diagrams that show in a precise and concise way what the architecture is.

This section introduces the core concepts that make up the TOGAF content metamodel, through the following subsections:

第 34 章
内容元模型

34.1 概述

TOGAF 架构开发方法（ADM）提供在 ENTERPRISE 内创建和管理架构的流程生命周期。在 ADM 内各个阶段，对输入、输出和步骤的探讨描述了许多架构工作产物或制品，如流程和应用。此处提供的内容元模型为这些术语定义了正式的结构，以确保 ADM 内的一致性，也为希望在架构工具内实施其架构的组织提供指南。

34.2 内容元模型愿景和概念

本节提供内容元模型目标的概述、支持元模型的概念以及元模型本身的概述。然后，后续章节将更详细地继续论述元模型的各个部分。本节内容如下：

- 核心内容元模型概念（见 34.2.1 节）识别核心内容元模型内的关键概念，包括：
  - 核心和扩展内容
  - 正式和非正式的建模
  - 核心元模型实体
  - 目录集、矩阵和图概念
- TOGAF 内容元模型的概述（见 34.2.2 节）提供元模型内容的高层级概述。

34.2.1 核心内容元模型概念

TOGAF 架构基于在架构目录集内定义多个架构构建块，指定架构矩阵内那些构建块之间的关系，然后表达通信图，以一种精确、简明的方式说明架构是什么。

本节通过以下小节介绍了构成 TOGAF 内容元模型的核心概念。

- **Core and Extension Content** provides an introduction to the way in which TOGAF employs a basic core metamodel and then applies a number of extension modules to address specific architectural issues in more detail.
- **Core Metamodel Entities** introduces the core TOGAF metamodel entities, showing the purpose of each entity and the key relationships that support architectural traceability.
- **Catalog, Matrix, and Diagram Concept** describes the concept of catalogs, matrices, and diagrams.

Core and Extension Content

The role of TOGAF is to provide an open standard for architecture that is applicable in many scenarios and situations. In order to meet this vision, it is necessary to provide a fully featured enterprise architecture metamodel for content and also to provide the ability to avoid carrying out unnecessary activities by supporting tailoring.

The metamodel must provide a basic model with the minimum feature set and then support the inclusion of optional extensions during engagement tailoring.

The core TOGAF content metamodel and its extensions are illustrated in Figure 34-1.

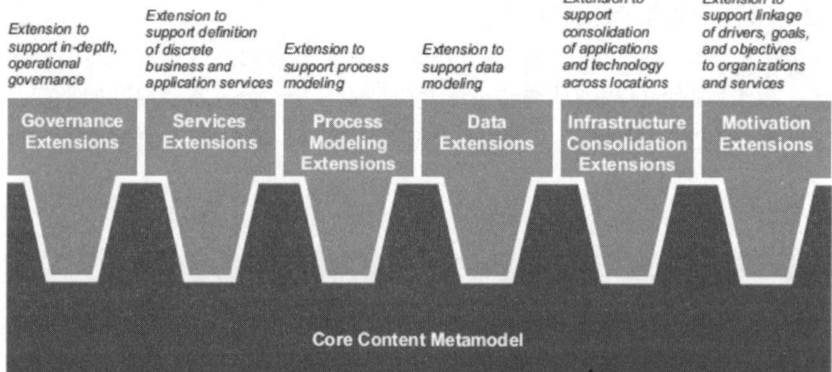

Figure 34-1 TOGAF Content Metamodel and its Extensions

The core metamodel provides a minimum set of architectural content to support traceability across artifacts. Additional metamodel concepts to support more specific or more in-depth modeling are contained within a group of extensions that logically cluster extension catalogs, matrices, and diagrams, allowing focus in areas of specific interest and focus.

All extension modules are optional and should be selected during the Preliminary Phase of the architecture development to meet the needs of the organization. Additionally, the extension groupings described by the content metamodel are only a suggestion and further tailoring may be carried out to suit the specific needs at the discretion of the architects.

This core and extension concept is intended as a move towards supporting formal method extension approaches within TOGAF, such as the method plug-in concept found within the Software Process Engineering Metamodel (SPEM) developed by the Object Management Group (OMG).[4]

4. Refer to www.omg.org/spec/SPEM.

核心和扩展内容对 TOGAF 使用基本核心元模型的方式提供简介，然后应用多个扩展模块更详细地处理特定的架构问题。

- **核心元模型实体**介绍了核心 TOGAF 元模型实体，以表明每个实体的目的和支持架构可追溯性的关键关系。
- **目录集、矩阵和图概念**描述目录集、矩阵和图的概念。

核心和扩展内容

TOGAF 的作用是为适用于多种场景和情况的架构提供开放标准。为实现这一愿景，有必要提供一个功能全面的 Enterprise Architecture 内容元模型，并通过支持剪裁来提供避免执行不必要的活动的能力。

元模型必须提供一个具有最小特征集的基本模型，并在剪裁工作期间支持可选扩展项的加入。

图 34-1 阐明核心 TOGAF 内容元模型及其扩展。

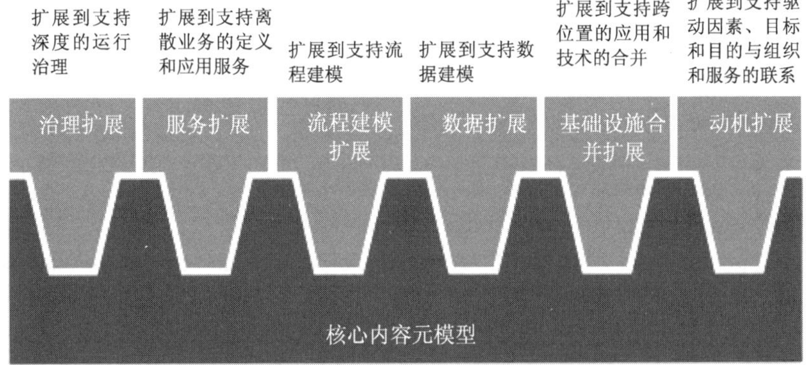

图 34-1　TOGAF 内容元模型及其扩展

核心元模型提供架构内容的最小集合，支持跨制品的可追溯性。其他元模型概念包含在一个扩展群组内，以支持更具体或更深层的建模，这些扩展在逻辑上聚集了扩展目录集、矩阵和图，从而能聚焦于特定兴趣和聚焦点的领域。

所有扩展模块都是可选的，且应在架构开发的预备阶段被选定，以满足组织的需要。此外，内容元模型所描述的扩展分组只是一个建议，可随架构师的意见进行进一步的剪裁以适应特定需要。

本核心和扩展概念旨在趋于支持 TOGAF 内正式方法的扩展途径，例如由对象管理组（OMG）开发的软件流程工程元模型（SPEM）内建立的插件概念方法。[4]

4. 见 www.omg.org/spec/SPEM。

Core Metamodel Entities

The content metamodel uses the terminology discussed within the TOGAF ADM as the basis for a formal metamodel. The following core terms are used:

- **Actor**: A person, organization, or system that is outside the consideration of the architecture model, but interacts with it.
- **Application Component**: An encapsulation of application functionality that is aligned to implementation structuring.
- **Business Service**: Supports business capabilities through an explicitly defined interface and is explicitly governed by an organization.
- **Data Entity**: An encapsulation of data that is recognized by a business domain expert as a discrete concept. Data entities can be tied to applications, repositories, and services and may be structured according to implementation considerations.
- **Function**: Delivers business capabilities closely aligned to an organization, but not explicitly governed by the organization.
- **Information System Service**: The automated elements of a business service. An information system service may deliver or support part or all of one or more business services.
- **Organization Unit**: A self-contained unit of resources with goals, objectives, and measures. Organization units may include external parties and business partner organizations.
- **Platform Service**: A technical capability required to provide enabling infrastructure that supports the delivery of applications.
- **Role**: An actor assumes a role to perform a task.
- **Technology Component**: An encapsulation of technology infrastructure that represents a class of technology product or specific technology product.

A more in-depth definition of terms used within the content metamodel can be found in Part I, Chapter 3.

Some of the key relationship concepts related to the core metamodel entities are described below:

- **Process should normally be used to describe flow.**

  A process is a flow of interactions between functions and services and cannot be physically deployed. All processes should describe the flow of execution for a function and therefore the deployment of a process is through the function it supports; i.e., an application implements a function that has a process, not an application implements a process.

- **Function describes units of business capability at all levels of granularity.**

  The term "function" is used to describe a unit of business capability at all levels of granularity, encapsulating terms such as value chain, process area, capability, business function, etc. Any bounded unit of business function should be described as a function.

- **Business services support organizational objectives and are defined at a level of granularity consistent with the level of governance needed.**

核心元模型实体

内容元模型使用 TOGAF ADM 内论述的术语用作正式元模型的基础。使用下列核心术语：

- **施动者**：架构模型考量因素以外、但与架构模型进行交互的个人、组织或系统。
- **应用组件**：与实施结构化一致的应用功能的封装。
- **业务服务**：通过明确定义的界面支持各种业务能力，并由组织明确管控。
- **数据实体**：一种数据封装，业务领域专家将之视为一种独立完整的概念。可以将数据实体与应用、存储库以及服务进行绑定，并可按照实施考虑对其进行结构化处理。
- **功能**：交付与一个组织紧密结合的业务能力，但不由该组织明确管控。
- **信息系统服务**：业务服务的自动化元素。一个信息系统服务可以交付或支持一种或多种业务服务的部分或全部服务。
- **组织单元**：拥有目标、目的和测度的资源自主单元。组织单元可包括外部各方和业务伙伴组织。
- **平台服务**：一种提供能够支持应用交付的基础设施所需的技术能力。
- **角色**：施动者担任执行任务的角色。
- **技术组件**：一种技术基础设施的封装，代表某类技术产品或某个特定的技术产品。

内容元模型内使用的术语的更深入定义可在第一部分第 3 章找到。

与核心元模型实体相关的一些关键关系概念描述如下：

- **流程应通常用于描述流。**

  一个流程是功能和服务之间的交互流且不能被物理部署。所有流程应描述执行一个功能的流，因此流程的部署是通过它所支持的功能完成的；即，一个应用实施具有一个流程的一个功能，而不是应用实施一个流程。

- **功能描述所有粒度层级的业务能力单元。**

  术语“功能”用于描述在所有粒度层级上的业务能力的一个单元，封装诸如价值链、流程领域、能力和业务功能等术语。业务功能的任何有界单元都应被描述为一个功能。

- **业务服务支持组织的目标，且在符合所需治理层级的粒度层级被定义。**

A business service operates as a boundary for one or more functions. The granularity of business services is dependent on the focus and emphasis of the business (as reflected by its drivers, goals, and objectives). A service in Service Oriented Architecture (SOA) terminology (i.e., a deployable unit of application functionality) is actually much closer to an application service, application component, or technology component, which may implement or support a business service.

- **Business services are deployed onto application components.**

  Business services may be realized by business activity that does not relate to IT, or may be supported by IT. Business services that are supported by IT are deployed onto application components. Application components can be hierarchically decomposed and may support one or more business services. It is possible for a business service to be supported by multiple application components, but this is problematic from a governance standpoint and is symptomatic of business services that are too coarse-grained, or application components that are too fine-grained.

- **Application components are deployed onto technology components.**

  An application component is implemented by a suite of technology components. For example, an application, such as "HR System" would typically be implemented on several technology components, including hardware, application server software, and application services.

Figure 34-2 illustrates the core entities and their relationships.

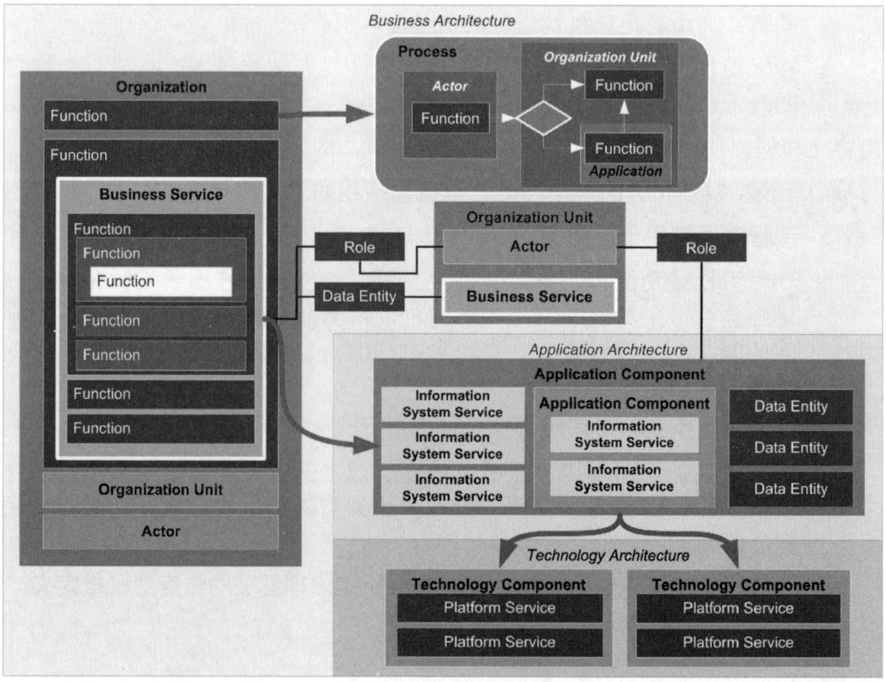

Figure 34-2 Core Entities and their Relationships

业务服务作为一个或多个功能的一个边界进行运作。业务服务的颗粒度取决于业务的聚焦点和重点（由其驱动因素、目标和目的来反映）。面向服务的架构（SOA）术语中的服务（即，应用功能性的可部署单元）实际上更接近于可实施或支持业务服务的应用服务、应用组件或技术组件。

- **将业务服务部署到应用组件**。

  业务服务可通过与 IT 不相关的业务活动实现，或者可由 IT 支持。由 IT 支持的业务服务被部署到应用组件。应用组件可分层级分解，并且可支持一个或多个业务服务。一个业务服务可能由多个应用组件支持，但从管控角度来看这是有问题的，这可能是因为业务服务颗粒度太粗，或是应用组件颗粒度太细。

- **将应用组件部署到技术组件**。

  一个应用组件通过一套技术组件实施。例如，典型情况下，诸如“HR 系统”应用组件将在多个技术组件上实施，包括硬件、应用服务软件和应用服务。

图 34-2 阐明核心实体及其关系。

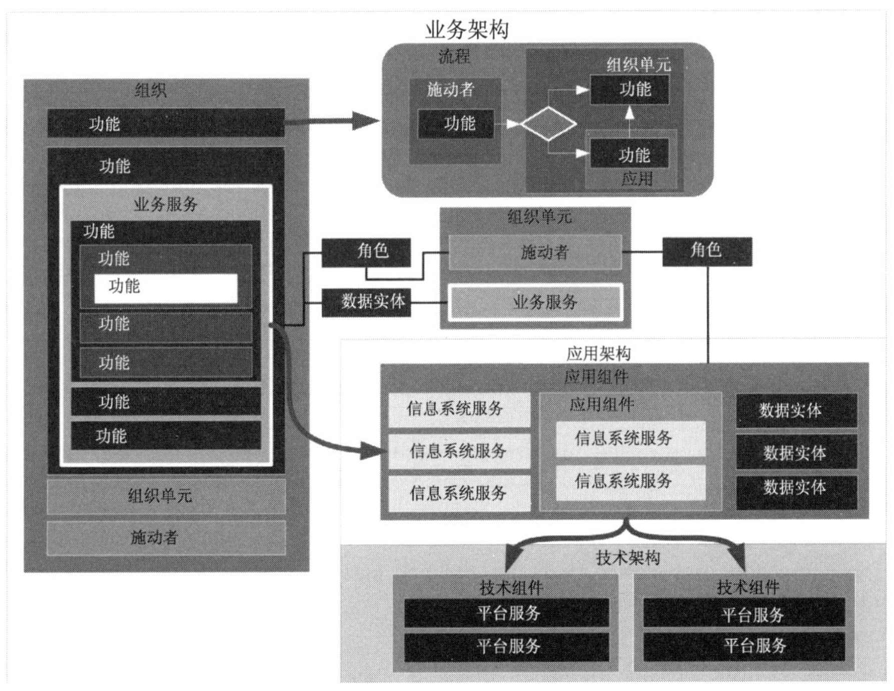

图 34-2 核心实体及其关系

Catalog, Matrix, and Diagram Concept

The content metamodel is used as a technique to structure architectural information in an ordered way so that it can be processed to meet the stakeholder needs. The majority of architecture stakeholders do not actually need to know what the architecture metamodel is and are only concerned with specific issues, such as "what functionality does this application support?", "which processes will be impacted by this project?", etc. In order to meet the needs of these stakeholders, the TOGAF concepts of building blocks, catalogs, matrices, and diagrams are used.

Building blocks are entities of a particular type within the metamodel (for example, a business service called "Purchase Order"). Building blocks carry metadata according to the metamodel, which supports query and analysis. For example, business services have a metadata attribute for owner, which allows a stakeholder to query all business services owned by a particular organization. Building blocks may also include dependent or contained entities as appropriate to the context of the architecture (for example, a business service called "Purchase Order" may implicitly include a number of processes, data entities, application components, etc.).

Catalogs are lists of building blocks of a specific type, or of related types, that are used for governance or reference purposes (for example, an organization chart, showing locations and actors). As with building blocks, catalogs carry metadata according to the metamodel, which supports query and analysis.

Matrices are grids that show relationships between two or more model entities. Matrices are used to represent relationships that are list-based rather than graphical in their usage (for example, a CRUD matrix showing which applications Create, Read, Update, and Delete a particular type of data is difficult to represent visually).

Diagrams are renderings of architectural content in a graphical format to allow stakeholders to retrieve the required information. Diagrams can also be used as a technique for graphically populating architecture content or for checking the completeness of information that has been collected. TOGAF defines a set of architecture diagrams to be created (e.g., organization chart). Each of these diagrams may be created several times for an architecture with different style or content coverage to suit stakeholder concerns.

Building blocks, catalogs, matrices, and diagrams are all concepts that are well supported by leading enterprise architecture tools. In environments where tools are used to model the architecture, such tools typically support mechanisms to search, filter, and query the Architecture Repository.

On-demand querying of the Architecture Repository (such as the business service ownership example mentioned above) can be used to generate *ad hoc* catalogs, matrices, and diagrams of the architecture. As this type of query is by nature required to be flexible, it is therefore not restricted or defined within the content metamodel.

The interactions between metamodel, building blocks, diagrams, and stakeholders are shown in Figure 34-3.

目录集、矩阵和图概念

内容元模型被用作一种技术，以有序的方式对架构信息进行结构化，以便处理到能够以满足利益攸关者需要。大多数架构的利益攸关者实际上不需要知道什么是架构元模型，他们只关注某些特定的问题，如“这种应用支持什么功能？”“哪些流程会受该项目的影响？”等。为了满足这些利益攸关者的需要，使用了构建块、目录集、矩阵和图等 TOGAF 概念。

构建块是元模型内特定类型的实体（例如，被称作“采购订单”的业务服务）。构建块按照支持查询和分析的元模型来携带元数据。例如，对于所有者而言，业务服务具有元数据属性，这使得利益攸关者能够查询特定组织所拥有的所有业务服务。构建块还可包括适合架构背景环境的依赖性实体或包含的实体（例如，被称为“采购订单”的业务服务可隐含地包括多个流程、数据实体、应用组件等）。

目录集是特定类型或相关类型的构建块的列表，用于管控或参考的目的（例如，组织图用以表明位置和施动者）。与构建块相同，目录集按照支持查询和分析的元模型携带元数据。

矩阵是表明两个或多个模型实体之间关系的网格。矩阵被用于表示基于列表而不是图形的关系（例如，表明哪些应用创建、读取、更新和删除特定类型数据的 CRUD 矩阵很难可视化地表达出来）。

图是采用图形格式对架构内容的描绘，以使利益攸关者能够检索所需信息。图还可用作以图形式填充架构内容或检查已收集信息的完整性的一种技术。TOGAF 定义一系列要创建的架构图（如组织图）。为适合利益攸关者的关注点，而使一个架构具有不同风格和内容涵盖，这些图的每一个也许要创建多次。

构建块、目录集、矩阵和图是得到由领先的 Enterprise Architecture 工具的良好支持的全部概念。在使用架构工具进行架构建模的环境中，这类工具通常支持用于搜索、过滤和查询架构库的机制。

架构库的按需查询（如上述业务服务所有者示例）可用于生成架构的临时目录集、矩阵和图。由于本质上要求这种类型的查询具有灵活性，因此没有在内容元模型内对其限制或定义。

元模型、构建块、图和利益攸关者之间的交互如图 34-3 所示。

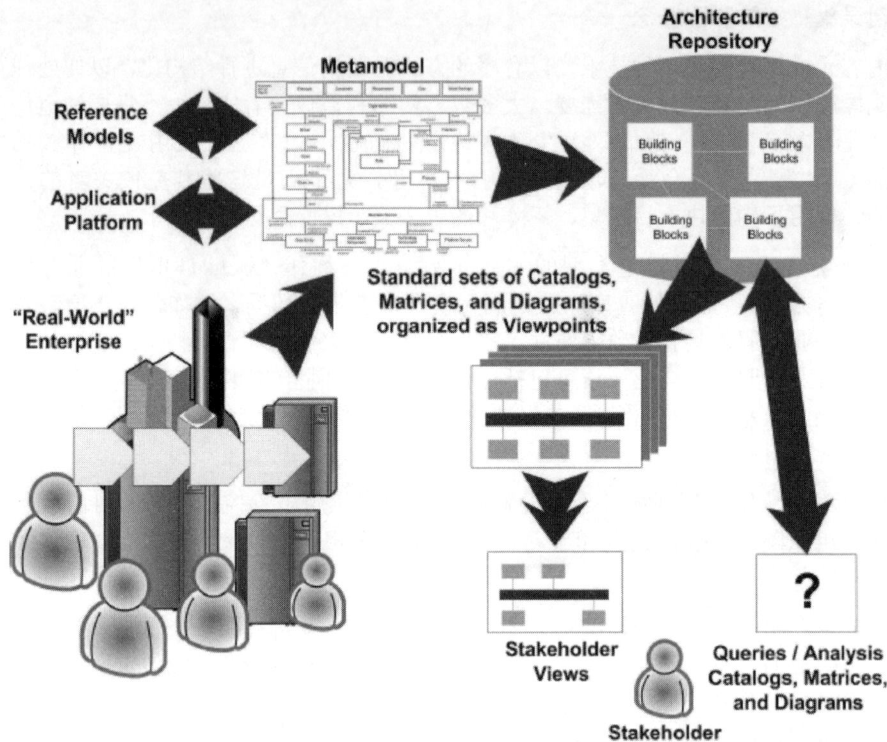

Figure 34-3 Interactions between Metamodel, Building Blocks, Diagrams, and Stakeholders

34.2.2 Overview of the Content Metamodel

The content metamodel defines a set of entities that allow architectural concepts to be captured, stored, filtered, queried, and represented in a way that supports consistency, completeness, and traceability.

At the highest level, the content framework is divided up in line with the TOGAF ADM phases, as shown in Figure 34-4.

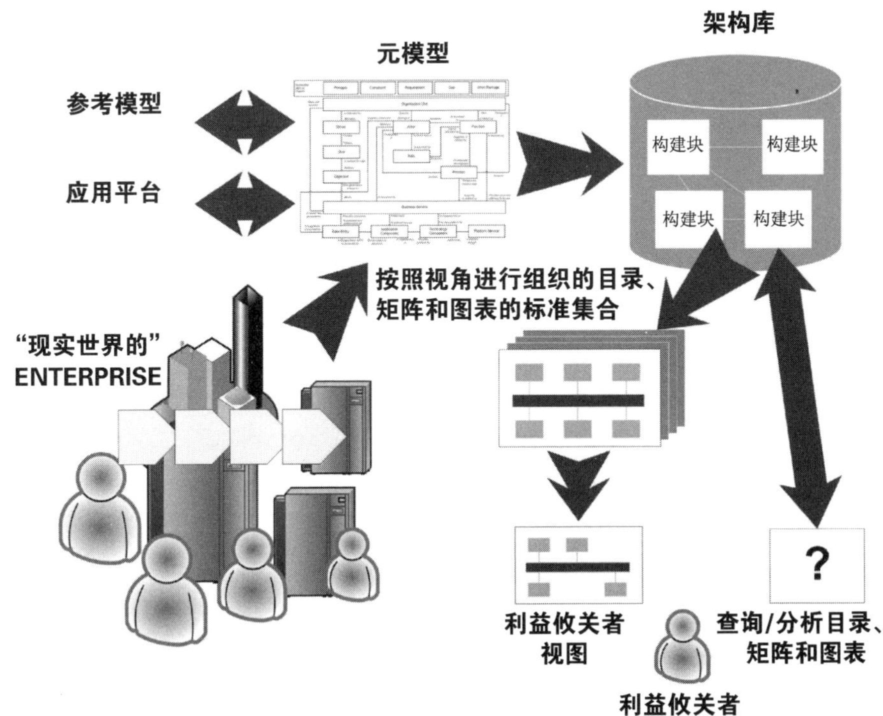

图 34-3　元模型、构建块、图和利益攸关者之间的交互作用

34.2.2　内容元模型的概述

内容元模型定义了一系列实体，这些实体使得能够以支持一致性、完整性和可追溯性的方式获取、存储、过滤、查询和表达架构概念。

在最高层级，按照 TOGAF ADM 阶段划分内容框架，如图 34-4 所示。

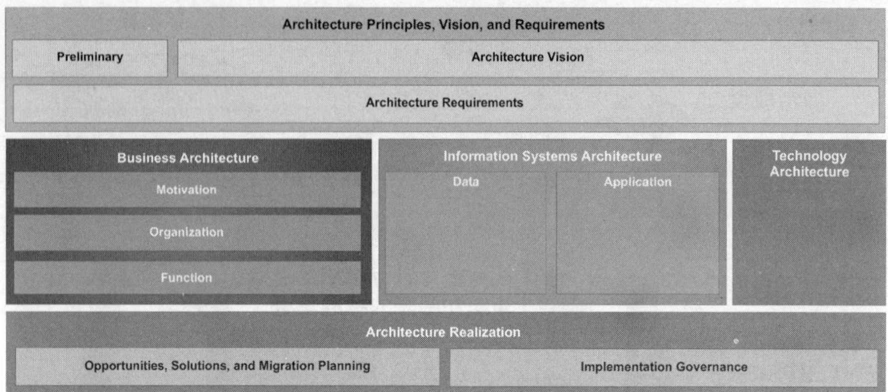

Figure 34-4 Content Framework by ADM Phases

- **Architecture Principles, Vision, and Requirements** artifacts are intended to capture the surrounding context of formal architecture models, including general architecture principles, strategic context that forms input for architecture modeling, and requirements generated from the architecture. The architecture context is typically collected in the Preliminary and Architecture Vision phases.
- **Business Architecture** artifacts capture architectural models of business operation, looking specifically at factors that motivate the enterprise, how the enterprise is organizationally structured, and also what functional capabilities the enterprise has.
- **Information Systems Architecture** artifacts capture architecture models of IT systems, looking at applications and data in line with the TOGAF ADM phases.
- **Technology Architecture** artifacts capture procured technology assets that are used to implement and realize information system solutions.
- **Architecture Realization** artifacts capture change roadmaps showing transition between architecture states and binding statements that are used to steer and govern an implementation of the architecture.

A more detailed representation of the content metamodel is shown in Figure 34-5.

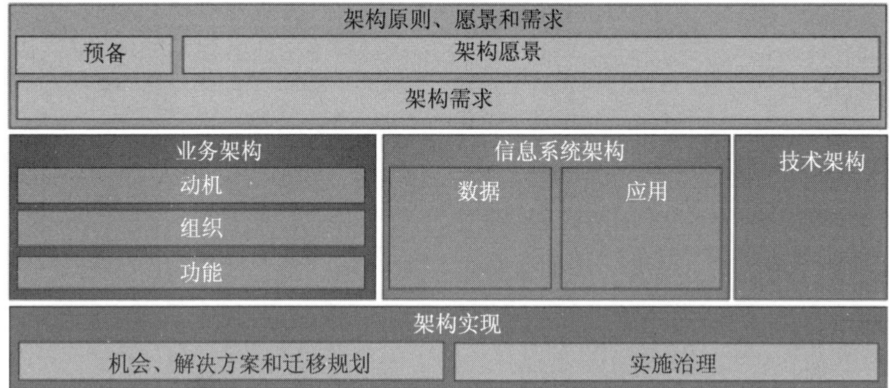

图 34-4　ADM 阶段的内容框架

- **架构原则、愿景和需求**制品旨在获取正式架构模型的周围背景环境，包括一般架构原则、形成架构建模输入的战略背景环境和由架构产生的需求。架构背景环境通常在预备阶段和架构愿景阶段进行收集。
- **业务架构**制品获取业务运作的架构模型，特别关注激励 ENTERPRISE 的因素、ENTERPRISE 在组织上如何被结构化以及 ENTERPRISE 还具有哪些功能性能力。
- **信息系统架构**制品获取 IT 系统的架构模型，关注与 TOGAF ADM 各个阶段相符合一致的应用和数据。
- **技术架构**制品获取用于实施和实现信息系统解决方案的已采购的技术资产。
- **架构实现**制品获取变更路线图，表明用于指导和管控架构实施的架构状态和约束性说明之间的过渡。

内容元模型的更详细的表达形式如图 34-5 所示。

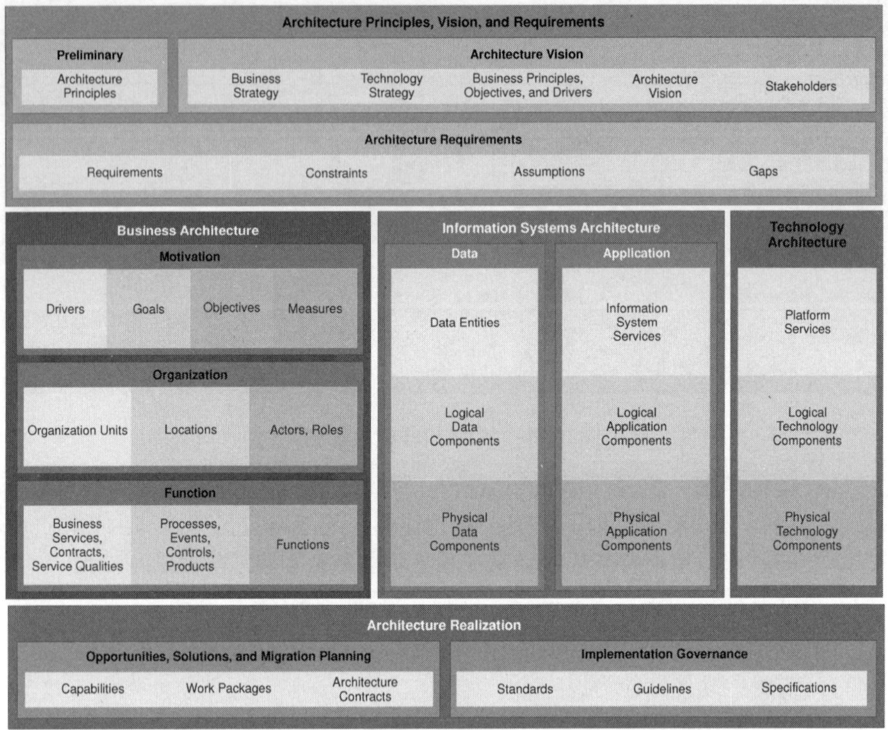

Figure 34-5 Detailed Representation of the Content Metamodel

34.3 Content Metamodel in Detail

This section contains the following subsections:

- Core Content Metamodel (see Section 34.3.1) describes the metamodel entities that form the core content metamodel.
- Core Architecture Artifacts (see Section 34.3.2) lists the set of artifacts intended to accompany the core content metamodel.
- Full Content Metamodel (see Section 34.3.3) describes the metamodel entities that form extensions to the content metamodel.

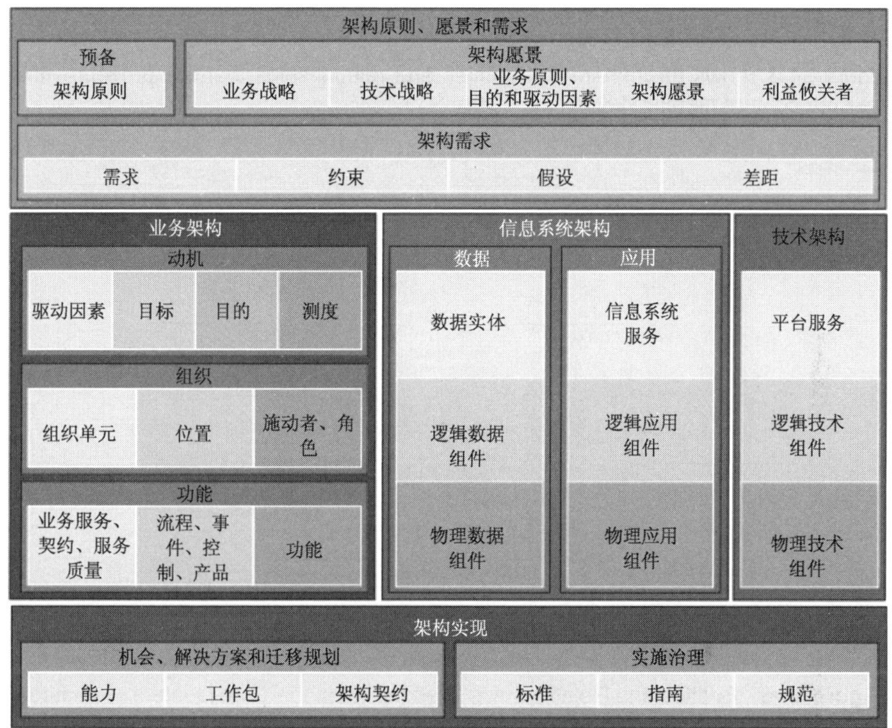

图 34-5　内容元模型的详细表达形式

34.3　详细的内容元模型

本节包含下列小节：

- 核心内容元模型（见 34.3.1 节）描述形成核心内容元模型的元模型实体。
- 核心架构制品（见 34.3.2 节）列出了旨在补充核心内容元模型的制品集。
- 完整内容元模型（见 34.3.3 节）描述了构成内容元模型扩展的元模型实体。

34.3.1 Core Content Metamodel

Figure 34-6 shows the metamodel entities and relationships that are present within the core content metamodel.

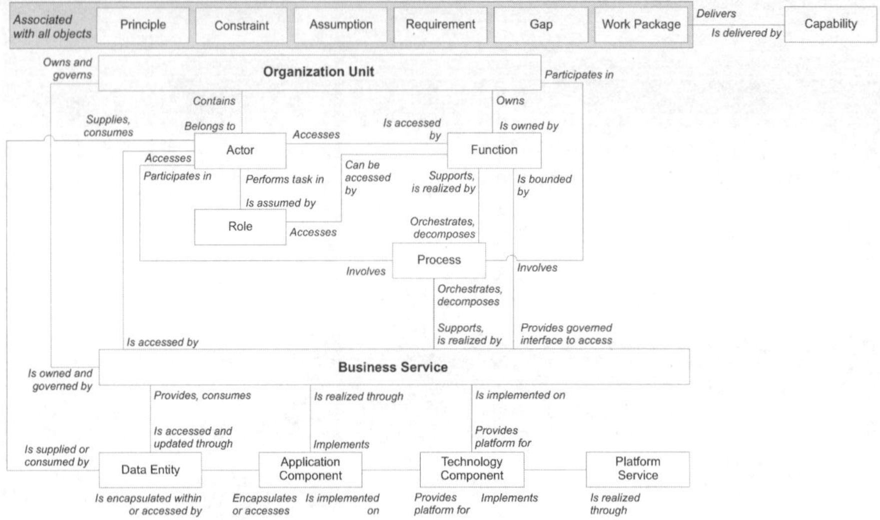

Figure 34-6 Entities and Relationships Present within the Core Content Metamodel

34.3.2 Core Architecture Artifacts

Chapter 35 discusses in detail the way in which the underlying content metamodel can be used to present a set of catalogs, matrices, and diagrams to address stakeholder concerns.

The following set of artifacts are intended to accompany the core content metamodel:

ADM Phase	Artifacts
Preliminary	Principles Catalog
Architecture Vision	Stakeholder Map Matrix Value Chain Diagram Solution Concept Diagram
Business Architecture	Organization/Actor Catalog Role Catalog Business Service/Function Catalog Business Interaction Matrix Actor/Role Matrix Business Footprint Diagram Business Service/Information Diagram Functional Decomposition Diagram Product Lifecycle Diagram

34.3.1 核心内容元模型

图 34-6 表明核心内容元模型内表达的元模型实体和关系。

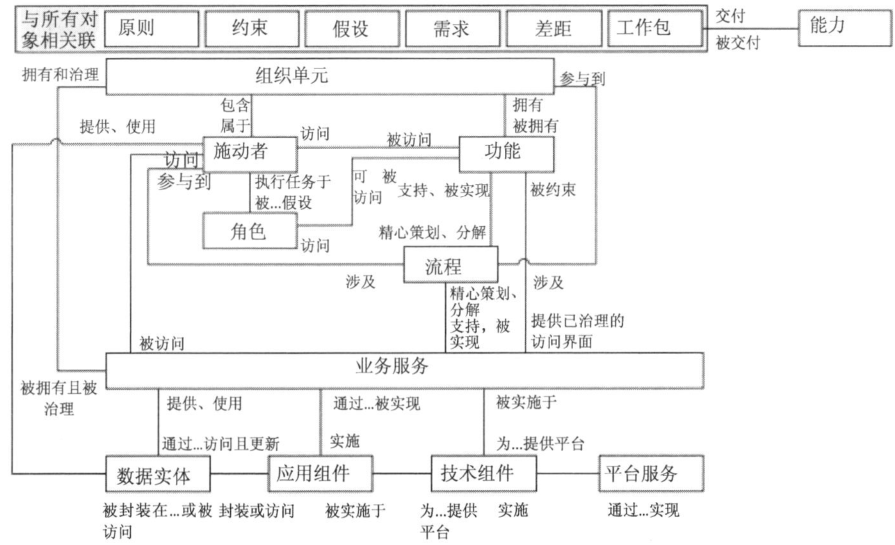

图 34-6 核心内容元模型内表达的实体和关系

34.3.2 核心架构制品

第 35 章详细论述了使用基础内容元模型表达一系列目录集、矩阵和图以应对利益攸关者关注点的方式。

下列制品集旨在补充核心内容元模型：

ADM 阶段	制品
预备	原则目录集
架构愿景	利益攸关者映射矩阵 价值链图 解决方案概念图
业务架构	组织/施动者目录集 角色目录集 业务服务/功能目录集 业务交互矩阵 施动者/角色矩阵 业务轨迹图 业务服务/信息图 功能分解图 产品生命周期图

ADM Phase	Artifacts
Information Systems (Data Architecture)	Data Entity/Data Component Catalog Data Entity/Business Function Matrix Application/Data Matrix Conceptual Data Diagram Logical Data Diagram Data Dissemination Diagram
Information Systems (Application Architecture)	Application Portfolio Catalog Interface Catalog Application/Organization Matrix Role/Application Matrix Application/Function Matrix Application Interaction Matrix Application Communication Diagram Application and User Location Diagram Application Use-Case Diagram
Technology Architecture	Technology Standards Catalog Technology Portfolio Catalog Application/Technology Matrix Environments and Locations Diagram Platform Decomposition Diagram
Opportunities and Solutions	Project Context Diagram Benefits Diagram
Requirements Management	Requirements Catalog

34.3.3 Full Content Metamodel

When all extensions are applied to the core content metamodel, a number of new metamodel entities are introduced. Figure 34-7 shows which entities are contained in the core content metamodel and which new entities are introduced by which extension.

ADM 阶段	制品
信息系统（数据架构）	数据实体/数据组件目录集 数据实体/业务功能矩阵 应用/数据矩阵 概念数据图 逻辑数据图 数据分发图
信息系统（应用架构）	应用谱系目录集 界面目录集 应用/组织矩阵 角色/应用矩阵 应用/功能矩阵 应用交互矩阵 应用通信图 应用和用户位置图 应用用例图
技术架构	技术标准目录集 技术谱系目录集 应用/技术矩阵 环境和位置图 平台分解图
机会和解决方案	项目背景环境图 效益图
需求管理	需求目录集

34.3.3 完整内容元模型

当所有扩展都应用于核心内容元模型时，大量新的元模型实体将被引入。图 34-7 表明哪些实体包含在核心内容元模型中，以及哪些新实体是通过扩展引入的。

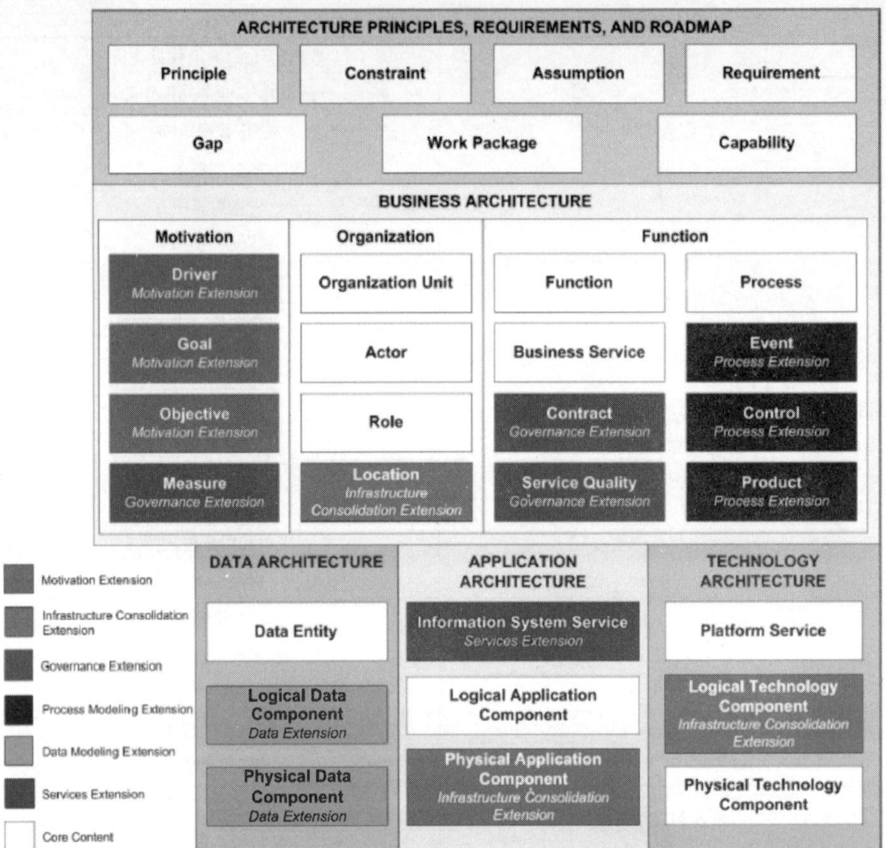

Figure 34-7 Content Metamodel with Extensions

The relationships between entities in the full metamodel are shown in Figure 34-8.

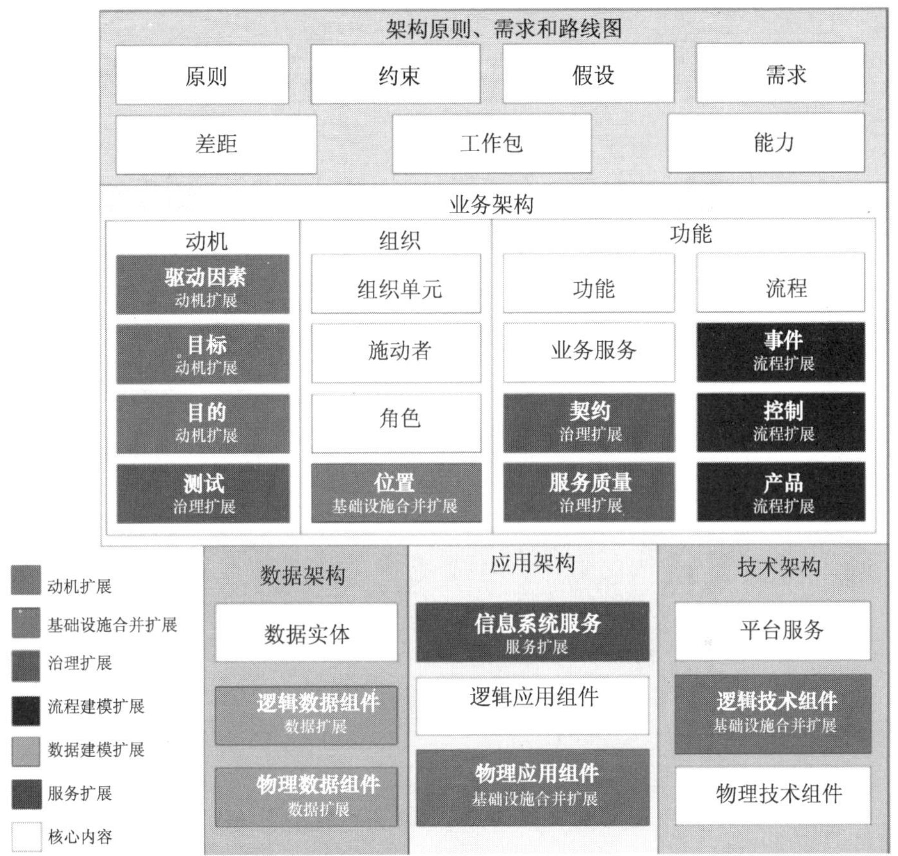

图 34-7 扩展内容元模型

见彩色插图iv页

完整元模型内实体之间的关系如图 34-8 所示。

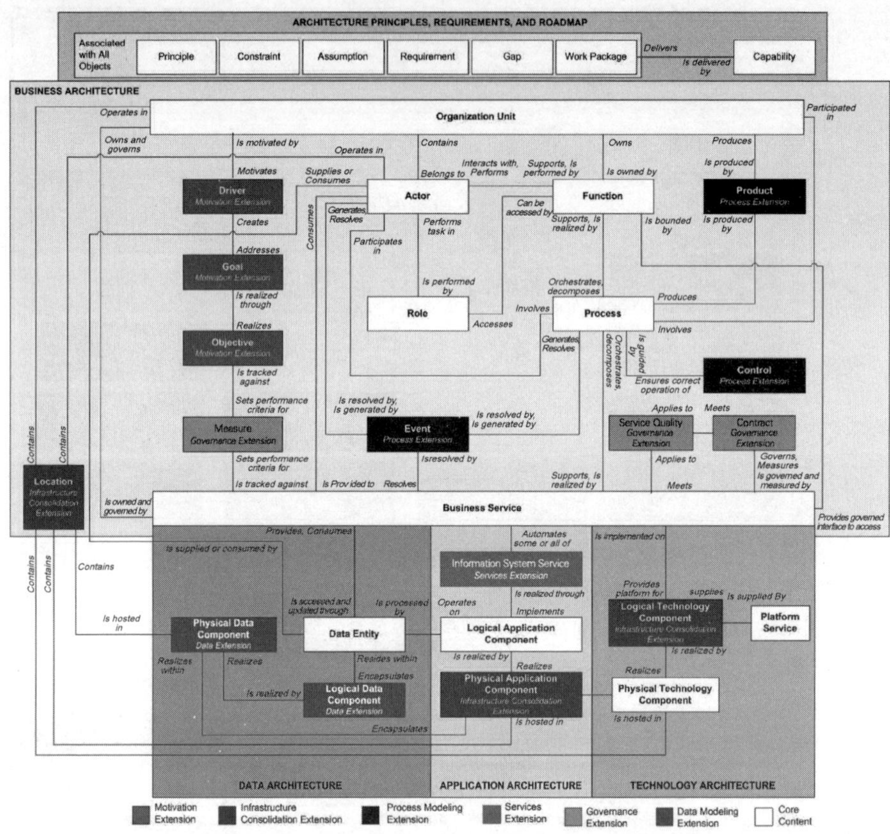

Figure 34-8 Relationships between Entities in the Full Metamodel

34.4 Content Metamodel Extensions

As discussed earlier, the TOGAF content metamodel supports a number of extension modules that allow more in-depth consideration for particular architecture concerns. Figure 34-9 shows the core content metamodel and predefined extension modules.

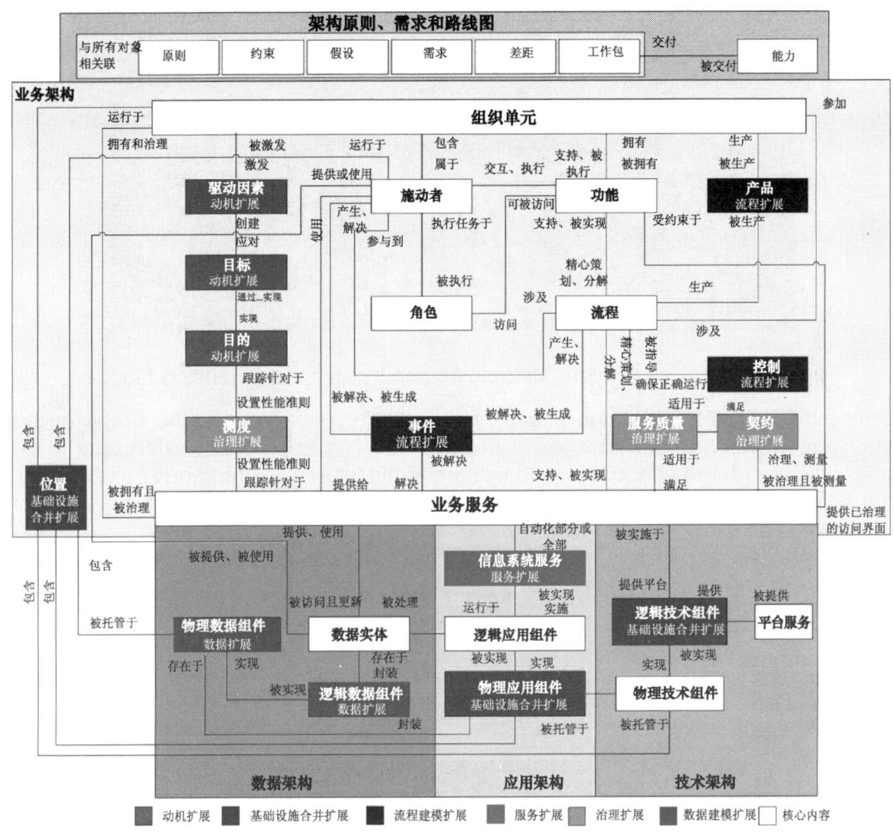

图 34-8 完整元模型内实体之间的关系

见彩色插图vi页

34.4 内容元模型扩展

如上所述，TOGAF 内容元模型支持多个扩展模块，这些扩展模块允许更深入地考虑特定的架构关注点。图 34-9 表明核心内容元模型和预定义的扩展模块。

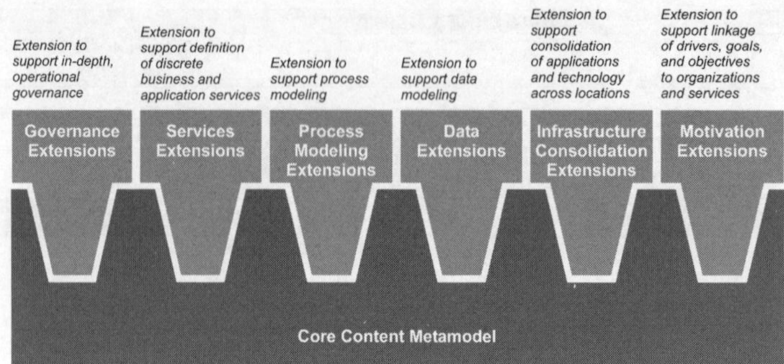

Figure 34-9 Core Content Metamodel and Predefined Extension Modules

During the Architecture Vision phase of a particular engagement, the scope of the engagement will be used to make a determination on appropriate extensions to be employed in order to adequately address the architecture requirements. For example, the scope of an engagement could be defined as core content, plus the governance extensions, as shown in Figure 34-10.

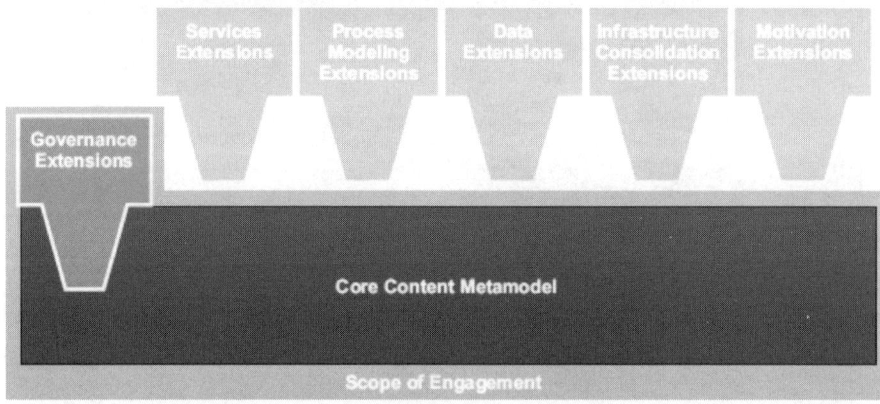

Figure 34-10 Core Content with Governance Extensions

The following sections provide a more detailed description of the purpose and content of each of the extension modules.

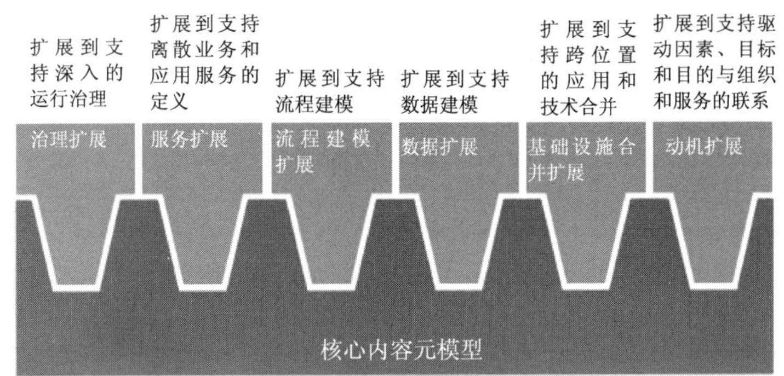

图 34-9　核心内容元模型和预定义的扩展模块

在特定介入的架构愿景阶段，介入范围将用于确定待采用的适当扩展，以便充分地应对架构需求。例如，介入范围可被定义为核心内容加上治理扩展，如图 34-10 所示。

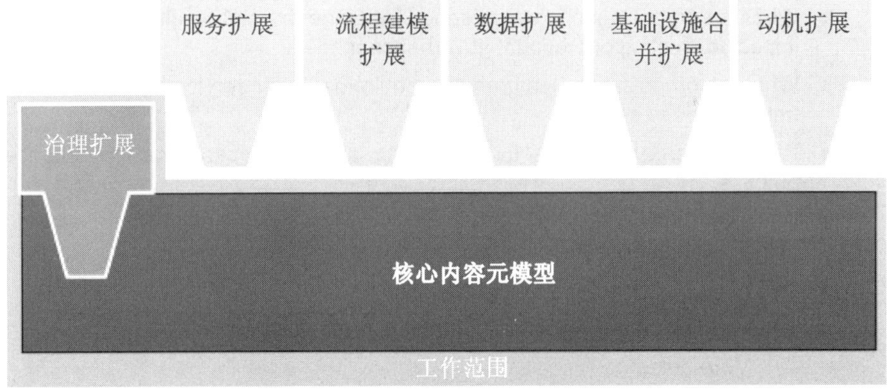

图 34-10　具有治理扩展的核心内容

下列几节对每个扩展模块的目的和内容提供更详细的描述。

34.4.1 Governance Extensions

Purpose

The governance extension is intended to allow additional structured data to be held against objectives and business services, supporting operational governance of the landscape.

The scope of this extension is as follows:

- The ability to apply measures to objectives and then link those measures to services.
- The ability to apply contracts to service communication or service interactions with external users and systems.
- The ability to define re-usable service qualities defining a service-level profile that can be used in contracts.
- Creation of additional diagrams to show ownership and management of systems.

This extension should be used in the following situations:

- When an organization is considering IT change that will result in a significant impact to existing operational governance models.
- When an organization has granular requirements for service levels that differ from service to service.
- When an organization is looking to transform its operational governance practice.
- When an organization has very strong focus on business drivers, goals, and objectives and how these trace to service levels.

The benefits of using this extension are as follows:

- Service levels are defined in a more structured way, with:
  - More detail
  - The ability to re-use service profiles across contracts
  - Stronger tracing to business objectives
- Impacts to operations and operational governance models are considered in a more structured way, with:
  - Additional diagrams of system and data ownership
  - Additional diagrams of system operation and dependencies on operations processes

In addition to the extensions described here, organizations wishing to focus on architecture governance should also consult:

- The COBIT framework for IT governance provided by the Information Systems Audit and Control Association (ISACA); refer to www.isaca.org.
- The IT Portfolio Management Facility (ITPMF) from the OMG; refer to www.omg.org/spec/ITPMF.

34.4.1 治理扩展

目的

治理扩展旨在按照目的和业务服务保存增加的结构化数据，从而支持全景的运行治理。

本扩展的范围如下：

- 将测度应用于目的，然后将这些测度与服务联系起来的能力。
- 将契约应用于与外部用户和系统的服务沟通或服务交互的能力。
- 定义可复用服务质量的能力，该服务质量可定义契约中可使用的服务层级概要。
- 创建附加图以表明系统的所有权和管理。

这种扩展应当用于下列情况：

- 当组织正考虑 IT 变更，这一变更可能对现有运行治理模型产生显著影响时。
- 当组织对服务与服务之间不同的服务层级具有粒度要求时。
- 当组织期待转变其运行治理实践时。
- 当组织非常强烈地关注业务驱动因素、目标、目的以及它们如何追溯到服务层级时。

使用这一扩展的好处如下：

- 以更加结构化的方式定义服务层级，会：
  - 更加详细
  - 跨契约复用服务概要的能力
  - 对业务目的更强的追溯
- 以更加结构化的方式考虑对运行及运行治理模型的影响，会：
  - 增加了系统和数据所有权图
  - 增加了系统运行和其对运行流程的依赖性图

除了本文描述的扩展外，想要关注架构治理的组织还应咨询：

- 信息系统审计与控制协会（ISACA）提供的 IT 治理的 COBIT 框架，见 www.isaca.org。
- 来自 OMG 的 IT 项目谱系管理工具（ITPMF），见 www.omg.org/spec/ITPMF。

Required Changes to the Metamodel

Changes to the metamodel entities and relationships are shown in Figure 34-11.

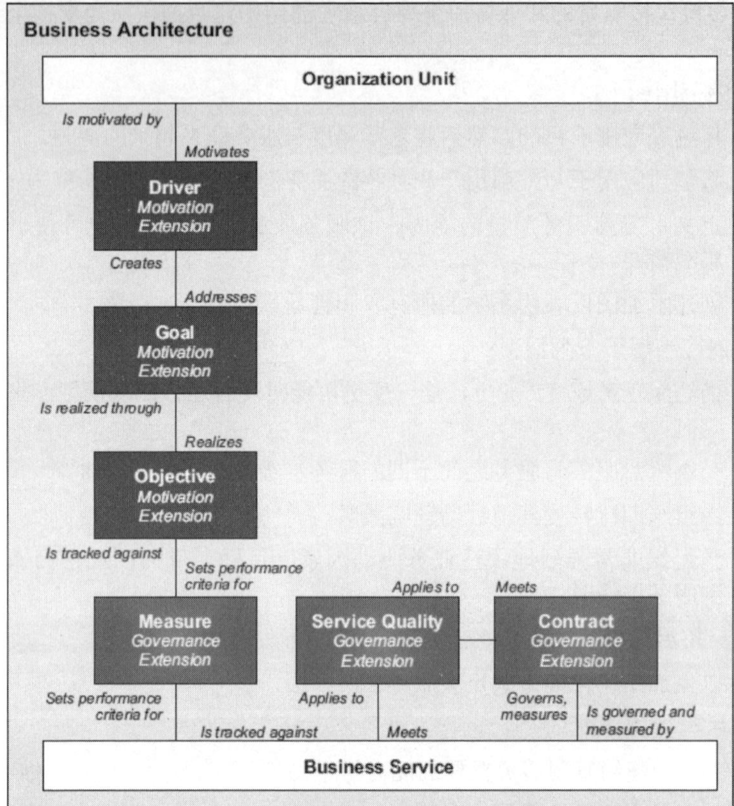

Figure 34-11 Governance Extensions: Changes to Metamodel

Changes to the metamodel entities and relationships are as follows:

- Measure is added as a new entity that links objective and business service.
- Service Quality is added as a new entity that provides a generic service profile template to be applied to business services or contracts.
- Contract is added as a new entity that formalizes the functional and non-functional characteristics of a service interaction with other services, external applications, or users.

元模型所需的变更

元模型实体和关系的变更如图 34-11 所示。

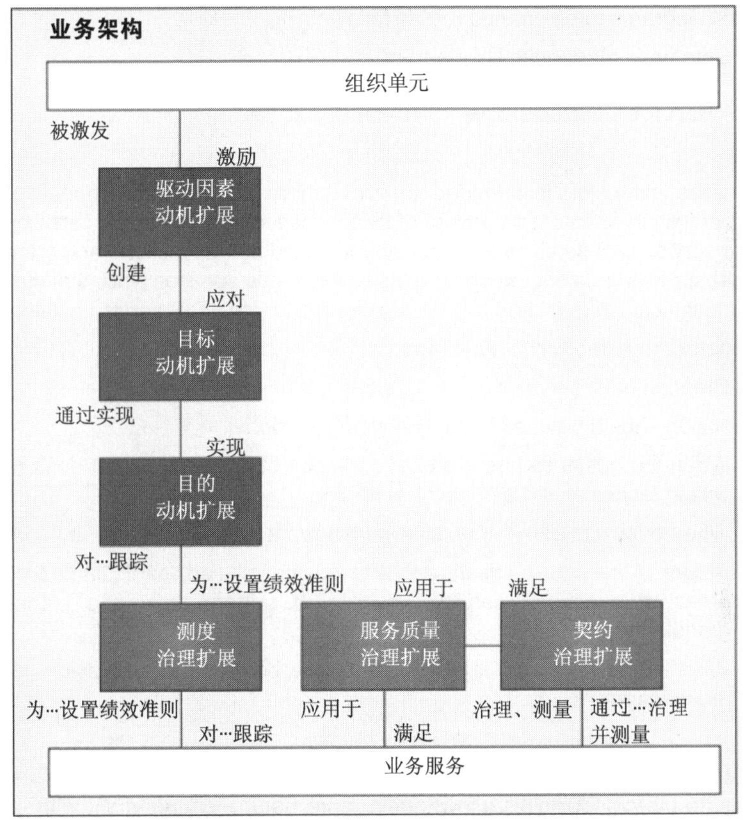

图 34-11 治理扩展：元模型的变更

元模型实体和关系的变更如下：

- 增加测度，作为将目的和业务服务联系起来的一个新实体。
- 增加服务质量，作为提供在业务服务或契约中待应用的一般服务概要模板的一个新实体。
- 增加契约，作为对服务与其他服务、外部应用或用户交互的功能和非功能特征进行正式处理的一个新实体。

Changes to the metamodel attributes are as follows:

- Attributes are added for the new metamodel entities of Measure, Service Quality, and Service Contract.

Additional diagrams to be created are as follows:

- Enterprise Manageability diagram.

34.4.2 Services Extensions

Purpose

The services extension is intended to allow more sophisticated modeling of the service portfolio by creating a concept of IS services in addition to the core concept of business services. IS services are directly supported by applications and creating the layer of abstraction relaxes the constraints on business services while simultaneously allowing technical stakeholders to put more formality into an IS service catalog.

The scope of this extension is as follows:

- Creation of IS services as an extension of business service.

This extension should be used in the following situations:

- When the business has a preset definition of its services that does not align well to technical and architectural needs.
- When business and IT use different language to describe similar capabilities.
- Where IT service is misaligned with business need, particularly around the areas of quality of service, visibility of performance, and management granularity.
- Where IT is taking initial steps to engage business in discussions about IT architecture.

The benefits of using this extension are as follows:

- Business services can be defined outside of the constraints that exist in the core metamodel. This allows for a more natural engagement with business stakeholders.
- IS services can be defined according to a model that maps closely to implementation, providing a more realistic solution abstraction to support IT decision-making.
- Business and IS service relationships show where the business view aligns with the ISview and where there are misalignments.

In addition to the extensions described here, organizations wishing to focus on services-centric architectures should also consult:

- The Service Component Architecture (SCA) specification developed by the Open Service Oriented Architecture (OSOA) collaboration; refer to www.osoa.org/display/Main/Service+Component+Architecture+Home.
- The Service Data Objects (SDO) specification developed by the Open Service Oriented Architecture(OSOA)collaboration;refer to www.osoa.org/display/Main/Service+Data+Objects+Home.

元模型属性的变更如下：

- 为测度、服务质量和服务契约的新元模型实体增加属性。

待创建的附加图如下：

- ENTERPRISE 可管理性图。

34.4.2 服务扩展

目的

服务扩展的目的在于通过创建除业务服务核心概念之外的 IS 服务概念，从而使得能够对服务谱系进行更复杂的建模。IS 服务由应用直接支持，创建抽象层，以放宽对业务服务的约束，并同时使得技术利益攸关者能够使 IS 服务目录集更加正式。

此扩展的范围如下：

- 创建 IS 服务，作为业务服务的扩展。

这种扩展应当用于下列情况：

- 当业务服务的预设定义不太符合技术需要和架构需要时。
- 当业务和 IT 使用不同的语言描述相似能力时。
- 在 IT 服务不符合业务需要的情况下，特别是在服务质量、性能可见性和管理粒度领域。
- 在 IT 正采取初始步骤，将业务加入到关于 IT 架构的论述时。

使用此扩展的好处如下：

- 可在核心元模型中存在的约束范围以外定义业务服务。这使得与业务利益攸关者进行更自然的对接。
- 可按照紧密地映射到实施的一个模型来定义 IS 服务，从而提供更实际的解决方案抽象概念，以支持 IT 决策。
- 业务和 IS 服务的关系表明哪些业务视图与 IS 视图相匹配，哪些地方不匹配。

除了本文描述的扩展外，想要聚焦于以服务为中心的架构的组织还应咨询：

- 开放式面向服务的架构（OSOA）协作开发的服务组件架构（SCA）规范，见 www.osoa.org/display/Main/Service+Component+Architecture+Home。
- 开放式面向服务的架构（OSOA）协作开发的服务数据对象（SDO）规范，见 www.osoa.org/display/Main/Service+Data+Objects+Home。

Required Changes to the Metamodel

Changes to the metamodel entities and relationships are shown in Figure 34-12.

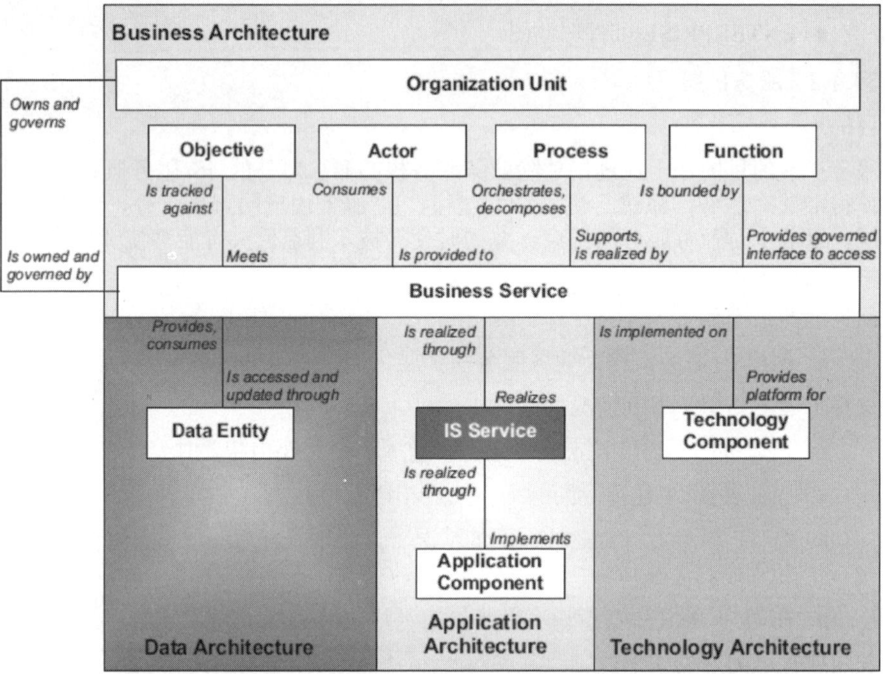

Figure 34-12 Services Extension: Changes to Metamodel

Changes to the metamodel entities and relationships are as follows:

- IS Service is added as a new metamodel entity, extending business service.
- IS Service inherits all the relationships of a business service.
- A new relationship is created linking an IS service to a business service.

Changes to the metamodel attributes are as follows:

- IS Service is added as a new type of business service.

Additional diagrams to be created are as follows:

- Business Use-Case Diagram.
- Organization Decomposition Diagram.

元模型所需的变更

元模型实体和关系的变更如图 34-12 所示。

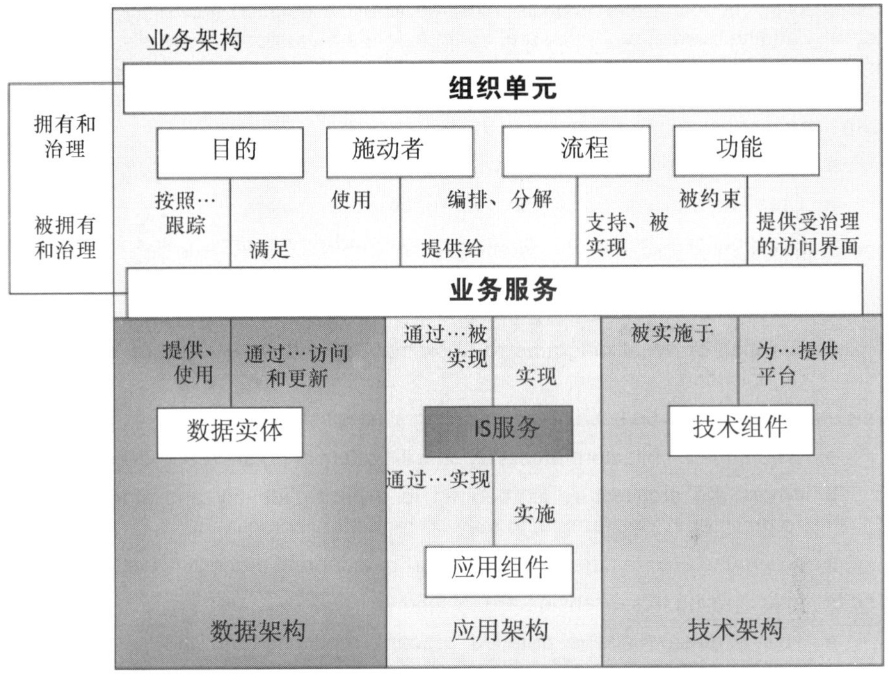

图 34-12　服务扩展：元模型的变更

元模型实体和关系的变更如下：

- 增加“IS 服务”，作为扩展业务服务的新元模型实体。
- “IS 服务”继承业务服务的所有关系。
- 创建了将 IS 服务与业务服务联系起来的新关系。

元模型属性的变更如下：

- 增加了“IS 服务”，作为新业务服务类型。

待创建的附加图如下：

- 业务用例图。
- 组织分解图。

34.4.3 Process Modeling Extensions

Purpose

The process modeling extension is intended to allow detailed modeling of process flows by adding events, products, and controls to the metamodel. Typically, enterprise architecture does not drill into process flow, but in certain process-centric or event-centric organizations it may be necessary to elaborate process in a much more formal manner using this extension module.

The scope of this extension is as follows:

- Creation of events as triggers for processes.
- Creation of controls that business logic and governance gates for process execution.
- Creation of products to represent the output of a process.
- Creation of event diagrams to track triggers and state changes across the organization.

This extension should be used in the following situations:

- Where the architecture must pay specific attention to state and events.
- Where the architecture is required to explicitly identify and store process control steps; for example, to support regulatory compliance.
- Where the architecture features critical or elaborate process flows.

The benefits of using this extension are as follows:

- This extension allows detailed process modeling and the cataloging of process artifacts.
- May be used to support regulatory compliance activities.
- May be used to re-purpose legacy or non-architectural process decomposition analysis.

In addition to the extensions described here, organizations wishing to focus on process-centric architectures should also consult:

- The Business Process Modeling Notation (BPMN) specification, provided by the OMG;refer to www.bpmn.org.
- The Software Process Engineering Metamodel (SPEM) specification, provided by theOMG; refer to www.omg.org/spec/SPEM.

Required Changes to the Metamodel

Changes to the metamodel entities and relationships are shown in Figure 34-13.

34.4.3 流程建模扩展

目的

流程建模扩展旨在通过在元模型中增加事件、产品和控制项，从而使得能够对过程流进行详细建模。典型情况下，Enterprise Architecture 不会深入到过程流中，但在某些以流程为中心的组织或以事件为中心的组织中，可能有必要使用这个扩展模块以更加正式的方式详细阐明流程。

此扩展的范围如下：

- 创建事件，作为流程触发器。
- 创建控制项，用于流程执行的业务逻辑和治理门。
- 创建表达流程输出的产出物。
- 创建事件图，以便跨组织追踪触发器和状态变更。

这种扩展应当用于下列情况：

- 架构必须对状态和事件给予特别关注的情况。
- 架构需要明确地识别和存储流程控制步骤的情况；例如支持法规合规性。
- 当架构特征很关键或详细阐明过程流时。

使用此扩展的好处如下：

- 这种扩展使得能够进行详细的流程建模，以及对流程制品进行分类。
- 可用于支持法规合规性活动。
- 可用于对遗留的或非架构流程的分解分析重新设计目的。

除了本文描述的扩展外，想要聚焦于以流程为中心的架构的组织还应咨询：

- OMG 提供的业务流程建模标注（BPMN）规范，见 www.bpmn.org。
- OMG 提供的软件流程工程元模型（SPEM）规范，见 www.omg.org/spec/SPEM。

元模型所需的变更

元模型实体和关系的变更如图 34-13 所示。

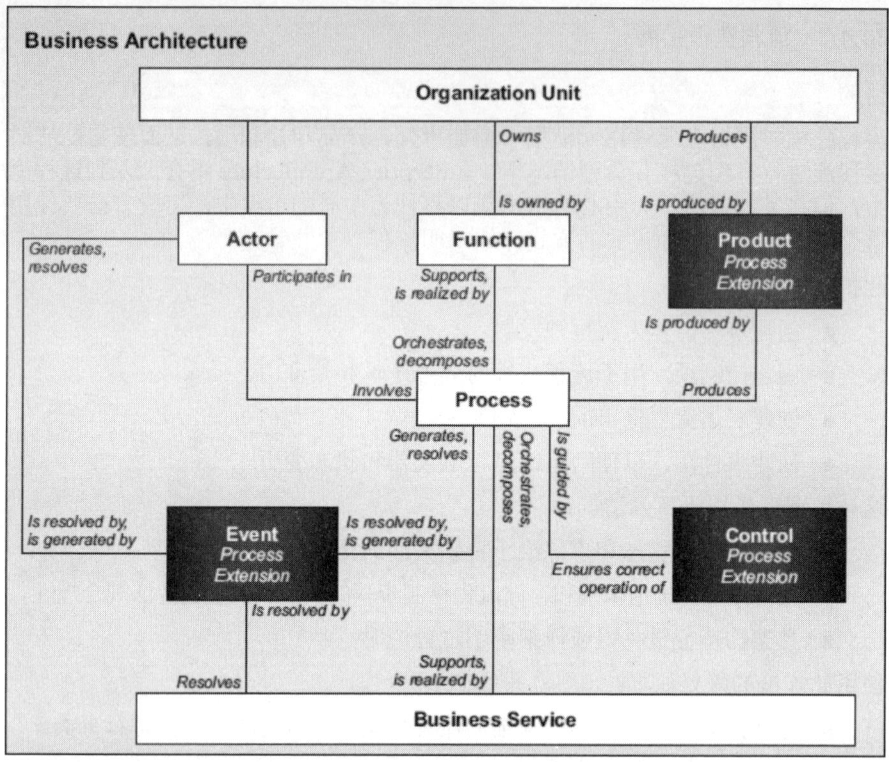

Figure 34-13 Process Modeling Extensions: Changes to Metamodel

Changes to the metamodel entities and relationships are as follows:

- Event is added as a metamodel entity, sitting between Actor, Process, and Service
- Control is added as a metamodel entity, relating to a Process.
- Product is added as a metamodel entity, linking Organization and Processes.

Changes to the metamodel attributes are as follows:

- Attributes are added for the new metamodel entities of Event, Control, and Product.

Additional diagrams to be created are as follows:

- Process Flow diagrams, showing the way in which business functions, events, controls, and products are linked to support a particular business scenario.
- Event diagrams, showing events, were they are received from, and what processes they trigger.

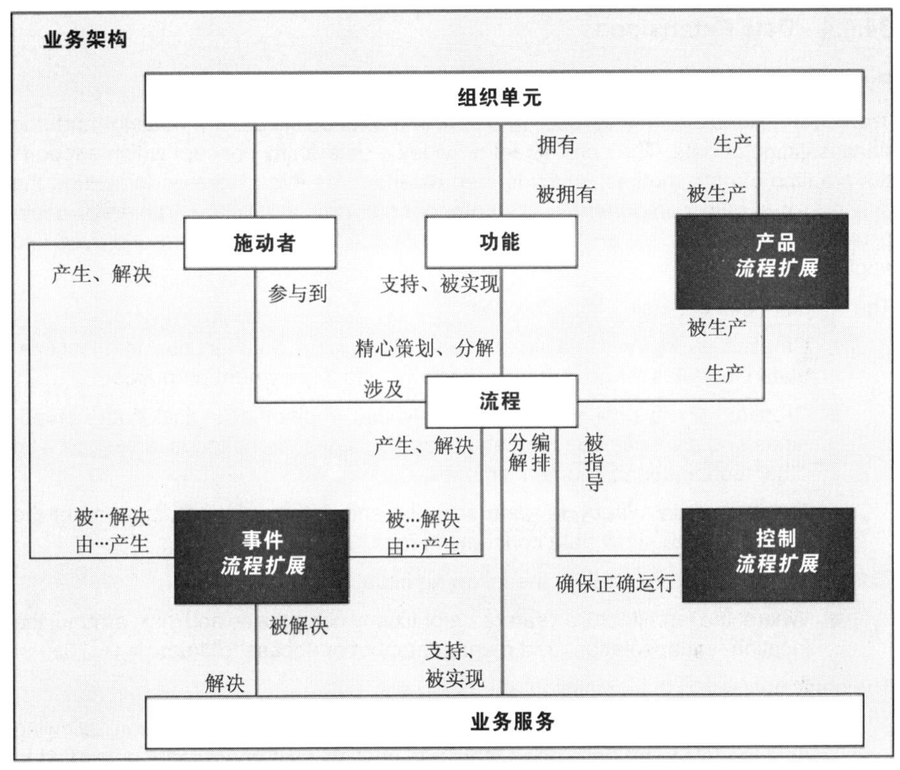

图 34-13　流程建模扩展：元模型的变更

元模型实体和关系的变更如下：

- 增加事件作为元模型实体，位于施动者、流程和服务之间。
- 增加控制项，作为与流程有关的元模型实体。
- 增加产品，作为将组织和流程联系起来的元模型实体。

元模型属性的变更如下：

- 为事件、控制项和产品的新元模型实体添加属性。

待创建的附加图如下：

- 过程流图，表明为了支持特定的业务场景，业务功能、事件、控制项和产品相互联系的方式。
- 事件图，表明事件、从何处接收事件以及事件触发了哪些流程。

34.4.4 Data Extensions

Purpose

The data extension is intended to allow more sophisticated modeling and the encapsulation of data. The core model provides a data entity concept which supports the creation of data models, which is then extended by this extension to include the concept of a data component. Data components form a logical or physical encapsulation of abstract data entities into units that can be governed and deployed into applications.

The scope of this extension is as follows:

- Creation of logical data components that group data entities into encapsulated modules for governance, security, and deployment purposes.
- Creation of physical data components that implement logical data components and are analogous to databases, registries, repositories, schemas, and other techniques of segmenting data.
- Creation of data lifecycle, data security, and data migration diagrams of the architecture to show data concerns in more detail.

This extension should be used in the following situations:

- Where the architecture features significant complexity and risk around the location, encapsulation, and management of or access to data.

The benefits of using this extension are as follows:

- The structure of data is modeled independently from its location, allowing data models to be developed that span multiple systems without being tied to physical concerns.
- Logical groupings of data can be used to set governance, security, or deployment boundaries around data, providing a much more holistic appreciation of data issues surrounding the architecture.

Required Changes to the Metamodel

Changes to the metamodel entities and relationships are shown in Figure 34-14.

34.4.4 数据扩展

目的

数据扩展旨在支持更复杂的建模并进行数据封装。核心模型提供了数据实体概念，此概念支持创建数据模型，然后通过将数据组件的概念纳入进来以进行扩展。数据组件构成逻辑或物理的封装，将抽象数据实体封装进在应用中被管控和部署的单元。

此扩展的范围如下：

- 创建逻辑数据组件，出于治理、安保和部署的目的，将数据实体分组成封装模块。
- 创建物理数据组件，这些物理数据组件实施逻辑数据组件，且与分段数据的数据库、登记表、存储库、模式及其他技术相类似。
- 创建架构的数据生命周期图、数据安保图和数据迁移图，以更详细地表明数据关注点。

这种扩展应当用于下列情况：

- 架构在数据的位置、封装和管理或访问方面具有高复杂性和高风险特征。

使用此扩展的好处如下：

- 数据结构建模独立于其位置，这就能够跨越多个系统开发数据模型，而不与物理关注点绑定。
- 数据的逻辑分组可用于围绕数据设置治理、安保或部署边界，从而对架构周围的数据问题提供更整体的评价。

元模型所需的变更

元模型实体和关系的变更如图 34-14 所示。

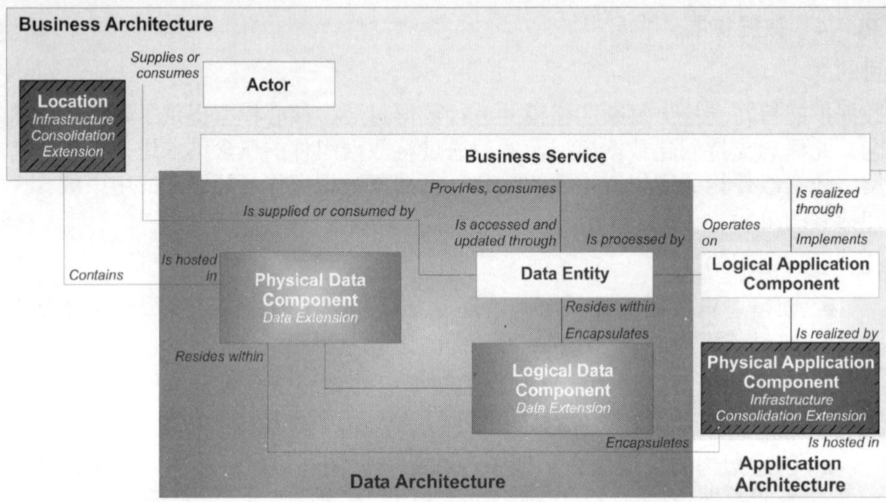

Figure 34-14 Data Extensions: Changes to Metamodel

Changes to the metamodel entities and relationships are as follows:

- Logical Data Component is added as a new metamodel entity, encapsulating data entities.
- Physical Data Component is added as a new metamodel entity, extending Logical Data Component.
- A relationship is created between Physical Data Component and Application Component. If the infrastructure consolidation extension is applied, this should be to Physical Application Component.
- If the infrastructure consolidation extension is applied, Physical Data Components will have a relationship with Location.

Changes to the metamodel attributes are as follows:

- Attributes are added for the new metamodel entities of Logical Data Component and Physical Data Component.

Additional diagrams to be created are as follows:

- Data Security diagram.
- Data Migration diagram.
- Data Lifecycle diagram.

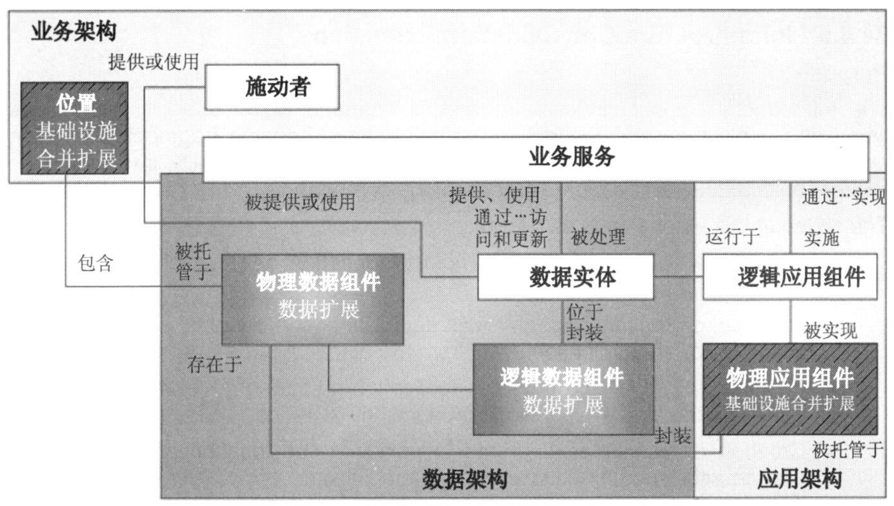

图 34-14　数据扩展：元模型的变更

元模型实体和关系的变更如下：

- 增加了逻辑数据组件，作为封装数据实体的新元模型实体。
- 增加了物理数据组件，作为扩展逻辑数据组件的新元模型实体。
- 在物理数据组件和应用组件之间创建关系。如果应用基础设施合并扩展，则对物理应用组件也应如此。
- 如果应用了基础设施合并扩展，物理数据组件将与位置有关系。

元模型属性的变更如下：

- 为逻辑数据组件和物理数据组件的新元模型实体添加了属性。

待创建的附加图如下：

- 数据安保图。
- 数据迁移图。
- 数据生命周期图。

34.4.5 Infrastructure Consolidation Extensions

Purpose

The infrastructure consolidation extension is intended to be used in landscapes where the application and technology portfolios have become fragmented and the architecture seeks to consolidate the business as usual capability into a smaller number of locations, applications, or technology components.

The scope of this extension is as follows:

- Creation of a location entity to hold the location of IT assets and external consumers of service.
- Creation of logical and physical application components to abstract the capability of an application away from the actual applications in existence.
- Creation of logical and physical application components to abstract product type from the actual technology products in existence.
- Creation of additional diagrams focusing on the location of assets, compliance with standards, structure of applications, application migration, and infrastructure configuration.

This extension should be used in the following situations:

- Where many technology products are in place with duplicate or overlapping capability.
- Where many applications are in place with duplicate or overlapping functionality.
- Where applications are geographically dispersed and the decision logic for determining the location of an application is not well understood.
- When applications are going to be migrated into a consolidated platform.
- When application features are going to be migrated into a consolidated application.

The benefits of using this extension are as follows:

- Allows visibility and analysis of redundant duplication of capability in the application and technology domains.
- Supports analysis of standards compliance.
- Supports analysis of migration impact of application or technology consolidation.
- Supports detailed architectural definition of application structure.

In addition to the extensions described here, organizations wishing to focus on infrastructure consolidation should also consult:

- The Unified Modeling Language (UML), provided by the OMG; refer to www.uml.org.
- The Systems Modeling Language (SysML) — www.sysml.org — which reduces the complexity and software engineering focus of UML for the purposes of systems modeling.
- The IT Portfolio Management Facility (ITPMF) from the OMG; refer to www.omg.org/spec/ITPMF.

34.4.5 基础设施合并扩展

目的

基础设施合并扩展的目的是用于全景图，其中，应用谱系和技术谱系已分段，且架构力求将业务作为普通能力合并到更少的位置、应用或技术组件中。

此扩展的范围如下：

- 创建位置实体，以保存 IT 资产和外部的服务消费者的位置。
- 创建逻辑和物理应用组件，将应用的能力从实际应用中抽象出来。
- 创建逻辑和物理应用组件，将产品类型从现有实际技术产品中抽象出来。
- 创建附加图，聚焦于资产位置、与标准的合规性、应用的结构、应用迁移和基础设施构型。

这种扩展应当用于下列情况：

- 多个技术产品具有重复或重叠的能力的情况。
- 多个应用具有重复或重叠的功能的情况。
- 应用的地理位置分散且用于确定应用位置的决策逻辑没有被很好理解的情况。
- 当应用即将被迁移到已合并的平台时。
- 当应用特征即将被迁移到已合并的应用时。

使用此扩展的好处如下：

- 使应用和技术领域的冗余重复能力可见并可分析。
- 支持对标准合规性的分析。
- 支持对应用或技术合并的迁移影响的分析。
- 支持对应用结构的详细架构定义。

除了本文描述的扩展外，想要关注基础设施合并的组织还应咨询：

- OMG 提供的统一建模语言（UML），见 www.uml.org。
- 系统建模语言（SysML）——www.sysml.org——出于系统建模的目的，降低了 UML 的复杂性及其对软件工程的聚焦。
- 来自 OMG 的 IT 项目谱系管理工具（ITPMF），见 www.omg.org/spec/ITPMF。

Required Changes to the Metamodel

Changes to the metamodel entities and relationships are shown in Figure 34-15.

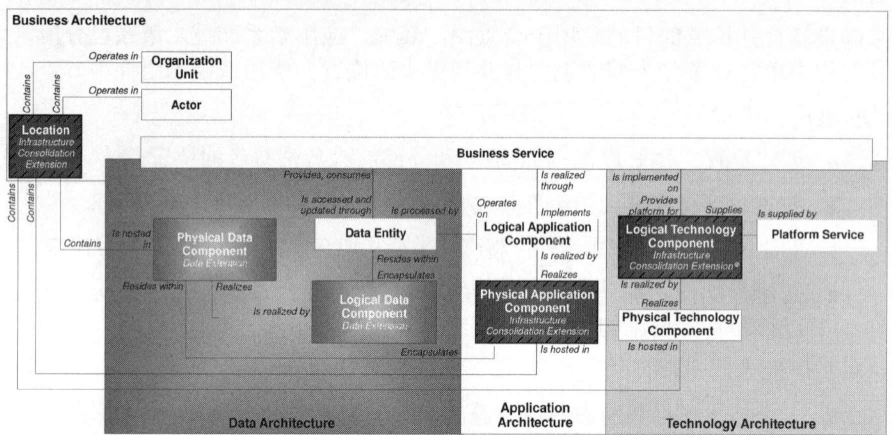

Figure 34-15 Infrastructure Consolidation Extensions: Changes to Metamodel

Changes to the metamodel entities and relationships are as follows:

- Location attributes on Organization, Actor, Application Component, Data Component, and Technology Component are enhanced to create a location entity within the metamodel.
- Application Components are extended to include Logical Application Components (a class of application) and Physical Application Components (an actual application).
- Technology Components are extended to include Logical Technology Components (a class of technology product) and Physical Technology Components (an actual technology product).

Changes to the metamodel attributes are as follows:

- Creation of attributes for the new Metamodel entities of Logical Application Component, Physical Application Component, Logical Technology Component, Physical Technology Component, and Location.
- Removal of Location as an attribute of entities that have a location and replacement with a relationship with the Location entity.

Additional diagrams to be created are as follows:

- Process/Application Realization diagram.
- Software Engineering diagram.
- Application Migration diagram.
- Software Distribution diagram.
- Processing diagram.

元模型所需的变更

元模型实体和关系的变更如图 34-15 所示。

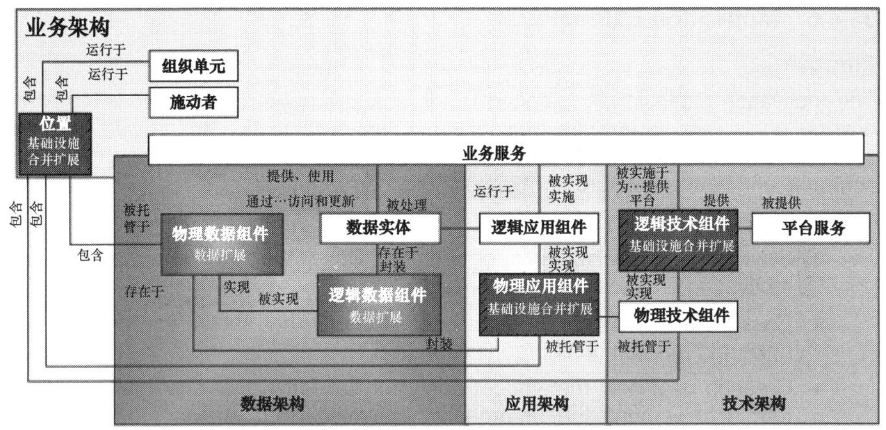

图 34-15　基础设施合并扩展：元模型的变更

元模型实体和关系的变更如下：

- 加强了组织、施动者、应用组件、数据组件和技术组件上的位置属性，以便在元模型内创建位置实体。
- 扩展了应用组件，以包括逻辑应用组件（应用类）和物理应用组件（实际应用）。
- 扩展了技术组件，以包括逻辑技术组件（技术产品类）和物理技术组件（实际技术产品）。

元模型属性的变更如下：

- 创建逻辑应用组件、物理应用组件、逻辑技术组件、物理技术组件和位置的新元模型实体的属性。
- 删除作为实体（该实体有一个位置）属性的位置属性并替换为与位置实体的关系。

待创建的附加图如下：

- 流程/应用实现图。
- 软件工程图。
- 应用迁移图。
- 软件分布图。
- 处理图。

- Networked Computing/Hardware diagram.
- Communications Engineering diagram.

34.4.6 Motivation Extensions

Purpose

The motivation extension is intended to allow additional structured modeling of the drivers, goals, and objectives that influence an organization to provide business services to its customers. This in turn allows more effective definition of service contracts and better measurement of business performance.

The scope of this extension is as follows:

- Creation of a new metamodel entity for Driver that shows factors generally motivating or constraining an organization.
- Creation of a new metamodel entity for Goal that shows the strategic purpose and mission of an organization.
- Creation of a new metamodel entity for Objective that shows near to mid-term achievements that an organization would like to attain.
- Creation of a Goal/Objective/Service diagram showing the traceability from drivers, goals, and objectives through to services.

This extension should be used in the following situations:

- When the architecture needs to understand the motivation of organizations in more detail than the standard business or engagement principles and objectives that are informally modeled within the core content metamodel.
- When organizations have conflicting drivers and objectives and that conflict needs to be understood and addressed in a structured form.
- When service levels are unknown or unclear.

The benefits of using this extension are as follows:

- Highlights misalignment of priorities across the enterprise and how these intersect with shared services (e.g., some organizations may be attempting to reduce costs, while others are attempting to increase capability).
- Shows competing demands for business services in a more structured fashion, allowing compromise service levels to be defined.

In addition to the extensions described here, organizations wishing to focus on architecture modeling of business motivation should also consult:

- The Business Motivation Model (BMM) specification, provided by the OMG; refer to www.omg.org/technology/documents/bms_spec_catalog.htm.

- 网络计算/硬件图。
- 通信工程图。

34.4.6 动机扩展

目的

动机扩展旨在对影响组织向其客户提供业务服务的驱动因素、目标和目的进行附加的结构化建模，转而更有效地定义服务契约并更好地衡量业务绩效。

此扩展的范围如下：

- 为驱动因素创建新元模型实体，表明通常情况下激励或约束一个组织的因素。
- 为目标创建新元模型实体，表明一个组织的战略目标和任务。
- 为目的创建新元模型实体，表明了一个组织到中期想要达成的成就。
- 创建目标/目的/服务图，表明从驱动因素、目标和目的直到服务的可追溯性。

这种扩展应当用于下列情况：

- 当与核心内容元模型内非正式建模的标准业务或参与原则和目的相比，架构需要更加详细地理解组织的动机时。
- 当组织具有相冲突的驱动因素和目的，且这种冲突需要以结构化的形式理解和应对时。
- 当服务层级未知或不明确时。

使用此扩展的好处如下：

- 强调优先级在整个 ENTERPRISE 内部的不一致性，以及这些不一致性如何与共享服务相互作用（如某些组织可能力求降低成本，而其他组织力求提高能力）。
- 以更为结构化的方式展示对业务服务的相互竞争的需求，从而能够折中处理待定义的服务层级。

除了本文描述的扩展外，想要聚焦于业务动机的架构建模的组织还应咨询：

- OMG 提供的业务动机模型（BMM）规范，见 www.omg.org/technology/documents/bms_spec_catalog.htm。

Required Changes to the Metamodel

Changes to the metamodel entities and relationships are shown in Figure 34-16.

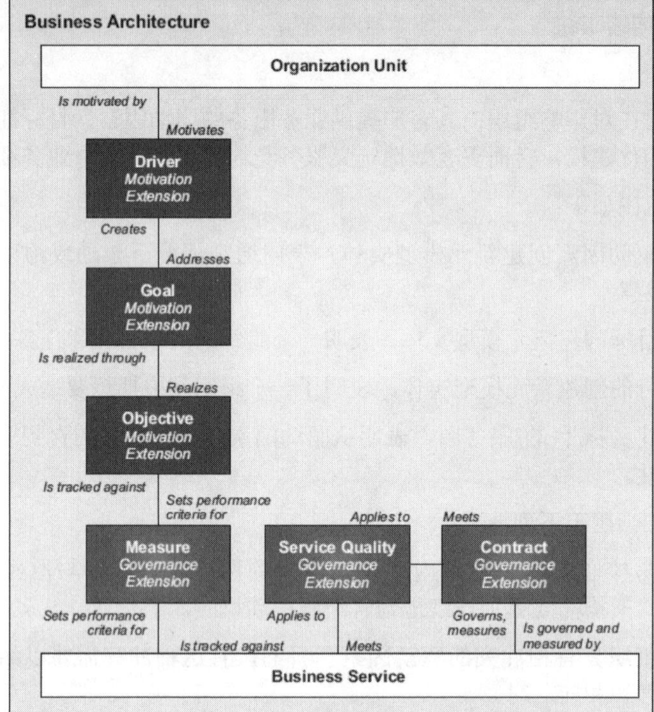

Figure 34-16 Motivation Extensions: Changes to Metamodel

Changes to the metamodel entities and relationships are as follows:

- Driver, Goal, and Objective are added as new entities that link Organization Unit to Business Service.

Changes to the metamodel attributes are as follows:

- Attributes are added for the new metamodel entities of Driver, Goal, and Objective.

Additional diagrams to be created are as follows:

- Goal/Objective/Service diagram.

元模型所需的变更

元模型实体和关系的变更如图 34-16 所示。

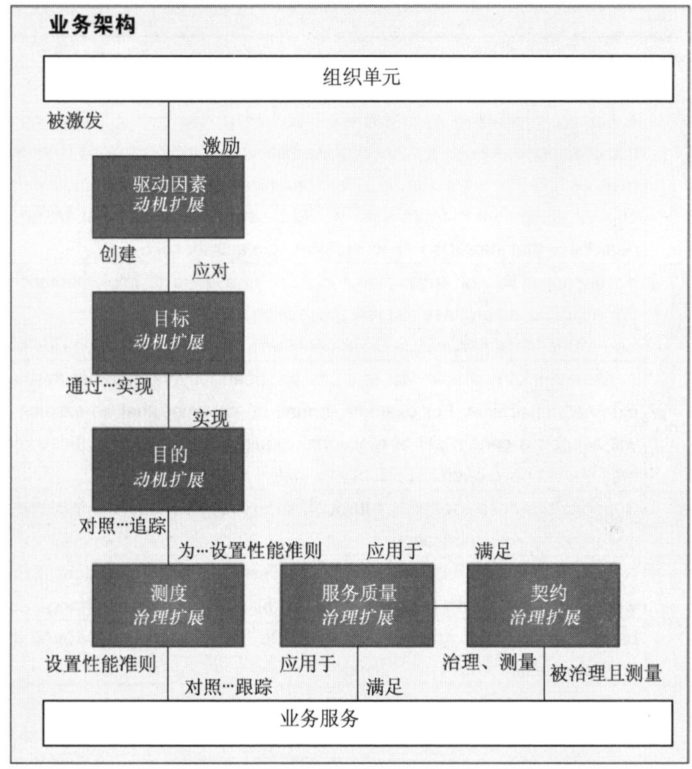

图 34-16　动机扩展：元模型的变更

元模型实体和关系的变更如下：

- 增加了驱动因素、目标和目的，将其作为将组织单元与业务服务联系起来的新实体。

元模型属性的变更如下：

- 为驱动因素、目标和目的的新元模型实体增加属性。

待创建的附加图如下：

- 目标/目的/服务图。

34.5 Content Metamodel Entities

The following table lists and describes the entities within the content metamodel.

Metamodel Entity	Description
Actor	A person, organization, or system that has a role that initiates orinteracts with activities; for example, a sales representative who travels to visit customers. Actors may be internal or external to an organization. In the automotive industry, an original equipment manufacturer would be considered an actor by an automotive dealership that interacts with its supply chain activities
Application Component	An encapsulation of application functionality aligned to implementation structure. For example, a purchase request processing application. See also *Logical Application Component* and *Physical Application Component*
Assumption	A statement of probable fact that has not been fully validated at thisstage, due to external constraints. For example, it may be assumed that an existing application will support a certain set of functional requirements, although those requirements may not yet have been individually validated
Business Service	Supports business capabilities through an explicitly defined interfaceand is explicitly governed by an organization
Capability	A business-focused outcome that is delivered by the completion of one or more work packages. Using a capability-based planning approach, change activities can be sequenced and grouped in order to provide continuous and incremental business value
Constraint	An external factor that prevents an organization from pursuing particular approaches to meet its goals. For example, customer data is not harmonized within the organization, regionally or nationally, constraining the organization's ability to offer effective customer service
Contract	An agreement between a service consumer and a service provider that establishes functional and non-functional parameters for interaction
Control	A decision-making step with accompanying decision logic used to determine execution approach for a process or to ensure that a process complies with governance criteria. For example, a sign-off control on the purchase request processing process that checks whether the total value of the request is within the sign-off limits of the requester, or whether it needs escalating to higher authority
Data Entity	An encapsulation of data that is recognized by a business domain expert as a thing. Logical data entities can be tied to applications, repositories, and services and may be structured according to implementation considerations
Driver	An external or internal condition that motivates the organization todefine its goals. An example of an external driver is a change in regulation or compliance rules which, for example, require changes to the way an organization operates; i.e., Sarbanes-Oxley in the US

34.5 内容元模型实体

下表列出并描述了内容元模型内的实体。

元模型实体	描述
施动者	以某种角色发起活动或与活动进行交互的个人、组织或系统；例如，出差访问客户的销售代表。对一个组织而言，施动者可以是内部或外部的。在汽车行业，汽车经销商认为原始设备制造商是与其供应链活动进行交互的一个施动者
应用组件	与实施结构相一致的应用功能的封装。例如，采购要求处理应用。 另参见《逻辑应用组件》和《物理应用组件》
假设	由于外部约束，对在此阶段尚未被充分确认的可能事实的申明。例如，可以假设现有应用将支持功能需求的某一集合，尽管那些需求可能尚未被单独确认
业务服务	通过明确定义的界面支持各种业务能力，并由一个组织来明确地管控
能力	以业务为中心的成果，通过完成一个或多个工作包来交付。使用基于能力的规划途径，可对变革活动进行排序和分组，以便提供持续且递增的业务价值
约束	阻碍组织寻求特殊途径实现其目标的外部因素。例如，在组织内部，各地区或全国范围内的客户数据不一致，约束了组织提供有效客户服务的能力
契约	服务消费者和服务提供者之间达成的协议，它设立了双方交互的功能性参数和非功能性参数
控制	一个伴有决策逻辑的决策步骤，用于确定流程的执行途径或确保流程符合治理准则。例如，对采购要求处理流程的签署控制，用于检查要求的总价值是否在提出要求者的签署限制内，或是否需要逐步升级到较高权限
数据实体	一种数据的封装，业务领域专家将之视为一种独立完整的事物。可以将逻辑数据实体与应用、存储库以及服务进行绑定，并且按照实施考量因素对其进行结构化处理
驱动因素	激发组织定义其目标的一个内部或外部条件，例如，法规或合规条例的变更（如美国的索克斯法案）要求组织改变其经营方式。这是一种外部驱动因素

Metamodel Entity	Description
Event	An organizational state change that triggers processing events; may originate from inside or outside the organization and may be resolved inside or outside the organization
Function	Delivers business capabilities closely aligned to an organization, but not necessarily explicitly governed by the organization. Also referred to as "business function"
Gap	A statement of difference between two states. Used in the context of gap analysis, where the difference between the Baseline and Target Architecture is identified. **Note:** Gap analysis is described in Part III, Chapter 27
Goal	A high-level statement of intent or direction for an organization. Typically used to measure success of an organization
Information SystemService	The automated elements of a business service. An information system service may deliver or support part or all of one or more business services
Location	A place where business activity takes place and can be hier archaically decomposed
Logical Application Component	An encapsulation of application functionality that is independent of a particular implementation. For example, the classification of all purchase request processing applications implemented in an enterprise
Logical Data Component	A boundary zone that encapsulates related data entities to form alogical location to be held; for example, external procurement information
Logical Technology Component	An encapsulation of technology infrastructure that is independent of a particular product. A class of technology product; for example, supply chain management software as part of an Enterprise Resource Planning (ERP) suite, or a Commercial Off-The-Shelf (COTS) purchase request processing enterprise service
Measure	An indicator or factor that can be tracked, usually on an ongoingbasis, to determine success or alignment with objectives and goals
Objective	A time-bounded milestone for an organization used to demonstrate progress towards a goal; for example, "Increase capacity utilizationby 30% by the end of 2009 to support the planned increase in market share"
Organization Unit	A self-contained unit of resources with goals, objectives, and measures. Organization units may include external parties and business partner organizations
Physical Application Component	An application, application module, application service, or other deployable component of functionality. For example, a configured and deployed instance of a Commercial Off-The-Shelf (COTS) Enterprise Resource Planning (ERP) supply chain management application
Physical Data Component	A boundary zone that encapsulates related data entities to form a physical location to be held. For example, a purchase order business object, comprising purchase order header and item business object nodes

元模型实体	描述
事件	触发处理事件的一种组织状态变化；事件可能起源于组织内部或外部，并且可以在组织内部或外部得到解决
功能	交付与某个组织紧密一致的业务能力，但这些能力并非必须受该组织明确治理。也可被称为“业务功能”
差距	两种状态之间差异的陈述。用于差距分析的背景环境中，识别基线架构和目标架构之间的差异。 注：第三部分第 27 章描述了差距分析
目标	对组织的意图或方向的高层级陈述。 典型情况下，用于衡量组织的成功程度
信息系统服务	业务服务的自动化元素。信息系统服务可以交付或支持一种或多种业务服务的部分或全部服务
位置	业务活动发生并可按层级分解之处
逻辑应用组件	一种与特定实施无关的应用功能的封装。例如，将在 ENTERPRISE 内部实施的全部采购要求处理应用进行分类
逻辑数据组件	封装相关数据实体的一个有界区域，形成用来容纳数据实体的逻辑位置；例如，外部采购信息
逻辑技术组件	与特定产品无关的技术基础设施的一种封装。逻辑技术组件是一类技术产品；例如，作为企业资源规划（ERP）套件组成部分的供应链管理软件，或商用货架（COTS）采购要求处理的 ENTERPRISE 服务
测度	通常可持续追踪的指标或因素，以确定目的和目标达成的成功程度或者与目的、目标的一致性
目的	一个组织用于展现其趋近目标的进程中具有时限的里程碑；例如，“截至 2009 年年底将产能利用率提高 30%，以支持市场份额按计划增长”
组织单元	具有目标、目的和测度的资源自包含单元。组织单元可包括外部各方和业务合作伙伴组织
物理应用组件	应用、应用模块、应用服务或其他可部署的功能性组件。例如，商用货架（COTS）企业资源规划（ERP）的供应链管理应用的一个已配置和部署的实例
物理数据组件	封装相关数据实体的一个有界区域，形成要占用的物理位。例如，一个由采购订单抬头和业务对象节点组成的采购订单业务对象

Metamodel Entity	Description
Physical Technology Component	A specific technology infrastructure product or technology infrastructure product instance. For example, a particular product version of a Commercial Off-The-Shelf (COTS) solution, or a specific brand and version of server
Platform Service	A technical capability required to provide enabling infrastructure that supports the delivery of applications
Principle	A qualitative statement of intent that should be met by the architecture. Has at least a supporting rationale and a measure of importance. **Note:** A sample set of architecture principles is defined in Part III, Chapter 23
Process	A process represents flow of control between or within functions and/or services (depends on the granularity of definition). Processes represent a sequence of activities that together achieve a specified outcome, can be decomposed into sub-processes, and can show operation of a function or service (at next level of detail). Processes may also be used to link or compose organizations, functions, services, and processes
Product	Output generated by the business. The business product of the execution of a process
Requirement	A quantitative statement of business need that must be met by a particular architecture or work package
Role	The usual or expected function of an actor, or the part somebody or something plays in a particular action or event. An actor may have a number of roles. See also *Actor*
Service	An element of behavior that provides specific functionality inresponse to requests from actors or other services. A service delivers or supports business capabilities, has an explicitly defined interface, and is explicitly governed. Services are defined for business, information systems, and platforms
Service Quality	A preset configuration of non-functional attributes that may beassigned to a service or service contract
Technology Component	An encapsulation of technology infrastructure that represents a class of technology product or specific technology product
Work Package	A set of actions identified to achieve one or more objectives for thebusiness. A work package can be a part of a project, a complete project, or a program

元模型实体	描述
物理技术组件	一种特定的技术基础设施产品或技术基础设施产品的实例。例如，某个商用货架（COTS）解决方案的一个特定产品版本，或服务器的一个特定品牌和版本
平台服务	使基础设施能够提供支持应用交付所需的一种技术能力
原则	对架构应满足的意图的定性陈述。一个原则至少具备一个支持的理由依据和一项重要性测度。 注：第三部分第 23 章定义了架构原则的样本集
流程	流程表示功能和/或服务之间或内部的控制流（取决于定义的粒度）。 流程表示共同达成某种特定结果的一连串活动，一个流程可被分解为若干子流程，并且，能够展示某项功能或服务的运行过程（在下一个详细层级）。流程也可用于联系或组成组织、功能、服务和流程
产品	业务产生的输出。执行流程的业务产出物
需求	对特定架构或工作包必须满足的业务需要的定量陈述
角色	施动者具有的通常或预期的功能，或某个人或事物在特定行动或事件中扮演的角色。一名施动者可具有多种角色。 另见施动者
服务	根据施动者的要求或其他服务提供特定功能的一种行为要素。服务可交付或支持业务能力，具有明确定义的界面，并且接受明确管控。服务是针对业务、信息系统和平台所定义的
服务质量	非功能属性的一种预设配置，可指派给服务或服务契约
技术组件	技术基础设施的一种封装，代表某类技术产品或某个特定的技术产品
工作包	达成一个或多个业务目的的一组确定的活动。工作包可以是某个项目的一部分，也可以是一个完整项目或一个项目群

34.6 Content Metamodel Attributes

The following table shows typical attributes for each of the metamodel entities described previously.

Metamodel Entity Attribute	Description	
All Metamodel Entities	ID	Unique identifier for the architecture entity
	Name	Brief name of the architecture entity
	Description	Textual description of the architecture entity
	Category	User-definable categorization taxonomy for each metamodel entity
	Source	Location from where the information was collected
	Owner	Owner of the architecture entity
Capability	Business value	Describes how this capability provides value to the enterprise.
	Increments	Lists possible maturity/quality levels for the capability
Constraint	No additional attributes	This metamodel entity has onlybasic attributes
Gap	No additional attributes	This metamodel entity has onlybasic attributes
Location	Category	The following categories of Location apply: Region (applies to a grouping of countries or territory; e.g., South East Asia, UK, and Ireland), Country (applies to a single country; e.g., US), Building (applies to a site of operation; where several offices are collected in a singlecity, this category may represent a city), and Specific Location (applies to any specific location within a building, such as a server room). The nature of the business may introduce other Locations: Ship or Port for a ferry company, Mine for a gold company, Car for a police force, Hotel for any firm's traveling workers, and so on

34.6 内容元模型属性

下表表明上述每个元模型实体的典型属性。

元模型实体属性	描述	
所有元模型实体	ID	架构实体的唯一标识符
	名称	架构实体的简称
	描述	架构实体的文字描述
	类别	每个元模型实体的用户可定义的分类法
	来源	收集信息的位置
	所有者	架构实体的所有者
能力	业务价值	描述了此能力如何向 ENTERPRISE 提供价值
	增量	列出能力的可能的成熟度/质量水平
约束	无附加属性	该元模型实体只有基本属性
差距	无附加属性	该元模型实体只有基本属性
位置	类别	位置应用如下：地区（适用于国家或领土分组；如东南亚、英国和爱尔兰）、国家（适用于一个国家；如，美国）、建筑物（适用于工作场地；在一个城市有多个办公室的地方，这个类别可代表一个城市）和特定位置（适用于一个建筑物内的任何特定位置，如服务器室）。业务的本质可引入其他位置：渡轮公司的船舶或港口、黄金公司的矿山、警察部门的汽车、任何公司的差旅员工的旅馆等

Metamodel Entity Attribute	Description	
Principle	Category	The following categories of principle apply: Guiding Principle, Business Principle, Data Principle, Application Principle, Integration Principle, Technology Principle
	Priority	Priority of this principle relative to other principles
	Statement of principle	Statement of what the principle is
	Rationale	Statement of why the principle is required and the outcome to be reached
	Implication	Statement of what the principle means in practical terms
	Metric	Identifies mechanisms that will be used to measure whether the principle has been met or not
Requirement	Statement of requirement	Statement of what the requirement is, including a definition of whether the requirement shall be met, should be met, or may be met
	Rationale	Statement of why the requirement exists
	Acceptance criteria	Statement of what tests will be carried out to ensure that the requirement will be met
Actor	# FTEs	Estimated number of FTEs that operate as this Actor
	Actor goal	Objectives that this actor has, in general terms
	Actor tasks	Tasks that this actor performs, in general terms
Business Service	Standards class	Non-Standard, Proposed Standard, Provisional Standard, Standard, Phasing-Out Standard, Retired Standard
	Standard creation date	If the product is a standard, when the standard was created
	Last standard review date	Last date that the standard was reviewed
	Next standard review date	Next date for the standard to be reviewed
	Retire date	Date when the standard was/will be retired
Contract	Behavior characteristics	Functional behavior to be supported within the scope of the contract
	Service name “caller”	Consuming service

元模型实体属性	描述	
原则	类别	下列原则的类别适用：指导原则、业务原则、数据原则、应用原则、综合原则、技术原则
	优先级	该原则相对于其他原则的优先级
	原则陈述	关于原则是什么的陈述
	理由依据	关于为什么需要原则的陈述以及将要达成的结果
	含义	关于原则实际上是什么意思的陈述
	衡量标准	识别出用于衡量原则是否已得到满足的机制
需求	需求陈述	关于需求是什么的陈述，包括关于需求是否将要得到满足、是否应该得到满足或是否可以得到满足的定义
	理由依据	关于需求为什么存在的陈述
	验收准则	关于为确保需求得到满足而要执行什么试验的陈述
施动者	# FTE	作为该施动者工作的 FTE 的预计数目
	施动者目标	一般来说，是指该施动者所具有的目的
	施动者任务	一般来说，是指该施动者所执行的任务
业务服务	标准类别	非标准、建议标准、临时标准、标准、淘汰标准、退役标准
	标准创建日期	如果产品是一种标准，则指的是该标准被创建的时间
	上次标准审视日期	标准被审视的上一个日期
	下次标准审视日期	审视标准的下一个日期
	退役日期	标准曾经/将要被退役的日期
契约	行为特征	在契约范围内需要支持的功能行为
	服务名称“主叫”	消费服务

Metamodel Entity Attribute	Description	
	Service name “called”	Providing service
	Service quality characteristics	Non-functional behavior to be supported within the scope of the contract
	Availability characteristics	Degree to which something is available for use
	Service times	Hours during which the service must be available
	Manageability characteristics	Ability to gather information about the state of something and control it
	Serviceability characteristics	Ability to identify problems and take corrective action, such as to repair or upgrade acomponent in a running system
	Performance characteristics	Ability of a component to perform its tasks in an appropriate time
	Response requirements	Response times that the service provider must meet for particular operations
	Reliability characteristics	Resistance to failure
Contract	Quality of information required	Contracted requirements on accuracy and completeness of information
	Contract control requirements	Level of governance and enforcement applied to the contractual parameters for overall service
	Result control requirements	Measures in place to ensure that each service request meets contracted criteria
	Recoverability characteristics	Ability to restore a system to a working state after an interruption
	Locatability characteristics	Ability of a system to be found when needed
	Security characteristics	Ability of a system to prevent unauthorized access to functions and data
	Privacy characteristics	Protection of data from unauthorized access
	Integrity characteristics	Ability of a system to ensure that data has not been corrupted
	Credibility characteristics	Ability of a system to ensure that the service request originates from an authorized source

元模型实体属性	描述	
契约	服务名称“被叫”	提供服务
	服务质量特征	契约范围内需要支持的非功能性行为
	可供使用性特征	某件事物可以使用的程度
	服务时间	服务必须保持可用的时间（小时）
	可管理性特征	收集某件事物的状态信息，以及控制该信息的能力
	可服务性特征	提出问题并采取纠正措施的能力，如修复或升级运行系统中的一个组件
	绩效特征	组件在适当时间内执行其任务的能力
	响应需求	服务提供商针对特定运行必须满足的响应时间
	可靠性特征	抗故障能力
	所需信息的质量	对信息精确度和完整性的契约要求
	契约控制需求	适用于总体服务的契约参数的管控和执行水平
	结果控制需求	确保每个服务要求满足契约准则的恰当的测度
	可恢复性特征	中断后将系统恢复到工作状态的能力
	可定位性特征	在需要时系统能被发现的能力
	安保性特征	系统阻止未经授权访问功能和数据的能力
	保密特征	防止数据经受未经授权的访问
	完整性特征	系统确保数据未被损坏的能力
	可信度特征	系统确保服务要求源于已授权来源的能力

Metamodel Entity Attribute	Description	
Contract	Localization characteristics	Ability of a service to support localized variants for different consumer groups
	Internationalization characteristics	Ability of a service to support international variations in business logic and data representation (such as character set)
	Interoperability characteristics	Ability of the service to interoperate with different technical environments, inside and outside of the organization
	Scalability characteristics	Ability of the service to grow or shrink its performance or capacity appropriately to the demands of the environment in which it operates
	Portability characteristics	Of data, people, applications, and components
	Extensibility characteristics	Ability to accept new functionality
	Capacity characteristics	Contracted capacity of the service provider to meet requests
	Throughput	Required throughput capacity
	Throughput period	Time period needed to deliver through put capacity
	Growth	Expected future growth rate of service request
	Growth period	Time period needed to reach the expected growth rate
	Peak profile short term	Short-term profile of peak service traffic
	Peak profile long term	Long-term profile of peak service traffic
Control	No additional attributes	This metamodel entity has only basic attributes
Driver	No additional attributes	This metamodel entity has only basic attributes
Event	No additional attributes	This metamodel entity has only basic attributes
Function	Standards class	Non-Standard, Proposed Standard, Provisional Standard, Standard, Phasing-Out Standard, Retired Standard
	Standard creation date	If the product is a standard, when the standard was created
	Last standard review date	Last date that the standard was reviewed

元模型实体属性	描述	
契约	局部化特征	服务支持局部不同的消费者群组变体的能力
	国际化特征	服务支持业务逻辑和数据表达形式（如字符集）国际性变化的能力
	互用性特征	服务与组织内外的不同技术环境互用的能力
	可伸缩性特征	服务按其运行环境的需求适当地增加或减少其性能或生产力的能力
	可移植性特征	关于数据、人员、应用和组件
	可扩展性特征	接受新功能性的能力
	能力特征	服务提供商满足要求的已契约化的能力
	吞吐量	所需的吞吐能力
	吞吐周期	交付吞吐能力所需的时间区间
	增长	服务要求的预期未来增长率
	增长周期	达到预期增长率所需的时间区间
	短期峰值概要	峰值服务流量的短期概要
	长期峰值概要	峰值服务流量的长期概要
控制	无附加属性	该元模型实体只有基本属性
驱动因素	无附加属性	该元模型实体只有基本属性
事件	无附加属性	该元模型实体只有基本属性
功能	标准类别	非标准、建议标准、临时标准、标准、淘汰标准、退役标准
	标准创建日期	如果产品是一种标准，则指的是该标准被创建的时间
	上次标准审视日期	标准被审视的上一个日期

Metamodel Entity Attribute	Description	
Function	Next standard review date	Next date for the standard to bereviewed
	Retire date	Date when the standard was/will be retired
Goal	No additional attributes	This metamodel entity has only basic attributes
Measure	No additional attributes	This metamodel entity has only basic attributes
Objective	No additional attributes	This metamodel entity has only basic attributes
Organization Unit	Headcount	Number of FTEs working within the organization
Process	Standards class	Non-Standard, Proposed Standard, Provisional Standard, Standard, Phasing-Out Standard, Retired Standard
	Standard creation date	If the product is a standard, when the standard was created
	Last standard review date	Last date that the standard was reviewed
	Next standard review date	Next date for the standard to be reviewed
	Retire date	Date when the standard was/will be retired
	Process criticality	Criticality of this process to business operations
	Manual or automated	Whether this process issupported by IT or is a manual process
	Process volumetrics	Data on frequency of process execution
Product	No additional attributes	This metamodel entity has only basic attributes
Role	Estimated number of FTEs that operate in this Role	This metamodel entity has only basic attributes
Service Quality	No additional attributes	This metamodel entity has only basic attributes
Service	Standards class	Non-Standard, Proposed Standard, Provisional Standard, Standard, Phasing-Out Standard, Retired Standard
	Standard creation date	If the product is a standard, when the standard was created
	Last standard review date	Last date that the standard was reviewed
	Next standard review date	Next date for the standard to be reviewed
	Retire date	Date when the standard was/will be retired

元模型实体属性	描述	
功能	下次标准审视日期	审视标准的下一个日期
	退役日期	标准已/要退役的日期
目标	无附加属性	该元模型实体只有基本属性
测度	无附加属性	该元模型实体只有基本属性
目的	无附加属性	该元模型实体只有基本属性
组织单元	总人数	在组织内工作的 FTE 数目
流程	标准类别	非标准、建议标准、临时标准、标准、淘汰标准、退役标准
	标准创建日期	如果产品是一种标准，则指的是该标准被创建的时间
	上次标准审视日期	标准被审视的上一个日期
	下次标准审视日期	审视标准的下一个日期
	退役日期	标准已/要退役的日期
	流程关键性	该流程对业务运作的关键程度
	手动或自动	该流程是由 IT 支持还是作为一种手动流程
	流程容量说明	关于流程执行频率的数据
产品	无附加属性	该元模型实体只有基本属性
角色	以该角色工作的预计数目的 FTE	该元模型实体只有基本属性
服务质量	无附加属性	该元模型实体只有基本属性
服务	标准类别	非标准、建议标准、临时标准、标准、淘汰标准、退役标准
	标准创建日期	如果产品是一种标准，则指的是该标准被创建的时间
	上次标准审视日期	标准被审视的上一个日期
	下次标准审视日期	审视标准的下一个日期
	退役日期	标准已/要退役的日期

Metamodel Entity Attribute	Description	
Application Component	Standards class	Non-Standard, Proposed Standard, Provisional Standard, Standard, Phasing-Out Standard, Retired Standard
	Standard creation date	If the product is a standard, when the standard was created
	Last standard review date	Last date that the standard was reviewed
	Next standard review date	Next date for the standard to be reviewed
	Retire date	Date when the standard was/will be retired
Information SystemService	Standards class	NonStandard, Proposed Standard, Provisional Standard, Standard, Phasing-Out Standard, Retired Standard
	Standard creation date	If the product is a standard, when the standard was created
	Last standard review date	Last date that the standard was reviewed
	Next standard review date	Next date for the standard to be reviewed
	Retire date	Date when the standard was/will be retired
Logical Application Component	Standards class	Non-Standard, Proposed Standard, Provisional Standard, Standard, Phasing-Out Standard, Retired Standard
	Standard creation date	If the product is a standard, when the standard was created
	Last standard review date	Last date that the standard was reviewed
	Next standard review date	Next date for the standard to be reviewed
	Retire date	Date when the standard was/will be retired
Physical Application Component	Lifecycle status	Proposed, In Development,Live, Phasing Out, Retired
	Standards class	Non-Standard, Proposed Standard, Provisional Standard, Standard, Phasing-Out Standard, Retired Standard
	Standard creation date	If the product is a standard, when the standard was created
	Last standard review date	Last date that the standard was reviewed
	Next standard review date	Next date for the standard to be reviewed
	Retire date	Date when the standard was/will be retired

元模型实体属性	描述	
应用组件	标准类别	非标准、建议标准、临时标准、标准、淘汰标准、退役标准
	标准创建日期	如果产品是一种标准，则指的是该标准被创建的时间
	上次标准审视日期	标准被审视的上一个日期
	下次标准审视日期	审视标准的下一个日期
	退役日期	标准已/要退役的日期
信息系统服务	标准类别	非标准、建议标准、临时标准、标准、淘汰标准、退役标准
	标准创建日期	如果产品是一种标准，则指的是该标准被创建的时间
	上次标准审视日期	标准被审视的上一个日期
	下次标准审视日期	审视标准的下一个日期
	退役日期	标准已/要退役的日期
逻辑应用组件	标准类别	非标准、建议标准、临时标准、标准、淘汰标准、退役标准
	标准创建日期	如果产品是一种标准，则指的是该标准被创建的时间
	上次标准审视日期	标准被审视的上一个日期
	下次标准审视日期	审视标准的下一个日期
	退役日期	标准已/要退役的日期
物理应用组件	生命周期状态	提议的、开发中的、现行的、淘汰的、退役的
	标准类别	非标准、建议标准、临时标准、标准、淘汰标准、退役标准
	标准创建日期	如果产品是一种标准，则指的是该标准被创建的时间
	上次标准审视日期	标准被审视的上一个日期
	下次标准审视日期	审视标准的下一个日期
	退役日期	标准已/要退役的日期

Metamodel Entity Attribute	Description	
Physical Application Component	Initial live date	Date when the first release of the application was/will be released into production
	Date of last release	Date when the last release of the application was released into production
	Date of next release	Date when the next release of the application will be released into production
	Retirement date	Date when the application was/will be retired
	Availability characteristics	Degree to which something is available for use
	Service times	Hours during which the application must be available
	Manageability characteristics	Ability to gather information about the state of something and control it
	Serviceability characteristics	Ability to identify problems and take corrective action, such as to repair or upgrade acomponent in a running system
	Performance characteristics	Ability of a component to perform its tasks in an appropriate time
	Reliability characteristics	Resistance to failure
	Recoverability characteristics	Ability to restore a system to a working state after an interruption
	Locatability characteristics	Ability of a system to be found when needed
	Security characteristics	Ability of a system to prevent unauthorized access to functions and data
	Privacy characteristics	Protection of data from unauthorized access
	Integrity characteristics	Ability of a system to ensure that data has not been corrupted
	Credibility characteristics	Ability of a system to ensure that the service request originates from an authorized source
	Localization characteristics	Ability of a service to support localized variants for different consumer groups
	Internationalization characteristics	Ability of a service to support international variations in business logic and data representation (such as character set)

元模型实体属性	描述	
物理应用组件	初始使用日期	应用的第一个版本曾经/将要投入生产时的日期
	上一次发布的日期	应用的上一个版本投入生产时的日期
	下一次发布的日期	应用的下一个版本将要投入生产时的日期
	退役日期	应用已/要退役的日期
	可供使用性特征	某件事物可供使用的程度
	服务时间	应用必须可用的小时数
	可管理性特征	收集某件事物的状态信息以及控制该信息的能力
	可服务性特征	提出问题并采取纠正措施的能力，如修复或升级运行系统中的一个组件
	性能特征	组件在适当时间内执行其任务的能力
	可靠性特征	抗故障能力
	可恢复性特征	中断后将系统恢复到工作状态的能力
	可定位性特征	在需要时系统能被发现的能力
	安保性特征	系统防止未经授权访问功能和数据的能力
	保密特征	防止数据经受未经授权的访问
	完整性特征	系统确保数据没有被损坏的能力
	可信度特征	系统确保服务要求源于已授权来源的能力
	局部化特征	服务支持局部不同的消费者群组变体的能力
	国际化特征	服务支持业务逻辑和数据表达形式（如字符集）国际性变化的能力

Metamodel Entity Attribute	Description	
Physical Application Component	Interoperability characteristics	Ability of the service to interoperate with different technical environments, inside and outside of the organization
	Scalability characteristics	Ability of the service to grow or shrink its performance or capacity appropriately to the demands of the environment in which it operates
	Portability characteristics	Of data, people, applications, and components
	Extensibility characteristics	Ability to accept new functionality
	Capacity characteristics	Contracted capacity of the service provider to meet requests
	Throughput	Required throughput capacity
	Throughput period	Time period needed to deliver throughput capacity
	Growth	Expected future growth rate of service request
	Growth period	Time period needed to reach the expected growth rate
	Peak profile short term	Short-term profile of peak service traffic
	Peak profile long term	Long-term profile of peak service traffic
Data Entity	Category	The following categories of dataentity apply: Message, Internally Stored Entity
	Privacy classification	Level of restriction placed on access to the data
	Retention classification	Level of retention to be placed on the data
Logical Data Component	Standards class	Non-Standard, ProposedStandard, Provisional Standard, Standard, Phasing-Out Standard, Retired Standard
	Standard creation date	If the product is a standard, when the standard was created
	Last standard review date	Last date that the standard was reviewed
	Next standard review date	Next date for the standard to be reviewed
	Retire date	Date when the standard was/will be retired
Physical Data Component	Standards class	Non-Standard, ProposedStandard, Provisional Standard, Standard, Phasing-Out Standard, Retired Standard

元模型实体属性	描述	
物理应用组件	互用性特征	服务与组织内外的不同技术环境互用的能力
	可伸缩性特征	服务按其运行环境的需求适当地增加或减少其性能或生产力的能力
	可移植性特征	关于数据、人员、应用和组件
	可扩展性特征	接受新功能的能力
	能力特征	服务提供商满足要求的契约能力
	吞吐量	所需的吞吐能力
	吞吐周期	交付吞吐能力所需的时间区间
	增长	服务要求的预期未来增长率
	增长周期	达到预期增长率所需的时间区间
	短期峰值概要	峰值服务流量的短期概要
	长期峰值概要	峰值服务流量的长期概要
数据实体	类别	下列数据实体的类别适用：消息、内部存储实体
	隐私分类	对数据访问设置的限制水平
	保留分类	对数据设置的保留水平
逻辑数据组件	标准类别	非标准、建议标准、临时标准、标准、淘汰标准、退役标准
	标准创建日期	如果产品是一种标准，则指的是该标准被创建的时间
	上次标准审视日期	标准被审视的上一个日期
	下次标准审视日期	审视标准的下一个日期
	退役日期	标准已/要退役的日期
物理数据组件	标准类别	非标准、建议标准、临时标准、标准、淘汰标准、退役标准

Metamodel Entity Attribute	Description	
Physical Date Component	Standard creation date	If the product is a standard, when the standard was created
	Last standard review date	Last date that the standard was reviewed.
	Next standard review date	Next date for the standard to be reviewed
	Retire date	Date when the standard was/will be retired
Logical Technology Component	Standards class	Non-Standard, Proposed Standard, Provisional Standard, Standard, Phasing-Out Standard, Retired Standard
	Standard creation date	If the product is a standard, when the standard was created
	Last standard review date	Last date that the standard was reviewed
	Next standard review date	Next date for the standard to be reviewed
	Retire date	Date when the standard was/will be retired
	Category	Logical Technology Components are categorized according to the TOGAF TRM, which may be extended to meet the needs of an individual organization
Physical Technology Component	Standards class	Non-Standard, Proposed Standard, Provisional Standard, Standard, Phasing-Out Standard, Retired Standard
	Standard creation date	If the product is a standard, when the standard was created
	Last standard review date	Last date that the standard was reviewed
	Next standard review date	Next date for the standard to be reviewed
	Retire date	Date when the standard was/will be retired
	Category	Physical Technology Components are categorized according to the TOGAF TRM, which may be extended to meet the needs of an individual organization
	Product name	Name of the product making up the technology component
	Module name	Module, or other sub-product, name making up the technology component

元模型实体属性	描述	
物理数据组件	标准创建日期	如果产品是一种标准，则指的是该标准被创建的时间
	上次标准审视日期	标准被审视的上一个日期
	下次标准审视日期	审视标准的下一个日期
	退役日期	标准已/要退役的日
逻辑技术组件	标准类别	非标准、建议标准、临时标准、标准、淘汰标准、退役标准
	标准创建日期	如果产品是一种标准，则指的是该标准被创建的时间
	上次标准审视日期	标准被审视的上一个日期
	下次标准审视日期	审视标准的下一个日期
	退役日期	标准已/要退役的日期
	类别	按照 TOGAF TRM 对逻辑技术组件进行分类，其中 TOGAF TRM 可对逻辑技术组件进行扩展以满足个别组织的需要
物理技术组件	标准类别	非标准、建议标准、临时标准、标准、淘汰标准、退役标准
	标准创建日期	如果产品是一种标准，则指的是该标准被创建的时间
	上次标准审视日期	标准被审视的上一个日期
	下次标准审视日期	审视标准的下一个日期
	退役日期	标准已/要退役的日期
	类别	按照 TOGAF TRM 对物理技术组件进行分类，其中 TOGAF TRM 可对物理技术组件进行扩展以满足个别组织的需要
	产品名称	构成技术组件的产品的名称
	模块名称	构成技术组件的模块或其他子产品的名称

Metamodel Entity Attribute	Description	
Physical Technology Component	Vendor	Vendor providing the technology component
	Version	Version of the product making up the technology component
Platform Service	Standards class	Non-Standard, Proposed Standard, Provisional Standard, Standard, Phasing-Out Standard, Retired Standard
	Category	Platform Services are categorized according to the TOGAF TRM, which may be extended to meet the needs of an individual organization
Technology Component	Standards class	Non-Standard, Proposed Standard, Provisional Standard, Standard, Phasing-Out Standard, Retired Standard
Work Package	Category	The following categories of work package apply: Work Package, Work Stream, Project, Program, Portfolio
	Capability delivered	Describes the contribution this work package makes to capability delivery

34.7 Metamodel Relationships

Source Entity	Target Entity	Name	Extension Module
Actor	Event	Generates	Process
Actor	Event	Resolves	Process
Actor	Function	Interacts with	Core
Actor	Function	Performs	Core
Actor	Location	Operates in	Infrastructure Consolidation
Actor	Organization Unit	Belongs to	Core
Actor	Process	Participates in	Core
Actor	Role	Performs task in	Core
Actor	Service	Consumes	Core
Actor	Actor	Decomposes	Core
Actor	Data Entity	Supplies/Consumes	Core
Capability	Work Package	Is delivered by	Core
Contract	Service	Governs and Measures	Governance
Contract	Service Quality	Meets	Governance
Control	Process	Ensures correct operation of	Process

元模型实体属性	描述	
物理技术组件	厂商	提供技术组件的厂商
	版本	构成技术组件的产品的版本
平台服务	标准类别	非标准、建议标准、临时标准、标准、淘汰标准、退役标准
	类别	按照 TOGAF TRM 对平台服务进行分类，其中 TOGAF TRM 可对平台服务进行扩展以满足个别组织的需要
技术组件	标准类别	非标准、建议标准、临时标准、标准、淘汰标准、退役标准
工作包	类别	下列工作包的类别适用：工作包、工作流、项目、项目群、项目谱系
	所交付的能力	描述该工作包对能力交付的贡献

34.7 元模型关系

源实体	目标实体	名称	扩展模块
施动者	事件	产生	流程
施动者	事件	解决	流程
施动者	功能	交互	核心
施动者	功能	执行	核心
施动者	位置	运行于	基础设施合并
施动者	组织单元	属于	核心
施动者	流程	参与到	核心
施动者	角色	执行任务于	核心
施动者	服务	使用	核心
施动者	施动者	分解	核心
施动者	数据实体	提供/使用	核心
能力	工作包	被交付	核心
契约	服务	治理和衡量	治理
契约	服务质量	满足	治理
控制	流程	确保正确运行	流程

Source Entity	Target Entity	Name	Extension Module
Data Entity	Logical Application Component	Is processed by	Core
Data Entity	Logical Data Component	Resides within	Data
Data Entity	Service	Is accessed and updated through	Core
Data Entity	Data Entity	Decomposes	Core
Data Entity	Data Entity	Relates to	Core
Driver	Goal	Creates	Motivation
Driver	Organization Unit	Motivates	Motivation
Driver	Driver	Decomposes	Motivation
Event	Actor	Is resolved by	Process
Event	Actor	Is generated by	Process
Event	Process	Is resolved by	Process
Event	Process	Is generated by	Process
Event	Service	Is resolved by	Process
Function	Actor	Supports	Core
Function	Actor	Is performed by	Core
Function	Organization Unit	Is owned by	Core
Function	Process	Supports	Core
Function	Process	Is realized by	Core
Function	Role	Can be accessed by	Core
Function	Service	Is bounded by	Core
Function	Function	Decomposes	Core
Function	Function	Communicates with	Core
Goal	Driver	Addresses	Motivation
Goal	Objective	Is realized through	Motivation
Goal	Goal	Decomposes	Motivation
Location	Actor	Contains	Infrastructure Consolidation
Location	Organization Unit	Contains	Infrastructure Consolidation
Location	Physical Application Component	Contains	Infrastructure Consolidation
Location	Physical Data Component	Contains	Infrastructure Consolidation
Location	Physical Technology Component	Contains	Infrastructure Consolidation
Location	Location	Decomposes	Infrastructure Consolidation
Logical Application Component	Data Entity	Operates on	Core
Logical Application Component	Physical Application Component	Is extended by	Infrastructure Consolidation
Logical Application Component	Service	Implements	Core
Logical Application Component	Logical Application Component	Decomposes	Core

源实体	目标实体	名称	扩展模块
数据实体	逻辑应用组件	被处理	核心
数据实体	逻辑数据组件	存在于	数据
数据实体	服务	通过…访问和更新	核心
数据实体	数据实体	分解	核心
数据实体	数据实体	关联	核心
驱动因素	目标	创建	动机
驱动因素	组织单元	激发	动机
驱动因素	驱动因素	分解	动机
事件	施动者	被解决	流程
事件	施动者	被产生	流程
事件	流程	被解决	流程
事件	流程	被产生	流程
事件	服务	被解决	流程
功能	施动者	支持	核心
功能	施动者	被执行	核心
功能	组织单元	被拥有	核心
功能	流程	支持	核心
功能	流程	被实现	核心
功能	角色	可被访问	核心
功能	服务	被约束	核心
功能	功能	分解	核心
功能	功能	沟通	核心
目标	驱动因素	应对	动机
目标	目的	通过…实现	动机
目标	目标	分解	动机
位置	施动者	包含	基础设施合并
位置	组织单元	包含	基础设施合并
位置	物理应用组件	包含	基础设施合并
位置	物理数据组件	包含	基础设施合并
位置	物理技术组件	包含	基础设施合并
位置	位置	分解	基础设施合并
逻辑应用组件	数据实体	运行于	核心
逻辑应用组件	物理应用组件	被扩展	基础设施合并
逻辑应用组件	服务	实施	核心
逻辑应用组件	逻辑应用组件	分解	核心

Source Entity	Target Entity	Name	Extension Module
Logical Application Component	Logical Application Component	Communicates with	Core
Logical Data Component	Data Entity	Encapsulates	Data
Logical Data Component	Physical Data Component	Is extended by	Data
Logical Technology Component	Physical Technology Component	Is extended by	Infrastructure Consolidation
Logical Technology Component	Platform Service	Supplies	Core
Logical Technology Component	Service	Provides platform for	Core
Logical Technology Component	Logical Technology Component	Decomposes	Core
Logical Technology Component	Logical Technology Component	Is dependent on	Core
Measure	Objective	Sets performance criteria for	Governance
Measure	Service	Sets performance criteria for	Governance
Measure	Measure	Decomposes	Governance
Objective	Goal	Realizes	Motivation
Objective	Measure	Is tracked against	Governance
Objective	Objective	Decomposes	Motivation
Organization Unit	Actor	Contains	Core
Organization Unit	Driver	Is motivated by	Core
Organization Unit	Function	Owns	Core
Organization Unit	Location	Operates in	Core
Organization Unit	Product	Produces	Core
Organization Unit	Service	Owns and Governs	Core
Organization Unit	Organization Unit	Decomposes	Core
Physical Application Component	Location	Is hosted in	Infrastructure Consolidation
Physical Application Component	Logical Application Component	Extends	Infrastructure Consolidation
Physical Application Component	Physical Data Component	Encapsulates	Data Modeling
Physical Application Component	Physical Technology Component	Is realized by	Core
Physical Application Component	Physical Application Component	Decomposes	Core
Physical Application Component	Physical Application Component	Communicates with	Core
Physical Data Component	Location	Is hosted in	Infrastructure Consolidation
Physical Data Component	Logical Data Component	Extends	Data
Physical Data Component	Physical Data Component	Decomposes	Core
Physical Data Component	Physical Application Component	Encapsulates	Data Modeling

源实体	目标实体	名称	扩展模块
逻辑应用组件	逻辑应用组件	与…沟通	核心
逻辑数据组件	数据实体	封装	数据
逻辑数据组件	物理数据组件	被扩展	数据
逻辑技术组件	物理技术组件	被扩展	基础设施合并
逻辑技术组件	平台服务	提供	核心
逻辑技术组件	服务	为…提供平台	核心
逻辑技术组件	逻辑技术组件	分解	核心
逻辑技术组件	逻辑技术组件	取决于	核心
测度	目的	设置性能准则	治理
测度	服务	设置性能准则	治理
测度	测度	分解	治理
目的	目标	实现	动机
目的	测度	按照…跟踪	治理
目的	目的	分解	动机
组织单元	施动者	包含	核心
组织单元	驱动因素	被激发	核心
组织单元	功能	拥有	核心
组织单元	位置	运行于	核心
组织单元	产品	生产	核心
组织单元	服务	拥有和治理	核心
组织单元	组织单元	分解	核心
物理应用组件	位置	被托管于	基础设施合并
物理应用组件	逻辑应用组件	扩展	基础设施合并
物理应用组件	物理数据组件	封装	数据建模
物理应用组件	物理技术组件	被实现	核心
物理应用组件	物理应用组件	分解	核心
物理应用组件	物理应用组件	与…沟通	核心
物理数据组件	位置	被托管于	基础设施合并
物理数据组件	逻辑数据组件	扩展	数据
物理数据组件	物理数据组件	分解	核心
物理数据组件	物理应用组件	封装	数据建模

Source Entity	Target Entity	Name	Extension Module
PhysicalTechnology Component	Location	Is hosted in	Infrastructure Consolidation
Physical Technology Component	Physical Application Component	Realizes	Core
Physical Technology Component	Logical Technology Component	Extends	Infrastructure Consolidation
Physical Technology Component	Physical Technology Component	Decomposes	Core
Physical Technology Component	Physical Technology Component	Is dependent on	Core
Platform Service	Logical Technology Component	Is supplied by	Core
Process	Actor	Involves	Core
Process	Control	Is guided by	Process
Process	Event	Generates	Process
Process	Event	Resolves	Process
Process	Function	Orchestrates	Core
Process	Function	Decomposes	Core
Process	Product	Produces	Process
Process	Service	Orchestrates	Core
Process	Service	Decomposes	Core
Process	Process	Decomposes	Core
Process	Process	Precedes/Follows	Core
Product	Organization Unit	Is produced by	Process
Product	Process	Is produced by	Process
Role	Actor	Is performed by	Core
Role	Function	Accesses	Core
Role	Role	Decomposes	Core
Service	Actor	Is provided to	Core
Service	Contract	Is governed and measured by	Governance
Service	Data Entity	Provides	Core
Service	Data Entity	Consumes	Core
Service	Event	Resolves	Process
Service	Function	Provides governed interface to access	Core
Service	Logical Application Component	Is realized through	Core
Service	Logical Technology Component	Is implemented on	Core
Service	Measure	Is tracked against	Governance
Service	Organization Unit	Is owned and governed by	Core
Service	Process	Supports	Core
Service	Process	Is realized by	Core
Service	Service Quality	Meets	Governance
Service	Service	Consumes	Core
Service	Service	Decomposes	Core
Service Quality	Contract	Applies to	Governance
Service Quality	Service	Applies to	Governance
Work Package	Capability	Delivers	Core

源实体	目标实体	名称	扩展模块
物理技术组件	位置	被托管于	基础设施合并
物理技术组件	物理应用组件	实现	核心
物理技术组件	逻辑技术组件	扩展	基础设施合并
物理技术组件	物理技术组件	分解	核心
物理技术组件	物理技术组件	取决于	核心
平台服务	逻辑技术组件	被提供	核心
流程	施动者	涉及	核心
流程	控制	被指导	流程
流程	事件	产生	流程
流程	事件	解决	流程
流程	功能	编排	核心
流程	功能	分解	核心
流程	产品	生产	流程
流程	服务	编排	核心
流程	服务	分解	核心
流程	流程	分解	核心
流程	流程	先于/其后	核心
产品	组织单元	被生产	流程
产品	流程	被生产	流程
角色	施动者	被执行	核心
角色	功能	访问	核心
角色	角色	分解	核心
服务	施动者	提供给	核心
服务	契约	被治理并被测量	治理
服务	数据实体	提供	核心
服务	数据实体	使用	核心
服务	事件	解决	流程
服务	功能	提供已治理的访问界面	核心
服务	逻辑应用组件	通过…实现	核心
服务	逻辑技术组件	被实施于	核心
服务	测度	按照…跟踪	治理
服务	组织单元	被拥有且治理	核心
服务	流程	支持	核心
服务	流程	被实现	核心
服务	服务质量	满足	治理
服务	服务	使用	核心
服务	服务	分解	核心
服务质量	契约	应用于	治理
服务质量	服务	应用于	治理
工作包	能力	交付	核心

Chapter 35
Architectural Artifacts

This chapter discusses the concepts surrounding architecture artifacts and then describes the artifacts that are recommended to be created for each phase within the Architecture Development Method (ADM). It also presents guidance for developing a set of views, some or all of which may be appropriate in a particular architecture development.

35.1 Basic Concepts

Architectural artifacts are created in order to describe a system, solution, or state of the enterprise. The concepts discussed in this section have been adapted from more formal definitions contained in ISO/IEC 42010: 2007 and illustrated in Figure 35-1.[5]

Note: The notation used is from the Unified Modeling Language (UML) specification.

5.Figure 35-1 is reprinted, with permission, from IEEE Std 1471-2000, Systems and Software Engineering — Recommended Practice for Architectural Description of Software-intensive Systems, Copyright© 2000, by IEEE. The IEEE disclaims any responsibility or liability resulting from the placement and use in the described manner.

第 35 章
架构制品

本章论述架构制品相关的概念，并描述在架构开发方法（ADM）内的每个阶段建议创建的制品。本章还提供开发一系列视图的引导，其中部分或全部视图可适用于特殊架构开发。

35.1 基本概念

架构制品的创建是为了描述 ENTERPRISE 的系统、解决方案或状态。本节论述的概念改编自 ISO/IEC 42010: 2007 所包含的更正式的定义，且如图 35-1 所示。[5]

注：所用注释来自于统一建模语言（UML）规范。

5.图 35-1 是在经允许的情况下从 IEEE 标准 1471-2000，“系统和软件工程——软件密集型系统的架构描述的推荐做法，版权©2000”转载的。IEEE 不承担以所述方式安排和使用所产生的任何责任或义务。

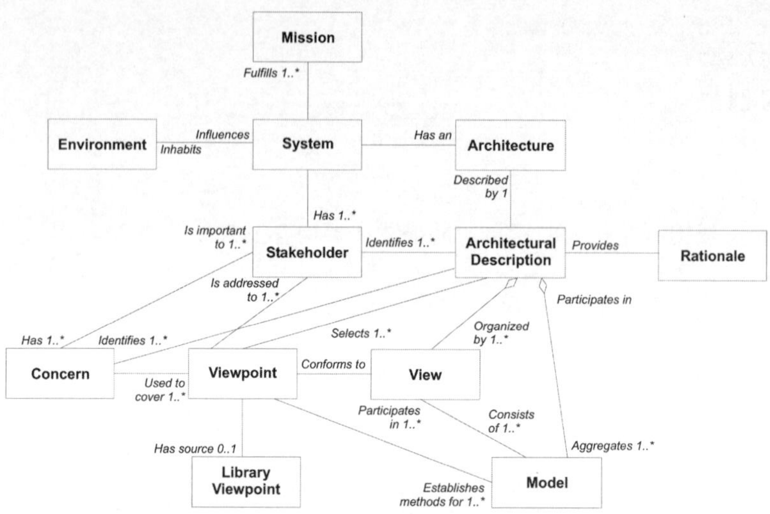

Figure 35-1 Basic Architectural Concepts

A "system" is a collection of components organized to accomplish a specific function or set of functions.

The "architecture" of a system is the system's fundamental organization, embodied in its components, their relationships to each other and to the environment, and the principles guiding its design and evolution.

An "architecture description" is a collection of artifacts that document an architecture. In TOGAF, architecture views are the key artifacts in an architecture description.

"Stakeholders" are people who have key roles in, or concerns about, the system; for example, as users, developers, or managers. Different stakeholders with different roles in the system will have different concerns. Stakeholders can be individuals, teams, or organizations (or classes thereof).

"Concerns" are the key interests that are crucially important to the stakeholders in the system, and determine the acceptability of the system. Concerns may pertain to any aspect of the system's functioning, development, or operation, including considerations such as performance, reliability, security, distribution, and evolvability.

A "view" is a representation of a whole system from the perspective of a related set of concerns. In capturing or representing the design of a system architecture, the architect will typically createone or more architecture models, possibly using different tools. A view will comprise selectedparts of one or more models, chosen so as to demonstrate to a particular stakeholder or group of stakeholders that their concerns are being adequately addressed in the design of the system architecture.

A "viewpoint" defines the perspective from which a view is taken. More specifically, a viewpoint defines: how to construct and use a view (by means of an appropriate schema or template); the information that should appear in the view; the modeling techniques for expressing and analyzing the information; and a rationale for these choices (e.g., by describing the purpose and intended audience of the view).

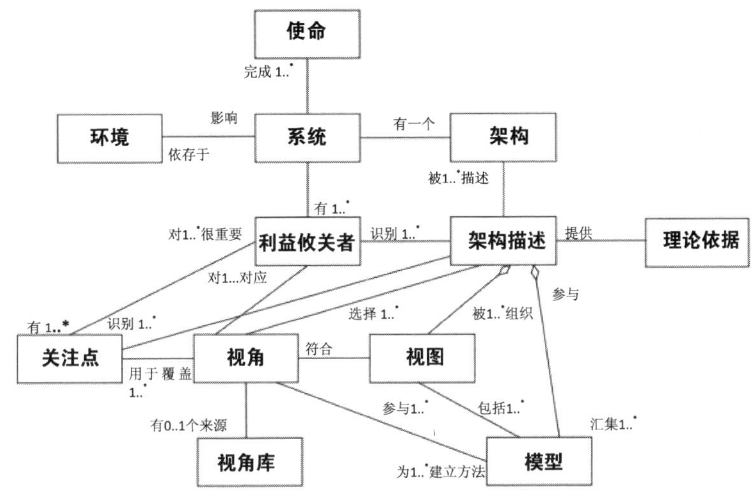

图 35-1　基本架构概念

一个“系统”是为实现一个特定功能或功能集所组织起来的组件的集合。

系统的“架构”是系统的基础组织，体现在其组件、各组件之间以及组件与环境之间的相互关系，以及指导系统设计和演进的原则。

“架构描述”是对一个架构进行文件化的制品的集合。在 TOGAF 中，架构视图是架构描述中的关键制品。

“利益攸关者”是在系统中担任关键角色或关注系统的人员；例如，用户、开发人员或管理人员。在系统中，担任不同角色的不同利益攸关者会有不同的关注点。利益攸关者可以是个人、团队或组织（或诸如此类的）。

“关注点”是对系统中的利益攸关者而言至关重要的关键兴趣点，并决定系统的可接受性。关注点可能与系统的功能、开发或运行的任一方面相关，包括诸如性能、可靠性、安保性、分布特点和可演进性等考量因素。

“视图”是从一系列相关关注点关注的层级出发的、对整个系统的一种表达。在获取或表达系统架构的设计时，架构师通常可能使用不同的工具创建一个或多个架构模型。视图将由一个或多个模型的选定部分组成，视图被选用来向特定利益攸关者或利益攸关者群组展示其关注点在系统架构的设计中得到了充分应对。

“视角”定义获得视图的关注层级。更具体地说，一个视角定义了：如何构建和使用一个视图（借助于合适的模式或模板）；应该出现在视图中的信息；表达和分析信息的建模技术；以及做出这些选择的理由依据（例如，通过描述视图的目的和预期读者）。

- A view is what you see. A viewpoint is where you are looking from — the vantage point or perspective that determines what you see.
- Viewpoints are generic, and can be stored in libraries for re-use. A view is always specific to the architecture for which it is created.
- Every view has an associated viewpoint that describes it, at least implicitly. ISO/IEC42010: 2007 encourages architects to define viewpoints explicitly. Making this distinction between the content and schema of a view may seem at first to be an unnecessary overhead, but it provides a mechanism for re-using viewpoints across different architectures.

In summary, then, architecture views are representations of the overall architecture in terms meaningful to stakeholders. They enable the architecture to be communicated to and understood by the stakeholders, so they can verify that the system will address their concerns.

Note: The terms "concern" and "requirement" are not synonymous. A concern is an area of interest.So, system reliability might be a concern/area of interest for some stakeholders. The reason why architects should identify concerns and associate them with viewpoints, is to ensure that those concerns will be addressed in some fashion by the models of the architecture. For example, if the only viewpoint selected by an architect is a structural viewpoint, then reliability concerns are almost certainly not being addressed, since they cannot be represented in a structural model. Within that concern, stakeholders may have many distinct requirements: different classes of users may have very different reliability requirements for different capabilities of the system.

Concerns are the root of the process of decomposition into requirements. Concerns are represented in the architecture by these requirements. Requirements should be SMART (e.g., specific metrics).

35.1.1 Simple Example of a Viewpoint and View

For many architectures, a useful viewpoint is that of business domains, which can be illustrated by an example from The Open Group itself.

The viewpoint is specified as follows:

Viewpoint Element	Description
Stakeholders	Management Board, Chief Executive Officer
Concerns	Show the top-level relationships between geographical sites and business functions.
Modeling technique	Nested boxes diagram. Outer boxes = locations; inner boxes = business functions. Semantics of nesting = functions performed in the locations.

The corresponding view of The Open Group (in 2008) is shown in Figure 35-2.

- 视图是你所看到的。视角是你从哪里看——决定你看到什么的有利的点或关注层级。
- 视角是一般性的，可以储存在视角库中，以供复用。视图对于从中创建的架构而言总是特定的。
- 每个视图都具有——至少隐含地具有——描述它的相关视角。ISO/IEC 42010:2007 鼓励架构师明确地定义视角。最初看起来，在视图的内容和模式之间做出这种区分似乎是一笔不必要的负担，但它提供一种跨不同架构复用视角的机制。

总之，架构视图以对利益攸关者有意义的方式表现了总体架构。视图使架构可以被传达给利益攸关者并被其理解，因此他们能够验证系统将考虑其关注点。

注：术语“关注点”和“需求”不是同义的。关注点是所感兴趣之领域。因此，系统可靠性可以是某些利益攸关者所感兴趣之关注点/领域。架构师应识别关注点，并将其与视角联系起来，原因是为了确保那些关注点会以某种方式通过架构模型来被考虑。例如，如果架构师所选择的唯一视角是结构性视角，那么，可靠性关注点几乎肯定不会被考虑，因为它们不能在结构性模型中被表达出来。在该关注点范围内，利益攸关者可能具有多种独特的需求：不同种类的用户可能对系统的不同能力有截然不同的可靠性需求。

关注点是将流程分解成需求的根源。关注点在架构中是通过这些需求表达的。需求应是 SMART 的（如，特定的衡量标准）。

35.1.1 视角和视图的简单示例

对于许多架构而言，一个有用的视角是业务领域的视角，它可通过 The Open Group 本身的示例详细阐明。

视角详述如下：

视角元素	描述
利益攸关者	管理委员会、首席执行官
关注点	表明地理位置和业务功能之间的顶层关系。
建模技术	嵌套框图。 外部框＝位置；内部框＝业务功能。 嵌套的语义＝在这些位置上执行的功能。

The Open Group（2008 年）的对应视图如图 35-2 所示。

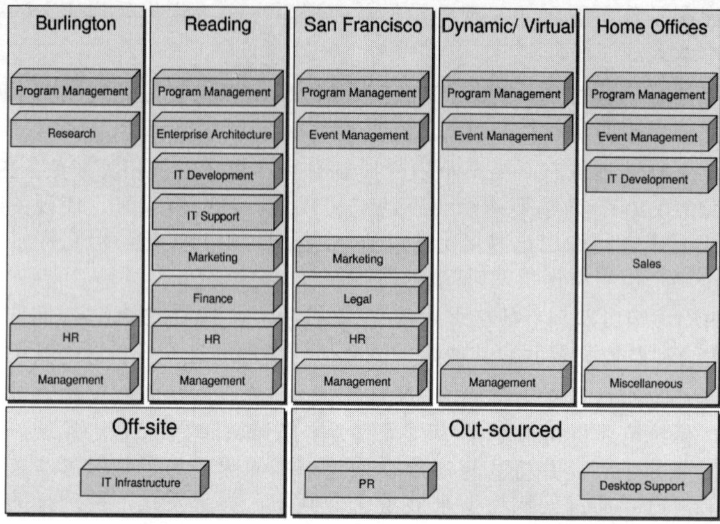

Figure 35-2 Example View — The Open Group Business Domains in 2008

35.2 Developing Views in the ADM

35.2.1 General Guidelines

The choice of which particular architecture views to develop is one of the key decisions that the architect has to make.

The architect has a responsibility for ensuring the completeness (fitness-for-purpose) of the architecture, in terms of adequately addressing all the pertinent concerns of its stakeholders; and the integrity of the architecture, in terms of connecting all the various views to each other, satisfactorily reconciling the conflicting concerns of different stakeholders, and showing the trade-offs made in so doing (as between security and performance, for example).

The choice has to be constrained by considerations of practicality, and by the principle of fitness-for-purpose (i.e., the architecture should be developed only to the point at which it is fit-for-purpose, and not reiterated *ad infinitum* as an academic exercise).

As explained in Part II: Architecture Development Method (ADM), the development of architecture views is an iterative process. The typical progression is from business to technology, using a technique such as business scenarios (see Part III, Chapter 26) to properly identify all pertinent concerns; and from high-level overview to lower-level detail, continually referring back to the concerns and requirements of the stakeholders throughout the process.

Moreover, each of these progressions has to be made for two distinct environments: the existing environment (referred to as the baseline in the ADM) and the target environment. The architect must develop pertinent architecture views of both the Baseline Architecture and the Target Architecture. This provides the context for the gap analysis at the end of Phases B, C, and D of the ADM, which establishes the elements of the Baseline Architecture to be carried forward and the elements to be added, removed, or replaced.

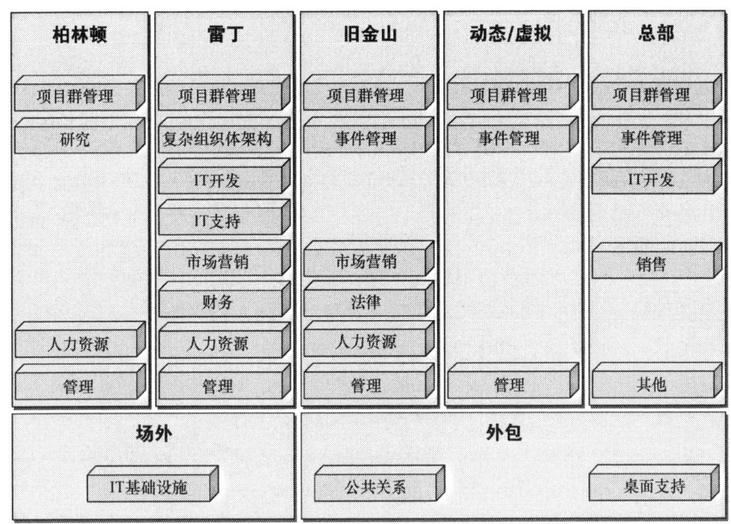

图 35-2 视图示例 — 2008 年 The Open Group 的业务领域

35.2 采用 ADM 开发视图

35.2.1 一般指南

选择开发哪些特殊架构视图是架构师必须做的关键决策之一。

在充分考虑其利益攸关者的所有相关关注点方面，架构师负责确保架构的完备性（适用性），在连接所有不同视图方面，架构师负责确保架构的完整性，从而以令人满意的方式，协调不同利益攸关者的相互冲突的关注点，并表明这么做所做出的权衡（例如，在安保和绩效之间做出权衡）。

选择必须受实用性考量因素和适用性原则约束（即，架构应仅开发至适用的程度，而不是作为一种学术训练被无限地反复进行）。

按照“第二部分：架构开发方法（ADM）”中的说明，架构视图的开发是一个迭代过程。典型的迭代进程是从业务到技术，使用诸如业务场景（见第三部分第 26 章）的技术，恰当地识别所有相关关注点；以及从高层级概述到低层级细节，在整个流程中不断回溯到利益攸关者的关注点和需求。

而且，每个进程必须在两种不同环境下做出：现有环境（称为 ADM 中的基线）和目标环境。架构师必须开发基线架构和目标架构两者的相关架构视图。这可为 ADM 的阶段 B、阶段 C 和阶段 D 末尾的差距分析提供背景环境，建立待向前推进的基线架构的元素和需要添加、删除或替换的元素。

This whole process is explained in Part III, Chapter 27.

35.2.2 View Creation Process

As mentioned above, at the present time TOGAF encourages but does not mandate the use of ISO/IEC 42010: 2007. The following description therefore covers both the situation where ISO/IEC 42010: 2007 has been adopted and where it has not.

ISO/IEC 42010: 2007 itself does not require any specific process for developing viewpoints or creating views from them. Where ISO/IEC 42010: 2007 has been adopted and become well-established practice within an organization, it will often be possible to create the required views for a particular architecture by following these steps:

1. Refer to an existing library of viewpoints.
2. Select the appropriate viewpoints (based on the stakeholders and concerns that need to be covered by views).
3. Generate views of the system by using the selected viewpoints as templates.

This approach can be expected to bring the following benefits:

- Less work for the architects (because the viewpoints have already been defined and therefore the views can be created faster).
- Better comprehensibility for stakeholders (because the viewpoints are already familiar).
- Greater confidence in the validity of the views (because their viewpoints have a known track record).

However, situations can always arise in which a view is needed for which no appropriate viewpoint has been predefined. This is also the situation, of course, when an organization has not yet incorporated ISO/IEC 42010: 2007 into its architecture practice and established a library of viewpoints.

In each case, the architect may choose to develop a new viewpoint that will cover the outstanding need, and then generate a view from it. (This is ISO/IEC 42010: 2007 recommended practice.) Alternatively, a more pragmatic approach can be equally successful: the architect can create an *ad hoc* view for a specific system and later consider whether a generalized form of the implicit viewpoint should be defined explicitly and saved in a library, so that it can be re-used. (This is one way of establishing a library of viewpoints initially.)

Whatever the context, the architect should be aware that every view has a viewpoint, at least implicitly, and that defining the viewpoint in a systematic way (as recommended by ISO/IEC42010: 2007) will help in assessing its effectiveness; i.e., does the viewpoint cover the relevant stakeholder concerns?

第三部分第 27 章解释了整个流程。

35.2.2 视图创建流程

如上所述，目前 TOGAF 鼓励但不强制使用 ISO/IEC 42010: 2007。因此，下列描述涵盖 ISO/IEC 42010: 2007 中已被采用和尚未被采用这两种情况。

ISO/IEC 42010: 2007 本身不要求从中开发视角或创建视图的任何特定流程。在 ISO/IEC 42010: 2007 已被组织采用并成为组织内已建立好的实践时，可能常常按以下步骤为特定架构创建所需视图：

1. 参见现有视角库。
2. 选择恰当的视角（基于视图中要求涵盖的利益攸关者和关注点）。
3. 使用所选视角作为模板来生成系统视图。

预期这种实施途径会带来下列好处：

- 减轻架构师的工作（由于视角已经被定义，因此可更快地创建视图）。
- 更有助于利益攸关者理解（因为视角是已经熟悉的）。
- 视图正确性的可信度更大（因为他们的视角具有已知的追踪记录）。

然而，总会出现需要视角却没有预定义适当视角的情况。当然，当组织尚未将 ISO/IEC 42010: 2007 纳入其架构实践中并建立视角库时，也会出现这种情况。

在上述各种情况下，架构师都可以选择开发一个涵盖未解决需要的新视角，然后根据这个新视角生成一个视图（这是 ISO/IEC 42010: 2007 的推荐实践）。或者，一种更实用的实施途径也同样能够成功：架构师可以为一个特定系统创建一个临时视图，随后考虑是否应明确定义该隐含视角的一般形式并保存在视角库中，以便它可以被复用。（这是最初建立视角库的一种方式。）

无论背景环境是什么，架构师都应意识到：每一个视图都有一个视角，哪怕是隐含视角；以及以系统的方式定义视角（如 ISO/IEC 42010: 2007 中的建议）会有助于评估其有效性；即，视角涵盖相关利益攸关者关注点吗？

35.3 Views, Tools, and Languages

The need for architecture views, and the process of developing them following the ADM, are explained above. This section describes the relationships between architecture views, the tools used to develop and analyze them, and a standard language enabling interoperability between the tools.

35.3.1 Overview

In order to achieve the goals of completeness and integrity in an architecture, architecture views are usually developed, visualized, communicated, and managed using a tool.

In the current state of the market, different tools normally have to be used to develop and analyze different views of the architecture. It is highly desirable that an architecture description be encoded in a standard language, to enable a standard approach to the description of architecture semantics and their re-use among different tools.

A viewpoint is also normally developed, visualized, communicated, and managed using a tool, and it is also highly desirable that standard viewpoints (i.e., templates or schemas) be developed, so that different tools that deal in the same views can interoperate, the fundamental elements of an architecture can be re-used, and the architecture description can be shared among tools.

Issues relating to the evaluation of tools for architecture work are discussed in detail in Part V, Chapter 42.

35.4 Views and Viewpoints

35.4.1 Example of Views and Viewpoints

To illustrate the concepts of views and viewpoints, consider the example of a very simple airport system with two different stakeholders: the pilot and the air traffic controller.

One view can be developed from the viewpoint of the pilot, which addresses the pilot's concerns. Equally, another view can be developed from the viewpoint of the air traffic controller. Neither view completely describes the system in its entirety, because the viewpoint of each stakeholder constrains (and reduces) how each sees the overall system.

The viewpoint of the pilot comprises some concerns that are not relevant to the controller, such as passengers and fuel, while the viewpoint of the controller comprises some concerns not relevant to the pilot, such as other planes. There are also elements shared between the two viewpoints, such as the communication model between the pilot and the controller, and the vital information about the plane itself.

A viewpoint is a model (or description) of the information contained in a view. In our example, one viewpoint is the description of how the pilot sees the system, and the other viewpoint is how the controller sees the system.

Pilots describe the system from their perspective, using a model of their position and vector toward or away from the runway. All pilots use this model, and the model has a specific language that is used to capture information and populate the model.

Controllers describe the system differently, using a model of the airspace and the locations and vectors of aircraft within the airspace. Again, all controllers use a common language derived from the common model in order to capture and communicate information pertinent to their viewpoint.

35.3 视图、工具和语言

上面解释了对架构视图的需要和按照 ADM 开发视图的流程。本节描述架构视图之间的关系、用于开发和分析视图的工具以及使工具之间互用性的标准语言。

35.3.1 概述

为了达到架构完备性和完整性的目的，通常使用一种工具来开发、可视化、沟通和管理架构视图。

在当前市场情形下，通常不得不使用不同的工具来开发和分析不同的架构视图。以一种标准语言来对架构描述进行编码是非常可取的，使架构语义能用标准途径来描述，并能在不同工具之间复用。

通常还使用工具来开发、可视化、沟通和管理视角，并且开发标准视角（即模板或模式）也是非常可取的，从而使处理相同视图的不同工具可互用，架构的基础元素可以被复用，并且架构描述可在多个工具之间共享。

第五部分第 42 章详细论述与架构工作工具的评价相关的议题。

35.4 视图和视角

35.4.1 视图和视角示例

为详细阐明视图和视角的概念，参考一个由两名不同的利益攸关者（飞行员和空中交通管制员）组成的非常简单的机场系统的示例。

一个视图可从飞行员的视角开发，应对飞行员的关注点。同样地，另一个视图可从空中交通管制员的视角开发。两个视图都没有从整体上完整地描述系统，因为每个利益攸关者的视角约束（并简化）其如何看待总体系统。

飞行员的视角包括与管制员无关的一些关注点，如乘客和燃油，而管制员的视角包括与飞行员无关的一些关注点，如其他飞机。两个视角之间还存在共享的元素，如飞行员和管制员之间的通信模型以及关于飞机本身的至关重要信息。

视角是视图中所包含的信息的一个模型（或描述）。在我们的示例中，一个视角是描述飞行员如何看待系统的，另一个视角是描述管制员如何看待系统的。

飞行员从他们的关注层级利用他们的位置和驶向或驶离跑道的航线的模型来描述系统。所有飞行员都使用这个模型，该模型具有用于获取信息并充实该模型的特定语言。

管制员以不同方式利用空域的模型和空域内飞机的位置及航向的模型来描述系统。另外，为了获取和沟通与他们的视角相关的信息，所有管制员都使用源自于常见模型的公共语言。

Fortunately, when controllers talk with pilots, they use a common communication language. (In other words, the models representing their individual viewpoints partially intersect.) Part of this common language is about location and vectors of aircraft, and is essential to safety.

So in essence each viewpoint is an abstract model of how all the stakeholders of a particular type — all pilots, or all controllers — view the airport system.

Tools exist to assist stakeholders, especially when they are interacting with complex models such as the model of an airspace, or the model of air flight.

The interface to the human user of a tool is typically close to the model and language associated with the viewpoint. The unique tools of the pilot are fuel, altitude, speed, and location indicators. The main tool of the controller is radar. The common tool is a radio.

To summarize from the above example, we can see that a view can subset the system through the perspective of the stakeholder, such as the pilot *versus* the controller. This subset can be described by an abstract model called a viewpoint, such as an air flight *versus* an air space model. This description of the view is documented in a partially specialized language, such as

"pilot-speak" *versus* "controller-speak" . Tools are used to assist the stakeholders, and they interface with each other in terms of the language derived from the viewpoint ("pilot-speak" *versus'* "controller-speak").

When stakeholders use common tools, such as the radio contact between pilot and controller, a common language is essential.

35.4.2 Views and Viewpoints in Enterprise Architecture

Now let us map this example to the enterprise architecture. Consider two stakeholders in a new small computing system: the users and the developers.

The users of the system have a viewpoint that reflects their concerns when interacting with the system, and the developers of the system have a different viewpoint. Views that are developed to address either of the two viewpoints are unlikely to exhaustively describe the whole system, because each perspective reduces how each sees the system.

The viewpoint of the user is comprised of all the ways in which the user interacts with the system, not seeing any details such as applications or Database Management Systems (DBMS).

The viewpoint of the developer is one of productivity and tools, and doesn't include things such as actual live data and connections with consumers.

However, there are things that are shared, such as descriptions of the processes that are enabled by the system and/or communications protocols set up for users to communicate problems directly to development.

In this example, one viewpoint is the description of how the user sees the system, and the other viewpoint is how the developer sees the system. Users describe the system from their perspective, using a model of availability, response time, and access to information. All users of the system use this model, and the model has a specific language.

Developers describe the system differently than users, using a model of software connected to hardware distributed over a network, etc. However, there are many types of developers (database, security, etc.) of the system, and they do not have a common language derived from the model.

幸运的是，在管制员与飞行员交谈时，他们使用了公共通信语言。（换言之，表达他们各自视角的模型相交部分。）此公共语言的一部分是关于飞机的位置和航向的，且对于安全而言是最基本的。

因此，在本质上，每个视角都是某个特定类型的所有利益攸关者——所有飞行员或所有管制员——如何看待机场系统的一种抽象模型。

有一些工具可帮助利益攸关者，尤其是在利益攸关者与诸如空域模型或空中飞行模型等复杂模型交互时。

典型情况下，工具的界面对人员用户而言接近于与视角相关联的模型和语言。飞行员独有的工具是燃油指示器、高度指示器、速度指示器和位置指示器。管制员的主要工具是雷达。公共工具是无线电设备。

从上述示例做出总结，我们可以看到，视图可通过诸如飞行员 VS 管制员这样的利益攸关者关注层级，来划分出系统的子集。这种子集可通过一个被称为视角的抽象模型来描述，如空中飞行模型 VS 空域模型。采用部分专业化语言对视图的这种描述进行文件化，如“飞行员讲的语言”VS“管制员讲的语言”。工具用于帮助利益攸关者，它们根据来自视角的语言（“飞行员讲的语言”VS“管制员讲的语言”）进行彼此交互。

当利益攸关者使用公共工具时，如飞行员与管制员之间的无线电设备联系，公共语言是最基本的。

35.4.2 Enterprise Architecture 中的视图和视角

现在，让我们把这个示例映射到 Enterprise Architecture 中。考虑一个新的小型计算系统中的两名利益攸关者：用户和开发人员。

系统用户具有反映其与系统交互时的关注点的视角，而系统开发人员具有不同的视角。被开发用于应对两个视角中任意一个视角的视图不可能详尽地描述整个系统，因为每个关注层级都简化了每个利益攸关者看待系统的方式。

用户的视角包括用户与系统交互的所有方式，不会看到诸如应用或数据库管理系统（DBMS）等任何细节。

开发人员的视角是生产率和工具中的一个，不包括如实际的实时数据和与消费者的联系等内容。

然而，有一些东西是共享的，例如流程描述，它由为用户建立来与开发直接沟通问题的系统和/或通信协议使能。

在本示例中，一个视角是用户如何看待系统的描述，另一个视角是开发人员如何看待系统的描述。用户使用可用性、响应时间和信息访问的模型从他们的关注层级描述系统。系统的所有用户都使用该模型，且这个模型具有特定语言。

开发人员使用分布于网络中的软件连接硬件的模型，以区别于用户的方式来描述系统。然而，系统开发人员（数据库、安保性等）的类型很多，而且他们没有来自模型的公共语言。

35.4.3 Need fora Common Language and Interoperable Tools for Architecture Description

Tools exist for both users and developers. Tools such as online help are there specifically for users, and attempt to use the language of the user. Many different tools exist for different types of developers, but they suffer from the lack of a common language that is required to bring the system together. It is difficult, if not impossible, in the current state of the tools market to have one tool interoperate with another tool.

Issues relating to the evaluation of tools for architecture work are discussed in detail in Part V, Chapter 42.

35.5 Conclusions

This section attempts to deal with views in a structured manner, but this is by no means a complete treatise on views.

In general, TOGAF embraces the concepts and definitions presented in ISO/IEC 42010: 2007, specifically the concepts that help guide the development of a view and make the view actionable. These concepts can be summarized as:

- Selecting a key stakeholder.
- Understanding their concerns and generalizing/documenting those concerns.
- Understanding how to model and deal with those concerns.

35.6 Architectural Artifacts by ADM Phase

Figure 35-3 shows the artifacts that are associated with the core content metamodel and each of the content extensions.

35.4.3 需要用于架构描述的常用语言和可互用性工具

用户和开发人员都应具有工具。一些诸如在线帮助的工具，专门用于用户，并力求使用用户语言。不同的开发工具供不同类型的开发人员使用，但他们遭受的痛苦是缺少一种把系统合起来所需的公共语言。在工具市场的现状中，使一个工具与另一个工具互用不是不可能，但是很困难。

第五部分第 42 章详细论述了与架构工作所用工具的评价相关的议题。

35.5 结论

本节尝试以结构化的方式处理视图，但本节决不意味着对视图的完整论述。

一般来说，TOGAF 包括在 ISO/IEC 42010: 2007 中表达的概念和定义，特别是有助于指导视图开发和使视图可实施的概念。这些概念可总结为：

- 选择关键利益攸关者。
- 了解他们的关注点并使那些关注点一般化/文件化。
- 了解如何建模和处理那些关注点。

35.6 ADM 阶段的架构制品

图 35-3 表明与核心内容元模型和每个内容扩展相关联的制品。

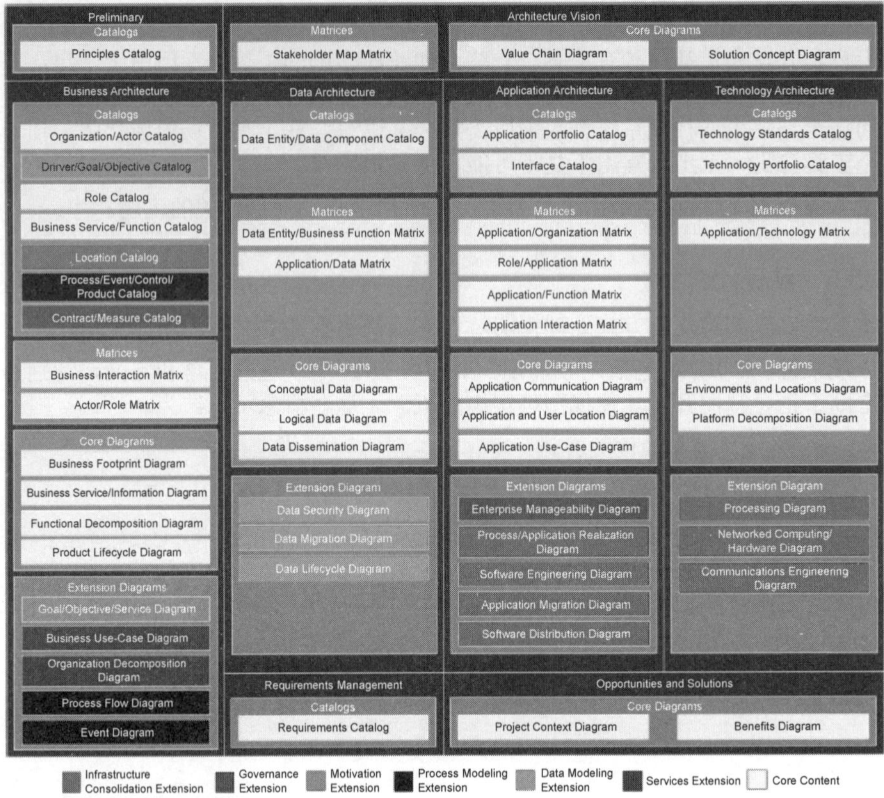

Figure 35-3 Artifacts Associated with the Core Content Metamodel and Extensions

The specific classes of artifact are as follows:

- **Catalogs** are lists of building blocks.
- **Matrices** show the relationships between building blocks of specific types.
- **Diagrams** present building blocks plus their relationships and interconnecttions in a graphical way that supports effective stakeholder communication.

The recommended artifacts for production in each ADM phase are as follows.

图 35-3　与核心内容元模型和扩展相关联的制品

见彩色插图viii页

制品的特定类别如下：

- **目录集**是构建块的列表。
- **矩阵**表明特定类型构建块之间的关系。
- **图**以一种支持利益攸关者有效沟通的图形化方式展现构建块及其之间的关系和相互连接。

在每个 ADM 阶段中推荐的制品如下。

35.6.1 Preliminary Phase

The following describes catalogs, matrices, and diagrams that may be created within the Preliminary Phase, as listed in Part II, Section 6.5.

Principles Catalog

The Principles catalog captures principles of the business and architecture principles that describe what a "good" solution or architecture should look like. Principles are used to evaluate and agree an outcome for architecture decision points. Principles are also used as a tool to assist in architectural governance of change initiatives.

The Principles catalog contains the following metamodel entities:

- Principle

35.6.2 Phase A: Architecture Vision

The following describes catalogs, matrices, and diagrams that may be created within Phase A (Architecture Vision) as listed in Section 7.5.

Stakeholder Map Matrix

The purpose of the Stakeholder Map matrix is to identify the stakeholders for the architecture engagement, their influence over the engagement, and their key questions, issues, or concerns that must be addressed by the architecture framework.

Understanding stakeholders and their requirements allows an architect to focus effort in areas that meet the needs of stakeholders (see Part III, Chapter 24).

Due to the potentially sensitive nature of stakeholder mapping information and the fact that the Architecture Vision phase is intended to be conducted using informal modeling techniques, no specific metamodel entities will be used to generate a stakeholder map.

Value Chain Diagram

A Value Chain diagram provides a high-level orientation view of an enterprise and how it interacts with the outside world. In contrast to the more formal Functional Decomposition diagram developed within Phase B (Business Architecture), the Value Chain diagram focuses on presentational impact.

The purpose of this diagram is to quickly on-board and align stakeholders for a particular change initiative, so that all participants understand the high-level functional and organizational context of the architecture engagement.

Solution Concept Diagram

A Solution Concept diagram provides a high-level orientation of the solution that is envisaged in order to meet the objectives of the architecture engagement. In contrast to the more formal and detailed architecture diagrams developed in the following phases, the solution concept represents a "pencil sketch" of the expected solution at the outset of the engagement.

This diagram may embody key objectives, requirements, and constraints for the engagement and also highlight work areas to be investigated in more detail with formal architecture modeling.

Its purpose is to quickly on-board and align stakeholders for a particular change initiative, so that all participants understand what the architecture engagement is seeking to achieve and how it is expected that a particular solution approach will meet the needs of the enterprise.

35.6.1 预备阶段

下面描述了在预备阶段内可能被创建的目录集、矩阵和图，如第二部分 6.5 节中所列。

原则目录集

原则目录集捕获业务原则和架构原则，这些原则描述“好的”解决方案或架构应该是什么样子。原则用于评价和商定架构决策点的结果。原则还被用作帮助对变革举措进行架构治理的工具。

原则目录集包含下列元模型实体：

- 原则

35.6.2 阶段 A：架构愿景

下面描述了在阶段 A（架构愿景）内可能被创建的目录集、矩阵和图，如 7.5 节中所列。

利益攸关者映射矩阵

利益攸关者映射矩阵的目的在于识别参与架构的利益攸关者、其对参与的影响以及架构框架必须应对利益攸关者的关键问题、议题或关注点。

了解利益攸关者及其需求，使架构师能将精力集中于满足利益攸关者需要的领域（见第三部分第 24 章）。

由于利益攸关者映射信息的潜在敏感本质以及架构愿景阶段是用非正式的建模技术进行的这一事实，所以没有特定的元模型实体会被用来生成利益攸关者映射。

价值链图

价值链图提供 ENTERPRISE 的高层级定位视图以及视图与外界的交互方式。与阶段 B（业务架构）内开发的更正式的功能分解图相反，价值链图集中于表象的影响。

该图的目的在于，使利益攸关者快速就绪并对特殊的变革举措达成一致，从而使所有参与者了解架构工作的高层级功能和组织的背景环境。

解决方案概念图

解决方案概念图提供解决方案高层级定位，该解决方案被设想来满足架构工作的目的。与下列阶段中开发的更正式和详细的架构图相反，解决方案概念表达在工作伊始对预期解决方案进行的“铅笔素描”。

该图可以体现架构工作的关键目的、需求和约束，还强调将采用正式的架构建模进行更多细节研究的工作领域。

其目的在于使利益攸关者快速就绪，并对特殊的变革举措达成一致，以便使所有参与者理解架构工作力求达成什么，以及如何预期特殊解决方案的实施途径会满足 ENTERPRISE 的需要。

35.6.3 Phase B: Business Architecture

The following describes catalogs, matrices, and diagrams that may be created within Phase B (Business Architecture) as listed in Section 8.5.

Organization/Actor Catalog

The purpose of the Organization/Actor catalog is to capture a definitive listing of all participants that interact with IT, including users and owners of IT systems.

The Organization/Actor catalog can be referenced when developing requirements in order to test for completeness.

For example, requirements for an application that services customers can be tested for completeness by verifying exactly which customer types need to be supported and whether there are any particular requirements or restrictions for user types.

The Organization/Actor catalog contains the following metamodel entities:

- Organization Unit
- Actor
- Location (may be included in this catalog if an independent Location catalog is not maintained)

Driver/Goal/Objective Catalog

The purpose of the Driver/Goal/Objective catalog is to provide a cross-organizational reference of how an organization meets its drivers in practical terms through goals, objectives, and (optionally) measures.

Publishing a definitive breakdown of drivers, goals, and objectives allows change initiatives within the enterprise to identify synergies across the organization (e.g., multiple organizations attempting to achieve similar objectives), which in turn allow stakeholders to be identified and related change initiatives to be aligned or consolidated.

The Driver/Goal/Objective catalog contains the following metamodel entities:

- Organization Unit
- Driver
- Goal
- Objective
- Measure (may optionally be included)

Role Catalog

The purpose of the Role catalog is to provide a listing of all authorization levels or zones within an enterprise. Frequently, application security or behavior is defined against locally understood concepts of authorization that create complex and unexpected consequences when combined on the user desktop.

If roles are defined, understood, and aligned across organizations and applications, this allows for a more seamless user experience and generally more secure applications, as administrators do not need to resort to work arounds in order to enable users to carry out their jobs.

In addition to supporting security definition for the enterprise, the Role catalog also forms a key input to identifying organizational change management impacts, defining job functions, and executing end-user training.

35.6.3 阶段 B：业务架构

下面描述了在阶段 B（业务架构）内可能被创建的目录集、矩阵和图，如 8.5 节中所列。

组织/施动者目录集

组织/施动者目录集的目的在于获取与 IT 交互的所有参与者的明确列表，包括 IT 系统的用户和所有者。

在开发需求时为了测试完备性，可引用组织/施动者目录集。

例如，通过准确地验证哪些客户类型需要被支持以及是否存在对用户类型的任何特殊需求或限制，可测试服务客户的应用需求的完备性。

组织/施动者目录集包含下列元模型实体：

- 组织单元
- 施动者
- 位置（如果没有保留单独的位置目录集，可包含在该目录集中）

驱动因素/目标/目的目录集

驱动因素/目标/目的目录集的目的在于提供关于一个组织在实践中如何通过目标、目的和（可选地）测度来满足其驱动因素的跨组织引用。

发布驱动因素、目标和目的的明确细目，使得 ENTERPRISE 内的变革举措能够跨组织（如，尝试达成类似目的的多个组织）识别协同性，进而识别利益攸关者并且对准或合并相关变革举措。

驱动因素/目标/目的目录集包含下列元模型实体：

- 组织单元
- 驱动因素
- 目标
- 目的
- 测度（可选择性地包括）

角色目录集

角色目录集的目的在于提供 ENTERPRISE 内所有授权层级或区域的列表。往往定义应用的安保性或行为来防止对于授权的局部理解概念，这些概念在应用被结合到用户桌面上时会造成复杂且无法预期的后果。

如果跨组织和应用的角色被定义、理解和对准，则可以执行更加无缝的用户体验和通常更安全的应用，因为管理员不需要依靠变通方案也可以使用户进行工作。

除了支持 ENTERPRISE 的安保性定义外，角色目录集还形成识别组织变革管理影响、定义工作职能和执行最终用户培训的关键输入。

As each role implies access to a number of business functions, if any of these business functionsare impacted, then change management will be required, organizational responsibilities may need to be redefined, and retraining may be needed.

The Role catalog contains the following metamodel entities:

- Role

Business Service/Function Catalog

The purpose of the Business Service/Function catalog is to provide a functional decomposition in a form that can be filtered, reported on, and queried, as a supplement to graphical Functional Decomposition diagrams.

The Business Service/Function catalog can be used to identify capabilities of an organization and to understand the level that governance is applied to the functions of an organization. This functional decomposition can be used to identify new capabilities required to support business change or may be used to determine the scope of change initiatives, applications, or technology components.

The Business Service/Function catalog contains the following metamodel entities:

- Organization Unit
- Business Function
- Business Service
- Information System Service (may optionally be included here)

Location Catalog

The Location catalog provides a listing of all locations where an enterprise carries out business operations or houses architecturally relevant assets, such as data centers or end-user computing equipment.

Maintaining a definitive list of locations allows change initiatives to quickly define a location scope and to test for completeness when assessing current landscapes or proposed target solutions. For example, a project to upgrade desktop operating systems will need to identify all locations where desktop operating systems are deployed.

Similarly, when new systems are being implemented, a diagram of locations is essential in order to develop appropriate deployment strategies that comprehend both user and application location and identify location-related issues, such as internationalization, localization, time zone impacts on availability, distance impacts on latency, network impacts on bandwidth, and access.

The Location catalog contains the following metamodel entities:

- Location

由于每个角色意味着访问多种业务功能，如果任何一个业务功能受到影响，则需要变革管理，组织的职责可能需要被重新定义，且可能需要进行重新培训。

角色目录集包含下列元模型实体：

- 角色

业务服务/功能目录集

业务服务/功能目录集的目的在于，以一种能够被过滤、被报告和被查询的形式提供功能分解，作为图形化功能分解图的补充。

业务服务/功能目录集可用于识别组织的能力并了解在组织中该功能的治理水平。该功能分解可用于识别支持业务变革所需的新能力或者可用于确定变革举措、应用或技术组件的范围。

业务服务/功能目录集包含下列元模型实体：

- 组织单元
- 业务功能
- 业务服务
- 信息系统服务（此处可选择性地包括）

位置目录集

位置目录集提供 ENTERPRISE 开展业务运行或存放架构相关的资产（如数据中心或最终用户计算设备）所在的所有位置的列表。

保存明确的位置列表可在评估当前全景或提出目标解决方案时，使得变革举措能够迅速地定义位置范围以及测试完备性。例如，升级桌面操作系统的项目需要识别部署桌面操作系统的所有位置。

同样，当正在实施新系统时，为了开发同时考虑用户和应用位置二者并识别与位置相关的问题（如国际化、本地化、对可用性的时区影响、距离对等待时间的影响、对带宽的网络影响及访问）的恰当部署方针，位置图是必不可少的。

位置目录集包含下列元模型实体：

- 位置

Process/Event/Control/Product Catalog

The Process/Event/Control/Product catalog provides a hierarchy of processes, events that trigger processes, outputs from processes, and controls applied to the execution of processes. This catalog provides a supplement to any Process Flow diagrams that are created and allows an enterprise to filter, report, and query across organizations and processes to identify scope, commonality, or impact.

For example, the Process/Event/Control/Product catalog allows an enterprise to see relationships of processes to sub-processes in order to identify the full chain of impacts resulting from changing a high-level process.

The Process/Event/Control/Product catalog contains the following metamodel entities:

- Process
- Event
- Control
- Product

Contract/Measure Catalog

The Contract/Measure catalog provides a listing of all agreed service contracts and (optionally) the measures attached to those contracts. It forms the master list of service levels agreed to across the enterprise.

The Contract/Measure catalog contains the following metamodel entities:

- Business Service
- Information System Service (optionally)
- Contract
- Measure

Business Interaction Matrix

The purpose of this matrix is to depict the relationship interactions between organizations and business functions across the enterprise.

Understanding business interaction of an enterprise is important as it helps to highlight value chain and dependencies across organizations.

The Business Interaction matrix shows the following metamodel entities and relationships:

- Organization
- Business Function
- Business Service
- Business Service *communicates with* Business Service relationships
- Business Service *is dependent on* Business Service relationships

流程/事件/控制/产品目录集

流程/事件/控制/产品目录集提供流程的层级结构、触发流程的事件、来自流程的输出和用于执行流程的控制。该目录集为已创建的任何过程流图提供补充，并使得 ENTERPRISE 能够跨组织和流程进行过滤、报告和查询，以识别范围、通用性或影响。

例如，流程/事件/控制/产品目录集使得 ENTERPRISE 能够查看流程与子流程之间的关系，以便识别出由于改变高层级流程而引起的完整影响链。

流程/事件/控制/产品目录集包含下列元模型实体：

- 流程
- 事件
- 控制
- 产品

契约/测度目录集

契约/测度目录集提供所有已商定的服务契约和（可选的）与那些契约相关的测度的列表。它构成了跨 ENTERPRISE 达成的服务水平总清单。

契约/测度目录集包含下列元模型实体：

- 业务服务
- 信息系统服务（可选的）
- 契约
- 测度

业务交互矩阵

该矩阵的目的在于描述跨 ENTERPRISE 的组织与业务功能之间的关系交互。

理解 ENTERPRISE 的业务交互是非常重要的，因为它有助于突出跨多个组织的价值链和依赖性。

业务交互矩阵表明下列元模型实体和关系：

- 组织
- 业务功能
- 业务服务
- 业务服务与业务服务通信关系
- 业务服务依赖于业务服务关系

Actor/Role Matrix

The purpose of this matrix is to show which actors perform which roles, supporting definition of security and skills requirements.

Understanding Actor-to-Role relationships is a key supporting tool in definition of training needs, user security settings, and organizational change management.

The Actor/Role matrix shows the following metamodel entities and relationships:

- Actor
- Role
- Actor *performs* Role relationships

Business Footprint Diagram

A Business Footprint diagram describes the links between business goals, organizational units, business functions, and services, and maps these functions to the technical components delivering the required capability.

A Business Footprint diagram provides a clear traceability between a technical component and the business goal that it satisfies, while also demonstrating ownership of the services identified.

A Business Footprint diagram demonstrates only the key facts linking organization unit functions to delivery services and is utilized as a communication platform for senior-level (CxO) stakeholders.

Business Service/Information Diagram

The Business Service/Information diagram shows the information needed to support one or more business services. The Business Service/Information diagram shows what data is consumed by or produced by a business service and may also show the source of information.

The Business Service/Information diagram shows an initial representation of the information present within the architecture and therefore forms a basis for elaboration and refinement within Phase C (Data Architecture).

Functional Decomposition Diagram

The purpose of the Functional Decomposition diagram is to show on a single page the capabilities of an organization that are relevant to the consideration of an architecture. By examining the capabilities of an organization from a functional perspective, it is possible to quickly develop models of what the organization does without being dragged into extended debate on how the organization does it.

Once a basic Functional Decomposition diagram has been developed, it becomes possible to layer heat-maps on top of this diagram to show scope and decisions. For example, the capabilities to be implemented in different phases of a change program.

施动者/角色矩阵

这个矩阵的目的在于，表明哪些施动者扮演哪些角色，从而支持安保性和技能需求的定义。

理解施动者与角色的关系是定义培训需要、用户安保性设置和组织变革管理中的一个关键支持工具。

施动者/角色矩阵表明下列元模型实体和关系：

- 施动者
- 角色
- 施动者执行角色关系

业务轨迹图

业务轨迹图描述业务目标、组织单元、业务功能以及服务两两之间的联系，并将这些功能映射到交付所需能力的技术组件中。

业务轨迹图提供技术组件和其所满足的业务目标之间的清晰的可追溯性，同时还表明所识别的服务所有权。

业务轨迹图仅表明将组织单元功能与交付服务相联系的关键事实，并用作高级（CxO）利益攸关者的沟通平台。

业务服务/信息图

业务服务/信息图表明支持一项或多项业务服务所需的信息。业务服务/信息图表明业务服务所使用或产生的是什么数据，还可表明信息源。

业务服务/信息图表明架构内存在的信息的初始表达形式，因此构成了在阶段C（数据架构）内进行详细阐述和细化的基础。

功能分解图

功能分解图的目的在于，在单个页面上表明一个组织的与架构考量因素相关的能力。通过从功能的关注层级审查组织的能力，在没有深入地拓展讨论组织如何做的情况下，快速地开发组织做什么的模型是有可能的。

一旦已经开发了基本的功能分解图，在此图顶部对热点图分层以表明范围和决策将成为可能。例如，在变革计划的不同阶段实现的能力。

Product Lifecycle Diagram

The purpose of the Product Lifecycle diagram is to assist in understanding the lifecycles of key entities within the enterprise. Understanding product lifecycles is becoming increasingly important with respect to environmental concerns, legislation, and regulation where products must be tracked from manufacture to disposal. Equally, organizations that create products that involve personal or sensitive information must have a detailed understanding of the product lifecycle during the development of Business Architecture in order to ensure rigor in design of controls, processes, and procedures. Examples of this would include credit cards, debit cards, store/loyalty cards, smart cards, user identity credentials (identity cards, passports, etc.).

Goal/Objective/Service Diagram

The purpose of a Goal/Objective/Service diagram is to define the ways in which a service contributes to the achievement of a business vision or strategy.

Services are associated with the drivers, goals, objectives, and measures that they support, allowing the enterprise to understand which services contribute to similar aspects of business performance. The Goal/Objective/Service diagram also provides qualitative input on what constitutes high performance for a particular service.

Business Use-Case Diagram

A Business Use-Case diagram displays the relationships between consumers and providers of business services. Business services are consumed by actors or other business services and the Business Use-Case diagram provides added richness in describing business capability by illustrating how and when that capability is used.

The purpose of the Business Use-Case diagram is to help to describe and validate the interaction between actors and their roles to processes and functions. As the architecture progresses, the use-case can evolve from the business level to include data, application, and technology details. Architectural business use-cases can also be re-used in systems design work.

Organization Decomposition Diagram

An Organization Decomposition diagram describes the links between actor, roles, and location within an organization tree.

An organization map should provide a chain of command of owners and decision-makers in the organization. Although it is not the intent of the Organization Decomposition diagram to link goal to organization, it should be possible to intuitively link the goals to the stakeholders from the Organization Decomposition diagram.

Process Flow Diagram

The purpose of the Process Flow diagram is to depict all models and mappings related to the process metamodel entity.

Process Flow diagrams show sequential flow of control between activities and may utilize swim-lane techniques to represent ownership and realization of process steps. For example, the application that supports a process step may be shown as a swim-lane.

In addition to showing a sequence of activity, process flows can also be used to detail the controls that apply to a process, the events that trigger or result from completion of a process, and also the products that are generated from process execution.

Process Flow diagrams are useful in elaborating the architecture with subject specialists, as they allow the specialist to describe "how the job is done" for a particular function. Through this process, each process step can become a more fine-grained function and can then in turn be elaborated as a process.

产品生命周期图

产品生命周期图的目的在于，帮助理解 ENTERPRISE 内关键实体的生命周期。理解产品生命周期正变得越来越重要，包括遵守环境的关注点、法律和法规，在这些方面产品从生产到退出必须被追踪。同样，创建涉及私人或敏感信息的产品的组织必须在业务架构开发期间详细理解产品生命周期，以便确保严格设计控制、流程和程序。这种例子包括信用卡、借记卡、（商店）专用赊购卡/积分卡、智能卡、用户身份凭证（身份证、护照等）。

目标/目的/服务图

目标/目的/服务图的目的在于定义服务有助于业务愿景或战略达成的方式。

服务与其所支持的驱动因素、目标、目的和测度相关联，使得 ENTERPRISE 能够了解哪些服务可促成类似方面的业务绩效。目标/目的/服务图还提供构成特定服务的高绩效方面的定性输入。

业务用例图

业务用例图显示出业务服务的使用者与提供者之间的关系。业务服务由施动者或其他业务服务使用，业务用例图通过详细阐明能力如何以及何时使用能力，更加丰富地描述了业务能力。

业务用例图的目的在于，帮助描述和确认施动者及其在流程和功能方面的作用之间的交互。随着架构的进展，用例可由业务层演进而成，包括数据、应用和技术细节。架构的业务用例还可在系统设计工作中复用。

组织分解图

组织分解图描述组织树内的施动者、角色和位置之间的联系。

组织机构图应提供组织中的所有者和决策者的指令链。尽管组织分解图并不旨在将目标与组织联系起来，但应能从组织分解图将目标与利益攸关者直观地联系起来。

过程流图

过程流图的目的在于，描述与流程元模型实体相关的所有模型和映射。

过程流图表明活动之间的控制顺序流，并可使用泳道技术表达流程步骤的所有权和实现方式。例如，支持一个流程步骤的应用可表示为一个泳道。

除了表明活动顺序外，过程流还可用于详细描述应用于流程的控制、触发流程或因完成流程而引发的事件以及在流程执行中产生的产品。

过程流图在由学科领域专家详细阐明的架构中是有用的，因为过程流图使得专家能够针对某一特定功能描述“工作是如何做的”。通过该过程，每个流程步骤可成为更细粒度的功能，然后可反过来作为流程被详细阐明。

Event Diagram

The purpose of the Event diagram is to depict the relationship between events and process. Certain events — such as arrival of certain information (e.g., customer submits sales order) or acertain point in time (e.g., end of fiscal quarter) — cause work and certain actions need to be undertaken within the business. These are often referred to as "business events" or simply "events" and are considered as triggers for a process. It is important to note that the event has to trigger a process and generate a business response or result.

35.6.4 Phase C: Data Architecture

The following describes catalogs, matrices, and diagrams that may be created within Phase C (Data Architecture) as listed in Section 10.5.

Data Entity/Data Component Catalog

The purpose of the Data Entity/Data Component catalog is to identify and maintain a list of all the data use across the enterprise, including data entities and also the data components where data entities are stored. An agreed Data Entity/Data Component catalog supports the definition and application of information management and data governance policies and also encourages effective data sharing and re-use.

The Data Entity/Data Component catalog contains the following metamodel entities:

- Data Entity
- Logical Data Component
- Physical Data Component

Data Entity/Business Function Matrix

The purpose of the Data Entity/Business Function matrix is to depict the relationship between data entities and business functions within the enterprise. Business functions are supported by business services with explicitly defined boundaries and will be supported and realized by business processes. The mapping of the Data Entity-Business Function relationship enables the following to take place:

- Assign ownership of data entities to organizations
- Understand the data and information exchange requirements business services
- Support the gap analysis and determine whether any data entities are missing and need to be created
- Define application of origin, application of record, and application of reference for data entities
- Enable development of data governance programs across the enterprise (establish data steward, develop data standards pertinent to the business function, etc.)

The Data Entity/Business Function matrix shows the following entities and relationships:

事件图

事件图的目的在于描述事件和流程之间的关系。某些事件——例如，某一信息的到达（如，客户提交销售订单）或某一时间点的出现（如，财政季度末）——产生工作并需要在业务内开始某些行动。这些事件通常被称为“业务事件”或简单地被称为“事件”，并且被认为是流程的触发条件。重要的是，注意到事件必须触发流程并产生业务响应或结果。

35.6.4 阶段 C：数据架构

下面描述了在阶段 C（数据架构）内可能被创建的目录集、矩阵和图，如 10.5 节中所列。

数据实体/数据组件目录集

数据实体/数据组件目录集的目的在于，识别和维护跨 ENTERPRISE 使用的所有数据的列表，包括数据实体以及用于存储数据实体的数据组件。经商定的数据实体/数据组件目录集支持信息管理和数据治理方针的定义和应用，并且还鼓励有效的数据共享和复用。

数据实体/数据组件目录集包含下列元模型实体：

- 数据实体
- 逻辑数据组件
- 物理数据组件

数据实体/业务功能矩阵

数据实体/业务功能矩阵的目的在于，描述 ENTERPRISE 内数据实体和业务功能之间的关系。业务功能由具有明确定义的边界的业务服务所支持，并将由业务流程来支持和实现。数据实体—业务功能的关系映射使以下事件能够发生：

- 向组织分派数据实体的所有权
- 理解数据和信息交换需求的业务服务
- 支持差距分析并确定数据实体是否缺失以及是否需要创建
- 为数据实体定义应用起源、应用记录和应用参考
- 能够跨 ENTERPRISE 制定数据治理计划（设立数据管理员，制定与业务功能相关的数据标准等）

数据实体/业务功能矩阵表明下列实体和关系：

- Data Entity
- Business Function
- Data Entity relationship to owning Organization Unit

Application/Data Matrix

The purpose of the Application/Data matrix is to depict the relationship between applications (i.e., application components) and the data entities that are accessed and updated by them.

Applications will create, read, update, and delete specific data entities that are associated with them. For example, a CRM application will create, read, update, and delete customer entity information.

The data entities in a package/packaged services environment can be classified as master data, reference data, transactional data, content data, and historical data. Applications that operate on the data entities include transactional applications, information management applications, and business ware house applications.

The mapping of the Application Component-Data Entity relationship is an important step as it enables the following to take place:

- Assign access of data to specific applications in the organization
- Understand the degree of data duplication within different applications, and the scale of the data lifecycle
- Understand where the same data is updated by different applications
- Support the gap analysis and determine whether any of the applications are missing and as a result need to be created

The Application/Data matrix is a two-dimensional table with Logical Application Component on one axis and Data Entity on the other axis.

Conceptual Data Diagram

The key purpose of the Conceptual Data diagram is to depict the relationships between critical data entities within the enterprise. This diagram is developed to address the concerns of business stakeholders.

Techniques used include:

- Entity relationship models
- Simplified UML class diagrams

Logical Data Diagram

The key purpose of the Logical Data diagram is to show logical views of the relationships between critical data entities within the enterprise. This diagram is developed to address the concerns of:

- Application developers
- Database designers

- 数据实体
- 业务功能
- 数据实体与拥有组织单元的关系

应用/数据矩阵

应用/数据矩阵的目的在于，描述应用（即应用组件）及其所访问和更新的数据实体之间的关系。

应用将创建、读取、更新和删除与其相关联的特定数据实体。例如，CRM 应用将创建、读取、更新和删除客户实体信息。

在包/打包服务环境中的数据实体可被归类为主数据、引用数据、交易数据、内容数据和历史数据。在数据实体上运行的应用包括事务应用、信息管理应用和商业仓库应用。

应用组件—数据实体的关系映射是一个重要步骤，因为它使以下事件能够发生：

- 向组织中的特定应用分派数据访问
- 理解不同应用内的数据重复程度以及数据生命周期的规模
- 理解在何处相同数据被不同应用更新
- 支持差距分析并确定应用是否缺失以及是否因此需要创建应用

应用/数据矩阵是一个二维表，其在一个轴上是逻辑应用组件，在另一个轴上是数据实体。

概念数据图

概念数据图的主要目的在于，描述 ENTERPRISE 内关键数据实体之间的关系。该图被开发用于应对业务利益攸关者的关注点。

所使用的技术包括：

- 实体关系模型
- 简化的 UML 类图

逻辑数据图

逻辑数据图的主要目的在于，表明 ENTERPRISE 内关键数据实体之间关系的逻辑视图。该图被开发用于应对下列人员的关注点：

- 应用开发人员
- 数据库设计人员

Data Dissemination Diagram

The purpose of the Data Dissemination diagram is to show the relationship between data entity, business service, and application components. The diagram shows how the logical entities are to be physically realized by application components. This allows effective sizing to be carried out and the IT footprint to be refined. Moreover, by assigning business value to data, an indication of the business criticality of application components can be gained.

Additionally, the diagram may show data replication and application ownership of the master reference for data. In this instance, it can show two copies and the master-copy relationship between them. This diagram can include services; that is, services encapsulate data and they reside in an application, or services that reside on an application and access data encapsulated within the application.

Data Security Diagram

Data is considered as an asset to the enterprise and data security simply means ensuring that enterprise data is not compromised and that access to it is suitably controlled.

The purpose of the Data Security diagram is to depict which actor (person, organization, or system) can access which enterprise data. This relationship can be shown in a matrix form between two objects or can be shown as a mapping.

The diagram can also be used to demonstrate compliance with data privacy laws and other applicable regulations (HIPAA, SOX, etc). This diagram should also consider any trust implications where an enterprise's partners or other parties may have access to the company's systems, such as an outsourced situation where information may be managed by other people and may even be hosted in a different country.

Data Migration Diagram

Data migration is critical when implementing a package or packaged service-based solution. This is particularly true when an existing legacy application is replaced with a package or an enterprise is to be migrated to a larger packages/packaged services footprint. Packages tend to have their own data model and during data migration the legacy application data may need to be transformed prior to loading into the package.

Data migration activities will usually involve the following steps:

- Extract data from source applications (baseline systems)
- Profile source data
- Perform data transformation operations, including data quality processes:
  - Standardize, normalize, de-duplicate source data (data cleansing)
  - Match, merge, and consolidate data from different source(s)
  - Source-to-target mappings
- Load into target applications (target systems)

The purpose of the Data Migration diagram is to show the flow of data from the source to the target applications. The diagram will provide a visual representation of the spread of sources/targets and serve as a tool for data auditing and establishing traceability. This diagram can be elaborated or enhanced as detailed as necessary. For example, the diagram can contain just an overall layout of migration landscape or could go into individual application metadata element level of detail.

数据分发图

数据分发图的目的在于展示数据实体、业务服务和应用组件之间的关系。该图表明逻辑实体将如何由应用组件物理实现。这能够执行有效的大小调整并细化 IT 足迹。而且，通过将业务价值分派到数据，可获得应用组件的业务关键性指标。

此外，该图可展示主引用数据的数据复制和应用所有权。在这种情况下，它可显示两个副本以及这两个副本之间的主副关系。该图可包括服务，即服务封装数据且它们属于应用中，或者服务位于应用中且访问该应用内所封装的数据。

数据安保图

数据被认为是 ENTERPRISE 的资产，数据安保仅意味着确保 ENTERPRISE 数据不受损害且数据访问得到恰当地控制。

数据安保图的目的在于，描述哪位施动者（个人、组织或系统）可访问哪些 ENTERPRISE 数据。这种关系可在两个对象之间以矩阵形式展示，或可展示为一种映射。

该图还可用于论证与数据保密法及其他适用法规（HIPAA、SOX 等）的合规性。该图还应考虑 ENTERPRISE 合作伙伴或其他各方可以访问公司系统时的任何信任影响，例如信息可能由其他人管理甚至可能托管在不同国家的外包情况。

数据迁移图

在实施基于包或打包服务的解决方案时，数据迁移非常关键。在现有的遗留应用被替换为包或 ENTERPRISE 将被迁移到较大的包/打包服务覆盖区中时，尤为如此。包往往具有其自己的数据模型，并且在数据迁移期间，遗留的应用数据可能需要在载入包之前被转换。

数据迁移活动将通常涉及下列步骤：

- 从源应用（基线系统）中抽取数据
- 概要源数据
- 执行数据转换操作，包括数据质量流程：
  - 源数据的标准化、规范化、去重（数据清洗）
  - 匹配、合并和统一不同来源的数据
  - 源—目标映射
- 载入目标应用（目标系统）

数据迁移图的目的在于，表明从源应用到目标应用的数据流动。该图将提供源数据/目标数据的传播的可视化表达，并作为数据审核和建立可追溯性的工具。该图可根据需要被详细阐明或者改进。例如，该图可以只包含迁移全景的总体布局或者可进入单独应用元数据元素的细节层级。

Data Lifecycle Diagram

The Data Lifecycle diagram is an essential part of managing business data throughout its lifecycle from conception until disposal within the constraints of the business process.

The data is considered as an entity in its own right, decoupled from business process and activity. Each change in state is represented on the diagram which may include the event or rules that trigger that change in state.

The separation of data from process allows common data requirements to be identified which enables resource sharing to be achieved more effectively.

35.6.5 Phase C: Application Architecture

The following describes catalogs, matrices, and diagrams that may be created within Phase C (Application Architecture) as listed in Section 11.5.

Application Portfolio Catalog

The purpose of this catalog is to identify and maintain a list of all the applications in the enterprise. This list helps to define the horizontal scope of change initiatives that may impact particular kinds of applications. An agreed Application Portfolio allows a standard set of applications to be defined and governed.

The Application Portfolio catalog provides a foundation on which to base the remaining matrices and diagrams. It is typically the start point of the Application Architecture phase.

The Application Portfolio catalog contains the following metamodel entities:

- Information System Service
- Logical Application Component
- Physical Application Component

Interface Catalog

The purpose of the Interface catalog is to scope and document the interfaces between applications to enable the overall dependencies between applications to be scoped as early as possible.

Applications will create, read, update, and delete data within other applications; this will be achieved by some kind of interface, whether via a batch file that is loaded periodically, a direct connection to another application's database, or via some form of API or web service.

The mapping of the Application Component-Application Component entity relationship is an important step as it enables the following to take place:

- Understand the degree of interaction between applications, identifying those that are central in terms of their dependencies on other applications.
- Understand the number and types of interfaces between applications.
- Understand the degree of duplication of interfaces between applications.
- Identify the potential for simplification of interfaces when considering the target Application Portfolio.
- Support the gap analysis and determine whether any of the applications are missing and as a result need to be created.

数据生命周期图

数据生命周期图是在业务流程约束内从概念直到退出的整个生命周期内管理业务数据的一个基本部分。

数据被认为是一个有自己权限的实体，从业务流程和活动中解耦出来。每个状态的变化都可在图上表达，该图可包括触发状态变化的事件或规则。

将数据从流程中分离，使得公共数据需求能够被识别，以更有效地实现资源共享。

35.6.5 阶段 C：应用架构

下面描述了在阶段 C（应用架构）内可能被创建的目录集、矩阵和图，如 11.5 节中所列。

应用谱系目录集

该目录集的目的在于识别和维护 ENTERPRISE 内所有应用的列表。该列表有助于定义可能会影响某些特定类型应用的变更举措的横向范围。商定的应用谱系使得一套标准的应用能够被定义和管控。

应用谱系目录集提供建立其余矩阵和图所依据的基础。它通常是应用架构阶段的起点。

应用谱系目录集包含下列元模型实体：

- 信息系统服务
- 逻辑应用组件
- 物理应用组件

界面目录集

界面目录集的目的在于确定应用之间的界面范围并将其文件化，使应用之间的总体依赖性范围能够被尽早界定。

应用将创建、读取、更新和删除其他应用内的数据；这将通过某种类型的界面实现，无论是通过定期加载的批处理文件与另一个应用的数据库直接连接，还是通过某种形式的 API 或网络服务。

应用组件与应用组件实体关系的映射是一个重要的步骤，因为它使以下事件能够发生：

- 理解应用之间的交互程度，根据它们对其他应用的依赖性识别主要的那些。
- 理解应用之间的界面数量和类型。
- 理解应用之间界面的重复程度。
- 在考虑目标应用谱系时识别界面简化的可能性。
- 支持差距分析并确定应用是否缺失，以及是否因此需要创建应用。

The Interface catalog contains the following metamodel entities:

- Logical Application Component
- Physical Application Component
- Application *communicates with* application relationship

Application/Organization Matrix

The purpose of this matrix is to depict the relationship between applications and organizational units within the enterprise.

Business functions are performed by organizational units. Some of the functions and services performed by those organizational units will be supported by applications. The mapping of the Application Component-Organization Unit relationship is an important step as it enables the following to take place:

- Assign usage of applications to the organization units that perform business functions.
- Understand the application support requirements of the business services and processes carried out by an organization unit.
- Support the gap analysis and determine whether any of the applications are missing and as a result need to be created.
- Define the application set used by a particular organization unit.

The Application/Organization matrix is a two-dimensional table with Logical/Physical Application Component on one axis and Organization Unit on the other axis.

The relationship between these two entities is a composite of a number of metamodel relationships that need validating:

- Organization Units *own* Services.
- Actors that *belong to* Organization Units *use* Services.
- Services are *realized by* Logical/Physical Application Components.

Role/Application Matrix

The purpose of the Role/Application matrix is to depict the relationship between applications and the business roles that use them within the enterprise.

People in an organization interact with applications. During this interaction, these people assume a specific role to perform a task; for example, product buyer.

The mapping of the Application Component-Role relationship is an important step as it enables the following to take place:

- Assign usage of applications to the specific roles in the organization.
- Understand the application security requirements of the business services and processes supporting the function, and check these are in line with current policy.
- Support the gap analysis and determine whether any of the applications are missing and as a result need to be created.
- Define the application set used by a particular business role; essential in any move to role-based computing.

The Role/Application matrix is a two-dimensional table with Logical Application Component on one axis and Role on the other axis.

界面目录集包含下列元模型实体：

- 逻辑应用组件
- 物理应用组件
- 应用与应用关系相通

应用/组织矩阵

该矩阵的目的在于描述ENTERPRISE内应用与组织单元之间的关系。

业务功能由组织单元执行。这些组织单元所执行的一些功能和服务将由多个应用支持。应用组件与组织单元关系的映射是一个非常重要的步骤，因为它使以下事件能够发生：

- 向执行业务功能的组织单元分派应用的使用。
- 理解组织单元所执行的业务服务和流程的应用支持需求。
- 支持差距分析并确定应用是否缺失，以及是否因此需要创建应用。
- 定义特定组织单元所使用的应用集。

应用/组织矩阵是一个二维表，其在一个轴上是逻辑/物理应用组件，在另一个轴上是组织单元。

这两个实体之间的关系是许多的元模型关系的组合，需要确认的是：

- 组织单元拥有服务。
- 属于组织单元的施动者使用服务。
- 服务由逻辑/物理应用组件实现。

角色/应用矩阵

角色/应用矩阵的目的在于，描述应用与在ENTERPRISE内使用应用的业务角色之间的关系。

组织内的人员与应用进行交互。在该交互期间，这些人员承担特定的角色去执行某项任务，例如，产品买方。

应用组件与角色的关系映射是一个非常重要的步骤，因为它使以下事件能够发生：

- 向组织内特定角色分派应用的使用。
- 理解对功能提供支持的业务服务和流程的应用安保需求，并检查这些需求是否符合当前仿真。
- 支持差距分析并确定应用是否缺失，以及是否因此需要创建应用。
- 定义特殊业务角色所使用的应用集；这在向基于角色计算的迁移中是最有必要的。

角色/应用矩阵是一个二维表，其在一个轴上是逻辑应用组件，在另一个轴上是角色。

The relationship between these two entities is a composite of a number of metamodel relationships that need validating:

- Role *accesses* Function.
- Function *is bounded by* Service.
- Services are *realized by* Logical/Physical Application Components.

Application/Function Matrix

The purpose of the Application/Function matrix is to depict the relationship between applications and business functions within the enterprise.

Business functions are performed by organizational units. Some of the business functions and services will be supported by applications. The mapping of the Application Component-Function relationship is an important step as it enables the following to take place:

- Assign usage of applications to the business functions that are supported by them.
- Understand the application support requirements of the business services and processes carried out.
- Support the gap analysis and determine whether any of the applications are missing and as a result need to be created.
- Define the application set used by a particular business function.

The Application/Function matrix is a two-dimensional table with Logical Application Component on one axis and Function on the other axis.

The relationship between these two entities is a composite of a number of metamodel relationships that need validating:

- Function *is bounded by* Service.
- Services are *realized by* Logical/Physical Application Components.

Application Interaction Matrix

The purpose of the Application Interaction matrix is to depict communications relationships between applications.

The mapping of the application interactions shows in matrix form the equivalent of the InterfaceCatalog or an Application Communication diagram.

The Application Interaction matrix is a two-dimensional table with Application Service, Logical Application Component, and Physical Application Component on both the rows and the columns of the table.

The relationships depicted by this matrix include:

- Application Service *consumes* Application Service.
- Logical Application Component *communicates with* Logical Application Component.
- Physical Application Component *communicates with* Physical Application Component.

这两个实体之间的关系是许多的元模型关系的组合，需要确认的是：

- 角色访问功能。
- 功能受服务的约束。
- 服务由逻辑/物理应用组件实现。

应用/功能矩阵

应用/功能矩阵的目的在于，描述 ENTERPRISE 内应用和业务功能之间的关系。

业务功能由组织单元执行。某些业务功能和服务将由应用支持。应用组件与功能的关系映射是一个非常重要的步骤，因为它使以下事件能够发生：

- 向应用所支持的业务功能分派应用的使用。
- 理解所执行的业务服务和流程的应用支持需求。
- 支持差距分析并确定应用是否缺失，以及是否因此需要创建应用。
- 定义特定业务功能所使用的应用集。

应用/功能矩阵是一个二维表，其在一个轴上是逻辑应用组件，在另一个轴上是功能。

这两个实体之间的关系是许多的元模型关系的组合，需要确认的是：

- 功能受服务的限制。
- 服务由逻辑/物理应用组件实现。

应用交互矩阵

应用交互矩阵的目的在于描述应用之间的通信关系。

应用交互的映射以矩阵形式展示界面目录集或应用通信图的等价物。

应用交互矩阵是一个二维表，表的各行各列上具有应用服务、逻辑应用组件，以及物理应用组件。

该矩阵所描述的关系包括：

- 应用服务使用应用服务。
- 逻辑应用组件与逻辑应用组件通信。
- 物理应用组件与物理应用组件通信。

Application Communication Diagram

The purpose of the Application Communication diagram is to depict all models and mappings related to communication between applications in the metamodel entity.

It shows application components and interfaces between components. Interfaces may be associated with data entities where appropriate. Applications may be associated with business services where appropriate. Communication should be logical and should only show intermediary technology where it is architecturally relevant.

Application and User Location Diagram

The Application and User Location diagram shows the geographical distribution of applications. It can be used to show where applications are used by the end user; the distribution of where the host application is executed and/or delivered in thin client scenarios; the distribution of where applications are developed, tested, and released; etc.

Analysis can reveal opportunities for rationalization, as well as duplication and/or gaps.

The purpose of this diagram is to clearly depict the business locations from which business users typically interact with the applications, but also the hosting location of the application infrastructure.

The diagram enables:

- Identification of the number of package instances needed to sufficiently support the user population that may be spread out geographically.
- Estimation of the number and the type of user licenses for the package or other software.
- Estimation of the level of support needed for the users and location of support center.
- Selection of system management tools, structure, and management system required to support the enterprise users/customers/partners both locally and remotely.
- Appropriate planning for the technological components of the business, namely server sizing and network bandwidth, etc.
- Performance considerations while implementing application and technology architecture solutions.

Users typically interact with applications in a variety of ways; for example:

- To support the operations of the business day-to-day.
- To participate in the execution of a business process.
- To access information (look-up, read).
- To develop the application.
- To administer and maintain the application.

Application Use-Case Diagram

An Application Use-Case diagram displays the relationships between consumers and providers of application services. Application services are consumed by actors or other application services and the Application Use-Case diagram provides added richness in describing application functionality by illustrating how and when that functionality is used.

The purpose of the Application Use-Case diagram is to help to describe and validate the interaction between actors and their roles with applications. As the architecture progresses, the use-case can evolve from functional information to include technical realization detail.

应用通信图

应用通信图的目的在于，描述元模型实体中与应用之间的通信相关的所有模型和映射。

它表明应用组件及组件之间的界面。若合适，界面可与数据实体相关联。若合适，应用可与业务服务相关联。通信应符合逻辑，并且应只表明在架构上相关的中间技术。

应用和用户位置图

应用和用户位置图表明应用的地理分布。它可用于表明应用在何处被最终用户所使用；在瘦客户端场景中主应用在何处被执行和/或交付的分布；应用在何处被开发、测试和发布的分布；等等。

分析可揭示合理化的机会，以及重复度和/或差距。

该图的目的在于清晰地描述业务用户与应用进行典型的交互所在的业务位置，以及应用基础设施的托管位置。

该图能够：

- 识别出充分支持可能在地理上分散的用户群体所需的包实例的数量。
- 估计包或其他软件的用户许可证的数量和类型。
- 估计用户所需的支持水平和支持中心的位置。
- 选择对 ENTERPRISE 用户/客户/合作伙伴进行本地和远程支持所需的系统管理工具、结构和管理系统。
- 适当地规划业务的技术组件，即服务器大小调整和网络带宽等。
- 考虑绩效，同时实施应用和技术架构解决方案。

典型情况下，用户以各种方式与应用进行交互；例如：

- 支持日常的业务运作。
- 参与业务流程的执行。
- 访问信息（查找，读取）。
- 开发应用。
- 管理和维护应用。

应用用例图

应用用例图显示出应用服务的消费者和提供者之间的关系。应用服务由施动者或其他应用服务所使用，应用用例图通过详细阐明如何以及何时使用功能性来更加丰富地描述应用功能性。

应用用例图的目的在于，帮助描述和确认施动者及其角色与应用之间的交互。随着架构的进展，用例可由功能信息向包括技术实现细节演进。

Application use-cases can also be re-used in more detailed systems design work.

Enterprise Manageability Diagram

The Enterprise Manageability diagram shows how one or more applications interact with application and technology components that support operational management of a solution.

This diagram is really a filter on the Application Communication diagram, specifically for enterprise management class software.

Analysis can reveal duplication and gaps, and opportunities in the IT service management operation of an organization.

Process/Application Realization Diagram

The purpose of the Process/Application Realization diagram is to clearly depict the sequence of events when multiple applications are involved in executing a business process.

It enhances the Application Communication diagram by augmenting it with any sequencing constraints, and hand-off points between batch and real-time processing.

It would identify complex sequences that could be simplified, and identify possible rationalization points in the architecture in order to provide more timely information to business users. It may also identify process efficiency improvements that may reduce interaction traffic between applications.

Software Engineering Diagram

The Software Engineering diagram breaks applications into packages, modules, services, and operations from a development perspective.

It enables more detailed impact analysis when planning migration stages, and analyzing opportunities and solutions.

It is ideal for application development teams and application management teams when managing complex development environments.

Application Migration Diagram

The Application Migration diagram identifies application migration from baseline to target application components. It enables a more accurate estimation of migration costs by showing precisely which applications and interfaces need to be mapped between migration stages.

It would identify temporary applications, staging areas, and the infrastructure required to support migrations (for example, parallel run environments, etc).

Software Distribution Diagram

The Software Distribution diagram shows how application software is structured and distributed across the estate. It is useful in systems upgrade or application consolidation projects.

This diagram shows how physical applications are distributed across physical technology and the location of that technology.

This enables a clear view of how the software is hosted, but also enables managed operations staff to understand how that application software is maintained once installed.

应用用例还可在更详细的系统设计工作中被复用。

ENTERPRISE 可管理性图

ENTERPRISE 可管理性图展示一个或多个应用如何与应用和支持解决方案运作管理的技术组件进行交互。

该图实际上是应用通信图上的过滤器，特别用于 ENTERPRISE 管理类软件。

分析可揭示重复度和差距，以及组织的 IT 服务管理运作方面的机会。

流程/应用实现图

流程/应用实现图的目的在于，当多个应用都涉及执行一个业务流程时，清晰地描述事件顺序。

通过用排序约束以及批处理和实时处理之间的切换点，对该图进行补充，来增强应用通信图。

它将识别可能被简化的复杂顺序，并识别架构中可能的合理化点，以便向业务用户提供更及时的信息。它还可识别可减少应用之间交互流量的流程效率改进措施。

软件工程图

软件工程图从开发的关注层级将应用分成包、模块、服务和运行。

在规划迁移阶段和分析机会与解决方案时，它促使能够进行更详细的影响分析。

在管理复杂开发环境时，此图对于应用开发团队和应用管理团队而言是非常理想的。

应用迁移图

应用迁移图识别从基线应用组件到目标应用组件的应用迁移。通过准确地表明哪些应用和界面需要在迁移阶段之间被映射，能够更准确地估计迁移成本。

它将识别支持迁移所需的临时应用、分段区和基础设施（例如，并行运行环境等）。

软件分布图

软件分布图表明应用软件如何被跨地区构建和分布。它用于系统升级或应用合并项目。

该图表明物理应用如何跨物理技术和该技术的位置被分布。

该图能够清晰地查看软件如何被托管，而且使被管理的操作人员能够理解应用软件在安装后该如何被维护。

35.6.6 Phase D: Technology Architecture

The following section describes catalogs, matrices, and diagrams that may be created within Phase D (Technology Architecture) as listed in Section 12.5.

Technology Standards Catalog

The Technology Standards catalog documents the agreed standards for technology across the enterprise covering technologies, and versions, the technology lifecycles, and the refresh cycles for the technology.

Depending upon the organization, this may also include location or business domain-specific standards information.

This catalog provides a snapshot of the enterprise standard technologies that are or can be deployed, and also helps identify the discrepancies across the enterprise.

If technology standards are currently in place, apply these to the Technology Portfolio catalog to gain a baseline view of compliance with technology standards.

The Technology Portfolio catalog contains the following metamodel entities:

- Platform Service
- Logical Technology Component
- Physical Technology Component

Technology Portfolio Catalog

The purpose of this catalog is to identify and maintain a list of all the technology in use across the enterprise, including hardware, infrastructure software, and application software. An agreed technology portfolio supports lifecycle management of technology products and versions and also forms the basis for definition of technology standards.

The Technology Portfolio catalog provides a foundation on which to base the remaining matrices and diagrams. It is typically the start point of the Technology Architecture phase.

Technology registries and repositories also provide input into this catalog from a baseline and target perspective.

Technologies in the catalog should be classified against the TOGAF Technology Reference Model (TRM) — see Part VI, Chapter 43 — extending the model as necessary to fit the classification of technology products in use.

The Technology Portfolio catalog contains the following metamodel entities:

- Platform Service
- Logical Technology Component
- Physical Technology Component

35.6.6 阶段 D：技术架构

下一节描述了在阶段 D（技术架构）内可能被创建的目录集、矩阵和图，如 12.5 节中所列。

技术标准目录集

技术标准目录集记录了跨 ENTERPRISE 的经商定的技术标准，涵盖技术、版本、技术生命周期和技术的刷新周期。

取决于组织，技术标准目录集还可包括位置或业务特定领域的标准信息。

该目录集对已被部署或可被部署的 ENTERPRISE 标准技术提供快照，而且有助于识别跨 ENTERPRISE 的差异。

如果技术标准目前合适，则将这些技术标准应用于技术谱系目录集，以获得符合技术标准的基线视图。

技术谱系目录集包含下列元模型实体：

- 平台服务
- 逻辑技术组件
- 物理技术组件

技术谱系目录集

该目录集的目的在于识别和维护跨 ENTERPRISE 在用的所有技术的列表，包括硬件、基础设施软件和应用软件。协定的技术谱系支持技术产品和版本的生命周期管理，而且为定义技术标准奠定了基础。

技术谱系目录集提供建立其余矩阵和图所依据的基础。它通常是技术架构阶段的起点。

技术注册表和存储库还从基线和目标的关注层级提供该目录集中的输入。

该目录集中的技术应按照 TOGAF 技术参考模型（TRM）进行分类——见第六部分第 43 章——从而根据需要扩展模型以适配在用的技术产品的分类。

技术谱系目录集包含下列元模型实体：

- 平台服务
- 逻辑技术组件
- 物理技术组件

Application/Technology Matrix

The Application/Technology matrix documents the mapping of applications to technology platform.

This matrix should be aligned with and complement one or more platform decomposition diagrams.

The Application/Technology matrix shows:

- Logical/Physical Application Components
- Services, Logical Technology Components, and Physical Technology Components
- Physical Technology Component *realizes* Physical Application Component relationships

Environments and Locations Diagram

The Environments and Locations diagram depicts which locations host which applications, identifies what technologies and/or applications are used at which locations, and finally identifies the locations from which business users typically interact with the applications.

This diagram should also show the existence and location of different deployment environments, including non-production environments, such as development and pre production.

Platform Decomposition Diagram

The Platform Decomposition diagram depicts the technology platform that supports the operations of the Information Systems Architecture. The diagram covers all aspects of the infrastructure platform and provides an overview of the enterprise's technology platform. The diagram can be expanded to map the technology platform to appropriate application components within a specific functional or process area. This diagram may show details of specification, such as product versions, number of CPUs, etc. or simply could be an informal "eye-chart" providing an overview of the technical environment.

The diagram should clearly show the enterprise applications and the technology platform for each application area can further be decomposed as follows:

- Hardware:
  - Logical Technology Components (with attributes)
  - Physical Technology Components (with attributes)
- Software:
  - Logical Technology Components (with attributes)
  - Physical Technology Components (with attributes)

Depending upon the scope of the enterprise architecture work, additional technology cross-platform information (e.g., communications, telco, and video information) may be addressed.

应用/技术矩阵

应用/技术矩阵记录了应用到技术平台的映射。

该矩阵应符合并补充一个或多个平台分解图。

应用/技术矩阵表明：

- 逻辑/物理应用组件
- 服务、逻辑技术组件和物理技术组件
- 物理技术组件实现物理应用组件的关系

环境和位置图

环境和位置图描述哪些位置托管哪些应用，识别在哪些位置使用什么技术和/或应用，并最终识别业务用户与应用进行典型的交互所在的位置。

该图还应表明不同部署环境的存在方式和位置，包括非生产环境，如开发和预生产。

平台分解图

平台分解图描述支持信息系统架构运行的技术平台。该图涵盖基础设施平台的所有方面，并提供 ENTERPRISE 技术平台的概述。该图可被扩展，用于在特定的功能或流程区内将技术平台映射到恰当的应用组件里。该图可表明规范的细节，如产品版本、CPU 数量等，或者可以只是一个提供技术环境概述的非正式的“视觉图”。

该图应清晰地表明 ENTERPRISE 应用，且每个应用领域的技术平台可进一步分解如下：

- 硬件：
  - 逻辑技术组件（具有属性）
  - 物理技术组件（具有属性）
- 软件：
  - 逻辑技术组件（具有属性）
  - 物理技术组件（具有属性）

根据 Enterprise Architecture 工作的范围，可应对附加的技术跨平台信息（如，通信、电信和视频信息）。

Processing Diagram

The Processing diagram focuses on deployable units of code/configuration and how these are deployed onto the technology platform. A deployment unit represents grouping of business function, service, or application components. The Processing diagram addresses the following:

- Which set of application components need to be grouped to form a deployment unit.
- How one deployment unit connects/interacts with another (LAN, WAN, and the applicable protocols).
- How application configuration and usage patterns generate load or capacity requirements for different technology components.

The organization and grouping of deployment units depends on separation concerns of the presentation, business logic, and data store layers and service-level requirements of the components. For example, presentation layer deployment unit is grouped based on the following:

- Application components that provide UI or user access functions.
- Application components that are differentiated by location and user roles.

There are several considerations to determine how application components are grouped together. Each deployment unit is made up of sub-units, such as:

- **Installation**: Part that holds the executable code or package configuration (in case of packages).
- **Execution**: Application component with its associated state at run time.
- **Persistence**: Data that represents the persistent state of the application component.

Finally, these deployment units are deployed on either dedicated or shared technology components (workstation, web server, application server, or database server, etc.). It is important to note that technology processing can influence and have implications on the services definition and granularity.

Networked Computing/Hardware Diagram

Starting with the transformation to client-server systems from mainframes and later with the advent of e-Business and J2EE, large enterprises moved predominantly into a highly network-based distributed network computing environment with firewalls and demilitarized zones. Currently, most of the applications have a web front-end and, looking at the deployment architecture of these applications, it is very common to find three distinct layers in the network landscape; namely a web presentation layer, an business logic or application layer, and a back-end data store layer. It is a common practice for applications to be deployed and hosted in a shared and common infrastructure environment.

So it becomes highly critical to document the mapping between logical applications and the technology components (e.g., server) that supports the application both in the development and production environments. The purpose of this diagram is to show the "as deployed" logical view of logical application components in a distributed network computing environment. The diagram is useful for the following reasons:

- Enable understanding of which application is deployed where in the distributed network computing environment.
- Establishing authorization, security, and access to these technology components.

流程图

流程图聚焦于代码/构型的可部署单元以及它们如何部署到技术平台上。部署单元代表业务功能、服务或应用组件的分组。流程图应对以下几个问题：

- 哪组应用组件需要被分组以形成部署单元。
- 一个部署单元如何与另一个（LAN、WAN和适用协议）进行连接/交互。
- 应用构型和使用模式如何产生对不同技术组件的负荷或能力需求。

部署单元的组织及分组，取决于展现层、业务逻辑层和数据存储层及组件服务层级需求的分别关注点。例如，展现层部署单元基于以下内容分组：

- 提供UI或用户访问功能的应用组件。
- 按位置和用户角色区分的应用组件。

有一些考量因素决定应用组件如何被分组在一起。每个部署单元由子单元组成，如：

- **安装**：包含可执行代码或包配置（如果有包）的部分。
- **执行**：在运行时具有与其状态相关联的应用组件。
- **持续性**：代表应用组件持续状态的数据。

最后，这些部署单元被部署在专用的或者共享的技术组件上（工作站、网络服务器、应用服务器或数据库服务器等）。重要的是，注意到技术处理可影响并作用于服务定义和颗粒度。

网络计算/硬件图

从中央处理机转换为客户端服务器系统开始，后来随着电子商务和 J2EE 的出现，大型 ENTERPRISE 主要转移到具有防火墙和非军事区的高度基于网络的分布式网络计算环境中。目前，多数应用都具有网络前端，并且查看这些应用的部署架构，在网络全景中找到三个不同分层是很常见的，即网页展现层、业务逻辑层或应用层及后端数据存储层。在共享的公共基础设施环境中对应用进行部署和托管是一种普遍做法。

因此，将支持开发环境和生产环境中的应用的逻辑应用和技术组件（如，服务器）之间的映射进行文件化变得极其关键。该图的目的在于表明分布式网络计算环境中逻辑应用组件的“按部署”逻辑视图。该图是有用的，原因如下：

- 能够了解在分布式网络计算环境的何处部署哪个应用。
- 建立这些技术组件的授权、安保和访问。

- Understand the Technology Architecture that support the applications during problem resolution and troubleshooting.
- Isolate performance problems encountered by applications, determine whether it is application code-related or technology platform-related, and perform necessary upgrade to specific physical technology components.
- Identify areas of optimization as and when newer technologies are available which will eventually reduce cost.
- Enable application/technology auditing and prove compliance with enterprise technology standards.
- Serve as an important tool to introduce changes to the Technology Architecture, thereby supporting effective change management.
- Establish traceability and changing application end-point address while moving application either from a shared environment to a dedicated environment or *vice versa.*

The scope of the diagram can be appropriately defined to cover a specific application, business function, or the entire enterprise. If chosen to be developed at the enterprise level, then the network computing landscape can be depicted in an application agnostic way as well.

Communications Engineering Diagram

The Communications Engineering diagram describes the means of communication — the method of sending and receiving information — between these assets in the Technology Architecture; insofar as the selection of package solutions in the preceding architectures put specific requirements on the communications between the applications.

The Communications Engineering diagram will take logical connections between client and server components and identify network boundaries and network infrastructure required to physically implement those connections. It does not describe the information format or content, but will address protocol and capacity issues.

35.6.7 Phase E: Opportunities and Solutions

The following section describes catalogs, matrices, and diagrams that may be created withinPhase E (Opportunities & Solutions) as listed in Section 13.5.

Project Context Diagram

A Project Context diagram shows the scope of a work package to be implemented as a part of a broader transformation roadmap. The Project Context diagram links a work package to the organizations, functions, services, processes, applications, data, and technology that will be added, removed, or impacted by the project.

The Project Context diagram is also a valuable tool for project portfolio management and project mobilization.

- 理解在解决问题和故障排除期间，支持应用的技术架构。
- 隔离应用所遇到的性能问题，确定是否与应用代码相关或与技术平台相关，并对特定的物理技术组件执行必要的升级。
- 在较新的技术可用时应识别优化区，这将最终降低成本。
- 能够进行应用/技术审计并证明与ENTERPRISE技术标准的合规性。
- 作为向技术架构中引入变更的一个重要工具，从而支持有效的变更管理。
- 将应用从共享环境移至专用环境（或反之）时，建立可追溯性和变更应用终端地址。

可恰当地定义该图的范围，以涵盖特定应用、业务功能或整个ENTERPRISE。如果选择在ENTERPRISE层级开发，则也可采用与应用无关的方式来描述网络计算全景。

通信工程图

通信工程图描述了在技术架构的这些资产之间的通信手段——发送和接收信息的方法；在先前架构中解决方案包的选择范围内，在应用之间的通信上提出特定要求。

通信工程图将在客户端和服务器组件之间采用逻辑连接，并识别物理上实施这些连接所需的网络边界和网络基础设施。它不描述信息格式或内容，但会涉及协议和能力议题。

35.6.7 阶段E：机会和解决方案

下一节描述了在阶段E（机会和解决方案）内可能被创建的目录集、矩阵和图，如13.5节中所列。

项目背景环境图

项目背景环境图表明作为更广泛的转型路线图的一部分而有待被实施的工作包范围。项目背景环境图将工作包与项目要增加、删除或影响的组织、功能、服务、流程、应用、数据和技术联系起来。

项目背景环境图也是用于项目谱系管理和项目动员的一个有价值的工具。

Benefits Diagram

The Benefits diagram shows opportunities identified in an architecture definition, classified according to their relative size, benefit, and complexity. This diagram can be used by stakeholders to make selection, prioritization, and sequencing decisions on identified opportunities.

35.6.8 Requirements Management

The following section describes catalogs, matrices, and diagrams that may be created within the

Requirements Management phase as listed in Section 17.5.

Requirements Catalog

The Requirements catalog captures things that the enterprise needs to do to meet its objectives. Requirements generated from architecture engagements are typically implemented through change initiatives identified and scoped during Phase E (Opportunities & Solutions). Requirements can also be used as a quality assurance tool to ensure that a particular architecture is fit-for-purpose (i.e., can the architecture meet all identified requirements).

The Requirements catalog contains the following metamodel entities:

- Requirement
- Assumption
- Constraint
- Gap

35.7 Recommended Architecture Views to be Developed

Part III, Chapter 24 provides an outline of the major stakeholder groups that are typically encountered when developing enterprise architecture. The likely concerns of each stakeholder group are also identified together with relevant artifacts (catalogs, matrices, and diagrams).

The architecture views, and corresponding viewpoints, that may be created to support each of these stakeholders fall into the following categories:

- Business Architecture views, which address the concerns of the users of the system, and describe the flows of business information between people and business processes.
- Data Architecture views, which address the concerns of database designers and database administrators, and system engineers responsible for developing and integrating the various database components of the system.
- Application Architecture views, which address the concerns of system and software engineers responsible for developing and integrating the various application software components of the system.
- Technology Architecture views, which address the concerns of acquirers (procurement personnel responsible for acquiring the Commercial Off-The-Shelf (COTS) software and hardware to be included in the system), operations staff, systems administrators, and systems managers.

效益图

效益图表明在架构定义中所识别的机会按照其相对大小、效益和复杂性分类。该图可由利益攸关者用于对所识别的机会进行选择、优先化并做出排序决策。

35.6.8 需求管理

下一节描述了在需求管理阶段内可能被创建的目录集、矩阵和图，如 17.5 节中所列。

需求目录集

需求目录集捕获 ENTERPRISE 为满足其目的需要完成的事情。在架构工作中产生的需求，通常通过在阶段 E（机会和解决方案）期间所识别和确定范围的变更举措来实现。需求还可用作质量保证工具，以确保特定架构的适用性（即，架构可满足所有所识别的需求）。

需求目录集包含下列元模型实体：

- 需求
- 假设
- 约束
- 差距

35.7 待开发的推荐架构视图

第三部分第 24 章提供了在开发 Enterprise Architecture 时通常遇到的主要利益攸关者群组。每个利益攸关者群组的可能的关注点也与相关制品（目录集、矩阵和图）一起被识别。

为支持每个利益攸关者而创建的架构视图和对应视角属于下列类别：

- 业务架构视图，应对系统用户的关注点并描述人员和业务流程之间的业务信息流。
- 数据架构视图，应对数据库设计人员和数据库管理人员以及负责开发和综合各种系统数据库组件的系统工程师的关注点。
- 应用架构视图，应对系统及负责开发和综合各种系统应用软件组件的软件工程师的关注点。
- 技术架构视图，应对采办方［负责采办系统内包括的商用货架（COTS）软件和硬件的采购人员］、操作人员、系统管理员和系统经理的关注点。

In the following subsections TOGAF presents some recommended views, some or all of which may be appropriate in a particular architecture development. This is not intended as an exhaustive set of views, but simply as a starting point. Those described may be supplemented by additional views as required. This material should be considered as guides for the development and treatment of a view, not as a full definition of a viewpoint. The artifacts identified in Section 35.6 can be used to address specific concerns of the stakeholders, and in some instances the artifacts can be used with the view of the same name; for example, the Software Engineering diagram, Communications Engineering diagram, and Enterprise Manageability diagram.

Each subsection describes the stakeholders related to the view, their concerns, and the entities modeled and the language used to depict the view (the viewpoint). The viewpoint provides architecture concepts from the different perspectives, including components, interfaces, and allocation of services critical to the view. The viewpoint language, analytical methods, and modeling methods associated with views are typically applied with the use of appropriate tools.

35.7.1 Developing a Business Architecture View

The Business Architecture view is concerned with addressing the concerns of users.

35.7.1.1 Stakeholders and Concerns

This view should be developed for the users. It focuses on the functional aspects of the system from the perspective of the users of the system.

Addressing the concerns of the users includes consideration of the following:

People	The human resource aspects of the system. It examines the human actors involved in the system.
Process	Deals with the user processes involved in the system.
Function	Deals with the functions required to support the processes.
Business Information	Deals with the information required to flow in support of the processes.
Usability	Considers the usability aspects of the system and its environment.
Performance	Considers the performance aspects of the system and its environment.

35.7.1.2 Developing the View

Business scenarios (see Part III, Chapter 26) are an important technique that may be used prior to, and as a key input to, the development of the Business Architecture view, to help identify and understand business needs, and thereby to derive the business requirements and constraints that the architecture development has to address. Business scenarios are an extremely useful way to depict what should happen when planned and unplanned events occur. It is highly recommended that business scenarios be created for planned change, and for unplanned change.

The following section describe some of the key issues that the architect might consider when constructing business scenarios.

在下列小节中，TOGAF 提出一些推荐视图，其中部分或全部视图在特定架构开发中可能是合适的。其目的不是作为视图的穷举集，而仅作为一个起点。以上描述可按需要补充附加视图。该资料应被认为是开发和处理视图的指南，而非视角的完整定义。35.6 节所识别的制品可用于应对利益攸关者的特定关注点，在某些情况下，制品可与相同名称的视图配合使用；例如，软件工程图、通信工程图和 ENTERPRISE 可管理性图。

每个小节描述与视图相关的利益攸关者、利益攸关者的关注点、已建模的实体和用于描述视图（视角）的语言。视角从不同的关注层级提供架构概念，包括对视图很关键的组件、界面和服务分配。与视图相关联的视角语言、分析方法和建模方法通常与合适的工具配合使用。

35.7.1 开发业务架构视图

业务架构视图涉及用户关注点的处理。

35.7.1.1 利益攸关者和关注点

该视图应针对用户来开发。它从系统用户的关注层级聚焦于系统的功能方面。

应对用户关注点包括下列考量因素：

人员	系统的人力资源方面。它审查与系统相关的人员施动者。
流程	处理与系统相关的用户流程。
功能	处理支持流程所需的功能。
业务信息	处理支持流程的流转所需的信息。
可用性	考虑系统及其环境的可用性方面。
绩效	考虑系统及其环境的绩效方面。

35.7.1.2 开发视图

业务场景（见第三部分第 26 章）是在开发业务架构视图之前使用且作为其关键输入的一种重要技术，以帮助识别和理解业务需要，并因此衍生出架构开发必须应对的业务需求和约束。业务场景是在出现计划性和非计划性事件时来描述应发生什么的一个极其有用的方式。强烈建议分别针对计划性变更和非计划性变更创建业务场景。

下一节描述在建立业务场景时架构师可能考虑的一些关键问题。

35.7.1.3 Key Issues

The Business Architecture view considers the functional aspects of the system; that is, what the new system is intended to do. This can be built up from an analysis of the existing environment and of the requirements and constraints affecting the new system.

The new requirements and constraints will appear from a number of sources, possibly including:

- Existing internal specifications and lists of approved products
- Business goals and objectives
- Business process re-engineering activities
- Changes in technology

What should emerge from the Business Architecture view is a clear understanding of the functional requirements for the new architecture, with statements like: "Improvements in handling customer enquiries are required through wider use of computer/telephony integration" .

The Business Architecture view considers the usability aspects of the system and its environment. It should also consider impacts on the user such as skill levels required, the need for specialized training, and migration from current practice. When considering usability the architect should take into account:

- The ease-of-use of the user interface, and how intuitive it is.
- Whether or not there is transparent access to data and applications, irrespective of location.
- Ease-of-management of the user environment by the user.
- Application interoperability through means such as drag-and-drop.
- Online help facilities.
- Clarity of documentation.
- Security and password aspects, such as avoiding the requirement for multiple sign-on and password dialogs.
- Access to productivity applications, such as mail or a spreadsheet.

Note that, although security and management are thought about here, it is from a usability and functionality point of view. The technical aspects of security and management are considered in the Enterprise Security view (see Section 35.7.2) and the Enterprise Manageability view (see Section 35.7.7).

35.7.2 Developing an Enterprise Security View

The Enterprise Security view is concerned with the security aspects of the system.

35.7.2.1 Stakeholders and Concerns

This view should be developed for security engineers of the system. It focuses on how the system is implemented from the perspective of security, and how security affects the system properties. It examines the system to establish what information is stored and processed, how valuable it is, what threats exist, and how they can be addressed.

Major concerns for this view are understanding how to ensure that the system is available to only those that have permission, and how to protect the system from unauthorized tampering.

35.7.1.3 关键问题

业务架构视图考虑到系统的功能方面；即，新系统想要做什么。它可根据对现有环境以及影响新系统的需求和约束进行的分析来构建。

新的需求和约束将出自多个来源，可能包括：

- 现有内部规范和已批准的产品的列表
- 业务目标和目的
- 业务流程重组活动
- 技术变革

从业务架构视图中产生的是对新架构功能需求的清晰理解，附有诸如“需要通过更广泛地使用计算机/电话综合来改进对客户查询的处理”的说明。

业务架构视图考虑到系统及其环境的可用性方面。它还应考虑对用户的影响（如所需的技术水平）、专业培训的需要及从当前实践中的迁移。在考虑可用性时，架构师应考虑到：

- 用户界面的易用性，以及直观程度。
- 不考虑位置，是否存在对数据和应用的透明访问。
- 用户对用户环境的易管理性。
- 通过某种手段（如拖放）的应用互用性。
- 在线帮助工具。
- 文件清晰度。
- 安保性和口令方面，如避免对多个开始指令和口令对话的需求
- 生产率应用的访问，如邮件或电子表格。

注意，尽管本文考虑了安保性和管理，但它是从可用性和功能性的观点出发的。安保和管理的技术方面在 ENTERPRISE 安保视图（见 35.7.2 节）和 ENTERPRISE 可管理性视图（见 35.7.7 节）中考虑。

35.7.2 开发 ENTERPRISE 安保视图

ENTERPRISE 安保视图涉及系统的安保方面。

35.7.2.1 利益攸关者和关注点

该视图应针对系统的安保工程师来开发。它聚焦于如何从安保的关注层级实施系统，以及安保如何影响系统特性。它对系统进行审查以确定存储和处理什么信息、有多大价值、存在什么威胁，以及可如何应对。

该视图的主要关注点是，理解如何确保系统只用于经许可的内容，以及如何保护系统不被未经授权篡改。

35.7.2.2 Developing the View

The subjects of the general architecture of a "security system" are components that are secured, or components that provide security services. Additionally Access Control Lists (ACLs) and security schema definitions are used to model and implement security.

35.7.2.3 Basic Concepts

This section presents basic concepts required for an understanding of information system security.

The essence of security is the controlled use of information. The purpose of this section is to provide a brief overview of how security protection is implemented in the components of an information system. Doctrinal or procedural mechanisms, such as physical and personnel security procedures and policy, are not discussed here in any depth.

Figure 35-4 depicts an abstract view of an Information Systems Architecture, which emphasizes the fact that an information system from the security perspective is either part of a Local Subscriber Environment (LSE) or a Communications Network (CN). An LSE may be either fixed or mobile. The LSEs by definition are under the control of the using organization. In an open system distributed computing implementation, secure and non-secure LSEs will almost certainly be required to interoperate.

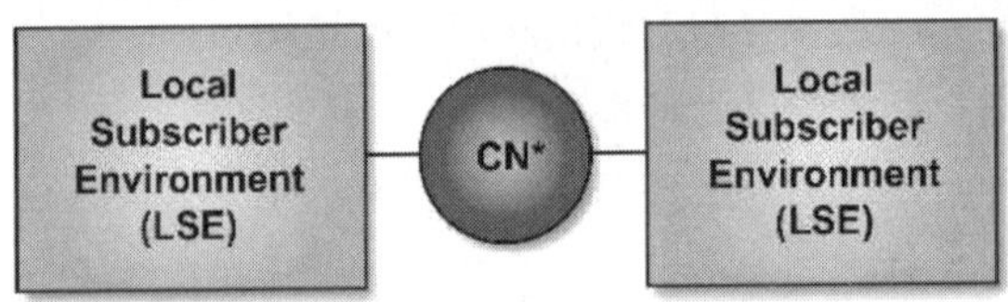

Figure 35-4 Abstract Security Architecture View

Information Domains

The concept of an information domain provides the basis for discussing security protection requirements. An information domain is defined as a set of users, their information objects, and a security policy. An information domain security policy is the statement of the criteria for membership in the information domain and the required protection of the information objects. Breaking an organization's information down into domains is the first step in reducing the task of security policy development to a manageable size.

The business of most organizations requires that their members operate in more than one information domain. The diversity of business activities and the variation in perception of threats to the security of information will result in the existence of different information domains within one organization security policy. A specific activity may use several information domains, each with its own distinct information domain security policy.

Information domains are not necessarily bounded by information systems or even networks of systems. The security mechanisms implemented in information system components may be evaluated for their ability to meet the information domain security policies.

35.7.2.2 开发视图

“安保系统”的一般架构主题是受保护的组件或提供安保服务的组件。此外，访问控制列表（ACL）和安保模式定义用于对安保建模并实施。

35.7.2.3 基本概念

本节提供了解信息系统安保性所需的基本概念。

安保性的本质是信息的受控使用。本节的目的在于提供如何在信息系统的组件内实施安保性保护的简要概述。诸如物理和人员安保程序和方针等教条性或程序性的机制，没有被进行任何程度的论述。

图 35-4 描述了信息系统架构的抽象视图，强调了从安保的关注层级而言信息系统是本地用户环境（LSE）或通信网络（CN）的一部分这一事实。LSE 可以是固定的或移动的。按照定义，LSE 处于使用组织的控制之中。在开放系统分布式计算的实施中，安全和非安全 LSE 几乎肯定需要互用。

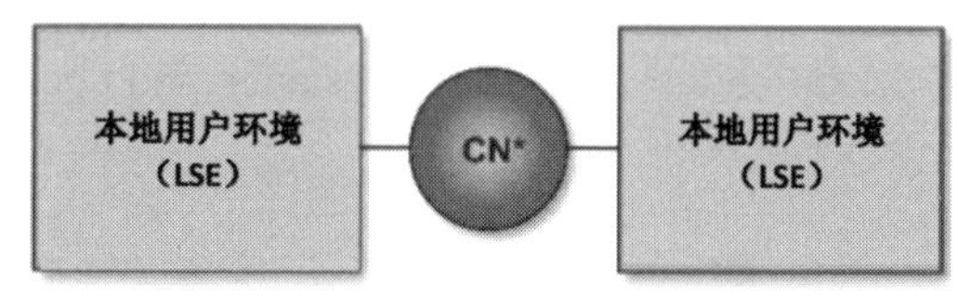

图 35-4 抽象的安保架构视图

信息域

信息域的概念提供了论述安保性保护需求的基础。信息域被定义为用户及其信息对象和安保方针的集合。信息域安保方针，是对信息域内会员资格准则和对信息对象所需的保护的说明。将组织的信息分解为多个领域，是将安保方针开发任务缩小到可管理规模的第一步。

多数组织的业务都要求其成员在一个以上信息域内工作。业务活动的多样性和对信息安保的威胁的感知变化，将导致在一个组织安保方针内存在不同的信息域。一个特定活动可使用多个信息域，每个信息域具有各自不同的信息域安保方针。

信息域不一定受信息系统或甚至系统网络的约束。信息系统组件内所实施的安保机制，可通过满足信息域安保方针的能力被评估。

Strict Isolation

Information domains can be viewed as being strictly isolated from one another. Information objects should be transferred between two information domains only in accordance with established rules, conditions, and procedures expressed in the security policy of each information domain.

Absolute Protection

The concept of "absolute protection" is used to achieve the same level of protection in all information systems supporting a particular information domain. It draws attention to the problems created by interconnecting LSEs that provide different strengths of security protection. This interconnection is likely because open systems may consist of an unknown number of heterogeneous LSEs. Analysis of minimum security requirements will ensure that the concept of absolute protection will be achieved for each information domain across LSEs.

35.7.2.4 Security Generic Architecture View

Figure 35-5 shows a generic architecture view which can be used to discuss the allocation of security services and the implementation of security mechanisms. This view identifies the architectural components within an LSE. The LSEs are connected by CNs. The LSEs include end systems, relay systems, and Local Communications Systems (LCSs), described below.

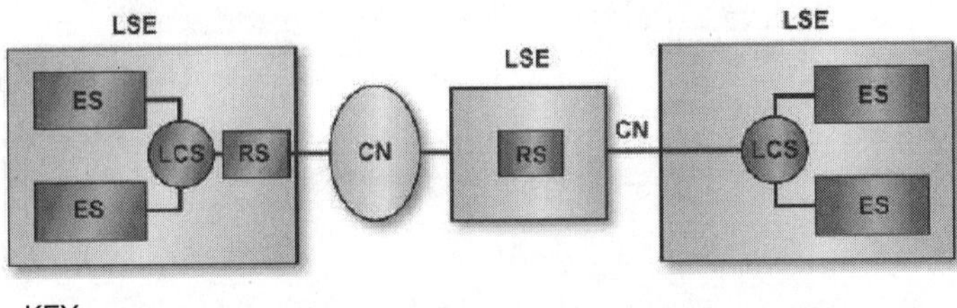

KEY

CN Communications Network

ES End System

LCS Local Communications System

LSE Local Subscriber Environment

RS Relay System

Figure 35-5 Generic Security Architecture View

- **Relay System (RS)**: The component of an LSE, the functionality of which is limited to information transfer and is only indirectly accessible by users (e.g., router, switch, multiplexor, Message Transfer Agent (MTA)). It may have functionality similar to an end system, but an end user does not use it directly. Note that relay system functions may be provided in an end system.
- **Local Communication System (LCS)**: A network that provides communications capabilities between LSEs or within an LSE with all of the components under control of an LSE.

严格隔离

信息域可被视为彼此严格的隔离。应仅按照各信息域安保方针内所表达的已建立的规则、条件和程序，在两个信息域之间传输信息对象。

绝对保护

“绝对保护”的概念用于在支持特定信息域的所有信息系统中达成相同的保护等级。它关注于对提供不同强度的安保性保护的 LSE 进行互连所产生的问题。这种互连是可能的，因为开放系统可由未知数量的异构的 LSE 组成。分析最低安保需求将确保跨 LSE 针对每个信息域达成绝对保护的概念。

35.7.2.4 通用安保架构视图

图 35-5 表明一个一般架构视图，可用于论述安保服务的分配和安保机制的实施。该视图识别 LSE 内的架构组件。LSE 由 CN 连接。LSE 包括终端系统、中继系统和本地通信系统（LCS），描述如下。

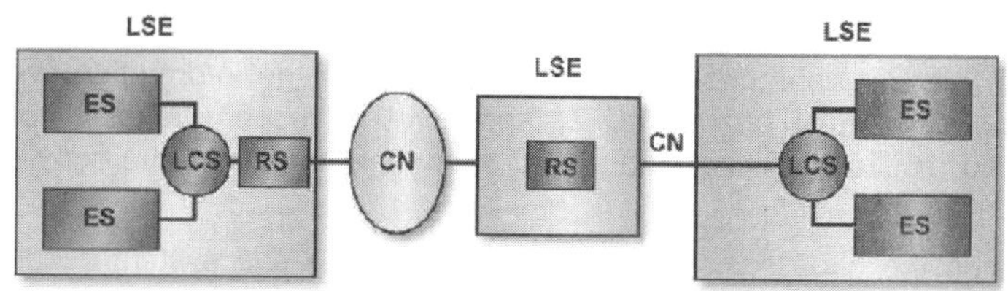

KEY

CN 通信网络

ES 终端系统

LCS 本地通信系统

LSE 本地用户环境

RS 中继系统

图 35-5 一般安保架构视图

- 中继系统（RS）：LSE 的组件，其功能性仅限于信息传输且可由用户［如，路由器、开关、多路复用器、消息传输代理（MTA）］间接地访问。它具有与终端系统相似的功能性，但最终用户不直接使用它。注意，可在终端系统中提供中继系统功能。
- 本地通信系统（LCS）：在多个 LSE 之间或一个 LSE 内提供通信能力的网络，其所有组件处于一个 LSE 的控制之中。

- **Communications Network (CN)**: A network that provides inter-LSE communications capabilities, but is not controlled by LSEs (e.g., commercial carriers).

The end system and the relay system are viewed as requiring the same types of security protection. For this reason, a discussion of security protection in an end system generally also applies to a relay system. The security protections in an end system could occur in both the hardware and software.

35.7.2.5 Security Services Allocation

Security protection of an information system is provided by mechanisms implemented in the hardware and software of the system and by the use of doctrinal mechanisms. The mechanisms implemented in the system hardware and software are concentrated in the end system or relay system. This focus for security protection is based on the open system, distributed computing approach for information systems. This implies use of commercial common carriers and private common-user communications systems as the CN provider between LSEs. Thus, for operation of end systems in a distributed environment, a greater degree of security protection can be ensured from implementation of mechanisms in the end system or relay system.

However, communications networks should satisfy the availability element of security in order to provide appropriate security protection for the information system. This means that CNs must provide an agreed level of responsiveness, continuity of service, and resistance to accidental and intentional threats to the communications service availability.

Implementing the necessary security protection in the end system occurs in three system service areas of TOGAF. They are operating system services, network services, and system management services.

Most of the implementation of security protection is expected to occur in software. The hardware is expected to protect the integrity of the end-system software. Hardware security mechanisms include protection against tampering, undesired emanations, and cryptography.

Operating System Services

A "security context" is defined as a controlled process space subject to an information domain security policy. The security context is therefore analogous to a common operating system notion of user process space. Isolation of security contexts is required. Security contexts are required for all applications (e.g., end-user and security management applications). The focus is on strict isolation of information domains, management of end-system resources, and controlled sharing and transfer of information among information domains. Where possible, security-critical functions should be isolated into relatively small modules that are related in well-defined ways.

The operating system will isolate multiple security contexts from each other using hardware protection features (e.g., processor state register, memory mapping registers) to create separate address spaces for each of them. Untrusted software will use end-system resources only by invoking security-critical functions through the separation kernel. Most of the security-critical functions are the low-level functions of traditional operating systems.

- 通信网络（CN）：提供 LSE 间通信能力，但不受 LSE 控制的网络（如，商业载体）。

终端系统和中继系统被认为需要相同类型的安保性保护。为此，终端系统中安保性保护的论述一般还适用于中继系统。硬件和软件中，都可出现终端系统中的安保性保护。

35.7.2.5 安保服务分配

通过系统硬件和软件中实施的机制以及使用教条性的机制来提供信息系统的安保性保护。系统硬件和软件中实施的机制集中在终端系统或中继系统中。这个安保性保护的聚焦点是基于开放系统和系统分布式计算实施途径。这意味着，使用商业公共载体和私有普通用户通信系统作为 LSE 之间的 CN 提供者。因此，为了终端系统在分布式环境中的运行，可在终端系统或中继系统中的机制实施中确保更大程度的安保性保护。

然而，通信网络应满足安保的可用性元素，以便为信息系统提供恰当的安保性保护。这意味着，CN 必须提供商定的响应水平、服务连续性以及对通信服务可用性的意外和蓄意威胁的抵抗能力。

在 TOGAF 的三个系统服务区对终端系统实施必要的安保性保护。三个系统服务区是操作系统服务、网络服务和系统管理服务。

预计多数安保性保护的实施发生在软件中，硬件会保护终端系统软件的完整性。硬件安保机制包括防止篡改、不希望的扩散和密码系统。

操作系统服务

“安保背景环境”被定义为遵守信息域安保方针的受控流程空间。因此，安保背景环境类似于用户流程空间的公共操作系统概念。安保背景环境需要隔离。所有应用（如，最终用户和安保管理应用）都需要安保背景环境。聚焦点是信息域的严格隔离、终端系统资源的管理以及信息域之间信息的受控共享和传输。若可能，应将安保关键功能分隔成以明确定义的方式相关联的相对较小的模块。

操作系统将使用硬件保护特征（如，处理器状态寄存器、内存映射寄存器）将多重安保背景环境彼此隔离，以便为每个安保背景环境创建单独的地址空间。通过分离核心来仅调用安保关键功能，不可信软件将使用终端系统资源。多数安保关键功能是传统操作系统的低级功能。

Network Services

Two basic classes of communications are envisioned for which distributed security contexts may need to be established. These are interactive and staged (store and forward) communications.

The concept of a "security association" forms an interactive distributed security context. A security association is defined as all the communication and security mechanisms and functions that extend the protections required by an information domain security policy within an end system to information in transfer between multiple end systems. The security association is an extension or expansion of an OSI application layer association. An application layer association is composed of appropriate application layer functions and protocols plus all of the underlying communications functions and protocols at other layers of the OSI model. Multiple security protocols may be included in a single security association to provide for a combination of security services.

For staged delivery communications (e.g., email), use will be made of an encapsulation technique (termed "wrapping process") to convey the necessary security attributes with the data being transferred as part of the network services. The wrapped security attributes are intended to permit the receiving end system to establish the necessary security context for processing the transferred data. If the wrapping process cannot provide all the necessary security protection, interactive security contexts between end systems will have to be used to ensure the secure staged transfer of information.

System Security Management Services

Security management is a particular instance of the general information system management functions discussed in earlier chapters. Information system security management services are concerned with the installation, maintenance, and enforcement of information domain and information system security policy rules in the information system intended to provide these security services. In particular, the security management function controls information needed by operating system services within the end system security architecture. In addition to these core services, security management requires event handling, auditing, and recovery. Standardization of security management functions, data structures, and protocols will enable interoperation of Security Management Application Processes (SMAPs) across many platforms in support of distributed security management.

35.7.3 Developing a Software Engineering View

The Software Engineering view is concerned with the development of new software systems.

35.7.3.1 Stakeholders and Concerns

Building a software-intensive system is both expensive and time-consuming. Because of this, it is necessary to establish guidelines to help minimize the effort required and the risks involved. This is the purpose of the Software Engineering view, which should be developed for the software engineers who are going to develop the system.

Major concerns for these stakeholders are:

- Development approach
- Software modularity and re-use
- Portability

网络服务

设想了两种基本类型的通信，可能需要为其建立分布式安保背景环境。这两种基本类型是交互的和分段的（存储和转发）通信。

“安保关联”的概念构成交互的分布式安保背景环境。安保关联被定义为所有通信和安保机制与功能，它们将终端系统内的信息域安保方针所需的保护扩展至多个终端系统之间传输的信息。安保关联是 OSI 应用层关联的扩展或扩充。应用层关联由恰当的应用层功能和协议加上所有 OSI 模型其他层的基础通信功能和协议构成。单个安保关联可包括多重安保协议，以提供给安保服务组合。

对于分段的传递通信（如电子邮件），将使用封装技术（称作“包装工艺”）传输必要的安保属性，同时数据作为网络服务的一部分被传输。所包装的安保属性，旨在允许接收终端系统以建立必要的安保背景环境来处理所传输的数据。如果包装过程不能提供所有必要的安保性保护，则必须使用终端系统之间的交互性安保背景环境来确保信息的安全分段传输。

系统安保管理服务

安保管理是之前章节中论述的一般信息系统管理功能的一个特定实例。信息系统安保管理服务涉及用于提供这些安保服务的信息系统中的信息域和信息系统安保方针规则的安装、维护和执行。特别是，安保管理功能对终端系统安保架构内的操作系统服务所需的信息进行控制。除了这些核心服务外，安保管理需要进行事件处理、审核和恢复。安保管理功能、数据结构和协议的标准化，将使安保管理应用流程（SMAP）能够在跨多个支持分布式安保管理的平台上进行互用。

35.7.3 开发软件工程视图

软件工程视图涉及新的软件系统的开发。

35.7.3.1 利益攸关者和关注点

构建软件密集型系统既昂贵而且耗费时间。正因为如此，所以有必要建立指南以帮助最小化所需工作和相关风险。这是软件工程视图的目的，软件工程视图应针对参加开发系统的软件工程师来开发。

这些利益攸关者的主要关注点是：

- 开发途径
- 软件模块化和复用
- 可移植性

- Migration and interoperability

Development Approach

There are many lifecycle models defined for software development (waterfall, prototyping, etc.).A consideration for the architect is how best to feed architectural decisions into the lifecycle model that is going to be used for development of the system.

Software Modularity and Re-Use

As a piece of software grows in size, so the complexity and inter-dependencies between different parts of the code increase. Reliability will fall dramatically unless this complexity can be brought under control.

Modularity is a concept by which a piece of software is grouped into a number of distinct and logically cohesive sub-units, presenting services to the outside world through a well-defined interface. Generally speaking, the components of a module will share access to common data, and the interface will provide controlled access to this data. Using modularity, it becomes possible to build a software application incrementally on a reliable base of pre-tested code.

A further benefit of a well-defined modular system is that the modules defined within it may be re-used in the same or on other projects, cutting development time dramatically by reducing both development and testing effort.

In recent years, the development of object-oriented programming languages has greatly increased programming language support for module development and code re-use. Such languages allow the developer to define "classes" (a unit of modularity) of objects that behave in a controlled and well-defined manner. Techniques such as inheritance — which enables parts of an existing interface to an object to be changed — enhance the potential for re-usability by allowing predefined classes to be tailored or extended when the services they offer do not quite meet the requirement of the developer.

If modularity and software re-use are likely to be key objectives of new software developments, consideration must be given to whether the component parts of any proposed architecture may facilitate or prohibit the desired level of modularity in the appropriate areas.

Portability

Software portability — the ability to take a piece of software written in one environment and make it run in another — is important in many projects, especially product developments. It requires that all software and hardware aspects of a chosen Technology Architecture (not just the newly developed application) be available on the new platform. It will, therefore, be necessary to ensure that the component parts of any chosen architecture are available across all the appropriate target platforms.

Migration and Interoperability

Interoperability is always required between the component parts of a new architecture. It may also, however, be required between a new architecture and parts of an existing legacy system; for example, during the staggered replacement of an old system. Interoperability between the new and old architectures may, therefore, be a factor in architectural choice.

- 迁移和互用性

开发途径

针对软件开发而定义的生命周期模型有很多（如瀑布、原型等）。架构师考虑的是，如何最好地向即将用于系统开发的生命周期模型提供架构决策。

软件模块化和复用

由于一个软件的规模增加，因此不同部分的代码之间的复杂性和相互依赖性也在增加。除非复杂性可以得到控制，否则可靠性将大幅下降。

模块化是一个软件被分组为多个不同的逻辑内聚子单元所用的概念，它通过明确定义的界面向外界提供服务。一般而言，一个模块的多个组件将共享访问公共数据，而且界面将提供对该数据的受控访问。使用模块化，在可靠的预测试代码基础上递增地构建软件应用成为可能。

明确定义的模块化系统的其他好处是，其内部定义的模块可在相同的或其他项目中复用，通过减少开发和试验工作大幅来减少开发时间。

近年来，面向对象的编程语言的发展，大幅增加了对模块开发和代码复用的编程语言的支持。此类语言使得开发人员能够对遵循受控和明确定义方式的对象“类”（模块化单元）进行定义。一些技术，如继承——使一个对象的部分现有界面能够变化——在他们所提供的服务无法完全满足开发人员的要求时，通过允许剪裁或扩展预定义的类来提高可复用性的潜力。

如果模块化和软件复用可能是新软件开发的关键目标，则必须考虑，提出的任何架构的组件是否会促进或阻碍在恰当区域中所期望的模块化水平。

可移植性

软件可移植性——在一个环境下编写一个软件并使其在另一个环境中运行的能力——在许多项目中都非常重要，尤其是在产品开发中。它要求所选择的技术架构的所有软件和硬件方面（不只是新开发的应用）在新的平台上可用。因此，有必要确保所选择的任何架构的组件部分可用于跨所有适当的目标平台。

迁移和互用性

新架构的组件之间总是需要互用性。然而，新架构与部分现有遗留系统之间也需要互用性；例如，在旧系统的交错更替期间。因此，新旧架构之间的互用性可能是架构选择中的一个因素。

35.7.3.2 Key Issues

- Data-intensive *versus* information-intensive software systems
- Achieving interoperability
- Software tiers
- Uses of a data access tier
- Distribution

Data-Intensive versus Information-Intensive Software Systems

This view considers two general categories of software systems. First, there are those systems that require only a user interface to a database, requiring little or no business logic built into the software. These systems can be called "data-intensive". Second, there are those systems that require users to manipulate information that might be distributed across multiple databases, and to do this manipulation according to a predefined business logic. These systems can be called "information-intensive"

Data-intensive systems can be built with reasonable ease through the use of 4GL tools. In these systems, the business logic is in the mind of the user; i.e., the user understands the rules for manipulating the data and uses those rules while doing his work.

Information-intensive systems are different. Information is defined as "meaningful data"; i.e., data in a context that includes business logic. Information is different from data. Data is the tokens that are stored in databases or other data stores. Information is multiple tokens of data combined to convey a message. For example, "3" is data, but "3 widgets" is information. Typically, information reflects a model. Information-intensive systems also tend to require information from other systems and, if this path of information passing is automated, usually some mediation is required to convert the format of incoming information into a format that can be locally used. Because of this, information-intensive systems tend to be more complex than others, and require the most effort to build, integrate, and maintain.

This view is concerned primarily with information-intensive systems. In addition to building systems that can manage information, though, systems should also be as flexible as possible. This has a number of benefits. It allows the system to be used in different environments; for example, the same system should be usable with different sources of data, even if the new data store is a different configuration. Similarly, it might make sense to use the same functionality but with users who need a different user interface. So information systems should be built so that they can be reconfigured with different data stores or different user interfaces. If a system is built to allow this, it enables the enterprise to re-use parts (or components) of one system in another.

Achieving Interoperability

The word "interoperate" implies that one processing system performs an operation on behalf of or at the behest of another processing system. In practice, the request is a complete sentence containing a verb (operation) and one or more nouns (identities of resources, where the resources can be information, data, physical devices, etc.). Interoperability comes from shared functionality.

Interoperability can only be achieved when information is passed, not when data is passed. Most information systems today get information both from their own data stores and other information systems. In some cases the web of connectivity between information systems is quite extensive. The US Air Force, for example, has a concept known as "A5 Interoperability". This means that the required data is available Anytime, Anywhere, by Anyone, who is Authorized, in Any way. This requires that many information systems are architecturally linked and provide information to each other.

35.7.3.2 关键问题

- 数据密集型软件系统与信息密集型软件系统的对比
- 达成互用性
- 软件级
- 数据访问级的使用
- 分布

数据密集型软件系统与信息密集型软件系统的对比

该视图考虑到两大类软件系统。第一，那些仅需要数据库用户界面的系统，软件中几乎不需要构建业务逻辑。这些系统可称为“数据密集型系统”。第二，那些需要用户操纵可能跨多个数据库分布的信息并按照预定义的业务逻辑进行此操纵的系统。这些系统可称为“信息密集型系统”。

可通过使用 4GL 工具，以合理的难易程度构建数据密集型系统。在这些系统中，业务逻辑是用户的想法；即，用户理解操纵数据的规则并在工作时使用那些规则。

信息密集型系统则不同。信息被定义为“有意义的数据”；即，在背景环境内包括业务逻辑的数据。信息与数据不同。数据是存储在数据库或其他数据存储器中的标识。信息是为传递消息而组合的多个数据标识。例如，“3”是数据，但“3 个小装置”是信息。典型情况下，信息反映一个模型。信息密集型系统还往往会需要其他系统中的信息，如果这个信息传递路径是自动的，通常需要进行某种“中介处理”，以便将输入信息的格式转换为本地可使用的格式。正因为如此，信息密集型系统往往会比其他系统更加复杂，且需要付出最大的努力来构建、集成和维护。

该视图主要涉及信息密集型系统。除了构建可管理信息的系统外，系统还应尽可能灵活。这有许多好处。它使得系统能够被用于不同的环境；例如，即使新的数据存储配置不同，同一个系统对不同数据源应该都是可用的。同样，使用相同的功能性但其用户需要不同用户界面是有意义的。因此，应构建信息系统，从而使它们可以根据不同的数据存储或不同的用户界面被重新配置。如果系统构建后允许重新配置，则该系统使 ENTERPRISE 能够复用另一个 ENTERPRISE 中的一个系统的某些部分（或组件）。

达成互用性

“互用”一词意指，一个处理系统代表另一个处理系统或在另一个处理系统的命令下执行一项操作。实际上，要求是一个完整的句子，包含一个动词（操作）及一个或多个名词（资源标识，其中资源可以是信息、数据、物理设备等）。互用性来自共享的功能性。

互用性只有在传递信息而不是传递数据时才可达成。如今，大多数信息系统既从其自身数据存储也从其他信息系统中获得信息。在某些情况下，信息系统之间的连接网络是相当广泛的。例如，美国空军有一个被称为“A5 互用性”的概念，意味着所需数据可在任何时候、任何地方被任何已授权的人以任何方式获得。这就要求多个信息系统在架构上相关联并为彼此提供信息。

There must be some kind of physical connectivity between the systems. This might be a Local Area Network (LAN), a Wide Area Network (WAN), or, in some cases, it might simply be the passing data storage media between systems. Assuming a network connects the systems, there must be agreement on the protocols used. This enables the transfer of bits.

When the bits are assembled at the receiving system, they must be placed in the context that the receiving system needs. In other words, both the source and destination systems must agree on an information model. The source system uses this model to convert its information into data to be passed, and the destination system uses this same model to convert the received data into information it can use.

This usually requires an agreement between the architects and designers of the two systems. In the past, this agreement was often documented in the form of an Interface Control Document (ICD). The ICD defines the exact syntax and semantics that the sending system will use so that the receiving system will know what to do when the data arrives. The biggest problem with ICDs is that they tend to be unique solutions between two systems. If a given system must share information with n other systems, there is the potential need for n^2 ICDs. This extremely tight integration prohibits flexibility and the ability of a system to adapt to a changing environment. Maintaining all these ICDs is also a challenge.

New technology, such as eXtensible Markup Language (XML), has the promise of making data "self describing" . Use of new technologies such as XML, once they become reliable and well documented, might eliminate the need for an ICD. Further, there would be Commercial Off-The-Shelf (COTS) products available to parse and manipulate the XML data, eliminating the need to develop these products in-house. It should also ease the pain of maintaining all the interfaces.

Another approach is to build "mediators" between the systems. Mediators would use metadata that is sent with the data to understand the syntax and semantics of the data and convert it into a format usable by the receiving system. However, mediators do require that well-formed metadata be sent, adding to the complexity of the interface.

Software Tiers

Typically, software architectures are either two-tier or three-tier.[6]

Each tier typically presents at least one capability.

Two-Tier

In a two-tier architecture, the user interface and business logic are tightly coupled while the data is kept independent. This gives the advantage of allowing the data to reside on a dedicated data server. It also allows the data to be independently maintained. The tight coupling of the user interface and business logic ensure that they will work well together, for this problem in this domain. However, the tight coupling of the user interface and business logic dramatically increases maintainability risks while reducing flexibility and opportunities for re-use.

---

6. These are different from two and three-tiered system architectures in which the middle tier is usually middleware. In the approach being presented here, middleware is seen as an enabler for the software components to interact with each other. See Section 35.7.3.2 for more details.

系统之间必须具有某种类型的物理连接。它可能是局域网（LAN）、广域网（WAN），或者，在某些情况下，它可能仅仅是系统之间的传递数据存储介质。假设用一个网络连接这些系统，则必须针对所使用的协议达成一致，使得能够进行比特传输。

当在接收系统上组合字节时，必须将其放在接收系统需要的背景环境中。换言之，源系统和目标系统都必须就信息模型达成一致。源系统使用这个模型将其信息转换为需要传递的数据，目标系统使用同一模型将接收到的数据转换为它可以使用的信息。

这通常需要在两个系统的架构师和设计者之间达成协议。在过去，该协议通常以界面控制文件（ICD）的形式被文件化。ICD 定义了发送系统将要使用的确切的语法和语义，以便接收系统在数据到达时知道做什么。ICD 的最大问题是，它们往往是两个系统之间唯一的解决方案。如果一个特定系统必须与 n 个其他系统共享信息，则可能需要 n^2 个 ICD。这种极其紧密的集成阻碍了系统的灵活性和系统适应不断变化的环境的能力。维护所有这些 ICD 也是一种挑战。

新技术，如可扩展标记语言（XML），保证数据进行“自描述”。一旦新技术变得可靠且被很好地文件化，这些新技术（如 XML）的使用可能消除对 ICD 的需要。而且，商用现货（COTS）产品可供 XML 数据进行语法分析和操纵，从而消除在内部开发这些产品的需要。它还应缓解维护所有界面的“痛苦”。

另一个实施途径是在系统之间构建“中介者”。中介者将使用数据发送的元数据来理解数据的语法和语义，并将其转换为接收系统可用的格式。然而，中介者确实要求发送格式良好的元数据，从而增加界面的复杂性。

软件级

典型情况下，软件架构是二级的或三级的。[6]

每一级通常提供至少一种能力。

二级

在二级架构中，用户界面和业务逻辑紧密耦合，而数据保持独立。其优点是，使得数据能够位于专用数据服务器上。它还使得数据能够被独立地维护。用户界面和业务逻辑的紧密耦合可确保在该领域的问题上很好地合作。然而，用户界面和业务逻辑的紧密耦合大幅增加了可维护性风险，同时减少了复用的灵活性和机会。

6. 它们不同于中间级，通常就是中间件的两到三级的系统架构。在此提出的实施途径中，中间件被视为软件组件彼此交互的使能项。更多细节见 35.7.3.2 节。

Three-Tier

A three-tier approach adds a tier that separates the business logic from the user interface. This in principle allows the business logic to be used with different user interfaces as well as with different data stores. With respect to the use of different user interfaces, users might want the same user interface but using different COTS presentation servers; for example, Java Virtual Machine (JVM). Similarly, if the business logic is to be used with different data stores, then each data store must use the same data model[7] (data standardization), or a mediation tier must be added above the data store (data encapsulation).

Five-Tier

To achieve maximum flexibility, software should utilize a five-tier scheme for software which extends the three-tier paradigm (see Figure 35-6). The scheme is intended to provide strong separation of the three major functional areas of the architecture. Since there are client and server aspects of both the user interface and the data store, the scheme then has five tiers.[8]

The presentation tier is typically COTS-based. The presentation interface might be an X Server, Win32, etc. There should be a separate tier for the user interface client. This client establishes the look-and-feel of the interface; the server (presentation tier) actually performs the tasks by manipulating the display. The user interface client hides the presentation server from the application business logic.

The application business logic (e.g., a scheduling engine) should be a separate tier. This tier is called the "application logic" and functions as a server for the user interface client. It interfaces to the user interface typically through callbacks. The application logic tier also functions as a client to the data access tier.

If there is a user need to use an application with multiple databases with different schema, thena separate tier is needed for data access. This client would access the data stores using the appropriate COTS interface[9] and then convert the raw data into an abstract data type representing parts of the information model. The interface into this object network would then provide a generalized Data Access Interface (DAI) which would hide the storage details of the data from any application that uses that data.

Each tier in this scheme can have zero or more components. The organization of the components within a tier is flexible and can reflect a number of different architectures based on need. For example, there might be many different components in the application logic tier (scheduling, accounting, inventory control, etc.) and the relationship between them can reflect whatever architecture makes sense, but none of them should be a client to the presentation server.

This clean separation of user interface, business logic, and information will result in maximum flexibility and componentized software that lends itself to product line development practices. For example, it is conceivable that the same functionality should be built once and yet be usable by different presentation servers (e.g., on PCs or UNIX system boxes), displayed with different looks and feels depending on user needs, and usable with multiple legacy databases. Moreover, this flexibility should not require massive rewrites to the software whenever a change is needed.

---

7. If, for example, SQL statements are to be embedded in the business logic.
8. Note that typical "layered" architectures require each layer to be a client of the layer below it and a server to the layer above it. The scheme presented here is not compliant with this description and therefore we have used the word "tier" instead of "layer".
9. The interface to the data store might utilize embedded SQL. A more flexible way would be to use the Distributed Relational Database Architecture (DRDA) or ODBC since either of these standards would enable an application to access different DBMSs in a location-independent manner using the same SQL statements.

三级

三级实施途径增加了一级，将业务逻辑与用户界面分开。这在原则上使得业务逻辑与不同的用户界面以及不同的数据存储能够一起使用。至于不同用户界面的使用，用户可能想要相同的用户界面，但使用了不同的 COTS 展示服务器；例如，Java 虚拟机（JVM）。同样，如果业务逻辑与不同的数据存储一起使用，那么每个数据存储器必须使用相同的数据模型[7]（数据标准化），或必须在数据存储之上增加中介级（数据封装）。

五级

为达成最大的灵活性，软件应使用五级软件模式，其扩展了三级范式（见图 35-6）。该模式旨在严格分离架构的三个主要功能领域。由于存在用户界面和数据存储的客户端和服务器，因此该模式有五级。[8]

展现级通常是基于 COTS 的。展现界面可能是 X 服务器、Win32 等。应存在用户界面客户端的单独层级。此客户端确定了界面的外观；服务器（展现级）实际上通过操纵其显示来执行这些任务。用户界面客户端对应用业务逻辑隐藏了展现服务器。

应用业务逻辑（如，调度引擎）应当是一个单独层级。该级被称作“应用逻辑”，且起到用户界面客户端的服务器的作用。它通常通过回调与用户界面连接。应用逻辑级还起到数据访问级的客户端的作用。

如果用户需要使用具有不同模式的多重数据库的应用，那么需要一个单独层级用于数据访问。该客户端将使用恰当的 COTS 界面[9]来访问数据存储器，并将原始数据转换为代表部分信息模型的抽象数据类型。然后，接入该对象网络之中的界面，将提供广义的数据访问界面（DAI），它会对使用该数据的任何应用隐藏数据的存储细节。

该模式中的每一层级可具有零个或更多个组件。单个层级内组件的组织较灵活，且可基于需要来反映多个不同的架构。例如，在应用逻辑级中，可能具有多个不同组件（调度、会计、库存控制等），它们之间的关系可反映无论什么架构都是有意义的，但是它们都不应当是展现服务器的客户端。

用户界面、业务逻辑和信息的这种完全分离，将会产生最大灵活性和适用于产品线开发实践的组件化软件。例如，可以想象，相同的功能性只被构建一次，却可由不同的展现服务器使用（如，在 PC 或 UNIX 系统框上），依据用户需要，以不同的界面外观来显示并可与多重遗留数据库一起使用。而且，每当需要变化时，这种灵活性应不需要大规模重写软件。

---

7. 例如，如果 SQL 语句需要嵌入到业务逻辑中。
8. 注意，典型的“分层”架构要求每一层都应当是其下面那层的客户端以及其上面那层的服务器。这里提出的模式不符合这种描述，因此我们使用了词语“级”（tier）而不是“层”（layer）。
9. 数据存储器的界面可使用嵌入式 SQL。一种更灵活的方式是使用分布式关系数据库架构（DRDA）或 ODBC，因为这两个标准中的任何一个都使应用能够使用相同的 SQL 语句以与位置无关的方式访问不同的 DBMS。

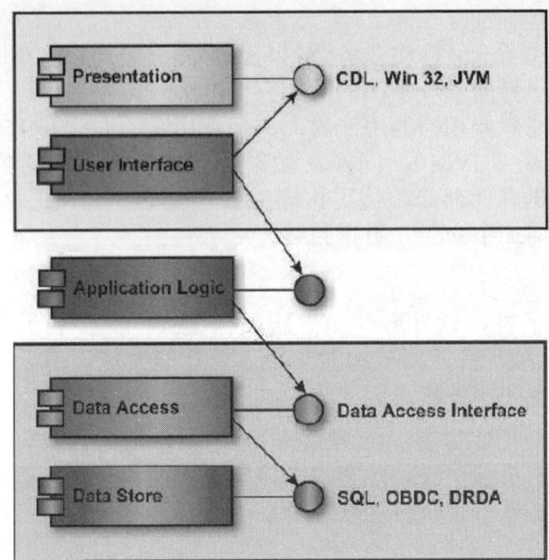

Figure 35-6 The Five-Tier Organization

Some Uses of a Data Access Tier

The data access tier provides a standardized view of certain classes of data, and as such functions as a server to one or more application logic tiers. If implemented correctly, there would be no need for application code to "know" about the implementation details of the data. The application code would only have to know about an interface that presents a level of abstraction higher than the data. This interface is called the Data Access Interface (DAI).

For example, should a scheduling engine need to know what events are scheduled between two dates, that query should not require knowledge of tables and joins in a relational database. Moreover, the DAI could provide standardized access techniques for the data. For example, the DAI could provide a Publish and Subscribe (P&S) interface whereby systems which require access to data stores could register an interest in certain types of data, perhaps under certain conditions, and the DAI would provide the required data when those conditions occur.

One Possible Instantiation of a DAI

One means to instantiate a data access component is with three layers, as shown in Figure35-7. This is not the only means to build a DAI, but is presented as a possibility.

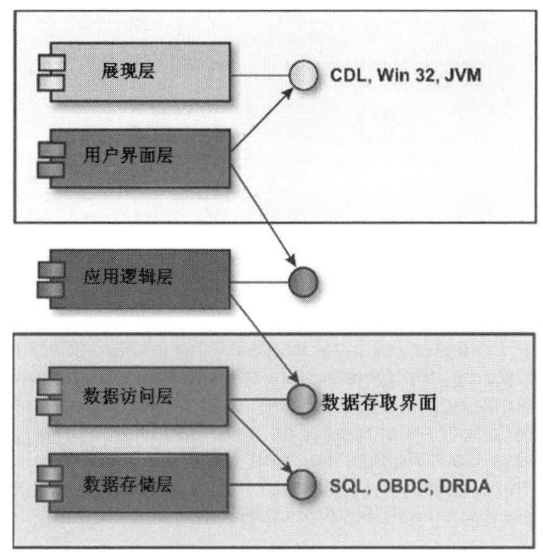

图 35-6　五级组织

数据访问级的某些用途

数据访问级提供某些类别数据的标准化视图，正因为如此，它起到一个或多个应用逻辑级的服务器的作用。如果正确地实施，则应用代码不需要“了解”数据的实施细节。应用代码仅需要了解可提供比数据更高的抽象层次的界面。这个界面被称作数据访问界面（DAI）。

例如，如果调度引擎需要了解两个日期之间调度了什么事件，则该查询应不需要掌握关系数据库中的表格和连接。而且，DAI 应为数据提供标准化的访问技术。例如，DAI 可提供发布和订阅（P&S）界面，借助该界面需要访问数据存储的系统也许在某些条件下可以注册对某些类型数据的兴趣，并且当那些条件出现时，DAI 会提供所需数据。

DAI 的一种可能的实例

举例说明，数据访问组件的一个手段是通过三个层级，如图 35-7 所示。这并不是构建 DAI 的唯一手段，但作为一种可能性进行表达。

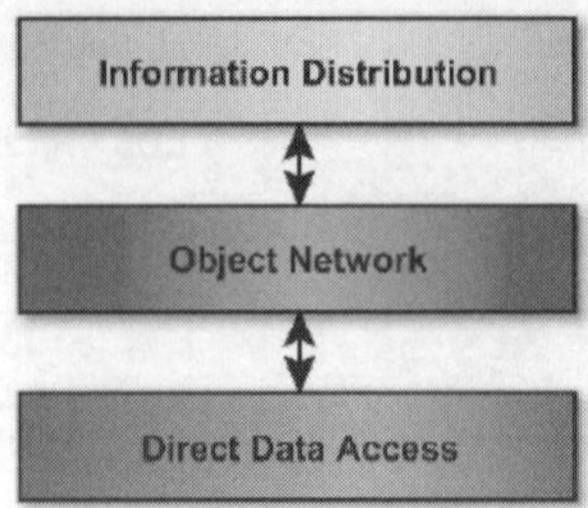

Figure 35-7 Data Access Interface (DAI)

Whereas the Direct Data Access layer contains the implementation details of one or more specific data stores, the Object Network and the Information Distribution layer require no such knowledge. Instead, the upper two layers reflect the need to standardize the interface for a particular domain. The Direct Data Access layer spans the gap between the Data Access tier and the Data Store tier, and therefore has knowledge of the implementation details of the data. SQL statements, either embedded or via a standard such as DRDA or ODBC, are located here.

The Object Network layer is the instantiation in software of the information model. As such, it is an efficient means to show the relationships that hold between pieces of data. The translation of data accesses to objects in the network would be the role of the Direct Data Access layer.

Within the Information Distribution layer lies the interface to the "outside world" . This interface typically uses a data bus to distribute the data (see below).[10] It could also contain various information-related services; for example, a P&S registry and publication service or an interface to a security server for data access control.[11] The Information Distribution layer might also be used to distribute applications or applets required to process distributed information. Objects in the object network would point to the applications or applets, allowing easy access to required processing code.

DAIs Enable Flexibility

The DAI enables a very flexible architecture. Multiple raw capabilities can access the same or different data stores, all through the same DAI. Each DAI might be implemented in many ways, according to the specific needs of the raw capabilities using it. Figure 35-8 illustrates a number of possibilities, including multiple different DAIs in different domains accessing the same database, a single DAI accessing multiple databases, and multiple instantiations of the same DAI access the same database.

It is not always clear that a DAI is needed, and it appears to require additional work during all phases of development. However, should a database ever be redesigned, or if an application is to be re-used and there is no control over how the new data is implemented, using a DAI saves time in the long run.

---

10. Although it could use other mechanisms. For example, the DAI could be built as a shared library to be linked with the application logic at compile time.

11 The security server itself would use a five-tier architecture. The security application logic tier would interface with the DAI of other systems to provide data access control.

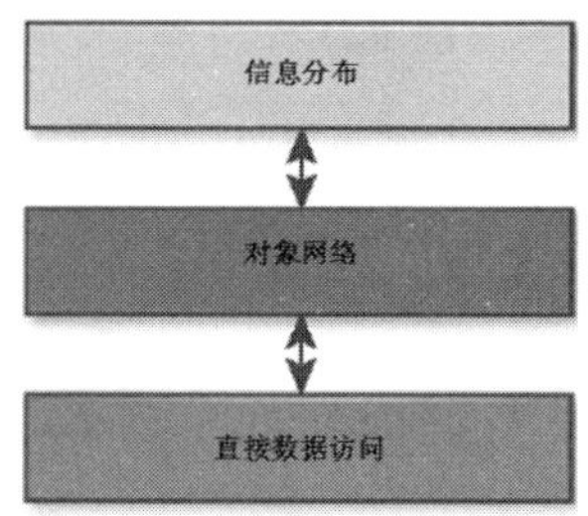

图 35-7 数据访问界面（DAI）

鉴于直接数据访问层包含一个或多个特定数据存储的实施细节，对象网络和信息分布层不需要此类知识。相反，上面两层反映了对特定域的界面进行标准化的需要。直接数据访问层跨越了数据访问级和数据存储级之间的差距，因此具有数据实施细节的知识。SQL 语句，无论是被嵌入还是通过一个标准（如 DRDA 或 ODBC），都位于此处。

对象网络层是信息模型软件中的实例。正因如此，它是表明数据块之间所保持关系的一种有效手段。直接数据访问层的角色将是从数据访问到网络对象的转换。

在信息分布层中设置了与“外界”的界面。这个界面通常使用数据总线来分发数据（参见下文）。[10] 它还可包含各种信息相关的服务；例如，P&S 注册和发布服务或用于数据访问控制的与安保服务器的界面。[11] 信息分布层还可用于对处理分布式信息所需的应用或小应用程序进行分布。对象网络中的对象可指向应用或小应用程序，从而便于访问所需处理代码。

DAI 实现灵活性

DAI 实现非常灵活的架构。多种原始能力可全部通过相同的 DAI 访问相同或不同的数据存储。按照原始能力使用它的特定需要，每个 DAI 可采用多种方式实施。图 35-8 详细阐明多种可能性，包括不同域中的多个不同 DAI 访问同一个数据库、单个 DAI 访问多个数据库以及相同的 DAI 的多个实例访问相同数据库。

我们并不总是很清楚是否需要 DAI，在开发的所有阶段，似乎都需要附加工作。然而，如果数据库需要被重新设计，或如果应用将要被复用且没有对如何实现新数据进行控制，从长远来看，使用 DAI 可节省时间。

10. 尽管它可使用其他机制。例如，可将 DAI 构建为在编译时与应用逻辑联系在一起的共享库。

11. 安保服务器本身将使用五级架构。安保应用逻辑级将与其他系统的 DAI 连接，以提供数据访问控制。

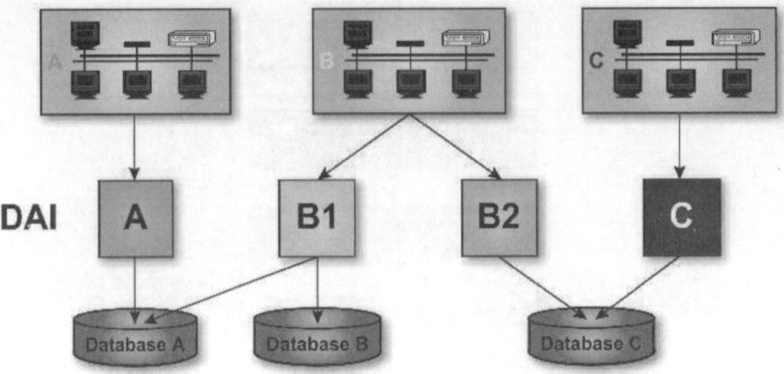

Figure 35-8 Multiple Uses of a Data Access Interface (DAI)

Distribution

The ISO Reference Model for Open Distributed Processing (RM-ODP) offers a meta-standard that is intended to allow more specific standards to emerge. The RM-ODP Reference Model defines a set of distribution transparencies that are applicable to the TOGAF Software Engineering view.

- **Access Transparency** masks differences in data representation and invocation mechanisms to enable interworking between objects. This transparency solves many of the problems of interworking between heterogeneous systems, and will generally be provided by default.
- **Failure Transparency** masks from an object the failure and possible recovery of other objects (or itself) to enable fault tolerance. When this transparency is provided, the designer can work in an idealized world in which the corresponding class of failures does not occur.
- **Location Transparency** masks the use of information about location in space when identifying and binding to interfaces. This transparency provides a logical view of naming, independent of actual physical location.
- **Migration Transparency** masks from an object the ability of a system to change the location of that object. Migration is often used to achieve load balancing and reduce latency.
- **Relocation Transparency** masks relocation of an interface from other interfaces bound to it. Relocation allows system operation to continue even when migration or replacement of some objects creates temporary inconsistencies in the view seen by their users.
- **Replication Transparency** masks the use of a group of mutually behaviorally compatible objects to support an interface. Replication is often used to enhance performance and availability.
- **Transaction Transparency** masks co-ordination of activities amongst a configuration of objects to achieve consistency.

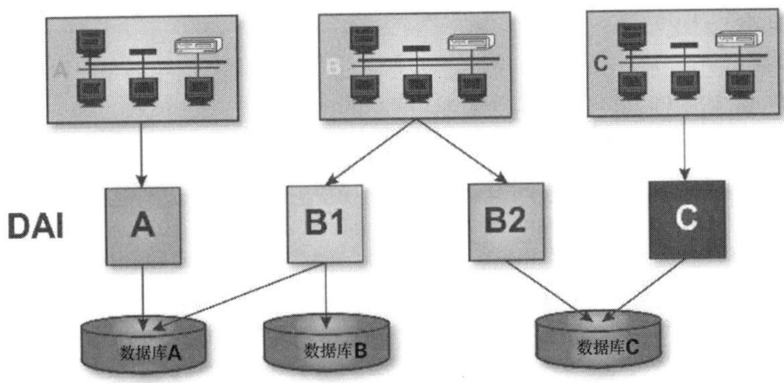

图 35-8　数据访问界面（DAI）的多个用途

分布

ISO 开放分布式处理参考模型（RM-ODP）提供了元标准，旨在呈现更具体的标准。RM-ODP 参考模型定义了适用于 TOGAF 软件工程视图的一系列分布透明性。

- **访问透明性**掩盖了数据表达和调用机制的差异，以实现对象之间的互相配合。这种透明性解决了异构系统之间的许多互相配合问题，一般被默认提供。
- **故障透明性**向一个对象掩盖其他对象（或其自身）的故障和可能的恢复，以实现容错。当提供了这种透明性时，设计人员可在一个不会出现相应故障类型的理想化世界里工作。
- 在识别界面和与界面绑定时，**位置透明性**掩盖了空间位置的信息的使用。这种透明性提供了命名的逻辑视图，独立于实际的物理位置。
- **迁移透明性**对一个对象掩盖系统改变该对象位置的能力。迁移通常用于达成负载平衡并减少等待时间。
- **重新定位透明性**向绑定到一个界面的其他界面掩盖该界面的重新定位。当某些对象的迁移或替换使其用户看到的视图出现暂时不一致时，重新定位使得系统能够继续操作。
- **复制透明性**掩盖了一组行为上相互兼容的对象的使用，以支持界面。复制通常用于提高性能和可用性。
- **事务透明性**掩盖了对象构型之间的活动的协调，以达成一致性。

Infrastructure Bus

The infrastructure bus represents the middleware that establishes the client/server relationship. This commercial software is like a backplane onto which capabilities can be plugged. A system should adhere to a commercial implementation of a middleware standard. This is to ensure that capabilities using different commercial implementations of the standard can interoperate. If more than one commercial standard is used (e.g., COM and CORBA), then the system should allow for interoperability between implementations of these standards via the use of commercial bridging software.[12] Wherever practical, the interfaces should be specified in the appropriate Interface Description Language (IDL). Taken this way, every interface in the five-tier scheme represents an opportunity for distribution.

Clients can interact with servers via the infrastructure bus. In this interaction, the actual network transport (TCP/IP, HTTP, etc.), the platform/vendor of the server, and the operating system of the server are all transparent.

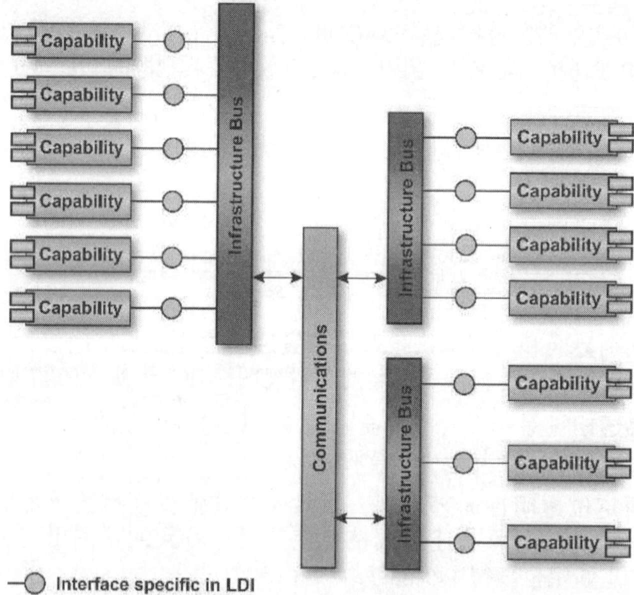

Figure 35-9 Notional Distribution Model

12. For example, many people believe that the user interface should be built on COM, while the data access tiers should be built on CORBA.

基础设施总线

基础设施总线代表建立客户端/服务器关系的中间件。这个商业软件如同可安插多个能力的一个背板。系统应遵循中间件标准的商业化实施。这可确保使用标准的不同商业化实施的能力可以互用。如果使用一个以上的商业标准（如，COM 和 CORBA），那么系统应允许通过使用商业桥接软件实现这些标准的实施之间的互用性。[12] 无论实际上什么情况，均应以恰当的界面描述语言（IDL）详细说明界面。通过采取这种方式，五级模式中的每个界面代表一个分布机会。

客户端可通过基础设施总线与服务器进行交互。在这种交互中，实际网络传输（TCP/IP、HTTP 等）、服务器的平台/厂商和服务器的操作系统全部都是透明的。

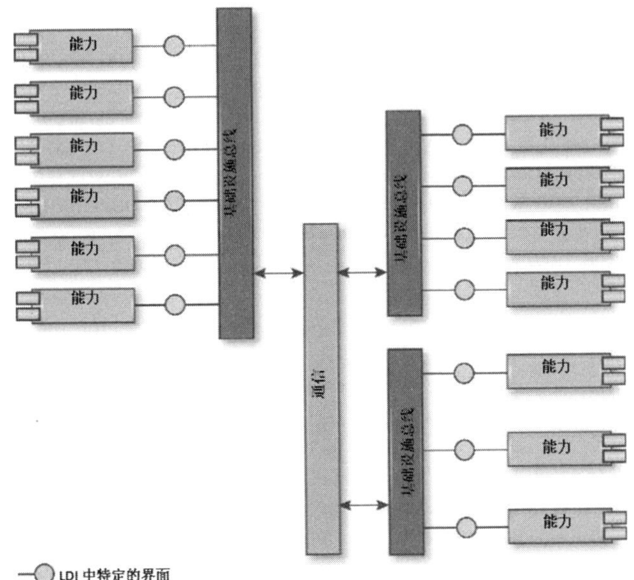

图 35-9 理论上的分布模型

12. 例如，许多人认为用户界面应构建于 COM 上，而数据访问级应构建于 CORBA 上。

35.7.3.3 Conclusion

The Software Engineering view gives guidance on how to structure software in a very flexible manner. By following these guidelines, the resulting software will be componentized. This enables the re-use of components in different environments. Moreover, through the use of an infrastructure bus and clean interfaces, the resulting software will be location-independent, enabling its distribution across a network.

35.7.4 Developing a System Engineering View

The System Engineering view is concerned with assembling software and hardware components into a working system.

35.7.4.1 Stakeholders and Concerns

This view should be developed for the systems engineering personnel of the system, and should focus on how the system is implemented from the perspective of hardware/software and networking.

Systems engineers are typically concerned with location, modifiability, re-usability, and availability of all components of the system. The System Engineering view presents a number of different ways in which software and hardware components can be assembled into a working system. To a great extent, the choice of model determines the properties of the final system. It looks at technology which already exists in the organization, and what is available currently or in the near future. This reveals areas where new technology can contribute to the function or efficiency of the new architecture, and how different types of processing platform can support different parts of the overall system.

Major concerns for this view are understanding the system requirements. In general these stakeholders are concerned with ensuring that the appropriate components are developed and deployed within the system in an optimal manner.

Developing this view assists in the selection of the best configurations for the system.

35.7.4.2 Key Issues

This view of the architecture focuses on computing models that are appropriate for a distributed computing environment. To support the migration of legacy systems, this section also presents models that are appropriate for a centralized environment. The definitions of many of the computing models (e.g., host-based, master/slave, and three-tiered) historically preceded the definition of the client/server model, which attempts to be a general-purpose model. In most cases the models have not been redefined in the computing literature in terms of contrasts with the client/server model. Therefore, some of the distinctions of features are not always clean. In general, however, the models are distinguished by the allocation of functions for an information system application to various components (e.g., terminals, computer platforms). These functions that make up an information system application are presentation, application function, and data management.

35.7.3.3 结论

软件工程视图在如何以非常灵活的方式对软件进行结构化处理方面提供引导。通过遵循这些指南，产生的软件会是组件化的。这使得组件能够在不同环境中被复用。而且，通过使用基础设施总线和清晰的界面，使得由此产生的软件将与位置无关，从而使软件的分布能够跨网络实现。

35.7.4 开发系统工程视图

系统工程视图涉及在工作系统中组装软件和硬件组件。

35.7.4.1 利益攸关者和关注点

这个视图应针对系统的系统工程人员来开发，并应聚焦于如何从硬件/软件和网络的关注层级实施系统。

系统工程师通常关注系统所有组件的位置、可修改性、可复用性和可用性。系统工程视图提出软件和硬件组件在工作系统中组装的多种不同方式。在很大程度上，模型的选择决定了最终系统的性能。它着眼于组织内已经存在的技术，以及当前或在不久的将来可用什么技术。这揭示了新技术在哪些领域有助于新架构的功能和效率，以及不同类型的处理平台可如何支持总体系统的不同部分。

这个视图的主要关注点是理解系统需求。一般说来，这些利益攸关者关注确保恰当的组件以最优的方式在系统内被开发和部署。

开发这个视图可帮助选择系统的最佳配置。

35.7.4.2 关键问题

架构的这个视图聚焦于适合分布式计算环境的计算模型。为了支持遗留系统的迁移，本节还提出适合集中环境的模型。许多计算模型（如，基于主机的模型、主/从模型和三级模型）的定义在历史上先于客户端/服务器模型的定义，客户端/服务器模型力求成为一个一般模型。在多数情况下，在计算文献中没有根据与客户端/服务器模型的对比而对模型进行重新定义。因此，某些特征差异并不总是很清晰。然而，一般说来，我们根据信息系统应用的功能在各种组件（如，终端和计算机平台）上的分配来区分模型。展示、应用功能和数据管理等功能构成了信息系统应用。

Client/Server Model

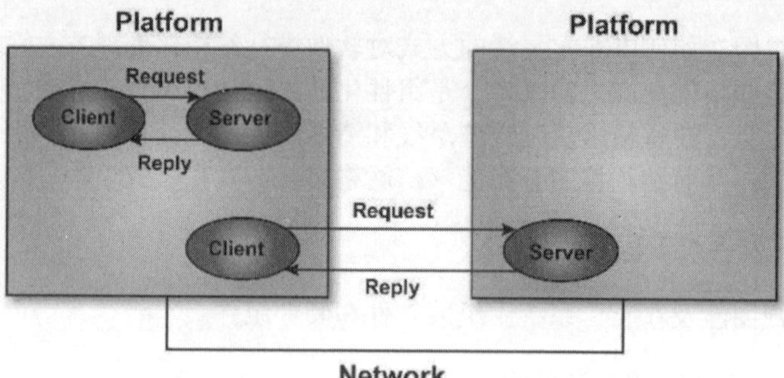

Figure 35-10 Basic Client/Server Model

Client/server processing is a special type of distributed computing termed "co-operative processing" because the clients and servers co-operate in the processing of a total application (presentation, functional processing, data management). In the model, clients are processes that request services, and servers are processes that provide services. Clients and servers can be located on the same processor, different multi-processor nodes, or on separate processors at remote locations. The client typically initiates communications with the server. The server typically does not initiate a request with a client. A server may support many clients and may act as a client to another server. Figure 35-10 depicts a basic client/server model, which emphasizes the request-reply relationships. Figure 35-11 shows the same model drawn following the TOGAF TRM, showing how the various entities and interfaces can be used to support a client/server model, whether the server is local or remote to the client. In these representations, the request-reply relationships would be defined in the API.

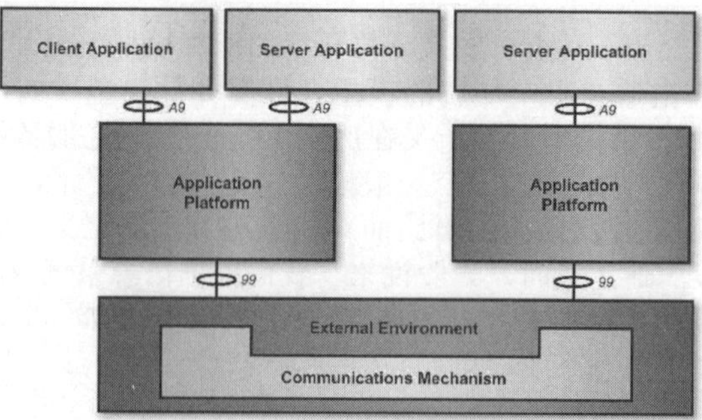

Figure 35-11 Reference Model Representation of Client/Server Model

Clients tend to be generalized and can run on one of many nodes. Servers tend to be specialized and run on a few nodes. Clients are typically implemented as a call to a routine.

客户端/服务器模型

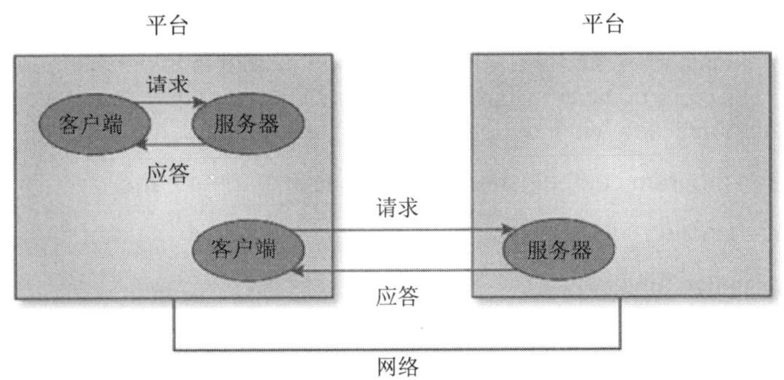

图 35-10 客户端/服务器模型的参考模型表达

客户端/服务器处理是被称为“合作处理”的一种特殊类型的分布式计算，因为客户端和服务器在总体应用的处理（展现、功能处理、数据管理）中合作。在模型中，客户端是要求服务的流程，服务器是提供服务的流程。客户端和服务器可位于同一个处理器、不同的多处理器节点或位于远程位置的单独处理器上。客户端通常发起与服务器的通信。服务器通常不向客户端提出要求。服务器可支持多个客户端，并可用作另一个服务器的客户端。图 35-10 描述了一个基本的客户端/服务器模型，强调了要求—应答关系。图 35-11 展示了按照 TOGAF TRM 绘制的相同的模型，表明了各种不同的实体和界面可如何用于支持客户端/服务器模型，无论服务器对于客户端而言是本地的还是远程的。在这些表达形式中，要求—应答关系将在 API 中进行定义。

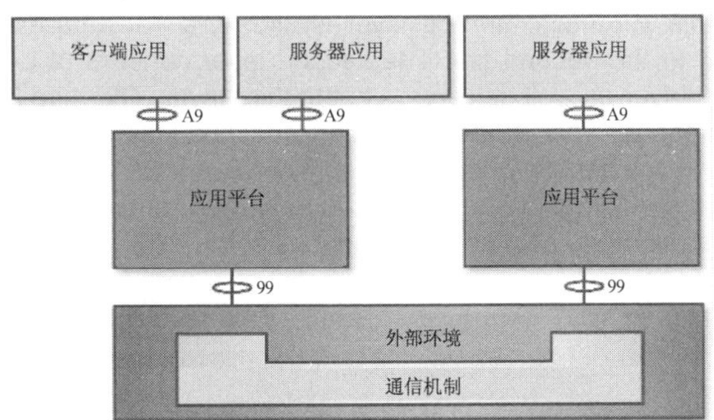

图 35-11 客户端/服务器模型的参考模型表达

客户端往往是广义的，且可在多个节点之一上运行。服务器往往是专用的，可在少数节点上运行。客户端通常作为对例程的调用来实施。

Servers are typically implemented as a continuous process waiting for service requests (from clients). Many client/server implementations involve remote communications across a network. However, nothing in the client/server model dictates remote communications, and the physical location of clients is usually transparent to the server. The communication between a client and a server may involve a local communication between two independent processes on the same machine.

An application program can be considered to consist of three parts:

- Data handling
- Application function
- Presentation

In general, each of these can be assigned to either a client or server application, making appropriate use of platform services. This assignment defines a specific client/server configuration.

Master/Slave and Hierarchic Models

In this model, slave computers are attached to a master computer. In terms of distribution, the master/slave model is one step up from the host-based model. Distribution is provided in one direction — from the master to the slaves. The slave computers perform application processing only when directed to by the master computer. In addition, slave processors can perform limited local processing, such as editing, function key processing, and field validation. A typical configuration might be a mainframe as the master with PCs as the slaves acting as intelligent terminals, as illustrated in Figure 35-12.

The hierarchic model is an extension of the master/slave model with more distribution capabilities. In this approach, the top layer is usually a powerful mainframe, which acts as a server to the second tier. The second layer consists of LAN servers and clients to the first layer as well as servers to the third layer. The third layer consists of PCs and workstations. This model has been described as adding true distributed processing to the master/slave model. Figure35-12 shows an example hierarchic model in the third configuration, and below, Figure 35-13 shows the hierarchic model represented in terms of the entities and interfaces of the TRM.

服务器通常作为等待服务要求（来自客户端）的连续流程来实施。许多客户端/服务器的实施涉及跨网络远程通信。然而，在客户端/服务器模型中没有规定远程通信，客户端的物理位置通常对于服务器而言是透明的。一个客户端和一个服务器之间的通信，可能涉及相同机器上两个独立流程之间的本地通信。

一个应用程序由三个部分组成：

- 数据处理
- 应用功能
- 展示

一般说来，每个部分可被分派到客户端或服务器应用，从而恰当地使用平台服务。这种分派，定义了特定的客户端/服务器配置。

主/从模型和层级模型

在这个模型中，从属计算机附属于主计算机。根据分布情况，主/从模型比基于主机的模型高一级。在单一方向上提供分布，即从主到从方向。从属计算机只有在被主计算机指挥时才进行应用处理。此外，从属处理器可执行有限的本地处理，如编辑、功能键处理和字段确认。典型的构型可能是主机作为主模型而个人计算机（PC）作为从模型用作智能终端，如图 35-12 所示。

层级模型是主/从模型的扩展，具有更多分布能力。在这个实施途径中，顶层通常是一个强大的主机，用作第二级的服务器。第二层由第一层的 LAN 服务器和客户端以及第三层的服务器组成。第三层由 PC 和工作站组成。该模型被描述为在主/从模型上增加真正的分布式处理。图 35-12 表明第三个构型中的层级模型示例，图 35-13 表明以 TRM 实体和界面表达的层级模型。

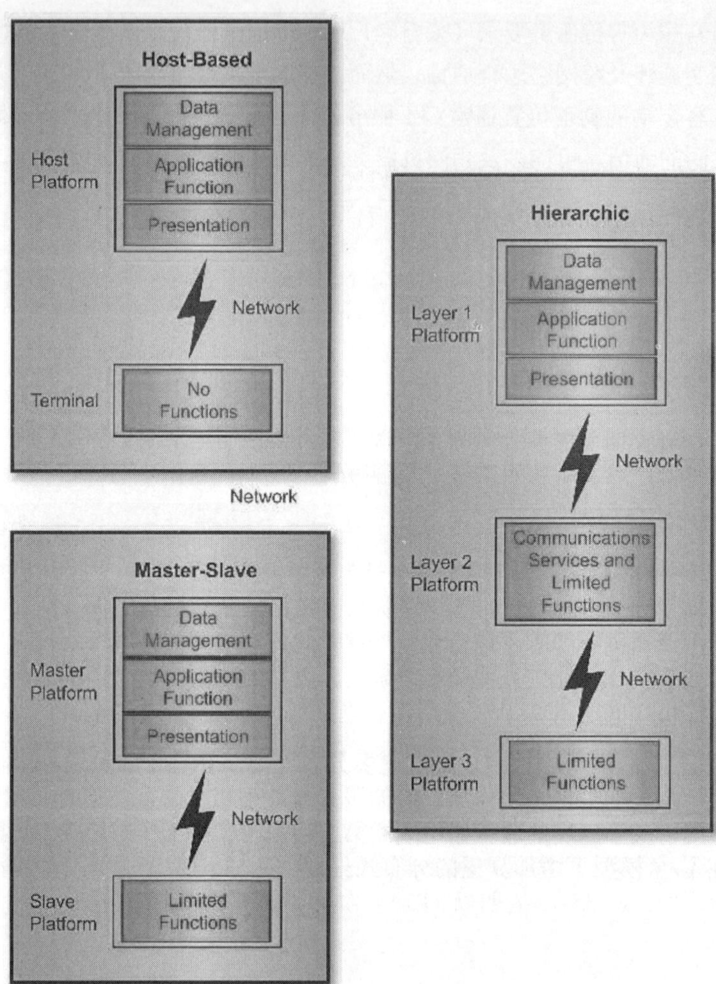

Figure 35-12 Host-Based, Master/Slave, and Hierarchic Models

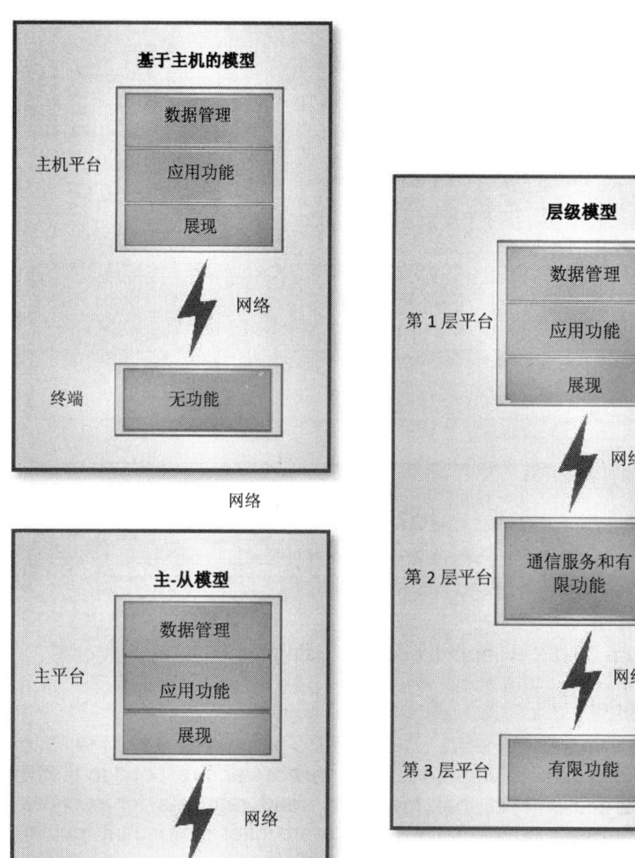

图 35-12　基于主机的模型、主/从模型和层级模型

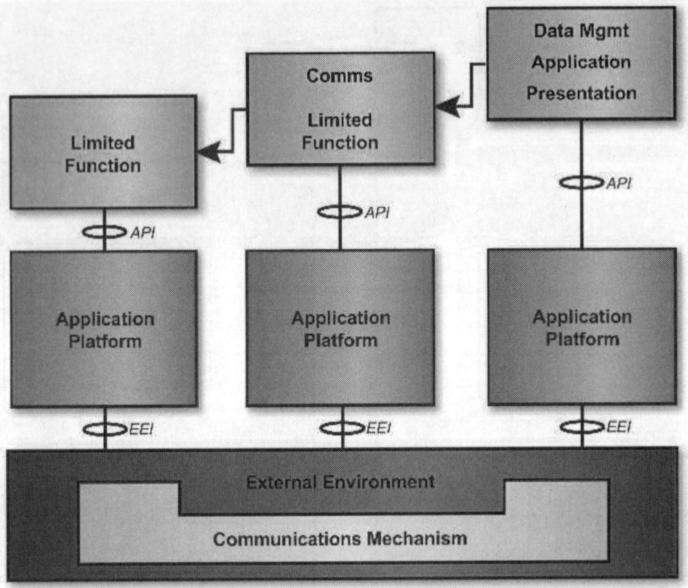

Figure 35-13 Hierarchic Model Using the Reference Model

Peer-to-Peer Model

In the peer-to-peer model there are co-ordinating processes. All of the computers are servers in that they can receive requests for services and respond to them; and all of the computers are clients in that they can send requests for services to other computers. In current implementations, there are often redundant functions on the participating platforms.

Attempts have been made to implement the model for distributed heterogeneous (or federated) database systems. This model could be considered a special case of the client/server model, in which all platforms are both servers and clients. Figure 35-14 (A) shows an example peer-to-peer configuration in which all platforms have complete functions.

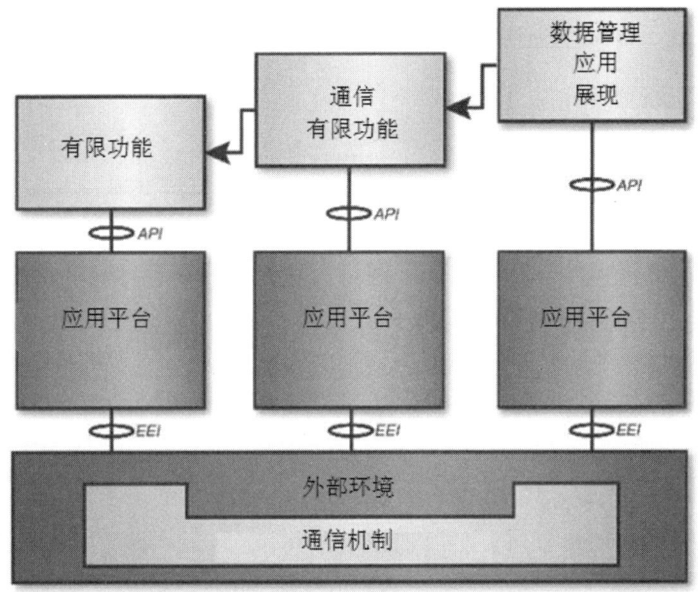

图 35-13 使用参考模型的层级模型

点对点模型

在点对点模型中具有协作流程。所有计算机都是服务器，因为它们可接收服务要求并响应这些要求；所有计算机都是客户端，因为它们可向其他计算机发送服务要求。在当前实施中，参与其中的平台通常具有冗余功能。

已经有对实施分布式异构（或联邦）数据库系统的模型的尝试。该模型可被认为是客户端/服务器模型的一个特例，其中所有平台既是服务器也是客户端。图 35-14（A）展示了点对点构型示例，其中所有平台都具有完整的功能。

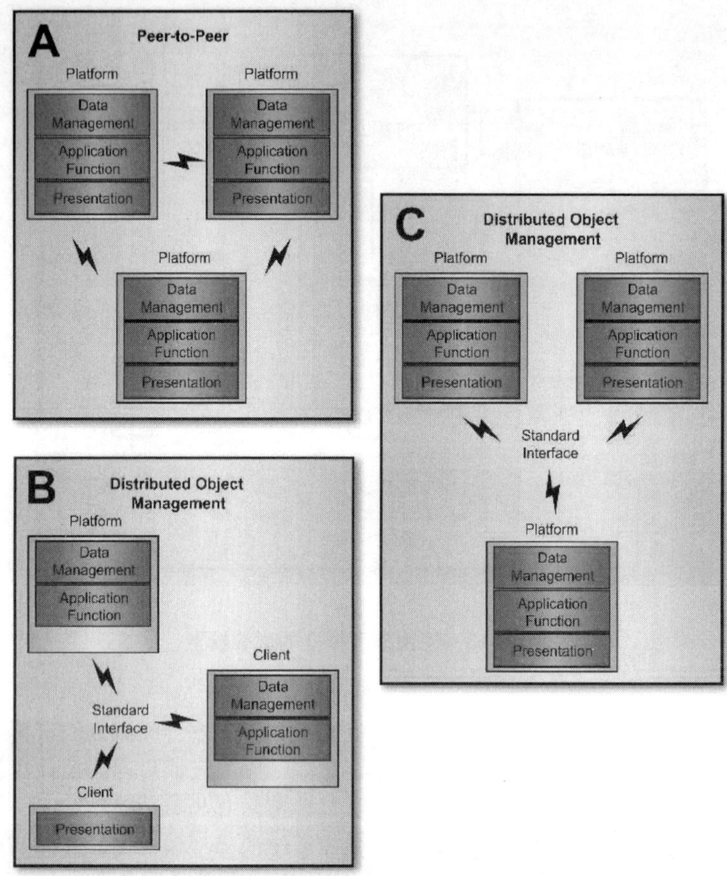

Figure 35-14 Peer-to-Peer and Distributed Object Management Models

Distributed Object Management Model

In this model the remote procedure calls typically used for communication in the client/server and other distributed processing models are replaced by messages sent to objects. The services provided by systems on a network are treated as objects. A requester need not know the details of how the object is configured. The approach requires:

- A mechanism to dispatch messages
- A mechanism to co-ordinate delivery of messages
- Applications and services that support a messaging interface

This approach does not contrast with client/server or peer-to-peer models but specifies a consistent interface for communicating between co-operating platforms. It is considered by someas an implementation approach for client/server and peer-to-peer models. Figure 35-14 presents two distributed object model examples. Example B shows how a client/server configuration would be altered to accommodate the distributed object management model. Example C shows how a peer-to-peer model would be altered to accomplish distributed object management.

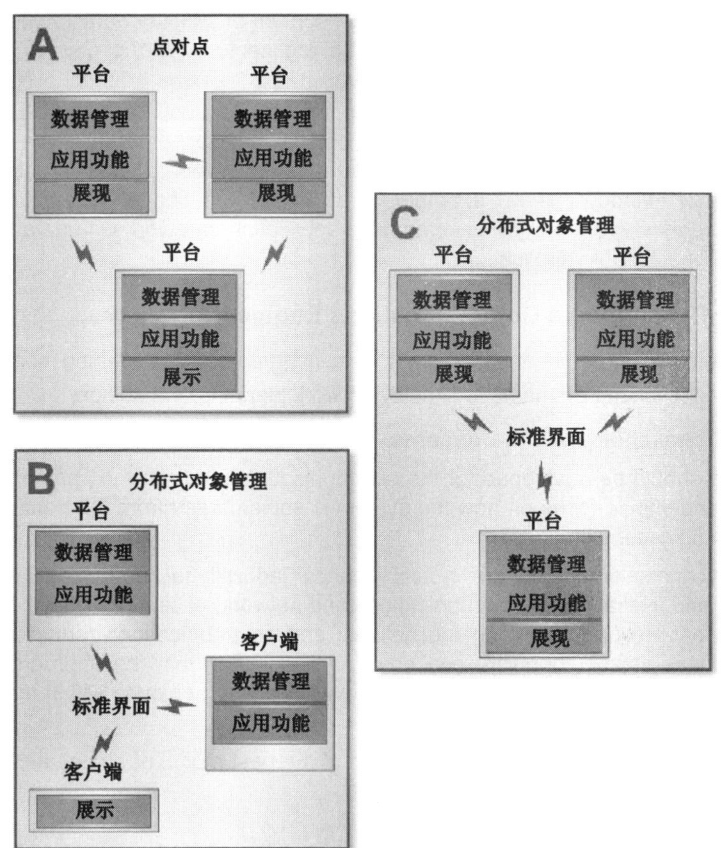

图 35-14　点对点模型和分布式对象管理模型

分布式对象管理模型

在此模型中，通常用于客户端/服务器和其他分布式处理模型通信的远程程序调用被发送给对象的消息所替代。由网络上的系统所提供的服务被视为对象。提出要求者不需要了解如何配置对象的细节。该实施途径需要：

- 发送消息的机制
- 协调消息传递的机制
- 支持消息传送界面的应用和服务

本实施途径与客户端/服务器或点对点模型没有差别，但规定了协作平台之间一致的通信界面。有些人将此方法视为客户端/服务器和点对点模型的实施途径。图 35-14 提出了两个分布式对象模型示例。示例 B 表明应如何改变客户端/服务器构型以适应分布式对象管理模型。示例 C 表明将如何改变点对点模型以实现分布式对象管理。

The Object Management Group (OMG), a consortium of industry participants working toward object standards, has developed an architecture — the Common Object Request Broker Architecture (CORBA) — which specifies the protocol a client application must use to communicate with an Object Request Broker (ORB), which provides services. The ORB specifies how objects can transparently make requests and receive responses. In addition, Microsoft's Object Linking and Embedding (OLE) standard for Windows is an example of an implementation of distributed object management, whereby any OLE-compatible application can work with data from any other OLE-compatible application.

35.7.5 Developing a Communications Engineering View

The Communications Engineering view is concerned with structuring communications and networking elements to simplify network planning and design.

35.7.5.1 Stakeholders and Concerns

This view should be developed for the communications engineering personnel of the system, and should focus on how the system is implemented from the perspective of the communications engineer.

Communications engineers are typically concerned with location, modifiability, reusability, and availability of communications and networking services. Major concerns for this view are understanding the network and communications requirements. In general these stakeholders are concerned with ensuring that the appropriate communications and networking services are developed and deployed within the system in an optimal manner.

Developing this view assists in the selection of the best model of communications for the system.

35.7.5.2 Key Issues

Communications networks are constructed of end devices (e.g., printers), processing nodes, communication nodes (switching elements), and the linking media that connect them. The communications network provides the means by which information is exchanged. Forms of information include data, imagery, voice, and video. Because automated information systems accept and process information using digital data formats rather than analog formats, the TOGAF communications concepts and guidance will focus on digital networks and digital services. Integrated multimedia services are included.

The Communications Engineering view describes the communications architecture with respect to geography, discusses the Open Systems Interconnection (OSI) reference model, and describes a general framework intended to permit effective system analysis and planning.

对象管理组（OMG），是从事对象标准工作的行业参与者联合体，已开发了一个架构——公共对象要求代理架构（CORBA）——规定了客户端应用与提供服务的对象要求代理（ORB）进行通信所必须使用的协议。ORB 规定了对象可如何透明地产生要求并接收响应。此外，微软用于 Windows 的对象连接与嵌入（OLE）标准是实施分布式对象管理的一个示例，任何与 OLE 兼容的应用，可以与来自任何其他与 OLE 兼容的应用的数据一起使用。

35.7.5 开发通信工程视图

通信工程视图涉及结构化通信和网络元素，以简化网络规划和设计。

35.7.5.1 利益攸关者和关注点

本视图应针对系统的通信工程人员而开发，并应聚焦于如何从通信工程师的关注层级实施系统。

典型情况下，通信工程师关注通信和网络服务的位置、可修改性、可复用性和可用性。本视图的主要关注点是理解网络和通信需求。一般来说，这些利益攸关者关注于确保以最佳方式在系统内开发和部署恰当的通信和网络服务。

开发此视图有助于为系统选择最佳的通信模型。

35.7.5.2 关键问题

通信网络由终端设备（如，打印机）、处理节点、通信节点（切换元件）和连接它们的链接介质组成。通信网络提供了信息交换的手段。信息的形式包括数据、图像、语音和视频。由于自动化信息系统使用数字化数据格式而非模拟格式来接受和处理信息，TOGAF 通信概念和指南将聚焦于数字化网络和数字化服务。包括综合多媒体服务。

通信工程视图描述关于地理方面的通信架构，论述开放系统互连（OSI）参考模型，并描述用于允许有效的系统分析和规划的一般框架。

Communications Infrastructure

The Communications Infrastructure may contain up to three levels of transport — local, regional/metropolitan, and global — as shown in Figure 35-15. The names of the transport components are based on their respective geographic extent, but there is also a hierarchical relationship among them. The transport components correspond to a network management structure in which management and control of network resources are distributed across the different levels.

The local components relate to assets that are located relatively close together geographically. This component contains fixed communications equipment and small units of mobile communications equipment. LANs, to which the majority of end devices will be connected, are included in this component. Standard interfaces will facilitate portability, flexibility, and interoperability of LANs and end devices.

Regional and Metropolitan Area Networks (MANs) are geographically dispersed over a large area. A regional or metropolitan network could connect local components at several fixed bases or connect separate remote outposts. In most cases, regional and metropolitan networks are used to connect local networks. However, shared databases, regional processing platforms, and network management centers may connect directly or through a LAN. Standard interfaces will be provided to connect local networks and end devices.

Global or Wide Area Networks (WANs) are located throughout the world, providing connectivity for regional and metropolitan networks in the fixed and deployed environment. In addition, mobile units, shared databases, and central processing centers can connect directly to the global network as required. Standard interfaces will be provided to connect regional and metropolitan networks and end devices.

通信基础设施

通信基础设施可包含多达三个传输层级——本地、地区/城市和全球，如图35-15 所示。传输组件的名称基于它们各自地理上的范围，但它们之间还存在层级关系。传输组件对应于网络管理结构，在该结构中网络资源的管理和控制跨不同层级分布。

本地组件涉及地理位置上分布相对较近的资产。该组件包含固定通信设备以及移动通信设备的较小单元。将与大多数终端设备连接的 LAN 也包括在该组件内。标准界面将促进 LAN 和终端设备的可移植性、灵活性和互用性。

区域网和城域网（MAN）在地理位置上散布于较大地区内。区域网或城域网可在多个固定基地上连接本地组件或连接单独的远程前哨。多数情况下，区域网和城域网用于连接本地网络。然而，共享数据库、区域处理平台和网络管理中心可直接地或通过 LAN 进行连接。将提供标准界面，以连接本地网络和终端设备。

全球网或广域网（WAN）遍布全世界，从而在固定环境和部署环境内为区域网和城域网提供连接性。此外，移动单元、共享数据库和中央处理中心可按需直接连接到全球网。标准界面将被提供以连接区域网和城域网以及终端设备。

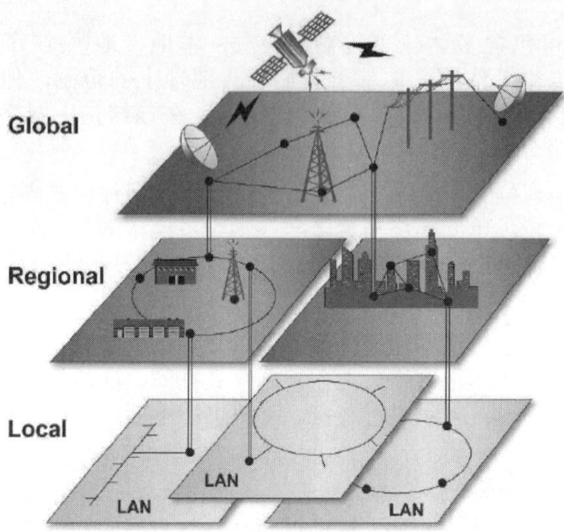

Figure 35-15 Communications Infrastructure

Communications Models

The geographically divided infrastructure described above forms the foundation for an overall communications framework. These geographic divisions permit the separate application of different management responsibilities, planning efforts, operational functions, and enabling technologies to be applied within each area. Hardware and software components and services fitted to the framework form the complete model.

The following sections describe the OSI Reference Model and a grouping of the OSI layers that facilitates discussion of interoperability issues.

The OSI Reference Model

The Open Systems Interconnection (OSI) Reference Model, portrayed in Figure 35-16, is the model used for data communications in TOGAF. Each of the seven layers in the model represents one or more services or protocols (a set of rules governing communications between systems), which define the functional operation of the communications between user and network elements. Each layer (with the exception of the top layer) provides services for the layer above it. This model aims at establishing open systems operation and implies standards-based implementation. It strives to permit different systems to accomplish complete interoperability and quality of operation throughout the network.

The seven layers of the OSI model are structured to facilitate independent development within each layer and to provide for changes independent of other layers. Stable international standard protocols in conformance with the OSI Reference Model layer definitions have been published by various standards organizations. This is not to say that the only protocols which fit into TOGAF are OSI protocols. Other protocol standards such as SNA or TCP/IP can be described using the OSI seven layer model as a reference.

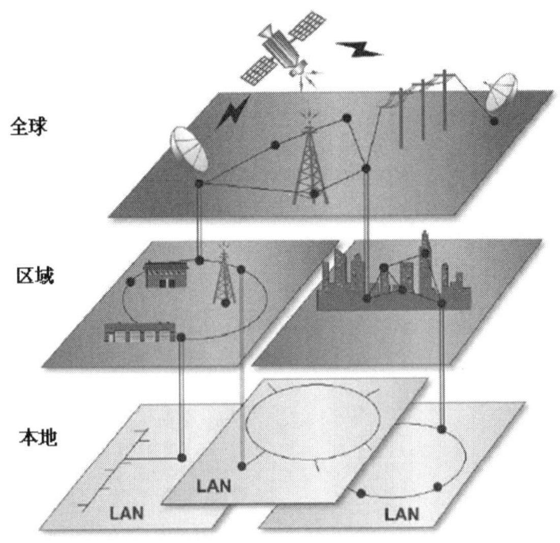

图 35-15　通信基础设施

通信模型

上述在地理上划分的基础设施构成总体通信框架的基础。这些地理划分允许单独应用的不同管理职责、规划工作和运作功能，并使技术能够在每个地区被应用。同框架匹配的硬件和软件组件与服务构成完整模型。

下面几节描述 OSI 参考模型和 OSI 层的分组，以促进互用性问题的论述。

OSI 参考模型

图 35-16 描述的开放系统互连（OSI）参考模型是 TOGAF 中用于数据通信的模型。模型的七层中的每一层代表一个或多个服务或协议（用于管控系统之间通信的规则集），定义了用户和网络元件之间通信的功能操作。每一层（顶层除外）都为其上一层提供服务。本模型旨在建立开放系统操作，并意味着基于标准的实施。它力求允许不同的系统在整个网络内实现完全的互用性和运行质量。

对 OSI 模型的七层进行结构化，以促进每一层内的独立开发并提供独立于其他层的变更。各类标准组织已经发布了与 OSI 参考模型层定义一致的稳定的国际标准协议。这并不是说唯一与 TOGAF 适配的协议是 OSI 协议。也可使用 OSI 七层模型作为参考来描述其他诸如 SNA 或 TCP/IP 等协议标准。

Support and business area applications, as defined in TOGAF, are above the OSI Reference Model protocol stack and use its services via the applications layer.

Communications Framework

A communications system based on the OSI Reference Model includes services in all the relevant layers, the support and business area application software which sits above the application layer of the OSI Reference Model, and the physical equipment carrying the data. These elements may be grouped into architectural levels that represent major functional capabilities, such as switching and routing, data transfer, and the performance of applications.

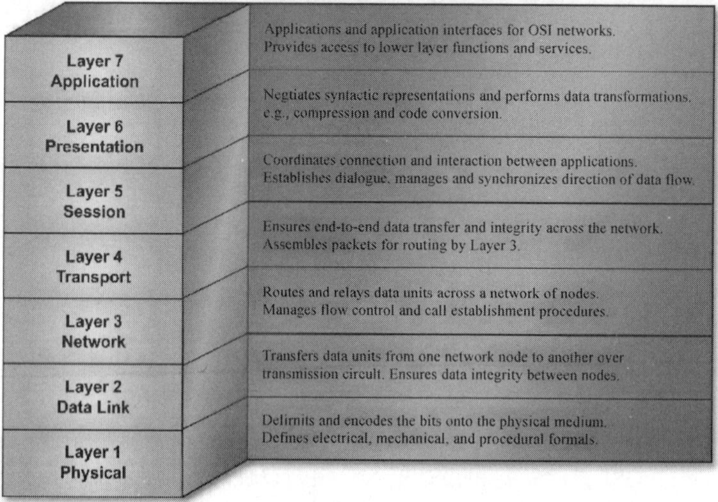

Figure 35-16 OSI Reference Model

These architectural levels are:

- The **Transmission level** (below the physical layer of the OSI Reference Model) provides all of the physical and electronic capabilities, which establish a transmission path between functional system elements (wires, leased circuits, interconnects, etc.).
- The **Network Switching level** (OSI layers 1 through 3) establishes connectivity through the network elements to support the routing and control of traffic (switches, controllers, network software, etc.).
- The **Data Exchange level** (OSI layers 4 through 7) accomplishes the transfer of information after the network has been established (end-to-end, user-to-user transfer) involving more capable processing elements (hosts, workstations, servers, etc.).

In the TRM, OSI application layer services are considered to be part of the application platform entity, since they offer standardized interfaces to the application programming entity.

TOGAF 中所定义的支持和业务领域的应用，在 OSI 参考模型协议栈之上，并通过应用层使用其服务。

通信框架

基于 OSI 参考模型的通信系统，包括所有相关层中的服务、位于 OSI 参考模型的应用层之上的支持和业务领域应用软件以及携带数据的物理设备。这些元素可以被分组为代表主要功能能力的架构层级，如切换和路由传送、数据传送和应用性能。

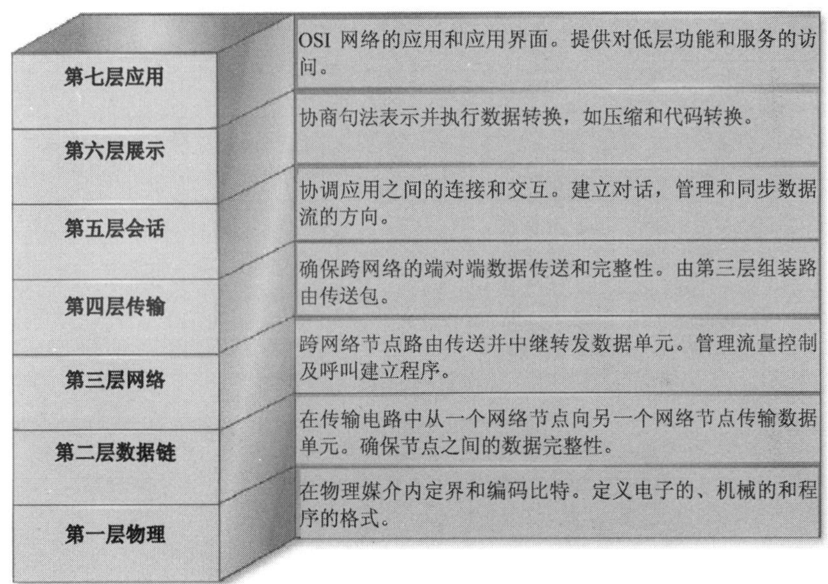

第七层应用
OSI 网络的应用和应用界面。提供对低层功能和服务的访问。
第六层展示
协商句法表示并执行数据转换，如压缩和代码转换。
第五层会话
协调应用之间的连接和交互。建立对话，管理和同步数据流的方向。
第四层传输
确保跨网络的端对端数据传送和完整性。由第三层组装路由传送包。
第三层网络
跨网络节点路由传送并中继转发数据单元。管理流量控制及呼叫建立程序。
第二层数据链
在传输电路中从一个网络节点向另一个网络节点传输数据单元。确保节点之间的数据完整性。
第一层物理
在物理媒介内定界和编码比特。定义电子的、机械的和程序的格式。

图 35-16　OSI 参考模型

这些架构层级是：

- **传输层级**（OSI 参考模型的物理层之下）提供了所有物理和电子能力，在功能系统元素之间，建立了传输路径（电线、租赁线路、连接线等）。
- **网络切换层级**（OSI 第一层至第三层）通过网络元素建立连接性，以支持流量的路由传送和控制（开关、控制器、网络软件等）。
- **数据交换层级**（OSI 第四层至第七层）在网络建立后完成了信息传输（端对端、用户对用户传输），涉及更有能力的处理元素（主机、工作站、服务器等）。

在 TRM 中，OSI 应用层服务被认为是应用平台实体的一部分，因为它们提供应用编程实体的标准化界面。

- The **Applications Program level** (above the OSI) includes the support and business area applications (non-management application programs).

The communications framework is defined to consist of the three geographical components of the Communications Infrastructure (local, regional, and global) and the four architectural levels (Transmission, Network Switching, Data Exchange, and Applications Program), and is depicted in Figure 35-17. Communications services are performed at one or more of these architectural levels within the geographical components. Figure 35-17 shows computing elements (operating at the Applications Program level) with supporting data exchange elements, linked with each other through various switching elements (operating at the Network Switching level), each located within its respective geographical component. Figure 35-17 also identifies the relationship of TOGAF to the communication architecture.

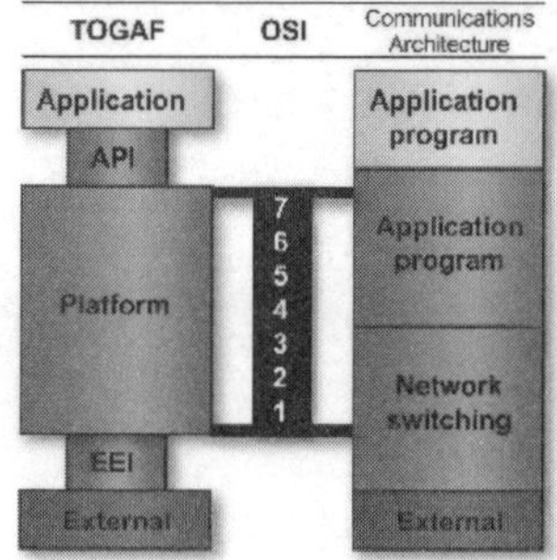

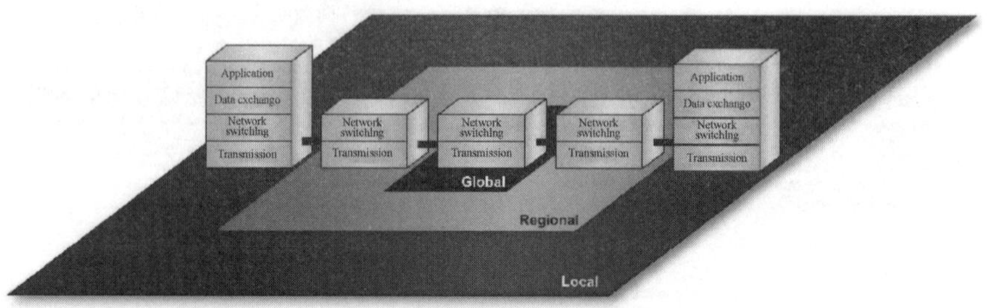

Figure 35-17 Communications Framework

Allocation of Services to Components

The Communications Infrastructure consists of the local, regional, and global transport components.

The services allocated to these components are identical to the services of the Application Program, Data Exchange, Network Switching, or Transmission architectural levels that apply to a component. Data Exchange and Network Switching level services are identical to the services of the corresponding OSI Reference Model layers.

Typically, only Network Switching and Transmission services are allocated to the regional and global components, which consist of communications nodes and transmission media. All services may be performed in the local component, which includes end devices, processing nodes, communications nodes, and linking media. Transmission, switching, transport, and applications are all performed in this component.

- **应用程序层级**（OSI 之上）包括支持性应用和业务领域应用（非管理应用程序）。

定义了通信框架，由通信基础设施的三个地理组件（本地的、地区的和全球的）和四个架构层级（传输、网络切换、数据交换和应用程序）组成，如图 35-17 所述。在地理组件内的一个或多个架构层级上执行通信服务。图 35-17 表明具有支持数据交换元素的计算元素（在应用程序层级上运行），它们通过各种切换元素（在网络切换层级上运行）彼此连接在一起，每个元素位于其各自的地理组件内。图 35-17 还识别了 TOGAF 与通信架构的关系。

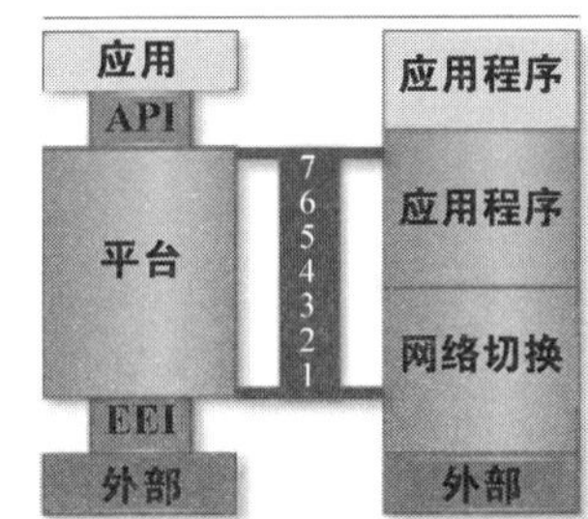

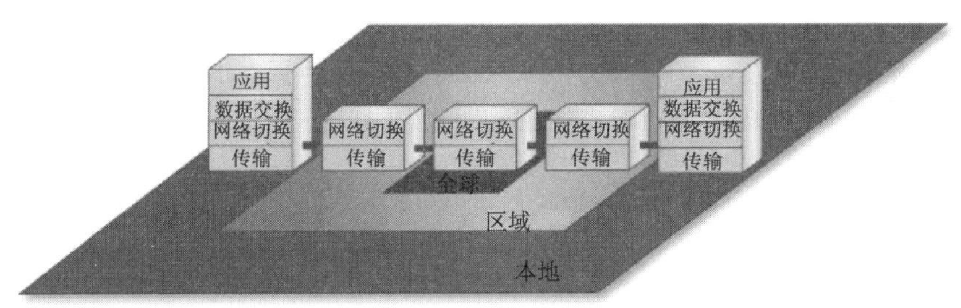

图 35-17 通信框架

服务到组件的分配

通信基础设施由本地传输组件、区域传输组件和全球传输组件组成。

分配给这些组件的服务与应用于一个组件的应用程序、数据交换、网络切换或传输架构层级的服务完全相同。数据交换和网络切换层级服务与对应的 OSI 参考模型层的服务完全相同。

典型情况下，只将网络切换和传输服务分配给由通信节点和传输介质组成的地区和全球组件。所有服务可在本地组件中执行，包括终端设备、处理节点、通信节点和链接介质。传输、切换、传送和应用全部都在该组件中执行。

35.7.6 Developing a Data Flow View

The Data Flow view is concerned with storage, retrieval, processing, archiving, and security of data.

35.7.6.1 Stakeholders and Concerns

This view should be developed for database engineers of the system.

Major concerns for this view are understanding how to provide data to the right people and applications with the right interfaces at the right time. This view deals with the architecture of the storage, retrieval, processing, archiving, and security of data. It looks at the flow of data as it is stored and processed, and at what components will be required to support and manage both storage and processing. In general, these stakeholders are concerned with ensuring ubiquitous access to high quality data.

35.7.6.2 Developing the View

The subjects of the general architecture of a "database system" are database components or components that provide database services.

The modeling of a "database" is typically done with entity-relationship diagrams and schema definitions, including document type definitions.

35.7.6.3 Key Issues

Data management services may be provided by a wide range of implementations. Some examples are:

- Mega-centers providing functionally-oriented corporate databases supporting local and remote data requirements.
- Distributed DBMSs that support the interactive use of partitioned and partially replicated databases.
- File systems provided by operating systems, which may be used by both interactive and batch processing applications.

Data management services include the storage, retrieval, manipulation, backup, restart/recovery, security, and associated functions for text, numeric data, and complex data such as documents, graphics, images, audio, and video. The operating system provides file management services, but they are considered here because many legacy databases exist as one or more files without the services provided by a DBMS.

Major components that provide data management services that are discussed in this section are:

- Database Management Systems (see Section 35.7.6.3)

35.7.6 开发数据流视图

数据流视图涉及数据的存储、检索、处理、存档和安保性。

35.7.6.1 利益攸关者和关注点

该视图应针对系统的数据库工程师来开发。

该视图的主要关注点是，了解如何在适当的时间向正确的人和具有正确界面的应用提供数据。该视图处理数据存储、检索、处理、存档和安保性的架构。它着眼于所存储和处理的数据流，以及需要什么组件对存储和处理进行支持和管理。一般说来，这些利益攸关者还关注确保对高质量数据的无所不在的访问。

35.7.6.2 开发视图

“数据库系统”的一般架构主题是数据库组件或提供数据库服务的组件。

“数据库”建模通常使用实体关系图和模式定义来完成，包括文件类型定义。

35.7.6.3 关键问题

数据管理服务可由宽泛的实施方式提供。一些示例包括：

- 提供支持本地和远程数据需求的面向功能的公司级数据库的特大中心。
- 支持已划分的且部分重复的数据库的交互使用的分布式 DBMS。
- 操作系统所提供的可被交互和批量处理应用使用的文件系统。

数据管理服务包括文本、数字数据和复杂数据（如文件、图形、图像、音频和视频）的存储、检索、操纵、备份、重启/恢复、安保性和相关功能。操作系统提供文件管理服务，但此处将这些服务考虑在内，是因为许多遗留数据库作为一个或多个文件存在，而没有 DBMS 提供的服务。

提供本节论述的数据管理服务的主要组件是：

- 数据库管理系统（见 35.7.6.3 节）

- Data Dictionary/Directory Systems (see Section 35.7.6.3)
- Data Administration (see Section 35.7.6.3)
- Data Security (see Section 35.7.6.3)

These are critical aspects of data management for the following reasons. The DBMS is the most critical component of any data management capability, and a data dictionary/directory system is necessary in conjunction with the DBMS as a tool to aid the administration of the database. Data security is a necessary part of any overall policy for security in information processing.

Database Management Systems

A Database Management System (DBMS) provides for the systematic management of data. This data management component provides services and capabilities for defining the data, structuring the data, accessing the data, as well as security and recovery of the data. A DBMS performs the following functions:

- Structures data in a consistent way.
- Provides access to the data.
- Minimizes duplication.
- Allows reorganization; that is, changes in data content, structure, and size.
- Supports programming interfaces.
- Provides security and control.

A DBMS must provide:

- Persistence; the data continues to exist after the application's execution has completed.
- Secondary storage management.
- Concurrency.
- Recovery.
- Data Definition/Data Manipulation Language (DDL/DML), which may be a graphical interface.

Database Models

The logical data model that underlies the database characterizes a DBMS. The common logical data models are as follows:

- **Relational Model**: A Relational Database Management System (RDBMS) structures data into tables that have certain properties:
  - Each row in the table is distinct from every other row.
  - Each row contains only atomic data; that is, there is no repeating data or such structures as arrays.
  - Each column in the relational table defines named data fields or attributes.

A collection of related tables in the relational model makes up a database. The mathematical theory of relations underlies the relational model — both the organization of data and the languages that manipulate the data. Edgar Codd, then at IBM, developed the relational model in 1973. It has been popular, in terms of commercial use, since the early1980s.

- 数据字典/目录系统（见 35.7.6.3 节）
- 数据监管（见 35.7.6.3 节）
- 数据安保（见 35.7.6.3 节）

这些是数据管理的关键方面，原因如下：DBMS 是任何数据管理能力的最关键的组件，数据字典/目录系统有必要连同 DBMS 作为帮助监管数据库的工具。数据安保是信息处理中的总体安保方针的必要组成部分。

数据库管理系统

数据库管理系统（DBMS）提供数据的系统性管理。该数据管理组件提供了定义数据、结构化数据、访问数据以及数据安保和恢复的服务和能力。DBMS 执行以下功能：

- 以一致的方式对数据进行结构化处理。
- 提供数据访问。
- 最小化重复。
- 允许重新组织，即数据内容、结构和大小中的变更。
- 支持编程界面。
- 提供安保和控制。

DBMS 必须提供：

- 持续性；在已经完成了应用执行后，数据继续存在。
- 二级存储管理。
- 并发性。
- 恢复。
- 数据定义/数据操纵语言（DDL/DML），其可以是一个图形化界面。

数据库模型

构成数据库基础的逻辑数据模型描述了 DBMS 的特征。常见逻辑数据模型如下：

- **关系模型**：关系数据库管理系统（RDBMS）将数据结构化为具有某些特性的表：
  - 表中的每行都与其他行截然不同。
  - 每行仅包含原子数据，即没有重复数据或此类结构作为数组。
  - 关系表中的每列定义了给定名称的数据字段或属性。

关系模型中相关表的集合构成数据库。关系的数学理论构成关系模型的基础——数据组织和操纵数据的语言。当时在 IBM 的 Edgar Codd 于 1973 年开发了关系模型。自 20 世纪 80 年代初以来，它在商业用途方面很普遍。

- **Hierarchical Model**: The hierarchical data model organizes data in a tree structure. There is a hierarchy of parent and child data segments. This structure implies that a record can have repeating information, generally in the child data segments. For example, an organization might store information about an employee, such as name, employee number, department, salary. The organization might also store information about an employee's children, such as name and date of birth. The employee and children data forms a hierarchy, where the employee data represents the parent segment and the children data represents the child segment. If an employee has three children, then there would be three child segments associated with one employee segment. In a hierarchical database the parent-child relationship is one-to-many. This restricts a child segment to having only one parent segment. Hierarchical DBMSs were popular from the late 1960s, with the introduction of IBM's Information Management System (IMS) DBMS, through the 1970s.
- **Network Model**: The popularity of the network data model coincided with the popularity of the hierarchical data model. Some data was more naturally modeled with more than one parent per child. So, the network model permitted the modeling of many-to-many relationships in data. In 1971, the Conference on Data Systems Languages (CODASYL) formally defined the network model. The basic data modeling construct in the network model is the set construct. A set consists of an owner record type, a set name, and a member record type. A member record type can have that role in more than one set, hence the multi-parent concept is supported. An owner record type can also be a member or owner in another set. The CODASYL network model is based on mathematical set theory.
- **Object-Oriented Model**: An Object-Oriented Database Management System (OODBMS) must be both a DBMS and an object-oriented system. As a DBMS it must provide the capabilities identified above. OODBMSs typically can model tabular data, complex data, hierarchical data, and networks of data. The following are important features of an object-oriented system:
  - Complex objects: e.g., objects may be composed of other objects.
  - Object identity: each object has a unique identifier external to the data.
  - Encapsulation: an object consists of data and the programs (or methods) that manipulate it.
  - Types or classes: a class is a collection of similar objects.
  - Inheritance: subclasses inherit data attributes and methods from classes.
  - Overriding with late binding: the method particular to a subclass can override the method of a class at run time.
  - Extensibility: e.g., a user may define new objects.
  - Computational completeness: a general-purpose language (such as Ada, C, or C++) is computationally complete. The special-purpose language SQL is not. Most OODBMSs incorporate a general-purpose programing language.
- **Flat Files**: A flat file system is usually closely associated with a storage access method. An example is IBM's Indexed Sequential Access Method (ISAM). The models discussed earlier in this section are logical data models; flat files require the user to work with the physical layout of the data on a storage device. For example, the user must know the exact location of a data item in a record. In addition, flat files do not provide all of the services ofa DBMS, such as naming of data, elimination of redundancy, and concurrency control. Further, there is no independence of the data and the application program. The application program must know the physical layout of the data.

- **层级模型**：层级数据模型以一个树形结构来组织数据。它具有一个父数据段和子数据段的层级结构。该结构意味着一个记录可具有重复信息，这一般是在子数据段中。例如，组织可存储关于员工的信息，如姓名、员工编号、部门、薪金。组织还可存储关于员工子女的信息，如姓名和出生日期。员工数据和子女数据形成层级结构，其中员工数据代表父数据段，子女数据代表子数据段。如果一名员工有三个子女，那么将具有与一个员工数据段相关联的三个子数据段。在层级数据库中，父—子关系是一对多的。这将子数据段限制为只具有一个父数据段。随着 IBM 的信息管理系统（IMS）DBMS 的引入，自 20 世纪 60 年代末直到 20 世纪 70 年代，层级 DBMS 一直很普遍。
- **网络模型**：网络数据模型的普及程度与层级数据模型的普及程度一致。一些数据以每个子数据段有一个以上的父数据段的方式更自然地建模。因此，网络模型允许数据的多对多关系建模。1971 年，数据系统语言会议（CODASYL）正式定义了网络模型。网络模型中，基本的数据建模构造是集合构造。一个集合由所有者记录类型、集合名称和成员记录类型组成。成员记录类型可在一个以上的集合中具有该角色，因此，支持多父体概念。所有者记录类型还可以是另一个集合中的成员或所有者。CODASYL 网络模型基于数学集合理论。
- **面向对象的模型**：面向对象的数据库管理系统（OODBMS）必须既是 DBMS，又是面向对象的系统。作为 DBMS，它必须提供上面所识别的能力。OODBMS 通常可对表格数据、复杂数据、层级数据和数据网络进行建模。以下是面向对象的系统的重要特征：
  - 复杂对象：如，对象可由其他对象构成。
  - 对象标识：每个对象具有数据外部的唯一标识符。
  - 封装：一个对象由数据和操纵数据的程序（或方法）组成。
  - 类型或类：类是同类对象的集合。
  - 继承：子类从类中继承数据属性和方法。
  - 后期绑定的重载：子类的特定方法可以在运行时重载父类方法。
  - 可扩展性：如，用户可定义新的对象。
  - 计算完整性：一般语言（如 Ada、C 或 C++）在计算上是完整的。专用语言 SQL 则不然。多数 OODBMS 包含一般编程语言。
- **平面文件**：平面文件系统通常与存储器访问方法密切相关。一个示例是 IBM 的索引顺序存取法（ISAM）。本节此前论述的模型是逻辑数据模型；平面文件要求用户工作用到存储设备上的数据的物理布局。例如，用户必须知道记录中数据项的精确位置。此外，平面文件不提供 DBMS 的所有服务，如数据命名、冗余消除和并发控制。而且数据和应用程序没有独立性。应用程序必须知道数据的物理布局。

Distributed DBMSs

A distributed DBMS manages a database that is spread over more than one platform. The database can be based on any of the data models discussed above (except the flat file). The database can be replicated, partitioned, or a combination of both. A replicated database is one in which full or partial copies of the database exist on the different platforms. A partitioned database is one in which part of the database is on one platform and parts are on other platforms. The partitioning of a database can be vertical or horizontal. A vertical partitioning puts some fields and the associated data on one platform and some fields and the associated data on another platform. For example, consider a database with the following fields: employee ID, employee name, department, number of dependents, project assigned, salary rate, tax rate. One vertical partitioning might place employee ID, number of dependents, salary rate, and tax rate on one platform and employee name, department, and project assigned on another platform. A horizontal partitioning might keep all the fields on all the platforms but distribute the records. For example, a database with 100,000 records might put the first 50,000 records on one platform and the second 50,000 records on a second platform.

Whether the distributed database is replicated or partitioned, a single DBMS manages the database. There is a single schema (description of the data in a database in terms of a data model; e.g., relational) for a distributed database. The distribution of the database is generally transparent to the user. The term "distributed DBMS" implies homogeneity.

Distributed Heterogeneous DBMSs

A distributed, heterogeneous database system is a set of independent databases, each with its own DBMS, presented to users as a single database and system. "Federated" is used synonymously with "distributed heterogeneous". The heterogeneity refers to differences in data models (e.g., network and relational), DBMSs from different suppliers, different hardware platforms, or other differences. The simplest kinds of federated database systems are commonly called "gateways". In a gateway, one vendor (e.g., Oracle) provides single-direction access through its DBMS to another database managed by a different vendor's DBMS (e.g., IBM's DB2). The two DBMSs need not share the same data model. For example, many RDBMS vendors provide gateways to hierarchical and network DBMSs.

There are federated database systems both on the market and in research that provide more general access to diverse DBMSs. These systems generally provide a schema integration component to integrate the schemas of the diverse databases and present them to the users asa single database, a query management component to distribute queries to the different DBMSs in the federation, and a transaction management component, to distribute and manage the changes to the various databases in the federation.

Data Dictionary/Directory Systems

The second component providing data management services, the Data Dictionary/ Directory System (DD/DS), consists of utilities and systems necessary to catalog, document, manage, and use metadata (data about data). An example of metadata is the following definition: a six-character long alphanumeric string, for which the first character is a letter of the alphabet and each of the remaining five characters is an integer between 0 and 9; the name for the string is "employee ID". The DD/DS utilities make use of special files that contain the database schema. (A schema, using metadata, defines the content and structure of a database.) This schema is represented by a set of tables resulting from the compilation of Data Definition Language (DDL) statements. The DD/DS is normally provided as part of a DBMS but is sometimes available from alternate sources. In the management of distributed data, distribution information may also be maintained in the network directory system. In this case, the interface between the DD/DS and the network directory system would be through the API of the network services component on the platform.

分布式 DBMS

分布式 DBMS 管理在一个以上平台分布的数据库。数据库可基于以上论述的任何数据模型（平面文件除外）。数据库可以被复制、划分或同时被复制和划分。复制的数据库是在不同的平台上存在数据库的完整或部分副本的数据库。划分的数据库是在一个平台上存在其部分数据库而其他平台上存在其余部分的数据库。数据库的划分可以是垂直的或水平的。垂直划分将一些字段和相关数据放在一个平台上，并将一些字段和相关数据放在另一个平台上。例如，考虑具有下列字段的数据库：员工 ID、员工姓名、部门、家属人数、分派的项目、薪金率、税率。一个垂直划分可在一个平台上放置员工 ID、家属人数、薪金率和税率，在另一个平台上放置员工姓名、部门和分派的项目。水平划分可在所有平台上保留所有字段，但分布记录。例如，具有 100 000 条记录的数据库可在一个平台上放置前 50 000 条记录，在第二个平台上放置另外的 50 000 条记录。

无论分布式数据库被复制还是划分，都由单个 DBMS 管理数据库。分布式数据库有一个单一的模式（依照数据模型对数据库中的数据的描述；如，关系模型）。数据库的分布对用户一般是透明的。术语“分布式 DBMS”意味着同质性。

分布式异构 DBMS

分布式异构数据库系统是一系列独立的数据库，每个独立的数据库具有其自己的 DBMS，作为单个数据库和系统提供给用户。“联邦”的使用与“分布式异构”同义。异构指的是数据模型（如，网络模型和关系模型）、来自不同供应商的 DBMS 和不同硬件平台的差异，或者其他差异。最简单种类的联邦数据库系统通常被称为“网关”。在网关中，一个厂商（如，Oracle 公司）通过其 DBMS 向不同厂商的 DBMS（如，IBM 的 DB2）所管理的另一个数据库提供单向访问。两个 DBMS 不需要共享相同的数据模型。例如，多个 RDBMS 厂商提供层级 DBMS 和网络 DBMS 的网关。

市场和研究中均存在对不同 DBMS 提供更普遍访问的联邦数据库系统。这些系统一般提供模式综合组件以综合不同数据库的模式，并将它们以单个数据库、一个向联合数据库中的不同 DBMS 分配查询的查询管理组件、一个事务管理组件以及以分布和管理联合数据库中各种数据库的变更的形式提供给用户。

数据字典/目录系统

提供数据管理服务的第二个组件，即数据字典/目录系统（DD/DS），包括对元数据（关于数据的数据）编目录集、文件化、管理和使用所必需的实用程序和系统。元数据的一个示例定义如下：六字符长度的字母数字串，其中第一个字符是字母表中的一个字母，且其余各字符分别是 0 和 9 之间的整数；字符串的名称是“员工 ID”。DD/DS 实用程序使用包含数据库模式的专用文件。（模式使用元数据定义了数据库的内容和结构）。该模式由数据定义语言（DDL）的语句编译而产生的一系列表来表达。DD/DS 通常作为 DBMS 的一部分来提供，但有时可从备用源中获得。在分布式数据的管理中，分布信息还可保留在网络目录系统中。在这种情况下，DD/DS 和网络目录系统之间的界面将通过平台上网络服务组件的 API 来实现。

In current environments, data dictionaries are usually integrated with the DBMS, and directory systems are typically limited to a single platform. Network directories are used to expand the DD/DS realms. The relationship between the DD/DS and the network directory is an intricate combination of physical and logical sources of data.

Data Administration

Data administration properly addresses the Data Architecture, which is outside the scope of TOGAF. We discuss it briefly here because of areas of overlap. It is concerned with all of the data resources of an enterprise, and as such there are overlaps with data management, which addresses data in databases. Two specific areas of overlap are the repository and database administration, which are discussed briefly below.

Repository

A repository is a system that manages all of the data of an enterprise, which includes data and process models and other enterprise information. Hence, the data in a repository is much more extensive than that in a DD/DS, which generally defines only the data making up a database.

Database Administration

Data administration and database administration are complementary processes. Data administration is responsible for data, data structure, and integration of data and processes. Database administration, on the other hand, includes the physical design, development, implementation, security, and maintenance of the physical databases. Database administration is responsible for managing and enforcing the enterprise's policies related to individual databases.

Data Security

The third component providing data management services is data security. This includes procedures and technology measures implemented to prevent unauthorized access, modification, use, and dissemination of data stored or processed by a computer system. Data security also includes data integrity (i.e., preserving the accuracy and validity of the data), and protecting the system from physical harm (including preventative measures and recovery procedures).

Authorization control allows only authorized users to have access to the database at the appropriate level. Guidelines and procedures can be established for accountability, levels of control, and type of control. Authorization control for database systems differs from that in traditional file systems because, in a database system, it is not uncommon for different users to have different rights to the same data. This requirement encompasses the ability to specify subsets of data and to distinguish between groups of users. In addition, decentralized control of authorizations is of particular importance for distributed systems.

Data protection is necessary to prevent unauthorized users from understanding the content of the database. Data encryption, as one of the primary methods for protecting data, is useful for both information stored on disk and for information exchanged on a network.

在当前环境中，数据字典通常与 DBMS 综合，且目录系统通常限于单个平台。网络目录用于扩展 DD/DS 领域。DD/DS 和网络目录之间的关系是物理和逻辑数据源的错综复杂的组合。

数据监管

数据监管恰当地应对数据架构，属于 TOGAF 范围之外。由于有重叠的区域，我们在此处作简短论述。它涉及 ENTERPRISE 的所有数据资源，正因如此，与应对数据库中数据的数据管理存在重叠。两个具体的重叠区域是存储库和数据库监管，下面将简要论述。

存储库

存储库是管理 ENTERPRISE 所有数据的系统，包括数据和流程模型以及其他 ENTERPRISE 信息。因此，存储库中的数据比 DD/DS 中的数据广泛得多，DD/DS 一般仅对构成数据库的数据进行定义。

数据库监管

数据监管和数据库监管是互补的流程。数据监管负责数据、数据结构以及数据和流程的综合。另一方面，数据库监管包括物理数据库的物理设计、开发、实施、安保和维护。数据库监管负责管理和执行与单独数据库相关的 ENTERPRISE 方针。

数据安保

提供数据管理服务的第三个组件是数据安保。它包括防止计算机系统所存储或处理的数据被未授权访问、修改、使用和分发而实施的程序和技术措施。数据安保还包括数据完整性（即，保留数据的准确性和有效性）以及保护系统免受物理损害（包括预防性测度和恢复程序）。

授权控制只允许经授权的用户在恰当的层级上访问数据库。可针对责任、控制层级和控制类型建立指南和程序。数据库系统的授权控制不同于传统文件系统，因为在数据库系统中，不同用户对相同数据具有不同权限的情况并不少见。这种需求包括详细说明数据子集和在用户群组之间区分的能力。此外，授权的分散控制对分布式系统特别重要。

为防止未被授权的用户掌握数据库内容，数据保护是必要的。数据加密作为保护数据的主要方法之一，既可用于硬盘上存储的信息，也可用于网络上交换的信息。

35.7.7 Developing an Enterprise Manageability View

The Enterprise Manageability view is concerned with operations, administration, and management of the system.

35.7.7.1 Stakeholders and Concerns

This view should be developed for the operations, administration, and management personnel of the system.

Major concerns for these stakeholders are understanding how the system is managed as a whole, and how all components of the system are managed. The key concern is managing change in the system and predicting necessary preventative maintenance.

In general, these stakeholders are concerned with ensuring that the availability of the system does not suffer when changes occur. Managing the system includes managing components such as:

- Security components
- Data assets
- Software assets
- Hardware assets
- Networking assets

35.7.7.2 Developing the View

Business scenarios are an extremely useful way to depict what should happen when planned and unplanned events occur. It is highly recommended that business scenarios be created for planned change, and for unplanned change.

The following paragraphs describe some of the key issues that the architect might consider when constructing business scenarios.

35.7.7.3 Key Issues

The Enterprise Manageability view acts as a check and balance on the difficulties and day-to-day running costs of systems built within the new architecture. Often, system management is not considered until after all the important purchasing and development decisions have been taken, and taking a separate management view at an early stage in architecture development is one way to avoid this pitfall. It is good practice to develop the Enterprise Manageability view with close consideration of the System Engineering view since, in general, management is difficult to retrofit into an existing design.

Key elements of the Enterprise Manageability view are:

- The policies, procedures, and guidelines that drive your management requirements (such as a policy to restrict downloading software from the Internet).
- How your shop measures system availability.
- The management services and utilities required.
- The likely quantity, quality, and location of management and support personnel.

35.7.7 开发 ENTERPRISE 可管理性视图

ENTERPRISE 可管理性视图涉及系统的运行、监管和管理。

35.7.7.1 利益攸关者和关注点

该视图应针对系统的运行、监管和管理人员来开发。

这些利益攸关者的主要关注点是了解如何将系统作为一个整体来管理，以及如何管理系统的所有组件。关键关注点是管理系统变更并预测必要的预防性维护。

一般来说，这些利益攸关者关注的是确保发生变更时系统可用性不受影响。对系统的管理包括对如下组件的管理：

- 安保组件
- 数据资产
- 软件资产
- 硬件资产
- 网络资产

35.7.7.2 开发视图

业务场景是描述出现计划性和非计划性事件时应发生什么事件的一个极其有用的方式。强烈建议分别针对计划性变化和非计划性变化创建业务场景。

下列段落描述了架构师在构造业务场景时可能考虑的一些关键问题。

35.7.7.3 关键问题

ENTERPRISE 可管理性视图起到了检查和平衡新架构内构建的系统的难度和日常运行成本的作用。通常，在所有重要的采购和开发都已做出决策后，才考虑系统管理，在架构开发的早期，采取单独管理视图是避免这种陷阱的一种方式。通过仔细考虑系统工程视图来开发 ENTERPRISE 可管理性视图是良好的实践，因为一般来说，管理很难改进到现有设计中。

ENTERPRISE 可管理性视图的关键元素是：

- 驱动管理需求的方针、程序和指南（如限制从互联网下载软件的方针）。
- 您的业务如何衡量系统可用性。
- 所需的管理服务和实用程序。
- 管理和支持人员的可能的数量、质量和位置。

- The ability of users to take on system management tasks, such as password maintenance.
- The manageability of existing and planned components in each of the component categories.
- Whether management should be centralized or distributed.
- Whether security is the responsibility of system managers or a separate group, bearing in mind any legal requirements.

Key technical components categories that are the subject of the Enterprise Manageability view deal with change, either planned upgrades, or unplanned outages. The following table lists specific concerns for each component category.

Component Category	Planned Change Considerations	Unplanned Change Considerations
Security Components	How is a security changepropagated throughout the system? Who is responsible for making changes; end users, or security stewards?	What should happen whensecurity is breached? What should happen if a security component fails?
Data Assets	How are new data elements added? How is data imported/exported or loaded/ unloaded? How is backup managed while running continuously? How is data change propagated in a distributed environment?	What are the backup procedures and are all the system capabilities there to backup in time?
Software Assets	How is a new application introduced into the systems? What procedures are there to control software quality? How are application changes propagated in a distributed environment? How is unwanted software introduction restricted given the Internet?	What do you want to happen when an application fails? What do you want to happen when a resource of the application fails?
Hardware Assets	How do you assess the impactof new hardware on the system, especially network load?	What do you want to happen when hardware outages occur?
Networking Assets	How do you assess the impactof new networking components? How do you optimize your networking components?	

- 用户在承担系统管理任务（如口令维护）上的能力。
- 每个组件目录中的现有组件和已计划组件的可管理性。
- 管理应当是集中式的还是分布式的。
- 安保是系统管理者的职责还是单独群组的职责，要考虑到任何法律要求。

关键技术组件类别是 ENTERPRISE 可管理性视图的主题，其处理变化，即计划性升级或非计划性停用。下表列出了每个组件类别的特定关注点。

组件类别	计划性变更考量因素	非计划性变更考量因素
安保组件	安保变更如何在整个系统内扩散？ 谁负责做出变更；最终用户或安保管理员？	违反安保性时应发生什么？ 如果安保组件出现故障，应发生什么？
数据资产	如何添加新的数据元素？ 如何输入/输出或加载/卸载数据？ 连续运行时如何管理备份？ 如何在分布式环境中扩散数据变更？	什么是备份程序以及需要及时备份的所有系统能力是什么？
软件资产	如何将新的应用引入系统中？ 控制软件质量的是什么程序？ 如何在分布式环境中扩散应用变更？ 考虑到互联网，如何限制引入无用的软件？	应用故障时你想要发生什么？ 应用资源故障时你想要发生什么？
硬件资产	你如何评估新的硬件对系统，特别是对网络负载的影响？	出现硬件停用时你希望发生什么？
网络资产	你如何评估新的网络组件的影响？ 你如何优化你的网络组件？	

35.7.8 Developing an Acquirer View

The Acquirer view is concerned with acquiring Commercial Off-The-Shelf (COTS) software and hardware.

35.7.8.1 Stakeholders and Concerns

This view should be developed for personnel involved in the acquisition of any components of the subject architecture.

Major concerns for these stakeholders are understanding what building blocks of the architecture can be bought, and what constraints (or rules) exist that are relevant to the purchase. The acquirer will shop with multiple vendors looking for the best cost solution while adhering to the constraints (or rules) applied by the architecture, such as standards.

The key concern is to make purchasing decisions that fit the architecture, and thereby to reduce the risk of added costs arising from non-compliant components.

35.7.8.2 Developing the View

The Acquirer view is normally represented as an architecture of Solution Building Blocks (SBBs), supplemented by views of the standards to be adhered to by individual building blocks.

35.7.8.3 Key Issues

The acquirer typically executes a process similar to the one below. Within the step descriptions we can see the concerns and issues that the acquirer faces.

Procurement Process Steps	Step Description and Output
Acquisition Planning	Creates the plan for the purchase of some component. For IT systems, the following considerations are germane to building blocks. This step requires access to Architecture Building Blocks(ABBs) and SBBs. ■ The procurer needs to know which ABBs apply constraints (standards) for use in assessment and for creation of RFP/RFIs. ■ The procurer needs to know which candidate SBBs adhere to these standards. ■ The procurer also needs to know which suppliers provide accepted SBBs and where they have been deployed. ■ The procurer needs to know what budget this component was given relative to the over all system cost

35.7.8 开发采办方视图

采办方视图涉及采办商用货架（COTS）的软件和硬件。

35.7.8.1 利益攸关者和关注点

该视图应针对参与主题架构任何组件的采办的人员来开发。

这些利益攸关者的主要关注点是了解可购买架构的哪些构建块以及存在哪些与采购相关的约束（或规则）。采办方将与多个厂商一起采购，寻找最佳成本解决方案，同时遵循架构所应用的约束（或规则），如标准。

关键关注点是，做出适合架构的采购决策，从而减少由不合规组件所引起的成本增加的风险。

35.7.8.2 开发视图

采办方视图通常表示为解决方案构建块（SBB）的架构，并被单独构建块需要遵循的标准视图进行补充。

35.7.8.3 关键问题

采办方通常执行与下面的流程相似的流程。在步骤描述中，我们可以看到采办方面临的关注点和问题。

采购流程步骤	步骤描述和输出
采办规划	创建采购某一组件的计划。对于 IT 系统而言，下列考量因素与构建块密切相关。 这个步骤需要访问架构构建块（ABB）和 SBB。 ■ 采购方需要知道哪些 ABB 将约束（标准）应用于评估以及创建 RFP/RFI。 ■ 采购方需要知道哪些候选 SBB 遵循这些标准。 ■ 采购方还需要知道哪些供应商提供已接受的 SBB 以及它们已部署在何处。 ■ 采购方需要知道相较于总体系统成本，给予该组件多少预算

Procurement Process Steps	Step Description and Output
Concept Exploration	In this step the procurer looks at the viability of the concept. Building blocks give the planner a sense of the risk involved; if many ABBs or SBBs exist that match the concept, the risk is lower. This step requires access to ABBs and SBBs. The planner needs to know which ABBs apply constraints (standards), and needs to know which candidate SBBs adhere to these standards
Concept Demonstration and Validation	In this step, the procurer works with development toprototype an implementation. The procurer recommends the re-usable SBBs based upon standards fit, and past experience with suppliers. This step requires access to re-usable SBBs
Development	In this step the procurer works with development to manage the relationship with the vendors supplying the SBBs. Building blocks that are proven to be fit-for-purpose get marked as approved. This step requires an update of the status to "procurement approved" of an SBB
Production	In this step, the procurer works with development to manage the relationship with the vendors supplying the SBBs. Building blocks that are put into production get marked appropriately. This step requires an update of the status to "in production" of SBBs, with the system identifier of where the building block is being developed
Deployment	In this step, the procurer works with development to manage the relationship with the vendors supplying the SBBs. Building blocks that are fully deployed get marked appropriately. This step requires an update of the status to "deployed" of SBBs, with the system identifier of where the building block was deployed

采购流程步骤	步骤描述和输出
概念探索	在这个步骤中，采购方着眼于概念的可行性。 构建块给予计划人员一种相关风险的感觉；如果存在多个与概念匹配的 ABB 或 SBB，则风险较低。 该步骤需要使用 ABB 和 SBB。计划人员需要知道哪些 ABB 应用约束（标准），还需要知道哪些候选 SBB 遵循这些标准
概念演示和确认	在该步骤中，采购方开展开发工作以便使实施原型化。采购方基于标准适合性以及供应商过去的经验来建议使用可复用的 SBB。 该步骤需要访问可复用的 SBB
开发	在该步骤中，采购方开展开发工作以便管理与供应 SBB 的厂商的关系。已被证明适用的构建块被标记为“批准”。 该步骤需要将 SBB 的状态更新为“批准采购”
生产	在该步骤中，采购方开展开发工作以管理与供应 SBB 的厂商的关系。对投入生产的构建块进行恰当的标记。 该步骤需要将 SBB 的状态更新为“生产中”，并使用构件块所在开发位置的系统标识符
部署	在该步骤中，采购方开展开发工作以管理与供应 SBB 的厂商的关系。对全面部署的构建块进行恰当的标记。 该步骤需要将 SBB 的状态更新为“已部署”，并使用构件块所在部署位置的系统标识符

Chapter 36
Architecture Deliverables

This chapter provides descriptions of deliverables referenced in the Architecture Development Method(ADM).

36.1 Introduction

This chapter defines the deliverables that will typically be consumed and produced across the TOGAF ADM cycle. As deliverables are typically the contractual or formal work products of an architecture project, it is likely that these deliverables will be constrained or altered by any overarching project or process management for the enterprise (such as CMMI, PRINCE2, PMBOK, or MSP).

This chapter therefore is intended to provide a typical baseline of architecture deliverables in order to better define the activities required in the ADM and act as a starting point for tailoring within a specific organization.

The TOGAF Content Framework (see Part IV, Chapter 33) identifies deliverables that are produced as outputs from executing the ADM cycle and potentially consumed as inputs at other points in the ADM. Other deliverables may be produced elsewhere and consumed by the ADM.

Deliverables produced by executing the ADM are shown in the table below.

Deliverable	Output from...	Input to...
Architecture Building Blocks (see Section 36.2.1)	F, H	A, B, C, D, E
Architecture Contract (see Section 36.2.2)	—	—
Architecture Definition Document (see Section 36.2.3)	B, C, D, E, F	C, D, E, F, G, H
Architecture Principles (see Section 36.2.4)	Preliminary, A, B, C, D	Preliminary, A, B, C, D, E, F, G, H
Architecture Repository (see Section 36.2.5)	Preliminary	Preliminary, A, B, C, D, E, F, G, H, Requirements Management
Architecture Requirements Specification (see Section 36.2.6)	B, C, D, E, F, Requirements Management	C, D, Requirements Management
Architecture Roadmap (see Section 36.2.7)	B, C, D, E, F	B, C, D, E, F
Architecture Vision	A, E	B, C, D, E, F, G, H,

第 36 章 架构交付物

本章提供在架构开发方法（ADM）中提及的交付物的描述。

36.1 简介

本章定义了通常贯穿 TOGAF ADM 周期使用和生产的交付物。由于交付物通常是架构项目的契约的或正式的工作成果，因此这些交付物有可能受到 ENTERPRISE 的任何影响全局的项目或流程管理（如 CMMI、PRINCE2、PMBOK 或 MSP）的约束或被它们改变。

因此，本章旨在提供架构交付物的典型基线，以便更好地定义 ADM 中所需的活动并充当特定组织内剪裁的起点。

“TOGAF 内容框架”（见第四部分第 33 章）识别出产自执行 ADM 周期时的输出，且可能被用作 ADM 中其他点上输入的交付物。其他交付物可在其他地方产生并由 ADM 使用。

通过执行 ADM 所生产的交付物如下表所示。

交付物	从……输出	输入到……
架构构建块（见 36.2.1 节）	F、H	A、B、C、D、E
架构契约（见 36.2.2 节）	—	—
架构定义文件（见 36.2.3 节）	B、C、D、E、F	C、D、E、F、G、H
架构原则（见 36.2.4 节）	预备阶段、A、B、C、D	预备阶段、A、B、C、D、E、F、G、H
架构库（见 36.2.5 节）	预备	预备阶段、A、B、C、D、E、F、G、H、需求管理
架构需求规范（见 36.2.6 节）	B、C、D、E、F、需求管理	C、D、需求管理
架构路线图（见 36.2.7 节）	B、C、D、E、F	B、C、D、E、F
架构愿景	A、E	B、C、D、E、F、G、H、

Deliverable	Output from...	Input to...
(see Section 36.2.8)		Requirements Management
Business Principles, Business Goals, and Business Drivers (see Section 36.2.9)	Preliminary, A, B	A, B
Capability Assessment (see Section 36.2.10)	A, E	B, C, D, E, F
Change Request (see Section 36.2.11)	F, G, H	—
Communications Plan (see Section 36.2.12)	A	B, C, D, E, F
Compliance Assessment (see Section 36.2.13)	G	H
Implementation and Migration Plan (see Section 36.2.14)	E, F	F
Implementation Governance Model (see Section 36.2.15)	F	G, H
Organizational Model for Enterprise Architecture (see Section 36.2.16)	Preliminary	Preliminary, A, B, C, D, E, F, G, H, Requirements Management
Request for Architecture Work (see Section 36.2.17)	Preliminary, F, H	A, G
Requirements Impact Assessment (see Section 36.2.18)	Requirements Management	Requirements Management
Solution Building Blocks (see Section 36.2.19)	G	A, B, C, D, E, F, G
Statement of Architecture Work (see Section 36.2.20)	A, B, C, D, E, F, G, H	B, C, D, E, F, G, H, Requirements Management
Tailored Architecture Framework (see Section 36.2.21)	Preliminary, A	Preliminary,A, B, C, D, E, F, G, H, Requirements Management

36.2 Deliverable Descriptions

The following sections provide example descriptions of deliverables referenced in the ADM.

Note that not all the content described here need be contained in a particular deliverable. Rather, it is recommended that external references be used where possible; for example, the strategic plans of a business should not be copied into a Request for Architecture Work, but rather the title of the strategic plans should be referenced.

Also, it is not suggested that these descriptions should be followed to the letter. However, each element should be considered carefully; ignoring any input or output item may cause problems downstream.

交付物	从……输出	输入到……
（见 36.2.8 节）		需求管理
业务原则、业务目标和业务驱动因素（见 36.2.9 节）	预备阶段、A、B	A、B
能力评估（见 36.2.10 节）	A、E	B、C、D、E、F
变革要求（见 36.2.11 节）	F、G、H	—
沟通计划（见 36.2.12 节）	A	B、C、D、E、F
合规性评估（见 36.2.13 节）	G	H
实施和迁移计划（见 36.2.14 节）	E、F	F
实施管控模型（见 36.2.15 节）	F	G、H
Enterprise Architecture 的组织模型（见 36.2.16 节）	预备	预备阶段、A、B、C、D、E、F、G、H、需求管理
架构工作要求书（见 36.2.17 节）	预备阶段、F、H	A、G
需求影响评估（见 36.2.18 节）	需求管理	需求管理
解决方案构建块（见 36.2.19 节）	G	A、B、C、D、E、F、G
架构工作说明书（见 36.2.20 节）	A、B、C、D、E、F、G、H	B、C、D、E、F、G、H、需求管理
剪裁的架构框架（见 36.2.21 节）	预备阶段、A	预备阶段、A、B、C、D、E、F、G、H、需求管理

36.2 交付物描述

下面几节提供在 ADM 中提及的交付物的描述示例。

需要注意的是，不是本文描述的所有内容都有必要包含在特定交付物中。相反，如果可能，建议使用外部参考文献；例如，业务的战略计划不应拷贝到架构工作要求书中，而应引用战略计划的标题。

同时，不建议严格地遵循这些描述。然而，每个元素应被仔细地考虑，忽略任何输入或输出项可能导致下游出现问题。

36.2.1 Architecture Building Blocks

Architecture documentation and models from the enterprise's Architecture Repository; seePart IV, Chapter 37.

36.2.2 Architecture Contract

Purpose

Architecture Contracts are the joint agreements between development partners and sponsors on the deliverables, quality, and fitness-for-purpose of an architecture. Successful implementation of these agreements will be delivered through effective architecture governance (see Part VII, Chapter 50). By implementing a governed approach to the management of contracts, the following will be ensured:

- A system of continuous monitoring to check integrity, changes, decision-making, and audit of all architecture-related activities within the organization.
- Adherence to the principles, standards, and requirements of the existing or developing architectures.
- Identification of risks in all aspects of the development and implementation of the architecture(s) covering the internal development against accepted standards, policies, technologies, and products as well as the operational aspects of the architectures such that the organization can continue its business within a resilient environment.
- A set of processes and practices that ensure accountability, responsibility, and discipline with regard to the development and usage of all architectural artifacts.
- A formal understanding of the governance organization responsible for the contract, their level of authority, and scope of the architecture under the governance of this body.

Content

Typical contents of an Architecture Design and Development Contract are:

- Introduction and background
- The nature of the agreement
- Scope of the architecture
- Architecture and strategic principles and requirements
- Conformance requirements
- Architecture development and management process and roles
- Target Architecture measures
- Defined phases of deliverables
- Prioritized joint workplan
- Time window(s)
- Architecture delivery and business metrics

36.2.1 架构构建块

来自 Enterprise Architecture 库的架构文件和模型；见第四部分第 37 章。

36.2.2 架构契约

目的

架构契约是开发合作伙伴和发起人就架构的交付物、质量和适用性而达成的联合协议。这些协议的成功实施，将通过有效的架构治理来实现（见第七部分第 50 章）。通过实施已治理的契约管理途径，以下将得到保证：

- 对系统连续监控，以检查完整性、变革、决策以及组织内所有架构相关活动的审计。
- 遵循现有的或开发中的架构原则、标准和需求。
- 识别架构开发和实施的所有方面的风险，这些风险涵盖了按照公认的标准、方针、技术和产品所进行的内部开发以及架构的运行方面，使得组织可在一个弹性环境内继续执行其业务。
- 一系列流程和实践，确保实现有关所有架构制品开发和使用的责任、职责和规程。
- 正式了解对契约负责的治理组织及其权限级别以及在该机构治理下的架构范围。

内容

架构设计和开发契约的典型内容是：

- 简介和背景
- 协议的本质
- 架构范围
- 架构及战略的原则和需求
- 合规性需求
- 架构开发和管理流程与角色
- 目标架构测度
- 交付物的已定义阶段
- 根据优先级排序的联合工作计划
- 时间窗
- 架构交付和业务衡量标准

Typical contents of a Business Users' Architecture Contract are:

- Introduction and background
- The nature of the agreement
- Scope
- Strategic requirements
- Conformance requirements
- Architecture adopters
- Time window
- Architecture business metrics
- Service architecture (includes Service Level Agreement (SLA))

For more detail on the use of Architecture Contracts, see Part VII, Chapter 49.

36.2.3 Architecture Definition Document

Purpose

The Architecture Definition Document is the deliverable container for the core architectural artifacts created during a project and for important related information. The Architecture Definition Document spans all architecture domains (business, data, application, and technology) and also examines all relevant states of the architecture (baseline, transition, and target).

A Transition Architecture shows the enterprise at an architecturally significant state between the Baseline and Target Architectures. Transition Architectures are used to describe transitional Target Architectures necessary for effective realization of the Target Architecture.

The Architecture Definition Document is a companion to the Architecture Requirements Specification, with a complementary objective:

- The Architecture Definition Document provides a qualitative view of the solution and aims to communicate the intent of the architects.
- The Architecture Requirements Specification provides a quantitative view of the solution, stating measurable criteria that must be met during the implementation of the architecture.

Content

Typical contents of an Architecture Definition Document are:

- Scope
- Goals, objectives, and constraints
- Architecture principles
- Baseline Architecture
- Architecture models (for each state to be modeled):
  - Business Architecture models
  - Data Architecture models

业务用户的架构契约的典型内容是：

- 简介和背景
- 协议的本质
- 范围
- 战略需求
- 合规性需求
- 架构采纳
- 时间窗
- 架构业务衡量标准
- 服务架构［包括服务水平协议（SLA）］

关于使用架构契约的更多细节，见第七部分第 49 章。

36.2.3 架构定义文件

目的

架构定义文件是在项目期间所创建的核心架构制品和重要相关信息的交付物容器。架构定义文件跨越所有架构领域（业务、数据、应用和技术），并审查架构的所有相关状态（基线、过渡和目标）。

过渡架构表明 ENTERPRISE 处于基线架构和目标架构之间的一种架构上的重要状态。过渡架构用于描述有效实现目标架构所必需的过渡的目标架构。

架构定义文件是架构需求规范的伴随物，具有互补的目的：

- 架构定义文件提供解决方案的定性视图，旨在沟通架构师的意图。
- 架构需求规范提供解决方案的定量视图，说明在架构的实施期间必须满足的可衡量的准则。

内容

架构定义文件的典型内容是：

- 范围
- 目标、目的和约束
- 架构原则
- 基线架构
- 架构模型（对待建模的每个状态）：
  - 业务架构模型
  - 数据架构模型

  - — Application Architecture models
  - — Technology Architecture models
- Rationale and justification for architectural approach
- Mapping to Architecture Repository:
  - — Mapping to Architecture Landscape
  - — Mapping to reference models
  - — Mapping to standards
  - — Re-use assessment
- Gap analysis
- Impact assessment
- Transition Architecture:
  - — Definition of transition states
  - — Business Architecture for each transition state
  - — Data Architecture for each transition state
  - — Application Architecture for each transition state
  - — Technology Architecture for each transition state

36.2.4 Architecture Principles

Purpose

Principles are general rules and guidelines, intended to be enduring and seldom amended, that inform and support the way in which an organization sets about fulfilling its mission.

In their turn, principles may be just one element in a structured set of ideas that collectively define and guide the organization, from values through to actions and results.

Content

See Part III, Chapter 23 for guidelines and a detailed set of generic architecture principles, including:

- Business principles (see Section 23.6.1)
- Data principles (see Section 23.6.2)
- Application principles (see Section 23.6.3)
- Technology principles (see Section 23.6.4)

  - 应用架构模型
  - 技术架构模型
- 架构实施途径的理由依据和合理性
- 映射到架构库：
  - 映射到架构全景
  - 映射到参考模型
  - 映射到标准
  - 复用评估
- 差距分析
- 影响评估
- 过渡架构：
  - 过渡状态的定义
  - 每个过渡状态的业务架构
  - 每个过渡状态的数据架构
  - 每个过渡状态的应用架构
  - 每个过渡状态的技术架构

36.2.4 架构原则

目的

原则是传达并支持组织履行其任务的方式的一般规则和指南，是持久的且很少修改。

从而，这些原则可能只是一套结构化思想中的一个元素，它们从价值观到行动和结果上共同定义和指导组织。

内容

关于一般架构原则的指南和详细集合，见第三部分第23章，包括：

- 业务原则（见23.6.1节）
- 数据原则（见23.6.2节）
- 应用原则（见23.6.3节）
- 技术原则（见23.6.4节）

36.2.5 Architecture Repository

Purpose

The Architecture Repository acts as a holding area for all architecture-related projects within the enterprise. The repository allows projects to manage their deliverables, locate re-usable assets, and publish outputs to stakeholders and other interested parties.

Content

See Part V, Chapter 41 for a detailed description of the content of an Architecture Repository.

36.2.6 Architecture Requirements Specification

Purpose

The Architecture Requirements Specification provides a set of quantitative statements that outline what an implementation project must do in order to comply with the architecture. An Architecture Requirements Specification will typically form a major component of an implementation contract or contract for more detailed Architecture Definition.

As mentioned above, the Architecture Requirements Specification is a companion to the Architecture Definition Document, with a complementary objective:

- The Architecture Definition Document provides a qualitative view of the solution and aims to communicate the intent of the architect.
- The Architecture Requirements Specification provides a quantitative view of the solution, stating measurable criteria that must be met during the implementation of the architecture.

Content

Typical contents of an Architecture Requirements Specification are:

- Success measures
- Architecture requirements
- Business service contracts
- Application service contracts
- Implementation guidelines
- Implementation specifications
- Implementation standards
- Interoperability requirements
- IT Service Management requirements
- Constraints
- Assumptions

36.2.5 架构库

目的

架构库充当 ENTERPRISE 内所有架构相关项目的保存区域。存储库使得项目能管理其交付物，确定可复用资产的位置以及向利益攸关者和其他感兴趣的各方发布输出。

内容

关于架构库内容的详细描述，见第五部分第 41 章。

36.2.6 架构需求规范

目的

架构需求规范提供一系列定量说明，概述了实施的项目为了遵从架构必须做什么。架构需求规范通常构成实施契约或更详细的架构定义契约的主要部分。

如上所述，架构需求规范是架构定义文件的伴随物，具有互补的目的：

- 架构定义文件提供解决方案的定性视图，旨在沟通架构师的意图。
- 架构需求规范提供解决方案的定量视图，说明在架构的实施期间必须满足的可衡量的准则。

内容

架构需求规范的典型内容是：

- 成功测度
- 架构需求
- 业务服务契约
- 应用服务契约
- 实施指南
- 实施规范
- 实施标准
- 互用性需求
- IT 服务管理需求
- 约束
- 假设

36.2.7 Architecture Roadmap

Purpose

The Architecture Roadmap lists individual work packages that will realize the Target Architecture and lays them out on a timeline to show progression from the Baseline Architecture to the Target Architecture. The Architecture Roadmap highlights individual work packages' business value at each stage. Transition Architectures necessary to effectively realize the Target Architecture are identified as intermediate steps. The Architecture Roadmap is incrementally developed throughout Phases E and F, and informed by readily identifiable roadmap components from Phase B, C, and D within the ADM.

Content

Typical contents of an Architecture Roadmap are:

- Work package portfolio:
  - Work package description (name, description, objectives, deliverables)
  - Functional requirements
  - Dependencies
  - Relationship to opportunity
  - Relationship to Architecture Definition Document and Architecture Requirements Specification
  - Business value
- Implementation Factor Assessment and Deduction matrix, including:
  - Risks
  - Issues
  - Assumptions
  - Dependencies
  - Actions
  - Inputs
- Consolidated Gaps, Solutions, and Dependencies matrix, including:
  - Architecture domain
  - Gap
  - Potential solutions
  - Dependencies
- Any Transition Architectures
- Implementation recommendations:
  - Criteria measures of effectiveness of projects
  - Risks and issues
  - Solution Building Blocks (SBBs)

36.2.7 架构路线图

目的

架构路线图列出了实现目标架构的单独的工作包，并将它们布置在时间表上，以表明从基线架构到目标架构的进展。架构路线图强调各阶段单独的工作包的业务价值，有效实现目标架构所必需的过渡架构识别为中间步骤。架构路线图在阶段 E 和阶段 F 期间被渐进地开发，并在 ADM 内以阶段 B、C 和 D 中可识别的路线图组件作为依据。

内容

架构路线图的典型内容是：

- 工作包谱系：
  - 工作包描述（名称、描述、目标、交付物）
  - 功能需求
  - 依赖性
  - 与机会的关系
  - 与架构定义文件及架构需求规范的关系
  - 业务价值
- 实施因素评估和推导矩阵，包括：
  - 风险
  - 问题
  - 假设
  - 依赖性
  - 活动
  - 输入
- 合并的差距、解决方案和依赖性矩阵，包括：
  - 架构领域
  - 差距
  - 潜在的解决方案
  - 依赖性
- 任何过渡架构
- 实施建议：
  - 项目有效性的准则测度
  - 风险和问题
  - 解决方案构建块（SBB）

36.2.8 Architecture Vision

Purpose

The Architecture Vision is created early on in the ADM cycle. It provides a summary of the changes to the enterprise that will accrue from successful deployment of the Target Architecture. The purpose of the Architecture Vision is to provide key stakeholders with a formally agreed outcome. Early agreement on the outcome enables the architects to focus on the detail necessary to validate feasibility. Providing an Architecture Vision also supports stakeholder communication by providing a summary version of the full Architecture Definition.

Content

Typical contents of an Architecture Vision are:

- Problem description:
  - Stakeholders and their concerns
  - List of issues/scenarios to be addressed
- Objective of the Statement of Architecture Work
- Summary views necessary for the Request for Architecture Work and the Version 0.1 Business, Application, Data, and Technology Architectures created; typically including:
  - Value Chain diagram
  - Solution Concept diagram
- Mapped requirements
- Reference to Draft Architecture Definition Document

36.2.9 Business Principles, Business Goals, and Business Drivers

Purpose

Business principles, business goals, and business drivers provide context for architecture work, by describing the needs and ways of working employed by the enterprise. Many factors that lie outside the consideration of architecture discipline may nevertheless have significant implications for the way that architecture is developed.

Content

The content and structure of business context for architecture is likely to vary considerably from one organization to the next.

36.2.8 架构愿景

目的

架构愿景在 ADM 周期早期被创建。它向将从目标架构的成功部署中获益的 ENTERPRISE 提供变更概要。架构愿景的目的在于向关键利益攸关者提供正式商定的结果。早期对结果达成一致使架构师能够聚焦于确认可行性所必需的细节。通过提供完整架构定义的概要版本，提供架构愿景还支持利益攸关者沟通。

内容

架构愿景的典型内容是：

- 问题描述：
  - 利益攸关者及其关注点
  - 将应对的问题/场景的列表
- 架构工作说明书的目的
- 架构工作要求书和所创建的 0.1 版本的业务、应用、数据和技术架构所必需的概要视图，通常包括：
  - 价值链图
  - 解决方案概念图
- 映射的需求
- 架构定义文件草案的参考资料

36.2.9 业务原则、业务目标和业务驱动因素

目的

业务原则、业务目标和业务驱动因素通过描述 ENTERPRISE 采用的工作需要和方式来提供架构工作的背景环境。然而，置于架构修炼考量因素以外的多个因素对架构的开发方式可能具有重要意义。

内容

架构的业务背景环境的内容和结构在不同组织之间可能变化相当大。

36.2.10 Capability Assessment

Purpose

Before embarking upon a detailed Architecture Definition, it is valuable to understand the baseline and target capability level of the enterprise. This Capability Assessment can be examined on several levels:

- What is the capability level of the enterprise as a whole? Where does the enterprise wish to increase or optimize capability? What are the architectural focus areas that will support the desired development of the enterprise?
- What is the capability or maturity level of the IT function within the enterprise? What are the likely implications of conducting the architecture project in terms or design governance, operational governance, skills, and organization structure? What is an appropriate style, level of formality, and amount of detail for the architecture project to fit with the culture and capability of the IT organization?
- What is the capability and maturity of the architecture function within the enterprise? What architectural assets are currently in existence? Are they maintained and accurate? What standards and reference models need to be considered? Are there likely to be opportunities to create re-usable assets during the architecture project?
- Where capability gaps exist, to what extent is the business ready to transform in order to reach the target capability? What are the risks to transformation, cultural barriers, and other considerations to be addressed beyond the basic capability gap?

Content

Typical contents of a Capability Assessment are:

- Business Capability Assessment, including:
  - Capabilities of the business
  - Baseline state assessment of the performance level of each capability
  - Future state aspiration for the performance level of each capability
  - Baseline state assessment of how each capability is realized
  - Future state aspiration for how each capability should be realized
  - Assessment of likely impacts to the business organization resulting from the successful deployment of the Target Architecture
- IT Capability Assessment, including:
  - Baseline and target maturity level of change process
  - Baseline and target maturity level of operational processes
  - Baseline capability and capacity assessment
  - Assessment of the likely impacts to the IT organization resulting from the successful deployment of the Target Architecture
- Architecture maturity assessment, including:
  - Architecture governance processes, organization, roles, and responsibilities
  - Architecture skills assessment

36.2.10 能力评估

目的

在着手详细的架构定义之前，了解 ENTERPRISE 的基线和目标能力水平是很有价值的。可在多个等级上审查这种能力评估：

- 总的来说，什么是 ENTERPRISE 的能力水平？ENTERPRISE 希望在哪方面增加或优化能力？支持 ENTERPRISE 希望的开发的架构焦点领域是什么？
- ENTERPRISE 内，IT 功能的能力或成熟度水平是多少？根据设计治理、运行治理、技能和组织结构来执行架构项目可能的意义是什么？为匹配 IT 组织的文化和能力，架构项目的恰当样式、正式程度以及细节数量是什么？
- ENTERPRISE 内架构功能的能力和成熟度是什么？当前存在的架构资产是什么？它们是否被维护并且是准确的？需要考虑哪些标准和参考模型？在架构项目期间是否具有创建可复用资产的机会？
- 何处存在能力差距，为达到目标能力，业务转换已经准备到什么程度？在基本能力差距以外需要应对的转型、文化障碍和其他考量因素的风险是什么？

内容

能力评估的典型内容是：

- 业务能力评估，包括：
  - 业务能力
  - 每个能力的绩效水平的基线状态评估
  - 每个能力的绩效水平将来的状态的强烈渴望
  - 关于如何实现每个能力的基线状态评估
  - 关于应如何实现每个能力将来的状态的强烈渴望
  - 因成功部署目标架构而引起的对业务组织的可能影响的评估
- IT 能力评估，包括：
  - 变更流程的基线和目标成熟度水平
  - 运行流程的基线和目标成熟度水平
  - 基线能力和能力评估
  - 因成功部署目标架构而引起的对 IT 组织的可能影响的评估
- 架构成熟度评估，包括：
  - 架构治理流程、组织、角色和职责
  - 架构技能评估

  - Breadth, depth, and quality of landscape definition with the Architecture Repository
  - Breadth, depth, and quality of standards definition with the Architecture Repository
  - Breadth, depth, and quality of reference model definition with the Architecture Repository
  - Assessment of re-use potential
- Business Transformation Readiness Assessment, including:
  - Readiness factors
  - Vision for each readiness factor
  - Current and target readiness ratings
  - Readiness risks

36.2.11 Change Request

Purpose

During implementation of an architecture, as more facts become known, it is possible that the original Architecture Definition and requirements are not suitable or are not sufficient to complete the implementation of a solution. In these circumstances, it is necessary for implementation projects to either deviate from the suggested architectural approach or to request scope extensions. Additionally, external factors — such as market factors, changes in business strategy, and new technology opportunities — may open up opportunities to extend and refine the architecture.

In these circumstances, a Change Request may be submitted in order to kick-start a further cycle of architecture work.

Content

Typical contents of a Change Request are:

- Description of the proposed change
- Rationale for the proposed change
- Impact assessment of the proposed change, including:
  - Reference to specific requirements
  - Stakeholder priority of the requirements to date
  - Phases to be revisited
  - Phase to lead on requirements prioritization
  - Results of phase investigations and revised priorities
  - Recommendations on management of requirements
- Repository reference number

  - 具有架构库的全景定义的广度、深度和质量
  - 具有架构库的标准定义的广度、深度和质量
  - 具有架构库的参考模型定义的广度、深度和质量
  - 可复用可能性的评估
- 业务转型准备度评估，包括：
  - 准备度因素
  - 每个准备度因素的愿景
  - 当前的和目标准备度等级
  - 准备度风险

36.2.11 变更要求

目的

在架构实施期间，由于更多的事项变得已知，原始架构定义和需求有可能不合适或不足以完成解决方案的实施。在这些情况下，实施项目有必要偏离所建议的架构实施途径或要求范围扩展。此外，外部因素——如市场因素、业务战略变更和新的技术机会——可开拓扩展和改进架构的机会。

在这些情况下，为启动架构工作的另外的周期，可提交变更要求。

内容

变更要求的典型内容是：

- 所提出变更的描述
- 所提出变更的理由依据
- 所提出变更的影响评估，包括：
  - 特定需求的参考资料
  - 到目前为止利益攸关者的需求优先级
  - 待回顾的阶段
  - 导致需求进行优先级排序的阶段
  - 阶段研究的结果和修订的优先级
  - 对需求管理的建议
- 存储库参考数量

36.2.12 Communications Plan

Purpose

Enterprise architectures contain large volumes of complex and inter-dependent information. Effective communication of targeted information to the right stakeholders at the right time is a critical success factor for enterprise architecture. Development of a Communications Plan for architecture allows for this communication to be carried out within a planned and managed process.

Content

Typical contents of a Communications Plan are:

- Identification of stakeholders and grouping by communication requirements.
- Identification of communication needs, key messages in relation to the Architecture Vision, communication risks, and Critical Success Factors (CSFs).
- Identification of mechanisms that will be used to communicate with stakeholders and allow access to architecture information, such as meetings, newsletters, repositories, etc..
- Identification of a communications timetable, showing which communications will occur with which stakeholder groups at what time and in what location.

36.2.13 Compliance Assessment

Purpose

Once an architecture has been defined, it is necessary to govern that architecture through implementation to ensure that the original Architecture Vision is appropriately realized and that any implementation learnings are fed back into the architecture process. Period compliance reviews of implementation projects provide a mechanism to review project progress and ensure that the design and implementation is proceeding in-line with the strategic and architectural objectives.

Content

Typical contents of a Compliance Assessment are:

- Overview of project progress and status
- Overview of project architecture/design
- Completed architecture checklists:
  - Hardware and operating system checklist
  - Software services and middleware checklist
  - Applications checklists
  - Information management checklists
  - Security checklists
  - System management checklists
  - System engineering checklists

36.2.12 沟通计划

目的

Enterprise Architecture 包含大量复杂且相互依赖的信息。在适当的时候与适合的利益攸关者有效沟通目标信息是 Enterprise Architecture 的关键成功因素。制定架构的沟通计划，使得能够在已计划且接受管理的流程内执行这种沟通。

内容

沟通计划的典型内容是：

- 按沟通需求确认利益攸关者并进行分组。
- 确认沟通需要、与架构愿景有关的关键消息、沟通风险和关键成功因素（CSF）。
- 确认用于与利益攸关者沟通并允许访问架构信息的机制（如会议、内部通讯、存储库等）。
- 确认沟通时间表，从而表明在何时以及什么位置与哪些利益攸关者群组进行哪些沟通。

36.2.13 合规性评估

目的

一旦定义了一个架构，则有必要通过实施来治理该架构，以确保恰当地实现原始架构愿景且所有实施知识被反馈回架构流程中。实施项目的定期合规性审视提供了一种机制，以审视项目进展并确保设计和实施符合战略目的和架构目的。

内容

合规性评估的典型内容是：

- 项目进展和状态的概述
- 项目架构/设计的概述
- 已完成的架构检查单：
  - — 硬件和操作系统检查单
  - — 软件服务和中间件检查单
  - — 应用检查单
  - — 信息管理检查单
  - — 安保检查单
  - — 系统管理检查单
  - — 系统工程检查单

— Methods and tools checklists

36.2.14 Implementation and Migration Plan

Purpose

The Implementation and Migration Plan provides a schedule of the projects that will realize the Target Architecture. The Implementation and Migration Plan includes executable projects grouped into managed portfolios and programs. The Implementation and Migration Strategy identifying the approach to change is a key element of the Implementation and Migration Plan.

Content

Typical contents of an Implementation and Migration Plan are:

- Implementation and Migration Strategy:
  - Strategic implementation direction
  - Implementation sequencing approach
- Project and portfolio breakdown of implementation:
  - Allocation of work packages to project and portfolio
  - Capabilities delivered by projects
  - Milestones and timing
  - Work breakdown structure
  - May include impact on existing portfolio, program, and projects

It may contain:

- Project charters:
  - Included work packages
  - Business value
  - Risk, issues, assumptions, dependencies
  - Resource requirements and costs
  - Benefits of migration, determined (including mapping to business requirements)
  - Estimated costs of migration options

— 方法和工具检查单

36.2.14 实施和迁移计划

目的

实施和迁移计划针对可实现目标架构的项目提供了进度表。实施和迁移计划包括可执行项目并将其分组成被管理的项目谱系和项目群。确认变更实施途径的实施和迁移策略是实施和迁移计划的关键元素。

内容

实施和迁移计划的典型内容是：

- 实施和迁移方针：
  — 战略实施方向
  — 实施排序途径
- 实施的项目和项目谱系的分解：
  — 给项目和项目谱系分配工作包
  — 项目交付的能力
  — 里程碑和时机
  — 工作分解结构
  — 可包括对现有项目谱系、项目群和项目的影响

它可包含：

- 项目章程：
  — 包含的工作包
  — 业务价值
  — 风险、问题、假设、依赖性
  — 资源需求和成本
  — 经确定的迁移好处（包括映射到业务需求）
  — 迁移选项的估算成本

36.2.15 Implementation Governance Model

Purpose

Once an architecture has been defined, it is necessary to plan how the Transition Architecture that implements the architecture will be governed through implementation. Within organizations that have established architecture functions, there is likely to be a governance framework already in place, but specific processes, organizations, roles, responsibilities, and measures may need to be defined on a project-by-project basis.

The Implementation Governance Model ensures that a project transitioning into implementation also smoothly transitions into appropriate architecture governance.

Content

Typical contents of an Implementation Governance Model are:

- Governance processes
- Governance organization structure
- Governance roles and responsibilities
- Governance checkpoints and success/failure criteria

36.2.16 Organizational Model for Enterprise Architecture

Purpose

In order for an architecture framework to be used successfully, it must be supported by the correct organization, roles, and responsibilities within the enterprise. Of particular importance is the definition of boundaries between different enterprise architecture practitioners and the governance relationships that span across these boundaries.

Content

Typical contents of an Organizational Model for enterprise architecture are:

- Scope of organizations impacted
- Maturity assessment, gaps, and resolution approach
- Roles and responsibilities for architecture team(s)
- Constraints on architecture work
- Budget requirements
- Governance and support strategy

36.2.15 实施治理模型

目的

一旦定义了一个架构，就有必要针对如何通过实施来治理实施该架构的过渡架构而制订计划。在已经建立了架构功能的组织内，可能已经存在一个治理框架，但可能需要以逐个项目为基础来定义特定的流程、组织、角色、职责和测度。

实施治理模型，确保一个过渡到实施中的项目还可平滑地过渡到恰当的架构治理。

内容

实施治理模型的典型内容是：

- 治理流程
- 治理组织结构
- 治理角色和职责
- 治理检查点和成功/失败准则

36.2.16 Enterprise Architecture 的组织模型

目的

为了成功地使用架构框架，必须由 ENTERPRISE 内正确的组织、角色和职责来支持架构框架。不同 Enterprise Architecture 的实践者之间边界的定义以及跨越这些边界的管控关系尤为重要。

内容

Enterprise Architecture 的组织模型的典型内容是：

- 受影响的组织范围
- 成熟度评估、差距和解决方案实施途径
- 架构团队的角色和职责
- 对架构工作的约束
- 预算需求
- 治理和支持方针

36.2.17 Request for Architecture Work

Purpose

This is a document that is sent from the sponsoring organization to the architecture organization to trigger the start of an architecture development cycle. Requests for Architecture Work can be created as an output of the Preliminary Phase, a result of approved architecture Change Requests, or terms of reference for architecture work originating from migration planning.

In general, all the information in this document should be at a high level.

Content

Requests for Architecture Work typically include:

- Organization sponsors
- Organization's mission statement
- Business goals (and changes)
- Strategic plans of the business
- Time limits
- Changes in the business environment
- Organizational constraints
- Budget information, financial constraints
- External constraints, business constraints
- Current business system description
- Current architecture/IT system description
- Description of developing organization
- Description of resources available to developing organization

36.2.18 Requirements Impact Assessment

Purpose

Throughout the ADM, new information is collected relating to an architecture. As this information is gathered, new facts may come to light that invalidate existing aspects of the architecture. A Requirements Impact Assessment assesses the current architecture requirements and specification to identify changes that should be made and the implications of those changes.

Content

Typical contents of a Requirements Impact Assessment are:

- Reference to specific requirements
- Stakeholder priority of the requirements to date
- Phases to be revisited
- Phase to lead on requirements prioritization

36.2.17 架构工作要求书

目的

它是发起组织发送给架构组织以触发开始架构开发周期的文件。可创建架构工作要求书，作为预备阶段的输出、已批准的架构变更要求的结果或源于迁移规划的架构工作的参考项。

一般来说，本文件中的所有信息应处于一个较高的层级。

内容

架构工作要求书通常包括：

- 组织发起人
- 组织的任务说明
- 业务目标（和变更）
- 业务的战略计划
- 时间限制
- 业务环境的变更
- 组织的约束
- 预算信息、财务约束
- 外部约束、业务约束
- 当前业务系统描述
- 当前架构/IT 系统描述
- 开发组织的描述
- 开发组织可得到的资源的描述

36.2.18 需求影响评估

目的

在整个 ADM 内收集与架构有关的新信息。由于收集了这种信息，可能会出现新的事实而使架构的现有各方面失效。需求影响评估可评估当前架构需求和规范，以确认应当做的变更以及那些变更的意义。

内容

需求影响评估的典型内容是：

- 特定需求的参考资料
- 到目前为止利益攸关者的需求优先级
- 待回顾的阶段
- 导致需求优先级排序的阶段

- Results of phase investigations and revised priorities
- Recommendations on management of requirements
- Repository reference number

36.2.19 Solution Building Blocks

Implementation-specific building blocks from the enterprise's Architecture Repository; see Part IV, Chapter 37.

36.2.20 Statement of Architecture Work

Purpose

The Statement of Architecture Work defines the scope and approach that will be used to complete an architecture development cycle. The Statement of Architecture Work is typically the document against which successful execution of the architecture project will be measured and may form the basis for a contractual agreement between the supplier and consumer of architecture services.

Content

Typical contents of a Statement of Architecture Work are:

- Title
- Architecture project request and background
- Architecture project description and scope
- Overview of Architecture Vision
- Specific change of scope procedures
- Roles, responsibilities, and deliverables
- Acceptance criteria and procedures
- Architecture project plan and schedule
- Approvals

36.2.21 Tailored Architecture Framework

Purpose

TOGAF provides an industry standard framework for architecture that may be used in a wide variety of organizations. However, before TOGAF can be effectively used within an architecture project, tailoring at two levels is necessary.

Firstly, it is necessary to tailor the TOGAF model for integration into the enterprise. This tailoring will include integration with project and process management frameworks, customization of terminology, development of presentational styles, selection, configuration, and deployment of architecture tools, etc. The formality and detail of any frameworks adopted should also align with other contextual factors for the enterprise, such as culture, stakeholders, commercial models for enterprise architecture, and the existing level of Architecture Capability.

Once the framework has been tailored to the enterprise, further tailoring is necessary in order to tailor the framework for the specific architecture project. Tailoring at this level will select appropriate deliverables and artifacts to meet project and stakeholder needs.

- 阶段研究的结果和修订的优先级
- 对需求管理的建议
- 存储库参考数量

36.2.19 解决方案构建块

来自 Enterprise Architecture 库的特定于实施的构建块；见第四部分第 37 章。

36.2.20 架构工作说明书

目的

架构工作说明书定义了用于完成架构开发周期的范围和实施途径。架构工作说明书通常是对架构项目的成功执行而进行测量所依据的文件，并且可构成架构服务的供应商和消费者之间的契约协议的基础。

内容

架构工作说明书的典型内容是：

- 标题
- 架构项目要求和背景
- 架构项目描述和范围
- 架构愿景的概述
- 范围程序的特定变更
- 角色、职责和交付物
- 验收准则和程序
- 架构项目计划和进度表
- 批准

36.2.21 剪裁的架构框架

目的

TOGAF 提供可在多种组织中使用的架构的行业标准框架。然而，在 TOGAF 可有效用于架构项目之前，有必要在两个层级上进行裁剪。

首先，有必要剪裁 TOGAF 模型，以便集成到 ENTERPRISE 内。这种剪裁将包括与项目和流程管理框架的集成、术语定制、展现风格的开发以及架构工具的选择、配置和部署等。所采用的任何框架的正式程度和细节还应符合 ENTERPRISE 其他的背景环境因素，如文化、利益攸关者、Enterprise Architecture 的商业模型及架构能力的现有水平。

一旦按 ENTERPRISE 剪裁了框架，为了按特定架构项目剪裁框架，有必要进行进一步剪裁。这个层级上的剪裁将选择恰当的交付物和制品，以满足项目和利益攸关者的需要。

See Part II, Section 6.4.5 for further considerations when selecting and tailoring the architecture framework.

Content

Typical contents of a Tailored Architecture Framework are:

- Tailored architecture method
- Tailored architecture content (deliverables and artifacts)
- Configured and deployed tools
- Interfaces with governance models and other frameworks:
  - Corporate Business Planning
  - Enterprise Architecture
  - Portfolio, Program, Project Management
  - System Development/Engineering
  - Operations (Services)

关于选择和剪裁架构框架时的更多考量因素，见第二部分 6.4.5 节。

内容

剪裁的架构框架的典型内容是：

- 剪裁的架构方法
- 剪裁的架构内容（交付物和制品）
- 已配置和部署的工具
- 与治理模型和其他框架的界面：
  - — 公司业务规划
  - — Enterprise Architecture
  - — 项目谱系、项目群、项目管理
  - — 系统开发/工程
  - — 运行（服务）

Chapter 37
Building Blocks

This chapter explains the concept of building blocks.

37.1 Overview

This section is intended to explain and illustrate the concept of building blocks in architecture. Following this overview, there are two main parts:

- Introduction to Building Blocks (see Section 37.2), discusses the general concepts of building blocks, and explains the differences between Architecture Building Blocks (ABBs) and Solution Building Blocks (SBBs).
- Building Blocks and the ADM (see Section 37.3), summarizes the stages at which building block design and specification occurs within the TOGAF Architecture Development Method (ADM).

37.2 Introduction to Building Blocks

This section is an introduction to the concept of building blocks.

37.2.1 Overview

This section describes the characteristics of building blocks. The use of building blocks in the ADM is described separately in Section 37.3.

37.2.2 Generic Characteristics

Building blocks have generic characteristics as follows:

- A building block is a package of functionality defined to meet the business needs across an organization.
- A building block has a type that corresponds to the TOGAF content metamodel (such as actor, business service, application, or data entity).
- A building block has a defined boundary and is generally recognizable as "a thing" by domain experts.

第 37 章
构建块

本章解释了构建块的概念。

37.1 概述

本节用于解释和详细阐明架构中构建块的概念。按照此概述，有两个主要部分：

- 构建块的简介（见 37.2 节），论述了构建块的一般概念并解释了架构构建块（ABB）和解决方案构建块（SBB）之间的差异。
- 构建块和 ADM（见 37.3 节），总结了在 TOGAF 架构开发方法（ADM）内出现构建块设计和规范的阶段。

37.2 构建块的简介

本节是对构建块概念的简介。

37.2.1 概述

本节描述构建块的特征。37.3 节中单独描述了构建块在 ADM 中的用途。

37.2.2 一般特征

构建块具有如下一般特征：

- 构建块是为满足跨组织业务需要所定义的功能包。
- 构建块具有与 TOGAF 内容元模型（如施动者、业务服务、应用或数据实体）相对应的类型。
- 构建块具有已定义的边界，且一般可被领域专家识别为“一种事物”。

- A building block may interoperate with other, inter-dependent, building blocks.
- A good building block has the following characteristics:
  - It considers implementation and usage, and evolves to exploit technology and standards.
  - It may be assembled from other building blocks.
  - It may be a subassembly of other building blocks.
  - Ideally a building block is re-usable and replaceable, and well specified.

A building block's boundary and specification should be loosely coupled to its implementation; i.e., it should be possible to realize a building block in several different ways without impacting the boundary or specification of the building block. The way in which assets and capabilities are assembled into building blocks will vary widely between individual architectures. Every organization must decide for itself what arrangement of building blocks works best for it. A good choice of building blocks can lead to improvements in legacy system integration, interoperability, and flexibility in the creation of new systems and applications.

Systems are built up from collections of building blocks, so most building blocks have to interoperate with other building blocks. Wherever that is true, it is important that the interfaces to a building block are published and reasonably stable.

Building blocks can be defined at various levels of detail, depending on what stage of architecture development has been reached.

For instance, at an early stage, a building block can simply consist of a name or an outline description. Later on, a building block may be decomposed into multiple supporting building blocks and may be accompanied by a full specification.

The level of detail to which a building block should be specified is dependent on the objectives of the architecture and, in some cases, less detail may be of greater value (for example, when presenting the capabilities of an enterprise, a single clear and concise picture has more value than a dense 100-page specification).

The OMG have developed a standard for Re-usable Asset Specification (RAS),[13] which provides a good example of how building blocks can be formally described and managed.

37.2.3 Architecture Building Blocks

Architecture Building Blocks (ABBs) relate to the Architecture Continuum (see Part V, Section 39.4.1), and are defined or selected as a result of the application of the ADM.

37.2.3.1 Characteristics

ABBs:

- Capture architecture requirements; e.g., business, data, application, and technology requirements.
- Direct and guide the development of SBBs.

---

13. Refer to www.omg.org/spec/RAS.

- 构建块可与其他相互依赖的构建块进行互用。
- 一个好的构建块具有下列特征：
  - 它考虑到实施和使用，并进行演进以利用技术和标准。
  - 它可由其他构建块组装。
  - 它可以是其他构建块的子组件。
  - 理想情况下，构建块是可复用和可更换的，并可被明确规定。

构建块的边界和规范应与其实施松耦合；即，在不影响构建块的边界或规范的情况下以不同的方式实现构建块应是可能的。资产和能力组合成构建块的方式在单独架构之间变化很大。每个组织必须为自身决定哪种构建块排列对其工作效果最佳。构建块的合理选择可在创建新系统和应用的过程中促使改进遗留系统的集成、互用性和灵活性。

系统从构建块的集合中被构建，因此大多数构建块必须与其他构建块进行互用。无论是否真实，发布构建块的界面以及界面的合理稳定性是非常重要的。

可以在不同细节层级上定义构建块，这取决于架构开发已达到何种阶段。

例如，在初期阶段，构建块可以只包括名称或概述。随后，构建块可分解成多个支持构建块，并可随附一份完整的规范。

构建块需要被规定的细节层级取决于架构的目的，且在某些情况下，较少的细节可能具有更大的价值（例如，当表达 ENTERPRISE 能力时，单个清晰且简洁的图像比密集的 100 页规范更有价值）。

OMG 已制定了可复用资产规范（RAS）的标准[13]，为如何正式地描述和管理构建块提供了良好示例。

37.2.3 架构构建块

架构构建块（ABB）涉及架构统一体（见第五部分 39.4.1 节），并且通过应用 ADM 而被定义或选择。

37.2.3.1 特征

ABB：

- 捕获架构需求；如，业务、数据、应用和技术需求。
- 指引和指导 SBB 的开发。

---

13. 见 www.omg.org/spec/RAS。

37.2.3.2 Specification Content

ABB specifications include the following as a minimum:

- Fundamental functionality and attributes: semantic, unambiguous, including security capability and manageability
- Interfaces: chosen set, supplied
- Interoperability and relationship with other building blocks
- Dependent building blocks with required functionality and named user interfaces
- Map to business/organizational entities and policies

37.2.4 Solution Building Blocks

Solution Building Blocks (SBBs) relate to the Solutions Continuum (see Part V, Section 39.4.2), and may be either procured or developed.

37.2.4.1 Characteristics

SBBs:

- Define what products and components will implement the functionality
- Define the implementation
- Fulfil business requirements
- Are product or vendor-aware

37.2.4.2 Specification Content

SBB specifications include the following as a minimum:

- Specific functionality and attributes
- Interfaces; the implemented set
- Required SBBs used with required functionality and names of the interfaces used
- Mapping from the SBBs to the IT topology and operational policies
- Specifications of attributes shared across the environment (not to be confused with functionality) such as security, manageability, localizability, scalability
- Performance, configurability
- Design drivers and constraints, including the physical architecture
- Relationships between SBBs and ABBs

37.2.3.2 规范内容

ABB 规范至少包括以下内容：

- 基本功能性和属性：具有明确语义的，包括安保能力和可管理性
- 界面：已提供的选定集合
- 与其他构建块的互用性和关系
- 具有所需功能性和已命名用户界面的从属构建块
- 映射到业务/组织实体和方针

37.2.4 解决方案构建块

解决方案构建块（SBB）涉及解决方案统一体（见第五部分 39.4.2 节），并且可以被采购或开发。

37.2.4.1 特征

SBB：

- 定义什么产品和组件将实施功能性
- 定义实施
- 满足业务需求
- 有产品意识或厂商意识

37.2.4.2 规范内容

SBB 规范至少包括以下内容：

- 特定功能性和属性
- 界面；实施集合
- 具有所需功能性和所用界面名称的已使用的所需 SBB
- 从 SBB 到 IT 拓扑和运行方针的映射
- 跨环境共享属性的规范（不要与功能性相混淆），如安保性、可管理性、局部化能力、可伸缩性
- 性能、可配置性
- 设计驱动因素和约束，包括物理架构
- SBB 和 ABB 之间的关系

37.3 Building Blocks and the ADM

37.3.1 Basic Principles

This section focuses on the use of building blocks in the ADM. General considerations and characteristics of building blocks are described in Section 37.2.

37.3.1.1 Building Blocks in Architecture Design

An architecture is a set of building blocks depicted in an architectural model, and a specification of how those building blocks are connected to meet the overall requirements of the business.

The various building blocks in an architecture specify the scope and approach that will be used to address a specific business problem.

There are some general principles underlying the use of building blocks in the design of specific architectures:

- An architecture need only contain building blocks that are relevant to the business problem that the architecture is attempting to address.
- Building blocks may have complex relationships to one another. One building block may support multiple building blocks or may partially support a single building block (for example, the business service of "complaint handling" would be supported by many data entities and possibly multiple application components).
- Building blocks should conform to standards relevant to their type, the principles of the enterprise, and the standards of the enterprise.

37.3.1.2 Building Block Design

The process of identifying building blocks includes looking for collections of capabilities or assets that interact with one another and then drawing them together or making them different:

- Consider three classes of building blocks:
  - Re-usable building blocks, such as legacy items.
  - Building blocks to be the subject of development, such as new applications.
  - Building blocks to be the subject of purchase; i.e., Commercial Off-The-Shelf (COTS) pplications.
- Use the desired level of integration to bind or combine functions into building blocks. For instance, legacy elements could be treated as large building blocks to avoid breaking them apart.

In the early stages and during views of the highest-level enterprise, the building blocks are often kept at a broad integration definition. It is during these exercises that the services definitions can often be best viewed. As implementation considerations are addressed, more detailed views of building blocks can often be used to address implementation decisions, focus on the critical strategic decisions, or aid in assessing the value and future impact of commonality and reusability.

37.3 构建块和 ADM

37.3.1 基本原则

本节聚焦于 ADM 中构建块的使用。37.2 节描述了构建块的一般考量因素和特征。

37.3.1.1 架构设计中的构建块

架构是架构模型中所描述的构建块集合，以及关于如何连接那些构建块以满足总体业务需求的规范。

架构中的各种构建块规定了用于应对特定业务问题的范围和实施途径。

以下一般原则构成在特定架构的设计中使用构建块的基础：

- 架构仅需包含与架构力求应对的业务问题相关的构建块。
- 构建块彼此可能具有复杂的关系。一个构建块可支持多个构建块或部分地支持单个构建块（例如，“投诉处理”的业务服务将由多个数据实体和可能多个应用组件来支持）。
- 构建块应符合与其类型相关的标准、ENTERPRISE 原则和 ENTERPRISE 标准。

37.3.1.2 构建块设计

识别构建块的过程，包括寻找彼此相互作用的能力或资产的集合，然后将它们聚集在一起或将其区分开：

- 考虑三类构建块：
  - 可复用的构建块，如遗留项。
  - 作为开发主题的构建块，如新的应用。
  - 作为采购主题的构建块；即商用货架（COTS）的应用。
- 使用期望的集成层级将功能绑定或合并到构建块中。例如，遗留元素可被当作大构建块以避免将它们分开。

在早期阶段和最高层级 ENTERPRISE 的视图内，构建块通常保持在一个广泛的集成定义上。正是在这些训练期间，服务定义通常可更好辨认。由于实施考量因素被应对，更详细的构建块视图通常可用于应对实施决策，聚焦于关键的战略性决策，或帮助评估通用性和可复用性的价值和未来的影响。

37.3.2 Building Block Specification Process in the ADM

The process of building block definition takes place gradually as the ADM is followed, mainly in Phases A, B, C, and D. It is an iterative process because as definition proceeds, detailed information about the functionality required, the constraints imposed on the architecture, and the availability of products may affect the choice and the content of building blocks.

The key parts of the ADM at which building blocks are designed and specified are summarized below.

The major work in these steps consists of identifying the ABBs required to meet the business goals and objectives. The selected set of ABBs is then refined in an iterative process to arrive at a set of SBBs which can either be bought off-the-shelf or custom developed.

The specification of building blocks using the ADM is an evolutionary and iterative process. The key phases and steps of the ADM at which building blocks are evolved and specified are summarized below, and illustrated in Figure 37-1.

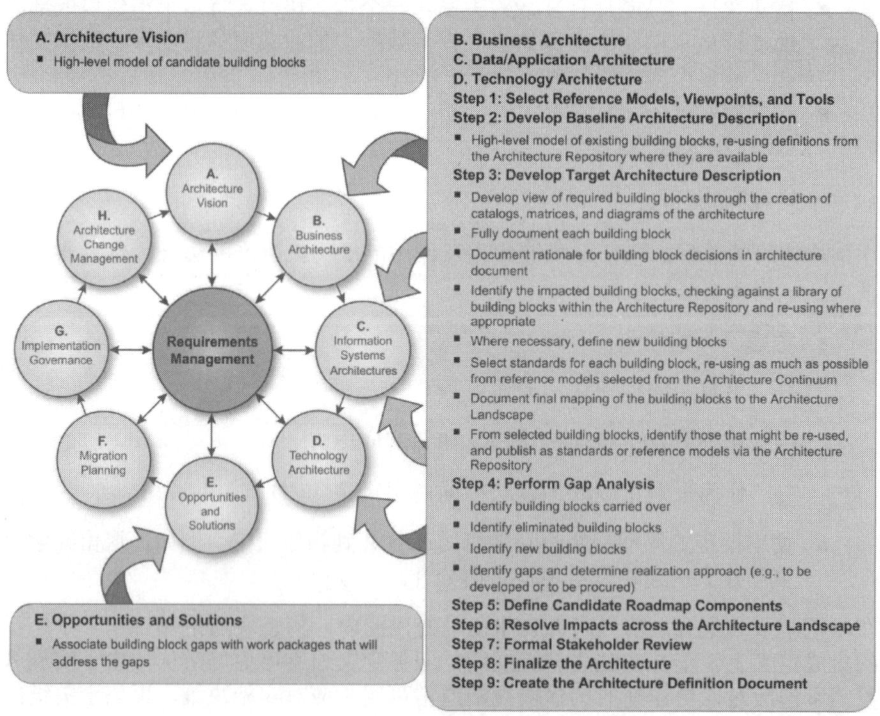

Figure 37-1 Key ADM Phases/Steps at Which Building Blocks AreEvolved/Specified

37.3.2 ADM 中的构建块规范流程

遵循 ADM，构建块定义的流程逐步地进行，主要在 A、B、C、D 四个阶段。它是一种迭代过程，因为随着定义的进行，所需功能性的详细信息、对架构施加的约束以及产品的可用性可能影响构建块的选择和内容。

设计和规定构建块所在的 ADM 的关键部分总结如下。

这些步骤中的主要工作包括确认满足业务目标和目的所需的 ABB。然后，在迭代过程中改进 ABB 的选定集，以获得可现货购买或定制开发的 SBB 集。

通过使用 ADM 来构建块规范是一种演进式迭代的过程。演进和规定构建块所在的 ADM 的关键阶段和步骤总结如下，并如图 37-1 所示。

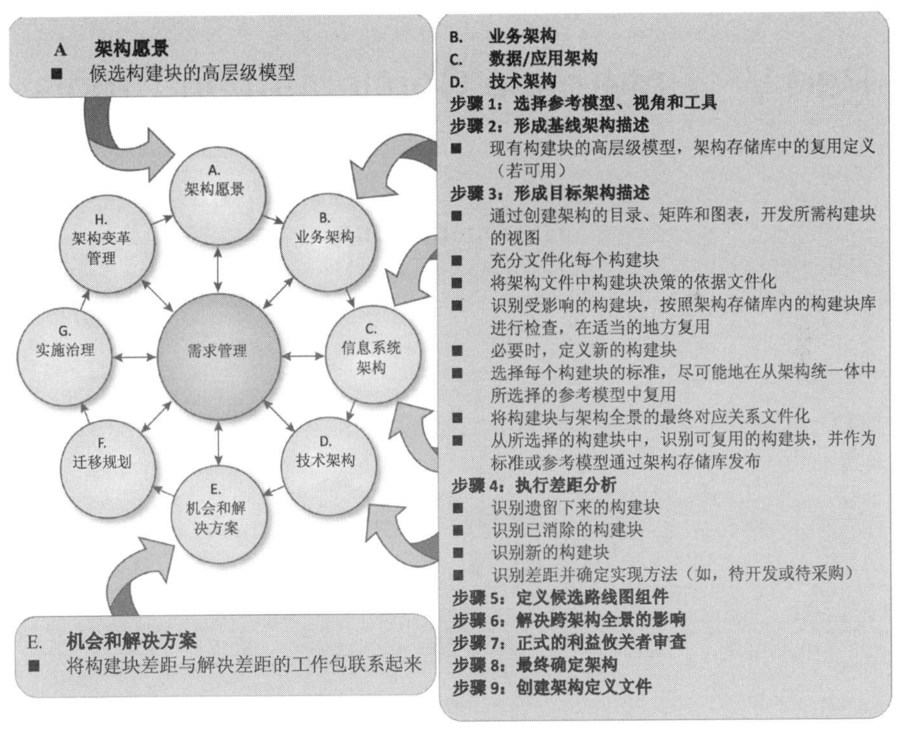

图 37-1 演进/规定构建块所处的 ADM 的关键阶段/步骤

TOGAF Version 9.1

Part V Enterprise Continuum and Tools

The Open Group

TOGAF 9.1 版本

第五部分　ENTERPRISE 的连续统一体和工具

The Open Group

Chapter 38
Introduction

This chapter provides an introduction to and an overview of the contents of Part V: Enterprise Continuum & Tools.

38.1 Introduction

It is usually impossible to create a single unified architecture that meets all requirements of all stakeholders for all time. Therefore, the enterprise architect will need to deal not just with a single enterprise architecture, but with many related enterprise architectures.

Each architecture will have a different purpose and architectures will relate to one another. Effectively bounding the scope of an architecture is therefore a critical success factor in allowing architects to break down a complex problem space into manageable components that can be individually addressed.

The Enterprise Continuum provides a view of the Architecture Repository that shows the evolution of these related architectures from generic to specific, from abstract to concrete, and from logical to physical.

This part of TOGAF discusses the Enterprise Continuum; including the Architecture Continuum and the Solutions Continuum. It describes how architectures can be partitioned and organized within a repository. It also describes tools for architecture development.

38.2 Structure of Part V

Part V: Enterprise Continuum & Tools is structured as follows:

- Introduction (this chapter).
- The Enterprise Continuum (see Chapter 39) describes a view of the Architecture Repository that provides methods for classifying architecture and solution artifacts, showing how the different types of artifact evolve, and how they can be leveraged and re-used.

第 38 章
引　言

本章提供“第五部分：ENTERPRISE 的连续统一体和工具”内容的简介和概述。

38.1　简介

创建一个永远满足所有利益攸关者所有需求的统一架构通常是不可能的。因此，ENTERPRISE 架构师需要处理的不只是某个单一 Enterprise Architecture，还需要处理多个关联的 Enterprise Architecture。

每个架构会具有不同的目的，且架构彼此相关联。因此，有效地限制架构的范围，是使得架构师能将复杂的问题空间分解成可单独应对的多个可管理部分的一个关键成功因素。

ENTERPRISE 的连续统一体提供一个架构库视图，它表明这些相关架构从一般到特定、从抽象到具体以及从逻辑到物理方面的演进。

本部分 TOGAF 论述 ENTERPRISE 的连续统一体；包括架构连续统一体和解决方案连续统一体。本部分 TOGAF 描述如何在存储库内划分和组织架构，还描述用于架构开发的各类工具。

38.2　第五部分的结构

“第五部分：ENTERPRISE 的连续统一体和工具”的结构如下：

- “简介”（本章）。
- “ENTERPRISE 的连续统一体”（见第 39 章）描述架构库的视图，该视图提供对架构和解决方案制品进行分类的方法，表明不同类型的制品如何演进及其如何被更好地利用和复用。

- Architecture Partitioning (see Chapter 40) describes the various characteristics that can be applied to classify and then partition architectures.
- The Architecture Repository (see Chapter 41) shows how the abstract classifications of architecture can be applied to a repository structure so that architectures can be organized and easily accessed.
- Tools for Architecture Development (see Chapter 42) provides guidelines on selecting a toolset to create and manage architectural artifacts.

- “架构划分”（见第 40 章）描述可用于对架构分类然后对架构进行划分的各种特征。
- “架构库”（见第 41 章）表明架构的抽象分类可以如何应用于存储库结构，以使架构可以被组织起来且易于访问。
- “架构开发工具”（见第 42 章）提供关于选择一套用于创建和管理各类架构制品的工具的指南。

Chapter 39
Enterprise Continuum

39.1 Overview

The Enterprise Continuum provides methods for classifying architecture and solution artifacts, both internal and external to the Architecture Repository, as they evolve from generic Foundation Architectures to Organization-Specific Architectures.

The Enterprise Continuum enables the architect to articulate the broad perspective of what, why, and how the enterprise architecture has been designed with the factors and drivers considered. The Enterprise Continuum is an important aid to communication and understanding, both within individual enterprises, and between customer enterprises and vendor organizations. Without an understanding of "where in the continuum you are", people discussing architecture can often talk at cross-purposes because they are referencing different points in the continuum at the same time, without realizing it.

Any architecture is context-specific; for example, there are architectures that are specific to individual customers, industries, subsystems, products, and services. Architects, on both the buy side and supply side, must have at their disposal a consistent language to effectively communicate the differences between architectures. Such a language will enable engineering efficiency and the effective leveraging of Commercial Off-The-Shelf (COTS) product functionality. The Enterprise Continuum provides that consistent language.

The Enterprise Continuum enables the organization of re-usable architecture artifacts and solution assets to maximize the enterprise architecture investment opportunities.

39.2 Enterprise Continuum and Architecture Re-Use

The simplest way of thinking of the Enterprise Continuum is as a view of the repository of all the architecture assets. It can contain architecture descriptions, models, building blocks, patterns, viewpoints, and other artifacts — that exist both within the enterprise and in the IT industry at large, which the enterprise considers to have available for the development of architectures for the enterprise.

Examples of internal architecture and solution artifacts are the deliverables of previous architecture work, which are available for re-use. Examples of external architecture and solution artifacts are the wide variety of industry reference models and architecture patterns that exist, and are continually emerging, including those that are highly generic (such as the TOGAF Technical Reference Model (TRM)); those specific to certain aspects of IT (such as a web services architecture, or a generic manageability architecture); those specific to certain types of information processing, such as e-Commerce, supply chain management, etc.; and those specific to certain vertical industries, such as the models generated by vertical consortia like TMF (in the Telecommunications sector), ARTS (Retail), Energistics (Petrotechnical), etc.

第 39 章 ENTERPRISE 的连续统一体

39.1 概述

ENTERPRISE 的连续统一体，提供对架构库内部和外部的架构制品和解决方案制品进行分类的方法，因为这些制品是从一般基础架构到组织特定架构演进而成的。

ENTERPRISE 的连续统一体，使架构师能够清楚地表达在考虑到一些因素和驱动因素的情况下设计了什么 Enterprise Architecture、为什么要设计以及如何设计等方面的广泛观点。ENTERPRISE 的连续统一体，是个别 ENTERPRISE 内以及在客户 ENTERPRISE 和供应商组织之间一个重要的沟通和理解辅助手段。如果不理解“你在连续统一体中的位置”，讨论架构的人员通常会在谈话时存在观点分歧，因为他们在同一时间引用的是连续统一体中的不同点，而且并未意识到。

任何架构都有特定的背景环境；例如，特定于个别客户、行业、子系统、产品和服务的架构。买方和供应方的架构师必须自主决定使用一致的语言有效地沟通架构之间的差异。这样的语言能够确保工程效率并更好地有效利用商用货架（COTS）产品的功能性。ENTERPRISE 的连续统一体提供这种一致的语言。

ENTERPRISE 的连续统一体，使具有各类可复用架构制品和解决方案资产的组织能够使 Enterprise Architecture 的投资机会最大化。

39.2 ENTERPRISE 的连续统一体和架构复用

考虑 ENTERPRISE 的连续统一体的最简单方式是，将其作为所有架构资产的存储库的视图。它可包含整体上在 ENTERPRISE 内和 IT 行业中同时存在的架构描述、模型、构建块、特征模式、视角和其他制品，ENTERPRISE 认为它们可用于开发 ENTERPRISE 的架构。

内部架构制品和解决方案制品的示例是之前架构工作的交付物，可以加以复用。外部架构制品和解决方案制品的示例是现有的和正在不断兴起的各种各样的行业参考模型和架构特征模式，包括高度通用的模型（如 TOGAF 技术参考模型，TRM）；特定于 IT 某些方面的架构（如网络服务架构，或一般可管理性架构）；特定于某些类型的信息处理的模型，如电子商务、供应链管理等；以及特定于某些垂直行业的模型，诸如 TMF（电信部门）、ARTS（零售）、能源（石油技术）等垂直联合体产生的模型。

The enterprise architecture determines which architecture and solution artifacts an organization includes in its Architecture Repository. Re-use is a major consideration in this decision.

39.3 Constituents of the Enterprise Continuum

An overview of the context and constituents of the Enterprise Continuum is shown in Figure 39-1.

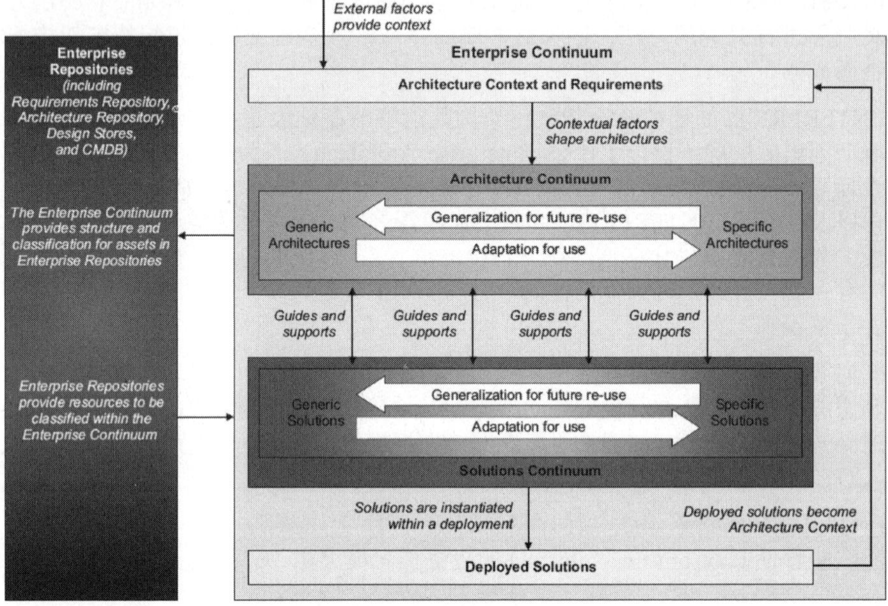

Figure 39-1 Enterprise Continuum

The Enterprise Continuum is partitioned into three distinct continue as follows:

- The **Enterprise Continuum** (see Section 39.4) is the outermost continuum and classifies assets related to the context of the overall enterprise architecture. The Enterprise Continuum classes of assets may influence architectures, but are not directly used during the ADM architecture development. The Enterprise Continuum classifies contextual assets used to develop architectures, such as policies, standards, strategic initiatives, organizational structures, and enterprise-level capabilities. The Enterprise Continuum can also classify solutions (as opposed to descriptions or specifications of solutions). Finally, the Enterprise Continuum contains two specializations, namely the Architecture and Solutions Continua.

Enterprise Architecture 决定一个组织在其架构库中包括哪些架构制品和解决方案制品。复用是这一决定中主要的考量因素。

39.3 ENTERPRISE 的连续统一体的构成要素

ENTERPRISE 的连续统一体的背景环境和构成要素的概述如图 39-1 所示。

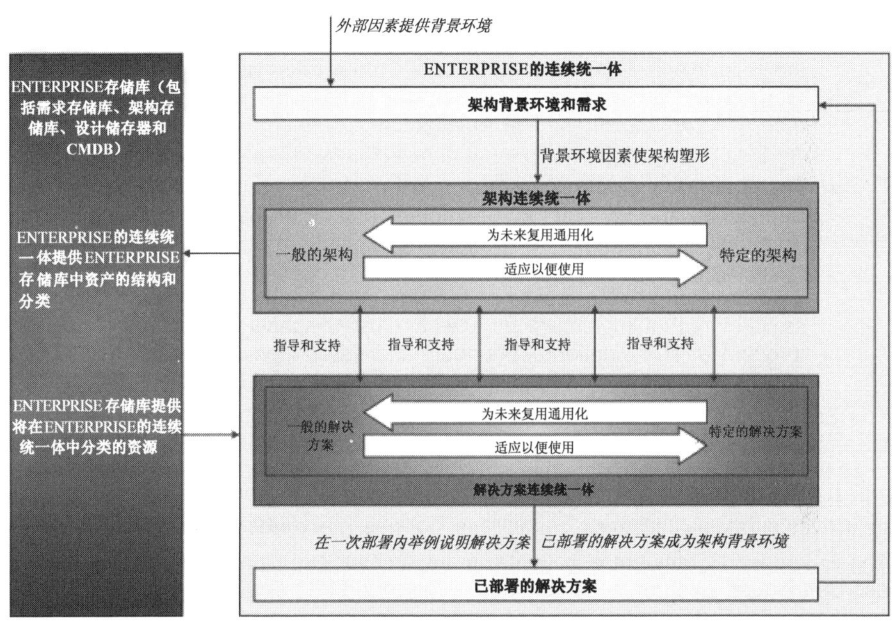

图 39-1　ENTERPRISE 的连续统一体

ENTERPRISE 的连续统一体被划分成如下三个截然不同的连续统一体：

- ENTERPRISE 的连续统一体（见 39.4 节）是最外层的连续统一体，并对与总体 Enterprise Architecture 的背景环境相关的资产进行分类。ENTERPRISE 的连续统一体的资产类别可影响架构，但在 ADM 架构开发期间不直接使用。ENTERPRISE 的连续统一体对用于开发架构的背景环境资产进行分类，如方针、标准、战略举措、组织结构和 ENTERPRISE 层级的能力。ENTERPRISE 的连续统一体还可对解决方案进行分类（而不是对解决方案的描述或规范进行分类）。最后，ENTERPRISE 的连续统一体包含两个专门领域，即架构连续统一体和解决方案连续统一体。

- The **Architecture Continuum** (see Section 39.4.1) offers a consistent way to define and understand the generic rules, representations, and relationshipps in an architecture, including traceability and derivation relationships (e.g., to show that an Organization-Specific Architecture is based on an industry or generic standard). The Architecture Continuum represents a structuring of Architecture Building Blocks (ABBs) which are re-usable architecture assets. ABBs evolve through their development lifecycle from abstract and generic entities to fully expressed Organization-Specific Architecture assets. The Architecture Continuum assets will be used to guide and select the elements in the Solutions Continuum (see below). The Architecture Continuum shows the relationships among foundational frameworks (such as TOGAF), common system architectures (such as the III-RM), industry architectures, and enterprise architectures. The Architecture Continuum is a useful tool to discover commonality and eliminate unnecessary redundancy.
- The **Solutions Continuum** (see Section 39.4.2) provides a consistent way to describe and understand the implementation of the assets defined in the Architecture Continuum. The Solutions Continuum defines what is available in the organizational environment as re-usable Solution Building Blocks (SBBs). The solutions are the results of agreements between customers and business partners that implement the rules and relationships defined in the architecture space. The Solutions Continuum addresses the commonalities and differences among the products, systems, and services of implemented systems.

The Enterprise Continuum classifies architecture assets that are applicable across the entire scope of the enterprise architecture. These assets, which may be referred to as building blocks, can represent a variety of elements that collectively define and constrain the enterprise architecture. They can take the form of business goals and objectives, strategic initiatives, capabilities, policies, standards, and principles.

The Enterprise Continuum also contains the Architecture Continuum and the Solutions Continuum. Each of these continua is described in greater detail in the following sections.

39.4 Enterprise Continuum in Detail

The Enterprise Continuum is intended to represent the classification of all assets that are available to an enterprise. It classifies assets that exist within the enterprise along with other assets in the wider environment that are relevant to the enterprise, such as products, research, market factors, commercial factors, business strategies, and legislation.

TOGAF is intended to be a framework for conducting enterprise architecture and as a result many of the assets that reside within the Enterprise Continuum are beyond the specific consideration of the TOGAF framework. However, architectures are fundamentally shaped by concerns outside the practice of architecture and it is therefore of paramount importance that any architecture must accurately reflect external context.

The specific contextual factors to be identified and incorporated in an architecture will vary from architecture to architecture. However, typical contextual factors for architecture development are likely to include:

- External influencing factors, such as regulatory change, technological advances, and competitor activity.
- Business strategy and context, including mergers, acquisitions, and other business transformation requirements.

- 架构连续统一体（见 39.4.1 节）提供一致的方式来定义和理解架构中的一般规则、表达方式和关系，包括可追溯性和衍生关系（如，表明组织特定架构是以行业标准或通用标准为基础的）。架构连续统一体代表架构构建块（ABB）的结构化，架构构建块是可复用的架构资产。ABB 在其整个开发生命周期中从抽象和一般的实体演进为完整表达的组织特定的架构资产。架构连续统一体资产将用于指导和选择解决方案连续统一体中的元素（见下文）。架构连续统一体表明基本框架（如 TOGAF）、公共系统架构（如 III-RM）、行业架构和 Enterprise Architecture 之间的关系。架构连续统一体是发现通用性并消除不必要冗余的有用工具。
- 解决方案连续统一体（见 39.4.2 节）提供一致的方式来描述和理解架构连续统一体中所定义的资产的实施过程。解决方案连续统一体定义在组织环境中什么可作为可复用的解决方案构建块（SBB）。解决方案是实施架构空间中所定义的规则和关系的客户与业务合作伙伴之间的协议的结果。解决方案连续统一体涉及所实施系统的产品、系统和服务之间的通用性和差异。

ENTERPRISE 的连续统一体对可贯穿 Enterprise Architecture 整个范围适用的架构资产进行分类。这些资产可能被称为构建块，可代表共同定义和约束 Enterprise Architecture 的各种元素。它们可采取业务目标和目的、战略举措、能力、方针、标准和原则的形式。

ENTERPRISE 的连续统一体还包含架构连续统一体和解决方案连续统一体。下面几节非常详细地描述了每个连续统一体。

39.4 详细的 ENTERPRISE 的连续统一体

ENTERPRISE 的连续统一体旨在表达可供 ENTERPRISE 使用的所有资产的分类。它对 ENTERPRISE 内存在的资产连同更广泛环境中的与 ENTERPRISE 相关的其他资产进行分类，如产品、研究、市场因素、商业因素、业务战略和法律。

TOGAF 旨在用作进行 Enterprise Architecture 的框架，因此，ENTERPRISE 的连续统一体内存在的多种资产都不在 TOGAF 框架的特定考量因素之内。然而，架构基本上是由架构实践以外的关注点所塑形的，因此，任何架构必须准确地反映出外部背景环境，这一点是至关重要的。

在架构中待识别和合并的特定背景环境因素在架构和架构之间会有所不同。然而，架构开发的典型背景环境因素可能包括：

- 外部影响因素，如法规变更、技术进步和竞争活动。
- 业务战略和背景环境，包括合并、采办和其他业务转型需求。

- Current business operations, reflecting deployed architectures and solutions

By observing the context for architecture, it can be seen that architecture development activity exists within a wider enterprise lifecycle of continuous change.

ABBs are defined in relation to a set of contextual factors and then realized through SBBs. SBBs are deployed as live solutions and become a part of the baseline operating model of the enterprise. The operating model of the enterprise and empiric information on the performance of the enterprise shapes the context and requirements for future change. Finally, these new requirements for change create a feedback-loop to influence the creation of new Target Architectures.

39.4.1 Architecture Continuum

The Architecture Continuum illustrates how architectures are developed and evolved across a continuum ranging from Foundation Architectures, such as the one provided by TOGAF, through Common Systems Architectures, and Industry Architectures, and to an enterprise's own Organization-Specific Architectures.

The arrows in the Architecture Continuum represent the relationship that exists between the different architectures in the Architecture Continuum. The leftwards direction focuses on meeting enterprise needs and business requirements, while the rightwards direction focuses on leveraging architectural components and building blocks.

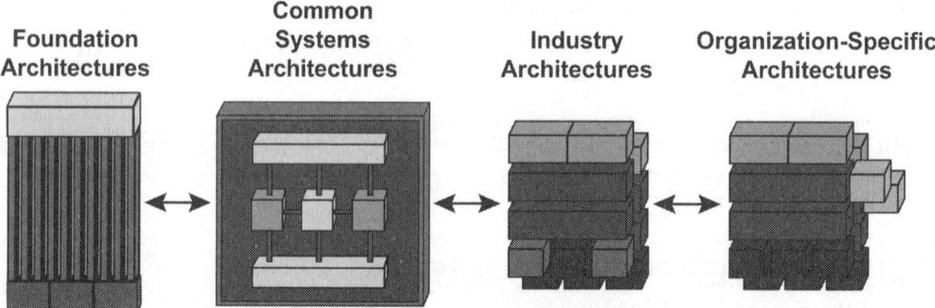

Figure 39-2 Architecture Continuum

The enterprise needs and business requirements are addressed in increasing detail from left to right. The architect will typically look to find re-usable architectural elements toward the left of the continuum. When elements are not found, the requirements for the missing elements are passed to the left of the continuum for incorporation. Those implementing architectures within their own organizations can use the same continuum models specialized for their business.

The four particular architecture types illustrated in Figure 39-2 are intended to indicate the range of different types of architecture that may be developed at different points in the continuum; they are not fixed stages in a process.

Many different types of architecture may occur at points in between those illustrated in Figure 39-2. Although the evolutionary transformation continuum illustrated does not represent a formal process, it does represent a progression, which occurs at several levels:

- 当前业务运作，反映已部署的架构和解决方案

通过观察架构的背景环境，可以看出架构开发活动存在于持续变更的、更广泛的 ENTERPRISE 生命周期之内。

ABB 相对于一系列背景环境因素而被定义，然后通过 SBB 实现。SBB 作为正在使用的解决方案而被部署，并成为 ENTERPRISE 的基线运行模型的一部分。ENTERPRISE 的运行模型和 ENTERPRISE 绩效方面的经验信息形成将来变更的背景环境和需求。最后，这些新的变更需求创建一个反馈环路，以影响新的目标架构的创建。

39.4.1 架构连续统一体

架构连续统一体阐明如何贯穿连续统一体从基础架构（如 TOGAF 提供的基础架构）经过公共系统架构和行业架构再到 ENTERPRISE 自己的组织特定架构对各类架构进行开发和演进。

架构连续统一体中的箭头代表架构连续统一体中不同架构之间存在的关系。向左方向聚焦于满足 ENTERPRISE 需要和业务需求，而向右方向聚集于更好地利用架构组件和构建块。

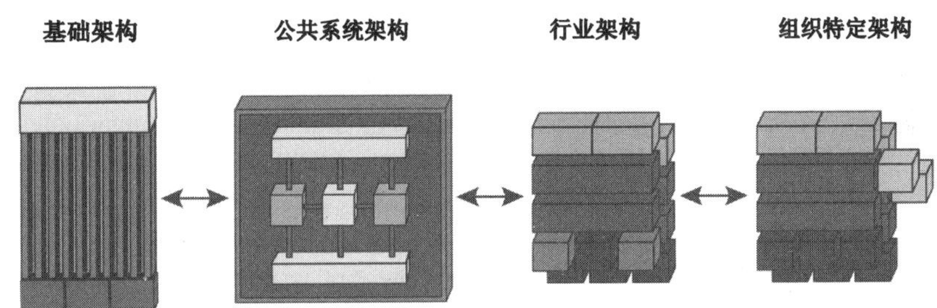

图 39-2 架构 连续统一体

ENTERPRISE 需要和业务需求从左到右越来越详细。架构师通常期待在连续统一体的左侧找到可复用的架构元素。当未找到元素时，对缺失元素的需求转到连续统一体的左侧，以便纳入这些需求。他们自己组织内的那些实施架构可使用其业务专用的相同的连续统一体模型。

图 39-2 中所阐明的四种特定架构类型，旨在指明可在连续统一体的不同点开发的不同类型架构的范围；它们不是一个流程中的固定阶段。

许多不同类型的架构可能在图 39-2 中所阐明的那些架构类型之间的点上出现。虽然所阐明的演进式转换连续统一体不代表正式的流程，但它确实代表几个层级上发生的演变：

- Logical to physical
- Horizontal (IT-focused) to vertical (business-focused)
- Generalization to specialization
- Taxonomy to complete and specific architecture specification

At each point in the continuum, an architecture is designed in terms of the design concepts and building blocks available and relevant to that point.

The four architectures illustrated in Figure 39-2 represent main classifications of potential architectures, and will be relevant and familiar to many architects. They are analyzed in detail below.

Foundation Architecture

A Foundation Architecture consists of generic components, inter-relationships, principles, and guidelines that provide a foundation on which more specific architectures can be built. The TOGAF ADM is a process that would support specialization of such Foundation Architectures in order to create organization-specific models.

The TOGAF TRM describes a fundamental architecture upon which other, more specific architectures can be based. See Chapter 43 for more details.

Common Systems Architectures

Common Systems Architectures guide the selection and integration of specific services from the Foundation Architecture to create an architecture useful for building common (i.e., highly re-usable) solutions across a wide number of relevant domains.

Examples of Common Systems Architectures include: a security architecture, a management architecture, a network architecture, an operations architecture, etc. Each is incomplete in terms of overall system functionality, but is complete in terms of a particular problem domain (security, manageability, networking, operations, etc.), so that solutions implementing the architecture constitute re-usable building blocks for the creation of functionally complete operating states of the enterprise.

Other characteristics of Common Systems Architectures include:

- Reflects requirements specific to a generic problem domain
- Defines building blocks specific to a generic problem domain
- Defines business, data, application, or technology standards for implementing these building blocks
- Provides building blocks for easy re-use and lower costs

The TOGAF Integrated Information Infrastructure Reference Model (III-RM) — see Part VI, Chapter 44 — is a reference model that supports describing Common Systems Architecture in the Application Domain that focuses on the requirements, building blocks, and standards relating to the vision of Boundaryless Information Flow.

- 逻辑到物理
- 水平（聚焦于 IT）到垂直（聚焦于业务）
- 一般化到特定化
- 从分类法到完整的和特定的架构规范

在连续统一体的每个点上，按照在该点可用且与该点相关的设计概念和构建块来设计架构。

图 39-2 中所阐明的四种架构代表潜在架构的主要分类，并会与多个架构师有关且为其所熟悉。下面详细地分析了这四种架构。

基础架构

基础架构由一般组件、相互关系、原则和指南组成，这些组成部分提供了可构建更多特定架构的基础。TOGAF ADM 是一种为了创建组织特定的模型而支持此类基础架构专业化的流程。

TOGAF TRM 描述其他更特定的架构可依据的基础性架构。更多细节见第 43 章。

公共系统架构

公共系统架构指导从基础架构中选择和综合特定服务，以便创建一个用于跨大量相关域构建公共（即，高度可复用的）解决方案的架构。

公共系统架构的示例包括：安保架构、管理架构、网络架构、运行架构等。按照总体系统功能性，每个架构都是不完整的，但按照某一特定的问题域（安保性、可管理性、网络、运行等），每个架构都是完整的，以便使实施架构的解决方案构成可复用的构建块，用于创建功能完整的 ENTERPRISE 运行状态。

公共系统架构的其他特征包括：

- 反映特定于一般问题域的需求
- 定义特定于一般问题域的构建块
- 定义实施这些构建块的业务、数据、应用或技术标准
- 提供复用方便且成本较低的构建块

TOGAF 集成信息基础设施参考模型（III-RM）——见第六部分第 44 章——是一种支持在应用域中描述公共系统架构的参考模型，它聚焦于与无边界信息流的愿景相关的需求、构建块和标准。

Industry Architectures

Industry Architectures guide the integration of common systems components with industry-specific components, and guide the creation of industry solutions for targeted customer problems within a particular industry.

A typical example of an industry-specific component is a data model representing the business functions and processes specific to a particular vertical industry, such as the Retail industry's "Active Store" architecture, or an Industry Architecture that incorporates the Energistics Data Model (refer to www.energistics.org).

Other characteristics of Industry Architectures include:

- Reflects requirements and standards specific to a vertical industry
- Defines building blocks specific to a generic problem domain
- Contains industry-specific logical data and process models
- Contains industry-specific applications and process models, as well as industry-specific business rules
- Provides guidelines for testing collections of systems
- Encourages levels of interoperability throughout the industry

Organization-Specific Architectures

Organization-Specific Architectures describe and guide the final deployment of solution components for a particular enterprise or extended network of connected enterprises.

There may be a variety of Organization-Specific Architectures that are needed to effectively cover the organization's requirements by defining the architectures in increasing levels of detail. Alternatively, this might result in several more detailed Organization-Specific Architectures for specific entities within the global enterprise. Breaking down Organization-Specific Architectures into constituent pieces is addressed in Chapter 40.

The Organization-Specific Architecture guides the final customization of the solution, and has the following characteristics:

- Provides a means to communicate and manage business operations across all four architectural domains
- Reflects requirements specific to a particular enterprise
- Defines building blocks specific to a particular enterprise
- Contains organization-specific business models, data, applications, and technologies
- Provides a means to encourage implementation of appropriate solutions to meet business needs
- Provides the criteria to measure and select appropriate products, solutions, and services
- Provides an evolutionary path to support growth and new business needs

行业架构

行业架构指导公共系统组件与行业特定组件的综合，并指导在某一特定行业内创建针对目标客户问题的行业解决方案。

行业特定组件的一个典型示例是数据模型，其表达特定于某一特殊垂直行业的业务功能和流程，如零售行业的“主动式存储”架构或包含能源数据模型的行业架构（见 www.energistics.org）。

行业架构的其他特征包括：

- 反映特定于垂直行业的需求和标准
- 定义特定于一般问题领域的构建块
- 包含行业特定的逻辑数据和流程模型
- 包含行业特定的应用和流程模型，以及行业特定的业务规则
- 提供测试系统集合的指南
- 鼓励整个行业内的互用性层级

组织特定的架构

组织特定的架构描述和指导针对某一特定 ENTERPRISE 或相关 ENTERPRISE 的扩展网络的解决方案组件的最终部署。

通过在越来越详细的层面定义架构，可能需要各种组织特定的架构来有效地涵盖组织需求。或者，这可导致在全球 ENTERPRISE 内产生特定实体的多个更详细的组织特定架构。第 40 章涉及将组织特定架构分解成多个构成部分。

组织特定的架构指导解决方案的最终定制，并具有下列特征：

- 提供一种跨所有四种架构域沟通和管理业务运行的手段
- 反映特定于某一特殊 ENTERPRISE 的需求
- 定义特定于某一特殊 ENTERPRISE 的构建块
- 包含组织特定的业务模型、数据、应用和技术
- 提供一种鼓励实施适当的解决方案的手段以满足业务需要
- 提供衡量和选择适当的产品、解决方案和服务的准则
- 提供一种支持增长的业务需要和新的业务需要的演进式途径

39.4.2 Solutions Continuum

The Solutions Continuum represents the detailed specification and construction of the architectures at the corresponding levels of the Architecture Continuum. At each level, the Solutions Continuum is a population of the architecture with reference building blocks — either purchased products or built components — that represent a solution to the enterprise's business need expressed at that level. A populated repository based on the Solutions Continuum can be regarded as a solutions inventory or re-use library, which can add significant value to the task of managing and implementing improvements to the enterprise.

The Solutions Continuum is illustrated in Figure 39-3.

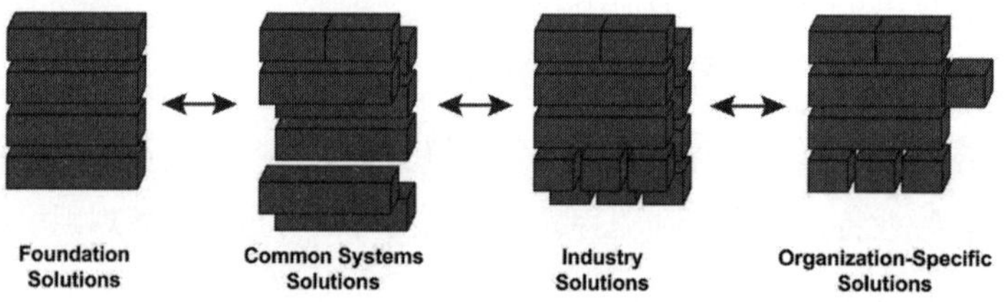

Figure 39-3 Solutions Continuum

"Moving to the right" on the Solutions Continuum is focused on providing solutions value (i.e., foundation solutions provide value in creating common systems solutions; common systems solutions are used to create industry solutions; and industry solutions are used to create organization-specific solutions). "Moving to the left" on the Solutions Continuum is focused on addressing enterprise needs.

These two viewpoints are significant for a company attempting to focus on its needs while maximizing the use of available resources through leverage.

The following subsections describe each of the solution types within the Solutions Continuum.

Foundation Solutions

Foundation Solutions are highly generic concepts, tools, products, services, and solution components that are the fundamental providers of capabilities. Services include professional services — such as training and consulting services — that ensure the maximum investment value from solutions in the shortest possible time; and support services — such as Help Desk — that ensure the maximum possible value from solutions (services that ensure timely updates and upgrades to the products and systems).

Example Foundation Solutions would include programming languages, operating systems, foundational data structures (such as EDIFACT), generic approaches to organization structuring, foundational structures for organizing IT operations (such as ITIL), etc.

39.4.2 解决方案连续统一体

解决方案连续统一体，代表架构连续统一体对应层级上的架构的详细规范和结构。在每个层级，解决方案连续统一体是具有参考构建块（采购的产品或构建的组件）的架构群——代表在该层级上所表达的 ENTERPRISE 业务需要的解决方案。基于解决方案连续统一体的已充实存储库可以被视为解决方案存储清单或复用库，其可为管理和实施 ENTERPRISE 改进措施的任务增加重要的价值。

图 39-3 阐明解决方案连续统一体。

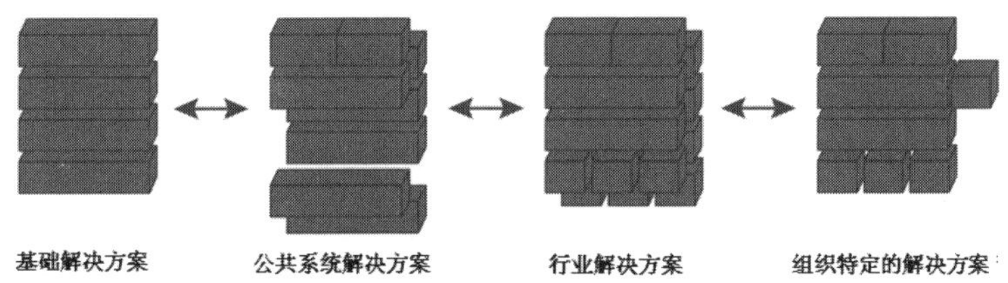

图 39-3 解决方案连续统一体

在解决方案连续统一体上，“向右移动”聚焦于提供解决方案价值（即，基础解决方案提供创建公共系统解决方案的价值；公共系统解决方案用于创建行业解决方案；行业解决方案用于创建组织特定的解决方案）。在解决方案连续统一体上，“向左移动”聚焦于应对 ENTERPRISE 需要。

对于试图聚焦其需要同时通过更好地发挥作用以最大程度使用可用资源的公司而言，这两个视角非常重要。

下列小节描述了解决方案连续统一体内的每个解决方案类型。

基础解决方案

基础解决方案是高度通用的作为能力基本提供者的概念、工具、产品、服务和解决方案组件。服务包括确保在可能的最短时间内从解决方案中获得最大投资价值的专业服务，如培训和咨询服务；并且支持确保从解决方案中获得可能的最大价值的服务（确保对产品和系统及时更新并升级的服务），如服务台。

基础解决方案的示例将包括编程语言、操作系统、基础数据结构（如 EDIFACT）、组织结构化的一般途径、组织 IT 运行的基本结构（如 ITIL）等。

Common Systems Solutions

A Common Systems Solution is an implementation of a Common Systems Architecture comprised of a set of products and services, which may be certified or branded. It represents the highest common denominator for one or more solutions in the industry segments that the Common Systems Solution supports.

Common Systems Solutions represent collections of common requirements and capabilities, rather than those specific to a particular customer or industry. Common Systems Solutions provide organizations with operating environments specific to operational and informational needs, such as high availability transaction processing and scalable data warehousing systems. Examples of Common Systems Solutions include: an enterprise management system product or a security system product.

Computer systems vendors are the typical providers of technology-centric Common Systems Solutions. "Software as a service" vendors are typical providers of common application solutions. Business process outsourcing vendors are typical provides of business capability-centric Common Systems Solutions.

Industry Solutions

An Industry Solution is an implementation of an Industry Architecture, which provides re-usable packages of common components and services specific to an industry.

Fundamental components are provided by Common Systems Solutions and/or Foundation Solutions, and are augmented with industry-specific components. Examples include: a physical database schema or an industry-specific point-of-service device.

Industry Solutions are industry-specific, aggregate procurements that are ready to be tailored to an individual organization's requirements.

In some cases an industry solution may include not only an implementation of the Industry Architecture, but also other solution elements, such as specific products, services, and systems solutions that are appropriate to that industry.

Organization-Specific Solutions

An Organization-Specific Solution is an implementation of the Organization-Specific Architecture that provides the required business functions. Because solutions are designed for specific business operations, they contain the highest amount of unique content in order to accommodate the varying people and processes of specific organizations.

Building Organization-Specific Solutions on Industry Solutions, Common Systems Solutions, and Foundation Solutions is the primary purpose of connecting the Architecture Continuum to the Solutions Continuum, as guided by the architects within an enterprise.

An Organization-Specific Solution will be structured in order to support specific Service Level Agreements (SLAs) to ensure support of the operational systems at desired service levels. For example, a third-party application hosting provider may offer different levels of support for operational systems. These agreements would define the terms and conditions of that support.

Other key factors to be defined within an Organization-Specific Solution are the key operating parameters and quality metrics that can be used to monitor and manage the environment.

The Enterprise Continuum can provide a key link between architecture, development, and operations personnel by allowing them to communicate and reach agreement on anticipated operational support requirements. Operations personnel can in turn access the Enterprise Continuum to obtain information regarding the operation concepts and service support requirements of the deployed system.

公共系统解决方案

公共系统解决方案是公共系统架构的实施方式，包括可能被认证或有品牌的一系列产品和服务。它代表公共系统解决方案所支持的行业部门中的一个或多个解决方案的最大共同之处。

公共系统解决方案代表公共需求和能力的集合，而不是特定于某一特殊客户或行业的那些需求和能力。公共系统解决方案向组织提供特定于运行需要和信息需要的操作环境，如高可用性事务处理系统和可升级数据存储系统。公共系统解决方案的示例包括：ENTERPRISE 管理系统产品或安保系统产品。

计算机系统厂商是以技术为中心的公共系统解决方案的典型提供者。“作为服务的软件”的厂商是公共应用解决方案的典型供应者。业务流程外包厂商是以业务能力为中心的公共系统解决方案的典型提供者。

行业解决方案

行业解决方案是行业架构的实施，提供特定于某一行业的公共组件和服务的可复用包。

基本组件由公共系统解决方案和/或基本解决方案提供，并增加行业特定的组件。示例包括：物理数据库模式或行业特定的服务点装置。

行业解决方案是行业特定的总采购方式，可以针对个别组织的需求而进行剪裁。

在某些情况下，行业解决方案可能不仅包括行业架构的实施，而且还包括其他解决方案元素，如适合该行业的特定产品、服务和系统解决方案。

组织特定的解决方案

组织特定的解决方案是组织特定的架构的实施，提供所需的业务功能。由于解决方案设计用于特定的业务运行，因此它们包含最大数量的独特内容，以便适应特定组织不断变化的人员和流程。

在 ENTERPRISE 内架构师的指导下，在行业解决方案、公共系统解决方案和基础解决方案上构建组织特定的解决方案，是将架构连续统一体与解决方案连续统一体联系起来的主要目的。

将组织特定的解决方案结构化，以便支持特定服务水平协议（SLA），以确保在期望的服务水平上支持运行系统。例如，第三方应用托管提供者可提供对运行系统的不同层级的支持。这些协议将定义该支持的条款和条件。

在组织特定的解决方案内，待定义的其他关键因素是可用于监控和管理环境的关键运行参数和质量衡量标准。

ENTERPRISE 的连续统一体通过使得架构、开发和运行人员能在预期的运行支持需求方面进行沟通并达成共识，从而在他们之间提供一个关键的连接。反过来，运行人员可使用 ENTERPRISE 的连续统一体来获得关于已部署系统的运行概念和服务支持需求方面的信息。

39.5 The Enterprise Continuum and the ADM

The TOGAF ADM describes the process of developing an enterprise-specific architecture and an enterprise-specific solution(s) which conform to that architecture by adopting and adapting (where appropriate) generic architectures and solutions (left to right in the continuum classification). In a similar fashion, specific architectures and solutions that prove to be credible and effective will be generalized for re-use (right to left in the continuum classification).

At relevant places throughout the TOGAF ADM, there are pointers to useful architecture assets at the relevant level of generality in the continuum classification. In some cases — for example, in the development of a Technology Architecture — this may be the TOGAF TRM Foundation Architecture (see below). In other cases — for example, in the development of a Business Architecture — it may be a reference model for e-Commerce taken from the industry at large.

TOGAF itself provides two reference models for consideration for use in developing an organization's architecture:

1. The **TOGAF Foundation Architecture**, which comprises a TRM of generic services and functions that provides a firm foundation on which more specific architectures and architectural components can be built.
2. The **Integrated Information Infrastructure Reference Model** (III-RM), which is based on the TOGAF Foundation Architecture, and is specifically designed to help the realization of architectures that enable and support the vision of Boundaryless Information Flow.

However, in developing architectures in the various domains within an overall enterprise architecture, the architect will need to consider the use and re-use of a wide variety of different architecture assets, and the Enterprise Continuum provides an approach for categorizing and communicating these different assets.

39.6 The Enterprise Continuum and Your Organization

The preceding sections have described the Enterprise Continuum, the Architecture Continuum, and the Solutions Continuum. The following sections describe the relationships between each of the three continua and how these relationships should be applied within your organization.

39.6.1 Relationships

Each of the three continua contains information about the evolution of the architectures during their lifecycle:

- The Enterprise Continuum provides an overall context for architectures and solutions and classifies assets that apply across the entire scope of the enterprise.
- The Architecture Continuum provides a classification mechanism for assets that collectively define the architecture at different levels of evolution from generic to specific.
- The Solutions Continuum provides the classification for assets to describe specific solutions for the organization that can be implemented to achieve the intent of the architecture.

The relationships between the Architecture Continuum and Solutions Continuum are shown in Figure 39-4.

39.5 ENTERPRISE 的连续统一体和 ADM

TOGAF ADM 描述了开发 ENTERPRISE 特定架构和 ENTERPRISE 特定解决方案的流程，ENTERPRISE 特定架构和 ENTERPRISE 特定解决方案通过采用和调整（若合适）一般架构和解决方案（在连续统一体分类中从左到右）以符合该架构。以类似的方式，对已证明可信且有效的特定架构和解决方案进行归纳，以便复用（在连续统一体分类中从右到左）。

在整个 TOGAF ADM 的相关位置，对连续统一体分类的相关一般性层级上的有用架构资产提供了一些建议。在某些情况下——例如，在技术架构的开发过程中——可能是 TOGAF TRM 基础架构（见下文）。在其他情况下——例如，在业务架构的开发过程中——可能是用于整个行业内的电子商务参考模型。

TOGAF 本身提供了两个参考模型，以供考虑用于开发组织的架构：

1. **TOGAF 基础架构**，包括通用服务和功能的 TRM，提供了可构建更多特定的架构和架构组件所依据的坚实基础。

2. **集成信息基础设施参考模型**（III-RM），其基于 TOGAF 基础架构，专门设计用于帮助实现启动和支持无边界信息流愿景的架构。

然而，在开发总体 Enterprise Architecture 内各种域的架构的过程中，架构师会需要考虑各种不同架构资产的使用和复用，且 ENTERPRISE 的连续统一体提供分类和沟通这些不同资产的实施途径。

39.6 ENTERPRISE 的连续统一体和你的组织

前面几节已经描述了 ENTERPRISE 的连续统一体、架构连续统一体和解决方案连续统一体。下列几节描述每个连续统一体之间的关系以及应如何在你的组织内应用这些关系。

39.6.1 关系

三个连续统一体分别包含有关在其生命周期内进行架构演进的信息：

- ENTERPRISE 的连续统一体，提供架构和解决方案的总体背景环境，并对贯穿 ENTERPRISE 整个范围应用的资产进行分类。

- 架构连续统一体提供资产的分类机制，这些资产共同定义了从一般到特定的不同演进层级的架构。

- 解决方案连续统一体提供资产分类，以描述组织的特定解决方案，这些解决方案可被实施以达成架构意图。

架构连续统一体和解决方案连续统一体之间的关系如图 39-4 所示。

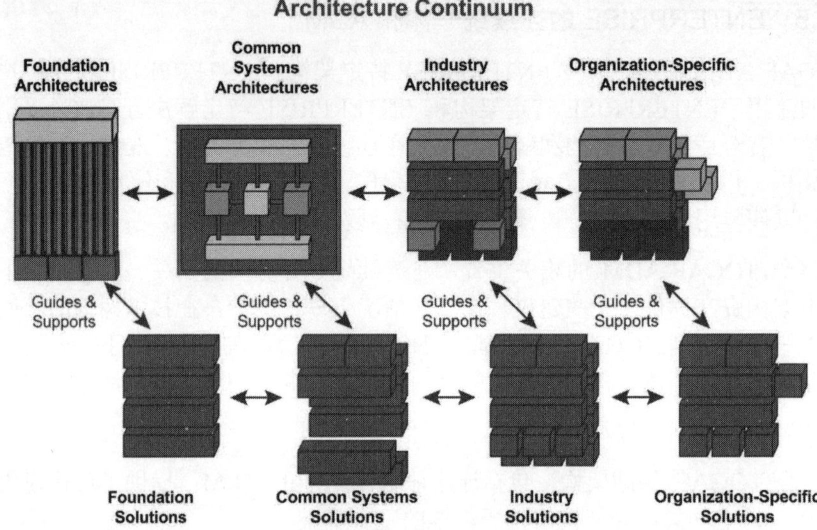

Figure 39-4 Relationships between Architecture and Solutions Continua

The relationship between the Architecture Continuum and the Solutions Continuum is one of guidance, direction, and support. For example, Foundation Architectures guide the creation or selection of Foundation Solutions. Foundation Solutions support the Foundation Architecture by helping to realize the architecture defined in the Architecture Continuum. The Foundation Architecture also guides development of Foundation Solutions, by providing architectural direction, requirements and principles that guide selection, and realization of appropriate solutions. A similar relationship exists between the other elements of the Enterprise Continuum.

The Enterprise Continuum presents mechanisms to help improve productivity through leverage. The Architecture Continuum offers a consistent way to understand the different architectures and their components. The Solutions Continuum offers a consistent way to understand the different products, systems, services, and solutions required.

The Enterprise Continuum should not be interpreted as representing strictly chained relationships. Organization-Specific Architectures could have components from a Common Systems Architecture, and Organization-Specific Solutions could contain Foundation Solutions. The relationships depicted in Figure 39-1 are an illustration showing opportunities for leveraging architecture and solution components.

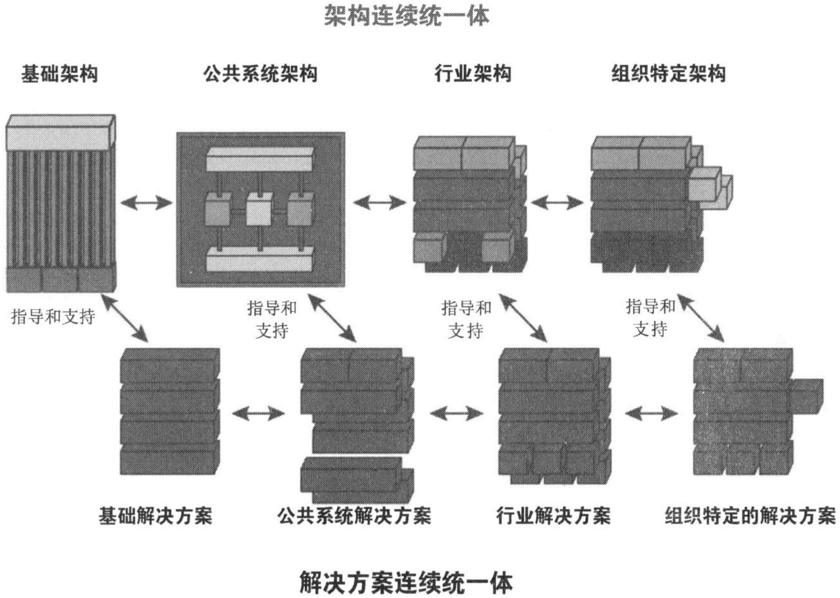

图 39-4　架构连续统一体和解决方案连续统一体之间的关系

架构连续统一体和解决方案连续统一体之间的关系是指导、引导和支持之一。例如，基础架构指导基础解决方案的创建或选择。基础解决方案通过帮助实现在架构连续统一体中所定义的架构来支持基础架构。基础架构还通过提供用于指导适当解决方案的选择和实现的架构方向、需求和原则来指导基础解决方案的开发。ENTERPRISE 的连续统一体的其他元素之间存在类似关系。

ENTERPRISE 的连续统一体表达通过更好地发挥作用来帮助提高生产率的机制。架构连续统一体提供了理解不同架构及其组件的一致的方式。解决方案连续统一体提供了理解所需不同产品、系统、服务和解决方案的一致的方式。

ENTERPRISE 的连续统一体不应被解释为代表严格链接的关系。组织特定架构可具有公共系统架构中的组件，组织特定解决方案可包含基础解决方案。图 39-1 所描述的关系是一个表明更好地利用架构和解决方案组件的机会的图解说明。

39.6.2 Your Enterprise

TOGAF provides a method for you to "architect" the systems in your enterprise. Your architecture organization will have to deal with each type of architecture described above. For example, it is recommended that you have your own Foundation Architecture that governs all of your systems. You should also have your own Common Systems Architectures that govern major shared systems — such as the networking system or management system. You may have your own industry-specific architectures that govern the way your systems must behave within your industry. Finally, any given department or organization within your business may need its own individual Organization-Specific Architecture to govern the systems within that department.

Your architecture organization will either adopt or adapt existing architectures, or will develop its own architectures from the ground up. In either case, TOGAF is a tool to help. It provides a method to assist you in generating/maintaining any type of architecture within the Architecture Continuum while leveraging architecture assets already defined, internal or external to your organization. The TOGAF ADM helps you to re-use architecture assets, making your architecture organization more efficient and effective.

39.6.2 你的 ENTERPRISE

TOGAF 为你提供一种在你的 ENTERPRISE 内对系统进行“架构设计”的方法。你的架构组织必须要处理上述每种类型的架构。例如，建议你具有自己的管控所有系统的基础架构。你还应具有自己的管控主要共享系统的公共系统架构——如网络化系统或管理系统。你可以具有自己的对你的系统在所处行业必须表现出的方式进行管控的行业特定架构。最后，你的业务内的任何指定部门或组织可能需要其自己的单独的组织特定的架构来管控该部门内的系统。

你的架构组织将采用或调整现有架构，或从头开始开发其自己的架构。不论哪种情况，TOGAF 都是一个提供帮助的工具。它提供一种方法，辅助你产生/维护架构连续统一体内任何类型的架构，同时更好地利用已在你的组织内部或外部定义的架构资产。TOGAF ADM 帮助你复用架构资产，使你的架构组织更有效率、更有成效。

Chapter 40
Architecture Partitioning

40.1 Overview

Partitions are used to simplify the development and management of the enterprise architecture. Partitions lie at the foundation of Architecture Governance and are distinct from levels and the organizing concepts of the Architecture Continuum (see Chapter 39).

Architectures are partitioned because:

- Organizational unit architectures conflict with one another.
- Different teams need to work on different elements of architecture at the same time and partitions allow for specific groups of architects to own and develop specific elements of the architecture.
- Effective architecture re-use requires modular architecture segments that can be taken and incorporated into broader architectures and solutions.

It is impractical to present a definitive partitioning model for architecture. Each enterprise needs to adopt a partitioning model that reflects its own operating model.

This chapter discusses the classification criteria that are generally applied to architectures and how these can be leveraged to partition the enterprise into a set of architectures with manageable complexity and effective governance.

40.2 Applying Classification to Create Partitioned Architectures

For the reasons outlined in the previous section, it is valuable to partition and organize the Enterprise Continuum into a set of related solutions and architectures with:

- Manageable complexity for each individual architecture or solution.
- Defined groupings.
- Defined hierarchies and navigation structures.
- Appropriate processes, roles, and responsibilities attached to each grouping.

The following table shows how suitable classification criteria can be used to support partitioning of solutions:

第 40 章
架构划分

40.1 概述

划分用于简化 Enterprise Architecture 的开发和管理。划分是架构治理的基础，且与架构连续统一体的层级和组织概念（见第 39 章）截然不同。

划分架构的原因是：

- 组织单元架构彼此冲突。
- 不同团队需要针对不同的架构元素同时工作，划分使特定的架构师群组能拥有并开发特定的架构元素。
- 有效的架构复用要求模块化的分部架构可以被采用并纳入更广泛的架构和解决方案中。

为架构提出一个明确划分的模型是不切实际的。每个 ENTERPRISE 都需要采用反映其自身运行模型的一个划分模型。

本章论述了一般应用于架构的分类准则，以及如何更好地利用这些准则将 ENTERPRISE 划分成具有可管理的复杂性和有效管控的一系列架构。

40.2 应用分类来创建所划分的架构

由于上一节所概括的原因，将 ENTERPRISE 的连续统一体划分和组织成一系列具有下列内容的相关解决方案和架构是有价值的：

- 每个单独的架构或解决方案的可管理的复杂性。
- 已定义的分组。
- 已定义的层级结构和导航结构。
- 每个分组所附带的恰当的流程、角色和职责。

下表表明可如何使用恰当的分类准则来支持解决方案的划分：

Characteristic	Usage to Support Solution Partitioning
Subject Matter (Breadth)	Solutions are naturally organized into groups to support operational management and control. Examples of solution partitions according to subject matter would include applications, departments, divisions, products, services, service centers, sites, etc. Solution decomposition by subject matter is typically the fundamental technique for structuring both solutions and the architectures that represent them.
Time	Solution lifecycles are typically organized around a timeline, which allows the impact of solution development, introduction, operation, and retirement to be managed against other business activity occurring in similar time periods.
Maturity/Volatility	The maturity and volatility of a solution will typically impact the speed of execution required for the solution lifecycle. Additionally, volatility and maturity will shape investment priorities. Solutions existing in highly volatile environments may be better suited to rapid, agile development techniques.

The following table shows how each classification criteria can be used to support partitioning of architectures:

Characteristic	Usage to Support Architecture Partitioning
Depth	The level of detail within an architecture has a strong correlation to the stakeholder groups that will be interested in the architecture. Typically less detailed architectures will be of interest to executive stakeholders. As architectures increase in detail, their relevance to implementation and operational personnel will also increase.

In practical terms, architecture discipline is used to support a number of different types of architecture that are used for different objectives. The classification criteria described above can be used in different ways to support the achievement of each objective.

The following characteristics are generally not used to partition an Architecture Landscape:

- Architectures used to describe the Architecture Landscape are generally not abstract.
- Solution volatility generally prevents architectures from being defined that are far in the future. Volatility also reduces the accuracy of historic architectures over time, as the organization changes and adapts to new circumstances.

Using the criteria above, architectures can be grouped into partitions.

特征	支持解决方案划分的使用
主题（广度）	解决方案被自然地组织成支持运行管理和控制的群组。按照主题进行的解决方案划分的示例包括应用、部门、分部、产品、服务、服务中心、场地等。典型情况下，按主题进行的解决方案分解是对解决方案和代表解决方案的架构进行结构化的基本技巧
时间	解决方案生命周期通常围绕一个时间表进行组织，使得解决方案开发、引入、运行和退役的影响能根据类似时间区间内所发生的其他业务活动进行管理
成熟度/波动性	解决方案的成熟度和波动性通常会影响解决方案生命周期所需的执行速度。此外，波动性和成熟度会形成投资优先级。存在于波动较大的环境的解决方案可能更适合快速、敏捷的开发技术

下表表明可如何使用每个分类准则来支持架构的划分：

特征	支持架构划分的使用
深度	架构内的细节层级与对架构感兴趣的利益攸关者群组密切相关。 典型情况下，利益攸关者管理人员对不太详细的架构感兴趣。随着架构的细节增加，它们与实施和运行人员的关联性也随之增加

实际上，架构规程用来支持用于不同目的的多种不同类型的架构。上述分类准则可采用不同方式使用，以支持每个目的的达成。

下列特征一般不用于划分架构全景：

- 用于描述架构全景的架构一般不是抽象的。
- 解决方案波动性通常防止架构在遥远的将来被定义。随着组织变革并适应新的环境，波动性还会随时间推移而降低历史架构的准确性。

使用以上准则，架构可被分组成多个部分。

40.2.1 Activities within the Preliminary Phase

The key objective of the Preliminary Phase is to establish the Architecture Capability for the enterprise. In practical terms this activity will require the establishment of a number of architecture partitions, providing defined boundaries, governance, and ownership.

Generally speaking, each team carrying out architecture activity within the enterprise will own one or more architecture partitions and will execute the ADM to define, govern, and realize their architectures.

If more than one team is expected to work on a single architecture, this can become problematic, as the precise responsibilities of each team are difficult to establish. For this reason, it is preferable to apply partitioning to the architecture until each architecture has one owning team.

Finally, it is worth considering the distinction between standing capabilities of the enterprise and temporary teams mobilized to support a particular change initiative. Although the remit of standing teams within the enterprise can be precisely defined, it is more difficult to anticipate and specify the responsibilities of (possibly unknown) temporary architecture teams. In the cases of these temporary teams, each team should come under the governance of a standing architecture team and there should be a process within the ADM cycle of these teams to establish appropriate architecture partitioning.

Steps within the Preliminary Phase to support architecture partitioning are as follows:

- **Determine the organization structure for architecture within the enterprise**: The various standing teams that will create the architecture should be identified. For each of these teams, appropriate boundaries should be established, including:
  - Governance bodies that are applicable to the team.
  - Team membership.
  - Team reporting lines.
- **Determine the responsibilities for each standing architecture team**: For each architecture team, the responsibilities should be identified. This step applies partitioning logic to the enterprise architecture in order to firstly identify the scope of each team and secondly to partition the architecture under the remit of a single team. Once complete, this step should have partitioned the entire scope of the enterprise and should have assigned responsibility for each partitioned architecture to a single team. Partitioning should create a definition of each architecture that includes:
  - Subject matter areas being covered.
  - Level of detail that the team will work at.
  - Time periods to be covered.
  - Stakeholders.
- **Determine the relationships between architectures**: Once a set of partitioned architectures has been created, the relationships between architectures should be developed. This step allows governance relationships to be formalized and also shows where artifacts from one architecture are expected to be re-used within other architectures. Areas of consideration include:
  - Where do different architectures overlap/dovetail/drill-down?
  - What are the compliance requirements between architectures?

40.2.1 预备阶段内的活动

预备阶段的关键目的是建立 ENTERPRISE 的架构能力。实际上，该活动需要建立多个架构划分，提供已定义的边界、治理和所有权。

一般而言，执行 ENTERPRISE 内架构活动的每个团队都会拥有一个或多个架构划分，并执行 ADM 以定义、管控和实现他们的架构。

如果预计一个以上团队针对一个单一架构进行工作，这可能会出问题，因为难以建立每个团队的确切职责。由于这一原因，更好的做法是在架构上应用划分，直到每个架构都具有一个自己的团队。

最后，ENTERPRISE 和被动员来支持特定变更举措的临时团队的固定能力之间的区别是值得考虑的。尽管 ENTERPRISE 内固定团队的职权范围可被确切定义，但更难的是，预期到并规定临时架构团队的职责（可能未知的）。对于这些临时团队而言，每个团队都应受到固定架构团队的治理，且这些团队的 ADM 周期内应具有一个流程以建立恰当的架构划分。

预备阶段内支持架构划分的步骤如下：

- 确定 ENTERPRISE 内架构的组织结构：应识别创建架构的各个固定团队。对于每个团队而言，应建立恰当的边界，包括：
  - 适用于团队的治理机构。
  - 团队成员。
  - 团队报告程序。
- 确定每个固定架构团队的职责：对于每个架构团队而言，应识别职责。该步骤将划分逻辑应用于 Enterprise Architecture，以便首先识别每个团队的范围，其次在单个团队的职权范围下划分架构。一旦完成，该步骤应已经划分了 ENTERPRISE 的整个范围，并且应已向单个团队指派了对每个已划分架构的职责。划分应创建每个架构的定义，包括：
  - 所涵盖的主题领域。
  - 团队将钻研的细节层级。
  - 待涵盖的时间区间。
  - 利益攸关者。
- 确定架构之间的关系：一旦创建所划分的系列架构，就应形成架构之间的关系。此步骤使治理关系正式化，还表明了预计一个架构中的制品在其他架构内的何处被复用。考虑范围包括：
  - 不同的架构在哪方面重叠/吻合/往下深入？
  - 架构之间的合规需求是什么？

Once the Preliminary Phase is complete, the teams conducting the architecture should be understood. Each team should have a defined scope and the relationships between teams and architecture should be understood. Allocation of teams to architecture scope is illustrated in Figure 40-1.

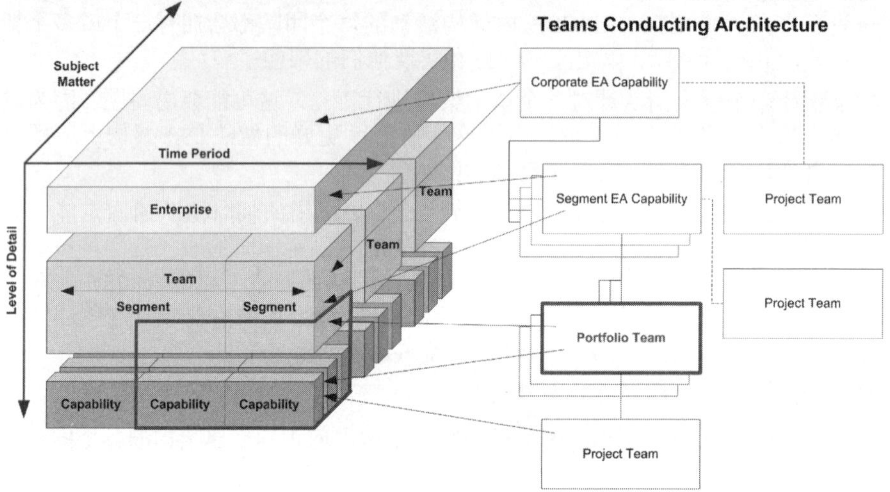

Figure 40-1 Allocation of Teams to Architecture Scope

40.3 Integration

Creation of partitioned architectures runs the risk of producing a fragmented and disjointed collection of architectures that cannot be integrated to form an overall big picture (see Part II, Section 5.6).

For large complex enterprises, federated architectures — independently developed, maintained, and managed architectures that are subsequently integrated within an integration framework — are typical. Federated architectures typically are used in governments and conglomerates, where the separate organizational units need separate architectures. Such a framework specifies the principles for interoperability, migration, and conformance. This allows specific business units to have architectures developed and governed as stand-alone architecture projects. More details and guidance on specifying the interoperability requirements for different solutions can be found in Part III, Chapter 29.

In order to mitigate against this risk, standards for content integration should be defined and architecture governance should address content integration as a condition of architectural compliance. Content frameworks, such as the TOGAF content framework (refer to Part IV: Architecture Content Framework) can be used to specify standard building blocks and artifacts that are the subject of content integration standards.

For example, a standard catalog of business processes can be agreed for an enterprise. Subsequent architectures can then ease integration by using the same process list and cross-referencing other aspects of the architecture to those standard processes.

一旦完成了预备阶段，应了解执行架构的团队。每个团队应具有一个已定义的范围，并且应了解各团队与架构之间的关系。图 40-1 阐明团队在架构范围的分配。

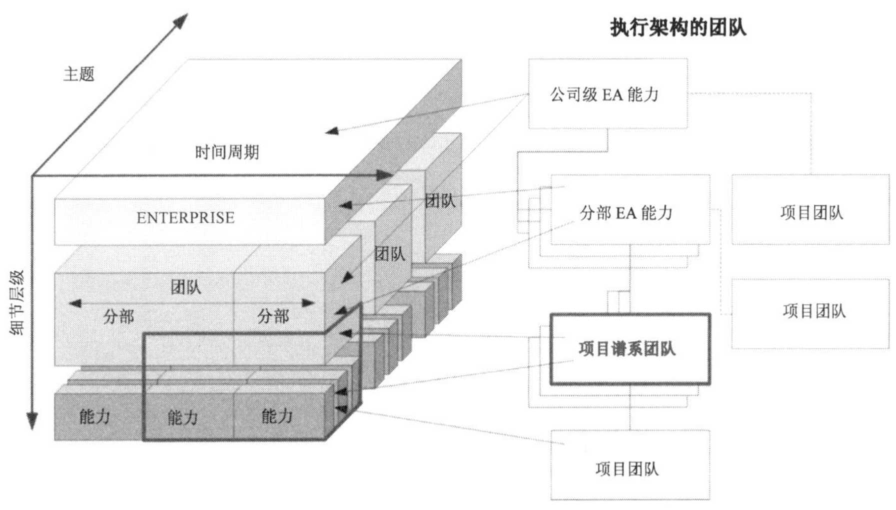

图 40-1 团队在架构范围的分配

40.3 综合

创建已划分的架构面临的风险是产生碎片化的、不连贯的架构集，不能被整合为一个大的总体大图像（见第二部分 5.6 节）。

对于大型复杂的 ENTERPRISE 而言，联邦架构是具有代表性的架构——随后在一个综合框架内进行综合的独立开发、维护和管理的架构。联邦架构通常用于政府和企业集团中单独的组织单元需要单独的架构的情况。这样的框架规定互用性、迁移和一致性的原则，这使得特定业务单元能以这些架构作为独立的架构项目进行开发和管控。更多关于规定不同解决方案互用性需求的详细说明和指南可在第三部分的第 29 章中找到。

为了减轻这种风险，应定义内容综合标准，架构治理应作为架构合规的条件应对内容综合。诸如 TOGAF 内容框架（见第四部分：架构内容框架）等内容框架可用于规定标准构建块和制品，这些标准构建块和制品是内容综合标准的主题。

例如，可为一个 ENTERPRISE 议定业务流程的标准目录集。然后，后续架构可通过使用相同的流程列表并在那些标准流程中相互参照架构的其他方面来使综合变得容易。

Integration can be addressed from a number of dimensions:

- Integration across the architectural domains provides a cross-domain view of the state of a segment of the enterprise for a point in time.
- Integration across the organizational scope of the business provides a cross-segment view of the enterprise.
- The Architecture Vision provides an integrated summary of Architecture Definitions, which provide an integrated summary of Transition Architectures.

Figure 40-2 shows how architectural content can be aggregated using a variety of techniques.

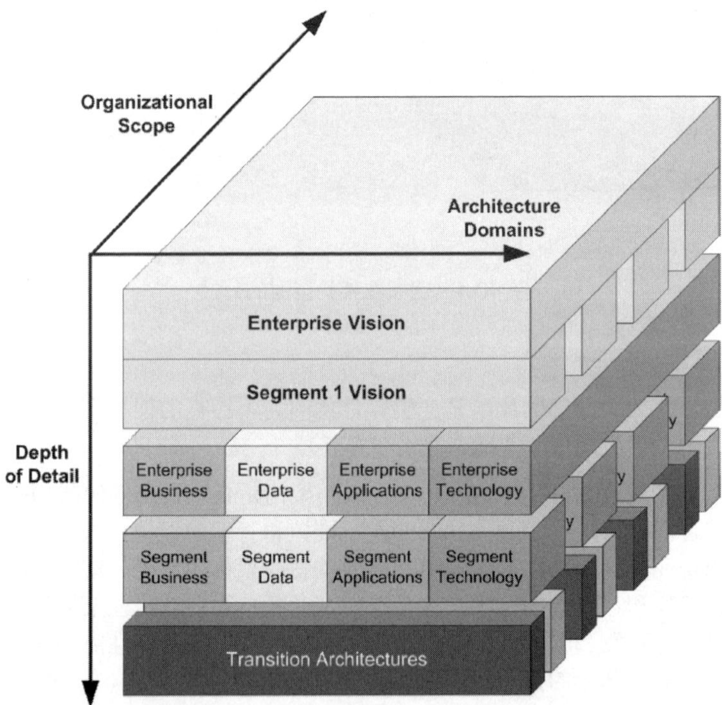

Figure 40-2 Architecture Content Aggregation

综合可从多个方面进行论述：

- 跨架构域的综合提供在某一时点 ENTERPRISE 的分部状态的跨领域视图。
- 穿越业务组织范围的整合（一体化）提供 ENTERPRISE 的交叉视图。
- 架构愿景提供架构定义的综合概要，架构定义提供过渡架构的综合概要。

图 40-2 表明可如何通过使用各种技巧来集合架构内容。

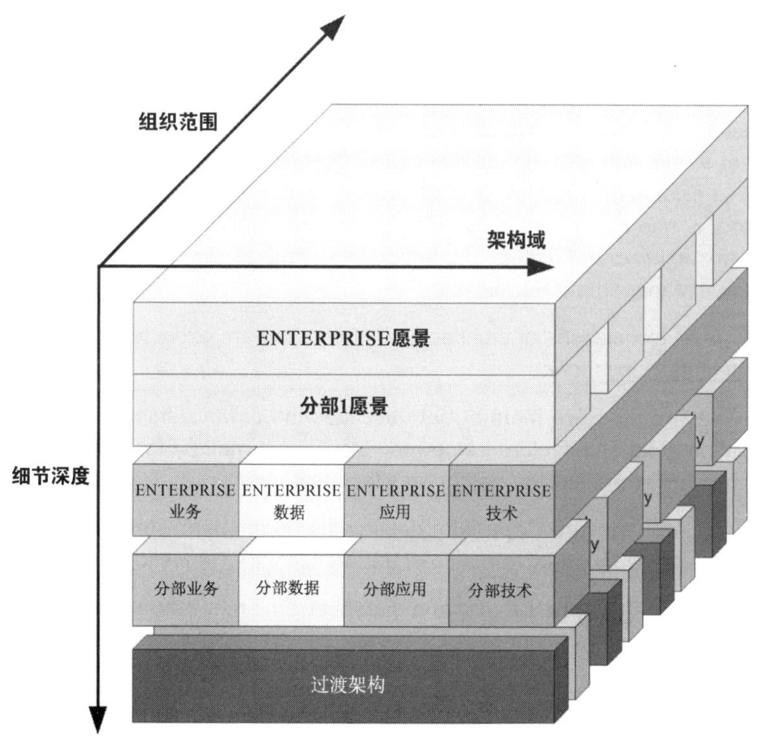

图 40-2　架构内容集合

Chapter 41
Architecture Repository

41.1 Overview

Operating a mature Architecture Capability within a large enterprise creates a huge volume of architectural output. Effective management and leverage of these architectural work products require a formal taxonomy for different types of architectural asset alongside dedicated processes and tools for architectural content storage.

This section of TOGAF provides a structural framework for an Architecture Repository that allows an enterprise to distinguish between different types of architectural assets that exist at different levels of abstraction in the organization. This Architecture Repository is one part of the wider Enterprise Repository, which provides the capability to link architectural assets to components of the Detailed Design, Deployment, and Service Management Repositories.

At a high level, six classes of architectural information are expected to be held within an Architecture Repository:

- The **Architecture Metamodel** describes the organizationally tailored application of an architecture framework, including a method for architecture development and a metamodel for architecture content.
- The **Architecture Capability** defines the parameters, structures, and processes that support governance of the Architecture Repository.
- The **Architecture Landscape** presents an architectural representation of assets in use, or planned, by the enterprise at particular points in time.
- The **Standards Information Base** captures the standards with which new architectures must comply, which may include industry standards, selected products and services from suppliers, or shared services already deployed within the organization.
- The **Reference Library** provides guidelines, templates, patterns, and other forms of reference material that can be leveraged in order to accelerate the creation of new architectures for the enterprise.
- The **Governance Log** provides a record of governance activity across the enterprise.

The relationships between these areas of the Architecture Repository are shown in Figure 41-1.

第 41 章
架构库

41.1 概述

在大型 ENTERPRISE 内运行成熟的架构能力可创建大量的架构输出。对这些架构工作产物的有效管理和更好的利用，需要一种用于不同类型的架构资产连同用于架构内容存储的专用流程和工具的正式分类法。

本节 TOGAF 提供架构库的结构框架，其使得 ENTERPRISE 能对组织的不同抽象层级上存在的不同类型的架构资产进行区分。此架构库是更大的 ENTERPRISE 存储库的一部分，其提供将架构资产与详细设计、部署和服务管理存储库的组件联系起来的能力。

在高层级上，预计架构库内存在六类架构信息：

- **架构元模型**描述一个架构框架的在组织上被剪裁过的应用，包括架构开发方法和架构内容元模型。
- **架构能力**定义了支持架构库治理的参数、结构和流程。
- **架构全景**提供 ENTERPRISE 在特定时点正在使用的和已计划的资产的架构表达。
- **标准信息库**获取新架构必须遵守的标准，可能包括行业标准、从供应商选定的产品和服务或已经部署在该组织内的共享服务。
- **参考库**提供指南、模板、特征模式和可更好地发挥作用的其他参考资料形式，以便加速 ENTERPRISE 新架构的创建。
- **治理日志**提供整个 ENTERPRISE 内的治理活动记录。

架构库的这些区域之间的关系如图 41-1 所示。

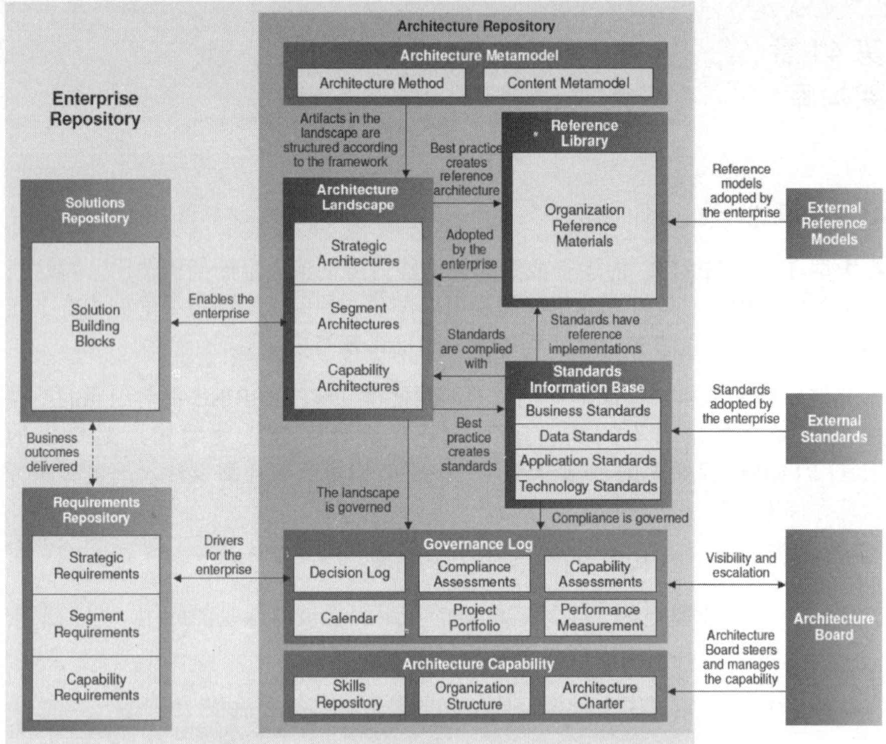

Figure 41-1 Overview of Architecture Repository

This section of TOGAF describes the structure and content of the repository areas that hold the output of projects, namely the Architecture Landscape, the Reference Library, the Standards Information Base, and the Governance Log.

This section also discusses requirements to be considered when selecting tools to manage an Architecture Repository.

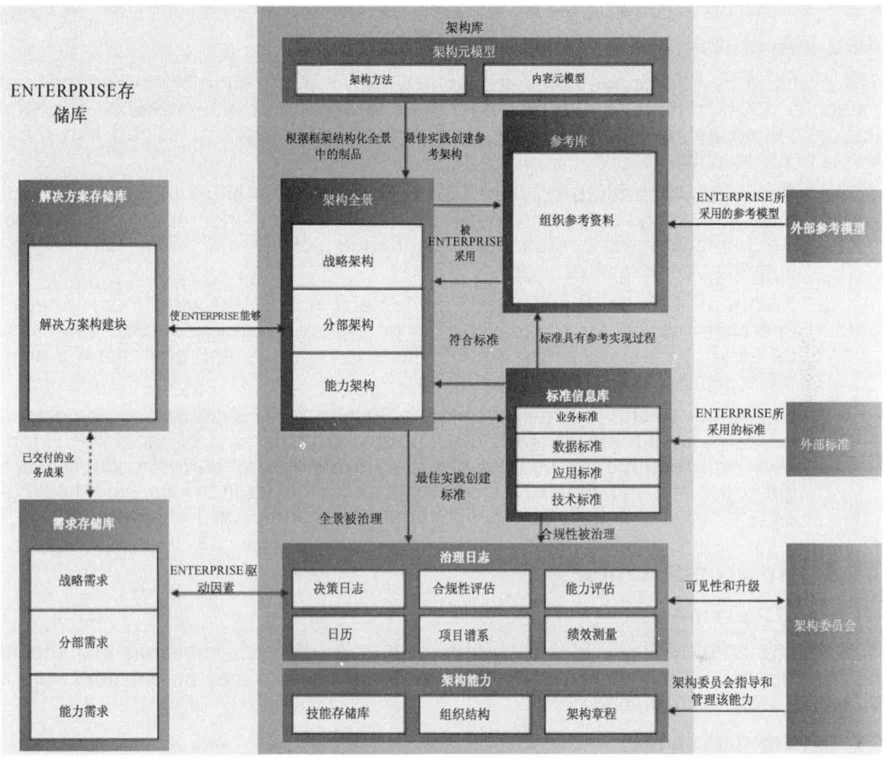

图 41-1　架构库的概述

本节 TOGAF 描述保存项目输出的存储库区域的结构和内容，即架构全景、参考库、标准信息库和治理日志。

本节还论述在选择管理架构库的工具时需要考虑的需求。

41.2 Architecture Landscape

The Architecture Landscape holds architectural views of the state of the enterprise at particular points in time. Due to the sheer volume and the diverse stakeholder needs throughout an entire enterprise, the Architecture Landscape is divided into three levels of granularity:

1. **Strategic Architectures** (see Part I, Section 3.70) show a long-term summary view of the entire enterprise. Strategic Architectures provide an organizing framework for operational and change activity and allow for direction setting at an executive level.
2. **Segment Architectures** (see Part I, Section 3.62) provide more detailed operating models for areas within an enterprise. Segment Architectures can be used at the program or portfolio level to organize and operationally align more detailed change activity.
3. **Capability Architectures** (see Part I, Section 3.27) show in a more detailed fashion how the enterprise can support a particular unit of capability. Capability Architectures are used to provide an overview of current capability, target capability, and capability increments and allow for individual work packages and projects to be grouped within managed portfolios and programs.

41.3 Reference Library

41.3.1 Overview

The Reference Library provides a repository to hold reference materials that should be used to develop architectures. Reference materials held may be obtained from a variety of sources, including:

- Standards bodies
- Product and service vendors
- Industry communities or forums
- Standard templates
- Enterprise best practice

The Reference Library should contain:

- Reference Architectures
- Reference Models
- Viewpoint Library
- Templates

Note: The terms *reference architecture* and *reference model* are not used carefully in most literature. Reference architecture and reference model have the same relationship as architecture and model. Either can exist as either generic or an organization-specific state. Typically, a generic reference architecture provides the architecture team with an outline of their organization-specific reference architecture that will be customized for a specific organization. For example, a generic reference architecture may identify that there is a need for data models. An organization that selects the TMF's SID as a reference data model is creating an organization-specific reference architecture.

In order to segregate different classes of architecture reference materials, the Reference Library can use the Architecture Continuum as a method for classification.

41.2 架构全景

架构全景存有 ENTERPRISE 在特定时点上状态的架构视图。由于在整个 ENTERPRISE 内具有大量且不同的利益攸关者需要，因此把架构全景划分为三个粒度层级：

1. **战略架构**（见第一部分 3.70 节）表明整个 ENTERPRISE 的长期概要视图。战略架构为运行和变更活动提供一个组织框架并使得能在执行层级上设置方向。
2. **分部架构**（见第一部分 3.62 节）为 ENTERPRISE 内各区域提供更详细的运行模型。分部架构可用在项目群或项目谱系层级上，以组织更详细的变更活动并使其在运行上协调一致。
3. **能力架构**（见第一部分 3.27 节）以更详细的方式表明 ENTERPRISE 可如何支持特定的能力单元。能力架构被用于提供对当前能力、目标能力和能力增量的概述，并使得受管理的项目谱系和项目群内能对单独工作包和项目进行组合。

41.3 参考库

41.3.1 概述

参考库提供一个存储库，以保存用于开发架构的参考资料。保存的参考资料可从各种来源获得，包括：

- 标准机构
- 产品和服务厂商
- 行业团体或论坛
- 标准模板
- ENTERPRISE 最佳实践

参考库应包含：

- 参考架构
- 参考模型
- 视角库
- 模板

注：术语“参考架构”和“参考模型”在多数文献中未得到审慎使用。参考架构和参考模型的关系与架构和模型的关系相同，每一个都能以一般的或组织特定的状态存在。典型情况下，一般的参考架构为架构团队提供针对组织特定参考架构（为特定组织定制）的大纲。例如，一般的参考架构可识别出对数据模型的需要。选择 TMF 的 SID 作为参考数据模型的组织正在创建组织特定的参考架构。

为了分开不同类别的架构参考资料，参考库可使用架构连续统一体作为分类方法。

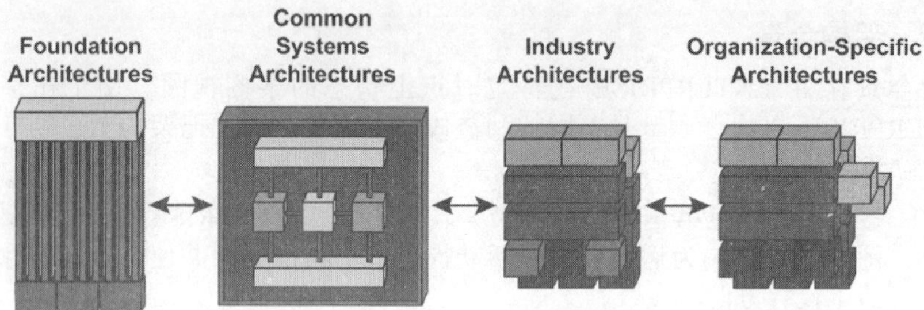

Figure 41-2 Architecture Continuum

The Architecture Continuum, as shown in Figure 41-2, can be viewed as a Reference Library classification scheme. As such it illustrates how reference architectures can be organized across a range — from Foundation Architectures, and Industry-Specific Architectures, to an Organization-Specific Architecture.

The enterprise needs and business requirements are addressed in decreasing abstraction from left to right. The architect will typically find more re-usable architectural elements toward the left of the range. When elements are not found, the requirements for the missing elements are passed to the left of the range for incorporation.

Through this exercise it is important to keep in mind the concepts of levels and partitions. At different levels of granularity there may exist reference materials appropriate to the level, and partitions within the Architecture Landscape can be expected to use different reference material (see Chapter 40 and Part III, Chapter 20).

41.4 Standards Information Base

41.4.1 Overview

The Standards Information Base provides a repository area to hold a set of specifications, to which architectures must conform. Establishment of a Standards Information Base provides an unambiguous basis for architectural governance because:

- The standards are easily accessible to projects and therefore the obligations of the project can be understood and planned for.
- Standards are stated in a clear and unambiguous manner, so that compliance can be objectively assessed.

41.4.2 Types of Standard

Standards typically fall into three classes:

- **Legal and Regulatory Obligations**: These standards are mandated by law and therefore an enterprise must comply or face serious consequences.
- **Industry Standards**: These standards are established by industry bodies, such as The Open Group, and are then selected by the enterprise for adoption. Industry Standards offer potential for interoperation and sharing across enterprises, but also fall outside of the control of the enterprise and therefore must be actively monitored.

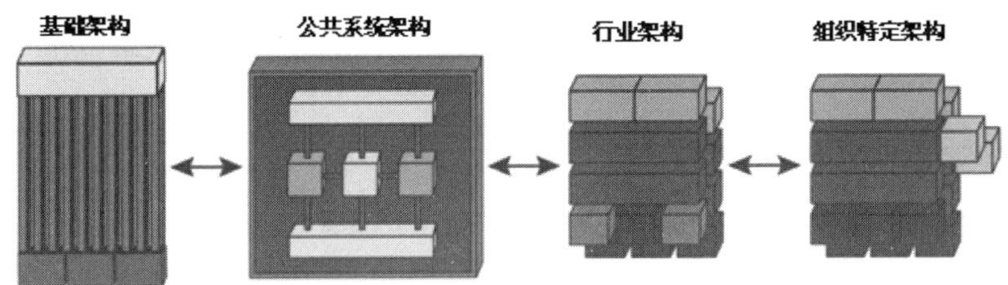

图 41-2 架构连续统一体

架构连续统一体如图 41-2 所示，可被看作一个参考库的分类方案。正因如此，它阐明参考架构可如何穿越一个范围而被组织起来——从基础架构和行业特定架构到组织特定架构。

以抽象程度从左至右降低的方式描述 ENTERPRISE 需要和业务需求。在该范围的左侧通常会找到更多可复用的架构元素。当未找到这些元素时，对这些缺失元素的需求将传递至该范围的左侧，以便纳入这些需求。

通过这一训练，重要的是记住层级和划分的概念。在不同的粒度层级，可能存在适合该层级的参考资料，架构全景内的划分会被期望使用不同的参考资料（见第 40 章和第三部分第 20 章）。

41.4 标准信息库

41.4.1 概述

标准信息库提供一个存储库区域来保存架构必须遵守的一系列规范。标准信息库的建立为架构治理提供了一个明确的基础，因为：

- 标准可便于项目使用，因此，项目的责任可以被理解和规划。
- 标准是以清晰且明确的方式陈述的，从而能够客观地评估合规性。

41.4.2 标准类型

标准通常分为以下三类：

- **法律法规的责任**：这些标准是根据法律规定的，因此 ENTERPRISE 必须遵守，否则须面对严重后果。
- **行业标准**：这些标准是由诸如 The Open Group 的行业机构建立，然后由 ENTERPRISE 选择采纳的。行业标准提供跨 ENTERPRISE 互操作和共享的潜在能力，而且还在 ENTERPRISE 的控制之外，因此必须被主动地监控。

- **Organizational Standards**: These standards are set within the organization and are based on business aspiration (e.g., selection of standard applications to support portfolio consolidation). Organizational Standards require processes to allow for exemptions and standards evolution.

41.4.3 Standards Lifecycle

Standards do not generally exist for all time. New standards are identified and managed through a lifecycle process. Typically, standards pass through the following stages:

- **Proposed Standard**: A potential standard has been identified for the organization, but has not yet been evaluated for adoption.
- **Provisional Standard** (also known as a **Trial Standard**): A Provisional Standard has been identified as a potential standard for the organization, but has not been tried and tested to a level where its value is fully understood. Projects wishing to adopt Provisional Standards may do so, but under specific pilot conditions, so that the viability of the standard can be examined in more detail.
- **Standard** (also known as an **Active Standard**): A Standard defines a mainstream solution that should generally be used as the approach of choice.
- **Phasing-Out Standard** (also known as a **Deprecated Standard**): A Phasing-Out Standard is approaching the end of its useful lifecycle. Projects that are re-using existing components can generally continue to make use of Phasing-Out Standards. Deployment of new instances of the Phasing-Out Standard are generally discouraged.
- **Retired Standard** (also known as an **Obsolete Standard**): An Retired Standard is no longer accepted as valid within the landscape. In most cases, remedial action should be taken to remove the Retired Standard from the landscape. Change activity on a Retired Standard should only be accepted as a part of an overall decommissioning plan.

All standards should be periodically reviewed to ensure that they sit within the right stage of the standards lifecycle. As a part of standards lifecycle management, the impact of changing the lifecycle status should be addressed to understand the landscape impact of a standards change and plan for appropriate action to address it.

41.4.4 Standards Classification within the Standards Information Base

Standards within the Standards Information Base are categorized according to the building blocks within the TOGAF content metamodel. Each metamodel entity can potentially have standards associated with it (e.g., Business Service, Technology Component).

Standards may relate to "approved" building blocks (e.g., a list of standard Technology Components) or may specify appropriate use of a building block (e.g., scenarios where messaging infrastructure is appropriate, application communication standards are defined).

At the top level, standards are classified in line with the TOGAF architecture domains, including the following areas:

- Business Standards:
  - Standard shared business functions
  - Standard role and actor definitions

- **组织标准**：这些标准是在组织内设置的，并且基于业务渴望（如，选择标准应用，以支持项目谱系合并）。组织标准要求流程考虑到豁免和标准的演进。

41.4.3 标准生命周期

标准通常不会永远存在。新的标准在整个生命周期内得到识别和管理。典型情况下，标准经过下列阶段：

- **建议标准**：已经为组织识别了潜在标准，但尚未对采纳进行评价。
- **临时标准**（也称为**试用标准**）：临时标准已被组织识别为潜在标准，但尚未在全面理解其价值的水平上试用和测试。对于一些项目，可能希望选取某个临时标准，但在特定的试验性条件下，可以更详细地审查标准的可行性。
- **标准**（也称为**现行标准**）：标准定义了一般被用作选择途径的主流解决方案。
- **淘汰标准**（也称为**弃用标准**）：淘汰标准接近其有用生命周期的末期。正在复用现有组件的项目，一般可继续使用淘汰标准。一般不鼓励部署淘汰标准的新实例。
- **退役标准**（也称为**作废标准**）：退役标准在全景内不再被认为有效。多数情况下，应采取补救措施以便从全景中删除退役标准。关于退役标准的变更活动，应仅被作为总体退役计划的一部分。

所有标准应被定期审视，以确保它们处于标准生命周期的正确阶段。作为标准生命周期管理的一部分，改变生命周期状态的影响应当被描述，以了解标准变更和计划的全景影响，并采取恰当的措施来应对该影响。

41.4.4 标准信息库内的标准分类

按照 TOGAF 内容元模型内的构建块对标准信息库内的标准进行分类。每个元模型实体可能具有与其相关联的标准（如业务服务、技术组件）。

标准可涉及“经批准的”构建块（如标准技术组件列表）或者可规定对构建块的恰当使用（如消息发送基础设施恰当且定义应用通信标准的场景）。

在顶层，按照 TOGAF 架构域对标准进行分类，包括下列区域：

- 业务标准：
  - 标准共享的业务功能
  - 标准的角色和施动者的定义

  - Security and governance standards for business activity
- Data Standards:
  - Standard coding and values for data
  - Standard structures and formats for data
  - Standards for origin and ownership of data
  - Restrictions on replication and access
- Applications Standards:
  - Standard/shared applications supporting specific business functions
  - Standards for application communication and interoperation
  - Standards for access, presentation, and style
- Technology Standards;
  - Standard hardware products
  - Standard software products
  - Standards for software development

41.5 Governance Log

41.5.1 Overview

The Governance Log provides a repository area to hold shared information relating to the ongoing governance of projects. Maintaining a shared repository of governance information is important, because:

- Decisions made during projects (such as standards deviations or the rationale for a particular architectural approach) are important to retain and access on an ongoing basis. For example, if a system is to be replaced, having sight of the key architectural decisions that shaped the initial implementation is highly valuable, as it will highlight constraints that may otherwise be obscureed.
- Many stakeholders are interested in the outcome of project governance (e.g., other projects, customers of the project, the Architecture Board, etc.).

41.5.2 Contents of the Governance Log

The Governance Log should contain the following items:

- **Decision Log**: A log of all architecturally significant decisions that have been made in the organization. This would typically include:
  - Product selections
  - Justification for major architectural features of projects
  - Standards deviations
  - Standards lifecycle changes

  — 业务活动的安保标准和治理标准

- 数据标准：
  — 数据的标准编码和价值
  — 数据的标准结构和格式
  — 数据的来源和所有权标准
  — 对复制和访问的限制
- 应用标准：
  — 支持特定业务功能的标准/共享应用
  — 应用通信和互操作的标准
  — 访问、展现和风格的标准
- 技术标准：
  — 标准硬件产品
  — 标准软件产品
  — 软件开发标准

41.5 治理日志

41.5.1 概述

治理日志提供一块存储库区域，用以保存与正在进行的项目治理相关的共享信息。维护治理信息的共享存储库非常重要，因为：

- 在项目期间做出的决策（如某一特殊架构途径的标准的偏差或理由依据），对于持续地进行保存和访问而言是非常重要的。例如，如果系统将要被替换，发现已形成初步实施的关键架构决策是非常有价值的，因为它强调约束，否则这些约束可能不会被发现。
- 许多利益攸关者对项目治理的成果感兴趣（如，其他项目、项目客户、架构委员会等）。

41.5.2 治理日志的内容

治理日志应包含下列内容：

- **决策日志**：包含有在组织内做出的所有架构方面重要决策的一个日志。它通常包括：
  — 产品选择
  — 项目的主要架构特征的解释
  — 标准的偏差
  — 标准生命周期变更

— Change request evaluations and approvals

— Re-use assessments

- **Compliance Assessments**: At key checkpoint milestones in the progress of a project, a formal architecture review will be carried out. This review will measure the compliance of the project to the defined architecture standards. For each project, this log should include:

  — Project overview

  — Progress overview (timeline, status, issues, risks, dependencies, etc.)

  — Completed architecture checklists

  — Standards compliance assessment

  — Recommended actions

- **Capability Assessments**: Depending on their objectives, some projects will carry out assessments of business, IT, or Architecture Capability. These assessments should be periodically carried out and tracked to ensure that appropriate progress is being made. This log should include:

  — Templates and reference models for executing Capability Assessments

  — Business Capability Assessments

  — IT capability, maturity, and impact assessments

  — Architecture maturity assessments

- **Calendar**: The Calendar should show a schedule of in-flight projects and formal review sessions to be held against these projects.

- **Project Portfolio**: The Project Portfolio should hold summary information about all in-flight projects that fall under architectural governance, including:

  — The name and description of the project

  — Architectural scope of the project

  — Architectural roles and responsibilities associated with the project

- **Performance Measurement**: Based on a charter for the architecture function, a number of performance criteria will typically be defined. The Performance Measurement log should capture metrics relating to project governance and any other performance metrics relating to the architecture charter so that performance can be measured and evaluated on an ongoing basis.

— 变更要求的评价和审批

— 复用评估

- **合规性评估**：在项目进展中关键检查点的里程碑中，要执行正式的架构审视。该审视会衡量项目与已定义的架构标准的合规性。对于每个项目而言，该日志应包括：

— 项目概述

— 进展概述（时间表、状态、议题、风险、依赖性等）

— 已完成的架构检查单

— 标准合规性评估

— 建议的行动

- **能力评估**：根据项目目的，会对某些项目执行业务、IT 或架构能力的评估。应定期地执行和跟踪这些评估，以确保项目正取得进展。该日志应包括：

— 执行能力评估的模板和参考模型

— 业务能力评估

— IT 能力、成熟度和影响评估

— 架构成熟度评估

- **日历**：日历应表明正在执行的项目，以及对这些项目执行正式审视的进度表。

- **项目谱系**：项目谱系应保存包含在架构治理之下的所有正在执行的项目的概要信息，包括：

— 项目的名称和描述

— 项目的架构范围

— 与项目相关联的架构角色和职责

- **绩效测量**：根据章程中对架构功能的描述，通常会定义多个架构绩效标准。绩效测量日志应获取与项目治理相关的衡量标准以及与架构章程相关的任何绩效衡量标准，从而持续地测量和评价架构绩效。

41.6 The Enterprise Repository

While the Architecture Repository holds information concerning the enterprise architecture and associated artifacts there are a considerable number of enterprise repositories that support the architecture. These include the Requirements Repository storing requirements and the Solutions Repository storing Solution Building Blocks (SBBs). See Figure 41-1.

The business outcomes for requirements will be reflected in the Solutions Repository over time. When this occurs the requirements are met and archived for audit purposes.

41.6.1 Requirements Repository

The Requirements Repository is used by the Requirements Management Phase of the Architecture Development Method (ADM) to record and manage all information relevant to the architecture requirements. The requirements address the many types of architecture requirements; i.e., strategic, segment and capability requirements which are the major drivers for the enterprise architecture.

Requirements can be gathered at every stage of the architecture development lifecycle and need to be approved through the various phases and governance processes.

41.6.2 Solutions Repository

The Solutions Repository holds the Solution Building Blocks (SBBs).

41.7 External Repositories

41.7.1 External Reference Models

There are many industry reference models available which may assist in understandding the role of and developing the Reference Architectures. Examples include MDA from OMG, FEA for US Government, TMF from the Telecoms Industry, SOA reference models from OASIS and The Open Group.

41.7.2 External Standards

These relate to industry, best practice, or formal defined standards used by leading organizations. Examples include ISO, IEEE, and Government standards.

41.7.3 Architecture Board Approvals

Decisions made by the Architecture Board which affect the enterprise architecture are often recorded in the minutes of meetings. These minutes are often held in documentation archives which are excluded from the Architecture Repository for legal or regulatory reasons.

41.6 ENTERPRISE 存储库

尽管架构库保存关于 ENTERPRISE 的信息和相关的架构制品，但还存在大量的支持架构的 ENTERPRISE 存储库。它们包括存储需求的需求存储库和存储解决方案构建块（SBB）的解决方案存储库。见图 41-1。

关于需求的业务成果，随时间反映在解决方案存储库中。这种情况发生时，可以满足并实现出于审核目的的需求。

41.6.1 需求存储库

在架构开发方法（ADM）的需求管理阶段使用需求存储库，以记录和管理与架构需求相关的所有信息。需求涉及多种类型的架构需求；即战略需求、分部需求和能力需求，它们是 Enterprise Architecture 的主要驱动因素。

可在架构开发生命周期的每个阶段收集需求，并且需要通过各阶段和治理流程来审批这些需求。

41.6.2 解决方案存储库

解决方案存储库保存解决方案构建块（SBB）。

41.7 外部存储库

41.7.1 外部参考模型

有很多行业参考模型可以帮我们理解参考架构的作用，并开发参考架构。例子包括来自 OMG 的 MDA、美国政府的 FEA、来自电信业的 TMF、来自 OASIS 和 The Open Group 的 SOA 参考模型。

41.7.2 外部标准

外部标准是由行业领先的组织所使用的，关于行业标准、最佳实践或已正式定义的标准。例子包括 ISO、IEEE 和政府标准。

41.7.3 架构委员会的审批

架构委员会做出的影响 Enterprise Architecture 的决策，通常记录在会议记录中。这些记录通常保存在文件档案中，出于法律或法规的原因，这些文件档案不包括在架构库中。

Chapter 42
Tools for Architecture Development

42.1 Overview

As an enterprise architecture framework, TOGAF provides a basis for developing architectures in a uniform and consistent manner. Its purpose in this respect is to ensure that the various architecture descriptions developed within an enterprise, perhaps by different architects or architecture teams, support the comparison and integration of architectures within and across architecture domains (business, data, application, technology), and relating to different business area scopes within the enterprise.

To support this goal, TOGAF defines numerous deliverables in the form of architectures, represented as architecture models, architecture views of those models, and other artifacts. Over time, these artifacts become a resource that needs to be managed and controlled, particularly with a view to re-use. This concept is referred to in TOGAF as the "Enterprise Continuum".

Architecture models and views are discussed in detail separately in Part IV, Chapter 35. This section discusses considerations in choosing automated tools in order to generate such architecture models and views, and to maintain them over time.

42.2 Issues in Tool Standardization

In the current state of the tools market, many enterprises developing enterprise architectures struggle with the issue of standardizing on tools, whether they seek a single "one size fits all" tool or a multi-tool suite for modeling architectures and generating the different architecture views required.

There are ostensible advantages associated with selecting a single tool. Organizations following such a policy can hope to realize benefits such as reduced training, shared licenses, quantity discounts, maintenance, and easier data interchange. However, there are also reasons for refusing to identify a single mandated tool, including reasons of principle (endorsing a single architecture tool would not encourage competitive commercial innovation or the development of advanced tool capability); and the fact that a single tool would not accommodate a variety of architecture development "maturity levels" and specific needs across an enterprise.

Successful enterprise architecture teams are often those that harmonize their architecture tools with their architecture maturity level, team/organizational capabilities, and objectives or focus. If different organizations within an enterprise are at different architecture maturity levels and have different objectives or focus (e.g., Enterprise *versus* Business *versus* Technology Architecture), it becomes very difficult for one tool to satisfy all organizations' needs.

第 42 章 架构开发工具

42.1 概述

作为 Enterprise Architecture 框架，TOGAF 提供以均匀一致的方式开发架构的基础。TOGAF 在这方面的目的是，确保可能由不同架构师或架构团队在 ENTERPRISE 内开发的各种架构描述，能够支持对架构域（业务、数据、应用、技术）内和跨越架构域的、与 ENTERPRISE 内的不同业务领域范围有关的架构进行比较和综合。

为了支持该目标，TOGAF 定义了很多架构形式的交付物，表现为架构模型、那些模型的架构视图及其他制品。经过一段时间后，这些制品变成了一种需要管理和控制的资源，尤其是复用的视图。该概念被称为 TOGAF 中的“ENTERPRISE 的连续统一体”。

在第四部分第 35 章分别详细地论述了架构模型和视图。本节对选择自动化工具的考量因素进行论述，以便生成此类架构模型和视图，并在一段时间后对它们进行维护。

42.2 工具标准化问题

在工具市场的当前状态下，很多开发 Enterprise Architecture 的 ENTERPRISE 都与工具标准化问题“斗争”，它们在寻求一种对架构进行建模并生成所需不同架构视图的单一“一刀切”工具或寻求多个工具组成的工具包。

选择单一工具有明显的优势。遵循这样一种方针的组织可能希望得到减少培训、共享许可、批量折扣、维护和易于数据交换等好处。但是，也有拒绝识别单一强制性工具的原因，包括原则性原因（支持某单一架构工具将不利于鼓励竞争性的商业创新或先进工具能力的开发），以及单一工具不能适应 ENTERPRISE 范围内各种各样的架构开发“成熟度等级”和特殊需要的这一事实。

成功的 Enterprise Architecture 团队，通常是那些使其架构工具与架构成熟度等级、团队/组织能力以及目标或聚焦点一致的团队。如果在 ENTERPRISE 内不同组织的架构成熟度等级和目标或聚焦点（如，ENTERPRISE VS 业务 VS 技术架构）均有不同，则一个工具很难满足所有组织的需要。

TOGAF Version 9.1

Part VI　TOGAF Reference Models

The Open Group

TOGAF 9.1 版本

第六部分　TOGAF 参考模型

The Open Group

Chapter 43
Foundation Architecture: Technical Reference Model

This chapter describes the Technical Reference Model (TRM), including core taxonomy, graphical representation, and the detailed platform taxonomy.

The detailed platform taxonomy is described in Section 43.5.

43.1 Concepts

This section describes the role of the TRM, the components of the TRM, and using other TRMs.

43.1.1 Role of the TRM in the Foundation Architecture

The TOGAF Foundation Architecture is an architecture of generic services and functions that provides a foundation on which more specific architectures and architectural components can be built. This Foundation Architecture is embodied within the Technical Reference Model (TRM), which provides a model and taxonomy of generic platform services.

The TRM is universally applicable and, therefore, can be used to build any system architecture.

43.1.2 TRM Components

Any TRM has two main components:

1. A **taxonomy**, which defines terminology, and provides a coherent description of the components and conceptual structure of an information system.
2. An associated **TRM graphic**, which provides a visual representation of the taxonomy, as an aid to understanding.

The objective of the TOGAF TRM is to provide a widely accepted core taxonomy, and an appropriate visual representation of that taxonomy. The TRM graphic is illustrated in Section 43.3, and the taxonomy is explained in Section 43.4.

第 43 章
基础架构：技术参考模型

本章描述技术参考模型（TRM），包括核心分类法、图形表达和详细的平台分类法。

详细的平台分类法将在 43.5 节中描述。

43.1 概念

本节描述 TRM 的角色、TRM 的组件以及对其他 TRM 的使用。

43.1.1 TRM 在基础架构中的角色

TOGAF 基础架构是一般服务与功能的架构，它提供可以构建更多特定架构和架构组件的基础。该基础架构体现在提供通用平台服务的模型和分类法的技术参考模型（TRM）中。

TRM 是普遍适用的，因此可以用于构建任何系统架构。

43.1.2 TRM 组件

任何 TRM 都具有两个主要组件：

1. **分类法**，它定义术语并对信息系统的组件和概念结构提供清晰的描述。
2. 相关的 **TRM 图形**，作为一种帮助理解的手段，它提供分类法的直观展示。

TOGAF TRM 的目的是提供一种被广泛认可的核心分类法以及该分类法的适当直观表达。TRM 图形将在 43.3 节中阐述，分类法将在 43.4 节中解释。

43.1.3 Other TRMs

One of the great difficulties in developing an architecture framework is in choosing a TRM that works for everyone.

The TOGAF TRM was originally derived from the Technical Architecture Framework for Information Management (TAFIM) TRM (which in turn was derived from the IEEE 1003.0 model). This TRM is "platform-centric" : it focuses on the services and structure of the underlying platform necessary to support the use and re-use of applications (i.e., on application portability). In particular, it centers on the interfaces between that platform and the supported applications, and between the platform and the external environment.

The current TOGAF TRM is an amended version of the TAFIM TRM, which aims to emphasize the aspect of interoperability as well as that of portability.

The objective of the TRM is to enable structured definition of the standardized application platform and its associated interfaces. The other entities, which are needed in any specific architecture, are only addressed in the TRM insofar as they influence the application platform. The underlying aim in this approach is to ensure that the higher-level building blocks which make up business solutions have a complete, robust platform on which to run.

Other architectural models — taxonomies and/or graphics — not only are possible, but may be preferable for some enterprises. For example, such an enterprise-specific model could be derived by extension or adaptation of the TOGAF TRM. Alternatively, a different taxonomy may be embodied in the legacy of previous architectural work by an enterprise, and the enterprise may prefer to perpetuate use of that taxonomy. Similarly, an enterprise may prefer to represent the TOGAF taxonomy (or its own taxonomy) using a different form of graphic, which better captures legacy concepts and proves easier for internal communication purposes.

In addition to its use as a reference model for the development of technology architecture, the TRM can be used as a taxonomy to develop a Standards Information Base (SIB) within a specific organization. The core of TOGAF is its ADM: the TRM is a tool used in applying the ADM in the development of specific architectures. Provided consistency between TRM and SIB are maintained, the TOGAF ADM is valid whatever the choice of specific taxonomy, TRM graphic, or SIB toolset.

43.2 High-Level Breakdown

This section describes the major elements of the TRM.

43.2.1 Overview

The coarsest breakdown of the TRM is shown in Figure 43-1, which shows three major entities (Application Software, Application Platform, and Communications Infrastructure) connected by two interfaces (Application Platform Interface and Communications Infrastructure Interface).

43.1.3 其他 TRM

开发架构框架的一大困难是选择一种适用于每个人的 TRM。

TOGAF TRM 最初起源于信息管理技术架构框架（TAFIM）TRM（TAFIM TRM 依次来源于 IEEE 1003.0 模型）。该 TRM“以平台为中心”：它聚焦于支持应用的使用和复用所必需的基础平台的服务和结构（即，聚焦于应用的可移植性）。特别是，它重点关注该平台与所支持应用之间以及该平台与外部环境之间的界面。

当前的 TOGAF TRM 是 TAFIM TRM 的修正版本，旨在强调互用性及可移植性两个方面。

TRM 的目的是促进标准化应用平台及其相关界面的结构化定义。任何特定架构所必需的其他实体，只要影响应用平台就只能在 TRM 中处理。该实施途径的基本目标是，确保组成业务解决方案的较高层级构建块具有可在其上运行的完整的稳健的平台。

其他架构模型，即分类法和/或图形，对于一些 ENTERPRISE 而言不仅是可能的，而且可能更为可取。例如，这样一种 ENTERPRISE 特定的模型，可以通过 TOGAF TRM 的扩展或调整推导得出。或者，不同的分类法可以由 ENTERPRISE 体现在之前架构工作的遗留物中，且 ENTERPRISE 可能更愿意延续该分类法的使用。同样，ENTERPRISE 可能更愿意利用不同形式的图形来展示 TOGAF 分类法（或它自己的分类法），以更好地获取遗留概念并证明更易于实现内部通信的目的。

除了用作技术架构开发的参考模型，还可将 TRM 用作在特定组织内开发标准信息库（SIB）的分类法。TOGAF 的核心是 ADM：TRM 是一种在开发特定架构中应用 ADM 时所使用的工具。假如保持 TRM 与 SIB 之间的一致性，则无论选择什么特定分类法、TRM 图形或 SIB 工具箱，TOGAF ADM 都是有效的。

43.2 高层级分解

本节描述 TRM 的主要元素。

43.2.1 概述

TRM 的最粗粒度的分解如图 43-1 所示，其显示通过两个界面（应用平台界面和通信基础设施界面）连接的三个主要实体（应用软件、应用平台和通信基础设施）。

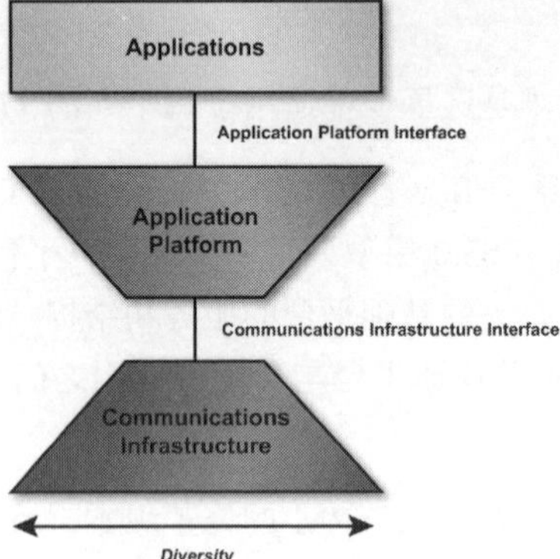

Figure 43-1 Technical Reference Model — High-Level View

The diagram says nothing about the detailed relationships between the entities; only that they exist.

Each of the elements in this diagram is discussed in detail in Section 43.3.

43.2.2 Portability and Interoperability

The high-level TRM seeks to emphasize two major common architectural objectives:

1. **Application Portability**, via the Application Platform Interface — identifying the set of services that are to be made available in a standard way to applications via the platform.

2. **Interoperability**, via the Communications Infrastructure Interface — identifying the set of Communications Infrastructure services that are to be leveraged in a standard way by the platform.

Both of these goals are essential to enable integration within the enterprise and trusted interoperability on a global scale between enterprises.

In particular, the high-level model seeks to reflect the increasingly important role of the Internet as the basis for inter- and intra-enterprise interoperability.

The horizontal dimension of the model in Figure 43-1 represents diversity, and the shape of the model is intended to emphasize the importance of minimum diversity at the interface between the Application Platform and the Communications Infrastructure.

This in turn means focusing on the core set of services that can be guaranteed to be supported by every IP-based network, as the foundation on which to build today's interoperable enterprise computing environments.

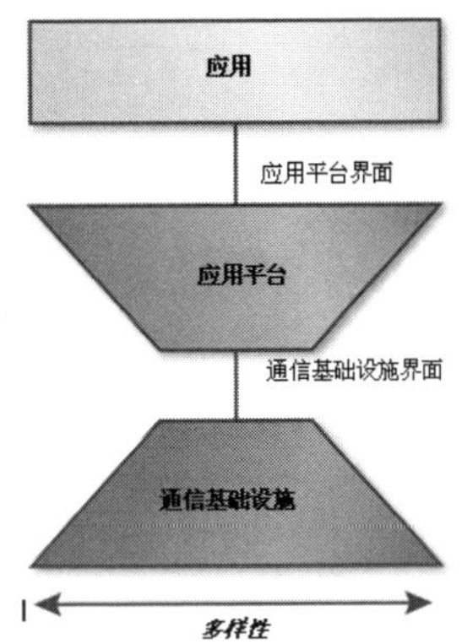

图 43-1 技术参考模型——高层级视图

图上并未提及两个实体之间的详细关系，只是说它们存在关系。

在 43.3 节中详细论述该图上的每个元素。

43.2.2 可移植性和互用性

高层级 TRM 旨在强调两个主要的公共架构目的：

1. 通过应用平台界面实现的**应用可移植性**——识别通过平台以标准方式可用于应用的服务集。
2. 通过通信基础设施界面实现的**互用性**——识别通过平台以标准方式更强有力地发挥作用的通信基础设施服务集。

这两个目标对于使得在 ENTERPRISE 内能够进行综合以及在全球范围内 ENTERPRISE 之间能够赢得可信任的互用性而言是必要的。

特别是，高层级模型旨在反映互联网作为 ENTERPRISE 间和 ENTERPRISE 内部实现互用性的、基础的、日益重要的角色。

图 43-1 中的模型的水平尺寸表达多样性，模型的形状旨在强调最低程度的多样性在应用平台与通信基础设施之间的界面处的重要性。

这反过来意味着，聚焦于可以确保被每个基于 IP 的网络支持的核心服务集，作为构建当今可互操作的 ENTERPRISE 计算环境的基础。

43.3 TRM in Detail

This section describes the TRM in detail, including platform service categories and external environment sub-entities.

43.3.1 Introduction

Figure 43-2 expands on Figure 43-1 to present the service categories of the Application Platform and the two categories of Application Software.

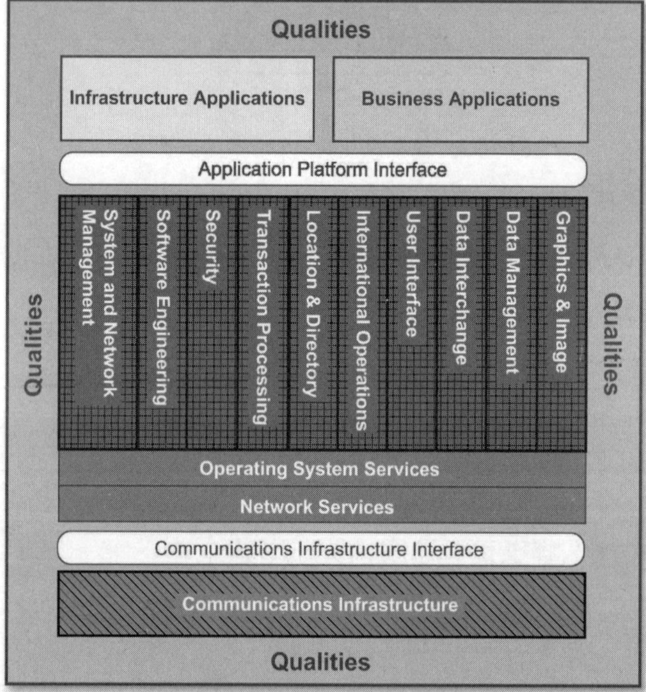

Figure 43-2 Detailed Technical Reference Model (Showing Service Categories)

Figure 43-2 is only a depiction of the TRM entities: it neither implies nor inhibits interrelationships among them.

IT architectures derived from TOGAF may differ greatly depending on the requirements of the information system. In practice, many architectures will not include all of the services discussed here, and many will include additional services to support Application Software that is specific to the organization or to its vertical industry.

In building an architecture, users of TOGAF should assess their own requirements and select the services, interfaces, and standards that satisfy their own business needs.

43.3 TRM 的详述

本节详细地描述 TRM，包括平台服务类别和外部环境子实体。

43.3.1 简介

图 43-2 对图 43-1 进行扩展，以表达应用平台的服务类别及两类应用软件。

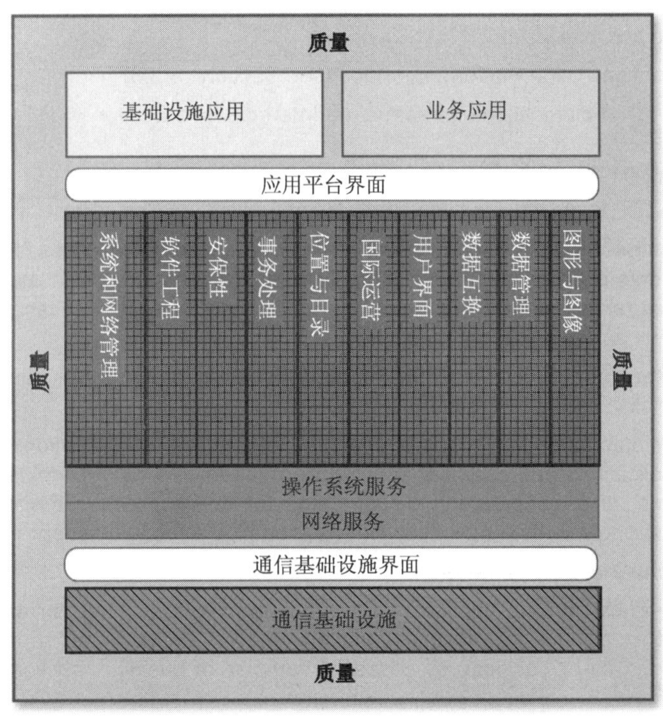

图 43-2 详细的技术参考模型（表明服务类别）

图 43-2 仅是 TRM 实体的描述：既没有暗示，也没有禁止 TRM 实体之间的相互关系。

根据信息系统的需求，源于 TOGAF 的 IT 架构会有很大不同。实际上，很多架构将不包括在此论述的所有服务，而很多架构将包括一些附加服务，以支持组织或其垂直行业特定的应用软件。

在构建架构过程中，TOGAF 的用户应评估各自的需求，并选择满足各自业务需要的服务、界面和标准。

43.3.2 TRM Entities and Interfaces

The following sections discuss in detail each element of the TRM illustrated in Figure 43-2. They are dealt with in the following order:

- The three entities:
  - Application Software (see Section 43.3.3)
  - Application Platform (see Section 43.3.4)
  - Communications Infrastructure (see Section 43.3.5)
- The two interfaces:
  - Application Platform Interface (see Section 43.3.6)
  - Communications Infrastructure Interface (see Section 43.3.7)

43.3.3 Application Software

The detailed TRM recognizes two categories of Application Software:

1. **Business Applications**, which implement business processes for a particular enterprise or vertical industry. The internal structure of business applications relates closely to the specific application software configuration selected by an organization.
2. **Infrastructure Applications**, which provide general-purpose business functionality, based on infrastructure services.

During development of the Technology Architecture, business applications and infrastructure applications are important sources of requirements for Technology Architecture services, and the selection of standards for the Application Platform will be influenced strongly by the Application Software configuration to be supported.

43.3.3.1 Business Applications

Business applications are applications that are specific to a particular enterprise or vertical industry. Such applications typically model elements of an enterprise's domain of activity or business processes. Examples of business applications might include:

- Patient record management services used in the Medical industry
- Inventory management services used in the Retail industry
- Geological data modeling services used in the Petroleum industry

Over time, particular business applications may become infrastructure applications, if they become sufficiently ubiquitous, interoperable, and general-purpose to be potentially useful to a broad range of enterprise IT users.

43.3.3.2 Infrastructure Applications

Infrastructure applications are applications that have all, or nearly all, of the following characteristics:

- Widespread availability as Commercial Off-The-Shelf (COTS) software means that it is uneconomic to consider custom implementation.

43.3.2 TRM 实体和界面

下列几节详细地论述了如图 43-2 所示的 TRM 的各个元素。按照下述顺序进行论述：

- 三个实体：
  - — 应用软件（见 43.3.3 节）
  - — 应用平台（见 43.3.4 节）
  - — 通信基础设施（见 43.3.5 节）
- 两个界面：
  - — 应用平台界面（见 43.3.6 节）
  - — 通信基础设施界面（见 43.3.7 节）

43.3.3 应用软件

详细的 TRM 认可两类应用软件：

1. **业务应用**，它实施特殊 ENTERPRISE 或垂直行业的业务流程。业务应用的内部结构与组织选择的特定应用软件构型密切相关。
2. **基础设施应用**，它基于基础设施服务提供通用的业务功能。

在技术架构开发期间，业务应用和基础设施应用是技术架构服务需求的重要来源，且应用平台标准的选择将受到待支持的应用软件构型的强烈影响。

43.3.3.1 业务应用

业务应用是特定于特殊 ENTERPRISE 或垂直行业的应用。典型情况下，此类应用对某个 ENTERPRISE 的活动或业务流程领域的元素进行建模。业务应用的示例可以包括：

- 用于医疗行业的病人记录管理服务
- 用于零售行业的库存管理服务
- 用于石油行业的地质数据建模服务

经过一段时间之后，特殊的业务应用如果变得足够普遍、可互操作且通用，并对大范围的 ENTERPRISE IT 用户是可能有用的，则可以成为基础设施应用。

43.3.3.2 基础设施应用

基础设施应用为具有全部或几乎全部下述特征的应用：

- 作为商用货架（COTS）软件的普遍可用性，意味着考虑定制实施是不经济的。

- User interaction is an important part of the application's function.
- Implementations are based on infrastructure services.
- Implementations may include significant extensions beyond that needed to use the underlying infrastructure services.
- Interoperability is a strong requirement.

Examples of applications in this cate-gory include:

- Electronic payment and funds transfer services.
- Electronic mail client services.
- Publish and subscribe.
- Intelligent agents.
- Calendaring and scheduling services.
- Groupware services.
- Workflow services.
- Spreadsheets.
- Presentation software.
- Document editing and presentation.
- Management applications, performing general-purpose system and network management functions for the system administrator.
- Software engineering tools, providing software development functions for systems development staff.

Infrastructure applications have strong dependencies on lower-level services in the architecture. For example, a workflow application may use platform services such as messaging or transaction processing to implement the flow of work among tasks. Similarly, a groupware application is likely to make extensive use of both data and communication services for the structure of documents, as well as the mechanics of storing and accessing them.

Infrastructure applications by definition are applications that are considered sufficiently ubiquitous, interoperable, and general-purpose within the enterprise to be effectively considered as part of the IT infrastructure. Just as business applications may over time come to be regarded as infrastructure applications, so infrastructure applications are normally candidates for inclusion as infrastructure services in future versions of an IT architecture.

43.3.4 Application Platform

43.3.4.1 Platform Concept

The term "platform" is used in many different ways within the IT industry today. Because of the different usages, the term is often qualified; for example, "application platform", "standardized" and "proprietary platforms", "client" and "server platforms", "distributed computing platform", "portability platform". Common to all these usages is the idea that someone needs a set of services provided by a particular kind of platform, and will implement a "higher-level" function that makes use of those services.

The TOGAF TRM focuses on the Application Platform, and the "higher-level function" is the set of Application Software, running on top of the Application Platform, that is needed to address the enterprise's business requirements.

- 用户交互是应用功能的一个重要部分。
- 实施以基础设施服务为基础。
- 实施可以包括超出使用底层基础设施服务所需以外的重大扩展。

该类别中的应用示例包括：

- 电子支付和资金转账服务。
- 电子邮件客户端服务。
- 发布和订阅。
- 智能代理。
- 日程和进度安排服务。
- 群件服务。
- 工作流程服务。
- 电子表格。
- 演示软件。
- 文件编辑和演示。
- 管理应用，由系统管理员执行通用系统和网络管理功能。
- 软件工程工具，为系统开发人员提供软件开发功能。

基础设施应用对架构中的低层级服务具有很强的依赖性。例如，工作流程应用可以使用诸如消息发送或事务处理等平台服务来实施任务之间的工作流程。同样，群件应用可将数据服务和通信服务广泛地用于文件的结构以及存储和访问这些文件的机制。

从定义上看，基础设施应用是在 ENTERPRISE 内部被视为足够普遍、可互操作且通用的，并被有效视为 IT 基础设施一部分的应用。正如业务应用可能经过一段时间后才被视为基础设施应用，所以基础设施应用通常是 IT 架构未来版本中作为基础设施服务而包含的候选应用。

43.3.4 应用平台

43.3.4.1 平台概念

现如今，术语“平台”在 IT 行业内部有多种使用方式。因为用法不同，所以该术语通常有所限定；例如，“应用平台”“标准化平台”“专有平台”“客户端平台”“服务器平台”“分布式计算平台”“可移植性平台”。所有这些用法的共性是一种观念，即有人需要一组由特殊类型的平台提供的服务，并且将实施使用这些服务的“较高层级”功能。

TOGAF TRM 聚焦于应用平台，“较高层级功能”是在应用平台之上运行的且处理 ENTERPRISE 的业务需求所需的一组应用软件。

It is important to recognize that the Application Platform in the TOGAF TRM is a single, generic, conceptual entity. From the viewpoint of the TOGAF TRM, the Application Platform contains all possible services. In a specific Target Architecture, the Application Platform will contain only those services needed to support the required functions.

Moreover, the Application Platform for a specific Target Architecture will typically not be a single entity, but rather a combination of different entities for different, commonly required functions, such as desktop client, file server, print server, application server, Internet server, database server, etc., each of which will comprise a specific, defined set of services necessary to support the specific function concerned.

It is also important to recognize that many of the real-world IT systems that are procured and used today to implement a Technology Architecture come fully equipped with many advanced services, which are often taken for granted by the purchaser. For example, a typical desktop computer system today comes with software that implements services from most if not all of the service categories of the TOGAF TRM. Since the purchaser of such a system often does not consider anything "smaller" than the total bundle of services that comes with the system, that service bundle can very easily become the "platform". Indeed, in the absence of a Technology Architecture to guide the procurement process, this is invariably what happens. As this process is repeated across an enterprise, different systems purchased for similar functions (such as desktop client, print server, etc.) can contain markedly different bundles of services.

Service bundles are represented in a Technology Architecture in the form of "building blocks". One of the key tasks of the IT architect in going from the conceptual Application Platform of the TRM to an enterprise-specific Technology Architecture is to look beyond the set of real-world platforms already in existence in the enterprise. The IT architect must analyze the services actually needed in order to implement an IT infrastructure that meets the enterprise's business requirements in the optimal manner, and to define the set of optimal Solution Building Blocks (SBBs) — real-world "platforms" — to implement that architecture.

43.3.4.2 Extending the TRM

The TOGAF TRM identifies a generic set of platform services, and provides a taxonomy in which these platform services are divided into categories of like functionality. A particular organization may need to augment this set with additional services or service categories which are considered to be generic in its own vertical market segment.

The set of services identified and defined for the Application Platform will change over time. New services will be required as new technology appears and as application needs change.

43.3.4.3 Interfaces between Services

In addition to supporting Application Software through the Application Platform Interface (API), services in the Application Platform may support each other, either by openly specified interfaces which may or may not be the same as the API, or by private, unexposed interfaces. A key goal of architecture development is for service modules to be capable of replacement by other modules providing the same service functionality via the same service API. Use of private, unexposed interfaces among service modules may compromise this ability to substitute. Private interfaces represent a risk that should be highlighted to facilitate future transition.

重要的是，认识到 TOGAF TRM 中的应用平台是单一通用概念实体。从 TOGAF TRM 的视角看，应用平台包含所有可能的服务。在特定目标架构中，应用平台将仅包含支持要求的功能所需要的那些服务。

此外，典型情况下，特定目标架构的应用平台不是单一实体，而是实现通常需要的不同功能的不同实体的组合，例如桌面客户端、文件服务器、打印服务器、应用服务器、因特网服务器、数据库服务器等，其中的每一个都将包含一个特定的支持相关特定功能所必需的已定义的服务集。

同样重要的是，认识到现如今很多已经购买和使用的实施技术架构的现实的 IT 系统已经完全具备了多项先进服务，买方通常认为这些服务是理所当然的。例如，现如今典型的台式计算机系统都带有实施 TOGAF TRM 服务类别中的大部分（并非全部）服务的软件。因为这样一种系统的采购方通常不会考虑比整体打包在系统里的服务更“小”的任何事，所以服务包可能极易成为“平台”。的确，缺少用于指导采购流程的技术架构时，这样的事必然会发生。当该流程在整个 ENTERPRISE 内重复时，采购用于类似功能（例如桌面客户端、打印服务器等）的不同系统可能包含明显不同的服务包。

在技术架构中，以“构建块”的形式表示服务包。从 TRM 的概念应用平台到 ENTERPRISE 特定技术架构，IT 架构师的关键任务之一是展望 ENTERPRISE 中已经存在的现实的平台集的发展。IT 架构师必须分析实际需要的服务，以便以最佳方式实施满足 ENTERPRISE 业务需求的 IT 基础设施，并定义该组最佳解决方案构建块（SBB），即现实的“平台”，以实施该架构。

43.3.4.2 扩展 TRM

TOGAF TRM 识别一组通用平台服务，并提供可将这些平台服务分为几个功能性相似的类别的分类法。某一特殊组织可能需要在该组服务中增加在其自身垂直市场区域中视为通用的附加服务或服务类别。

为应用平台识别和定义的该服务集将随时间变化。随着新技术的出现和应用需要的变化，也需要新的服务。

43.3.4.3 服务间的界面

除了通过应用平台界面（API）支持应用软件之外，应用平台中的服务可能既可通过公开指定的可能与 API 相同也可能不相同的界面，也可通过未公开的私有界面互相支持。架构开发的关键目标在于，使服务模块能由通过相同的服务 API 提供相同服务功能性的其他模块代替。在服务模块之间使用未公开的私有界面可能会有损这种代替能力。私有界面代表了一个为促进未来转变而应被重点强调的风险。

43.3.4.4 Future Developments

The TRM deals with future developments in the Application Platform in two ways. Firstly, as interfaces to services become standardized, functionality which previously formed part of the Application Software entity migrates to become part of the Application Platform. Secondly, the TRM may be extended with new service categories as new technology appears.

Examples of functional areas which may fall into Application Platform service categories in the future include:

- Spreadsheet functions, including the capability to create, manipulate, and present information in tables or charts; this capability should include fourth generation language- like capabilities that enable the use of programming logic within spreadsheets.
- Decision support functions, including tools that support the planning, administration, and management of projects.
- Calculation functions, including the capability to perform routine and complex arithmetic calculations.
- Calendar functions, including the capability to manage projects and coordinate schedules via an automated calendar.

A detailed taxonomy of the Application Platform is given in Section 43.4.

43.3.5 Communications Infrastructure

The Communications Infrastructure provides the basic services to interconnect systems and provide the basic mechanisms for opaque transfer of data. It contains the hardware and software elements which make up the networking and physical communications links used by a system, and of course all the other systems connected to the network. It deals with the complex world of networks and the physical Communications Infrastructure, including switches, service providers, and the physical transmission media.

A primary driver in enterprise-wide Technology Architecture in recent years has been the growing awareness of the utility and cost-effectiveness of the Internet as the basis of a Communications Infrastructure for enterprise integration. This is causing a rapid increase in Internet usage and a steady increase in the range of applications linking to the network for distributed operation.

This is considered further in Section 43.3.7.

43.3.6 Application Platform Interface

The Application Platform Interface (API) specifies a complete interface between the Application Software and the underlying Application Platform across which all services are provided. A rigorous definition of the interface results in application portability, provided that both platform and application conform to it. For this to work, the API definition must include the syntax and semantics of not just the programmatic interface, but also all necessary protocol and data structure definitions.

Portability depends on the symmetry of conformance of both applications and the platform to the architected API. That is, the platform must support the API as specified, and the application must use no more than the specified API.

The API specifies a complete interface between an application and one or more services offered by the underlying Application Platform. An application may use several APIs, and may even use different APIs for different implementations of the same service.

43.3.4.4 未来开发

TRM 在应用平台中以两种方式处理未来开发。首先，随着服务界面的标准化，之前构成应用软件实体一部分的功能性迁移成为应用平台的一部分。其次，随着新技术的出现，TRM 可以拓展出新服务类别。

未来可能归入应用平台服务类别的功能领域的示例包括：

- 电子表格功能，包括创建、操作和表达表格或图表中信息的能力；这种能力应包括能在电子表格内使用编程逻辑的类似第四代语言的能力。
- 决策支持功能，包括支持项目的规划、监管和管理的工具。
- 计算功能，包括执行常规的和复杂的算数计算的能力。
- 日历功能，包括通过自动日历来管理项目并协调进度的能力。

43.4 节给出应用平台的详细分类法。

43.3.5 通信基础设施

通信基础设施提供互连系统的基本服务，还提供对数据进行不透明传送的基本机制。通信基础设施包含组成该系统，还有所有连接至网络的其他系统所使用的网络和物理通信链路的硬件和软件元素。它处理复杂的网络世界和物理通信基础设施，包括交换机、服务提供商和物理传输媒介。

近年来，整个 ENTERPRISE 范围技术架构的主要驱动因素已经是互联网在实用性和成本效益方面日益成熟的意识，作为通信基础设施进行 ENTERPRISE 综合的基础。这正导致互联网使用率的快速增长，以及联系到分布运行网络的应用范围的稳定增长。

这一点在 43.3.7 节中进一步论述。

43.3.6 应用平台界面

应用平台界面（API）规定应用软件与提供所有服务的基础应用平台之间的完整界面。界面的严格定义带来应用可移植性，但条件是平台和应用都符合该定义。为了能正常工作，API 定义必须不只是包括编程界面的语法和语义，还要包括所有必要的协议和数据结构定义。

可移植性取决于应用和平台与架构 API 相符的对称性。换言之，该平台必须支持规定的 API，且应用必须仅使用规定的 API。

API 规定应用与由基础应用平台提供的一项或多项服务之间的完整界面。应用可以使用若干个 API，甚至对于同一项服务的不同实施可以使用不同的 API。

43.3.7 Communications Infrastructure Interface

The Communications Infrastructure Interface is the interface between the Application Platform and the Communications Infrastructure.

Figure 43-1 seeks to reflect the increasingly important role of the Internet as the basis for inter- and intra-enterprise interoperability. The horizontal dimension of the model in Figure 43-1 represents diversity, and the shape of the model is specifically intended to emphasize minimum diversity at the interface between the Application Platform and the Communications Infrastructure.

In particular, the model emphasizes the importance of focusing on the core set of services that can be guaranteed to be supported by every IP-based network, as the foundation on which to build today's interoperable enterprise computing environments.

43.3.8 Qualities

Besides the set of components making up the TRM, there is a set of attributes or qualities that are applicable across the components. For example, for the management service to be effective, manageability must be a pervasive quality of all platform services, applications, and Communications Infrastructure services.

Figure 43-2 captures this concept by depicting the TRM components sitting on a backplane of qualities.

Another example of a service quality is security. The proper system-wide implementation of security requires not only a set of Security services, corresponding to the security services category shown in the platform, but also the support (i.e., the "security awareness") of software in other parts of the TRM. Thus, an application might use a security service to mark a file as read-only, but it is the correct implementation of the security quality in the operating system services which prevents write operations on the file. Security and operating system services must co-operate in making the file secure.

Qualities are specified in detail during the development of a Target Architecture. Some qualities are easier than others to describe in terms of standards. For instance, support of a set of locales can be defined to be part of the specification for the international operation quality. Other qualities can better be specified in terms of measures rather than standards. An example would be performance, for which standard APIs or protocols are of limited use.

43.3.7 通信基础设施界面

通信基础设施界面是应用平台与通信基础设施之间的界面。

图 43-1 旨在反映互联网作为 ENTERPRISE 间和 ENTERPRISE 内部实现互用性的基础的日益重要的角色。图 43-1 中模型的横向维度代表多样性，模型的形状特别用来强调应用平台与通信基础设施之间界面的最低程度的多样性。

特别是，该模型强调聚焦于可以确保由每个基于 IP 的网络支持的核心服务集的重要性，作为构建当今可互操作的 ENTERPRISE 计算环境的基础。

43.3.8 质量

除了组成 TRM 的组件集，还存在跨组件适用的属性或质量集。例如，为了使管理服务有效，可管理性必须是全部平台服务、应用和通信基础设施服务的普遍质量。

图 43-2 通过描述置于在质量背板之上的 TRM 组件捕获这一概念。

服务质量的另一个示例是安保性。适当的全系统安保实施不仅需要一组对应于平台所示安保服务类别的安保服务，还需要 TRM 的其他部分中的软件支持(即，“安保意识”)。因此，应用可以使用安保服务来标记只读文件，但是，操作系统服务中安保质量的正确实施却阻止在文件上进行写入操作。安保和操作系统服务必须合作，确保文件安全。

质量在目标架构开发期间被详细地规定。有些质量比其他质量更易于依据标准进行描述。例如，可将对一组语言环境的支持定义为国际运营质量规范的一部分。依照测度，而非标准，可以更好地规定其他质量。例如，标准 API 或协议的使用受到限制的性能。

43.4 Application Platform — Taxonomy

This section describes the Application Platform taxonomy, including basic principles and a summary of services and qualities. A detailed taxonomy of platform services and qualities can be found in Section 43.5.

43.4.1 Basic Principles

The TOGAF TRM has two main components:

1. A **taxonomy**, which defines terminology, and provides a coherent description of the components and conceptual structure of an information system.
2. An associated **TRM graphic**, which provides a visual representation of the taxonomy, as an aid to understanding.

This section describes in detail the taxonomy of the TOGAF TRM. The aim is to provide a core taxonomy that provides a useful, consistent, structured definition of the Application Platform entity and is widely acceptable.

No claims are made that the chosen categorization is the only one possible, or that it represents the optimal choice.

Indeed, it is important to emphasize that the use of TOGAF, and in particular the TOGAF ADM, is in no way dependent on use of the TOGAF TRM taxonomy. Other taxonomies are perfectly possible, and may be preferable for some organizations.

For example, a different taxonomy may be embodied in the legacy of previous architectural work by an organization, and the organization may prefer to perpetuate use of that taxonomy. Alternatively, an organization may decide that it can derive a more suitable, organization-specific taxonomy by extending or adapting the TOGAF TRM taxonomy.

In the same way, an organization may prefer to depict the TOGAF taxonomy (or its own taxonomy) using a different form of TRM graphic, which better captures legacy concepts and proves easier for internal communication purposes.

43.4.2 Application Platform Service Categories

The major categories of services defined for the Application Platform are listed below.

Note that "Object Services" does not appear as a category in the TRM taxonomy. This is because all the individual object services are incorporated into the relevant main service categories. However, the various descriptions are also collected into a single subsection (see Section 43.4.2.1) in order to provide a single point of reference which shows how object services relate to the main service categories.

- Data Interchange Services (see Section 43.5.1):
  - Document generic data typing and conversion services
  - Graphics data interchange services
  - Specialized data interchange services
  - Electronic data interchange services
  - Fax services

43.4 应用平台—分类法

本节描述应用平台分类法，包括服务和质量的基本原则及概要。平台服务和质量的详细分类法可见 43.5 节。

43.4.1 基本原则

TOGAF TRM 具有两个主要组件：

1. **分类法**，它定义术语，并对信息系统的组件和概念结构提供一致的描述。
2. 相关的 **TRM 图形**，作为一种帮助理解的手段，它提供分类法的直观表达。

本节详细地描述 TOGAF TRM 的分类法。目的是提供一种得到广泛认可的核心分类法，这种分类法提供应用平台实体的有用、一致和结构化的定义。

不做出任何关于所选分类是唯一一种可能或者所选分类代表最佳选择的声明。

实际上，重要的是强调 TOGAF 的使用，尤其是 TOGAF ADM，绝不依赖于 TOGAF TRM 分类法的使用。其他分类法是完全有可能的，而且对一些组织而言也更为可取。

例如，不同的分类法可以由组织体现在之前架构工作的遗留物中，而且组织可能更愿意延续使用该分类法。另一方面，组织可以决定其能够通过扩展或调整 TOGAF TRM 分类法的方式取得更为适当的组织特定的分类法。

同样，组织可能更愿意利用不同形式的 TRM 图形描述 TOGAF 分类法（或它自己的分类法），以更好地获取遗留概念并证明更易于实现内部通信。

43.4.2 应用平台服务类别

下面列出为应用平台定义的主要服务类别。

需要注意，“对象服务”未作为一个类别出现在 TRM 分类法中。这是因为，所有单独对象服务均被包含到相关的主要服务类别中。但是，不同的描述还是会整理到一个小节（见 43.4.2.1 节）中，以便提供单一的参考点，表明对象服务是如何与主要服务类别相关联的。

- 数据交换服务（见 43.5.1 节）：
  - 文件化通用数据键入和转换服务
  - 图形数据交换服务
  - 专有数据交换服务
  - 电子数据交换服务
  - 原始图形界面功能

- — Raw graphics interface functions
- — Text processing functions
- — Document processing functions
- — Publishing functions
- — Video processing functions
- — Audio processing functions
- — Multimedia processing functions
- — Media synchronization functions
- — Information presentation and distribution functions
- — Hypertext functions

- Data Management Services (see Section 43.5.2):
  - Data dictionary/repository services
  - Database Management System (DBMS) services
  - Object-Oriented Database Management System (OODBMS) services
  - File management services
  - Query processing functions
  - Screen generation functions
  - Report generation functions
  - Networking/concurrent access functions
  - Warehousing functions
- Graphics and Imaging Services (see Section 43.5.3):
  - Graphical object management services
  - Drawing services
  - Imaging functions
- International Operation Services (see Section 43.5.4):
  - Character sets and data representation services
  - Cultural convention services
  - Local language support services
- Location and Directory Services (see Section 43.5.5):
  - Directory services
  - Special-purpose naming services
  - Service location services
  - Registration services
  - Filtering services

- 文本处理功能
- 文件处理功能
- 发布功能
- 视频处理功能
- 音频处理功能
- 多媒体处理功能
- 媒介同步功能
- 信息展示和分配功能
- 超文本功能

■ 数据管理服务（见 43.5.2 节）：
- 数据字典/存储库服务
- 数据库管理系统（DBMS）服务
- 面向对象的数据库管理系统（OODBMS）服务
- 文件管理服务
- 查询处理功能
- 屏蔽生成功能
- 报表生成功能
- 联网/并发访问功能
- 入库存储功能

■ 图形和成像服务（见 43.5.3 节）：
- 图形对象管理服务
- 绘图服务
- 成像功能

■ 国际运营服务（见 43.5.4 节）：
- 字符集和数据表达服务
- 文化习俗服务
- 本地语言支持服务

■ 位置和目录服务（见 43.5.5 节）：
- 目录服务
- 专用命名服务
- 服务位置服务
- 注册服务
- 过滤服务

  - Accounting services
- Network Services (see Section 43.5.6):
  - Data communications services
  - Electronic mail services
  - Distributed data services
  - Distributed file services
  - Distributed name services
  - Distributed time services
  - Remote process (access) services
  - Remote print spooling and output distribution services
  - Enhanced telephony functions
  - Shared screen functions
  - Video conferencing functions
  - Broadcast functions
  - Mailing list functions
- Operating System Services (see Section 43.5.7):
  - Kernel operations services
  - Command interpreter and utility services
  - Batch processing services
  - File and directory synchronization services
- Software Engineering Services (see Section 43.5.8):
  - Programming language services
  - Object code linking services
  - Computer-aided software engineering (CASE) environment and tools services
  - Graphical user interface (GUI) building services
  - Scripting language services
  - Language binding services
  - Run-time environment services
  - Application binary interface services
- Transaction Processing Services (see Section 43.5.9):
  - Transaction manager services
- User Interface Services (see Section 43.5.10):
  - Graphical client/server services
  - Display objects services

  - 账户服务
- 网络服务（见 43.5.6 节）：
  - 数据通信服务
  - 电子邮件服务
  - 分布式数据服务
  - 分布式文件服务
  - 分布式名称服务
  - 分布式时间服务
  - 远程进程（访问）服务
  - 远程打印排队和输出分配服务
  - 增强的通话功能
  - 共享屏幕功能
  - 视频会议功能
  - 广播功能
  - 邮件列表功能
- 操作系统服务（见 43.5.7 节）：
  - 核运算服务
  - 命令解释器和实用程序服务
  - 批量处理服务
  - 文件和目录同步服务
- 软件工程服务（见 43.5.8 节）：
  - 编程语言服务
  - 对象代码链接服务
  - 计算机辅助软件工程（CASE）环境和工具服务
  - 用户图形界面（GUI）构建服务
  - 脚本语言服务
  - 语言绑定服务
  - 运行时环境服务
  - 应用二进制界面服务
- 事务处理服务（见 43.5.9 节）：
  - 事务管理程序服务
- 用户界面服务（见 43.5.10 节）：
  - 图形客户端/服务器服务
  - 显示对象服务

  - Window management services
  - Dialog support services
  - Printing services
  - Computer-based training and online help services
  - Character-based services
- Security Services (see Section 43.5.11):
  - Identification and authentication services
  - System entry control services
  - Audit services
  - Access control services
  - Non-repudiation services
  - Security management services
  - Trusted recovery services
  - Encryption services
  - Trusted communication services
- System and Network Management Services (see Section 43.5.12):
  - User management services
  - Configuration management (CM) services
  - Performance management services
  - Availability and fault management services
  - Accounting management services
  - Security management services
  - Print management services
  - Network management services
  - Backup and restore services
  - Online disk management services
  - License management services
  - Capacity management services
  - Software installation services
  - Trouble ticketing services

43.4.2.1 Object-Oriented Provision of Services

A detailed description of each of these service categories is given in Section 43.5.13.

- Object Request Broker (ORB) Services:

- — 窗口管理服务
- — 对话支持服务
- — 打印服务
- — 基于计算机的培训和在线帮助服务
- — 基于字符的服务

■ 安保服务（见 43.5.11 节）：

- — 识别和认证服务
- — 系统入口控制服务
- — 审核服务
- — 访问控制服务
- — 反拒认服务
- — 安保管理服务
- — 可信恢复服务
- — 加密服务
- — 可信通信服务

■ 统和网络管理服务（见 43.5.12 节）：

- — 用户管理服务
- — 构型管理（CM）服务
- — 性能管理服务
- — 可用性和故障管理服务
- — 账户管理服务
- — 安保管理服务
- — 打印管理服务
- — 网络管理服务
- — 备份与恢复服务
- — 网盘管理服务
- — 许可管理服务
- — 容量管理服务
- — 软件安装服务
- — 故障标签服务

43.4.2.1 面向对象的服务提供

43.5.13 节提供每种服务类别的详细描述。

■ 对象要求代理（ORB）服务：

  - Implementation repository services
  - Installation and activation services
  - Interface repository services
  - Replication services
- Common Object Services:
  - Change management services
  - Collections services
  - Concurrency control services
  - Data interchange services
  - Event management services
  - Externalization services
  - Licensing services
  - Lifecycle services
  - Naming services
  - Persistent object services
  - Properties services
  - Query services
  - Relationship services
  - Security services
  - Start-up services
  - Time services
  - Trading services
  - Transaction services

43.4.3 Application Platform Service Qualities

43.4.3.1 Principles

Besides the platform service categories delineated by functional category, service qualities affect Information Systems Architectures. A service quality describes a behavior such as adaptability or manageability. Service qualities have a pervasive effect on the operation of most or all of the functional service categories.

In general a requirement for a given level of a particular service quality requires one or more functional service categories to co-operate in achieving the objective. Usually this means that the software building blocks that implement the functional services contain software which contributes to the implementation of the quality.

For the quality to be provided properly, all relevant functional services must have been designed to support it. Service qualities may also require support from software in the Application Software entity and the External Environment as well as the Application Platform.

  - 实施储存库服务
  - 安装和激活服务
  - 界面存储库服务
  - 拷贝服务
- 公共对象服务：
  - 变更管理服务
  - 集合服务
  - 并行控制服务
  - 数据交换服务
  - 事件管理服务
  - 外部化服务
  - 许可服务
  - 生命周期服务
  - 命名服务
  - 持久化对象服务
  - 特性服务
  - 查询服务
  - 关系服务
  - 安保服务
  - 启动服务
  - 时间服务
  - 交易服务
  - 事务服务

43.4.3 应用平台服务质量

43.4.3.1 原则

除了按照功能类别描绘的平台服务类别之外，服务质量还影响信息系统架构。服务质量描述诸如适应性或可管理性等特性。服务质量对大部分或全部功能服务类别的运行具有广泛影响。

通常，对给定层级的特殊服务质量的要求需要一个或多个功能服务类别合作以实现该目的。通常，这意味着，实施功能服务的软件构建块包含有助于实现该质量的软件。

为了恰当提供该质量，所有相关功能服务必须设计成支持该质量的。服务质量可能还需要从应用软件实体和外部环境以及应用平台的软件中获取支持。

In some cases, a service quality affects each of the service categories in a similar fashion, while in other cases, the service quality has a unique influence on one particular service category. For instance, international operation depends on most of the service categories in the same way, both providing facilities and needing their co-operation for localization of messages, fonts, and other features of a locale, but it may have a more profound effect on the software engineering services, where facilities for producing internationalized software may be required.

During the process of architecture development, the architect must be aware of the existence of qualities and the extent of their influence on the choice of software building blocks used in implementing the architecture. The best way of making sure that qualities are not forgotten is to create a quality matrix, describing the relationships between each functional service and the qualities that influence it.

43.4.3.2 Taxonomy of Service Qualities

The service qualities presently identified in the TRM taxonomy are:

- **Availability** (the degree to which something is available for use), including:
  - **Manageability**, the ability to gather information about the state of something and to control it
  - **Serviceability**, the ability to identify problems and take corrective action, such as to repair or upgrade a component in a running system
  - **Performance**, the ability of a component to perform its tasks in an appropriate time
  - **Reliability**, or resistance to failure
  - **Recoverability**, or the ability to restore a system to a working state after an interruption
  - **Locatability**, the ability of a system to be found when needed
- **Assurance**, including:
  - **Security**, or the protection of information from unauthorized access
  - **Integrity**, or the assurance that data has not been corrupted
  - **Credibility**, or the level of trust in the integrity of the system and its data
- **Usability**, or ease-of-operation by users, including:
  - **International Operation**, including multi-lingual and multi-cultural abilities
- **Adaptability**, including:
  - **Interoperability**, whether within or outside the organization (for instance, interoperability of calendaring or scheduling functions may be key to the usefulness of a system)
  - **Scalability**, the ability of a component to grow or shrink its performance or capacity appropriately to the demands of the environment in which it operates
  - **Portability**, of data, people, applications, and components
  - **Extensibility**, or the ability to accept new functionality
  - The ability to offer access to services in new paradigms such as object-orientation

在一些情况下，服务质量以相似的方式影响每个服务类别，但在其他情况下，服务质量对一种特殊服务类别有独特的影响。例如，国际运营依赖于相同方式的大部分服务类别，既提供设施也需要它们合作，以便本地化当地语言环境的消息、字体和其他特征，但是在可能需要制造国际化软件的设施的情况下，可能对软件工程服务有更深远的影响。

在架构开发过程中，架构师必须意识到，质量的存在以及质量对选择用于实施架构中的软件构建块的影响程度。确保质量不被忽视的最佳方式是创建一个质量矩阵，描述每个功能服务与影响该服务的质量之间的关系。

43.4.3.2 服务质量的分类法

目前在 TRM 分类法中识别的服务质量为：

- **可用性**（某物可加以利用的程度），包括：
  - **可管理性**，收集某物状态信息并对其控制的能力
  - **可服务性**，识别问题并采取纠正措施的能力，诸如修复或升级运行系统中的一个组件
  - **性能**，组件在适当的时间内执行任务的能力
  - **可靠性**，或抗故障能力
  - **可恢复性**，或系统中断后将其恢复到工作状态的能力
  - **可定位性**，在需要时定位系统的能力
- **保障性**，包括：
  - **安保性**，或者防止信息被未经授权访问
  - **完整性**，或者确保数据未被破坏
  - **可信度**，或在系统及其数据完整性方面值得信任的级别
- **使用性**，或用户的易于操作性，包括：
  - **国际运营**，包括多种语言及多种文化的能力
- **适应性**，包括：
  - **互用性**，无论是在组织之内还是之外（例如，日程或进度安排功能的互操作性可能对系统有用性而言非常关键）
  - **可缩放性**，组件根据其所处操作环境适当提高或缩减其性能或容量的能力
  - 数据、人员、应用和组件的**可移植性**
  - **可扩展性**，或接受新功能性的能力
  - 对新范式（如面向对象）中的服务进行访问的能力

43.5 Detailed Platform Taxonomy

This section provides a detailed taxonomy of platform services and qualities.

43.5.1 Data Interchange Services

Data interchange services provide specialized support for the exchange of information between applications and the external environment. These services are designed to handle data interchange between applications on the same platform and applications on different (heterogeneous) platforms. An analogous set of services exists for object-oriented data interchange, which can be found under Data Interchange services and Externalization services in Section 43.5.13.

- **Document Generic Data Typing and Conversion** services are supported by specifications for encoding the data (e.g., text, picture, numeric, special character) and both the logical and visual structures of electronic documents, including compound documents.
- **Graphics Data Interchange** services are supported by device-independent descriptions of picture elements for vector-based graphics and descriptions for raster-based graphics.
- **Specialized Data Interchange** services are supported by specifications that describe data used by specific vertical markets. Markets where such specifications exist include the Medical, Library, Dental, Assurance, and Oil industries.
- **Electronic Data Interchange** services are used to create an electronic (paperless) environment for conducting commerce and achieving significant gains in quality, responsiveness, and savings afforded by such an environment. Examples of applications that use electronic commerce services include: vendor search and selection; contract award; product data; shipping, forwarding, and receiving; customs; payment information; inventory control; maintenance; tax-related data; and insurance-related data.
- **Fax** services are used to create, examine, transmit, and/or receive fax images.

The following functional areas are currently supported mainly by Application Software, but are progressing towards migration into the Application Platform:

- **Raw Graphics Interface** functions support graphics data file formats such as TIFF, JPEG, GIF, and CGM.
- **Text Processing** functions, including the capability to create, edit, merge, and format text.
- **Document Processing** functions, including the capability to create, edit, merge, and format documents. These functions enable the composition of documents that incorporate graphics, images, and even voice annotation, along with stylized text. Included are advanced formatting and editing functions such as style guides, spell checking, use of multiple columns, table of contents generation, headers and footers, outlining tools, and support for scanning images into bit-mapped formats. Other capabilities include compression and decompression of images or whole documents.
- **Publishing** functions, including incorporation of photographic quality images and color graphics, and advanced formatting and style features such as wrapping text around graphic objects or pictures and kerning (i.e., changing the spacing between text characters). These functions also interface with sophisticated printing and production equipment. Other capabilities include color rendering and compression and decompression of images or whole documents.

43.5 详细的平台分类法

本节提供平台服务和质量的详细分类法。

43.5.1 数据交换服务

数据交换服务为应用与外部环境之间的信息交换提供专门的支持。这些服务被设计成用于处理相同平台上的应用与不同（异构的）平台上的应用之间的数据交换。面向对象的数据交换中存在一组类似的服务，它们可以在 43.5.13 节中的数据交换服务和外部化服务下找到。

- **文件通用数据键入和转换**服务，由数据（例如，文本、图片、数值、特殊字符）的编码规范以及电子文件（包括复合文件）的逻辑结构和视觉结构支持。
- **图形数据交换**服务，由与设备无关的关于基于向量的图形的图像元素的描述以及对基于光栅的图形的描述支持。
- **专用数据交换**服务，由描述特定垂直市场使用的数据的规范支持。存在此类规范的市场包括医疗、图书馆、牙科、保险和石油等行业。
- **电子数据交换**服务，用于创建一种电子（无纸）环境，以开展电子商务，并在由这样一种环境提供的质量、响应能力和节约等方面得到显著提高。使用电子商务服务的应用示例包括：厂商搜索和选择；契约签订；产品数据；装运、转发和接收；关税；付款信息；库存控制；维护；税务相关的数据；以及保险相关的数据。
- **传真**服务，用于创建、审查、传送和/或接收传真图像。

下述功能领域目前主要由应用软件提供支持，但是正迁移入应用平台：

- **原始图形界面**功能，支持如 TIFF、JPEG、GIF 和 CGM 等图形数据文件格式。
- **文本处理**功能，包括创建、编辑、合并和格式化文本的能力。
- **文件处理**功能，包括创建、编辑、合并和格式化文件的能力。这些功能使得包含图形、图像甚至是语音标注以及形式化文本的文件组合变得可能。包括先进的格式化和编辑功能，诸如样式指南、拼写检查、使用多列、生成目录、页眉和页脚、概要工具以及对将图像扫描成位映像格式的支持。其他能力包括对图像或全部文件的压缩和解压。
- **出版**功能，包括摄影质量的图像与彩色图形的合并，以及先进的格式化和样式特征，例如对图形对象或图像周围的文字进行换行及字距调整（即，改变文本字符之间的间距）。这些功能还与复杂的印刷和生产设备连接。其他能力包括颜色再现以及对图像或全部文件的压缩和解压。

- **Video Processing** functions, including the capability to capture, compose, edit, compress, and decompress video information using formats such as MPEG. Still graphics and title generation functions are also provided.
- **Audio Processing** functions, including the capability to capture, compose, edit, compress, and decompress audio information.
- **Multimedia Processing** functions, including the capability to store, retrieve, modify, sort, search, and print all or any combination of the above-mentioned media. This includes support for microfilm media, optical storage technology that allows for storage of scanned or computer produced documents using digital storage techniques, a scanning capability, and data compression and decompression.
- **Media Synchronization** functions allow the synchronization of streams of data such as audio and video for presentation purposes.
- **Information Presentation and Distribution** functions are used to manage the distribution and presentation of information from batch and interactive applications. These functions are used to shield business area applications from how information is used. They allow business area applications to create generic pools of information without embedding controls that dictate the use of that information. Information distribution and presentation functions include the selection of the appropriate formatting functions required to accomplish the distribution and presentation of information to a variety of business area applications and users. Information presentation and distribution functions also include the capability to store, archive, prioritize, restrict, and recreate information.
- **Hypertext** functions support the generation, distribution, location, search, and display of text and images either locally or globally. These functions include searching and browsing, hypertext linking, and the presentation of multimedia information.

43.5.2 Data Management Services

Central to most systems is the management of data that can be defined independently of the processes that create or use it, maintained indefinitely, and shared among many processes. Data management services include:

- **Data Dictionary/Repository** services allow data administrators and information engineers to access and modify data about data (i.e., metadata). Such data may include internal and external formats, integrity and security rules, and location within a distributed system. Data dictionary and repository services also allow end users and applications to define and obtain data that is available in the database. Data administration defines the standardization and registration of individual data element types to meet the requirements for data sharing and interoperability among information systems throughout the enterprise. Data administration functions include procedures, guidelines, and methods for effective data planning, analysis, standards, modeling, configuration management, storage, retrieval, protection, validation, and documentation. Data dictionaries are sometimes tied toa single Database Management System (DBMS), but heterogeneous data dictionaries will support access to different DBMSs. Repositories can contain a wide variety of information including Management Information Bases (MIB) or CASE-related information. Object-oriented systems may provide repositories for objects and interfaces, described under Implementation Repository services and Interface Repository services in Section 43.5.13.
- **Database Management System** (DBMS) services provide controlled access to structured data. To manage the data, the DBMS provides concurrency control and facilities to combine data from different schemas. Different types of DBMS support different data models, including relational, hierarchical, network, object-oriented, and flat-file models.

- **视频处理**功能，包括截获、组成、编辑、压缩和解压使用诸如 MPEG 格式的视频信息的能力。还提供了图形和标题生成功能。
- **音频处理**功能，包括截获、组成、编辑、压缩和解压音频信息的能力。
- **多媒介处理**功能，包括存储、检索、修改、分类、搜索和打印上述介质的全部或任意组合的能力。包括对缩微胶片介质、允许使用数字存储技术存储扫描的或计算机产生的文件的光学存储技术、扫描能力以及数据压缩和解压的支持。
- **介质同步**功能，它使得诸如音频和视频等数据流能同步，方便展示。
- **信息展示和分配**功能，它用于管理对来自于批量应用和交互应用的信息的分配和展示。这些功能用于保护业务领域应用，以免受到信息使用方式的影响。它们使得业务领域应用能创建通用信息池，无需嵌入指令使用的该信息的控制器。信息分配和展示功能包括选择适当的格式化功能，这些格式化功能是完成向各种业务领域应用和用户分配和展示信息所需的功能。信息展示和分配功能还包括存储、存档、按优先序排列、限制和重新创建信息的能力。
- **超文本功能**，支持文本及图像的局部或全局生成、分配、定位、搜索和展示。这些功能包括搜索和浏览、超文本链接及显示多媒体信息。

43.5.2 数据管理服务

多数系统的核心是，对可以独立于创建或使用信息的流程进行定义、对可以无限期地保持并在多个流程中共享的数据进行管理。数据管理服务包括：

- **数据字典/存储库**服务，它使得数据管理员和信息工程师能访问并修改关于数据的数据（即元数据）。此类数据可以包括内外格式、完整性和安保性规则及在分布式系统之内的位置。数据字典和存储库服务还允许终端用户及应用定义并获得在数据库中可用的数据。数据管理定义各个数据元素类型的标准化和注册，以满足对贯穿于 ENTERPRISE 的多个信息系统间的数据共享和互用性的要求。数据管理功能包括进行有效数据规划、分析、标准、建模、构型管理、存储、检索、保护、确认和文件化的程序、指南和方法。数据字典有时被绑定到单一数据库管理系统（DBMS），但是不同种类的数据字典将支持对不同 DBMS 的访问。存储库可以包含各类信息，包括管理信息库（MIB）或 CASE 相关的信息。面向对象的系统可以提供在 43.5.13 节中的实施存储库服务和界面存储库服务下描述的对象和界面存储库。
- **数据库管理系统**（DBMS）服务，它向结构化数据提供受控访问。为了管理数据，DBMS 提供并发控制和设施，以组合来源于不同方案的数据。不同类型的 DBMS 支持不同的数据模型，包括关系模型、层级结构模型、网络模型、面向对象的模型以及平面文件模型。

Some DBMSs are designed for special functions such as the storage of large objects or multimedia data. DBMS services are accessible through a programming language interface, an interactive data manipulation language interface (such as SQL), or an interactive/fourth-generation language interface. Look-up and retrieval services for objects are described separately under Query services in Section 43.5.13. For efficiency, DBMSs often provide specific services to create, populate, move, backup, restore, recover, and archive databases, although some of these services could be provided by the general file management capabilities described in Section 43.5.7 or a specific backup service. Some DBMSs support distribution of the database, including facilities for remotely updating records, data replication, locating and caching data, and remote management.

- **Object-Oriented Database Management System** (OODBMS) services provide storage for objects and interfaces to those objects. These services may support the Implementation Repository, Interface Repository, and Persistent Object services in Section 43.5.13.
- **File Management** services provide data management through file access methods including indexed sequential (ISAM) and hashed random access. Flat file and directory services are described in Section 43.5.7.

The following functional areas are currently supported mainly by Application Software, but are progressing towards migration into the Application Platform:

- **Query Processing** functions that provide for interactive selection, extraction, and formatting of stored information from files and databases. Query processing functions are invoked via user-oriented languages and tools (often referred to as fourth generation languages), which simplify the definition of searching criteria and aid in creating effective presentation of the retrieved information (including use of graphics).
- **Screen Generation** functions that provide the capability to define and generate screens that support the retrieval, presentation, and update of data.
- **Report Generation** functions that provide the capability to define and generate hardcopy reports composed of data extracted from a database.
- **Networking/Concurrent Access** functions that manage concurrent user access to Database Management System (DBMS) functions.
- **Warehousing** functions that provide the capability to store very large amounts of data — usually captured from other database systems — and to perform online analytical processing on it in support of *ad hoc* queries.

43.5.3 Graphics and Imaging Services

Graphics services provide functions required for creating, storing, retrieving, and manipulating images. These services include:

- **Graphical Object Management** services, including defining multi-dimensional graphic objects in a form that is independent of output devices, and managing hierarchical structures containing graphics data. Graphical data formats include two-and three-dimensional geometric drawings as well as images.
- **Drawing** services support the creation and manipulation of images with software such as GKS, PEX, PHIGS, or OpenGL.

The following functional areas are currently supported mainly by Application Software, but are progressing towards migration into the Application Platform:

有些 DBMS 被设计用于执行诸如存储大型对象或多媒体数据的特殊功能。DBMS 服务可以通过编程语言界面、交互数据操作语言界面（例如 SQL）或交互式/第四代语言界面访问。在 43.5.13 节的查询服务下具体地描述对象的查找和检索服务。为了提高效率，DBMS 通常提供创建、充实、移动、备份、还原、恢复和存档数据库的特定服务，虽然这些服务中的一些服务可以由 43.5.7 节中描述的一般文件管理能力或特定的备份服务提供。有些 DBMS 支持数据库的分配，包括进行远程更新记录、数据拷贝、定位和高速缓存数据以及远程管理的设施。

- **面向对象的数据库管理系统**（OODBMS）服务提供对对象的存储以及这些对象的界面。这些服务可以支持 43.5.13 节中的实施存储库服务、界面存储库服务和持久化对象服务。
- **文件管理服务**通过包括索引顺序的文件访问方法（ISAM）和散列的随机访问提供数据管理。在 43.5.7 节中描述了平面文件和目录服务。

下述功能领域目前主要由应用软件提供支持，但是正在朝着向应用平台的迁移前进：

- **查询处理**功能，为来自于文件和数据库的存储信息提供交互式选择、提取和格式化。查询处理功能通过面向用户的语言和工具（通常被称为第四代语言）调用，简化了搜索准则的定义，并且有助于创建检索到的信息的有效展示（包括使用图形）。
- **屏幕生成**功能，提供对支持数据检索、展示和更新的屏幕进行定义和生成的能力。
- **报表生成**功能，提供对由从数据库中提取的数据构成的硬拷贝报表进行定义和生成的能力。
- **联网/并发访问**功能，管理对数据库管理系统（DBMS）功能的并发用户访问。
- **入库存储**功能，提供存储大量数据（通常从其他数据库系统中获取），并在临时查询的支持下对数据进行在线分析处理的能力。

43.5.3 图形和成像服务

图形服务提供创建、存储、检索和操纵图像所需的功能。这些服务包括：

- **图形对象管理**服务，包括定义独立于输出设备形式的多维图形对象，及管理含有图形数据的层级结构。图形数据格式包括二维和三维的几何图形以及图像。
- **绘图**服务，支持使用诸如 GKS、PEX、PHIGS 或 OpenGL 的软件创建和操纵图像。

下述功能领域目前主要由应用软件提供支持，但是正在迁移入应用平台：

- **Imaging** functions providing for the scan, creation, edit, compression, and decompression of images in accordance with recognized image formatting standards; for example, PIKS/IPI, OpenXIL, or XIE.

43.5.4 International Operation Services

As a practice, information system developers have generally designed and developed systems to meet the requirements of a specific geographic or linguistic market segment, which may be a nation or a particular cultural market. To make that information system viable, or marketable, to a different segment of the market, a full re-engineering process was usually required. Users or organizations that needed to operate in a multi-national or multi-cultural environment typically did so with multiple, generally incompatible information processing systems.

International operation provides a set of services and interfaces that allow a user to define, select, and change between different culturally-related application environments supported by the particular implementation. In general, these services should be provided in such a way that internationalization issues are transparent to the application logic.

- **Character Sets and Data Representation** services include the capability to input, store, manipulate, retrieve, communicate, and present data independently of the coding scheme used. This includes the capability to maintain and access a central character set repository of all coded character sets used throughout the platform. Character sets will be uniquely identified so that the end user or application can select the coded character set to be used. This system-independent representation supports the transfer (or sharing) of the values and syntax, but not the semantics, of data records between communicating systems. The specifications are independent of the internal record and field representations of the communicating systems. Also included is the capability to recognize the coded character set of data entities and subsequently to input, communicate, and present that data.
- **Cultural Convention** services provide the capability to store and access rules and conventions for cultural entities maintained in a cultural convention repository called a "locale". Locales should be available to all applications. Locales typically include date and currency formats, collation sequences, and number formats. Standardized locale formats and APIs allow software entities to use locale information developed by others.
- **Local Language Support** services provide the capability to support more than one language concurrently on a system. Messages, menus, forms, and online documentation can be displayed in the language selected by the user. Input from keyboards that have been modified locally to support the local character sets can be correctly interpreted.

The proper working of international operation services depends on all the software entities involved having the capability to:

- Use locales
- Switch between locales as required
- Maintain multiple active locales
- Access suitable fonts

This requires software entities to be written to a particular style and to be designed from the outset with internationalization in mind.

- **成像**功能，按照得到认可的图像格式化标准，对图像提供扫描、创建、编辑、压缩和解压；例如，PIKS/IPI、OpenXIL 或 XIE。

43.5.4 国际运营服务

作为一项实践，信息系统开发者一般已经设计并开发了满足特定的地理或语言市场区域（可能是某个国家或某个特殊文化市场）需求的系统。为了使信息系统在市场的不同区域可行或适销，通常需要全面的重建流程。需要在多个国家的或多种文化的环境中运行的用户或组织在重建时使用多个通常互不兼容的信息处理系统。

国际运营提供一组服务和界面，使用户能在由特殊实施支持的不同的文化相关应用环境之间定义、选择和变化。通常应以国际化问题对于应用逻辑而言，都是透明的这样一种方式提供这些服务。

- **字符集和数据表达**服务，包括不依赖于所用编码方案输入、存储、操纵、检索、交流和表达数据的能力。这包括维护和访问在整个平台使用的所有编码字符集的中心字符集存储库的能力。字符集会被唯一识别，以使得最终用户或应用可以选择将使用的编码字符集。这种独立于系统的表达，支持通信系统之间的数据记录的值和语法（不是语义）的传输（或共享）。这些规范独立于通信系统的内部记录和字段表达。还包括识别数据实体的编码字符集并随后输入、传送和显示该数据的能力。
- **文化习俗**服务，提供存储和访问保留在称为“语言环境”的文化习俗储存库中的文化实体的规则和习惯。语言环境应可用于所有应用。典型情况下，语言环境包括日期和货币格式、排序规则以及数字格式。标准化语言环境格式和 API 使得软件实体能使用其他实体开发的语言环境信息。
- **本地语言支持**服务，提供在一个系统上同时支持多种语言的能力。消息、菜单、格式和线上文件能用由用户选取的语言显示。可以准确地解释已在本地修改以支持本地字符集的来自键盘的输入。

国际运营服务的适当工作取决于所涉及的具备下述能力的全部软件实体：

- 使用语言环境
- 按要求在两种语言环境之间转换
- 维护多个活跃的语言环境
- 使用适当的字体

这就要求以特殊的样式编写软件实体并从一开始就有国际化意识。

43.5.5 Location and Directory Services

Location and directory services provide specialized support for locating required resources and for mediation between service consumers and service providers.

The World Wide Web, based on the Internet, has created a need for locating information resources, which currently is mainly satisfied through the use of search engines. Advancements in the global Internet, and in heterogeneous distributed systems, demand active mediation through broker services that include automatic and dynamic registration, directory access, directory communication, filtration, and accounting services for access to resources.

- **Directory** services provide services for clients to establish where resources are, and by extension how they can be reached. "Clients" may be humans or computer programs, and "resources" may be a wide variety of things, such as names, email addresses, security certificates, printers, web pages, etc.
- **Special-Purpose Naming** services provide services that refer names (ordered strings of printable characters) to objects within a given context (namespaces). Objects are typically hierarchically organized within namespaces. Examples are:
  - — File systems
  - — Security databases
  - — Process queues
- **Service Location** services provide access to "Yellow Pages" services in response to queries based on constraints.
- **Registration** services provide services to register identity, descriptions of the services a resource is providing, and descriptions of the means to access them.
- **Filtering** services provide services to select useful information from data using defined criteria.
- **Accounting** services provide services such as account open, account update, account balance, account detail, account close, account discounts, account bill/usage tally, account payment settlement based on message traffic, and/or connection time, and/or resource utilization, and/or broker-specific (e.g., value-based).

43.5.6 Network Services

Network services are provided to support distributed applications requiring data access and applications interoperability in heterogeneous or homogeneous networked environments.

A network service consists of both an interface and an underlying protocol.

- **Data Communications**, which include interfaces and protocols for reliable, transparent, end-to-end data transmission across communications networks. Data communications services include both high-level functions (such as file transfer, remote login, remote process execution, or PC integration services) and low-level functions (such as a sockets API) giving direct access to communications protocols.
- **Electronic Mail** services include the capability to send, receive, forward, store, display, retrieve, prioritize, authenticate, and manage messages. This includes the capability to append files and documents to messages. Messages may include any combination of data, text, audio, graphics, and images and should be capable of being formatted into standard data interchange formats. This service includes the use of directories and distribution lists for routing information, the ability to assign priorities, the use of preformatted electronic forms, and the capability to trace the status of messages. Associated services include a summarized listing of incoming messages, a log of messages received and read, the ability to file or print messages, and the ability to reply to or forward messages.

43.5.5 位置和目录服务

位置和目录服务，为所需资源的定位以及服务消费者与服务提供者之间的调解提供专门的支持。

基于互联网的万维网已经创建了定位信息资源的需要，目前主要通过使用搜索引擎来满足这一需求。在全球互联网以及在异构分布式系统中的改进需要通过代理服务主动调解，代理服务包括访问资源时自动的和动态的注册、目录访问、目录通信、过滤和账户服务。

- **目录**服务，它为客户端提供服务以确定资源在哪，乃至如何到达。“客户端”可以是人，也可以是计算机程序，“资源”可以是诸如姓名、电子邮件地址、安保证书、打印机、网页等各种各样的事物。
- **专用命名**服务，它提供在规定背景环境（命名空间）内为对象指定名称（有序的可印字符串）的服务。典型情况下，对象在命名空间内是分层级组织的。示例为：
  — 文件系统
  — 安保性数据库
  — 流程队列
- **服务定位**服务，它提供到“黄页”服务的访问，以基于约束对查询做出响应。
- **注册**服务，它提供注册身份的服务、关于资源正在提供的服务的描述以及关于访问这些资源的手段的描述。
- **过滤**服务，它提供利用定义准则从数据中选取有用信息的服务。
- **账户**服务，它提供诸如账户开立、账户更新、账户结余、账户明细、账户关闭、账户折扣、账户清单/使用的统计情况、基于消息流量的账户支付结算、和/或接通时间、和/或资源利用、和/或代理特定的（如，基于价值的）等各项服务。

43.5.6 网络服务

提供网络服务，以支持在异构或同构的网络环境中需要的数据访问和应用互用性的分布式应用。

一个网络服务由一个界面和一个底层协议组成。

- **数据通信**，它包括跨通信网络进行可靠的、透明的、端对端数据传输的界面和协议。数据通信服务包括高层级功能（如文件传输、远程登录、远程进程执行或 PC 综合服务）和低层级功能（例如，套接字 API），以直接访问通信协议。
- **电子邮件**服务，它包括发送、接收、转发、存储、显示、检索、按优先序排列、验证和管理消息的能力。电子邮件服务包括向消息中添加文件和文档的能力。消息可以包括数据、文本、音频、图形和图像的任意组合，还应能格式化成标准的数据互换格式。该项服务包括使用目录和分发列表发送信息、指派优先级的能力、使用预先格式化的电子表格以及追踪消息状态的能力。相关的服务包括输入消息的汇总清单、接收并读取的消息日志、归档或打印消息的能力以及回复或转发消息的能力。

- **Distributed Data** services provide access to, and modification of, data/metadata in remote or local databases. In a distributed environment, data not available on the local database is fetched from a remote data server at the request of the local client.
- **Distributed File** services provide for transparent remote file access. Applications have equivalent access to data regardless of the data's physical location. Ancillary services for this function can include transparent addressing, cached data, data replication, file locking, and file logging.
- **Distributed Name** services provide a means for unique identification of resources within a distributed computing system. These services are available to applications within the network and provide information that can include resource name, associated attributes, physical location, and resource functionality. Note that all system resources should be identifiable, in all information systems, by the distributed name. This permits physical location to change, not only to accommodate movement, but also load balancing, system utilization, scaling (adding processors and moving resources to accommodate the increased resources), distributed processing, and all aspects of open systems. Distributed name services include directory services such as X.500 and network navigation services. Distributed name services include ways to locate data objects both by name and by function. Section 43.5.13 describes equivalent services under Naming services and Trading services, respectively.
- **Distributed Time** services provide synchronized time co-ordination as required among distributed processes in different timezones. An equivalent service is described under Time services in Section 43.5.13.
- **Remote Process (Access)** services provide the means for dispersed applications to communicate across a computer network. These services facilitate program-to-program communications regardless of their distributed nature or operation on heterogeneous platforms. Remote process services including remote procedure call (RPC) and asynchronous messaging mechanisms underpin client/server applications.
- **Remote Print Spooling and Output Distribution** services provide the means for printing output remotely. The services include management of remote printing including printer and media selection, use of forms, security, and print queue management.

The following functional areas are currently supported mainly by Application Software, but are progressing towards migration into the Application Platform:

- **Enhanced Telephony** functions, including call set-up, call co-ordination, call forwarding, call waiting, programmed directories, teleconferencing, automatic call distribution (useful for busy customer service categories), and call detail recording.
- **Shared Screen** functions that provide audio teleconferencing with common workstation windows between two or more users. This includes the capability to refresh windows whenever someone displays new material or changes an existing display. Every user is provided with the capability to graphically annotate or modify the shared conference window.
- **Video-Conferencing** functions that provide two-way video transmission between different sites. These functions include call set-up, call co-ordination, full motion display of events and participants in a bidirectional manner, support for the management of directing the cameras, ranging from fixed position, to sender directed, to receiver directed, to automated sound pickup.

- **分布式数据**服务，它提供对远程或本地数据库中的数据/元数据的访问及修改。在分布式环境中，根据本地客户端的要求从远程数据服务器中提取出在本地数据库上没有的数据。
- **分布式文件**服务，它提供透明的远程文件访问。不管数据在什么物理位置，应用对数据的访问都是等效的。该功能的辅助服务可以包括透明寻址、缓存数据、数据拷贝、文件锁定和文件记录。
- **分布式名称**服务，它提供在分布式计算系统之内对资源进行唯一识别的手段。这些服务可用于网络之内的应用，并且提供可以包括资源名称、联合属性、物理位置和资源功能性的信息。需要注意的是，所有系统资源在所有信息系统中都应可通过分布式名称识别。这允许物理位置变化，不仅仅是适应移动，还要适应负载平衡、系统利用率、缩放比例（增加处理器并移动资源以适应增加的资源）、分布式处理以及开放系统的所有方面。分布式名称服务包括诸如 X.500 和网络导航服务的目录服务。分布式名称服务包括通过名称和通过功能定位数据对象的方式。43.5.13 节分别描述在命名服务和交易服务下的等效服务。
- **分布式时间**服务，它按要求提供在属于不同时区的多个分布式流程间的同步时间协调。等效服务在 43.5.13 节中的时间服务下描述。
- **远程进程（访问）**服务，它提供分散应用跨计算机网络进行通信的手段。不管在异构平台上的分布式属性或运行如何，这些服务都促进程序间的通信。远程进程服务包括远程程序调用（RPC），且异步消息接发机制支持客户端/服务器应用。
- **远程打印排队和输出分配**服务，它提供进行远程打印输出的方式。该服务包括管理远程打印（包括打印机和介质选择）、使用表单、安保性和打印队列管理。

下述功能领域目前主要由应用软件支持，但是正在迁移入应用平台：

- **增强的通话**功能，它包括呼叫建立、呼叫协调、呼叫转移、呼叫等待、程序目录、远程会议、自动呼叫分配（用于繁忙的客户服务类别）和呼叫详细记录。
- **共享屏幕**功能，它利用公用工作站窗口提供在两个或更多用户之间的音频远程会议。包括每当有人演示新资料或变更现有显示画面时更新窗口的能力。每个用户都具有用图表注释或修改共享会议窗口的能力。
- **视频会议**功能，它提供不同现场之间的双向视频传输。这些功能包括呼叫建立、呼叫协调，以双向方式全面动态显示事件和参与者，支持对摄像机定向的管理，从固定位置延伸到定向的发送器、定向的接收器和自动的拾音器。

- **Broadcast** functions that provide one-way audio or audio/video communications functions between a sending location and multiple receiving locations or between multiple sending and receiving locations.
- **Mailing List** functions that allow groups to participate in conferences. These conferences may or may not occur in real time. Conferees or invited guests can drop in or out of conferences or subconferences at will. The ability to trace the exchanges is provided. Functions include exchange of documents, conference management, recording facilities, and search and retrieval capabilities.

43.5.7 Operating System Services

Operating system services are responsible for the management of platform resources, including the processor, memory, files, and input and output. They generally shield applications from the implementation details of the machine. Operating system services include:

- **Kernel Operations** provide low-level services necessary to:
  - Create and manage processes and threads of execution
  - Execute programs
  - Define and communicate asynchronous events
  - Define and process system clock operations
  - Implement security features
  - Manage files and directories
  - Control input/output processing to and from peripheral devices

  Some kernel services have analogues described in Section 43.5.13, such as concurr-ency control services.
- **Command Interpreter and Utility** services include mechanisms for services at the operator level, such as:
  - Comparing, printing, and displaying file contents
  - Editing files
  - Searching patterns
  - Evaluating expressions
  - Logging messages
  - Moving files between directories
  - Sorting data
  - Executing command scripts
  - Local print spooling
  - Scheduling signal execution processes
  - Accessing environment information

- **广播**功能，它提供在一个发送位置与多个接收位置之间或者在多个发送位置和接收位置之间的单向音频或音频/视频通信功能。
- **邮件列表**功能，它使得群组能参加会议。这些会议可以实时召开也可以不必如此。参会者或受邀请的客人可以随意参加或不参加会议或分组会议。提供追踪交换的能力。功能包括文件交换、会议管理、记录设备以及搜索和检索能力。

43.5.7 操作系统服务

操作系统服务负责管理平台资源，包括处理器、存储器、文件以及输入和输出。它们通常根据该机器的实施细节保护应用。操作系统服务包括：

- **核运算**，它提供执行下述操作所需的低层级服务：
  - 创建并管理执行的流程和线程的执行
  - 执行程序
  - 定义并传达异步事件
  - 定义并处理系统时钟操作
  - 实现安保特性
  - 管理文件和目录
  - 控制往返于外部设备的输入/输出进程

  在 43.5.13 节中描述核服务的一些类似服务，如并发控制服务。
- **命令解释程序和实用程序**服务，包括操作员层级的服务机制，例如：
  - 比较、打印和显示文件内容
  - 编辑文件
  - 搜索特征模式
  - 对表达式求值
  - 记录消息
  - 在目录之间移动文件
  - 对数据分类
  - 执行命令脚本
  - 本地打印排队
  - 安排信号执行流程进度
  - 访问环境信息

- **Batch Processing** services support the capability to queue work (jobs) and manage the sequencing of processing based on job control commands and lists of data. These services also include support for the management of the output of batch processing, which frequently includes updated files or databases and information products such as printed reports or electronic documents. Batch processing is performed asynchronously from the user requesting the job.
- **File and Directory Synchronization** services allow local and remote copies of files and directories to be made identical. Synchronization services are usually used to update files after periods of offline working on a portable system.

43.5.8 Software Engineering Services

The functional aspect of an application is embodied in the programming languages used to code it. Additionally, professional system developers require tools appropriate to the development and maintenance of applications. These capabilities are provided by software engineering services, which include:

- **Programming Language** services provide the basic syntax and semantic definition for use by a software developer to describe the desired Application Software function. Shell and executive script language services enable the use of operating system commands or utilities rather than a programming language. Shells and executive scripts are typically interpreted rather than compiled, but some operating systems support compilers for executive scripts. In contrast, some compilers produce code to be interpreted at run time. Other tools in this group include source code formatters and compiler compilers.
- **Object Code Linking** services provide the ability for programs to access the underlying application and operating system platform through APIs that have been defined independently of the computer language. It is used by programmers to gain access to these services using methods consistent with the operating system and specific language used. Linking is operating system-dependent, but language-independent.
- **Computer-Aided Software Engineering (CASE) Environment and Tools** services include systems and programs that assist in the automated development and maintenance of software. These include, but are not limited to, tools for requirements specification and analysis, for design work and analysis, for creating, editing, testing, and debugging program code, for documenting, for prototyping, and for group communication. The interfaces among these tools include services for storing and retrieving information about systems and exchanging this information among the various components of the system development environment. An adjunct to these capabilities is the ability to manage and control the configuration of software components, test data, and libraries to record changes to source code or to access CASE repositories. Other language tools include code generators and translators, artificial intelligence tools, and tools like the UNIX system command *make*, which uses knowledge of the inter-dependencies between modules to recompile and link only those parts of a program which have changed.
- **Graphical User Interface (GUI) Building** services assist in the development of the Human Computer Interface (HCI) elements of applications. Tools include services for generating and capturing screen layouts, and for defining the appearance, function, behavior, and position of graphical objects.
- **Scripting Language** services provide interpreted languages which allow the user to carry out some complicated function in a simple way. Application areas served by special-purpose scripting languages include calculation, graphical user interface development, and development of prototype applications.

- **批量处理**服务，它支持使工作排队并基于工作控制命令和数据列表管理处理顺序的能力。这些服务还包括支持对批量处理输出的管理，往往包括更新的文件或数据库，以及诸如打印的报表或电子文件的信息产品。批量处理是由要求该项工作的用户异步完成的。
- **文件和目录同步**服务，它使得文件和目录的本地和远程拷贝能一致。通常在对可移植系统进行脱机工作后利用同步服务更新文件。

43.5.8 软件工程服务

应用的功能方面体现于用来对该应用进行编码的编程语言。此外，职业系统开发人员需要适于开发和维护应用的工具。这些能力由软件工程服务提供，包括：

- **编程语言**服务，它提供由软件开发人员用来描述期望应用软件功能的基本语法和语义定义。Shell 和执行脚本语言服务使得使用操作系统命令或实用程序而不是编程语言成为可能。典型情况下，Shell 和执行脚本可以解析，而不可编译，但是有些操作系统支持执行脚本的编译程序。相反，有些编译程序在运行时产生待解释的代码。该群组中的其他工具包括源代码格式器和编译程序的编译器。
- **对象代码链接**服务，它提供由程序通过已经独立于计算机语言定义的 API 来访问基础应用和操作系统平台的能力。通过使用该项服务，程序员可以利用与所使用的操作系统和特有的语言符合的方法获取这些服务。链接取决于操作系统，但不取决于语言。
- **计算机辅助软件工程（CASE）环境和工具**服务，它包括有助于自动开发和维护软件的系统和程序。这些服务包括但不限于：需求说明和分析工具，设计工作和分析工具，创建、编辑、测试和调试程序代码的工具，文件化工具，模型开发工具以及群组通信工具。这些工具之间的界面，包括存储和检索系统相关信息的服务，以及在系统开发环境的不同组件之间交换该信息的服务。这些能力的附属物是管理和控制软件组件构型、测试数据及记录源代码变更或访问 CASE 存储库的库的能力。其他语言工具包括代码生成器和翻译器、人工智能工具以及其他工具，例如 UNIX 系统命令 make，它利用模块间的相互依赖的知识重新编译并链接程序中已经变更的部分。
- **用户图形界面（GUI）构建**服务，它帮助开发应用的人机界面（HCI）元素。工具包括生成和获取屏幕布局的服务以及定义图形对象的外观、功能、特性和位置的服务。
- **脚本语言**服务，它提供使得用户能以简单的方式执行一些复杂功能的解释语言。由专用脚本语言服务的应用领域包括计算、用户图形界面开发和原型应用的开发。

- **Language Binding** services provide mappings from interfaces provided by programming languages onto the services provided by the Application Platform. In many cases the mapping is straightforward since the platform supplies analogous services to those expected by the application. In other cases the language binding service must use a combination of Application Platform services to provide a fully functional mapping.
- **Run-Time Environment** services provide support for Application Software at run time.This support includes locating and connecting dynamically linked libraries, or even emulation of an operating environment other than the one which actually exists.
- **Application Binary Interface** services provide services that make the Application Platform comply with defined application binary interface standards.

43.5.9 Transaction Processing Services

Transaction Processing (TP) services provide support for the online processing of information in discrete units called "transactions", with assurance of the state of the information at the end of the transaction. This typically involves predetermined sequences of data entry, validation, display, and update or inquiry against a file or database. It also includes services to prioritize and track transactions. TP services may include support for distribution of transactions to a combination of local and remote processors.

A transaction is a complete unit of work. It may comprise many computational tasks, which may include user interface, data retrieval, and communications. A typical transaction modifies shared resources. Transactions must also be able to be rolled back (that is, undone) if necessary, at any stage. When a transaction is completed without failure, it is committed. Completion of a transaction means either commitment or rollback.

Typically a TP service will contain a transaction manager, which links data entry and display software with processing, database, and other resources to form the complete service.

The sum of all the work done anywhere in the system in the course of a single transaction is called a "global transaction". Transactions are not limited to a single Application Platform.

- **Transaction Manager** services, which allow an application to demarcate transactions, and direct their completion. Transaction manager services include:
  - Starting a transaction
  - Co-ordination of recoverable resources involved in a transaction
  - Committing or rolling back transactions
  - Controlling timeouts on transactions
  - Chaining transactions together
  - Monitoring transaction status

Some transaction manager services have equivalents described in Section 43.5.13, under Transaction services.

- **语言绑定**服务，它提供从由编程语言提供的界面到由应用平台所提供服务的映射。在很多情况下，映射是最直截了当的，因为平台提供与该应用期望的服务类似的服务。在其他情况下，语言绑定服务必须利用应用平台服务的组合来提供全面的功能性映射。
- **运行时环境**服务，它在应用软件运行时为其提供支持。这种支持包括定位和连接动态链接库，乃至模拟除实际存在的操作环境外的某一操作环境。
- **应用二进制界面**服务，它提供使应用平台符合所定义的应用二进制界面标准的服务。

43.5.9 事务处理服务

事务处理（TP）服务对被称为“事务”的独立完整单元中的信息进行在线处理提供支持，并确保信息在事务结束时的状态。典型情况下，这涉及针对文件或数据库进行数据输入、确认、显示和更新或查询数据的预定顺序。还包括对事务进行优先排序和追踪的服务。TP 服务可包括对将事务分配至本地和远程处理器组合的支持。

一项事务是一整套工作。它由多个计算任务组成，可能包括用户界面、数据检索和通信。一个典型的事务修改共享的资源。必要时，事务还必须能够在任何阶段回滚（即，撤销）。当毫无故障地完成了某项事务时，提交该事务。事务的完成意味着提交或回滚。

典型情况下，TP 服务会包括事务管理程序，它将进程、数据库和其他资源与数据输入和显示软件联系起来形成整套的服务。

在单个事务期间，系统中的任何地方所做工作的总和被称为“全局事务”。事务不仅限于单个应用平台。

- **事务管理程序**服务，它使得应用能够划分事务并指导事务的完成。事务管理程序服务包括：
  - 开始事务
  - 协调参与事务的可恢复资源
  - 提交或回滚事务
  - 控制事务的超时
  - 将事务链接在一起
  - 监控事务状态

在 43.5.13 节中的事务服务下，描述了一些事务管理程序服务的等效服务。

43.5.10 User Interface Services

User interface services define how users may interact with an application. Depending on the capabilities required by users and the applications, these interfaces may include the following:

- **Graphical Client/Server** services that define the relationships between client and server processes operating graphical user interface displays, usually within a network. In this case, the program that controls each display unit is a server process, while independent user programs are client processes that request display services from the server.
- **Display Objects** services that define characteristics of display elements such as color, shape, size, movement, graphics context, user preferences, font management, and interactions among display elements.
- **Window Management** services that define how windows are created, moved, stored, retrieved, removed, and related to each other.
- **Dialog Support** services translate the data entered for display to that which is actually displayed on the screen (e.g., cursor movements, keyboard data entry, and external data entry devices).
- **Printing** services support output of text and/or graphical data, including any filtering or format conversion necessary. Printing services may include the ability to print all or part of a document, to print and collate more than one copy, to select the size and orientation of output, to choose print resolution, colors, and graphical behavior, and to specify fonts and other characteristics.
- **Computer-Based Training and Online Help** services provide an integrated training environment on user workstations. Training is available on an as-needed basis for any application available in the environment. Electronic messages are provided at the stroke of a key from anywhere within the application. This includes tutorial training on the application in use and the availability of offline, on-site interactive training.
- **Character-Based** services, which deal with support for non-graphical terminals.

Character-based services include support for terminal type-independent control of display attributes, cursor motions, programmable keys, audible signals, and other functions.

The services associated with a window system include the visual display of information on a screen that contains one or more windows or panels, support for pointing to an object on the screen using a pointing device such as a mouse or touch-screen, and the manipulation of a set of objects on the screen through the pointing device or through keyboard entry. Other user interfaces included are industrial controls and virtual reality devices.

43.5.11 Security Services

Security services are necessary to protect sensitive information in the information system. The appropriate level of protection is determined based upon the value of the information to the business area end users and the perception of threats to it.

To be effective, security needs to be made strong, must never be taken for granted, and must be designed into an architecture and not bolted on afterwards. Whether a system is stand-alone or distributed, security must be applied to the whole system. It must not be forgotten that the requirement for security extends not only across the range of entities in a system but also through time.

In establishing a security architecture, the best approach is to consider what is being defended, what value it has, and what the threats to it are. The principal threats to be countered are:

43.5.10 用户界面服务

用户界面服务定义用户可以与应用如何交互。根据用户和应用需要的能力，这些界面可以包括下述服务：

- **图形客户端/服务器**服务，通常定义在一个网络之内运行的图形用户界面显示器的客户端进程与服务器进程之间的关系。在这种情况下，控制每个显示单元的程序是服务器进程，单独的用户程序是从服务器中要求显示服务的客户端进程。
- **显示对象**服务，它定义显示元素的特征，如颜色、形状、尺寸、移动、图形背景环境、用户偏好、字体管理以及显示元素间的相互作用。
- **窗口管理**服务，它定义窗口是如何被创建、移动、存储、检索、清除且相互关联的。
- **对话支持**服务，它将为了显示而输入的数据转换成在屏幕上实际显示的数据（如，光标移动、键盘数据输入和外部数据输入装置）。
- **打印**服务，它支持文本和/或图形数据的输出，包括任何必要的过滤或格式转换。打印服务可以包括打印整个文件或其中一部分的能力，打印并分类整理多份复件的能力，选择输出大小和方向的能力，选择打印分辨率、颜色和图形特性的能力，以及指定字体和其他特征的能力。
- **基于计算机的培训和在线帮助**服务，它提供关于用户工作站的综合培训环境。培训可根据需要，用于在该环境下有效的任何应用。从应用之内的任何地方敲击按键时提供电子信息。包括对使用中的应用以及脱机现场交互培训的有效性的辅导培训。
- **基于字符**的服务，它处理对非图形终端的支持。

基于字符的服务包括支持对显示属性、光标移动、程控键、可听信号和其他功能进行独立于终端类型的控制。

与窗口系统相关的服务包括信息在包含一个或更多窗口或面板的屏幕上的直观显示，对利用诸如鼠标或触摸屏等定点设备指出屏幕上的某一对象的支持，以及通过定点设备或键盘输入处理屏幕上的一组对象。所包括的其他用户界面是行业控制器和虚拟真实设备。

43.5.11 安保服务

对保护信息系统中的敏感信息而言，安保服务是必不可少的。基于业务领域终端用户的信息价值和对它造成威胁的认识，确定适当的保护等级。

为了有效，安保性需要加强，不得掉以轻心，必须设计到架构中，而不是之后再连接到架构上。无论系统是独立的还是分布式的，安保性必须应用于整个系统。不能忽略的是，对安保性的要求不仅延伸跨越某个系统中的各实体的整个范围，还要在时间上贯穿始终。

在建立安保架构的过程中，最好的实施途径是，考虑正在保护什么、它具有什么价值以及对它造成什么威胁。需要考虑的主要威胁有：

- Loss of confidentiality of data
- Unavailability of data or services
- Loss of integrity of data
- Unauthorized use of resources

Counters to these threats are provided by the following services:

- **Identification and Authentication** services provide:
  — Identification, accountability, and audit of users and their actions
  — Authentication and account data
  — Protection of authentication data
  — Active user status information
  — Password authentication mechanisms
- **System Entry Control** services provide:
  — Warning to unauthorized users that the system is security-aware
  — Authentication of users
  — Information, displayed on entry, about previous successful and unsuccessful login attempts
  — User-initiated locking of a session preventing further access until the user has been re-authenticated
- **Audit** services provide authorized control and protection of the audit trail, recording of detailed information security-relevant events, and audit trail control, management, and inspection.
- **Access Control** services provide:
  — Access control attributes for subjects (such as processes) and objects (such as files)
  — Enforcement of rules for assignment and modification of access control attributes
  — Enforcement of access controls
  — Control of object creation and deletion, including ensuring that re-use of objects does not allow subjects to accidentally gain access to information previously held in the object

Access control services also appear under Security services in Section 43.5.13.

- **Non-Repudiation** services provide proof that a user carried out an action, or sent or received some information, at a particular time. Non-repudiation services also appear under Security services in Section 43.5.13.
- **Security Management** services provide secure system set-up and initializetion, control of security policy parameters, management of user registration data, and system resources and restrictions on the use of administrative functions.
- **Trusted Recovery** services provide recovery facilities such as restoring from backups in ways that do not compromise security protection.
- **Encryption** services provide ways of encoding data such that it can only be read by someone who possesses an appropriate key, or some other piece of secret information. As well as providing data confidentiality for trusted communication, encryption services are used to underpin many other services including identification and authentication, system entry control, and access control services.

- 失去数据保密性
- 数据或服务无效
- 数据完整性受损
- 未经授权使用资源

通过下述服务提供对这些威胁的对抗：

- **识别和认证**服务提供：
  — 用户及其行动的识别、问责和审计
  — 认证和账户数据
  — 保护认证数据
  — 活跃用户的状态信息
  — 口令认证机制
- **系统入口控制**服务提供：
  — 警告未经授权的用户：系统是有安保意识的
  — 用户的认证
  — 在入口显示的关于之前成功或不成功的登录尝试的信息
  — 在用户得到重新认证之前，用户发起的会话锁定，防止进一步的访问
- **审核**服务提供对审核跟踪的授权控制和保护，记录与安保性无关的事件的详细信息，以及审核跟踪控制、管理和验收。
- **访问控制**服务提供：
  — 对主题（如流程）和对象（如文件）的访问控制属性
  — 对指派和修改访问控制属性的规则的执行
  — 访问控制的执行
  — 对象创建和删除的控制，包括确保对象的复用不会使主题意外访问该对象之前所保存的信息。

访问控制服务还出现在 43.5.13 节中的安保服务下面。

- **反拒认**服务提供关于用户在特殊时期采取某个行动或者发送或接收到某些信息的证明。反拒认服务也出现在 43.5.13 节中的安保服务下面。
- **安保管理**服务提供可靠系统的建立和初始化、安保策略参数的控制、用户注册数据的管理以及关于使用管理功能的系统资源及限制。
- **可信恢复**服务提供恢复措施，如以不损害安保性保护的方式从备份中恢复。
- **加密**服务提供对数据进行编码的方式，这样只有拥有适当的密钥或一些其他秘密信息的人才能够读取。除了提供数据保密以进行可信通信外，加密服务还用来支撑多个其他服务，包括识别和认证、系统入口控制以及访问控制等服务。

- **Trusted Communication** services provide:
  - A secure way for communicating parties to authenticate themselves to each other without the risk of an eavesdropper subsequently masquerading as one of the parties
  - A secure way of generating and verifying check values for data integrity
  - Data encipherment and decipherment for confidentiality and other purposes
  - A way to produce an irreversible hash of data for support of digital signature and non-repudiation functions
  - Generation, derivation, distribution, storage, retrieval, and deletion of cryptographic keys

Security services require other software entities to co-operate in:

- Access control for resources managed by the entity
- Accounting and audit of security-relevant events
- The import and export of data
- Potentially all other security services depending on the particular implementation approach Security services are one category where a wide view is particularly important, as a chain is only as strong as its weakest link. This is one category of services where the external environment has critical implications on the Application Platform. For instance, the presence of a firewall may provide a single point of access onto a network from the outside world, making it possible to concentrate access control in one place and relax requirements behind the firewall.

43.5.12 System and Network Management Services

Information systems are composed of a wide variety of diverse resources that must be managed effectively to achieve the goals of an open system environment. While the individual resources (such as printers, software, users, processors) may differ widely, the abstraction of these resources as managed objects allows for treatment in a uniform manner. The basic concepts of management — including operation, administration, and maintenance — may then be applied to the full suite of information system components along with their attendant services.

System and network management functionality may be divided in several different ways; one way is to make a division according to the management elements that generically apply to all functional resources. This division reduces as follows:

- **User Management** services provide the ability to maintain a user's preferences and privileges.
- **Configuration Management** (CM) services address four basic functions:
  - Identification and specification of all component resources
  - Control, or the ability to freeze configuration items, changing them only through agreed processes
  - Status accounting of each configuration item
  - Verification through a series of reviews to ensure conformity between the actual configuration item and the information recorded about it

- **可信通信**服务提供：
  - — 通信双方相互证实而不会有偷听者随后冒充成其中一方的风险的安保方式
  - — 生成和验证检查值的数据完整性的安保方式
  - — 为了保密和其他目的而进行的数据加密及解密
  - — 生成一个不可逆数据散列，以支持数字签名和不可否认功能的方式
  - — 密钥的生成、衍生、分配、存储、检索和删除

安保服务要求其他软件实体在以下几个方面进行合作：

- 由实体管理对资源的访问控制
- 对安保性相关事件的问责和审核
- 数据的输入和输出
- 安保服务是在各个环节都特别重要的一类服务，正如链条的强度是由最薄弱的环节决定的。这是一类外部环境对应用平台有重要含义的服务。例如，防火墙的存在可以提供从外部世界对网络进行的单点访问，使访问控制集中在一个地方并且放宽防火墙后的要求成为可能。

43.5.12 系统和网络管理服务

信息系统由各种各样必须有效管理才能实现开放系统环境目标的不同资源构成。虽然资源（如打印机、软件、用户、处理器）可能大不相同，但将这些资源抽象为受管理对象，就能够以一种统一的方式进行处理。管理（包括运行、监管和维护）的基本概念则可以应用于一整套信息系统组件及其附带服务。

系统和网络管理功能性可以用若干不同的方式划分；一种方式是，根据通常适用于所有功能资源的管理要素进行划分。这种划分归纳如下：

- **用户管理**服务，它提供保持用户偏好和特权的能力。
- **构型管理**（CM）服务，它涉及四个基本功能：
  - — 识别和规范所有组件资源
  - — 控制，或者冻结构型项使它们仅通过协商的流程改变的能力
  - — 每个构型项目的状态统计
  - — 通过一系列审查进行审视，以确保实际构型项目及其相关记录信息之间的一致性

These services include: Processor CM, Network CM, Distributed System CM, Topology CM, and Application CM. Processor CM takes a platform-centric approach. Network CM and Distributed System CM services allow remote systems to be managed and monitored including the interchange of network status. Topology CM is used to control the topology of physical or logical entities that are distributed. Application CM focuses on applications. Configuration management also appears as Change Management services in Section 43.5.13.

- **Performance Management** services monitor performance aspects of hardware, platform and application software, and network components and provide ways to tune the system to meet performance targets.
- **Availability and Fault Management** services allow a system to react to the loss or incorrect operation of system components including hardware, platform software, and application software.
- **Accounting Management** services provide the ability to cost services for charging and reimbursement.
- **Security Management** services control the security services in accordance with applicable security policies.
- **Print Management** services provide the ability to manage both local and remote print spooling services.
- **Network Management** services comprise elements of all the services described above, but are often treated as a separate service.
- **Backup and Restore** services provide a multi-level storage facility to ensure continued data security in case of component or subsystem failure.
- **Online Disk Management** services manage the utilization of disk storage against threshold values and invoke corrective action.
- **License Management** services support the effective enforcement of software license agreements. Licensing services for objects are described under Licensing services in Section 43.5.13.
- **Capacity Management** services address three basic functions:
  - Capacity management analyzing current and historic performance and capacity
  - Workload management to identify and understand applications that use the system
  - Capacity planning to plan required hardware resources for the future
- **Software Installation** services support distribution, installation, removal, relocation, activation, and automatic update of software or data packages from transportable media or over networks. Similar services for objects are described under Installation and Activation services in Section 43.5.13.

The following functional areas are currently supported mainly by Application Software, but are progressing towards migration into the Application Platform:

- **Trouble Ticketing** services support the generation, processing, and tracking of problem reports. Trouble ticketing is a term originating in the telecommunications world, referring to the ability to pass fault reports both within and between telecommunications service providers. In this environment, faults are often found by a customer of one provider, while the cause of the problem lies within the administrative domain of another provider. Trouble ticketing is a common service that may be useful to an increasing range of applications if the necessary work is done to extend it from telecommunications into wider areas of distributed applications such as email.

这些服务包括：处理器 CM、网络 CM、分布式系统 CM、拓扑结构 CM 和应用 CM。处理器 CM 采取以平台为中心的实施途径。网络 CM 和分布式系统 CM 服务使得能管理和监控远程系统，包括网络状态的互换。拓扑结构 CM 用于控制被分布的实际或逻辑实体的拓扑结构。应用 CM 聚焦于应用。构型管理还作为变更管理服务出现在 43.5.13 节中。

- **性能管理**服务，它监控硬件、平台和应用软件以及网络组件的性能情况，并提供调整系统以达到性能目标的方式。
- **可用性和故障管理**服务，它使系统能对系统组件（包括硬件、平台软件和应用软件）的损耗或不当操作做出反应。
- **账户管理**服务，它提供记账和报销服务成本的能力。
- **安保管理**服务，它按照适用的安保策略控制安保服务。
- **打印管理**服务，它提供管理本地和远程打印排队服务的能力。
- **网络管理**服务，它包括上述所有服务的元素，但是通常作为独立服务被处理。
- **备份与恢复**服务，它提供多层级存储设施，以确保在组件或子系统发生故障时能继续确保数据安全。
- **网盘管理**服务，它根据阈值管理磁盘存储器的利用率并调用纠正措施。
- **许可管理**服务，它支持软件许可协议的有效执行。在 43.5.13 节中的许可服务描述了各个对象的许可服务。
- **容量管理**服务，它涉及三个基本功能：
  — 容量管理，分析当前和历史的性能及容量
  — 工作负荷管理，识别并理解使用该系统的各类应用
  — 容量规划，计划未来所需的硬件资源
- **软件安装**服务，它支持来自于移动式媒介或网络上的软件或数据包的分配、安装、删除、重新定位、激活和自动更新。在 43.5.13 节中的安装和激活服务下描述对象的类似服务。

下述功能领域目前主要由应用软件提供支持，但是正在迁移入应用平台：

- **故障标签**服务，它支持问题报告的生成、处理和跟踪。故障标签是源于电信领域的一个术语，指的是在电信服务提供者内部或之间递交故障报告的能力。在这种环境中，故障一般是由一家供应商的客户发现的，而问题的原因属于另一家供应商的管理领域。故障标签是一项普通的服务，如果为了将这项服务从远程通信扩展到更广泛的分布式应用领域（例如电子邮件）而做了必要工作，则这些普通服务可用于范围不断扩大的应用。

This breakout of system and network management services parallels the breakout of emerging OSI network management, thereby presenting an overall coherent framework that applies equally to whole networks and the individual nodes of the networks.

One important consideration of the standards supporting the services in this category is that they should not enforce specific management policies, but rather enable a wide variety of different management policies to be implemented, selected according to the particular needs of the end-user installations.

System and network management services require the co-operation of other software entities in:

- Providing status information
- Notifying events
- Responding to management instructions

43.5.13 Object-Oriented Provision of Services

This section shows how services are provided in an object-oriented manner. "Object Services" does not appear as a category in the Technical Reference Model (TRM) since all the individual object services are incorporated as appropriate in the given service categories.

An object is an identifiable, encapsulated entity that provides one or more services that can be requested by a client. Clients request a service by invoking the appropriate method associated with the object, and the object carries out the service on the client's behalf. Objects provide a programming paradigm that can lead to important benefits, including:

- Increased modularity
- A reduction in errors
- Ease of debugging

Object management services provide ways of creating, locating, and naming objects, and allowing them to communicate in a distributed environment. The complete set of object services identified so far is listed below for the sake of completeness. Where a particular object service is part of a more generally applicable service category, a pointer to the other service category is given. Object services include:

- **Object Request Broker** (ORB) services, which enable objects to transparently make and receive requests and responses in a distributed environment. ORB services include:
  - **Implementation Repository** services support the location and management of object implementations. The services resemble those provided by the Data Dictionary/Repository services in Section 43.5.2.
  - **Installation and Activation** services provide ways to distribute, install, activate, and relocate objects. This corresponds to the Software Installation services in Section 43.5.12.
  - **Interface Repository** services support the storage and management of information about interfaces to objects. The services resemble those provided by the Data Dictionary/Repository services in Section 43.5.2.
  - **Replication** services support replication of objects in distributed systems, including management of consistency between the copies.

系统和网络管理服务的中断与新兴 OSI 网络管理的中断并行发生，从而提出一种同样适用于整个网络和网络各个节点的总体一致框架。

支持该类服务的标准的一个重要考量因素是，它们不应实施特定的管理策略，而是使多种多样的不同管理策略按照最终用户安装的特殊需要进行选择。

系统和网络管理服务要求在下述方面与其他软件实体合作：

- 提供状态信息
- 通知事件
- 对管理指令做出响应

43.5.13 面向对象的服务提供

本节表明如何以面向对象的方式提供服务。“对象服务”不作为一个类别出现在技术参考模型（TRM）中，因为所有单独的对象服务均已根据具体情况纳入到了规定的服务类别中。

对象是可识别的封装实体，它提供客户端可能要求的一项或多项服务。客户端通过调用与该对象相关的适当方法来要求一项服务，该对象代表客户端执行该项服务。对象提供一个可以带来以下重大效益的编程范例：

- 增加模块性
- 减少误差
- 易于调试

对象管理服务提供创建、定位并命名对象的方式，以及使这些对象能在分布式环境中通信的方式。为了完整起见，下面列出到目前为止识别的一整套对象服务。在特殊对象服务作为更普遍适用的服务类别的一部分的情况下，提供一种对其他服务类别的提示。对象服务包括：

- **对象要求代理**（ORB）服务，使对象能够在分布式环境中透明地提出和接收要求及响应。ORB 服务包括：
  - — **实施存储库**服务，支持对象实施的定位和管理。该服务类似于那些由 43.5.2 节中的数据字典/存储库服务提供的服务。
  - — **安装和激活**服务，提供分配、安装、激活和重新定位对象的方式。该服务与 43.5.12 节中的软件安装服务对应。
  - — **界面存储库**服务，支持对象界面信息的存储和管理。该服务类似于由 43.5.2 节中的数据字典/存储库服务提供的服务。
  - — **复制**服务，支持对分布式系统中的对象的拷贝，包括管理两个副本之间的一致性。

- **Common Object** services, which provide basic functions for using and implementing objects. These are the services necessary to construct any distributed application. Common object services include:
  - **Change Management** services provide for version identification and configuration management of object interfaces, implementations, and instances. This corresponds to the Configuration Management services described in Section 43.5.12.
  - **Collections** services provide operations on collections of objects, such as lists, trees, stacks, or queues. Services include establishing, adding objects to, or removing them from collections, testing set membership, forming unions and intersections of sets, and so on.
  - **Concurrency Control** services enable multiple clients to co-ordinate their access to shared resources. Synchronization like this is normally provided using the Kernel services provided in Section 43.5.7.
  - **Data Interchange** services support the exchange of visible state information between objects. Depending on the kind of object involved, this corresponds to one or more of the services provided in Section 43.5.1.
  - **Event Management** services provide basic capabilities for the management of events, including asynchronous events, event "fan-in", notification "fan-out", and reliable event delivery.
  - **Externalization** services define protocols and conventions for externalizing and internalizing objects. Externalizing means recording the object state in a stream of data, and internalizing means recreating an object state from a data stream. This is one example of the Information Presentation and Distribution functions in Section 43.5.1.
  - **Licensing** services support policies for object licensing, and measurement and charging for object use. This corresponds to the License Management services in Section 43.5.12.
  - **Lifecycle** services define conventions for creating, deleting, copying, and moving objects. The creation of objects is defined in terms of factory objects, which are objects that create other objects.
  - **Naming** services provide the ability to bind a name to an object, and to locate an object by its name. This is analogous to the Distributed Name service described in Section 43.5.6.
  - **Persistent Object** services provide common interfaces for retaining and managing the persistent state of objects. Objects are often stored in an OODBMS, described as one of the services in Section 43.5.2.
  - **Properties** services support the creation, deletion, assignment, and protection of dynamic properties associated with objects.
  - **Query** services support indexing and query operations on collections of objects that return a subset of the collection. This is similar to database look-up, a part of the DBMS functions in Section 43.5.2.
  - **Relationship** services allow relationships between objects (such as ownership or containment) to be explicitly represented as objects.
  - **Security** services support access control on objects and non-repudiation of operations on objects. Access control is defined as a security service (see Section 43.5.11). Non-repudiation, which is also a Security service, provides proof that an action was carried out by a particular user at a particular time.

- **公共对象**服务，提供使用和实施对象的基本功能。公共对象服务是构建任何分布式应用所必需的服务。公共对象服务包括：
  - — **变更管理**服务，提供对象界面、实施和实例的版本识别及构型管理。变更管理服务与 43.5.12 节中描述的构型管理服务对应。
  - — **集合**服务，提供对对象集合的操作，例如清单、树形结构、存储栈或队列。集合服务包括建立对象、将对象添加到集合中、或从集合中移除对象、测试集合成员、形成集合的并集和交集，等等。
  - — **并行控制**服务，使多个客户端协调它们对共享资源的访问。通常利用 43.5.7 节中提供的内核服务提供诸如此类的同步。
  - — **数据交换**服务，支持在对象之间交换可视状态信息。根据所涉及的这种对象，数据交换服务与 43.5.1 节中提供的服务中的一项或多项服务对应。
  - — **事件管理**服务，提供管理事件的基本能力，包括异步事件、事件“扇入”、通知“扇出”及可靠的事件交付。
  - — **外部化**服务，定义使对象外表化和内在化的协议及协定。外部化意味着将对象状态记录到数据流中，而内在化则意味着根据数据流重新创建对象状态。外部化服务是 43.5.1 节中的信息展示和分配功能的一个示例。
  - — **许可**服务，支持对象许可及对象使用测量和记账的策略。许可服务与 43.5.12 节中的许可管理服务对应。
  - — **生命周期**服务，定义创建、删除、拷贝和移动对象的协定。根据工厂对象来定义对象的创建，工厂对象可创建其他对象。
  - — **命名**服务，提供将一个名称绑定到一个对象并通过其名称定位对象的能力。该服务类似于 43.5.6 节中描述的分布式名称服务。
  - — **持久化对象**服务，提供保持和管理对象的持久状态的公用界面。通常将对象存储在 OODBMS 中，描述为 43.5.2 节中的服务之一。
  - — **特性**服务，支持创建、删除、指派和保护与对象相关的动态特性。
  - — **查询**服务，支持对返回集合子集的对象集合的索引和查询操作。该服务类似于数据库查找，是 43.5.2 节中的 DBMS 功能的一部分。
  - — **关系**服务，使对象之间的关系（如所有权关系或包含关系）能明确地表示为各个对象。
  - — **安保**服务，支持对对象的访问控制及对对象的操作的反拒认。访问控制被定义为一项安保服务（见 43.5.11 节）。反拒认也是一项安保服务，提供某个特殊用户曾在某一特殊时间执行某一动作的证明。

— **Start-Up** services support automatic start-up and termination of object services at ORB start-up or termination.

— **Time** services support synchronization of clocks in a distributed system. This is the same as the Distributed Time service in Section 43.5.6.

— **Trading** services allow clients to locate objects by the services the objects provide, rather than by name. This is similar to the Distributed Name service in Section 43.5.6.

— **Transaction** services provide facilities for grouping operations into atomic units, called "transactions", with the certainty that a transaction will be carried out in its entirety or not at all. This corresponds to some of the Transaction Manager services in Section 43.5.9.

— **启动**服务，支持对象服务在 ORB 启动或终止时的自动启动和终止。
— **时间**服务，支持时钟在分布式系统中的同步。该服务与 43.5.6 节中的分布式时间服务相同。
— **交易**服务，使客户端能根据对象提供的服务而非名称来定位对象。该服务类似于 43.5.6 节中的分布式名称服务。
— **事务**服务，提供将操作分成若干原子单元（称为“事务”）的设施，确定的是一项事务将全部执行或根本未执行。该服务与 43.5.9 节中的一些事务管理程序服务对应。

Chapter 44
Integrated Information Infrastructure Reference Model

This chapter describes the Integrated Information Infrastructure Reference Model (III-RM), in terms of its concepts, an overview, and taxonomy.

44.1 Basic Concepts

This section looks at the basic concepts of the III-RM, including background, components, and drivers.

44.1.1 Background

With the emergence of Internet-based technologies in recent years, for many organizations the main focus of attention, and the main return on investment in architecture effort, has shifted from the Application Platform space to the Application Software space. (Indeed, this has been one of the drivers behind the migration of TOGAF itself from a framework and method for Technology Architecture to one for overall enterprise architecture.)

The TOGAF Technical Reference Model (TRM) described in Chapter 43 focuses on the Application Platform space.

This section describes a reference model that focuses on the Application Software space, and "Common Systems Architecture" in Enterprise Continuum terms. This is the Integrated Information Infrastructure Reference Model (III-RM).

The III-RM is a subset of the TOGAF TRM in terms of its overall scope, but it also expands certain parts of the TRM — in particular, the business applications and infrastructure applications parts — in order to provide help in addressing one of the key challenges facing the enterprise architect today: the need to design an integrated information infrastructure to enable Boundaryless Information Flow. These concepts are explained in detail below.

This introductory section examines the concept of Boundaryless Information Flow; why an integrated information infrastructure is necessary to enable it; and how the III-RM can help the architect in designing an integrated information infrastructure for their enterprise.

第 44 章 综合信息基础设施参考模型

本章在概念、概述和分类法方面描述综合信息基础设施参考模型（III-RM）。

44.1 基本概念

本节介绍 III-RM 的基本概念，包括背景、组件和驱动因素。

44.1.1 背景

近年来，随着基于互联网的技术的出现，对许多组织而言，主要关注焦点及架构工作投资的主要回报已经从应用平台空间转移至应用软件空间。（实际上，这一转移已经成为 TOGAF 从一种技术架构框架和方法迁移至总体 Enterprise Architecture 的框架和方法背后的驱动因素之一。）

第 43 章中描述的 TOGAF 技术参考模型（TRM）聚焦于应用平台空间。

本节描述一种参考模型，它聚焦于应用软件空间，以及 ENTERPRISE 的连续统一体各项中的“公用系统架构”。这就是综合信息基础设施参考模型（III-RM）。

III-RM 就其总体范围而言是 TOGAF TRM 的子集，但 III-RM 还扩展 TRM 的某些部分，特别是业务应用和基础设施应用的各个部分，以便为应对 ENTERPRISE 架构师现如今面临的关键挑战中的其中之一提供帮助：设计实现无边界信息流的综合信息基础设施的需要。下面详细解释这些概念。

本介绍性章节探讨无边界信息流的概念，为什么综合信息基础设施对实现无边界信息流而言必不可少，以及 III-RM 如何才能帮助架构师为 ENTERPRISE 设计综合信息基础设施。

44.1.2 Components of the Model

Like the TOGAF TRM, the III-RM has two main components:

1. A **taxonomy**, which defines terminology, and provides a coherent description of the components and conceptual structure of an integrated information infrastructure.
2. An associated **III-RM graphic**, which provides a visual representation of the taxonomy, and the inter-relationship of the components, as an aid to understanding.

The model assumes the underlying existence of a computing and network platform, as described in the TRM; these are not depicted in the model.

44.1.3 Relationship to Other Parts of TOGAF

The relationship of the III-RM to the TRM is explained above.

Although the III-RM is intended as a useful tool in the execution of the TOGAF Architecture Development Method (ADM), it is important to emphasize that the ADM is in no way dependent on use of the III-RM (any more than it is dependent on use of the TRM). Other taxonomies and reference models exist in this space that can be used in conjunction with the ADM, and indeed may be preferable for some organizations.

44.1.4 Key Business and Technical Drivers

44.1.4.1 Problem Space: The Need for Boundaryless Information Flow

The Boundaryless Information Flow problem space is one that is shared by many customer members of The Open Group, and by many similar organizations worldwide. It is essentially the problem of getting information to the right people at the right time in a secure, reliable manner, in order to support the operations that are core to the extended enterprise.

In General Electric, Jack Welch invented the term "the Boundaryless Organization", not to imply that there are no boundaries, but that they should be made permeable.

Creating organizational structures that enabled each individual department to operate at maximum efficiency was for a long time accepted as the best approach to managing a large enterprise. Among other benefits, this approach fostered the development of specialist skills in staff, who could apply those skills to specific aspects of an overall activity (such as a manufacturing process), in order to accomplish the tasks involved better, faster, and cheaper.

As each overall activity progressed through the organization, passing from department to department (for example, from Design to Production to Sales), each department would take inputs from the previous department in the process, apply its own business processes to the activity, and send its output to the next department in line.

In today's world where speed, flexibility, and responsiveness to changing markets make all the difference between success and failure, this method of working is no longer appropriate. Organizations have been trying for some time to overcome the limitations imposed by traditional organization structures. Many business process re-engineering efforts have been undertaken and abandoned because they were too ambitious, while others cost far more in both time and money than originally intended.

However, organizations today recognize that they need not abandon functional or departmental organization altogether. They can enable the right people to come together in cross-functional teams so that all the skills, knowledge, and expertise can be brought to bear on any specific problem or business opportunity.

44.1.2 模型的组件

与 TOGAF TRM 一样，III-RM 也具有两个主要组件：

1. **分类法**，它定义术语并对综合信息基础设施的组件和概念结构提供一致的描述。
2. 相关的 **III-RM 图形**，作为一种帮助理解的手段，它提供组件的分类法及相互关系的直观表达。

该模型假定可能存在计算和网络平台（如 TRM 所描述），但未在该模型中描述。

44.1.3 与 TOGAF 其他部分的关系

III-RM 与 TRM 的关系如上所述。

虽然试图将 III-RM 作为执行 TOGAF 架构开发法（ADM）的有用工具，但重要的是强调 ADM 绝不依赖于 III-RM 的使用（仅仅依赖于 TRM 的使用）。在这种情况中，存在其他分类法和参考模型，它们可以与 ADM 结合使用，而且事实上对一些组织而言可能更为可取。

44.1.4 关键业务和技术驱动因素

44.1.4.1 问题空间：对无边界信息流的需要

无边界信息流的问题空间，是被 The Open Group 的许多客户成员及全世界范围内的许多类似组织共享的。该问题空间本质上是恰当的人在适当的时间以安全可靠的方式获取信息，以便支持作为扩展的 ENTERPRISE 核心的运作的问题。

在通用电气公司，杰克·韦尔奇发明了术语"无边界组织"，并不是暗指边界不存在，而是应使边界可渗透。

很长时间以来，创建能使各部门以最大效率运行的组织结构一直被视为管理大型 ENTERPRISE 的最佳途径。除其他效益外，这种实施途径促进员工专业技能的发展，这些员工可以将这些技能应用于所有活动的特定方面（如制造流程），以便更好、更快地以更低的成本完成所涉及的任务。

随着每个总体活动在整个组织中的不断发展，即从一个部门传递至另一个部门（例如，从设计到生产再到销售），每个部门都在该流程中接收之前部门的输入，将其自己的业务流程应用于该活动，然后将其输出有序地发送至下一个部门。

当今世界，市场变化的速度、灵活性和响应能力对于成功和失败而言关系重大，这种工作方法不再适用。一段时间以来，组织一直努力克服传统组织结构强加的限制条件。因为他们太过雄心勃勃，已经从事并承担了很多业务流程重组工作，与此同时在时间和金钱方面的其他成本也远远超出了最初的预期。

但是，今天各组织都认识到，他们无需放弃全部职能或部门组织。他们可以让合适的人共同加入跨职能团队，以便所有技能、知识和经验可以得到足够的重视，以瞄准任何特定问题或业务机会。

But this in turn poses its own challenges. CIOs are under enormous pressure to provide access to information to each cross-functional team on an as-required basis, and yet the sources of this data can be numerous and the volumes huge.

Even worse, the IT systems, which have been built over a period of 20 or 30 years at a cost of many billions of dollars, and are not about to be thrown out or replaced wholesale, were built for each functional department. So although it may be possible to get people to work together effectively (no minor achievement in itself), the IT systems they use are designed to support the old-style thinking. The IT systems in place today do not allow for information to flow in support of the boundaryless organization. When they do, then we will have Boundaryless Information Flow.

44.1.4.2 Solution Space: The Need for Integrated Information Infrastructure

The Open Group's Interoperable Enterprise Business Scenario[14]originally published in 2001, crystallizes this need for Boundaryless Information Flow and describes the way in which this need drives IT customers' deployment of their information infrastructure.

In this scenario, the customer's problem statement says that I (as the customer enterprise) could gain significant operational efficiencies and improve the many different business processes of the enterprise — both internal processes, and those spanning the key interactions with suppliers, customers, and partners — if only I could provide my staff with:

- **Integrated information** so that different and potentially conflicting pieces of information are not distributed throughout different systems.
- **Integrated access to that information** so that staff can access all the information they need and have a right to, through one convenient interface.

The infrastructure that enables this vision is termed the " integrated information infrastructure" .

As an example, one current approach to integrated information infrastructure is to provide " enterprise portals" that allow integrated access to information from different applications systems enterprise-wide, via a convenient, web-enabled interface (one of the colored segments in the ends of the cylinder in Figure 44-1).

14. Available at www.opengroup.org/bookstore/catalog/k022.htm.

但是，反之也会带来独特的挑战。由于要根据需要为每个跨职能团队提供信息访问，然而数据源却可以有很多，数据量也会很大，因此 CIO 仍面临着巨大的压力。

更糟的是，已过去的 20 或 30 年间，为每个职能部门建立了花费几十亿美元建成的并且不会被大规模抛弃或取代的 IT 系统。所以，虽然可以与人们有效地合作（本身没有小成就），但是他们使用的 IT 系统被设计成用于支持旧思维模式。今天拥有的 IT 系统在支持无边界组织时不允许信息流动。当允许信息流动时，那么我们将具有无边界信息流。

44.1.4.2 解决方案空间：对综合信息基础设施的需要

由 The Open Group 最初于 2001 年出版的《可互操作的 ENTERPRISE 业务场景》[14]明确对无边界信息流的需要，并描述该需要驱动 IT 客户部署信息基础设施的方式。

在该场景中，消费者的问题申明中提到：我方（作为客户 ENTERPRISE）可以获得重要的运行效率并改善 ENTERPRISE 的很多不同业务流程，即内部流程及包括与供应商、客户和合作伙伴的关键相互作用的流程，但前提是，只有当我方可以为员工提供：

- **综合信息**，以便不同的且潜在可能冲突的信息不会在不同系统间到处分布。
- **对综合信息的综合访问**，以便员工可以通过一个方便的界面访问他们需要的和享有的全部信息。

实现该愿景的基础设施被称为“综合信息基础设施”。

例如，综合信息基础设施的一个现有途径是，提供允许通过一个方便的、能连接网络的界面（图 44-1 中的圆柱体端部的彩色部分之一），对来自于不同的整个 ENTERPRISE 应用系统的信息进行综合访问的“ENTERPRISE 门户”。

14. 详情可登陆：www.opengroup.org/bookstore/catalog/k022.htm。

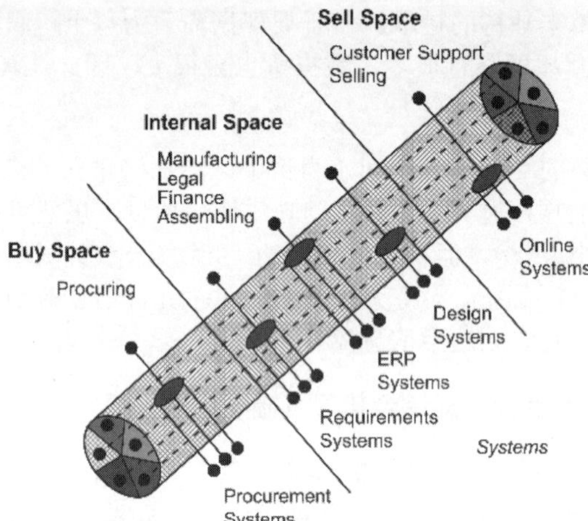

Figure 44-1 An approach to Boundaryless Information Flow (Enterprise Portals)

One of the key challenges for the architect in today's enterprise is to work out, and then communicate to senior management, how far technologies such as web services, application integration services, etc., can go toward achieving an integrated information infrastructure, and realizing the vision of Boundaryless Information Flow, in the enterprise concerned.

The Open Group's follow-up analysis of the Interoperable Enterprise Business Scenario has resulted in the development of an integrated information infrastructure model (the III-RM), which depicts the major components required to address the Boundaryless Information Flow problem space, and can help the architect in this task.

The III-RM thus provides insights related to customer needs for Boundaryless Information Flow in enterprise environments. The model also points to rules and standards to assist in leveraging solutions and products within the value chain.

The following subsections discuss the model in detail.

44.1.5 Status of the III-RM

The III-RM is documented as it stands today, and is by no means considered a finished article. However, it is a model that has been developed and approved by the members of The Open Group as a whole, in response to the Interoperable Enterprise Business Scenario, which itself was developed in response to an urgent need articulated by the customer members of The Open Group for assistance in this field.

The Business Scenario and the Reference Model thus represent a problem and a solution approach that The Open Group membership as a whole fully endorses.

It is hoped that publication of the model as part of TOGAF will encourage its widespread adoption and use, and provide a channel of communication whereby experience with use of the model can be fed back, improvement points assimilated, and the model refined and republished as necessary.

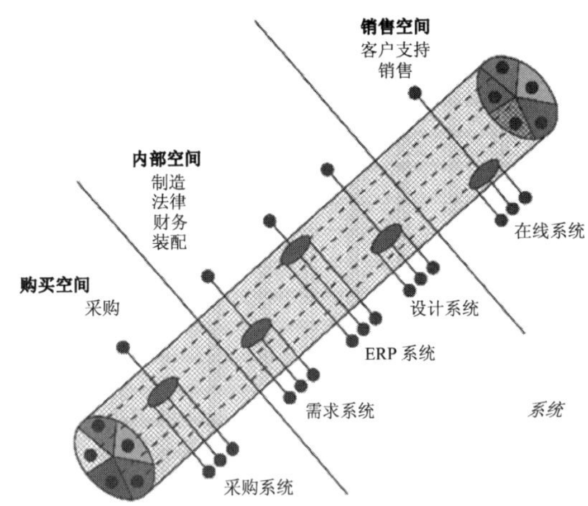

图 44-1　无边界信息流的实施途径（ENTERPRISE 门户）

见彩色插图ix页

在今天的 ENTERPRISE 中，架构师的关键挑战之一是，找出诸如网络服务、应用集成服务的技术到什么程度才能达到综合信息基础设施并实现相关 ENTERPRISE 的无边界信息流愿景，然后将其传达给高级管理层。

The Open Group 对可互操作的 ENTERPRISE 业务场景的跟踪分析已经引发对描述处理无边界信息流问题空间所需主要组件的综合信息基础设施模型（III-RM）的开发，并且可以帮助架构师执行该任务。

因此，III-RM 提供关于在 ENTERPRISE 环境中对无边界信息流的客户需要的洞察。该模型还指出有助于更好地利用价值链中的解决方案和产品的规则和标准。

下列小节详细地论述该模型。

44.1.5　III-RM 的状态

将目前状态的 III-RM 文件化，而且绝不将其视为一个成品。但是，这是一个由 The Open Group 的成员根据可互操作的 ENTERPRISE 业务场景作为一个整体开发并予以批准的模型，其本身是根据支持该领域的 The Open Group 客户成员明确表达的急迫需求而开发的。

因此，业务场景和参考模型代表 The Open Group 全体会员作为一个整体完全赞同的一个问题和一个解决方案途径。

希望该模型作为 TOGAF 的一部分公布会鼓励其广泛采用和使用，并提供一种沟通渠道，通过该沟通渠道可以反馈使用该模型的经验，融会贯通改进之处并根据需要细化和重新发布该模型。

44.2 High-Level View

This section provides a high-level view of the III-RM, including derivation of the model, high-level graphic, and components.

44.2.1 Derivation of the III-RM from the TRM

The III-RM is a model of the major component categories for developing, managing, and operating an integrated information infrastructure. It is a model of a set of applications that sits on top of an Application Platform. This model is a subset of the TOGAF TRM, and it uses a slightly different orientation.

Consider Figure 44-2 where two views of the TOGAF TRM are presented. The left side is the familiar view of the TOGAF TRM; it is a side view, where we look at the model as if looking at a house from the side, revealing the contents of the "floors". The top-down view on the right-hand side depicts what one might see if looking at a house from the "roof" down.

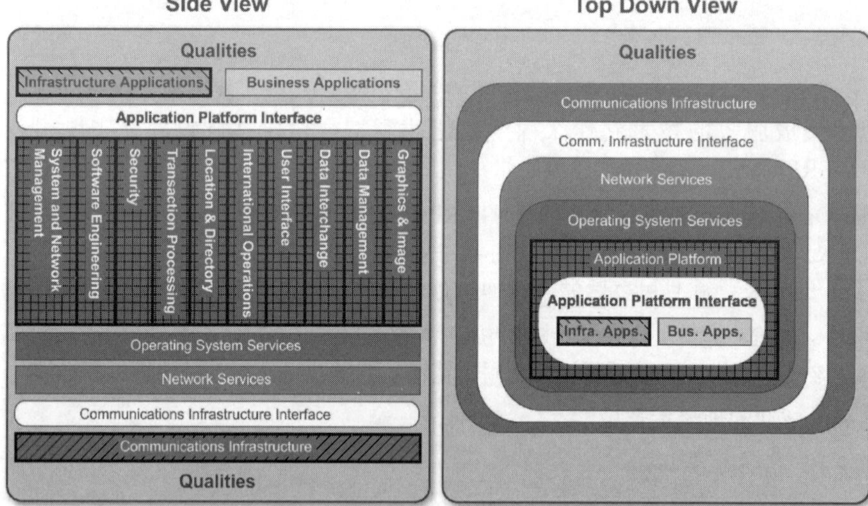

Figure 44-2 TOGAF TRM Orientation Views

The subset of the TRM that comprises the III-RM is depicted in Figure 44-3, in which those parts of the TRM not relevant to the III-RM are "greyed out".

Figure 44-3 illustrates that the focus is on the Application Software, Application Platform, and qualities subset of the TOGAF TRM.

44.2 高层级视图

本节提供 III-RM 的高层级视图，包括该模型的衍生品、高层级图形及组件。

44.2.1 III-RM 衍生自 TRM

III-RM 是开发、管理和运行综合信息基础设施的主要组件类别的一个模型，是设置在应用平台之上的一组应用的一个模型。该模型是 TOGAF TRM 的子集，它使用稍微不同的方向。

图 44-2 呈现出两个 TOGAF TRM 视图。左侧是熟悉的 TOGAF TRM 视图；该视图是一个侧视图，我们看该模型就像从侧面看一座房子，露出了“地板”上的内容。右手边的俯视图描述一个人如果从“屋顶”向下看房子可以看到的内容。

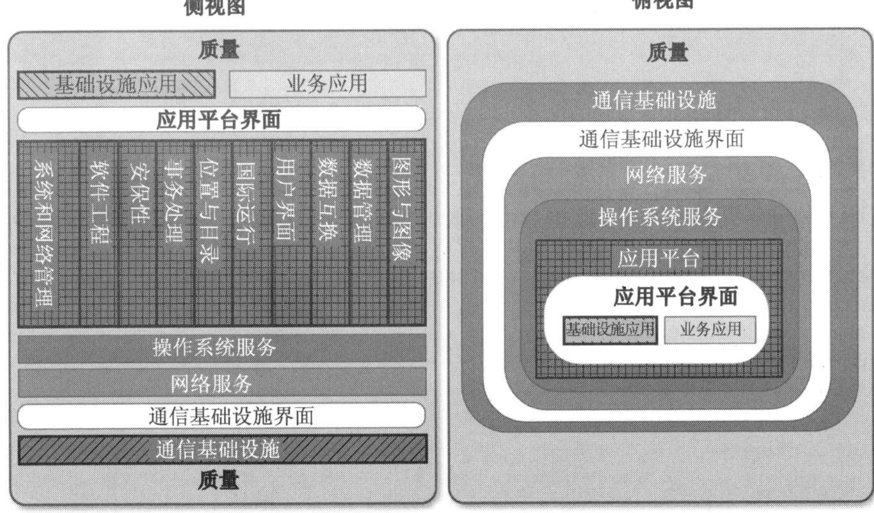

图 44-2　TOGAF TRM 方向视图

图 44-3 描述包括 III-RM 的 TRM 的子集，其中与 III-RM 无关的那些 TRM 部分都是“灰色的”。

图 44-3 阐明，聚焦点是 TOGAF TRM 的应用软件、应用平台及质量子集。

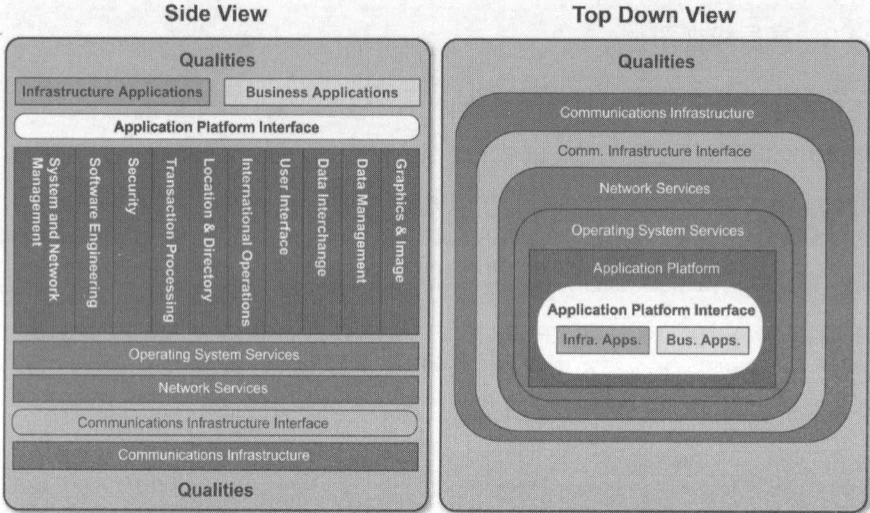

Figure 44-3 Focus of the III-RM

44.2.2 High-Level III-RM Graphic

The resulting III-RM itself is depicted in Figure 44-4. It is fundamentally an Application Architecture reference model — a model of the application components and application services software essential for an integrated information infrastructure. (There are more business applications and infrastructure applications than these in the environment, of course, but these are the subsets relevant to the Boundaryless Information Flow problem space.)

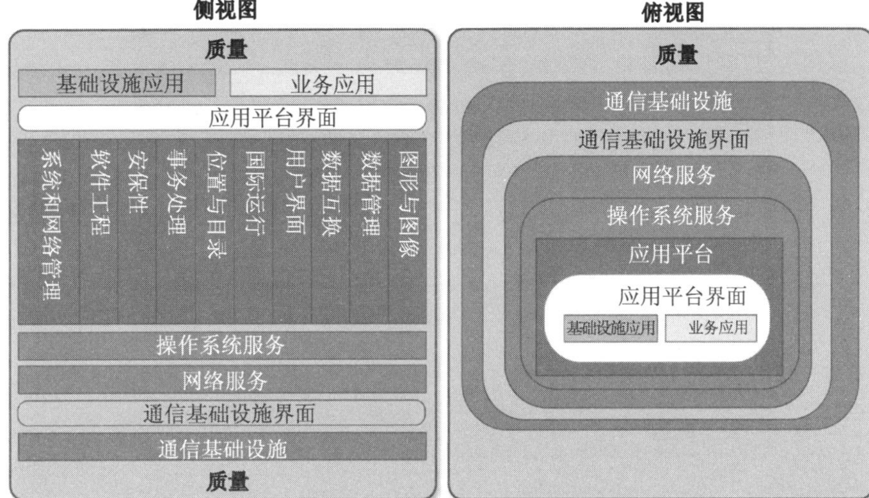

图 44-3 III-RM 的聚焦点

见彩色插图 x 页

44.2.2 高层级 III-RM 图形

图 44-4 描述最终形成的 III-RM 本身。从根本上看，III-RM 是一个应用架构参考模型——对综合信息基础设施至关重要的应用组件和应用服务软件的模型。（当然，业务应用和基础设施应用比该环境中的这些多，但是这些业务应用和基础设施应用是与无边界信息流问题空间有关的子集。）

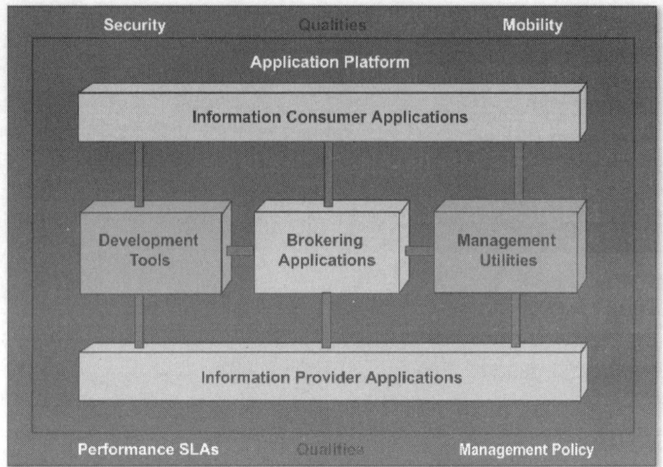

Figure 44-4 III-RM — High-Level

As explained above, the model assumes the underlying existence of a computing and network platform, and does not depict them explicitly.

Although the computing and network platform are not depicted, there may be requirements on them that must be met, in addition to requirements on the components of the III-RM, in order to fully address the Boundaryless Information Flow problem space.

44.2.3 Components of the High-Level III-RM

The III-RM has the following core components:

- **Business Applications**, denoted by the yellow boxes in the high-level model (corresponding to the "Business Applications" box in the TRM graphic). There are three types of Business Application in the model:
  - **Brokering Applications**, which manage the requests from any number of clients to and across any number of Information Provider Applications.
  - **Information Provider Applications**, which provide responses to client requests and rudimentary access to data managed by a particular server.
  - **Information Consumer Applications**, which deliver content to the user of the system, and provide services to request access to information in the system on the user's behalf.
- **Infrastructure Applications**, denoted by the orange boxes in the high-level model (corresponding to the "Infrastructure Applications" box in the TRM graphic). There are two types of Infrastructure Application in the model:

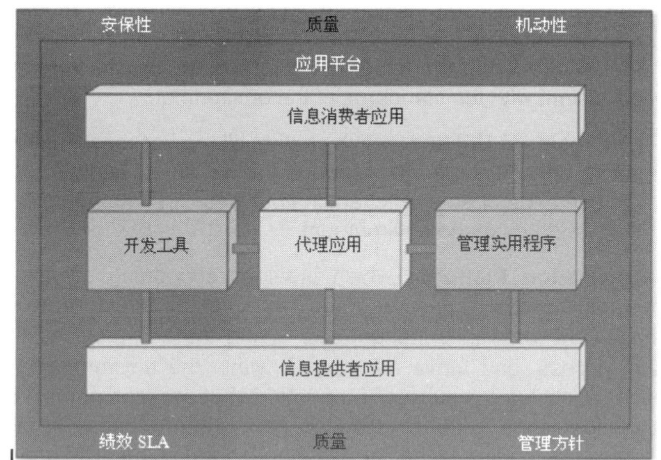

图 44-4 III-RM—高层级

见彩色插图 xi 页

如上所述，该模型假定可能存在计算和网络平台，但并未明确地描述。

虽然未描述计算和网络平台，但除了关于 III-RM 组件的需求，还可能有关于该平台的并且必须满足的需求，以便完全应对无边界信息流问题空间。

44.2.3 高层级 III-RM 的组件

III-RM 具有下述核心组件：

- **业务应用**，它在高层级模型中用黄色方框表示（对应于 TRM 图形中的“业务应用”方框）。该模型有三种类型的业务应用：
  - — **代理应用**，它管理从任意数量的客户端向跨任意数量的信息提供者提出的要求。
  - — **信息提供者应用**，它提供对客户端要求的响应及由特殊服务器管理的数据的初步访问。
  - — **信息消费者应用**，它向系统用户交付内容并代表用户提供对系统中信息要求访问的服务。
- **基础设施应用**，它在高层级模型中用橙色方框表示（对应于 TRM 图形中的“基础设施应用”方框）。该模型有两种类型的基础设施应用：

- **Development Tools**, which provide all the necessary modeling, design, and construction capabilities to develop and deploy applications that require access to the integrated information infrastructure, in a manner consistent with the standards of the environment.
- **Management Utilities**, which provide all the necessary utilities to understand, operate, tune, and manage the run-time system in order to meet the demands of an ever-changing business, in a manner consistent with the standards of the environment.

- An **Application Platform**, which provides supporting services to all the above applications — in areas such as location, directory, workflow, data management, data interchange, etc.— and thereby provides the ability to locate, access, and move information within the environment. This set of services constitutes a subset of the total set of services of the TRM Application Platform, and is denoted by the dark green underlay in the high-level model (corresponding to the Application Platform in the TRM graphic).
- The **Interfaces** used between the components. Interfaces include formats and protocols, application programming interfaces, switches, data values, etc. Interfaces among components at the application level are colored red. Interfaces between any application-level components and their supporting services in the Application Platform are colored white (corresponding to the API box in the TRM graphic).
- The **Qualities** backplane, denoted by the brown underlay in the high-level model (corresponding to the Qualities backplane in the TRM graphic). The Application Software and Application Platform must adhere to the policies and requirements depicted by the qualities backplane.

— **开发工具**，以符合环境标准的方式提供开发和部署需要访问综合信息基础设施的应用所需的所有建模、设计和构建能力。

— **管理实用程序**，以符合环境标准的方式提供了解、操作、调整和管理运行时系统所需的所有实用程序，以便满足不断变化的业务需求。

- **应用平台**，它向所有上述应用提供支持服务，诸如定位、目录、工作流程、数据管理、数据互换等方面，从而提供在该环境之内定位、访问和移动信息的能力。该组服务构成 TRM 应用平台的整组服务的子集，在高层级模型中用碧绿色衬底表示（对应于 TRM 图形中的应用平台）。

- 在组件之间使用的**界面**。界面包括格式和协议、应用编程界面、转换器、数据值等。在应用层级中组件之间的界面用红色表示。在应用平台间，任何应用层级组件与其支持服务之间的界面都用白色表示（对应于 TRM 图形中的 API 方框）。

- **质量背板**，它在高层级模型中用棕色衬底表示（对应于 TRM 图形中的质量背板）。应用软件和应用平台必须遵守质量背板描述的策略和需求。

44.3 Detailed Taxonomy

This section provides a detailed taxonomy of the III-RM, including detailed graphic, platform service categories, and external environment sub-entities.

44.3.1 Detailed III-RM Graphic

The detailed III-RM is depicted in Figure 44-5.

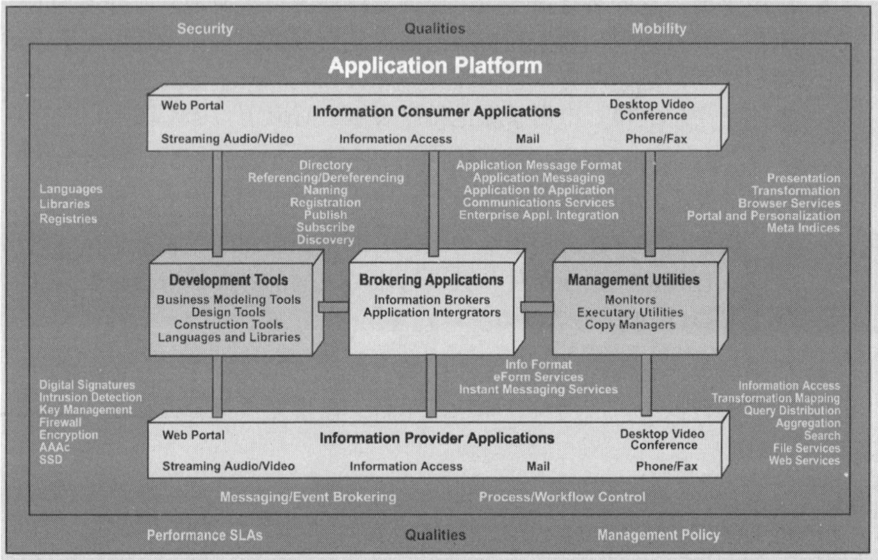

Figure 44-5 III-RM — Detailed

The remaining subsections expand on the taxonomy/component detail shown in Figure 44-5.

44.3.2 Business Applications

There are three types of business application in the model:

- **Information Provider Applications**, which provide responses to client requests and rudimentary access to data managed by a particular server.
- **Brokering Applications**, which manage the requests from any number of clients to and across any number of service providers.
- **Information Consumer Applications**, which deliver content to the user of the system, and provide services to request access to information in the system on the user's behalf.

The overall set of Information Provider, Information Consumer, and Brokerage Applications collectively creates an environment that provides a rich set of end-user services for transparently accessing heterogeneous systems, databases, and file systems.

44.3 详细的分类法

本节提供 III-RM 的详细分类法，包括详细的图形、平台服务类别及外部环境子实体。

44.3.1 详细的 III-RM 图形

在图 44-5 中描述了详细的 III-RM。

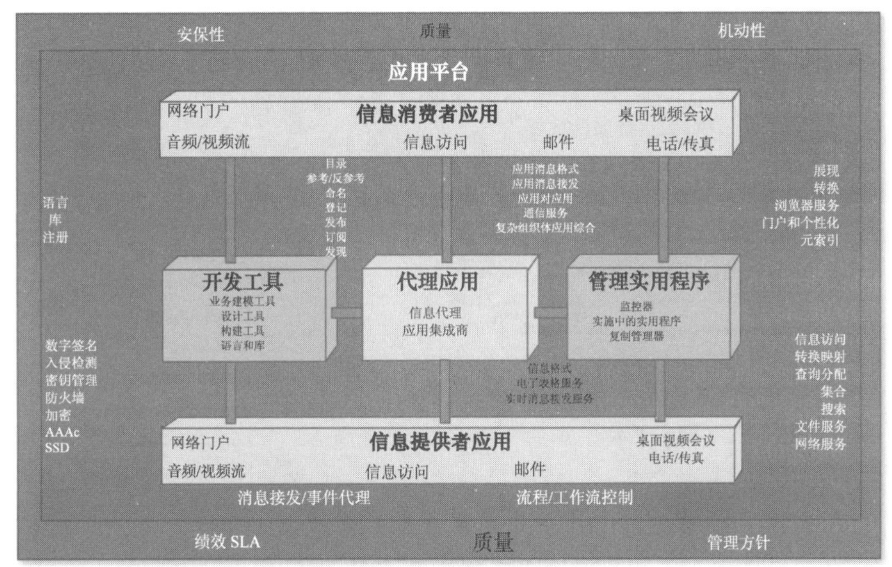

图 44-5 III-RM—细节说明

见彩色插图 xii 页

剩余小节详述分类法/组件细节，如图 44-5 所示。

44.3.2 业务应用

该模型有三种类型的业务应用：

- **信息提供者应用**，它提供对客户端要求的响应及由特殊服务器管理的数据的初步访问。
- **代理应用**，它管理从任意数量的客户端向跨任意数量的服务提供者提出的要求。
- **信息消费者应用**，它向系统用户传递内容并代表用户提供对系统中信息要求访问的服务。

信息提供者、信息消费者及代理应用的总体集合共同创建了一种环境，这种环境为透明地访问异构型系统、数据库和文件系统提供了丰富的最终用户服务集。

44.3.2.1 Information Provider Applications

To the extent that information today can be regarded as being "held hostage", as depicted in Figure 44-6, Information Provider Applications are those applications that "liberate" data from their silos.

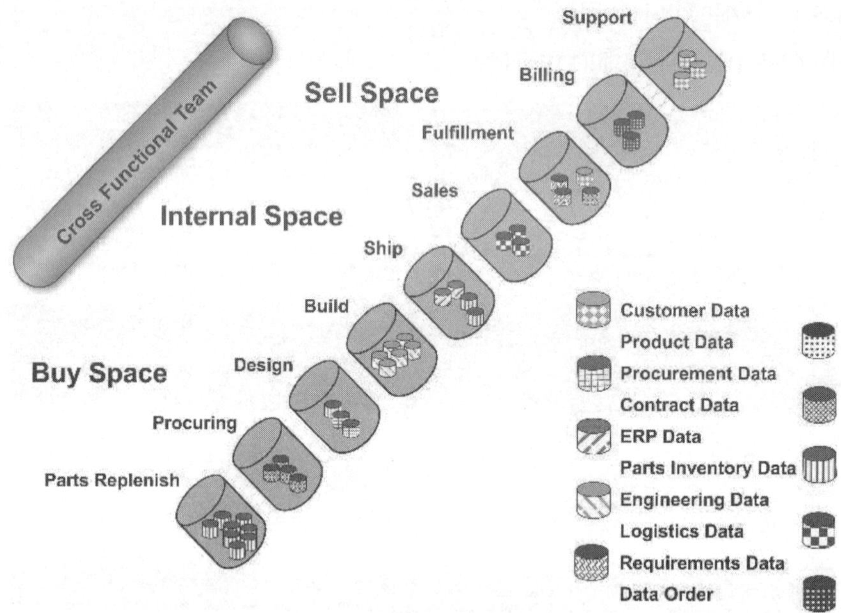

Figure 44-6 Liberate Data Silos to Meet Information Needs of Cross-Functional Enterprise Teams

Information Provider Applications achieve this by providing an open interface to a potentially proprietary silo interface, as illustrated in Figure 44-7, where the interfaces on the left of the Information Provider Applications are open interfaces and the interfaces between the Information Provider Applications and silo data are proprietary interfaces.

44.3.2.1 信息提供者应用

在一定程度上，信息在今天可被视为“被劫持的人质”，如图 44-6 所示，信息提供者应用是那些“释放”数据孤岛中的数据的应用。

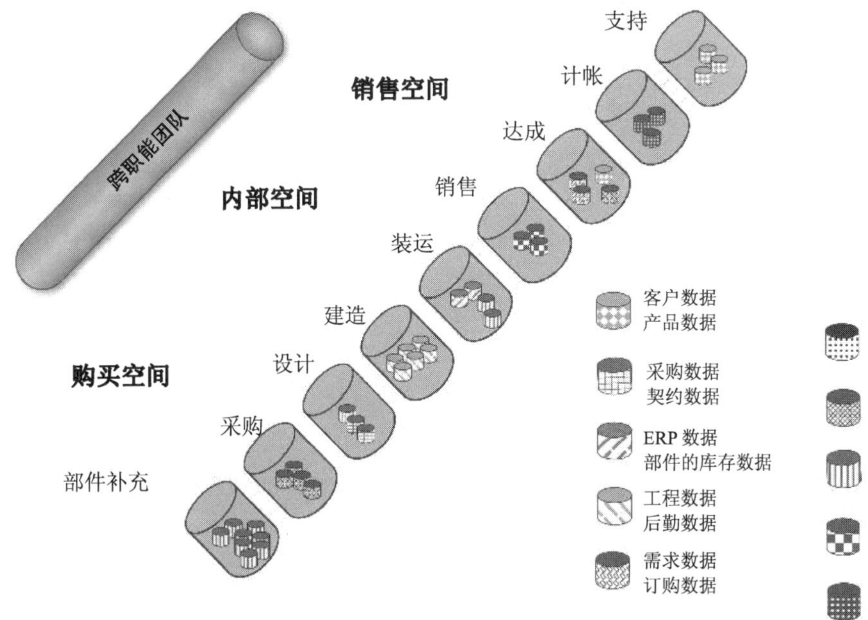

图 44-6 释放数据孤岛以满足跨职能的 ENTERPRISE 团队的信息需要

信息提供者应用通过向潜在专有竖井界面提供一个开放界面来达成该释放，如图 44-7 所示，其中在信息提供者应用左侧的界面为开放界面，信息提供者应用与竖井数据之间的界面为专有界面。

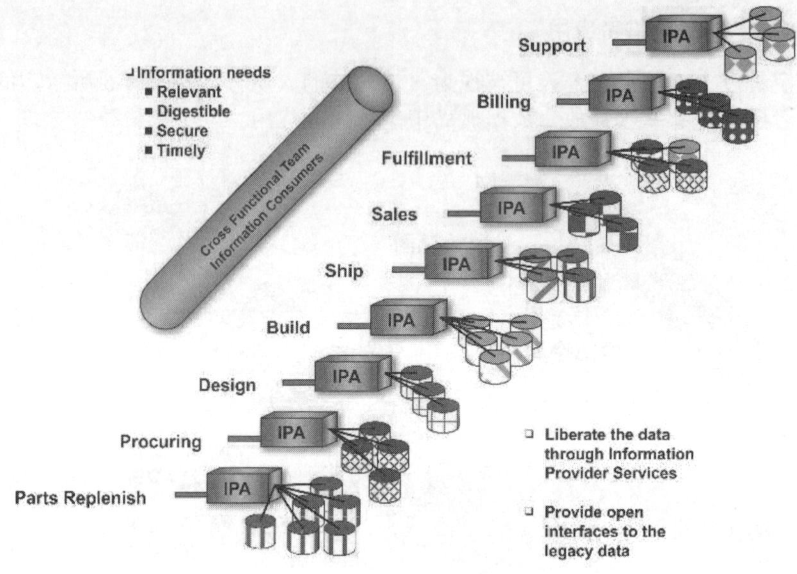

Figure 44-7 Information Provider Applications Liberate Data by Providing Open Interfaces to Data Silos

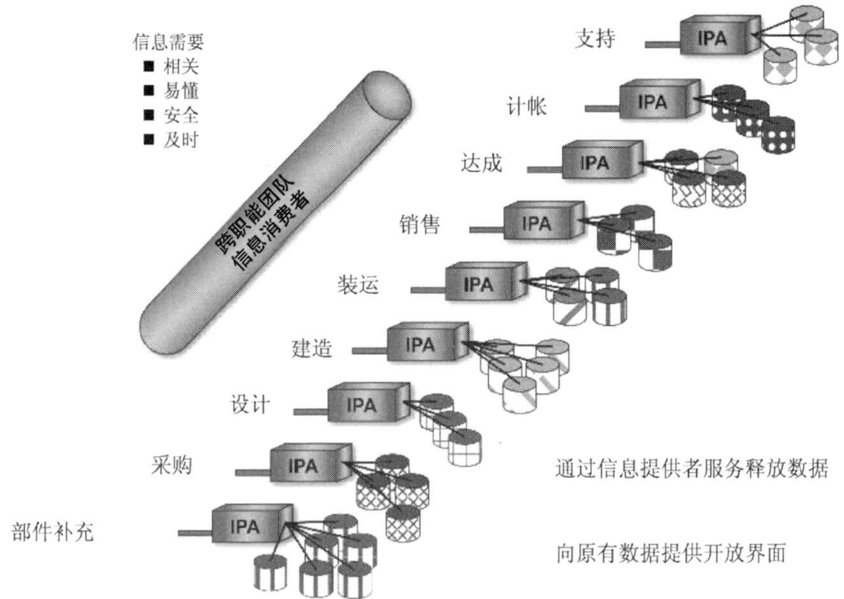

图 44-7 信息提供者应用通过向数据孤岛提供开放界面释放数据

44.3.2.2 Brokerage Applications

Brokerage Applications serve up single requests that require access to multiple information sources. A Brokerage Application breaks down such a request, distributes the request to multiple information sources, collects the responses, and sends a single response back to the requesting client.

Brokerage Applications access Information Provider Applications using the open interfaces provided by the Information Provider Applications (as described above); they integrate information from multiple Information Provider Applications and pass the integrated information to Information Consumer Applications using open interfaces.

Brokerage Applications also enable access to information within the enterprise by strategic partners.

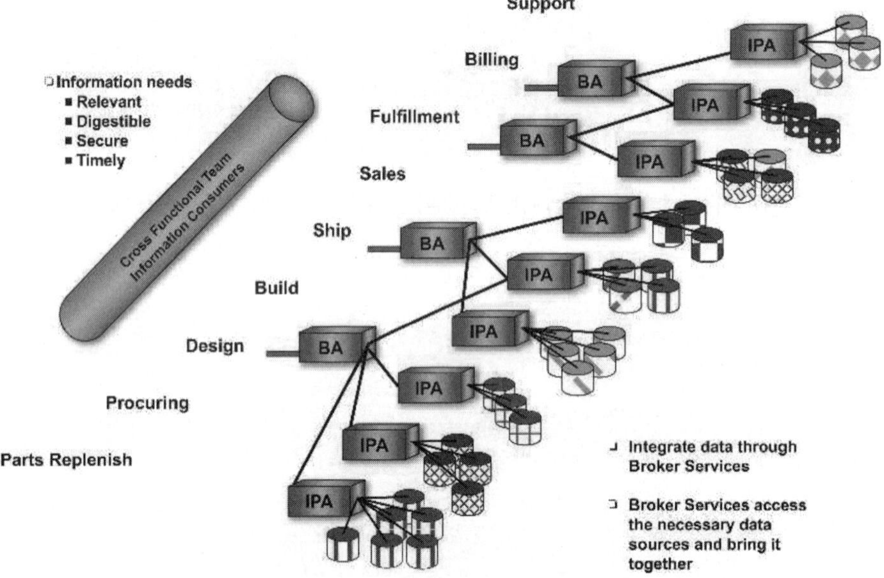

Figure 44-8 Brokerage Applications Integrate Information from Information Provider Applications

44.3.2.2 代理应用

代理应用提供需要访问多重信息源的单个要求。代理应用分解这样一种要求，将要求分发给多重信息源，收集响应并将单个响应发送回要求客户端。

代理应用利用信息提供者应用提供的开放界面（如上所述）访问信息提供者应用；代理应用综合多重信息提供者应用的信息并利用开放界面将综合信息传送至信息消费者应用。

代理应用还使战略性合作伙伴能够访问 ENTERPRISE 内部信息。

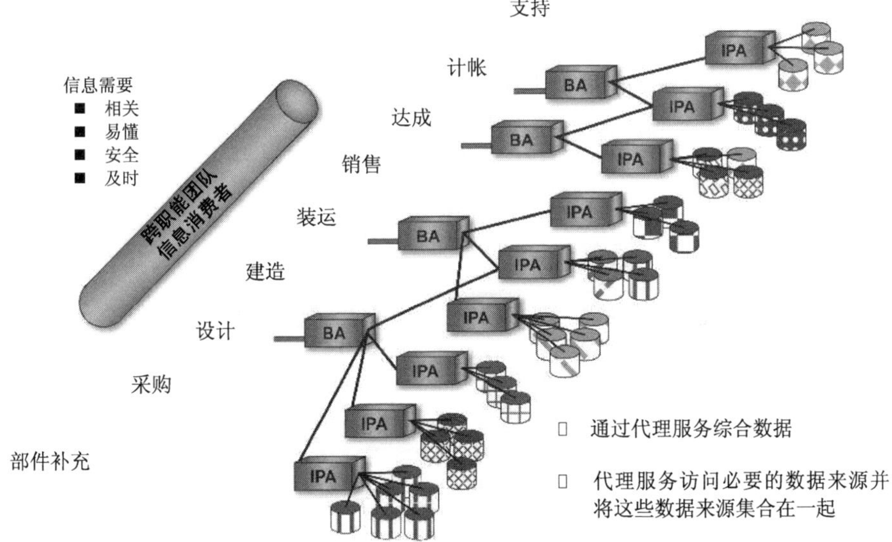

图 44-8　代理应用综合信息提供者应用的信息

44.3.2.3 Information Consumer Applications

Information Consumer Applications provide information to end users in the form in which they need it, when they need it, and in a secured manner. This includes providing the information in text, video, audio, English, German, etc.

Information Consumer Applications communicate with Brokerage Applications or Information Provider Applications using the open interfaces that the Brokerage and Information Provider Applications provide. Security is provided through the firewalls and/or security services.

Figure 44-9 depicts the Information Consumer Applications with the security services depicted as the brick pattern.

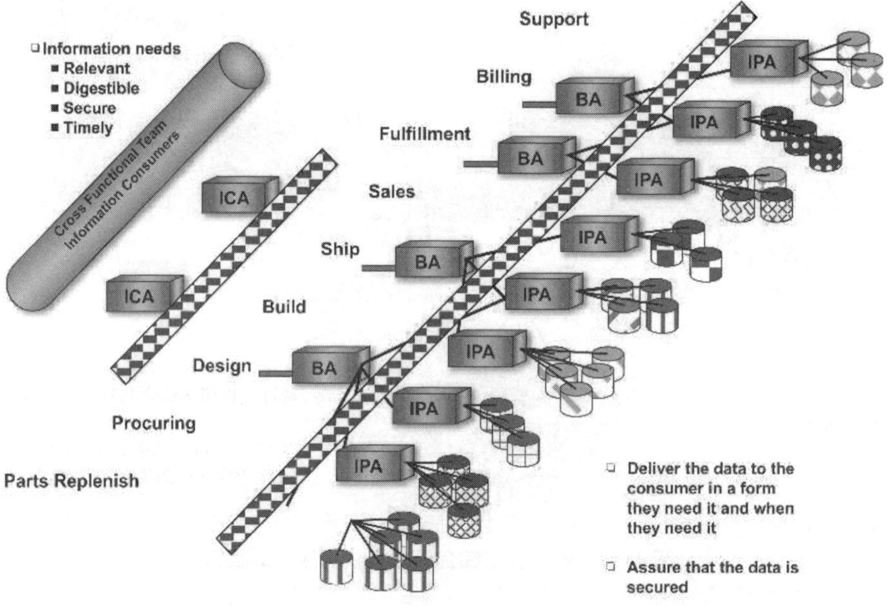

Figure 44-9 Information Consumer Applications Communicate Using Open Interfaces

44.3.2.3 信息消费者应用

信息消费者应用以最终用户需要的形式、在其需要的时间并以安保的方式向最终用户提供信息，包括提供文本、视频、音频、英语、德语等形式的信息。

信息消费者应用利用代理应用和信息提供者应用提供的开放界面与代理应用或信息提供者应用进行通信。通过防火墙和/或安保服务提供安保性。

图 44-9 描述信息消费者应用以及以砖块形式描述的安保服务。

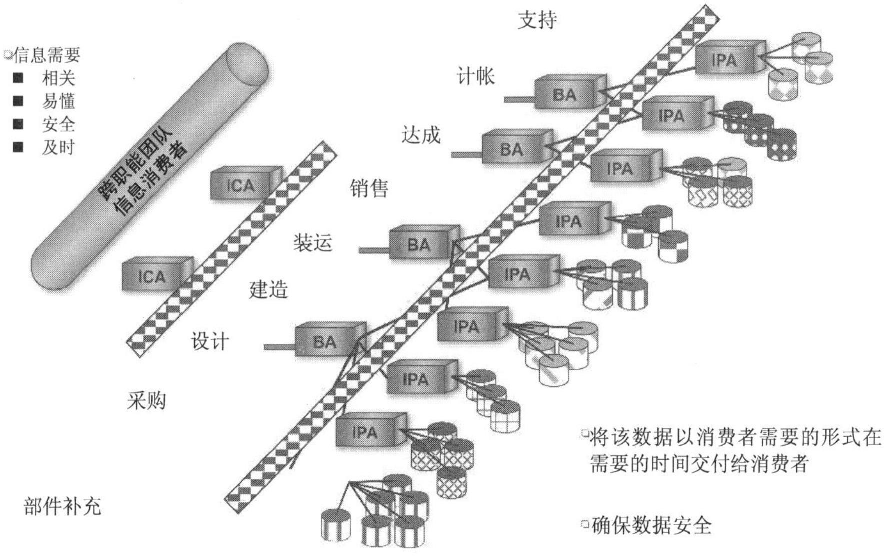

图 44-9 信息消费者应用通信采用开放界面

44.3.3 Infrastructure Applications

There are two types of Infrastructure Application in the model:

- **Development Tools**, which provide all the necessary modeling, design, and construction capabilities to develop and deploy applications that require access to the integrated information infrastructure, in a manner consistent with the standards of the environment.
- **Management Utilities**, which provide all the necessary utilities to understand, operate, tune, and manage the run-time system in order to meet the demands of an ever-changing business, in a manner consistent with the standards of the environment.

44.3.3.1 Development Tools

The Development Tools component of the model comprises applications that take the form of tools for modeling, designing, and constructing the integrated information infrastructure. Specifically, it includes tools for business, process, and data modeling, as well as the traditional application construction tools that transform the business model into software that automates the business processes revolving around information.

Note that each set of tools will be logically connected through a directory, allowing one tool to be driven by data from another. The following sections describe the requirements for components of Development Tools. The tool set also includes a repository.

Business Modeling Tools

This category covers tools for the modeling of business rules and business process rules.

Business modeling describes and documents the business in a comprehensive knowledge base. It establishes a consensus among general management of the business direction, organization, processes, information requirements, and the current environment of the business. Perhaps most importantly, this understanding is documented in a common, business-oriented format to be utilized for subsequent enhancement.

Design Modeling Tools

This category covers tools for designing, defining, and documenting the most pertinent IT elements of the business based upon the business and business process rules. Examples of elements to be designed include: connections between people, organizations, workflows and computers; data and object models; physical data translation and translation rules; and constraints.

Implementation and Construction Tools

Implementation tools enable timely development of re-usable processes, applications, and application services. Such tools include intelligent browsers, data manipulation language compilers and optimizers, distributed application compilers and debuggers, heterogeneous client and server development tools, policy definition tools, and workflow script generation tools.

44.3.3 基础设施应用

该模型有两种类型的基础设施应用：

- **开发工具**，以符合环境标准的方式提供开发和部署需要访问综合信息基础设施的应用所需的所有建模、设计和构建能力。
- **管理实用程序**，以符合环境标准的方式提供理解、操作、调整和管理运行时系统所需的所有实用程序，以便满足不断变化的业务需求。

44.3.3.1 开发工具

模型的开发工具组件，包括采取工具的形式对综合信息基础设施进行建模、设计和构建的应用。具体地说，它包括用于业务、流程和数据建模的工具以及传统的应用构建工具，传统的应用构建工具将业务模型转换成以信息为中心的业务流程自动化的软件。

注意，每组工具都会通过目录从逻辑上连接，使一个工具能由另一个工具的数据驱动。下面几节描述开发工具组件的需求。该成套工具还包括存储库。

业务建模工具

该类别包括对业务规则和业务流程规则进行建模的工具。

业务建模描述综合知识库中的业务，并使其文件化。它在业务方向、组织、流程、信息需求及业务的当前环境的共用管理之间建立一个共识。或许最重要的是，以普通的面向业务的格式使这种认识文件化，以供后续增加内容使用。

设计建模工具

该类别包括基于业务和业务流程规则对该业务的大部分相关 IT 元素进行设计、定义和文件化的工具。待设计的元素的示例包括：人员之间、组织之间、工作流程之间及计算机之间的连接，数据和对象模型，物理数据转换和转换规则，以及约束。

实施和构建工具

实施工具促进可复用流程、应用和应用服务的及时开发。此类工具包括智能浏览器、数据操作语言编译程序和优化程序、分布式应用编译程序和调试程序、不同种类的客户端和服务器开发工具、策略定义工具及工作流程脚本生成工具。

Data Modeling Tools

Deployment Tools

Deployment tools are necessary to move implemented software from the development environment into the operational environment.

Libraries

This component includes re-usable libraries of software that use the standards of the operational environment.

44.3.3.2 Management Utilities

This category covers applications that take the form of utilities for operations, administration, and systems management, and for the management of data based on availability and cost requirements. Such utilities may execute in an attended or an unattended environment.

Operations, Administration, and Management (OA&M) Utilities

The OA&M component covers traditional systems management and administration utilities that manage business rules and information objects. Examples include: utilities for installation, copyright and license management; and miscellaneous administration, configuration, and registration functions. Additionally there are utilities for the control of service billing, service triggering, and account management.

Quality of Service Manager Utilities

These include health monitoring and management utilities.

Copy Management Utilities

Copy Management utilities are those that manage data movement from any given operational system to necessary distribution points in the enterprise, in order to ensure the maximum leverage of operational systems data. They also include tools that detect and flag poor quality data.

Storage Management Utilities

These are utilities that provide least-cost data storage management. Storage management utilities support the wide variety of storage mechanisms and are connected to file, object, and database systems.

44.3.4 Application Platform

All the different types of application described above are built on top of the services provided by the Application Platform.

The Application Platform component of the III-RM comprises a subset of all the services defined in the TOGAF TRM, the subset that pertains to integrated information infrastructure. Specifically, it comprises all those services in the TRM Application Platform that allow applications to focus on understanding and processing the information required, rather than understanding the form, format, and/or location of the information.

The services of the Application Platform component can be used to support conventional applications as well as Brokerage, Information Consumer, and Information Provider applications.

数据建模工具

部署工具

部署工具对于将实施的软件从开发环境移动到运行环境中而言必不可少。

库

该组件包括使用运行环境标准的可复用软件库。

44.3.3.2 管理实用程序

该类别包括采取实用程序的形式进行运行、监管和系统管理及基于有效性和成本需求进行数据管理的应用。此类实用程序可以在有人值守或无人值守的环境中执行。

运行、监管与管理（OA&M）实用程序

OA&M 组件包括管理业务规则及信息对象的传统系统管理和监管实用程序。示例包括：用于安装、版权及许可管理的实用程序；以及其他监管、构型和注册功能。此外，还有控制服务记账、服务触发和账户管理的实用程序。

服务质量管理人员的实用程序

这些实用程序包括健康监控和管理实用程序。

拷贝管理实用程序

拷贝管理实用程序是那些管理数据从任何给定运行系统移动至 ENTERPRISE 中的必要分配点，以便确保更好地最大化利用运行的系统数据的实用程序。它们还包括检测并标记劣质数据的工具。

存储管理实用程序

存在提供最低成本的数据存储管理的实用程序。存储管理实用程序支持各种各样的存储机制并连接至文件、对象和数据库系统。

44.3.4 应用平台

上述所有不同类型的应用均建立在应用平台提供的服务之上。

III-RM 的应用平台组件包括 TOGAF TRM 中定义的所有服务的子集，该子集属于综合信息基础设施。更具体地说，它包括 TRM 应用平台中的全部服务，这些服务使得应用聚焦于对所需信息的理解和处理，而不关注对该信息的形式、格式和/或位置的理解。

应用平台组件的服务，可用于支持常规的应用以及代理、信息消费者和信息提供者等应用。

When used as part of an overall Application Architecture in this way, such an approach enables maximum leverage of a single operational environment that is designed to ensure effective and consistent transfer of data between processes, and to support fast and efficient development, deployment, and management of applications.

The Application Platform component comprises the following categories of service.

44.3.4.1 Software Engineering Services

- Languages
- Libraries
- Registries

44.3.4.2 Security Services

- Authentication, authorization, and access control
- Single sign-on
- Digital signature
- Firewall
- Encryption
- Intrusion detection
- Identity management
- Key management

44.3.4.3 Location and Directory Services

Location and directory services provide access facilities for name, location, description, and relationship data that describes the integrated information infrastructure.

Directory services support the deployment and enterprise-wide availability of an integrated information infrastructure directory. The data in the directory is made available to all other components in the architecture model.

Figure 44-10 depicts the juxtaposition of location and directory services to the other components.

当以该方式用作总体应用架构的一部分时，这样一种实施途径使单一运行环境能够得到更好的最大化利用，该环境旨在确保在流程之间高效一致地传输数据并支持快速有效的应用开发、部署和管理。

应用平台组件包括下述服务类别。

44.3.4.1 软件工程服务

- 语言
- 库
- 注册表

44.3.4.2 安保服务

- 认证、授权和访问控制
- 单点登录
- 数字签名
- 防火墙
- 加密
- 入侵检测
- 身份管理
- 密钥管理

44.3.4.3 位置和目录服务

位置和目录服务提供访问描述综合信息基础设施的名称、位置、说明和关系数据的设施。

目录服务支持综合信息基础设施目录的部署及整个 ENTERPRISE 范围的有效性。目录中的数据可供架构模型的所有其他组件使用。

图 44-10 描述位置和目录服务与其他组件的并置。

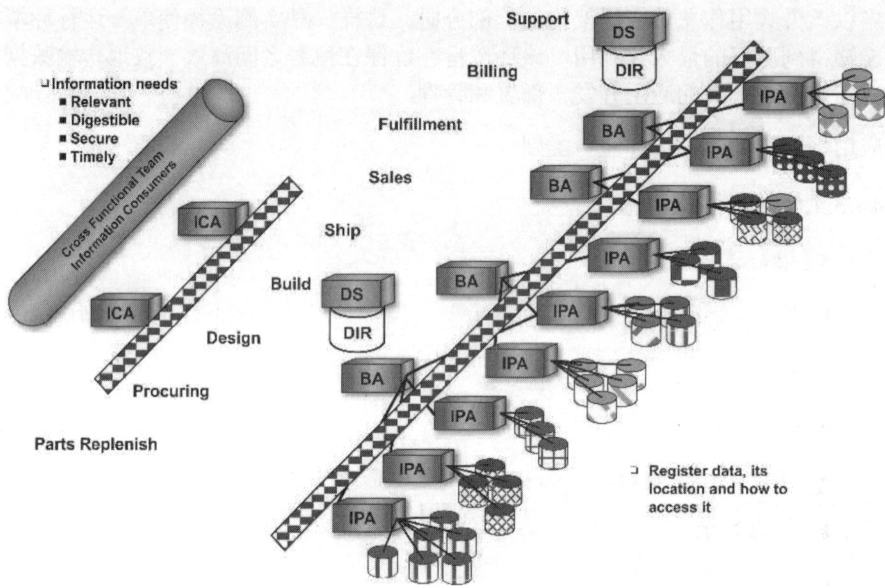

Figure 44-10 Juxtaposition of Location and Directory Services to Other Components

Specific services include:

- Directory
- Registration
- Publish/subscribe
- Discovery
- Naming
- Referencing/dereferencing

44.3.4.4 Human Interaction Services

Human Interaction services provide the means to consistently present data to the end user in the appropriate format. They comprise services that assist in the formulation of customer data requests and enable visualization and presentation of the data accessed.

Specific services include:

- Presentation
- Transformation
- Browser
- Meta indices
- Portal and personalization

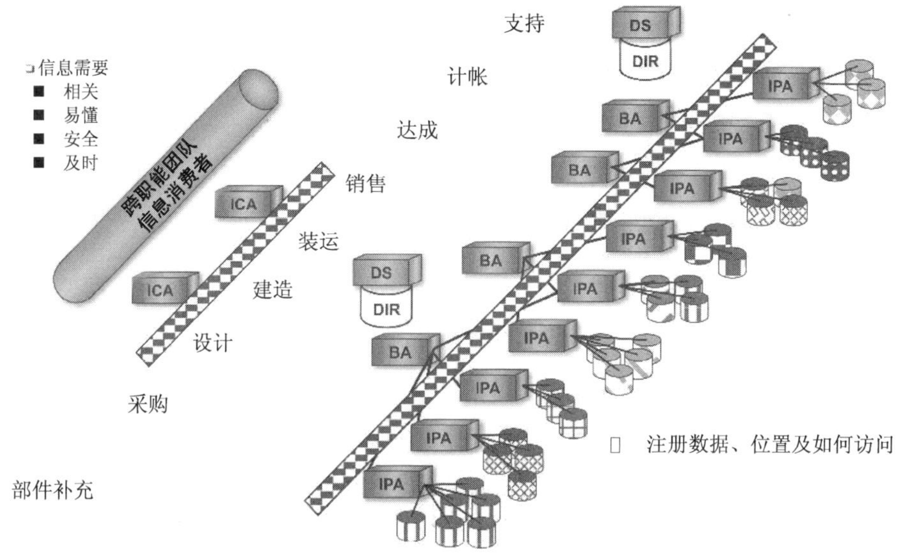

图 44-10　位置和目录服务与其他组件的并置

特定服务包括：

- 目录
- 注册
- 发布/订阅
- 发现
- 命名
- 参考/反参考

44.3.4.4　人机交互服务

人机交互服务提供始终以适当格式向最终用户表达数据的手段。人机交互服务包括帮助满足公式化客户数据要求并促进所访问数据的可视化及展示的服务。

特定服务包括：

- 展示
- 转换
- 浏览器
- 元索引
- 门户和个性化

44.3.4.5 Data Interchange Services

Specific services include:

- Information format
- eForm
- Instant messaging
- Application messaging
- Application-to-application communications
- Enterprise application integration

44.3.4.6 Data Management Services

Specific services include:

- Information and data access
- Transformation mapping
- Query distribution
- Aggregation
- Search
- File

Information access services provide the ability for an application to access an integrated view of data, regardless of whether the data exists in a mainframe system or in a distributed system. The information access services ensure that data integrity is maintained among multiple databases, and also provide online data cleansing (whereby data is checked against data rules for each access).

Data access services provide open interfaces to legacy data, provide new applications standard database access services to vast amounts of existing data, and provide standard access services to new data types.

44.3.4.7 Additional Operating System Services

Specific services include:

- Event brokering
- Workflow

These additional services enable the flow of information, as depicted in Figure 44-11.

44.3.4.5 数据交换服务

特定服务包括：

- 信息格式
- 电子表单
- 实时消息接发
- 应用消息接发
- 应用到应用的通信
- ENTERPRISE 应用综合

44.3.4.6 数据管理服务

特定服务包括：

- 信息和数据访问
- 转换映射
- 查询分配
- 聚集
- 搜索
- 归档

信息访问服务提供应用访问综合数据视图的能力，不管数据是存在于主机系统中还是存在于分布式系统中。信息访问服务确保在多个数据库之间保持数据完整性，还提供在线数据清理（从而在每次访问时按照数据规则检查数据）。

数据访问服务为遗留数据提供开放界面，为大量现有数据提供新应用的标准数据库访问服务，还为新数据类型提供标准访问服务。

44.3.4.7 附加的操作系统服务

特定服务包括：

- 事件代理
- 工作流程

这些附加服务使信息流成为可能，如图 44-11 所示。

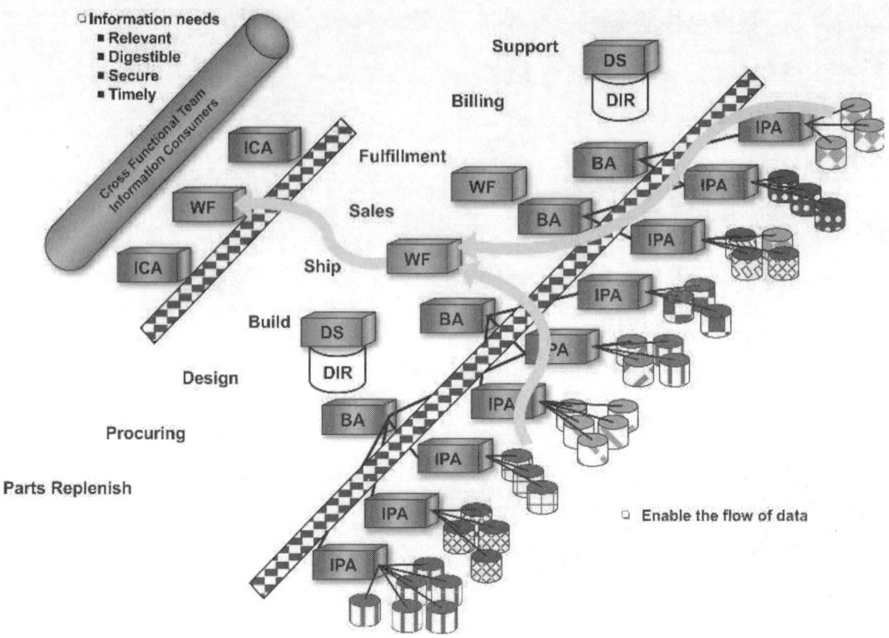

Figure 44-11 Workflow Services Enable Information Flow

Workflow denotes the concept of automating processes by facilitating user interactions and executing applications according to a process map. Workflow services enable integration of enterprise applications, resulting in applications of extended value.

Workflow services also address the needs of managing an environment where legacy systems are prevalent.

Workflow services also provide a means to encapsulate existing applications, thereby supporting customer needs for leverage of existing assets.

44.3.5 Qualities

The qualities component of the model is supported by quality of service services, including the various services required to maintain the quality of the system as specified in Service Level Agreements (SLAs).

Included in this are the services to post conditions to, and react to requests from, the Quality of Service Manager.

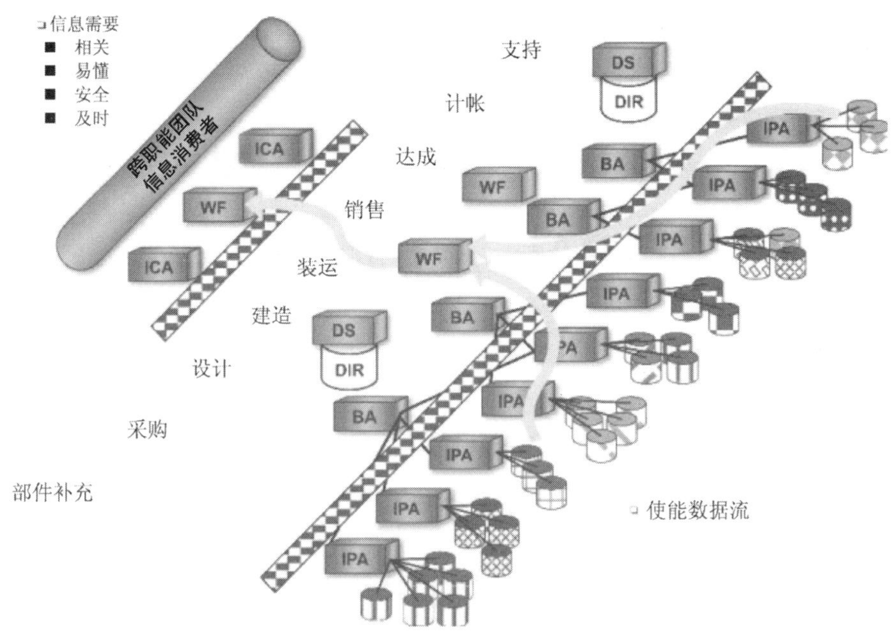

图 44-11　工作流程服务使能信息流

工作流程按照流程图指出通过促进用户交互和执行应用使流程自动化的概念。工作流程服务促使对 ENTERPRISE 应用进行综合，带来有附加值的应用。

工作流程服务还应对遗留系统普遍存在的环境的管理需要。

工作流程服务还提供一种封装现有应用的手段，从而支持客户最大程度地发挥现有资产作用的需要。

44.3.5　质量

该模型的质量组件由服务质量等服务支持，包括将系统质量保持在服务水平协议（SLA）指定水平所需的各种不同服务。

其中，还包括将各个条件发送给服务质量管理人员并对服务质量管理人员的要求作出反应的服务。

TOGAF Version 9.1

Part VII Architecture Capability Framework

The Open Group

TOGAF 9.1 版本

第七部分　架构能力框架

The Open Group

Chapter 45
Introduction

This chapter provides an introduction to and an overview of the contents of Part VII: Architecture Capability Framework.

45.1 Overview

In order to successfully operate an architecture function within an enterprise, it is necessary to put in place appropriate organization structures, processes, roles, responsibilities, and skills to realize the Architecture Capability.

Part VII: Architecture Capability Framework provides a set of reference materials for how to establish such an architecture function. Readers should note that although this part contains a number of guidelines to support key activities, in its current form, the Architecture Capability Framework is not intended to be a comprehensive template for operating an enterprise Architecture Capability.

An overall structure for the Architecture Capability Framework is shown in Figure 45-1.

第 45 章
简　介

本章提供关于“第七部分：架构能力框架”内容的简介和概述。

45.1　概述

为了在 ENTERPRISE 内成功地运行架构功能，有必要将恰当的组织结构、流程、角色、职责和技能落实到位，以实现架构能力。

“第七部分：架构能力框架”对于如何建立这样一种架构功能提供一系列参考资料。读者应注意，尽管这一部分包括许多支持关键活动的指南，但就其目前的形式来说，架构能力框架还未计划用作运行 ENTERPRISE 的架构能力的综合性模板。

架构能力框架的总体结构如图 45-1 所示。

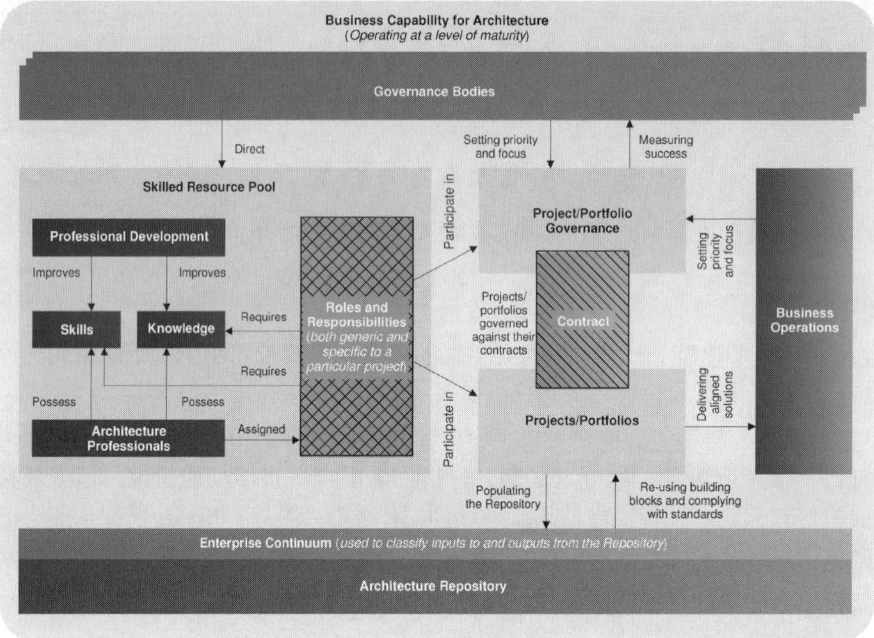

Figure 45-1 Mature Architecture Capability

45.2 Structure of Part VII

Part VII: Architecture Capability Framework is structured as follows:

- Introduction (this chapter)
- Establishing an Architecture Capability (see Chapter 46)
- Architecture Board (see Chapter 47)
- Architecture Compliance (see Chapter 48)
- Architecture Contracts (see Chapter 49)
- Architecture Governance (see Chapter 50)
- Architecture Maturity Models (see Chapter 51)
- Architecture Skills Framework (see Chapter 52)

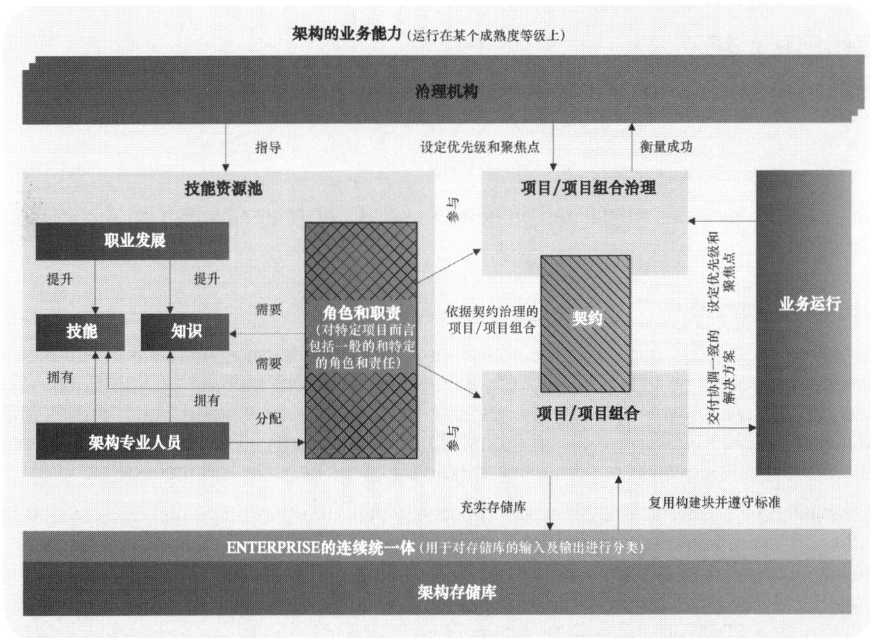

图 45-1　成熟的架构能力

45.2　第七部分的结构

“第七部分：架构能力框架”的结构如下：

- 简介（本章）
- 建立架构能力（见第 46 章）
- 架构委员会（见第 47 章）
- 架构合规性（见第 48 章）
- 架构契约（见第 49 章）
- 架构治理（见第 50 章）
- 架构成熟度模型（见第 51 章）
- 架构技能框架（见第 52 章）

Chapter 46
Establishing an Architecture Capability

This chapter provides guidelines on how to use the ADM to establish an Architecture Capability.

46.1 Overview

As with any business capability, the establishment of an enterprise Architecture Capability can be supported by the TOGAF Architecture Development Method (ADM). Successful use of the ADM will provide a customer-focused, value-adding, and sustainable architecture practice that enables the business, helps maximize the value of investments, and pro-actively identifies opportunities to gain business benefits and manage risk.

Establishing a sustainable architecture practice within an organization can be achieved by adhering to the same approach that is used to establish any other capability — such as a business process management capability — within an organization. The ADM is an ideal method to be used to architect and govern the implementation of such a capability. Applying the ADM with the specific Architecture Vision to establish an architecture practice within the organization would achieve this objective.

This shouldn't be seen as a phase of an architecture project, or a one-off project, but rather as an ongoing practice that provides the context, environment, and resources to govern and enable architecture delivery to the organization. As an architecture project is executed within this environment it might request a change to the architecture practice that would trigger another cycle of the ADM to extend the architecture practice.

Implementing any capability within an organization would require the design of the four domain architectures: Business, Data, Application, and Technology. Establishing the architecture practice within an organization would therefore require the design of:

- The **Business Architecture** of the architecture practice that will highlight the architecture governance, architecture processes, architecture organizational structure, architecture information requirements, architecture products, etc..
- The **Data Architecture** that would define the structure of the organization's Enterprise Continuum and Architecture Repository.
- The **Application Architecture** specifying the functionality and/or applications services required to enable the architecture practice.
- The **Technology Architecture** that depicts the architecture practice's infrastructure requirements and deployment in support of the architecture applications and Enterprise Continuum.

第 46 章 建立架构能力

本章对如何利用 ADM 建立架构能力提供指南。

46.1 概述

与其支持任何业务能力一样，TOGAF 架构开发方法（ADM）可支持 ENTERPRISE 的架构能力的建立。ADM 的成功使用将提供以客户为中心的、增值的且可持续的架构实践，该架构实践可使得业务能够实现，有助于最大化投资价值，并且主动识别多个获取业务收益和管理风险的机会。

通过遵守与用于建立任何其他能力（如业务流程管理能力）相同的实施途径，可以达成在组织内建立可持续的架构实践。对架构开发和对实施此类能力进行管控而言，ADM 是所用的一种理想方法。应用这种具有特定架构愿景的 ADM 在组织内部建立架构实践会达成此目的。

这不应被视为架构项目的一个阶段或一次性项目，而应视为一项持续进行的实践，向组织提供管控和使能架构交付的背景、环境和资源。当在这种环境内执行架构项目时，可能要求架构实践的变更，该变更会触发 ADM 的另一个周期，以扩展架构实践。

在组织内，实现任何能力都需要设计如下四个领域的架构：业务、数据、应用和技术。因此，在组织内建立架构实践将需要如下设计：

- 架构实践的**业务架构**，强调架构治理、架构流程、架构组织结构、架构信息需求和架构产品等。
- **数据架构**，定义组织的 ENTERPRISE 的连续统一体和架构库的结构。
- **应用架构**，规定使架构实践可行所需的功能性和/或应用服务。
- **技术架构**，描述支持架构应用和 ENTERPRISE 的连续统一体的架构实践基础设施需求和部署。

The steps in establishing an architecture practice are explained below, against the context of the ADM phases. The reader should therefore refer to the relevant ADM phase in Part II: Architecture Development Method (ADM), to understand the complete scope of each step. In this section, key aspects will be highlighted for each ADM phase that should be considered and are specific to establishing an architecture practice. The intent is therefore not to repeat each ADM phase description, but to guide the reader to apply each ADM phase within the context of establishing an architecture practice.

46.2 Phase A: Architecture Vision

The purpose of this phase within the context of establishing an architecture practice is to define or review the vision, stakeholders, and principles of the architecture practice. The focus in this phase would be on the architecture practice as a whole and not on a particular architecture project.

The following should be considered in terms of understanding the steps in the context of establishing an architecture practice:

- **Establish the Project**: This step should focus on defining the stakeholders in the architecture practice. The stakeholders would include the roles and organization units participating in the architecture practice, as well as those that will benefit from the deliverables generated by the architecture practice that can therefore be defined as customers of the architecture practice.
- **Identify Stakeholders and Concerns, Business Requirements, and Architecture Vision**: This step generates the first, very high-level definitions of the baseline and target environments, from a business information systems and technology perspective for the architecture practice.
- **Identify Business Goals and Business Drivers**: This would be more relevant for the architecture practice than for a particular architecture project. An understanding of the business goals and drivers is essential to align the architecture practice to the business.
- **Define Scope**: Defining the scope of the architecture practice would be a high-level project plan of what should be addressed in terms of architecture for the next period.
- **Define Constraints**: The focus in this step should be on the enterprise-wide constraints that would impact on all architecture projects.
- **Review Architecture Principles, including Business Principles**: The intent in this step should be to define the principles that would govern and guide the running of the architecture practice. Where architecture principles usually govern the architecture deliverables, the architecture practice principles would address the architecture practice organization, content, tools, and process.
- **Develop Statement of Architecture Work and Secure Approval**: This step should generate the architecture practice vision and scope.

Another step that can be considered during this phase is to conduct an architecture maturity assessment. Refer to Chapter 51 for guidance on this topic.

下面，针对 ADM 阶段的背景环境，解释建立架构实践的步骤。因此，读者应参照“第二部分：架构开发方法（ADM）”中相关的 ADM 阶段来理解每个步骤的完整范围。本节将强调应在每个 ADM 阶段考虑的并且对于建立架构实践特定的一些关键方面。因此，意图不是重复每个 ADM 阶段的描述，而是指导读者在建立架构实践的背景环境内应用每个 ADM 阶段。

46.2 阶段 A：架构愿景

在建立架构实践的背景环境下，本阶段的目的是定义或审视架构实践的愿景、利益攸关者和原则。本阶段的聚焦点是作为一个整体的架构实践，而非特殊的架构项目。

为理解在建立架构实践的背景中的步骤，应考虑以下几点：

- **建立项目**：该步骤应聚焦在架构实践中定义利益攸关者。利益攸关者将包括参与架构实践的角色和组织单元，以及将从构架实践产生的交付物中受益并因此可定义为架构实践客户的角色和组织单元。
- **识别利益攸关者和关注点、业务需求以及架构愿景**：该步骤从架构实践的业务信息系统和技术的关注层面，产生基线和目标环境的第一个超高层级定义。
- **识别各类业务目标和业务驱动因素**：这一步对于架构实践比对于特殊架构项目更为相关。理解业务目标和驱动因素，对使架构实践对准业务而言是根本性的。
- **定义范围**：定义架构实践的范围对于下一阶段的架构而言是一个应该处理什么问题的高层级项目计划。
- **定义约束**：该步骤的聚焦点应是会影响所有架构项目的整个 ENTERPRISE 范围的约束。
- **审视架构原则，包括业务原则**：该步骤意图定义将管控和指导架构实践运行的原则。在架构原则经常管控架构交付物的情况下，架构实践原则将涉及架构实践组织、内容、工具和流程。
- **制定架构工作说明书并获得批准**：该步骤应产生架构实践愿景和范围。

在本阶段中可以考虑的另一个步骤是进行架构成熟度评估。关于该主题的引导，见第 51 章。

46.3 Phase B: Business Architecture

Key areas of focus during this phase of establishing or refining the Business Architecture of the architecture practice are:

- An **Architecture Ontology** defining the architectural terms and definitions that will be used in the organization in order to establish a common understanding of these terms.
- The **Architecture Process** where the ADM would form the base of the process and need to be customized to meet the organization's requirements and architecture practice vision. Refer to Section 5.3 for guidance on developing this process. The required architecture governance processes should be included in the overall architecture process.
- The **Architecture Viewpoints and Views** that lists all the viewpoints and views that should be addressed by the architecture practice. The identified architecture practice stakeholders would guide the development of this definition. One of the viewpoints to be included is the architecture governance viewpoint; refer to Part IV, Chapter 35 for guidance on this output.
- The **Architecture Framework** describing the various architecture deliverables that will be generated by the architecture practice, the inter-relationships and dependencies between the architecture deliverables, as well as the rules and guidelines governing the design of these deliverables. The defined architecture viewpoints and views should be used to guide the definition of the architecture framework. Part II: Architecture Development Method (ADM) and Chapter 36 are useful references that will assist in describing the architecture framework.
- The **Architecture Accountability Matrix** defining the roles in the architecture practice and allocating accountability of the roles to architecture deliverables and processes. This matrix would include the required architecture governance structures and roles. Part II: Architecture Development Method (ADM) as well as Chapter 47, Chapter 50, and Chapter 52 would provide guidance on this output.
- The **Architecture Performance Metrics** identifying and describing the metrics that will be used to monitor the performance of the architecture practice against its stated architecture practice vision and objectives.
- The **Architecture Governance Framework** which is a specific view of the defined architecture process and Architecture Accountability Matrix.

46.4 Phase C: Data Architecture

The Data Architecture of the architecture practice would specify and govern the structure of the organization's Enterprise Continuum and Architecture Repository. The Data Architecture should be defined based on the architecture framework. The Data Architecture is sometimes referred to as the metamodel of the architecture practice.

46.3 阶段 B：业务架构

在建立或细化架构实践的业务架构这一阶段中聚焦的关键领域有：

- **架构本体论**，它定义将在组织中使用的架构术语及定义，以便对这些架构术语建立共识。
- **架构流程**，在其中 ADM 会构成流程基础并需要定制，以满足组织的需求及架构实践愿景。关于开发该流程的引导，见 5.3 节。所需的架构治理流程应包括在所有架构流程中。
- **架构视角和视图**，列出架构实践应当涉及的所有视角和视图。所识别的架构实践利益攸关者将指导该定义的制定。应包括的视角之一是架构治理视角；关于该输出的引导，见第四部分第 35 章。
- **架构框架**，描述将由架构实践产生的各种架构交付物、架构交付物之间的相互关系和依赖性以及管控这些交付物设计的规则和指南。所定义的架构视角和视图应用来指导架构框架的定义。“第二部分：架构开发方法（ADM）”和第 36 章是帮助描述架构框架的有用参考。
- **架构责任矩阵**，定义架构实践中的角色并将角色的责任分配到架构交付物和流程。本矩阵将包括所需的架构治理结构和角色。“第二部分：架构开发方法（ADM）”以及第 47 章、第 50 章和第 52 章将对本输出提供引导。
- **架构绩效衡量标准**，识别并描述根据申明的架构实践愿景和目标而监控架构实践绩效的衡量标准。
- **架构治理框架**，这是所定义的架构流程和架构责任矩阵的一个特定视图。

46.4 阶段 C：数据架构

架构实践的数据架构将规定并管控组织的 ENTERPRISE 的连续统一体和架构库的结构。应基于架构框架定义数据架构。数据架构有时被称为架构实践的元模型。

46.5 Phase C: Application Architecture

The Application Architecture of the architecture practice defines the functionality required to generate, maintain, publish, distribute, and govern the architecture deliverables as defined in the architecture framework. A key focus should be on the modeling toolsets required for modeling, but it should not be the only focus. Refer to Chapter 42 for guidance on selecting a toolset. Publishing the architecture deliverables to address specific views in the architecture framework would sometimes require specialized or customized functionality and should not be neglected.

46.6 Phase D: Technology Architecture

The Technology Architecture of the architecture practice should define technology infrastructure supporting the architecture practice.

46.7 Phase E: Opportunities & Solutions

A critical factor to consider during this phase of planning the establishment of the architecture practice is the organizational change that is required and how this will be achieved.

46.8 Phase F: Migration Planning

The focus should not only be on the Information Systems Architecture components in this phase, but include the Business Architecture. The adoption of the architecture process and framework will have a major impact on the overall establishment of the architecture practice in the organization.

46.9 Phase G: Implementation Governance

The implementation of the Business Architecture of the architecture practice should be the focus of this phase. Changing practices within the organization to adopt a more structured and disciplined approach will be a challenge and should be addressed by the appropriate organizational change techniques.

46.5 阶段 C：应用架构

架构实践的应用架构，对架构框架中定义的架构交付物进行生成、维护、发布、分配和管控所需的功能性进行定义。一个关键的聚焦点应是建模所需的建模工具套件，但不应将其作为唯一的聚焦点。关于选择工具套件的引导，参见第 42 章。发布处理架构框架中特定视图的架构交付物有时需要专门的或定制的功能，而且不应被忽略。

46.6 阶段 D：技术架构

架构实践的技术架构应定义支持架构实践的技术基础设施。

46.7 阶段 E：机会和解决方案

在对建立架构实践进行规划的这一阶段中考虑的一个关键因素是，所需的组织变革以及如何达成该变革。

46.8 阶段 F：迁移规划

在本阶段，不应仅聚焦于信息系统架构组件，还应包括业务架构。架构流程和框架的采用将对架构实践在组织中的全面建立具有重要影响。

46.9 阶段 G：实施治理

架构实践中业务架构的实施应是本阶段的聚焦点。变革组织内的实践以采用更结构化、更严格的实施途径会是一个挑战，应通过适当的组织变革技术予以应对。

46.10 Phase H: Architecture Change Management

Changes to the architecture of the architecture practice should be managed by this phase. These changes are usually triggered during the execution of architecture projects. A typical change would be the requirement for a new architecture deliverable. This would impact on all the architecture domains of the architecture practice.

46.11 Requirements Management

Understanding and managing the requirements for the architecture practice is crucial. Requirements should be clearly articulated and align to the architecture practice vision.

46.10 阶段 H：架构变更管理

架构实践的架构变更应在本阶段进行管理。通常，会在执行架构项目时触发这些变更。一种典型的变更是新架构交付物的需求。这会对架构实践的所有架构领域产生影响。

46.11 需求管理

理解并管理架构实践的需求是至关重要的。需求应被清晰地表达并且对准架构实践愿景。

Chapter 47
Architecture Board

This chapter provides guidelines for establishing and operating an Enterprise Architecture Board.

47.1 Role

A key element in a successful architecture governance strategy (see Chapter 50) is a cross- organization Architecture Board to oversee the implementation of the strategy. This body should be representative of all the key stakeholders in the architecture, and will typically comprise a group of executives responsible for the review and maintenance of the overall architecture.

Architecture Boards may have global, regional, or business line scope. Particularly in larger enterprises, Architecture Boards typically comprise representatives from the organization at a minimum of two levels:

- Local (domain experts, line responsibility)
- Global (organization-wide responsibility)

In such cases, each board will be established with identifiable and articulated:

- Responsibilities and decision-making capabilities
- Remit and authority limits

47.2 Responsibilities

The Architecture Board is typically made responsible, and accountable, for achieving some or all of the following goals:

- Providing the basis for all decision-making with regard to the architectures.
- Consistency between sub-architectures.
- Establishing targets for re-use of components.
- Flexibility of enterprise architecture:
  — To meet changing business needs.
  — To leverage new technologies.
- Enforcement of Architecture Compliance.
- Improving the maturity level of architecture discipline within the organization.

第 47 章
架构委员会

本章对建立并运作 Enterprise Architecture 委员会提供指南。

47.1 角色

成功的架构治理战略（见第 50 章）中的一个关键要素是有一个交叉组织架构委员会，以便对策略实施进行监督。该机构应代表架构中的所有关键利益攸关者，并且通常应包括一组负责审视和维护总体架构的管理人员。

架构委员会可以覆盖全球、区域或业务线范围。特别是在大型 ENTERPRISE 中，架构委员会通常包括来自于至少两个层级的组织的代表：

- 本地（领域专家、直线职责）
- 全球（整个组织范围的职责）

在这样的情况下，每个委员会都将拥有可识别且可清楚表达的：

- 职责和决策能力
- 职权范围和权力限制

47.2 职责

架构委员会通常负责实现部分或全部下述目标并就此承担责任：

- 为所有关于架构的决策提供基础。
- 子架构之间的一致性。
- 建立组件复用的目标。
- Enterprise Architecture 的灵活性：
  - 满足变化的业务需要。
  - 更好地利用新技术。
- 架构合规性的执行。
- 提高组织内架构修炼的成熟度等级。

- Ensuring that the discipline of architecture-based development is adopted.
- Supporting a visible escalation capability for out-of-bounds decisions.

Further responsibilities from an operational perspective should include:

- All aspects of monitoring and control of the Architecture Contract.
- Meeting on a regular basis.
- Ensuring the effective and consistent management and implementation of the architectures.
- Resolving ambiguities, issues, or conflicts that have been escalated.
- Providing advice, guidance, and information.
- Ensuring compliance with the architectures, and granting dispensations that are in keeping with the technology strategy and objectives.
- Considering policy (schedule, Service Level Agreements (SLAs), etc.) changes where similar dispensations are requested and granted; e.g., new form of service requirement.
- Ensuring that all information relevant to the implementation of the Architecture Contract is published under controlled conditions and made available to authorized parties.
- Validation of reported service levels, cost savings, etc..

From a governance perspective, the Architecture Board is also responsible for:

- The production of usable governance material and activities.
- Providing a mechanism for the formal acceptance and approval of architecture through consensus and authorized publication.
- Providing a fundamental control mechanism for ensuring the effective implementation of the architecture.
- Establishing and maintaining the link between the implementation of the architecture, the architectural strategy and objectives embodied in the enterprise architecture, and the strategic objectives of the business.
- Identifying divergence from the architecture and planning activities for realignment through dispensations or policy updates.

47.3 Setting Up the Architecture Board

47.3.1 Triggers

One or more of the following occurrences typically triggers the establishment of an ArchitectureBoard:

- New CIO
- Merger or acquisition
- Consideration of a move to newer forms of computing
- Recognition that IT is poorly aligned to business
- Desire to achieve competitive advantage via technology

- 确保采用了基于架构的开发的规程。
- 对超出界限的决策提供可见的升级能力。

从运行的关注层面看，架构委员会的更多职责应包括：

- 监测并控制架构契约的所有方面。
- 定期举行会议。
- 确保有效和一致的架构管理与实施。
- 解决已经升级的歧义、问题或冲突。
- 提供建议、引导及信息。
- 确保符合架构，并给予与技术战略和目的保持一致的特许。
- 在要求并给予相似特许的情况下，考虑策略［进度表、服务水平协议（SLA）等］的变更；例如新形式的服务需求。
- 确保与架构契约实施相关的所有信息在受控条件下发布，并可供被授权方使用。
- 确认已报告的服务水平、成本节约等。

从治理的关注层面看，架构委员会还负责：

- 可用管控资料的生产及相关活动。
- 通过一致和经授权的发布，提供正式认可和批准架构的一种机制。
- 提供一项确保架构有效实施的基础性控制机制。
- 在实施架构、架构战略、体现在 Enterprise Architecture 中的目标以及业务战略目标之间建立并保持联系。
- 识别与架构的偏离并通过特许或策略更新来规划各项重新对准活动。

47.3 成立架构委员会

47.3.1 触发条件

下述一个或多个事件通常会触发架构委员会的建立：

- 新 CIO
- 合并或采办
- 考虑向较新的计算形式转变
- 认识到 IT 与业务的对准性较差
- 希望通过技术获取竞争优势

- Creation of an enterprise architecture program
- Significant business change or rapid growth
- Requirement for complex, cross-functional solutions

In many companies, the executive sponsor of the initial architecture effort is the CIO (or other senior executive). However, to gain broad corporate support, a sponsoring body has more influence. This sponsoring body is here called an Architecture Board, but the title is not important. Whatever the name, it is the executive-level group responsible for the review and maintenance of the strategic architecture and all of its sub-architectures.

The Architecture Board is the sponsor of the architecture within the enterprise, but the Architecture Board itself needs an executive sponsor from the highest level of the corporation. This commitment must span the planning process and continue into the maintenance phase of the architecture project. In many companies that fail in an architecture planning effort, there is a notable lack of executive participation and encouragement for the project.

A frequently overlooked source of Architecture Board members is the company's Board of Directors. These individuals invariably have diverse knowledge about the business and its competition. Because they have a significant impact on the business vision and objectives, they may be successful in validating the alignment of IT strategies to business objectives.

47.3.2 Size of the Board

The recommended size for an Architecture Board is four or five (and no more than ten)permanent members.

In order to keep the Architecture Board to a reasonable size, while ensuring enterprise-wide representation on it over time, membership of the Architecture Board may be rotated, giving decision-making privileges and responsibilities to various senior managers. This may be required in any case, due to some Architecture Board members finding that time constraints prevent long-term active participation.

However, some continuity must exist on the Architecture Board, to prevent the corporate architecture from varying from one set of ideas to another. One technique for ensuring rotation with continuity is to have set terms for the members, and to have the terms expire at different times.

In the ongoing architecture process following the initial architecture effort, the Architecture Board may be re-chartered. The executive sponsor will normally review the work of the Architecture Board and evaluate its effectiveness; if necessary, the Architecture Compliance review process is updated or changed.

47.3.3 Board Structure

The TOGAF Architecture Governance Framework (see Section 50.2) provides a generic organizational framework that positions the Architecture Board in the context of the broader governance structures of the enterprise. This structure identifies the major organizational groups and responsibilities, as well as the relationship between each group. This is a best practice structure, and may be subject to change depending on the organization's form and existing structures.

Consideration must be given to the size of the organization, its form, and how the IT functions are implemented. This will provide the basis for designing the Architecture Board structure within the context of the overall governance environment. In particular, consideration should be given to the concept of global ownership and local implementation, and the integration of new concepts and technologies from all areas implementing against architectures.

- 创建 Enterprise Architecture 项目群
- 重要的业务变革或迅速的业务增长
- 需要复杂的交叉功能解决方案

在很多公司，初始架构工作的执行发起人是 CIO（或其他高级管理人员）。然而，为了获得广泛的公司级支持，一个发起机构具有更大的影响。发起机构在此被称为架构委员会，但头衔并不重要。无论用什么名称，它都是负责审视和维护战略架构及其所有子架构的执行层级的群组。

架构委员会是 ENTERPRISE 内架构的发起人，但架构委员会本身需要来自公司最高层的一个执行发起人。这一委任必须跨越规划流程，并且延续到架构项目的维护阶段。很多未能在架构规划工作中取得成功的公司明显缺乏对该项目的行政参与和鼓励。

架构委员会成员的一个经常被忽视的来源是公司董事会。这些个体无不在业务和竞争方面有着各种各样的知识。因为他们对业务愿景和目的有重要影响，所以可以成功地确认 IT 战略与业务目标的对准性。

47.3.2 委员会规模

架构委员会的建议规模是 4 个或 5 个（不超过 10 个）常任成员。

为了将架构委员会保持在合理规模，同时确保其在一段时间内代表整个 ENTERPRISE，架构委员会的成员资格可以采用轮流制，将决策特权和职责提供给不同的高级经理。由于有些架构委员会成员发现时间约束阻碍了长期的主动参与，所以在任何情况下都可能需要这种制度。

但是，为了防止公司架构由一套理念变化到另一套理念，架构委员会必须存在一定的连续性。一个确保轮流制具有连续性的技巧是为成员设定期限，并将每个期限设置在不同的时间到期。

在紧随初始架构工作之后进行的架构流程中，可以重新委任架构委员会。执行发起人通常审视架构委员会的工作并评价其有效性；必要时，更新或变更架构合规性审视流程。

47.3.3 委员会结构

TOGAF 架构治理框架（见 50.2 节）提供一种一般组织框架，将架构委员会置于 ENTERPRISE 的广泛治理结构背景环境下。这种结构识别主要的组织群组及其职责以及群组之间的关系。这是一种最佳实践结构，且可以根据组织的形式和现有结构进行变革。

必须考虑组织的规模、形式以及如何实现 IT 功能。这将为在总体治理环境的背景下设计架构委员会结构提供基础。尤其是，还应考虑全球所有权和本地实施的概念，以及来自于根据架构实施的所有领域的新概念和技术的综合。

The structure of the Architecture Board should reflect the form of the organization. The architecture governance structure required may well go beyond the generic structures outlined in the TOGAF Architecture Governance Framework (see Section 50.2). The organization may need to define a combination of the IT governance process in place and the existing organizational structures and capabilities, which typically include the following types of body:

- Global governance board
- Local governance board
- Design authorities
- Working parties

47.4 Operation of the Architecture Board

This section describes the operation of the Architecture Board particularly from the governance perspective.

47.4.1 General

Architecture Board meetings should be conducted within clearly identified agendas with explicit objectives, content coverage, and defined actions. In general, board meetings will be aligned with best practice, such as given in the COBIT framework (see Section 50.1.4.1).

These meetings will provide key direction in:

- Supporting the production of quality governance material and activities.
- Providing a mechanism for formal acceptance through consensus and authorized publication.
- Providing a fundamental control mechanism for ensuring the effective implementation of the architectures.
- Establishing and maintaining the link between the implementation of the architectures and the stated strategy and objectives of the organization (business and IT).
- Identifying divergence from the contract and planning activities to realign with the contract through dispensations or policy updates.

47.4.2 Preparation

Each participant will receive an agenda and any supporting documentation — e.g., dispensation requests, performance management reports, etc. — and will be expected to be familiar with the contents of each.

Where actions have been allocated to an individual, it is that person's responsibility to report on progress against these.

Each participant must confirm their availability and attendance at the Architecture Board meeting.

架构委员会的结构应反映组织的形式。所需架构治理结构很可能超出 TOGAF 架构治理框架（见 50.2 节）中概述的一般结构。组织可能需要定义正在运行的 IT 治理流程与现有组织结构及能力的组合形态，通常包括下述几类机构：

- 全球治理委员会
- 本地治理委员会
- 设计局
- 工作组

47.4 架构委员会的运作

本节特别从治理的关注层面描述架构委员会的运作。

47.4.1 概述

应在清晰识别的且具有明确的目的、内容覆盖范围和所定义活动的议程内召开架构委员会会议。通常，委员会会议将与最佳实践对准，如 COBIT 框架中所给出的（见 50.1.4.1 节）。

这些会议将提供下述事项的关键方向：

- 支持质量管控资料的制作及相关活动。
- 通过统一和经授权的发布提供一种正式认可的机制。
- 提供一种确保架构有效实施的基础性控制机制。
- 在架构实施与组织申明的战略和目的（业务和 IT）之间建立并保持联系。
- 识别与契约的偏离，并通过特许或策略更新来规划各项活动，以重新对准契约。

47.4.2 准备

每名与会者都会收到一份议程和所有支持性文件，如特许要求、绩效管理报告等，而且希望每名与会者都能熟悉各项内容。

当行动被指派给个人时，此人的职责是汇报这些行动的进展。

每名与会者必须确认这些文件的可用性并出席架构委员会会议。

47.4.3 Agenda

This section outlines the contents of a Architecture Board meeting agenda. Each agenda item is described in terms of its content only.

Minutes of Previous Meeting

Minutes contain the details of previous Architecture Board meeting as per standard organizational protocol.

Requests for Change

Items under this heading are normally change requests for amendments to architectures, principles, etc., but may also include business control with regard to Architecture Contracts; e.g., ensure that voice traffic to premium numbers, such as weather reports, are barred and data traffic to certain web sites is controlled.

Any request for change is made within agreed authority levels and parameters defined by theArchitecture Contract.

Dispensations

A dispensation is used as the mechanism to request a change to the existing architectures, contracts, principles, etc. outside of normal operating parameters; e.g., exclude provision of service to a subsidiary, request for unusual service levels for specific business reasons, deploy non-standard technology or products to support specific business initiatives.

Dispensations are granted for a given time period and set of identified services and operational criteria that must be enforced during the lifespan of the dispensation. Dispensations are not granted indefinitely, but are used as a mechanism to ensure that service levels and operational levels, etc. are met while providing a level flexibility in their implementation and timing. The time- bound nature of dispensations ensures that they are a trigger to the Architecture Compliance activity.

Compliance Assessments

Compliance is assessed against SLAs, Operational Level Agreements (OLAs), cost targets, and required architecture refreshes. These assessments will be reviewed and either accepted or rejected depending on the criteria defined within the Architecture Governance Framework. The Architecture Compliance assessment report will include details as described.

Dispute Resolution

Disputes that have not been resolved through the Architecture Compliance and dispensation processes are identified here for further action and are documented through the Architecture Compliance assessments and dispensation documentation.

Architecture Strategy and Direction Documentation

This describes the architecture strategies, direction, and priorities and will only be formulated by the global Architecture Board. It should take the form of standard architecture documentation.

47.4.3 议程

本节概述架构委员会会议议程的内容。仅依照各项议程的内容描述其事项。

上次会议的会议记录

按照标准组织协议，会议记录包含上次架构委员会会议的详细内容。

变更要求

本标题下的事项通常是对修正架构、原则等的变更要求，但可能还包括关于架构契约的业务控制，如确保禁止收费号码产生的语音流量（如天气报告），并且控制特定网站的数据流量。

任何变更要求都在已商定的权力层级和架构契约所定义的参数内做出。

特许

特许是对正常运行参数之外的现有架构、契约、原则等要求做出更改的机制，如拒绝向子公司提供服务、由于特殊业务原因而要求例外服务水平、部署非标准技术或产品以支持特定的业务举措。

在规定时间区间内，对一组必须在特许有效期间执行的已识别服务和操作准则给予特许。特许不会被无限期地给予，但是可作为一种机制来确保在满足服务水平和操作水平等的同时，还在实施与时间安排中提供同等的灵活性。特许的时效本质确保其是架构合规性活动的一个触发条件。

合规性评估

针对 SLA、运行水平协议（OLA）、成本目标和所需架构更新进行合规性评估。审视这些评估结果，并依据架构治理框架中定义的准则或接受或拒绝。架构合规性评估报告将包括如下所述的详细内容。

争端的解决

在此对尚未通过架构合规和特许流程解决的争端进行标识，以采取进一步的行动，并通过架构合规性评估和特许文档将这些争端文件化。

架构策略和方向文档

架构策略和方向文档描述架构的策略、方向和优先级，并将仅由全球架构委员会制定。其应采取标准架构文档的形式。

Actions Assigned

This is a report on the actions assigned at previous Architecture Board meetings. An action tracker is used to document and keep the status of all actions assigned during the Architecture Board meetings and should consist of at least the following information:

- Reference
- Priority
- Action description
- Action owner
- Action details
- Date raised
- Due date
- Status
- Type
- Resolution date

Contract Documentation Management

This is a formal acceptance of updates and changes to architecture documentation for onward publication.

Any Other Business (AOB)

Description of issues not directly covered under any of the above. These may not be described in the agenda but should be raised at the beginning of the meeting. Any supporting documentation must be managed as per all architecture governance documentation.

Schedule of Meetings

All meeting dates detail should be detailed and published.

活动指派

这是关于在上次架构委员会会议上所指派活动的一份报告。利用活动跟踪系统来记录并保留在架构委员会会议期间指派的所有活动的状态，且应包括至少下述信息：

- 基准
- 优先级
- 活动描述
- 活动负责人
- 活动细节
- 提出日期
- 到期日
- 状态
- 类型
- 解决日期

契约文档管理

这是对之前公布的架构文档的更新和更改的正式认可。

任何其他业务（AOB）

对上述任何一项未直接覆盖的议题的描述。这些议题可能未在议程中描述，但应在会议开始时提出。任何支持性文档都必须按照所有架构治理文档管理。

会议日程表

应详细说明并公布所有会议日期细节。

Chapter 48
Architecture Compliance

This chapter provides guidelines for ensuring project compliance to the architecture.

48.1 Introduction

Ensuring the compliance of individual projects with the enterprise architecture is an essential aspect of architecture governance (see Chapter 50). To this end, the IT governance function within an enterprise will normally define two complementary processes:

- The **Architecture** function will be required to prepare a series of Project Architectures; i.e., project-specific views of the enterprise architecture that illustrate how the enterprise architecture impacts on the major projects within the organization. (See ADM Phases A to F.)
- The **IT Governance** function will define a formal Architecture Compliance review process(see Section 48.3) for reviewing the compliance of projects to the enterprise architecture.

Apart from defining formal processes, the architecture governance (see Chapter 50) function may also stipulate that the architecture function should extend beyond the role of architecture definition and standards selection, and participate also in the technology selection process, and even in the commercial relationships involved in external service provision and product purchases. This may help to minimize the opportunity for misinterpretation of the enterprise architecture, and maximize the value of centralized commercial negotiation.

48.2 Terminology: The Meaning of Architecture Compliance

A key relationship between the architecture and the implementation lies in the definitions of the terms "conformant", "compliant", etc. While terminology usage may differ between organizations, the concepts of levels of conformance illustrated in Figure 48-1 should prove useful in formulating an IT compliance strategy.

第 48 章 架构合规性

本章提供确保项目对架构合规的指南。

48.1 简介

确保单个项目与 Enterprise Architecture 合规是架构治理（见第 50 章）的一个根本性的方面。为此，ENTERPRISE 内的 IT 治理职能部门通常定义两个互补的流程：

- 要求**架构**职能部门准备一系列项目架构；即，Enterprise Architecture 的项目特定视图，这些视图将展现 Enterprise Architecture 如何影响组织内的主要项目。（见 ADM 的阶段 A 至阶段 F。）
- **IT 治理**职能部门将定义正式的架构合规性审视流程（见 48.3 节），以审视项目与 Enterprise Architecture 的合规性。

除了定义正式的流程，架构治理（见第 50 章）职能部门还可以规定：架构职能部门应超越架构定义和标准选择的角色，还应参与技术选择流程，甚至是外部服务提供和产品采购所涉及的商业关系。这可能有助于最小化 Enterprise Architecture 被曲解的可能，并使集中商业谈判的价值最大化。

48.2 术语：架构合规性的含义

架构与实施之间的关键关系在于“符合”“合规”等术语的定义。由于组织之间术语的使用不同，如图 48-1 所示的合规性层级的概念应证明其在制定 IT 合规战略方面有用。

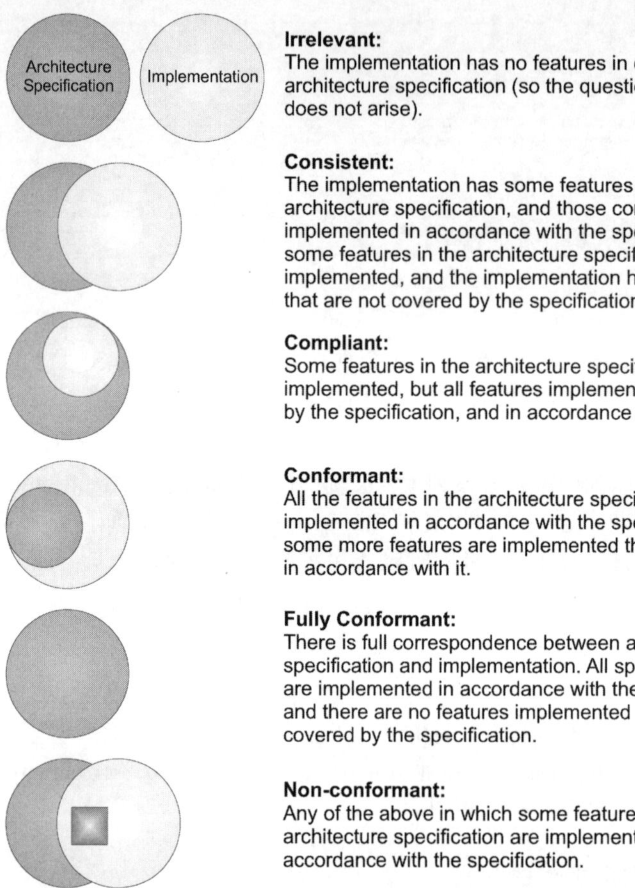

Architecture Specification
Implementation
Irrelevant:
The implementation has no features in common with the architecture specification (so the question of conformance does not arise).
Consistent:
The implementation has some features in common with the architecture specification, and those common features are implemented in accordance with the specification. However, some features in the architecture specification are not implemented, and the implementation has other features that are not covered by the specification.
Compliant:
Some features in the architecture specification are not implemented, but all features implemented are covered by the specification, and in accordance with it.
Conformant:
All the features in the architecture specification are implemented in accordance with the specification, but some more features are implemented that are not in accordance with it.
Fully Conformant:
There is full correspondence between architecture specification and implementation. All specified features are implemented in accordance with the specification, and there are no features implemented that are not covered by the specification.
Non-conformant:
Any of the above in which some features in the architecture specification are implemented not in accordance with the specification.

Figure 48-1 Levels of Architecture Conformance

The phrase "In accordance with" in Figure 48-1 means:

- Supports the stated strategy and future directions.
- Adheres to the stated standards (including syntax and semantic rules specified).
- Provides the stated functionality.
- Adheres to the stated principles; for example:
  - Open wherever possible and appropriate.
  - Re-use of component building blocks wherever possible and appropriate.

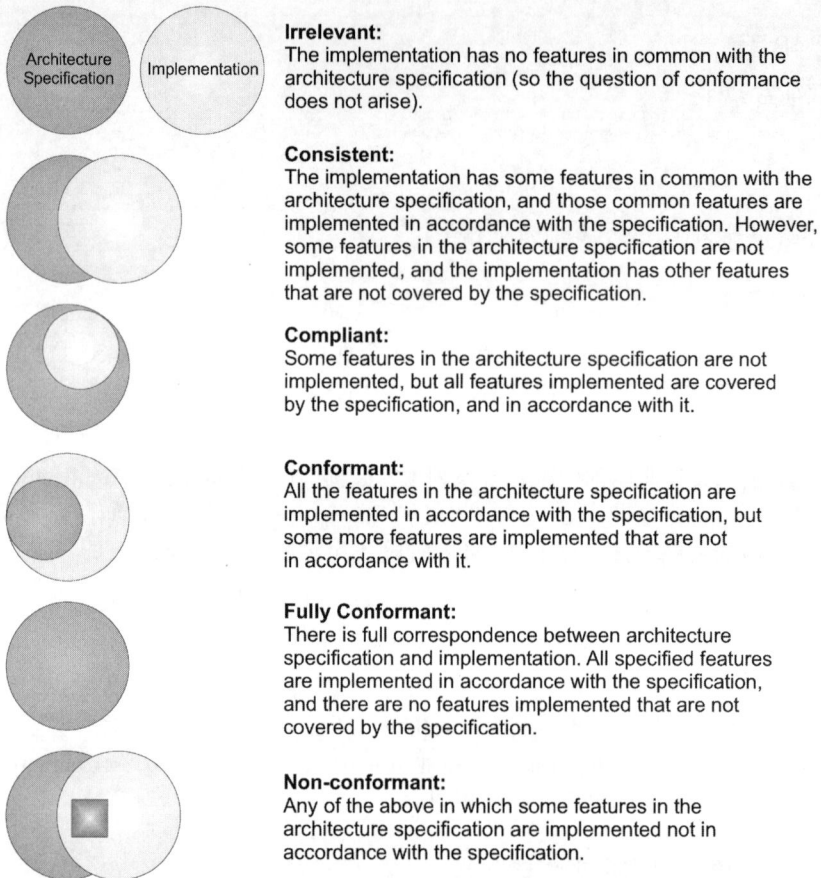

架构规范
实施
不相关：
实施与架构规范没有共同特征（所以未出现合规问题）。
相容：
实施与架构规范有一些共同特征，并且按照规范实施这些共同特征。但是，架构规范中的有些特征未实施，并且实施具有规范未涵盖的其他特征。
合规：
架构规范中的有些特征并没有实施，但所有实施的特征均涵盖在规范中并符合规范。
符合：
架构规范中的所有特征都均被实施，但是还有一些特征的实施超出架构规范之外。
完全符合：
架构规范与实施完全对应。所有规定特征均按照规范实施，不实施规范不涵盖的特征。
不符合：
以上所有中，架构规范中的有些特征不是按照规范实施。

图 48-1 架构符合性等级

图 48-1 中的短语“按照”意味着：

- 支持申明的策略和未来的方向。
- 遵守申明的标准（包括指定的语法和语义规则）。
- 提供申明的功能性。
- 遵守规定的原则；例如：
  - 可能且适当时打开。
  - 在可能且适合的地方复用组件构建块。

48.3 Architecture Compliance Reviews

An Architecture Compliance review is a scrutiny of the compliance of a specific project against established architectural criteria, spirit, and business objectives. A formal process for such reviews normally forms the core of an enterprise Architecture Compliance strategy.

48.3.1 Purpose

The goals of an Architecture Compliance review include some or all of the following:

- First and foremost, catch errors in the project architecture early, and thereby reduce the cost and risk of changes required later in the lifecycle. This in turn means that the overall project time is shortened, and that the business gets the bottom-line benefit of the architecture development faster.
- Ensure the application of best practices to architecture work.
- Provide an overview of the compliance of an architecture to mandated enterprise standards.
- Identify where the standards themselves may require modification.
- Identify services that are currently application-specific but might be provided as part of the enterprise infrastructure.
- Document strategies for collaboration, resource sharing, and other synergies across multiple architecture teams.
- Take advantage of advances in technology.
- Communicate to management the status of technical readiness of the project.
- Identify key criteria for procurement activities (e.g., for inclusion in Commercial Off-The-Shelf (COTS) product RFI/RFP documents).
- Identify and communicate significant architectural gaps to product and service providers.

Apart from the generic goals related to quality assurance outlined above, there are additional,more politically-oriented motivations for conducting Architecture Compliance reviews, which maybe relevant in particular cases:

- The Architecture Compliance review can be a good way of deciding between architectural alternatives, since the business decision-makers typically involved in the review can guide decisions in terms of what is best for the business, as opposed to what is technically more pleasing or elegant.
- The output of the Architecture Compliance review is one of the few measurable deliverables to the CIO to assist in decision-making.
- Architecture reviews can serve as a way for the architecture organization to engage with development projects that might otherwise proceed without involvement of the architecture function.
- Architecture reviews can demonstrate rapid and positive support to the enterprise business community:
  - The enterprise architecture and Architecture Compliance helps ensure the alignment of IT projects with business objectives.

48.3 架构合规性审视

架构合规性审视是按照已建立的架构准则、精髓和业务目的，对特定项目合规性仔细检查。此类审视的正式流程通常形成 ENTERPRISE 的架构合规性策略的核心。

48.3.1 目的

架构合规性审视的目标包括部分或全部下述内容：

- 首先也是最重要的是，捕获早期项目架构中的错误，从而降低在生命周期后期所需变更的成本和风险。这也相应地意味着缩短了总体项目时间，并使业务更快获得架构开发的实际好处。
- 确保将最佳实践应用于架构工作。
- 提供关于架构与指令性 ENTERPRISE 标准的合规性的概述。
- 识别其自身可能需要修改的标准。
- 识别目前特定于应用但可能作为 ENTERPRISE 基础设施的一部分而提供的服务。
- 将跨越多个架构团队的协作、资源共享和其他协同合作的策略进行文件化。
- 充分利用技术进步。
- 与管理层沟通项目的技术准备度的状态。
- 识别采购活动的关键准则［例如，纳入商用货架（COTS）产品 RFI/RFP 文件］。

除了与上述质量保证相关的通用目标外，进行架构合规性审视还具有在下述特殊情况下相关的更多政治导向的附加动机：

- 架构合规性审视可能是在架构选项之间做出选择的一个良好方式，因为通常涉及审视的业务决策者可以按照对业务最有益的方式指导决策，而不是依照在技术上更满意的或更简洁的方式进行。
- 架构合规性审视的输出是交付给 CIO 的帮助决策的几个可测量的交付物之一。
- 架构审视可作为架构组织参与开发项目的一种途径，否则这些开发项目可能会在没有架构职能部门参与的情况下继续进行。
- 架构审视可以展示对 ENTERPRISE 团体的快速积极的支持：
    - — Enterprise Architecture 和架构合规性有助于确保 IT 项目对准业务目的。

— Architects can sometimes be regarded as being deep into technical infrastructure and far removed from the core business.

— Since an Architecture Compliance review tends to look primarily at the critical risk areas of a system, it often highlights the main risks for system owners.

While compliance to architecture is required for development and implementation, non- compliance also provides a mechanism for highlighting:

- Areas to be addressed for realignment.
- Areas for consideration for integration into the architectures as they are uncovered by the compliance processes.

The latter point identifies the ongoing change and adaptability of the architectures to requirements that may be driven by indiscipline, but also allows for changes to be registered by faster moving changes in the operational environment. Typically dispensations (see Section 50.1.4) will be used to highlight these changes and set in motion a process for registering, monitoring, and assessing the suitability of any changes required.

48.3.2 Timing

Timing of compliance activities should be considered with regard to the development of the architectures themselves.

Compliance reviews are held at appropriate project milestones or checkpoints in the project's lifecycle. Specific checkpoints should be included as follows:

- Development of the architecture itself (ADM compliance)
- Implementation of the architecture(s) (architecture compliance)

Architecture project timings for assessments should include:

- Project initiation
- Initial design
- Major design changes
- Ad hoc

The Architecture Compliance review is typically targeted for a point in time when business requirements and the enterprise architecture are reasonably firm, and the project architecture is taking shape, well before its completion.

The aim is to hold the review as soon as practical, at a stage when there is still time to correct any major errors or shortcomings, with the obvious proviso that there needs to have been some significant development of the project architecture in order for there to be something to review.

Inputs to the Architecture Compliance review may come from other parts of the standard project lifecycle, which may have an impact on timing.

— 架构师有时可能被认为深入到技术基础设施而远离了核心业务。

— 因为架构合规性审视往往主要着眼于系统的关键风险领域，所以它通常强调系统所有者的主要风险。

在需要架构合规性被开发和实施的同时，不合规性也提供了一种机制来强调下述内容：

- 待处理以便重新对准的领域。
- 集成到架构中需要考虑的领域（当合规性流程未涉及这些领域时）。

后一点对因缺少架构修炼而可能造成的架构的不断变化及其与需求的适应性进行识别，而且还使得能通过在运行环境中更快地移动变更而注册这些变更。典型情况下，特许（见 50.1.4 节）将被用来强调这些变更并调动注册、监控和评估任何所需变更的适用性的流程。

48.3.2 时间安排

应就架构本身的开发来考虑合规性活动的时间安排。

在项目生命周期内适当的项目里程碑或检查点进行合规性审视。应包括如下特定检查点：

- 架构本身的开发（ADM 合规性）
- 架构实施（架构合规性）

评估的架构项目时间安排应包括：

- 项目启动
- 初始设计
- 主要设计变更
- 临时安排

当业务需求和 Enterprise Architecture 合理可靠时，架构合规性审视通常以一个时间点为目标，而且在其结束之前形成项目架构。

目的是在仍然有时间校正所有主要错误或缺点的阶段，尽可能实际地进行审视，其中明显的限制条件是，为了审视某些事物，项目架构需要有重大进展。

架构合规性审视的输入可能来自标准项目生命周期的其他部分，这可能会影响时间安排。

48.3.3 Governance and Personnel Scenarios

In terms of the governance and conduct of the Architecture Compliance review, and the personnel involved, there are various possible scenarios:

- For smaller-scale projects, the review process could simply take the form of a series of questions that the project architects or project leaders pose to themselves, using the checklists provided below, perhaps collating the answers into some form of project report to management. The need to conduct such a process is normally included in overall enterprise-wide IT governance policies.
- Where the project under review has not involved a practicing or full-time architect to date (for example, in an application-level project), the purpose of the review is typically to bring to bear the architectural expertise of an enterprise architecture function. In such a case, the enterprise architecture function would be organizing, leading, and conducting the review, with the involvement of business domain experts. In such a scenario, the review is not a substitute for the involvement of architects in a project, but it can be a supplement ora guide to their involvement. It is probable that a database will be necessary to manage the volume of data that would be produced in the analysis of a large system or set of systems.
- In most cases, particularly in larger-scale projects, the architecture function will have been deeply involved in, and perhaps leading, the development project under review. (This is the typical TOGAF scenario.) In such cases, the review will be co-ordinated by the lead enterprise architect, who will assemble a team of business and technical domain experts for the review, and compile the answers to the questions posed during the review into some form of report. The questions will typically be posed during the review by the business and technical domain experts. Alternatively, the review might be led by a representative of an Architecture Board or some similar body with enterprise-wide responsibilities.

In all cases, the Architecture Compliance review process needs the backing of senior management, and will typically be mandated as part of corporate architecture governance policies (see Chapter 50). Normally, the enterprise CIO or enterprise Architecture Board (see Chapter 47) will mandate architec-ture reviews for all major projects, with subsequent annual reviews.

48.4 Architecture Compliance Review Process

48.4.1 Overview

The Architecture Compliance review process is illustrated in Figure 48-2.

48.3.3 治理和人员场景

在架构合规性审视的治理和实施以及涉及的人员方面，可能的多种不同场景如下：

- 对于小型项目，审视流程可能仅采取项目架构师或项目领导向自己提出一系列问题的形式，利用下面提供的检查单，或许可将答案整理成向管理层进行项目报告的某种形式。执行这种流程的需要通常包括在整个 ENTERPRISE 范围的 IT 治理方针中。
- 到目前为止，当正在审视的项目未牵涉实习或全职架构师时（例如，在应用层级的项目中），审视目的通常是运用 Enterprise Architecture 职能部门的架构专业知识。在此情况下，Enterprise Architecture 职能部门将在业务领域专家的参与下组织、领导并执行该审视。在此场景中，审视不能代替架构师对项目的参与，但可以作为架构师参与项目的补充或指导。在管理对大型系统或系统群进行分析而产生的大量数据方面，数据库可能必不可少。
- 在大部分情况下，特别是在大型项目中，架构职能部门已经深入参与或者指挥正在审视的开发项目。（这是典型的 TOGAF 场景。）在此情况下，将由首席 ENTERPRISE 架构师协调审视，他们将为此次审视组建业务和技术领域专家团队，并将审视期间所提问题的答案编制成某种形式的报告。问题通常由业务和技术领域专家在审视期间提出。或者，审视可以由架构委员会代表或由具有整个 ENTERPRISE 范围职责的某些相似机构来主导。

在所有情况下，架构合规性审视流程均需要高级管理层的支持，而且通常被强制作为公司架构治理方针（见第 50 章）的一部分。正常情况下，ENTERPRISE CIO 或 ENTERPRISE 的架构委员会（见第 47 章）将强制对所有重点项目进行架构审视，随后进行年度审视。

48.4 架构合规性审视流程

48.4.1 概述

图 48-2 说明架构合规性审视流程。

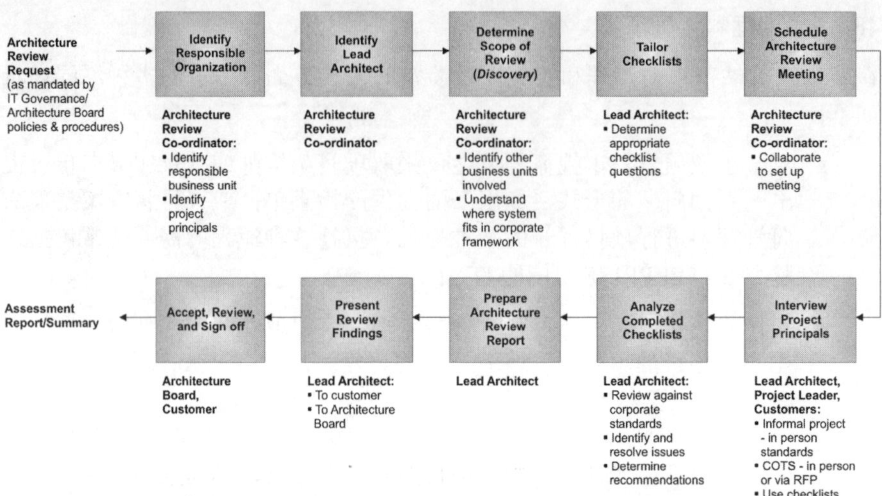

Figure 48-2 Architecture Compliance Review Process

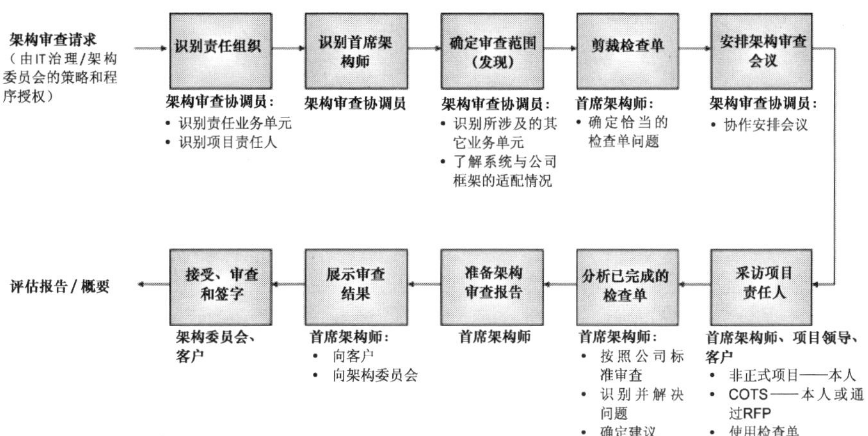

图 48-2　架构合规性审视流程

48.4.2 Roles

The main roles in the process are tabulated below.

No.	Role	Responsibilities	Notes
1	Architecture Board	To ensure that IT architectures are consistent and support overall business needs	Sponsor and monitor architecture activities
2	Project Leader (or Project Board)	Responsible for the whole project	
3	Architecture Review Co-ordinator	To administer the whole architecture development and review process	More likely to be business oriented than technology oriented
4	Lead Enterprise Architect	To ensure that the architecture is technically coherent and future-proof	An IT architecture specialist
5	Architect	One of the Lead Enterprise Architect's technical assistants	
6	Customer	To ensure that business requirements are clearly expressed and understood.	Manages that part of the organization that will depend on the success of the IT descrybed in the architecture
7	Business Domain Expert	To ensure that the processes tosatisfy the business requirements are justified and understood	Knows how the businessdomain operates; may also be the customer
8	Project Principals	To ensure that the architects havea sufficiently detailed understanding of the customer department's processes. They can provide input to the business domain expert or to the architects	Members of the customer's organization who have input to the business requirements that the architecture is to address

48.4.2 角色

流程主要角色在下表列出。

No.	角色	职责	注释
1	架构委员会	确保 IT 架构相容并支持全部业务需要	发起并监控架构活动
2	项目领导（或项目委员会）	对整个项目负责	
3	架构审视协调员	管理整个架构开发和审视流程	相较于以技术为导向，更可能以业务为导向
4	首席复杂组织体架构师	确保架构在技术上具有连贯性和前瞻性	IT 架构专家
5	架构师	首席 ENTERPRISE 架构师的技术助理之一	
6	客户	确保业务需求表达清晰，易于理解	对依赖于在架构中所描述的 IT 是否成功的部分组织进行管理
7	业务领域专家	确保满足业务需求的流程合理且易于理解	了解业务领域如何运行；可能还可作为客户
8	项目负责人	确保架构师充分详细地理解客户部门的流程。他们可以向业务领域专家或向架构师提供输入	对架构需要应对的业务需求具有输入的客户组织成员

48.4.3 Steps

The main steps in the process are tabulated below.

No.	Action	Notes	Who
1	Request architecture review	As mandated by IT governance policies and procedures	Anyone, whether IT or business-oriented, with an interest in or responsibility for the business area affected
2	Identify responsible part of organization and relevant project principals		Architecture Review Co-ordinator
3	Identify Lead Enterprise Architect and other architects		Architecture Review Co-ordinator
4	Determine scope of review	Identify which other business units/departments are involved Understand where the system fits in the corporate architecture framework	Architecture Review Co-ordinator
5	Tailor checklists	To address the business requirements	Lead Enterprise Architect
6	Schedule Architecture Review Meeting		Architecture Review Co-ordinatorwith collaboration of Lead Enterprise Architect
7	Interview project princepals	To get background and technical information: ■ For internal project: in person ■ For COTS: in person or via RFP Use checklists	Lead Enterprise Architect and/or-Architect, Project Leader, and Customers
8	Analyze completed checklists	Review against corporate standards.Identify and resolve issues. Determine recommendations	Lead Enterprise Architect
9	Prepare Architecture Compliance review report	May involve supporting staff	Lead Enterprise Architect
10	Present review findings	To Customer To Architecture Board	Lead Enterprise Architect
11	Accept review and sign off		Architecture Board and Customer
12	Send assessment report/ summary to Architecture Review Co-ordinator		Lead Enterprise Architect

48.4.3 步骤

下面列出了流程的主要步骤。

No.	活动	注释	人员
1	要求架构审视	由IT治理方针和程序强制执行	与受影响业务领域相关或负责该领域的任何人员，无论面向IT还是面向业务
2	识别组织负责的部分和相关的项目责任人		架构审视协调员
3	识别首席 ENTERPRISE 架构师和其他架构师		架构审视协调员
4	确定审视范围	识别所涉及的其他业务单元/部门 了解系统与公司架构框架的匹配情况	架构审视协调员
5	剪裁检查单	应对业务需求	首席 ENTERPRISE 架构师
6	安排架构审视会议		与首席 ENTERPRISE 架构师协作的架构审视协调员
7	与项目责任人面谈	获得背景和技术信息： ■ 对于内部项目：本人 ■ 对于 COTS：本人或通过 RFP 使用检查单	首席 ENTERPRISE 架构师和/或架构师、项目领导和客户
8	分析已完成的检查单	按照公司标准审视。确定建议	首席 ENTERPRISE 架构师
9	准备架构合规性审视报告	可能涉及支持人员	首席 ENTERPRISE 架构师
10	表达审视结果	向客户向架构委员会	首席 ENTERPRISE 架构师
11	接受审视并签字		架构委员会和客户
12	向架构审视协调员发送评估报告/摘要		首席 ENTERPRISE 架构师

48.5 Architecture Compliance Review Checklists

The following review checklists provide a wide range of typical questions that may be used in conducting Architecture Compliance reviews, relating to various aspects of the architecture. The organization of the questions includes the basic disciplines of system engineering, information management, security, and systems management. The checklists are based on material provided by a member of The Open Group, and are specific to that organization. Other organizations could use the following checklists with other questions tailored to their own particular needs.

The checklists provided contain too many questions for any single review: they are intended to be tailored selectively to the project concerned (see Section 48.6). The checklists actually used will typically be developed/selected by subject matter experts. They are intended to be updated annually by interest groups in those areas.

Some of the checklists include a brief description of the architectural principle that provokes the question, and a brief description of what to look for in the answer. These extensions to the checklist are intended to allow the intelligent re-phrasing of the questions, and to give the user of the checklist a feel for why the question is being asked.

Occasionally the questions will be written, as in RFPs, or in working with a senior project architect. More typically they are expressed orally, as part of an interview or working session with the project.

The checklists provided here are designed for use in individual architecture projects, not for business domain architecture or for architecture across multiple projects. (Doing an architecture review for a larger sphere of activity, across multiple business processes and system projects, would involve a similar process, but the checklist categories and their contents would be different.)

48.5.1 Hardware and Operating System Checklist

1. What is the project's lifecycle approach?
2. At what stage is the project in its lifecycle?
3. What key issues have been identified or analyzed that the project believes will drive evaluations of hardware and operating systems for networks, servers, and end-user devices?
4. What system capabilities will involve high-volume and/or high-frequency data transfers?
5. How does the system design impact or involve end-user devices?
6. What is the quantity and distribution (regional and global) of usage, data storage, and processing?
7. What applications are affinitized with your project by similarities in data, application services, etc.? To what degree is data affinitized with your project?
8. What hardware and operating system choices have been made before functional design of key elements of the system?
9. If hardware and operating system decisions were made outside of the project's control:
   — What awareness does the project have of the rationale for those decisi-ons?

48.5 架构合规性审视检查单

下述审视检查单提供范围广泛的典型问题，其与架构各方面相关且在架构合规性审视中使用。问题的组织结构包括系统工程、信息管理、安保性和系统管理等基础学科。检查单以 The Open Group 成员所提供的资料为基础，并特定于该组织。其他组织可以使用具有按其自身特殊需要进行剪裁的其他问题的下述检查单。

对于任何一次单独的审视，所提供的检查单都包含许多问题：往往根据所涉及的项目，对这些问题有选择性地进行剪裁（见 48.6 节）。实际使用的检查单通常由权威专家制定/选择。这些检查单往往由相关领域的兴趣群组每年进行更新。

一些检查单包括对引起问题的架构原则的简短描述，以及对所寻找的答案的简短描述。对检查单的这些扩展，旨在使得能对问题进行理解上的重新划分，并使检查单的用户理解为什么问这个问题。

这些问题偶尔是书面形式的，或如 RFP 中那样，或如与高级项目架构师合作时那样。更为典型的是口头表述这些问题，作为访谈或项目工作会的一部分。

此处提供的检查单被设计用于单个的架构项目，而非业务领域架构或跨多个项目的架构。（对跨越多个业务流程和系统项目的大范围活动进行架构审视将涉及相似的流程，但检查单目录及其内容不同。）

48.5.1 硬件和操作系统检查单

1. 什么是项目的生命周期法？
2. 项目处于生命周期的什么阶段？
3. 已经识别或分析出什么主要问题，其项目观点将驱动网络、服务器及终端用户设备的硬件和操作系统评估？
4. 什么系统能力将涉及大量和/或高频的数据传送？
5. 系统设计如何影响或涉及终端用户设备？
6. 什么是使用、数据存储和处理的数量和分布（区域的和全球的）？
7. 哪些应用在数据、应用服务等的相似性方面与用户项目相关联？数据与项目相关联的程度如何？
8. 在系统关键元件的功能设计之前已经选择什么硬件和操作系统？
9. 如果在项目控制之外做出硬件和操作系统决策：
   — 项目对那些决策的理由依据有什么认识？

— How can the project influence those decisions as system design takes shape?

10. If some non-standards have been chosen:
    - What are the essential business and technical requirements for not using corporate standards?
    - Is this supported by a business case?
    - Have the assumptions in the business case been subject to scrutiny?
11. What is your process for evaluating full lifecycle costs of hardware and operating systems?
12. How has corporate financial management been engaged in evaluation of lifecycle costs?
13. Have you performed a financial analysis of the supplier?
14. Have you made commitments to any supplier?
15. Do you believe your requirements can be met by only one supplier?

48.5.2 Software Services and Middleware Checklist

1. Describe how error conditions are defined, raised, and propagated between application components.
2. Describe the general pattern of how methods are defined and arranged in various application modules.
3. Describe the general pattern for how method parameters are defined and organized in various application modules. Are [in], [in/out], [out] parameters always specified in the same order? Do Boolean values returned by modules have a consistent outcome?
4. Describe the approach that is used to minimize the number of round-trips between client and server calls, particularly for out-of-process calls, and when complex data structures are involved.
5. Describe the major data structures that are passed between major system components.
6. Describe the major communication protocols that are used between major system components.
7. Describe the marshaling techniques that are used between various system components.Describe any specialized marshaling arrangements that are used.
8. Describe to what extent the system is designed with stateful and stateless components.
9. Describe how and when state is saved for both stateful and stateless com-ponents.
10. Describe the extent to which objects are created, used, and destroyed *versus* reused through object pooling.
11. Describe the extent to which the system relies on threading or critical section coding.
12. Describe the approach and the internal documentation that is used internally in the system to document the methods, methods arguments, and method functionality.
13. Describe the code review process that was used to build the system.
14. Describe the unit testing that has been used to test the system components.

— 形成系统设计时，项目如何才能影响这些决策？

10. 如果已经选择一些非标准件：

— 对不使用公司标准的根本业务需求和技术需求是什么？

— 是否被业务案例支持？

— 已经仔细检查了业务案例中的假设吗？

11. 评价硬件和操作系统的全部生命周期成本的流程是什么？

12. 公司财务管理层如何进行生命周期成本评价？

13. 是否已完成对供应商的财务分析？

14. 是否已向供应商做出承诺？

15. 是否相信只有一家供应商可以满足自身需求？

48.5.2 软件服务和中间件检查单

1. 描述错误条件是如何被定义、提出并在应用组件之间扩散的。
2. 描述如何在不同应用模块中定义方法并分类的一般性特征模式。
3. 描述如何在不同应用模块中定义并创建方法参数的一般性特征模式。参数[in]、[in/out]、[out]是否始终按相同的顺序规定？各模块返回的布尔值是否具有一致的结果？
4. 描述用来对客户端与服务器之间调用的往返次数进行最小化的实施途径，特别是对进程外调用且涉及复杂数据结构时。
5. 描述在主系统组件之间通过的主要数据结构。
6. 描述在主系统组件之间使用的主要通信协议。
7. 描述在不同系统组件之间所用的封送处理技术。描述所用的任何专门封送处理。
8. 描述有状态组件和无状态组件的系统被设计到何种程度。
9. 描述如何以及何时为有状态组件和无状态组件保存状态。
10. 描述通过对象集中来创建、使用和破坏或复用对象的程度。
11. 描述系统对线程或临界区编码的依赖程度。
12. 描述在系统内部对方法、方法论据和方法功能性进行文件化的实施途径以及内部文件。
13. 描述用于构建系统的代码审视流程。
14. 描述已经用于对系统组件进行测试的单元测试。

15. Describe the pre-and post-condition testing that is included in various system modules.
16. Describe the assertion testing that is included with the system.
17. Do components support all the interface types they need to support or are certain assumptions made about what types of components will call other components either in terms of language bindings or other forms of marshal-ing?
18. Describe the extent to which big-endian or little-endian data format problems need to be handled across different platforms.
19. Describe if numbers or strings need to be handled differently across different platforms.
20. Describe whether the software needs to check for floating-point round-off errors.
21. Describe how time and date functions manage dates so as to avoid improper handling of time and date calculation or display.
22. Describe what tools or processes have been used to test the system for memory leaks, reachability, or general robustness.
23. Describe the layering of the systems services software. Describe the general number of links between major system components. Is the system composed of a lot of point-to-point interfaces or are major messaging backbones used instead?
24. Describe to what extent the system components are either loosely coupled or tightly coupled.
25. What requirements does the system need from the infrastructure in terms of shared libraries, support for communication protocols, load balancing, transaction processing, system monitoring, naming services, or other infrastructure services?
26. Describe how the system and system components are designed for refac-toring.
27. Describe how the system or system components rely on common messaging infrastructure *versus* a unique point-to-point communication structure.

48.5.3 Applications Checklists

48.5.3.1 Infrastructure (Enterprise Productivity) Applications

1. Is there need for capabilities that are not provided through the enterprise's standard infrastructure application products? For example:
   - Collaboration
     - Application sharing
     - Video conferencing
     - Calendaring
     - Email
   - Workflow management
   - Publishing/word processing applications
     - HTML
     - SGML and XML

15. 描述不同系统模块包括的前置条件和后置条件测试。
16. 描述系统包括的断言测试。
17. 组件是否支持其需要支持的所有界面类型？或者是否依照语言绑定或其他形式的封送处理，做出了关于哪些类型的组件将调用其他组件的假设？
18. 描述需要跨越不同平台处理大端法或小端法数据格式问题的程度。
19. 描述是否需要对数字或字符串进行跨越不同平台的不同处理。
20. 描述软件是否需要检查浮点取整误差。
21. 描述时间与日期功能，如何管理日期才能避免对时间与日期的计算或显示的不恰当处理。
22. 描述已经使用什么工具或流程来测试系统的内存泄漏、可达性或一般稳健性。
23. 描述系统服务软件的分层。描述主要系统组件之间的总体链接数量。系统是否由许多点对点界面组成？还是使用主要消息传递中枢代替？
24. 描述系统组件松耦合或紧耦合的程度。
25. 系统需要从基础设施中获取共享存储库、通信协议支持、负载平衡、事务处理、系统监控、命名服务或其他基础设施服务等方面的哪些需求？
26. 描述系统和系统组件如何设计以便重构。
27. 描述系统或系统组件如何依赖公共消息传递基础设施和独特的点到点通信结构。

48.5.3 应用检查单

48.5.3.1 基础设施（ENTERPRISE 生产率）应用

1. 是否需要不通过 ENTERPRISE 标准基础设施应用产品而提供的能力？例如：
   - 协作
     - 应用共享
     - 视频会议
     - 安排日程
     - 电子邮件
   - 工作流管理
   - 发布/文字处理应用
     - HTML
     - SGML 和 XML

  — Portable document format
  — Document processing (proprietary format)
  — Desktop publishing
- Spreadsheet applications
- Presentation applications
  — Business presentations
  — Image
  — Animation
  — Video
  — Sound
  — CBT
  — Web browsers
- Data management applications
  — Database interface
  — Document management
  — Product data management
  — Data warehouses/mart
- Program management applications
  — Project management
  — Program visibility

2. Describe the business requirements for enterprise infrastructure application capabilities that are not met by the standard products.

48.5.3.2 Business Applications

1. Are any of the capabilities required provided by standard products supporting one or more line-of-business applications? For example:

- Business acquisition applications
  — Sales and marketing
- Engineering applications
  — Computer-aided design
  — Computer-aided engineering
  — Mathematical and statistics analysis
- Supplier management applications
  — Supply chain management
  — Customer relationship management

  - 便携式文件格式
  - 文件处理（专用格式）
  - 桌面发布
- 电子表格应用
- 演示应用
  - 业务演示
  - 图像
  - 动画
  - 视频
  - 声音
  - CBT
  - Web 浏览器
- 数据管理应用
  - 数据库界面
  - 文件管理
  - 产品数据管理
  - 数据仓库/集市
- 项目群管理应用
  - 项目管理
  - 项目群可见性

2. 对标准产品没有满足 ENTERPRISE 基础设施应用能力的业务需求进行描述。

48.5.3.2 业务应用

1. 所需任何能力是否都由支持一个或多个业务线应用的标准产品来提供？例如：

- 业务采办应用
  - 销售和营销
- 工程应用
  - 计算机辅助设计
  - 计算机辅助工程
  - 数学统计分析
- 供应商管理应用
  - 供应链管理
  - 客户关系管理

- Manufacturing applications
  - Enterprise Resource Planning (ERP) applications
  - Manufacturing execution systems
  - Manufacturing quality
  - Manufacturing process engineering
  - Machine and adaptive control
- Customer support applications
  - Airline logistics support
  - Maintenance engineering
- Finance applications
- People applications
- Facilities applications
- Information systems applications
  - Systems engineering
  - Software engineering
  - Web developer tools
  - Integrated development environments
  - Lifecycle categories
  - Functional categories
  - Specialty categories
- Computer-aided manufacturing
- e-Business enablement
- Business process engineering
  - Statistical quality control

2. Describe the process requirements for business application capabilities that are not met by the standard products.

48.5.3.3 Application Integration Approach

1. What integration points(business process/activity, application, data, computing environment) are targeted by this architecture?
2. What application integration techniques will be applied (common business objects [ORBs], standard data definitions [STEP, XML, etc.], common user interface presentation/desktop)?

- 制造应用
  - 企业资源规划（ERP）应用
  - 制造执行系统
  - 制造质量
  - 制造流程工程
  - 机器和自适应控制
- 客户支持应用
  - 航空公司后勤支持
  - 维修工程
- 财务应用
- 人员应用
- 设施应用
- 信息系统应用
  - 系统工程
  - 软件工程
  - Web 开发者工具
  - 集成开发环境
  - 生命周期类别
  - 功能性类别
  - 特性类别
- 计算机辅助制造
- 电子商务实现
- 业务流程工程
  - 统计质量控制

2. 对标准产品不满足的业务应用能力的流程需求进行描述。

48.5.3.3 应用集成途径

1. 本架构以哪些集成点（业务流程/活动、应用、数据、计算环境）为目标？
2. 将采用什么应用集成技术（公共业务对象[ORB]、标准数据定义[STEP、XML 等]、公共用户界面演示/桌面）？

48.5.4 Information Management Checklists

48.5.4.1 Data Values

1. What are the processes that standardize the management and use of the data?
2. What business process supports the entry and validation of the data? Use of the data?
3. What business actions correspond to the creation and modification of the data?
4. What business actions correspond to the deletion of the data and is it considered part of a business record?
5. What are the data quality requirements required by the business user?
6. What processes are in place to support data referential integrity and/or normalization?

48.5.4.2 Data Definition

1. What are the data model, data definitions, structure, and hosting options of purchased applications (COTS)?
2. What are the rules for defining and maintaining the data requirements and designs for all components of the information system?
3. What shareable repository is used to capture the model content and the supporting information for data?
4. What is the physical data model definition (derived from logical data models) used to design the database?
5. What software development and data management tools have been selected?
6. What data owners have been identified to be responsible for common data definitions, eliminating unplanned redundancy, providing consistently reliable, timely, and accurate information, and protecting data from misuse and destruction?

48.5.4.3 Security/Protection

1. What are the data entity and attribute access rules which protect the data from unintentional and unauthorized alterations, disclosure, and distribution?
2. What are the data protection mechanisms to protect data from unauthorized external access?
3. What are the data protection mechanisms to control access to data from external sources that temporarily have internal residence within the enter-prise?

48.5.4.4 Hosting, Data Types, and Sharing

1. What is the discipline for managing sole-authority data as one logical source with defined updating rules for physical data residing on different platforms?
2. What is the discipline for managing replicated data, which is derived from operational sole-authority data?
3. What tier data server has been identified for the storage of high or medium-critical operational data?

48.5.4 信息管理检查单

48.5.4.1 数据值

1. 对数据管理和使用进行标准化的流程是什么？
2. 什么业务流程支持数据的输入和确认？什么业务流程支持数据的使用？
3. 什么业务活动对应于数据的创建和修改？
4. 什么业务活动对应于数据的删除？是否将其视为业务记录的一部分？
5. 业务用户所需的数据质量需求是什么？
6. 正在运行什么流程以支持数据引用完整性和/或规范化？

48.5.4.2 数据定义

1. 所购应用（COTS）的数据模型、数据定义、结构和托管选项是什么？
2. 为信息系统所有组件定义并维护数据需求和设计的规则是什么？
3. 采用什么可分享存储库来获取模型内容和支持性数据信息？
4. 用于设计数据库的物理数据模型定义（源自逻辑数据模型）是什么？
5. 已经选择什么软件开发和数据管理工具？
6. 已经识别哪些数据所有者来负责公共数据定义，消除无计划的冗余码，提供一贯可靠、及时和精确的信息以及保护数据避免其遭到滥用和破坏？

48.5.4.3 安保/保护

1. 保护数据以免其受到无意和未经授权的改变、泄露和分配的数据实体及属性的访问规则是什么？
2. 保护数据使其免受未经授权的外部访问的数据保护机制是什么？
3. 对来自外部数据源且暂时存储在 ENTERPRISE 内部的数据进行访问控制的数据保护机制是什么？

48.5.4.4 托管、数据类型和共享

1. 利用所定义的对存储在不同平台上的物理数据进行更新的规则，将独立授权数据作为一个逻辑源进行管理的规程是什么？
2. 对来自独立授权操作数据的复制数据进行管理的规程是什么？
3. 已识别什么层级数据服务器来存储高临界或中间临界操作数据？

4. What tier data server has been identified for the storage of type C operational data?
5. What tier data server has been identified for the storage of decision support data contained in a data warehouse?
6. What Database Management Systems (DBMSs) have been implemented?

48.5.4.5 Common Services

1. What are the standardized distributed data management services (e.g., validation, consistency checks, data edits, encryption, and transaction management) and where do they reside?

48.5.4.6 Access Method

1. What are the data access requirements for standard file, message, and data management?
2. What are the access requirements for decision support data?
3. What are the data storage and the application logic locations?
4. What query language is being used?

48.5.5 Security Checklist

1. **Security Awareness**: Have you ensured that the corporate security policies and guidelines to which you are designing are the latest versions? Have you read them? Are you aware of all relevant computing security compliance and risk acceptance processes? (Interviewer should list all relevant policies and guidelines.)
2. **Identification/Authentication**: Diagram the process flow of how a user is identified to the application and how the application authenticates that the user is who they claim to be. Provide supporting documentation to the dia-gram explaining the flow from the user interface to the application/ database server(s) and back to the user. Are you compliant with corporate policies on accounts, passwords, etc.?
3. **Authorization**: Provide a process flow from beginning to end showing how a user requests access to the application, indicating the associated security controls and separation of duties. This should include how the request is approved by the appropriate data owner, how the user is placed into the appropriate access-level classification profile, how the user ID, password, and access is created and provided to the user. Also include how the user is informed of their responsibilities associated with using the application, given a copy of the access agreement, how to change password, who to call for help, etc.
4. **Access Controls**: Document how the user IDs, passwords, and access profiles are added, changed, removed, and documented. The documentation should include who is responsible for these processes.
5. **Sensitive Information Protection**: Provide documentation that identifies se-nsitive data requiring additional protection. Identify the data owners responsi-ble for this data and the process to be used to protect storage, transmission, printing, and distribution of this data. Include how the password file/field is protected. How will users be prevented from viewing someone else's sensi-tive information? Are there agreements with outside parties (partners, supp-liers, contractors, etc.) concerning the safeguarding of information? If so, what are the obligations?

4. 已识别什么层级数据服务器来存储C型操作数据？
5. 已识别什么层级数据服务器来存储数据仓库中所包含的决策支持数据？
6. 已经实施了什么数据库管理系统（DBMS）？

48.5.4.5 公用服务

1. 什么是标准化的分布式数据管理服务（如确认、一致性检查、数据编辑、加密和事务管理）及其在何处存储？

48.5.4.6 访问方法

1. 对标准文件、消息和数据管理的数据访问需求是什么？
2. 对决策支持数据的访问需求是什么？
3. 数据存储位置和应用逻辑位置是什么？
4. 正在使用的查询语言是什么？

48.5.5 安保检查单

1. **安保意识**：是否确保正在设计的公司安保策略和指南为最新版本？是否读过这些安保策略和指南？是否知道所有相关计算安保合规性和风险接受流程？（面谈者应列出所有相关方针和指南。）
2. **识别/认证**：将如何向应用识别用户以及应用如何证实该用户正是其所申明用户的处理流程进行图形化。为流程图提供支持性文件，以解释从用户界面到应用/数据库服务器并返回用户的流程。在账户、密码等方面是否与公司策略合规？
3. **授权**：提供一个自始至终的处理流程，展示用户如何要求对应用进行访问，表明关联的安保控制和职责分离。这应包括该要求如何被适当的数据所有者批准，如何将用户置入适当访问层级的分类概要，如何创建用户 ID、密码和访问以及如何提供给用户。还包括如何向用户告知与使用该应用相关的职责，如何提供一份访问协议，如何更改密码、谁来求助等。
4. **访问控制**：将如何添加、更改、删除和记录用户 ID、密码和访问概要进行文件化。文档应包括谁对这些流程负责。
5. **敏感信息保护**：提供对需要附加保护的敏感数据进行识别的文档。识别负责该数据的数据所有者，以及用于保护该数据的存储、传输、打印和分配的流程。包括如何保护密码文件/字段。如何防止用户看到其他人的敏感信息？是否与外部相关方（合作伙伴、供应商、承包商等）具有关于信息保护的协议？如果有，其义务是什么？

6. **Audit Trails and Audit Logs**: Identify and document group accounts requir-ed by the users or application support, including operating system group accounts. Identify and document individual accounts and/or roles that have superuser type privileges, what these privileges are, who has access to these accounts, how access to these accounts is controlled, tracked, and logged, and how password change and distribution are handled, including operating system accounts. Also identify audit logs, who can read the audit logs, who can modify the audit logs, who can delete the audit logs, and how the audit logs are protected and stored. Is the user ID obscured in the audit trails?
7. **External Access Considerations**: Will the application be used internally only? If not, are you compliant with corporate external access requirements?

48.5.6 System Management Checklist

1. What is the frequency of software changes that must be distributed?
2. What tools are used for software distribution?
3. Are multiple software and/or data versions allowed in production?
4. What is the user data backup frequency and expected restore time?
5. How are user accounts created and managed?
6. What is the system license management strategy?
7. What general system administration tools are required?
8. What specific application administration tools are required?
9. What specific service administration tools are required?
10. How are service calls received and dispatched?
11. Describe how the system is uninstalled.
12. Describe the process or tools available for checking that the system is properly installed.
13. Describe tools or instrumentation that are available that monitor the health and performance of the system.
14. Describe the tools or process in place that can be used to determine where the system has been installed.
15. Describe what form of audit logs are in place to capture system history, particularly after a mishap.
16. Describe the capabilities of the system to dispatch its own error messages to service personnel.

6. **审核跟踪和审计日志**：识别并记录用户或应用支持所需的群组账户，包括操作系统群组账户。识别并记录具有超级用户类型特权的个人账户和/或角色，这些特权是什么，谁访问这些账户，如何控制、跟踪并记录对这些账户的访问，以及如何处理密码更改和分配，包括操作系统账号。还识别审计日志，谁可以阅读审计日志，谁可以修改审计日志，谁可以删除审计日志，以及如何保护和存储审计日志。用户 ID 是否在审计跟踪中被隐藏?
7. **外部访问考量因素**：该应用是否将仅在内部使用？若不是，是否与公司外部访问需求合规?

48.5.6 系统管理检查单

1. 必须发布的软件更改频率是什么?
2. 什么工具用于软件分发?
3. 允许生产多个软件和/或数据版本吗？
4. 用户数据备份频率和期望的恢复时间是什么？
5. 如何创建和管理用户账户？
6. 系统许可证管理策略是什么？
7. 需要什么一般系统管理工具？
8. 需要什么特定应用管理工具？
9. 需要什么特定服务管理工具？
10. 如何接收并发送服务调用？
11. 描述如何卸载系统。
12. 描述用于检查系统是否恰当安装的流程或工具。
13. 描述用于监控系统健康及性能的工具或仪器。
14. 描述可用于确定已在何处安装系统的恰当工具或流程。
15. 描述什么形式的审计日志可适当地获取系统历史记录，特别是在发生事故之后。
16. 描述将系统错误信息迅速发送到服务人员的系统能力。

48.5.7 System Engineering/Overall Architecture Checklists

48.5.7.1 General

1. What other applications and/or systems require integration with yours?
2. Describe the integration level and strategy with each.
3. How geographically distributed is the user base?
4. What is the strategic importance of this system to other user communities inside or outside the enterprise?
5. What computing resources are needed to provide system service to users inside the enterprise? Outside the enterprise and using enterprise computing assets? Outside the enterprise and using their own assets?
6. How can users outside the native delivery environment access your applications and data?
7. What is the life expectancy of this application?
8. Describe the design that accommodates changes in the user base, stored data, and delivery system technology.
9. What is the size of the user base and their expected performance level?
10. What performance and stress test techniques do you use?
11. What is the overall organization of the software and data components?
12. What is the overall service and system configuration?
13. How are software and data configured and mapped to the service and system configuration?
14. What proprietary technology (hardware and software) is needed for this system?
15. Describe how each and every version of the software can be reproduced and redeployed over time.
16. Describe the current user base and how that base is expected to change over the next three to five years.
17. Describe the current geographic distribution of the user base and how that base is expected to change over the next three to five years.
18. Describe how many current or future users need to use the application in a mobile capacity or who need to work off-line.
19. Describe what the application generally does, the major components of the application, and the major data flows.
20. Describe the instrumentation included in the application that allows for the health and performance of the application to be monitored.
21. Describe the business justification for the system.
22. Describe the rationale for picking the system development language over other options in terms of initial development cost *versus* long-term maintena-nce cost.
23. Describe the systems analysis process that was used to come up with the system architecture and product selection phase of the system architecture.

48.5.7 系统工程/整体架构检查单

48.5.7.1 概述

1. 哪些其他应用和/或系统需要与你的应用和/或系统集成？
2. 描述与每个应用和/或系统的集成水平和集成策略。
3. 用户库在地理上如何分布？
4. 该系统对 ENTERPRISE 内部或外部的其他用户团体有什么战略重要性？
5. 需要什么计算资源来向 ENTERPRISE 内部用户提供系统服务？是在 ENTERPRISE 外部且使用 ENTERPRISE 计算资产？还是在 ENTERPRISE 外部使用其自身资产？
6. 本地交付环境外的用户如何才能访问你的应用和数据？
7. 该应用的预期寿命是什么？
8. 描述适应用户库、存储数据和交付系统技术方面变更的设计。
9. 用户库规模及其期望性能水平是什么？
10. 使用什么性能和压力测试技术？
11. 软件和数据组件的总体组织是什么？
12. 整体服务和系统配置是什么？
13. 如何配置软件和数据并将其映射到服务和系统构型？
14. 该系统需要什么专利技术（硬件和软件）？
15. 描述如何才能在一段时间之后复制并重新部署该软件的每一个版本。
16. 描述现有用户库以及期待该用户库在未来三到五年内如何更改。
17. 描述用户库的当前地理分布以及期待该用户库在未来三到五年内如何更改。
18. 描述有多少当前或未来用户需要使用移动应用，或谁需要离线工作。
19. 描述应用一般做什么、应用的主要组件以及主要数据流。
20. 描述应用中所包括并使得能监控应用健康及性能的仪器。
21. 描述系统的业务理由。
22. 根据初始开发成本和长期维修成本，描述在其他选项中选择系统开发语言的理由依据。
23. 描述用于提出系统架构及系统架构产品选择阶段的系统分析流程。

24. Who besides the original customer might have a use for or benefit from using this system?
25. What percentage of the users use the system in browse mode *versus* update mode?
26. What is the typical length of requests that are transactional?
27. Do you need guaranteed data delivery or update, or does the system tolerate failure?
28. What are the up-time requirements of the system?
29. Describe where the system architecture adheres or does not adhere to stan-dards.
30. Describe the project planning and analysis approach used on the project.

48.5.7.2 Processors/Servers/Clients

1. Describe the client/server Application Architecture.
2. Annotate the pictorial to illustrate where application functionality is executed.

48.5.7.3 Client

1. Are functions other than presentation performed on the user device?
2. Describe the data and process help facility being provided.
3. Describe the screen-to-screen navigation technique.
4. Describe how the user navigates between this and other applications.
5. How is this and other applications launched from the user device?
6. Are there any inter-application data and process sharing capabilities? If so, describe what is being shared and by what technique/technology.
7. Describe data volumes being transferred to the client.
8. What are the additional requirements for local data storage to support the application?
9. What are the additional requirements for local software storage/memory to support the application?
10. Are there any known hardware/software conflicts or capacity limitations caused by other application requirements or situations which would affect the application users?
11. Describe how the look-and-feel of your presentation layer compares to the look-and-feel of the other existing applications.
12. Describe to what extent the client needs to support asynchronous and/or synchronous communication.
13. Describe how the presentation layer of the system is separated from other computational or data transfer layers of the system.

48.5.7.4 Application Server

1. Can/do the presentation layer and application layers run on separate processors?
2. Can/do the application layer and data access layer run on separate processors?

24. 除了最初的客户，谁还可以使用该系统或者从中受益？
25. 以浏览模式和更新模式使用该系统的用户比例是多大？
26. 事务性要求的典型长度是多少？
27. 是否需要保证数据发送或更新？或者系统能否承受故障？
28. 系统的正常运行时间需求是什么？
29. 描述系统架构在哪些方面符合或不符合标准。
30. 描述该项目使用的项目规划和分析途径。

48.5.7.2 处理器/服务器/客户端

1. 描述客户端/服务器应用架构。
2. 在图上添加注释，以说明在何处执行应用功能性。

48.5.7.3 客户端

1. 用户设备是否执行了除演示外的功能？
2. 描述正在提供的数据和流程帮助设施。
3. 描述屏幕对屏幕的导航技术。
4. 描述用户如何在该应用与其他应用之间进行导航。
5. 如何从用户设备启动该应用和其他应用？
6. 是否具有应用间数据和流程共享能力？如果有，描述正在共享什么以及借助了什么技巧/技术。
7. 描述传送到客户端的数据量。
8. 支持该应用的本地数据存储的附加需求有哪些？
9. 支持该应用的本地软件存储/内存的附加需求有哪些？
10. 是否具有由影响应用用户的其他应用需求或情况引起的已知硬件/软件冲突或能力限制？
11. 描述如何对展现层的界面外观与其他现有应用的界面外观进行对比。
12. 描述客户端需要支持异步和/或同步通信的程度。
13. 描述如何将系统展现层与该系统其他计算层或数据传送层分开。

48.5.7.4 应用服务器

1. 展现层和应用层能否/是否在单独处理器上运行？
2. 应用层和数据访问层能否/是否在单独的处理器上运行？

3. Can this application be placed on an application server independent of all other applications? If not, explain the dependencies.
4. Can additional parallel application servers be easily added? If so, what is the load balancing mechanism?
5. Has the resource demand generated by the application been measured and what is the value? If so, has the capacity of the planned server been confirmed at the application and aggregate levels?

48.5.7.5 Data Server

1. Are there other applications which must share the data server? If so, identify them and describe the data and data access requirements.
2. Has the resource demand generated by the application been measured and what is the value? If so, has the capacity of the planned server been confirmed at the application and aggregate levels?

48.5.7.6 COTS (where applicable)

1. Is the vendor substantial and stable?
2. Will the enterprise receive source code upon demise of the vendor?
3. Is this software configured for the enterprise's usage?
4. Is there any peculiar A&D data or processes that would impede the use of this software?
   — Is this software currently available?
5. Has it been used/demonstrated for volume/availability/service-level requirements similar to those of the enterprise?
   — Describe the past financial and market share history of the vendor.

48.5.8 System Engineering/Methods & Tools Checklist

1. Do metrics exist for the current way of doing business?
2. Has the system owner created evaluation criteria that will be used to guide the project? Describe how the evaluation criteria will be used.
3. Has research of existing architectures been done to leverage existing work? Describe the method used to discover and understand. Will the architectures be integrated? If so, explain the method that will be used.
4. Describe the methods that will be used on the project:
   — For defining business strategies
   — For defining areas in need of improvement
   — For defining baseline and target business processes
   — For defining transition processes
   — For managing the project

3. 能否将该应用独立于所有其他应用放置在应用服务器上？如果不能，请解释依赖性。
4. 能否很容易地增加更多并行应用服务器吗？如果可以，负载平衡机制是什么？
5. 是否已测量该应用产生的资源需求？测量值是什么？如果已测量，是否已在应用层级和总体层级确认了计划服务器能力？

48.5.7.5 数据服务器

1. 是否具有必须共享数据服务器的其他应用？如果有，识别这些应用并描述数据和数据访问需求。
2. 是否已测量该应用产生的资源需求？测量值是什么？如果已测量，是否已在应用层级和总体层级确认了计划服务器能力？

48.5.7.6 COTS（若适用）

1. 厂商是否有实力且稳定？
2. 当厂商移交时 ENTERPRISE 能否收到源代码？
3. 本软件是否为 ENTERPRISE 使用而配置？
4. 是否具有会妨碍使用本软件的任何异常 A&D 数据或流程？
   — 本软件目前是否可用？
5. 是否已使用/证实了与 ENTERPRISE 类似的容量/可用性/服务层级需求？
   — 描述厂商的以往财务情况和市场份额历史情况。

48.5.8 系统工程/方法&工具检查单

1. 当前开展业务的方式是否存在衡量标准？
2. 系统所有者是否已创建用于指导该项目的评价准则？描述将如何使用这些评价准则。
3. 为了更好地利用现有工作，是否已对现有架构进行研究？描述用于研究和理解的方法。架构是否集成？如果集成，请解释将使用的方法。
4. 描述用于该项目的方法：
   — 用于定义业务战略
   — 用于定义需要改进的领域
   — 用于定义基线和目标业务流程
   — 用于定义过渡流程
   — 用于管理项目

- For team communication
- For knowledge management, change management, and configuration management
- For software development
- For referencing standards and statements of direction
- For quality assurance of deliverables
- For design reviews and deliverable acceptance
- For capturing metrics

5. Are the methods documented and distributed to each team member?
6. To what extent are team members familiar with these methods?
7. What processes are in place to ensure compliance with the methods?
8. Describe the infrastructure that is in place to support the use of the methods through the end of the project and anticipated releases.
   - How is consultation and trouble-shooting provided?
   - How is training co-ordinated?
   - How are changes and enhancements incorporated and cascaded?
   - How are lessons learned captured and communicated?
9. What tools are being used on the project? (Specify versions and platforms.) To what extent are team members familiar with these tools?
10. Describe the infrastructure that is in place to support the use of the tools through the end of the project and anticipated releases?
    - How is consultation and trouble-shooting provided?
    - How is training co-ordinated?
    - How are changes and enhancements incorporated and cascaded?
    - How are lessons learned captured and communicated?
11. Describe how the project will promote the re-use of its deliverables and deliverable content.
12. Will the architecture designs "live" after the project has been implemented? Describe the method that will be used to incorporate changes back into the architecture designs.
13. Were the current processes defined?
14. Were issues documented, rated, and associated to current processes? If not, how do you know you are fixing something that is broken?
15. Were existing/planned process improvement activities identified and associated to current processes? If not, how do you know this activity is not in conflict with or redundant to other Statements of Work?
16. Do you have current metrics? Do you have forecasted metrics? If not, how do you know you are improving something?
17. What processes will you put in place to gather, evaluate, and report metrics?

— 用于团队沟通
— 用于知识管理、变更管理和构型管理
— 用于软件开发
— 用于引用标准和指导说明
— 用于交付物的质量保证
— 用于设计审视和交付物验收
— 用于获取衡量标准

5. 该方法是否文件化并向每个团队成员发布这些方法？
6. 团队成员对这些方法的熟悉程度如何？
7. 什么流程适当地确保与这些方法合规？
8. 描述到项目和预期发布结束为止适当支持这些方法使用的基础设施。
   — 如何提供咨询和故障分析？
   — 如何协调培训？
   — 如何对变更及增强内容进行合并和级联？
   — 如何获取和交流经验教训？
9. 该项目正在使用什么工具？（规定版本和平台。）团队成员对这些工具的熟悉程度如何？
10. 描述到项目和预期发布结束为止适当支持这些工具使用的基础设施。
    — 如何提供咨询和故障分析？
    — 如何协调培训？
    — 如何对变更及增强内容进行合并和级联？
    — 如何获取和交流经验教训？
11. 描述该项目如何促进其交付物和可交付内容的复用。
12. 该项目实施后，架构设计还“有效”吗？描述将变更重新并入架构设计所用的方法。
13. 当前流程是否被定义？
14. 是否将这些问题进行文件化、评估并关联到当前流程？如果没有，如何知道你正在修理已被破坏的事物？
15. 是否识别现有的/计划的流程改进活动并将其关联到当前流程？如果没有，如何知道该活动不与其他工作说明书相互矛盾或者冗余？
16. 是否具有现行衡量标准？是否具有预测衡量标准？如果没有，你如何知道正在改善事物？
17. 用于适当收集、评价和报告衡量标准的流程是什么？

18. What impacts will the new design have on existing business processes, organizations, and information systems? Have they been documented and shared with the owners?

48.6 Architecture Compliance Review Guidelines

48.6.1 Tailoring the Checklists

- Focus on:
  - High risk areas
  - Expected (and emergent) differentiators
- For each question in the checklist, understand:
  - The question itself
  - The principle behind it
  - What to look for in the responses
- Ask subject experts for their views
- Fix the checklist questions for your use
- Bear in mind the need for feedback to the Architecture Board

48.6.2 Conducting Architecture Compliance Reviews

- Understand clearly the objectives of those soliciting the review; and stay on track and deliver what was asked for. For example, they typically want to know what is right or wrong with the system being architected; not what is right or wrong with the development methodology used, their own management structure, etc. It is easy to get off-track and discuss subjects that are interesting and perhaps worthwhile, but not what was solicited. If you can shed light and insight on technical approaches, but the discussion is not necessary for the review, volunteer to provide it after the review.
- If it becomes obvious during the discussion that there are other issues that need to be addressed, which are outside the scope of the requested review, bring it up with the meeting chair afterwards. A plan for addressing the issues can then be developed in accordance with their degree of seriousness.
- Stay "scientific" . Rather than: "We like to see large databases hosted on *ABC* rather than *XYZ*." , say things like: "The downtime associated with *XYZ* database environments is much greater than on *ABC* database environ-ments. Therefore we don't recommend hosting type *M* and *N* systems in an *XYZ* environment."
- Ask "open" questions; i.e., questions that do not presume a particular answer.
- There are often "hidden agendas" or controversial issues among those soliciting a review, which you probably won't know up-front. A depersona-lized approach to the discussions may help bridge the gaps of opinion rather than exacerbate them.
- Treat those being interviewed with respect. They may not have built the system "the way it should be" , but they probably did the best they could under the circumstances they were placed in.

18. 新设计会对现有业务流程、组织和信息系统产生什么影响？是否已将这些影响文件化并与所有者分享？

48.6 架构合规性审视指南

48.6.1 剪裁检查单

- 聚焦于：
  - 高风险领域
  - 预期的（和紧急的）差异
- 对于检查单中的每个问题，需理解：
  - 问题本身
  - 问题背后的原理
  - 寻求什么响应
- 询问学科专家的观点
- 确定可供使用的检查单问题
- 牢记向架构委员会进行反馈的必要性

48.6.2 进行架构合规性审视

- 清晰地理解请求该审视的人员的目的，并继续追踪和交付所要求的事物。例如，他们通常想知道，对于正在进行架构开发的系统来说什么是正确或错误的，而不是对所使用的开发方法及自身管理结构等方面来说什么是正确或错误的。很容易产生偏离，并讨论一些有趣且或许也有价值但并非所请求的话题。如果你能清楚明白地揭示并深入了解技术途径，但这些讨论对审视而言并非必须，请在审视之后自愿提供。
- 在讨论期间，如果需要处理的其他议题超出所需审视范围的情况已经变得非常明显，则留待以后与会议主席讨论。然后，可以按照其严重程度制定涉及这些议题的计划。
- 保持“科学性”，而非“我们愿意看到托管在 ABC 中而不是托管在 XYZ 中的大型数据库”，应是：“与 XYZ 数据库环境相关的停机时间远远大于 ABC 数据库环境下的停机时间。因此，我们不建议将 M 型系统和 N 型系统托管在 XYZ 环境中。”
- 提出“开放式”问题，即不能推导出特殊答案的问题。
- 在请求一项审视的那些问题之间，通常有“隐藏的日程”或争议性问题，这些可能无法提前预知。客观的讨论途径可帮助沟通意见分歧，而非扩大分歧。
- 尊重采访对象。他们可能没有以“应有的方式”构建系统，但是在其所处环境下他们可能尽了自己最大的努力。

- Help the exercise become a learning experience for you and the presenters.
- Reviews should include detailed assessment activities against the architectures and should ensure that the results are stored in the Enterprise Continuum.

- 将训练变成你和在座者的学习体验。
- 审视应包括针对架构而进行的详细评估活动，还应确保结果存储在ENTERPRISE的连续统一体中。

Chapter 49
Architecture Contracts

This chapter provides guidelines for defining and using Architecture Contracts.

49.1 Role

Architecture Contracts are the joint agreements between development partners and sponsors on the deliverables, quality, and fitness-for-purpose of an architecture. Successful implementation of these agreements will be delivered through effective architecture governance (see Chapter 50). By implementing a governed approach to the management of contracts, the following will be ensured:

- A system of continuous monitoring to check integrity, changes, decision-making, and audit of all architecture-related activities within the organization.
- Adherence to the principles, standards, and requirements of the existing or developing architectures.
- Identification of risks in all aspects of the development and implementation of the architecture(s) covering the internal development against accepted standards, policies, technologies, and products as well as the operational aspects of the architectures such that the organization can continue its business within a resilient environment.
- A set of processes and practices that ensure accountability, responsibility, and discipline with regard to the development and usage of all architectural artifacts.
- A formal understanding of the governance organization responsible for the contract, their level of authority, and scope of the architecture under the governance of this body.

The traditional Architecture Contract is an agreement between the sponsor and the architecture function or IS department. However, increasingly more services are being provided by systems integrators, applications providers, and service providers, co-ordinated through the architecture function or IS department. There is therefore a need for an Architecture Contract to establish joint agreements between all parties involved in the architecture development and delivery.

Architecture Contracts may occur at various stages of the Architecture Development Method(ADM); for example:

- The Statement of Architecture Work created in Phase A of Part II: Architecture Development Method (ADM) is effectively an Architecture Contract between the architecting organization and the sponsor of the enterprise architecture (or the IT governance function).
- The development of one or more architecture domains (business, data, application, technology), and in some cases the oversight of the overall enterprise architecture, may be contracted out to systems integrators, applications providers, and/or service providers.

第 49 章 架构契约

本章提供定义并使用架构契约的指南。

49.1 角色

架构契约是开发合作伙伴和发起人就架构的交付物、质量和适用性而达成的联合协议。这些协议的成功实施将通过有效的架构治理（见第 50 章）来交付。通过实施一种经管控的途径来进行契约管理，以下内容得到保证：

- 对系统连续监控，以检查组织内所有架构相关活动的完整性、变更、决策和审核。
- 遵循现有的或开发中的架构的原则、标准和需求。
- 根据已接受的标准、方针、技术和产品，识别架构开发和实施的所有方面风险（涵盖内部开发）和架构运行方面的风险，使得组织可在一个弹性环境内继续执行其业务。
- 一系列流程和实践，确保所有架构制品开发和使用过程中的追责性、责任性和纪律性。
- 正式了解负责契约的管控组织及其权限级别，以及在该机构管控下的架构范围。

传统架构契约是发起人与架构职能部门或 IS 部门之间的协议。但是，现在越来越多的服务正由系统集成商、应用提供者和服务提供者提供，并通过架构职能部门或 IS 部门协调。因此，需要一份架构契约，以在架构开发和交付涉及的所有相关方之间建立联合协议。

架构契约可以出现在架构开发方法（ADM）的不同阶段；例如：

- 在“第二部分：架构开发方法（ADM）”的阶段 A 中创建的架构工作说明书，是 Enterprise Architecture 的架构开发组织与发起人（或 IT 治理职能部门）之间的有效架构契约。
- 对一个或多个架构领域（业务、数据、应用、技术）的开发，以及在一些情况下对整体 Enterprise Architecture 的监督，都可外包给系统集成商、应用提供者和/或服务提供者。

Each of these arrangements will normally be governed by an Architecture Contract that defines the deliverables, quality, and fitness-for-purpose of the developed architecture, and the processes by which the partners in the architecture development will work together.

- At the beginning of Phase G (Implementation Governance), between the architecture function and the function responsible for implementing the enterprise architecture defined in the preceding ADM phases. Typically, this will be either the in-house systems development function, or a major contractor to whom the work is outsourced.
  - What is being "implemented" in Phase G of the ADM is the overall enterprise architecture. This will typically include the technology infrastructure (from Phase D), and also those enterprise applications and data management capabilities that have been defined in the Application Architecture and Data Architecture (from Phase C), either because they are enterprise-wide in scope, or because they are strategic in business terms, and therefore of enterprise-wide importance and visibility. However, it will typically not include non-strategic business applications, which business units will subsequently deploy on top of the technology infrastructure that is implemented as part of the enterprise architecture.
  - In larger-scale implementations, there may well be one Architecture Contract per implementation team in a program of implementation projects.
- When the enterprise architecture has been implemented (at the end of Phase G), an Architecture Contract will normally be drawn up between the architecting function (or the IT governance function, subsuming the architecting function) and the business users who will subsequently be building and deploying application systems in the architected environment.

It is important to bear in mind in all these cases that the ultimate goal is not just an enterprise architecture, but a dynamic enterprise architecture; i.e., one that allows for flexible evolution in response to changing technology and business drivers, without unnecessary constraints. The Architecture Contract is crucial to enabling a dynamic enterprise architecture and is key to governing the implementation.

Typical contents of these three kinds of Architecture Contract are explained below.

49.2 Contents

49.2.1 Statement of Architecture Work

The Statement of Architecture Work is created as a deliverable of Phase A, and is effectively an Architecture Contract between the architecting organization and the sponsor of the enterprise architecture (or the IT governance function, on behalf of the enterprise).

The typical contents of a Statement of Architecture Work are as defined in Part IV, Section 36.2.20.

通常，这些安排中的每一项都会通过架构契约来管控，架构契约中定义了已开发架构的交付物、质量和适用性，以及架构开发合作伙伴用来一起工作的流程。

- 在阶段 G（实施治理）开始时，在架构职能部门与负责实施之前 ADM 阶段中定义的 Enterprise Architecture 的职能部门之间。典型情况下，这要么是内部系统开发职能部门，要么是外包工作的主要承包商。
  - 在 ADM 的 G 阶段，正在“实施”的是整体 Enterprise Architecture。这通常包括技术基础设施（来自阶段 D），以及已经在应用架构和数据架构（来自阶段 C）中定义的那些 ENTERPRISE 应用和数据管理能力，因为它们是整个 ENTERPRISE 范围的，或者因为它们在业务方面是战略性的，从而在整个 ENTERPRISE 范围都具有重要性和可见性。但是，它通常不包括非战略性业务应用，这样业务单元随后部署在作为 Enterprise Architecture 一部分实施的技术基础设施之上。
  - 在大规模实施中，在多个实施项目的一个项目群中，每个实施团队很可能都有一个架构契约。
- 当 Enterprise Architecture 已经实施（在阶段 G 结束时）时，通常在架构开发职能部门（或 IT 治理职能部门，包括架构开发职能部门）与随后在架构环境中构建和部署应用系统的业务用户之间拟定架构契约。

重要的是，在所有这些情况下，都要牢记最终目标不仅仅是一个 Enterprise Architecture，而是一个动态的 Enterprise Architecture；即使得能根据不断变化的技术和业务驱动因素进行灵活演进的 Enterprise Architecture，没有多余的约束。架构契约对于实现动态 Enterprise Architecture 至关重要，对于管控实施也极为关键。

这三种架构契约的典型内容解释如下。

49.2 内容

49.2.1 架构工作说明书

架构工作说明书作为阶段 A 的交付物创建，它是架构开发组织与 Enterprise Architecture 发起人（或代表 ENTERPRISE 的 IT 治理职能部门）之间的有效架构契约。

第四部分 36.2.20 节定义架构工作说明书的典型内容。

49.2.2 Contract between Architecture Design and Development Partners

This is a signed statement of intent on designing and developing the enterprise architecture, or significant parts of it, from partner organizations, including systems integrators, applications providers, and service providers.

Increasingly the development of one or more architecture domains (business, data, application, technology) may be contracted out, with the enterprise's architecture function providing oversight of the overall enterprise architecture, and co-ordination and control of the overall effort. In some cases even this oversight role may be contracted out, although most enterprises prefer to retain that core responsibility in-house.

Whatever the specifics of the contracting-out arrangements, the arrangements themselves will normally be governed by an Architecture Contract that defines the deliverables, quality, and fitness-for-purpose of the developed architecture, and the processes by which the partners in the architecture development will work together.

Typical contents of an Architecture Design and Development Contract are:

- Introduction and background
- The nature of the agreement
- Scope of the architecture
- Architecture and strategic principles and requirements
- Conformance requirements
- Architecture development and management process and roles
- Target architecture measures
- Defined phases of deliverables
- Prioritized joint workplan
- Time window(s)
- Architecture delivery and business metrics

The template for this contract will normally be defined as part of the Preliminary Phase of the ADM, if not existing already, and the specific contract will be defined at the appropriate stage of the ADM, depending on the particular work that is being contracted out.

49.2.3 Contract between Architecting Function and Business Users

This is a signed statement of intent to conform with the enterprise architecture, issued by enterprise business users. When the enterprise architecture has been implemented (at the end of Phase F), an Architecture Contract will normally be drawn up between the architecting function (or the IT governance function, subsuming the architecting function) and the business users who will subsequently be building and deploying application systems in the architected environment.

Typical contents of a Business Users' Architecture Contract are:

- Introduction and background
- The nature of the agreement

49.2.2 架构设计与开发合作伙伴之间的契约

这是在合作组织（包括系统集成商、应用提供者和服务提供者）之间就设计和开发 Enterprise Architecture 或其重要部分而签署的意向书。

渐渐地，由 ENTERPRISE 的架构职能部门对整个 Enterprise Architecture 提供监督并对整个架构工作提供协调和控制，一个或多个架构领域（业务、数据、应用、技术）的开发都可以外包出去。在某些情况下，甚至这种监督角色都可以外包，尽管大部分 ENTERPRISE 更愿意保留其内部核心责任。

不管外包安排的特性是什么，这些安排本身都会通过架构契约来管控，架构契约定义已开发架构的交付物、质量和适用性，以及架构开发合作伙伴用来一起工作的流程。

架构设计和开发契约的典型内容是：

- 简介和背景
- 协议的本质
- 架构范围
- 架构及战略原则和需求
- 符合性需求
- 架构开发和管理流程与角色
- 目标架构测度
- 交付物的已定义阶段
- 经过优先级排序的联合工作计划
- 时间窗
- 架构交付和业务衡量标准

本契约的模板通常被定义为 ADM 预备阶段的一部分，如果还不存在，将在 ADM 的适当阶段根据外包的特殊工作内容来定义具体契约。

49.2.3 架构开发职能部门与业务用户之间的契约

这是一份已签署的、符合 Enterprise Architecture 的、由 ENTERPRISE 业务用户发出的意向书。当 Enterprise Architecture 已经实施（在阶段 F 结束时），架构契约通常在架构开发职能部门（或 IT 治理职能部门，包括架构开发职能部门）与随后在架构开发环境中构建和部署应用系统的业务用户之间拟定。

业务用户的架构契约的典型内容是：

- 简介和背景
- 协议的本质

- Scope
- Strategic requirements
- Architecture deliverables that meet the business requirements
- Conformance requirements
- Architecture adopters
- Time window
- Architecture business metrics
- Service architecture (includes Service Level Agreement (SLA))

This contract is also used to manage changes to the enterprise architecture in Phase H.

49.3 Relationship to Architecture Governance

The Architecture Contract document produced in Phase G of the ADM figures prominently in the area of architecture governance, as explained in Part VII, Chapter 50.

In the context of architecture governance, the Architecture Contract is often used as a means of driving architecture change.

In order to ensure that the Architecture Contract is effective and efficient, the following aspects of the governance framework may need to be introduced into Phase G:

- Simple processes
- People-centered authority
- Strong communication
- Timely responses and an effective escalation process
- Supporting organizational structures
- Status tracking of architecture implementation

- 范围
- 战略需求
- 满足业务需求的架构交付物
- 符合性需求
- 架构采纳者
- 时间窗
- 架构业务衡量标准
- 服务架构［包括服务水平协议（SLA）］

本契约还被用于管理 Enterprise Architecture 在阶段 H 中的变更。

49.3 与架构治理的关系

正如第七部分第 50 章所解释的一样，ADM 的阶段 G 中形成的架构契约文件在架构治理方面起显著作用。

在架构治理的背景环境下，架构契约通常作为一种驱动架构变更的方式。

为了确保架构契约有效并且高效，治理框架的下述方面可能需要引入到阶段 G：

- 简单的流程
- 以人为本的授权
- 较强的沟通能力
- 及时的响应以及有效的升级流程
- 支持组织结构
- 架构实施的状态跟踪

Chapter 50
Architecture Governance

This chapter provides a framework and guidelines for architecture governance.

50.1 Introduction

This section describes the nature of governance, and the levels of governance.

50.1.1 Levels of Governance within the Enterprise

Architecture governance is the practice and orientation by which enterprise architectures and other architectures are managed and controlled at an enterprise-wide level.

Architecture governance typically does not operate in isolation, but within a hierarchy of governance structures, which, particularly in the larger enterprise, can include all of the following as distinct domains with their own disciplines and processes:

- Corporate governance
- Technology governance
- IT governance
- Architecture governance

Each of these domains of governance may exist at multiple geographic levels — global, regional, and local — within the overall enterprise.

Corporate governance is thus a broad topic, beyond the scope of an enterprise architecture framework such as TOGAF.

This and related subsections are focused on architecture governance; but they describe it in the context of enterprise-wide governance, because of the hierarchy of governance structures within which it typically operates, as explained above.

In particular, this and following sections aim to:

- Provide an overview of the nature of governance as a discipline in its own right.
- Describe the governance context in which architecture governance typically functions within the enterprise.
- Describe an Architecture Governance Framework that can be adapted and applied in practice, both for enterprise architecture and for other forms of IT architecture.

第 50 章
架构治理

本章为架构治理提供框架和指南。

50.1 简介

本节描述治理的本质和治理的层级。

50.1.1 ENTERPRISE 内的治理层级

架构治理是在整个 ENTERPRISE 范围的层级下管理和控制 Enterprise Architecture 及其他架构所借助的实践和方向。

典型情况下，架构治理并非孤立地运行，而是在治理结构的层级内部运行，特别是在大型 ENTERPRISE 中，可以包括下述所有具有各自规程和流程的截然不同的领域：

- 公司治理
- 技术治理
- IT 治理
- 架构治理

整个 ENTERPRISE 内部的多重地理层级——全球、地区和本地都存在这些治理领域中的每个领域。

因此，公司治理是一个超出诸如 TOGAF 的 Enterprise Architecture 框架范围的广泛主题。

本节以及相关小节的重点都是架构治理，但它们在整个 ENTERPRISE 治理的背景环境下描述架构治理，这是因为架构治理通常在如上所述的治理结构层级中运行。

尤其是，本节和下面几节的目标是：

- 依照本身的规程提供关于治理本质的概述。
- 描述治理背景环境，在该背景环境中，架构治理通常在 ENTERPRISE 内发挥作用。
- 描述实际上可适应和可用于 Enterprise Architecture 也可用于其他形式的 IT 架构的架构治理框架。

50.1.2 Nature of Governance

50.1.2.1 Governance: A Generic Perspective

Governance is essentially about ensuring that business is conducted properly. It is less about overt control and strict adherence to rules, and more about guidance and effective and equitable usage of resources to ensure sustainability of an organization's strategic objectives.

The following outlines the basic principles of corporate governance, as identified by the Organization for Economic Co-operation and Development (OECD):

- Focuses on the rights, roles, and equitable treatment of shareholders.
- Disclosure and transparency and the responsibilities of the board.
- Ensures:
  - Sound strategic guidance of the organization.
  - Effective monitoring of management by the board.
  - Board accountability for the company and to the shareholders.
- Board's responsibilities:
  - Reviewing and guiding corporate strategy.
  - Setting and monitoring achievement of management's performance obj-ectives.

Supporting this, the OECD considers a traditional view of governance as: "... the system by which business corporations are directed and controlled. The corporate governance structure specifies the distribution of rights and responsibilities among different participants in the corporation — such as the board, managers, shareholders, and other stakeholders — and spells out the rules and procedures for making decisions on corporate affairs. By doing this, it also provides the structure through which the company objectives are set, and the means of attaining those objectives and monitoring performance" [OECD (1999)].

50.1.2.2 Characteristics of Governance

The following characteristics have been adapted from *Corporate Governance* (Naidoo, 2002) and are positioned here to highlight both the value and necessity for governance as an approach to be adopted within organizations and their dealings with all involved parties:

Discipline All involved parties will have a commitment to adhere to procedures, processes, and authority structures established by the organization.

Transparency All actions implemented and their decision support will be available for inspection by authorized organization and provider parties.

Independence All processes, decision-making, and mechanisms used will be established so as to minimize or avoid potential conflicts of interest.

Accountability Identifiable groups within the organization — e.g., governance boards who take actions or make decisions — are authorized and accountable for their actions.

Responsibility Each contracted party is required to act responsibly to the organization and its stakeholders.

Fairness All decisions taken, processes used, and their implementation will not be allowed to create unfair advantage to any one particular party.

50.1.2 治理的本质

50.1.2.1 治理：一般的关注层面

治理在根本上是关于确保业务被适当开展。治理较少地公然控制和严格地参照规则，较多地引导和有效公平地使用资源，以确保组织战略目的的持续性。

下面概述经济合作和发展组织（OECD）所识别的公司治理的基本原则：

- 关注股东的权利、角色和公平待遇。
- 委员会的公开和透明度以及职责。
- 确保：
  - 组织的良好战略引导。
  - 委员会管理的有效监控。
  - 委员会对公司以及对股东的责任。
- 委员会的职责：
  - 审视并指导公司战略。
  - 设定并监控管理绩效目标的达成。

为了支持这一点，OECD 将传统观点的治理视为：“……用来指导并控制公司业务系统。公司治理结构规定了公司的不同参与者之间（例如，委员会、经理、股东和其他利益攸关者）的权利和职责分配，并阐述了对公司事务做决策的规则和程序。通过这样做，还可提供设定公司目的所提供的结构，以及实现这些目的并监控绩效的方式” [OECD (1999)]。

50.1.2.2 治理的特点

下述特点摘自《公司治理》（Naidoo，2002），在这里引用是为了强调治理作为在组织内部采用的一种实施途径的价值和必要性及其与有关各方的关系：

纪律性 所有相关方承诺会坚持组织建立的程序、流程和授权结构。

透明性 所有已实施行动及其决策支持，随时可供授权组织和提供者各方检验。

独立性 建立所有会被使用流程、决策和机制，以便避免潜在利益冲突或使其最小化。

追责性 组织内的可识别群组——如采取行动或做决策的治理委员会——被授权采取行动并对行动负责。

负责性 每个契约方都需要向组织及其利益攸关者采取负责任的行动。

公平性 所采取的决策、所使用的流程及其实施都不允许任何特殊一方产生优势从而导致不公平。

50.1.3 Technology Governance

Technology governance controls how an organization utilizes technology in the research, development, and production of its goods and services. Although it may include IT governance activities, it often has broader scope.

Technology governance is a key capability, requirement, and resource for most organizations because of the pervasiveness of technology across the organizational spectrum.

Recent studies have shown that many organizations have a balance in favor of intangibles rather than tangibles that require management. Given that most of these intangibles are informational and digital assets, it is evident that businesses are becoming more reliant on IT: and the governance of IT — IT governance — is therefore becoming an even more important part of technology governance.

These trends also highlight the dependencies of businesses on not only the information itself but also the processes, systems, and structures that create, deliver, and consume it. As the shift to increasing value through intangibles increases in many industry sectors, so risk management must be considered as key to understanding and moderating new challenges, threats, and opportunities.

Not only are organizations increasingly dependent on IT for their operations and profitability, but also their reputation, brand, and ultimately their values are also dependent on that same information and the supporting technology.

50.1.4 IT Governance

IT governance provides the framework and structure that links IT resources and information to enterprise goals and strategies. Furthermore, IT governance institutionalizes best practices for planning, acquiring, implementing, and monitoring IT performance, to ensure that the enterprise's IT assets support its business objectives.

In recent years, IT governance has become integral to the effective governance of the modern enterprise. Businesses are increasingly dependent on IT to support critical business functions and processes; and to successfully gain competitive advantage, businesses need to manage effectively the complex technology that is pervasive throughout the organization, in order to respond quickly and safely to business needs.

In addition, regulatory environments around the world are increasingly mandating stricter enterprise control over information, driven by increasing reports of information system disasters and electronic fraud. The management of IT-related risk is now widely accepted as a key part of enterprise governance.

It follows that an IT governance strategy, and an appropriate organization for implementing the strategy, must be established with the backing of top management, clarifying who owns the enterprise's IT resources, and, in particular, who has ultimate responsibility for their enterprise- wide integration.

50.1.3 技术治理

技术治理控制组织如何在商品和服务的研究、开发和生产中使用技术。虽然技术治理可能包括 IT 治理活动，但其范围通常更广。

由于技术遍布整个组织范围，所以技术治理是大部分组织的关键能力、需求和资源。

最新研究已表明，很多组织在偏好于无形资产而非需要管理的有形资产之间取得平衡。假设这些无形资产中的大部分都是信息资产和数字资产，显然业务会变得越来越依赖 IT：因此对 IT 的治理，即 IT 治理，正在成为技术治理中一个更为重要的部分。

这些趋势还强调了业务不仅与信息本身具有相关性，而且与创建、交付和使用信息的流程、系统和结构具有相关性。在很多行业部门，因为通过无形资产向增加值的这一转变有所增加，所以必须将风险管理视为理解和缓和新挑战、新威胁和新机遇的关键。

不仅组织的运作和收益性越来越依赖 IT，而且组织的名誉、品牌和最终价值也依赖于这些信息和支持技术。

50.1.4 IT 治理

IT 治理提供将 IT 资源和信息联系到 ENTERPRISE 目标和战略的框架及结构。此外，IT 治理使规划、获取、实施和监控 IT 绩效的最佳实践制度化，以确保 ENTERPRISE 的 IT 资产支持其业务目的。

近年来，IT 治理已经成为有效治理现代 ENTERPRISE 不可或缺的一部分。业务越来越依赖于 IT，以支持关键的业务功能和流程；并成功地获得竞争优势，业务需要有效管理遍布组织内的复杂技术，以便快速并安全地响应业务需要。

此外，世界各地的监管环境受增加的信息系统故障和电子诈骗报告的驱动，越来越严格地强制 ENTERPRISE 控制信息。现在，对 IT 相关风险的管理被广泛视为 ENTERPRISE 治理的一个关键部分。

由此断定，IT 治理战略以及实施该策略的适合组织必须在高级管理层的支持下建立，明晰拥有 ENTERPRISEIT 资源的人员，特别是对全 ENTERPRISE 集成的最终负责的人员。

50.1.4.1 An IT Controls Framework — COBIT

As with corporate governance, IT governance is a broad topic, beyond the scope of an enterprise architecture framework such as TOGAF. A good source of detailed information on IT governance is the COBIT framework (Control OBjectives for Information and related Technology). This is an open standard for control over IT, developed and promoted by the IT Governance Institute, and published by the Information Systems Audit and Control Foundation (ISACF). COBIT controls may provide useful aides to running a compliance strategy. A comprehensive mapping between TOGAF and COBIT is available that guides the practitioner in implementing architecture governance aligned to IT governance: Mapping of TOGAF 8.1 With COBIT 4.0, by the IT Governance Institute (ITGI).[15]

50.1.5 Architecture Governance: Overview

50.1.5.1 Architecture Governance Characteristics

Architecture governance is the practice and orientation by which enterprise architectures and other architectures are managed and controlled at an enterprise-wide level. It includes the following:

- Implementing a system of controls over the creation and monitoring of all architectural components and activities, to ensure the effective introduction, implementation, and evolution of architectures within the organization.
- Implementing a system to ensure compliance with internal and external standards and regulatory obligations.
- Establishing processes that support effective management of the above processes within agreed parameters.
- Developing practices that ensure accountability to a clearly identified stakeholder community, both inside and outside the organization.

50.1.5.2 Architecture Governance as a Board-Level Responsibility

As mentioned above, IT governance has recently become a board responsibility as part of overall business governance. The governance of an organization's architectures is a key factor in effective IT/business linkage, and is therefore increasingly becoming a key board-level responsibility in its own right.

This section aims to provide the impetus for opening up IT and architecture governance so that the business responsibilities associated with architecture activities and artifacts can be elucidated and managed.

50.1.5.3 TOGAF and Architecture Governance

Phase G of the TOGAF ADM (see Part II, Chapter 15) is dedicated to implementation governance, which concerns itself with the realization of the architecture through change projects. Implementation governance is just one aspect of architecture governance, which covers the management and control of all aspects of the development and evolution of enterprise architectures and other architectures within the enterprise.

Architecture governance needs to be supported by an Architecture Governance Framework (described in Section 50.2) which assists in identifying effective processes so that the business responsibilities associated with architecture governance can be elucidated, communicated, and managed effectively.

---

15. Available at: www.opengroup.org/bookstore/catalog/w072.htm.

50.1.4.1 IT 控制框架—COBIT

正如公司治理一样，IT 治理是一个超出诸如 TOGAF 的 Enterprise Architecture 框架范围的广泛主题。关于 IT 治理的一个详细信息来源是 COBIT 框架（信息及相关技术的控制目标）。这是一个由 IT 治理协会制定并发起、由信息系统检查与控制协会（ISACF）公布的用来控制 IT 的公开标准。COBIT 控制项可能提供一些对运行合规性策略有用的帮助手段。TOGAF 与 COBIT 之间的综合映射有效地指导实践者实施与 IT 治理一致的架构治理：IT 治理协会（ITGI）进行的 COBIT 4.0 与 TOGAF 8.1 的映射。[15]

50.1.5 架构治理：概述

50.1.5.1 架构治理的特点

架构治理是在整个 ENTERPRISE 层级下管理和控制 Enterprise Architecture 及其他架构所借助的实践和方向。架构治理包括以下内容：

- 实施是对所有架构组件和活动创建与监控进行控制的系统，以确保架构在组织内的有效引入、实施和演进。
- 实施一个系统是为了确保与内外标准及监管义务合规。
- 在协议参数之内建立支持对上述流程进行有效管理的流程。
- 形成确保对组织内外的明确标识的利益攸关者团体负责的实践。

50.1.5.2 架构治理是委员会层级的职责

如上所述，IT 治理近年来已成为一项委员会职责，作为总体业务治理的一部分。组织架构的治理是有效 IT/业务联系的一个关键因素，因此其本身正逐渐成为关键委员会层级的职责。

本节旨在提供开辟 IT 和架构治理的推动力，以便可以阐明并管理与架构活动和制品相关的业务职责。

50.1.5.3 TOGAF 和架构治理

TOGAF ADM 的阶段 G（见第二部分第 15 章）致力于实施治理，这本身与通过变更项目以实现架构有关。实施治理恰恰是架构治理的一个方面，包括对 Enterprise Architecture 和 ENTERPRISE 之内的其他架构的开发和演进的所有方面进行的管理和控制。

架构治理需要有助于识别有效流程的架构治理框架（见 50.2 节的描述）的支持，以便可以有效地阐明、沟通和管理与架构治理相关的业务职责。

---

15. 详情可登录：www.opengroup.org/bookstore/catalog/w072.htm。

50.2 Architecture Governance Framework

This section describes a conceptual and organizational framework for architecture governance. As previously explained, Phase G of the TOGAF ADM (see Part II, Chapter 15) is dedicated to implementation governance, which concerns itself with the realization of the architecture through change projects.

Implementation governance is just one aspect of architecture governance, which covers the management and control of all aspects of the development and evolution of enterprise architectures and other architectures within the enterprise.

Architecture governance needs to be supported by an Architecture Governance Framework, described below. The governance framework described is a generic framework that can be adapted to the existing governance environment of an enterprise. It is intended to assist in identifying effective processes and organizational structures, so that the business responsibilities associated with architecture governance can be elucidated, communicated, and managed effectively.

50.2.1 Architecture Governance Framework — Conceptual Structure

50.2.1.1 Key Concepts

Conceptually, architecture governance is an approach, a series of processes, a cultural orientation, and set of owned responsibilities that ensure the integrity and effectiveness of the organization's architectures.

The key concepts are illustrated in Figure 50-1.

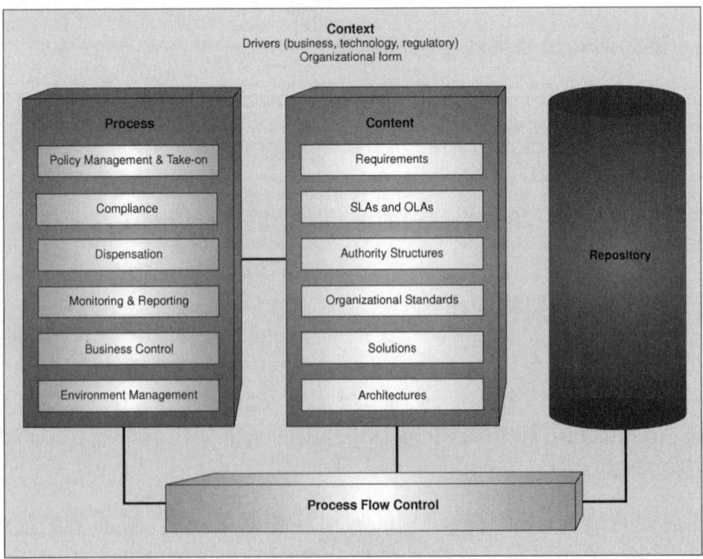

Figure 50-1 Architecture Governance Framework — Conceptual Structure

50.2 架构治理框架

本节描述架构治理的概念性组织框架。如前所述，TOGAF ADM 的阶段 G（见第二部分第 15 章）致力于实施治理，这本身与通过变更项目实现架构有关。

实施治理只是架构治理的一个方面，包括对 Enterprise Architecture 和 ENTERPRISE之内的其他架构的开发和演进的所有方面进行的管理和控制。

架构治理需要由架构治理框架支持，如下所述。所描述的治理框架是一种可适应 ENTERPRISE 现有治理环境的通用框架。旨在帮助识别有效的流程和组织结构，以便可以有效地阐述、沟通和管理与架构治理相关的业务职责。

50.2.1 架构治理框架——概念结构

50.2.1.1 主要概念

从概念上看，架构治理是确保组织架构完整和有效的一种实施途径、一系列流程、一种文化定位和一套特有责任。

主要概念如图 50-1 所示。

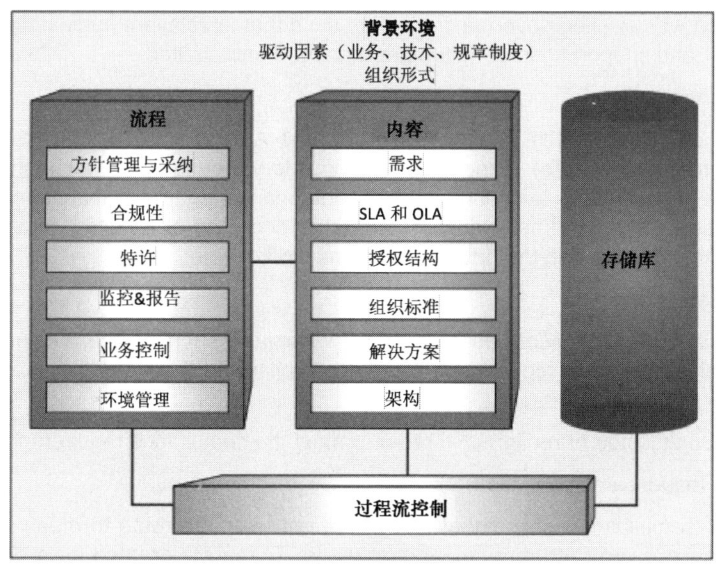

图 50-1 架构治理框架——概念结构

The split of process, content, and context are key to the support of the architecture governance initiative, by allowing the introduction of new governance material (legal, regulatory, standards-based, or legislative) without unduly impacting the processes. This content-agnostic approach ensures that the framework is flexible. The processes are typically independent of the content and implement a proven best practice approach to active governance.

The Architecture Governance Framework is integral to the Enterprise Continuum, and manages all content relevant both to the architecture itself and to architecture governance processes.

50.2.1.2 Key Architecture Governance Processes

Governance processes are required to identify, manage, audit, and disseminate all information related to architecture management, contracts, and implementation. These governance processes will be used to ensure that all architecture artifacts and contracts, principles, and operational-level agreements are monitored on an ongoing basis with clear auditability of all decisions made.

Policy Management and Take-On

All architecture amendments, contracts, and supporting information must come under governance through a formal process in order to register, validate, ratify, manage, and publish new or updated content. These processes will ensure the orderly integration with existing governance content such that all relevant parties, documents, contracts, and supporting information are managed and audited.

Compliance

Compliance assessments against Service Level Agreements (SLAs), Operational Level Agreements (OLAs), standards, and regulatory requirements will be implemented on an ongoing basis to ensure stability, conformance, and performance monitoring. These assessments will be reviewed and either accepted or rejected depending on the criteria defined within the governance framework.

Dispensation

A Compliance Assessment can be rejected where the subject area (design, operational, service level, or technology) are not compliant. In this case the subject area can:

1. Be adjusted or realigned in order to meet the compliance requirements.
2. Request a dispensation.

Where a Compliance Assessment is rejected, an alternate route to meeting interim conformance is provided through dispensations. These are granted for a given time period and set of identified service and operational criteria that must be enforced during the lifespan of the dispensation. Dispensations are not granted indefinitely, but are used as a mechanism to ensure that service levels and operational levels are met while providing a level of flexibility in their implementation and timing. The time-bound nature of dispensations ensures that they are a major trigger in the compliance cycle.

将流程、内容和背景环境分开，是支持架构治理举措的关键，使得在不对流程产生不当影响的情况下能引入新的治理资料（法律的、法规的、基于标准的或立法的）。这种与内容无关的实施途径确保框架是灵活的。这些流程通常独立于内容，并实施一种经证实的有效管控的最佳实践的途径。

架构治理框架是复杂组织连续统一体中不可或缺的一部分，管理与架构本身和架构治理流程相关的所有内容。

50.2.1.2 主要架构治理流程

要求治理流程识别、管理、审核并传播有关架构管理、契约和实施的全部信息。这些治理流程还用于确保持续地监控全部架构制品和契约、原则，以及运行水平协议，并且所做的全部决策具有明显的可审核性。

方针管理与采纳

所有架构修正案、契约和支持性信息必须通过一种正式流程进行治理，以便注册、确认、正式批准、管理和发布全新的或更新后的内容。这些流程会确保与现有治理内容的有序集成，以便管理和审核所有相关方、文件、契约和支持性信息。

合规性

持续地对服务水平协议（SLA）、运行水平协议（OLA）、标准和法规要求进行合规性评估，以确保稳定性、符合性和绩效监控。这些评估会接受审视，并依据治理框架中定义的准则予以接受或拒绝。

特许

在主题领域（设计、运行、服务水平或技术）不合规的情况下，可以拒绝合规性评估。在这种情况下，该主题领域可以：

1. 被调整或重新调整，以便达到合规性要求。
2. 要求特许。

在合规评估被拒绝的情况下，通过特许提供满足临时符合性的备用方式。在规定时间区间内给予特许，但只特许一组必须在特许有效期间实施的已识别服务和运行准则。并非无限期地给予特许，但是特许可用作一种确保在达到服务层级和运行层级的同时还在实施与时间安排方面提供灵活性层级的机制。特许的时限本质确保特许作为合规性周期的主要触发条件。

Monitoring and Reporting

Performance management is required to ensure that both the operational and service elements are managed against an agreed set of criteria. This will include monitoring against service and operational-level agreements, feedback for adjustment, and reporting.

Internal management information will be considered in Environment Management.

Business Control

Business Control relates to the processes invoked to ensure compliance with the organization's business policies.

Environment Management

This identifies all the services required to ensure that the repository-based environment underpinning the governance framework is effective and efficient. This includes the physical and logical repository management, access, communication, training, and accreditation of all users.

All architecture artifacts, service agreements, contracts, and supporting information must come under governance through a formal process in order to register, validate, ratify, manage, and publish new or updated content. These processes will ensure the orderly integration with existing governance content such that all relevant parties, documents, contracts, and supporting information are managed and audited.

The governance environment will have a number of administrative processes defined in order to effect a managed service and process environment. These processes will include user management, internal SLAs (defined in order to control its own processes), and management information reporting.

50.2.2 Architecture Governance Framework — Organizational Structure

50.2.2.1 Overview

Architecture governance is the practice and orientation by which enterprise architectures and other architectures are managed and controlled. In order to ensure that this control is effective within the organization, it is necessary to have the correct organizational structures established to support all governance activities.

An architecture governance structure for effectively implementing the approach described in this section will typically include the following levels, which may in practice involve a combination of existing IT governance processes, organizational structures, and capabilities. They will typically include the following:

- Global governance board
- Local governance board
- Design authorities
- Working parties

The architecture organization illustrated in Figure 50-2 highlights the major structural elements required for an architecture governance initiative. While each enterprise will have differing requirements, it is expected that the basics of the organizational design shown in Figure 50-2 will be applicable and implementable in a wide variety of organizational types.

监控和报告

需要绩效管理，以确保运行要素和服务要素按照已商定的准则集进行管理。这包括对服务和运行水平协议、调整反馈以及报告进行监控。

在环境管理中考虑内部管理信息。

业务控制

业务控制与所调用流程相关联，以确保与组织的业务方针合规。

环境管理

这识别确保支持治理框架的基于存储库的环境有效且高效所需的全部服务，包括对所有用户的物理和逻辑存储库的管理、访问、通信、培训和鉴定。

所有架构制品、服务协议、契约和支持性信息必须通过一种正式流程治理，以便注册、确认、正式批准、管理和发布全新的或更新的内容。这些流程要确保与现有治理内容的有序集成，以便管理和审核所有相关方、文件、契约和支持性信息。

治理环境会定义若干管理流程为了影响被管理的服务和流程环境。这些流程包括用户管理、内部 SLA（为了控制自己的流程而定义的 SLA）以及管理信息报告。

50.2.2 架构治理框架——组织结构

50.2.2.1 概述

架构治理是管理并控制 Enterprise Architecture 及其他架构的实践和方向。为了确保该控制在组织内有效，有必要建立正确的组织结构，以支持所有治理活动。

一个有效实施本节所描述的实施途径的架构治理结构通常包括下述层级，实际上可以包含现有 IT 治理流程、组织结构和能力的组合形态。它们通常包括下述内容：

- 全球治理委员会
- 本地治理委员会
- 设计局
- 工作组

图 50-2 所示的架构组织强调架构治理举措所需的主要结构元件。尽管每个 ENTERPRISE 都有不同的需求，但组织设计的最基本需求是在组织形式中适用并且可实施（如图 50-2 所示）。

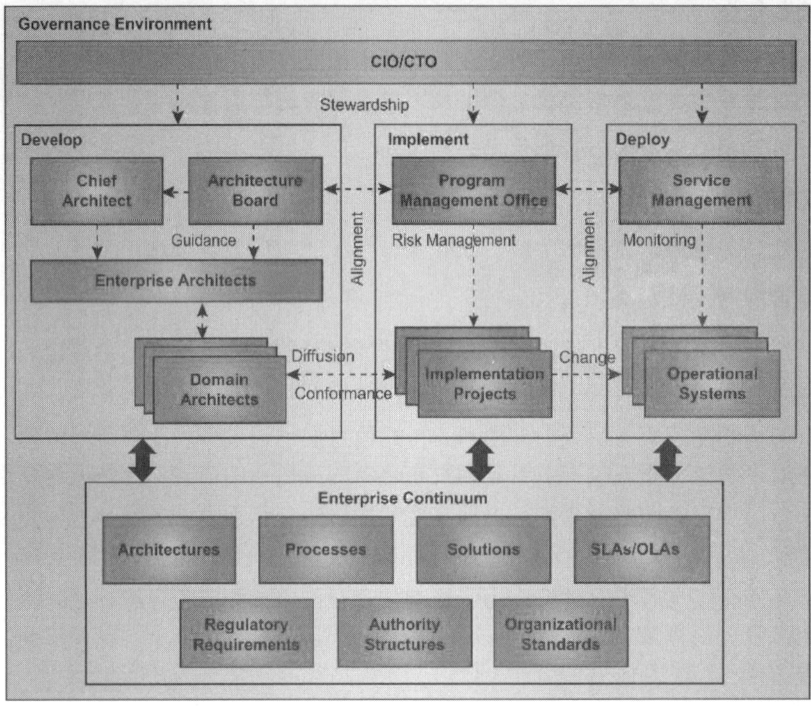

Figure 50-2 Architecture Governance Framework — Organizational Structure

50.2.2.2 Key Areas

Figure 50-2 identifies three key areas of architecture management: Develop, Implement, and Deploy. Each of these is the responsibility of one or more groups within the organization, while the Enterprise Continuum is shown to support all activities and artifacts associated with the governance of the architectures throughout their lifecycle.

The Develop responsibilities, processes, and structures are usually linked to the TOGAF ADM and its usage, while the Implement responsibilities, processes, and structures are typically linked to Phase G (see Part II, Chapter 15).

As mentioned above, the Architecture Governance Framework is integral to the Enterprise Continuum, and manages all content relevant both to the architectures themselves and to architecture governance processes.

50.2.2.3 Operational Benefits

As illustrated in Figure 50-2, the governance of the organization's architectures provides not only direct control and guidance of their development and implementation, but also extends into the operations of the implemented architectures.

The following benefits have been found to be derived through the continuing governance of architectures:

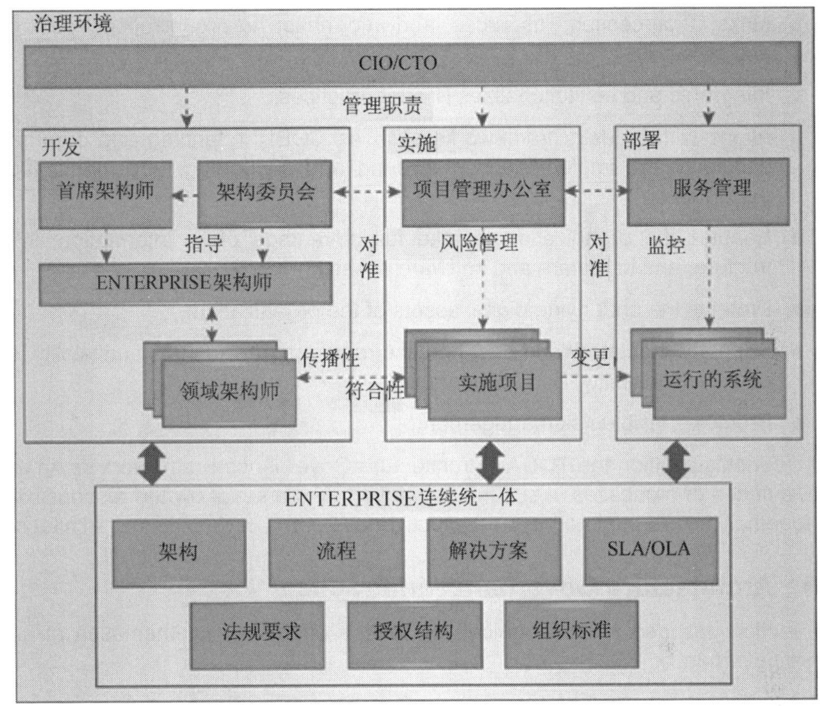

图 50-2 架构治理框架——组织结构

50.2.2.2 关键方面

图 50-2 识别架构管理的三个关键方面：开发、实施和部署。每个方面需要组织内的一个或多个群组同时负责，同时展示出了 ENTERPRISE 的连续统一体，以支持贯穿于生命周期的与架构治理相关的所有活动和制品。

开发的职责、流程和结构通常与 TOGAF ADM 及其使用有联系，而实施的职责、流程和结构通常与阶段 G（见第二部分第 15 章）有联系。

如上所述，架构治理框架是 ENTERPRISE 的连续统一体中不可或缺的一部分，并且管理与架构本身和架构治理流程的内容相关。

50.2.2.3 运行好处

如图 50-2 所示，组织架构的治理不仅仅对其开发和实施提供直接控制和引导，还扩展到所实施架构的运行。

已经发现通过架构的持续治理可获得下述好处：

- Links IT processes, resources, and information to organizational strategies and objectives.
- Integrates and institutionalizes IT best practices.
- Aligns with industry frameworks such as COBIT (planning and organizing, acquiring and implementing, delivering and supporting, and monitoring IT performance).
- Enables the organization to take full advantage of its information, infrastructure, and hardware and software assets.
- Protects the underlying digital assets of the organization.
- Supports regulatory and best practice requirements such as auditability, security, responsibility, and accountability.
- Promotes visible risk management.

These benefits position the TOGAF Architecture Governance Framework as an approach, a series of processes, a cultural orientation, and a set of owned responsibilities, that together ensure the integrity and effectiveness of the organization's architectures.

50.3 Architecture Governance in Practice

This section provides practical guidelines for the effective implementation of architecture governance.

50.3.1 Architecture Governance — Key Success Factors

It is important to consider the following to ensure a successful approach to architecture governance, and to the effective management of the Architecture Contract:

- Best practices for the submission, adoption, re-use, reporting, and retirement of architecture policies, procedures, roles, skills, organizational structures, and support services.
- Organizational responsibilities and structures to support the architecture governance processes and reporting requirements.
- Integration of tools and processes to facilitate the take-up of the processes, both procedurally and culturally.
- Criteria for the control of the architecture governance processes, dispensations, compliance assessments, SLAs, and OLAs.
- Internal and external requirements for the effectiveness, efficiency, confidentiality, integrity, availability, compliance, and reliability of all architecture governance-related information, services, and processes.

- 将 IT 流程、资源和信息与组织战略及目的联系起来。
- 集成 IT 最佳实践并使这些实践成为惯例。
- 与诸如 COBIT 的行业框架协调一致（规划并组织、获取并实施、交付并支持以及监控 IT 绩效）。
- 使组织能充分利用其信息、基础设施以及硬件和软件资产。
- 保护组织的基础数字资产。
- 支持符合法规的最佳实践需求，例如可审核性、安保性、责任性和问责制。
- 促进可见的风险管理。

这些好处将 TOGAF 架构治理框架定位为一种实施途径、一系列流程、一种文化定位和一套特有责任体系，以共同确保组织架构的完整性和有效性。

50.3 实践中的架构治理

本节为架构治理的有效实施提供实践指南。

50.3.1 架构治理—关键成功因素

重要的是考虑如下因素，以确保架构治理和架构契约有效管理的成功：

- 提交、采用、复用、报告及撤销架构的策略、程序、角色、技能、组织结构和支持服务的最佳实践。
- 支持架构治理流程以及报告需求的组织职责和结构。
- 从程序和文化角度，促进流程采纳的工具和流程的集成。
- 控制架构治理流程、特许、合规性评估、SLA 和 OLA 的准则。
- 对所有架构治理相关信息、服务和流程的效能、效率、机密性、完整性、有效性、合规性及可靠性的内部和外部的需求。

50.3.2 Elements of an Effective Architecture Governance Strategy

50.3.2.1 Architecture Governance and Corporate Politics

An enterprise architecture imposed without appropriate political backing is bound to fail. In order to succeed, the enterprise architecture must reflect the needs of the organization. Enterprise architects, if they are not involved in the development of business strategy, must at least have a fundamental understanding of it and of the prevailing business issues facing the organization. It may even be necessary for them to be involved in the system deployment process and to ultimately own the investment and product selection decisions arising from the implementation of the Technology Architecture.

There are three important elements of architecture governance strategy that relate particularly to the acceptance and success of architecture within the enterprise. While relevant and applicable in their own right apart from their role in governance, and therefore described separately, they also from an integral part of any effective architecture governance strategy.

- A cross-organizational Architecture Board (see Chapter 47) must be established with the backing of top management to oversee the implementation of the IT governance strategy.
- A comprehensive set of architecture principles (see Chapter 23) should be established, to guide, inform, and support the way in which an organization sets about fulfilling its mission through the use of IT.
- An Architecture Compliance (see Chapter 48) strategy should be adopted — specific measures (more than just a statement of policy) to ensure compliance with the architecture, including Project Impact Assessments, a formal Architecture Compliance review process, and possibly including the involvement of the architecture team in product procurement.

50.3.2 有效架构治理战略的要素

50.3.2.1 架构治理和公司方针

当 Enterprise Architecture 未得到适当政策支持时，它注定会失败。为了取得成功，Enterprise Architecture 必须反映组织的需要。如果 ENTERPRISE 架构师未参与到业务战略的定制中去，则必须基本了解该业务策略以及组织面对的普遍业务问题。对于架构师来说，甚至可能必须参与到系统部署流程中，并且最终承担技术架构实施引起的投资和产品选择的决策。

在 ENTERPRISE 内，架构治理战略获得认可与成功主要有三个重要因素。虽然与架构师自身的权利（除去他们的治理角色）相关并适用，并因此单独地描述，但他们仍然是任何有效架构治理战略的组成部分。

- 必须在高层管理人员的支持下建立跨组织架构委员会（见第 47 章），用于监督 IT 治理战略的实施。
- 应建立一套综合性架构原则（见第 23 章），用于指导、通知和支持组织通过使用 IT 开始执行其任务的方式。
- 应采用架构合规性（见第 48 章）策略，即确保与架构合规的具体措施（不仅仅是一项方针性的申明），包括项目影响评估、正式的架构合规性审视流程，可能还包括将架构团队加入产品采购。

Chapter 51
Architecture Maturity Models

This chapter provides techniques for evaluating and quantifying an organization's maturity in enterprise architecture.

51.1 Overview

Organizations that can manage change effectively are generally more successful than those that cannot. Many organizations know that they need to improve their processes in order to successfully manage change, but don't know how. Such organizations typically either spend very little on process improvement, because they are unsure how best to proceed; or spend a lot, on a number of parallel and unfocused efforts, to little or no avail.

Capability Maturity Models (CMMs) address this problem by providing an effective and proven method for an organization to gradually gain control over and improve its change processes. Such models provide the following benefits:

- They describe the practices that any organization must perform in order to improve its processes.
- They provide a yardstick against which to periodically measure improvement.
- They constitute a proven framework within which to manage the improvement efforts.
- They organize the various practices into levels, each level representing an increased ability to control and manage the development environment.

An evaluation of the organization's practices against the model — called an "assessment" — determines the level at which the organization currently stands. It indicates the organization's ability to execute in the area concerned, and the practices on which the organization needs to focus in order to see the greatest improvement and the highest return on investment. The benefits of CMMs to effectively direct effort are well documented.

第 51 章 架构成熟度模型

本章提供评价和量化 Enterprise Architecture 中组织成熟度的技术。

51.1 概述

可以有效管理变更的组织通常比那些不能管理变更的组织更为成功。很多组织都知道，必须改善流程才能成功地管理变更，但不知道如何做。此类组织通常要么在流程改进上花费很少，因为他们不确定怎样做才最好；要么在几乎或完全没用的大量平行和非重点的工作上花费很多。

能力成熟度模型（CMM）通过向组织提供一种有效并得到证实的方法来处理这一问题，从而逐步实现了对其变更流程的控制和改善。此类模型提供下述好处：

- 其描述任何组织为改进流程而必须实施的实践。
- 其提供用来定期测量改善情况的计算标准。
- 其构成一个得到证实的框架，在其内部管理改善工作。
- 它们将不同的实践组织成各个层级，每个层级代表一种控制和管理开发环境的提升能力。

根据模型对组织实践的评价——被称为“评估”——确定组织当前所处层级。该评价指出组织在所关注领域执行的能力，以及组织需要聚焦的实践，以便看到对投资的最大改进和最高回报。CMM 模型对有效指导工作的好处已被很好地文件化。

51.2 Background

The Software Engineering Institute (SEI) — www.sei.cmu.edu operated by Carnegie Mellon University — developed the original CMM (Capability Maturity Model) for Software (SWCMM) in the early 1990s, which is still widely used today. This CMM provided a framework to develop maturity models in a wide range of disciplines.

The increasing interest in applying these techniques to other fields has resulted in a series of template tools which assess:

- The state of the architecture processes
- The architecture
- The organization's buy-in to both

The main issues addressed by these models include:

- Process implementation and audit
- Quality measurements
- People competencies
- Investment management

They involve use of a multiplicity of models, and focus in particular on measuring business benefits and return on investment.

A closely related topic is the Architecture Skills Framework (see Chapter 52), which can be used to plan the target skills and capabilities required by an organization to successfully develop and utilize enterprise architecture, and to determine the training and development needs of individuals.

51.3 US DoC ACMM Framework

51.3.1 Overview

As an example of the trend towards increased interest in applying CMM techniques to enterprise architecture, all US federal agencies are now expected to provide maturity models and ratings as part of their IT investment management and audit requirements.

In particular, the US Department of Commerce (DoC) has developed an enterprise Architecture Capability Maturity Model (ACMM)[16] to aid in conducting internal assessments. ACMM Version 1.2 was published in December 2007. The ACMM provides a framework that represents the key components of a productive enterprise architecture process. The goal is to enhance the overall odds for success of enterprise architecture by identifying weak areas and providing a defined evolutionary path to improving the overall architecture process.

The ACMM comprises three sections:

1. The enterprise architecture maturity model.
2. Enterprise architecture characteristics of operating units' processes at different maturity levels.

16. Refer to ocio.os.doc.gov/ITPolicyandPrograms/Enterprise_Architecture/DEV01_003735.

51.2 背景

由美国卡耐基梅隆大学运行的软件工程研究院（SEI，网址 www.sei.cmu.edu）在 20 世纪 90 年代早期开发了原始的 CMM（能力成熟度模型）软件（SWCMM），至今仍然被人们广泛使用。该 CMM 提供了一种在众多规程中开发成熟度模型的框架。

将这些技术应用于其他领域的兴趣渐增，以致形成了一系列模板工具来评估如下方面：

- 架构流程的状态
- 架构
- 组织的双赢

这些模型涉及的主要议题包括：

- 流程实施和审核
- 质量测量
- 人员素质
- 投资管理

它们涉及大量模型的使用，并且特别聚焦于测量业务效益和投资回报。

一个密切相关的课题是“架构技能框架”（见第 52 章），可用于规划组织成功开发并利用 Enterprise Architecture 所需的目标技能和能力，并用于确定个人培训及发展需要。

51.3 美国商务部 ACMM 框架

51.3.1 概述

作为将 CMM 技术应用于 Enterprise Architecture 的兴趣增加的趋势的一个示例，期望所有美国联邦机构都提供成熟度模型和等级，以作为 IT 投资管理和审核需求的一部分。

特别是，美国商务部（DoC）已经开发了 Enterprise Architecture 的架构能力成熟度模型（ACMM）[16]，以帮助进行内部评估。ACMM 1.2 版本已于 2007 年 12 月份发布。ACMM 提供一种框架，表示一个高效的 Enterprise Architecture 流程的关键组件。目标是通过识别架构的薄弱环节，提供已定义的演进途径，从而提高 Enterprise Architecture 获得成功的总体概率，从而改善总体架构流程。

ACMM 包括以下三个章节：

1. Enterprise Architecture 成熟度模型。
2. 在不同成熟度等级运行单元流程的 Enterprise Architecture 特点。

16. 见 ocio.os.doc.gov/ITPolicyandPrograms/Enterprise_Architecture/DEV01_003735。

3. The enterprise architecture CMM scorecard.

The first two sections explain the Architecture Capability maturity levels and the corresponding enterprise architecture element and characteristics for each maturity level to be used as measures in the assessment process. The third section is used to derive the Architecture Capability maturity level that is to be reported to the DoC Chief Information Officer (CIO).

51.3.2 Elements of the ACMM

The DoC ACMM consists of six maturity levels and nine architecture elements. The six levels are:

0 None

1 Initial

2 Under development

3 Defined

4 Managed

5 Measured

The nine enterprise architecture elements are:

1. Architecture process
2. Architecture development
3. Business linkage
4. Senior management involvement
5. Operating unit participation
6. Architecture communication
7. IT security
8. Architecture governance
9. IT investment and acquisition strategy

Two complementary methods are used in the ACMM to calculate a maturity rating. The first method obtains a weighted mean enterprise architecture maturity level. The second method shows the percentage achieved at each maturity level for the nine architecture elements.

51.3.3 Example: Enterprise Architecture Process Maturity Levels

The following example shows the detailed characteristics of the enterprise architecture maturity levels as applied to each of the nine elements. For example, Level 3: Defined, point number 8 (Explicit documented governance of majority of IT investments) shows Maturity Level 3's state for Element 8 (Architecture Governance).

3. Enterprise Architecture CMM 记分卡。

前两节解释架构能力成熟度等级以及在评估流程中用作测度的成熟度等级的对应 Enterprise Architecture 要素和特征。第三节内容用于导出要上报给 DoC 首席信息官（CIO）的架构能力成熟度等级。

51.3.2 ACMM 的要素

DoC ACMM 由六大成熟度等级和九大架构要素组成：六大等级为：

0. 无
1. 初始
2. 开发中
3. 已定义
4. 已被管理
5. 已被测量

九大 Enterprise Architecture 元素为：

1. 架构流程
2. 架构开发
3. 业务联系
4. 高级管理层参与
5. 操作单元参与
6. 架构通信
7. IT 安保性
8. 架构治理
9. IT 投资和采办策略

在 ACMM 中，利用两个互补的方法计算成熟度等级。第一个方法获得加权平均后的 Enterprise Architecture 成熟度等级。第二个方法表明九大架构要素在每个成熟度等级下达到的百分比。

51.3.3 示例：Enterprise Architecture 流程成熟度等级

下述示例表明适用于九大要素中的每个要素的 Enterprise Architecture 成熟度等级的详细特征。例如，在“等级 3：已定义”中，第 8 部分内容（大多数 IT 投资的清晰且文件化的管控）表明用于要素 8（架构治理）在成熟度等级 3 达到的状态。

Level 0: None

No enterprise architecture program. No enterprise architecture to speak of.

Level 1: Initial

Informal enterprise architecture process underway.

1. Processes are *ad hoc* and localized. Some enterprise architecture processes are defined.There is no unified architecture process across technologies or business processes. Success depends on individual efforts.
2. Enterprise architecture processes, documentation, and standards are established by a variety of *ad hoc* means and are localized or informal.
3. Minimal, or implicit linkage to business strategies or business drivers.
4. Limited management team awareness or involvement in the architecture process.
5. Limited operating unit acceptance of the enterprise architecture process.
6. The latest version of the operating unit's enterprise architecture documentation is on the web. Little communication exists about the enterprise architecture process and possible process improvements.
7. IT security considerations are *ad hoc* and localized.
8. No explicit governance of architectural standards.
9. Little or no involvement of strategic planning and acquisition personnel in the enterprise architecture process. Little or no adherence to existing standards.

Level 2: Under Development

Enterprise architecture process is under development.

1. Basic enterprise architecture process is documented based on OMB Circular A-130 and Department of Commerce Enterprise Architecture Guidance. The architecture process has developed clear roles and responsibilities.
2. IT vision, principles, business linkages, Baseline, and Target Architecture are identified. Architecture standards exist, but not necessarily linked to Target Architecture. Technical Reference Model (TRM) and Standards Profile framework established.
3. Explicit linkage to business strategies.
4. Management awareness of architecture effort.
5. Responsibilities are assigned and work is underway.
6. The DoC and operating unit enterprise architecture web pages are updated periodically and are used to document architecture deliverables.
7. IT security architecture has defined clear roles and responsibilities.
8. Governance of a few architectural standards and some adherence to existing Standards Profile.
9. Little or no formal governance of IT investment and acquisition strategy. Operating unit demonstrates some adherence to existing Standards Profile.

等级 0：无

没有 Enterprise Architecture 项目群。没有提到 Enterprise Architecture。

等级 1：初始级

非正式的 Enterprise Architecture 流程正在进行中。

1. 流程是随意的和局部化的。一些 Enterprise Architecture 流程已被定义。没有跨技术或业务流程的统一架构流程。成功取决于个人努力。
2. 通过各种随意的手段建立 Enterprise Architecture 流程、文件和标准，它们是局部化或非正式的。
3. 与业务战略或业务驱动因素的联系很弱或没有显性化。
4. 管理团队在架构流程中的认识或参与程度很有限。
5. 架构运行组织对 Enterprise Architecture 流程的接受度很有限。
6. 架构运行组织 Enterprise Architecture 文件的最新版本公布在网上。几乎没有关于 Enterprise Architecture 流程和可能的流程改进的沟通。
7. IT 安保性考量因素是随意的和局部化的。
8. 没有对架构标准的明确管控。
9. 战略规划和采办人员很少参与或不参与 Enterprise Architecture 流程。几乎或完全不遵守现有标准。

等级 2：开发中

Enterprise Architecture 流程正在开发中。

1. 基于 OMB Circular A-130 和美国商务部 Enterprise Architecture 引导将基本的 Enterprise Architecture 流程文件化。架构流程已经形成了明确的角色和职责。
2. IT 愿景、原则、业务联系、基线和目标架构已被确定。存在架构标准，但不一定与目标架构有联系。建立技术参考模型（TRM）和标准概要框架。
3. 与业务战略明确联系。
4. 架构工作的管理意识。
5. 职责已被指派且工作正在进行。
6. DoC 和架构运行组织的 Enterprise Architecture 网页被定期更新并用于记录架构交付物。
7. IT 安保架构已经定义了明确的角色和职责。
8. 对少数架构标准进行管控，并部分遵守现有的标准文件。
9. 很少或根本没有对 IT 投资和采办策略进行正式管控。架构运行组织验证是否一定程度遵守现有标准概要。

Level 3: Defined

Defined enterprise architecture including detailed written procedures and TRM.

1. The architecture is well defined and communicated to IT staff and business management with operating unit IT responsibilities. The process is largely followed.
2. Gap analysis and Migration Plan are completed. Fully developed TRM and Standards Profile. IT goals and methods are identified.
3. Enterprise architecture is integrated with capital planning and investment control.
4. Senior management team aware of and supportive of the enterprise-wide architecture process. Management actively supports architectural standards.
5. Most elements of operating unit show acceptance of or are actively participating in the enterprise architecture process.
6. Architecture documents updated regularly on DoC enterprise architecture web page.
7. IT security architecture Standards Profile is fully developed and is integrated with enterprise architecture.
8. Explicit documented governance of majority of IT investments.
9. IT acquisition strategy exists and includes compliance measures to IT enterprise architecture. Cost benefits are considered in identifying projects.

Level 4: Managed

Managed and measured enterprise architecture process.

1. Enterprise architecture process is part of the culture. Quality metrics associated with the architecture process are captured.
2. Enterprise architecture documentation is updated on a regular cycle to reflect the updated enterprise architecture. Business, Data, Application, and Technology Architectures defined by appropriate *de jure* and *de facto* standards.
3. Capital planning and investment control are adjusted based on the feedback received and lessons learned from updated enterprise architecture. Periodic re-examination of business drivers.
4. Senior management team directly involved in the architecture review process.
5. The entire operating unit accepts and actively participates in the enterprise architecture process.
6. Architecture documents are updated regularly, and frequently reviewed for latest architecture developments/standards.
7. Performance metrics associated with IT security architecture are captured.
8. Explicit governance of all IT investments. Formal processes for managing variances feed back into enterprise architecture.
9. All planned IT acquisitions and purchases are guided and governed by the enterprise architecture.

等级 3：定义

包括详细书面程序和 TRM 的经过定义的 Enterprise Architecture。

1. 很好地定义了架构，并与具有架构运行组织 IT 职责的 IT 工作人员和业务管理人员沟通此架构且与 IT 人员和业务管理人员沟通过运行 IT 的责任。大体遵循该流程。
2. 完成差距分析和迁移计划。全面开发 TRM 和标准概要。IT 目标和方法被识别。
3. Enterprise Architecture 与资金规划和投资控制整合。
4. 高层管理团队知道并支持整个 ENTERPRISE 范围的架构流程。管理层积极地支持架构标准。
5. 架构运行组织的大部分成员都表示认可或者积极地参与 Enterprise Architecture 流程。
6. 定期在 DoC Enterprise Architecture 网页上更新架构文件。
7. IT 安保架构标准概要被充分开发并与 Enterprise Architecture 集成。
8. 大多数 IT 投资得到清晰且有记录的管控。
9. 存在 IT 采办策略并包括 IT Enterprise Architecture 的合规性检查措施。在识别项目的过程中考虑成本效益。

等级 4：管理

管理并测量了 Enterprise Architecture 流程。

1. Enterprise Architecture 流程是组织文化的一部分。与架构流程相关的质量衡量标准已被获取。
2. 定期更新 Enterprise Architecture 文档，以反映更新后的 Enterprise Architecture。根据适当的合法标准和实际标准定义了业务、数据、应用和技术架构。
3. 基于从更新后的 Enterprise Architecture 中收到的反馈和吸取的教训，调整资金规划和投资控制。定期重新审查业务驱动因素。
4. 高层管理团队直接地参与架构审视流程。
5. 整个架构运行组织接受并积极地参与 Enterprise Architecture 流程。
6. 定期地更新架构文件，并且频繁地对最新的架构开发/标准进行审视。
7. 与 IT 安保架构相关的绩效衡量标准被获取。
8. 所有 IT 投资得到明确地管控。管理差异的正式流程反馈到 Enterprise Architecture 中。
9. 所有计划的 IT 采办和采购都由 Enterprise Architecture 指导和管控。

Level 5: Optimizing

Continuous improvement of enterprise architecture process.

1. Concerted efforts to optimize and continuously improve architecture process.
2. A standards and waivers process is used to improve architecture development process.
3. Architecture process metrics are used to optimize and drive business linkages. Business involved in the continuous process improvements of enterprise architecture.
4. Senior management involvement in optimizing process improvements in architecture development and governance.
5. Feedback on architecture process from all operating unit elements is used to drive architecture process improvements.
6. Architecture documents are used by every decision-maker in the organization for every IT- related business decision.
7. Feedback from IT security architecture metrics are used to drive architecture process improvements.
8. Explicit governance of all IT investments. A standards and waivers process is used to make governance-process improvements.
9. No unplanned IT investment or acquisition activity.

51.4 Capability Maturity Models Integration (CMMI)

51.4.1 Introduction

The capability models that the SEI is currently involved in developing, expanding, or maintaining include the following:

- CMMI (Capability Maturity Model Integration)
- IPD-CMM (Integrated Product Development Capability Maturity Model)
- P-CMM (People Capability Maturity Model)
- SA-CMM (Software Acquisition Capability Maturity Model)
- SE-CMM (Systems Engineering Capability Maturity Model)
- SW-CMM (Capability Maturity Model for Software)

As explained in this chapter, in recent years the industry has witnessed significant growth in the area of maturity models. The multiplicity of models available has led to problems of its own, in terms of how to integrate all the different models to produce a meaningful metric for overall process maturity.

In response to this need, the SEI has developed a Framework called Capability Maturity ModelIntegration (CMMI), to provide a means of managing the complexity.

According to the SEI, the use of the CMMI models improves on the best practices of previous models in many important ways, in particular enabling organizations to:

- More explicitly link management and engineering activities to business objec-tives.

等级 5：优化

Enterprise Architecture 流程的持续改进。

1. 共同努力，以优化并连续改善架构流程。
2. 利用标准和豁免流程改善架构开发流程。
3. 利用架构流程衡量标准优化并驱动业务联系。业务包含在 Enterprise Architecture 的持续流程改进中。
4. 高级管理层参与优化架构开发和管控的流程改进。
5. 利用来自所有架构运行组织成员的架构流程反馈来驱动架构流程改进。
6. 组织中的每个决策者都利用架构文件做出每个 IT 相关业务决策。
7. 利用对 IT 安保架构衡量标准的反馈驱动架构流程改进。
8. 所有 IT 投资得到明确管控。利用标准和豁免流程进行管控流程的改进。
9. 没有未计划的 IT 投资或采办活动。

51.4 能力成熟度模型综合（CMMI）

51.4.1 简介

SEI 目前在开发、扩展或维护中涉及的能力模型包括：

- CMMI（能力成熟度模型综合）
- IPD-CMM（集成产品开发能力成熟度模型）
- P-CMM（人力资源能力成熟度模型）
- SA-CMM（软件采办能力成熟度模型）
- SE-CMM（系统工程能力成熟度模型）
- SW-CMM（软件能力成熟度模型）

正如本章所阐述的，近年来，业界已经见证了成熟度模型领域的显著增长。在如何集成所有不同模型以产生整个流程成熟度的衡量标准方面，多样化的可用模型都有其自身的问题。

根据这种需求，SEI 已经开发了称为能力成熟度模型综合（CMMI）的框架，从而提供一种管理复杂性的方式。

按照 SEI，CMMI 模型的使用可以在很多重要方面改善之前模型的最佳实践，特别是使组织能：

- 更加明确地将管理和工程活动联系到业务目的。

- Expand the scope of and visibility into the product lifecycle and engineering activities to ensure that the product or service meets customer expectations.
- Incorporate lessons learned from additional areas of best practice (e.g., measurement, risk management, and supplier management).
- Implement more robust high-maturity practices.
- Address additional organizational functions critical to its products and services.
- More fully comply with relevant ISO standards.

CMMI is being adopted worldwide.

51.4.2 SCAMPI Method

The Standard CMMI Appraisal Method for Process Improvement (SCAMPI) is the appraisal method associated with CMMI. The SCAMPI appraisal method is used to identify strengths, weaknesses, and ratings relative to CMMI reference models. It incorporates best practices found successful in the appraisal community, and is based on the features of several legacy appraisal methods. It is applicable to a wide range of appraisal usage modes, including both internal process improvement and external capability determinations.

The SCAMPI method definition document[17] describes the requirements, activities, and practices associated with each of the processes that compose the SCAMPI method.

51.5 Conclusions

This section has sought to introduce into TOGAF the topic of CMM-based methods and techniques for use in relation to enterprise architecture.

The benefits of using CMMs are well documented. Future versions of TOGAF may include a maturity model to measure adoption of TOGAF itself.

17. Available at www.sei.cmu.edu/publications/documents/01.reports/01hb001.html.

- 将范围和可视性扩展进产品的生命周期和工程活动中，以确保产品或服务达到客户期望。
- 从最佳实践的其他方面（如测量、风险管理和供应商管理）中获取教训。
- 实施更健壮的高成熟度实践。
- 提出对于其产品和服务关键的附加组织功能。
- 更全面地符合有关的 ISO 标准。

CMMI 在全球范围内被采用。

51.4.2 SCAMPI 方法

标准 CMMI 流程改进评价方法（SCAMPI）是与 CMMI 相关的评价方法。SCAMPI 评价方法用于识别与 CMMI 参考模型有关的优势、劣势及等级。这种评价方法结合被发现在评价团体方面取得成功的最佳实践，并以若干已有评价方法的特征为基础。它适用于各式各样的评价使用方式。它广泛适用于各类评价使用方式，包括内部流程改进和外部能力测定。

SCAMPI 方法定义文件[17]描述与构成 SCAMPI 方法的各个流程中的每个流程相关的需求、活动和实践。

51.5 结论

本节试图将有关 Enterprise Architecture 使用的基于 CMM 的方法和技术的主题引入 TOGAF。

使用 CMM 的好处已被很好地文件化。TOGAF 的未来版本可能包括衡量 TOGAF 本身采用情况的成熟度模型。

17. 详情可登录：www.sei.cmu.edu/publications/documents/01.reports/01hb001.html。

Chapter 52
Architecture Skills Framework

This chapter provides a set of role, skill, and experience norms for staff undertaking enterprise architecture work.

52.1 Introduction

Skills frameworks provide a view of the competency levels required for specific roles. They define:

- The roles within a work area
- The skills required by each role
- The depth of knowledge required to fulfil the role successfully

They are relatively common for defining the skills required for a consultancy and/or project management assignment, to deliver a specific project or work package. They are also widely used by recruitment and search agencies to match candidates and roles.

Their value derives from their ability to provide a means of rapidly identifying skill matches and gaps. Successfully applied, they can ensure that candidates are fit for the jobs assigned to them.

Their value in the context of enterprise architecture arises from the immaturity of the enterprise architecture discipline, and the problems that arise from this.

52.2 Need for an Enterprise Architecture Skills Framework

52.2.1 Definitional Rigor

"Enterprise Architecture" and "Enterprise Architect" are widely used but poorly defined terms in industry today. They are used to denote a variety of practices and skills applied in a wide variety of architecture domains. There is a need for better classification to enable more implicit understanding of what type of architecture/ architect is being described.

This lack of uniformity leads to difficulties for organizations seeking to recruit or assign/promote staff to fill positions in the architecture field. Because of the different usages of terms, there is often misunderstanding and miscommunication between those seeking to recruit for, and those seeking to fill, the various roles of the architect.

第 52 章 架构技能框架

本章为承担 Enterprise Architecture 工作的人员提供一套角色、技能和经验规范。

52.1 简介

技能框架提供特定角色需要的能力层级视图。其定义：

- 在工作区域内的角色
- 每个角色所需的技能
- 成功履行角色所需的知识深度

技能框架对定义咨询机构和/或项目管理层指派工作以交付特定项目或工作包所需的技能而言相对普遍，还被招聘和猎头机构广泛地用于对比候选人和角色。

技能框架的价值源于一种能够提供快速识别技能匹配度和差距的方式的能力。成功应用后，它们可以确保候选人胜任指派给他们的工作。

技能架构在 Enterprise Architecture 背景环境中的价值，起因于 Enterprise Architecture 修炼的不成熟以及这种不成熟所引起的问题。

52.2 对 Enterprise Architecture 技能框架的需要

52.2.1 定义的严密性

“Enterprise Architecture”和“ENTERPRISE 架构师”在当今业界被广泛应用，但一直未能很好地定义。它们常用来表示各种架构领域中所应用的各种实践和技能。这些实践或技能需要进行更好的分类，以便能够更精准地理解正在描述什么类型的架构/或架构师。

由于缺乏这种一致的定义，组织在招聘或指派/晋升职员以填补架构领域职位时，往往存在一些困难。由于对术语的使用不同，不当的沟通和误解往往存在于那些希望招聘架构师的组织和那些希望担任架构师的应聘者之间。

52.2.2 Basis of an Internal Architecture Practice

Despite the lack of uniform terminology, architecture skills are in increasing demand, as the discipline of architecture gains increasing attention within industry.

Many enterprises have set up, or are considering setting up, an enterprise architecture practice, as a means of fostering development of the necessary skills and experience among in-house staff to undertake the various architecting tasks required by the enterprise.

An enterprise architecture practice is a formal program of development and certifi-cation, by which an enterprise formally recognizes the skills of its practicing architects, as demonstrated by their work. Such a program is essential in order to ensure the alignment of staff skills and experience with the architecture tasks that the enterprise wishes to be performed.

The role and skill definitions on which such a program needs to be based are also required, by both recruiting and supplying organizations, in cases where external personnel are to be engaged to perform architecture work (for example, as part of a consultancy engagement).

An enterprise architecture practice is both difficult and costly to set up. It is normally built around a process of peer review, and involves the time and talent of the strategic technical leadership of an enterprise. Typically it involves establishment of a peer review board, and documentation of the process, and of the requirements for internal certification. Time is also required of candidates to prepare for peer review, by creating a portfolio of their work to demonstrate their skills, experiences, and contri-butions to the profession.

The TOGAF Architecture Skills Framework attempts to address this need by providing definitions of the architecting skills and proficiency levels required of personnel, internal or external, who are to perform the various architecting roles defined within the TOGAF Framework.

Because of the complexity, time, and cost involved, many enterprises do not have an internal enterprise architect certification program, preferring instead to simply interview and recruit architecture staff on an *ad hoc* basis. There are serious risks associated with this approach:

- Communication between recruiting organizations, consultancies, and employment agencies is very difficult.
- Time is wasted interviewing staff who may have applied in all good faith, but still lack the skills and/or experience required by the employer.
- Staff that are capable of filling architecture roles may be overlooked, or may not identify themselves with advertised positions and hence not even apply.
- There is increased risk of unsuitable personnel being employed or engaged, through no-one's fault, and despite everyone involved acting in good faith. This in turn can:
  - Increase personnel costs, through the need to rehire or reassign staff.
  - Adversely impact the time, cost, and quality of operational IT systems, and the projects that deliver them.

52.2.2 内部架构实践的基础

尽管缺乏一致的术语，但随着架构修炼在业界获得越来越多的关注，对架构技能的需要也越来越多。

很多ENTERPRISE已经开始或者正在考虑开始建立一项Enterprise Architecture实践，作为在内部员工之间促进承担ENTERPRISE所需不同架构开发任务的必备技能和经验发展的方式。

Enterprise Architecture实践是开发和认证的正式计划，通过该计划，ENTERPRISE可正式地根据实践架构师的工作表现认可其技能。为了确保员工的技能及经验与ENTERPRISE希望执行的架构任务协调一致，这种计划是根本性的。

在外部人员必须参与执行架构工作（例如，作为咨询工作的一部分介入）的情况下，该计划需要作为基础的角色和技能定义是招聘和劳动力供给组织所需的。

Enterprise Architecture实践不仅很难建立，而且成本很高。其通常围绕同级审视流程所建立，而且包括ENTERPRISE战略技术领导的时间和才能。典型情况下，它包括同级审视委员会的建立、流程的文件化以及对内部认证需求的文件化。候选人还需要时间通过创建工作项目谱系的方式为同级审视做准备，以表明他们的技能、经验以及对该职业的贡献。

TOGAF架构技能框架试图通过对在TOGAF框架之内定义的各类架构开发角色的人员（包括内部或外部的）所需的架构技能和熟练程度的水平提供定义来应对该需求。

考虑到复杂性、时间及成本，很多ENTERPRISE并没有内部ENTERPRISE架构师认证计划，反而更倾向于临时面试和招聘架构员工的方式。与该实施途径相关的严重风险有：

- 招聘组织、咨询机构和职业介绍所之间的沟通极其困难。
- 将时间浪费在面试那些可能已经真诚地提出请求但仍然缺乏雇主所需技能和/或经验的员工上。
- 有能力担任架构角色的人员可能被忽视，或由于认为自己可能不能从事所招聘的职位而没有提出申请。
- 尽管每个人都在努力地工作，即便没有个人过失，还是会增加正在雇佣或雇用不当工作人员的风险。相应地可能：
  - 由于需要重新雇用或重新任命职员，增加人事成本。
  - 对运行IT系统的时间、成本和质量以及交付系统的项目产生不利影响。

52.3 Goals/Rationale

52.3.1 Certification of Enterprise Architects

The main purpose behind an enterprise setting up an internal enterprise architect certification program is two-fold:

1. To formally recognize the skill of its practicing architects, as part of the task of establishing and maintaining a professional architecting organization.
2. To ensure the alignment of necessary staff skills and experience with the architecture tasks that the enterprise wishes to be performed, whether these are to be performed internally to the enterprise or externally; for example, as part of a consultancy engagement.

52.3.2 Specific Benefits

Specific benefits anticipated from use of the TOGAF Architecture Skills Framework include:

- Reduced time, cost, and risk in training, hiring, and managing architecture professionals, both internal and external:
  - Simplifies communication between recruiting organizations, consultancies, and employment agencies.
  - Avoids wasting time interviewing staff who may have applied in all good faith, but still lack the skills and/or experience required by the employer.
  - Avoids staff who are capable of filling architecture roles being overlooked, or not identifying themselves with advertised positions and hence not even applying.
- Reduced time and cost to set up an internal architecture practice:
  - Many enterprises do not have an internal architecture practice due to the complexity involved in setting one up, preferring instead to simply interview and recruit architecture staff on an *ad hoc* basis.
  - By providing definitions of the architecting skills and proficiency levels required of personnel who are to perform the various architecting roles defined within TOGAF, the Architecture Skills Framework greatly reduces the time, cost, and risk of setting up a practice for the first time, and avoids "re-inventing wheels".
  - Enterprises that already have an internal architecture practice are able to set enterprise-wide norms, but still experience difficulties as outlined above in recruiting staff, or engaging consultants, from external sources, due to the lack of uniformity between different enterprises. By aligning its existing skills framework with the industry-accepted definitions provided by The Open Group, an enterprise can greatly simplify these problems.
- Reduced time and cost to implement an architecture practice helps reduce the time, cost, and risk of overall solution development:
  - Enterprises that do not have an internal architecture practice run the risk of unsuitable personnel being employed or engaged, through no-one's fault, and despite everyone involved acting in good faith. The resultant time and cost penalties far outweigh the time and cost of having an internal architecture practice:

52.3 目标/理由依据

52.3.1 ENTERPRISE 架构师的认证

ENTERPRISE 建立一个内部的 ENTERPRISE 架构师认证项目群背后的主要意图有两个方面：

1. 为了正式地将架构师的实践技能视为建立和维护职业架构开发组织这项任务的一部分。
2. 为了确保员工的必备技能和经验与 ENTERPRISE 希望执行的架构任务协调一致，不管这些任务是在 ENTERPRISE 内部还是外部执行；例如，作为咨询工作的一部分介入。

52.3.2 具体益处

期望从 TOGAF 架构技能框架的使用中得到的具体益处包括：

- 缩短培训、雇用和管理内部及外部架构职业人员的时间，并降低成本和风险：
  - 简化招聘组织、咨询机构和招聘中介之间的沟通。
  - 避免将时间浪费在面试那些可能已经真诚地提出申请但仍然缺乏雇主所需技能和/或经验的员工上。
  - 避免有能力担任架构角色的人员被忽视，或由于认为自己可能不能从事所招聘的职位，没有提出申请的人员。
- 缩短建立内部架构实践的时间并降低成本：
  - 考虑到建立架构实践的复杂性，很多 ENTERPRISE 并未建立内部架构实践，反而更倾向于临时面试和招聘架构员工。
  - 通过提供履行在 TOGAF 之内定义的不同架构开发角色的员工所需架构开发技能和熟练程度的定义，架构技能框架极大地缩短了首次建立实践的时间，并降低了成本和风险，避免“多此一举”。
  - 已经具有内部架构实践的 ENTERPRISE 能设定整个 ENTERPRISE 范围的规范，但由于不同 ENTERPRISE 间缺乏一致性，其在招聘员工或雇用顾问等方面仍然面临着由外部来源或与经验的难题。通过使其现有技能框架与 The Open Group 提供的行业认可的定义协调一致，ENTERPRISE 可以极大地简化这些问题。
- 缩短实施架构实践的时间并降低成本，有助于缩短总体解决方案开发的时间并降低成本及风险。
  - 没有内部架构实践的 ENTERPRISE，尽管每个人都在努力地工作，即便没有个人过失还是会增加正在雇佣或雇用不当工作人员的风险。最终的时间和成本损失远远超过具有内部架构实践的 ENTERPRISE 的时间和成本：

  — Personnel costs are increased, through the occasional need to rehire or reassign staff.
  — Even more important is the adverse impact on the time, cost, and quality of operational IT systems, and the projects to deliver them, resulting from poor staff assignments.

52.4 Enterprise Architecture Role and Skill Categories

52.4.1 Overview

This section describes the role of an enterprise architect, the fundamental skills required, and some possible disciplines in which an enterprise architect might specialize.

TOGAF delivers an enterprise architecture, and therefore requires both business and IT-trained professionals to develop the enterprise architecture.

The TOGAF Architecture Skills Framework provides a view of the competency levels for specific roles within the enterprise architecture team. The Framework defines:

- The roles within an enterprise architecture work area
- The skills required by those roles
- The depth of knowledge required to fulfil each role successfully

The value is in providing a rapid means of identifying skills and gaps. Successfully applied, the Framework can be used as a measure for:

- Staff development
- Ensuring that the right person does the right job

52.4.2 TOGAF Roles

A typical architecture team undertaking the development of an enterprise architecture as described in TOGAF would comprise the following roles:

- Architecture Board Members
- Architecture Sponsor
- Architecture Manager
- Architects for:
  — Enterprise Architecture (which for the purpose of the tables shown below can be considered as a superset of Business, Data, Application, and Technology Architecture)
  — Business Architecture
  — Data Architecture
  — Application Architecture
  — Technology Architecture

— 由于偶尔需要重新雇用或重新任命员工，人事成本会不断增加。

— 更重要的是，对运行 IT 系统的时间、成本和质量以及交付这些系统的项目产生不利影响，造成人员指派效果欠佳。

52.4 Enterprise Architecture 角色和技能类别

52.4.1 概述

本节描述 ENTERPRISE 架构师的角色、所需基础技能及 ENTERPRISE 架构师可能专门研究的一些可能的规程。

TOGAF 交付 Enterprise Architecture，因此需要受过业务和 IT 培训的职业人员来开发 Enterprise Architecture。

TOGAF 架构技能框架为 Enterprise Architecture 团队之内的特殊角色提供资格层级视图。该框架定义：

- 在 Enterprise Architecture 工作领域之内的角色
- 这些角色需要的技能
- 成功履行每个角色所需的知识深度

价值在于提供一种快速识别技能和差距的方式。成功应用后，可以用该框架衡量：

- 员工发展
- 确保合适的人做合适的工作

52.4.2 TOGAF 角色

承担如 TOGAF 所述 Enterprise Architecture 的开发工作的典型架构团队包括下述角色：

- 架构委员会成员
- 架构发起人
- 架构经理
- 以下几个方面的架构师：
  - — Enterprise Architecture（适用于下述表格的架构可被视为业务架构、数据架构、应用架构和技术架构的扩展集）
  - — 业务架构
  - — 数据架构
  - — 应用架构
  - — 技术架构

- Program and/or Project Managers
- IT Designer
- And many others ...

The tables that follow show, for each of these roles, the skills required and the desirable level of proficiency in each skill.

Of all the roles listed above, the one that needs particularly detailed analysis and definition is of course the central role of enterprise architect. As explained above, "Enterprise Architecture" and "Enterprise Architect" are terms that are very widely used but very poorly defined in industry today, denoting a wide variety of practices and skills applied in a wide variety of architecture domains. There is often confusion between the role of an architect and that of a designer or builder. Many of the skills required by an enterprise architect are also required by the designer, who delivers the solutions. While their skills are complementary, those of the designer are primarily technology focused and translate the architecture into deliverable components.

The final subsection below therefore explores in some detail the generic characteristics of the role of enterprise architect, and the key skill requirements, whatever the particular architecture domain (Enterprise Architecture, Business Architecture, Data Architecture, Application Architecture, Technology Architecture, etc.).

52.4.3 Categories of Skills

The TOGAF team skill set will need to include the following main categories of skills:

- **Generic Skills**: — typically comprising leadership, teamworking, interpersonal skills, etc.
- **Business Skills & Methods**: — typically comprising business cases, business process, strategic planning, etc.
- **Enterprise Architecture Skills**: — typically comprising modeling, building block design, applications and role design, systems integration, etc.
- **Program or Project Management Skills**: — typically comprising managing business change, project management methods and tools, etc.
- **IT General Knowledge Skills**: — typically comprising brokering applications, asset management, migration planning, SLAs, etc.
- **Technical IT Skills**: — typically comprising software engineering, security, data interchange, data management, etc.
- **Legal Environment**: — typically comprising data protection laws, contract law, procurement law, fraud, etc.

The tables that follow illustrate each of these categories of skills.

The tables that follow show, for each of these skills, the roles to which they are relevant and the desirable level of proficiency in each skill.

- 项目群和/或项目经理
- IT 设计师
- 其他

下述表格示出这些角色中的每个角色所需的技能及对每项技能的理想熟练程度。

在上面列出的所有角色中，需要特殊详细分析和定义的当然是 ENTERPRISE 架构师的核心角色。如上所述，“Enterprise Architecture”和“ENTERPRISE 架构师”是当今广泛使用但在行业中未能很好地定义的术语，这表明在多种多样的架构领域中应用的各种各样的实践和技能。经常会将架构师的角色与设计师或建造者的角色混淆。交付解决方案的设计师也需要 ENTERPRISE 架构师所需的许多技能。尽管他们的技能是互补的，但设计师主要关注技术，并将架构转化成可交付组件。

因此，下面最后一个小节较详细地探究了 ENTERPRISE 架构师角色的一般特性和关键的技能需求，不管属于哪种特殊架构领域（Enterprise Architecture、业务架构、数据架构、应用架构、技术架构等）。

52.4.3 技能类别

TOGAF 团队技能集需要包括如下主要技能类别：

- **一般技能**：通常包括领导能力、团队合作、人际关系技能等。
- **业务技能与方法**：通常包括业务案例、业务流程、战略规划等。
- **Enterprise Architecture 技能**：通常包括建模、构建块设计、应用和角色设计、系统集成等。
- **项目群或项目管理技能**：通常包括管理业务变更、项目管理方法和工具等。
- **IT 常识技能**：通常包括代理应用、资产管理、迁移规划、SLA 等。
- **技术类 IT 技能**：通常包括软件工程、安保、数据交换、数据管理等。
- **法律环境**：通常包括数据保护法、合同法、采购法、反欺诈法等。

下述表格阐明这些技能类别中的每一类。

下述表格针对每种技能显示出了与这些技能相关的角色以及每项技能的理想熟练程度。

52.4.4 Proficiency Levels

The TOGAF Architecture Skills Framework identifies four levels of knowledge or proficiency in any area:

Level	Achievement	Description
1	Background	Not a required skill, though should be able to define and manage skill if required
2	Awareness	Understands the background, issues, and implications sufficiently to be able to understand how to proceed further and advise client accordingly
3	Knowledge	Detailed knowledge of subject area and capable of providing professional advice and guidance. Ability to integrate capability into architecture design
4	Expert	Extensive and substantial practical experience and applied knowledge on the subject

52.5 Enterprise Architecture Role and Skill Definitions

52.5.1 Generic Skills

Roles	Architecture Board Member	Architecture Sponsor	Enterprise Architecture Manager	Enterprise Architecture Technology	Enterprise Architecture Data	Enterprise Architecture Applications	Enterprise Architecture Business	Program/ Project Manager	IT Designer
Generic Skills									
Leadership	4	4	4	3	3	3	3	4	1
Teamwork	3	3	4	4	4	4	4	4	2
Interpersonal	4	4	4	4	4	4	4	4	2
Oral Communications	3	3	4	4	4	4	4	4	2
Written Communications	3	3	4	4	4	4	4	3	3
LogicalAnalysis	2	2	4	4	4	4	4	3	3
Stakeholder Management	4	3	4	3	3	3	3	4	2
Risk Management	3	3	4	3	3	3	3	4	1

52.4.4 熟练程度

TOGAF 架构技能框架识别在任何领域中 4 个层级的知识或熟练程度：

层级	成绩	描述
1	背景	当需要时应能够定义和管理技能，但不是必需的技能
2	认识	理解背景、议题和含义，从而足以能够理解如何进一步继续进行，并就此向客户提供建议
3	知识	关于主题领域的详细知识及能提供专业建议和引导。将能力集成到架构设计中的能力
4	专家	关于这一主题的广泛大量实践经验和应用知识

52.5 Enterprise Architecture 角色和技能定义

52.5.1 一般技能

角色	架构委员会成员	架构发起人	Enterprise Architecture 管理者	Enterprise Architecture 技术架构师	Enterprise Architecture 数据架构师	Enterprise Architecture 应用架构师	Enterprise Architecture 业务架构师	项目群/项目经理	IT 设计师
一般技能									
领导能力	4	4	4	3	3	3	3	4	1
团队合作	3	3	4	4	4	4	4	4	2
人际关系	4	4	4	4	4	4	4	4	2
口头沟通	3	3	4	4	4	4	4	4	2
书面沟通	3	3	4	4	4	4	4	3	3
逻辑分析	2	2	4	4	4	4	4	3	3
利益攸关者管理	4	3	4	3	3	3	3	4	2
风险管理	3	3	4	3	3	3	3	4	1

52.5.2 Business Skills & Methods

Roles	Architecture Board Member	Architecture Sponsor	Enterprise Architecture Manager	Enterprise Architecture Technology	Enterprise Architecture Data	Enterprise Architecture Applications	Enterprise Architecture Business	Program/ Project Manager	IT Designer
Business Skills & Methods									
Business Case	3	4	4	4	4	4	4	4	2
Business Scenario	2	3	4	4	4	4	4	3	2
Organization	3	3	4	3	3	3	4	3	2
Business Process	3	3	4	4	4	4	4	3	2
Strategic Planning	2	3	3	3	3	3	4	3	1
Budget Management	3	3	3	3	3	3	3	4	3
Visioning	3	3	4	3	3	3	4	3	2
Business Metrics	3	4	4	4	4	4	4	4	3
Business Culture	4	4	4	3	3	3	3	3	1
Legacy Investments	4	4	3	2	2	2	2	3	2
Business Functions	3	3	3	3	4	4	4	3	2

52.5.3 Enterprise Architecture Skills

Roles	Architecture Board Member	Architecture Sponsor	Enterprise Architecture Manager	Enterprise Architecture Technology	Enterprise Architecture Data	Enterprise Architecture Applications	Enterprise Architecture Business	Program/ Project Manager	IT Designer
Enterprise Architecture Skills									
Business Modeling	2	2	4	3	3	4	4	2	2
Business Process Design	1	1	4	3	3	4	4	2	2
Role Design	2	2	4	3	3	4	4	2	2
Organization Design	2	2	4	3	3	4	4	2	2
Data Design	1	1	3	3	4	3	3	2	3
Application Design	1	1	3	3	3	4	3	2	3
Systems Integration	1	1	4	4	3	3	3	2	2
IT Industry Standards	1	1	4	4	4	4	3	2	3
Services Design	2	2	4	4	3	4	3	2	2
Architecture Principles Design	2	2	4	4	4	4	4	2	2
Architecture Views & Viewpoints Design	2	2	4	4	4	4	4	2	2
Building Block Design	1	1	4	4	4	4	4	2	3
Solutions Modeling		1	4	4	4	4	4	2	3
Benefits Analysis	2	2	4	4	4	4	4	4	2
Business Interworking	3	3	4	3	3	4	4	3	1
Systems Behavior	1	1	4	4	4	4	3	3	2
Project Management	1	1	3	3	3	3	3	4	2

52.5.2 业务技能与方法

角色	架构委员会成员	架构发起人	Enterprise Architecture 管理者	Enterprise Architecture 技术架构师	Enterprise Architecture 数据架构师	Enterprise Architecture 应用架构师	Enterprise Architecture 业务架构师	项目群/项目经理	IT 设计师
业务技能与方法									
业务案例	3	4	4	4	4	4	4	4	2
业务场景	2	3	4	4	4	4	4	3	2
组织	3	3	4	3	3	3	4	3	2
业务流程	3	3	4	4	4	4	4	3	2
战略规划	2	3	3	3	3	3	4	3	1
预算管理	3	3	3	3	3	3	3	4	3
愿景	3	3	4	3	3	3	4	3	2
业务衡量标准	3	4	4	4	4	4	4	4	3
业务文化	4	4	4	3	3	3	3	3	1
已有投资	4	4	3	2	2	2	2	3	2
业务功能	3	3	3	3	4	4	4	3	2

52.5.3 Enterprise Architecture 技能

角色	架构委员会成员	架构发起人	Enterprise Architecture 管理者	Enterprise Architecture 技术架构师	Enterprise Architecture 数据架构师	Enterprise Architecture 应用架构师	Enterprise Architecture 业务架构师	项目群/项目经理	IT 设计师
Enterprise Architecture 技能									
业务建模	2	2	4	3	3	4	4	2	2
业务流程设计	1	1	4	3	3	4	4	2	2
角色设计	2	2	4	3	3	4	4	2	2
组织设计	2	2	4	3	3	4	4	2	2
数据设计	1	1	3	3	4	3	3	2	3
应用设计	1	1	3	3	3	4	3	2	3
系统集成	1	1	4	4	3	3	3	2	2
IT 行业标准	1	1	4	4	4	4	3	2	3
服务设计	2	2	4	4	3	4	3	2	2
架构原则设计	2	2	4	4	4	4	4	2	2
架构视图&视角设计	2	2	4	4	4	4	4	2	2
构建块设计	1	1	4	4	4	4	4	2	3
解决方案建模	1	1	4	4	4	4	4	2	3
效益分析	2	2	4	4	4	4	4	4	2
业务互通	3	3	4	3	3	4	4	3	1
系统行为	1	1	4	4	4	4	3	3	2
项目管理	1	1	3	3	3	3	3	4	2

52.5.4 Program or Project Management Skills

Roles	Architecture Board Member	Architecture Sponsor	Enterprise Architecture Manager	Enterprise Architecture Technology	Enterprise Architecture Data	Enterprise Architecture Applications	Enterprise Architecture Business	Program/ Project Manager	IT Designer
Program or Project Management Skills									
Program Management	1	2	3	3	3	3	3	4	2
Project Management	1	2	3	3	3	3	3	4	2
Managing Business Change	3	3	4	3	3	3	4	4	2
Change Management	3	3	4	3	3	3	4	3	2
Value Management	4	4	4	3	3	3	4	3	2

52.5.5 IT General Knowledge Skills

Roles	Architecture Board Member	Architecture Sponsor	Enterprise Architecture Manager	Enterprise Architecture Technology	Enterprise Architecture Data	Enterprise Architecture Applications	Enterprise Architecture Business	Program/ Project Manager	IT Designer
IT General Knowledge Skills									
IT Application Development Methodologies & Tools	2	2	3	4	4	4	2	3	3
Programming Languages	1	1	3	4	4	4	3	2	3
Brokering Applications	1	1	3	3	4	4	3	2	3
Information Consumer Applications	1	1	3	3	4	4	3	2	3
Information Provider Applications	1	1	3	3	4	4	3	2	3
Storage Management	1	1	3	4	4	2	2	2	3
Networks	1	1	3	4	3	2	2	2	3
Web-based Services	1	1	3	3	4	4	2	2	3
IT Infrastructure	1	1	3	4	3	2	2	2	3
Asset Management	1	1	4	4	3	3	3	2	3
Service Level Agreements	1	1	4	4	3	4	3	2	3
Systems	1	1	3	4	3	3	2	2	3
COTS	1	1	3	4	3	4	2	2	3
Enterprise Continuums	1	1	4	4	4	4	4	2	3
Migration Planning	1	1	4	3	4	3	3	2	3
Management Utilities	1	1	3	2	4	4	2	2	3
Infrastructure	1	1	3	4	3	4	2	2	3

52.5.4 项目群或项目管理技能

角色	架构委员会成员	架构发起人	Enterprise Architecture 管理者	Enterprise Architecture 技术架构师	Enterprise Architecture 数据架构师	Enterprise Architecture 应用架构师	Enterprise Architecture 业务架构师	项目群/项目经理	IT设计师
项目群或项目管理技能									
项目群管理	1	2	3	3	3	3	3	4	2
项目管理	1	2	3	3	3	3	3	4	2
管理业务变更	3	3	4	3	3	3	4	4	2
变更管理	3	3	4	3	3	3	4	3	2
价值管理	4	4	4	3	3	3	4	3	2

52.5.5 IT 常识技能

角色	架构委员会成员	架构发起人	Enterprise Architecture 管理者	Enterprise Architecture 技术架构师	Enterprise Architecture 数据架构师	Enterprise Architecture 应用架构师	Enterprise Architecture 业务架构师	项目群/项目经理	IT设计师
IT 常识技能									
IT 应用开发方法论与工具	2	2	3	4	4	4	2	3	3
编程语言	1	1	3	4	4	4	3	2	3
代理应用	1	1	3	3	4	4	3	2	3
信息消费者应用	1	1	3	3	4	4	3	2	3
信息提供者应用	1	1	3	3	4	4	3	2	3
存储管理	1	1	3	4	4	2	2	2	3
网络	1	1	3	4	3	2	2	2	3
基于 Web 的服务	1	1	3	3	4	4	2	2	3
IT 基础设施	1	1	3	4	3	2	2	2	3
资产管理	1	1	4	4	3	3	3	2	3
服务水平协议	1	1	4	4	3	4	3	2	3
系统	1	1	3	4	3	3	2	2	3
COTS	1	1	3	4	3	4	2	2	3
ENTERPRISE 的连续统一体	1	1	4	4	4	4	4	2	3
迁移规划	1	1	4	3	4	3	3	2	3
管理实用程序	1	1	3	2	4	4	2	2	3
基础设施	1	1	3	4	3	4	2	2	3

52.5.6 Technical IT Skills

Roles	Architecture Board Member	Architecture Sponsor	Enterprise Architecture Manager	Enterprise Architecture Technology	Enterprise Architecture Data	Enterprise Architecture Applications	Enterprise Architecture Business	Program/ Project Manager	IT Designer
Technical IT Skills									
Software Engineering	1	1	3	3	4	4	3	2	3
Security	1	1	3	4	3	4	3	2	3
Systems & Network Management	1	1	3	4	3	3	3	2	3
Transaction Processing	1	1	3	4	3	4	3	2	3
Location & Directory	1	1	3	4	4	3	3	2	3
User Interface	1	1	3	4	4	4	3	2	3
International Operations	1	1	3	4	3	3	2	2	2
Data Interchange	1	1	3	4	4	3	2	2	3
Data Management	1	1	3	4	4	3	2	2	3
Graphics & Image	1	1	3	4	3	3	2	2	3
Operating System Services	1	1	3	4	3	3	2	2	3
Network Services	1	1	3	4	3	3	2	2	3
Communications Infrastructure	1	1	3	4	3	3	2	2	3

52.5.7 Legal Environment

Roles	Architecture Board Member	Architecture Sponsor	Enterprise Architecture Manager	Enterprise Architecture Technology	Enterprise Architecture Data	Enterprise Architecture Applications	Enterprise Architecture Business	Program/ Project Manager	IT Designer
Legal Environment									
Contract Law	2	2	2	2	2	2	2	3	1
Data Protection Law	3	3	4	3	3	3	3	2	2
Procurement Law	3	2	2	2	2	2	2	4	1
Fraud	3	3	3	3	3	3	3	3	1
Commercial Law	3	3	2	2	2	2	3	3	1

52.5.6 技术类 IT 技能

角色	架构委员会成员	架构发起人	Enterprise Architecture 管理者	Enterprise Architecture 技术架构师	Enterprise Architecture 数据架构师	Enterprise Architecture 应用架构师	Enterprise Architecture 业务架构师	项目群/项目经理	IT 设计师
技术类 IT 技能									
软件工程	1	1	3	3	4	4	3	2	3
安保	1	1	3	4	3	4	3	2	3
系统与网络管理	1	1	3	4	3	3	3	2	3
事务处理	1	1	3	4	3	4	3	2	3
位置与目录	1	1	3	4	4	3	3	2	3
用户界面	1	1	3	4	4	4	3	2	3
国际运营	1	1	3	4	3	3	2	2	2
数据互换	1	1	3	4	4	3	2	2	3
数据管理	1	1	3	4	4	3	2	2	3
图形与图像	1	1	3	4	3	3	2	2	3
操作系统服务	1	1	3	4	3	3	2	2	3
网络服务	1	1	3	4	3	3	2	2	3
通信基础设施	1	1	3	4	3	3	2	2	3

52.5.7 法律环境

角色	架构委员会成员	架构发起人	Enterprise Architecture 管理者	Enterprise Architecture 技术架构师	Enterprise Architecture 数据架构师	Enterprise Architecture 应用架构师	Enterprise Architecture 业务架构师	项目群/项目经理	IT 设计师
法律环境									
合同法	2	2	2	2	2	2	2	3	1
数据保护法	3	3	4	3	3	3	3	2	2
采购法	3	2	2	2	2	2	2	4	1
反欺诈法	3	3	3	3	3	3	3	3	1
商业法	3	3	2	2	2	2	3	3	1

52.6 Generic Role and Skills of the Enterprise Architect

Of all the roles listed above, the one that needs particularly detailed analysis and definition is, of course, the central role of enterprise architect. As explained above, "Enterprise Architecture" and "Enterprise Architect" are terms that are very widely used but very poorly defined in industry today, denoting a wide variety of practices and skills applied in a wide variety of architecture domains.

This section therefore explores in some detail the generic characteristics of the role of enterprise architect, and some key skill requirements, whatever the particular architecture domain (Enterprise Architecture, Business Architecture, Data Architecture, Application Architecture, Technology Architecture, etc.).

52.6.1 Generic Role

Enterprise architects are visionaries, coaches, team leaders, business-to-technical liaisons, computer scientists, and industry experts.

The following is effectively a job description for an enterprise architect:

> "The architect has a responsibility for ensuring the completeness (fitness-for-purpose) of the architecture, in terms of adequately addressing all the pertinent concerns of its stakeholders; and the integrity of the architecture, in terms of connecting all the various views to each other, satisfactorily reconciling the conflicting concerns of different stakeholders, and showing the trade-offs made in so doing (as between security and performance, for example).
>
> The choice of which particular architecture views to develop is one of the key decisions that the enterprise architect has to make. The choice has to be constrained by considerations of practicality, and by the principle of fitness-for-purpose (i.e., the architecture should be developed only to the point at which it is fit-for-purpose, and not reiterated *ad infinitum* as an academic exercise)."

The role of the enterprise architect is more like that of a city planner than that of a building architect, and the product of the enterprise architect is more aptly characterized as a planned community (as opposed to an unconstrained urban sprawl), rather than as a well-designed building or set of buildings.

An enterprise architect does not create the technical vision of the enterprise, but has professional relationships with executives of the enterprise to gather and articulate the technical vision, and to produce the strategic plan for realizing it. This plan is always tied to the business plans of the enterprise, and design decisions are traceable to the business plan.

The strategic plan of the enterprise architect is tied to the architecture governance process (see Chapter 50) for the enterprise, so design decisions are not circumvented for tactical convenience.

The enterprise architect produces documentation of design decisions for application development teams or product implementation teams to execute.

An architect is involved in the entire process; beginning with working with the customer to understand real needs, as opposed to wants, and then throughout the process to translate those needs into capabilities verified to meet the needs. Additionally, the architect may present different models to the customer that commun-icate how those needs may be met, and is therefore an essential participant in the consultative selling process.

However, the architect is not the builder, and must remain at a level of abstraction necessary to ensure that they do not get in the way of practical implementation.

52.6 ENTERPRISE 架构师的一般角色和技能

在上述所有角色中，需要特殊详细分析和定义的当然是 ENTERPRISE 架构师的核心角色。如上所述，“Enterprise Architecture”和“ENTERPRISE 架构师”是在今天广泛使用但在行业中未能很好地定义的术语，表明在多种多样的架构领域中应用的各种各样的实践和技能。

因此，本节较为详细地探究了 ENTERPRISE 架构师角色的一般特性以及一些关键的技能需求，不管是在什么特殊架构领域（Enterprise Architecture、业务架构、数据架构、应用架构、技术架构等）。

52.6.1 一般角色

ENTERPRISE 架构师是有远见的人、教练、团队领导、业务与技术联络人、计算机科学家和行业专家。

下面实际上是一个 ENTERPRISE 架构师的工作描述：

> “架构师有责任充分地应对其利益攸关者的所有相关关注点方面并确保架构的完整性（适用性）；以及在相互连接所有各种视图方面，负责确保架构的完整性，从而按要求协调不同利益攸关者的冲突关注点并表明此举所做的权衡（例如，在安保性和绩效之间做出权衡）。
>
> 选择开发哪些特定架构视图是 ENTERPRISE 架构师必须要做的关键决策之一。选择会受到实用性考量因素和适用性原则的约束（即，仅应在其适用范围开发架构，而不是作为一种学术活动被无止境地反复迭代）。”

ENTERPRISE 架构师的角色与房屋建筑师相比更像是城市规划人员，ENTERPRISE 架构师的产品可被更形象地描述为一个规划的社区（与无约束的城市扩建截然相反），而不是描述为设计完善的建筑或建筑群。

一个 ENTERPRISE 架构师不创建 ENTERPRISE 的技术愿景，但是与 ENTERPRISE 的管理人员具有专业的合作关系，以收集并清晰地表达技术愿景，并为实现该愿景制定战略计划。该计划始终被绑定到 ENTERPRISE 的业务计划，而且设计决策可追溯到业务计划。

ENTERPRISE 架构师的战略计划被绑定到 ENTERPRISE 的架构治理流程（见第 50 章），所以设计决策不可避免地要实现战术上的便利。

ENTERPRISE 架构师制定了需要应用开发团队或产品实施团队执行的设计决策文件。

一个架构师参与整个流程；以与客户合作理解实际需要而不是客户想要的为开始，然后在整个流程中将这些需要转换成经验证满足需要的能力。此外，架构师可以向客户展示不同的模型，以沟通如何可能满足这些需求，因此，架构师是协商买卖流程的必需的参与者。

但是，架构师不是建造者，必须保持在一个必要的抽象层级上，以确保不妨碍实际实施。

The following excerpt from *The Art of Systems Architecting* depicts this notion:

"It is the responsibility of the architect to know and concentrate on the critical few details and interfaces that really matter, and not to become overloaded with the rest."

The architect's focus is on understanding what it takes to satisfy the client, where qualitative worth is used more than quantitative measures. The architect uses more inductive skills than the deductive skills of the builder. The architect deals more with guidelines, rather than rules that builders use as a necessity.

It also must be clear that the role of an architect may be performed by an engineer. A goal of this document is to describe the role — what should be done, regardless of who is performing it.

Thus, the role of the architect can be summarized as to:

- **Understand and interpret requirements**: probe for information, listen to information, influence people, facilitate consensus building, synthesize and translate ideas into actionable requirements, articulate those ideas to others. Identify use or purpose, constraints, risks, etc. The architect participates in the discovery and documentation of the customer's business scenarios that are driving the solution. The architect is responsible for requirements understanding and embodies that requirements understanding in the architecture specification.
- **Create a useful model**: take the requirements and develop well-formulated models of the components of the solution, augmenting the models as necessary to fit all of the circumstances. Show multiple views through models to communicate the ideas effectively. The architect is responsible for the overall architecture integrity and maintaining the vision of the offering from an architectural perspective. The architect also ensures leverage opportunities are identified, using building blocks, and is a liaison between the functional groups (especially development and marketing) to ensure that the leverage opportunities are realized. The architect provides and maintains these models as a framework for understanding the domain(s) of development work, guiding what should be done within the organization, or outside the organization. The architect must represent the organization view of the architecture by understanding all the necessary business components.
- **Validate, refine, and expand the model**: verify assumptions, bring in subject matter experts, etc. in order to improve the model and to further define it, adding as necessary new ideas to make the result more flexible and more tightly linked to current and expected requirements. The architect additionally should assess the value of solution-enhancing developments emanating from field work and incorporate these into the architecture models as appropriate.
- **Manage the architecture**: continuously monitor the models and update them as necessary to show changes, additions, and alterations. Represent architecture and issues during development and decision points of the program. The architect is an "agent of change", representing that need for the implementation of the architecture. Through this development cycle, the architect continuously fosters the sharing of customer, architecture, and technical information between organizations.

摘自《系统架构开发的艺术》的下述内容描述了这个概念：

“架构师的职责是了解并关注实际上关系重大但未变得过载的一些关键细节和界面。”

架构师关注于理解满足客户需要什么，哪些方面的定性价值比定量测度使用的更多。架构师使用建造者感应技能比使用推理技能更多。架构师更多的是处理指南，而不是建造者必需使用的规则。

还必须清楚的是，架构师的角色可以由工程师履行。本文件的目标是描述角色，即不管谁去履行和他应完成什么。

因此，可以将架构师的角色总结如下：

- **理解并解释需求**：探寻消息、听取信息、影响人员、促进共识达成、综合各种想法并将这些想法转换成可付诸实施的需求、可将想法清晰地表达给其他人。识别用途或目的、约束、风险等。架构师参与发现和文件化可驱动解决方案的客户业务场景。架构师负责理解需求并在架构规范中体现出对需求的理解。
- **创建有用的模型**：考虑需求并开发解决方案组件的成熟模型，以按照满足全部环境的需要增加模型。通过有效沟通各种想法的模型展示出多个视图。架构师负责总体架构的完整性并维护从架构关注层面提供的愿景。架构师还确保使用构建块识别进行更好利用的机会，架构师还是两个职能群组（特别是开发和市场）之间的联络员，以确保实现这些进行更好利用的机会。架构师提供并维护这些模型，作为理解开发工作的领域，指导在组织内部和外部应做什么样的框架。架构师必须通过理解所有必要业务组件的方式表达架构的组织视图。
- **确认、细化并扩展模型**：假设检验，引进要点问题专家等，以便改善模型和进一步定义模型，必要时需添加一些新想法，使结果更灵活且与当前需求和预期需求的联系更紧密。此外，架构师应评估源于现场工作的增强解决方案开发的价值，并根据具体情况将这些并入架构模型中。
- **管理架构**：连续监控模型，并在必要时更新模型，以表明变化、附加部分和改动。表示架构、开发期间的问题和项目群决策点。架构师是一个“促成改变的人”，代表架构实施的需要。通过该开发周期，架构师连续推动组织之间的客户、架构和技术信息的共享。

52.6.2 Characterization in Terms of the Enterprise Continuum

Under certain circumstances, the complexity of a solution may require additional architects to support the architecture effort. The different categories of architects are described below, but as they are architects, they all perform the tasks described above. Any combination of enterprise, enterprise solution, and solution architects may be utilized, as a team. In such cases each member may have a specific focus, if not specific roles and responsibilities, within the phases of the development process. In cases where a team of architects is deemed necessary, a lead enterprise architect should be assigned to manage and lead the team members.

- The **Enterprise Architect** has the responsibility for architectural design and documentation at a landscape and technical reference model level. The Enterprise Architect often leads a group of the Segment Architects and/or Solution Architects related to a given program. The focus of the Enterprise Architect is on enterprise-level business functions required.
- The **Segment Architect** has the responsibility for architectural design and documentation of specific business problems or organizations. A Segment Architect re-uses the output from all other architects, joining detailed technical solutions to the overall architectural landscape. The focus of the Segment Architect is on enterprise-level business solutions in a given domain, such as finance, human resources, sales, etc.
- The **Solution Architect** has the responsibility for architectural design and documentation at a system or subsystem level, such as management or security. A Solution Architect may shield the Enterprise/Segment Architect from the unnecessary details of the systems, products, and/or technologies. The focus of the Solution Architect is on system technology solutions; for example, a component of a solution such as enterprise data warehousing.

52.6.3 Key Characteristics of an Enterprise Architect

52.6.3.1 Skills and Experience in Producing Designs

An enterprise architect must be proficient in the techniques that go into producing designs of complex systems, including requirements discovery and analysis, formulation of solution context, identification of solution alternatives and their assessment, technology selection, and design configuration.

52.6.3.2 Extensive Technical Breadth, with Technical Depth in One or a Few Disciplines

An enterprise architect should possess an extensive technical breadth through experience in the IT industry. This breadth should be in areas of application development and deployment, and in the areas of creation and maintenance of the infrastructure to support the complex application environment. Current IT environments are heterogeneous by nature, and the experienced enterprise architect will have skills across multiple platforms, including distributed systems and traditional mainframe environments. Enterprise architects will have, as a result of their careers, skills in at least one discipline that is considered to be at the level of a subject matter expert.

52.6.3.3 Method-Driven Approach to Execution

Enterprise architects approach their job through the consistent use of recognized design methods such as the TOGAF Architecture Development Method (ADM). Enterprise architects should have working knowledge of more than one design method and be comfortable deploying parts of methods appropriate to the situation in which they are working working. This should be seen in the body of design work the enterprise architect has produced through repeated successful use of more than one design method. Proficiency in methodology use is in knowing what parts of methods to use in a given situation, and what methods not to use.

52.6.2 依照 ENTERPRISE 的连续统一体描述特性

在某些情况下，解决方案的复杂性可能需要更多的架构师支持架构工作。对不同类别的架构师描述如下，但因为他们是架构师，他们都履行上述任务。ENTERPRISE、ENTERPRISE 解决方案和解决方案架构师的任何组合形态都可以作为一个团队使用。在此类情况下，如果在开发流程的各个阶段没有特定的角色和职责，则每个成员都可能有一个特定聚焦点。在架构师团队被认为必要的情况下，应指派一个首席 ENTERPRISE 架构师来管理和领导团队成员。

- **ENTERPRISE 架构师**的职责是在一个全景和技术参考模型层级下进行架构设计和文档记录。ENTERPRISE 架构师通常领导一组与给定项目群相关的分部架构师和/或解决方案架构师。ENTERPRISE 架构师关注的是 ENTERPRISE 层级业务功能所需的。
- **分部架构师**的职责是对特定业务问题或组织进行架构设计和文件化。分部架构师复用所有其他架构师的输出，以将详细的技术解决方案加入总体架构全景。分部架构师关注的是在诸如财务、人力资源、销售等给定领域的 ENTERPRISE 层级业务解决方案。
- **解决方案架构师**的职责是在系统或子系统层级，例如管理或安保，进行架构设计和文件化。解决方案架构师可以使 ENTERPRISE/分部架构师避开关于系统、产品和/或技术的不必要细节。解决方案架构师关注的是系统技术解决方案；例如，解决方案（如 ENTERPRISE 数据入库存储）的一个组件。

52.6.3 ENTERPRISE 架构师的主要特点

52.6.3.1 产生设计的技能和经验

ENTERPRISE 架构师必须精通产生复杂系统设计的技巧，包括需求发现和分析、解决方案背景环境的表述、解决方案选项的识别及其评估、技术选择和设计构型。

52.6.3.2 在一个或几个学科中的广泛技术的广度以及技术深度

ENTERPRISE 架构师应通过在 IT 行业的经验拥有广泛的技术广度。该广度应在应用开发和部署的领域内以及基础设施的创建和维护领域内，以支持复杂的应用环境。当前 IT 环境的本质不同，而且有经验的 ENTERPRISE 架构师具有跨多个平台（包括分布式系统和传统的主框架环境）的技能。由于 ENTERPRISE 架构师职业的原因，他们在至少一个学科上拥有被认为是主题事项专家层级的技能。

52.6.3.3 方法驱动的执行途径

ENTERPRISE 架构师通过经认可的设计方法[诸如 TOGAF 架构开发方法（ADM）]的连贯一致的使用来完成他们的工作。ENTERPRISE 架构师应具有多种设计方法的工作知识，而且应熟悉如何部署适于他们正在处理的情况的部分方法。这应体现在 ENTERPRISE 架构师已经通过重复地成功使用多种设计方法的设计工作中。方法论使用的熟练程度，是知道在给定情况下使用方法的什么部分以及不使用什么方法。

52.6.3.4 Full Project Scope Experience

While enterprise architects are responsible for design and hand-off of the project to implementors, it is vital that they have experience with all aspects of a project from design through development, testing, implementation, and production. This scope of experience will serve to keep enterprise architects grounded in the notion of fitness-for-purpose and the practical nature of system implementation. The impact of full project scope experience should lead the enterprise architect to make better design decisions, and better inform the trade-offs made in those decisions.

52.6.3.5 Leadership

Communication and team building are key to the successful role of the enterprise architect. The mix of good technical skill and the ability to lead are crucial to the job. The enterprise architect should be viewed as a leader in the enterprise by the IT organization, the clients they serve, and management.

52.6.3.6 Personal and Professional Skills

The enterprise architect must have strong communications and relationship skills. A major task of the enterprise architect is to communicate complex technical information to all stakeholders of the project, including those who do not have a technical background. Strong negotiation and problem-solving skills are also required. The enterprise architect must work with the project management team to make decisions in a timely manner to keep projects on track.

52.6.3.7 Skills and Experience in One or More Industries

Industry skill and experience will make the task of gathering requirements and deciding priorities easier and more effective for the enterprise architect. Enterprise architects must understand the business processes of the enterprise in which they work, and how those processes work with other peer enterprises in the industry. They should also be able to spot key trends and correct flawed processes, giving the IT organization the capability to lead the enterprise, not just respond to requests. The mission of the enterprise architect is strategic technical leadership.

52.7 Conclusions

The TOGAF Architecture Skills Framework provides an assessment of the skills required to deliver a successful enterprise architecture.

It is hoped that the provision of this Architecture Skills Framework will help reduce the time, cost, and risk involved in training, recruiting, and managing IT architecture professionals, and at the same time enable and encourage more organizations to institute an internal IT architecture practice, hopefully based on (or at least leveraging) the role and skill definitions provided.

52.6.3.4 全部项目范围经验

虽然 ENTERPRISE 架构师负责设计和协调管制实施者的项目，但更重要的是，他们在项目的所有方面，即从设计到开发、试验、实施和生产都具有经验。其经验范围使 ENTERPRISE 架构师在系统实施的适用性概念和实用性质方面脚踏实地。全部项目范围经验的影响应致使 ENTERPRISE 架构师做出更好的设计决策，并更好地为在这些决策中做出权衡提供依据。

52.6.3.5 领导能力

沟通和团队建设是 ENTERPRISE 架构师取得成功的关键。良好的技术技能与领导能力的结合对于该项工作至关重要。ENTERPRISE 架构师应被 IT 组织、他们服务的客户以及管理层视作 ENTERPRISE 的领导。

52.6.3.6 个人技能和职业技能

ENTERPRISE 架构师必须有较强的沟通和处理人际关系的能力。ENTERPRISE 架构师的主要任务是与项目的所有利益攸关者，包括那些没有技术背景的人员，交流复杂的技术信息。还需要有较强的协商和解决问题的技能。ENTERPRISE 架构师必须与项目管理团队及时地共同做出决策，以保持项目正常进行。

52.6.3.7 在一个或多个行业的技能和经验

行业技能和经验会使 ENTERPRISE 架构师应对收集需求和决定优先级的任务更容易和更有效。ENTERPRISE 架构师必须理解他们工作的 ENTERPRISE 的业务流程以及这些流程如何帮助行业中的其他同等 ENTERPRISE。他们应该还能确定关键趋势并校正有缺陷的流程，从而为 IT 组织提供领导 ENTERPRISE 的能力，不只是响应要求。ENTERPRISE 架构师的使命是战略技术领导作用。

52.7 结论

TOGAF 架构技能框架提供对交付成功 Enterprise Architecture 所需技能的评估。

希望这种架构技能框架的提供有助于缩短 IT 架构职业人员的培训、招聘和管理时间，并降低成本和风险，同时希望基于（或至少更好地利用）所提供的角色和技能定义鼓励并使更多的组织能够建立内部 IT 架构实践。

TOGAF Version 9.1

Part VIII Appendices

The Open Group

TOGAF 9.1 版本

第八部分　附录

The Open Group

Appendix A
Glossary of Supplementary Definitions

This appendix contains additional definitions to supplement the definitions contained in Chapter 3.

A.1 Access Control (AC)

A security service that ensures only those users with the correct rights can access a specific device, application, or data.

A.2 Ada

A high-level computer programming language developed by the US Department of Defense (DoD) and widely used within the DoD and NATO countries. It is used for real-time processing, is modular in nature, and includes object-oriented features.

A.3 Application Component

An encapsulation of application functionality aligned to implementation structure. For example, a purchase request processing application.
See also Section A.50 and Section A.63.

A.4 Application Software

Software entities which have a specific business purpose.

A.5 Availability

In the context of IT systems, the probability that system functional capabilities are ready for use by a user at any time, where all time is considered, including operations, repair, administration, and logistic time. Availability is further defined by system category for both routine and priority operations.

附录 A
补充定义的词汇表

本附录包含一些附加定义，以补充第 3 章中包含的定义。

A.1 访问控制（AC）

一种安保服务，其确保只有那些拥有正确权限的用户才能访问特定设备、应用或数据。

A.2 Ada

一种由美国国防部（DoD）开发的高级计算机编程语言，广泛用于 DoD 和北约成员国。ADa 用于实时处理，本质上是模块化的，并且包括诸多面向对象的特征。

A.3 应用组件

与实施结构相对准的应用功能的封装形式。例如，采购要求处理应用。

还可参见 A.50 节和 A.63 节。

A.4 应用软件

具有特定业务用途的软件实体。

A.5 可用性

在 IT 系统的背景环境中，系统功能性能力已经就绪，以备用户随时使用的可能性。“随时”是指，包括运行时间、维护时间、管理时间和物流时间在内的所有时间。可以根据系统类别为日常运行和优先运行进一步地定义可用性。

A.6 Batch Processing

Processing data or the accomplishment of jobs accumulated in advance in such a manner that each accumulation thus formed is processed or accomplished in the same computer run.

A.7 Business System

Hardware, software, policy statements, processes, activities, standards, and people which together implement a business function.

A.8 Catalog

A structured list of architectural outputs of a similar kind, used for reference. For example, a technology standards catalog or an application portfolio.

A.9 Client

An application component which requests services from a server.

A.10 COBIT

An acronym for Control OBjectives for Information and related Technology, created by the Information Systems Audit and Control Association (ISACA) and the IT Governance Institute (ITGI), which provides a set of recommended best practices for the governance/management of information systems and technology.

A.11 Communications Network

A set of products, concepts, and services that enable the connection of computer systems for the purpose of transmitting data and other forms (e.g., voice and video) between the systems.

A.12 Communications Node

A node that is either internal to the communications network (e.g., routers, bridges, or repeaters)or located between the end device and the communications network to operate as a gateway.

A.13 Communications System

A set of assets (transmission media, switching nodes, interfaces, and control devices) that will establish linkage between users and devices.

A.6 批处理

以这样一种在同一次计算机运行中处理或完成每次积累的任务的方式处理数据或完成事先积累的工作。

A.7 业务系统

共同实现业务功能的硬件、软件、方针说明、流程、活动、标准和人员。

A.8 目录集

类似类别的构架产出的结构表，以供参考。例如，技术标准目录集或应用谱系。

A.9 客户端

从服务器要求服务的应用组件。

A.10 COBIT

信息及相关技术控制目标（Control Objectives for Information and related Technology）的缩写，由信息系统审核和控制协会（ISACA）和 IT 治理协会（ITGI）共同创建，为信息系统和技术的治理/管理提供一整套推荐的最佳实践。

A.11 通信网络

实现计算机系统互连的一组产品、概念和服务，以便在系统间传输数据和其他形式的信息（如语音和视频）。

A.12 通信节点

通信网络内部的节点（如路由器、网桥、中继器等）或位于终端设备和通信网络之间作为网关运行的节点。

A.13 通信系统

在用户和设备之间建立连接的一套资产（传输介质、转换节点、界面和控制设备）。

A.14 Composite Application

An application component that is created by composing other atomic or composite applications.

A.15 Configuration Management

A discipline applying technical and administrative direction and surveillance to:

- Identify and document the functional and physical characteristics of a configuration item.
- Control changes to those characteristics.
- Record and report changes to processing and implementation status.

Also, the management of the configuration of enterprise architecture practice (intellectual property) assets and baselines and the control of change over of those assets.

A.16 Connectivity Service

A service area of the external environment entity of the Technical Reference Model (TRM) that provides end-to-end connectivity for communications through three transport levels (global, regional, and local). It provides general and application-specific services to platform end devices.

A.17 Contract

An agreement between a service consumer and a service provider that establishes functional and non-functional parameters for interaction.

A.18 Control

A decision-making step with accompanying decision logic used to determine execution approach for a process or to ensure that a process complies with governance criteria. For example, a sign-off control on the purchase request processing process that checks whether the total value of the request is within the sign-off limits of the requester, or whether it needs escalating to higher authority.

A.19 CxO

The chief officer within a particular function of the business; e.g., Chief Executive Officer, Chief Financial Officer, Chief Information Officer, Chief Technology Officer.

A.14 复合应用

一种通过对其他原子应用或复合应用进行组合而创建的应用组件。

A.15 构型管理

一门将技术和管理指导以及监督应用到如下方面的规程：

- 识别配置项的功能特征和物理特征并使其文件化。
- 控制这些特征的变更。
- 记录并报告对处理和实施状态的变更。

此外，还包括对 Enterprise Architecture 实践（知识产权）资产和基线的配置管理以及对这些资产的变更控制。

A.16 连通性服务

技术参考模型（TRM）的外部环境实体中的一个服务区域，它通过三个传输级别（全球、区域和本地）为通信提供端对端的连通性。连通性服务为平台终端设备提供一般的和应用特定的服务。

A.17 契约

服务消费者和服务提供者之间达成的协议，它确立了双方交互的功能性参数和非功能性参数。

A.18 控制

一个随附决策逻辑的决策步骤，用于确定流程的执行途径或确保流程符合治理准则。例如，对采购要求处理流程的签收控制，用于检查申请的总价值是否在申请者的签收限制内或是否需要升级到较高权限。

A.19 首席×官

企业特定职能部门的首席主管，如首席执行官、首席财务官、首席信息官、首席技术官。

A.20 Data Dictionary

A specialized type of database containing metadata; a repository of information describing the characteristics of data used to design, monitor, document, protect, and control data in information systems and databases; an application system supporting the definition and management of database metadata.

A.21 Data Element

A basic unit of information having a meaning and that may have subcategories (data items) of distinct units and values.

A.22 Data Entity

An encapsulation of data that is recognized by a business domain expert as a thing. Logical data entities can be tied to applications, repositories, and services and may be structured according to implementation considerations.

A.23 Data Interchange Service

A service of the platform entity of the Technical Reference Model (TRM) that provides specialized support for the interchange of data between applications on the same or different platforms.

A.24 Data Management Service

A service of the platform entity of the Technical Reference Model (TRM) that provides support for the management, storage, access, and manipulation of data in a database.

A.25 Database

A structured or organized collection of data entities, which is be accessed by a computer.

A.26 Database Management System

A computer application program that accesses or manipulates the database.

A.20 数据字典

一种包含元数据的特殊类型的数据库；一种描述数据特征的信息存储库，用于设计、监控、文件化、保护及控制信息系统和数据库中的数据；一种支持数据库元数据定义和管理的应用系统。

A.21 数据元素

一种具有某种含义的基本信息单元，其可能具有截然不同的单位和值的子类别（数据项）。

A.22 数据实体

一种数据封装形式，业务领域专家将之视为一种事物。可以将逻辑数据实体与应用、存储库以及服务进行绑定，并且按照实施考量因素可对其进行结构化。

A.23 数据互换服务

技术参考模型（TRM）的平台实体的一种服务，为在同一平台或不同平台上的应用之间进行数据互换提供专门支持。

A.24 数据管理服务

技术参考模型（TRM）的平台实体的一种服务，为管理、存储、访问和操纵数据库中的数据提供支持。

A.25 数据库

一种可通过计算机访问的结构化或有组织的数据实体集合。

A.26 数据库管理系统

一种访问或操纵数据库的计算机应用程序。

A.27 Directory Service

A technology component that provides locator services that find the location of a service, or the location of data, or translation of a common name into a network-specific address. It is analogous to telephone books and may be implemented in centralized or distributed schemes.

A.28 Distributed Database

1. A database that is not stored in a central location but is dispersed over a network of interconnected computers.
2. A database under the overall control of a central Database Management System (DBMS)but whose storage devices are not all attached to the same processor.
3. A database that is physically located in two or more distinct locations.

A.29 Driver

An external or internal condition that motivates the organization to define its goals. An example of an external driver is a change in regulation or compliance rules which, for example, require changes to the way an organization operates; i.e., Sarbanes-Oxley in the US.

A.30 End User

Person who ultimately uses the computer application or output.

A.31 Enterprise Resource Planning (ERP) System

A complete suite of integrated applications that support the major business support functions of an organization; e.g., Financial (AP/AR/GL), HR, Payroll, Stock, Order Processing and Invoicing, Purchasing, Logistics, Manufacturing, etc.

A.32 Event

An organizational state change that triggers processing events may originate from inside or outside the organization and may be resolved inside or outside the organization.

A.33 External Environment Interface (EEI)

The interface that supports information transfer between the application platform and the external environment.

A.27 目录服务

一种提供定位服务的技术组件，这些定位服务能够发现服务位置或数据位置，或者将一个通用名称转换成网络特定地址。目录服务类似于电话簿，可以通过集中或分布的方式实现。

A.28 分布式数据库

1. 一种在互连计算机网络上分散而非存储在中央位置的数据库。
2. 一种由中央数据库管理系统（DBMS）进行总体控制的数据库，但其各存储设备并非完全连接到同一处理器上。
3. 一种在物理上位于两个或多个截然不同的位置的数据库。

A.29 驱动因素

激发组织定义其目标的某种外部或内部条件。例如，组织变革的一种外部驱动因素是监管或合规性规则的变更（如美国的索克斯法案），要求组织改变其经营方式。

A.30 最终用户

最终使用计算机应用或输出的人。

A.31 企业资源规划（ERP）系统

一整套综合应用，用以支持组织的主要业务支持性功能，如财务（AP/AR/GL）、人力资源、工资、库存、订单处理，以及发票、采购、物流、制造等。

A.32 事件

一种触发处理事件的组织状态变更，事件可能来源于组织内部或外部，并且可以在组织内部或外部得到解决。

A.33 外部环境界面（EEI）

支持应用平台与外部环境之间的信息传输的界面。

A.34 FORTRAN

An acronym for FORmula TRANslator, which is a high-level computer language used extensively in scientific and engineering applications.

A.35 Functional Decomposition

A hierarchy of the functions of an enterprise or organization.

A.36 Goal

A high-level statement of intent or direction for an organization. Typically used to measure success of an organization.

A.37 Guideline

An architectural document that provides guidance on the optimal ways to carry out design or implementation activities.

A.38 Hardware

The physical infrastructure needed to run software; e.g., servers, workstations, network equipment, etc.

A.39 Human Computer Interface (HCI)

Hardware and software allowing information exchange between the user and the computer.

A.40 Information Domain

Grouping of information (or data entities) by a set of criteria such as security classification, ownership, location, etc. In the context of security, information domains are defined as a set of users, their information objects, and a security policy.

A.41 Information System (IS)

The computer (or IT)-based portion of a business system.

A.34 FORTRAN

公式翻译器（FORmula TRANslator）的缩写，是一种广泛用于科学和工程应用的高级计算机语言。

A.35 功能分解

ENTERPRISE 或组织的功能层级。

A.36 目标

组织意图或方向的高层级申明。典型情况下，用于衡量一个组织的成功。

A.37 指南

一种针对开展设计或实施活动的最佳方式提供引导的架构文件。

A.38 硬件

运行软件所需的物理基础设施，如服务器、工作站、网络设备等。

A.39 人机界面（HCI）

使得能在用户与计算机之间进行信息交换的硬件和软件。

A.40 信息域

按照一组诸如安保等级、所有权、位置等准则分组的信息（或数据实体）。在安保背景环境中，信息域被定义为一组用户、用户信息对象以及一种安保方针。

A.41 信息系统（IS）

业务系统中基于计算机（或 IT）的部分。

A.42 Information System Service

The automated elements of a business service. An information system service may deliver or support part or all of one or more business services.

A.43 Interaction

A relationship between architectural building blocks (i.e., services or components) that embodies communication or usage.

A.44 Interaction Model

An architectural view, catalog, or matrix that shows a particular type of interaction. For example, a diagram showing application integration.

A.45 Interface

Interconnection and inter-relationships between, for example, people, systems, devices, applications, or the user and an application or device.

A.46 ITIL

An acronym for Information Technology Infrastructure Library, which provides a set of recommended best practices for the governance/management of information systems and technology.

A.47 Key Performance Indicator (KPI)

A way of quantifying the performance of the business or project.

A.48 Lifecycle

The period of time that begins when a system is conceived and ends when the system is no longer available for use.

A.49 Location

A place where business activity takes place and can be hierarchically decomposed.

A.42 信息系统服务

业务服务的自动化元素。信息系统服务可以交付或支持一种或多种业务服务的部分或全部。

A.43 交互

在架构构建块（即服务或组件）之间体现通信或使用的一种关系。

A.44 交互模型

表明特定类型交互的架构视图、目录集或矩阵。例如，一个表明应用整合的图。

A.45 界面

例如，人员间、系统间、设备间、应用间或者用户与应用或设备之间的互连和相互关系。

A.46 ITIL

信息技术基础设施库（Information Technology Infrastructure Library）的缩写，为信息系统和技术的治理/管理提供一套推荐的最佳实践。

A.47 关键绩效指标（KPI）

一种量化业务或项目绩效的方式。

A.48 生命周期

从系统构思开始到系统失去可用性结束的时间区间。

A.49 位置

业务活动发生并可按层级分解的地方。

A.50 Logical Application Component

An encapsulation of application functionality that is independent of a particular implementation. For example, the classification of all purchase request processing applications implemented in an enterprise.

A.51 Logical Data Component

A boundary zone that encapsulates related data entities to form a logical location to be held. For example, external procurement information.

A.52 Logical Technology Component

An encapsulation of technology infrastructure that is independent of a particular product. A class of technology product. For example, supply chain management software as part of an Enterprise Resource Planning (ERP) suite or a Commercial Off-The-Shelf (COTS) purchase request processing enterprise service.

A.53 Managing Successful Programs (MSP)

A best practice methodology for program management, developed by the UK Office of Government Commerce (OGC).

A.54 Matrix

A format for showing the relationship between two (or more) architectural elements in a grid format.

A.55 Measure

An indicator or factor that can be tracked, usually on an ongoing basis, to determine success or alignment with objectives and goals.

A.50 逻辑应用组件

一种与特定实施无关的应用功能性的封装形式。例如，在 ENTERPRISE 内所实施的全部采购要求处理应用可以归类为一种逻辑应用组件。

A.51 逻辑数据组件

一种对相关数据实体进行封装以形成需占用逻辑位置的边界区域。例如，外部采购信息。

A.52 逻辑技术组件

与特定产品无关的技术基础设施的封装形式。一类技术产品，例如，作为企业资源规划（ERP）套件一部分的供应链管理软件或商用货架（COTS）采购要求处理的企业服务。

A.53 成功项目群管理（MSP）

一种由英国政府商务办公室（OGC）制定的项目群管理的最佳实践方法论。

A.54 矩阵

一种以网格形式表明两个（或多个）架构元素之间关系的格式。

A.55 测度

一种通常可持续追踪的指标或因素，旨在确定成功程度或者与目的和目标的对准性。

A.56 Metaview

A metaview acts as a pattern or template of the view, from which to develop individual views. A metaview establishes the purposes and audience for a view, the ways in which the view is documented (e.g., for visual modeling), and the ways in which it is used (e.g., for analysis).

See also Section 3.76 in Chapter 3.

A.57 Multimedia Service

A service of the Technical Reference Model (TRM) that provides the capability to manipulate and manage information products consisting of text, graphics, images, video, and audio.

A.58 Open Specifications

Public specifications that are maintained by an open, public consensus process to accommodate new technologies over time and that are consistent with international standards.

A.59 Open System

A system that implements sufficient open specifications for interfaces, services, and supporting formats to enable properly engineered application software:

- To be ported with minimal changes across a wide range of systems.
- To interoperate with other applications on local and remote systems.
- To interact with users in a style that facilitates user portability.

A.60 Operational Governance

Operational governance looks at the operational performance of systems against contracted performance levels, the definition of operational performance levels, and the implementation of systems that ensure effective operation of systems.

See also Section 3.39 in Chapter 3.

A.61 Operating System Service

A core service of the application platform entity of the Technical Reference Model (TRM) that is needed to operate and administer the application platform and provide an interface between the application software and the platform (for example, file management, input/output, print spoolers).

A.56 元视图

元视图是视图的特征模式或模板，由此形成各种视图。元视图确定视图的目的、受众、视图的文件化方式（如可视化建模）以及使用视图的方式（如用于分析）。

还可参见第 3 章中的 3.76 节。

A.57 多媒体服务

技术参考模型（TRM）的服务，提供操纵和管理由文字、图形、图像、视频和音频构成信息产物的能力。

A.58 开放规范

按照开放的公认流程进行维护的公共规范，以随时间推移接纳各种新技术。开放规范始终与国际标准保持一致。

A.59 开放系统

一种充分执行针对各种界面与服务的开放规范和支持格式的系统，以使设计适当的应用软件能够：

- 以最小的修改实现跨各种系统的移植。
- 与本地和远程系统上的其他应用进行互操作。
- 以促进用户可移植性的方式与用户进行交互。

A.60 运行治理

运行治理对比契约规定的绩效水平、运行绩效水平的定义和系统的实施来评判系统的运行绩效，确保系统有效运行。

还可参见第 3 章中的 3.39 节。

A.61 操作系统服务

技术参考模型（TRM）的应用平台实体的核心服务，这是一项运行和管理应用平台以及提供应用软件与平台（例如，文件管理、输入/输出、打印后台任务）之间的界面都需要的服务。

A.62 Packaged Services

Services that are acquired from the market from a Commercial Off-The-Shelf (COTS) vendor, rather than being constructed via code build.

A.63 Physical Application Component

An application, application module, application service, or other deployable component of functionality. For example, a configured and deployed instance of a Commercial Off-The-Shelf (COTS) Enterprise Resource Planning (ERP) supply chain management application.

A.64 Physical Data Component

A boundary zone that encapsulates related data entities to form a physical location to be held. For example, a purchase order business object, comprising purchase order header and item business object nodes.

A.65 Physical Technology Component

A specific technology infrastructure product or technology infrastructure product instance. For example, a particular product version of a Commercial Off-The-Shelf (COTS) solution, or a specific brand and version of server.

A.66 Portability

1. The ease with which a system, component, data, or user can be transferred from one hardware or software environment to another.
2. A quality metric that can be used to measure the relative effort to transport the software for use in another environment or to convert software for use in another operating environment, hardware configuration, or software system environment.

A.67 Portfolio

The complete set of change activities or systems that exist within the organization or part of the organization. For example, application portfolio and project portfolio.

A.68 PRINCE2

An acronym for PRojects IN Controlled Environments, which is a standard project management method.

A.62 服务包

从商用货架（COTS）厂商处购得，而非通过代码构建而构造的服务。

A.63 物理应用组件

应用、应用模块、应用服务或其他可部署的功能性组件。例如，已经配置和部署的某个商用货架（COTS）的企业资源规划（ERP）的供应链管理应用的一个实例。

A.64 物理数据组件

对相关数据实体进行封装，以形成需占用物理位置的边界区域。例如，一个采购订单业务对象，包括采购订单表头和业务对象节点的子项。

A.65 物理技术组件

特定的技术基础设施产物或技术基础设施产物的实例。例如，某个商用货架（COTS）解决方案的特殊产品版本或服务器的特定品牌和版本。

A.66 可移植性

1. 系统、组件、数据或用户可从一个硬件或软件环境转移到另一个环境的难易程度。
2. 质量衡量标准，可用于衡量将软件转移到另一个环境中使用的相对难度，或者用于衡量对软件进行转换，使之能够在另一个操作环境、硬件构型或软件系统环境中使用的相对难度。

A.67 谱系

存在于整个组织或部分组织内的整套变革活动或系统。例如，应用谱系和项目谱系。

A.68 PRINCE2

受控环境下的项目管理（PRojects IN Controlled Environment）的缩写，是一种标准的项目管理方法。

A.69 Process

A process represents a sequence of activities that together achieve a specified outcome, can be decomposed into sub-processes, and can show operation of a function or service (at next level of detail). Processes may also be used to link or compose organizations, functions, services, and processes.

A.70 Product

Output generated by the business. The business product of the execution of a process.

A.71 Profile

A set of one or more base standards and, where applicable, the identification of those classes, subsets, options, and parameters of those base standards, necessary for accomplishing a particular function.

A.72 Profiling

Identifying standards and characteristics of a particular system.

A.73 Program

A co-ordinated set of change projects that deliver business benefit to the organization.

A.74 Project

A single change project which delivers business benefit to the organization.

A.69 流程

流程代表一连串可共同取得某种特定结果的活动，可以被分解成若干个子流程，还可以表明某项功能或服务（更详细）的运行。流程也可用于连接或组成组织、功能、服务和流程。

A.70 产物

业务产生的输出。流程执行的业务产物。

A.71 概要

一个或多个基础标准的集合，以及（如适用）对这些基础标准的类别、子集、选项和参数的识别，是完成某种特殊功能的必要条件。

A.72 概要分析

识别特定系统的标准和特征。

A.73 项目群

给组织带来业务效益的一组相互协作的变革项目。

A.74 项目

给组织带来业务效益的单个变革项目。

A.75 Risk Management

The management of risks and issues that may threaten the success of the enterprise architecture practice and its ability to meet is vision, goals, and objectives, and, importantly, its service provision.

Note: Risk management is described in Part III, Chapter 31.

A.76 Scalability

The ability to use the same application software on many different classes of hardware/software platforms from PCs to super-computers (extends the portability concept). The capability to grow to accommodate increased work loads.

A.77 Security

Services which protect data, ensuring its confidentiality, availability, and integrity.

A.78 Server

An application component which responds to requests from a client.

A.79 Service

A logical representation of a repeatable business activity that has a specified outcome. A service is self-contained, may be composed of other services, and is a “black box” to its consumers. Examples are “check customer credit”, “provide weather data”, and “consolidate drilling reports”.

A.80 Service Quality

A preset configuration of non-functional attributes that may be assigned to a service or service contract.

A.81 SMART

An acronym for Specific, Measurable, Attainable, Realistic, and Time-bound, which is an approach to ensure that targets and objectives are set in a way that can be achieved and measured.

A.75 风险管理

对可能威胁 Enterprise Architecture 实践成功与否的风险和问题的管理，其具有满足愿景、目标和目的的能力；更为重要的是其提供服务的能力。

注：第三部分第 31 章描述了风险管理。

A.76 可伸缩性

在从 PC 到超级计算机的很多不同类别的硬件/软件平台上使用相同应用软件的能力（扩展可移植性概念），随工作负荷增加而扩展的能力。

A.77 安保

保护数据以确保数据机密性、可用性和完整性的服务。

A.78 服务器

应对客户端要求的应用组件。

A.79 服务

对产生特定结果的可重复业务活动的逻辑表达。服务自身是独立完整的，可由其他服务组成，并且对其消费者来说是一个“黑匣子”。例如，“检查客户信用”“提供气象数据”以及“合并数据钻取报告”。

A.80 服务质量

非功能属性的预设配置，可指派给服务或服务契约。

A.81 SMART

SMART 是特定（Specific）、可衡量（Measurable）、可付诸行动（Attainable）、切实可行（Realistic）和有时限（Time-bound）五个单词的首字母缩写，是一种确保以可达成及可衡量的方式来设定目标和目的的实施途径。

A.82 Supplier Management

The management of suppliers of products and services to the enterprise architecture practice in concert with larger corporate procurement activities.

A.83 System

A collection of components organized to accomplish a specific function or set of functions(source: ISO/IEC 42010: 2007).

A.84 System and Network Management Service

A cross-category service of the application platform entity of the Technical Reference Model (TRM) that provides for the administration of the overall information system. These services include the management of information, processors, networks, configurations, accounting, and performance.

A.85 System Stakeholder

An individual, team, or organization (or classes thereof) with interests in, or concerns relative to, a system (source: ISO/IEC 42010: 2007).

A.86 Technology Component

An encapsulation of technology infrastructure that represents a class of technology product or specific technology product.

A.87 Time Period

The timeframe over which the potential impact is to be measured.

A.88 Transaction

Interaction between a user and a computer in which the user inputs a command to receive a specific result from the computer.

A.89 Transaction Sequence

Order of transactions required to accomplish the desired results.

A.82 供应商管理

对向 Enterprise Architecture 实践提供产品和服务的供应商的管理，适用于较大的公司级采购活动。

A.83 系统

为完成某一特定功能或一组功能而组织起来的组件集合（来源：ISO/IEC 42010:2007）。

A.84 系统和网络管理服务

技术参考模型（TRM）中应用平台实体的一种跨类别服务，对总体信息系统提供管理。这些服务包括对信息、处理器、网络、配置、计费和绩效的管理。

A.85 系统利益攸关者

具有系统利益或具有与系统相关的关注点的个体、团队或组织（或其类别）（来源：ISO/IEC 42010:2007）。

A.86 技术组件

技术基础设施的封装形式，其代表某类技术产物或某个特定的技术产物。

A.87 时间区间

对潜在影响进行测量的时间段。

A.88 事务

用户与计算机之间的交互，在交互中，用户输入指令以接收计算机返回的特定结果。

A.89 事务序列

达到期望结果需要的事务顺序。

A.90 Use-Case

A view of organization, application, or product functionality that illustrates capabilities in context with the user of that capability.

A.91 User

1. Any person, organization, or functional unit that uses the services of an information processing system.
2. In a conceptual schema language, any person or any thing that may issue or receive commands and messages to or from the information system.

A.92 User Interface Service

A service of the application platform entity of the Technical Reference Model (TRM) that supports direct human-machine interaction by controlling the environment in which users interact with applications.

A.90 用例

组织、应用或产品功能性的视图，其说明在背景环境中用户对能力的可用性。

A.91 用户

1. 使用信息处理系统服务的任何人、组织或功能单元。
2. 在概念模式语言中，可以向信息系统发出或从信息系统接收命令和消息的任何人或事物。

A.92 用户界面服务

技术参考模型（TRM）的应用平台实体的一种服务，通过控制用户与应用交互的环境支持直接的人机交互。

Appendix B
Abbreviations

ABB	Architecture Building Block
AC	Access Control
ACL	Access Control List
ACMM	Architecture Capability Maturity Model
ACSE	Association Control Service Element
ADM	Architecture Development Method
ANSI	American National Standards Institute
API	Application Platform Interface
ARTS	Association for Retail Technology Standards
BMM	Business Motivation Model
BPM	Business Process Management
BPMN	Business Process Modeling Notation
BTEP	The Canadian Government Business Transformation Enablement Program
CAB	Change Advisory Board
CCITT	Consultative Committee on International Telegraph and Telephone, now known as theInternational Telecommunication Union (ITU)
CI	Configuration Item
CIPR	Central Information Process
CM	Configuration Management
CMIP	Common Management Information Protocol
CMIS	Common Management Information Service
CMM	Capability Maturity Models
CMMI	Capability Maturity Model Integration
CN	Communications Network
COBIT	Control OBjectives for Information and related Technology
CODASYL	Conference on Data Systems Languages
CORBA	Common Object Request Broker Architecture
COTS	Commercial Off-The-Shelf applications

附录 B
缩略语

ABB	架构构建块
AC	访问控制
ACL	访问控制列表
ACMM	架构能力成熟度模型
ACSE	关联控制服务元素
ADM	架构开发方法
ANSI	美国国家标准协会
API	应用平台界面
ARTS	零售技术标准协会
BMM	业务动机模型
BPM	业务流程管理
BPMN	业务流程建模标注
BTEP	加拿大政府业务转型使能计划
CAB	改革咨询委员会
CCITT	国际电话电报咨询委员会，现称为国际电信联盟（ITU）
CI	配置项
CIPR	中央信息处理
CM	构型管理
CMIP	公共管理信息协议
CMIS	公共管理信息服务
CMM	能力成熟度模型
CMMI	能力成熟度模型集成
CN	通信网络
COBIT	信息及相关技术控制目标
CODASYL	数据系统语言会议
CORBA	公用对象要求代理架构
COTS	商用货架应用

CRM	Customer Relationship Management
CRUD	Create/Read/Update/Delete
CSF	Critical Success Factor
DAI	Data Access Interface
DBA	Database Administrator
DBMS	Database Management System
DCE	Distributed Computing Environment
DDL	Data Definition Language
DISA	US Department of Defense Information Systems Agency
DMF	Data Management Facility
DML	Data Manipulation Language
DMTF	Distributed Management Task Force
DNS	Domain Name System
DoC	US Department of Commerce
DoD	US Department of Defense
DoDAF	Department of Defense Architecture Framework
DRDA	Distributed Relational Database Architecture
EA	Enterprise Architecture
EAI	Enterprise Application Integration
EDI	Electronic Data Interchange
EEI	External Environment Interface
ERP	Enterprise Resource Planning
ES	End System
ESB	Enterprise Service Bus
ETL	Extract, Transform, Load
FEAF	Federal Enterprise Architecture Framework
FICO	Fair Isaac Corporation
FORTRAN	FORmula TRANslator
FTE	Full-Time Equivalent
GOTS	Government Off-The-Shelf applications
GUI	Graphical User Interface
HIPAA	Health Insurance Portability and Accountability Act
ICAM	Integrated Computer Aided Manufacturing
ICD	Interface Control Document

CRM	客户关系管理
CRUD	创建/读取/更新/删除
CSF	关键成功因素
DAI	数据存取界面
DBA	数据库管理员
DBMS	数据库管理系统
DCE	分布式计算环境
DDL	数据定义语言
DISA	美国国防部信息系统机构
DMF	数据管理设备
DML	数据操纵语言
DMTF	分布式管理任务组
DNS	域名系统
DoC	美国商务部
DoD	美国国防部
DoDAF	国防部架构框架
DRDA	分布式关系型数据库架构
EA	Enterprise Architecture
EAI	ENTERPRISE 应用整合
EDI	电子数据互换
EEI	外部环境界面
ERP	企业资源规划
ES	终端系统
ESB	企业服务总线
ETL	抽取、转型、加载
FEAF	联邦 Enterprise Architecture 框架
FICO	费尔艾克公司
FORTRAN	公式翻译器
FTE	全时当量
GOTS	政府成品应用
GUI	图形用户界面
HIPAA	美国医治保险携带和责任法案
ICAM	集成计算机辅助制造
ICD	界面控制文件

ICOM	Inputs, Controls, Outputs, and Mechanisms/Resources
IDEF	Integrated Computer Aided Manufacturing (ICAM) DEFinition
IDL	Interface Description Language
IEC	International Electrotechnical Commission
IEEE	Institute of Electrical and Electronic Engineers
III	Integrated Information Infrastructure
III-RM	Integrated Information Infrastructure Reference Model
IMS	Information Management System
ISA	Information Systems Architecture
ISACA	Information Systems Audit and Control Association
ISACF	Information Systems Audit and Control Foundation
ISAM	Indexed Sequential Access Method
ISO	International Standards Organization
IT	Information Technology
ITGI	IT Governance Institute
ITIL	Information Technology Infrastructure Library
ITPMF	IT Portfolio Management Facility
ITU	International Telecommunication Union
JMS	Java Message Service
JVM	Java Virtual Machine
KPI	Key Performance Indicator
LAN	Local Area Network
LCS	Local Communications System
LIPR	Local Information Process
LSE	Local Subscriber Network
MAN	Metropolitan Area Network
MDA	Model Driven Architecture
MIB	Management Information Bases
MIS	Management Information Systems MLS Multi-Level Security
MTA	Message Transfer Agent
NASCIO	National Association of State Chief Information Officers
NIST	National Institute of Standards and Technology
OAG	Open Applications Group

ICOM	输入、控制、输出和机制/资源
IDEF	集成计算机辅助制造（ICAM）的定义
IDL	界面描述语言
IEC	国际电子技术委员会
IEEE	电气与电子工程师协会
III	综合信息架构
III-RM	综合信息基础设施参考模型
IMS	信息管理系统
ISA	信息系统架构
ISACA	信息系统审核和控制协会
ISACF	信息系统审核和控制基金会
ISAM	指数顺序存取法
ISO	国际标准组织
IT	信息技术
ITGI	IT 治理协会
ITIL	信息技术基础设施库
ITPMF	IT 谱系管理设施
ITU	国际电信联盟
JMS	Java 消息服务
JVM	Java 虚拟机
KPI	关键绩效指标
LAN	局域网
LCS	本地通信系统
LIPR	本地信息处理
LSE	本地用户网络
MAN	城域网
MDA	模型驱动架构
MIB	管理信息库
MIS	管理信息系统
MLS	多层级安保
MTA	消息传送代理
NASCIO	美国州政府首席信息官协会
NIST	国家标准和技术研究所
OAG	开放应用群组

OAGIS	Open Applications Group Integration Specification
ODBC	Open Database Connectivity
OECD	Organization for Economic Co-operation and Development
OGC	UK Office of Government Commerce
OLA	Operational Level Agreement
OMB	Office of Management and Budget
OMG	Object Management Group
OODBMS	Object-Oriented Database Management System
ORB	Object Request Broker
OS	Operating System
OSE	Open System Environment
OSI	Open Systems Interconnection
OSOA	Open Service Oriented Architecture
P-CMM	People Capability Maturity Model
PDA	Personal Digital Assistant
PDF	Portable Document Format
PEX	PHIGS Extension to the X Window system
PHIGS	Programmer's Hierarchical Interactive Graphics System
PMI	Project Management Initiative
PMBOK	Project Management Body of Knowledge
PRINCE	PRojects in Controlled Environments
QoS	Quality of Service
RACI	Responsible, Accountable, Consulted, Informed
RAS	Remote Access Services
RDA	Remote Database Access
RDBMS	Relational Database Management System
REA	Resource-Event-Agent
RFC	Request For Change
RFI	Request for Information
RFP	Request for Proposal
RFQ	Request for Quotation
RM	Reference Model
RM-ODP	ISO Reference Model for Open Distributed Processing
RPC	Remote Procedure Call

OAGIS	开放应用群组整合规范
ODBC	开放式数据库连通性
OECD	经济合作和发展组织
OGC	英国政府商务办公室
OLA	运行水平协议
OMB	管理和预算办公室
OMG	对象管理组
OODBMS	面向对象的数据库管理系统
ORB	对象要求代理
OS	操作系统
OSE	开放系统环境
OSI	开放系统互连
OSOA	面向开放服务的架构
P-CMM	人力资源成熟度模型
PDA	个人数字助理
PDF	便携式文件格式
PEX	PHIGS 对 X Window 系统的扩展
PHIGS	程序员层次交互式图形系统
PMI	项目管理举措
PMBOK	项目管理知识体系
PRINCE	受控环境下的项目
QoS	服务质量
RACI	负责、批准、咨询、告知
RAS	远程访问服务
RDA	远程数据库访问
RDBMS	关系数据库管理系统
REA	资源—事件—主体
RFC	变更要求
RFI	信息要求
RFP	建议要求
RFQ	报价要求
RM	参考模型
RM-ODP	开放分布式处理 ISO 参考模型
RPC	远程过程调用

RS	Relay System
SA-CMM	Software Acquisition Capability Maturity Model
SBB	Solution Building Block
SCAMPI	Standard CMMI Appraisal Method for Process Improvement
SDO	Service Data Objects
SEI	Software Engineering Institute
SGML	Standard Generalized Markup Language
SIB	Standards Information Base
SCA	Service Component Architecture
SCAMPI	CMMI Appraisal Method for Process Improvement
SLA	Service Level Agreement
SMAP	Security Management Application Process
SMART	Specific, Measurable, Attainable, Realistic, and Time-bound
SMTP	Simple Mail Transfer Protocol
SNA	System Network Architecture
SNMP	Simple Network Management Protocol
SOA	Service Oriented Architecture
SPEM	Software Processing Engineering Metamodel
SQL	Structured Query Language
STEP	STandard for the Exchange of Product model data
SWG	Special Working Group
SysML	Systems Modeling Language
TADG	Treasury Architecture Development Guidance
TAFIM	Technical Architecture Framework for Information Management
TCP/IP	Transmission Control Protocol/Internet Protocol
TISAF	Treasury Information System Architecture Framework
TRM	Technical Reference Model
TFA	Transparent File Access
TLSP	Transport Layer Security Protocol
TMF	TeleManagement Forum
TP	Transaction Processing
UML	Unified Modeling Language
UN/CEFACT	United Nations Centre for Trade Facilitation and Electronic Business
UN/EDIFACT	United Nations/Electronic Data Interchange For Administration, Commerce, and Transport

RS	中继系统
SA-CMM	软件采办能力成熟度模型
SBB	解决方案构建块
SCAMPI	标准 CMMI 流程改进评价法
SDO	服务数据对象
SEI	软件工程协会
SGML	标准通用化标记语言
SIB	标准信息库
SCA	服务组件架构
SCAMPI	CMMI 流程改进评价法
SLA	服务水平协议
SMAP	安保管理应用流程
SMART	特定、可衡量、可付诸行动、切实可行以及有时限
SMTP	简单邮件传送协议
SNA	系统网络架构
SNMP	简单网络管理协议
SOA	面向服务架构
SPEM	软件处理工程元模型
SQL	结构查询语言
STEP	产品模型数据交换标准
SWG	特别工作组
SysML	系统建模语言
TADG	财政部架构开发引导原则
TAFIM	信息管理技术架构框架
TCP/IP	传输控制协议/互联网协议
TISAF	财政部信息系统架构框架
TRM	技术参考模型
TFA	透通式文件访问
TLSP	传输层安保协议
TMF	电信管理论坛
TP	事务处理
UML	统一建模语言
UN/CEFACT	联合国贸易促进和电子商务中心
UN/EDIFACT	联合国/行政、商业和运输电子数据互换

WAN	Wide Area Network
WSDL	Web Services Description Language
XML	Extensible Markup Language
XSD	XML Schema Definition

WAN	广域网
WSDL	Web 服务描述语言
XML	可扩展标记语言
XSD	XML 模式定义

Index

索引